Tasha Tudor:

The Direction of Her Dreams

[Tasha with apple blossoms]

Tasha Tudor
The Direction of Her Dreams

The Definitive Bibliography
and Collectors' Guide

Including the Books of
Thomas L. McCready, Jr.
Bethany Tudor
Efner Holmes

Illustrations by Bethany Tudor
Photographs by Nell Dorr

Wm John Hare
Priscilla T. Hare

Oak Knoll Press
New Castle, Delaware

First edition/second printing - 2000 by:
Oak Knoll Press 310 Delaware Street, New Castle, DE 19720 USA

Copyright © 1998 by Wm John Hare and Priscilla T. Hare

ISBN: 1-884718-59-0 Oak Knoll Press

Publishing Director: John von Hoelle
Typographer for the Essays: Michael Höhne
Dustjacket, Cartouche, and Section Head Designs: Mary Torosian Graves

Library of Congress Cataloging-in-Publication Data

Hare, Wm John (William John), 1944–
Hare, Priscilla T.
     Tasha Tudor : the direction of her dreams / Wm John Hare, Priscilla T. Hare
         p.   cm.
     Includes bibliographical references and index.
     ISBN 1-884718-59-0 (H/B)
     1. Tudor, Tasha 1915– . 2. Tudor, Bethany W., 1940– . 3. Holmes, Efner Tudor,
1949– . 4. McCready, Thomas Leighton, Jr., 1907–1964. 5. Illustrators—United States—
Bio-bibliography. 6. Illustrated books, Children's—United States. I. Hare, Priscilla T., 1945–.
II. Tudor, Tasha. III. Title.
NC975.5.T82H37 1998
741.6'42'092—dc21
[B]   98-23806
                                                      CIP

Printed in the United States of America on 60# archival paper by Braun-Brumfield Printing Co.

TABLE OF CONTENTS

The Bibliography

(in numero-alphabetical order)

Photographs by Nell Dorr
ca. 1940–45

from nitrate negatives
Amon Carter Museum, Fort Worth, Texas

Selected Covers and Dustjackets
(color photographs)

ACKNOWLEDGMENTS

Researchers build on the foundations of others. Here is where we try to even the score a little bit and say thank you to many friends and associates who encouraged and helped at all the right times.

There are not enough ways to thank Efner Holmes and Bethany Tudor for their graciousness and recollections. For their first-person insights, their suggesting the correct person to consult, and their allowing us to examine unique paintings, the book world is eternally grateful. They provided the warp for our woof. Their beams are the strong underpinning that keep this structure from tumbling. We thank them for sharing rare examples of their mother's artistry.

Barbara Howe, Mary Lightner, Hugh Sanborn, and Yvonne Snyder each had information that has helped make this a more complete book. Each reflects an aspect of Tudor's associations and activities.

Thank you Patricia Gauch and Dorothy Haas for your written reminiscences. Thanks, also, to Ann Beneduce and Beth Mathers for kindness extended and support given. Donna Slawsky opened the HarperCollins library to us and buoyed our spirits when they needed a real boost. We had suspected such a place existed but had not explored one until casually walking past Ms Slawsky's book exhibit at 10 East 53rd Street in Manhattan. (Be sure to view Donna's current exhibit, the next time you are on 53rd Street. You won't be disappointed.) Louise Bates, we are honored to have made your acquaintance. You have handled more Tudor books in your role at the Permissions Desk at Putnam's than any other person save Henry Z. Walck, who filed the first Tudor copyright for Oxford University Press, New York, Inc. in 1938. John von Hoelle has been amazingly trusting and extremely encouraging at Oak Knoll Press.

We extend our gratitude to these people who assisted at some important phase. Marilyn Bousquin at The Horn Book. L. James Hannan, President, Hilltop Press, Indianapolis, Indiana for specifications of The Jenny Wren Press publications. Sally Wimberley for information about art on pages 134 and 153 in *Take Joy!* Stephanie Clayton, Jeanette Knazek, and Charlotte Pierce for many things. Marian E. Miller provided interesting clues to dolls.

Thank you Lee Burt (Barn Loft Bookshop, 96 Woodland Avenue, Laconia, NH 03246-2228, 603-524-4839) for finding books during your most trying of times. Lee has been a jewel and a delight among book dealers. She found us stacks of out-of-print material always saying, "Nothing new here. Just the old familiar titles." And always, there were several new states that we had not seen before. Helen Younger and Jo Ann Reisler had choice pieces; Kevin Ransom always had a surprise or two; Jean Kulp sold us nice old calico books; Gary Overmann has been helpful, especially suggesting printings or points of which we were unaware. Carol Docheff, Jeanette Kirkland, Charles and Frances Mague, Richard Mori, Audra Nelson, Cathy Ten Eyck, and Elaine Woodford were encouraging, always.

Joan Malfait and Charlene Dondero at the New Hampshire Technical Institute borrowed other libraries' books for us, and our other co-workers must have tired of this Tudor conversation years ago. Thank you Charlotte, Barbara, Steve and Deb. Donna Gilbreth and the reference staff, New Hampshire State Library, David Devries, Kalamazoo (Mi.) Public Library, and Debra Jop, the Rochester (N.Y.) Public Library aided the cause. Angeline Moscatt and Karen Ulric kept finding Tudor books at the Donnell Library Center, New York Public Library; and Dr. Anna Lou Ashby, the Pierpont Morgan Library, was most helpful, and interested. Amy Moore of the Fordham Library Center, New York Public Library, and Teresa Hunt also provided help at the ultimate hour.

Remembering the testamentary phrase, "Being not unmindful...," we regret that we have yet to visit these children's collections: de Grummond, University of Southern Mississippi; Kerwin, University of Minnesota; Lillian H. Smith, Toronto Public Library; and the Alice M. Jordan Collection, Boston Public Library. We're sure there will be surprises when we have the opportunity to examine their books.

Now, to appreciate this paragraph, consider my culinary habit of savoring the lobster tail last. Here it is then that I affectionately acknowledge my "partner in crime," my companion "bounder" and interloper, my collaborating author, my wife Jill. She alone has shared this abiding passion. She pulled me deeper into the thicket as we untangled the biblio-mysteries together. And then, she was pulling me out again, reminding me that we truly want to do something else in our lives. Jill's is the eye that scanned a thousand books while I was still reading the first preface. From Palo Alto to East Gloucester, she browsed bookshop and website and found treasures while I was hooked by some serendipitous piece that was rarely on subject.

For years, Ruth Schmocker has provided bushels of tangible support, always looking and digging for anything pertinent. A retired journalist, she has a sharp eye for detail and accuracy. Reggie Bacon rode shotgun until he had saddlesores always scouting for any different printing. Dr. Elizabeth G. Russell and Kay D. Harrison provided advice and editing assistance at crucial stages (especially the last one). Our daughter Susan also did those things as well as becoming an M.D. waiting for this book to end. And of course, our sons Jeff and Stott Hare kept upgrading computers to provide better tools. Every time we lost a computer file, they joined in a singular mantra—Back up, Back up, Back up, Back up, Back up.

It's a strange but meaningful prayer. Michelle, Thank You, too, for your understanding and appreciation and assistance at book fairs.

Your contributions have meant the difference between success and failure. We appreciate all your assistance, encouragement, and faith in the unbelievable. We willingly admit that any mistakes are our own. Our sincere and grateful Thank You to you all!

For My Beloved
Jill Hare
and to My Parents
T. N. (Chief) and Barbara Hare
Who started me
—wjh

To John for a Life of Love
Sue, Jeff and Stott
For their love and encouragement
and
To my family
—pth

Our deepest gratitude
To Trudy Huntington, Bill and Jane Stott
Ruth Schmocker and Reggie Bacon
For their love and kindness

And there were flying squirrels in the brick oven
Who kept me company through the winter night hours
—wjh

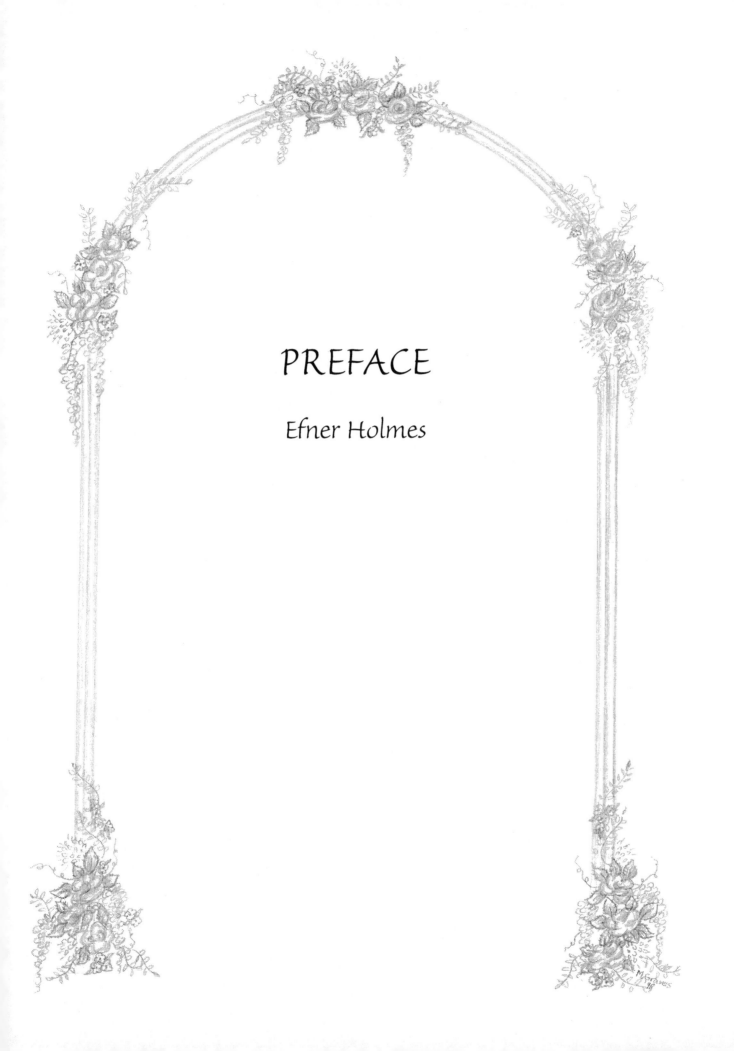

PREFACE

Efner Holmes

[Tasha at Villa Serena]

n November 1996 John and Jill Hare attended the "Take Joy" exhibition at the Abby Aldrich Rockefeller Folk Art Museum in Williamsburg, Virginia, an event celebrating the life and work of my mother, Tasha Tudor. They brought with them the manuscript of *Tasha Tudor: The Direction of Her Dreams*. When greeting my mother they laid the thick manuscript in her hands and said, "Here, Mrs. Tudor, is your life's work."

My mother was silent for a moment as she felt its weight.

"This is all me?" she asked in a childlike voice.

"Yes," John replied.

"My goodness," Mum answered demurely, "I've been quite busy, haven't I!"

Even at 82 years of age, with nearly one hundred books graced by her art, Tasha Tudor still regards her accomplishments with a mixture of amused amazement and modest indifference.

"I was simply trying to keep the wolf from the door," she'll say with a shrug. And so she did, often with an Herculean effort. Her adoring public envisions my mother sitting at her New Hampshire farm where we grew up and later in her Vermont garden peacefully drawing in her own beautiful world untouched by today's frantic pace. But my childhood memories are dominated by her small figure sitting in our big kitchen at the drop leaf table covered with its red and white cloth, a messy array of books, bouquets, and unfinished doll clothes. A corgi lays against her bare feet and the sound of her paint brush clinks as she quickly rinses from color to color in an old jelly jar of water.

Outside, her gardens called to her. And left to our own devices, the four of us children ran in and out with our needs and demands. We must have been a constant interruption to the concentration and her desperate need to get a book finished. Without a completed book there would be no checks. The royalty checks arrived only twice a year, and they were essential to feed her children and pay the taxes on 485 acres and a seventeen-room house. What my mother accomplished as a single woman would have sent many women into a total collapse of body and spirit. Yet she persevered to become famous for her pictures of her beloved New England countryside and scenes of blissful family life that only exist in fairy tales.

My mother's sense of fantasy both sustains and delights her, fueling a creative spirit and energy that has no bounds. The birthday parties with the candlelit cakes floating down the dark waters of the river at night in *Becky's Birthday*. The magical Christmas seasons that lasted from December 6 to New Year's Day. Her love of animals and her delight in their antics evident in all her books and crowned by *Corgiville Fair*. Her well-known love of her dolls as shown in *The Dolls' Christmas*. All these are evidence of a woman who never abandoned her childhood, yet who has faced life with courage, dignity, and a single-minded determination to live by the beauty in this world.

"I've always wanted to find the pot of gold at the end of the rainbow," she often says.

I wonder if she knows it has been in her hands all her life.

Whether you have collected Tasha Tudor's work for a long time or if you're just beginning, this book should be of invaluable help in your collecting and identifying editions. It is the first comprehensive bibliography to record Mum's sixty years in publishing.

The Hares have been working on *Tasha Tudor: The Direction of Her Dreams* for fifteen years. Their interest in my mother's work has now grown from this book to redirect the business of their twenty-five-year-old antiquarian book service. To my knowledge, their Cellar Door Books is now the country's largest source of Tasha Tudor books, both old and new, as well as an extensive collection of her early art. Their catalog is available by writing Cellar Door Books, 61 Borough Road, Concord, New Hampshire 03303.

It has been my pleasure to introduce John and Jill Hare and *Tasha Tudor: The Direction of Her Dreams.* Enjoy!

Efner Holmes
Contoocook, New Hampshire
March 1997

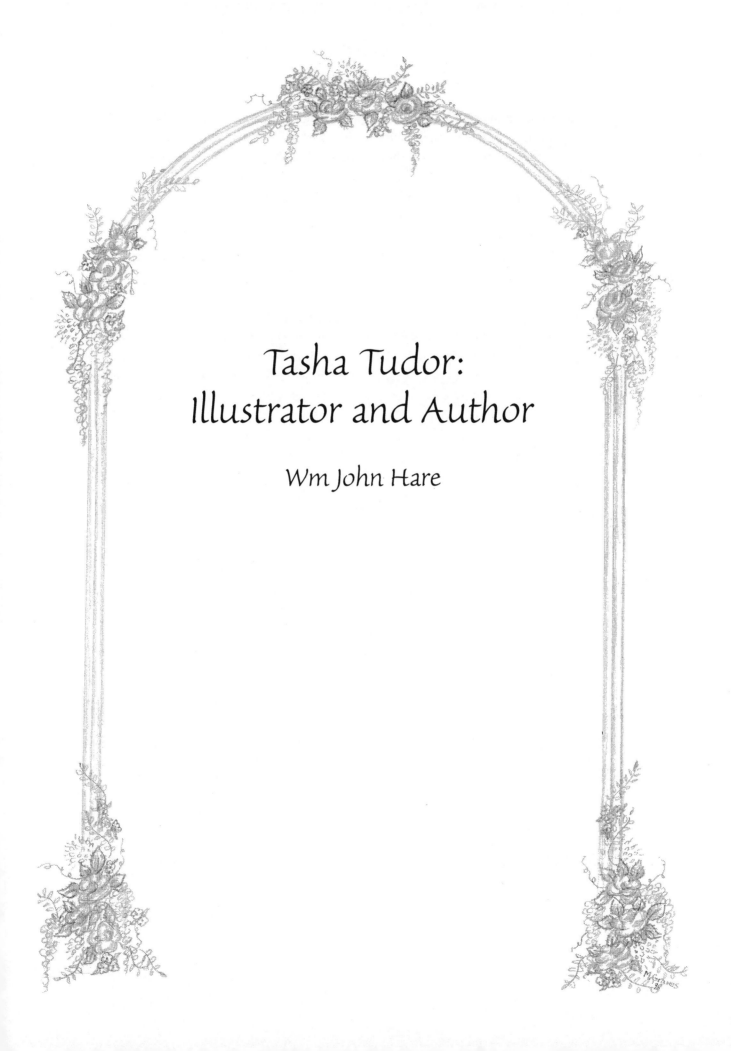

Tasha Tudor:
Illustrator and Author

Wm John Hare

[Tasha in costume]

Tasha Tudor! She is a gardener. She is an octogenarian entrepreneur. And she is a New England artist who has been writing and illustrating books with superlative images since at least 1934. Many in her worldwide audience knew her books as children—in a childhood left many years ago. But in a sense, they remain children always, reliving their younger days through Tasha Tudor's eyes and reminiscing on the scenes she paints. This audience is intrigued not only by her original magical stories, but also by her particular romantic rendering of the New England countryside depicted in those stories. These have often been experiences from her own family life. Nineteen ninety-eight marks her sixtieth year writing and illustrating a quaint and lovely, quiet-paced (generally), mostly agrarian life. Her work is published in more than ninety books that stand the test of time. There have been many printings and re-publications. Tudor travels to book fairs to meet her fans and autograph her books. Her business company of the moment stages other publicity events to maintain her public accessibility. She has worked ceaselessly to generate and maintain interest in her product (her art and her books). One is led to believe that she would just as soon walk down her country lane, close a gate, and leave the world behind her. There are numerous clues in her books that she has worked very hard to create her personal haven on a south-facing hillside in Vermont. To maintain her pace and meet her public as she does at eighty-two years of age demonstrates the stamina of the farmer (which she is) and the dignity and grace instilled by her Beacon Hill heritage. She is at once a product and a proponent of the New England she emulates.

One of Tasha Tudor's earliest appearances in print was March 26, 1924, when the *Boston Herald* ran a picture of a demure eight-year-old girl holding roses at the launching of the yacht *Argyll* in Salem, Massachusetts. She is identified as Miss Natasha Burgess, the sponsor at the launching and daughter of naval architect W. Starling Burgess. Tudor speaks fondly of her father's wonderful storytelling when she was a little girl. That aside, her parents divorced when she was still a child and her father remarried. Subsequently two more daughters were born making Tudor the middle of her father's five children. Tudor and her father were mostly separated in her later youth, but she certainly appreciated his engineering skill and applied it to her paintings and her houses; her perspective is true. Her lines are confident, solid, and traditional New England construction with a flair and a wit which must have been instilled by her father. From her mother, the noted portrait painter Rosamond Tudor, Tasha learned color and composition and how to draw. She first learned to paint with her mother, and later attended the museum school at Boston's Museum of Fine Arts.

Tudor was named for her father Starling Burgess. Later she was called Natasha to memorialize Tolstoy's heroine in *War and Peace*. In spite of subsequent name changes with marriages and divorces, Starling 'Tasha' Burgess has been known to the children's book world as Tasha Tudor since her first book, *Pumpkin Moonshine,* was published in 1938.[1] She used the matrilineal Tudor name for artistic purposes at a young age, and inscribed her 1934 *Hitty's Almanac* with that name. Her own children would later change their names from McCready to Tudor also reflecting the maternal heritage.

As a child, Tudor was influenced by two quite different *milieux*—the social life of Boston (the port city and political capital) and seafaring Marblehead, and rural Connecticut (her father's engineering accomplishments versus her mother's life as a bohemian painter with country friends). The young Tasha absorbed the atmosphere of the Tudor house on Beacon Hill amid constant reminders of an ancestor's voyages to the Orient. She became especially enraptured by the life of the 1830s; the journey back a hundred years is vital in her art and life, making her a favorite illustrator for stories of that decade. Not only does she illustrate stories of that time; but she long ago adopted the costume as well. Her home and drawings are evocative of daily life 150 years in the past. *A Brighter Garden* (1990), *Little Women* (1969), and *The Night Before Christmas* (1962, 1975) all transport the reader to New England in the years before the American War Between the States. Tudor's wardrobe and household furniture are the models for these time travels. One sees them throughout her books.

Tudor spent most of her formative years on a Connecticut farm, an experience never far from view in her thousands of illustrations. She dreamed of living on a farm of her own. When she was but nineteen years old, she interpreted her agrarian dreams in her first tiny manuscript, *Hitty's Almanac.* It remains unpublished, but it presages scenes that appear in numerous later books—*Around the Year* (1957), *A Time to Keep* (1977), and, *Tasha Tudor's Seasons of Delight* (1986), for example. The theme is repetitive but each new interpretation still delights the senses.

Tasha Burgess and Thomas Leighton McCready, Jr. were married May 28, 1938, at her mother's house in Redding, Connecticut, where they initially lived. Their two older children Bethany and Seth were born there. Tudor's experience of country life as a young girl is reflected in her books from the Connecticut years before World War II. Bethany, Tom, and Seth are names she uses in her stories. She portrays strong farmers, small children, sheep, goats, cows, pumpkins, geese, and dogs. Her earliest "calico" books of this period are *Pumpkin Moonshine* (1938), *Alexander the Gander* (1939), *The County Fair* (1940), *Dorcas Porkus* (1942), and *Linsey Woolsey* (1946). They are miniatures of color and charm, in high demand today. Fine copies command hundreds of dollars in the used book trade. These books are only five by four inches and were designed for children to carry in their small pockets. They *were* carried, they were loved, and sixty years later they are uncommon in very good condition. To find them with fine dust jackets as well is a rare occurrence. Some of the best copies to be seen are at the

Pierpont Morgan Library in New York City. There they are housed among the rarest of cultural treasures. Warner Books, responding to requests for the scarce titles, had planned to re-issue the set of five calico books in the Spring of 1998. They changed their plans, however, and the books will not be reprinted by them.

In the Spring of 1945, the McCready family moved north and settled into "Uncle" Ed Gerrish's large 1790s "colonial" frame house in Webster, New Hampshire. The house was in disrepair, and so its extensive refurbishment became one more artistic labor of love shoehorned among the other aspects of living and writing and painting. Children Tom and Efner were born after the New Hampshire move, and there the stable of farm animals continued to increase, as did the books they inspired.[2]

Now, please indulge us for this small geography lesson from "Uncle Henry-Adam-John."[3] The McCready/Tudor family lived in the town (township, for those west of the Hudson River) of *Webster*, New Hampshire. But, they were close enough to the village of *Contoocook* (on the north-flowing river of the same name) that mail was addressed as a rural route of that village. Three miles downstream from Contoocook, the river is increased by the Blackwater River, that stream flowing by the McCready farm and commemorated in *Becky's Birthday* (1960) and other paintings from the Webster period. Contoocook, itself, is a village in the northwestern part of the town[ship] of *Hopkinton* (the political entity and neighboring town to Webster). *Warner*, another adjoining town becomes the family name in Thomas McCready's books of the 1950s which Tudor illustrated. Since those New Hampshire years, Tudor has lived for twenty-five years in Marlboro, Vermont. Again, however, her mailing address becomes a rural route of the nearby village of West Brattleboro.

But, back to our story. By 1945, Tudor had published eight books. Her illustrations for *Mother Goose* (1944) paid for the house in Webster. Tudor's early "calico books" had captured children's imaginations with a lamb named Linsey Woolsey and a goose named Alexander. Encouraged by his wife's success, Thomas McCready also began to write children's books about the farm animals in New Hampshire. McCready found his animal protagonists in the family's own barnyard—*Biggity Bantam* (1954), the story of an irascible banty rooster who, like the McCreadys, moves north from Connecticut, *Pekin White* (1955), a particularly adventurous duck, *Mr. Stubbs* (1956), a cat with virtually no tail, *Increase Rabbit* (1958), and the *Adventures of a Beagle* (1959) named May Day Warner. Tasha Tudor brought all these family stories to life through her vivid and honest paintings. A final volume about *Flatfoot*, a Toulouse goose, was never published. But in these books Tudor's very active family first crosses the bibliographic stage and here the parents and children are introduced under various thinly disguised names. Sometimes, not disguised at all.

The proliferate household activities and barnyard chores are well documented in Tudor's watercolors. The greening of Spring in the south pasture is depicted on the endpapers of *Biggity Bantam,* and birthday cakes glow in the night as they float down the Blackwater River in *Becky's Birthday.* Throughout her books Tudor records the hills and flowers and local animals (Merrimack County scenes from the artist's dooryard and her own farmhouse domesticity). Family friends such as Nell Dorr and Ann Beneduce also focused their cameras' lenses on that life and captured loving vignettes published in *Mother and Child* (1954) and *Tasha Tudor* (1971), Beneduce's small photo booklet.

One of the most charming of Tudor's Webster books, *Thistly B* (1949), features a yellow canary, one among many birds that lived—indeed, flew—in the McCready home. *Thistly B* makes his home in a doll house which was a famous feature of the New Hampshire home. The doll inhabitants appear here and in several other books. *The Dolls' Christmas* (1950) features favorite dolls Sethany Ann and Nicey Melinda. McCready marionettes first appear here and will reappear in several of Tudor's stories. A fanciful article from *Life* magazine (September 12, 1955) reported the wedding of McCready dolls Lieut. Thaddeus Crane and Melissa Shakespeare, ably assisted by real children of the neighborhood. A set of photographic postal cards from the 1950s portrays daily events in the lives of the six-doll Shakespeare family.

The postal cards were one of many products distributed through The Ginger and Pickles Store, the family's home business whose name derives from a Beatrix Potter book. Here the McCreadys sold home-grown produce, books, and other gifts. The shop was a favorite destination for fans of the day, despite the interruption these visits caused Tudor. As a home enterprise, The Ginger and Pickles Store provided revenue to help pay the bills of a growing family. As a marketing strategy, it allowed many people the opportunity to shop and visit at *Tasha Tudor's home.* In 1957–58 the family made an extended visit to England during which they visited Beatrix Potter's home and her bibliographer Leslie Linder. The visit is manifested in a number of ways in Tudor's art including unpublished Advent calendars. The home store was disrupted when the McCreadys divorced in 1961, and closed following Thomas McCready's death in London in 1964.

Tudor (she always published under this name) and the children lived in the New Hampshire house until 1972. Oldest daughter Bethany recalls that "My most vivid memories of my mother in those early New Hampshire years are related to her art ... At an old-fashioned table by the east window, she would be busily drawing and illustrating ... bits of nature collected from field or garden (flowers, berries, and seedpods stuck in a glass, or perhaps a mouse or a frog, captive for a few hours only, in a large glass jar arranged with moss, tiny ferns, and dried grass). I am sure my own passionate love of nature must have been greatly inspired by that wonderful table and my mother's love of beauty."[4] Readers can still find these kitchen table interpretations throughout her books. It is just such gentle evocations of country loveliness that so enthrall Tudor's admirers around the world. She has never claimed to be more than an illustrator, yet she has created many inventive stories distinctly her own. She does this in words; she does this in paint. See *The Dolls' Christmas*, *Edgar Allan Crow*, and *Becky's Birthday*. Not least, she skillfully, cleverly paints impish mischief into the faces of corgi dogs and little boys; her angelic girls capture as many nuances of character as the best written prose can do. She has been honored for her work with the Catholic Library Association's Regina Medal, and with an honorary doctorate in humane letters from the University of Vermont. *Mother Goose* was named a Caldecott Honor Book in competition for the year's outstanding illustrated children's book. Tudor has never been awarded either the Caldecott Medal nor its literary counterpart, the Newbery Medal, for best children's book of the year.

Tasha Tudor still lives in New England, still with cats and goats and canaries and corgyn. The latter term, she has taught us, is the Welsh plural for the corgi dogs she has owned since the 1958 trip to England. In 1972 she realized a long-time goal of living in Vermont. Her son Seth built her "cape" and barn, inspired by the Concord, New Hampshire, hilltop house of a friend. She named her new Vermont home Corgi Cottage. It is seen in *The Night Before Christmas* (1976) and has frequently been painted in whole or in minute detail in Tudor's art. It appears regularly in her later books, and even pops up at us from *Tasha Tudor's Seasons of Delight*. The house and gardens have been amply described in recent books by Tovah Martin and lavishly photographed by fellow-Vermonter Richard Brown, a former son-in-law of Charles and Anne Lindbergh. Tudor's pride in her flower gardens is also evidenced in numerous magazine articles of the last ten years, especially *Victoria* with which Martin is associated. Tudor obviously thrives on much publicity although *Horticulture*, August/September 1995, carried this 'Word [to the contrary] from Tasha Tudor.'

> Since the May 1995 publication of "A Spring Visit with Tasha Tudor," Tasha Tudor has received so many requests to visit her garden that she cannot possibly respond to them all. Although she was delighted to share her garden with kindred spirits through Horticulture, she regrets that she cannot entertain the public at Corgi Cottage. —Ed.[5]

Once published and allowed to go out-of-print, Tudor's books have sometimes re-appeared in different forms. Three of her early books were later published as the anthology *Tasha Tudor's Sampler* (1977). *First Delights, A Book About the Five Senses* (1966) was rewritten by the original publisher and simplified for young readers in 1988. The most common event has been the movement of Tudor's many books from publisher to publisher (the conglomerate effect of publishers' general regrouping through purchase and sale). The very popular

Mother Goose began at Oxford University Press, transferred to Henry Z. Walck, passed on to David McKay and more recently to Random House. Sales and acquisitions are still occurring as evidenced by the merging of Penguin and Putnam in 1997. Both publish Tudor titles and distribute them worldwide, for Tudor is known in many countries. Translations of *The Book of Christmas* (1979) have been published in Denmark, France, Germany, Italy, Japan, Sweden; *Amy's Goose* can be found in Afrikaans, Dutch, and Swedish.

Books, while common and visible, have not been the sole arena for Tudor's art. She designed and illustrated Christmas cards for many years. They are lovely vignettes of the holiday season. A sub-culture of the Tudor phenomenon exists for the collecting and trading of these cards, most of them from the Irene Dash greeting card company. And a sub-culture of that group could concentrate only on Tudor's portrayals of young Madonnas. Tudor has illustrated post cards, tin cans, jig-saw puzzles, and soaps. She designed porcelain figurines for The Franklin Mint, and porcelain boxes. Her hand-made toys also have been recreated that others might try the magic that touched the Tudor children as they were growing up. There are posters and many art prints of her paintings. Those of recent years have some limited few pieces with an extra original drawing in the margin. Her publisher, Corgi Cottage Industries, calls these extra drawings "remarques." This is, however, a technical misnomer. A true remarque is normally drawn into the margin of a printing plate by the artist and reproduced on each print to be drawn from the stone or press. It might or might not be eradicated during the edition. Tudor's images are original drawings added after the prints are made; the images vary.

Throughout her life, Tudor has allied herself with kindred spirits wherever they might find one another. The "Stillwaters" denotes her quasi-religious circle of friends who seek to live a self-sustaining life with the earth. See Sarah Ban Breathnach's *Simple Abundance: A Daybook of Comfort and Joy* (1995). And those who feel themselves to be kindred spirits have always sought out Tudor.

We have already alluded to the Nell Dorr collaboration recorded in *Mother and Child* (1954) and *The Family Of Man* (1955). Many people have long enjoyed the books Tudor created with Mary Mason Campbell (a friend and neighbor from up the road in New Hampshire), *The New England Butt'ry Shelf Cookbook* (1968) and *...Almanac* (1970). Tudor illustrated reprints of the Henry Augustus Shute books, *The Real Diary of a Real Boy* (1967) and *Brite and Fair* (1968), stories of New Hampshire of a hundred years earlier. *A Brighter Garden* (1990), a selection of Emily Dickinson's poems with illustrations has subsequently been interpreted in audio and video tape. Each of these transports the listener to mid-nineteenth century New England. Tudor tolerates the twentieth century despite her adherence to nineteenth century technology. She will travel by air when necessary. But she revels in her natural setting where Sarah Kerruish captured her for the videotapes *Take Joy! The Magical World of Tasha Tudor* (1996) and *Take Peace, A Corgi Cottage Christmas with Tasha Tudor* (1997).

Tudor's influence has been a powerful one within her own family. Her children and grandchildren regularly served as models for her to paint. They appear throughout her books. In the last decade, Tudor has several times dipped into her source material and published sketchbooks capturing these visual records of her children growing. Mothers, children, and animals abound; fathers are rare. Both Tudor daughters have written books of their own, naturally enough about animals with whom they have lived their lives. Bethany wrote of ducklings and owls in *Samantha's Surprise* (1964) and *Skiddycock Pond* (1965). Teaming with her mother, Efner Holmes gave us the story of a cat lost in the winter, *The Christmas Cat* (1976). Her mother's paintings for this book introduced Efner's family to readers. More recently, Efner has written of domestic horses in *My Sadie* (1993), and wild animals in *Deer in the Hollow* (1993). But these books were published with other artists' illustrations. In the last year, Tudor's sons and other family members have written for *Take Joy!* a bi-monthly Tudor magazine published from January 1997 through April 1998.

Tudor has influenced the way *many* people live. One of the earliest examples was the Lock Haven State Teachers College English professor and Mill Hall, Pennsylvania, collector and shop owner Edward "Ned" Hills. When the official Tudor biography is written, a large chapter will need to address Hills' role, first in collecting, and then marketing the art of Tudor's first forty years. I will attempt no more here than to say that a strong friendship bound the two for many years. Hills made a profound effort to introduce Tudor directly to a larger audience than she might otherwise have found. Tudor reciprocated by painting him as Santa Claus into her *Night Before Christmas* (Achille J. St. Onge). Indeed, she dedicated the book to him. Hills was joined at a later date by his niece Gretchen Brown McKeever. The connections between the McCready family and the Hills-Brown family are alluded to in the periodical literature.

In the 1970s, Linda Allen and Tudor jointly authored two books, *Tasha Tudor's Favorite Christmas Carols* (1978) and *Tasha Tudor's Old-fashioned Gifts* (1979). A recent Tudor protégé is New Yorker Paul Peabody whom she encouraged to write and illustrate *Blackberry Hollow* (1993). Tudor has appeared publicly for many years, drawing, demonstrating her marionettes, and generally playing the role of raconteur. She continues to do so and her fans will travel long distances to an announced presentation to participate, however vicariously, in the Tudor mystique.

The Books and The Bibliography

We were snared by Tudor's books innocently enough. (Many book collectors would say as much about their chosen subjects.) Mrs. Hare admired the paintings! She appreciated the childhood innocence. She was warmed by Tudor's delivery of New England culture during our years living in the mid-West. And so, we bought some Tudor books, enjoyed them and put them on a shelf. And then we bought some more, and still some more. After duplicating a few purchases, we observed that some books were near-duplicates, but with small and interesting differences.

We intended to jot down a few notes that might serve as a guide for our visits to book shops. But by 1979, the microcomputer had appeared, and a librarian with an Apple II (64K memory!) could really record details twenty years ago! So began this "short" bibliographic study. In the ensuing years, we have attempted to unravel details which publishers seem not to have recorded, or discarded long ago. Our research into Tudor's publishing history began to reflect the personalities and frenetic activity of publishing since 1950. We sought out information on cloths, papers, copyrights. We visited libraries to examine children's books looking for more variations. We made the acquaintance of production managers at publishing houses. These are the people who really know the materials used to produce a book. It is they who know the production order for a title at any given moment and which printer will bring ink to paper and books to glorious life.

And in the end, we determined that Tasha Tudor's publishing history runs like this:

Under Eunice Blake's editorship, Oxford University Press, New York, Inc. published Tudor's first book, *Pumpkin Moonshine,* in 1938. This followed rejections from other publishers and the important children's editor May Massee. Having teamed and succeeded, Tudor and Blake averaged better than a book a year for the next twenty years with Oxford, until its manager-president Henry Z. Walck left to establish his own firm. And with his 1958 departure, Walck bought the inventory, authors' contracts, and copyrights of Oxford's 250 children's titles. These included, of course, the total work Tudor had produced for that house.[6] The new company, Henry Z. Walck, Inc., produced books with moderate success until publishing's massive corporate reorganization of the 1970s caused him to merge his firm with the David McKay Co., then owned by Ken Rawson. Rawson and Walck both began their publishing careers at Putnam's in the 1930s. Putnam has survived as a publishing group so that many of Tudor's books ironically have found their home under Putnam's roof in recent years.

Walck initially managed McKay's list of children's books, but he had retired from McKay by 1980, leaving his imprint as a McKay subsidiary.[7] Tudor's books follow this corporate path. Printings of *Pumpkin Moonshine* can be found in several Oxford issues, enlarged copies from Walck and as one of the titles anthologized in McKay's *Tasha Tudor's Sampler*. Random House was still issuing *Pumpkin Moonshine* in paperback in 1989. The Jenny Wren Press, Mooresville, Indiana, issued a 55th Anniversary Edition in 1993, including a limited number of copies in pumpkin-colored leather. Lastly, Warner Books planned to re-issue the first "calico" sized reprint in the Spring of 1998. They abandoned the idea.

Henry Z. Walck's exodus from Oxford with its children's list created the most tortuous aspect of Tudor bibliography. Walck, quite naturally, began issuing books with his own imprint. But he did not *renew* copyright in his new company's name nor did he specify *reprinting* dates in his company's books. Instead, Walck, Inc. printed its copyright statement with the date of the original Oxford edition, e.g. "Copyright 1939, Henry Z. Walck, Inc." and "Henry Z. Walck, Inc., 1956." Neither of those statements comes from a book manufactured in those years. Nor did Henry Z. Walck, Inc. obtain copyrights for the books in those years, or ever. (There is, however, one neat irony buried in these peregrinations. Henry Z. Walck was the Oxford official who signed and filed the 1938 copyright application for *Pumpkin Moonshine*, Tudor's first published book.) To the uninitiated, Walck books appear to be legitimate first editions dating from the 1930s, '40s and '50s, when in fact they are reprints dating from 1958 into the 1980s, generally on whiter paper. Other clues to their actual production dates exist in ISBNs and Cataloging-In-Publication data, neither of which was used in the 1940s and 1950s. Although Library of Congress card numbers can be found in post–World War II books, their inclusion did not become common until the 1950s. Then a great deal of attention was given to helping librarians catalog their books faster by national standards. I would like to date each of these Walck printings to a precise year, but it is impossible to do so. One makes an educated guess at best.

Walck's misleading statement about copyright appears in many Tudor books. One is warned, erroneously, in many copies of *Pumpkin Moonshine*: "Copyright by Henry Z. Walck, 1938". Most distressing, The Jenny Wren Press, in which Tudor partnered for a few years with Beth Mathers, perpetuates the error in its 55th anniversary edition, 1993. Here again, the statement is repeated on the verso (the left hand page) of the title page: "1st Edition Copyright 1938 Henry Z. Walck, Inc." Two recent title lists perpetuate the wrong attribution, in *Drawn from New England* (Philomel, 1979), and in the *Tasha Tudor Bibliography* (Elaine's Upper Story, 1989). Henry Z. Walck, Inc. didn't exist in 1938; in fact, no books could have been published with the Walck name until after 1957. Yet, many booksellers and unsuspecting book buyers, ignorant of this vagary have routine-

ly traded Walck's books as "first editions" not suspecting their true age. No wonder their condition seems so good, their paper so white! A simple caution is in
order. Oxford is the name to prove a first edition of most Tudor books before
1958. Furthermore, Oxford University Press carefully numbered its successive
printings, another point which Walck failed to follow. The *only title* which Walck
published as a true first edition, its initial entrance to the market, is *More Prayers*
(1967). This is the only evidence that Tudor and Walck collaborated on any publication after 1957.

With the dispersal of children's books at Oxford, Eunice Blake brought
Tudor to J. B. Lippincott Company, in Philadelphia, where Tudor illustrated new
editions of the perennial sellers *The Secret Garden* (1962) and *A Little Princess*
(1963). Despite their lasting popularity, or actually because of it, these books
present a vexing bibliographic problem. They have been continuously in print
for thirty-five years, but Lippincott never, and its successor HarperTrophy only
once, has ascribed a printing date. Indeed, the best clues to their sequence come
from the manufacturing details: jacket price and text, the color of paper and
binding, and the thickness of the book. We have thirty copies of *The Secret
Garden* sitting on our shelves (see S, below). We *think* they are all unique printings. Attempting to determine the gradations of carmine, rose, scarlet and red—
through varying amounts of soil—came closest to ending this whole project.
Other Blake/Tudor products from Lippincott include *Wings from the Wind* (1964)
and *Tasha Tudor's Favorite Stories* (1965), a book Tudor dislikes.

Tudor maintained friendships with other writers. From one of those came
new illustrations for Rumer Godden's *The Dolls' House* (1962). May Massee, pre-
eminent children's editor at the Viking Press, had retired by that time. But she
also had been responsible for introducing Tudor and Godden. Viking originally
published *The Dolls' House* in 1948 with color illustrations by Dana Saintsbury.
The Saintsbury and Tudor images are similar; they were both drawing from a
descriptive text. In at least one instance, a rebinder has graced the front cover of
the Tudor version of the book with Saintsbury's house. Viking had previously
published Tudor's *Becky's Birthday* (1960) and *Becky's Christmas* (1961) and would
next issue *A Round Dozen* (1963), an anthology of Louisa May Alcott's stories.

Ann K. Beneduce first met Tudor when Beneduce was working for Eunice
Blake at J. B. Lippincott Company. An affinity for art brought them together.
The affinity grew to a friendship which continues today as Tudor's strongest and
most enduring professional alliance. So, when Beneduce became principle editor
at Blake's retirement, she and Tudor were soon working on a topic dear to both
of them—the Christmas season. Their work together created the enchanting
Take Joy! The Tasha Tudor Christmas Book (1966), an anthology of poems, stories,
songs and activities centered on this end-of-the-year Christian celebration. The
title is taken from a quotation attributed to Fra Giovanni, 1513. Tudor dedicated

the book to her friend and editor Beneduce, an interesting contrast to the practice Dorothy Haas mentions in her essay concerning books from Rand McNally. *Take Joy!* is a *tour de force* of Tudor's skills. There is new art, pages 10-11, 30. There are twig frames, pages 30, 89, 152. There are alternating black and white and color illustrations. Older greeting cards are reproduced, pages 91, 111, 135. Page 65 suggests friend Pamela Sampson's *A Mouse Family Album*. There are real places; the hall pictured on page 99 is in Hudson, Ohio, and was featured on an earlier Christmas card. A Santa Lucia makes her premiere here on page 131. This was before her mechanical version reappeared in *A Book of Christmas* (1979). There are botanical borders, the title page and page 117, and seasonal decorations on many pages. And there are corgis, or as Tudor prefers, corgyn.

Tudor and Beneduce would produce a number of books together. *Corgiville Fair* (1971), Tudor's own favorite, most inventive book and the title most sought by her collector-admirers, was published by Thomas Y. Crowell Company when Beneduce was head of that house's children's book department. *Corgiville Fair* gives us a world with no people, although there is plenty of action carried on by Welsh corgi dogs, other animals, and Tudor's interpretations of "boggarts," (trollish creatures who "smoke cigars and are apt to be wild").[8] Beneduce helped provide us, too, with daughter Bethany Tudor's *Drawn from New England* (1979)—the only biography to date. This came from William Collins Publishers where Beneduce worked following Harper & Row's purchase of Crowell. This was a short venture, and in 1980 Beneduce established her own publishing unit, Philomel Books, of the Putnam Publishing Group.[9] Philomel continued to publish a number of books by Tudor during the 1980s, including mechanical books derived from the Tudor family tradition of Advent calendars. These have opening doors and surprises. Capitalizing on the recent interest in moving books, Tudor designs appear in *Tasha Tudor's Seasons of Delight* and *A Book of Christmas* (in several languages), pop-up books from the same time and publisher. By mid-decade Beneduce had stepped back from her role at Philomel and was succeeded by Patricia Gauch who now edits Philomel material. Their special friendship kept Beneduce as uniquely responsible for Tudor's books. But with Beneduce's guidance, Gauch brought two more Tudor books to market over the Philomel name, *Tasha Tudor's Advent Calendar: A Wreath of Days* (1988) and *A Brighter Garden* (1990). We've already mentioned Paul Peabody's *Blackberry Hollow*, also edited by Gauch.

Another publisher to present Tudor during the Beneduce years is Universal Publishing and Distributing Corporation/Scribner's. Its *Betty Crocker's Kitchen Gardens* (1971) presents more Mary Mason Campbell country recipes for native foods and herbs. *Kitchen Gardens* was reprinted in several sizes after the original. One issue enlarges the book's dimensions, and the dust jacket, by adding an olive band at top and bottom edges of the previous jacket design. Golden Press published paperbacks of the title in which they first reduced the page size, and then in a 1979 reprint enlarged beyond the original and created a new photographic cover.

Among the fascinating aspects of Tudor iconography is how many forms her art, and even her books, have taken. We have mentioned pop-up and other mechanical books and puzzles. Her first two books, *Hitty's Almanac* and *New England Wild Flowers,* which exist in unique manuscripts, demonstrate a knowledge of flowers and a sensitive beauty in the miniature. She has followed these themes all her life. She shares her floral knowledge in a number of almanacs. Tudor illustrated for the Worcester, Massachusetts, miniaturist Achille St. Onge who published two small leather-bound books, *The Night Before Christmas* (1962) and *The Twenty-third Psalm* (1965). These lovely little volumes take up almost no shelf space and would delight any child who appreciates life at a child's scale. Unfortunately, their regular prices run between fifty and one hundred dollars, and therefore out of consideration for most children's gift books—top shelf.

From about 1988 through 1996, Beth Mathers promoted Tudor's arts, crafts and various ephemera through their joint Jenny Wren Press. The name derives from an old verse relating the tale of Christopher Robin and Miss Jenny Wren. As the McCready children were growing up, Jenny Wren was but one of the fantastic creatures their mother employed for their entertainment. And Jenny Wren's re-creations became stock in trade for the 1980s enterprise in Mooresville, Indiana. Indeed, Miss Jenny Wren was the "spokesbird" for the Press. Old art was recycled into new cards and art prints. Attempts were made to market a new doll at several thousand dollars. Books were reprinted and made available to a new generation of collectors. One failed attempt was made at reprinting *Mother and Child* from the second edition. The reports at the time said that the Press wished to eliminate certain photographs of nude children, but could not obtain copyright permission to do so. At the last, the Jenny Wren Press offered miniature doll furniture for sale patterned after pieces in Tudor's home.

By 1996 the Jenny Wren Press had been dissolved by the principals and Tudor had created a new business with Harry Davis of Richmond, Virginia. Tudor announced her plans to continue playing an active role in publishing in this 1995 letter to her collectors: "As an artist, I have long lamented the fact that, quite often, the artist sends her work out into the world with very little control over how it is presented or distributed. I wished that I could oversee what happened to my work once I had completed it. My wish has been granted, or to be more precise, I have made my wish reality. I have created a new company, Corgi Cottage Industries, which will produce fine quality art prints, cards, books, and a great variety of other items—all personally overseen by the artist—me!"[10] We heard her say much the same thing in Burlington, Vermont, in 1989 relative to The Jenny Wren Press.

With the Corgi Cottage notice, she included announcements of a new print, new Christmas cards, and a sketchbook, each copy of which she would autograph. The latter seems to be a reaction against the inflation of her signature on many recent books. Her autograph is far from rare, and has even been found on adhesive stickers applied to books sold by The Jenny Wren Press. The latest version is her squarish signature, *T. Tudor*, reproduced on the front free endpaper of Simon and Schuster's *The Night Before Christmas* (1997). Here, the reproduction is printed so well that it appears to be an authentic signature. But, it is just another decoration on the page.

Book dealers have known for a long time; Tasha Tudor is a durable seller. Her books are common and yet those who own them don't often let go of them. When they are offered by antiquarian dealers, the books move quickly, commanding respectable prices. They are collectable and they are sought after—with a fervor which has been growing for sixty years.

1 Tudor, Bethany, *Drawn From New England*. Collins: 1979, pp. 10-13
2 Ibid., pp. 26-29
3 A reference to teachers, the real-life Uncle Henry and his fictional counter-part Uncle Adam of *Snow Before Christmas* who are depicted in *Drawn from New England,* page 18; and the bibliographer, also an educator.
4 Tudor, p. 33
5 *Horticulture: The Magazine of American Gardening,* August/September 1995. 73:7 p. 6
6 Tebbel, John, *A History of Book Publishing in The United States*. Bowker: 1981. IV:479
7 Ibid.
8 Tudor, Tasha, *CORGIVILLE FAIR*. Crowell: 1971, p. [viii]
9 Tebbel, IV: 217
10 Undated letter postmarked Richmond, Va., September 30, 1995

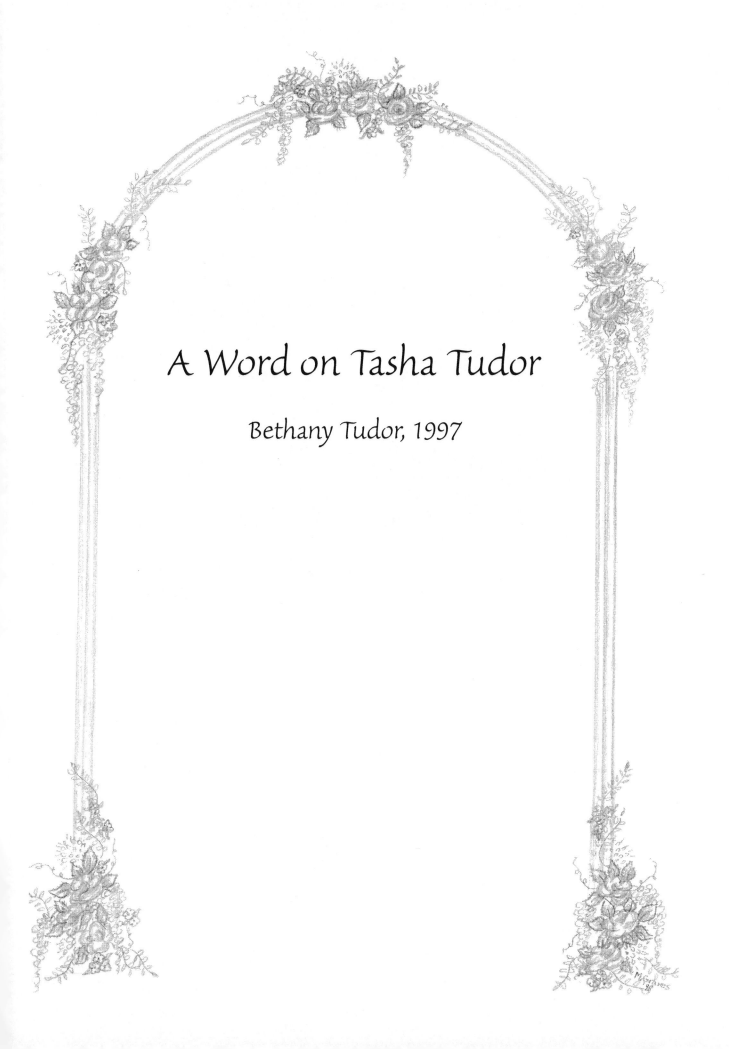

A Word on Tasha Tudor

Bethany Tudor, 1997

[Tasha in bonnet, profile]

y mother always loved to draw and, by the age of seven, knew she wanted to become an artist. Today she says these words of Thoreau sum up the way she has lived her life: "If one advances confidently in the direction of his dreams, and endeavors to live the life which he has imagined, he will meet with a success unexpected in common hours."

She has also said to me in the past, "Part of my success is due to choosing the right parents." Her mother was an accomplished portrait painter, her father a well-known designer of yachts.

Starling Burgess, later Tasha Tudor, was born in Boston on August 28, 1915, when her brother Frederic was nine years old. Tasha grew up as might an only child, since Frederic was away at school during many of her early years. I think being alone fostered her growing imagination and a desire to create pictures of her inner world—which she loved best. This special world had characters of the early 19th century with country lifestyles. The costumes of that time so appealed to my mother that she fashioned her own clothes like them as soon as she learned to sew.

Until she was nine years old, her home was in or near Marblehead, Massachusetts. A Scottish nanny, Mary D. Burnett, helped care for her. Burnett, affectionately called "Dady," had a great influence on Tasha's early learning and interests. Tasha learned the domestic arts from Dady. To this day, she loves and practices them and they play a great part in her books and illustrations.

My grandparents were divorced when Tasha was nine years old. Her mother wanted to continue painting and lived in Greenwich Village in the 1920s. Tasha was sent to live with family friends in Redding, Connecticut. "It was the best thing that ever happened to me—it changed my whole life," says my mother. The family and their friends were creative and imaginative, and the young Tasha throve in an unconventional environment, learning from home schooling, nature, and farm life.

Tasha didn't much care for the formal city life of Beacon Hill in Boston, where her mother sometimes took her to visit relatives. Even as a very young child Tasha was more strongly drawn to the animals and country living.

Tasha spent much of her time painting and drawing during these growing-up years. By the age of fifteen her formal schooling was over and art was her one passion. At nineteen she decided to collect and paint all the Connecticut wildflowers in the area. It took two or three summers but the resulting book, *New England Wildflowers,* though never published, remains a thing of beauty. Her tiny 1934 book, *Hitty's Almanac,* was also unpublished, but it hints of her great latent talent.

In 1938 my mother married Thomas McCready from Redding, Connecticut. My father's little niece, Sylvie Ann, came from Scotland to visit her grandmother in Connecticut every summer and developed a fondness for my mother. As a gift to Sylvie, Mother wrote and bound the little calico story book, *Pumpkin*

Moonshine. My mother decided to show *this* book to publishers. The book was initially turned down by every New York publisher she visited but, unwilling to be defeated, she went around a second time, found Eunice Blake, a newly-hired editress at Oxford University Press, and the book was published that year. It was the first success for both women.

My brother Seth (two years younger) and I lived in Connecticut from 1940 to 1945. Because my grandmother was away, she let our family use the old home in Redding for a time. My mother really wanted to live on a farm in Vermont but my father thought that was "too far from civilization and good schools." They compromised and finally settled for an old farm in Webster, New Hampshire, and we moved there in April 1945.

When we moved to New Hampshire, Seth and I shared Mother's delight in the animals, birds, and flowers. We were given sketchbooks, pencils, and crayons, but no serious lessons. We just had fun doing what we wanted. At a very early age we were exposed to beautifully illustrated books from my mother's collection. Beatrix Potter (the source for Ginger and Pickles) was my favorite but I also liked Arthur Rackham, Edmund Dulac, E.H. Shepard, Jessie Wilcox Smith, and many others.

When I became old enough to use water colors, my mother and I went on sketching trips to garden, woods, or fields. I learned a lot but never really wanted to become an illustrator. I did give it a try when my *Gooseberry Lane* stories were accepted for publication by Lippincott in the 1960s. But I have never pursued art lessons beyond a few months in London in 1957 and at a Boston art school in 1963.

Inspiration for my mother's work has always been drawn from the things she loves most—antiques, her lifetime collection of costumes, gardening, pets (particularly corgi dogs), and nature. Her art gave all four of us a greater appreciation for the beauty in this world as well. We are all creatively inclined, due to her influence. Efner is an accomplished author. And even though my brothers don't have books published, they are both fine writers too.

I love my mother's early books. Some of my favorites are *The Doll's Christmas, Thistly B, Springs of Joy, Corgiville Fair,* and her illustrated edition of Robert Louis Stevenson's *A Child's Garden of Verses* (1947). I am also particularly fond of *Around the Year*. My mother painted the illustrations for that book when the movie *Friendly Persuasion* was first released. We loved the movie, and one week saw it every night at the Concord Theater. You can see the film's influence on the house and the endpapers in *Around the Year*.

Fantasy and our doll family played a large part in our lives as young children. It was like living in another century most of the time. My mother always wore long skirts and made the clothes we wore as children. Her earlier stories and pictures reflect much of this and Seth and I were often a part of it. If my mother was doing a book and needed models, we would wear the costumes while she sketched us. My mother claims that before we were born she drew little boys and girls who looked amazingly similar to us as we grew up.

We actually used the antiques and some of the old home implements that appear in my mother's illustrations. Cooking was done on the cast iron cookstove, "Black Maria." For years the Webster farmhouse had no central heat and only limited electricity and running water. It took years of hard work and determination to transform the old farm. But during those years my mother did what I consider some of her finest illustrations at the same time she was restoring our house. Earnings from her illustrated *Mother Goose* paid for the farm and five hundred acres of land.

Corgi dogs can almost be considered my mother's "trade mark," they feature so frequently in her illustrations. Mr. B, the original Corgi, came into her life in 1958 after we returned from a year in England. My brother Tom remained in school abroad for a few months more and during that time he saw some corgis and decided that he wanted one. Tom looked through ads in the paper to find the name of an old vicar in Wales (the Corgi's native homeland). The man had corgis for sale and picked out the best pup in his litter for Tom. This puppy was sent to us in a tea chest which we had to pick up at the airport in Concord, New Hampshire. My mother was immediately charmed by him and she has kept corgis ever since.

Mr. B grew up and acquired a lovely wife. Together they are the "Browns" in *Corgiville Fair.* My mother claims this book is a masterpiece and her favorite. Their son Caleb is the protagonist of my mother's newest book *The Great Corgiville Kidnapping.*

By the late sixties the old farmhouse had become lovely and tasteful, both inside and out. The gardens with herbs and flowers were works of art such as only my mother's hands and imagination could create. Everything she touches is done with a great sense of appreciation for beauty. Although the house in New Hampshire was beautiful and a reflection of my mother's creativity, she had never given up her dream of living in Vermont; and in 1971 she acquired the land that would eventually make her dream come true.

My brother, Seth, was living in a house he had built on several acres in the southern part of Vermont. My mother bought some adjoining land— mostly pine trees but with a small field. Seth was willing to build a "new old house" for his mother, once he had cleared the pine trees from the area where she wanted to build. The resulting house is a copy of one belonging to Doris Purvis, a close friend in Concord. The only change was a reversal of an ell to fit the house to the lay of the land.

The Vermont house took several years of planning and building. Seth built everything by hand with no power tools. Mother planned and designed the gardens and grounds. A stone retaining wall and various terraces were also part of her plan, and were built by a neighbor and his sons.

The move from our seventeen-room farmhouse in New Hampshire was a worthwhile challenge. The new place with its gardens and woods was the beginning of a new and even happier part of my mother's life and artistic career. Now that the children were grown and on their own, she could pursue talents and interests to their fullest potential.

During all the moving and building Mother still managed to write or illustrate more books, always incorporating her beloved corgis. The corgi dogs loved their new home in Vermont as well. It wasn't long before the name "Corgi Cottage" seemed perfect for the cozy Cape Cod house. My mother dotes on her dogs and I've heard her claim that she's part Corgi herself.

Small grandchildren loved the new place, too, particularly after pets were acquired. Baby goats were a favorite. My mother recreated for her grandchildren many of the wonderful times we had as children. Since the move from New Hampshire she has made a lot of marionettes and occasionally puts on marionette shows in which the children participate.

In Vermont, besides reading and caring for her animals, she is much involved in handicrafts—spinning, weaving, knitting, sewing clothes for herself and her doll, Emma, basket weaving, making stuffed corgis and cut-wool animals. She still collects antiques and tea sets, all of which eventually find their way into her sketchbooks and illustrations. She also enjoys entertaining close friends and is famous for her cooking. A firm believer in living self-sufficiently, she has a garden and fruit trees to provide much of her food which she preserves and stores for winter. And she bakes all her own bread.

Friends who visit Corgi Cottage often speak of the aura of peace and contentment. A cup of tea by the fire with Tasha is a most soothing escape from the cares and stresses of everyday living out in the world—a world into which Tasha steps occasionally but not one in which she feels at home.

Mother made much of holidays and traditions as we were growing up. Although she loved all the holidays, Christmas was her favorite. Every year before Christmas we learned to make presents for friends and relatives. Mother loves to do things with her hands and we grew up feeling that the gifts we made meant more to people than something we might have bought. Our tree was decorated with family ornaments dating back to great-grandmother Tudor and had real candles which were lighted when we opened presents on Christmas night. Some of the prettiest decorations for our tree were Mother's lifelike gingerbread animals decorated with white frosting. Christmas inspired many of my mother's greeting cards. She has made twelve every year since the late thirties and several books have also been inspired by the holiday.

Even the dolls had a tree and their own special party. One of my favorite stories, *The Dolls' Christmas,* tells about two of our dolls preparing for their party. As children, my sister Efner and I spent many hours playing with the characters Sethany Ann and Nicey Melinda in the wonderful house described in this book. (The house in *Thistly B* was made by my grandmother and is for small dolls.)

My mother never liked "man dolls" as she called them; but, deciding that Sethany Ann needed a husband, she created Captain Shakespeare. We never saw her working on him because his arrival had to be a complete surprise one Christmas. He is wonderful in Civil War uniform and cap. My mother has always loved making dolls' clothes, so he owns quite a wardrobe.

All of us enjoyed Valentine's Day and spent much time making pretty cards of decorated hearts for the Valentine Tea Party held for our dolls and our friends' dolls, bears, and other stuffed animals. I learned a lot about painting from these Valentines. We were all encouraged to use our paints and pencils and imaginations. Mother always made each of us children a wonderfully painted card with clever verses appropriate to our interests in birds, ducks, bears, bogarts, rabbits, or dolls. I have saved every one of mine and a favorite is a large heart with a group of flower pots in each of which is a pretty flower, separately cut and fitted into a slot in the top of each pot, as if growing. When removed each flower has a little heart-shaped "ball of earth" with words on it. (This valentine appears in my book *Drawn from New England.)*

My favorite holiday is Easter. It comes at such a lovely time of year. Mother always made an Easter egg tree. Our ducks, geese, and chickens provided eggs in abundance around this time. Mother and I decorated them with pretty little stickers of flowers in lovely colors, added tiny gold-paper-chain trim, then fine ribbon. We had fun competing to see who could make the most original or decorative egg and the egg tree was lovely. My canaries contributed tiny blue eggs for the very top branch of the tree.

During all these holidays, my mother drew and painted between farm and housework. I recall quite a few of my mother's books in progress. The most memorable are *Corgiville Fair* and *Around the Year.* I was home at the time and remember the work involved. My mother was enjoying it, but there always seemed to be deadlines from the publishers and farm care to interfere with meeting them. The distracting allure of gardening usually created a last-minute rush to complete a book.

Mother would paint for hours at the old kitchen table, with the ever-present corgi models playing happily on the braided rug by the cook stove. I washed dishes, prepared meals, baked bread, and cleaned. It was cozy and enjoyable, and perhaps a few of Dady's skills come alive through me.

Some of my mother's publishers and editors became valued family friends after several trips from New York to the New Hampshire farm. They would come to discuss the business of editing and publishing a new book but Mother's graciousness made them feel immediately at home. Occasionally one of them would try on an outfit from my mother's collection of old dresses. It was fun to watch the transformation of a sophisticated New Yorker into a bonneted lady of 1830. Some said they felt immediately transported to another century.

Among these people, Eunice Blake and Ann Beneduce bring back the fondest memories. Eunice was my mother's first editress at Oxford University Press, the woman who saw in *Pumpkin Moonshine* what none of the other publishers had seen and gave this new writer a chance. She edited my own *Gooseberry Lane* books in the 1960s. Ann edited *Drawn from New England* and *Samuel's Treehouse*. I sometimes visited her in New York when working on one of my books. When the business day was over, she would treat me to experiences I never had as a country girl—experiences such as dining in fine Chinese or French restaurants, seeing a play or movie, or going to an art museum.

Other special people I remember are Elizabeth Yates whom we visited in her lovely home in Peterborough, New Hampshire, and Rumer Godden who came to our New Hampshire home once or twice and whom we visited in London during our year in England. My mother illustrated her book, *The Dolls' House,* for The Viking Press.

Seth, Efner, Tom and I are in many of mother's cards and books. *The Dolls' Christmas* features my cousins Rico and Mary Tudor and school friends, Judy and Susie Moulton, Alice, Sally, and Peter Smith. The story *Amanda and the Bear* is written about the Smith children's grand-mother as a young girl and is a true story. Some of Tasha's grandchildren are in a few Christmas cards, *A Time to Keep, Drawn from New England,* and *The Christmas Cat*. Efner's two oldest sons, Nate and Jason, feature in *The Christmas Cat,* as does her husband Pete. Their son Seth had not been born when Efner wrote that book. My daughter Laura is in my mother's favorite card, "Laura on snow shoes with black cats." The Jenny Wren Press sold this as a print entitled "Laura in the Snow." She is also in cards done for the Jenny Wren Press and in books and sketch books. My book has photos of young Laura on her grandmother's farm and a photo of Seth and Marjorie's children—Jennifer, Julie, and Winslow who appear in Mother's art. (Their Benjamin hadn't been born yet.)

The grandchildren were not used for models as much as were my siblings and I. None of the grandchildren who lived close by were much interested in dressing up in the old costumes although they might occasionally pose for sketches, bribed with my mother's promise of hot tea and brownies. Tom's children Jan, Kim, Mia, and Rani appear almost not at all because they have lived outside the United States for a long time.

At various times over the years my mother has been involved in several business ventures relating to her work. The first was the Ginger and Pickles Store, operated by my father at our house in the early 1950s. He sold Mother's books and Christmas cards, along with quality imported gifts and the Beatrix Potter stories.

The Ginger and Pickles Store featured a museum-doll house that was a great attraction. It was a doll house a neighbor had built for our doll family and was furnished with our childhood collections and playthings and even had a greenhouse designed by my mother for real plants in tiny pots. The doll house is photographed in Nell Dorr's *The Golden Key* which is about a doll wedding we celebrated in 1955.

There were many tourists and visitors to the Ginger and Pickles Store but my mother was not in the store nor was she available to meet with those visitors—she was busy raising a family, farming, painting, and writing. The shop lasted about five years and then operated five or six years more as a mail order business until my parents divorced. Although popular, it wasn't a great financial success.

Another business venture began in 1988 when my mother gave permission for Beth Mathers of Mooresville, Indiana, to use the name "Jenny Wren Press"—a name which we had made up for our doll, bear, and duckling families when I was fifteen. We drew and painted sheets of tiny cards that could be cut and folded, each card having "Jenny Wren Press" printed on the back. We used them ourselves and shared them with friends who had dolls.

Mother did special greeting cards, Advent calendars and other assorted work for the Indiana Jenny Wren Press but it did not generate the business and advertising my mother had hoped for. She and Ms. Mathers dissolved their business relationship in 1995.

At that time, my mother began a new venture with her current business manager, Harry Davis, from Richmond, Virginia. They called the business Corgi Cottage Industries. In the last two years, she has made a lot of public appearances and has produced Christmas cards, new prints, calendars, a new book, *The Great Corgiville Kidnapping,* and has branched out into fashioning stuffed Corgi dogs. *The Great Corgiville Kidnapping* was actually written while Mother was in southern France in 1985 but the illustrations were made in 1996. She said she was waiting until the right moment in her life to publish this, her second masterpiece.

As she matured into later years, Mother's art techniques changed somewhat. She was always improving her techniques and trying new and different ways to make her subjects attractive. She is now secure in her ability to paint whatever is envisioned in her head, without first sketching the subject. She also does lovely flowers and garden scenes by applying water color to paper which has been dampened, thus producing a wonderful soft effect to her work. She says her colors show a greater strength than in the past, due to years of practice and experience.

Mother has worked hard all her life and continues to do so. Today I believe my mother is fully enjoying the realization of her dream—living the life she has imagined and "meeting with success unexpected in common hours."

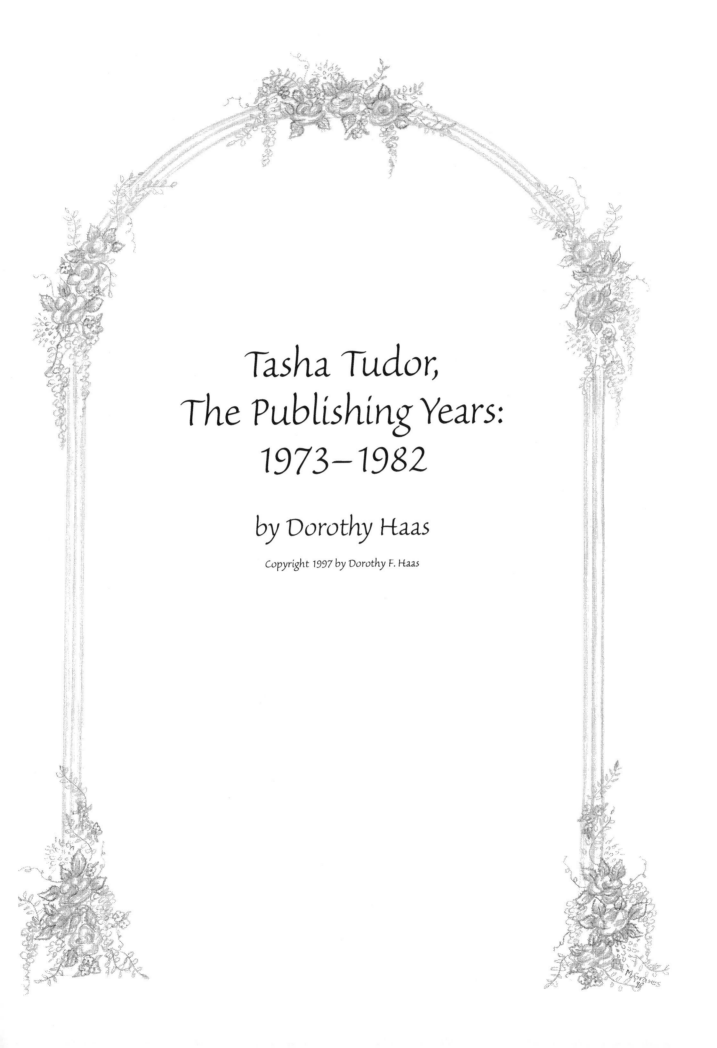

Tasha Tudor, The Publishing Years: 1973–1982

by Dorothy Haas

[Bethany on stairs]

K nowing and admiring Tasha Tudor's books, I wrote to her in May of 1973 asking whether she would be interested in doing a book for Rand McNally where I held forth as editor of children's books. I suggested she call me, that I would accept the charges. And then I sat back and waited. And waited. Nothing came by way of response. June passed, and I pretty much gave up hope of hearing from her.

And then the letter arrived, dated July 9. She wrote that she had just taken my letter out of her mending basket. She regretted not being able to call, but she had not been in her new home in Vermont very long and did not have a telephone. Yes, she might be interested in doing a book for Rand McNally, but of course certain of her expectations would have to be met. She had to like the story. She did not care to do modern-day subject matter. Her artwork was to be returned in pristine condition at the end of the project. And more.

I wrote at once telling of my delight. I would do the necessary paperwork for the project and get back to her with story suggestions for discussion.

I gave considerable thought to the project. I wanted the best she had to offer—subject matter suited to the delicacy of her style and to settings of the past century. And I wanted as well a subject that would appeal to book buyers. After in-depth research into the classic tales, I wrote asking whether she would be interested in doing "the" edition of Clement Clark Moore's "A Visit From St. Nicholas," written in 1822 and known ever afterward as "The Night Before Christmas." Or, what about her own version of "Mary Had a Little Lamb"? Or, we could consider a special edition combining the most favored of the so-called old favorites—"The Three Bears," "The Three Little Pigs," and "Little Red Riding Hood." Or, I asked, did she have a particular favorite she was yearning to do? I particularly liked the thought of the Clement Clark Moore classic.

She wrote at once. *The Night Before Christmas* was very much to her taste. It was decided. That would be her/our subject. We had more than a year to work on the book. It would be scheduled for 1975.

Most people have some idea of what an editor does, of the dialogue between the creator and the editor, of the exchange of ideas and the critique of material. The editor watches the book grow into the best the creator has to offer. But there is more to the process, having to do with the physical aspects of the book-to-be, than the casual observer knows.

What will the book's dimensions be? Six by eight inches in oblong format, perhaps? Or a vertical nine by twelve? How many pages will it contain? What will the charges be for typesetting the text? What the cost of camera separation of artwork into the primary colors used in printing? What the cost of printing plates made from those separations? Paper has to be considered, too. What quality? How much will be needed, and at what cost? Finally, the book will have to go through the binding process. What will those charges be?

Those considerations and more occupy the editor's mind, as well as, finally, the retail price to be charged. The selling price must cover all production expenses as well as the author/artist's royalty. Too high a price will turn off potential purchasers. Knowing the buyer appeal of larger books, I wanted the 9 x 12 format if it could be managed. Many were the conferences with the production department as we juggled figures and possible printing quantities.

I finally determined that the large format book could be done if color was used only on alternating spreads. I presented my proposal to the publishing committee: *The Night Before Christmas,* a 9 x 12 book, 64 pages long, with alternating full color and black and white spreads. The production costs distributed over 40,000 copies would make an appealing $6.95 selling price possible. Corporate approval was swift in coming.

I returned to Tasha with the dimensions she required for her artwork and the project was underway.

Tasha and I got to know each other in the course of our work. I visited her Vermont farm home in July 1975 and again in October. The house, constructed on plans of one built in 1740, was familiar. It appeared, snow cloaked, in the opening and closing illustrations of the book. I felt as though I was stepping into one of her illustrations. Inside I was introduced to the doll, doll carriage, rocking horse, and other period toys that appear in the book. Outdoors, I strolled about the tumble-of-flowers English style garden. I met the corgis, the chicks, saw the goats milked. Tasha and I became comfortable with each other in that serene setting.

A hundred and fifty years separate author Clement Clark Moore and Tasha Tudor. Their talents spanned the years and joined in a charmingly whimsical treat for children of today. *The Night Before Christmas* touches the hearts of adults and children alike.

The book appeared in time for the fall 1975 selling season, and I accompanied her on several promotional tours. I was frequently bemused by the attitudes of some of the autograph seekers. Seeming to think they knew and understood her through her illustrations, they imposed upon her a sentimentality bordering on the saccharine. They could not have been farther from the truth. As Tasha's editor, I was keenly aware of the dedicated work she put into her illustrations. And having visited her home, I was aware as well of how she toiled to attain and maintain a lifestyle patterned on the ways of the mid-nineteenth century. I have rarely known anyone who worked as hard as Tasha Tudor does to achieve a personal lifestyle.

The Night Before Christmas sold out almost at once. No question but that another book was wanted. This one, it was decided, would use the same appealing format, would be modestly priced. And this one—the company was willing to take a chance at covering the costs—would use full color artwork throughout.

It was Tasha's thought to do a book based on a child's request to know what life was like when "Mummy" was a little girl. It would be a book of days, months, seasons, the celebration of holidays and family events. There was a flurry of telephone calls—she had acquired a phone—and letters.

The project moved along smoothly. But as it developed it became apparent that Tasha was uneasy. She had a number of titles in mind, none of which was quite right. I visited her in the summer of 1976 and she ran titles past me. "A Joy for All Seasons?" "Days to Delight?" "A Delight of Days?" We mulled them over, talked at length. Then while she went about her daily chores, I settled down in the parlor with one of the best sources of literary phrases, the Bible. In time I turned to Ecclesiastes, to "To every thing there is a season, and a time to every purpose…" I called to her. She came into the parlor. "Is there something here?" I asked. She looked over my shoulder, scanning the wonderful lines. Her finger came down instantly on one phrase. "There it is!" she exclaimed, "A Time to Keep." It was as a title singularly right for her book.

It was a joy to watch this book develop. Tasha put much of herself into it, from memories of her childhood that she recreated for her own children. She reveals herself as the passionate gardener that she is, the omnivorous reader, the weaver, spinner, seamstress. She translates her joy in a flower, her happiness in a task performed well, her pleasure in the turning of the seasons, her appreciation of traditional values into visual forms that speak eloquently to readers everywhere.

A Time to Keep appeared in the bookstores in 1977. Its strength, its quality, immediately touched the public's interest. It was a sell-out.

Tasha had produced two highly successful books. What was to follow? It would be hard to match the popularity of *The Night Before Christmas* and *A Time to Keep.*

I well remember the thinking that led to the third book. We tossed ideas back and forth. I suggested it might be interesting to illustrate outstanding moments in her life. Did she, for example, recall her first awareness of beauty? Could that moment be illustrated? And were there other equally significant events? Such a collection would, I felt, be welcome, a pictorial autobiography.

Tasha listened, neither rejecting the idea nor wholly accepting it. A short time later an illustration arrived in the mail, not the rough sketch that might be expected for a book still in the thinking stage, but a finished piece of art. It depicted a small girl, her back to the viewer, standing in an open doorway looking out into the out-of-doors. In the far distance was a suggestion of the sun rising over misted hills, picking up the colors of trees, of a lake. The interior of the room behind the child was shadowed, contained a churn, canning jars, cooking implements hung on the wall. Under the floor was one of Tasha's tiny mouse households teeming with activity, with spinning, weaving, food cooking on an iron range. The child, unaware of the room behind her, was about to step out into a world of grace, of beauty, to find who knew what wonders. I was enchanted, studying the painting.

But Tasha was not satisfied, as became apparent in a phone call that soon followed. She did not say she was uncomfortable with the thought of exposing her inner self to the world at large, but I sensed as much. I had come to recognize her deeply cherished reserve, and I had to respect that need for privacy. She could not launch herself into a book that made her ill at ease. I as an editor knew that the best books are those that grow out of the creator's inner sense of rightness about a given project. And I wanted her best. She decided, finally, that she could do a book of her favorite quotations, "Other men's flowers" as she would later call them in a foreword to the book. Reluctantly I gave up thoughts of an autobiography. With a last appreciative look at the child in the doorway, I had the picture wrapped and returned to her. I sat back to await the illustrations that would come.

They did arrive, illustrations of children at play and at work, in snow, rain, and sunshine, and under rainbows. The scenes were all recognizable, set in and around her home or in variations of those scenes. Rabbits, kittens, chicks, goats, and frolicking kids were there. As were the corgis, of course. The collection of quotations that accompanied the illustrations reveal much of Tasha as a reader of wide ranging tastes—John Donne, Henry David Thoreau, Sarah Orne Jewett, Edward Fitzgerald, Ralph Waldo Emerson, Elizabeth Barrett Browning. The collection says something of Tasha Tudor the person as well as Tasha Tudor the reader. Her joys and values can be discerned.

One quotation in particular caused a mild corporate ruckus. The poem from *Leaves of Grass* expresses Walt Whitman's appreciation of animals and reflects Tasha's feelings as well.

> I think I could turn and live with animals
> they are so placid and self-contain'd,
> I stand and look at them long and long.
> They do not sweat and whine about their condition,
> They do not lie awake in the dark and weep for their sins.
> They do not make me sick discussing their duty to God.

The last two lines raised vice-presidential hackles.

I do not subscribe to censorship and have fought many battles on that issue. My feeling was that the quotation was Tasha's choice and her right to use it unquestionable. I did feel that the poem was intellectually mature—as were many in the collection—and beyond the comprehension of the children at whom the book was beamed. That's the sort of thing an editor points out to an author and then rests with the author's final judgment. But such was not to be. Word came down from on high that the two "troubling" lines had to be deleted.

A notice on the copyright page would state, "In deference to the sensibilities of some readers, the publisher has deleted several lines from the Walt Whitman poem contained herein."

The book would be called *The Springs of Joy.*

History repeated itself. This book, too, was eagerly received.

That Christmas, a package arrived in the mail at my home. In it was the painting of the little girl looking out of the doorway into a bright world waiting to be explored. Tasha sent Christmas greetings with the painting. I treasure it still.

Between *The Springs of Joy* and Tasha's fourth book, we took an interesting short detour. I suggested she do an advent calendar, a Christmas scene with the typical little doors to be opened on successive days leading up to the holiday. The calendar would be sold with its own envelope so that it could be mailed as a greeting card. My thinking was that if the calendar met with popular approval, she might do a series of such greeting cards at two year intervals. Each would appear for several seasons and then be retired. At some distant future time they could be reissued. She liked the idea.

The first advent calendar was published in 1978, a second in 1980, and a third in 1982. An amusing incident touched on one of the calendars.

At some time in the development of the three previous books, Tasha had suggested that she would like to dedicate one of them—I forget which—to me. I was hugely pleased and would have liked to say yes. But the realities of corporate life are such that I knew the dedication would ruffle a whole array of corporate feathers, would not add ease to my life. Much as I hated to do so, I declined the honor.

I was amused, then, when the art for the second advent calendar arrived on my desk. Entitled "The Days Before Christmas," the scene was a Christmasy street lined with shops. One of the shops bore the name "Haas's Bakery." It was Tasha's quiet response to the corporate realities that hedged my life. I don't think anyone in the company studied the illustration, noted the name. It was and remains still one of my private amusements.

As Tasha's artwork had spanned and closed the decades between the present and Clement Clark Moore's lifetime in *The Night Before Christmas,* so again did her styled artwork bridge the gap in the century that separated her from another classic author, Robert Louis Stevenson. *A Child's Garden of Verses* would be her next book. It would be published in 1981, nearly a hundred years after the collection's first appearance. It was a natural for Tasha's children in their period clothing, caught up in activities of that earlier day—lamplighters making their rounds, railway carriages, children tucked into bed by mothers in long gowns. Room interiors, dress, toys, and activities were drawn with the loving attention to detail that is so typical of her work.

A favorite of my childhood, this book especially pleased me. And I was delighted when The American Library Association later notified me that their publication *Booklist* would include it in their 1982 "Reviewer's Choice List."

At the close of 1982, Tasha Tudor's four wonderful books and three charming advent calendars had impressive records. *The Night Before Christmas* had had seven printings and there were 215,000 copies in print. *A Time to Keep* had had five printings, with 145,000 copies in print. *The Springs of Joy* and *A Child's Garden of Verses* had each had a single printing, *Joy* of 65,000 copies and *Garden* with 70,000 copies. The first advent calendar had had two printings of 122,000 copies, and the second and third had each had single printings of 50,000 copies each.

And so ends the tale of Tasha Tudor's association with Rand McNally. I left the company at the close of 1982. I still recall with pleasure and a degree of editorial pride the unique books that resulted from that association.

A Remembrance

Patricia Lee Gauch

[Bethany with dipper]

1 met Tasha Tudor during the earliest days of my tenure at Philomel Books, the winter of 1986. Her longtime editor and friend, Ann Beneduce, had retired, and Ann accompanied me and Philomel president Clay Winters to her Vermont home. We did not arrive until night, and as there had been snow aplenty in the days before we came, we had to park the car at the end of the road to her house, and walk what seemed like a mile through the cold, starless Vermont night to her home.

I still remember the lights of the windows across the last field, and remember Tasha coming out to greet us, her cape-like coat blowing in the gusty wind. She was most interested in seeing once again Ann Beneduce who greeted her with some kind of friendly package.

The editor-artist relationship is an amazing one. A close one. If there are people and animals who mate for life, there are certainly editors and artists who bond for life. It is as if, once given, the gift of trusting and sharing creatively cannot be given again. That first night Ann was led to the guest room under the eaves on the second floor; our president, Clay Winters, was led to the room next to that, both to sleep in great feathery beds. As the new presuming editor, I was led to the "milking room," an unheated room between the 1840s-like mainhouse and the barn. I was grateful! It was kind of Tasha to take strangers in, particularly ones who threatened her long-standing relationship, and, indeed, her creative process.

To walk into the Tudor farmhouse is to walk into one of Tasha's storybooks: back in time. At night gentle candles flicker, lighting up the portraits of family that came to this country during the 1600 and 1700s. In the back room, the bench by the fire and the low-slung chairs with cushions padded by time welcome the nighttime traveler, as do the smells of lamb roasting in the oven, the nighttime stirrings of the parrots, whose cages are hooded for the night. All of it welcomed this nighttime traveler.

The question for me that early visit was what kind of an editor-artist relationship could I manage. I, having been an author for twenty years, was new to editing as a profession. Would Tasha Tudor, the great Tasha Tudor, accept that newness, my middle western openness?

In many ways she did. For the next six years I and my husband Ronald were welcomed into the Tudor home. Though it is a crucial task of the editor to create suggestions or encourage new stories from an artist-author, this was never an easy task with Tasha. Mostly, when one visited, one entered her world. I cleaned carrots and washed dishes; Ronald stacked more than one season's wood. We watched her milk the Nubian goats, and helped her feed the prize pigeons. It always felt as if the matter at hand was living in that other time. Preparing to eat —and eating—supper at the coffee table in a living room lit with twenty or more candles. Enjoying good talk. Good ideas. Savoring the place and Tasha herself, whose family stories came from her—always unexpected—in her wonderful and magical 1800s New England accent.

Whenever there was a free moment, I would browse her small library, looking to see what books she collected in order to better understand her interests, her preferences: tales abound on her shelves. I looked at her back room with its giant loom, investigated the dolls that lived with her, and the doll room, where a handsome lieutenant courted a beautiful young thing. In the summer, I walked the gardens that clung to a rock wall in front of her weathered frame house, marking the giant, salmon-colored poppies that she raised with such care. Always looking for a story. But savoring the grace of the place, too. The peace of it. And Tasha's place in that world.

The agreement had been that Ann Beneduce, while retired, would continue to edit Tasha's books. While I was at Philomel, Tasha and Ann completed *The Lord Is My Shepherd*. A smallish book, the Tudor touch is so evident on every page. The country empire style dress that places it in the last century, the humility that places it among simple people. But, most important, it is bathed in Tudor light, the light of candles reflected on the face of a mother saying good night to a child. Always that golden light, which evokes such warmth.

Early in my tenure, perhaps 1987, I suggested *A Brighter Garden*, a collection of Emily Dickinson poems, be illustrated by Tasha. I brought the suggestion to Ann, of course. Through Ann, I was told Tasha loved the idea, but soon after, Ann took a position at the then new Orchard Books with editor Richard Jackson, and so the project was left to me to finish.

This was a great joy for me. Tasha decided that she would use her own collection of dresses to feature young women and children who would have lived in Emily Dickinson's time. And this is what she did. This is a living collection, in many ways, because Tasha and her young friends wear these dresses on an afternoon. Enjoy them. Again, everything in Tasha's house lives. And so, for the book, a friend—perhaps more than one—donned the dresses, and Tasha sketched.

Then, Tasha, in her back window by the table—in north light—settled into her low-wooden armchair with the warmly-worn cushion (blue plaid, I believe) and began to draw, then paint. Tasha is scrupulously frugal, using the back of watercolor paper that had already been used for another sketch, if she can, and so I would come to visit her, and would go through the new *Brighter Garden* paintings. Painting after painting: young girls by the gate, or near a stream, or in a meadow, their long skirts billowing, sun on their faces. And on the back of the painting, I'd often find some earlier drawing.

I never saw Tasha paint. Her palette always sat delicately—showing diligent use—on the table near the window, along with a small box of paints as I recall, as if she had just stepped away for a moment.

How can I explain the delight of turning each picture up, and reading the Dickinson text that went with it? And when I would come again to visit, there would be the additional paintings to discover. I was always enchanted by the light and color in her work: that, I remember most of all.

Other people, other students, even relatives, have tried to imitate Tasha Tudor's work. But, it seems to me that the beauty of it comes from her own invincible spirit. Her playfulness. Her dear and wry, frequently mischievous, way of viewing the world. She is at play! And that lightness and joy is evident in every painting she has ever made.

But, ironically, again, when I was with her, it always seemed amazing there was any time for her to paint at all, as she was so busy with her life: her goats, her pigeons, the seemingly hundreds of finches and canaries that lived in the wooden cages in her home, the parrots, those comedians that amused her so. The corgis that lay by the fire or barked at each visitor, the gardens that grew and grew, and became in their artistry and beauty an equal vocation to her painting. Another kind of art in her strong and creative hands.

The other book that I edited with Tasha, perhaps the first after Ann left, was *Tasha Tudor's Advent Calendar, A Wreath of Days*. This would have a paper-engineering surprise, and Tasha would make it come alive, using the recollections of her own Christmases, not as a child, but with her own children.

I remember when I first received her text. It had lovely spots in it, but it was irregular. Her memories went their own way. As a new editor, I noted sentences which might be more efficient. Sentences which might be written more efficiently. But Tasha let me know, in no uncertain terms—but always kindly—that it might be better the way that I was suggesting, but then it would not be her Voice. She intended to tell her own story, with her own Voice.

Of course, she was absolutely right! An artist's Voice is aberrant. It is not governed by neat, grammatical laws. Indeed, such laws can devastate Voice. I still hear Tasha, sitting next to the fireplace in the back room she called the "summer kitchen" in her low hearth chair, telling me stories of play at her Uncle Henry's home, the place she went to live when there was illness in her family. The words fell rhythmically, warmly, with quaint juxtapositions and asides. Entirely Tasha. What an affront to consider changing her words! And what a bad thing for the book that would have been, since now readers can be assured that they are hearing Tasha's own, wonderful Voice in this calendar book.

I believe Tasha came to trust my editing. She was very fond of my husband Ronald, a gentle, quiet man who fit well into her 1840s world. He liked helping her, and enjoyed her mischievous humor. She probably liked my ingenuousness. She would call me with wonderfully imaginative requests—like to help her find sealing wax, or an out-of-print book. She haunts old book stores, particularly looking for coming-of-age books that were given to mid-1800s young men and women on the verge of going into the world.

We had a wonderful Publication Party for *A Brighter Garden* in Marblehead, Massachusetts—the town where Tasha had lived as a child and in which her father gained some fame as a designer of yachts. The party was held at a narrow, five-story mansion, and friends from all over the country came to celebrate this event. Her original paintings were displayed in one room and drew the admiring visitors. It was the right place and the right time, and I was terribly proud of her and the book.

But somehow, either in the matting of the paintings or in some mysterious place that we have never been able to discover, some of her original art was cut. That is, when someone made ovals of the art, a worker cut into the original art. It is unlikely that a designer would do this, so respectful of original art are they; the framer absolutely denied responsibility. How could this happen? Tasha was, understandably, furious; I was distraught. And we have never found the culprit. But this affected our relationship.

It was after this, that Tasha began to create adult books, such as *The Private World of Tasha Tudor* (Little, Brown) and *Tasha Tudor's Garden* (Houghton Mifflin). And perhaps it was the right time for her to do so. Her children had grown, even grandchildren were only occasionally at her home. Her gardens, her kitchen, her animals, these after all were what made the texture of her life.

When I visited Tasha, only at the end of a visit would I mention books or what she might create next. In the springtime or fall, we would have tea under the bower at the end of her home. You could hear birds there, persistent wrens, saucy chickadees, some raucous crows. The wind blew through the vines around the bower. It was an enchanted place. Tasha is an enchanted lady. Not of this century, but of the last. Yet bringing that beauty and warmth of time and place and person into this century. I miss her, but cherish the few years when I was her friend and editor, and Philomel was her publisher.

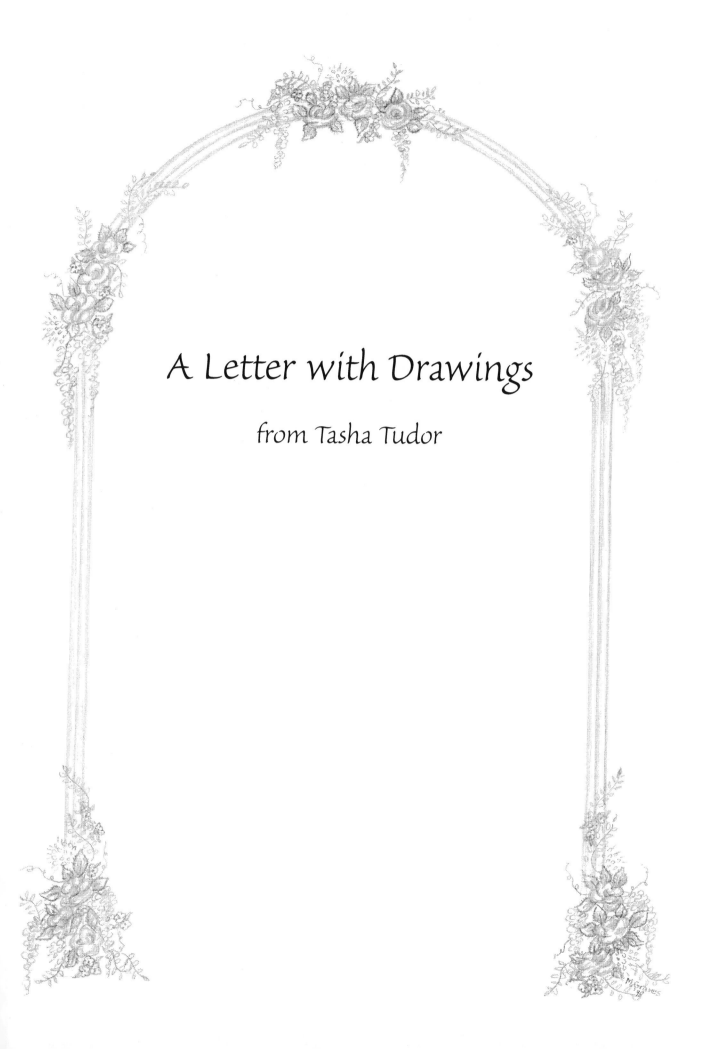

A Letter with Drawings

from Tasha Tudor

Melissa Dove Crane at her correspondence

N ot many Beatrix Potter enthusiasts realize the debt they owe to Leslie Linder. I for one was entirely unaware of this unusual person until Bertha Mahony Miller told me of him last August just before we sailed for England, yet our family and friends had been inspired and delighted by his book, *The Art of Beatrix Potter,* since its publication by Warne in 1955.

It seems a pity that this wonderful book should be enjoyed by many Beatrix Potter admirers who do not know that it was through the imagination and efforts of Leslie Linder that it came into print. Mrs. Miller kindly wrote Mr. Linder of our being in England, but it was not until after Easter that we met him.

During the Spring Holidays my husband, two of my children, and I paid a short visit to Sawrey. The sun was shining when we arrived and walked through Tom Kitten's gate and up the garden path. I'm sure I felt then what the old-time pilgrims felt on visiting a shrine. Beatrix Potter's books have always been such a familiar part of our lives and our children's that to realize we were actually walking up her path and looking across the village to the very lane that could be seen from the roof-top where Tom Kitten hoped to catch sparrows before his plans went awry, was far too exciting to describe in words. I know we all felt it and were armed by an inner glow in spite of the cold March wind which more than stirred the dancing daffodils.

We were greeted at the door by Mrs. Ludbrook, a very friendly person, who showed us through the house and left us to feast our eyes on the originals from *Jemima Puddle-Duck* and *Tom Kitten.* These are two of our favorites, and to have them laid out as if to order capped the enjoyment of the day.

I was particularly interested to see that Beatrix Potter had two French Fashion dolls very like some of mine. I wonder if she really loved them? They lie now in a case looking rather forlorn. One is in an undignified position with her dress turned back to show her underclothing. How embarrassing for her!

We saw Hunca Munca's ham which "Underneath the paint was nothing but plaster," Tom Kitten's stairway with the clock, and many other little things that reminded us of the stories.

It was through Mrs. Ludbrook that we again heard of Mr. Linder. We left Sawrey with our minds set on following up Mrs. Miller's suggestion that we meet him. We hadn't long to wait. A few days later a letter arrived from Mr. Linder, inviting us to spend a day with him and see his collection of Beatrix Potter's art.

A day was chosen, and we were at the Buckhurst Hill Station at the appointed time where Mr. Linder met us and drove us to his home. It was a large house of the period of 1900, surrounded by a garden full of lilacs and azaleas which were covered with bloom.

Here we were greeted by Miss Linder and Miss Moppet, the cat, who has, I believe, the finest set of whiskers of any cat in England. We enjoyed lunch and then were taken to the study where a world of enchantment was opened before us. Folio after folio of Potter drawings and sketches, from the exquisitely finished to the rougher type, were laid before our eyes to study and admire. It was truly like a dream.

The care and interest that has been lavished by Mr. Linder in mounting and preserving these treasures is amazing. Even the tiniest sketches have been devotedly put into folders.

We were also impressed by his knowledge of the editions of her books. I had never known that in certain editions of *The Tale of Benjamin Bunny* there were different drawings, or that in early copies of *Peter Rabbit* there were extra drawings which were removed to allow for endpapers.

We learned many things about Beatrix Potter we had not known; one of the most interesting of which was that from about the age of fifteen and for many years thereafter she kept a record of conversations and experiences of special interest which she wanted to remember. These were written on loose sheets of paper and in odd exercise books, in a self-invented code. Mr. Linder had discovered the key to the code a short while before our visit and had been working on the translation of many of the pages. The writing is so minute that he has to use a magnifying glass to read it. No wonder Beatrix Potter could draw such delicate whiskers on her mice! Mr. Linder explained that he discovered the code's key through a date, the date of the execution of Louis XVI.

How fortunate it is for the memory of Beatrix Potter, and all those who love her work, that such a man as Leslie Linder was captivated by the inimitable charm of her art and writing.

We were extremely interested to learn from Mr. Linder that he is working on another book. He says it will most probably be of the same format as that of *The Art of Beatrix Potter*, but while combining some further unpublished drawings and water colors, the main emphasis will be on her work as a writer. He hopes that this book can be published for her centenary in 1966, and I hope that the name of Leslie Linder will appear beneath the title so that those who read and enjoy the book will realize what a great deal of credit goes to the author for his persistence and interest in his subject.

The hours of that afternoon raced by; before we knew it Miss Linder, who shares her brother's enthusiasm, had gathered us out of this delightful dream and was graciously serving us tea.

We parted from the Linders full of gratitude and admiration for what they have done, and aware that we had met two very special people indeed.

Since that unforgettable day we have exchanged many letters, or rather I might say that Mr. Linder and our favorite doll, Melissa Dove Crane, have been correspondents. She is particularly devoted to him because he has the consideration to write her doll-size letters that she doesn't need a reducing glass to read. The printing of these letters "is so small, *so* small, that it looks as if it had been made by little mice."

A lane in Sawrey

(Reprinted courtesy of HORN BOOK MAGAZINE, 35:1, pp. 4-5 February 1959)

Interpreting
the Bibliography

[Bethany at window with bird cage]

This is a book about books—the direct output and the books inspired by one artist's work. We have recorded the information that distinguishes the many reprintings of Tasha Tudor's books from each other. We have done this largely by direct examination of our own books. Only at the HarperCollins archives and the U. S. Copyright Office did we find substantial data concerning the actual publication of the books described here.

We call the reader's attention immediately to two excellent bibliographies which have been our inspiration. First, *A Bibliography of Booth Tarkington, 1869–1946* by Dorothy Ritter Russo and Thelma L. Sullivan (Indiana Historical Society, 1949). It is a fine delineation of an author's work. The title page is a true beauty and we have tried to follow the descriptive pattern employed by Russo and Sullivan. We knew we were on solid ground after reading Russo's note in the preface: ". . . it is my desire here to express again my gratitude to Jacob Blanck for his help in 1943 in preparing a bibliographical pattern." We could aspire to no better advise than that of Blanck, America's bibliographer.

The second title is *Printed Kate Greenaway, A Catalogue Raisonn,* by Thomas E. Schuster & Rodney Engen (London, T.E. Schuster, 1986). When Stephanie Clayton loaned us her copy late in the research, we were immediately taken by the illustrative photography. Its inspiration will be seen especially in the photographs which appear here. Thank you Stephanie for opening that avenue. We are indebted. We were also encouraged by reading Tasha Tudor's appreciation of Leslie Linder. It provided the strength to finish the task knowing that our subject recognized the true worth of the bibliographer's efforts!

On the order of things; early on we decided to list titles alphabetically. It seemed the simplest approach because people refer to books by their titles. We appreciate the instruction of a chronologic bibliography, and have seen many. Such a bibliography presents the author's works logically and sequentially in the order the public first saw them. Gary Overmann uses that arrangement in his Tudor lists. Indeed, Russo and Sullivan followed the same scheme in their Tarkington bibliography. But it is not an easy format to use. So for us, an alphabetical sequence is best for a true working reference volume. The book serves as an encyclopedia of the author's *oeuvre.* And then we settled on an alpha-numeric coding of the titles, giving each entry a simple reference number. We would have preferred a continuous sequence like Schuster and Engen, above. But it was too restrictive when we considered the number of printings we haven't seen and the additions still to be made. This system gives me the latitude to insert new pieces with relative ease, and still provide a simple code.

We mean to describe every printing, binding, and state of each Tudor book. You will not find a more complete collection than is described here. Most bibliographies concentrate on the first appearances of books, and especially so when a popular book is reprinted over a number of years. But, we have not found the children's book market to be so discriminating that people concentrate exclusively on the first editions of titles. Certainly, some people and institutions do. But, many more are satisfied to have a clean readable example of a title for personal enjoyment. Both groups should appreciate knowing where a particular volume fits in the artist's pantheon and the publishers' chronology. At times, the differences among examples are minuscule, as in the case of changing prices on dust jackets. A book may have been recased by a firm that rebinds worn-out library books. The body seems to be unchanged; but in fact, plates may be missing, certainly the endpapers will not be as before, and there is the phenomenon of new cover designs introduced by the rebinder. This, too, is a fact of book life; and we record *some* of it here. Not the least of our efforts is to guide book dealers in knowing what they hold, and to guide customers in judging whether a price be fair, or not.

We cite a small sampling of book dealer's catalogs which have a particular Tudor interest. There are many other catalogs being issued monthly which will contain one or more out-of-print Tudor offerings. For a sense of the market, we refer the reader to one of the reports from the used book trade, perhaps *American Book Prices Current* or The Clique's *Annual Register of Book Values: Children's Books*. And now the world wide web offers daily listings of items for sale, as well as providing direct, rapid correspondence between book sellers and their customers world-wide.

We tell you, too, that we are on the trail of a Tudor "ghost." *The American Book Publishing Record* (Bowker: 1967, p. 88) says of *More Prayers* that it was *originally published in paperback in 1965*. We have yet to see such a copy. We appeal to those with Tudor collections to see who might first locate one. If it is truly a ghost as we suspect, you won't. All too often, we have had to rely on imperfect copies of the "real" books. Frequently, the original sale price has been clipped from a book jacket. We tell you if we have not seen a complete copy. And we appeal to your kindness if you have a complete copy. May we borrow the piece, or a photocopy, to complete the description? Also, if you can prove when you bought your copy new in a bookstore, it may be the nearest although imperfect way to date a particular printing. We've mentioned that fact on a few recent printings. Publishers, themselves, were not generally open in sharing the print dates or titles, or the size of the print run. Those small details also reveal part of the evolution of American children's books in this century.

Having chosen to describe all books, we also decided to include all pertinent descriptive text. We transcribe the title page and its verso, also called the copyright page. It is here that a publisher records copyright, may issue a warning, include addresses and indicate subsidiary relationships with other companies. Books published in the United States over the last forty years have generally included information from the Library of Congress to assist librarians in describing their books. This information changes through time, and by its wording provides clues to a book's age which publishers have not left us. Likewise, the text of covers and book jackets and various biographical sections provide more information and clues to the book's history. We describe unusual Tudor points. Tudor created all illustrations unless otherwise noted. She frequently is the author of the book as well. And there are instances where she serves as anthologist choosing and illustrating passages meaningful to herself.

This book has been compiled with a great deal of respect. We have only the highest regard for the body of work Tudor has created. In 1989, we met and advised Tudor of our intentions to compile this bibliography and asked if we might appoint a time to discuss aspects of her publishing history. She indicated that she never paid attention to those details, a declaration we accept to be true. We saw her at subsequent public appearances and continued to advise her of our progress.

There are omissions in the photography presented here, and out of respect to readers we regret that we could not lay out for you a complete pictorial review. Through its attorney, Kathryn L. Barrett, Corgi Cottage Industries in June 1997 denied us permission to reproduce book jacket illustrations over which Tudor maintains control, indicating that Tudor disapproves of this work.

We also meant to include a chapter in which Ann K. Beneduce would discuss her valuable insights into Tudor's art and publishing career. We conducted a friendly correspondence about the writing. But on Friday the thirteenth of June 1997, Tudor requested Beneduce not to cooperate with us. Out of respect for their long-standing friendship, Beneduce complied with the request. We also respect Beneduce for her decision. We are sorry that Tudor did not appreciate the effort we make in her behalf. This was especially disappointing when one considers Tudor's earlier acclaim in the *Horn Book* for Leslie Linder's work with Beatrix Potter's bibliography. Readers will reach your own conclusions concerning the book we put before you.

We have formulated these rules to guide our descriptions and use of standard terminology:

1   Describe the books, and items resembling books (as small as a few pages). We include videotapes and audiotapes. But flat art, greeting cards, puzzles, etc., are for another day—and another book.

2   Transcribe text as it is found, including italics, capitals and misspellings. When there was an error in the original, we follow the particular error with [*sic*] to indicate *We found it thus.*

3   Breaks between lines of type are indicated with a single 'pipe' | . When the space is more than a single typed space would be, we employ a "double pipe" || .

4   Repetitive text is replaced with an ellipsis . . . in the interests of space and attention.

5   A long ellipsis _____. indicates that a title page is repeated exactly, or to the point that a change occurs. A change in text or typeface will be indicated. Otherwise, the long ellipsis means this title page is like the previous entry in all details.

6   Square brackets [ ] set off the title page from [information found on the title page verso.] Secondly they indicate the editor's side comments (often about illustrations) interposing transcribed text. Sometimes the two uses concur creating a double set of square brackets. [[…]]

7   Measure books carefully in inches, reporting first the height and then the width. I have not reported the thickness of a book, except in cases where that dimension obviously varied. This breaks with decimal tradition, but does follow Russo and Sullivan (and Blanck).

8   Distinctions between printings are <u>underlined</u>.

9   When details do not change, we don't mention the repetition. Thus, many entries are silent concerning the PAGINATION or perhaps the COVER, because they duplicate the previous entry(ies). An item is re-introduced only when a detail changes, perhaps the design of the dust jacket, or the color and type of binding. The cover may not change through several printings.

10   We imply the type font in the examination piece by using a word processor font similar to the piece. We could not reproduce fonts exactly, and so we came as close as possible with the tools available. This was the most difficult decision; we were counseled against doing so. Our goal is to convey the look of the original as accurately as we can without photography. We have used smaller type to indicate the comparative size of fonts used.

11   *Half-paper* and *half-cloth* are our own corruptions from the traditional designation "half-leather," wherein a book's spine was bound in leather for beauty and durability. The leather continued onto both covers where it

joined the vellum or parchment binding glued over boards. A few Tudor titles demonstrate this mix of binding materials albeit they are usually cloth and not leather. See *Wings from the Wind,* or *Rosemary for Remembrance.*

12 It is often impossible to determine exact print dates. Publishers have not kept the information. The production manager is generally the only person who tracks that data. Thus, in the few Houghton Mifflin examples where we can report with certainty a print run and date, we are indebted to those who knew and were willing to share the information. We cite dated inscriptions because they give clues to an early date by which that state was being sold. How much earlier it may have been available is not known, but we are pleased to find books with an inscribed date. We solicit the help of readers in dating any printing by this method.

13 Librarian's notations. Many ex-library copies carry notations giving some indication of the true age of the physical book. Presuming that a library bought the book new, it is useful to know that an acquisition date and price might be penciled in the gutter of the title page verso. It is an indication of an early date when the book was being distributed.

14 Spine printing. Thin children's books usually demand lateral printing. Generally, the author's surname, the title, and the publisher's name are printed laterally running down the spine, i.e., the spine printing reads best with the book lying flat on a surface, face up. One reads straight on without having to cock the head. The commonest variation turns a publisher's logo ninety degrees and prints the logo straight across the base of the spine as the book is standing on its bottom edge. The author's first name may be included. The least common and most traditional type arrangement is for all words to be printed across the spine, probably one word to a line (see *A Little Princess*). In transcribing these spines, we use the pattern of separating the words with either a single or a double pipe to indicate a single-spaced line, or some space larger than single-spaced, e.g., BUR-NETT || A | LITTLE | PRINCESS || LIPPINCOTT.

15 Bands on the spine of a book. When books were constructed by hand, a cord was created across the spine at each place the signatures were sewn together. In the final stages of binding, these raised cords created a bump under the leather or cloth binding. It was impossible to smooth the binding material along the spine. The bumps are "raised bands" and are a positive point of decoration. The bands were often high-lighted by tooling a gold rule on either side, thus creating a parallel line decoration and repeating it down the spine. 'False bands' sometimes decorate modern bindings even though there is no built-up cord beneath the binding, only printed or stamped bars across the spine. See *First Poems of Childhood,*

A B C Go, The New England Butt'ry Shelf Cookbook (paperback) and the leather bound presentation copies of *Give Us This Day* and *Tasha Tudor's Seasons of Delight.*

16 The colophon was the final combined statement of a book's manufacture in the centuries before title pages became common. It was normally the last word from the scribe or the printer, placed on the last page. This is uncommon today, but see *Give Us This Day.* Today the word colophon can also indicate the publisher's logo or device.

17 Endpapers. The decorative finishing sheets at the front and back of a book. They may be two large sheets (or four, half size) serving two purposes: they finish the interior of the cover masking the boards and the edges where the binding material is folded over boards. If one large sheet is folded creating both the pasted and the free endpapers, then that sheet also adds strength to the binding. Indeed, there are cases where the free endpapers (not the two pasted to the boards) are actually the first and last leaves of the first and last signatures of the book. See *The Springs of Joy.* The endpapers are also a decorative welcome inside the book, frequently with a pattern, and in Tudor's case, paintings. We have used free endpapers to indicate the first and the last leaf in a book; ffep = front free endpaper, rfep = rear free endpaper. Pasted end papers are those glued to the binder's boards.

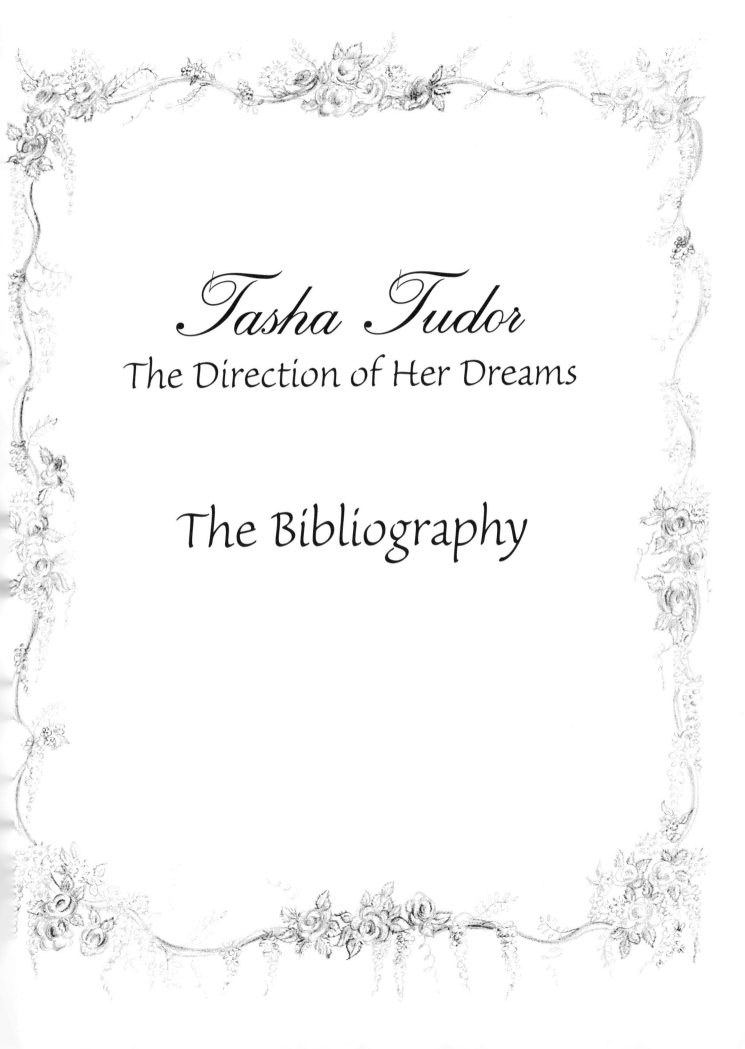

Tasha Tudor
The Direction of Her Dreams

The Bibliography

1-1 1 | is | One | By | **TASHA TUDOR** | New York   Oxford University Press
1956 [© Oxford University Press, Inc., 1956 | Library of Congress Catalog Card Number: 56-11381 |
PRINTED IN THE UNITED STATES OF AMERICA]

PAGINATION: [52] pp. including free endpapers in 2 signatures ivory paper. 7″ x 9 1/8″.

COVER: Pink gauze weave cloth, lightly painted in green. Front: mouse playing a guitar and sitting
on a toadstool (pencil drawing from "12"). Spine: Tudor   1 is One   Oxford.

Four identical endpapers: spiderwort [?]on a gray-green ground within a border of white violets.

DUST JACKET: Gray-mauve dust jacket. Front illustration features a small girl beside a lily pond; she
is sitting inside the O of the title watching a red-winged blackbird sitting on the i of the title, and
looking at the girl. All in a 5½ x 8¼″ rectangular border of lily pads. Title lettered in green;
below that in black: by Tasha Tudor. Spine: Tudor   1 is One   Oxford. White lily and pad
centered on back. Front flap: 1 is One | by Tasha Tudor || Designed as a companion
volume to Miss | Tudor's alphabet book, *A is for* | *Annabelle*, this charming book includes |
numbers one through twenty. Each number | is graphically illustrated by one of Miss |
Tudor's paintings and accompanied by an | original verse. ¶A variety of pictures—of animals,
chil- | dren, trees and flowers—as well as the easy- | to-remember verses will encourage the |
youngest readers to learn their numbers and | make them want to return to the book again | and
again. ¶The old-fashioned loveliness of Miss | Tudor's delicate illustrations make this a |
particularly inviting introduction to "how | to count." || **Oxford Books** | **for Boys and**
Girls | 30-60 $2.75. [Upper right corner clipped.]   Back flap: **A is for Annabelle** |
by Tasha Tudor || "The perfect gift for a little girl is this | enchanting new alphabet book,
which be- | gins: 'A is for Annabelle, Grandmother's | doll. B for her Box on the chest in the |
hall.' In verses and some of Tasha Tudor's | loveliest pictures two small girls dress the | quaint
doll in an elegant old time ward- | robe, each item of which starts with suc- | ceeding letters of
the alphabet, right thru | Z! Mothers and grandmothers will love | this one, too."—Chicago
Tribune

ILLUSTRATONS: Many illustrations signed "T. Tudor | 1956," some "56." Colored title page [5] in a
border of beauty bush and winter berries: a girl in a thicket looking at crow which is behind the
number 1. Illustration also contains a frog, a rabbit, an owl, a field mouse, a wren on a nest, and
Tudor's painted of the title into the whole.

CONTENTS: Dedication page [7]: [young robin on apple branch] | To Patricia Cummings. Patricia
Cummings was an editor. Text is 20 counting rhymes, 1 to 20. Each number verse is printed
across the verso and recto, but each page is a separate illustration within its own rectangular
floral border. Odd numbers beginning on pages [8-9] are colored illustrations; even numbers are
black and white. Blank pages: [2-4] [48-51]

OTHER: *1Is One* was a Randolph Caldecott Honor Medal winner in 1957, one of five runners-up when
Marc Simont received the Caldecott Medal for illustrating Janice Udry's *A Tree Is Nice.*

COPYRIGHT REGISTRATION: A 259131 granted to Oxford University Press, Inc., 114 Fifth Ave.,
N.Y. 11, N.Y. John A. Begg, agent for claimant, swears on Nov. 9, 1956:

1 IS ONE, by Tasha Tudor, Route 1, Contoocook, N.H., a U.S. citizen, was published Nov. 1, 1956.
The book was printed by Kellogg & Bulkeley, Hartford, Ct., and bound by H. Wolff Book Mfg.

Co., Inc., N.Y., N.Y. Fees charged to Oxford University Press, Inc. Application and affidavit and two deposit copies received at L.C. Nov. 16,1956.

1-2 _____. **Henry Z. Walck, Inc. New York** [© Henry Z. Walck, Inc., 1956 | Library of Congress Catalog Card Number: 56-11381 | PRINTED IN THE UNITED STATES OF AMERICA]

> PAGINATION: Saddle stitched through the end papers and two signatures before cover was applied.

> COVER: Spine: Tudor   1 is One   Walck.

> DUST JACKET: Examination copy had no jacket, but I examined another with this statement at the bottom of the front flap: Henry Z. Walck, Inc. | successor to | Oxford Books for Boys and Girls 30-60.

1-3 _____.

> COVER: Pink gauze weave cloth. Cloth hinges.

> DUST JACKET: Spine: Tudor   1 is One   Walck. Front flap: … to count." | **Henry Z. Walck, Inc.** || 30-60 $3.75. Have not examined a copy with upper corner intact.

1-4 _____. By | TASHA TUDOR || 1963 FIRST CADMUS EDITION | THIS SPECIAL EDITION IS PUBLISHED BY ARRANGEMENT WITH | THE PUBLISHERS OF THE REGULAR EDITION | HENRY Z. WALCK, INC. | BY | **E. M. HALE AND COMPANY** | EAU CLAIRE, WISCONSIN [© Henry Z. Walck, Inc., 1956. || Library of Congress Catalog Card Number: 56-11381 | This edition lithographed in USA by Wetzel Bros., Inc., Milwaukee 2, Wisconsin]

> COVER: Pictorial cloth with the images of the previous dust jacket. Back, lower left: There is a 3/4″ 'seal': a circle of hash lines enclosing the large initials CEB with a device above and its inverse below. Printed around the inside of the circle is CADMUS EDITORIAL BOARD • APPROVED • Spine: TUDOR   1 IS ONE   HALE-CADMUS. Endpapers have an overall Hale-Cadmus gray design.

> DUST JACKET: Have not examined one.

> CONTENTS: Half-title, page [3] is largely a biographical sketch of Tudor. **1 IS ONE** | *Written and illustrated by Tasha Tudor* || "7 is seven apples on a little apple tree. | 8 is eight daffodils you are picking for me . . . " | Here is a variety of paintings of numbers and animals that illustrate how to count for the | youngest readers. The easily remembered verses help, also. | **K** | Classification and Dewey: Easy [E] || ***About the Author and Illustrator*:** | TASHA TUDOR has been writing and illustrating books for boys and girls since 1938. Her mother | was a portrait painter who taught her to paint in water color. Later, she studied art in Boston. | Miss Tudor was also influenced by the beloved authors and artists of her childhood — Beatrix | Potter, Kate Greenaway, Randolph Caldecott, Walter Crane, as well as Edmund Dulac and | Arthur Rackham. The characters in her books are in her home, a lovely old farmhouse in New | Hampshire — Alexander the Gander, Edgar Allen Crow*[sic],* and Annabelle, the old-fashioned doll. | The children in her drawings are her own four children — Seth, Bethany, Efner and Thomas.

> OTHER: See also *First Delights*, F17, for another Hale imprint. There may be more, however, these are the only two we have examined. *School Library Journal* 17:7 refers to an edition from Hale.

1-5 _____.

> PAGINATION: Course buff paper.

COVER: Pink gauze weave cloth. Cloth hinges.

DUST JACKET: Have not examined a copy.

ILLUSTRATIONS: The green of endpapers is much deeper, without the yellow hue. The background is a dark gray, and the printing on the endpapers slightly out of registration to produce a fuzzy quality to the image. The colors are stronger throughout the book. "15" is on a yellow-flesh background in this printing; it has been a blush pink.

1-6 _____. [{An out-lined catalog card at top of page, enclosing: E Tudor, Tasha | 1 is one. Walck, 1956 | unp. Illus. || A counting book using both words and | figures; one to twenty and 1 to 20. || 1. Counting books 2. Numbers | I. Title [circle]} | This Main Entry catalog card may be reproduced without permission. || © Henry Z. Walck, Inc., 1956. | ISBN: 0-8098-1047-6 | Library of Congress Catalog Card Number: 56-11381 | Printed in the United States of America]

COVER: Pink linen with a stronger shade of green paint.

DUST JACKET: This copy lacks both corners of front flap, but I examined a copy printed $4.25 on the bottom flap.

1-7 _____. **TASHA TUDOR** || [globe and calipers logo] **Rand McNally &**
Company Chicago • New York • San Francisco [© Henry Z. Walck . . . States of America]

PAGINATION: [48] pp. on a thick ivory paper perfect bound. 6 3/4″ x 9 x ¼″.

COVER: Full color paper wrapper imprinted with illustration from the original dust jacket, and *impressed with buckram weave. Front upper right: $1.50, on the gray border. Spine: Tudor 1 is One [logo] Rand McNally. Back upper left: 82-1679; upper right: 30-60.

CONTENTS: B&W mouse-guitar-toadstool, p. [1]. Three of original endpaper illustrations on pages [2, 46 and 47]. Page [48] is a re-write of the original jacket blurb: A IS FOR ANNABELLE | *By Tasha Tudor* || "A is for Annabelle, Grand- | mother's doll..." in this charmingly | illustrated alphabet book. Two little | girls play with the elegant, old- | fashioned doll, whose clothes and | possessions complete the alphabet. | Annabelle's varied wardrobe, her | dresses and fan, her slippers and veil, | will please all little girls, as well as | Tasha Tudor fans. ¶The simple verse and delicate | drawings are Tasha Tudor at her best. | Young readers will find this a memor- | able introduction to the alphabet and | all those who love dolls will love | Annabelle."

OTHER: An inscription on page [1] is dated 1975.

1-8 _____.

COVER: Back upper left: 528-87679-1. A plain gold foil label (1/4 x 3/8″) has been attached over the $1.50 price on the front cover.

1-9 _____.

COVER: Front, upper right: $1.95.

1-10 _____.

COVER: Front, upper right: $2.95 in a white box.

1-11 _____.

PAGINATION: A thinner paper; book is 3/16″ thick.

COVER: For the first time, the spine is white, rather than gray.

1-12 _____.

PAGINATION: Whiter paper.

COVER: Gloss paper wrapper without the weave imprint . Front upper right, white box: $3.95.

1-13 _____. **TASHA TUDOR** ‖ **Checkerboard Press** • New York
[Copyright © 1956 Checkerboard Press, a division of Macmillan, Inc. | All rights reserved. | Library of Congress Catalog Number: 86-064059 | ISBN 0-02-688535-2 ‖ CHECKERBOARD PRESS and colophon are trademarks of Macmillan, Inc. ‖ Printed in Hong Kong]

PAGINATION: [48] pp. white matte paper, perfect bound. 6 3/4 x 9″.

COVER: Gloss paper wrapper as before. Front upper right, white box: $3.95. Back lower left, UPC bar code in a white box 1 3/8 x 2″: [bar code] and beneath it, 0 14121 88535 4 | ISBN 0-02-688535-2.

1-14 _____.

PAGINATION: [52] pp. including extra endpapers. 6 ¾″ x 9 1/16″

COVER: Library binding of the same interior as above. Illustrated gloss paper over boards. Where earlier versions had a taupe background, this cover is decidedly pink. Front upper right: a blue PERMA-BOUND book logo, PAT. NO. 3,161,423. Pink spine, printed in blue: Tudor 1 is One. No publisher listed on rounded spine.

1-15 _____. [Copyright © 1956 Checkerboard Press . . . trademarks of Macmillan, Inc.]

PAGINATION: Paper is a shinier finish.

COVER: Front upper right, white box: $4.95 . White square spine. Back, bar code as before, and upper right corner: >>$4.95 US | >>$6.50 CAN.

OTHER: Purchased new in February 1992.

1-16 _____. **TASHA TUDOR** ‖ **Aladdin Books** • New York [Copyright © 1956 Checkerboard Press, a division of Macmillan, Inc. ‖ All rights reserved. No part of this book may be reproduced or | transmitted in any form or by any means, electronic or | mechanical, including photocopying, recording, or by an | information storage and retrieval system, without permission in | writing from the Publisher. ‖ Aladdin Books | Macmillan Publishing Company | 866 Third Avenue | New York, NY 10022 ‖ Maxwell Macmillan Canada, Inc. | 1200 Eglinton Avenue East | Suite 200 | Don Mills, Ontario M3C 3N1 ‖ Macmillan Publishing Company is part of the Maxwell Communication | Group of Companies. ‖ Library of Congress Catalog Card Number: 86-064059 | ISBN 0-689-71743-1 ‖ Printed in the United States of America | 3 5 7 9 10 8 6 4]

COVER: Gloss wrapper. Front upper right, white box: $4.95. Spine: Tudor 1 is One Aladdin Books. Back lower left, 2 UPC bar codes in an inset white box: above the smaller right bar code, 90000>, and beneath the larger left code, 9 780689 717437 | ISBN 0-689-71743-1. Upper right corner: >>$4.95 US | >>$6.50 CAN.

1-17 _____. **TASHA TUDOR** ‖ Troll Associates [Copyright © 1956 Checkerboard Press . . . America | 10 9 8 7 6 5 4 3 2 1]

> COVER: Gloss wrapper is more gray than the taupe of the Aladdin imprint above. Front upper right, white box: $4.95. Lower left carries a photograph of the Caldecott Honor Book medallion superimposed over the illustration - not the normal foil medal. White spine: Tudor   1 is One Troll. Back lower left, previous bar codes have been eliminated leaving only the inset white box. Upper right corner: **$4.95** U.S. | $6.95 CAN. Lower right: **Troll Associates**.

> OTHER: In other respects this is a photoduplication of the Aladdin imprint. Although some versions of this book must exist with the Caldecott foil medal attached to the cover, I have not seen one. This photographic duplication of the medal is the only version I have examined. The book was printed circa 1997. Troll Associates is an imprint of Simon & Schuster.

1-18 1980 | Tasha Tudor | Calendar | [4 1/8″ rule] | with fourteen reproductions | of full-color paintings | from *A Time To Keep.*

> OTHER: See *A Time To Keep* for a full description of this derivative work.

1-19 *THE 1995 BIBLIOGRAPHY | AND PRICE GUIDE | TO BOOKS | ILLUSTRATED BY ‖ Tasha Tudor ‖ COMPILED | BY | GARY J. OVERMANN ‖ BOOKS OF THE AGES | BATAVIA , OHIO* [Copyright 1995 | Gary J. Overmann ‖ All rights reserved. No part of this book may | be reproduced in any form without permission | from the publisher. ‖ Books of the Ages | 4764 Silverwood Drive | Batavia, Ohio   45103 ‖ First Printing | December, 1995]

> PAGINATION: [1-48] on twelve sheets of white paper folder and stapled. 8 ½ x 5 3/8″

> COVER: Gray cover stock folded and stapled twice with the pages. Front cover as the title page, minus the business name and city. Back: *This Price Guide consists | of a list of Books | Illustrated | by Tasha Tudor | along with current | Market Values. | Included in the list are | Limited Editions, | First Trade Editions, | Early Reprints, | Later Printings | and Foreign Editions | with or without | Dust Wrappers | or an Autograph. ‖ $10.00*

> CONTENTS: Title page [1], Introduction and Use of the Guide, p. [3], Books Illustrated by Tasha Tudor, pp. [5-42], Calendars Illustrated by Tasha Tudor, pp. [43-44], Index, pp. [45-48]. Page [4] is blank.

> OTHER: There were earlier title lists, but this is the first attempt at listing multiple editions of Tudor books. Chronological listing, 1938-1995 (*Pumpkin Moonshine* through *The Tasha Tudor Sketchbook Series: Family and Friends.*) Editor does identify first editions by publisher, and a category "later editions" without indicating when those later editions were printed. No indications of the number of printings. Eight value ranges are given for each title, a first edition with and without a jacket, later printings with and without jackets, and autographs in all four categories. There are errors and many omissions. Authors are given second billing to Tudor throughout which we find to be odd since books are normally credited to their authors. Illustrators are normally given second ranking in bibliographic citations, even when they are the subjects of the work as in this instance. Further, we are left to wonder why Mary Mason Campbell is cited as Mary Campbell throughout, even though all three names always appear in her books. *Tasha Tudor's Treasure* is mistakenly cited, and placed in the wrong year of publication. Publishers' names are incorrectly cited: Little Brown, and MacMillan. Errors of fact cite the first printing of *Tasha Tudor's Sampler* to be in red boards, and black ink on the first printing of *Tasha Tudor's Seasons of Delight.* The cover ink of *Take Joy!* is incorrect. We

question Overmann's citing Tudor as the illustrator of *Drawn from New England* when the publisher did not say so, or supplying a title which does not appear on the piece for the miniature boxed set of the 23rd Psalm and the Lord's Prayer. At least one title is prominently misprinted, *The Tasha Tudor's Bedtime Book*. A title index refers to the year of entry. 'A' and 'The' are used as filing points, thereby losing those titles to the normal alphabetical sequencing. Eleven calendars (1978-1995) include nine Advent and valentine 'calendars.' There is no copyright notice on file at the Library of Congress.

1-20 *THE 1996 BIBLIOGRAPHY* . . . [Copyright 1995 . . . December, 1995]

PAGINATION: [1-72]   8 ½ x 5 3/8″

COVER: Blue cover stock. The only change is color or paper, and the date in the title.

CONTENTS: Text, pp. [5-59], Blank, [4, 60, 68], Calendars Illustrated by Tasha Tudor [61-62], Identification of First Editions of | Books | Illustrated by Tasha Tudor | Listed by Publisher [63-67], Index [69-72]. There are minor revisions to the text and values.   No new titles, no new calendars. Increasing the type font increased the number of pages and the legibility.

OTHER: The errors persist.

1-21 The 1998 Bibliography | and Price Guide to | Books Illustrated by ‖ **Tasha Tudor** ‖

Compiled by | **Gary J. Overmann** ‖ **Books of the Ages** ‖ Batavia, Ohio. [*Text Copyright 1995, 1998 | Gary J. Overmann | Books of the Ages | 4764 Silverwood Drive | Batavia, Ohio 45103 ‖Illustrations, including cover artwork entitled "Reading Aloud" Copyright 1998 | Tasha Tudor | Corgi Cottage Industries, L.L.C. | 121 Wyck Street, Suite 101 | Richmond, Virginia 23225 ‖ All rights reserved. No part of this book may be reproduced in any form without | permission from the publisher. ‖ Books of the Ages | 4764 Silverwood Drive | Batavia, Ohio 45103 ‖ First Printing, Revised Edition | January, 1998*]

PAGINATION: [i-vi] 1-86, plus wrapper.   8 ½ x 5 ½″

COVER: Paper wrapper, rust background on which are printed two color illustrations. A large (7 9/16 x 4 9/16″) tan panel on the front shows a boy in a ladder back chair reading to a girl holding a cat as she sits in a thumb-back chair. A corgi listens and two books resembling *Around the Year* and *Alexander the Gander* lie on the floor.   The boy is modeled after the often-pictured Rosamond Tudor painting of her son Frederick, Tasha Tudor's brother. Dated 97. Cover text: ***The 1998 Bibliography | and Price Guide to | Books Illustrated by* ‖ Tasha Tudor |** [illustration] | ***Compiled by Gary J. Overmann.*** Spine: The 1998 Bibliography and Price Guide to Books Illustrated by Tasha Tudor   Books of the Ages. Back cover: $16.95 ‖ *This price guide consists of a list of books illustrated by Tasha | Tudor along with current market values. Included in the list are | limited editions, early reprints, later printings and for- | eign editions with or without dust wrappers or an autograph.* | [2 15/16″ x 4 1/16″ cream panel with illustration of a child shaking paws with a rabbit. Dated 91]

CONTENTS: Title page, i; colophon, ii; Contents, iii; Acknowledgements, Introduction and | Use of this Guide, v; "To my wife Pam | and our children | Katie, Erin and Nathan," vi. The body of the booklet, pp. 1-86, Blank, [iv], Calendars Illustrated by | Tasha Tudor, pp. 75-77; Identification of First Editions of | Books Illustrated by Tasha Tudor — | Listed by Publisher, pp. 78-82; Index, pp. 83-86.

OTHER: Gary Overmann announced his third price guide in late Fall 1997 to contain original art especially for this edition, two color illustrations and 30+ black and white sketches. A large and expanded edition with information on limited editions, first editions, later printings, and some foreign editions. Advertised as item no. [BOTA] 1028 to be released in January 1998 at $16.95.

This revision of Overmann's list makes an important contribution; it publishes for the first time a collection of Tudor signatures, which one presumes to be authentic. We have heard that at various times people other than Tudor have signed her name to books. The examples under examination seem to be the reprinted inscriptions from various books; there are several personal inscriptions. We spotted the name of one of Overmann's children among them. Many of the signatures are dated 1970 - with most of them since 1985. One should use this guide with a healthy skepticism; errors which appeared in the first printing in 1995 are still here. There were some obvious errors in titles and copyrights which have not been corrected. Overmann has fallen into the entanglement of failing to define accurately the many printings of Tudor books. We are dismayed at inconsistent descriptions which do not place printings in their chronological order. Indeed, the print order of *The Secret Garden* and *A Little Princess* is arbitrary and bounces among publishers. He errs in transcribing foreign titles in *A Book of Christmas* and is unfamiliar with foreign publishing terminology. In fact fundamental English terminology causes problems when he refers to a 'forward' to *English Cottage Gardening*. We take issue with his market values finding some of them to be inflated, $50 for the Corgi Standard booklet for instance. As before, Overmann places a premium on Tudor's signature, which after all is a very common one, but always in demand by her fans. Tudor has generously signed her books throughout her career.

1-22 _____.

    OTHER: The Spring 1998 catalog from Corgi Cottage Industries advertises the *1998* list in a "SPECIAL LIMITED EDITION of 100, hardbound, each numbered and signed by | both Gary and Tasha. Of the 100, the first 10 are for presentation, 90 are for sale. | *Hardbound* (#224 BOK) $75.00 || *As both a collector and dealer of out-of-print books, Gary Overmann is an invaluable source | for Tasha's hard-to-find books. He's the one Tasha calls! You may contact Gary at BOOKS OF THE | AGES, Maple Ridge Manor, 4764 Silverwood Drive, Batavia, Ohio 45103*"

A1 **A** | **B** | **C** [mustard ink] | **GO!** [blue] | *A completely new selection of outstanding children's stories* | *and poems compiled for enrichment reading by a distinguished* | *editorial board of children's librarians.* || Series Editor | **MARGARET E. MARTIGNONI** | Former Superintendent | Work with Children | Brooklyn Public Library || Editor-in-Chief | **DR. LOUIS SHORES** | Dean, Library School | Florida State University || Managing Editor | **HARRY R. SNOWDEN, JR.** [black] | Volume Editor | **ROSEMARY E. LIVSEY** | Coordinator, Children's Services | Los Angels Public Library [blue] || Collier's *Junior* Classics Series || THE CROWELL-COLLIER PUBLISHING COMPANY • NEW YORK [black]. [A, B, C: GO! || Copyright © 1962 by the Crowell-Collier Publishing Company | Library of Congress Catalog Card Number 61-17993 | Printed in the United States of America | Twenty-first Printing || All rights to text and illustrations reprinted from other books or | sources are reserved to the respective copyright owners. The copy- | right ownership of prose selections is shown on the opening page of each selection. All copyright notices, including those for illus- | trations, appear in the Acknowledgments at the back of the book.]

PAGINATION: [I-iv] v-xv [xvi] [1-2] 3-9 [10] 11-17 [18-19] 20 [21] 22 [23] 24-25 [26-27] 28-30 [31-33] 34 [35-36] 37-42 [43] . . . 383-400, plus endpapers perfect bound. 9 ½" x 6 ¾".

COVER: Turquoise cloth with plastic coating, stamped in gilt, on front: [thick rule] | Collier's Junior Classics | [thick rule] | THE YOUNG FOLKS | SHELF OF BOOKS | [thick rule]. Spine: each of three navy bands is edged in a thick gilt border, a narrow one at the top and the bottom, and a two-inch wide band in the middle of the spine. Stamped on the spine between the two upper bands: COLLIER'S | Junior | Classics. On the wide navy band: A | B | C | GO! There is a navy silhouette of Little Bo Peep and one sheep in the wide lower turquoise band. Beneath it in gilt, the number 1. In gilt on the lower navy band: CROWELL-COLLIER. The back is turquoise with no imprint.

DUST JACKET: Have not examined a dust jacket.

ILLUSTRATIONS: Black and white Tudor illustrations, with original *Mother Goose* references in {}: 9 {48}, 13 {81} [21 {84}, 23 {65}] 25 {80} [27 {49}, 31 {72}]. Color Tudor ILLUSTRATIONS: [2] {10} 3 {86}, 6 {43} - 7 {39}, [10] {63} 11 {62}, 14 {51} - 15 {54}.

CONTENTS: The last paragraph of thirty-seven individual ACKNOWLEDGMENTS, pages 398-400, reads: HENRY Z. WALCK, INC. Illustrations by Tasha Tudor for "Baa, baa, black sheep," "Heigh diddle | diddle," [*sic*] "Hickety, pickety, my black hen," "Hickory dickory dock," "I had a little nut tree," "Little | Jack Horner," "Little Tommy Tucker," "Old King Cole," "One, two, buckle my shoe," "Pease por- | ridge hot," "Ride a cock-horse to Banbury Cross," "Ring-a-ring o' roses," "Sing a song of Six- | pence," "There was an old woman who lived in a shoe," and "Tom, Tom, the piper's son," from | *Mother Goose;* reprinted by permission of Henry Z. Walck, Inc.

OTHER: This is the first volume in a set of ten, the only volume with Tudor illustrations. The other volumes are:

Vol. 2 ONCE UPON A TIME

Vol. 3 MAGIC IN THE AIR

Vol. 4 JUST AROUND THE CORNER

Vol. 5 IN YOUR OWN BACKYARD

Vol. 6 HARVEST OF HOLIDAY

Vol. 7 LEGENDS OF LONG AGO

Vol. 8 ROADS TO GREATNESS

Vol. 9 CALL OF ADVENTURE

Vol. 10 GIFTS FROM THE PAST

COPYRIGHT REGISTRATION: A582101

A2 A | is | [a doll in a pink gingham dress] | for | ANNABELLE | By TASHA TUDOR |
NEW YORK OXFORD UNIVERSITY PRESS 1954 [COPYRIGHT 1954 | OXFORD
UNIVERSITY PRESS, INC. | PRINTED IN THE UNITED STATES OF AMERICA]

PAGINATION: [60] pp. in 4 signatures, including free endpapers. 7"x 9 ¼".

COVER: Yellow-green cloth. A is for ANNABELLE between two leaves stamped in gold on front; in
gold on spine [leaf] TUDOR [leaf] A is for ANNABELLE [leaf] OXFORD [leaf]. Each end
paper: small bunch of flowers, green wash in a large oval frame of lily of the valley.

DUST JACKET: Pink dust jacket, front illustration: Annabelle sitting within the title in an oval of
bleeding heart, roses and other flowers. Printing in black: A | is for | ANNA [a sitting doll]
BELLE | By TASHA TUDOR. Spine: [leaf] TUDOR [leaf] A is for ANNABELLE [leaf]
OXFORD [leaf]. Rose sprig on back. Front flap: A IS FOR ANNABELLE [apple green ink,
remaining text except publisher's series, black] || By Tasha Tudor || "A is for Annabelle, Grand- |
mother's doll..." in this charmingly | illustrated alphabet book. Two little | girls play with the
elegant, old- | fashioned doll, whose clothes and | possessions complete the alphabet. |
Annabelle's varied wardrobe, her | dresses and fan, her slippers and veil, | will please all little
girls, as well as | Tasha Tudor fans. ¶The simple verse and delicate | drawings are Tasha Tudor
at her best. | Young readers will find this a memor- | able introduction to the alphabet and | all
those who love dolls will love | Annabelle. || Oxford Books | for Boys and Girls [apple green] |
30-60 $2.50.   Back flap in black: [2 x 2 7/8" photograph of Tudor and Efner and
Annabelle sitting beside a tree] | On Tasha Tudor's New Hampshire | farm there is a nine room,
two-story | doll house where Annabelle lives. | This doll house is the setting for A | IS FOR
ANNABELLE and the clothes | and accessories mentioned in the al- | phabet book are part of
Annabelle's | wardrobe. Annabelle herself is shown | above with Tasha Tudor and Efner |
Tudor, one of the little girls in the | story. ¶Miss Tudor has always been inter- | ested in dolls.
She first wrote about | her collection in A DOLL'S [sic] | CHRISTMAS, a story of their doll's
[sic] | Christmas party, an annual event on | the Tudor farm.

CONTENTS: The oval floral frame around each illustration reflects the frames of H. Willebeek Le
Mair's Mother Goose (1911). This is an alphabet book of verses about Grandmother's doll
Annabelle; each letter's verse describes an article of her wardrobe and is printed across two
pages. Text begins on pages [4-5] in color. The black and white dedication page [3]: To
dearest | Muff | and | Aunt Middle Mary [Friends Marcia Cunningham of Hopkinton, NH, and
her sister Mary Davis.] Pages [5-6] and inside front and back endpapers are blank.

ILLUSTRATIONS: The title page is drawn with the oval theme divided. The top half of the oval is
floral: the bottom half is formed from the words ANNA and BELLE with the doll sitting
interposed and filling one-third of the oval illustration. Two pages of text alternate with two
pages of black and white illustrations throughout the book. Some illustrations show Tudor's
signature.

OTHER: Lea Pedersen, 7620 North El Dorado, Apt 69, Stockton, CA 95207 [and now of Lodi,
CA], a US citizen, born in 1921, obtained copyright registration VA 14-941 Dec. 14, 1978, for
ANNABELLE PATTERNS, scale line drawings for a 6 inch doll published Mar. 30, 1978, 17
pages, as part of the United Federation of Doll Clubs Regional Conference. The material is an
"adaptation of design in pattern form, with explicit instructions plus illustrations, original, from
the artist," [sic] based on the children's book "A IS FOR ANNABELLE" by Tasha Tudor.

There were actually nineteen sheets (12 ¼" x 9 ¼") of black ink drawings on white paper as
follows: Cover sheet ANNA BELLE PATTERNS, Pink Check A, Ball gown B in two pages,

Cloak C in two pages, Purple plaid day dress D in two pages, White and green morning dress E in two pages, Annabelles' [*sic*] jacket, Annabelles' [*sic*] party dress in two pages, Travel gown T, Visiting dress V in two pages, F fan and bonnet and tippet, Underwear, Nightie. The set was packaged in a manila envelope with a yellow sheet of paper imprinted with cover sheet design pasted on the front. Frankie Von Blomberg is credited for fan and bonnet patterns.

Freddie Chevreier reports in 1998 that a 6″ Annabelle doll was made for each of the 450 registrants of the 1978 Region 2 Doll Federation conference at Asilomar, Pacific Grove, Ca. The conference was hosted by the Stockton CAL Doll Club when Chevreier was president. Pederson was the design engineer. All the dolls were made by Gail Curry [Alter]. Mr. Alter published a souvenir *Annabelle Journal* as part of the registration package. [We have not examined a copy. Ed.] The dolls came unclothed, but with a small wooden trunk, a copy of *A is for Annabelle*, the dress patterns and a zither. To cloth the dolls became the attendees' next year's project. Many fulfilled the assignment, and Chevreier relates, the dolls appear on auction bills to this day. Chevreier also presented a slide show at the conference in which real children were depicted in the tableaux of Tudor's book.
The Children's Museum, Indianapolis, In., also used Tudor's design motif for card advertisements of its November 27, 1981 - January 3, 1982, exhibit. The cards feature a doll sitting in an oval of ivy but with the words *T is for Tasha Tudor* over the dates and museum name.

COPYRIGHT REGISTRATION: A 164880 granted to Oxford University Press, Inc., 114 Fifth Avenue, New York 11, NY., whose agent W.M. Gherton {illegible} swears on December 3, 1954:

A IS FOR ANNABELLE, by Tasha Tudor a United States citizen born 1910 of Contoocook, NH, was published October 21, 1954. The book was printed by Kellogg and Bulkeley, Hartford, Ct. from hand-lettering. Binding by American Book-Stratford Press, Inc., New York, NY. Application, affidavit and two copies of the book were received at the Library of Congress December 10, 1954.

COPYRIGHT RENEWAL REGISTRATION: RE 147-603 to the text and illustrations (with no changes from the original version) was granted to the author Tasha Tudor, Route 4, West Brattleboro, VT 05301 on December 10, 1982. Lisa Marrongelli, David McKay Co., 2 Park Avenue, New York, NY, 10016, filed as agent for Tasha Tudor [undated]. Although the application received December 2 ?, 1982, listed Tasha Tudor as the original copyright claimant, the Copyright Office amended the declaration to read Oxford University press, Inc.

A3 _____. [COPYRIGHT 1954 | OXFORD UNIVERSITY PRESS, INC. | PRINTED IN THE UNITED STATES OF AMERICA | SECOND PRINTING, 1957]

COVER: The cloth has a more yellow cast. Oversewn.

DUST JACKET: Have not examined one with price intact.

A4 A | is | [a doll in a pink gingham dress] | for | ANNABELLE | By TASHA TUDOR | NEW YORK HENRY Z. WALCK, INC. 1954. [COPYRIGHT 1954 | HENRY Z. WALCK, INC. | Library of Congress Catalog Card Number: 60-15911. PRINTED IN THE UNITED STATES OF AMERICA]

PAGINATION: [60] pp. in 4 signatures including free endpapers. Twelve stitches, topsewn. 7″x 9 ¼″.

COVER: Mint green cloth cover. Spine in gold: TUDOR [leaf] A is for ANNABELLE [leaf] WALCK.

OTHER: The text and illustrations of this edition match the Oxford printings, although the yellow and pink inks are stronger here.

A5 _____.

PAGINATION: Ten stitches, topsewn.

COVER: <u>Library binding</u> with cloth tape reinforced hinge.

DUST JACKET: Similar to Oxford first edition. Spine: [leaf] TUDOR [leaf] A is for ANNABELLE [leaf] <u>WALCK</u> [leaf]. Front flap: A IS FOR ANNABELLE . . . all those who love dolls will love | Annabelle. || *Henry Z. Walck, Inc.* | 30-60. {Have not examined one without the corners clipped.} Back flap <u>new text</u> in black: 1 is ONE || *By Tasha Tudor* | "This exquisite little counting book, | companion to her alphabet book, *A is* | *for Annabelle*, is alight with Tasha | Tudor's tender feeling for animals, | growing things, and small children. | Beginning with '1 is one duckling | swimming in a dish, 2 is two sisters | making a wish,' she makes the learn- | ing of numbers from 1 to 20 a happy | rhyming game. Each number takes | up two pages, each of which has a | border of lovely field flowers. And all | the pictures—alternating black and | white with delicate pastel colors— | have a warm, old-fashioned flavor | which will captivate all ages." | *—Chicago Tribune.*

OTHER: Examined a copy inscribed Christmas 1969.

A6 _____. . . . NEW YORK HENRY Z. WALCK, INC. [{Outlined catalog card} E Tudor, Tasha | A is for Annabelle. Walck, 1954 | unp. illus. | Annabelle, grandmother's doll, is | the center of this story built on | the letters of the alphabet. || 1. Alphabet books 2. Dolls - Fiction | I. Title. {below the card}: *This Main Entry catalog card may be reproduced without permission. || Copyright 1954. Henry Z. Walck, Inc. ISBN:0-8098-1040-9. Library of Congress | Catalog Card Number: 60-15911. Printed in the United States of America*]

COVER: Mint green cloth cover, title and two leaves stamped in <u>navy</u> on cover. Spine as before, but in <u>navy ink</u>. Library binding with buckram reinforcement tape. 7" x 9 ¼".

DUST JACKET: Examined copy with corners clipped, 3.40 | net penciled on the upper right front flap.

A7 A | is | [a doll in a pink gingham dress] | for | ANNABELLE | By TASHA TUDOR | Rand McNally & Company Chicago • New York • San Francisco [*Copyright 1954. Henry Z. Walck, Inc. ISBN: 0-8098-1040-9. Library of Congress | Catalog Card Number: 60-15911. Printed in the United States of America*]

PAGINATION: [64] pp. in paper wrapper. Thick paper, book is 5/16" thick, <u>perfect bound</u>. 9" w x 6 3/4"h.

COVER: Cover reproduces the dust jacket from the 1954 Walck edition, with these additions. <u>Front cover price: $ 1.50</u>. Back cover, upper left: <u>82-1678</u>; upper right, 30-60. Spine: [leaf] TUDOR [leaf] A is for ANNABELLE [leaf] [divider on globe] Rand McNally.

CONTENTS: Endpaper designs from hardback editions are printed on pages [1], [4], [60-61]. Pages [2] and [62] are blank. Page [3] has the band box sketch from "H". Title page is [5]. Text begins on page [8] and alternates with the same plates as before, two pages color, two pages black and white. Page [63] reproduces the front jacket flap from <u>1 is One</u>: 1 is One | by Tasha Tudor || Designed as a companion volume to Miss | Tudor's alphabet book, *A is for* | *Annabelle*, this charming book includes | numbers one through twenty. Each number | is graphically illustrated by one of Miss | Tudor's paintings and accompanied by an | original verse. || A variety of pictures—of animals, chil- | dren, trees and flowers—as well as the easy- | to remember verses will encourage the | youngest readers to learn their numbers and | make them want to return to the book again | and again. | The old-fashioned loveliness of Miss | Tudor's delicate illustrations make this a | particularly inviting introduction to "how | to count."

A8 _____.

>COVER: <u>Impressed weave more obvious on inside of wrapper.</u> Back cover, upper left: <u>528-87678-3</u>. Front cover upper right: $ 1.50.

A9 _____.

>COVER: The only change is the printed price on the front, which becomes <u>$1.95</u>.

A10 _____.

>COVER: In upper right hand corner of front cover: <u>$ 2.50</u>. Back cover upper left 528-87678-3, upper right 30-60.

A11 _____.

>COVER: Upper right front corner: $ 2.95. Book is 5/16″ thick.

A12 _____.

>COVER: <u>Upper right front corner: $ 2.95.</u> <u>Book is only 1/4″ thick</u> on a whiter paper. For the first time, <u>the spine is white,</u> but the rest of the cover is pink, as before.

A13 _____.

>COVER: <u>Upper right front corner: $ 3.95.</u> Printed on an ivory kid-finish paper.

A14 _____.

>COVER: Smooth gloss finish. Upper right front corner: $ 3.95. Ivory paper.

A15 _____.

>PAGINATION: <u>[68] pages</u> in four signatures, including free endpapers. <u>7 3/16″ x 9 11/32.″</u>

>COVER: Gloss finish paper over <u>boards</u>, square spine 13/32″, cloth hinges. Front carries only the central oval and title; the price and author's name are not printed. Spine: TUDOR A is for ANNABELLE CHILDRENS PRESS CHOICE [CP book logo]. Back, centered rose, and at lower left: [CP book logo] | CHILDRENS PRESS CHOICE | <u>REINFORCED BINDING</u>. Lower right in a ½ x 2″ white box: ISBN 0-516-09845-4.

>CONTENTS: All text and illustrations as above, plus two extra ivory endpapers.

A16 A | is | [a doll in a pink gingham dress] | for | ANNABELLE | By TASHA TUDOR | Checkerboard Press • New York [Copyright © 1954 Checkerboard Press, a division of Macmillan, Inc. | All rights reserved. | Library of Congress Catalog Card Number: 86-064058 | ISBN 0-02-688534-4 | CHECKERBOARD PRESS and colophon are trademarks of Macmillan, Inc. | Printed in Hong Kong]

>COVER: Smooth, gloss finish, illustration as before and a UPC code on back cover. Front cover price in upper right corner: $ 3.95. Back cover, lower left in a white box, 1 5/16″ x 2″: [bar code] | 0 14121 88534 7 | ISBN 0-02-688534-4. Spine: TUDOR A is for ANNABELLE Checkerboard Press. Book is 1/4″ thick.

A17 _____. [Copyright © 1954 . . . are trademarks of Macmillan, Inc.]

COVER: Front cover price is **$4.95**. Back cover upper right: >>$4.95 US | >>$6.50 CAN 1 3/8″ x 2″ white box at lower left, back cover: [bar code] | 0 14121 88534 7 | ISBN 0-02-688534-4. All numbers in 'computer' type font except those immediately beneath the bar code.

OTHER: No reference to Hong Kong in the colophon.

A18 _____.

PAGINATION: Book is 3/16″ thick, printed on thinner polished paper.

COVER: No price on front. Back cover upper right: >>$5.95 US | >>$7.50 CAN. Lower left has a 2″ x 1 3/8″ white box with 90000> [above the smaller right bar code] | [2 bar codes] | 9 780026 885348 [beneath the larger left bar code] | ISBN 0-02-688534-4.

A19 ADVENTURES | OF A | BEAGLE | [cat sitting and staring] | by T. L. McCready, Jr. | ILLUSTRATIONS | by Tasha Tudor | [rooster pecking at a bone] | ARIEL BOOKS • NEW YORK [*to Dr. Charles H. Endee* | [color illustration of 4 children examining newspaper] | Copyright © 1959 by Thomas L. McCready and Tasha Tudor | Library of Congress catalog card number 59-6211 | *Published simultaneously in Canada* | *by Ambassador Books, Ltd.* | MANUFACTURED IN THE U.S.A.]

PAGINATION: [52] pages including the fly leaves in 3 signatures. 8 1/8″ x 6 1/8″

COVER: Light olive green cloth cover printed in black: a left-facing beagle on the front; on the spine, McCready • ADVENTURES OF A BEAGLE • ARIEL. Full color endpapers (same scene front and back) show May Day in the pasture behind the barns at the Webster, N.H., property.

DUST JACKET: Lime green jacket with white flaps. Front: ADVENTURES | OF A | BEAGLE | [oval portrait of a beagle in a white and brown mat frame] | by T. L. McCready, Jr. | Pictures by Tasha Tudor. Spine: McCready ADVENTURES OF A BEAGLE Ariel. The back is green. Front flap: $ 2.75 | 428 || AN ARIEL EASY READING BOOK || ADVENTURES | OF A | BEAGLE | BY *T.L. McCready, Jr.* | PICTURES BY *Tasha Tudor* || May Day Warner, a beagle dog | named for the date of her arrival at | the Warner's New Hampshire farm, | proved to be one of the most popu- | lar pets the family ever owned. | Blessed with all the lovable (and | some *not* so lovable) characteristics | of the beagle breed, May has a | rather bumpy time adjusting to life | amidst the Warner menagerie of | geese, ducks, chickens, rabbits and | cats. She is led by her acute sense | of smell into all manner of mischief | and adventure, once almost getting | kidnapped as a result of her bound- | (*continued on back flap*) || ARIEL BOOKS | FARRAR, STRAUS AND CUDAHY | 101 Fifth Avenue, New York 3, N.Y. Back flap: (*continued from front flap*) | less curiosity. Actually, this all-bark | and no-bite beagle emerges as the | good-natured clown of Warner | Farm, easily outwitted by the terri- | ble Mr. Stubbs, the Warners' tail- | less tomcat, as well as the fearless | Biggity Bantam. The children love | her, however, and you will too. || May's escapades are depicted by | Tasha Tudor in black and white | and in full color, with the style and | charm which has helped to make | this series a favorite with children | and parents alike. | [rule] | If you enjoyed *Adventures of a* | *Beagle*, then you will want to own its | companion volumes. The following | is a complete listing of books by | T.L. McCready and Tasha Tudor | about the Warners and their pets: | BIGGITY BANTAM $ 2.75 | PEKIN WHITE $ 2.75 | MR. STUBBS $ 2.75 | INCREASE RABBIT $ 2.75 | ADVENTURES OF A BEAGLE $ 2.75 || ARIEL BOOKS | FARRAR, STRAUS AND CUDAHY | 101 Fifth Avenue, New York 3, N.Y.

ILLUSTRATIONS: Color illustrations on the endpapers, and pp. [1 (fly leaf), 4, 8, 9, 13, 17, 24-25, 29, 33, 37, 44, 45, 48, 49, 52 (fly leaf)]. Black and white ILLUSTRATIONS: pp. [2, 3, 6, 7, 10, 11, 14, 15, 19, 20, 21, 23, 27, 30, 35, 38, 39, 40, 41, 42, 43, 46, 47, 50]. Full page illustrations on pp. [17, 19, 29, 30, 33]. Pages with text only: [5, 12, 16, 18, 22, 26, 28, 31, 32, 34, 36]. Page [51] is blank.

OTHER: One notices a strong resemblance to the Dick and Jane illustrations of the 1950s. Dr. Endee was the McCready family's Boston dentist, who also had a "camp" not far from the Webster farm.

COPYRIGHT REGISTRATION: A 406333 granted to Thomas McCready and Tasha Tudor. Their agent Anne Brooks Murray, Farrar, Straus and Cudahy, Inc. swears on August 11,1959:

> ADVENTURES OF A BEAGLE, by Thomas McCready a United States citizen, was published August 11, 1959. The book was printed by Monitor Press, NY, NY., binding by H. Wolff Book Mfg., NY, NY. Application and affidavit were received at the Library of Congress August 14,1959, and two copies of the book were received August 17, 1959.

COPYRIGHT RENEWAL REGISTRATION: RE 354-076 granted to Seth Tudor, Box 247, Marlboro, VT 06344, claiming as son of the deceased author Thomas L. McCready, Jr. Dorothea Nelson, agent for Seth Tudor, swears on Nov. 12, 1987:

> The entire work ADVENTURES OF A BEAGLE, text by Thomas L. McCready and illustrations by Tasha Tudor is renewed. The original book was published Aug. 11, 1959 and assigned registration A 406333. Renewal application was received at LC Nov. 16, 1987 and charged against account DA 013366, Farrar, Straus & Giroux, Inc., Union Square West, 4th Floor, NY, NY 10003. Amended [inserting the phrase 'son of the deceased author'] by the Copyright Office; authority of telephone conversation with Dorothea Nelson of Farrar, Straus & Giroux, Dec. 3, 1987.

A20 _____. . . . by Tasha Tudor | [rooster pecking at a bone] | FREDERICK WARNE & CO. LTD. | LONDON [to Dr. Charles H. Endee | [color illustration of 4 children examining newspaper] || First Published 1954 *[sic]* | By Thomas Leighton McCready and Tasha Tudor McCready | Revised Edition | © FREDERICK WARNE & CO., LTD. | LONDON, ENGLAND, 1961 || Printed in Great Britain by | William Clowes and Sons Ltd. London and Beccles | 68.261]

PAGINATION: [i-ii, 1-2] 3-14 [15] 16 [17] 18-21 [22-23] 24-26 [27-28] 29-30 [31] 32-48 [49-50] including the fly leaves in 3 signatures. 8 1/16″ x 6 1/8″

COVER: Red paper, weave imprint over boards, printed in black: line drawing of the illustration from page [15], May Day jumping at a ball near a flower bed, above, ADVENTURES of a BEAGLE; on the spine, MᶜCREADY ● ADVENTURES of a BEAGLE ● TUDOR *WARNE*. Endpapers as above.

DUST JACKET: Pastel green dust jacket with white flaps. Front: [black line drawing from page 8] | ADVENTURES | of a BEAGLE [in red] || [irregular white wash area with illustration from page 11] | by T. L. | MᶜCREADY, JR. [green] | The Pictures by Tasha Tudor [red]. Spine: ADVENTURES OF A BEAGLE [red] by T. L. MᶜCREADY, JR. WARNE [green]. The back is green with the illustration from page [ii]. Front flap: ADVENTURES | OF A BEAGLE | *by T.L. McCready, Jnr.* | *Pictures by Tasha Tudor* || May Day Warner, a beagle dog named | after the date of her arrival at the | Warner's New Hampshire farm, proved | to be one of the most popular pets the | family ever owned. Blessed with all the | lovable (and some *not* so lovable) | characteristics | of the beagle breed, May | has a rather bumpy time adjusting to | life amidst the Warner menagerie of | geese, ducks, chickens, rabbits and cats. | She is led by her acute sense of smell | into all manner of mischief and adven- | ture, once almost getting kidnapped as | a result of her boundless curiosity. | Actually, this all-bark and no-bite | beagle emerges as the good-natured | clown of Warner Farm, easily outwitted | by the terrible Mr. Stubbs, the Warners' tailless tomcat, as well as the | fearless Biggity Bantam. The children | love her, however, and you will too. || PRINTED IN GREAT BRITAIN || 8/6. Back flap: You will enjoy the companion | to this book || **BIGGITY BANTAM** || * * * || **T. L. McCREADY, JNR.** || Tom McCready, descendant of a long and | illustrious New England family, is a Hamilton | College graduate who has turned farmer. He | lives with his beautiful wife, who has long been | a famous figure in the children's book world | (see below), and their four children high up on | a New Hampshire farm. There, in an old house | with huge fireplaces, slanting floorboards and | antique furniture, they work and play with | Seth, Bethany, Tom-Tom, and Efner. Outside | is a big barn full of animals, chickens and | banties, with many broad fields stretching down | to a river where they all go in swimming on | hot days. It is a good life—one, we hope, that will foster many books. || **TASHA TUDOR** || Tasha is well known in the book world. Young | readers should know how pleased she is to illus- | trate her husband's first book and how excited | the young McCreadys are to have their banty flock immortalized by their mother's brush. As | in Tasha's many other books, which she has | written and illustrated herself, the source of | inspiration has been her own family and her | surroundings. This is probably the basis for her splendid work, plus the fact that she can paint | in watercolours in such a beautiful way. || *Published by* | FREDERICK WARNE & CO., LTD | London, England.

ILLUSTRATIONS: Illustrations as in the Ariel edition, but the page numbering is less by two here where most pages are numbered.

A21 ALEXANDER | THE | GANDER | BY | TASHA TUDOR | OXFORD UNIVERSITY | PRESS || [a garden with hollyhocks on the left and a goose on the right] || LONDON NEW YORK TORONTO [COPYRIGHT, 1939 | OXFORD UNIVERSITY PRESS | NEW YORK, INC. | | PRINTED IN THE UNITED STATES OF AMERICA]

PAGINATION: [52] pp. flyleaf to flyleaf, in three signatures, ivory paper. 4¾″ x 3 15/16″.

COVER: Bright green cloth with white polka dots. Front: white panel in a red scalloped border encloses red text: ALEXANDER | THE | GANDER | BY | TASHA TUDOR.

DUST JACKET: Ivory dust jacket. Front: **ALEXANDER | THE | GANDER** in orange letters outlined in black. Scrolls above and below a picture of a gray goose with a pansy in his beak carry the first and last words of title. **THE** is placed between the illustration and the lower scroll. | **BY TASHA TUDOR**, in black lettering below the bottom scroll. Spine in black: TUDOR [scroll] ALEXANDER THE GANDER [scroll] OXFORD. Back cover, small illustration of a bird sitting on an iris stalk. Front flap: ALEXANDER | THE | GANDER | BY | TASHA TUDOR | MRS. FILLOW HAD PLANTED | SOME LOVELY HELIOTROPE | PANSIES THAT CAUGHT | ALEXANDER THE GANDER'S | EYES. "JUST RIGHT FOR DESSERT," | HE THOUGHT. SO WHEN SYLVIE | ANN WASN'T LOOKING HE | MADE OFF FOR MRS. FILLOW'S | GARDEN. HIS ADVENTURES | ARE DELIGHTFULLY TOLD IN | TEXT AND ILLUSTRATION. ¶ A TALE TO BE READ BY | FOUR TO SIX YEAR OLDS. | OXFORD BOOKS | FOR BOYS AND GIRLS. | $ .75. A cattail in black ink appears at either side of the title. Back flap: PUMPKIN | MOONSHINE | BY TASHA TUDOR | SYLVIE ANN WANTED | A PUMPKIN MOONSHINE | FOR HALLOWE'EN. SO SHE | STARTED OUT TO FIND | THE BIGGEST PUMPKIN | THAT SHE COULD. HER | ADVENTURES WITH THE | PUMPKIN ARE TOLD IN | ENCHANTING PICTURES | AND EASY TEXT FOR | VERY SMALL PEOPLE. | | OXFORD BOOKS | FOR BOYS AND GIRLS | | $ .75. Copies may be found with all four corners of the flaps slightly clipped, but with all text present.

CONTENTS: Pp. [2, 50, 51] are blank. Page [3] is title page with holly hock, goose and sparrows. The title is lettered in orange-filled letters out-lined in black. Remaining text is hand lettered in black. Page [4] is imprint statement. Page [5], dedication: ANOTHER WEE STORY | FOR | SYLVIE, pansies, two blue birds and watering can. Even numbered pages [6] through [48] have full color, full-page illustrations. Odd numbered pages [7] - [49] carry the lettered text, each page beginning with an orange embellished initial. The spine is rounded.

ILLUSTRATIONS: Front end paper: Sylvie in blue gingham standing at the right of a book plate which she is painting red/orange while Alexander looks on from the left. Front flyleaf and back endpaper are illustrated with red-wing black birds on cat tails. The rear fly leaf shows a wren sitting in a nest supported by cattails.

COPYRIGHT REGISTRATION: 132,955 granted to Tasha Tudor.

ALEXANDER THE GANDER, by Tasha Tudor a United States citizen, was published September 28, 1939 by Oxford University Press, 114 Fifth Ave., NY, NY. The book was printed by Jersey City Printing Company, Jersey City, N.J. Binding by Haddam Craftsmen, Camden, N.J. The printing of the text was completed on April 25, 1939. Application and affidavit were received at the Library of Congress October 16, 1939, and two copies of the book were received October 23, 1939.

COPYRIGHT RENEWAL: R-413852 to Tasha Tudor, Route 1, Contoocook, NH, the author. Application certified by Barbara L. Dammann for Henry Z. Walck, Inc., 19 Union Square West, NY, NY 10003, assignee of Oxford University Press. Filing fee charged to copyright account # 6694 for Walck. Application received July 14, 1967.

A22 _____. [...NEW YORK, INC. || SECOND PRINTING, 1943 | PRINTED IN THE UNITED STATES OF AMERICA]

PAGINATION: [52] pp. flyleaf to flyleaf, in three signatures on ivory paper. 4 ¾" x 3 15/16".

DUST JACKET: Have not examined a dust jacket.

CONTENTS: Text is hand-lettered as before, except for the PRINTING statement, page [4].

OTHER: Pages [6, 10, 22, 30, 36, 38, 40,] may be out of registration.

A23 _____.

COVER: Green paper printed with the same design as first edition.

DUST JACKET: Have not examined a dust jacket.

OTHER: Pages [6, 10, 14, 36] may not be in perfect registration on many copies.

A24 _____. Have not examined a Third Printing.

A25 _____. [...FOURTH PRINTING, 1945 || PRINTED IN THE UNITED STATES OF AMERICA]

PAGINATION: [52] pp. including flyleaves, in three signatures on ivory paper. 4 ¾" x 3 15/16".

COVER: Green polka dotted cloth.

A26 _____. [. . . NEW YORK, INC. || FIFTH PRINTING 1951 || PRINTED IN THE UNITED STATES OF AMERICA]

COVER: Lime green paper over boards, printed as before. Square spine.

DUST JACKET: Front flap clipped at bottom. Back flap: . . . || OXFORD BOOKS | FOR BOYS AND GIRLS | | $1.00.

A27 ALEXANDER I THE I GANDER || Tasha Tudor || [hollyhock, grass and goose] || HENRY Z. WALCK, INCORPORATED | New York [Copyright 1939. Henry Z. Walck, Inc. First published in this enlarged edition, 1961. Library | of Congress Catalog Card Number: 61-15646. Printed in the United States of America]

PAGINATION: [52] pp. including flyleaves, oversewn in a reinforced hinge. 6 3/4" x 6 1/8".

COVER: Mint green cloth, navy ink on spine: Tudor   ALEXANDER   THE GANDER   Walck. End papers as before. Square spine.

DUST JACKET: Dust jacket has been revised. Front flap has no illustrations, but for the first time the text is set type: ALEXANDER THE GANDER | by Tasha Tudor | Mrs. Fillow had planted some lovely he- | liotrope | pansies that caught Alexander the | Gander's eyes. "Just right for dessert," | he thought. So when Sylvie Ann wasn't | looking he made off for Mrs. Fillow's | garden. His adventures are delightfully | told in text and illustration. ¶A reissue, in an enlarged format, of the | 1939 edition. || HENRY Z. WALCK, INC. | 30-60 $2.75. Corners clipped. Back flap: Books by Tasha Tudor || A IS FOR ANNABELLE | AMANDA AND THE BEAR | AROUND THE YEAR | THE COUNTY

FAIR | THE DOLLS' CHRISTMAS | DORCAS PORKUS | EDGAR ALLAN CROW | FIRST GRACES | FIRST PRAYERS | LINSEY WOOLSEY | 1 IS ONE | PUMPKIN MOONSHINE | A TALE FOR EASTER | THISTLY B.
Spine: Tudor   ALEXANDER THE GANDER   Walck.

CONTENTS: Pp. [2, 50, 51] are blank. Page [3], title page as before, except, the black calligraphy has been replaced by type "Tasha Tudor" within the illustration, and publisher's credit beneath.

OTHER: <u>BOOK PUBLISHING RECORD 1960-1964</u>, IV:5067. TUDOR, Tasha   *JUV* | *Alexander the gander*. [Enl.ed.] New York, Walck | [1961, c.1939] unpaged, col. illus. 61-15646 2.75 | Ages 3-6.

A28 _____. Warner Books, Inc. planned to reprint *Alexander the Gander* in a 4 ¼ x 3 7/8″ paper over boards edition in April 1998. Part of the *Warner Treasures* series, the book, ISBN 0-446-91253-0, was announced to retail for $ 6.95. http:// www.warnerbooks.com did not list the title as of March 3, 1998.   A company spokesperson confirmed a few days later that Warner would not be reprinting the series. Another employee speculated the calico books might be reprinted by Little, Brown.

A29 *All for Love* | SELECTED, EDITED AND ILLUSTRATED BY | *Tasha Tudor* | | *Philomel Books* | *New York* [*Copyright Acknowledgments* || The editor and Philomel Books herewith render thanks to the | following authors, publishers, and agents whose interest, cooper- | ation, and permission to reprint have made possible the prepara- | tion of *All for Love*. All possible care has been taken to trace the | ownership of every selection included and to make full acknowl- | edgment for its use. If any errors have accidentally occurred, they | will be corrected in subsequent editions, provided notification is | sent to the publishers. || Farrar, Straus & Giroux, Inc., for an excerpt from *Break of Day*, | by Colette. Copyright © 1961 by Martin Secker and Warburg Ltd. | Reprinted by permission of Farrar, Straus & Giroux, Inc. || Houghton Mifflin Company for an excerpt from "Kokoro," by | Lafcadio Hearne. || Hutchinson Publishing Group Ltd. for an extract from "The | Corner of the Field," from *Collected Poems of Frances Cornford*. | Reprinted by permission of Hutchinson Publishing Group Ltd. || J.M. Dent & Sons Ltd. for lines from the essay "A Love That | Lasts," from *Searchlights and Nightingales*, by Robert Lynd. Re- | printed by permission of J.M. Dent & Sons Ltd. || Macmillan Publishing Co., Ltd. for "Come," by Sara Teasdale, | from *The Collected Poems of Sara Teasdale*. Reprinted by permission | {to next column} of Macmillan Publishing Co. Copyright © 1915 by Macmillan | Publishing Co., Inc., renewed 1943 by Mamie T. Wheless. || Michael Yeats and Macmillan London Limited for the poem | "The Song of Wandering Aengus," by W. B. Yeats. Reprinted by | permission of A. P. Watt Ltd., agents, and Michael Yeats. || Norma Millay Ellis for the poem "Recuerdo," by Edna St. Vin- | cent Millay, from *Collected Poems*, Harper & Row. Copyright © | 1922, 1950 by Edna St. Vincent Millay. Reprinted by permission | of Norma Millay Ellis. || Oxford University Press for the poem "Music I Heard," by | Conrad Aiken, from *Collected Poems*. Copyright © 1953, 1970 by | Conrad Aiken; renewed 1981 by Mary Aiken. Reprinted by per- | mission of Oxford University Press, Inc. || Random

House, Inc., and Alfred A. Knopf, Inc. for an extract | from "Argonauta," from *Gift From the Sea*, by Anne Morrow | Lindbergh. Copyright © 1955 by Anne Morrow Lindbergh. Re- | printed by permission of Pantheon Books, a division of Random | House, Inc. || Wesleyan University press for "The Beautiful." Copyright © | 1963 by W. H. Davies. Reprinted from *The Complete Poems of W. | H. Davies* by permission of Wesleyan University Press. || [painting of a white dove with rose in beak] || Published by Philomel books | a division of The Putnam Publishing Group | 51 Madison Ave., New York, N.Y. 10010 | Text copyright © 1984 by Philomel Books | Illustrations copyright © 1984 by Tasha Tudor | All rights reserved. No part of this book may be reproduced in any form | without written permission from the publisher, except for brief passages | included in a review appearing in a newspaper or magazine. | Printed in the United States of America | Designed by Nanette Stevenson/Calligraphy by Jeanyee Wong || Library of Congress Cataloging in Publication Data | Main entry under title: All for love. | Includes index. | Summary: An anthology of poems, stories, songs, letters, and | miscellaneous facts describing various aspects of love. | 1. Love—Literary collections. [1. Love—Literary collections] I. Tudor, Tasha. | PN6071.L7A4 1984 808.8'354 83-21959 | ISBN 0-399-21012-1]

PAGINATION: Three signatures, [96] pages, front cover to back cover numbered thus: [1] front cover, [2-3] front endpapers, [4] blank, [5] half-title, [6] blank, [7] title page, [8] imprint page, [9-10] Contents, [11] dedication *F.B.S.* | | *For my beloved* [Judge Frederick B. Smillie as revealed on page 82], [12] color wash full page illustration, [13] color wash full page illustration with William Blake verse, 14-15 [16] 17-27 [28] 29-33 [34-35] 36-42 [43-45] 46 [47-49] 50-53 [54] 55 [56] 57-66 [67] 68-86 [87] 88-93 [94-95] rear endpapers, [96] rear cover. 8 ¾" x 11 1/8".

COVER: Half cloth. Natural linen wraps the spine and one-third of the covers and is overlapped by mauve paper, over boards. The front cover is blind stamped with a small bouquet tied with a ribbon. Spine is stamped in a green metallic ink: TASHA TUDOR *All for Love* PHILOMEL.

DUST JACKET: Green. On the front: a floral heart-shaped wreath encloses the calligraphic *All for Love* [in pink] | *Tasha | Tudor* [white]. Back cover has a tussie-mussie centered, and printed in black in lower right: ISBN 0-399-21012-1. Calligraphy on spine: *TASHA TUDOR* [white] *All for Love* [pink] *Philomel* [white]. Front white flap, black type except for title in pink calligraphy: $15.95 | *All for Love | Selected and Illustrated* | by TASHA TUDOR | Love is the eternally appealing theme | of this rich and varied collection of | poems, letters, songs, stories, folklore | and customs, all assembled and en- | chantingly illustrated by distinguished | artist Tasha Tudor. || In addition to romantic love, this | book celebrates love of friends, of | family and even of pets, empathizes | with secret and unspoken love, and | offers solace to those whose love is un- | requited. The enduring sentiment of | a sonnet by Elizabeth Barrett Brown- | ing, the wry and touching charm of a | story by Colette, the passion of Cathy | in Emily Bronte's *Wuthering Heights,* | the poignancy of a letter from Na- | poleon to his adored Josephine—these | and many other eloquent expressions | of love are exquisitely interpreted in | Ms. Tudor's watercolors. || Love is, of course, not confined to | any season, but in the Tudor family it is | especially celebrated on Valentine's | Day, and, in a fascinating section of | this book, Ms. Tudor describes the cus- | toms and traditions that have grown | around this special day in several | generations of her own family. She also | gives clear and inspiring directions for | making uniquely beautiful greeting | cards, delectable cakes and cookies, | and fragrant nosegays for the delight | of those you love. || *(continued on back flap)* || *ISBN-399-21012-1.* Back white flap, black type except for TASHA TUDOR in pink: *(continued from front flap)* | All the classic expressions of ro- | mance are here, as well as many more | contemporary selections. In words and | pictures, Tasha Tudor has created the | perfect anthology for everyone of any age to cherish, the ideal memento or | gift for every loving occasion. || TASHA TUDOR | is known the world over for her glow- | ing watercolor depictions of the | American rural scene of a century or | so ago, and for her exquisite paintings | of flowers, children and animals. In | this book, she widens and deepens her | range of subjects, while retaining the | affectionate warmth and the delicacy | and freshness of color for which she is | famous. Ms. Tudor has illustrated | many beloved classics of children's lit- | erature, as well as a number of books | she herself has compiled or written, | such as *Take Joy!: The Tasha Tudor Christ-* | *mas Book; Rosemary for Remembrance: A* | *Keepsake Book;* and *Christmas Village: An* | *Advent Calendar.* She is also the subject | of a biography written by her daughter | Bethany Tudor, *Drawn from New En-* | *gland: Tasha Tudor, a Portrait in Words* | *and Pictures.* In this new book she | shares with readers young and old her | own loving and romantic view of life. || Calligraphy by Jeanyee Wong | Floral heart on front cover, painted by | Tasha Tudor from the original wreath | created by Frank Holder. || PHILOMEL BOOKS | *a member of The Putnam Publishing Group* | 51 Madison Avenue | New York, NY 10010.

ILLUSTRATIONS: There is a different bouquet on each of the four endpapers, on a yellow wash field. Nearly every page has a color illustration from a small turtle dove with rose on the copyright page to full page ILLUSTRATIONS: [12-13] 19, 22, 27, 32, 33, [34-35] 46, 51, 58, [67] 80 [87]. Page 92 has *Index* penned in pink. Many pages are framed in ribbons or vines.

CONTENTS: The title page is in a calligraphic script. An anthology of quotations about love in all its guises, including 12 love songs with music, and "Loving Gifts and Celebrations of Tasha Tudor and Her Family," pp. 79-91. An Index is printed on pp. 92-93. Jeanette Knazek reports these errors is the first printing Table of Contents which were corrected in the third printing: On Love (page 16) isn't listed, two selections listed for page 32 are on page 30, Shall I compare thee . . . listed on page 30 is on page 32, four selections listed on page 33 are printed on page 31, White and from The Anatomy of Melancholy are switched between their listings - pages 37 and 36 - and their opposite printings, pages 40 and 41 are transposed from the Contents, How to Make . . . is on page 85 not 84, the Tudor Family's Valentine Cake is on page 90 and has a typographical error listing "1 cup milk, room temperature" twice, How to Make Valentine . . . is listed on page 90 not 91, Frosting and Festive Punch aren't in the Contents, Valentine Cookies are listed but not included in the text.

A four-page full-color advertising piece (11″ x 28″) folded vertically features the page 46 illustration within a single line frame and with *Tasha Tudor* inside the loop of ribbon. Above the box: From one of America's | most beloved artists *All for Love* The perfect anthology | of the language of love . . . Page [2], three paragraphs of text *To Treasure . . . To Inspire . . . To Give* . . . Page [3]: *Contents* . . . with all the text of the book, pages [9-10], but the order is slightly different. Page [4] reproduces page 15 from the book but in more muted colors. At lower left back: [bird in circle logo] | PHILOMEL | BOOKS | (*a member of the Putnam Publishing Group*) | 51 Madison Avenue, New York, N.Y. 10010. Lower right back: THE•PUTNAM•PUBLISHING•GROUP | [horse and rider logo] | BOOKS FOR YOUNG READERS || Nonfiction•All ages• October 1984 | 11″ x 8 ½″ (oblong) •96 pages | Full-color illustrations throughout | Hardcover Trade ISBN (0-399-21012-1):$14.95.

OTHER: Tudor has recognized her grandchildren on page 79 by addressing a valentine to each of them.

COPYRIGHT REGISTRATION: TX 1-473-036 granted to Philomel Books, employer for hire. Louise Bates, agent for Philomel Books, swears on Nov. 14, 1984:

ALL FOR LOVE, compilation and additional text by Philomel Books, 51 Madison Ave., NY, NY, 10010, was published Oct. 22, 1984. Application and two deposit copies were received at LC Nov. 23, 1984, the effective date of registration. Registration was charged to account DA 038288, Putnam Publishing Group at the same address. The book was manufactured by Book Press, Putney, VT.

COPYRIGHT REGISTRATION: VA 173-158 for illustrations granted to Tasha Tudor, RFD # 4, West Brattleboro, VT 05301. Louise Bates, agent for Putnam Publishing Group, 51 Madison Ave., NY, NY 10010, swears on Nov. 14, 1984:

ALL FOR LOVE, illustrations by Tasha Tudor, a US citizen, was published Oct. 22, 1984. Application and deposit were received at LC Nov., 23, 1984, charged to account DA 038288, Putnam Publishing Group (Phil). Tudor's address was added by the Copyright Office; authority of a telephone call with Louis Bates, Jan. 8, 1985, the effective date of registration.

A30 _____. [*Copyright Acknowledgments* . . . a division of The <u>Putnam & Grosset Book Group</u> | 200 <u>Madison</u> Avenue, New York, <u>NY 10016</u> | Text copyright © 1984 by Philomel Books | <u>Art</u> copyright © 1984 by Tasha Tudor | All rights reserved. <u>This book, or parts thereof,</u> | may <u>not</u> be reproduced in any <u>form without</u> written permission <u>in writing</u> | from the publisher. <u>Published simultaneously in Canada</u> | Printed in <u>Hong Kong</u> | Designed by . . . ISBN 0-399-21012-1 | <u>Second impression</u>]

PAGINATION: <u>Six</u> signatures, [96] pages, front cover to back cover.

COVER: Wine paper imprinted with a fine weave, over boards. Same front blind stamp and imprint as before, but the <u>spine is stamped in gilt</u>.

DUST JACKET: A slightly <u>deeper green</u> color. <u>A yellow box</u> 1 3/8″ x 1 15/16″ at lower right back is imprinted with bar code: ISBN 0-399-21012-1, above bar code, and beneath it, 0 48228 21012 2. Have not examined a copy with prices intact. Remaining text has small changes from the first printing. Back flap:…PHILOMEL BOOKS | *a division of The Putnam & Grosset Book Group* | 200 Madison Avenue | New York, NY 10016 || <u>Printed in Hong Kong</u>.

CONTENTS: The previous errors in the Table of Contents and on page 90 have been corrected. Festive Punch is listed out of order in the Contents. The colors are generally brighter in this printing.

A31 _____. [*Copyright Acknowledgments*…ISBN 0-399-21012-1 | <u>3</u> 5 7 9 10 8 6 4]

DUST JACKET: Front flap: <u>$18.95</u> | [rule] | (<u>$24.95 CAN</u>), at top. Remaining text has small changes from the first printing. The ISBN has been deleted from the bottom of front flap.

A32 _____. [*Copyright Acknowledgments*…ISBN 0-399-21012-1 | 5 7 9 10 8 6 <u>4</u>] [The print numbers have been re-spaced. - *Ed.*]

DUST JACKET: Dust jacket has a <u>white box</u> 1 3/8″ x 1 15/16″ imprinted with bar code: <u>90000></u> | [2 bar codes] | 9 780399 210129 | ISBN 0-399-21012-1. Front flap: <u>$19.95</u> | [rule] | (<u>$25.95 CAN</u>), at top.

A33 *Amanda* | AND THE | *Bear* | BY | *Tasha Tudor* | OXFORD UNIVERSITY PRESS | NEW YORK **1951** [Copyright 1951 | OXFORD UNIVERSITY PRESS, INC. || PRINTED IN THE UNITED STATES OF AMERICA]

PAGINATION: Two signatures, [36] pp. including free endpapers. 6 23/32″ x 6 1/8″

COVER: Blue cloth over boards, buckram weave imprint. White paste-down label (2 11/32″ x 4 11/32″) on front cover, black type within an orange watercolor line: *Amanda* | *and the Bear* | BY TASHA TUDOR. Oak leaves inside each corner of lined box. Spine printed in orange: TUDOR *Amanda and the Bear* OXFORD. First and last endpapers show the bear cub with geraniums; second and third endpapers, just the geranium pots.

DUST JACKET: Blue dust jacket with a white panel front and back. The front white panel fills most of the front and shows Amanda walking off the left side in a sailor dress and carrying a red-orange banner with her name written on it in reverse white. She is followed by Adam bearing his own banner with the single word *Bear.* AND THE . . . BY | *Tasha Tudor* appear as on the title page. Blue spine, black ink: TUDOR *Amanda and the Bear* OXFORD. A 1 ¼″ white medallion in the middle of the back is painted with a sprig of three oak leaves. Front flap: *Amanda* | *and the Bear* [blue] | BY TASHA TUDOR [red] | Amanda was a little girl who had | as a pet a baby bear named Adam. | Adam was very friendly but some- | times visitors did not understand | this and were badly frightened | when they discovered a bear in their | bedroom. ¶Adam was a real bear and the | real | Amanda told Tasha Tudor the story. | Small boys and girls will love the | pictures and laugh over Adam's ad- | ventures which actually happened. [black] | *Oxford Books* | *for Boys and Girls* [blue] || 40-100 [black] Back flap: *Thistly B* [blue] || BY TASHA TUDOR [red] || "This well-loved artist tells in | quaint and lovely pictures and sim- | ple text the story of a small yellow | canary, Thistly B, who was the only | one of five eggs to hatch in the | teacup which was his first home. | Then came his cage, but he pre- | ferred the children's doll house, as | did his plump little wife, who lays | her eggs in the doll's bathtub after | Thistly B has built a beautiful nest | there. A charming story which will | fascinate small readers." | —*Boston Herald.*

CONTENTS: Page [5] is title page with Amanda holding an orange banner with her name on it, helping the bear hold his banner with *Bear* on it. Page [7], Dedication in an orange line box with bear and geraniums: To | Alice | Sally | and | Peter | to whose | Grandmother | the bear really belonged. These are the Smith family children who lived at St. Paul's School in Concord, New Hampshire. Text is printed in black type on versos [8] - [30]. Blank pages: [2-4], [32-35].

ILLUSTRATIONS: Twelve full-page unframed color illustrations on the rectos [9] - [31].

OTHER: Copies sold through the McCreadys' Ginger & Pickles Store have a paper label (1 ½ x 7/8″) printed in brown ink at the lower left inside back cover: TASHA TUDOR | — | RFD No. 1 Contoocook | New Hampshire | *Autographed Books* | *Christmas Cards* | *Correspondence Notes*

COPYRIGHT REGISTRATION: A 62378 granted to Oxford University Press, 114 Fifth Ave., N.Y., N.Y. Its agent [illegible M Garston?] swears on November 19, 1951:

AMANDA AND THE BEAR, by Tasha Tudor (a United States citizen, of Contoocook, NH, born approx. 1910), was published August 16, 1951. The book was printed by Kellogg and Bulkeley, Hartford, Ct. from their type setting. Binding by H. Wolff Book Mfg. Co. Inc., N.Y., N.Y. Application and affidavit were received at LC November 20, 1951, and two copies of the book received October 22, 1951.

COPYRIGHT RENEWAL: RE 31-663 for the entire text and illustrations was granted to the author Tasha Tudor, Route 4, West Brattleboro, VT, 05301, on August 20, 1979. Renewal fee charged to account DA050830, David McKay Co., Inc., 2 Park Ave., N.Y., N.Y. 10016. H.J. Rabinovitz certified the application August 17, 1979, for David McKay and Tasha Tudor. Certificate mailed 5 September 1979.

A34 _____.

COVER: Blue paper over boards, buckram weave imprint. Label and endpapers as above.

A35 *Efner Tudor Holmes* | AMY'S GOOSE || [three geese flying left] || *illustrated by Tasha Tudor* | THOMAS Y. CROWELL COMPANY   NEW YORK [Copyright © 1977 by Efner Tudor Holmes | Illustrations copyright © 1977 by Tasha Tudor | All rights reserved. Except for use in a review, | the reproduction or utilization of this work in | any form or by any electronic, mechanical, or | other means, now known or hereafter invented, | including xerography, photocopying, and record- | ing, and in any information storage and retrieval | system is forbidden without the written permission | of the publisher. Published simultaneously in | Canada by Fitzhenry & Whiteside Limited, Toronto. | Manufactured in the United States of America || *Library of Congress Cataloging in Publication Data* | Holmes, Efner Tudor. | Amy's Goose. | SUMMARY: Amy nurses a wild goose back to | health and struggles to decide whether to keep it | on the farm or let it be free. | [1. Geese—Fiction. 2. Farm life—Fiction] | I. Tudor, Tasha. II. Title. PZ7.H735Am   [E]   77-3027 | ISBN 0-690-03800-3 | ISBN 0-690-03801-1 (lib. bdg.) | 1 2 3 4 5 6 7 8 9 10]

PAGINATION: Two signatures of white paper: [36] pages including free endpapers. 7¼″ x 7 7/8″.

COVER: Illustrated paper over board covers, orange watercolor of clouds, front and back. At the top of the front cover, printed in black: AMY'S GOOSE | Efner Tudor Holmes | [Amy kneels petting the goose] | illustrated by Tasha Tudor. Back cover shows a goose flying to the left, and at the lower right corner: 0-690-03800-3. Spine: Holmes/Tudor AMY'S GOOSE Crowell. Blank endpapers.

DUST JACKET: Like cover plus a second ISBN beneath the first at lower right back: 0-690-03801-1 (CQR). Front white flap: 0-690-03800-3 | 0-690-03801-1 (CQR) [in the upper left corner] $5.95 [in the upper right corner] || AMY'S GOOSE || *by Efner Tudor Holmes | illustrated by Tasha Tudor* || The beautiful wild goose was nearly well | again. Amy and her father had rescued it | from the jaws of a hungry fox, and Amy had | nursed it back to health. An only child, Amy | had no playmates on her family's farm, so she | had a special fondness for all animals. But her | feeling for the wild geese was different. | Something in Amy responded deeply to their | haunting cry, their beautiful strong wings, | their wild freeness. She loved them more than | any of the familiar creatures of farm and field | and nearby woods. Now she had one of her | own; the injured goose was almost tame. It | would be her companion, her loving friend. || This moving story will strike a responsive | chord in all young readers who have ever | longed to befriend and tame a wild creature | for a pet. They will empathize with Amy as | she struggles with the difficult decision of | whether to keep "her" goose or let it go | free—and they will exult with the great wild | bird as Amy makes the right choice. | *(continued on back flap).* Back flap: *(continued from front flap)* | In this quietly told, skillfully understated | story, the author of *The Christmas Cat* dem- | onstrates once more her deep love for animals | and her respect for the integrity of all living | things. Tasha Tudor's radiant watercolor | illustrations are rendered with realism infused | with feeling, and reveal this distinguished and | beloved artist at the peak of her powers. || EFNER TUDOR HOLMES comes by her talent | naturally, for, as Tasha Tudor's daughter, she | was brought up in an atmosphere that en- | couraged creativity and a love of nature. She | now lives on a real farm in New Hampshire | with her husband and their two young sons. || TASHA TUDOR is one of America's best-loved | author-artists. She has won the Regina Medal | and many other awards for her beautiful | books for children. Mrs. Tudor loves the | traditions and handcrafts, the architecture, | gardens, farms, and way of life of her native | New England, and shares her delight with the | readers of her books. Tasha Tudor lives in | Marlboro, Vermont. || *Thomas Y. Crowell Company | New York • Established 1834* [The same biographies are printed on the dust jacket of *The Christmas Cat*.]

ILLUSTRATIONS: Full-page color illustrations on pages [4-5, 7, 9-10, 10-14, 16, 18-21, 23-33]. Pages [4-5] and [32-33] are the same two page spread of 7 geese in flight over the lake and farm of the story. Color vignettes on pages [9, 24, 25]. Pages [1-3, 33-36] are blank. Pages [6, 8, 15, 17, 22] have only text.

CONTENTS: Page [6]: BY EFNER TUDOR HOLMES | AND TASHA TUDOR | *The Christmas Cat* | *Amy's Goose*; Title page, [7]; copyright, [8]; Dedication, [9]: *For a very special person, | Jeanette Holmes | ...more lovingly known as | Great Grammie* | [a goose looking over its shoulder to the right].

OTHER: See W1 *The Way of the World* for an adaptation of this story in a classroom reading textbook with illustrations by Jane Clark.

COPYRIGHT REGISTRATION: A 915709 granted to Efner Tudor Holmes, Route 1, Concord, N.H. Mary D. Agnes, agent for Harper & Row, Publishers, Inc., 10 East 53rd St., N.Y., N.Y. 10022 swears on November 17, 1977:

AMY'S GOOSE, by Efner Tudor Holmes a United States citizen, illustrated by Tasha Holmes [*sic*], was published October 14, 1977. The book was lithographed by Federate Lithographers, Inc. [*sic*], Providence, R.D. [*sic*] and bound by Book Press, Brattleboro, VT. Application and affidavit, and two copies of the book were received at the Library of Congress November 25, 1977. Fee paid and certificates sent to the Copyright Department, Harper & Row.

COPYRIGHT REGISTRATION: A 915710 granted to Tasha Tudor, R.F.D., West Brattleboro, VT. 05301 for the illustrations. Mary D. Agnes swears as above, and typed more accurately: The book was illustrated by Tasha Tudor, and printed by Federated Lithographers, Inc., Providence, R.I.

A36 _____. Author's presentation copy.

    OTHER: Blue marbled endpapers glued to one ivory laid paper sheet. Pages [3-4, 5-6] are that ivory laid paper. Page [7] is blank white, and page [8] is geese flying - the pasted endpaper from the trade edition. Same treatment repeated at rear. 7 ¼ x 7 31/32″

    COVER: Blue leather binding stamped in gilt on spine: [two horizontal rules]   HOLMES • TUDOR - AMY'S GOOSE - CROWELL   [2 horizontal rules]

A37 _____.

    COVER: A gold foil label (7/8 x 3 5/8″) applied around the spine near bottom is imprinted: Crowell Quality Reinforced Binding CQR CQR [feather]

A38 _____. [Copyright © 1977 by Efner...(lib. bdg.) 2 3 4 5 6 7 8 9 10]

    DUST JACKET: Front white flap upper corner clipped, but carries an applied round sticker: <u>7.95</u>.

A39 _____. [... 2 3 4 5 6 7 8 9 10] [1-36] pp. including free endpapers.

    COVER: <u>Library binding</u>. <u>Gray-green painted cloth</u> imprinted with a small weave. Spine stamped in <u>white</u>: Holmes/Tudor AMY'S GOOSE Crowell. Reinforced white cloth hinge.

    DUST JACKET: A gold foil label (¾ x 4″) applied around the spine 1 3/8″ above bottom: A line of leaves [rule] *Library Binding*.

A40 _____. [... 3 4 5 6 7 8 9 10]

    PAGINATION: [1-28] pp. including free endpapers. The two-page geese flying illustration has become the end papers in this printing, otherwise as before.

    COVER: The illustrated paper over board cover is now under <u>gloss film lamination</u>. <u>No ISBN</u> printed on the back.

    DUST JACKET: <u>Price and ISBNs have been omitted</u> from the front flap. Publisher's name has been reset on the back flap to: <u>*Thomas Y. Crowell | New York.*</u>

A41 *Efner Tudor Holmes* | AMY'S GOOSE ‖ [three geese flying left] ‖ *illustrated by Tasha Tudor* | A HARPER TROPHY BOOK | *Harper & Row, Publishers* [Amy's Goose | Text copyright © 1977 by Efner Tudor Holmes | Illustrations copyright © 1977 by Tasha Tudor | Printed in the U.S.A. All rights reserved. | First Harper Trophy edition, 1986. | Published in hardcover by | Thomas Y. Crowell, New York. [rule] *Library of Congress Cataloging in Publication Data...*77-3027 | ISBN 0-690-03800-3 | ISBN 0-690-03801-1 (lib. bdg.) 85-45391 | "A Harper Trophy book" | ISBN 0-06-443091-X (pbk) [rule]]

    PAGINATION: As in second trade edition. 7 x 7 ½″

    COVER: <u>Blue paper wrapper, white inside, no endpapers</u>. An extract of the original front cover illustration of Amy and goose is inset in a yellow frame on blue. Printed in black: HARPER | TROPHY, upper left; *Efner Tudor Holmes*, centered; $3.95 in upper right; *illustrated by Tasha Tudor* below picture. Title is printed in 5/8″ white Roman letters outlined in black, just above the picture frame. Back cover has white square (5 1/16″ x 4 5/8″) in 1/8″ yellow frame on the blue field. Text within the square is black except for the title which is now <u>blue</u> Roman letters outlined in black: AMY'S GOOSE | Ages 4 to 8 | Every fall Amy waits for the geese to arrive on the lake. | This year, when the flock lands, a goose is badly wounded | by a fox. Amy rescues it, and the two become close | friends. But winter is nearing, and the geese must continue | south. Amy's goose has recovered fully, and Amy knows if | she loves her wild goose, she must be willing to set it free. | "[The author's and artist's] warmth and joy in nature shine | through."

—ALA *Booklist* | "An outstanding, tender story." | —*Children's Book Review Service* | 0586 |
[UPC bar code] (0 on left, 9 on right) | 46594 00395 | ISBN 0-06-443091-X.   Spine: JP091
Holmes/Tudor   Amy's Goose   Harper & Row.

A42 _____. . . . *Tudor* | [torch logo] HarperTrophy | *A Division of* HarperCollins*Publishers*.   [Copyright © 1977 by Efner
Tudor Holmes | Illustrations copyright © 1977 by Tasha Tudor || All rights reserved. No part of this book may be used or
reproduced in any manner | whatsoever without written permission except in the case of brief quotations embodied | in critical
articles and reviews. Printed in the United States of America. For information | address HarperCollins Children's Books, a
division of HarperCollins Publishers, 10 East | 53rd Street, New York, NY 10022. || *Library of Congress Cataloging in
Publication Data.* | Holmes, Efner Tudor. | Amy's Goose. | SUMMARY: Amy nurses a wild goose back to | health and struggles
to decide whether to keep it | on the farm or let it be free. | [1. Geese—Fiction. 2. Farm life—Fiction] | I. Tudor, Tasha. II. Title.
PZ7.H735Am   [E]   77-3027 | ISBN 0-690-03800-3 | ISBN 0-690-03801-1 (lib.bdg.) | ISBN 0-06-443091-X (pbk.)]

PAGINATION: 7″ x 7 ½″

COVER: $5.95 US | $7.95 CDN, upper right front flap. Back cover with redesigned bar codes: . . .
Children's Book Review Service | [2 UPC bar codes], above the smaller right one, 43091.
Beneath the larger left one, 0 46594 00595 3 | ISBN 0-06-443091-X.   Spine: Holmes/Tudor
Amy's Goose   HarperTrophy.   A different bar code array is printed at lower left inside the front
cover: beneath the larger code on the left, 9 780064 430913; above the smaller bar code on the
right, 50595>. Beneath both of them: ISBN 0-06-443091-X.

A43 Efner Tudor Holmes | **BETTYS GÅS** | illustreret af Tasha Tudor | [three geese flying] | ...*fra* CARLSEN
if — {from page [4]} [AMY'S GOOSE . Copyright © 1977 by Efner Tudor Holmes . Illustrations copyright © 1977 by Tasha Tudor. | All rights
reserved. Except for use in a review, the reproduction or utilization of this work in | any form or by any electronic, mechanical, or other means, now known
or hereafter invented, | including xerography, photocopying, and recording, and in any information storage and retrieval | system is forbidden without the
written permission of the publisher. || Dansk udgave © Carlsen if, Copenhagen · Dansk tekst: Karl Nielsen. | Printed in Italy 1978 | 1.03.79/06 ISBN 87-562-
1496-0]
PAGINATION: Two signatures: [32] pp., cover to cover. 8 x 9″
CONTENTS: Page [1] is front cover under gloss lamination, pp. [2-3] are front endpapers with flying
geese illustration, page [4] white with black text cited above, page [5] one white goose, page [6]
blank, [7] title page, [8] Amy looking across field, 9-11 geese and text begins *Betty stod I haven.
Hun havde* ... , [12] Betty and her father, 13 text without illustration, [14] the family at table, 15
text without illustration, 16 text and tree, [17] fox chasing geese, 18-19 Betty and father with
wounded goose, 20 text but no illustration, 21 Betty and goose in barn, 22-24 text and illustrations,
[25-27] text and Betty and goose, [28] Betty watching ... , 29 goose flying above text *Betty stod
alene tilbage,* [30-31] rear endpapers, [32] back cover.
COVER: Cover is the orange cloud wash with same illustrations as the first U.S. dust jacket, but
proportionately enlarged. Black text, on the front cover: Efner Tudor Holmes | BETTYS GÅS |
illustreret af Tasha Tudor | [illustration] | ...fra CARLSEN if— Spine: Holmes/Tudor   BETTYS
GÅS   ...fra CARLSEN if. Back cover, beneath the illustration: ...fra CARLSEN if   ISBN 87-562-
1496-0.

A44 Efner Tudor Holmes | ELMA SE GANS | *Illustrasies deur Tasha Tudor* || [three geese
flying left] || HUMAN & ROUSSEAU •KAAPSTAD EN PRETORIA [Oorsponklike titel: *Amy's Goose* |
Kopiereg in teks © 1977 deur Efner Tudor Holmes | Kopiereg in illustrasies © 1977 deur Tasha Tudor | Afrikaans deur Katrien
Webb | Eerste Afrikaanse uitgawe in 1978 deur | Human & Rousseau Uitgewers (Edmns.) Bpk., | Stategebou, Roostraat 3-9,
Kaapstad; | Pretoriusstraat 239, Pretoria | Uigegee in medeproduksie met Carlsen van Kopenhagen en in Italië gedruk || ISBN 0
7981 0877 0]

PAGINATION: Two signatures of ivory paper, [28] pp. 7 15/16″ x 8 15/16″

COVER: Gloss film laminate paper over boards. Printing in black. Efner Tudor Holmes | ELMA SE
GANS above front picture of Amy and goose; Illustrasies deur Tasha Tudor, below. Spine:
Holmes/Tudor ELMA SE GANS [H&R logo]. Lone goose in flight on back cover. In lower
right back: ISBN 0 7981 0877 0.

DUST JACKET: Have not examined a dust jacket, probably not issued with one.

CONTENTS: Dedication on [3]: *Vir 'n baie besondere mens | Jeanette Holmes | [goose]*. Page [4] is a 2 paragraph synopsis and this third paragraph: As kunstenares, o.m. van geliefde boekies soos *Eerste gebede* en *Eerste dankgebede*, is | Tasha Tudor by die Afrikaanse leser reeds bekend. In *Elma se gans* verskyn sy as illustreer- | der in geselskap van haar dogter, Efner Tudor Holmes, wat die boek geskryf het. Die fyn | aanvoeling wat hulle vir mekaar se werk het, blyk duidelik uit hierdie fraai publikasie. Title page, [5].

ILLUSTRATIONS: Same color illustrations as A32, but first pages have been rearranged. Two page spread of 7 geese in flight form the end paper and flyleaf in this edition. [2] is copyright statement.

OTHER: Elsa Naude', Editor, Children's Books, Human & Rousseau (PTY) LTD, writing 16 March 1992: "This edition has been out of print for many, many years and we do not have any copies available for sale...the Afrikaans edition was produced for us by Carlsen If in Denmark and the royalty agreement was with Harper & Row | William Crowell in the States."

A45 VILDGÅSEN | Text: Efner Tudor Holmes / Bild: Tasha Tudor | Svensk text: Ingrid Norrman || [three geese flying left] || Carlsen if [*if* in a box] [AMY'S GOOSE . Copyright © 1977 by Efner Tudor Holmes. Illustrations copyright © 1977 by Tasha Tudor. | all rights reserved. Except for use in a review, the reproduction or utilization of this work in | any form or by any electronic, mechanical, or other means, now known or hereafter invented, | including xerography, photocopying, and recording, and in any information storage and retrieval | system is forbidden without the written permission of the publisher. || Printed 1978 in Italy . 1.03.79/06 . ISBN 91-510-2250-8]

PAGINATION: Two signatures of ivory paper, [30] pp. 8 1/16″ x 8 15/16″

COVER: Gloss film laminate paper over boards. Printing in black. VILDGÅSEN || Text: Efner Tudor Holmes / Bild: Tasha Tudor | Svensk text: Ingrid Norrman above front picture of Amy and goose; Carlsen if, below.   Lone goose in flight on back cover, centered above Carlsen if . In lower right back: ISBN 91-510-2250-8.

DUST JACKET: Have not examined a dust jacket, probably not issued with one.

CONTENTS: Colophon, page [2], title page [3].

OTHER: Swedish language edition.

A46 [dandelions] | AND IT WAS SO | *Illustrated by Tasha Tudor* | [boy and girl reading this book] | THE WESTMINSTER PRESS | PHILADELPHIA. [COPYRIGHT, MCMLVIII, BY W. L. JENKINS || *All rights reserved*—no part of this book may be reproduced in any | form without permission in writing from the publisher, except | by a reviewer who wishes to quote brief passages in connection | with a review in magazine or newspaper. || *Giving Thanks:* from *Prayers for Little Children*, by Lucy W. | Peabody. Used by permission of Friendship Press. || Scripture quotations, unless otherwise indicated, are from | the Revised Standard Version of the Bible copyright, 1946 and | 1952, by the Division of Christian Education of the National | Council of Churches, and are used by permission. || Scripture quotations from the American Standard Edition of | the Revised Bible, copyright, 1929, by the International Coun- | cil of Religious Education, are used by permission. || PRINTED IN THE UNITED STATES OF AMERICA]

PAGINATION: [1-2] 3-48 pp. in 4 signatures, plus endpapers. 8 1/8″ x 8″

COVER: Green-gray cloth over boards; light green stamped title on front cover: *And | It Was So* | [sprig of leaves]. Front and back end papers are mint green shading around two pencil drawings in green on a white field, centered: a boy on a bench with cat and bird, and four children on a day bed.

DUST JACKET: Green with cream arched title panel on front; photograph and biography of Tudor on back, buff flaps. Front text in black: *And | It Was So* | ILLUSTRATED BY | TASHA TUDOR. The cover is reproduced in miniature on the title page which pictures a young girl reading this book to a smaller boy. Spine printed in yellow: AND IT WAS SO   WESTMINSTER. Back printing, yellow: *Tasha Tudor* | Born in Boston, Massachusetts, this noted illus- | trator, portrait painter, author, and lecturer | lives with her husband, Thomas L. McCready, | Jr., and their four children on a farm in Webster, | New Hampshire. Miss Tudor was educated | mostly by private tutor up to the time that she | attended the Boston Museum School of Fine | Arts. All available time, she reports, is spent | with the family enjoying the woods, fields, and | river (swimming and skating) on their property, | her love of the farm and outdoors clearly show- | ing in her art. When she is not illustrating either | her own or her husband's books, Miss Tudor is | very likely to be creating Christmas cards, | giving illustrated talks, caring for the farm | animals, or pursuing one of the many interests | —spinning, weaving, cooking, making doll's | clothes—that help form her enviable pattern of | the good life. | *Photograph by Nell Dorr* [at right under 6x4″ black and white photo of Tudor, seated, holding a cat] | THE WESTMINSTER PRESS • PHILADELPHIA. Front flap: *And It Was So* | illustrated by | TASHA TUDOR || Tasha Tudor's feeling for the warm, | eternal unity of man with man and of | mankind with the great natural world | —God's creation, all—could not mani- | fest itself more beautifully or more | clearly than in this book. Here she illu- | minates for the youngest children the | Bible's most basic meanings, "trans- | lating" brief, carefully selected Scrip- | tural passages into the language of | her sensitive, unique, timeless art. || A child's first questions are also | those of the thoughtful adult his life | long: Who made us? Where do we | come from? Why? What can we do? | For each of these the Bible has ultimate | answers, in some of the most thrilling | words ever written. Now Tasha Tudor | illustrates the words in a way to remain | memorable for child and adult. They | speak of God, the Creator and Sus- | tainer of life, of our praise to him for | his goodness, of Jesus and his teaching | and why he came to us, of the church | in which we learn about God and | worship him. || 46-1223 $2.50. Back flap: *The Lord* | *Will Love Thee* | illustrated by | TASHA TUDOR | *Text by Sara Klein Clarke* || In this vivid companion volume to | AND IT WAS SO, Tasha Tudor departs | from the whimsical, delicately tinted, | inexpressibly personal style of draw- | ing that so typifies and endears her | work to countless admirers of all ages | everywhere. Now, revealing her ver- | satility, the present illustrations are | boldly defined and brilliantly colored | — dramatic accompaniments to the Old | Testament incidents retold here briefly | and simply, yet in the Biblical tone, to | help pre-schoolers understand that it is | only through God's love that all other | love becomes possible. || The passages selected for retelling | enable the young child to identify such | family incidents as moving to a new | home, visiting grandfather, going to | worship as a family, bringing gifts to | the church, working together in the | church; they also show ways of being | thoughtful, kind, and concerned for | those in need.

ILLUSTRATIONS: All illustrations are set in an arched twig frame. Color illustrations: title page (title printed in green), 3, 6-7, 10, 12-13, 15, 18-19, 22, 24-25, 27, 30-31, 36-37, 42-43, 46, 48. Black and white illustrations: 4-5, 8-9, 11, 14, 16-17, 20-21, 23, 26, 28-29, 32-35, 38-41, 44-45, 47. Most illustrations are signed and dated, "T. Tudor, 1957." Helen Younger points out **01 at lower left, page 48**.

COPYRIGHT REGISTRATION: A 341311 granted to W. L. Jenkins, 915 Witherspoon Bldg., Philadelphia, PA. Ralph E. Moon Jr., agent for the Board of Christian Education of the Presbyterian Church in the U.S.A., at 929 Witherspoon Bldg. swears on August 20th, 1958:

AND IT WAS SO, a work done for hire for The Board of Christian Education of the Presbyterian Church in the U.S.A., 1319 Walnut Street, Philadelphia 7, PA. was published April 29, 1958. Portions of Revised Standard Version of the Holy Bible editorially revised with illustrations by Tasha Tudor (Mrs. T. L. McCready), Route #1, Contoocook, N.H., a United States citizen. The book was printed by R.R. Donnelley & Sons Co., Chicago, Il. and Crawfordsville, In. Application and affidavit were received at LC August 27, 1958, and two copies of the book were received July 21, 1959.

COPYRIGHT RENEWAL: RE 280-681, 23 January 1986.

A47 _____.

COVER: Green paper wrappers, mint green inside. Two staples through covers and 4 signatures and then wrapped with a one-inch wide tan paper over spine. Back cover, two paragraphs in yellow on either side of a church/home illustration: *To the mothers and fathers who will use this book:* A child has many questions | to ask of life, and many demands | to make upon it; in the main, | they are also our questions and | our demands. "Who made it | (me)?" "Where did it (I) come | from?" "Why?" "What can I | do?" For each of these the Bible | has ultimate answers, {next column} in some of | the most beautiful words ever | written. In this book the words | are illustrated in a way that will | help your child to understand | them. It is important for him | to know that they are from the | Bible *you* read; and that you | share with him other great | verses and passages. [Between the two paragraphs is an image of a square tower, above the words *Christian | Faith | And Life | A Program for | Church and Home.* Beneath the words is a cape cod house with an outside chimney centered on the front. At bottom left corner: 45-1223. Inside front cover this five-verse grace is printed in green in two columns above a pre-printed book plate. I thank Thee for the sunshine | That makes it light; | I thank Thee for the moon and starts | That shine at night; | For soft, white snow in winter | and rain in spring, | For flowers and trees, and birds | That fly and sing; | For ev'ry little creature | In the green wood, | That looks to Thee, our Father, | For daily food; | {second column} I thank Thee for my parents | Who are so dear, | And ev'ry one who loves me, | Both far and near. |I thank Thee for myself, too, | Thy child, so blest, | For all Thou hast given me, | And now, for rest. | AMEN | [A white box and frame with green text: *My Book and My Name* | [rule] A white box inside back cover lists the Bible verse origin of each page. 7 7/8" x 7 7/8".

ILLUSTRATION: Front cover is the same as dust jacket above; title in large black letters, AND | IT WAS | SO.

A48 _____.

CONTENTS: As above, but lacking the 01 on page 48.

A49 _____.

COVER: With green paper wrapping the spine.

A50 [dandelions] | AND IT WAS SO [green ink, remaining text black] | Words from the Scripture | [girl and boy reading this book] | *ILLUSTRATED BY TASHA TUDOR* | THE WESTMINSTER PRESS | PHILADELPHIA. [First published by The Westminster Press 1958 || © 1958 W. L. Jenkins | © 1988 The Westminster Press || *All rights reserved*—no part of this book may be reproduced in any form without | permission in writing from the publisher, except by a reviewer who wishes to quote | brief passages in connection with a review in a magazine or newspaper. || The verses in this book, with certain adaptations and omissions, are scripture | quotations from the Revised Standard Version of the Bible, copyright 1946, 1952, | © 1971, 1973 by the Division of Christian Education of the National Council of the | Churches of Christ in the U.S.A., and are used by permission. || The references are: p.3, Gen. 1:1... | 18:1a, 49b. || Second edition | Published by The Westminster Press | Philadelphia, Pennsylvania || Library of Congress Cataloging-in-Publication Data || And it was so. || SUMMARY: An illustrated collection of Bible verses, some of which have been | adapted. | 1. Creation—Biblical teaching—Juvenile literature. | 2. Jesus Christ—Juvenile literature. [1. Bible—Selections] I. Tudor, Tasha, ill. | BS651.A56 1988   220.5'20426   87-16130 | ISBN 0-664-32724-9 || Printed in Singapore]

PAGINATION: Four signatures, white matte paper: [1-2] 3-48 pp. plus white endpapers. 8 ¼" x 8 ¼"

COVER: Gloss film laminate green printed covers, white endpapers. Illustration on both covers is same as the first edition dust jacket. Front cover text in black: *And | It Was So* | Words from the Scripture | *ILLUSTRATED BY | TASHA TUDOR*. Spine lettering white: AND IT WAS SO   Tasha Tudor   [W | P logo in a double-line frame]. Back cover text black inside arched frame: Tasha Tudor's feeling for the warm relationship of | persons with one another and with the great | natural world—God's creation—all could not | manifest itself more beautifully or more clearly | than in this book. Here she illuminates for even the | youngest children brief, carefully selected | Scripture passages which answer questions like | Who made us? Where do we come from? What | was Jesus like? What can we do? Parents and | children alike will enjoy this book. | THE WESTMINSTER PRESS | ISBN 0-664-32724-9.

DUST JACKET: Same illustrations and text as cover, but a lighter green and minus the ISBN as last line. Spine printed in black, and single black line around logo. Front flap: And It Was So | Words from the Scriptures | *Illustrated by Tasha Tudor* || Acclaimed artist, author, and lecturer | Tasha Tudor speaks to the profound | questions that children ask and | adults ponder. In this book she | illustrates beautifully the words of | Scripture, telling of the greatness of | God from creation to the story of | Jesus' love. || The delightful illustrations that are | Tasha Tudor's signature speak of | God, the Creator and Sustainer of | life, of our response to God's | goodness, of Jesus and his | teaching, and of the church where | we learn to know and praise God. || AND IT WAS SO is a timeless book | that will help children understand | how "God saw everything that was | made, and it was very good." | (Continued on back flap) || ISBN 0-664-32724-9. Back flap reproduces 3 ¼ x 2 ½" Nell Dorr black and white photograph from the first edition, but not attributed: Tasha Tudor lives in West | Brattleboro, Vermont. She was | educated by private tutors and also | studied at the Boston Museum of | Fine Arts. In over forty books written | throughout her lifetime, she has | demonstrated an uncommon ability | to portray the earth and all living | creatures with great warmth and | affection.

ILLUSTRATIONS: Illustrations are identical to those in the first edition.

CONTENTS: There are numerous textual changes from the first edition, largely changing *he* to *God* in various passages: pp. 6-7, 18-24, 31. Page 28 changed from, *God loved us and sent his Son.* to, *For to us a child is born, | to us a son is given. | And you shall call his name Jesus.* Page 37 changed from, *And he taught them many things, and the people heard him gladly.* to, *And Jesus taught them many things.* Page 42 changed *teaching* to *teach.* Page 46 changed from, *And many shall say, "Come, let us go to the house of God"*; to, *Be still, and know that I am God.* Page 47 changed from, *and he will teach us of his ways, and we will walk | in his paths.* to, *I am exalted in the earth.* Page 48 changed from, *thy* to, *your.* The end paper illustrations were not included in this edition. In both editions, page 25 includes the line: *a time to keep,* and *a time to cast away;.* Only page 29 in both editions has an illustration without text.

A51 _____. [First published . . . 18:1a, 49b. | 2 3 4 5 6 7 8 9 || Second edition . . . Singapore]

COVER: Back cover space between boy and girl is whiter than before.

CONTENTS: Inks are brighter than before.

A52 _____. [First published . . .18:1a, 49b. | 3 4 5 6 7 8 9 | Second edition . . . | Printed in Mexico]

DUST JACKET: Gloss film laminate; back flap, a new bottom line: Printed in Mexico.

A53 _____. [First published . . .18:1a, 49b. | 4 5 6 7 8 9 | Second edition . . . | PRINTED IN MEXICO.

DUST JACKET: Gummed label on the back of jacket between girl and boy: [Bar code] | 9780664327248 | AND IT WAS SO   (2

A54 _____. . . . *TASHA TUDOR* | LUTTERWORTH PRESS | CAMBRIDGE. [**Lutterworth Press** | **PO Box 60** | **Cambridge CB1 2NT** || *British Library Cataloguing in Publication Data* | And it was so. | 1. Bible—Picture bibles—Juvenile literature | I. Tudor, Tasha | 220'.022'2   BS560 || ISBN 0-7188-2691-4 || Copyright © W. L. Jenkins 1958 | Copyright © The Westminster Press 1988 || First published in UK 1988 by Lutterworth Press || The verses in this book . . . Council of | the . . . permission. || The references are: p.3, Gen. 1:1... | 18:1a, 49b. || All rights reserved. No part of this book may be reproduced, stored in a | retrieval system, or transmitted in any form or by any means, electronic, | mechanical, photocopying, recording, or otherwise, without the prior permission | in writing of the publisher. || Printed in Singapore]

PAGINATION: 8 3/16" x 8 5/16"

COVER: Cover illustrations as above, variant text. Front cover text in black: ... Words from the Bible . . . Spine lettering white: AND IT WAS SO   Tasha Tudor   [L in a circle logo]. Back cover text black inside arched frame: Verses from the bible telling the story of God's | creation, singing praise from the psalms and | showing God's love from the Gospels. Tasha | Tudor's beautiful illustrations accompany the text. | Parents and children alike will enjoy this book. ||

Lutterworth Press, P.O. Box 60 | Cambridge CB1 2NT || £4.95 net || ISBN 0-7188-2691-4 | [bar code] | 9 780718 826918.

DUST JACKET: Have not examined one.

OTHER: Examination copy had an extra label applied over the printed price, and was imprinted: PUBLISHERS PRICE [in red] | £6.99.

A55 Animal | Magnetism | [oval cameo of dog's head] | *At Home with Celebrities* | *& Their Animal Companions* || *Patti Denys & Mary Holmes* | [SMITHMARK S logo] [Half title page: Earl McDonnell | title page: Matuschka with Liberty, Voler Wyeth || Copyright © 1998 by SMITHMARK Publishers || All rights reserved. No part of this publication may be reproduced, stored in a retrieval | system, or transmitted in any form or by any means, electronic, mechanical, photocopying, | recording or otherwise, without prior permission of the copyright holders. || SMITHMARK books are available for bulk purchase for sales promotion and premium | use. For details, write or call the manager of special sales, SMITHMARK Publishers, | 115 West 18th Street, New York, NY 10011. || Produced by SMITHMARK PUBLISHERS | 115 West 18th Street, New York, NY 10011. || Photography: Pattii Denys and Mary Holmes | Photo Editor: William Wegman | Design: Leah S. Carlson | Editor: Kristen Schilo, Gato & Maui Productions || 0-7651-9051-6 || Library of Congress Catalog Card Number: 97-62147 || Printed in Hong Kong || 10 9 8 7 6 5 4 3 2 1

PAGINATION: [1-5] 6-16 [17-155, versos are numbered, but rectos are full bleed black and white photographs without page numbers] 156-160 plus free endpapers on 128 grams per square meter matt artpaper, white. 9 x 9″

COVER: Printed 140 gsm woodfree paper over boards. Text is superimposed over screened photographs on the front and back and an animal design on the spine. All front text is printed on a 9″ x 7″ brown image of Michelle Phillips and her dog Mika. **animal** [black] | *at home with celebrities and their animal companions* [white] | **magnetism** || patti denys & mary holmes || *Foreword by Linda McCartney | Introductions by Jane Goodall & Ingrid Newkirk | Photography editing by William Wegman* [black] || A PORTION OF THE PROCEEDS FOR THIS BOOK WILL BE DONATED TO THE JANE GOODALL INSTITUTE AND PETA [brown on a horizontal black bar]. A vertical black bar separates this panel from a 9″ x 1 15/16″ column composed of five photographs and which reaches to the spine. [see identifications on dust jacket back flap] Spine, brown over a gray animal pattern on black: **animal magnetism   denys & holmes** S | SMITHMARK [logo, black letters on white ground]. Back cover, enlarged close-up of a part of a William Wegman Weimeraner, over-printed in white: animal magnetism is a heart-warming collection | of never-before-seen photographs, fabulous | works of art, and insightful quotes about the | emotional connection that exists between | celebrities and their favorite animal companions.   In a white box (1 3/8″ x 2″) at the lower right: 90000> [above the smaller right of | [two bar codes]] | 9 780765 190512 [beneath the larger left bar code] || ISBN 0-7651-9051-6 [beneath both codes]. Gray endpapers carry the names in black of seventy-two of the seventy-six people featured in the book. Each name is separated from its neighbor by a small white cat or dog figure.

DUST JACKET: Reproduces the cover, and both covers extend to a full bleed across the flaps. Front flap text in black: *Animal Magnetism* is a celebration of the deep | emotional connection that exists between people | and their animal companions. In over 150 black- | and-white photographs, photographers and animal | advocates Patti Denys and Mary Holmes not only | lovingly portray athletes, artists, actors, comedians, | musicians, cartoonists, and other people of note in | the company of their animal friends, but capture | the uniqueness and intimacy of these cross-species | relationships. Accompanying each portrait is a brief | reflection of each celebrity's view of the meaning | and importance of animals in all of our lives. Mickey | Rooney, Martina Navratilova, Robert Raushchenberg, | Michelle Phillips, and Bob Hope are among the | celebrities who come together in the pages of | Animal Magnetism to illustrate the meaning of | animal companionship in their own words. Many | profiles are adorned with paintings, drawings, | and photographs, lent by the artists themselves | especially for this distinguished compilation. ¶With a touching foreword by

Linda McCartney | and introductions by Jane Goodall, noted Ph.D. | animal and primate behaviorist and Ingrid Newkirk, | president of People for the Ethical Treatment of | Animals (PETA), there has never been a more | compassionate testament to the world of human- | animal relationships. William Wegman, noted | photographer of Weimeraners, serves as the | photography editor of this unforgettable collection. | Animal lovers and celebrity watchers alike will | delight in the pages of this beautiful book. || [continuation of black bar from front]. Back flap, printed in white: [photograph, and to its right this paragraph] California photographer | and educator Patti Denys | has always known a | house full of animals. She | is an adamant activist for | animal rights. || [photograph, and to its left this paragraph] Photographer Mary Holmes | has been an animal rights activist and rescuer since | the 1980s, and has always lived with animals. She | lives in Southern California. || *Pictured on front jacket:* Michelle Phillips and Mika; | Roy Rogers and Dale Evans with Charlie; Beverly | Johnson with Flame; James Cromwell with Piri; Rue | McClanahan with Polly, Winston, Angie, Belle, and Ginger; Tasha Tudor with Rebecca and Owyn | *Pictured on back jacket:* Fay Wegman || E-mail: synergydog@earthlink.net | Web: http://:home.earthlink.net/~synergydogs/ || Jacket Design: HOTFOOT Studio || S SMITHMARK | [rule] | PUBLISHERS [LOGO] | *a division of U.S. Media Holdings, Inc.* | 115 West 18th Street, New York, NY 10011 || Printed in Hong Kong.

CONTENTS: Half-title, Page [1]; frontispiece, [2]; title page, [3]; colophon, [4]; *Acknowledgments*, signed by Denys and Holmes, [5]; *Contents, 6-7; Dedication, 8; Foreword, 9; Introduction, 10-11; Introduction, 12-15;* [body of the book], *16*-[155]; *Sources, 156-159; Credits, 160.*

OTHER: Tudor is pictured with her corgis Owen and Rebecca on page [137]; a smaller copy of the photograph appears on the cover and dust jacket. "DON'T PEOPLE LOOK LIKE THEIR DOGS?" by Tudor, page 136. ". . . I have had Corgis for about fifty years. My dogs come from the Swedish Valhund. . ." She then recounts the family's English year, 1957-58, and son Tom's introduction to the corgi dogs. With a charcoal drawing 'Gingersnap,' 1997.

Ellen Hogan, Smithmark Publishers, reports the paper types and that 25,000 copies were printed for the April 1998 publication date. There were no cloth-bound nor paperback copies issued.

A56 **AROUND** | **the** | **YEAR** | TASHA TUDOR. [NEW YORK OXFORD UNIVERSITY PRESS 1957 (from page [4])] [*© Oxford University Press, Inc., 1957 | Library of Congress Catalog Card Number: 57-11451 | Printed in the United States*]

PAGINATION: Unpaged. [60] pp. including free endpapers, topsewn. 7" x 9 ¼".

COVER: Yellow cloth stamped in mustard, **AROUND** | **the** | **YEAR**, on front. Spine: **TUDOR AROUND the YEAR   OXFORD**. The letters are photoengraved from Tudor's fanciful Victorian painted letters of the dust jacket.

DUST JACKET: Front and back of jacket are identical: yellow watercolor wash with centered title from cover. The title is drawn in large elaborate out-lined letters mimicking the printing of Victorian book covers. Beneath the title: by Tasha Tudor. Surrounding the title are twelve framed medallions, each labeled and with a vignette depicting a month. Similar illustrations in each corner represent the four seasons. Spine in mustard outlined letters: **TUDOR AROUND tɧe YEAR OXFORD**. Both corners of front flap have been clipped without removing text. AROUND THE YEAR | by Tasha Tudor | Delicate pictures, enriched with fine de- | tails that children love, form the setting | for Miss Tudor's simple verses about each | month of the year. Holidays, the changes | in nature from month to month and season | to season, the variety of good times chil- | dren have around the year combined with | the charming paintings make this book a | storehouse of the year's joys. || The old-fashioned loveliness of Miss Tu- | dor's verse and art gives young children | a memorable invitation to reading and | storytelling time. || A companion volume to *1 Is One* and | *A Is for Annabelle*. || OXFORD BOOKS | FOR BOYS AND GIRLS | 30-60 $3.00. Back flap: *Also by Tasha Tudor* || 1 IS ONE || "This exquisite little counting book...is | alight with Tasha Tudor's tender feeling | for animals, growing things, and small | children....All the pictures—alternating | black and white with delicate pastel colors | —have a warm, old-fashioned flavor which | will captivate all ages."—*Chicago Tribune* || A IS FOR ANNABELLE || "In the delicate penciled lines and water- | colors which her name evokes for her many | devotees Tasha Tudor draws an alphabet | around the wardrobe of Grandmother's | doll, Annabelle...."—*New York Times*. Corners of the flap were trimmed slightly in the manufacturing process.

CONTENTS: Half-title: page [3]. Blank pages: [2, 56-59]. Dedication page [7] is also printed with a pencil medallion design: To | a certain person | for whom this country | in the hills beyond | has a special meaning.

ILLUSTRATIONS: The title page is an oval emanating from the centered title in the same mustard-color "Victorian" letters as the cover and dust jacket. This is the most elaborate of the three versions. Two rabbits, two mice, and a singing meadowlark embellish the title, itself. Below the title is: TASHA [dandelion] TUDOR, in black lettering. Each of twelve small medallions encircling the title depicts a different bird. A frame of flowers and greens reflecting all seasons encircles the entire grouping. The endpapers are white with two designs repeated front and back: the same country bridge scene in summer and in winter. These and each of the illustrations in the book are framed in an eight-sided scalloped medallion, the border of which changes to reflect the season of the year. Sheets for this book were printed in full color on one side and black and white illustrations on the reverse. The illustrated text comprises a verse, four pages and four illustrations to each month of the year beginning on page [8]. Most illustrations have text superimposed and are signed T. Tudor and either 1957 or 57. The first two illustrations introduce the month in color, the third and fourth are in black and white. For example, page [20] "April sees the birds return, " [oxen plowing], page [21] [girl at well with fowl], page [22] "scatters showers" [fiddleheads, fox and chipmunk beside a freshet], page [23] "on leaf and fern." [boy and girl running along stone fence in a shower].

OTHER: This cover often displays a blotchy foxing from the binding boards. Bethany Tudor relates that during the time her mother was creating this book, William Wyler's motion picture *Friendly Persuasion* was very popular, and especially so in the McCready home. The endpapers reflect the setting of the farmstead in the 1956 film. The book is dedicated to Bethany. The editor judges this to be one of Tudor's finest works. The lovely scenes are true to their rural settings, and the colors are vibrant.

COPYRIGHT REGISTRATION: 309126 granted to Oxford University Press, Inc., 114 Fifth Ave., NY 11, NY. Its agent John A. Begg swears October 31, 1957:

AROUND THE YEAR, by Tasha Tudor, ROUTE #1, Contoocook, N.H., a United States citizen, was published October 31, 1957. The book was printed Kellogg & Bulkeley, Hartford, Ct., and Chas H. Bohn, N.Y., N.Y. Application and affidavit, and two copies of the book were received at LC November 8, 1957.

A57 _____. [HENRY Z. WALCK, INCORPORATED *(from page [4])*] [*© Henry Z. Walck, Inc. 1957 | Library of Congress Catalog Card Number: 60-7419 | Printed in the United States of America*]

PAGINATION: Buff paper, 11 stitches visible between rear endpapers.

COVER: Yellow cloth. The spine text has been reset to Roman letters.

DUST JACKET: Corners have been clipped slightly in trimming. Wording changed from Oxford editions, bottom of front flap: ... HENRY Z. WALCK, INC. | FOR BOYS AND GIRLS || 30-60 [price clipped]. Back flap as before. TUDOR and WALCK, on the spine, are printed in Caslon Open Face capitals.

OTHER: Examined one signed by Tudor with a wide nib fountain pen.

A58 _____.

PAGINATION: A lighter buff paper, 20 stitches visible at rear endpapers.

DUST JACKET: Bottom of front flap, ... HENRY Z. WALCK, INC. | FOR BOYS AND GIRLS || 30-60 $3.00.

A59 _____.

PAGINATION: Seventeen stitches visible at back endpapers.

DUST JACKET: Have not examined one for this printing.

OTHER: Tudor inscribed a copy to Paige Biggers Rorick with best wishes! Tudor infrequently inscribed her books to specific people.

A60 _____.

PAGINATION: Ivory paper, 18 stitches visible at rear endpapers.

DUST JACKET: Trimmed corners; have not examined one with price intact.

A61 _____.

PAGINATION: Ivory paper, 22 stitches visible at rear endpapers.

DUST JACKET: Top line of front flap: $3.25. Publisher statement on flap shortened to: HENRY Z. WALCK, INC. | 30-60. Lower corner was clipped at a deep angle.

OTHER: Examined a copy inscribed by Tudor to New Hampshire seacoast author Rose Labrie on the upper right corner of ffep and with an extra drawing of a rose.

A62 _____.

PAGINATION: [64] pp. white paper with the addition of blank white endpapers. Previous pasted endpaper illustrations are now on pp. [2, 63]. 10 stitches.

COVER: Reinforced cloth hinge.

DUST JACKET: Corners have been clipped slightly in trimming. Bottom of front flap: … HENRY Z. WALCK, INC. || 30-60 $3.75.

A63 _____.

PAGINATION: Four signatures white paper, oversewn through the endpapers, 11 stitches. [60] pp., including free white endpapers. The previous <u>illustrated endpapers have been deleted</u> from this printing. Page [3] is the half title.

COVER: Yellow <u>plastic-filled paper</u> with the same stamping, front and spine, in brown paint.

DUST JACKET: Examined copy with all corners clipped and an applied store label from Marshall Field & Company coded <u>86   4.95</u>.

A64 **AROUND** | t̲h̲e̲ | **YEAR** | TASHA TUDOR. [Copyright © 1994 by The Jenny Wren Press | All Rights Reserved | No part of this book may be reproduced in any form | without permission from the Publisher. ‖ Library of Congress number in publication data | ISBN-09621753-32 ‖ Re-printed in the U.S.A. | First printing in 1957 by Oxford Press, New York]

PAGINATION: [<u>72</u>] pp. including free endpapers. 7″ x 9 ¼″.

COVER: Green leather stamped in <u>gilt</u>, with the central design of the title page, minus the wrens sitting on "u" and "h": **AROUND** | t̲h̲e̲ | **YEAR** | TASHA TUDOR, on front. The previous fine line embellishment has been removed from letters. The left rabbit is the reverse of the right. Spine: <u>TASHA</u> TUDOR **AROUND** t̲h̲e̲ **YEAR** <u>The JENNY WREN PRESS</u>. Back cover, lower right: <u>ISBN-09621753-32</u>

DUST JACKET: As before except, author and publisher on spine which are <u>printed in small caps in black ink</u>: TASHA TUDOR   The JENNY WREN PRESS. <u>ISBN-09621753-32, in black ink, lower right of jacket back.</u>   Front jacket flap has been reset. **AROUND THE YEAR** | by Tasha Tudor | Delicate pictures, enriched with | tiny details that children love, form | the setting for Miss Tudor's simple | verses about each month of the year. | Holidays, the changes in nature from | month to month and season to sea- | son, the variety of good times children | have around the year combined with | the charming paintings make this | book a storehouse of the year's joys. ‖ The old-fashioned loveliness of Miss | Tudor's verse and art gives young chil- | dren a memorable invitation to read- | ing and storytelling time. | THE JENNY WREN PRESS.   Back flap: ***About the Author*** | TASHA TUDOR is one of America's | most loved and respected illustrators | of Children's Books. Her wondrous | illustrations take one to a quieter, sim- | pler time and place...where enchant- | ing children enjoy the joyful surround- | ings of the countryside, animals, | friendships and loving celebrations. ‖ Tasha Tudor has over 80 books to | her credit. When she is not in the gar- | den, she is moving ahead with joyful | enthusiasm into her second half cen- | tury of illustrating. Her fans, whom | she considers as "special friends," | cover the globe as far away as Russia. | | Enjoy her Magical World that she | herself lives...the world that we | all yearn for...that we all become a | part of every time we open one of her books. | [miniature pencil sketch, the reverse image of the 'March pond scene'] | The Jenny Wren Press | P.O. Box 505 | 11 E. Main Street | Mooresville, Indiana 46158

CONTENTS: Text on pp. [14-61]. Blank pages: [1-5, 8, 62, 64-65, 68-72]. The previous endpaper illustrations are now pp. [6-7, 66-67]. These white endpapers are blank with <u>reinforced hinges</u>.

Half-title, page [9]: A Special Edition of | **AROUND** | t̲h̲e̲ | **YEAR** | TASHA TUDOR, again, reproducing the central motif of the title page.   Page [10]: [heart] OUR HEARTFELT GRATITUDE TO OUR JENNY WREN PRESS FRIENDS | FOR MAKING OUR DREAM A REALITY [heart] ‖ THE JENNY WREN PRESS, INCORPORATED.   Page [63] sets this new text inside the February pencil sketch of table, lamp and letter writing: If interested in other Tasha Tudor creations—calendars, | Christmas cards, Valentines, reprints of early miniature | books made for her children, replicas of her sketch | books, lithographs, paper dolls, illustrated books | and other treasures—send for our catalogue. | The Jenny Wren Press | P.O. Box 505 | Mooresville, Indiana 46158.

OTHER: This limited edition has a gummed sticker (Item no. S036 from the Jenny Wren Press catalog) on page [8], signed in the center <u>Tasha Tudor</u>; numbered outside the right edge of sticker in pencil, 112/150. Jenny Wren Press mixes two references and completes neither on the verso of title page. Library of Congress catalog card number, and Cataloging-in-publication data, have become "Library of Congress number in publication data" followed by an ISBN. Neither the LC card number nor CIP data is present. Also an incorrect reference to the original publisher as "Oxford Press."

A65 _____.

COVER: <u>Yellow cloth</u> stamped in <u>gold</u>, as above.

CONTENTS: <u>Page [8] is blank</u> without signature and numbering.

A66 THE ART OF | MAKING | FURNITURE | IN | MINIATURE | WRITTEN AND ILLUSTRATED BY | Harry W. Smith [rule] KALMBACH PUBLISHING CO.   REVISED EDITION. [Copyright° 1982 by Harry W. Smith. Revised edition 1993. All rights | reserved. This book may not be reproduced in part or in whole without | written permission from the publisher, except in the case of brief quota- | tions used in reviews. Published in the United States by Kalmbach | Publishing Co., 21027 Crossroads Circle, P.O. Box 1612, Waukesha, | Wisconsin 53187. || Library of Congress Cataloging-in-Publication Data || Smith, Harry W. | The art of making furniture in miniature / written and illustrated | by Harry W. Smith.—[Rev. ed.] || p. cm. | ISBN 0-89024-159-7 (softcover) | 1. Miniature furniture. I. Title. | TT178.S64 1993 | 749'.1'0228—dc20]

PAGINATION: [xiv] 288 [289-290] pp. Eight pp. of full-color illustrations on enameled paper inserted between pp. 146 and 147. 11″ x 8 ½″

COVER: Green paper wrapper with photograph of a bombe chest on the front.

CONTENTS: "World-renowned miniaturist Harry Smith reveals the techniques and secrets of mastering the construction of furniture in miniature." Patterns, black and white illustrations, instructions.

OTHER: On pages 9-10 Smith describes receiving a tiny letter from Mr. And Mrs. T. Crane requesting that he craft a *proper* spinning wheel for their home. "Mrs. Tasha Tudor will send you some scale drawings." A further project was creating eight musical instruments to be played by an orchestra of corgi dogs in the Tudor marionette production of *The Rose and the Ring*. Although none of the items are pictured in this book, Smith does show them in his gate-fold brochure *Barnstable Originals Studios of Harry W. Smith, Artist, Author, Silversmith, Master Miniaturist*. Black and white photographs show 8 musical instruments and Melissa and another doll at the spinning wheel for Tasha Tudor.

COPYRIGHT REGISTRATION: TX 1-049-888 granted to Harry W. Smith, 50 Harden Avenue, Camden, Maine 04843. Judith Morse, E. P. Dutton, Inc., 2 Park Avenue, New York, New York 10016 agent for Harry W. Smith, swears on January 7, 1983:

THE ART OF MAKING FURNITURE IN MINIATURE, the entire work by Harry W. Smith, a U.S.A. citizen and not a work for hire, was published November 19, 1982. The book was completed in 1982. The book was printed by Vail Ballou, New York, New York. The Library of Congress was granted non-exclusive permission to make copies and phonorecords for the blind and physically handicapped. Fees charged to account DA 015938, E.P. Dutton, Inc., attention Judith Morse, 212-725-1818 x306. Application and two deposit copies were received at LC January 10, 1983, the effective date of registration.

B1 **A BASKET OF HERBS** ‖ *A Book of* | [1 3/8″ rule] | *American Sentiments* ‖ ILLUSTRATED BY |
TASHA TUDOR ‖ PRESENTED BY | THE NEW ENGLAND UNIT, INC., | OF THE HERB SOCIETY OF
AMERICA, INC. ‖ EDITED BY | MARY MASON CAMPBELL, DEBORAH WEBSTER GREELEY, |
PRISCILLA SAWYER LORD, AND ELISABETH W. MORSS ‖ THE STEPHEN GREENE PRESS |
Brattleboro, Vermont | Lexington, Massachusetts [*Because of space limitations, the material on pages
175-184* [sic] *should be con-* | *sidered as part of this copyright page.* ‖ *Calligraphy appearing on the
book plate is by Helen Merena.* ‖ First Edition ‖ Text copyright © 1983 by The New England Unit, Inc.
of The Herb Society of | America, Inc. ‖ Illustrations copyright © 1983 by Tasha Tudor ‖ All rights
reserved. No part of this book may be reproduced | without written permission from the publisher,
except by | a reviewer who may quote brief passages or reproduce illustrations | in a review; nor may any
part of this book be reproduced, | stored in a retrieval system, or transmitted in any form or by | any
means electronic, mechanical, photocopying, recording, or | other, without written permission from the
publisher. ‖ This book is manufactured in the United States of America. It is published | by The Stephen
Greene Press, Fessenden Road, Brattleboro, Vermont 05301. ‖ Library of Congress Cataloging in Publication
Data | Main entry under title: | A Basket of herbs. | Bibliography. | 1. Herbs—United States—Miscellanea.   I. Campbell, | Mary
Mason.   II. Tudor, Tasha.   III. Herb Society of | America.   New England Unit. | QK98.4.U6B33 1983   582′.06′3
82-21130 | ISBN 0-8289-0500-2]

> PAGINATION: Eight signatures of ivory kid paper. [i-ii, 1-6] 7-9 [10] 11 [12] 13-29 [30] 31-55 [56] 57-
> 65 [66] 67-87 [88] 89-101 [102] 103-107 [108] 109-119 [120] 121-125 [126] 127-131 [132] 133-
> 141 [142] 143-149 [150] 151-155 [156] 157-173 [174] 175-185 [186-194]   7 7/16″ x 6 ½″.

> COVER: Moss green paper in cloth weave pattern over boards. Spine stamped in gilt, double rule
> frame enclosing all text: CAMPBELL | et al. ‖ A Basket of Herbs: | A BOOK OF AMERICAN
> SENTIMENTS [title printed laterally] ‖ Illustrated | by | Tasha Tudor ‖ S | GP. Ivory kid
> endpapers.

91

DUST JACKET: Gloss-finish, printed mint green front and back; text in magenta and black. A single white panel with a Tudor color illustration of a basket of herbs is centered front and back and is overlaid with a narrow within a wider magenta line, and a thin black line border around all.

Front text above the panel: A Basket of Herbs: | A BOOK OF AMERICAN SENTIMENTS [magenta] | ILLUSTRATED WITH ORIGINAL DRAWINGS BY | Tasha Tudor. Below panel: edited by Mary Mason Campbell, | Deborah Webster Greeley, Priscilla Sawyer Lord, Elisabeth W. Morss [black]. Spine lettering on a white box bordered in a magenta line within a thin black line. CAMPBELL | et al. [black] || A Basket of Herbs: | A BOOK OF AMERICAN SENTIMENTS [magenta] || Illustrated | by | Tasha | Tudor || S | GP [black]. Back upper right in black: NATURE; lower right: ISBN 0-8289-0500-2. Front flap: B.O.H. $12.95 | 0-8289-0500-2 || A Basket of Herbs: | A BOOK OF AMERICAN SENTIMENTS | ILLUSTRATED WITH ORIGINAL DRAWINGS BY | Tasha Tudor || Speak in the language of herbs and you | speak with all the sentiment and fascination | their lore and history bring: there is Saffron | for Mirth . . . Dill for Good Spirits . . . Ivy | brings Undying Affection . . . Betony will | heal your wounds . . . and Chervil warms | old hearts. . . . ¶ This enchanting collection, in praise of | over sixty herbs and their significance, goes | well beyond the four-leaf clover's good | luck we all once learned. There are quotes | from diaries brimming with wisdom; po- | etry from classic works on herbs; age-old | advice on practical, medicinal uses. And | those who cook with herbs will discover a | world of new meaning in those dried, | crushed or freshly plucked garden herbs. || TASHA TUDOR—known and loved so | long as a children's book illustrator—graces | this unique book with original black and | white drawings, a color frontispiece and | full-color jacket, which she created espe- | cially as a gift to the Herb Society of Amer- | ica, Inc. Here, in familiar Tudor style, she | brings life and charm to the herbs of her | choice. Miss Tudor continues to work and | live in New England. || A BASKET OF HERBS has been a labor of | love for Mary Mason Campbell, Deborah | Webster Greeley, Priscilla Sawyer Lord, || *(continued on back flap)* | Back flap: *(continued from front flap)* || and Elisabeth W. Morss, all of whom are | members of the New England Unit, Inc., of | the Herb Society of America, Inc. Mary | Mason Campbell lives in New England and | divides her time between New Hampshire | and Rhode Island. She is the author of The | New England BUTT'RY SHELF COOK- | BOOK, also illustrated by Tasha Tudor | (SGP 1982). || *Jacket illustration by Tasha Tudor | Jacket design by Marjorie Merena | ©1983 The Stephen Greene Press. Printed in U.S.A.*

CONTENTS: Blank pages: [ii, 12, 174, 186-194] Pages [i-2] are enameled paper tipped-in. Page [i] is a large brown bookplate, "Ex Libris" and a rule in a floral frame, single thin line border around all. Page [2] is a full-color plate featuring a tussie-mussie with red-orange nasturtiums, lavender and other herbs. Title page, [3]. Page [5]: *This book is dedicated to | Herb Lovers Everywhere || "For Use and for Delight" || The New England Unit, Inc., of The | Herb Society of America, Inc. especially | thanks Tasha Tudor for her gracious | gift of illustrations.* The book is an anthology of verses and other thoughts relating to herbs; alphabetized, Aloe through Yarrow. *Bibliographical References,* pp. 175-182 lists 139 sources of quotations used throughout the book. *Acknowledgments,* pp. 183-185 lists 20 other citations by copyright owner.

ILLUSTRATIONS: Illustrations are black and white, either full page showing a person(s) with herbs or a half page sketch of the herb. Sweet bay, [30]; dill [56] and 57 (1/2); lavender [88] and 89 (1/2); nasturtium [102]; pansy [108] and 109 (1/2); rose [120]; rosemary [126] and 128 (1/2); sage [132] and 133 (1/2); (wild) strawberry [142] and 144 (1/2); thyme [150] and 153 (1/2); lemon verbena [156].

Copyright registration: TX 1-083-006 granted to The New England Unit Inc. of The Herb Society of America, Inc., Horticultural Hall, 300 Massachusetts Ave., Boston, MA. 02115. Janet A. Bergmann, agent for The Stephen Green Press, Box 1000, Fessenden Road, Brattleboro, VT 05301, swears on March 11, 1983:

A BASKET OF HERBS: A BOOK OF AMERICAN SENTIMENTS, by Mary Mason Campbell, Deborah Webster Greeley and Priscilla Sawyer Lord, coeditors of the entire text and not a work for hire, was published February 17, 1983. The book is a compilation of herb poetry and additional new material. The book was completed in 1982 and the copyright claimant obtained ownership by contractual agreement. The book was printed by Maple Vail MFG Group, Binghamton, NY, from type set by Yankee Typesetters, Biddeford, ME. The Library of Congress was granted non-exclusive permission to make copies and phonorecords for the blind and physically handicapped. Application and two deposit copies were received at LC March 15, 1983, the effective date of registration.

B2 _____.

CONTENTS: <u>Limited edition</u>. The illustration of the *Ex Libris*, page [i], is the same; but the text has changed to "*This is copy no.* [rule] | *of a limited edition of 1500.*" Printed text is brown, but the two numbers are hand lettered in gold ink.

B3 _____. [*Because of* ... ISBN 0-8289-0500-2 ‖ PUBLISHED FEBRUARY 1983 | *Second printing November 1983*]

CONTENTS: This printing on a smoother paper with a <u>yellow cast</u>.

B4 _____. [*Because of* ... ISBN 0-8289-0500-2 ‖ PUBLISHED FEBRUARY 1983 | *Third printing June 1985*]

COVER: The cover paper is a darker <u>Lincoln green</u>.

DUST JACKET: Have not examined a copy with price intact. Dust jacket lower right back now has an <u>overprinted white ½″ x 2″ rectangle</u>, within which is printed in square 'computer' type: ISBN 0-8289-0500-2.

B5 **Battered** /produced by Michael Jaffe; directed by Peter Werner. Written by Karen Grassle, Cynthia Lovelace Sears; music by Don Peake, director of photography, John Bailey. Cast: Karen Grassle, Levar Burton, Mike Farrell, *et alia*.

FORMAT: Motion picture, 2 videocassettes (ca. 97 minutes); sound, color; ¾″.

OTHER: The copyright deposit includes a 1 page synopsis. Applicant identifies excerpts from Shingebill [*sic*], a story from Bedtime book by Tasha Tudor as pre-existing material. Have not examined a copy.

COPYRIGHT REGISTRATION PA-77-456: granted to Jaffe Productions, 1420 North Beachwood Drive, Los Angeles, Ca. 90028. Michael Jaffe, swears on April 18, 1980:

BATTERED, a motion picture completed in 1978, was published 11 September 1978. Excerpts from SHINGEBILL [*sic*], a story from Tasha Tudor's BEDTIME BOOK, used with permission, all other being new material added to this work. Application and deposit received 22 April 1980, remittance number 334997, 7 August 1980. Registered 7 August 1980. Certificate mailed 6 October 1980.

B6 *Becky's Birthday* | WRITTEN AND ILLUSTRATED BY | *Tasha Tudor* | [cake in a ring of flowers] | *The Viking Press* | NEW YORK [Copyright © 1960 by Tasha Tudor McCready | First published in 1960 by The Viking Press, Inc. | 625 Madison Avenue, New York 22, N.Y. | Published simultaneously in Canada | by The Macmillan Company of Canada Limited || LITHOGRAPHED IN THE U.S.A. BY KELLOGG & BULKELEY.

PAGINATION: 3 signatures ivory paper: [i-ii, 1-6] 7 [8] 9-10 [11-12] 13 [14] 15-16 [17-18] 19-20 [21-22] 23-24 [25-26] 27 [28] 29 [30] 31 [32] 33-34 [35-38] 39-40 [41-42] 43 [44] 45 [46] 47 [48-50] plus paste-down endpapers. 10 x 8 ¼″.

COVER: Yellow cloth over board covers printed in red. Front: Detail of page [37], a wren on a rock holding a slip of paper in its beak bearing the word BECKY; in a circle of bachelor buttons and daisies. Spine: *Tasha Tudor* BECKY'S BIRTHDAY *Viking*. Identical endpapers are full illustrations: yellow wash, with a frame of golden rod and a ladybug. A wren on each page faces the other across the gutter. Both have paper banners in their beaks, verso reading HAPPY, recto, BIRTHDAY.

DUST JACKET: Same illustration on front and back of dust jacket. Yellow wash, golden rod framing a white-iced cake decorated with blue, yellow and orange flowers and 11 green candles. Above this in brick red script: *Becky's* | *Birthday*. Below, also in brick script: *Tasha Tudor*. Spine: **Tasha Tudor** [black] **BECKY'S BIRTHDAY** [brick] **The Viking Press** [black] Black text on flaps, front: $ 3.00 | Becky's Birthday | *Story and Pictures by* | TASHA TUDOR | "Thank all of you, even Cow, for just | the most magic birthday I've ever had," | ten-year-old Becky says at the very end | of this book. || What a truly magical birthday it is! | It would be wonderful if every child | could have one such day, but since that | is unlikely the next best thing is to share | Becky's birthday with her—in story and | pictures full of fresh country air. || From the first moment when the sun | awakens Becky, all through the whole | August day, and into the blue evening, | you can hear bird song, smell sun-soaked | flowers and growing things, feel the | good cool earth on bare feet, and see | and taste the tantalizing farm food. But | the *surprise* is the best part of all—a real | surprise to the reader as well as to the | birthday girl! || It is all delight—like going back a | generation in time for a summer holiday | with an affectionate, closely knit family | group, well-loved animals, no modern | "improvements"—just simple fun and | pure contentment. || 08011. Back flap: ***About the Author*** || TASHA TUDOR writes and paints con- | vincingly of the old-fashioned country- | side because she has always lived there. | She was one of five children on a Con- | necticut farm, who "ran wild over the | countryside when not having lessons. We | spent most of our time being people out | of the books which were read to us." || Now she lives with her four children | on an old farm in New Hampshire "with | lots of animals, all very badly behaved, | like the goat and the pony who come in | any door left open by mistake." || According to the last census there are | seventy-nine pets (including one starling | and three crows), and people and pets all | "have a glorious time." || THE VIKING PRESS | *625 Madison Ave., New York, N.Y.* | LITHOGRAPHED IN U.S.A.

CONTENTS: Page [1] is half title; pages [2, 6, 48] and inside both fly leaves are blank; [3] is title page; [5] is dedication: *To | Marcia, Katharine, and Jim, | to read when they are older.*

ILLUSTRATIONS: Half-page watercolors on title page and pages 7, 10 [11, 14] 15 [26] 27 [30] 31, 34 [35, 38] 39 [42] 43 [46]. Full-page watercolors on pages [18, 22]. Half-page black and white drawings on pages 8-9 [12] 13, 16 [17] 20 [21] 24 [25, 28] 29 [32] 33 [36-37] 40 [41, 44] 45. Pages 19, 23 and 47 are text only. The dust jacket illustration includes one candle "to grow on." The birthday cake is painted with eleven candles even though there are ten on the title page, and the opening paragraph states, "I am ten years old!"

OTHER: This is the first appearance of the ice cream making and birthday cake floating down the Blackwater River in Webster, N.H. In Efner Holmes' copy, [i-ii, 1-6] ... Page 7 is first page of text. Both end papers are blank, so [50] is [48]. Efner Holmes identifies the dedicatees to be the grandchildren of Hopkinton, N.H., friend Marcia Cunningham.

The description of this book in *Book Publishing Record, 1960-1964*, volume IV, page 5067, reads: TUDOR, Tasha   JUV | Becky's birthday; written and illustrated by Tasha | Tudor. New York, Viking Press [c.1960] 47p. illus. | 23cm. 60-4441 bds. 3.00 | Children from 8-11 will enjoy this portrayal of a ten-year- | old girl's birthday which takes place a generation ago on | an old fashioned farm in New Hampshire.

Copyright registration A 463534, granted to Tasha Tudor McCready, Route 1, Contoocook, N.H. Charles Tupper, agent for The Viking Press, Inc., 625 Madison Ave., N.Y. 22, N.Y., swears on September 21, 1960:

BECKY'S BIRTHDAY, written and illustrated by Tasha Tudor, a United States citizen, was published August 15, 1960. The book was printed by Kellogg & Bulkeley, 55 Granby St., Bloomfield, Conn. The book was bound by George McKibbin & Son, 87- 34th St., Brooklyn, N.Y. Application and affidavit were received at the Library of Congress September 23, 1960, and two copies of the book were received September 26, 1960.

Copyright renewal registration RE 375 593 granted to Tasha Tudor, Route #4, Box # 250, West Brattleboro, VT 05301. Tsuyako Uehara, agent for Tudor, swears on February 5, 1988:

BECKY'S BIRTHDAY, written and illustrated by Tasha Tudor was originally published August 15, 1960; registration A 463534 granted to Tasha Tudor McCready. Registration fee charged to account DA 018074 for Viking Penguin, Inc., 40 West 23rd St., NY, NY 10010. Application received at LC Feb. 9, 1988, the effective date of renewal.

B7 _____.

PAGINATION: [i-iv, 1-6] 7...47 [48-52] including fly leafs in 5 signatures, buff paper. 10 ¼″ x 8 1/8″.

COVER: Green painted cover, library binding. Blue paint on front: Beck's | Birthday, above and, Tasha Tudor, below, a yellow, blue and black line drawing of a cake, the illustration from the front of the trade dust jacket. On spine in black: BECKY'S BIRTHDAY   Tasha Tudor   A GUILD BOOK. Hinges reinforced with white buckram. White end papers and fly leaves.

DUST JACKET: Have not examined a copy.

OTHER: Original yellow end papers with golden rod and two wrens holding ribbons on which are written "Happy" and "Birthday" are bound in as pp. [ii-iii] and [50-51].

B8 _____. Have not examined a second printing.

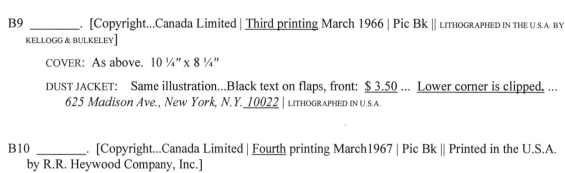

B9 _____. [Copyright...Canada Limited | <u>Third printing</u> March 1966 | Pic Bk || LITHOGRAPHED IN THE U.S.A. BY KELLOGG & BULKELEY]

COVER: As above. 10 ¼″ x 8 ¼″

DUST JACKET: Same illustration...Black text on flaps, front: <u>$ 3.50</u> ... <u>Lower corner is clipped.</u> ... *625 Madison Ave., New York, N.Y. 10022* | LITHOGRAPHED IN U.S.A.

B10 _____. [Copyright...Canada Limited | <u>Fourth</u> printing March1967 | Pic Bk || Printed in the U.S.A. by R.R. Heywood Company, Inc.]

PAGINATION: 3 signatures <u>plus an extra folded sheet front and back on</u> ivory paper: [i-vi, 1-6] 7 [8] 9-10 [11-12] 13 [14] 15-16 [17-18] 19-20 [21-22] 23-24 [25-26] 27 [28] 29 [30] 31 [32] 33-34 [35-38] 39-40 [41-42] 43 [44] 45 [46] 47 [48-54]. Pages [iv-v, 50-51] are the previous illustrated endpapers with extra ivory sheets before and after. 10 ¼″ x 8 1/8″.

COVER: Reproduces the dust jacket on cloth. In addition, the ship logo and <u>VIKING | Library Binding</u> | 2 wavy lines, printed in black at bottom center of back cover. Reinforced hinge. Ivory endpapers.

DUST JACKET: As before, but with <u>an added gold foil label 5/8″ above the bottom left front with the same logo as on back cover printed in black. The ¾″ x 2 ¾″ label isimprinted in black, [ship logo] and VIKING | Library Binding, above two wavy lines. Printed sideways on the label as it wraps the spine: VIKING | Library | Binding.</u> Text as above. Have not examined a copy with the corners of the front flap intact.

B11 _____.

PAGINATION: 10 1/32″ x 8 1/8″.

COVER: A Treasure Trove rebinding bound in mint green buckram. Front reproduces the jacket and cover illustration from above, but reduced to 8 ½″ x 7″. Spine printed in teal: BECKY'S BIRTHDAY • TUDOR. Back has a darker mottled green pattern and near the top right, TT in a circle. This is the subtle monogram for Treasure Trove, not Tasha Tudor.

B12 *Becky's Birthday* | WRITTEN AND ILLUSTRATED BY | *Tasha Tudor* | The Jenny Wren Press | Mooresville, Indiana [Copyright © 1992 by The Jenny Wren Press | All Rights Reserved | No part of this book may be reproduced in any form without permission from the publisher. || Re-printed in the U.S.A. | First Printed in 1961 by Viking Press, New York | Library of Congress Catalog Card Number | 92-080849 || ISBN #0962175359 || LITHOGRAPHED IN THE U.S.A. BY SHEPARD POORMAN]

PAGINATION: As first edition. 10 1/8″ x 8 1/16″.

COVER: Green cloth, stamped in gold: the same medallion of wren holding ribbon in beak surrounded by flowers. The spine text has been reset, in gold: TASHA TUDOR   BECKY'S BIRTHDAY   The JENNY WREN PRESS.

DUST JACKET: New design. Front and spine on a green field. A festoon of ribbons and flowers drapes the top and sides of front. A center medallion depicts the night-time cake floating on the Blackwater River, within a wreath of honeysuckle. Black script above the medallion: *Becky's Birthday*, and below: *Tasha | Tudor*. Vignettes at lower right and left depict the making of ice cream and the testing of same. Spine text also black: TASHA TUDOR   BECKY'S BIRTHDAY   The JENNY WREN PRESS. The jacket back is white and has inset a reproduction of the original yellow jacket front. Extra text in black, arched above: A Limited Edition of; at right just below illustration: [heart] Cover From Original Book [heart]. Lower right: **ISBN: 0962175359.** [Even though text says 'cover,' it is the <u>original dust jacket</u> that is pictured.] Black text on flaps, front has been reset and is nearly identical to earlier jackets: Becky's Birthday | *Story and Pictures by* | TASHA TUDOR. | "Thank all of you, even Cow, for just the ⌋ most magic birthday I've ever had," ten- ⌋ year-old Becky says at the very end of ⌋ this book. ¶What a truly magical birthday it is! It ⌋ would be wonderful if every child | could have one such day, but since that | is unlikely the next best thing is to share | Becky's birthday with her—in story and | pictures full of fresh country air. ¶From the first moment when the sun | awakens Becky, all through the whole | August day, and into the blue evening, | you can hear bird song, smell sun- ⌋ soaked flowers and growing things, feel ⌋ the good cool earth on bare feet, and see | and taste the tantalizing farm food. But | the surprise is the best part of all—a ⌋ real surprise to the reader as well as to ⌋ the birthday girl! ¶It is all delight—like going back a | generation in time for a summer holiday | with an affectionate, closely knit family | group, well-loved animals, no modern | "improvements"—just simple fun and | pure contentment.

Back flap: ***About the Author*** | TASHA TUDOR is one of America's most | loved and respected illustrators of Chil- | dren's Books. Her wondrous illustra- | tions take one to a quieter, simpler time | and place ... where enchanting chil- | dren enjoy the joyful surroundings of | the countryside, animals, friendships | and loving celebrations. Tasha's book of | *Becky's Birthday* is a true story of a | birthday celebration Tasha herself cre- | ated for her oldest daughter! ¶Tasha Tudor has over 80 books to her | credit. When she is not in the garden, | she is moving ahead with joyful enthusi- | asm into her second half century of | illustrating. Her fans, whom she consid- | ers as "special friends", cover the globe | as far away as Russia. ¶Enjoy her Magical world that she her- | self lives ... the world that we all | yearn for ... that we all become a part | of everytime [*sic*] we open one of her books. ‖ [pencil sketch of wren from end paper] ‖ [heart] | The Jenny Wren Press | P.O. Box 505 | 11 E. Main Street | Mooresville, Indiana | 46158 [heart]

CONTENTS: There is extra text in this edition, although no more pages. The half-title has added above the title the same arched words as the jacket back: A Limited Edition of. Page [2] previously blank now has this text: [heart] OUR HEARTFELT GRATITUDE TO OUR JENNY WREN PRESS FRIENDS | FOR MAKING OUR DREAM A REALITY [heart] ‖ LITHOGRAPHED IN THE U.S.A. | BY SHEPARD POORMAN, INDIANAPOLIS, INDIANA. Page [48] now has a black and white half-tone version of the endpaper wren with BIRTHDAY ribbon above: [heart] This Book and other Tasha Tudor Treasures | can be ordered from: ‖ The Jenny Wren Press | P.O. Box 505 | 11 E. Main Street | Mooresville, Indiana | 46158 | [heart]

OTHER: Some copies were sold at $32.95 with an <u>autograph on the front free fly leaf</u>: Tasha Tudor | 1992. Without the autograph, the book was advertised at $ 17.95. The copyright statement incorrectly states this book was first printed in 1961. It should be 1960.

B13 *Becky's Christmas* | WRITTEN AND ILLUSTRATED BY | *Tasha Tudor* | *The Viking Press* | NEW YORK. [Copyright © 1961 by Tasha Tudor | All rights reserved | First published in 1961 by The Viking Press, Inc. | 625 Madison Avenue, New York 22, N.Y. | Published simultaneously in

Canada | by The Macmillan Company of Canada Limited || Library of Congress catalog card number: 61-11667 || LITHOGRAPHED IN THE U.S.A. BY KELLOGG & BULKELEY]

PAGINATION: Three signatures, [i-ii, 1-5] 6 [7] 8-9 [10] 11 [12] 13-14 [15] 16-17 [18] 19-24 [25-26] 27-28 [29] 30 [31] 32 [33-34] 35-36 [37] 38-42 [43] 44-45 [46-48] plus fly leaves. 10 1/4″ x 8 3/16″.

COVER: Rose cloth cover imprinted in black. Front cover: a decorated Christmas tree with gifts centered within a border of evergreens and ornaments around the perimeter of the cover. Spine: *Tasha Tudor   BECKY'S CHRISTMAS   Viking*. Back cover is plain.

DUST JACKET: Front and spine of dust jacket are fully decorated on a blue ground. Front in a full frame of greens, ornaments and other objects. Centered in an oval evergreen wreath, a red colonial farmhouse and barn set before snow covered mountains. [This is essentially the Webster, N.H. home. -ed.] Title above and below this wreath, yellow ornamented letters outlined in purple. At bottom center in a small evergreen wreath: **Tasha Tudor,** in purple. The ornamented title is repeated on the spine, between (in purple) **Tasha Tudor   Viking**. Back cover and flaps are white. A full color Christmas tree with gifts is centered on the back, a tableau similar to the front cover of the book minus the border. Front flap: $3.00 || Becky's Christmas [blue] || *Story and Pictures by* | **TASHA TUDOR** || Christmas coming! Christmas coming! | The words sang in the ten-year-old Becky's | mind through all the wintry days of | preparation on the farm. ¶There was so much to be done: spicy | fruit cakes and gingerbread ornaments | to be made with the whole family help- | ing; knitting and weaving to be finished; | all the presents to be made except the | ones for the stockings; spruce boughs | and ground pine to be gathered in the | woods and made into wreaths; the beau- | tiful little creche to be set up in the an- | cient unused brick oven—just hundreds | of fascinating things to be accomplished | before the Day of Days. All these excit- | ing things had to be fitted in between | chores and school, which luckily would | soon be recessed for the holidays. ¶But most exciting of all to Becky were | the whispers and the consultations go- | ing on almost, but not quite, out of ear- | shot. It was clear that father and the | boys were planning a surprise for her, | with Mother and Kitty helping. And | Becky could hardly wait for them to see | the surprises *she* was preparing for *them*. ¶Every little girl will share Becky's | breathless delight when her surprise | finally comes, and will agree with her | that she couldn't possibly have had a | more wonderful Christmas! || 09011.   Back flap: Becky's Birthday [in blue] || *Story and Pictures by* | TASHA TUDOR || "Thank all of you, even Cow, for just | the most magic birthday I've ever had," | ten-year-old Becky says at the very end | of this book. ¶What a truly magical birthday it is! | It would be wonderful if every child | could have one such day, but since that | is unlikely the next best thing is to share | Becky's birthday with her—in story and | pictures of fresh country air. ¶From the first moment when the sun | awakens Becky, all through the whole | August day, and into the blue evening, | you can hear bird song, smell sun-soaked | flowers and growing things, feel the | good cool earth on bare feet, and see | and taste the tantalizing farm food. But | the *surprise* is the best part of all—a real | surprise to the reader as well as to the | birthday girl! ¶It is all delight—like going back a | generation in time for a summer holiday | with an affectionate, closely knit family | group, well-loved animals, no modern | "improvements"—just simple fun and | pure contentment. || THE VIKING PRESS | *625 Madison Ave., New York 22, N.Y.* || LITHOGRAPHED IN U.S.A.

ILLUSTRATIONS: Full color illustrations: Endpapers, [3] 6 [7, 10] 11, 14 [15, 18] 19, 22-23 [26] 27, 30 [31, 34] 35, 38-39, 42 [43, 46] Pencil drawings: [5] 9 [12] 13, 16-17, 21, 24 [25] 28 [29] 32 [33] 36 [37] 40-41, 44-45.

CONTENTS: Half-title, [1]; *Also by Tasha Tudor* | BECKY'S BIRTHDAY, [2]; title page [3]; colophon, page [4]; dedication "TO SOMEONE | VERY SPECIAL" beneath a child [Efner] on a galloping pony [Tone pome] and within an evergreen wreath. Text ends on page [46]. Front and back end papers repeat the same two full-color Tudor Advent calendars; vertical rectangles framed with greens, ornaments and gifts. The verso panel shows the impact of the McCready English period. A beamed and plastered shoppe front, diamond pane casement windows and one of the earliest manifestations of

98

the Corgi theme. The business is advertised to be CORGI'S CANDY SHOP, W. Brown | and | Puppies | Candy | Merchand [*sic*]. The recto is a large tree labeled POST OFFICE with woodland animals and birds dressed and performing human activities. [Efner Holmes confirmed the book is dedicated to her. -Ed., 2/22/1992.]

Copyright registration A 548337, granted to Tasha Tudor, Route 1, Contoocook, N.H. Marshall A. Best, agent for The Viking Press, Inc., 625 Madison Ave., N.Y. 22, N.Y., (attention Phyllis Gelbman) swears on February 24, 1962:

BECKY'S CHRISTMAS, written and illustrated by Tasha Tudor, a United States citizen, was published October 23, 1961. The book was printed by Kellogg & Bulkeley, 85 Trumball St., Hartford 1, Conn. from type set by The Composing Room, 130 West 46th St., N.Y. , N.Y. The book was bound by The H. Wolff Book Mfg. Co., 526 West 26th St., N.Y., N.Y. Application and affidavit were received at the Library of Congress February 26, 1962, and two copies of the book were received February 23, 1962.

Copyright renewal registration RE 430 719 granted to Tasha Tudor, Rt. 4, Box 205, W. Brattleboro, VT 05301, author, artist of said book. Tudor swears on Feb. 10, 1989:

BECKY'S CHRISTMAS, written and illustrated by Tasha Tudor was originally published Oct. 23, 1961, registration A 548337 granted to Tasha Tudor. Tudor hand wrote this entire application. Application received at LC Feb. 17, 1989, the effective date of renewal.

B14 _____. [Published simultaneously in Canada | by The Macmillan Company of Canada Limited.] Have not examined a copy.

B15 _____. Rebound library copies.

PAGINATION: [i-vi, 1-5] 6 [7] 8-9 [10] 11 [12] 13-14 [15] 16-17 [18] 19-24 [25-26] 27-28 [29] 30 [31] 32 [33-34] 35-36 [37] 38-42 [43] 44-45 [46-54].   The pasted endpapers were lost with the covers, only the free endpapers are still bound in.   10 1/16″ x 8″.

COVER: Reproduces the dust jacket illustration on the light blue buckram cover.

B16 _____. [Copyright © 1961... 61-11667 || Second printing May 1962 || LITHOGRAPHED ...]

PAGINATION: Illustrated endpapers and first 5 pages un-numbered as in first printing. 10 ¼ x 8 ¼.″

COVER: Rose cloth, as in first trade edition.

DUST JACKET: Front flap: $3.25 || ... Have not examined a copy with the bottom corner intact. Back flap: ... THE VIKING PRESS | *625 Madison Ave., New York, N.Y. 10022* || LITHOGRAPHED IN U.S.A.

OTHER: The publisher's address on dj flap indicates that Viking had changed to 5-digit zip codes between these two printings: 1961 and May 1962. But the next entry for this 2nd printing still preserves the New York 22, a case of two versions of the same printing being issued with variant dust jackets.

B17 _____. [Copyright © 1961... 61-11667 || Second printing May 1962 || LITHOGRAPHED ...]

PAGINATION: As above, pasted endpapers, [i-ii, 1-5] ...   10 ¼ x 8 ¼.″

COVER: Viking Library Binding with the cover colors basically reversed. The cover is a finer cloth and mint green. The previous cover illustration of Christmas tree and evergreen border are stamped in green ink, as are Tasha Tudor and Viking on the spine. But red ink is used for the title on the spine and on the front cover below the Christmas tree. The Viking Library Binding logo of ship on the waves and name are stamped <u>in red ink near the lower right corner of the back</u> <u>cover</u>.

DUST JACKET: Complete with a considerable amount of blue printing as follows: Net $ 3.19 | Becky's Christmas . . . and printed at the right edge of flap running perpendicular to the rest of the text and facing the gutter: *This is a VIKING LIBRARY BINDING, designed for maximum* *pleasure in use as well as maximum durability.* It opens flat, | but is strongly reinforced at every point of wear or tear, without marring the centers of endpapers or double-page drawings. | Boards, cloth, paper, thread, and reinforcing fabrics are selected to meet the most exacting requirements of multiple use. Back flap, as before: ...THE VIKING PRESS | *625 Madison Ave.,* *New York 22, N.Y.* ‖ LITHOGRAPHED IN U.S.A.

B18 _____. [Copyright © 1961... 61-11667 ‖ <u>Third printing February 1966</u> ‖ Fic 1. Christmas stories | 2. Family ‖ LITHOGRAPHED ...]

Have not examined a trade printing.

B19 _____. [Copyright © 1961... 61-11667 ‖ <u>Third printing February 1966</u> ‖ Fic 1. Christmas stories | 2. Family ‖ LITHOGRAPHED ...]

PAGINATION: [i-iv, 1-5] 6 . . . 45 [46-<u>52</u>] 10 ¼ x 8 ¼."

COVER: Viking Library Binding with the cloth <u>cover printed</u> with the former <u>dust jacket illustration</u>. The white back features a Christmas tree with gifts, centered. At the lower right back <u>the</u> <u>publisher's logo</u>: a Viking ship sailing on a two-line ocean to the right toward VIKING | Library Binding. The covers have reinforced cloth hinges and white end papers. The advent calendar "endpapers" are now pp. [ii-iii, 50-51].

DUST JACKET: Have not examined a copy.

B20 _____. [Copyright © 1961... 61-11667 ‖ <u>Fourth printing</u> November 1967 . . .

A book dealer cites a [trade] copy in <u>red cloth</u> which I have not examined.

B21 _____. [Copyright © 1961... 61-11667 ‖ <u>Fourth printing</u> November 1967 ‖ Fic 1. Christmas stories | 2. Family ‖ LITHOGRAPHED IN THE U.S.A. BY AFFILIATED LITHOGRAPHERS.]

PAGINATION: [i-iv, 1-5] 6 . . . 45 [46-<u>54</u>] 10 ¼" x 8 1/8"

COVER: Viking Library Binding, exactly like B17.

DUST JACKET: Have not examined one, although the exlib described has part of the front flap pasted inside the rear cover. The blue title, and four paragraphs of text match the flap from the first edition.

B22 _____. [Copyright © 1961... 61-11667 ‖ <u>Fourth printing</u> November 1967 ‖ Fic 1. Christmas stories | 2. Family ‖ LITHOGRAPHED IN THE U.S.A. BY AFFILIATED LITHOGRAPHERS.]

COVER: This description is from a rebound, ex-library copy. The cover is cream buckram, painted with the original dust jacket illustration. Spine printed in blue: BECKY'S CHRISTMAS • TUDOR. There is no text on the back. Endpapers are imprinted with the logo HUNTTING BOUND: a small child sitting and a short stool reading. Only the two free endpaper illustrations remain, the missing pair would have been discarded with the original covers.

B23 _____. Have not examined a <u>fifth printing</u>.

B24 _____. [Copyright © 1961 by Tasha Tudor | All rights reserved | First published in 1961 by The Viking Press, Inc. | 625 Madison Avenue, New York, N.Y.10022 | Published simultaneously in Canada | by The Macmillan Company of Canada Limited || Library of Congress catalog card number: 61-11667 || 6 7 8 9 10 76 75 74 73 72 | VLB 670-15426-1   Trade 670-15425-3 || Fic 1.... AFFILIATED LITHOGRAPHERS]

PAGINATION: 10 1/8" x 8 3/16".

COVER: Black bordered box at lower right, back cover: $5.95 | 670-15425-3 | Reinforced | Binding. Numbers are printed black on white, the words are reverse printed white on black.

B25 _____. Another state. Colophon page exactly as above, i.e., 6th printing, 1972.

PAGINATION: Extra white sheets have been added, creating pagination [i-vi] [1-5]...[46-54] including flyleaves..End papers are white with cloth reinforcing hinge. Advent calendars become pages [iv-v] and [50-51]

COVER: Continuous plasticized paper cover with cloth imprint carries the jacket illustrations from B10 above on a light blue field. Tasha Tudor, on front in purple; but Tasha Tudor and Viking are light blue on spine, title is yellow letters outlined in blue also. May have faded. White back cover has Christmas tree decoration, and boxed logo at lower right: VLB $4.31 | 670-15426-1 | Reinforced | Binding [in black frame]. Reinforced Library binding.

B26 *Becky's Christmas* | WRITTEN AND ILLUSTRATED BY | *Tasha Tudor* | THE JENNY WREN PRESS | MOORESVILLE, INDIANA [Copyright © 1991 by The Jenny Wren Press | All rights reserved | No part of this book may be reproduced | in any form without permission from the | publisher || Re-Printed in the U.S.A. || First published in 1961 by The Viking Press, Inc. | New York || Library of Congress Catalog Card Number: 91-61679 || I.S.B.N. 09621753-5-8 || LITHOGRAPHED IN THE U.S.A. | BY HILLTOP PRESS, INDIANAPOLIS, INDIANA]

PAGINATION: 48 pages. 80# Finch opaque Vellum Offset, white paper. 10 ¼ x 8 1/8"

COVER: Black ink on red cloth as before except spine lettering: *Tasha Tudor   BECKY'S CHRISTMAS   The Jenny Wren Press*.   B Cloth and 88 pt. Austell Board.

DUST JACKET: Illustrations and front as in first edition. The ornamented title is repeated on the spine, between (in purple) TASHA TUDOR [and] The JENNY WREN PRESS Back cover and flaps are white, black text:. THIRTIETH ANNIVERSARY EDITION [arching above] full color Christmas tree with gifts centered on back, from the first edition; [in lower right corner] I.S.B.N. 09621753-5-8. Flaps are complete with no printed price. Color and text like the first edition, with these exceptions: the code number has been dropped from bottom of front flap. Publisher's name at bottom of back flap now reads: [heart] TO BE REISSUED IN 1992 [heart] | THE JENNY WREN PRESS | P.O. BOX 505, MOORESVILLE, IND. | 46158 ||LITHOGRAPHED IN THE U.S.A.

CONTENTS: THIRTIETH ANNIVERSARY EDITION | *Becky's Christmas* [1]; [heart] OUR SINCERE GRATITUDE TO OUR JENNY WREN PRESS | FRIENDS FOR MAKING OUR DREAM A REALITY [heart] [2]; title page [3]; colophon, page [4]; dedication. Text ends on page [46].

ILLUSTRATIONS: Illustrations as in first edition.

OTHER: The Jenny Wren Press Spring-Summer 1993 catalog advertises a "limited printing of 5000 books of this [special 30th Anniversary] edition." They are listed at $17.95, and $32.95 with Tudor's autograph. According to the printer, 5,150 copies were printed, the job completed June 24, 1995 [*sic*].

B27 𝐵𝑒𝑡𝑡𝑦 𝐶𝑟𝑜𝑐𝑘𝑒𝑟'𝑠 | KITCHEN | GARDENS | by MARY MASON CAMPBELL | pictures
by TASHA TUDOR | [pencil sketch of a bunny reaching to sniff a tomato plant in a basket] |
UNIVERSAL PUBLISHING INC. upd [initials in a box] NEW YORK | DISTRIBUTED BY CHARLES
SCRIBNER'S SONS   [*THANK YOU* | from the author who extends her grateful | appreciation to those
who have given | valuable help and encouragement in the | research and writing of this book. | [sketch of
a little girl walking and lifting her skirt] | Copyright © 1971 by Universal Publishing and | Distributing
Corporation. All rights reserved. | No part of this book may be reproduced in any form | without the
written permission of the publishers. || Recipes for Herb Vinegar, Italian Dressing, and | Herb Jelly
reprinted from *Betty Crocker's Cookbook* | © copyright 1969 by General Mills, Inc., | Minneapolis,
Minnesota. || Printed in the United States of America || Library of Congress Catalog Card Number 79-
153734. || Betty Crocker is a trademark of General Mills, Inc., | which is licensed for use to Universal
Publishing | and Distributing Corporation.]

    PAGINATION: [i-ii] iii-v [vi] 1-8 [9-10] 11-26 [26a-26b] 27-58 [58a-58b] 59-91 [92] 93-106 [106a-
        106b] 107-138 [138a-138b] 139 [140] 141-170. 8 ¾" x 6 ½".

    COVER: <u>Perfect bound</u>. White end papers. Light green imprinted linen weave paper over board
        covers. Front cover text in black: 𝐵𝑒𝑡𝑡𝑦 𝐶𝑟𝑜𝑐𝑘𝑒𝑟'𝑠 | KITCHEN GARDENS above an illustration of
        vegetables and pottery on a red cloth, all within a circle of herbs; and this statement below: *A
        year 'round guide to growing and using herbs and vegetables.* | by Mary Mason Campbell |
        pictures by Tasha Tudor. Spine: [a bunch of fresh onions] | THE | 𝐵𝑒𝑡𝑡𝑦 | 𝐶𝑟𝑜𝑐𝑘𝑒𝑟 | HOME |
        LIBRARY | KITCHEN GARDENS || UPD | SCRIBNERS [bunch of radishes]. Back cover forms a grid
        of 16 panels each containing an oval with the hand lettered name and an illustration of an herb or
        vegetable. A 17th oval with a tussie-mussie of herbs is centered in this design. Sprigs of thyme
        and marjoram are also identified at two vertical intersections. In black at the bottom right: SBN
        684-12613-3.

    DUST JACKET: Exactly reproduces the cover. Front flap: $6.95 | 𝐵𝑒𝑡𝑡𝑦 𝐶𝑟𝑜𝑐𝑘𝑒𝑟'𝑠 | KITCHEN |
        GARDENS || *A year-round guide to growing and* | *using herbs and vegetables* || by Mary Mason
        Campbell | Pictures by Tasha Tudor || This is a book for the gardener who loves | to cook and the
        cook who loves to garden; | for the beginner who has never turned a | spade and for the
        experienced gardener | whose "green thumb" is itching to try an | exciting new project. It offers a
        treasury of | suggestions to help you choose the site of | your kitchen garden, plan it (it can be
        large | or small; indoors or outdoors), prepare the | soil, plant the garden, and reap a bountiful |
        harvest. You will learn how to capture and | enjoy the peak flavor of the herbs and vege- | tables
        you grow and how to dry, freeze | and store herbs so that your cooking need | not suffer when
        fresh snippings are not | available. | The Betty Crocker tested recipes for | several dishes in which
        herbs play an im- | portant role, a collation of herbal culinary | terms, and a glossary for
        gardeners make | this an exceptionally useful year-round | guide for anyone who delights in the
        flavor | and fragrance of fresh-picked herbs, the taste | and texture of crisp, tender vegetables, |
        and the look of a well-ordered and beauti- | ful garden. || *"Betty Crocker's KITCHEN GARDENS*

| *by Mary Mason Campbell is botanically and | horticulturally accurate and ranks with the | best books in its field."* | —Thomas H. Everett | Senior Horticulture Specialist | New York Botanical Garden. Back flap: [A heavy and a light rule] | THE 𝓑𝑒𝓽𝓉𝓎 𝒞𝓇𝑜𝒸𝓀𝑒𝓇 | HOME LIBRARY | 𝓑𝑒𝓽𝓉𝓎 𝒞𝓇𝑜𝒸𝓀𝑒𝓇'𝓈 KITCHEN GARDENS | is the first volume in this series of beautifully | illustrated books on gardening, needlepoint, | crewel embroidery, sewing, knitting, crafts, | home repairs and many other subjects of | special interest to women. | [a light and a heavy rule] || *About the Author and Artist* | MARY MASON CAMPBELL lives with | her husband in a beautiful 18th century | farmhouse in New Hampshire where they | enjoy their old-fashioned herb, vegetable, | and flower gardens. ¶Mrs. Campbell is the author of *The New | England Butt'ry Shelf Cookbook* and *The | New England Butt'ry Shelf Almanac.* She | is a member of the Massachusetts Horticul- | tural Society, the Herb Society of America | and the Audubon Society of New Hamp- | shire. || TASHA TUDOR is also a New Englander | and a gardener. Her talent as an artist and | illustrator has made her name well known | and well loved in the world of books. Paint- | ings of the gardens that surround her own | charming farmhouse as well as Mary Camp- | bell's lovely gardens were used to illustrate | this book.

ILLUSTRATIONS: Black & white drawings are grouped 1, 2, or 3 to a page as follows: Title page, verso of title page, 4, [9]. [10], 11, 12, 18, 27, 31, 36, 38, 40, 43, 45, 47, 49, 53, 55, 59, 61, 65, 67, 71, 73, 75, 78, 80, 83, 86, 87, 88, 89, 90, 91, [92], 94, 96, 97, 99, 102, 105, 107, 109, 114, 116, 118, 120, 122, 124 repeats the title page illustration, 129, 133, 135, 136, 139, [140], 144, 148, 151, 153, 158, 164 repeats one illustration from page 53. There are four sheets [26a, 26b, 58a, 58b, 106a, 106b, 138a, 138b] of full page color illustrations on kid paper. Altogether, 91 b&w and 8 color illustrations.

OTHER: Some Sources for | Seeds, Plants, and Garden Needs, pp. 165-166.

Copyright registration A 278501, granted to Universal Publishing and Distributing Corporation, 235 East 45th St. N.Y., N.Y. Ruth M. Shair, agent for Universal Publishing and Distributing Corporation, swears on October 18, 1971:

BETTY CROCKER'S KITCHEN GARDENS, by Mary Mason Campbell, South Road, Salisbury, N.H., 03268, and Tasha Tudor, Route 1, Contoocook, N.H., 03229, both United States citizens, was published October 18, 1971. The book was printed by Elgin Press, 18-06 130th St., College Point, N.Y. from type set by Hallmark Typographers, 52 East 19th St., N.Y., N.Y. The book was bound by Colonial Press, Clinton, Massachusetts. Application, affidavit and two deposit copies of the book were received at the Library of Congress October 21, 1971.

B28 _____.

PAGINATION: Another issue on larger paper.   10 signatures.   9 ½″ x 6 3/8″.

COVER: is light green cloth stamped in black on spine: 𝓑𝑒𝓽𝓉𝓎 𝒞𝓇𝑜𝒸𝓀𝑒𝓇'𝓈 || KITCHEN GARDENS || UPD | SCRIBNERS. Green and yellow <u>head band and tail bands</u>.

DUST JACKET: Jacket has been <u>enlarged with an olive bands</u> 3/8″ wide at top and 7/16″ wide across the bottom. Front flap of jacket as before, and has added at bottom: *Book Club | Edition.* Back flap carries the two biographies as before, followed by: PRINTED IN THE U.S.A. | 5280. The 'Home Library' <u>statement is omitted</u>. The <u>SBN does not appear</u> on the lower right of dj.

ILLUSTRATIONS: Identical. Color plates are printed on an enameled paper.

B29 _____.

PAGINATION: Ivory paper.

COVER: <u>Plastic-filled olive paper</u> imprinted <u>leather-pattern</u> over boards. Spine text as above.

OTHER: This might be a third printing.

B30 _____. [*THANK YOU...* | which is licensed for use to Universal Publishing | and Distributing Corporation || 15 14 13 12 11 10]

DUST JACKET: Last line of back flap: <u>PRINTED IN THE U.S.A.</u> Jacket back, lower right in olive border: <u>5280</u>.

OTHER: I have not found evidence to prove there were nine printings before this one.

B31 _____.

PAGINATION: <u>8 ½″ x 6 ¼″</u>

COVER: Paper wrapper printed with same illustrations as the first edition, glossy finish. <u>Spine text varies</u>: UPD | SCRIBNERS is larger and is printed vertically, rather than horizontally as before. <u>SBN number is absent</u> from back cover. Inside front cover reprints original front dust jacket flap <u>headed by this one line</u>: *(Original Hardcover Edition $6.95)*... Inside back cover revised from previous dust jacket back flap. THE *Betty* *Crocker* | HOME LIBRARY | <u>A series of beautifully illustrated books on | gardening, needlepoint, crewel embroidery, | sewing, knitting, crafts, home repairs and | many other subjects of special interest | to women. ||</u> ALREADY PUBLISHED: | *Betty Crocker's KITCHEN GARDENS* | by Mary Mason Campbell | *PLEASURES OF NEEDLEPOINT* | by Inman Cook and Daren Pierce | *PLEASURES OF CREWEL* | by Jo Springer | *GOOD & EASY SEWING BOOK* | by Joanne Schreiber and Carter Houck. || *About the Author and Artist of* | *Betty Crocker's KITCHEN GARDENS* | MARY MASON CAMPBELL lives ... to illustrate | this book.

CONTENTS: Same text as first edition. <u>Ivory paper</u>, as compared to the original which has a greenish cast. There are <u>no end papers</u>.

ILLUSTRATIONS: Color illustrations are on <u>semi-gloss paper.</u>

B32 *Betty Crocker's* | KITCHEN | GARDENS by MARY MASON CAMPBELL | pictures by TASHA TUDOR | [pencil sketch of a bunny reaching to sniff a tomato plant in a basket] | [lion logo] <u>GOLDEN PRESS</u> • NEW YORK | <u>Western Publishing Company, Inc.</u> | <u>Racine, Wisconsin</u> [*THANK YOU* | from the author who extends her grateful | appreciation to those who have given | valuable help and encouragement in the | research and writing of this book. | [pencil sketch of a little girl] | Copyright © 1971 by Western Publishing Company, Inc. | Published under license from General Mills, Inc. | owner of the Betty Crocker trademark. All rights | reserved. No <u>portion</u> of this book may be reproduced in | any form <u>or any manner</u> without the written | permission of the publishers, <u>except by a reviewer who</u> | <u>wishes to quote brief passages in connection with a</u> | review. Produced in the U.S.A. || Recipes for Herb Vinegar, Italian Dressing, and Herb | Jelly reprinted from *Betty Crocker's Cookbook © 1969* | by General Mills, Inc., | Minneapolis, Minnesota. || Library of Congress Catalog Card Number: 79-153734. || GOLDEN and GOLDEN PRESS ® are trademarks | of Western Publishing Company, Inc.]

PAGINATION: In ten signatures. 8 7/16″ x 6 3/32″.

COVER: Paperback edition without endpapers. Printed covers reprint the jacket of the first edition. Trimming has removed some of the oval design at the left edge of the back cover. ISBN 0-307-09651-3 in black on lower right back cover. Spine: 09651 | THE | *Betty* | *Crocker* | HOME | LIBRARY | KITCHEN GARDENS || [logo] GOLDEN PRESS. Onions and radishes as before. Text previously on front flap of dust jackets is printed inside the front cover. Inside back cover: THE *Betty* *Crocker* | HOME LIBRARY ... *GOOD & EASY SEWING BOOK* | by Joanne Schreiber and Carter Houck. || The Modern Woman's | *FIX IT YOURSELF* | Handbook of Home Repair | by Harry Zarachy || *GIFTS TO MAKE FOR LOVE* | *OR MONEY* |by Janet and Alex D'Amota || <u>ABOUT THE AUTHOR AND ARTIST OF</u> | *Betty Crocker's*... MARY MASON CAMPBELL lives ...with | her husband in a beautiful 18th century | farmhouse in New Hampshire where they |

enjoy their old-fashioned herb, vegetable, | and flower gardens. || Mrs. Campbell is the author *of The New* | *England Butt'ry Shelf Cookbook* and *The* | *New England Butt'ry Shelf Almanac*. She | is a member of the Massachusetts Horticul- | tural Society and the Audubon Society of | New Hampshire. || TASHA TUDOR …book.

 ILLUSTRATIONS:. Color illustrations on matte paper are identical to previous entries.

B33 Betty Crocker's | Kitchen Gardens [black shadowed letters outlined in white] | A YEAR-ROUND GUIDE TO GROWING | AND USING HERBS AND VEGETABLES | by Mary Mason Campbell | Illustrations by | Tasha Tudor || [pencil sketch of a bunny reaching to sniff a tomato plant in a basket] | [lion logo] GOLDEN PRESS.NEW YORK | Western Publishing Company, Inc. | Racine, Wisconsin [THANK YOU… Copyright © 1979, 1971… GOLDEN® and GOLDEN PRESS ® are trademarks…]

 PAGINATION As above. Perfect bound. 11″ x 8 1/8″

 COVER: Front cover is a full-bleed color photograph of a wooden kitchen table top with various bottles and baskets of greens, vinegar, jelly etc. Text of front cover is largely a colored overlay of the title page: [in white] Betty Crocker's, by Mary Mason Campbell, [lion logo] GOLDEN [lower left] and Illustrations by | Tasha Tudor [lower right]. Kitchen Gardens: same font as title page, yellow letters outlined in white with green shading. Orange letters: A YEAR-ROUND GUIDE TO GROWING | AND USING HERBS AND VEGETABLES. Back cover and spine are green reverse-printed in white. Spine: 9550 | Betty Crocker's Kitchen Gardens || [lion logo] GOLDEN®. Back cover text revised: For the gardener who loves to cook... | for the cook who loves to garden... | Whether you're an experienced gardener whose green | thumb is itching to try an exciting new project or a begin- | ner who has never turned a spade before, you'll find that | *Betty Crocker's Kitchen Gardens* offers a treasury of | helpful suggestions. || You'll learn how to help you choose the most favorable site for | your kitchen garden (be it large or small, indoors or outdoors)... | how to plan it...how to prepare the soil...which herbs and | vegetables to select and how to arrange them attractively | ...what techniques of planting are best...and when and | how to harvest your herbs and vegetables so that you can | enjoy them at the peak of their flavor. Also included are | directions for drying, freezing and storing herbs for out- | of-season pleasure. || To add to your enjoyment, there is a special collection of kitchen garden recipes for Herb Jelly, Minted Fruits, Dilled | Cucumbers in Sour Cream and many more -- all tested in | the Betty Crocker Kitchens. || Mary Mason Campbell writes with authority, in language | every reader will understand. Tasha Tudor's charming | illustrations were inspired by two "real" kitchen gardens -- her own and Mrs. Campbell's. || Betty Crocker's | Kitchen Gardens [these two words in the font as on the title page] || *"Betty Crocker's Kitchen Gardens...ranks with the best* | *books in the field."* | —Thomas H. Everett | Senior Horticulture Specialist | New York Botanical Garden || 0495 ISBN:0-307-09550-9 [sic]. Inside covers are white.

 CONTENTS: A new issue in paperback. Pages are photographically enlarged so that text area is approximately 8 x 5 ¼″. A revision of "Some Sources for Seeds, Plants, and Garden Needs," pp. 165-166 omits these firms from the list published in the 1971 paperback: New England - Greene Herb Gardens Inc., South -Hilltop Farm & Garden Center, Midwest - Indiana Botanic Gardens, Inc., Sunny Brook Farms Nursery, West - Mail Box Seeds, Herb Products Company, Taylor's Gardens.

B34 BIGGITY | BANTAM ‖ *By T. L. McCready, Jr.* | ILLUSTRATIONS | *By Tasha Tudor* | [banties] ‖ ARIEL BOOKS • NEW YORK [*To* MY MOTHER *and* FATHER | *on Their Fiftieth Wedding Anniversary* | [Biggity in a flower bed] | COPYRIGHT, 1954, BY THOMAS LEIGHTON McCREADY, JR. | AND TASHA TUDOR McCREADY. ALL RIGHTS RESERVED. | LIBRARY OF CONGRESS CATALOG CARD NUMBER: 54-5202.]

PAGINATION: Three signatures ivory paper: [i-ii, 1-2] 3-16, [17] 18 [19] 20-22 [23] 24-26 [27] 28-30 [31] 32-34 [35] 36-40 [41] 42-44 [45] 46-49 [50]. 8″ x 6 1/4″.

COVER: Yellow cloth covers, navy stamping: front, BIGGITY BANTAM, under a right-facing rooster; spine, McCready • BIGGITY BANTAM • Ariel.

DUST JACKET: Light blue dust jacket with white flaps. Printed in black front and back, each in a scalloped yellow line: BIGGITY | BANTAM, above a full-color left-facing crowing rooster, and below the illustration, By T. L. McCready, Jr. | Pictures by Tasha Tudor. Spine: McCready BIGGITY BANTAM Ariel. There is a clump of dandelions in each bottom front corner and one centered on the back. Front flap: $2.50 | 40-80 ‖ BIGGITY BANTAM | *by T. L. McCready, Jr.* | *Pictures by Tasha Tudor* | Biggity was a bantam rooster who got | his name by acting very fierce in spite | of his small size. His spirit was cer- | tainly admirable but it got him into a | lot of trouble, as you will see when you | read this delightful picture book. ‖ It is about some real banty hens and | roosters on a real New Hampshire | farm. Needless to say, the children are | real, too, and very proud of their | banty flock. ‖ This is <u>Tom McCready's first book</u> | but we feel sure it will not be his last because he has the same feeling for | writing that his wife, the famous | Tasha Tudor, has for painting. Ariel | is indeed proud to present this, <u>their | first book together</u>. | **ARIEL BOOKS** | *Children's Division* | FARRAR, STRAUS & YOUNG, INC. | *101 Fifth Avenue, New York 3.* Back flap: [black and white photograph of McCready and (?) Efner outdoors in a chair above this text. **T. L. McCREADY, JR.** | Tom McCready, descendant of a long and il- | lustrious New England family, is a Hamilton | College graduate who has turned farmer. He | lives with his beautiful wife, who has long been | a famous figure in the children's book world | (see below), and their four children high up on | a New Hampshire farm. There, in an old house | with huge fireplaces, slanting floorboards and | antique furniture, they work and play with | Seth, Bethany, Tom-Tom, and Efner. Outside | is a big barn full of animals, chickens and | banties, with many broad fields stretching down to a river where they all go in swimming on | hot days. It is a good life — one, we hope, that | will foster many books. ‖ **TASHA TUDOR** | Tasha is almost too well known in the book | world to discuss here. However, we feel young | readers should know how pleased she is to il- | lustrate her husband's first book and how ex- | cited the young McCreadys are to have their | banty flock immortalized by their mother's brush. As in Tasha's many other books, which | she has written and illustrated herself, the | source of inspiration has been her own family | and her surroundings. This is probably the | basis for her splendid work plus the fact that | she can paint in watercolors in such a beautiful | way that the

Tasha Tudor shelves in public | libraries are among the most popular with little | folk and <u>there are Tasha Tudor collectors all | over the United States.</u>

ILLUSTRATIONS: Color illustrations on endpapers and pages [2] 11, 15 [23, 27, 31, 35] 42, 43, 46, 47. Pages [iii] 17 [19, 23, 27, 31, 35, 41, 45] carry illustrations only, without text. Black and white pencil drawings on pages [ii-1] 4, 5, 6-7, 8, 12, 13, [17], [19], 21, 25, 28, 29, 33, 36, 37, 38, 39 [41, 45] 48, 49. Endpapers depict the McCready/Tudor farm on Tyler Road in Webster, NH, with cows, house, barn. and the children on the pasture rock.

OTHER: A single sheet advertising piece (8 5/16 x 6 3/8″)reproduced the dust jacket front but with

changed text. Instead of the title at top this phrasing: *Ariel Books* | Children's Division

FARRAR, STRAUS & YOUNG, INC. | **FOR BOYS AND GIRLS** | Presents | BIGGITY BANTAM | By | T. L. McCready, Jr. At left of rooster's craw: Illustrated | By | TASHA TUDOR. Beneath the rooster's feet: **SPRING** | *1954* . Text on back of flyer: BIGGITY BANTAM is the name of the bantam rooster belonging | to the children of Mr. And Mrs. Thomas L. McCready, Jr., of Webster, New Hampshire (P.O. Contoocook). The book named after Biggity is | the first written by T. L. McCready, Jr., and is illustrated by his artist | wife, Tasha Tudor, who has illustrated some twenty books (published by | Oxford University Press, of New York and London) — juvenile classics | such as *Mother Goose Rhymes*; Robert Louis Stevenson's *A Child's | Garden of Verses*, etc., plus her own well known books — the five Calico | books known as *Pumpkin Moonshine, Alexander The Gander, The | County Fair, Dorcas Porkus, Linsey Woolsey*. Also *The Dolls' Christmas* | which tells about the Tasha Tudor dolls and the annual doll Christmas | party — their dinner and marionette show given for the dolls. Other | books written and illustrated by Tasha Tudor are *Thistly B*, about the | canaries raised by Bethany McCready; *Snow Before Christmas*; *Edgar | Allan Crow*, about the family's pet tame crow, and many others, include- | ing a book of prayers for young children entitled *First Prayers* which is | published in two editions (Protestant and Catholic). ‖ ◊ ◊ ◊ ‖ The illustrations in "BIGGITY BANTAM" depict scenes of the McCready | home and farm, the children and animals. 48 pages in color and black and white. For ages 4 to 8. ‖ "BIGGITY BANTAM" is The Junior Literary Guild selection for its | 7-8 year old members for May, 1954. ‖ Price $2.50 (*each copy autographed*)   ‖ Orders shipped by mail | GINGER & PICKLES STORE | R.F.D. No. 1 | CONTOOCOOK | NEW HAMPSHIRE ‖*A price list of titles of Tasha Tudor books sent on request. Announcement of her | new Christmas Cards and book for 1954 will be made in mid-summer.*

COPYRIGHT REGISTRATION: A127101, granted to Thomas Leighton McCready, Jr., Contoocook, N.H. and Tasha Tudor McCready, Route 1, Contoocook, N.H.

Patsy P. McLaughlin, agent for Farrar, Straus and Young , 101 Fifth Ave., NY, NY, swears on February 24, 1954:

BIGGITY BANTAM, by Thomas Leighton McCready and Tasha Tudor McCready both United States citizens, was published February 23, 1954. The book was printed by Brett Lithographing Co., Long Island City, NY. The book was bound by Country Life Press, Garden City, NJ. Application and affidavit were received at the Library of Congress March 1, 1954, and two copies of the book were received March1,1954.

COPYRIGHT RENEWAL REGISTRATION: RE 136-507 granted to Tasha Tudor McCready, R.D. #4, Box 144, West Brattleboro, VT 05301, widow of the deceased author Thomas Leighton McCready and as author, and Seth Tudor, Thomas Tudor, and Bethany Tudor, R.D. #4, Box 144, West Brattleboro, VT 05301, children of the deceased Author Thomas Leighton McCready, and Efner Tudor Holmes, Rt. #1, Concord, NH, daughter of the deceased author Thomas Leighton McCready. Elizabeth Besobrasow, agent for the named parties, swears on August 23, 1982:

BIGGITY BANTAM, by Thomas Leighton McCready, Jr. and Tasha Tudor McCready was originally published Feb. 23, 1954; registration A 127121 granted to Thomas Leighton McCready, Jr. and Tasha Tudor McCready. Charge deposit account DAO 13366, Farrar,

Straus and Giroux, Inc. Application received at LC Aug. 27, 1982, the effective date of renewal.

B35 _____. . . . NEW YORK | AND | THE JUNIOR LITERARY GUILD [*To* MY MOTHER . . . 54-5202].

> PAGINATION: [i-iv, 1-2] 3-16, [17] 18 [19] 20-22 [23] 24-26 [27] 28-30 [31] 32-34 [35] 36-40 [41] 42-44 [45] 46-49 [50-52]. 8 1/8″ x 6 1/8″.

> COVER: Red plasticized cover, pigskin imprint. Title printed in yellow at bottom of front cover, also a replica in yellow and aqua paint of the banty rooster crowing which appeared on the original dust jacket. Library binding with reinforced buckram hinge. Ivory endpapers. The previous endpapers are pages [ii-iii] and [50-51] in this binding.

> DUST JACKET: Spine publisher changed to: A GUILD | BOOK

> ILLUSTRATIONS: Color illustrations on pages [ii-iii], interior as , and [50-51]. Black and white pencil drawings as in trade binding, except verso before title page has become [iv].

B36 _____. WARNE, United Kingdom. Overmann reports a blue cloth binding. Have not examined a copy.

B37 _____. . . . [banties] || FREDERICK WARNE & CO. LTD. | LONDON. [*To* MY MOTHER *and* FATHER | *on Their Fiftieth Wedding Anniversary* [Biggity in a flower bed] || First Published 1954 | By Thomas Leighton McCready and Tasha Tudor McCready. Revised Edition | © FREDERICK WARNE & CO., LTD. | LONDON, ENGLAND, 1961 || Printed in Great Britain by | William Clowes and Sons Ltd, London and Beccles | 67.261.

> PAGINATION: Three signatures ivory paper, including free endpapers: [i-ii, 1-2] 3-16, [17] 18 [19] 20-22 [23] 24-26 [27] 28-30 [31] 32-34 [35] 36-40 [41] 42-44 [45] 46-49 [[50]. 8 1/8″ x 6 1/8″.

> COVER: Green-gray weave-imprinted paper over boards, no stamping or decoration. Endpapers, as in the U.S. edition.

> DUST JACKET: Redesigned with a predominantly yellow tone. There are two illustrations from the book, each in its own white area, from page 47 at the top left, and from page 43 at the bottom right. Text is similar with small changes. Lettering in blue, red and black: BIGGITY | BANTAM [blue] | by T. L. McCREADY, Jr. [red] | The Pictures by Tasha Tudor [black]. Spine: BIGGITY BANTAM [blue]   by T. L. McCREADY, Jr. [red]   WARNE [black]. Additionally, the pencil sketch of Biggity from page 25 (minus the fence) is printed at the upper right of the dj front. The pencil sketch from the title page is reproduced on the back of the jacket. Front flap: BIGGITY | BANTAM || *by T. L. McCready, Jr.* | *Pictures by Tasha Tudor* || Biggity was a bantam rooster who got | his name by acting very fierce in spite | of his small size. His spirit was certainly | admirable but it got him into a lot of | trouble, as you will see when you read | this delightful picture book. || It is about some real banty hens and | roosters on a real New Hampshire farm. | Needless to say the children are real too, and very proud of their banty flock. || This is Tom McCready's first book, | but we feel sure it will not be his last | because he has the same feeling for | writing that his wife, Tasha Tudor, has | for painting. It is their | first book together. || PRINTED IN GREAT BRITAIN   Back flap: You will enjoy the companion | to this book | **ADVENTURES OF A BEAGLE** || * * * || **T. L. McCREADY, JNR.** | Tom McCready, descendant of a long and | illustrious New England family, is a Hamilton | College graduate who has turned farmer. He | lives with his beautiful wife, who has long been | a famous figure in the children's book world | (see below), and their four children high up on | a New Hampshire farm. There, in an old house | with huge fireplaces, slanting floorboards and | antique furniture, they work and play with | Seth, Bethany, Tom-Tom, and Efner. Outside | is a big barn full of animals, chickens and | banties, with many broad fields stretching down | to a river where they all go in

swimming on | hot days. It is a good life -- one, we hope, that | will foster many books. ||
TASHA TUDOR | Tasha is well known in the book world. <u>Young</u> | <u>readers</u> should know how
pleased she is to illus- | trate her husband's first book and how excited | the young McCreadys are
to have their banty | flock immortalized by their mother's brush. As | in Tasha's many other
books, which she has | written and illustrated herself, the source of | inspiration has been her own
family and her | surroundings. This is probably the basis for her | splendid work, plus the fact
that she can paint | in <u>watercolours</u> in such a beautiful way. || *Published by* | FREDERICK
WARNE & CO.LTD | London, England.

B38 _____.

  PAGINATION: 8 1/16″ x 6 1/8″.

  COVER: Deep fleshy-orange paper over boards, imprinted with weave. Front is stamped in red, the
  illustration from page 25, Biggity on a stone wall and in the open space, BIGGITY BANTAM.

  DUST JACKET: As above, but with price 8/6 in lower corner, front flap.

  OTHER: Examined a copy autographed by McCready from "Biggity and both his wives."

B39 TASHA TUDOR | A Book of | CHRISTMAS | A THREE DIMENSIONAL
BOOK. [Copyright ©1979 by Tasha Tudor. All rights reserved. Published | in the United States by William Collins Publishers, Inc., | New
York and Cleveland, and in Great Britain by William Collins | Sons, Ltd., London and Glasgow. Printed in Colombia, S.A. for | Intervisual
Communications, Inc., Los Angles.]

  PAGINATION: [1-14] pages, including covers.

  COVER: Full color. Gloss film laminate paper over board covers. Both covers are blue-green
  background and show Her signature "T.Tudor, 1979" in the lower right corner. Front cover
  color illustration is children, cat and corgis around a Christmas tree within a gift-laden twig and
  ribbon border; TASHA TUDOR, red, rest of text is black. Spine, squirrel and nuts at top and
  bottom and between: Tasha Tudor A BOOK OF CHRISTMAS Collins [in black]. Back
  cover has same branch and ribbon border enclosing this black text: A Book of | CHRISTMAS ||
  Christmas is a time for the gathering together of families; for | the reuniting of old friends; for the
  giving of gifts to those we | love; and, above all, for celebrating the birthday of the Holy | Child.
  It is a time for recalling old traditions, and for the | creating of new ones - making joyful
  memories to shine | down the ensuing years like lighted candles in the heart. || There are two
  Christmases, of course — the secular one, | with all the happy activities of the Yuletide season;
  and the | religious one, a time for rejoicing anew each year in the | timeless and eternal miracle of
  the birth of Christ. || Tasha Tudor keeps both Christmases, and her beautiful, | three-dimensional
  illustrations in this unique book are a gift | of joy to all. | [a catalog card, box] Library of Congress
  (USA) Cataloging in Publication Data | Tudor, Tasha. A book of Christmas | "A three-dimensional book." |
  SUMMARY: The Christmas story and holiday traditions are | depicted in three-dimensional pictures. | 1.Christmas—
  Juvenile literature. | [1.Christmas] I. Title. | GT4985.T82 394.2'68282 78-31704 | ISBN 0-529-05532-5. Below the
  card: COLLINS | New York● Cleveland ● London ● Glasgow ● Sydney | USA <u>ISBN 0-529-
  05532-5 $5.95</u> | UK   <u>ISBN   0-00-183760-5 L2.95.</u> 10 ¾″ x 7 ¾″.

  CONTENTS: Each of six two-page spreads is a pop-up scene with Tudor signature printed: [2-3],
  Christmas tree with children decorating and making cookies; [4-5], a 17th century town scene Advent
  calendar; [6-7], a flip door with St. Nicholas, 18th century chimney with stockings, St. Lucia with a
  turning wheel halo; [8-9], shepherds, angel and turning wheel star; [10-11], three kings on their
  camels; [12-13], a manger scene with children.

  Copyright registration TX 359-335 granted to Tasha Tudor, RFD #4, West Brattleboro, Vt. 05301.
  Sarah W. Crane, agent for Tudor, swears on Oct. 16, 1979:

  A BOOK OF CHRISTMAS, text and illustrations by Tasha Tudor, a US citizen, was published
  September 5, 1979 in Colombia, South America. The work was completed in 1979 and the

book was manufactured by Caravajal [*sic*] S.A., Cali, Columbia. Charge deposit account DAO 34681, William Collins Publisher, Inc., 200 Madison Ave., N.Y., N.Y. 10016. Library of Congress was granted non-exclusive permission to make copies and phonorecords for the blind and physically handicapped. Application received at L.C. Oct. 25, 1979, the effective date of registration.

B40 _____.

> COVER: A printed blue and gold paper label 1″ x 1/2″ reading 6^{95} placed over the prices printed on the back cover.

B41 _____. [Copyright . . . United States by <u>Philomel Books,</u> ⌐New York. Printed⌐ in Colombia, S.A. for Intervisual ⌐ Communications, Inc., California.]

> PAGINATION: [1-14] pages, including covers. 10 7/8″ x 7¾″.

> COVER: Gloss film lamination over printed board covers, more blue than green. Front cover is identical to B31. Publisher's name on spine: <u>PHILOMEL BOOKS [a singing bird sits in the enlarged O of Philomel].</u> Back cover text varies. The ISBN has been removed from within the catalog card box. Beneath the card: [bird in circle logo] | PHILOMEL BOOKS | ISBN 0-399-21475-5 US >>$12.95   CAN >> $18.25. The last line is in 'computer' font.

B42 _____. [Copyright . . . Philomel Books, | New York. <u>Published simultaneously in Canada.</u> Printed ⌐ in Colombia, S.A. for Intervisual Communications, Inc.,⌐ California. <u>Third impression.</u>]

> COVER: Cover is more blue than green in this printing. Front cover is identical to B31. Publisher's name on spine is <u>PHILOMEL, [singing bird sits in the O].</u> Back cover text varies thus: The <u>catalog card is moved to the left, and there is no ISBN in within the card.</u> To the right of the card box is a <u>black bar code with text:</u> ISBN 0-399-21475-5 | 90000 | 9 780399 214752 | $13.95 / $18.50 (CAN). Centered at bottom within the border: <u>PHILOMEL BOOKS, the same bird logo from the spine positioned above the name.</u>

B43 TASHA TUDOR ‖ Een boek voor de **KERSTTIJD.** All designs and colors match the Collins edition. Text has been changed beginning with the cover: TASHA TUDOR [in red]‖ Een boek voor de | **KERSTTIJD** ‖ PANORAMABOEK MET ADVENTKALENDER [in the bottom margin, black]. … Back: VAN REEMST | [dog logo] | KINDERBOEKEN ‖ Van Reemst Panorama boeken ‖ Met Kertmis vieren we de terugkeer | van het licht en de geboorte van | Jesus Christus. Dit panorama boek | laat in drie dimensies zien wat er | allemaal in de kersttijd gebeurt. Het | is een lees- en kijkboek met daarin | een prachtige adventkalender. ‖ Andere Van Reemst panorama boeken heten: ‖ PADDINGTON | DIERENKERMIS | WERELD OP WIELEN | SNEEUWWITJE EN DE ZEVEN DWERGEN | PINOKKIO ‖ derde druk | © 1979 Tasha Tudor | © 1980 Unieboek BV/Uitgeverij Van Reemst, | Bussum-Holland | Verspreiding voor Beldie:Standaard Uitgeverij, | Antwerpen | ISBN 90 269 0795 8 | Printed and Bound in Cali, Colombia, S.A. by Caravajal S.A. | for Intervisual Communications, Inc., Los Angeles, CA 90045.] [14] pages including covers.   10 13/16″ x 7 ¾″

Gloss film lamination over printed board covers. The 12 inner pages are printed on three sheets of light board. Each board is folded three times to form the pages with these mechanical additions nine pop-ups, one wheel, one flipper door. Spine: Tasha Tudor   Een boek voor de Kersttijd   **VAN REEMST-BUSSUM**.

Page [2]: Het kerstfeest brengt wat licht en gezelligheid in de | donkere decembermaand. Iedereen is druk in de weer | met de voorbereidingen: er worden cadeautjes gekocht, | kerstkransen gebakken, het huis wordt versierd en op . . .

Page [12]: *Komt allen tezamen* | *Komt verheugd van harte* | *Bethlehem stal in den geest bezocht.* || En de wijzen gingen het huis binnen en | zagen het kind met Maria, zijn moeder,

Page [13]: Zien wij dat kindje, ons tot heil geboren | O, laten wij aanbidden, o, laten wij aanbidden | O, laten wij aanbidden die Koning. || en zij vielen neder en bewezen hem | hulde. En zij boden hem geschenken aan. | (VRIJ NAAR MATTHEUS 2, VER 11)

B44 TASHA TUDOR || **BUON | NATALE**   All designs and colors match the Collins edition. Text has been changed beginning with the cover: TASHA TUDOR [in red]|**BUON | NATALE** || **Arnoldo Mondadori Editore** [in the bottom margin]. [©1979 by Tasha Tudor | © 1980 Arnoldo Mondadori Editore S.p.A., Milano, per l'edizione italiana | Titolo dell'opera originale: *A Book of Christmas* | Traduzione di Francesco Saba Sardi | Prima edizione ottobre 1980 | Stampato da Carvajal S.A., Cali, Colombia] [The following text is printed on the back cover] **UN | LIBRO | ANIMATO | MONDADORI** [LOGO] || Natale e illustration and description tempo in cui le famiglie si riu- | niscono, ci si ritrova con I vecchi amici, | si offrono doni a color che si amano; ma | e soprattutto illustration and description tempo in cui si celebra la | nascita del Santo Bambino. E un'occasio- | ne per riportare in vita vecchie tradizioni | e crearne di nuove, che resteranno quali | gioiosi ricordi a illuminare gli anni che | verranno, come tante candeline accese | nei nostri cuori. Di Natali pero ce ne sono due: uno profano, con tutte le gio- | iose attivita delle grani occasioni; e uno | religioso, ed e illustration and description momento in cui ogni | anno si torna a celebrare l'eterno miraco- | lo della nascita di Cristo. In questo splen- | dido libro Tasha Tudor li illustra tutti e | due con belle immagini tridmensionali. || Lire 7000 | *(6603)*]

PAGINATION: [14] pages including covers.   10 13/16″ x 7 ¾″

COVER: Gloss lamination over printed board covers. The 12 inner pages are printed on three sheets of light board. Each board is folded three times to form the pages with these mechanical additions nine pop-ups, one wheel, one flipper door. Spine: **BUON NATALE**   AM [logo].

CONTENTS: Text, page [2]: Natale arriva nel freddo dicembre a riscaldarci I cuori | con buoni pensieri. E il temp dell'anno in cui si da e si fa | per gli altri, un tempo dioiosi preparativi: scegliere doni, . . .

B45 TASHA TUDOR || Julboken: med adventskalender och julkrubba. New York: Carlsen, 1980. [*sic*] ISBN 91-510-2472-8.

OTHER: Brit Østerud reports a Swedish translation. Have not examined a copy.

B46 TASHA TUDOR || poppu appu bukka | **kurisumasu ni tsuite** | tasha= chuudaa bun e. [from the back: kaiseisya no poppu appu bukku kurisumasu NDC196 | tasha= chuudaa bun e / KUMAGAYA, Ikue yaku | hakkousha IMAMURA, Hiroshi 1980nen issatsu 1988nen nanasatsu | hakkousho KAISEI-SHA, Tokyo-to Shinjuku-ku Ichigaya sadoharachou, Shinjuku, 3-5]

COVER: Title is taken from front. Tasha Tudor, at top, in English; remaining Japanese text translates to: pop-up book | Christmas | Tasha Tudor sentences & pictures. Back, text transliterated from the Kanji by Satoshi Nakamura: [kurisumasu ni tsuite | [rule] | kurisumasu wa kazoku sorotte danransuru toki desu。 mata mukashi no | tomodachi ni saikaishitari aisuru hito ni okurimono wo suru toki demo arimasu。| keredomo kurisumasu de ichiban taisetsuna no wa iesu=kirisuto no tanjou wo | iwaukoto nanodesu。 kono hi hitobito wa furuku kara tsutawaru kurisumasu | no gyouji wo omoiokosu to douji ni kurisumasu wo iwau atarashii gyouji mo kufuu | shimasu。 soshite tanoshii omoide wo ippai nokoshi te itsumo kokoro ni ai no | tomoshibi ga kagayaiteiru youna subarashii mainichi ga korekara mo otozu | reru koto wo inorunodesu。 ¶kurisumasu ni wa futa toori no kurisumasu ga aru koto ni minasan wa | okizuki de syou。 hitotsu wa omatsuri toshite iroirona moyooshi wo tano | shimu kurisumasu。 mouhitotsu wa kyoukai no gishiki toshite iesu=kirisuto | ga oumareninattakoto wo minna de yorokobi ai yasashii kokoro | de tasuke au kurisumasu desu。 || [in a single rule box. 9/16″ x 3 3/8″: gaka tasha=chuudaa wa 1915nen bosuton ni umare bosuton bi | jutsu gakkou de e wo mananda。 ehon kurisumasu no mae no ban (kaiseisha kan) | nado kurashikkuna sutairu no suisai ni yoru sakuhin ga tasuu aru。 || [pop-up book of KAISEI-SHA   Christmas] NDC196 | [Tasha Tudor   Sentences/Paintings /KUMAGAYA, Ikue   Translation | Publisher IMAMURA, Hiroshi   1980 First Impression/1988 Seventh Impression | Publishing Company KAISEI-SHA   3-5, Ichigayasadoharachou, Shinjuku-ku, Tokyo] | [rule] || A BOOK OF CHRISTMAS BY Tasha Tudor © 1979 | originally published in the United States by William Collins Publishers Inc., New York . | Japanese edition published by KAISEI-SHA Co., Ltd. Tokyo © 1980 | arranged by Intervisual Communications Inc., Los Angeles, | printed and bound in Colombia S.A. || ISBN 4-03-321010-5 C8716   [in black, on a silver impression] P1600E [the price 1,600 yen | the price without a consumption tax 1,553 yen]

OTHER: The Japanese text was graciously translated by Satoshi Nakamura: About Christmas | [rule] | Christmas is a time when all the family sit in a happy home. It is also a time for the reuniting of old friends and for the giving of the gifts to those we love. But the most important thing to do on the Christmas day is to celebrate the birth of Jesus Christ. On this day people recall events of Christmas which has come down from the olden times and at the same time, create new events to celebrate Christmas with various ideas. And they leave many joyful memories and pray that the wonderful days in which candles of love are always shining in our hearts, will come in the future. ¶ Of course you know that there are two types of Christmas. One is Christmas as a festival where we enjoy many kinds of activities. Another is Christmas as a ceremony at a church where we all congratulate each other on the birth of Jesus Christ and help each other with a gentle heart. || [single rule box]: the painter, Tasha Tudor was born in Boston in 1915, and has studied the painting at Boston Art School. There are many classical-style water-painting works, for example a picture book "The night before Christmas," published by KAISEI-SHA.

ILLUSTRATIONS: As in the English language edition.

B47 TASHA TUDOR || El Libro de | NAVIDAD || EDITORIAL | NORMA.   [© 1979 Tasha Tudor | Publicado por Edinorma Ltda. & Cia. S.C.A. Bogata, Colombia | previo acuerdo con Intervisual Communications Inc., | Todos los derechos reservados | Impreso y ensamblado por Carajal S.A., Cali, Colombia]

PAGINATION: [14] pages including covers. 10 13/16″ x 7 ¾″

COVER: Back cover: El Libro de | NAVIDAD || La Navidad es la época más hermosa del año. | Es la manifestació del amor y de la unidad | familiar. La oportunidad para el reencuentro | con las viejas amistades yu para el intercambio | de alegrías y regalos con nuestros seres | queridos. Pero ante todo, son días especiales | para conmemorar el nacimiento del Niño | Dios. El tiempo para revivir antiguas tradi- | ciones y crear otras nuevas, haciendo que los | tiernos recueros fulguren en imperecedera | alegría como rayos de luz en el corazón. | Hay dos Navidades, desde luego; la profana | con todas las felices actividades prorpias de la | Pascua de Navidad; y la religiosa que es el |tiempo para renovar, cada año, el jubilo del | máximo y eterno milagro del nacimiento de | Cristo. | Tasha Tudor conserva ambas Navidades, y la | belleza de las ilustraciones tridimensionales | en este único libro son un regalo de felicidad | para todos.

B48 TASHA TUDOR || Le livre de | NOËL | en relief et anime | un livre en relief FERNAND NATHAN   [Copyright © 1979 by Tasha Tudor. Tous droits réservés. | Imprimé en Colombie | d'ordre d'Intervisual

Communications, Inc., Los Angeles USA | pour Fernand Nathan et Cie, Paris | Texte français: © Fernand Nathan et Cie, Paris, 1980 | Numéro d'éditeur: O 27 195 | ISBN 2 09 263 021 0]

PAGINATION: [14] pages including covers. 10 13/16" x 7 ¾"

COVER:. Gloss lamination over printed board covers. Title from cover: TASHA TUDOR [in red], remaining text black. Spine: Tasha Tudor LE LIVRE DE NOëL Fernand Nathan. Back cover: Le livre de | NOëL ‖ en relief et animé ‖ Noel est la plus belle fête de l'année. | Les families se réunissent. Les amis se retrouvent. | Le monde chrétien célèbre la naissance de l'Enfant Jésus. | C'est l'époque où revivent les vielles traditions, | différentes de pays en pays. | Ce livre de Tasha Tudor | au très belles illustrations | en trois dimensions | sera une joie pour tous. ‖ **FERNAND NATHAN, PARIS** ‖ ISBN 2 09 **263 021** 0.

CONTENTS: The 12 inner pages are printed on three sheets of light board. Each board is folded three times to form the pages with these mechanical additions—nine pop-ups, one wheel, one flipper door.
Text, page [2]: C'est bientôt Noël! Les enfants font la ronde | autour du grand sapin, merveilleusement décoré. Autour de la table, garçons et filles préparent des gâteaux. . . .

B49 TASHA TUDOR ‖ Min julebok: billedbok med adventkalender. Oslo: Lunde, 1980. ISBN 82-520-5312-2

OTHER: Brit Østerud reports a Norwegian translation. Have not examined a copy.

B50 TASHA TUDOR ‖ WENN | WEIHNACHTEN | IST ... Carlsen Verlag GmbH

Reinbek bei Hamburg 1980 | Aus dem Amerikanischen A BOOK OF CHRISTMAS | Copyright © 1979 by Tasha Tudor | Originalverlag: William Collins Publishers, Inc., | New York and Cleveland | Created by Intervisual Communications Inc., Los Angeles CA 90045 | Alle deutschen Rechte vorbehalten | 10088097 ISBN 3 - 551 - 12059-5 Bestellnummer 12059 ‖ Carlsen Verlag.

PAGINATION: [14] pages including covers. 10 13/16" x 7 ¾"

COVER:. Gloss lamination over printed board covers. Text has been changed beginning with the cover: TASHA TUDOR [in red]‖ WENN | WEIHNACHTEN | IST ... ‖ Carlsen Verlag [in the bottom margin]. ... [The following text is printed on the back cover.] KM ab 3 J. ‖ Mitten im kalten Dezember gibt es jedes Jahr etwas, auf das | wir uns freuen konnen: das Weihnachsfest. | Es wird gebastelt und gebacken, Advents- und Weihnachts- | lieder werden gesungen, und alte Brouche werden mit neuem | Leben erfollt. | Tasha Tudor hat den Zauber der Weihnachtszeit in stim- | mungsvollen dreidimensionalen Bildern festgehalten. Und sie | erinnert auch an den eigentlichen Anlas des Festes: die Ge- | burt Christi im Stall von Bethlehem. ‖ {Then the copyright paragraph from above.}].

CONTENTS: The 12 inner pages are printed on three sheets of light board. Each board is folded three times to form the pages with these mechanical additions—nine pop-ups, one wheel, one flipper door.

Text, page [2]: Mitten im kalten Dezember gibt es jedes Jahr etwas, . . .

Text is loosely translated, specific scriptural references have been omitted. Four text blocks are not reproduced at all, revealing more of Tudor's illustrations in the German edition. The four places are the copyright paragraph at the top of page [2] , the block at the bottom of page [7], the two blocks at the bottom of pages [12] and [13].

ILLUSTRATIONS: All designs and colors match the Collins edition

OTHER: A white store label is affixed at the bottom right of page [2]: 191 15.80 [15 deutsch marks ?]

B51 **The** | **BouQuet** | Christmas Issue | 1962 | A | Journal for the | Lady of Fashion | Price twenty buttons. [From the base of the back cover: Published by The Jenny Wren Press, Box 505, Mooresville, Indiana 46158 | Copyright

PAGINATION: [i-ii] 1 [2] 3-28 [29] 30-33 [34] pages including the wrapper on 80# Mohawk Superfine Softwhite Text. 4 x 3″

CONTENTS: The entire booklet is printed on a buff paper, printed both sides, folded and stapled twice in the gutter. There is no jacket. The title is taken from the cover which is from a full-color hand-painted original: a rectangular holly border encasing a mistletoe wreath in its upper half. The wreath encircles red outlined letters **The | BouQuet** and is topped with a red bow; a sash of ribbon is draped on the bottom of the wreath bearing the words **Christmas Issue**; the sash supports a burning red candle in holly. The lower half of the panel carries the remaining text centered between two gold stars and eight other stars drawn as asterisks. The back cover has a drawing of holly and mistletoe in the center above a printed signature: Tasha Tudor. Some copies have an extra real signature above this: Tasha Tudor | 1989.

With the exception of the colophon on the back cover, and the ISBN printed at the bottom right of page 33, the booklet is completely hand printed and decorated by Tudor. This is the first publicly printed version of a piece that was created and shared with family and friends in 1962. Tudor drew a single line frame around each page, added the text to it, and numbered most pages, usually within the ruled frame at the upper right. Pages 6-7, 12, 25-27 are numbered outside the frame. Small drawings decorate pages [ii] 4, 6-7, 10-11, 16-18, 28, 30-31, 33 and [34]. The front cover, and pages 12-15 are in color after the style of nineteenth century fashion plate magazines. Page 29 is a full-page sepia watercolor of Christmas carolers. A 'boggart' holds a poled lantern to light the way.

OTHER: 5,150 copies were printed, the job completed October 31, 1989. The booklet was first advertised in a mailing from the Jenny Wren Press in mailings of October 18 and 24, 1989, thus: ⑦ Christmas bouquet | 3″ x 4″ | Jenny Wren's newest re- | lease . . . this enchanting | tiny book will make the per- | fect Christmas present! | Filled with the latest Holi- | day fashions, Christmas | Music, cookie recipe of the | month, Poetry, other | treasures & an editorial by | Miss Jenny Wren — Made | over 30 years ago by Tasha | . . . | Regularly $8.95 | with signature $ 12.95 | ♥Holiday Special $6.95 / | $10.95. Another order form for wholesale customers was dated Oct. 14, 1989 and lists The Bouquet - Christmas Edition Suggest Retail Unsigned $ 6.95, Suggested Retail Signed $10.95, Wholesale Unsigned $ 4.20, Wholesale Signed $ 9.40.   Copies were sold with Tudor's signature printed beneath a spring of holly on the back. Others were countersigned with a real signature above: Tasha Tudor | 1989.

Bethany Tudor speaks of this title in *Drawn From New England*, page [75], " . . . Her doll family subscribes to a wonderful magazine known | as *The Bouquet* in which is shown some of the latest fashions | for dolls. Included is also a social column, some short stories | and pictures, children's word games, and more. My mother used to put out a new issue of this magazine four times a year . . . " A Spring 1963 issue with hand-sewn binding is pictured on the same page, but only the Christmas issue discussed here has been published. Many biographical and artistic references familiar to Tudor fans can be found in its pages. It was published by Greenwillow, East of the Sun and West of the Moon (from Asbjörnsen and Moe's *East of the Sun and West of the Moon*), and would emerge in *Corgiville Fair* as 'West of New Hampshire and East of Vermont.' Jenny Wren is the Editress. Edward B. H. Bear [which belonged to Gretchen Brown, niece of Ned Hills] edited the poetry selections, and Merton Bogart, M.P. the Science section. Miss Lucy Bugs, pet beagle of the Brown family, was the Pennsylvania News Correspondent. A notice of a lending library includes books by Rumer Godden, Tasha Tudor and John Gruel. The Dutch Inn [Ned Hills] and the Jenny Wren Press placed ads. A news column describes a new house for Araminta Duckling on Gooseberry Lane [Bethany Tudor's book], and an exhibit of the Timothy [who belonged to Tasha Brown] and Edward Bear, Jr. families of Larchrise, Pennsylvania, at Bucknell University in February. Larchrise was the name given to the Brown home near Montandon and only a few miles from the Bucknell campus. The widow Shakespeare and her three daughters are moving to Marion, Ohio, [Virginia Lightner] "a place she has always loved. Her niece, Miss Rosemary Tudor came on from Ohio to help her Aunt and cousins with the move . . . Her portrait which was painted by Augustus Sparrow in 1950 . . . now hangs in the Lightner Museum of Marion." Reference is made to new furniture for the Bear family recently presented by Mrs. James Ward Thorne of Chicago. Mr. and Mrs. Thaddeus Crane *[dolls] have been on a tour of "Hartford, Philadelphia [Lippincott], Mill Hall [Hills and Brown], Detroit, Marion, Chicago, Cleveland and Corning, where they attended many cultural meetings and entertainments."

COPYRIGHT REGISTRATION: TX 402 768 granted to The Jenny Wren Press/by written agreement between Tasha Tudor and Beth Mathers, co-owners of The Jenny Wren Press. Beth Mathers (317-831-1415), other copyright claimant and agent for Tasha Tudor, swears on Jan. 15, 1990:

THE BOUQUET CHRISTMAS ISSUE, a Christmas magazine for small children by Tasha Tudor, born 1916, was completed in 1962. The author's contribution to the work was anonymous. Certificate to be mailed to The Jenny Wren Press, P.O. Box 505, Mooresville, IN 46158. Application and two deposit copies received at LC Jan. 23, 1990, the effective date of registration. *[This application entirely in Mathers' hand writing.]*

B52 **A Brighter Garden** [teal] | *Poetry by* Emily Dickinson | *Collected by Karen Ackerman* | *Paintings by* Tasha Tudor | Philomel Books | New York [black]. [Original text copyright © 1990 by Karen Ackerman. | Illustrations copyright © 1990 by Tasha Tudor. | Published by Philomel Books, | a division of The Putnam and Grosset Group. | 200 Madison Avenue, New York, NY 10016. | All rights reserved. Published simultaneously in Canada. | Printed in Hong Kong by South China Printing Co. (1988) Ltd | The text is set in Bembo with Centaur Display. | Book design by Nanette Stevenson. | Library of Congress Cataloging-in-Publication Data | Dickinson, Emily, 1830-1886. A brighter garden. | Summary: An illustrated collection of poems | by the famous nineteenth-century poet. | [1.American poetry] I. Ackerman, Karen, | II. Tudor, Tasha, ill. III. Title. | PS1541.A6 1989 811'.4 88-5849 | ISBN 0-399-21490-9 | First impression]

PAGINATION: Four signatures on white paper: [1-5] 6-7 [8-9] 10 [11] 12 [13-14] 15-16 [17] 18 [19] 20 [21-23] 24 [25-26] 27-28 [29-30] 31 [32] 33-34 [35-37] 38 [39] 40 [41-42] 43-44 [45] 46 [47-50] 51 [52] 53-54 [55] 56 [57] 58 [59] 60-61 [62] 63 [64] 10 ¼"x 8 ¾"

COVER: Half paper (mint green) over boards lapped over green linen spine stamped in gold: Dickinson/Tudor A Brighter Garden Philomel. Mint green end papers.

DUST JACKET: White jacket with garden scene filling both the front and the back. Front of jacket: Emily | Dickinson [black] | A Brighter | Garden [teal] | Tasha Tudor | *Poetry collected by* | *Karen Ackerman* [black]. Spine: Dickinson / Tudor [black] A Brighter Garden [teal] Philomel [black]. Back of jacket text, black: ...Here *is a little forest,* | *Whose leaf is ever green;* | *Here is a brighter garden,* | *Where not a frost has been;* | *In its unfading flowers* | *I hear the bright bee hum;* | *Prithee, my brother,* | *Into my garden come!* UPC bar code at bottom center surmounted by ISBN 0-399-21490-9 | 90000 | and below, 9 780399 214905. Text of jacket flaps is all black. Front flap: $17.95 | [rule] | $23.50 CAN || Just a hundred years ago, the extraordi- | nary poetry of Emily Dickinson was pub- | lished for the first time. *A Brighter Garden* | celebrates this anniversary in a special col- | lection made particularly for young people | by Karen Ackerman and illustrated by re- | nowned artist Tasha Tudor. || There is a childlike innocence and sim- | plicity in Dickinson's work. Here, in po- | etry always personal and engaging, she | explores the seasons through the small- | est nuance: two Gabriels in a winter | tree, summer's busy bee, the "nobody" | of a spring pond, the apparel of autumn. | And it is this delicacy and subtlety of mo- | ment that Tasha Tudor touches so bril- | liantly in her moving cameo of watercolor | paintings. || This remarkable volume of twenty- | three poems and paintings, conceived by | Karen Ackerman and combining the ex- | traordinary talents of Emily Dickinson | and Tasha Tudor, is a book exquisite in its | artistry and interpretation, a classic to be | shared by generations. || Philomel Books | *a division of The Putnam & Grosset Group* | 200 Madison Avenue | New York, NY 10016 | 9010. Back flap: EMILY DICKINSON began writing as a | young woman, but was never published | in her own lifetime. Born in 1830 and | raised in Amherst, Massachusetts, she | wrote over seventeen hundred poems. It | was not until her death in 1886 that her | sister discovered a box containing nine | hundred of these poems. And in 1890, a | hundred years ago, *Poems of Emily Dickin-* | *son* was made available to the public by | Roberts Brothers of Boston. ‖ Artist TASHA TUDOR'S illustrations are | treasured by people of all ages. Among the | over sixty books she has illustrated are | *Give Us This Day* and *The Lord Is My* | *Shepherd*, as well as such classics as *The* | *Wind in the Willows* by Kenneth Grahame | and *Little Women* by Louisa May Alcott. | A New Englander like Emily Dickin- | son, Ms. Tudor has always felt an affinity | for the mid-1800s, the era in which Dick- | inson lived, and maintains her home in | that period. On a Vermont farm, not too | far from Dickinson's Amherst home, she | divides her time between chores, paint- | ing, and working in her own lush and | bountiful "brighter garden." ‖ Compiler KAREN ACKERMAN is the author | of over fifteen books for children and | young adults. Her book *Song and Dance* | *Man*, illustrated by Stephen Gammell, | won the esteemed Caldecott Award for | 1989. ‖ *Jacket art © 1990 by Tasha Tudor* | [rule] | *Reinforced for library use* ‖ Printed in Hong Kong.

CONTENTS: Half-title [1], Title page [3], colophon [4], dedication: *For Carly and Daniel,* | *and, with Possibility, for Carol.* | K A | *These illustrations are dedicated to Miss. Dickinson* | *with profound respect.* | T T [5], Introduction pp. 6-7, Index of First Lines 60-61. About Tasha Tudor, 63: Born in Boston in 1915, Tasha Tudor spent part of her childhood in rural | Connecticut and quickly discovered her love of the New England coun- | tryside and its simple life. Her mother, Rosamond Tudor, was a skilled | portrait artist, and her father, William Starling Burgess, was a brilliant | and innovative naval architect and pioneer in early aviation, as well as a | talented storyteller. Both parents encouraged and inspired their daughter | to pursue her love of painting, and at the age of twenty-three she published her first book, *Pumpkin Moonshine*. ‖ Since then she has continued to live and work in the old-fashioned and | rustic style that first attracted her as a child. The eighteenth-century New Hampshire farmhouse in which her four children were raised | provided many of the scenes and much of the inspiration for her books. | Both her children and grandchildren have served as models for Ms. | Tudor's illustrations, dressing up in vintage costumes from the attic. Her prized Welsh corgis have had a book, *Corgiville Fair*, devoted to them. ‖ Ms. Tudor has long felt a kinship with Emily Dickinson, sharing her | love and sensitivity for the ever-changing seasons and the natural world | around her. It has been a particular delight for Ms. Tudor to interpret the | poetry that she has loved and appreciated since she was a child.

ILLUSTRATIONS: Blank pages: [8, 22, 36, 48, 64, 22 oval water color illustrations measure 7⅛″ high x 6 1/8″ wide within a two-line border: [11, 13, 14, 17, 19, 21, 25, 26, 29, 30, 32, 35, 39, 41, 42, 45, 47, 50, 52, 55, 57, 59] Smaller ovals within a line border introduce the four seasons, frontispiece and page [62], 3 1/8″ high x 4 ½″ wide on pages [2, 9, 23, 37, 49, 62].

OTHER: The Index of First Lines lists 23 poems, but 'Here is a little forest' appears in the Introduction on page 6 and on the back of the jacket, not in the main body of the book.

Patricia Gauch, Tudor's editor at Philomel suggested that Tudor illustrate poems of Dickinson.

Corgi Cottage Industries, Spring 1998 catalog advertised a set of blank note cards (12 cards for $12.95) with three of the images from this book.

COPYRIGHT REGISTRATION: TX 2 898 361granted to Karen Ackerman, 1403 Corvalis Ave., Cincinnati, Oh. 45237. Louise Bates, agent for Karen Ackerman, swears on Sept. 5, 1990:

A BRIGHTER GARDEN, by Karen Ackerman, a U.S. citizen, as author of original text and editorial selection and compilation of public domain poems by Emily Dickinson, was published Sept. 5, 1990. The book is a derivative of Poems by Emily Dickinson in public domain. Library of Congress is granted non-exclusive permission to make copies and phonorecords for the blind and physically handicapped. Charge deposit account DAO38288, the Putnam Publishing Group, 200 Madison, Ave., N.Y., N.Y. 10016. Application and two deposit copies were received at L.C. Sept, 7, 1990, the effective date of registration.

COPYRIGHT REGISTRATION: VA 415 671 granted to Tasha Tudor, RFD #4, Box 205, Brattleboro, Vt. 05301. Louise Bates, agent for Tasha Tudor, swears on Sept. 5, 1990:

A BRIGHTER GARDEN, with illustrations by Tasha Tudor, a U.S. citizen, was published Sept. 5, 1990. Charge deposit account DAO38288, the Putnam Publishing Group, 200 Madison, Ave., N.Y., N.Y. 10016. Application and two deposit copies were received at L.C. Sept, 7, 1990, the effective date of registration.

B53 _____. Published simultaneously in Canada. Have not examined a copy.

B54 _____. [Original text … | Second impression]

> DUST JACKET: Varies only in the bar codes of the dust jacket. There is a single bar code on the back of the dust jacket beneath the ISBN, and below it, a new code, 0 48228 21490 8. The two bar code array with ISBN and matching numbers which were on the back of the first impression dust jacket, now appear on the front flap between "generations" and "Philomel Books."

B55 _____. [Original text … | ISBN 0-399-21490-9 | 4 6 8 10 9 7 5 3]

> DUST JACKET: Varies only in the price at top of front flap: $18.95 USA | [rule] | $25.50 CAN.

> OTHER: Verso of title page printed in changed type face.

B56 SAV 9050 | A BRIGHTER GARDEN | Poetry by Emily Dickinson | Compiled by Karen Ackerman| Narrated by Frances Sternhagen | 14:58 | Unauthorized reproduction prohibited by law | [rule] | **SPOKEN ARTS** ® | *Knowledge Through Multimedia* | [rule] | 801 94th Ave. N. • St. Petersburg, Florida 33702 • 1-800-326-4090.

> CONTENTS: 1/2″ videotape cassette accompanied by: **SA** | SPOKEN ARTS ® | [rule] | **A Brighter | Garden** | Poetry by Emily Dickinson | Collected by Karen Ackerman | Paintings by Tasha Tudor | [woman and girl in garden] | TEACHER'S GUIDE. | [rule] | 12pp. pamphlet in paper wrapper. Inside back cover: ENJOY THESE OTHER...Teacher's Guide Copyright © 1991, SPOKEN ARTS, INC.

B57 **A BRIGHTER GARDEN** | Emily Dickinson's Poetry Collected by Karen Ackerman | Narrated by Frances Sternhagen | Music by Wayne Abravanel | SAC | 6587 | Side One | 16:33 | With Tones | ISBN | 0-8045-6587-2 | Text copyright © 1990 by Karen Ackerman. | Reproduced with the permission of Philomel Books, | a division of The Putnam & Grosset Group. | **SA** | SPOKEN | [rule] | ARTS. Reverse is not visible without breaking shrink-wrap, but this is visible: ISBN | 0-8045-6587-2 | P SPOKEN ARTS, INC., 1991 | Unauthorized reproduction prohibited by law. | **SA** | SPOKEN | [rule] | ARTS.

> OTHER: This is an audiotape sold with a second edition of Ackerman's book, both in one plastic bag.

B58 Henry A. Shute || BRITE AND FAIR | A SEQUEL TO | THE REAL DIARY OF A REAL BOY || Illustrated by | Tasha Tudor || Noone House | PETERBOROUGH, NEW HAMPSHIRE | 1968. [COPYRIGHT © 1968 BY WILLIAM L. BAUHAN, INC. | LIBRARY OF CONGRESS CATALOG CARD NO. 68-22886 | ALL RIGHTS RESERVED || PUBLISHED BY WILLIAM L. BAUHAN, INC. AT | THE NOONE HOUSE, PETERBOROUGH, NEW | HAMPSHIRE (FORMERLY THE RICHARD R. | SMITH CO., INC.). THIS BOOK IS SET IN LINO- | TYPE OLD STYLE AND WAS PRINTED AND BOUND | BY THE COLONIAL PRESS, CLINTON, MASS., ON | PAPER PROVIDED BY THE MONADNOCK PAPER | COMPANY, BENNINGTON, N.H. | MANUFACTURED IN THE UNITED STATES OF AMERICA]

> PAGINATION: [i-iv] v [vi] vii-xii [xiii-xiv] 1-14 [15] 16-26 [27] 28-55 [56] 57-95 [96] 97-110 [111] 112-124 [125] 126-174 [175] 176-194 [195] 196-217 [218] 219-244 [245] 246-264 [265] 266-282 [283] 284-286 [287-290] 7 5/8″ x 5 3/8″.

COVER: Light blue cloth over board covers, stamped in black: script "Diry" on front; on the spine, SHUTE ‖ Brite and Fair (in a box) | Tasha | Tudor ‖ NOONE | HOUSE. Moss green endpapers carry same 2-page chalk sketch front and back: 2 children fishing from a boat in a river with village in background. Half-title: page [i].

DUST JACKET: Yellow dust jacket printed in navy and red. Front, a thin red line within a broader navy line border enclosing: Henry A. Shute | ANOTHER DIARY BY THE AUTHOR OF | THE REAL DIARY OF A REAL BOY (navy) | BRITE AND FAIR (red) ‖ [illustration from page [175] of "Plupy" in a tub] ‖ (red) ILLUSTRATED BY | Tasha Tudor. Spine text in red: SHUTE | Brite and Fair [in a black line box] | Tasha Tudor | [pen and inkwell sitting on a book] | NOONE HOUSE. Back text, red, WHAT THE CRITICS SAID ABOUT THE "REAL DIARY" ‖ [remaining text is navy] "One of the very few genuinely funny accounts of boyhood... | and that in this age is rare indeed. There isn't a dull page in the | book. Plupy Shute remains for all time the epitome of boyhood, | his adventures a joy to read forever." | —NEW BEDFORD STANDARD-TIMES ‖ "In these troublesome times, what a relief to savor the delightful | days of an age gone by. Plupy and his friends remind us that there | is a good case for 'boys being boys', and that perhaps we should | not be too discouraged if the present young ones don't always per- | form in accordance with the precepts of their elders." | —WALTER CRONKITE ‖ "One of the classics of New England boyhood, reissued in a | new format, and we've been enjoying again the same sort of laughs | as we did reading it some forty years ago. The publisher is con- | sidering reissuing _Brite and Fair_ and here is one New England | boy who certainly hopes he does." | — _NEW HAVEN REGISTER_ ‖ "Funnier that Mark Twain's _Huck Finn_ or _Tom Sawyer_ and it's | about time we let the public in on the secret." | —AL CAPP ‖ "Hoo Raw. A new edition of Plupy. With Pikchers. Buly. I | first read this book a long long time ago when I was at Exeter | Academy...I suppose since then I've read this dum book 25 times | and although it is a completely stoopid book, once started I can't | stop until I come to: "father hasn't asked once about my diry, so i | aint going to wright enny more."...Al Capp says this book is | funnier than Huck Finn or Tom Sawyer... _The Real Diary_ is way | beyond funny. It tells the story of a sweet forgotten America that | makes you want to cry, especially when you take a look at New | England today. The "funny" stuff is all about "fites" and bean shoot- | ers and getting licked and other antics...The real woolen goods | is the straight story this kid comes over with about 'How it really | was' in a small New England town in the mid-19th century." | — RICHARD BISSELL IN THE NEW YORK TIMES ‖ Jacket printed by Sim's Press, Inc. | Peterborough, N.H. Front flap: $4.50 [upper corner in navy. Next four lines and book title are printed in red.]   HENRY A. SHUTE'S | BRITE AND FAIR | Another diary by the author of | The Real Diary of a Real boy | _Brite and Fair_ [remaining text in navy] is a book about Plupy, | Beany and Pewt — "the Terible 3" — | growing up in Exeter, New Hampshire a | century ago — a good time and place to | be young in. ‖ It is also about some disgruntled citi- | zens whose cats were shipped off on the | night freight to Haverhill; and old Billy | Tilton who encountered a snapping tur- | tle suspended on his front door; and the | pious Mr. Barrows whose views about | the reading of _Wild Mag the Trapers_ | _Bride_ were dark indeed; and the discom- | fiture of some overweight ladies when | an eel attended the annual church pic- | nic; and J. Albert Clark who became the | unfortunate target of "the Terible 3". ‖ _Brite and Fair_ [in red] was actually, or so its | author implied, his own diary as an elev- | en-or-twelve-year-old boy — "discovered" | years later in the shed chamber of his | house in Exeter, New Hampshire. Plupy | Shute could spell only an occasional | word correctly, but he told what it's like | to be a boy with accuracy, with humor, | and some irreverent barbs at the preten- | sions of the adult world. ‖ The original edition of this book was | published some fifty years ago, has been | out-of-print for many years, and is now | revived with delightful illustrations by | Tasha Tudor. _Brite and Fair_ [not in red, but navy as is the bulk of text] continues | (_Continued on back flap_) | [Back flap text is mostly navy](_Continued from front flap_) ‖ the chronicles of Plupy which were be- | gun in the classic _Real Diary of a Real_ | _Boy_. When we reissued the _Real Diary_ | last year (also with drawings by Miss | Tudor), many nostalgic old timers wrote | to tell us this "diry" was even funnier. | We hope you'll agree. ‖ _Judge Henry Augustus Shute_ [in red] (1856- | 1943) who wore all his substantial fame | lightly, was by all accounts a delightful | man, and his writings have brought to | generations of readers, young and old, | a degree of pleasure remarkable both in | quantity and quality. A widely respected | jurist, a life-long resident of Exeter, and | an energetic member of the town band, | Judge Shute has been compared with | Mark Twain for his authentic and hum- | orous chronicles of boyhood. || *Tasha Tudor*, [in red] who illustrated the new | edition of *The Real Diary of a Real Boy* | last year, has enhanced this book with | another set of charming drawings. Miss | Tudor lives in New Hampshire on a farm | she manages herself. She is an expert | cook, an avid gardener, and the mother | of four children. But most of her many | friends know her — from book after book | —as one of the world's foremost illustra- | tors, a lady with a magic pencil. || This new edition of *Brite and Fair* has | a warm and appreciative foreword by | George A Woods, children's book editor | of *The New York Times*. | [A sketch of a colonial four-square house with two chimneys, two dormers and an ell [Noone House], and to the right: William L. Bauhan, Inc. | *NOONE HOUSE* | *Peterborough, New Hampshire*.

ILLUSTRATIONS: Twelve black and white drawings on the un-numbered Arabic pages [15, 27, 56, 96, 111, 125, 175, 195, 218, 245, 265, 283], plus a boy fishing, p. [ii], and the end papers. Pages [287-290] are blank.

OTHER: Typographical error last line of page viii: "where" for "were." Earlier editions had been illustrated by Worth Brehm. One unpublished Tudor pencil drawing of a tomato hitting an old gentleman right in the kisser seems inspired by Brehm's published illustration of the scene.

COPYRIGHT REGISTRATION: A31013 granted to William L. Bauhan, Inc. Publishers, Noone House, Peterborough, N.H. William L. Bauhan, President, swears on Oct. 28, 1968:

BRITE AND FAIR: A SEQUEL TO THE REAL DIARY OF A REAL BOY, by Henry A. Shute (deceased) 1856-1943, a U.S. citizen, was domiciled in Exeter, N.H., and Tasha Tudor (Illustrator) a US citizen of RFD, Contoocook, N.H., and William L. Bauhan, Publisher, a U.S. citizen, of Peterborough, N.H. was published October 15, 1968. New matter in this version are 14 illustrations plus endleaf by Tasha Tudor" New Foreword; New Front Matter. Small text changes on pages: 20, 21, 41, 85, 94, 100, 145, 148, 149, 150-151, 161, 162-63, 166-168, 171, 174, 177, 206, 217, 237, 242, 243, 248, 254. The book was printed by Colonial Press, Inc., Clinton, Ma, from new composition by Atlantic Typesetters, Boston, Ma. Application and two deposit copies were received at L.C. Nov. 1, 1968; affidavit received Nov.22, 1968.

COPYRIGHT REGISTRATION RENEWAL: RE-740-241 granted to Tasha Tudor, c/o Corgi Cottage Industries, P.O. Box 7281, Richmond, Va 23221-0281, claiming as author (illustrator). Kathryn L. Barrett, 235 East 22nd Street, Apt. 11C, New York, New York 10010, agent for Tasha Tudor, swears on June 21, 1996:

BRITE AND FAIR *by Henry A. Shute [a Copyright Office correction]. Tasha Tudor claims as author of the renewable matter: illustrations, editorial matter and revisions. The book was originally copyright October 15, 1968, under registration A31013 by William L. Bauhan, Inc. Renewal Application was received at LC August 9, 1996, the effective date of this registration. A Copyright Office worker has subsequently lined out the August 9, 1996 received date, and stamped in Dec 12, 1996, instead. Correspondence to be addressed to Kathryn L. Barrett, Esq., 212-684-6689.

B59 _____.

COVER: <u>Robin's egg blue</u> cloth cover. Spine: SHUTE | Brite and Fair (in a box) | Tasha | Tudor | WLB [5/8″ broad].

DUST JACKET: Yellow dust jacket printed in navy and red. Back text <u>all in navy</u> varies: <u>What the critics say about *The Real Diary of a Real Boy*... || "Us professional humorists have always known that Henry Shute's | *Real Diary of a Real Boy* was funnier than Mark Twain's *Huck Finn* | or *Tom Sawyer*, and it's about time we let the public in on the secret." | —AL CAPP</u> | "In these troublesome times, what a relief to savor the delightful | days of an age gone by. Plupy and his friends remind us that there | is a good case for 'boys being boys', and that perhaps we should | not be too discouraged if the present young ones don't always per- | form in <u>acordance</u> [*sic*] with the precepts of their elders." | —WALTER CRONKITE | "One of the classics of New England boyhood, reissued in a new | format, and we've been enjoying again the same sort of laughs as | we did reading it some forty years ago." | —NEW HAVEN REGISTER | "Hoo Raw. A new edition of Plupy. With Pikchers .... *The* | *Real Diary* is way beyond funny. The funny stuff is all about 'fites' | and bean shooters and getting licked and other antics.... The real | woolen goods is the straight story this kid comes over with about | 'How it really was' in a small New England town in the mid-19th | century."   — RICHARD BISSELL IN THE NEW YORK TIMES | ....and its sequel *Brite and Fair*: | "*Brite and Fair* is a delightful book ... recreating childhood life | in the 1860's. Plupy and his two friends have all the innocence, | imagination and ingenuity as they create havoc among the towns- | people and their own families." — PUBLISHER'S WEEKLY || *Brite and Fair* adds up to a fine and funny helping of nostalgia | for the simple, sunny summer days of old-time America. | —THE NEW YORK TIMES || "Tasha Tudor's illustrations capture perfectly the feeling of the | diary." — PROVIDENCE JOURNAL || *Both editions available from* | William L. Bauhan Publisher, Dublin, New Hampshire | (formerly Richard R. Smith Co., Noone House, Peterborough, N.H.) Front flap identical to B44; corner is clipped removing the price. Back flap varies only that a William L. Bauhan, Inc. and black bar overprint the previous statement: NOONE HOUSE | Peterborough, New Hampshire.

OTHER: One probably will never find this state, nor the next, without clipped corners on dj. The corners were clipped to remove the original $ 4.50 price.

B60 _____.

COVER: The same light blue cloth as B54 above, not like B55. The WLB at base of spine is a smaller closer spaced type measuring 7/16" across. (71/2" x 53/8")

DUST JACKET: New line of black text beneath the bar bottom of dj back flap: $8.95 / 0-87233-003-6

C1 *Carrie's Gift* | EFNER TUDOR HOLMES | Illustrated by TASHA TUDOR || COLLINS + WORLD | *New York and Cleveland* [**Library of Congress Cataloging in Publication Data** || Holmes, Efner Tudor. Carrie's gift. || SUMMARY: Carrie's attempts to befriend the | dour old man on the neighboring farm are resisted | until they save her dog from a trap together. | [1.Friendship—Fiction. 2.Country life—Fic- | tion] | I. Tudor, Tasha. II. Title. | PZ7.H735Car   [Fic]   78-8452 | ISBN 0-529-05428-0 | ISBN 0-529-05429-9 lib. bdg. || Published by William Collins + World Publishing Company, | New York and Cleveland, 1978. || Text Copyright © 1978 by Efner Tudor Holmes | Illustrations copyright © 1978 by Tasha Tudor | All rights reserved. | Printed in the United States of America.]

PAGINATION: 2 signatures of white paper, [28] pp. including free endpapers. Title page [3], half-title [5], text [6-27]. 7 1/4" x 7 5/8"

COVER: Yellow paper over board covers. Large illustration on front: Carrie and berry basket on rock, with dog. Text in black, above illustration: *Carrie's Gift*; and below: EFNER TUDOR HOLMES   Illustrated by TASHA TUDOR. Spine: Holmes/Tudor   CARRIE'S GIFT   Collins + World. Back cover: berry basket and daisies above center; at lower right: ISBN 529-05428-0 | 529-05429-9 (Lib. bdg.)

DUST JACKET: Reproduces the cover. Front flap: ISBN 529 05428-0 $5.95 || Why was Old Duncan so unfriendly? | Carrie and her brothers sometimes | caught a glimpse of their mysterious | neighbor, but he never talked to them. | The old man spoke only to the animals | that visited his yard; he had no human | friends. But, on a chance encounter | with him in the woods, Carrie thought | she glimpsed loneliness beneath Dun- | can's gruff manner. And when Carrie's | dog Heidi brings them together in an | emergency, Carrie has a chance to see | if she is right. ¶ This poignant account of a child's | spontaneous and natural reaching-out | to an older person is told in a quiet | prose that is all the more moving for | being simply-stated. Carrie's gift is | really a gift of love, of trust. This is a | story of the kind of small miracle that | can be wrought in human nature by the | affection of a child. It is given a perfect | setting by the sensitive and expressive | watercolor illustrations of Tasha |Tudor. [A 3 ¼" x 1 1/2" triangle has been snipped from the lower corner of every jacket I've seen. - *Ed.*] Back flap: ABOUT THE AUTHOR || Efner Tudor Holmes grew up in the | New England countryside of which | she writes so convincingly. The young- | est of Tasha Tudor's four children, she | finds writing and drawing a natural | part of her life. With her husband and | three young children, she lives on a | real farm in New Hampshire. This is | her third book. || ABOUT THE ARTIST || Tasha Tudor's beautiful evocations of | the New England landscape, people, | animals, and traditional way of life | have brought her widespread fame and | admiration. Her stories and pictures | based on her own family's very individ- | ual lifestyle are particularly beloved. In | addition to CARRIE'S GIFT, she also | illustrated Efner Tudor Holmes' two | earlier books. She is the author of | TAKE JOY! and more than twenty | other books, and she has, in addition, | illustrated many of the world's great | classics of children's literature, such as | THE WIND IN THE WILLOWS and | LITTLE WOMEN. Ms. Tudor lives in | Vermont. || COLLINS + WORLD | *New York and Cleveland.*

ILLUSTRATIONS: Twenty-four watercolor illustrations including covers. Each endpaper carries the same strawberry plant. Pages [2, 9, 13, 21, 25] and endpapers have only illustrations; pages [3-5, 12, 20] have only text.

OTHER: The book was named for Holmes' young niece Carrie, and the dog is her own Feisty. *Cf. The Concord Monitor*, December 8, 1978.

C2 _____.

COVER: <u>Linen imprinted yellow paper</u> over boards. All cover stamping in <u>red ink</u>: on front, Carrie's Gift; spine, Holmes/Tudor   CARRIE'S GIFT   Collins + World; back cover lower right, A STORYCRAFT BOOK | ISBN 529-05429-9 RB.

DUST JACKET: Outside of dust jacket as above with the addition of a ¾ x 3 ¾″ <u>gold foil label</u> wrapping from the front around the spine and onto the back, near the bottom. The label is printed with black ink, on the front: CWLB | COLLINS + WORLD LIBRARY BINDING, and five lines printed sidewise on the spine and back, CWLB | CWLB | CWLB | CWLB | CWLB. In this library binding the top corner has been clipped leaving the bottom corner intact with: <u>ISBN 529 05429-9 Lib $6.49</u>. This is an example of a jacket being printed with two prices for both trade and library bindings. The top or bottom corner of the front flap was clipped accordingly.

OTHER: <u>Library binding, topsewn.</u>

C3 *Childcraft* | IN FOURTEEN VOLUMES | • | VOLUME ONE | POEMS OF EARLY CHILDHOOD |
[painting of three children and a dog listening to "Mother Goose] | **FIELD ENTERPRISES, INC.,** | **CHICAGO.** [Childcraft | (Reg. U.S. Pat. Off.) || Copyright 1949, U.S.A. | by Field Enterprises, Inc. | Copyright 1947, 1945, 1942, 1939 by The Quarrie Corporation | Copyright 1937, 1935, 1934 by W. F. Quarrie & Company || THE CHILD'S TREASURY | Copyright 1931, 1923 by W. F. Quarrie & Company || International Copyright 1949 | by Field Enterprises, Inc. | International Copyright 1947 | by The Quarrie Corporation | [rule] | All rights reserved. This volume may not be | reproduced in whole or in part in any form | without written permission from the publishers. | [rule] | *Printed in the U.S.A.* | EBB]

COVER: All covers are an orange pebbled cloth, blank on the back and with different black, white and blue painted front cover illustrations on each volume. Matching spines have two sets of stripes in the upper and lower thirds of the spine. These are alternating blue-orange-white-orange thin stripes above and below a wide black band. CHILD- | CRAFT is printed in gilt on the upper black band throughout the set. A single gilt volume number is stamped on an orange band halfway down each spine. The black band in the lower grouping is stamped in gilt with a specific volume title in each case.

ILLUSTRATIONS: Volume 1 POEMS OF EARLY CHILDHOOD has four pages with paintings by Tasha Tudor. The illustrations are similar in style to those of MOTHER GOOSE in 1944, although these are new renditions. Page 54, HERE WE GO ROUND THE MULBERRY BUSH. Page 55, MARY'S LAMB by Sarah Josepha Hale. Here Tudor has signed her name on a schoolhouse slate and left it sitting on a desk. Page 144, HALFWAY DOWN. Page [145], VESPERS.

OTHER: We have seen evidence of another printing bearing the code DIA rather than EBB on the verso of the title page. Tudor is listed among 108 CONTRIBUTING ARTISTS on page [5]. These few examples are classic Tudor paintings featuring her telling humor, antique detailing and lovely New Hampshire color. She paints a volume of Beatrix Potter lying on the stairs beside the little boy "Halfway down." Christopher Robin peeks through his fingers while saying his prayers. True little treasures hidden in a much larger work.

COPYRIGHT REGISTRATION: A 11377 granted to The Quarrie Corporation, 35 East Wacker Drive, Chicago 1, Illinois. J. Morris Jones, agent for claimant, swears on March 20, 1947:

> CHILDCRAFT (in 14 volumes), retail price $59.50, by The Quarrie Corporation, Editorial Department, J. Morris Jones, managing Editor, a US citizen of Chicago born 1896 was published March 10, 1947. The book was printed and bound by Kingsport Press, Inc., Kingsport, Tenn. from type set by American Typesetting Corp., Chicago, Illinois, and Kingsport Press, Inc., Kingsport, Tenn. Application and affidavit were received at L.C. March 22, 1947; and two deposit copies March 16, 1947. Remittance no. 23641, March 26, 1947. This is "A new edition of a previously published book," to wit: approximately two-thirds of the material contained in volumes 9, 10, 11 and 12 (numbered 7, [illegible] and 12, respectively, in previous edition) has been entirely replaced with new text [illegible]; approximately 80 percent of the illustrations in these volumes has been replaced with new ones; and all four volumes have been completely re-set in a new type face and were [illegible] 3 new pages of text material have been added to each of volumes 7 and 8 (numbered 11 and 10 respectively, in previous edition.)

COPYRIGHT RENEWAL REGISTRATION: R 578611 granted to Field Enterprises Educational Corporation, 510 merchandise Mart Plaza, Chicago, Illinois 60654, claiming as proprietor of copyright in a work made for hire. H. M. Ross, secretary, swears [no date]:

> CHILDCRAFT (in 14 volumes), by J. Morris Jones of United States, Managing Editor, The Quarrie Corporation, was originally registered A 11377 and published March 10, 1947. The original copyright claimant was The Quarrie Corporation. Fee received at L.C. June 7, 1974.

Field Enterprises, Inc., 35 East Wacker Drive, Chicago, Illinois, also copyrighted (A 55160) CHILDCRAFT ..... A Complete and Integrated Plan of Child Guidance for Young Children, Their Parents, and Their Teachers, May 2, 1951.

c4 A I CHILD'S I GARDEN I OF I VERSES ‖ by I *Robert Louis Stevenson* ‖ *with pictures by* I *Tasha Tudor* ‖ NEW YORK [pansy plant] 1947 I OXFORD UNIVERSITY PRESS {all within a floral oval} [Copyright 1947 I OXFORD UNIVERSITY PRESS | New York, Inc. ‖ PRINTED IN THE UNITED STATES OF AMERICA]

PAGINATION: Eight signatures on buff matte paper: [1-12] 13-14 [15] 16-22 [23] 24-30 [31] 32-34 [35] 36-42 [43] 44-46 [47] 48-50 [51] 52-54 [55] 56-62 [63] 64-69 [70-72] 73-78 [79] 80-82 [83] 84-86 [87] 88-90 [91-92] 93-98 [99] 100-102 [103] 104-106 [107-108] 109-110 [111] 112-118 [119-120] pages plus endpapers. This book is always printed and bound so that the pasted endpapers are actually the first leaf of the first signature and the last leaf of the last signature. Threads binding the signatures are visible in the front and back gutters when the book is opened. 8 ½" x 6 ¼".

COVER: Dark green cloth cover; with a 4 ¼" x 3 5/8" paper label mounted in a blind-stamped indention on the front cover, calligraphic title in an oval of yellow primroses: A I *CHILD'S* I *GARDEN* | [a primrose plant] | *OF* I *VERSES*. Spine stamped in gilt: STEVENSON A CHILD'S GARDEN OF VERSES OXFORD. Each ivory end paper has a different colored illustration: an oval of heather framing a child in a garden.

DUST JACKET: Buff paper, printing in black. Front reproduces text of title page, less publisher, place and year, within an oval of lavender tied at the top with a green ribbon and supported by a boy

[Little Rob Tenery eating bread and butter]

and girl standing on either side of a sun dial in a garden. Same primrose from cover label appears on back of jacket. Spine: STEVENSON   A CHILD'S GARDEN OF VERSES OXFORD. Front flap has both corners slightly clipped, with no loss of text: A CHILD'S GARDEN | OF VERSES || *By Robert Louis Stevenson* || *Illustrated by Tasha Tudor* || One of the happy events of childhood | is one's first introduction to *A Child's | Garden of Verses*. Through succeeding | generations these poems continue to be | part of the heritage of all American | and English children. Stevenson's | memory of his own childhood never | grew dim, and because he was a poet | he was able to share with children the | happiness and wonder of his early | years. ¶ Tasha Tudor has loved these poems | always and has now given us one of | their loveliest interpretations. Through | the pages of this volume she has por- | trayed the same dark-haired, bright- | eyed small boy who might indeed be | R.L.S. || **OXFORD BOOKS** | **for BOYS and GIRLS** || $2.50. Back flap also has corners slightly clipped, so that a small portion of a 3 ½ " x 2 ½ " photograph of Tudor (by Nell Dorr, although not ascribed) has been trimmed at the top. This text: TASHA TUDOR is already beloved by | many children. They have had her | *Mother Goose* as one of their first books. | Her tiny *Calico Books* about Sylvie | Ann are just right to slip into a pocket, | and her *Tale for Easter* and *Snow Be- | fore Christmas* are part of these holi- | days' pleasures. *The White Goose* and | her pictures for *Hans Christian Ander- | sen* have the true fairy-tale quality. ¶ Ever since she was very small, Tasha | Tudor has made tiny books. Before she | was married, [*sic*] her first book, *Pumpkin | Moonshine*, which started the *Calico | Book* series, was published. Now she | has three children and lives in an old | house in New Hampshire. It is filled | with lovely old things and has the same | atmosphere of warmth and happiness | that her pictures have. Many of the | scenes in her books are glimpses of her | own home and the lovely countryside | that surrounds it. [There is no ascription for the photograph on the dust jacket, but it is obviously by Nell Dorr from the MOTHER AND CHILD period. The jacket is in error regarding marriage. Thomas McCready and Tasha Burgess were married May 28, 1938; *Pumpkin Moonshine* was published three months later, September 15. - *Ed.*]

CONTENTS: Title page [3]; dedication, To | Allison Cunningham | From Her Boy...R.L.S. [5]; Contents [7-10].   Registration marks are often showing on pages [3], 59, 67.

ILLUSTRATIONS: Section titles on full page color illustrations in 6 ½ x 5 " oval frames: pp. [11, 71, 91, 107] Full page color illustrations in oval frames to accompany poems: pp. [15, 23, 31, 35, 43, 47, 51, 55, 63, 79, 83, 87, 99, 103, 111] Black and white illustrations (tulips, Jack-in-the-pulpit and geraniums) only on pages: [1, 72, 119]. Black and white illustrations accompany text on pages: [5, 7, 9] 13, 16, 18, 20, 25-26, 29, 33, 36, 39-40, 45, 48, 52, 57, 59-60, 65-66, 69, 74, 77, 80, 84, 88, 93, 95, 97, 100, 104, 109, 113, 117-118. Blank pages: [2, 6, 12, 70, 92, 108, 120] Page [118] pictures a girl, sitting on a cushion, reading what might be a copy of this book. The sundial on page 48 is the same as the one from the front cover.

The color plates show the influence of H. Willebeek Le Mair in *OUR OLD NURSERY RHYMES*, 1911. Tudor mirrors Le Mair's borders of tightly spaced repeating floral designs. See examples in *The Glorious MOTHER GOOSE*, Selected by Cooper Edens with illustrations by the best artists from the past. N.Y., Atheneum, 1988.

The boy on page 33 is drawn from Nell Dorr's photograph of her grandson Rob Tenery. See *Mother and Child*, p. [64].

Compare the similarity of the wallpaper on page 83 to the Art Guild Greetings, Inc., Heritage No. P643 greeting card.

OTHER: Have examined a copy with Tudor's personalized inscription in which she regrets not being able to write like Stevenson, but states her love and gratitude to her nanny Dady.

COPYRIGHT REGISTRATION: A 17117 granted to Oxford University Press, New York, Inc., 114 Fifth Ave., N.Y. 11, N.Y. Henry Z. Walck, agent for claimant, swears on Sept. 25, 1947:

A CHILD'S GARDEN OF VERSES, retail price $2.50, by Tasha Tudor, Contoocook, Webster, N.H., [*sic*] born approx. 1914, a U.S. citizen, was published September 25, 1947. The book was printed by Kipe Offset Company from type set by the Kipe Offset Company, N.Y., N.Y., and bound by American Book-Stratford Press, N.Y., N.Y. Application and affidavit were received at L.C. Sept. 26, 1947; and two deposit copies Sept -7, 1947 [*sic*]. Walck did not check the box indicating this to be "A new edition of a previously published book," nor did he "give title and author of original publication. . .and a brief statement of the nature of the new matter in this edition:"

COPYRIGHT RENEWAL REGISTRATION: R 613505 granted to Tasha Tudor, Marlboro, Vt. 05344, author/artist. Barbara L. Dammann, agent for Henry Z. Walck, 750 Third Ave., N.Y., N.Y. 10017, failed to sign the certificate swearing:

A CHILD'S GARDEN OF VERSES, by Tasha Tudor, was originally registered A 17117 and published September 25, 1947. The original copyright claimant was Henry Z. Walck, Inc. However, this company's name has been X'ed out and above it typed, Oxford University Press, Inc.* A note at the bottom of the certificate indicates this amendment was typed by the Copyright Office. Registration fee to be charged against Walck, Henry Z. Inc. #6694. Application was received at L.C. Sept. 4, 1975. There is no record that a fee was received.

C5 _____.

COVER: The cloth is slightly more khaki green.

C6 _____.

COVER: The cloth is coarser, dark-green.

C7 _____.

COVER: The cloth is coarser, moss-green.

C8 _____.

COVER: Forest green cloth.

DUST JACKET: Stephanie Clayton reports a copy with a jacket price of $3.00.

C9 *A | CHILD'S | GARDEN | OF | VERSES* | *by* | *Robert Louis Stevenson* | *with pictures by* | *Tasha Tudor* | [pansy plant] | *HENRY Z. WALCK, INC.* [Copyright 1947 | **HENRY Z. WALCK, INC.** || **Library of Congress Catalog Card Number: 59-8079** || PRINTED IN THE UNITED STATES OF AMERICA]

COVER: Sea green cloth, courser weave than Oxford editions. The green ink of the label is lighter than originally. Spine stamped in gilt: STEVENSON   A CHILD'S GARDEN OF VERSES   WALCK.

DUST JACKET: Have not examined a copy.

OTHER: Examined one with a Christmas 1959 inscription.

C10 _____.

PAGINATION: Eight signatures on a courser ivory paper.

COVER: Mint green cloth, cheesecloth weave.

DUST JACKET: Buff paper, printing in black. Spine: STEVENSON   A CHILD'S GARDEN OF VERSES   WALCK.   Front flap: **A CHILD'S GARDEN | OF VERSES** | . . . small boy who might indeed be | R.L.S. || HENRY Z. WALCK, INC. | *successor to* | OXFORD BOOKS FOR BOYS AND

GIRLS. [Have not examined a copy with front flap corners present.] Back flap has corners slightly clipped: Other books | by Tasha Tudor || MOTHER GOOSE || FIRST GRACES | FIRST PRAYERS || A IS FOR ANNABELLE | AROUND THE YEAR | 1 IS ONE || ALEXANDER THE GANDER | THE COUNTY FAIR | DORCAS PORKUS | LINSEY WOOLSEY | PUMPKIN MOONSHINE.

CONTENT: Although text and pagination are identical to the first edition, the quality of the color plates is diminished with poorer detail. Plates are often out of registration on the front end papers and pp. [3], [11].

C11 _____.

PAGINATION: Smoother ivory paper. ½″ thick.

COVER: Mint green cloth. Free endpapers are often out-of-registration.

DUST JACKET: Front upper corner clipped. Front flap: **A CHILD'S GARDEN** . . . HENRY Z. WALCK, INC. || $3.75

OTHER: Examined a copy inscribed: Jan. 30, 1963.

C12 _____.

COVER: Bright green cloth, without the label, gilt spine stamping on spine as before. Endpapers out of registration.

DUST JACKET: Front flap, upper corner clipped. Price changed to $ 4.25. Back flap: **FAIRY TALES | from | Hans Christian Andersen** || *Illustrated by Tasha Tudor* || "★★ Tasha Tudor has selected thirty- | one of her favorite Andersen tales to | illustrate. Ten exquisite illustrations in | color and thirty-one in black and white | and a beautiful design make this a gift | book to be cherished by young and old. | The E.V. Lucas translation has been | used for the majority of the tales, that | of the Oxford Standard Authors for | the balance. . . One of the truly dis- | tinguished books . . ."—*Library Journal*.

C13 _____. [Copyright 1947, Henry Z. Walck, Inc. ISBN: 0-8098-1902-3. Library of Congress | Catalog Card Number: 59-8079. Printed in the United States of America.]

PAGINATION: Four signatures buff kid paper.

COVER: Bright green pebbled plastic-filled paper over boards, no front label, spine printed in black.

DUST JACKET: Front flap: lower corner clipped; the upper corner is present with no printing. Back flap text reset: *Books illustrated* | *by Tasha Tudor* | FIRST GRACES | FIRST PRAYERS | *Catholic and Protestant* | MORE PRAYERS | MOTHER GOOSE | A CHILD'S GARDEN OF VERSES | *by Robert Louis Stevenson* || *Books written and illustrated* | *by Tasha Tudor* | A IS FOR ANNABELLE | AROUND THE YEAR | THE COUNTY FAIR | THE DOLLS' CHRISTMAS | 1 IS ONE | PUMPKIN MOONSHINE | A TALE FOR EASTER | THISTLY B.

OTHER: This would have been printed after September 20, 1967, the publication date for *More Prayers* referred to on the dust jacket.

C14 A | Child's Garden | of Verses || by Robert Louis Stevenson | Illustrated by Tasha Tudor | [boy, girl and sundial in a garden] | Rand McNally & Company | Chicago • New York • San Francisco [[child with dandelion] | To me, fair friend, you never can be old, | For as you were when first your eye I ey'd, | Such seems your beauty still. | *Shakespeare's Sonnet CIV* || Library of Congress Cataloging in Publication Data | Stevenson, Robert Louis, 1850-1894. | A child's garden of verses. || Summary: A collection of poems evoking the world and | feelings of childhood. | 1. Children's poetry, English. [1. English poetry] | I. Tudor, Tasha. II. Title | PR5489.C5 1981

821'.8 81-7317 | ISBN 0-528-82401-5 AACR2 | ISBN 0-528-80073-6 (lib. bdg.) || Copyright © 1981 by Rand McNally & Company | All rights reserved | Printed in the United States of America by Rand McNally & Company | First printing, 1981]

PAGINATION: Four signatures and a center gathering [1-3] 4 [5-9] 10-67 [68-72] pages including covers. 12″ x 9 3/8″.

COVER: White paper over boards stamped with a fine weave and printed with large garden scenes. Black text, front: A | Child's Garden | of Verses || by Robert Louis Stevenson | Illustrated by Tasha Tudor. Spine: A Child's Garden of Verses Stevenson • Tudor Rand McNally. Back cover, upper left: 528-82401-5. End papers each carry a different garden scene in a twig border.

CONTENTS: Dedication, page [7]. Page [68]: **Robert Louis Stevenson . . .** [Two paragraphs] Page [69]: **Tasha Tudor** | Scenes set in the nineteenth century — dress, interiors, toys, | activities drawn with loving attention to detail—are the hallmark | of Tasha Tudor's artwork. It is singularly appropriate, then, that | her talents should be here joined to those of the poet who wrote | so poignantly of childhood in that period. || Tasha Tudor shares with Stevenson, too, loving memories of a | devoted Scottish nanny. Stevenson had his "Cummy." Tasha | Tudor had her "Dady," Mary Denny Burnett, the nurse who cared | for her in infancy and childhood, sang the old Scottish songs to | her, accompanied her to dancing class and parties. "She lavished | a world of love on me," Tasha Tudor recalls. || Tasha Tudor was born in New England, her father a naval | architect, her mother a portrait painter. She has remained | faithful to her roots and today makes her home on a Vermont | farm, surrounded by the antiques she loves, pets of every | description, and gardens that bloom in artful profusion. One of | the most loved artists of our day, she has illustrated nearly | seventy books, among them THE NIGHT BEFORE CHRISTMAS, | A TIME TO KEEP, and THE SPRINGS OF JOY. | She was recently | awarded an honorary doctorate of humane letters by the | University of Vermont for her contributions to the field of | illustration.

ILLUSTRATIONS: Most pages carry text and illustrations within a 9 x 7″ twig border. Only page [8] which is most of the Table of Contents lacks illustration.

OTHER: Examined a copy which has been stamped on front fly leaf in red: REGISTER OF COPYRIGHTS | LIBRARY OF CONGRESS | WASHINGTON, D.C. || Certificate No. TX 1-028-347. The number itself has been written in hand. There are two publisher's gummed price labels on the upper right of front cover: gold, masked in black to reveal $7^{95}.

COPYRIGHT REGISTRATION: TX 1-028-347 granted to Rand McNally & Company, P.O. Box 7600, Chicago, Il. 60680. Arlene Clark, Mgr. Contracts & Copyrights and agent for Rand McNally & Company, 312-673-9100 Ext. 421, swears on [no date]:

A CHILD'S GARDEN OF VERSES, completed in 1980, illustrations by Tasha Tudor, a U.S. citizen, was published August 1, 1981. The book is derived from A CHILD'S GARDEN OF VERSES (in the public domain) with new illustrations and biographical information about the author and illustrator. The book was manufactured by Rand McNally & Company, Versailles, Ky. Fees to be charged against account DA 019712, Rand McNally & Company. Application and two deposit copies were received at L.C. Oct. 19, 1982. A second stamp on the application received line reads Dec. 23, 1982.

C15 _____. [To me . . . ISBN 0-528-82401-5 AARC2 Copyright © 1981 by Rand McNally & Company | All rights reserved | Printed in the United States of America by Rand McNally & Company | First printing, 1981 | Second printing, 1983]

PAGINATION: Five signatures.   12″ x 9 1/4″.

COVER: Black on gold gummed label (3/8 X 3/4″) at top right front: $9.95.

C16 _____. [To me . . . ISBN 0-528-82401-5 AARC2 Copyright © 1981 by Rand McNally & Company | All rights reserved | Printed in the United States of America by Rand McNally & Company | First printing, 1981 | <u>Second printing, 1985</u> | <u>Printed in Italy</u>]

PAGINATION: Six signatures. 12″ x 9 3/16″

COVER: Cover is continuous <u>gloss film laminate</u> over illustrated paper over boards. Black on gold gummed label (3/8 X 3/4″) at top right front: <u>$9.95</u>.

C17 _____. Have not examined a 3rd Rand McNally printing. Considering that the previous entry really was the third appearance, it is probable the error was corrected in the next entry and that no numbered third printing actually exists.

C18 _____. [To me . . . ISBN 0-528-82401-5 AARC2 Copyright © 1981 by Rand McNally & Company | All rights reserved || First printing, 1981 | <u>Second printing 1983</u> | <u>Third printing, 1985</u> | <u>Fourth printing, 1985</u> || <u>Printed in Italy</u>]

PAGINATION: <u>Page [4] is not numbered</u>.

COVER: Gold and black seal, upper right front cover: $ 9⁹⁵.

C19 A | Child's Garden | of Verses || by Robert Louis Stevenson | Illustrated by Tasha

Tudor [checked open book logo] CHECKERBOARD PRESS | NEW YORK   [[Child with dandelions] To me...*Shakespeare's Sonnet CIV* || Copyright © 1981 <u>Checkerboard Press, a division of Macmillan, Inc.</u> 098765 | Checkerboard Press and colophon are trademarks of Macmillan, Inc. All rights reserved. | No part of this book may be reproduced or transmitted in any form or by any means, | electronic or mechanical, including photocopying, recording, or by any | information storage | and retrieval system, without permission in writing from the Publisher. || <u>Printed in Italy</u>]

PAGINATION: <u>Six</u> signatures. <u>[1-9]</u> 10-67 [68-72] pages including front and back covers. <u>Page 4 is not numbered in this printing</u>. 12″ x 9 3/8″.

COVER: Black on gold gummed label (3/4″) at top right front: <u>$ 12.95</u>. Back, lower left: <u>UPC bar code [3/4″x1″]</u> | <u>0 14121 89093 8</u> | <u>ISBN 0-02-689093-3</u> [smaller type fits entire ISBN under the bar code]. Spine with new publisher: <u>CHECKERBOARD PRESS,</u> [open book logo].

OTHER: For the first time, the colophon is printed as a rectangular block of type near the bottom of page [6].

C20 _____. [[girl with dandelion] | To me... |<u>Printed in U.S.A.</u>]

PAGINATION: Five signatures. [<u>1-3</u>] 4 [<u>5-9</u>] 10-67 [68-72] pages including front and back covers. <u>Page 4 is numbered</u>.

COVER: Back cover, lower left: [UPC bar code [1″X1¼″] | 0 14121 89093 8 | ISBN 0-02-689093-3 [in large 'computer type']].   .

CONTENTS: For the first time, <u>there is no statement of publisher on the title page</u>.

C21 _____. Have not examined a 1st Macmillan printing. The second Checkerboard imprint may constitute the "first Macmillan."

C22 _____. [[Child with dandelions] To me...*Shakespeare's Sonnet CIV* | Copyright © 1981<u>, Macmillan Publishing Company</u>. | All rights reserved. No part of this book may be reproduced or | transmitted in any form or by any means, electronic or | mechanical, including photocopying, recording, or by any | information storage and retrieval system, without permission in | writing from the Publisher. | <u>Macmillan Publishing Company</u> | <u>866 Third Avenue</u> | <u>New York, NY 10022</u> | <u>Maxwell Macmillan Canada, Inc.</u> | <u>1200 Eglinton Avenue East</u> | <u>Suite 200</u> | <u>Don Mills, Ontario M3C 3N1</u> | <u>Macmillan Publishing Company is part of the Maxwell Communication</u> | <u>Group of Companies.</u> | <u>ISBN 0-02-788365-5</u> | <u>Printed in the United States of America</u> | 10 9 8 7 6 5 4 3 2]

PAGINATION: <u>Two</u> signatures and one folded sheet between them.

129

COVER: Back cover, lower left: <u>90000></u> | [2 UPC bar codes   7/8 "x 1 ¾"] | <u>9 780027 883657</u> | <u>ISBN 0-02-788365-5</u> [in large 'computer type']. A black circle label with $13.95 at upper right back cover near gutter. Spine has new publisher <u>MACMILLAN</u>.

C23 _____.   [Child with dandelions] To me...*Shakespeare's Sonnet CIV* || [Sower logo] | SIMON & SCHUSTER BOOKS FOR YOUNG READERS | An imprint of Simon & Schuster Children's Publishing Division | 1230 Avenue of the Americas | New York, New York 10020 || Copyright © 1981 by Macmillan Publishing Company | All rights reserved including the right of reproduction | in whole or in part in any form. | Simon & Schuster Books for Young Readers is a trademark of Simon & Schuster || ISBN 0-02-788365-5 || Printed in the United States of America | 10 9 8 7 6 5 4 3]

PAGINATION: <u>Three</u> signatures.   12" x 9 ¼".

COVER: Back cover, <u>upper right: $14.00 U.S. | $19.00 CAN</u>]. Spine has new publisher: [logo[Simon & Schuster.

OTHER: Printed about 1995?

C24 _____.   [[Child with dandelions] To me... United States of America | 10 9 8 7 6 5 4]]

PAGINATION: <u>Two</u> signatures.   12" x 9 ¼".

COVER: Back cover, <u>upper right: $15.00 U.S. | $20.00 CAN</u>].

OTHER: Printed 1997?   Purchased new January 1998.

C25 **Chip | the Chipmunk** | [brown and green illustration, chipmunk eating a pine cone] BY JESSIE BROWN MARSH | PICTURES BY BETHANY TUDOR || THE BETHANY PRESS   ST. LOUIS, MISSOURI [COPYRIGHT © 1962, BY THE BETHANY PRESS || LIBRARY OF CONGRESS CATALOG CARD NO. 61-16511. || DISTRIBUTED IN AUSTRALASIA BY THE AUSTRAL | PRINTING AND PUBLISHING COMPANY, MELBOURNE, | AND IN CANADA BY THE G.R. WELCH COMPANY, | TORONTO. || Manufactured in the United States of America]

PAGINATION: [1-4] 5-14 [15] 16-24 [25] 26-41 [42] 43-54 [55] 56-66 [67] 68-75 [76] 77-92 [93] 94-95 [96], plus endpapers. 6 signatures of ivory paper. 6 ¼ x 8 1/8 " x 7/16."

COVER: Green-brown linen over boards. Front cover has a brown illustration of 'Chip' curled up asleep in a ball, the same illustration as printed on page [96]. Spine, printed in brown: *Marsh* Chip the Chipmunk   [𝕭 logo of Bethany Press]. Yellow endpapers printed with seven chipmunks and a clump of grass.

DUST JACKET: Ivory dust jacket printed in brown and green, black type. **Chip** [chipmunk on a rock, from page 15] | **the Chipmunk** || [chipmunk on a root, half of the illustration from page 42] **by Jessie Brown Marsh** | *Illustrated by* | *Bethany Tudor*. Spine reproduces the book spine. Back cover, two chipmunks with pine cones, the illustration from page [67], and in the lower right corner: 10C830. Front flap: $2.50 | **Chip | the | Chipmunk** | by Jessie Brown Marsh | A twinkling whimsical story about a | delightfully impish chipmunk, his | friends, cousins, and adventures . . . | a lively little book. ¶Chip loves to play. He romps with Mickey, he scampers around | with his cousin Stripey, and he | watches Flay-Away whiz through the | air. Every day he plays the exciting | "get-up" game with his "special" | friend, the lady, who lives near the | lake. ¶Chip's life is not all fun, however. | One night he is awakened by an | earthquake's fearsome roar and | rumble. His cozy burrow is buried | by the shifting earth, and his winter | supply of nuts is lost. In replacing | them, Chip learns to work hard and | help himself. ¶Small readers will be enchanted | with the way Chip and the other | animals solve their problems, and | with the way in which Chip and | Mickey hitch-hike in the big red car | to a new home where peanuts are | plentiful and burrow digging easy. Rear flap: litho in U.S.A. || **about the author** | JESSIE BROWN MARSH, who | makes her home in Bozeman, Mon- | tana, specializes in children's stories. | Her tremendously warm understand- | ing of children reflects in her magic | little books. ¶ Mrs. Marsh has written articles | and stories for newspapers and mag- | azines and is the author of Chip's | Letters, a series issued by Artcraft | Printers, and of Chip's Corner, a | weekly column for the "Gallatin | Valley Tribune." Her book "The | New Little Fuzzy Green Worm" is | also published by Bethany Press. || **about the artist** | BETHANY TUDOR, the daughter | of TASHA TUDOR the well-known | illustrator, has created these tender, | charming drawings thoroughly at- | tuned to the child's understanding | and imagination. The influence of | a childhood spent on a farm in Web- | ster, New Hampshire, shows in her | sympathetic interpretations of the | small animals. She studied art in | England last year, and is now en- | rolled as an art student in the east. || Ages 005-008 || **THE BETHANY PRESS | ST. LOUIS, MO.**

ILLUSTRATIONS: The illustrations are painted completely in green and brown. Several of the same running chipmunk image appear throughout the book, including one on the dedication page [3]: To | Susan, David and Daniel Wolfe. Four more of the same painting appear on the first and third endpapers, three on the second and fourth endpapers. Each of these pages has one illustration about 2 ½ x 5″, and no text: [4, 15, 25, 42, 55, 67, 76, 93, 96]. These pages have a smaller running chipmunk placed with the text: 10, 16, 35. Page [14] is the same illustration as page [3], but it has been broken into two separate illustrations. Tudor signs her paintings very much like her mother, at the lower right edge of an illustration and her initial B., then Tudor.

COPYRIGHT REGISTRATION: A 556016 granted to The Bethany Press, M.P.O. Box 179, St. Louis 66, Missouri. Arnold C. Abrams, agent for claimant, swears on April 2, 1962:

CHIP THE CHIPMUNK by Jessie Brown Marsh, 916 south Third Ave., Bozeman, Montana, a US citizen, was published February 9, 1962. The book was type set and printed by Christian Board of Publication, M.P.O. Box 179, St. Louis 66, Mo. and cloth-bound by The Becktold Company, 1600 Macklind Ave., St. Louis 10, Missouri. Application and affidavit and two deposit copies were received at L.C. April 4, 1962.

[There is no copyright on file for Bethany Tudor for the book's illustrations.]

C26 *The* | **CHRISTMAS** | **CAT** | [cat creeping in snow] | by Efner Tudor Holmes | illustrated by Tasha Tudor | *Thomas Y. Crowell Company • New York* [The illustrations for this book were done in transparent | watercolor. Full-color separations were made in Italy | by Offset Separations Corp. of New York. | The book is set in Plantin Alphatype, and was printed | by Federated Lithographers in Providence, R.I. || [a cat peeking out of a basket] || Copyright © 1976 by Efner Tudor Holmes. | Illustrations copyright © 1976 by Tasha Tudor. | All rights reserved. Except for use in a review, the reproduction or utilization of this work | in any form or by any electronic, mechanical, or other means, now known | or hereafter invented, including xerography, photocopying, and recording, and in any | information storage and retrieval system is forbidden without the written permission | of the publisher. Published simultaneously in Canada by Fitzhenry &

Whiteside Limited, | Toronto. Manufactured in the United States of America. || *Library of Congress Cataloging in Publication Data* | Holmes, Efner Tudor. The Christmas Cat. | SUMMARY: On one cold Christmas eve, an abandoned cat | and a little boy receive a bit of seasonal magic. | [1. Christmas—Fiction] I. Tudor, Tasha. II. Title. PZ7.H735Ch | [E] 76-14802 ISBN 0-690-01267-5 ISBN 0-690-01268-3 (lib.bdg.) | 1 2 3 4 5 6 7 8 9 10]

PAGINATION: [28 pp.] in two signatures including front free endpapers. 7 3/8″ x 7 15/16″

COVER: Pink paper over boards imprinted in black. Efner Tudor Holmes | [a sleeping cat in a ring of oak leaves and acorns] | *The* | CHRISTMAS CAT | illustrated by Tasha Tudor. Spine: Holmes / Tudor THE CHRISTMAS CAT Crowell. Back: an oak leaf and acorn border around a creche, and in lower right corner: 0-690-01267-5 | 0-690-01268-3 (CQR).

DUST JACKET: Design is identical to cover, with white flaps. Front flap: 0-690-01267-5 $5.95 | 0-690-01268-3 (CQR) $6.95 || *The* | **CHRISTMAS CAT** | EFNER TUDOR HOLMES | ILLUSTRATED BY TASHA TUDOR || It was Christmas Eve. The little lost cat, | abandoned when its human family moved | away, could not survive much longer. The | forest was bitterly cold and filled with | hidden dangers. Not far away, in a small | warm farmhouse, a little boy anxiously | asked his older brother if Santa Claus | would be able to come in such bad weather. | Neither cat nor boys could know it, but a | small Christmas "miracle" was in the | making. ¶ Tasha Tudor's radiant full-color pic- | tures illuminate this story, perfectly | expressing the loving spirit that shines | through the simple text. Efner Tudor | Holmes skillfully combines down-to- | earth reality with the hint of just-possible | seasonal magic. ¶ Was it the work of Santa Claus, as Jason | would like to believe ? Or did some kindly | grownup know just the right home for a | little lost cat? However readers decide to | answer this question, they cannot fail to be | moved by the love and reverence for all || (*Continued on back flap*) Back flap: (*Continued from front flap*) | living creatures that permeate both story | and pictures. Love is the message of | Christmas. Love is what this beautiful | book is about. It is a book that could well | start a whole new Christmas tradition. || EFNER TUDOR HOLMES comes by her talent | naturally, for, as Tasha Tudor's daughter, | she was brought up in an atmosphere that | encouraged creativity and a love of nature. | She now lives on a real farm in New | Hampshire with her husband and their | two young sons. The Tudor family's | justly famous Christmas celebration is | still carried on in her own household— | and on Christmas Eve a special gift of | food is taken out to the wild animals in | the snowy woods. || TASHA TUDOR is one of America's best- | loved author-artists. She has won the | Regina Medal and many other awards for | her beautiful books for children. Mrs. | Tudor loves the traditions and handcrafts, | the architecture, gardens, farms, and way | of life of her native New England, and | shares her delight with the readers of her | books. Tasha Tudor lives in Marlboro, Vermont. || *Thomas Y. Crowell Company* | *New York • Established 1834*

CONTENTS: Dedication on page [5]: *For my mother, who has shown me the joys in life, | and | For my husband Pete, who is the embodiment of these joys*

ILLUSTRATIONS: All in full color. End papers are identical two page spread: a cat in snowy woods. Other two page spreads: pp. [6-7] [10-11] [12-13] [14-15] [16-17] [18-19] [20-21]. Single page illustrations: pp. [2 3 4 5 8 9 22 23 24 25 26 27]

OTHER: The front and rear pasted endpapers are the first and last leaves of the two signatures.

COPYRIGHT REGISTRATION: A 789950 granted to Efner Tudor Holmes, Route 1, Concord, N.H. 03301 for text only. Arlene Reisberg, agent for the claimant, swears on Sept. 29, 1976:

THE CHRISTMAS CAT, by Efner Tudor Holmes, a U.S. citizen, and illustrated by Tasha Tudor, was published Sept. 28, 1976. The book was manufactured by Modern Craftsmen Typographers, N.Y., N.Y., Federated Lithographers, Inc., Providence, R.I., and Book Press, Inc., N.Y.,N.Y. Fees to be charged to account of Thomas Y. Crowell Company, Inc., 666 Fifth Ave., N.Y., N.Y. 10019. Application, affidavit and two deposit copies were received at L.C. Oct., 15, 1976.

COPYRIGHT REGISTRATION: A 789951 granted to Tasha Tudor, R.F.D. #4, West Brattleboro, Vt. 05301 for illustrations only. Arlene Reisberg, agent for the claimant, swears as above on Sept. 29, 1976.

C27 _____.

> COVER: <u>Rose cloth</u> in a course weave. Gilt stamping, on front cover: cat inside a 1 7/8″ round ornament; and spine: Holmes / Tudor   THE CHRISTMAS CAT   Crowell. Back has no printing. This is the 'library binding.'

> DUST JACKET: As above. The examination copy had prices clipped, leaving ISBNs.

C28 _____. Publisher's <u>presentation copy</u> to Efner Tudor Holmes has no dust jacket.

> PAGINATION: Title page is page [9].

> COVER: 3/4 tan <u>leather binding</u> over green marbled covers and endpapers. Leather is edged in a gold bar. Three sheets tan laid paper before the blue 'endpaper' design from the trade printing. The blue sheet is glued to the last leaf in the book. Marble "end paper" glued to 1st sheet. Middle sheet is a single piece of the paper. Same array at the end of the book following the "blue endpaper" design. Spine has 4 gold bars and 2 raised 'bands.' | [band] | HOLMES • TUDOR - THE CHRISTMAS CAT - CROWELL | [band] |

C29 _____. [The illustrations for this book . . . <u>2</u> 3 4 5 6 7 8 9 10]

> PAGINATION: Two signatures <u>saddle-stitched</u>.

> COVER: <u>Paper over boards</u> printed like the first trade edition.

> DUST JACKET: As first edition.

C30 _____. [The illustrations for this book . . . <u>2</u> 3 4 5 6 7 8 9 10]

> PAGINATION: Two signatures <u>topsewn</u> into library binding.

> COVER: <u>Blue plastic-filled paper</u> (<u>fabric weave imprint</u>) over boards, gilt stamping as first edition.

> DUST JACKET: Have not examined one.

C31 _____. [The illustrations for this book . . . <u>3</u> 4 5 6 7 8 9 10]

> PAGINATION: Two signatures stitched into library binding.

> COVER: <u>Rose cloth imprinted</u> in gilt as above.

> DUST JACKET: Front flap: <u>$5.95</u> . . .

C32 _____.

> COVER: <u>Red plastic-filled paper imprinted with pigskin design</u> over boards imprinted in gilt as above. Library binding.

> DUST JACKET: Identical to 1ˢᵗ printing.

C33 _____. [The illustrations for this book . . . <u>3</u> 4 5 6 7 8 9 10]

> COVER: Rose cloth library binding, imprinted as before.

> DUST JACKET: Dust jacket prices identical to 1ˢᵗ printing. <u>A 13/16″ x 3 ¾″ gold foil label</u> is applied around the spine and 5/16″ from the bottom edge. The label is printed in brown with a thin rule border around the whole and on the back: *Crowell* | *Quality* [a feather] | *Reinforced Binding*. At

the right end CRQ is printed twice in a sideways column, one of which runs down the spine. The label conceals the ISBNs on the back of the jacket.

C34 _____. [The illustrations for this book . . . <u>4</u> 5 6 7 8 9 10]

COVER: <u>Coarse weave</u> rose cloth imprinted as before.

DUST JACKET: Have not examined one without the upper corner clipped.

C35 _____. . . . illustrated by Tasha Tudor ‖ <u>[flame logo] HarperCollins*Publishers*</u> [The illustrations for this book were done in transparent | watercolor. Full-color separations were made in Italy | by Offset Separations Corp. of New York. | The book is set in Plantin <u>Alphatype.</u> ‖ <u>[cat in basket]</u> ‖ Copyright © 1976 by Efner Tudor Holmes | Illustrations copyright © 1976 by Tasha Tudor | All rights reserved. <u>No part of this book may be used or reproduced in any | manner whatsoever</u> without written permission except in the case of brief | quotations embodied in critical articles and reviews. <u>Printed in the United | States of America. For information address HarperCollins Children's Books, | a division of HarperCollins Publishers, 10 East 53rd Street, New York, NY 10022.</u> ‖ *Library of Congress Cataloging-in-Publication Data* | Holmes, Efner Tudor. The Christmas cat. | SUMMARY: On one cold Christmas eve, an abandoned cat | and a little boy receive a bit of seasonal magic. | [1. Christmas—Fiction] I. Tudor, Tasha. II. Title. PZ7.H735Ch | [E] 76-14802   ISBN 0-690-01267-5   ISBN 0-690-01268-3 (lib.bdg.) | <u>4</u> 5 6 7 8 9 10]

PAGINATION: 7¼″ x 7 7/8″.

cover: <u>Half gray paper over boards, blind stamped</u> on front with same round cat ornament as before. Paper overlaps the red spine cloth. Spine stamped in silver: Holmes/Tudor THE CHRISTMAS CAT <u>HarperCollins.</u> Back is blank.

DUST JACKET: Base of spine: Harper | Collins. Lower right back: 90000 [above smaller right bar code] | [2 UPC bar codes] | 9 780690 012675 [beneath larger left bar code] | ISBN 0-690-01267-5 [beneath both]. Front flap lacks printed ISBNs and price, although 12.95 was penciled on examination copy. Remaining text same as the first edition. Back flap text: *(Continued from front flap)* | . . . shares her delights with the readers of her | books. <u>Tasha Tudor lives in Webster, | New Hampshire.</u> [*sic*] ‖ [flame logo] HarperCollins*Publishers*.

OTHER: This is at least the <u>5th</u> printing. The previous '4th' was from Crowell. Colophon changed from the Crowell. Examined a copy inscribed by Holmes, 1992. HarperCollins editor probably relied on earlier Collins or Crowell information about Tudor to change her residence from Marlboro, Vermont, back to Webster, New Hampshire.

C36 _____. . . . Tasha Tudor ‖ <u>A Harper Trophy Book | Harper & Row, Publishers.</u> [The Christmas Cat | Text copyright © 1976 by Efner Tudor Holmes | Illustrations copyright © 1976 by Tasha Tudor ‖ All rights reserved . . . articles and reviews. Printed in | the United States of America. For information address | <u>Harper & Row Junior Books,</u> 10 East 53rd Street, | New York, N.Y. 10022. ‖ [cat in basket] ‖ Library of Congress Cataloging-in-Publication Data...76-14802 | ISBN 0-690-01267-5 | ISBN 0-690-01268-3 (lib.bdg.) ‖ (A Harper Trophy book) | ISBN 0-06-443208-4 (pbk.) | [rule] | Published in hardcover by <u>Thomas Y. Crowell, New York.</u> | First Harper Trophy edition, 1989.]

PAGINATION: Increased by four to [32] pages. Previous pasted endpapers are the first and last leaves of the book in this printing. 6 15/16″ x 7 3/8″

COVER: <u>Paper wrappers</u>, white inside. A double bar code is printed sideways at lower left, inside front cover: 50450 [above the smaller right bar code] | 9 780064 432085 [beneath the larger left bar code]. Printed beneath both in a larger 'computer' type face: ISBN 0-06-443208-4. Front cover is original 1976 illustration. <u>Additional text to front cover</u>: HARPER | TROPHY, in upper left corner; and, $4.50 in upper right corner. Spine: <u>JP208</u> Holmes/Tudor THE CHRISTMAS CAT <u>Harper & Row</u>. Back cover: white square within a purple border, pink cover. Text in center: The Christmas Cat | Ages 4 to 8 ‖ It is Christmas Eve. A gray cat shivers in the woods. He is | hungry, and all alone in the bitter cold. But wait! There's the | sound of sleigh bells! Why are all the forest animals gathering | in the forest? And who is this kind man who has food for all the | animals — and just the perfect home for the little cat? ‖ **Efner Tudor Holmes** and Tasha Tudor collaborated on AMY'S | GOOSE, available in Harper Trophy. **Tasha Tudor** is the much | loved illustrator of the children's classics A LITTLE PRINCESS and | THE SECRET GARDEN by Frances Hodgson Burnett, both in | Harper Trophy editions. || 0989 || [2 bar codes] 50450 [above the smaller right one] | 9 780064 432085 [below the larger left bar code]. Printed beneath both: ISBN 0-06-443208-4. Below purple border at left: Cover art by Tasha Tudor.

OTHER: Examined one inscribed 1990.

C37 _____.

COVER: Two prices on the front cover: $4.50 US | $5.95 CDN. There is no longer a number on the back cover between the text and the bar codes.

C38 _____.   Overmann describes a red pictorial paperback from Harper Collins. I have not examined a copy.

C39 _____. . . . [flame emblem] HarperTrophy | *A Division of* HarperCollins*Publishers* [The Christmas Cat | Text copyright©1976 by Efner Tudor Holmes | Illustrations copyright © 1976 by Tasha Tudor || All rights reserved...articles and reviews. Printed in | the United States of America. For information address | HarperCollins Children's Books, a division of | HarperCollins Publishers, 10 East 53rd Street, | New York, NY 10022. || [cat in basket] || Library of Congress Cataloging-in-Publication Data...76-14802 ISBN 0-690-01267-5   ISBN 0-690-01268-3 (lib.bdg.) | (A Harper Trophy book) | ISBN 0-06-443208-4 (pbk.) | [rule] | Published in hardcover by Thomas Y. Crowell, New York. | First Harper Trophy edition, 1989.]

PAGINATION: [32] pp.

COVER: Paper wrappers. Front cover is original illustration from 1976 edition. Additional text: HARPER | TROPHY in upper left corner; and, $4.95 US | $6.95 CDN in upper right corner. Spine: Holmes/Tudor THE CHRISTMAS CAT HarperTrophy. Back: The Christmas Cat | Ages 4 to 8 . . . Harper Trophy editions. | 43208 | [2 bar codes] | 0 46594 00495 6 | ISBN 0-06-443208-4. Below purple border at left: Cover art by Tasha Tudor. UPC bar code and ISBN are also printed inside front cover, lower left: 50495> | [2 bar codes] | 9 780064 432085 | ISBN 0-06-443208-4.

C40 _____.

COVER: Front cover price: $4.95 US | $6.75 CDN in upper right corner. Spine as above. Back cover: The Christmas … | 50495> | [2 bar codes] | 9 780064 432085 | ISBN 0-06-443208-4. Same UPC bar code and ISBN on inside front cover; now they match the back cover, which they did not before

C41 _____.

HarperCollins plans to issue a reprint hard cover, enlarged and with brighter colors in Fall 1999.

C42 _____.

HarperCollins plans to issue a corresponding paperback edition in Fall 2000.

C43 Tasha Tudor [red] | *Christmas Village* | **A Three Dimensional Advent Calendar** | with 24 windows and doors to open—from December 1st to Christmas Eve! | | *No assembly needed   Sets up in an instant* [black] [Illustrations copyright © 1984 by Tasha Tudor. All rights | reserved. Published in the United States by Philomel | Books, a division of The Putnam Publishing Group, 51 | Madison Avenue, New York, N.Y. 10010. Printed and bound | in Singapore for Intervisual Communications, Inc., Los | Angeles, CAS 90045.]

PAGINATION: A diorama in a portfolio. This three-dimensional pop-up is comprised of two pieces of cardboard, ca. 31″ x 31″ slotted and interlaced.

COVER: The "cover" is a cardboard folder, 25 ¾″ x 17 ¼″, which folds to an 11 ½″ x 11 ¾″ envelope. The 'title page' text is transcribed from a cream box outlined in two red rules, the outer being thicker than the inner one. The letters of Christmas Village are edged in white, within a black outline. The opened construction is pictured below this text box. It was sprayed with an aerosol 'snow' before being photographed. The copyright statement comes from a flap at the bottom of the back. A 1 3/8″ x 2 1/8″ white box to the left of the statement is imprinted: 0-399-21088-1 >>$8.95. The larger back piece has three photographs of the 'village,' text below each of two photo groupings, and all printed on a large yellow box, again outlined in two red rules. [Beneath the larger photograph:] Festive crowds fill the streets of an old-fashioned village at Christmas-time and 24 flaps lift to open | doors and windows and reveal enchanting views of the townspeople preparing for the holidays in their | homes, stores and a charming church (where an exquisite crèche may be seen when the doors are | opened). Beloved American artist Tasha Tudor's tender and reverent watercolor illustrations make this | a treasure for the whole family to enjoy for many years to come. This unusual advent calendar folds flat | in its case, pops up in a second into a 3-D model village. ‖ [Beneath a second grouping:] No assembly needed. Calendar unfolds into a decorative dimen- | sional stand-up structure, approximately 10 x 20 inches. Easy to | display on table, mantelpiece or any flat surface. [Below the yellow box, above a 5 3/4″ slit for the tabbed flap:] PHILOMEL BOOKS.

ILLUSTRATIONS: The Tudor illustration is printed on both sides of the cardboard construction, the back side in reverse. This is evident from Tudor's signature which shows in reverse on one side. The illustration features two shops, a house and a stone church in a European street scene, a reference to the McCready's sojourn in England twenty-five years earlier. When pulled open, the scene has towers and doors, snow-covered roofs and chimneys, in addition to 24 flaps for the days of Advent.

OTHER: Printed at the bottom of the residence and near Tudor's signature is: © 1984 by Tasha Tudor. Printed in Singapore | for Intervisual Communications, Inc., Los Angeles, CA 90045. [I ultimately chose to include this piece because it is not *flat art*, includes brief text on the folder and it does tell a visual story of English village life at Christmastide. The piece is copyrighted, has many features of a book and resembles a pop-up book. *-Ed.*]

COPYRIGHT REGISTRATION: VA 166-413 granted to Tasha Tudor, Route #4, Box 144, West Brattleboro, Vt. 05301. Louise Bates, agent for Tasha Tudor, swears on Sept. 27, 1984:

CHRISTMAS VILLAGE Advent Calendar with illustrations completed in 1984 by Tasha Tudor, a U.S. citizen, was published Sept. 25, 1984. Fees to be charged to account DAO38288, Putnam Publishing Group, 51 Madison Ave., N.Y., N.Y. 10010 (212) 689-9200. Application, affidavit and two deposit copies were received at L.C. Oct. 4, 1984.

C44 _____.

COVER: The flap also has a 1 3/8″ x 2 1/8″ white box to the left of the statement. Printed in the box: 0-399-21088-1 >>$9.95.

C45 *Christmas with Tasha Tudor: Take Joy!*

Little, Brown, and Company has scheduled this book for publication September 1, 2000. It is to be a general revision of the 1966 *Take Joy!* edited by John Keller. Approximately 100 photographs and other illustrations. Corgi Cottage Industries announced it on its website July 9, 1998: "the most marvelous photographs."

C46 CORGIVILLE ǀ FAIR ‖ BY ǀ TASHA TUDOR ‖ THOMAS Y. CROWELL COMPANY ǀ NEW YORK [TASHA TUDOR lives in a lovely eighteenth-century farmhouse in | Webster, New Hampshire, a village that is not too unlike Corgiville. | Her fondness for the New England rural scene is reflected in all her illustrations, | many of which depict with loving accuracy the details of farm life as she observes them at firsthand. | Born in Connecticut [*sic*], she has lived in New England all her life, except for periods of travel in England and Europe. | One of the best known and most beloved of all American illustrators, | Tasha Tudor has won many honors and awards, including the 1971 Regina Medal | for her distinguished contribution to children's literature. || Copyright © 1971 by Tasha Tudor || All rights reserved. Except for use in a review, the reproduction or utilization of this work | in any form or by any electronic, mechanical, or other means, | now known or hereafter invented, including xerography, photocopying, and recording, | and in any information storage and retrieval system is forbidden | without the written permission of the publisher. | Published simultaneously in Canada by Fitzhenry & Whiteside Limited, Toronto. || Typography by Jack Jaget | Manufactured in the United States of America | L.C. Card 72—154042 ISBN 0-690-21791-9 | 0-690-21792-7 (LB) || 1 2 3 4 5 6 7 8 9 10]

PAGINATION: [52] pp. including free endpapers, in three signatures of matte white paper. 8 ½ x 10 5/8 ″.

COVER: Robin's egg blue cloth stamped in gilt: illustration from page [10] on front; spine printed laterally, Tudor   CORGIVILLE FAIR   0-690-21791-9 Crowell.

DUST JACKET: Water color illustration of arrivals lined up and entering the fair. Front: CORGIVILLE FAIR [in blue] arched above the MAIN GATE [in gold], TASHA TUDOR, at bottom [black]. Spine: Tudor [red] /[black] CORGIVILLE FAIR [blue] Crowell [black]. Back, lower right [in black]: 0-690-21791-9 | 0-690-21792-7 (LB)   Front flap: $4.95 || CORGIVILLE FAIR | TASHA TUDOR [blue, rest of text is black] || [] In Corgiville, as in many small towns | all over America, the biggest event of | the year is the Fair. And the most ex- | citing thing at the Corgiville Fair is | the goat race. Caleb Corgi had spent | many months training his goat Jose- | phine for the big event. But Edgar | Tomcat's goat was fast, too, and Caleb | knew that Edgar was not above in- | dulging in some foul play in order to | win. Caleb tried to guard Josephine | carefully before the race, but, even | so, an evil trick of Edgar's nearly put | her out of the running. ¶ The sights, sounds, and smells, the | fun and excitement of a typical small- | town fair, are captured with humor | and affection both in the text and in | the marvelously detailed watercolor | paintings. ¶ Tasha Tudor, one of America's most | beloved author-artists, has here | created her most original work, a mas- | terpiece of gentle satire, a loving ob- | servation of a particular segment of | rural American life couched in terms | of a rollicking story, and superbly | illustrated. || Back flap: TASHA TUDOR [in blue as are the last two publisher lines, remaining text, black] lives in a lovely | eighteenth-century farmhouse in Web- | ster, New Hampshire, a village that is | not too unlike Corgiville. | (One im- | portant difference is, of course, the | fact that Corgiville is inhabited not | by people, but by dogs, rabbits, cats, | boggarts, and other creatures.) || Her fondness for the New England | rural scene is reflected in all her illus- | trations, many of which depict with | loving accuracy the details of farm | life as she observes them at firsthand. | Born in Connecticut, she has lived in | New England all her life, except for | periods of travel in England and Eu- | rope. Mrs. Tudor's mother was a well- | known portrait artist, from whom she learned much about painting tech- | niques, and she has also studied art | in England. One of the best known | and most beloved of all American | illustrators, Tasha Tudor has won | many honors and awards, including | the 1971 Regina Medal for her dis- | tinguished contribution to children's | literature. || Thomas Y. Crowell Company | NEW YORK ESTABLISHED 1834.

CONTENTS: Pages [2] and [4] are blank; [3] is half-title; [5] title page; [6] colophon page; [7] dedication: To my beloved corgis || [illustration of 8 Corgis in a row] | Farley, Jr., Mr. B., Missus, Megan, Caleb, Snap, Farley, and Corey.

ILLUSTRATIONS: Watercolor illustrations on all pages and four endpapers, except the two blank pages. A double page spread opens the story on page [8] with the first text on page [9].

OTHER: Tudor speaks of this as being her greatest work. See also the 1997 sequel *The Great Corgiville Kidnapping*. She is her most inventive here in creating an entire town for her "beloved" corgi dogs, and her use of boggarts. She loosely designed buildings and village layout from the small mill village of Harrisville, New Hampshire. Tudor suggests that boggarts "come from Sweden, but I'm not sure." There is a Swedish community in Concord, New Hampshire, with which Tudor would have been familiar when she wrote this story. The *Oxford English Dictionary* (1933 I:966) defines a *boggard (boggart)* as a spectre, goblin, or bogy; in dialectal use, esp. a local goblin or sprite supposed to "haunt" a particularly gloomy spot, or scene of violence. The *OED* further cites this as "a word in popular use in Westmoreland, Lancashire, Cheshire, Yorkshire, and the north midlands, and of occasional appearance in literature since *c*1570. Burt (*c*1730) is quoted in *Letters from North Scotland* (1818): All that quarter of England is infested with boggarts of all sorts." Babe, the centerpiece rooster of *...Kidnapping*, appears in the grand parade on page [43]. Among other local elements of the illustrations are the Wells Fargo stage coach, a somewhat odd citing in a New England village, except that these vehicles known as Concord coaches were manufactured in Concord, New Hampshire. In their day, they were as prevalent on the coaching roads of the Northeast as Hollywood has taught us they were in traversing the West. Doc Tenney's powders on the last page of the book memorialize a well-known veterinarian of Peterborough, N.H. And Mary Mason Campbell's corgi S.A. Campbell also appears in several places. I viewed one misbound copy in which the left edge of the front pasted endpaper had been folded under leaving the glued board edge exposed. The front free endpaper thus became glued to this exposed left edge.

The manuscript of *Corgiville Fair* was placed on loan at the Pierpont Morgan Library, New York City, by its owner Thomas Strong Tudor, 8 May 1995. The Morgan Library describes the manuscript thus: 46 sheets of watercolor illustrations, 34 sheets of preparatory drawings on newsprint, in pencil, 80 sheets of preparatory drawings on transfer paper, in pencil, 3 drafts of text, 1 drawing on transfer paper, in pencil - perhaps not for this work. [I think it was drawn for this work, but not used. - *Ed*. 6/22/96] The 3 drafts of text cited above are: There was the Big Tent . . ., The spectators cheered . . ., and Such fireworks! . . .

An ephemeral book mark (3 x 11 7/16″) ivory laid paper is printed full color with the parade of fair-goers as pictured at the bottom of page [24]. Three blocks of text beneath the illustration at the left, middle and right. The left block: CORGIVILLE FAIR | BY TASHA TUDOR | ILLUSTRATED IN FULL COLOR | BY THE AUTHOR. Middle block: Harvard Cooperative Society | Harvard Square | Cambridge, Massachusetts 02138. Right block: Thomas Y. Crowell Company | 201 Park Avenue South | New York 10003. The right block is right justified; the other two are center justified.

COPYRIGHT REGISTRATION: A 270052 granted to Tasha Tudor, Route 1, Contoocook (webster) [*sic*], N.H. Arlene Reisberg, agent for Tudor, swears on Sept. 17, 1971:

CORGIVILLE FAIR, by Tasha Tudor, a US citizen, was published August 30, 1971. The book was manufactured by Westcott & Thomson, Inc., Phil., Pa., Federated Lithographers, Inc., Providence, R.I. and The Book Press, Inc., N.Y., N.Y. Fees to be charged against account of Thomas Y. Crowell, Inc., 201 Park Ave. South, N.Y., N.Y. 10003. Application, affidavit and two deposit copies were received at L.C. Sept. 27, 1971.

C47 _____.

COVER: Sealed cloth imprinted with the dust jacket illustration. Spine: Tudor [orange] / [black] CORGIVILLE FAIR [blue] Crowell [black]. Back, lower right in black: 0-690-21792-7 (LB).

DUST JACKET: Gold foil label (¾″ x 2 ¾″) added at base of spine: [feather] CROWELL | LIBRARY | BINDING [and four columns at the right end of label formed by printing CROWELL sideways four times]. Have not examined one with price intact.

C48 _____. [TASHA TUDOR . . . Born in Massachusetts . . . 2 3 4 5 6 7 8 9 10].

COVER: Blue cloth, other details like first printing.

DUST JACKET: Have not examined one for this printing.

OTHER: Rae Benedetto reports a copy rebound by Treasure Trove, thus: a pale yellow cloth with the dust jacket illustration on the front. The rear cover is patterned with blue striping over the same yellow cloth. Yellow spine, blue lettering. A small circled "TT" logo near the top front of the spine [*sic*]. The same logo, larger, on the rear cover, top right about 1″ down and 2″ from the spine.

C49 _____. [TASHA TUDOR . . . Born in Massachusetts . . . 2 3 4 5 6 7 8 9 10].

COVER: White paper over boards with prominent filaments overlapped by 1¼″ blue cloth spine wrap. The full width of the spine cloth is approximately 3 1/8″, but copies were not uniformly wrapped. Some have a wider application to the front cover and less fabric wrapped to the back cover. Dancing animals are stamped on the front cover in black. Spine imprinted black: Tudor CORGIVILLE FAIR   Crowell.

DUST JACKET: Have not examined a copy with the price intact. Back flap: TASHA TUDOR . . . she observes them at firsthand. | Born in Massachusetts . . .

C50 _____. [TASHA TUDOR . . . Born in Massachusetts . . . 2 3 4 5 6 7 8 9 10].

COVER: White paper over boards with medium filaments overlapping the blue cloth spine wrap.

DUST JACKET: Have not examined a copy.

C51 _____. [TASHA TUDOR . . . Born in Massachusetts . . . 2 3 4 5 6 7 8 9 10].

COVER: White paper over boards with very light filaments overlapping the blue cloth spine wrap.

DUST JACKET: Have not examined a copy with the price intact.

C52 _____. [TASHA TUDOR... 3 4 5 6 7 8 9 10].

COVER: Cloth spine overlapped by white paper, light filaments over boards. Black ink.

DUST JACKET: The jacket was not printed with a price or ISBN on flaps. The last two lines of back flap still in blue ink, but changed text: Thomas Y. Crowell | NEW YORK. ISBNs on back as before.

C53 _____. [TASHA TUDOR . . . 4 5 6 7 8 9 10].

COVER: As before.

DUST JACKET: Ivory jacket. Upper corner front flap: Ages 4-8   Back flap, bottom, added black text: TRADE printed sideways to left of: 90000 [above smaller right bar code] | [two UPC bar codes] | 9 780690 217919 [beneath the larger left bar code] | ISBN 0-690-21791-9. No ISBNs on back of jacket.

C54 _____. . . . TUDOR | [flame logo] HarperCollins *Publishers* [TASHA TUDOR... children's literature. || CORGIVILLE FAIR | Copyright © 1971 by Tasha Tudor | All rights reserved. No part of this book may be used or reproduced in any | manner whatsoever without written permission except in the case of brief | quotations embodied in critical articles and reviews. Printed in Hong Kong. | For information address HarperCollins Children's Books, a division | of HarperCollins Publishers, 10 East 53rd Street, New York, NY 10022. || Typography by Jack Jaget | Library of Congress Catalog Card Number 72-154042 | ISBN 0-690-21791-9.-ISBN 0-690-21792-7 (lib. bdg.) | 5 6 7 8 9 10]

PAGINATION: [52] pp. including flyleaves, in four signatures, matte white paper. 8 5/8″ x 10 ¾″

COVER: ½ light gray deckle paper over board covers, 2 ½″ robin's egg blue plastic spine wrap. Spine stamped in black: Tudor / CORGIVILLE FAIR   HarperCollins

DUST JACKET: Gloss film laminate jacket similar to previous. Spine: Tudor [red] /[black] CORGIVILLE FAIR [blue]   HarperCollins[black]. Front flap does not carry a price. Back flap text as before, but publisher's statement at bottom now reads: [flame logo] HarperCollins*Publishers* [in blue] | 90000 …

OTHER: Even though Crowell was acquired by Harper & Row in 1977, this is the first edition to appear under the Harper name. The firm, on 53rd Street since 1972, became HarperCollins in 1990. Examination copy purchased at a bookstore in June 1992.

C55 _____. Overmann lists a Harper Collins blue pictorial paperback. I have not examined a copy.

C56 _____.

COVER: Blue linen spine wrap.

OTHER: Examination copy purchased new March 1996.

C57 _____. TUDOR | [flame logo] HarperTrophy | *A Division of* HarperCollins*Publishers* [Corgiville Fair | Copyright © 1971 by Tasha Tudor | All rights reserved. No part of this book may be used or reproduced | in any manner whatsoever without written permission except in the | case of brief quotations embodied in critical articles and reviews. | Printed in the United States of America. For information address | HarperCollins Children's Books, a division of HarperCollins Publishers, | 10 East 53rd Street, New York, NY 10022. || LC Number 72-154042 | ISBN 0-690-21791-9 | ISBN 0-06-443236-X (pbk.) | First Harper Trophy edition, 1991.]

PAGINATION: [48] pages perfect bound; no endpaper illustrations.   8 ¼″ x 10 ¼″.

COVER: Paper wrapper, illustrations from former dust jacket: HARPER | TROPHY in upper left front; $5.95 US | $ 7.95 CDN in upper right front. Back cover text in black: **Ages 4 to 8** | It's time for the Corgiville Fair and the biggest event of all — the goat race! Caleb Bigbee Brown has worked | hard training his goat, Josephine, and she is fast. But Edgar Tomcat's goat is fast, too. And Edgar plans to win | at any cost. ¶ When Edgar decides to pull an evil trick that could put Josephine out of the running, Caleb has to think fast. Can | he come up with a trick of his own? || **Tasha Tudor** is the beloved illustrator of the children's classics THE SECRET GARDEN and A LITTLE PRINCESS, both | available in Harper Trophy editions.   White box at lower left back: 0191 [above the box, perhaps a print date, January 1991 ?] | 43236 [over smaller right bar code] | [2 UPC bar codes] | 0 46594 00595 3 | ISBN 0-06-443236-X [beneath the larger left bar code]. | Printed beneath the UPC box in small black letters: Cover art by Tasha Tudor. Orange spine: Tudor [black] CORGIVILLE FAIR [white] HarperTrophy [black]. UPC code printed to run vertically in the lower left inside front cover, facing out: 50595 [above smaller right bar code] | [2 bar codes] | 9 780064 432368 [beneath larger left bar code] | ISBN 0-06-443236.

CONTENTS: Page [1] is half-title; [2], blank ; [5] dedication page; page [48] is last page of text and book.

ILLUSTRATIONS: 74 illustrations plus covers. Two-page spreads on pp. [6-7, 24-25, 36-37, 40-41, 46-47]

C58 _____. Overmann lists a Collins, UK edition.   I have not examined a copy.

C59 **CORGIVILLE** | **FAIR** [blue, on covered bridge] || by Tasha Tudor [orange] || [*Ƶ B* and monument logo] Little, Brown and Company | BOSTON NEW YORK TORONTO LONDON [Also by Tasha Tudor: || *The Great Corgiville Kidnapping | The Tasha Tudor Cookbook | The Private World of Tasha Tudor* || [printer's swirl] || Copyright © 1971 by Tasha Tudor || All rights reserved. No part of this book may be reproduced in any form or by any electronic | or mechanical means, including information storage and retrieval systems, without permission | in writing from the publisher, except by a reviewer who may quote brief passages in a review. || First Little, Brown Edition || Originally published in 1971 by HarperCollins Children's Books || Library of Congress Cataloging-in-Publication Data || Tudor, Tasha. | Corgiville fair / by Tasha Tudor. — 1st Little, Brown ed. | p. cm. | Summary: Chronicles the events of the Corgiville Fair, especially the foul play by Edgar | Tomcat in his attempt to win the goat race. | ISBN 0-316-85312-7. — ISBN 0-316-85329-1 (pbk.) | [1. Dogs — Fiction. 2. Cats — Fiction. 3. Fairs — Fiction.] I. Title. | PZ7.T8228C1 1998 | [E] — dc 21   97-29665 || 10 9 8 7 6 5 4 3 2 1 || SC || Published simultaneously in Canada by Little, Brown & Company (Canada) Limited || Printed in Hong Kong]

PAGINATION: [52] pp. in three signatures of matte white paper. 9 5/16 x 12 1/8″.

COVER: Pictorial boards, gloss laminate finish, with reset type over the original dust jacket illustration which has been <u>enlarged and cropped</u>. At the top, only a portion of the balloon string remains at upper left; left, sign is cropped close to 'S'; bottom, picnicking corgi's right foot is 1/8″ from edge; right signs read "FARM MAC" and "21ST ANN." Single line blue title as on title page with a 11/2″ long orange line at both sides, TASHA TUDOR, in orange at bottom. Orange spine printed laterally: TUDOR [white]   CORGIVILLE FAIR [blue]   Little, Brown [white]. Back cover illustration is also enlarged and cropped; top, 5/8″ to red balloon; left, to "THE" and the blue falling cap; bottom, 5/8″ to the red wagon's wheels; right, "MERT" and "DEVILS." A white box at lower right corner covers the lower half of the rabbit pulling the red wagon and contains: ISBN 0-316-85329-1   9000 | EAN [printed laterally at left edge,   2 bar codes] 9 780316 853293 [under the larger left bar code]. Left of box in black: [2 vertical bars] LITTLE, BROWN | REINFORCED BINDING.

DUST JACKET: Reproduces the cover illustration exactly. Front cream-colored flap: **$15.95   FPT** | $21.95 in Canada || **CORGIVILLE** | **FAIR** [blue] | Tasha Tudor [orange] | **I**n Corgiville, as in many small | towns all over America, the | biggest event of the year is the | Fair. And the most exciting thing | at the Corgiville Fair is the goat | race. Caleb Corgi had <u>spent |</u> <u>months</u> training his goat Joseph- | ine for the big event. But Edgar Tomcat's goat <u>is</u> fast, too, and | Caleb <u>knows</u> that Edgar <u>is</u> not | above indulging in some <u>dirty |</u> <u>tricks</u> in order to <u>win</u>. ¶ The sights, sounds, smells, <u>and |</u> <u>all</u> the fun and excitement of a | typical small-town <u>fair are</u> cap- | tured with humor and affection | both in the text and <u>in mar- |</u> <u>velously</u> detailed watercolor | paintings. ¶ Tasha Tudor, one of America's | most beloved author-artists, has | here created her most original | work, a masterpiece of gentle | satire, a loving observation of a | <u>particular</u> segment of rural | American life couched in terms | of a rollicking <u>story and superb |</u> <u>illustrations.</u> || 04981545. Back flap: [color photograph of Tudor kneeling with corgi] Beside the photograph: Patti Denys. || **TASHA TUDOR** is a | member of the pantheon of the | most prolific and revered illustra- | tors of all time. She has written, | illustrated, or been the subject of | more than ninety books during a | career that has spanned nearly | three quarters of a century. ¶ While many of Tasha Tudor's | books are intended for children, | they have found a welcoming | audience among adults as well. | Many of these same adults have | also been inspired by Tasha | Tudor's unique vision of a life | lived in the style of the 1830s. || Printed in Hong Kong.

CONTENTS: Pages [2] and [4] are blank; [3] is half-title; [5] title page; [6] colophon page; [7] dedication: To my beloved corgis || [illustration of 8 Corgis in a row] | Farley, Jr., Mr. B., Missus, Megan, Caleb, Snap, Farley, and Corey.

ILLUSTRATIONS: These are the same illustrations as the earlier edition, but they have generally been much enlarged and cropped from the first edition. Page [8] the first full-page illustration, for example, clips the mountain tops, the left end of the boat on the river, includes only the top of the signpost at the bottom and abbreviates the store sign at the right to "MEGANS M." This reproduction maintains the essence of the illustrations but eliminates a good bit of detail. On the other hand, there is evidence on page [11] "This story is about . . . " that Little, Brown used the original illustrations for this reprint; <u>more of the barn</u> on the right is revealed even though only the dump rake is revealed at the left, clipping the dog raking. Pages [43, 45] also reveal more of the right side than was printed in the first edition. Of greatest significance is that Tudor's signature appears on nearly every illustration. Many of them did not appear in the first edition, but have been recently added in the newer style of Tudor's signature.

OTHER: The text has been reset throughout, and opens with a <u>large orange drop initial W</u>. Paragraphs are now indented. There are textual changes, thus:

p. [10] line 1	"…but you may not be familiar with corgis and	boggarts…"
p. [11] line 1	"Bigbee Browns" becomes "Bigby Browns" "…puppies: Caleb…"
p. [13] line 4	"…with the farm, he was…"
p. [14] line 4	"Every good day, Caleb…groom her, and…"
line 5	"…place, the Boggs…"
p. [16] line 1	"…loud-patterned…"
line 2	"…moonlit nights…"
p. [24] line 2	"…potatoes and hot dogs…"
p. [25] line 1	"…Mr. Bigby Brown…"
p. [29] line 3	"…Ice Cream Stall or the Cotton-Candy Stand…"
p. [30] line 1	"…lunchtime…"
line 2	"…He smelled baked beans and apple pie. .."
line 4	"…very moment, who…"
line 5	"…hot dogs…"
p. [31] lines 4, 6	"…hot dog."
p. [32] line 1	"…"man-to-man"…"
p. [37] line 6 is no longer spaced apart from the preceding paragraph
p. [38] line 1	"…soda-pop…"
p. [44] line 1	"After the parade, Josephine…"
p. [48] line 2	"…one never sees anymore…"

The publisher's colophon incorrectly credits the first edition to HarperCollins Children's Books, a further *current* testament to inadequate research on the part of editors. A check of the standard bibliographic tools would have shown that Crowell first published this work. As for HarperCollins Children's Books - no such company existed in 1971.

Corgi Cottage Industries, Spring 1988 catalog advertises this book and says "Orders placed now will feature a full color | bookplate designed just for this edition. The same catalog lists a "Special Edition of 100" Corgiville Prints. Sold in sets of four only. This set of off-prints were created in conjunction with the new edition: (#170 PRT) Souvenirs, (#172 PRT) Lemonade, (#174 PRT) Balloons, (#176 PRT) Ice Cream. Unsigned $15.00 each. Signed and numbered in the set of four $150. The same catalog also pictures and offers for sale two porcelain figurines 4 ¾" tall modeled on the two characters from the book Caleb Corgi and Edgar Tomcat. Each is $45. "A new character will be featured in our Christmas catalogue."

C60 _____.

PAGINATION: [50] pp. in three signatures.

COVER: At least one copy of the first printing was misbound without the front endpaper. The half-title page was glued to the front board and the title page is the first free leaf. The rear endpaper is present and correct.

C61 _____.

PAGINATION: [48] pp. in three signatures of matte white paper. 9 x 11 7/8".

COVER: Wrapper with the cover illustration as above.   Single line blue title as on title page with a 1¼″ long orange line at both sides.   Orange spine printed laterally: TUDOR [white]   CORGIVILLE FAIR [blue]   Little, Brown [white].   Back, overprinted in black at upper left: **$6.95   FPT** | $9.95 in Canada ‖ 04980670 | Printed in Hong Kong.   The bar code box at lower right masks the rabbit totally.   Text of the hardcover dust jacket flaps is reset and printed all black inside the back

cover: **I**n Corgiville, as in many small towns all over America, the biggest event of the year ⌊ is the Fair.   And the most exciting thing at the Corgiville Fair is the goat race.   Caleb ⌊ Corgi had spent months training his goat Josephine for the big event.   But Edgar | Tomcat's goat is fast, too, and Caleb knows that Edgar is not above indulging in some | dirty tricks in order to win.   ¶ The sights, sounds, smells, and all the fun and excitement of a typical small-town | fair are captured with humor and affection both in the text and in marvelously detailed watercolor paintings.   ¶ Tasha Tudor, one of America's most beloved author-artists, has here created her | most original work, a masterpiece of gentle satire, a loving observation of a particu- | lar segment of rural American life couched in terms of a rollicking story and superb | illustrations.   ‖ [printer's swirl] ‖

TASHA TUDOR is a member of the pantheon of the most prolific and revered | illustrators of all time.   She has written, illustrated, or been the subject of more than | ninety books during a career that has spanned nearly three quarters of a century.   ¶ While many of Tasha Tudor's books are intended for children, they have found a | welcoming audience among adults as well.   Many of these same adults have also been | inspired by Tasha Tudor's unique vision of a life lived in the style of the 1830s.

CONTENTS: Only the inside front cover and page [2] are blank.   Page [1] is half-title; [3] title page; [4] colophon page; [5] dedication.

C62 THE | COUNTY | FAIR | BY | TASHA TUDOR | OXFORD UNIVERSITY | PRESS | [vegetables and hen] | LONDON NEW YORK TORONTO [COPYRIGHT, 1940 | OXFORD UNIVERSITY PRESS | NEW YORK, INC. ‖ PRINTED IN THE UNITED STATES OF AMERICA]

PAGINATION: Three signatures ivory paper.   [52] pp. including flyleaves.   4 ¾″ x 4 1/16″.

COVER: Red polka-dot cloth (often faded to appear orange).   A scalloped oval framing a white title lozenge on which is imprinted almost like a child's printing in blue block letters: THE | COUNTY | FAIR | BY | TASHA TUDOR.   First endpaper, Sylvie Ann and Tom are nailing a book plate in a scalloped red border and red letters: THIS BOOK | BELONGS | [rule] | TO.   A dog jumps against the right side of the plate.   Second and fourth endpapers are the same aster and goldenrod illustrations with gold finches.   Third endpaper is a similar clump of flowers with a bunny.

DUST JACKET: Buff dust jacket with red outlined lettered title, remaining text is black.   COUNTY and FAIR lettered on arched scrolls above and below the illustration.   THE | COUNTY | [Illustration of a rooster crowing amid scattered vegetables and a blue ribbon] | FAIR | BY | TASHA TUDOR.   Spine: TUDOR [device] THE COUNTY FAIR [device] OXFORD.   Back cover: 5/8″ high color illustration of a mouse sitting on a toad stool.   Front flap with pencil drawings of a wild flower on either side of title and author: THE | COUNTY | FAIR | BY | TASHA TUDOR | THERE WAS GOING TO BE | A COUNTY FAIR. SYLVIE | ANN AND HER BROTHER, | TOM, DECIDED TO ENTER | ALEXANDER THE GANDER, | SOME STRAWBERRY JAM | AND BUTTERCUP, THE | CALF. EVERYONE HAD A | SUCCESSFUL TIME AT THE | FAIR AND CAME HOME | COVERED WITH GLORY. ¶A CHARMING TALE FOR | VERY SMALL READERS. ‖ OXFORD BOOKS | FOR BOYS AND GIRLS ‖ $.75.   Back flap: TWO OTHER BOOKS | ABOUT SYLVIE ANN | BY TASHA TUDOR ‖ ALEXANDER | THE | GANDER | A GREEDY GANDER | WHOSE FAVORITE FOOD | WAS HELIOTROPE PANSIES. ‖ PUMPKIN | MOONSHINE | ALL ABOUT SYLVIE ANN | AND A RUNAWAY PUMPKIN | THAT FINALLY BECAME | A PUMPKIN MOONSHINE. ‖ EACH $.75

ILLUSTRATIONS: The title page illustration is pile of fresh vegetables and a Plymouth Rock hen — contenders at the fair. The title is made of red-filled hand-lettered capitals outlined in black. Color illustrations on title page [3], dedication page "For the smallest Rosamond" [5], and 22 even-numbered pages [6] - [48]. Each text page [7] - [49] begins with a red initial embellished with flora and fauna. Pages [2, 50 and 51] are blank. Text is hand lettered capitals.

OTHER: All text is hand-lettered, and the title on title page and dust jacket are larger painted letters outlined in black. The editor has examined a set of rough-cut proof pages, folded into a red polka dot wrapper, a light oil cloth, apparently the binding material before being glued to boards. The set is missing four pages, which, one suspects, still hang framed in someone's personal space. The remaining sheets are paginated: Front endpapers, pp. [1-4] in one sheet. Pp. [5-6, 19-20] in one sheet Pp. [7-8, 17-18] were one sheet, but have been separated. Pp. [9-10, 15-16] in one sheet Pp. [11-14] in one sheet Pp. [21-22, {35-36}] were one sheet, have been separated. Pp. [23-24, 33-34] were one sheet, but have been separated, {33-34} are missing. Pp. [25-26, 31-32] in one sheet. Pp. [27-30] in one sheet. Pp. [37-38, 51-52] were one sheet, but have been separated. Pp. [39-40, 49-50] in one sheet. Pp. [41-42, 47-48] in one sheet. Pp. [43-46] in one sheet. Pp. [53-56] in one sheet.

COPYRIGHT REGISTRATION: 144760 granted to Oxford University Press, New York, Inc., 114 Fifth Ave., N.Y., N.Y.

THE COUNTY FAIR, by Tasha Tudor, a US citizen, was published Sept. 26, 1940. Printing was completed by the Jersey City Printing Co., Jersey City, N.J., May 2, 1940; binding was completed by Haddon Craftsmen, Camden, N.J., Sept. 26, 1940. Affidavit received at L.C. Oct. 5, 1940, and two deposit copies were received at L.C. Oct. 4, 1940.

COPYRIGHT RENEWAL REGISTRATION: R 437199 granted to the author Tasha Tudor, Route 1, Contoocook, N.H. 03229. Kuna Dolch, agent for the claimant, swears undated]:

THE COUNTY FAIR, by Tasha Tudor, was published September 26, 1940, under original registration A 144760. The original copyright claimant was Henry Z. Walck, Inc. However, that name has been X'ed out and beside it typed, Oxford University Press, Inc.* A note at the bottom of the certificate indicates this amendment was typed by the Copyright Office. Registration fee to be charged against Walck, Henry Z. Inc. #6694, 19 Union Square West, N.Y., N.Y. 10003. Application was received at L.C. June 6, 1968.

C63 _____. Have not examined a second printing.

C64 _____. [COPYRIGHT, 1940 || OXFORD UNIVERSITY PRESS | NEW YORK, INC. | THIRD PRINTING 1945 || PRINTED IN THE UNITED STATES OF AMERICA]

COVER: 4 ¾″ x 3 15/16″

ILLUSTRATIONS: Poor reproduction on several pages.

OTHER: In this printing, the THIRD PRINTING 1945 is typeset, rather than being hand-lettered as is the rest of the text.

C65 _____. [COPYRIGHT, 1940 || OXFORD UNIVERSITY PRESS | NEW YORK, INC. || FOURTH PRINTING 1945 || PRINTED IN THE UNITED STATES OF AMERICA]

DUST JACKET: Buff jacket as in the first edition.

ILLUSTRATIONS: Pages [ffep, 24, 40, 44, rfep] out of registration.

OTHER: FOURTH PRINTING 1945 is cut type, rather than being hand lettered.

C66 _____. [COPYRIGHT, 1940 || OXFORD UNIVERSITY PRESS | NEW YORK, INC. || <u>FIFTH PRINTING</u>
<u>1953</u> || PRINTED IN THE UNITED STATES OF AMERICA]

> COVER: White polka dot on <u>orange paper</u> over boards. Colors of title page less intense than in the 4th
> printing.

> DUST JACKET: Have not examined one with price intact.

C67 _____. . . . Tudor | [vegetables and hen] | HENRY Z. WALCK, INCORPORATED | New York
[Copyright 1940 Henry Z. Walck, Inc. <u>First published in this enlarged edition, 1964.</u> Library | of
Congress Catalog Card Number: 64-20584. Printed in the United States of America.]

> Have not examined a copy.

C68 _____. . . . Tudor | [vegetables and hen] | HENRY Z. WALCK, INCORPORATED | New York
[<u>Copyright 1940 Henry Z. Walck, Inc.</u> Copyright © renewed 1968 by Tasha Tudor. | All rights reserved. First
published in this enlarged edition, 1964. Library | of Congress Catalog Card Number: 64-20584. Printed in the
United States of America.]

> PAGINATION: Three signatures <u>buff</u> paper, topsewn. [52] pages including free endpapers. 6 ¾″ x 6 ¼″.

> COVER: Light blue cloth, "cheesecloth" weave. Blue printing, laterally on spine: Tudor   THE
> COUNTY FAIR   Walck. Cloth reinforced hinges. <u>Spine is 3/16″ wide.</u>

> DUST JACKET: The front and back illustrations are reproduced in the same size as the calico version.
> The illustrations are on two white free-form fields surround by a yellow wash on rest of jacket
> except the flaps. Spine printed in black: Tudor   THE COUNTY FAIR   Walck. Front flap with
> both corners clipped: THE COUNTY FAIR | *by Tasha Tudor* || Sylvie Ann's gander, Alexander,
> wins a | blue ribbon at the Fair, and so does But- | tercup, Tom's Jersey calf. Besides that, the |
> strawberry jam Sylvie Ann makes wins a | fourth prize! It's a glorious summer for | everyone, with
> honey bees in glass jars, a | merry-go-round and all the other won- | ders of a County Fair. Perfect
> pictures | compliment a happy story with a surprise | ending. || A reissue, in enlarged format, of the
> 1940 | edition. || HENRY Z. WALCK, INC. || *30-60.* BACK FLAP: *Also by Tasha Tudor* || PUMPKIN
> MOONSHINE || "For those 3-6's who like their Halloweens as | gentle and charming as late fall sunshine,
> there | is a new edition of Tasha Tudor's tale about | blue-bonnetted Sylvie….This tiny tale is made | delicate
> and delightful by Miss Tudor's own | water-color illustrations." | — *Christian Science Monitor* ||
> ALEXANDER THE GANDER || "Older children who loved to pieces their tiny | copies of this Tudor
> picture book with very | simple text will rejoice that their younger | brothers and sisters may now have it in
> slightly | larger format, looking somehow more bril- | liantly quaint and childlike than it ever did | before."
> — *Dallas Morning News* || DORCAS PORKUS || "…Dorcas was an unusually proper pig—so | thought
> her masters Sylvie Ann and Tom— | until the day their Mimmsy held a quilting bee. | Dorcas turned it into a
> most unconventional | afternoon, and the young reader will find the | doings entirely delightful. In the best
> tradition | of children's stories and pictures." | —*Chicago Daily News.* All corners clipped at an angle on
> the examination copy.

> OTHER: TUDOR, Tasha *JUV* | *The county fair.* [Enl. ed.] New York, Walck [1964, c.1940. 52]p. col.
> illus. 18cm. 64-20584 2.75 |Two children enter their pets for competition at the county | fair. An
> enlarged version of the 1940 edition. Younger | readers. (*Book Publishing Record, 1960-1964,*
> IV: 5067)

C69 _____.

> COVER: A darker blue cloth in a heavier weave, but still a light shade. Blue printing on spine is also
> darker than above. <u>Spine is 3/8″ wide.</u>

> DUST JACKET: Both corners clipped from front flap, but not back flap.

> OTHER: Examined copies with inked inscription on book plate, <u>4-22/79</u>, and $5.50 price sticker.

C70 _____. Warner Books planned to reprint *The County Fair* in a 4 ¼ x 3 7/8″ paper over boards edition in April 1998. Part of the *Warner Treasures* series, the book, ISBN 0-446-91249-2, would retail for $ 6.95. http:/www.warnerbooks.com did not list the title as of March 3, 1998.   A company spokesperson confirmed a few days later that Warner would not be reprinting the series; another employee speculated these "calico book" reprints might be published by Little, Brown.

D1 DEER | in | the | HOLLOW [green] | Efner Tudor Holmes | ILLUSTRATED BY Marlowe deChristopher || [oval painting of a fawn lying on the ground] || PHILOMEL BOOKS | NEW YORK. [gray ink] [Text copyright © 1993 by Efner Tudor Holmes | Illustrations copyright © 1993 by Marlowe deChristopher | Published by Philomel Books, a division of The Putnam & Grosset Group, | 200 Madison Avenue, New York, NY 10016. All rights reserved. | This book, or parts thereof, may not be reproduced without permission | in writing from the publisher. Published simultaneously in Canada. | Printed in Hong Kong by South China Printing Co. (1988) Ltd. | lettering by David Gatti. The text is set in Bembo. | The pictures for *Deer in the Hollow* were executed on canvas in alkyd oil paints | and regular oils, with a combination of direct painting, glazing, and scumbling. || Library of Congress Cataloging-in-Publication Data | Holmes, Efner Tudor. Deer in the hollow / | Efner Tudor Homes [*sic*]; illustrated by Marlowe deChristopher. P. cm. | Summary: A young boy's special relationship with the forest animals culminates | on the day before Christmas with the animals are able to repay his care. | [1.Forest animals– Fiction. 2. Animals–Fiction. 3. Christmas–Fiction.] | I. deChristopher, Marlowe, ill. II. Title. PZ7.H735De 1993 | [Fic]–dc19 88-29322 CIP AC ISBN 0-399-21735-5 || 1 3 5 7 9 10 8 6 4 2 || First Impression]

PAGINATION: [1-32] pages in two signatures on white eggshell paper. 10 x 8 11/16″

COVER: Gloss lamination on pictorial paper over board covers. The image is of a boy walking with a fawn in a snowy woods. The same typography as the title page is used here, although in different placement and color. The title and author are overprinted in white above the boy and deer. There is 4 ½″ red graduated tapered rule between the title and the author. At the bottom of the cover, in forest green: ILLUSTRATED BY | Marlowe deChristopher. Overprinted in white on the spine: Holmes/deChristopher DEER IN THE HOLLOW Philomel. Back cover, lower left, overprinted in black: ISBN 0-399-21735-5 || [two bar codes, and above the smaller one on the right] 90000> | [beneath the large left] 9 780399 217357. Printed sideways at the left of the codes: EAN. Forest green endpapers.

DUST JACKET: Dust jacket reproduces the book cover exactly. Front flap: $15.95 | [rule] | ($20.95 CAN) || Seth is a quiet boy, rarely speaking | to those around him, more at home in | the forest with the creatures who live | there. It is said that at midnight on | Christmas Eve, all the animals talk. | Yet even without this holiday miracle, | Seth seems to have a special gift of | understanding them. || But during the winter of the terrible | snowstorm, ill himself, Seth can do | nothing to help his animal friends. Until, | that is, late on Christmas Eve, when he | is awakened by the barking of a wild | dog chasing a doe and her fawn. Then | he rushes out into the night to help. || Only when his grandparents dis- | cover him missing and the villagers | find him do they see the real-life miracle | of his friendship with the creatures of | the wood. || Efner Tudor Holmes and artists | Marlowe deChristopher create a gentle, | heartwarming story of a young boy and | his unique relationship with the natural | world and its creatures. EFNER TUDOR HOLMES has always | had a deep appreciation of animals and | nature. The youngest daughter of illus- | trator Tasha Tudor, she grew up on the | family farm in New Hampshire, sur- | rounded by animals and growing plants. | She now lives on a beautiful country | farm of her own with her husband, | Peter, their three sons, Nathan, Jason, | and Seth, and a wide variety of animals. || *Deer in the Hollow* is her first book | for Philomel. || MARLOWE DECHRISTOPHER comes | from a family of artists: his grandfather | was a stonecarver in Italy; his father is | a graphics and product designer; his | brother is a sculptor. || Mr. deChristopher attended the | Rhode Island School of Design and | later taught there as well. He now lives | on a farm in Downeast Maine with his wife, Linda Allen. || Mr. deChristopher's first book | for Philomel was *Greencoat and the Swanboy*, | published in 1991. || *Lettering by David Gatti* | *Jacket art © 1993 by Marlowe deChristopher* | [rule] | *Reinforced for Library use* || PHILOMEL BOOKS | *a division of* | *The Putnam & Grosset Group* | 200 Madison Avenue | New York, NY 10016 | 9310 || Printed in Hong Kong.

CONTENTS: Dedication page [3]: *For Judy and Bill Egan* | ETH | *"Sometimes our inner light goes out, but it is blown | again into flame by an encounter with another | human being. Each of us owes the deepest thanks | to those who have rekindled this inner light."* | ALBERT SCHWEITZER || [printer's device] || *For my parents* | M deC.

ILLUSTRATIONS: Illustrations are all full-color and vary in size from small ovals, to full-page, to two-page spreads. Ovals: [1, 9, 13-14, 19, 32] Partial-page: [8, 15, 18] Full page: [4, 6, 12, 21-22, 26, 31] Two-page: [10-11, 16-17, 24-25, 28-29] These pages have text only: [2-3, 5, 7, 20, 23, 27, 30]

COPYRIGHT REGISTRATION: TX 3-636-964 granted to Efner Tudor Holmes, 725 Hatfield Road, Contoocook, N.H. 03229. Louise Bates, agent for Efner Tudor Holmes, swears on Oct. 27, 1993:

DEER IN THE HOLLOW, by Efner Tudor Holmes, a US citizen, was published Oct. 27, 1993. The book was completed in 1993. Non-exclusive right to make copies and phonorecords for the blind and physically handicapped is granted to the Library of Congress. Fees to be charged against account DAO38288, the Putnam Publishing Group, 200 Madison Ave., NY, NY 10016 (212) 951-8719. Application and two deposit copies were received at LC Oct. 28, 1993, the effective date of registration.

COPYRIGHT REGISTRATION: VA 595-822 granted to Marlowe deChristopher, R.R. -1, Box 5420, Lubec, Me. 04652-9715. Louise Bates, agent for Marlowe deChristopher, swears on Oct. 27, 1993:

DEER IN THE HOLLOW, by Efner Tudor Holmes, with illustrations by Marlowe deChristopher, a US citizen, was published Oct. 27, 1993. The book was completed in 1993. Fees to be charged against account DAO38288, the Putnam Publishing Group, 200 Madison Ave., NY, NY 10016 (212) 951-8719. Application and two deposit copies were received at LC Oct. 28, 1993, the effective date of registration.

D2 DIAPARENE [printed letter over letter down the spine] DIAPARENE | T.M. Reg. U.S. Pat. Off. | Patent no. 2,643,969 | All rights Reserved | Printed in U.S.A. [at base of spine] [ca. 1953]

PAGINATION: Printed pasteboard box in the form of a book with only "front cover" that opens. 7 7/8″ x 4½″

COVER: The box is sized and printed to look like a book with a printed spine, simulated pages at top, fore edge and bottom, and curved band top and bottom. The front cover has no text, but a large painted boot and general image of the old woman who lived in a shoe. She is pictured scrubbing one baby, with two more in a wash tub, and 15 miscellaneous children (mostly in diapers) throughout the scene. A stork has built a nest on the roof behind a brick chimney. Two babies are floating two balloons from the attic window. An apple tree in bloom also supports a clothesline with diapers drying. The spine is painted to resemble a leather bound book; text in green. Back cover shows the same domicile with a television antenna on the roof; a Diaparene truck has pulled up to the white picket fence. A delivery man brings fresh diapers to the door, the old woman is now lounging under a large umbrella, and the clothesline has been removed from the apple tree. The children seem to be much more orderly. A sample box has green text at the bottom of the panel: DIAPER SERVICE IMPRINT | GOES HERE, TOO! We have seen another imprinted BO-PEEP DIAPER SERVICE | Phone { Portsmouth [NH] GE 6-5500 | Dover SH 2-3517.

CONTENTS: Text inside the front cover above a domestic bedroom scene: There was an old woman who lived in a shoe; | She had so many children, she didn't know what to do. | Then she used diaper service, plus Diaparene; | No "home-laundry" rash, now all is serene. | For, direct to their door, antiseptic and white | Come didies to babies' and mommie's delight. The mother is sewing while rocking a cradle. Four more children are

148

asleep in their trundle beds. Pink gingham curtains at the window, two geraniums on the windowsill and two pictures and a coocoo clock on the wall. Other furniture includes an oval braided rug, a high-back Boston rocker, a three-legged candle stand with sewing supplies, and a wash stand complete with pitcher and bowl. The recto is fitted with two compartments that hold four small Diaparene samples: anti-bacterial baby lotion in a white plastic 1 ¼ ounce bottle, a metal tin of methyl benzethonium chloride dusting powder, two foil samples of Diaparene Peri-Anal and Diaparene Chloride Ointment. The lotion is credited to diaparene Products Div., Breon Laboratories, Inc., Subsidiary of Sterling Drug, Inc., New York 18, NY. The sleeve of Peri-Anal indicates 'Supplied by Homemakers products Division, George A. Breon & Co., New York 18, NY.

ILLUSTRATIONS: In addition to those already described, there are five babies in the borders around the sample tins, the interior recto.

OTHER: Although not technically a book, the box is designed to resemble a book with pages painted along the top, bottom and fore edges. It's cover opens like a book with the briefest of advertising rhymes inside. We include it for its book form and for its unique qualities. These sample kits were for local diaper services to imprint with their own name and supply to new mothers as an advertising medium. A 1 ¼" cardboard band slipped over the box to prevent the cover opening and spilling out its contents. The band is imprinted: **There was an old woman | Who lived in a shoe.**

D3 *The Dolls' Christmas* | [Antique locket, opened to two portraits, suspended by a red ribbon from an evergreen bough] | BY TASHA TUDOR [black] || New York [red] | *Oxford University Press* [black] | 1950 [red] [Copyright 1950 | OXFORD UNIVERSITY PRESS, INC. || PRINTED IN THE UNITED STATES OF AMERICA]

PAGINATION: [32] pp. in 2 signatures plus endpapers. 6 11/16" x 6 3/16".

COVER: Red linen cover with buff paste-on label, 3 ½" x 3 7/8": *The | Dolls' Christmas* | BY TASHA TUDOR within a green and red oval paper chain within a thick red line. Spine imprinted in black: TUDOR | *The Dolls' Christmas* | OXFORD.

DUST JACKET: Dust jacket is ivory with a green back. Printing in black, highlights in red. Front: *The Dolls' Christmas* [above] and BY TASHA TUDOR [below] an evergreen wreath surrounding two dolls sitting back-to-back. Spine: TUDOR [in red] | *The Dolls' Christmas* | OXFORD [in red]. Back: a 2 ½" ivory oval containing two candy canes and greens tied with a red ribbon, from page [1]. Front flap: *The | Dolls' Christmas* [red] || BY TASHA TUDOR || Sethany Ann and Nicey Melinda | were two very old dolls who lived in a | very handsome doll house and belonged | to two little girls. Every Christmas they | had a party for all the dolls of the neigh- | borhood at which a marionette show was given. ¶Tasha Tudor has told the story of this | Christmas party in lovely pictures and | delightful text. All small girls will revel | in this picture book of Christmas and | dolls, and agree with Nicey who says, | "Christmas is the most magic time in all | the year." [black] || *Oxford Books | for Boys and Girls* [red] || 40-80 $1.50 [black]. Back flap: *Also by Tasha Tudor* [red] || THISTLY B | A TALE FOR EASTER | SNOW BEFORE CHRISTMAS | THE WHITE GOOSE [black] || *The Calico Books* [red] | COUNTY FAIR | PUMPKIN MOONSHINE | DORCAS PORKUS | LINSEY WOOLSEY [black].

CONTENTS: The two dolls stand behind an open book on which is written this dedication: To all the | Children | and Dolls | who come | to the | Christmas | Party | and to | Rosabelle [Mauck]| for | helping | out, p. [5].

ILLUSTRATIONS: Full color, full-page watercolors on odd-numbered pages [1-29]. Buff endpapers have portraits of Sethany Ann and Nicey Melinda in antique oval frames with red bows.

Tudor's own dolls and two daughters (as well as their friends) served as models for these illustrations. See also *The Dolls of Yesterday.*

OTHER: Some copies, probably those sold at the Ginger and Pickles Store, bear a small paper label printed in brown ink inside the rear cover: TASHA TUDOR | [rule] | RFD No. 1 Contoocook | New Hampshire | *Autographed Books | Christmas Cards | Correspondence Notes.* In every instance, the title appears in a script with large capitals. See also *Dolls of Three Centuries* by St. George, page 65, below, for a photograph of Tudor's dolls Sethany Ann, Mr. Shakespeare and Nicey Melinda. And the dolls feature in a set of ten photographic postal cards sold by the Ginger & Pickles Store in the 1950s. See *Tasha Tudor's Dolls.*

Copyright registration A 48239 granted to Oxford University Press, Inc., 114 Fifth Ave., N.Y., N.Y. W. S. Gherton [illegible], agent for the claimant, swears on Oct. 8, 1950:

THE DOLLS' CHRISTMAS, by Tasha Tudor, of Contoocook, N.H., born 1910 [*sic*], a U.S. citizen, was published Oct. 5, 1950. The book was type-set and printed by Kellogg and Bulkeley Company, Hartford, Ct. and bound by H. Wolff Book Manufacturing Co., Inc., N.Y., N.Y. Application and two deposit copies were received at LC Oct. 10, 1950.

Copyright renewal registration RE 5-433 granted to the author Tasha Tudor, c/o David McKay Co. Inc., 750 Third Ave., N.Y., N.Y. 10017. H.J. Rabinovitz, agent for Tasha Tudor, swears on Aug. 9, 1978:

THE DOLLS' CHRISTMAS, text by Tasha Tudor, was originally registered as A 48239 by Oxford University Press and was published October 5, 1959. [However, that year has been X'ed out and beside it typed, 1950.* A note at the top of the certificate indicates this amendment was typed by the Copyright Office.] Charged to account DAO50830 DAVID MCKAY CO., INC. Renewal application received at LC Aug. 14, 1978, the effective date of the registration.

D4 _____.

COVER: Another binding in a rose cloth, cover label set in an impressed block.

D5 _____.

COVER: Scarlet cloth, course weave; cover label without the impressed block.

DUST JACKET: Have not examined one with price intact.

D6 _____. Have not examined a copy of <u>Second printing</u>.

D7 _____. [Copyright 1950 | OXFORD UNIVERSITY PRESS, INC. | <u>Third Printing, 1956</u> || PRINTED IN THE UNITED STATES OF AMERICA]

COVER: Rose cloth with no sheen, as on the first edition. 6 5/8"x 6 3/16".

DUST JACKET: Have not examined one with the price intact.

D8 _____.

COVER: A coarser woven carmine cloth.

DUST JACKET: Have not examined one with the price intact.

D9 *The Dolls' Christmas* | BY TASHA TUDOR [black] || New York [red] | *Henry Z. Walck,*
Incorporated [black] | 1950 [red] [Copyright 1950 | HENRY Z. WALCK, INC. || Library of Congress Catalog
Card Number: 59-12744 || PRINTED IN THE UNITED STATES OF AMERICA]

> PAGINATION: [32] pp. in 2 signatures buff paper plus endpapers. 6 11/16″ x 6 1/4″

> COVER: Carmine linen with the paste-on label. Hinges reinforced with white buckram. Spine
> imprinted in black: TUDOR *The Dolls' Christmas* WALCK. Buff endpapers as above.

> DUST JACKET: Spine: TUDOR [red] *The Dolls' Christmas* [black] WALCK [red]. Have not
> examined a copy with price intact. Last four lines of text vary: HENRY Z. WALCK, INC. |
> *successor to* | Oxford Books for Boys and Girls [red] | 40-80 [Price clipped]. Back flap text in
> black except for title: *Another holiday story by Tasha Tudor* | *A* | *Tale for Easter* ||
> "Children...take delight in the lovely | childlike character of this small book | which carries the thought of
> springtime. | ...Many delicate pictures of rabbits, | lambs, chickens and daffodils, in close as- | sociation
> with little children, are sprin- | kled over the pages, while a wonderful | fawn brings a happy climax to the
> story. | Precise in detail and exquisite in color, | Tasha Tudor's little books are truly Amer- | ican in tone,
> suggesting a loving obser- | vation akin to that of Beatrix Potter." | -*The Horn Book.*

D10 _____.

> PAGINATION: Brighter ivory paper.

> DUST JACKET: The dust jacket includes $2.50 lower corner of front flap; the upper corner is clipped

D11 _____.

> PAGINATION: The paper is whiter and a heavier stock.

> COVER: Carmine linen without the label. Buckram hinges.

> DUST JACKET: Have not examined front flap with corners present. *The* | *Dolls'* . . . the year." ||
> HENRY Z. WALCK, INC. [black] || 40-80 [corner clipped].

D12 _____. BY TASHA TUDOR [black] | New York [red] | *Henry Z. Walck, Incorporated* [black]
[A catalog card in top half: E Tudor, Tasha | The dolls' Christmas. Walck, 1950 | unp. Illus. || Each
Christmas two girls give a | party for all of the dolls of their | neighborhood. || 1. Christmas stories 2.
Dolls - Fiction | I. Title. Beneath the card: THIS MAIN ENTRY CATALOG CARD MAY BE REPRODUCED WITHOUT
PERMISSION. || COPYRIGHT 1950 HENRY Z. WALCK, INC. | ISBN: 0-8098-1026-3 (HARDCOVER) | ISBN: 0-8098-2912-6 (PAPERBACK) |
LIBRARY OF CONGRESS CATALOG CARD NUMBER: 59-12744 || PRINTED IN THE UNITED STATES OF AMERICA.]

> PAGINATION: [32] pp. in 2 signatures plus endpapers. 6 ¾ x 6 1/8″

> COVER: Carmine linen, no paste-on label. Buckram hinges.

> DUST JACKET: Front flap, bottom 40-80 $4.95.

> CONTENTS: There is no red date on the title page.

D13 _____.

> PAGINATION: [36] pp. including wrapper. 6 ½ x 5 7/8″

> COVER: White pasteboard, gloss finish, with design of previous dust jacket on front. There are also
> two prices, $1.50, in upper right corner, and $1.75 CAN., in lower right corner. Spine is printed in
> all Roman capitals, the only printing I have seen thus: TUDOR THE DOLLS' CHRISTMAS
> WALCK. Likewise, the back of the cover is the only example I have seen all white, no

decoration and two paragraphs of text: *The Dolls' Christmas* | by TASHA TUDOR || "For all little girls who still cherish dolls, this is a | perfect Christmas story. Sethany Ann and Nicey | Melinda were two very old dolls belonging to the little girls Laura and Efner. . . . Every year the little | girls had a party for their dolls and the other dolls | in the neighborhood." | —*The Instructor* || Tasha Tudor was born in Boston and grew up in | the Connecticut countryside. The mother of two | sons and two daughters, she now lives in Con- | toocook, New Hampshire, where she gardens, | housekeeps, sews and cooks, in addition to writing | and illustrating many children's books.

CONTENTS: Front cover [1-2], half-title [3], blank [4], title page [5], . . . last page of text [30], last illustration [31], blank pages [32-34], back cover [35-36].

D14 _____.

PAGINATION: [36] pp. <u>perfect bound</u> including free endpapers. 6 ½ x 6"

COVER: Red <u>pebbled</u> plastic-filled paper over boards, no label.

DUST JACKET: Top of front flap: <u>$5.95</u>.   Front flap, bottom 40-80

D15 _____. . . . Henry Z. Walck, <u>Inc. | New York</u> [3 ¾" printer's bar, broken] [black] [Copyright ©1950 <u>by Tasha Tudor</u> || All rights reserved, including the right to reproduce | this book, or parts thereof, in any form, except for | the inclusion of brief quotations in a review. || <u>Library of Congress Catalog Card Number: 59-12744</u> | <u>ISBN: 0-8098-1026-3</u> || 10 9 8 7 6 5 4 3 2 1 | MANUFACTURED IN THE UNITED STATES OF AMERICA]

PAGINATION: [<u>36</u>] pp. in 2 signatures plus endpapers. <u>6 13/16 x 6 7/8"</u>

COVER: <u>Royal blue paper</u> imprinted with fine weave over board covers. For the first time, endpapers are a heavier buff stock top sewn to the signatures and then glued into the casing. Only one set of the previous illustrated endpapers appear as pp. [32-33]. The printer's bar on the title page and the title on the dedication page are new to this printing.

DUST JACKET: Exterior of dust jacket as before, but the text on the flaps has been largely reset in italics. Front flap: $5.95 [black] | *The | Dolls' Christmas* [red] | BY TASHA TUDOR || *Sethany Ann and Nicey Melinda were* ⌊ *two very old dolls who lived in a very* ⌊ *handsome doll house and belonged to* ⌊ *two little girls. | Every Christmas they | had a party for all the dolls of the neigh- | borhood at which a marionette show was given.* ¶ *Tasha Tudor has told the story of this | Christmas party in lovely pictures and | delightful text. All small girls will revel | in this picture book of Christmas and | dolls, and agree with Nicey* ⌊ *who says, "Christmas is the most magic | time in all the year."* || Henry Z. Walck, Inc. | <u>a division of</u> | DAVID McKAY COMPANY, INC., | New York. Back flap: ANOTHER HOLIDAY STORY | BY TASHA TUDOR || A TALE FOR EASTER || *"Children...take delight in the lovely | childlike character of this small book | which carries the thought of springtime. | ...Many delicate pictures of rabbits, | lambs, chickens and daffodils, in close* ⌊ *association with little children, are sprin- | kled over the pages, while a wonderful | fawn brings a happy climax to the story. | Precise in detail and exquisite in color, | Tasha Tudor's little books are truly Amer- | ican in tone, suggesting a loving observa- | tion akin to that of Beatrix Potter."* | - Horn Book.

CONTENTS: Page [1] script print <u>title is much smaller</u> than earlier printings, and the <u>candy canes are printed in black</u>. Page [5], dedication, <u>now includes title</u>.

D16 _____.

PAGINATION: Front three leaves and last leaf, <u>buff paper</u>; remaining book on ivory matte.

COVER: <u>Moss green paper</u> over boards, fine weave pattern, shiny sprayed finish.

DUST JACKET: Have not examined a copy with price intact.

D17 _____.

PAGINATION: [32] pp. in a glossy white paper wrapper. 6 ½″ x 6 ½″

COVER: Approximates the first dust jacket design. Spine: TUDOR [red] | *The Dolls' Christmas* [black] | WALCK [red] Back cover upper right: $2.50 pre-printed in white || [two tied candy canes within a white oval] || Lower right: 0-8098-2912-6. [white on green]

D18 _____.

COVER: Back cover upper right, price has been obliterated by a metallic green overprinted rectangle.

D19 _____.

PAGINATION: [28] pp. The half-title and title pages were not bound into this copy.

D20 _____. Have not examined a second hard cover printing.

D21 _____. [. . . Library of Congress Catalog Card Number: 59-12744 | ISBN: 0-8098-1026-3 (Cloth) | ISBN: 0-8098-2912-6 (Paperback) || 10 9 8 7 6 5 4 3 2 | MANUFACTURED IN THE UNITED STATES OF AMERICA]

COVER: Price overprinted in the green metallic stamping.

D22 _____. Have not examined a third printing.

D23 _____. Have not examined a 4th printing hard cover.

D24 _____. [. . . 10 9 8 7 6 5 4 . . . UNITED STATES OF AMERICA]

PAGINATION: A smoother white paper.

COVER: Back cover upper right: $2.95 pre-printed in white.

D25 _____. Have not examined a 5th hard cover.

D26 _____. . . . Henry Z. Walck, Inc. | New York [. . . Library of Congress Catalog Card Number: 59-12744 || 10 9 8 7 6 5 | MANUFACTURED IN THE UNITED STATES OF AMERICA]

PAGINATION: [32] pp. 6 ½″ x 6 5/8″

COVER: Back cover upper right: $3.95 pre-printed in white on green.

OTHER: No printer's bar on the title page, verso lacks ISBNs.

D27 _____. [. . . Card Number: 59-12744 | ISBN: 0-8098-1026-3 (Cloth) | ISBN: 0-8098-2912-6 (Paperback) | 10 9 8 7 6 | MANUFACTURED IN THE UNITED STATES OF AMERICA]

PAGINATION: 36 pp. top sewn in one signature, including white endpapers without illustration. 6 11/16″ x 6 13/16″

COVER: <u>Green</u> cloth cover, <u>reset type</u> <u>stamped in gilt on spine</u>: TUDOR *The Doll's* [*sic*] *Christmas* WALCK.

DUST JACKET: White paper. Front image was reproduced from a damaged master print: <u>a scratch</u> runs vertically across the doll's brown dress.   Front flap: $6.95 [black] | *The . . .*

D28 _____. [. . . 1 0 9 8 7 6 | MANUFACTURED IN THE UNITED STATES OF AMERICA]

PAGINATION: [32] pp. <u>white paper</u>, in a glossy white <u>paper wrapper</u>.   6 ½″ x 6 5/8″

COVER: No scratch on front image. Back cover, upper right: <u>$4.50 printed in white against the green background</u>. Lower right: <u>0-8098-2912-6</u>. [white on green]

D29 _____. [. . . 1 0 9 8 7 6 | MANUFACTURED IN THE UNITED STATES OF AMERICA]

COVER: Back cover, upper right: <u>$4.95 stamped in black on a green round sticker,   attached over a pre-printed $4.50</u>. Examined copy with label cut smaller.

D30 _____. . . . BY TASHA TUDOR [. . . 1 0 9 8 7 | . . . UNITED STATES OF AMERICA]

PAGINATION: [36] pp.

COVER: Red-orange paper over boards, weave imprint.

DUST JACKET: $6.95, top of front flap. The jacket reverts to the design of the red-pebbled cover, D12. The front flap mentions <u>only Walck</u>, not McKay. Back flap title is in a large <u>red cursive</u> font.

OTHER: <u>Title page doesn't carry a publisher's name</u>. An ex-library copy is stamped Dec 5, 1986, suggesting this book was <u>manufactured in 1986</u>.

D31 _____. . . . BY TASHA TUDOR [. . . 1 0 9 8 7 | . . . UNITED STATES OF AMERICA]

PAGINATION: [32] pp.

COVER: Paper wrapper. Back cover, upper right: <u>$4.95</u>, white on green.

D32 *The Dolls' Christmas* | BY TASHA TUDOR ‖ Jenny Wren Press | Mooresville, Indiana [Copyright © 1994 by The Jenny Wren Press | All Rights Reserved | No part of this book may be reproduced in any form | without permission from the Publisher. ‖ Library of Congress number in publication data | ISBN 9621753-90 [*sic*] ‖ Re-printed in the U.S.A. | First printing in 1950 by Henry Z. Walck, Inc., New York]

PAGINATION: [36] pp. including free endpapers. 6 13/16″ x 7 1/8″

COVER: Red leather stamped in gilt. Front: the text and illustrations as they have always appeared on previous dust jackets. Spine: <u>TASHA</u> TUDOR | *The Dolls' Christmas* | THE JENNY WREN PRESS. Lower right, back cover: <u>9621753-90</u>. Ivory endpapers, white cloth hinges on covers.

ILLUSTRATIONS: Water color illustrations: pp. [3 (title), 5 (dedication), 7, 9, 11, 13, 15, 17, 19, 21, 23, 25, 27, 29-32.   Note: pp. [30-31] are the two oval doll portraits from the original endpapers. Page [32] carries the baking scene from page [15], slightly reduced, above this text: <u>If interested in other Tasha Tudor creations - calendars, Christmas cards, | Valentines, reprints of early miniature books made for her children, | replicas of her sketch books, lithographs, paper dolls, illustrated | books and other treasures - send for our catalogue. ‖ The Jenny Wren Press | P.O. Box 505 | Mooresville, Indiana 46158.</u>

CONTENT: Page [1] *The Dolls' Christmas* || [tied candy canes] || <u>The Jenny Wren Press, Incorporated |</u> <u>Mooresville, Indiana</u>. Page [2]: ♥ *OUR HEARTFELT GRATITUDE TO OUR JENNY WREN* *PRESS FRIENDS I FOR MAKING OUR DREAM A REALITY* ♥. The Press has applied a 2 5/8″ x 3 5/16″ oval gummed label in the center of the page. The label's color illustration depicts two girls at a tea party with three toys, a kitten and a corgi, within a border of pink ribbon and flowers. The label is <u>signed T. Tudor, 93</u> and at the left, <u>52/150</u> indicating the place of this copy in a limited edition of leather bound copies.

OTHER: Each copy was shipped in a plastic bag.

D33 _____.

OTHER: This item is actually a misprint of the following entry. One may assume, then, that as many errors were printed as were corrected copies. One also assumes that each customer who had preordered a copy actually received both copies. Beth Mathers mailed yellow postcards to customers from Indianapolis in October 1994 with this message: Sept, 1994 | Dear Customer, | The book the <u>Dolls Christmas</u> has a printing | error in the copy you have received. We ask that | you keep it (it may become collectable!) & by December | 15th — <u>No Later</u> we will be sending you another | copy in corrected form. We do so appreciate your | Kind understanding — for it was due to circumstances | beyond our control. Enjoy your free print in the | meantime! — Joyfully, | Beth Mathers.

Pages [12] and [18] were transposed in the erroneous printing.

D34 _____.

COVER: <u>Red cloth binding</u>.

OTHER: These copies were <u>not numbered,</u> but customers who wished to pay twice the normal price received copies with the same oval label used in the leather copies, with <u>the autograph T. Tudor, 93</u>. This Jenny Wren Press reprint was announced in the catalog, <u>The Jenny Wren Press Spring-Summer 1994</u>, page 2: **Another special Reprinting! Pre-order Now** <u>**A Doll's**</u> <u>**Christmas**</u> - This Enchanting book will be going on press in the late Summer just in time to add to your lists for Christmas presents! <u>A Doll's Christmas</u> is one of Tasha's most sought after & treasured by her fans - The book has been out of print for a very long time & can <u>now be yours!</u> <u>Pre-order now & a special surprise gift will be sent with your book in early Fall!!!</u> You'll be glad you did!!! - Also 125 leather copies are available with autographed bookplate & numbered! #B044 - A Doll's Christmas - $14.95 BB44 - Autographed with Bookplate - $29.95 BL44 - #1- 200 Leather - $85.00 <u>The Jenny Wren Press Fall-Winter 94-95</u>, page 3, pictures the jacket with this accompanying description. <u>The Doll's Christmas</u> - is one of Tasha's most sought after books & treasured by her fans - The book has been out of print for a very long time & can <u>now be yours!</u> - Also 150 leather copies are available with autographed bookplate & numbered! You will <u>love</u> the enchanted story! #B044 - A Doll's Christmas - $14.95 BL44 - -#1-150 Leather - $ 85.00. The title does not appear in <u>The Jenny Wren Press & Mrs. Fizziwigs Spring - Summer 1995</u>.

The book was photographically reproduced, and so the title appears correctly, THE DOLLS' CHRISTMAS as compared to the title given in the publisher's ad. More egregiously, the title page verso erroneously states that THE DOLLS' CHRISTMAS was first printed by Walck in 1950, ignoring the Oxford University Press publications. The publishers have also confused two common library control statements (Library of Congress Catalog Card Number, and Library of Congress Cataloging in Publication Data) and collapsed them into the single - Library of Congress number in publication data. But then, neither piece of information is given, only a partial ISBN.

Have examined a copy with a [Vermont?] store label on the dj back priced $14.95, 10/95 and 'VT-Tudor.' Copy was autographed on title page and carried a 1 ¾ x 3″ oval gold foil label with black printing: Autographed | Copy.

D35 *The Dolls' House* ‖ By Rumer Godden | ILLUSTRATED BY TASHA TUDOR ‖ [Tottie and Apple holding hands] ‖ NEW YORK | The Viking Press [COPYRIGHT 1947, © 1962 BY RUMER GODDEN | ALL RIGHTS RESERVED | TEXT FIRST PUBLISHED IN 1948 BY THE VIKING PRESS, INC. | THIS NEWLY ILLUSTRATED EDITION FIRST PUBLISHED IN 1962 | BY THE VIKING PRESS, INC. | 625 MADISON AVENUE, NEW YORK 22, NY. ‖ LIBRARY OF CONGRESS CATALOG CARD NUMBER: 62-18693 ‖ PRINTED IN THE U.S.A. BY KELLOGG & BULKELEY].

PAGINATION: Nine signatures of buff paper, pages [1-10] 11-127 [128] 129-136 [137-140] plus fly leaves. 8 1/8″ x 5 5/8″ x 3/4″.

COVER: Tan cloth imprinted in butterscotch: a line frame enclosing small vines in corners, and above the centered doll house The Dolls' House. Spine: GODDEN   THE DOLLS' HOUSE VIKING.

DUST JACKET: Buff paper dust jacket, red wash front and back except for a large oval on front on which 'the house' is printed in color. All letters, except VIKING which is black, are buff capitals against the red jacket: THE DOLLS' HOUSE [above] BY RUMER GODDEN | ILLUSTRATED BY TASHA TUDOR [below house]. Spine: GODDEN THE DOLLS' HOUSE VIKING. Front flap text, black, except <u>green title</u>: **$2.75** | *The Dolls' House* | By Rumer Godden | ILLUSTRATED BY TASHA TUDOR ‖ Bewitchingly beautiful drawings add | fresh delight to a book which *The Horn | Book* described (in its original edition) | as having "a lasting charm for readers of | any age." ‖ "The sensitive, penetrating art of | Rumer Godden has created the choicest | of all doll stories...Beautifully written, | *The Dolls' House* gives reality not only | to the leading characters but to others | who appear in the Exhibition opened | by the Queen. Tottie, a small wooden | Dutch doll who is the wisest of them all, | likes to think of the strength of the tree | from which she is made. 'It is an anx- | ious, sometimes a dangerous thing to be | a doll. Dolls cannot choose; they cannot | "do"; they can only be done by. They | can only wish hard for the right thing | to happen.' ‖ "Rumer Godden tells in this enchant- | ing story what two little girls did with | the Plantaganet family and how good | things and bad things came and passed." ‖ 07011. Back flap text, black but for green title and author on first two lines: STORIES ABOUT DOLLS | *by Rumer Godden* ‖ *Illustrated by Jean Primrose* | MISS HAPPINESS AND MISS FLOWER ‖ *Illustrated by Adrienne Adams* | THE STORY OF HOLLY AND IVY | THE FAIRY DOLL | CANDY FLOSS | IMPUNITY JANE ‖ [a red drawing of a circus bareback rider on a rearing circus horse] ‖ THE VIKING PRESS | 625 Madison Ave. | New York 22, N.Y. ‖ PRINTED IN THE U.S.A.

CONTENTS: Each brown printed end paper has a drawing "pinned" to it, each of a different character: Apple, Tottie, Birdie and Mr. Plantaganet. Page [1]: *The Dolls' House* ‖ *Also by Rumer Godden* | THE MOUSEWIFE | IMPUNITY JANE | THE FAIRY DOLL | MOUSE HOUSE | THE STORY OF HOLLY AND IVY | MISS HAPPINESS AND MISS FLOWER | CANDY FLOSS | ST. JEROME AND THE LION. Page [5]: For | *Janaki Paula Mary Foster* | WITH LOVE. Page [7]: *Fain am I to work these nosegays | Gathered from my tranquil days | In gentle rain, mild storm and sunny weather...* | FROM GREAT-GRANDMOTHER'S SAMPLER. Page [9]: *The Dolls' House*

ILLUSTRATIONS: There are color illustrations on pages [2] [3] title page, [10] and 11. Black and white illustrations on pages, 18, 29, 30, 35, 37, 38, 48, 53, 54, 63, 76, 77, 78, 82, 87, 92, 93, 98, 102, 103, 112, 115, 116, 119, 123, [128] 129, 132, 133, 134, 136. Pages [137-140] are blank.

COPYRIGHT REGISTRATION: A 587277 granted to Rumer Godden, Little Douce Grove, Northiam, East Sussex, England. Phyllis Gelbman, agent for claimant, swears on Oct. 5, 1962:

THE DOLLS' HOUSE, by Rumer Godden, a British citizen, and illustrated by Tasha Tudor, Route 1, Contoocook, NH, a US citizen, was published Oct. 5, 1962. Copyright is claimed on the illustrations and the work as a whole. The book was manufactured by Kellogg and

Bulkeley, 85 Trumbull St., Hartford 1, CT, Vail-Ballou Press, Inc., Binghamton, NY, and Montauk Book Mfg. Co., Inc., 419 Lafayette St., NY 3, NY. Charged to account of the Viking Press, Inc., 625 Madison Ave., NY 22, NY. Application and affidavit received at LC Oct. 8, 1962; two deposit copies received Oct. 15, 1962.

COPYRIGHT RENEWAL REGISTRATION: RE 467-889 granted to Rumer Godden (also known as Mrs. M.R. Haynes-Dixon), Ardnacloich, Moniaive, Thornhill, Dumfriesshire DG3 4HZ, Scotland, claiming as proprietor of copyright in a work made for hire. T. Uehara, agent for Rumer Godden, swears on Jan. 19, 1990:

THE DOLLS' HOUSE, by Rumer Godden*, Tasha Tudor was published Oct. 5, 1962, registration A 587277. Copyright is claimed on the illustrations and on the work as a whole.* However, 'and on the work as a whole' and Rumer Godden have been lined out and asterisked to a note at the top of page 2, "Amended by Copyright Office." Fees charged against account DA 018074, Viking Penguin Inc., 40 West 23rd St., NY, NY. Application received at LC Jan. 22, 1990, the effective date of registration.

D36 _____.

COVER: Another state with blood red paint imprinting cover and spine.

D37 _____. [COPYRIGHT 1947, 1962 BY RUMER GODDEN...62-18693 ‖ SECOND PRINTING JANUARY 1963 ‖ PRINTED IN THE U.S.A. BY KELLOGG & BULKELEY]

PAGINATION: Eight signatures of a smoother ivory paper.

D38 _____.

PAGINATION: A more buff and acidic paper, exhibiting minor foxing to edges in 1997.

COVER: Rust paint is less distinct than above.

OTHER: Inscribed April 19, 1972.

D39 _____.

COVER: Library binding of Second Printing. Stronger hinge, cover cloth is stronger, tighter weave and color has been added to cover painting. The frame line and house are red; title, vines and ivy on house are green. Spine: GODDEN [green] THE DOLLS' HOUSE [red] VIKING [green] Back, lower right: VIKING | Library Binding | with ship logo, all in red.

DUST JACKET: Have not examined a copy.

D40 _____. [COPYRIGHT 1947, 1962 BY RUMER GODDEN . . . 62-18693 ‖ THIRD PRINTING JULY 1965 ‖ FIC 1. DOLLS-STORIES | PRINTED IN THE U.S.A. BY KELLOGG & BULKELEY]

DUST JACKET: $3.00 price at top of front flap, bottom corner clipped at 45° angle.

CONTENTS: Page [1] includes two new title lines at bottom of page: LITTLE PLUM | HOME IS THE SAILOR, otherwise it is identical to first Tudor printing with butterscotch illustration on front cover.

D41 _____. [... THIRD PRINTING JULY 1965 . . .] Library binding. Have not examined one.

D42 _____. [... FOURTH PRINTING JULY 1966 ...] Trade binding. Have not examined one.

D43 _____. [COPYRIGHT 1947, © 1962 BY RUMER GODDEN ... NEW YORK 22, N.Y. | <u>FOURTH PRINTING JULY 1966</u> | <u>LIBRARY OF CONGRESS CATALOG CARD NUMBER:</u> 62-18693 | <u>FIC 1. DOLLS-STORIES</u> ‖ PRINTED IN THE U.S.A.]

    PAGINATION: [i-vi, 1-10] 11-127 [128] 129-136 [137-142] including free endpapers. Pagination as before, but with extra, heavier cream front endpapers. The previous illustrated endpapers are bound as pp. [iv-v], [142] and the rear pasted endpaper.

    COVER: Wine red cloth cover imprinted with the previous dust jacket illustration, cream printing, and added to the lower right back cover: [Viking ship on two waves sailing to the right toward ...] VIKING | _{Library Binding}. The front cover is attached with <u>white linen hinge</u> in this binding.

    DUST JACKET: Have not examined a copy.

D44 _____. [COPYRIGHT 1947, © 1962 BY RUMER GODDEN.. .NEW YORK 22, N.Y. | <u>FIFTH PRINTING JUNE 1968</u> | LIBRARY OF CONGRESS CATALOG CARD NUMBER: 62-18693 | FIC 1. DOLLS-STORIES | PRINTED IN THE U.S.A.]

    COVER: Tan cloth imprinted in butterscotch as in first printing.

    DUST JACKET: Have not examined one.

D45 _____. [... <u>FIFTH PRINTING JUNE 1968</u> ...] library binding. Have not examined one.

D46 _____. [. . . <u>FIFTH PRINTING</u> . . .]

    COVER: Examined an ex-lib, rebound by Treasure Trove [determined from the TT circular monogram on the back cover] with HUNTTING BOUND endpapers. This is the Tudor edition, but the binder has imprinted the front cover with the first edition dust jacket image by Dana Saintsbury from 1948.

D47 _____. [. . . SIXTH PRINTING NOVEMBER 1968. . .]

    PAGINATION: [i-ii, 1-10] 11-127 [128] 129-136 [137-146] including free endpapers

    COVER: As in fifth printing.

    DUST JACKET: <u>$3.95</u> . . . [<u>Lower corner</u> of front flap clipped at a 45° angle.] The dust jacket matches that of the 3rd printing with the red ink being a brighter scarlet.

D48 _____. [. . . <u>SIXTH PRINTING</u> . . .]

    PAGINATION: [i-vi, 1-10] 11-127 [128] 129-136 [137-146] including free endpapers. Interior pagination as before, but with extra, heavier cream endpapers. The previous illustrated endpapers are here bound in as pp. [iv-v] and [142-143].

    COVER: <u>Library binding</u> <u>brick</u> red cloth imprinted with the dust jacket illustration, cream printing, as in fourth printing. <u>White linen hinges</u>, front and back. <u>Top painted red.</u>

    DUST JACKET: <u>Upper corner</u> of front flap clipped at a 45° angle. Lower corner: <u>VLB $3.77</u>. Gold foil Viking Library Binding label (¾" x 2 5/8"), applied ½" from bottom edge, with the same logo as on back cover printed in black. <u>Printed sideways on the label as it wraps the spine:</u> <u>VIKING | Library | Binding.</u> The wave extends the full length of the label.

    OTHER: Examined a copy inscribed Christmas 1971.

D49 _____. [. . . <u>SIXTH PRINTING</u> . . .]

    COVER: <u>Library binding</u> <u>wine</u> red cloth. <u>Top edge is not painted.</u>

DUST JACKET: Have not examined a copy with price intact. <u>Upper corner</u> of front flap clipped at a 45° angle. Foil label no longer present.

OTHER: Examined a copy inscribed Nov. 16, 1973.

D50 _____. [FOR | *Janaki Paula Mary Foster* | WITH LOVE ‖ Copyright 1947, © 1962 by Rumer Godden | All rights reserved | Text first published in 1948 by The Viking Press, Inc. | First published <u>with these illustrations in</u> 1962 | <u>Viking Seafarer edition issued in 1970</u> by The Viking Press, Inc. | 625 Madison Avenue, New York, N.Y. <u>10022</u> | <u>Distributed in Canada by</u> | <u>The Macmillan Company of</u> <u>Canada Limited</u> | Library of Congress catalog card number: 62–18693 | Fic 1. Dolls–Stories | Printed in U.S.A. | <u>SBN 670–05048–2</u> [*sic*] <u>‖ 1 2 3 4 5   74 73 72 71 70</u>].

PAGINATION: Pages <u>[i-ii] 11</u>-127 [128] 129-136 in <u>paper wrapper, perfect bound.</u>   7 11/16″ x 5 5/16″ x 3/8″.

COVER: Reproduces previous red dust jacket illustration and white lettering. There is a vertical lozenge with ship logo and VIKING | SEAFARER | BOOKS, black ink, at upper right of house. Printed in white to the right of this logo: <u>95c</u>. Spine in white: VS-48 Rumer Godden   THE DOLLS' HOUSE   Viking. Back cover text in white: *The Dolls' House* ‖ by Rumer Godden | Illustrated by Tasha Tudor ‖ "A story about dolls and children that involves them | both in the mystery of human life. This book is for | little girls who love dolls, women who remember doll- | house days, and literary critics who can recognize a | masterpiece." — *The New York Times* ‖ "A memorable doll story, filled with the wisdom of | Tottie, a tiny farthing doll, who never forgets that part | of her was once a strong tree." — *Detroit Free Press* ‖ Selected by the American Library Association as a | Notable Book for Children ‖ Another Seafarer Book by Rumer Godden is | *Mouse House* | A Seafarer Book | 7-11 [centered between the two text blocks, lozenge logo: VIKING | SEAFARER | BOOKS] The Viking Press | New York 10022 ‖ SBN 670-05048-2.

CONTENTS: This paperback edition reproduces the text plates of the first edition without the color illustrations. Only the title page and verso precede page 11, Chapter 1; the half-titles and quote from great-grandmother's sampler were not printed in the paperback version. The book ends with page 136. Title page and text illustrations, pp. 11-136 match those of the first edition.

D51 _____. [FOR . . . SBN 670-05048-2 | <u>2 3 4 5   74 73 72</u>].

PAGINATION: Pages [i-ii] 11-127 [128] 129-136 in paper wrapper. 7 21/32″ x 5 9/ 32″ x 3/8″.

COVER: Back cover text in white: *The Dolls' House* ‖ . . . for Children ‖ <u>Other</u> Seafarer <u>Books</u> by Rumer Godden <u>are</u> | *Mouse House* | *The Mousewife* ‖ A Seafarer Book . . .

CONTENTS: This paperback edition reproduces the text plates of the first edition without the color illustrations. Only the title page and verso precede page 11, Chapter 1; the half-titles and quote from great-grandmother's sampler were not printed in the paperback version. The book ends with page 136. Title page and text illustrations, pp. 11-136 match those of the first edition.

D52 _____. Have not examined a 3rd paperback.

D53 _____. Have not examined a 4th paperback.

D54 _____. Have not examined a 5th paperback.

D55 _____. Have not examined a 6th paperback.

D56 _____. Have not examined a 7th paperback.

D57 _____. Have not examined an 8th paperback.

D58 _____. Have not examined a 9th paperback.

D59 *The Dolls' House* | By Rumer Godden | ILLUSTRATED BY TASHA TUDOR [Tottie and Apple holding hands] | Puffin Books [FOR | *Janaki Paula Mary Foster* | WITH LOVE || PUFFIN BOOKS | A Division of Penguin Books USA Inc. | 375 Hudson Street New York, New York 10014 | Penguin Books Ltd, 27 Wrights Lane, London W8 5TZ England | Penguin Books Australia Ltd., Ringwood, Victoria, Australia | Penguin Books Canada Ltd, 10 Alcorn Avenue, Toronto, Ontario, Canada M4V 3B2 | Penguin Books (N.Z.) Ltd, 182-190 Wairau Road, Auckland 10, New Zealand || Penguin Books Ltd, Registered Offices: Harmondsworth, Middlesex, England || Text first published by The Viking Press 1948 | First published with these illustrations in 1962 | Viking Seafarer Edition published in 1970 | Reprinted 1972 | Published in Puffin Books 1976 | 10 || Copyright 1947 by Rumer Godden | Copyright © renewed Rumer Godden, 1962 || All rights reserved | ISBN 0 14 03.0942X | Library of Congress catalog card number:62-18693 || Printed in the United States of America by | Offset Paperback Mfrs., Inc., Dallas, Pennsylvania | Set in Linotype Estienne || Except in the United States of America, this book is sold subject to the | condition that it shall not, by way of trade or otherwise, be lent, re-sold, hired | out, or otherwise circulated without the publisher's prior consent in any form of | binding or cover other than that in which it is published and without a similar | condition including this condition being imposed on the subsequent purchaser.]

PAGINATION: Pages [i-ii] 1-126 in paper wrapper. 7¾″ x 5 1/16″ x 3/8″.

COVER: New cover illustration, although inspired by the Tudor representations of the dolls who are pictured in their living room. A female face looks in at their window. The top of the front cover is a ¼″ brown band above a ¼″ violet band outlined with two red rules. A PUFFIN BOOK is printed on the violet band in black and superimposed at the right side is the puffin logo in a yellow oval in a black rule. On a 1¼″ brown band is printed [in white] RUMER GODDEN | [in yellow] *The Doll's* [sic] *House* | and superimposed at the top of the illustration, [in white] illustrated by Tasha Tudor. The violet band wraps around the spine and across the back. The spine is blue, imprinted [in black] GODDEN [violet]^{The} *Doll's House* [in black] ISBN 0 14 | 03.0942 X [puffin]. Back cover four-color text mostly on a white field, outlined with a light blue border. The white field is topped by the violet band on which is printed the same yellow puffin logo and A PUFFIN BOOK as the front cover. Text [blue] "For little girls who love dolls, women | who remember dollhouse days, and literary critics who can recognize a | masterpiece." —*The New York Times* || [black] For Tottie Plantaganet, a little wooden doll, belonging to | Emily and Charlotte Dane is wonderful. The only thing | missing is a dollhouse that Tottie and her family could call | their very own. But when the dollhouse finally does arrive, | Tottie's problems really begin. That dreadful doll | Marchpane comes to live with them, disrupting the har- | mony of the Plantaganet family with her lies and conceited | way. Will Tottie ever be able to call the dollhouse home? || [red] An ALA Notable Book || [violet] Also by Rumer Godden: | *Little Plum* | *Miss Happiness and Miss Flower* | *The Story of Holly and Ivy* [black] Cover illustration copyright © Robert Barrett, 1990 | Cover design by Rebecca Laughlin || At the lower left: [puffin logo in yellow oval] A PUFFIN BOOK | Ages 8-12 || $4.50. At the lower right: ISBN 0-14-030942-X, above one bar code, and below it: 9 780140 309423. Another similar bar code to the right has 90000 printed above it.

OTHER: This paperback edition carries the same illustrations, but with pages renumbered exactly ten numbers less than the second paperback. Purchased new, January <u>1996</u>.

D60 _____. [FOR | *Janaki* . . . 1976 | <u>15 14 13 12 11</u> || Copyright 1947 . . . purchaser.]

COVER: . . . Ages 8-12 || <u>$4.99</u> . . .

OTHER: Purchased new, August <u>1997</u>.

D61 _____. [FOR | *Janaki* . . . 1976 | <u>15 14 13 12</u> || Copyright 1947 . . . purchaser.]

PAGINATION: On a brighter ivory pulp paper; previous two printings were on buff paper.

OTHER: Purchased new, December <u>1997</u>.

D62 *Dolls | of | Three Centuries* || BY | ELEANOR ST. GEORGE || *"the world is so full of a number of things, | I'm sure we should all be as happy as kings." | -Robert Louis Stevenson* || CHARLES SCRIBNER'S SONS, NEW YORK | CHARLES SCRIBNER'S SONS, LTD., LONDON. [COPYRIGHT, 1951, BY | CHARLES SCRIBNER'S SONS | [3/8″ rule] | Printed in the United States of America || *All rights reserved. No part of this book | may be reproduced in any form without the permission of Charles Scribner's Sons*]

PAGINATION: [i-vi] vii-xviii [xix-xx] 1-205 [206-208] pp. 9 15/16″ x x 6 7/8″

COVER: Red cloth stamped in gilt on the spine: ELEANOR | ST. GEORGE || DOLLS OF THREE CENTURIES [laterally, in a decorative border] || *SCRIBNERS*

DUST JACKET: In black and red on white. Front carries the title DOLLS OF | THREE | CENTURIES printed inverse in a red rectangle (3 ¼ x 5″) near the top of the page. At left is a photograph of "Suzette, a musical Jumeau doll of about 1870, also shown on page 7. At its right: *Illustrated with Photographs | of more than 350 Dolls.* An inch and 3/16 black bank across the bottom is imprinted: by ELEANOR ST. GEORGE | AUTHOR OF [in red] *THE DOLLS OF YESTERDAY* [in white]. Black spine is decorated with the same device from the book spine but in a different array, two boxes above and below the centered text. [red box | two red rules] | DOLLS | OF | THREE | CENTURIES [white] | [two red rules] | ELEANOR | ST. GEORGE [white] | [two red rules | red box] | *SCRIBNERS*. Back: THE DOLLS OF YESTERDAY | *by* ELEANOR ST. GEORGE || *With photographs of over 450 dolls* || *The Dolls of Yesterday* is an indispensable book for the doll collector, | for it gives information about the kinds of dolls to look for, where | to find them, how to identify them and how to care for them. Material | for this book was gathered from doll collectors all over the country, | and there are data on almost every type of doll. There are photo- | graphs of over 450 dolls, including almost all of America's doll | celebrities as well as many less famous dolls. Although intended pri- | marily for collectors, *The Dolls of Yesterday* is written so entertain- | inly that it will appeal to anyone at all interested in dolls. || [printer's tapered rule] || "Mrs. St. George . . . has compiled what amounts to an encyclopedia | on dolls and a history of their invention and use."—*New York Times* || "For the collector of dolls, and also the non- collector, this book will | prove to be of tremendous interest, for not only does it give illustra- | tions and descriptions of many different types of dolls and informa- | tion about famous collections, but it is also a fascinating record of | their historical background . . . truly a most comprehensive coverage | of the doll world."—*Hobbies* || "Many illustrations and a full index make this book valuable. . . . | Then too it is a delightful volumes for casual inspection." | —*Library Journal* || "The illustrations in this big and handsome book are in themselves | enough to make a collector's eyes glisten!"—*Cleveland Plain Dealer* || CHARLES SCRIBNER'S

SONS, *New York.* Have not examined a copy with front flap upper corner intact: DOLLS OF | THREE | CENTURIES || *by* ELEANOR ST. GEORGE || With photographs of over 350 dolls || Eleanor St. George's previous books, *The | Dolls of Yesterday,* has become a standard | work for doll collectors. Now she has writ- | ten a companion volume, rich with the kind | of illustrations and new facts that made her | first work such a success. | ¶Mrs. St. George has gathered photographs | and information about outstanding modern | and antique collections in both this country | and Europe. Among the many items she | discusses are the life and work of Grace | Storey Putnam, creator of the Bye-lo baby; | Japanese festival dolls and the beautiful Vic- | toria and Albert Museum dolls' a solution | to the mystery of the Jumeau and Bru dolls; | and dolls with histories—among them "the | doll that went through the great flood," the | mysterious Hawthorne doll, "Miss flora | McFlimsey" (photographed with her in- | credible elaborate wardrobe), and "Jede- | diah," world traveller *[sic]* and mascot of the | Churchill family. | ¶Mrs. St. George is one of the foremost | authorities on dolls in America, and her own | collection is one of the country's finest. Her | aim is to enable doll owners to identify their | own dolls more accurately as well as to | understand the history of their manufacture. | The photographs of more than 350 dolls | in combination with the author's easy style | makes *Dolls of Three Centuries* of great | appeal to the casual doll owner as well as | to the veteran collector.   Back flap: CONTENTS || MUSICAL DOLLS || MECHANICAL DOLLS | THE SUBSEQUENT HISTORY OF THE | JUMEAU AND BRU DOLLS | GRACE STORY PUTNAM || DOLLS WITH A HISTORY || DOLLS IN THE VICTORIA AND | ALBERT MUSEUM || DOLLS IN THE MUSEUM OF THE CITY | OF NEW YORK || WOODEN DOLLS || FABRIC DOLLS || CHINA DOLLS || WAX DOLLS || PAPIER-MACHE DOLLS || MONTANARI DOLLS || PEDLAR DOLLS || PARIAN DOLLS || GERMAN BISQUES AND PORCELAINS || DOLL DRESSMAKING || THE LUDLOW, VERMONT, DOLL | CARRIAGES || DOLLS IN VISUAL EDUCATION.

ILLUSTRATIONS: Photographs including that (6 7/8 x 6″) on page 65 of Sethany Ann, Mr. Shakespeare, Nicey Melinda | Collection of Mrs. Thomas McCready, Jr., Contacook *[sic]*, New Hampshire.

OTHER: Dedication page v: TO FRANK || "There's rosemary, that's for remembrance".
          Page 64 discusses *MR. SHAKESPEARE ON HIS HONEYMOON* [see *Life* September 12, 1955, for comparable idea- ed.] "Tasha Tudor, the illustrator, who in private life is Mrs. Thomas | McCready, Jr., of Contacook, *[sic]* New Hampshire, created Mr. Shakespeare | in December of 1950 as a Christmas gift for her children and as a "hus- | band" for her porcelain-headed French fashion doll, "Sethany Ann." The paragraph further describes Sethany-Ann and Nicey Melinda, their wardrobes and their book *The Dolls' Christmas.*

Copyright registration A 60017 granted to Charles Scribner's Sons, 597 Fifth Avenue, N.Y. 17, N.Y. Elizabeth Youngstrom, agent for claimant, swears on Oct. 15, 1951:

DOLLS OF THREE CENTURIES, by (Mrs.) Eleanor St. George, a US citizen, Quechee, Vermont, was published Oct. 15, 1951. The book was printed by Affiliated Lithographers, Inc., New York, N.Y., from plates made from type set by Ruttle, Shaw & Wetherill, Philadelphia, Pa., bound by Scribner Press, New York. Application and affidavit and two deposit copies received at LC Oct. 16, 1951.

Copyright renewal registration RE 28-708 granted to Cynthia Carey Taylor, 23 Ardmore Road, Worcester, Ma., 01609, the next of kin of the deceased author, Eleanor St. George, there being no will. Providence Cicero, agent for Cynthia Carey Taylor, swears on July 19, 1979:

DOLLS OF THREE CENTURIES, by Eleanor St. George was originally copyright Oct. 15, 1951, registration A 60017.   Fees charged against account DA 050318, Charles Scribner's Sons, 597 Fifth Avenue, N.Y., N.Y. Application received at LC July 24, 1979, the effective date of registration. Certificate mailed 13 August 1979.

D63 ____.   Have not examined a first edition in a blue cloth, and different dust jacket than the one described below.

D64 THE DOLLS OF | YESTERDAY | [printer's Spencerian decoration] | by ELEANOR ST. GEORGE | [black and white photograph of Miss Madge, a doll wearing a tam o'shanter] | "The cabinet stood ajar and a large doll, rather oldish and | with a rivet in her neck, peeped out and said: 'Suppose | we play at human beings—that would be so charming!'" | *Hans Christian Andersen—*"THE MONEY BOX." || CHARLES SCRIBNER'S SONS [printer's leaf] NEW YORK. [COPYRIGHT, 1948, BY | CHARLES SCRIBNER'S SONS | GG-1.73 | PRINTED IN THE UNITED STATES OF AMERICA || ALL RIGHTS RESERVED. NO PART OF THIS BOOK | MAY BE REPRODUCED IN ANY FORM WITHOUT | THE PERMISSION OF CHARLES SCRIBNER'S SONS]

PAGINATION: 204 pp. 11 x 8 ¼"

COVER: Purple cloth. Spine stamped in silver: [printer's device] || [printer's device] | THE | DOLLS | OF | YESTERDAY | [printer's device] | ELEANOR | ST.GEORGE | [printer's device] || Scribners | [printer's device].

DUST JACKET: Raspberry dust jacket with white flaps. Front: *The | Dolls of | Yesterday* [in large cursive] | [a photographed group of ten milliners' model dolls] | by ELEANOR ST. GEORGE || DOLLS AND DOLL COLLECTING IN EUROPE | AND AMERICAN DURING THE PAST 200 YEARS || *ILLUSTRATED WITH PHOTOGRAPHS OF MORE THAN 450 DOLLS.* Spine: [doll photograph] | [printer's device] | THE | DOLLS | OF | YESTERDAY | [printer's device] | ELEANOR | ST. GEORGE | [printer's device] | [doll photograph] | SCRIBNERS | [printer's device]. Back cover, photographs of seven dolls form a circle around the white title in cursive: *The | Dolls of | Yesterday*. Front flap printed in black: $15.00 [printer's device] | THE DOLLS | OF YESTERDAY | [printer's device] || *Eleanor St. George* || This book was originally written for doll-collec- | tors, to tell them about the kinds of dolls to look | for, where to find them, and how to identify | them. The author, owner of an outstanding col- | lection of antique dolls, was well-qualified to | write such a definitive book. || From doll-collectors all over the country, | Mrs. St. George gathered information about | their collections and photographs of their favor- | ites. This material is in her book together with | data on almost every type of doll ever made. For | example, there is at last, the true story of the | rare Joel Ellis doll; a section on Black dolls; new | facts which have come to light about the Schoen- | huts; the history of the lovely Jumeaus, and more | new material on wax penny dolls, the English | pedlars, and the strange little poppets. || The various dolls described in each chapter | of the book are illustrated by photographs. Here | one will find pictures of all of America's doll | celebrities. Notable, for example, is "Mollie | Brinkerhoff" of Revolutionary War fame; | old "Peg Wooden," who belonged to John | Nott, founder of Springfield, Vermont; Mrs. | St., George's own "Ridiklis," and "Queen Vic- | toria," who had the honor of receiving an auto- | graph from Helen Hayes. Many other equally | famous dolls also have their photographs in the | book. || although written especially for doll-collec- | tors, the material is presented in such an enter- | taining fashion that others who chance upon it | are likely to be charmed into joining the ranks | of the doll-collecting enthusiasts. Back flap printed in black: [printer's device] | A HISTORY OF | DOLLS' HOUSES | [printer's device] || *Flora Gill Jacobs* || This fascinating account of dolls' houses | and miniature furnishings covers four cen- | turies in time and many countries. Included | are chapters on Dutch, German, French, | English, and American houses, with addi- | tional information on Scandinavian, Italian, | Swiss, and Japanese examples. Since dolls' | houses of the past reflect in great detail the | architectural furnishings and customs of | many countries and eras, this is a book not | only for the collector but for noncollectors | interested in social history as well. || Miniature shops, toy kitchens, and houses | for paper dolls have their place in the story, | as do the celebrated miniature rooms of | Mrs. James Ward Thorne, Madame Helena | Rubenstein, and the Duchess Dorothea of | Schwarzburg-Gotha. World-famous dolls' | houses described at length include Queen | Mary's Dolls' House, complete in every de- | tail down to miniature bottles of real cham- | pagne in the wine cellar; Colleen Moore's | spectacular Castle with its diamond chan- | delier and gold forks and knives (mono- | grammed!); Titania's Palace, which has been called "A Museum-in-Little of Italian | Art"; the Stettheimer Doll House with its | unique gallery of miniature originals by | famous modern artists. || *Jacket designed by Carol Callaway* || Published by | CHARLES SCRIBNER'S SONS | New York [Scribner's lamp logo]

OTHER: Four paragraphs spanning pages 82-83 describe the doll "Sethany Ann" and her wardrobe which belongs to Tasha Tudor, "the well-known illustrator of children's books…" A black and white reproduction of Tudor's watercolor painting of Sethany Ann appears with other photographs on page [60j].

Copyright registration A 21643 granted to Charles Scribner's Sons, 597 Fifth Avenue, N.Y. 17, N.Y. Gweneth P. Beam, agent for claimant, swears on April 9, 1948:

THE DOLLS OF YESTERDAY, by Eleanor St. George, a US citizen, Sybilholme, Quechee, Vermont, was published March 15, 1948. The book was printed and bound by Scribner Press., N.Y., N.Y., from type set by Brown Bros, Linotypers, N.Y., N.Y. Application and affidavit received at LC April 12, 1948; two deposit copies received March 3, 1948

Copyright renewal registration R 616316 granted to Margaret F. Carey, 38 Cedar Street, Worcester, Ma., 01609, the next of kin of the deceased author, Eleanor St. George, there being no will. Anne Sullivan, agent for Margaret F. Carey, swears, undated:

THE DOLLS OF YESTERDAY, by Eleanor St. George was originally PUBLISHED March 15, 1948, registration A 21643. Fees charged against account Scribner's (Charles) Sons, 597 Fifth Avenue, N.Y., N.Y. 10017 Application received at LC October 20, 1975.

D65 _____. *Hans Christian Andersen—"THE MONEY BOX."* || BONANZA BOOKS [printer's leaf] NEW YORK. [517108100 | Copyright © MCMXLVIII by Charles Scribner's Sons. | All rights reserved. No part of this book may be reproduced | or utilized in any form or by any means, electronic or mechanical, | including photocopying, recording, or by any information storage | and retrieval system, without permission in writing from the publisher. || This edition is published by BONANZA BOOKS, | a division of Crown Publishers, Inc. | by arrangement with Charles Scribner's Sons. | d e f g h | Manufactured in the United States of America.]

COVER: Half lavender paper over boards, with spine wrapped in magenta cloth. Spine stamped in white: [printer's device] || [printer's device] | THE | DOLLS | OF | YESTERDAY | [printer's device] | ELEANOR | ST.GEORGE | [printer's device] || BONANZA | [printer's device].

DUST JACKET: Lower right in black: ISBN: 0-517-108100. Front flap printed in black: [printer's device] | THE DOLLS | OF YESTERDAY . . . doll-collecting enthusiasts. || DJE. Back flap: Antiques of | American Childhood | by Katharine Morrison McClinton || with 380 illustrations || Collecting antiques of American child- | hood is fascinating fun. Whether I one is in- | terested in children's costumes, furniture, | books, or amusements, the fun increases in | proportion to the knowledge a collector | brings to the field. In this book, Katharine | Morrison McClinton applies her wide ex- | pertise as lecturer, author, and advisor to | indicate the fertile range of collectible items | and the relative availability and cost to the | collector. || In the early days of America, most of a | child's possessions came from England, but | by the early nineteenth century, they had | taken on a national character. For the infant, | there were coral and bells, silver porringers | and pap boats, and christening cradles of | wood and pottery. For the school-age child | there were slates and hornbooks, primers | and readers. Young girls had their needle- | work, and both boys and girls studied pen- | manship and "the three R's." Corseted, | capped, buttoned, and laced, the colonial | "young folk" must have been forced into | quiet or solitary activities as much by their | clothing as by the attitudes of their parents. | More than anything else, however, their | pastimes expose the lives they led. || Illustrations of toys and children have been | taken from contemporary portraits and from | books and magazines of the period, with fre- | quent quotations from the advertisements in | these first magazines for boys and girls. || *Jacket designed by Carol Callaway* || BONANZA BOOKS | a division of Crown Publishers, Inc. | 419 Park Avenue South | New York, N.Y. 10016 || ORPOO1500

D66 DORCAS | PORKUS | by Tasha Tudor ‖ [Dorcas rubbing against a stump] ‖ Oxford University Press ‖ London • New York • Toronto [COPYRIGHT 1942 | OXFORD UNIVERSITY PRESS | New York, Inc. | PRINTED IN THE UNITED STATES OF AMERICA | Calligraphy by Hilda Scott]

PAGINATION: [40] pages, plus endpapers. 4 11/16″ x 4″.

COVER: Yellow cloth with white polka dots. Printed in blue within a white oval outlined in a royal blue scalloped border on the front cover: **DORCAS** | **PORCAS** | BY | TASHA TUDOR. Inside front cover: Sylvie and Tom in blue supporting a book plate outlined in a red scalloped border with Dorcas standing on top. Free endpapers and inside back cover have black eyed Susans.

DUST JACKET: Have not examined a copy.

CONTENTS: Pages [1-2, 38-40] and inside both free endpapers are blank. Page [3] is hand drawn in red/orange with a towering sunflower and Dorcas by a stump. Page [5], dedication and illustrations of blue cup and saucer, a saucer of cookies, napkin embroidered P and a quilt with sewing supplies: *A Story | for | Ellen and Berty.* Versos [6-36] have full-color, full-page illustrations. The Hilda Scott-lettered text is printed on the rectos, pp. [7 - 37]. Tudor has painted a red embellished initial for the head of each page of text.

OTHER: Ellen and Berty are two (of three) children of one of Tudor's oldest friends Jeanie (Mrs. Albert) Thorndike, with whom Tudor grew up. See *The Tale of Little Pig Robinson* by Beatrix Potter for the source of this title. Pig Robinson, Potter opines, was that same pig discovered by Edward Lear's owl and pussy-cat in the land where the Bong-tree grows. They found him with a ring at the end of his nose. But, again in the words of Potter, he had grown up in Devonshire with his aunts [coincidentally, also pigs] Miss Dorcas and Miss Porcas.

Copyright registration A 167849 granted to Oxford University Press, Inc., 114 Fifth Ave., N.Y., N.Y.

DORCAS PORKUS, by Tasha Tudor, U.S.A., was published Oct. 1, 1942. The book was printed and produced by Jersey City Printing Co., Jersey City, N.J. Affidavit received at LC Oct. 12, 1942. Two deposit copies of the book were received June 16, 1942.

Copyright renewal registration R 478867 granted to the author Tasha Tudor, Route 1, Contoocook, N.H. 03229. Barbara L. Dammann, swears on Feb. 5, 1970:

DORCAS PORKUS, by Tasha Tudor, was published Oct. 1, 1942, registration A 167849. Original claimant was Henry Z. Walck, Inc.* [However, that name has been X'ed out, Oxford University Press typed above it and asterisked to a note at the bottom of page 2, "Amended by Copyright Office."] Fees to be charged to account 6694, Henry Z. Walck, Inc., Atten: Kuna Dolch, 19 Union Square West, N.Y., N.Y. 1003.

D67 _____. Have not examined a 2nd printing.

D68 _____. [THIRD PRINTING 1945 ‖ COPYRIGHT …]

COVER: Deeper shade of mustard cloth.

DUST JACKET: Have not examined a copy.

D69 _____. [FOURTH PRINTING 1945 | COPYRIGHT …]

PAGINATION: The paper is 'war-time,' thinner stock.

COVER: Bright mustard without the protective polish and the ink is navy blue.

DUST JACKET: Buff paper with a centered picture of Sylvie and Tom bathing Dorcas in a washtub. Two arched ribbons, above and below the illustration carry the red outlined letters of DORCAS, and PORKUS. Below the bottom ribbon: BY | TASHA TUDOR, printed to follow the

curve of the ribbon. A small clump of dandelions is centered on the back. Front flap: *DORCAS |*
PORKUS | by Tasha Tudor || Dorcas was an unusual | pig She wore a collar and | had
some manners. Sylvie | Ann and Tom decided to | give her a bath on the | same day that
a quilting | party was being held at | their house. The results | were rather surprising | and
disastrous. || A Calico Book for tiny | children. On the back flap | of this jacket are listed |
other Calico Books. || **OXFORD BOOKS | for BOYS and GIRLS | $.75.** Back flap:
CALICO BOOKS | ABOUT SYLVIE ANN | AND HER FRIENDS || PUMPKIN | MOONSHINE ||
ALEXANDER | THE GANDER || THE COUNTY FAIR || DORCAS PORKUS || EACH $.75 ||
ALSO BY TASHA TUDOR || SNOW BEFORE CHRISTMAS || A TALE FOR EASTER || EACH $
1.00

D70 _____. [**FIFTH PRINTING 1953** | COPYRIGHT …]

    COVER: Orange paper with white polka dots, cover printing in navy blue.

    DUST JACKET: Like the fourth printing. Have not examined a copy with price intact.

    OTHER: These pages are out of registration: [12, 24, 28, 32, 36]

D71 _____. [FIFTH PRINTING 1953 | COPYRIGHT …]

    OTHER: Examined a copy with an extra set of front endpapers, one bound at each end of the book,
and each pasted to the boards. The correct rear endpapers were present but were followed by the
second copy of the front endpaper.

D72 _____. . . . *Tudor* || HENRY Z. WALCK, INCORPORATED | New York

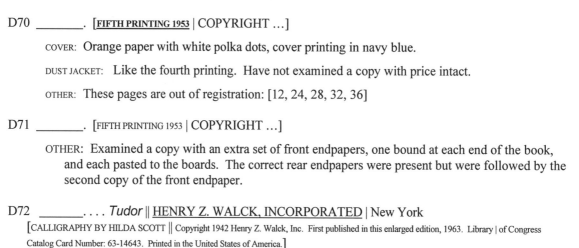

  [CALLIGRAPHY BY HILDA SCOTT || Copyright 1942 Henry Z. Walck, Inc. First published in this enlarged edition, 1963. Library | of Congress
Catalog Card Number: 63-14643. Printed in the United States of America.]

    PAGINATION: [48] pages in four signatures. 6 ¾″ x 6 1/8″

    COVER: Reinforced library binding in mint green cloth. Navy imprint on spine: Tudor   DORCAS
PORKUS   Walck.

    DUST JACKET: Reproduces the previous illustrations on an orange watercolor wash ground. The flaps
are white. Front: DORCAS | [illustration] | PORKUS | BY | TASHA TUDOR.
Spine, in black: Tudor   DORCAS PORKUS   Walck. Front flap has upper corner clipped
severely, and lower corner slightly: DORCAS PORKUS | *by Tasha Tudor* || Dorcas was an
unusual pig. She wore a | collar and had some manners. Sylvie Ann | and Tom decided to give
her a bath on | the same day that a quilting party was | being held at their house. The results |
were rather surprising and disastrous - | for everyone except Dorcas, who got just | exactly what
she wanted. ¶This is <u>a reissue, in an enlarged format</u>, | of the 1942 edition. || HENRY Z.
WALCK, INC. || 30-60 $2.75. Back flap: *Also by Tasha Tudor* || PUMPKIN MOONSHINE ||
"For those 3-6's who like their Halloweens as | gentle and charming as late fall sunshine, there |
is a new edition of Tasha Tudor's tale about | blue-bonnetted Sylvie….This tiny tale is made |
delicate and delightful by Miss Tudor's own | water-color illustrations." | — *Christian Science*
Monitor || ALEXANDER THE GANDER || "Older children who loved to pieces their tiny | copies
of this Tudor picture book with very | simple text will rejoice that their younger | brothers and
sisters may now have it in slightly | larger format, looking somehow more brilliant- | ly quaint and
childlike than it ever did before." | —*Dallas Morning News.* Both corners are slightly clipped.

    CONTENTS: Page [2] is former front pasted endpaper with book plate. Page [3], black-eyed Susans;
[7] is title page, etc. Rectos [10-40], centered illustrations without text. Versos [11-41], hand-
lettered black text. Embellished <u>orange</u> initial within a square orange frame on each text page.
Pages [46-47] reproduce original rear end papers. Blank pages: [42-45] and [48]. Blank end
papers.

OTHER: BOOK PUBLISHING RECORD 1960-1964, volume iv, page 5067:   TUDOR, Tasha
JUV | Dorcas Porkus. [Enl. ed.]   New York, Walck [1963, ©. | 1942] unpaged, col. illus. 17cm.
63-14643 2.75 | Ages 3-6.

D73 _____.

PAGINATION: [48] pages in four signatures. 6 ¾″ x 6 1/4″

COVER: Reinforced library binding in jade green cloth. Black imprint on spine, as before.

DUST JACKET: Have not examined one.

D74 _____.   Warner Books planned to reprint *Dorcas Porkus* in a 4 ¼ x 3 7/8″ paper over boards edition
in April 1998. Part of the *Warner Treasures* series, the book, ISBN 0-446-91247-6, was to retail for $
6.95.   http://www.warnerbooks.com did not list it in its on-line catalog as of March 3, 1998.   A
company spokesperson confirmed a few days later that Warner would not be reprinting the series;
another employee speculated they might be published by Little, Brown.

D75 DRAWN FROM NEW ENGLAND | Tasha Tudor || [Marjorie Tudor photograph of Tudor
sketching] || A Portrait In Words and Pictures By Bethany Tudor | COLLINS [*Acknowledgements* ||
The editor and William Collins Publishers, Incorporated | herewith render thanks to the following
authors, publishers, and | photographers whose interest, cooperation and permission to | reprint have
made possible the preparation of this book. All | possible care has been taken to trace the ownership of
every | selection or illustration included and to make full acknowledge- | ment for its use. If any errors
have accidentally occurred they will | be corrected in subsequent editions, provided notification is sent |
to the publishers. || Rand McNally & Company for the illustration on page 67 from | *A Time to Keep* by
Tasha Tudor, copyright © 1977 by Tasha Tudor. | Henry Z. Walck Inc./David McKay Inc. for the
illustration on | page 27 from *Pumpkin Moonshine* by Tasha Tudor, copyright © | 1958 by Tasha Tudor
(originally published in 1958 by Oxford | University Press, New York); for the illustration on page 46
from | *Alexander the Gander* by Tasha Tudor, copyright © 1939 by Tasha | Tudor (originally published
in 1939 by Oxford University Press, | New York); and for the illustration on page 18 from *Snow Before|
Christmas* by Tasha Tudor, copyright © 1949 by Tasha Tudor | (originally published in 1949 by Oxford
University Press, New | York). The Viking Press, for the illustration on page 64 from | *Becky's
Birthday*, by Tasha Tudor, copyright © 1947 by Tasha | Tudor. [second column] Irene Dash Greeting
Cards Inc. for the cards illustrated by Tasha | Tudor that appear on pages 30, 47, 60, 61, 64, 82, and 94.
All | copyright © by Tasha Tudor. || Linda Allen for the photographs on pages 68, 77 and 81; Bill |
Aller for the photograph on the jacket; Ann Beneduce for the | photographs on the half-title page and on pages
14, 40, 49, 51, | 73, 76, 78, 83, 87, 93 and 94; Bill Finney for the photographs on | pages 89 and 96; Bill
Lane for the photograph on page 90; Pete | Main for the photograph on page 88; Pamela Sampson for
the | photograph on page 44; Marjorie Tudor for the photographs on | the title page and on pages 84, 85,
92 and 93; Seth Tudor for the | photographs on pages 85 and 91; Tasha Tudor for the photographs | on
pages 41, 45, 48, 50, 52, 58, 59, 63, 64, 65, 73, 74, 77, 78, | and 91; Thomas Tudor for the photographs
on pages 31, 39, 50, | 54, 58, 66, 86, 87, and 90. || Particular gratitude is due to Nell Dorr, lifetime friend
and | distinguished photographer, for the use of the pictures on pages | 5, 21, 22, 24, 25, 28, 32, 34, 35,
36, 37, 38, 42, 43, 46, and 72. || And special thanks to photographer Schecter Lee for his color | pictures
on pages 23, 26, 27, 67, 70, 71, 75, and 79, and for his | expert preparation of nearly all the other
photographs in this | book, many of which were old, faded and extremely delicate. || **Library of Congress
Cataloging in Publication Data** || Tudor, Bethany. Drawn from New England || 1. Tudor, Tasha. 2. Illustrators— |
United States—Biography. I. Title. | NC975.5.T82T82 741'.092'4[B] 79-14230 | ISBN 0-529-05531-7 || Published by William
Collins Publishers, Inc., Cleveland and New York. | Copyright © 1979 by Bethany Tudor. All rights reserved. | No
part of this book may be reproduced | in any form without written permission from the publisher, except for brief
passages | included in a review appearing in a newspaper or magazine. | Printed in the United States of America. ||
DESIGNED BY SALLIE BALDWIN/ANTLER & BALDWIN STUDIO.]

PAGINATION: 6 signatures white paper: [1-7] 8 [9] 10-13 [14] 15-21 [22] 23-27 [28] 29-33 [34-36] 37 [38] 39-42 [43-44] 45-46 [47] 48 [49] 50-57 [58] 59-63 [64] 65 [66] 67-68 [69-70] 71-72 [73] 74 [75-76] 77-82 [83] 84 [85] 86-88 [89] 90-91 [92] 93-95 [96] plus free endpapers. 8¼" x 10¼".

COVER: Half-paper olive green deckled cover, wheat linen spine wrapped onto covers. Spine stamped in gilt: TUDOR | DRAWN FROM NEW ENGLAND | Collins. Lower back stamped in gilt on green: ISBN 0-529-05531-7. Yellow end papers.

DUST JACKET: Dust jacket is wheat with white flaps, black text. Wildflower oval (front) encloses a photograph of Tudor doing wood shaving splints on porch bench with Corgi. DRAWN FROM NEW ENGLAND | Tasha Tudor [above oval]; A Portrait In Words and Pictures By Bethany Tudor [below oval]. Spine: TUDOR DRAWN FROM NEW ENGLAND Collins. Back text within the same oval but reversed, and enclosing this text: *If one advances | confidently in the direction | of his dreams, and endeavors to live | the life which he has imagined, he will meet | with a success unexpected in common hours.* || (Henry David Thoreau) || Here, in a brief but charming text and a wealth of pictures, | is the life story of Tasha Tudor, an artist whose life and work | are interwoven to form a pattern of living that is itself a | work of art. Bethany Tudor has written a warm and | loving biography of her mother that provides the | reader with firm and joyous evidence that | dreams can and do come true. Lower right back: ISBN 0-529-05431-7. Front flap: $10.95 || DRAWN FROM | NEW ENGLAND | *Tasha Tudor,* | *A Portrait in Words and Pictures* | BY BETHANY TUDOR | Tasha Tudor's enchanting portrayals of | the New England rural scene in her many | stories and books have endeared her to | generations of readers. In this book | Bethany Tudor describes in affectionate | detail the special world that her mother | has created and made famous. The result | is not merely the portrait of an artist, but | also a celebration of her highly individual | way of life. ¶Photographs, snapshots from family | albums, book illustrations, paintings, | and drawings, most of which have never | been reproduced before, are an important | accompaniment to the text. They reveal | the true background of many of Tasha | Tudor's books and introduce her family, | as well as the Tudor's numerous house- | hold pets and farm animals. There are | photographs of Mrs. Tudor sketching her | children by the fireside, and color | reproductions of the first exquisite little | books she created for her own pleasure | (*continued on back flap*). Back flap: (*continued from front flap*) | when she was herself a child. We also see | her enjoying the many crafts at which she | excels—weaving, sewing, gardening, | making marionettes, and more. ¶Tasha Tudor has always lived according | to her own lights. Rejecting commer- | cialism, trends and fads in her life as in | her art, she has cultivated the virtues of | the simpler way of life of the country- | dweller of a hundred or so years ago. ¶Raising a family and pursuing her art | career while living in a centuries-old | farmhouse without running water or cen- | tral heating was arduous but, as this book | testifies eloquently, wonderfully reward- | ing. She and her family exemplify | without pretension a life-style that many | people dream of but do not know how to | realize. Readers of all ages will welcome | this book's insights into the life and work | of one of America's most beloved and | admired artists. || **Bethany Tudor,** herself a writer and | artist, is the eldest of Tasha Tudor's four | children. She and her own daughter | Laura live in Vermont, near the family | home so lovingly described in this book. || *Jacket illustration by Tasha Tudor* | *Photography by Bill Aller/New York Times.* | *Typography by Antler & Baldwin, Inc.* || COLLINS | *New York and Cleveland.*

CONTENTS: Half-title [1] with photograph of TT holding grandchild with Corgi. Page [2] blank. Acknowledgements, p. [4], lists sources of photographs in book. *"Books Illustrated by Tasha Tudor,"* pp. [6-7]. Page [6] lists *Pumpkin Moonshine,* through *Becky's Christmas,* page [7], *The Tasha Tudor Book of Fairy Tales* through *Springs of Joy,* 1979.

ILLUSTRATIONS: 98 black and white photographs of Tudor family including jacket, 24 color photographs of Tudors, 15 black and white reproductions of art, 30 color reproductions of art.

OTHER: Acknowledgments incorrectly cite *Pumpkin Moonshine* in 1958, *Snow Before Christmas* in 1949 and *Becky's Birthday* in 1947.

Copyright registration TX 420-471granted to Bethany Tudor, RFD #4, West Brattleboro, Vt. 05301. Sarah W. Crane, agent for Bethany Tudor, swears on February 13, 1980:

DRAWN FROM NEW ENGLAND: TASHA TUDOR, A PORTRAIT IN WORDS AND PICTURES, text by Bethany Tudor, a U.S. citizen, was completed in 1979 and published Nov. 19, 1979. The book was manufactured by Pearl Pressman, Philadelphia, Pa. Fees charged to account DAO 34681, William Collins Publishers, Inc., 200 Madison Ave., Room 1405, N.Y., N.Y. 10016. Deposit and application were received Nov. 19, 1979, the effective date of the registration. A second application was received Feb. 15, 1980.

D76 _____. Bethany Tudor | PHILOMEL BOOKS [*Acknowledgments* || The editor and Philomel Books herewith . . . the | following . . . inter- | est, . . . possible | the preparation . . . to | trace . . . included | and . . . acknowledgment . . . have | accidentally . . . edi- | tions, . . . publishers. || Rand McNally . . . © 1947 by Tasha | Tudor. || Irene Dash Greeting Cards Inc. for the cards illustrated by Tasha [second column] Tudor . . . pages 89 and 96; Steve J. Kovacs for the photograph on page 92, | top left; Bill Lane . . . Pete Main for | the . . . photograph | on page 44 . . . title page and | on pages 84 . . . on | pages 85 . . . 41, | 45 . . . 91; | Thomas . . . 58, | 66, 86, 87, and 90. || . . . ISBN 0-399-20835-6 (Previous ISBN 0-529-05531-7) || Published by Philomel Books, a division of The Putnam Publishing Group, | 200 Madison Avenue, New York, N.Y. 10010. Second Printing, 1981. | Copyright . . .]

COVER: White endpapers.

DUST JACKET: Spine: TUDOR   DRAWN FROM NEW ENGLAND Philomel. Lower right, back: ISBN 0-399-20835-6. Upper right front flap: ISBN 0-399-20835-6 $10.95 || DRAWN . . . [back flap, center bottom] Baldwin, Inc. || PHILOMEL BOOKS | *a division of* | The Putnam Publishing Group.

CONTENTS: Page [7] type has been reset so that the last line of column two now reads: **Amy's Goose** by Efner Tudor Holmes. Illus-. Third column: trated by Tasha Tudor. . . The final two title entries of the first printing have been replaced by **The Lord Is My Shepherd** and **Rosemary for Remembrance, A Keepsake Book.** *Tasha Tudor's Old-fashioned Gifts* and *Springs of Joy* were dropped from the list.

OTHER: Examined an autographed copy (no date) accompanied by a Friends of the Flint Public Library flyer and *The Flint Journal* book and author luncheon program featuring Tasha Tudor, May 4, 1982, 12:15 p.m. at the Hyatt Regency Hotel.

D77 _____. [*Acknowledgments* . . . Published by Philomel . . . Putnam Publishing Group, | 51 Madison Avenue, New York, N.Y. 10010. Third printing, 1984. | Copyright © 1979 . . .]

COVER: Yellow endpapers as in first printing. Dark green half-paper overlaps the wheat linen spine. The ISBN is not stamped on back cover.

DUST JACKET: Dust jacket price changes to >$13.95.

CONTENTS: Page [6] has title reduced and moved to head of left column. Type has been reset for page [6] with titles **Pumpkin Moonshine** through **A Little Princess** by Frances Hodgson Burnett. Page [7]: Illustrated by Tasha Tudor . . . Now the seven final titles in the list are: **The Springs of Joy; A Book of Christmas; The Lord Is My Shepherd: The Twenty-Third Psalm; A Child's Garden of Verses; Rosemary for Remembrance, a Keepsake Book; A Christmas Village; All For Love.**

D78 _____. [*Acknowledgments* . . .10010 Fourth printing . . .]

PAGINATION: Perfect bound.

COVER: White end papers.

DUST JACKET: Front flap, upper right: $16.95. ISBN is not printed on front flap. ISBN on back of jacket is printed in a square 'computer-style' font.

CONTENT: The last four entries on page [6] as repeated as the first four titles on page [7]. One new title, **Seasons of Delight:** A Year on an Old-Fash-| ioned Farm. Pop-up book written & illus. by | Tasha Tudor. Philomel Books, New York, | 1986.

OTHER: Examined a remaindered copy with P stamped on the front free endpaper, and a gummed price sticker between the printed price and the title on the front flap: $5.98.

D79 _____. [Acknowledgments . . .10010. Fifth printing. . . .]

DUST JACKET: Front flap, upper right: $17.95.

CONTENTS: ***Books illustrated by Tasha Tudor*** p. [6] has been reset and reduced to exactly the column width. Page [6] lists **Pumpkin Moonshine** through **First Delights**. Page [7] lists **Take Joy!** through **Give Us This Day** . . . 1987.

OTHER: Examined a production proof copy without dust jacket but with a rubber stamped approval box on the ffep where Exec. Editor, Mgr. Editor and Art Dir. all initialed O.K. 10/7. Also this hand written notation: Printing is uneven, register off in places. Two red arrows point to poor registration on page 23.]

D80 _____. [*Acknowledgments* . . . Published by Philomel Books, a division of The Putnam & Grosset Group, | 200 Madison Avenue, New York NY 10016. Published simultaneously in Canada. | Copyright © 1979. . .Printed in the United States of America. Sixth printing. | DESIGNED . . . BALDWIN STUDIO.]

DUST JACKET: Back, lower right corner, a white box, ISBN 0-399-20835-6 | 51795 [above right code] | [two barcodes] | 9 780399 208355 [beneath left code]. Front flap: $17.95 | [rule] | ($24.95 CAN) . . . Back flap bottom: PHILOMEL BOOKS | *a division of The Putnam &* *Grosset Group* | 200 Madison Avenue | New York, NY 10016

CONTENTS: Page [7] lists: **Take Joy!** through **Tasha Tudor's Advent Calendar** . . .1988.

D81 _____. [*Acknowledgments* . . . **Cataloging-in-Publication Data** | Tudor . . . England. | 1. Tudor, Tasha. 2. Illustrators—United States— | Biography. I. Title. NC975.5.T82T82 | 741'.092'4[B] 79-14230 | ISBN . . . Published simultaneously in | Canada. Copyright © 1979. . .newspaper or magazine. | Printed in Hong Kong. Seventh printing. | . . . BALDWIN STUDIO.]

PAGINATION: Six signatures.

COVER: Smoother, lighter green half-paper overlapping wheat spine.

DUST JACKET: Front flap: $18.95 | [rule] | $24.95 (CAN). Lower right corner of back,   ISBN 0-399-20835-6 | **90000** [over right code] | [two barcodes] | 9 780399 208355 [under left code]. Lower right corner of back flap, printed laterally near fold: PRINTED IN HONG KONG.

CONTENTS: Pages [6-7] as in the sixth printing.

D82 _____. [*Acknowledgments* . . . 05531-7) ‖ Bethany <u>Tudor. All Rights reserved.</u> | <u>This book, or parts thereof, may not be reproduced in any form</u> without | permission in writing from the publisher. Published by Philomel Books, | a division of The Putnam & Grosset Book Group, | 200 Madison Avenue, New York, NY 10016. | Published simultaneously in Canada. Printed in Hong Kong. | <u>9 10 8</u> ... BALDWIN STUDIO.]

> DUST JACKET: Front flap: <u>$19.95</u> | [rule] | (<u>$25.95</u> CAN). Lower right corner of back, ISBN 0-399-20835-6 | [UPC barcode] | 0 48228 20835 8.

> OTHER: Purchased new, with a store label imprinted 01/92.

D83 _____. [*Acknowledgments* ... Hong Kong. | <u>9 10</u> | ... BALDWIN STUDIO.]

> DUST JACKET: Front flap: <u>$22.95</u> | [rule] | <u>$29.95</u> (CAN). <u>Back flap, last line:</u> PRINTED IN HONG KONG.

> OTHER: Purchased new, July 1995.

D84 _____. [*Acknowledgments* . . . Hong Kong. | <u>10</u> | . . . BALDWIN STUDIO.]

> DUST JACKET: Back lower right, white box: 90000> [above the smaller right of two bar codes] | EAN [laterally] [two bar codes] | 9 780399 208355 [beneath larger left code] | ISBN 0-399-20835-6.

> OTHER: Purchased new, June 1996; but probably printed in late 1995.

D85 _____. [*Acknowledgments* . . . Hong Kong. | <u>11 13 15 17 19 20 18 16 14 12</u> | . . . BALDWIN STUDIO.]

> DUST JACKET: Front flap prices reset smaller: $24.95 USA | [rule] | $32.50 CAN.

> OTHER: Purchased new, April 1996.

D86 _____. [*Acknowledgments* . . . Hong Kong. | <u>13 15 17 19 20 18 16 14 12</u> | . . . BALDWIN STUDIO.]

> DUST JACKET: Front flap prices reset: <u>$25.95</u> USA | [rule] | <u>$34.95</u> CAN.

> OTHER: Purchased new, October 1997.

E1 EASTER at the WHITE HOUSE 1988. 11 x 8 ½″ [Washington, D.C, The White House, 1988 ?]

PAGINATION: [10] pages including wrapper in 1 signature of ivory paper. 11″ x 8 ½″

COVER: The title is set in teal ink across the bottom. An image of two rectangles, one superimposed slightly above and to the right of the lower one, carry the capital E of EASTER. A sparrow sits atop the rectangles and sings. Tudor's 9 x 8″ image resembles a large Easter egg with a painted scene. The egg is only suggested by an oval wire wrapped in pink ribbon similar to certain Christmas wire wreaths. The central image is a bare-foot girl in blue bonnet and smock on her hands and knees looking for eggs among the green grass and crocus. A rabbit stands with front paws on the girls hands as the two nearly rub noses. The image blends with the surrounding flowers beyond the wire, a scene incorporating chicks, ducklings, bunnies, birds and the blue New England hills typical of Tudor. At the lower right corner: ©1988 T. Tudor. The back cover in a thin-lined frame carries at the top of the page reduced copies of the title and a bouquet and ribbon from the front image. The rectangles form the majority of the back and are printed with the words to *Over the Rainbow* by E.T. Harburg and Harold Arlen. A rainbow arches over an engraving of the White House at the bottom.

CONTENTS: Page [2] Autographs, blank. Page [3] A letter Welcome to the White House Easter Egg Roll! printed with the signature of Nancy Reagan. Pages [4-5] A White House Tradition More than 100 Years Old and this boxed text: ON THE COVER | Each year a famous illustrator is invited to create the | front cover for the souvenir program. The 1988 | cover has been painted especially for the White House | Easter Egg Roll by renowned artist Tasha Tudor who | is known for her naturalistic and whimsical animals | and children. Mrs. Tudor lives and works in Vermont. Full-color reproductions are included of past White House Easters painted by Susan Northey Winch (1981), Christine Graf (1982), Milton Bond (1983), Kathy Jakobsen (1984) Lyda Revoire Wing Taylor (1986), Shari Hatchett (1987). Page [6-9] program of Events with six color photographs and images of thirteen decorated eggs. Pages [10-11] A stylized map of the south lawn indicating locations of activities. Pages [12-16] Coloring book. Page [17-19] Credits and Acknowledgements. "Thank you to Tasha Tudor of West Brattleboro, Vermont, for painting the cover especially for today's event. . . Programs were made possible thanks to a generous gift from James River Corporation. . . Be sure to see special guest artist, Jan Brett of Norwell, | Massachusetts, who is making sketches for a painting of this | year's Easter Egg Roll. Her painting, to be titled "EASTER AT | THE WHITE HOUSE 1988," will feature all of the color and | excitement of the day…perhaps she will add a figure that | looks like…YOU!" . . . THANK YOU TO ALL THE ARTISTS & CARTOONISTS WHO | PAINTED EGGS FOR THE 1988 ARTISTS' EGG EXHIBIT . . . Tudor is included with about 116 others. A Thank You also lists each artist since 1981 who created the Easter painting. Janet Munro's 1985 is not pictured in the program. . . Paper: Richmond Opaque-Text Basis 70 Vellum Finish.

OTHER: Easter egg rolls with the president are traced to the time of James and Dolley Madison, and have been celebrated as White House gatherings since the administration of Rutherford and Lucy Hayes, 1878. In recent years a prominent artist has been selected each year to design the official program.

Interested readers might consult "History of the White House Easter Egg Roll" at http://www.whitehouse.gov/WH/glimpse/Easter.

E2 Edgar Allan Crow | BY TASHA TUDOR || [Edgar] || **Oxford University Press** | NEW YORK 1953 [Copyright 1953 | OXFORD UNIVERSITY PRESS, INC. || PRINTED IN THE UNITED STATES OF AMERICA]

PAGINATION: [36] pages including free endpapers in 2 signatures of ivory paper. 6 3/4" x 6 1/8"

COVER: Navy paper, with buckram impression, over boards, paper label (3 3/4" x 4 23/32") on front impressed area. Front label printed in color with large oval of split leaf geranium leaves and flowers surrounding *Edgar Allan Crow* | BY | TASHA TUDOR. Spine, stamped in gilt: TUDOR EDGAR ALLAN CROW OXFORD.

DUST JACKET: Front and spine text in green ink, as are all titles on the flaps; remaining text in black. Front: Edgar Allan Crow | [Edgar with a cutworm in his mouth standing amongst petunias, encircled by a wreath of green split leaf geranium leaves and pink flowers] | BY TASHA TUDOR. Spine: TUDOR EDGAR ALLAN CROW OXFORD. There is a single green geranium leaf on back. Front flap: *Edgar Allan Crow* | **BY TASHA TUDOR** || Edgar Allan Crow's ambition | was to be useful to his adopted | human family. But sometimes this | got him into a great deal of trouble, | as his attempts were not always | understood and his mischievous | pranks not always appreciated! || The true story of how Edgar | found his place in the family and | Tasha Tudor's lovely water colors | will appeal to young children and | to anyone who has had a pet. || *Oxford Books* | *for Boys and Girls* || 40-80 $1.75. Back flap: Also by Tasha Tudor || *Thistly B* || A Canary and his family live in a | doll house. || *The Dolls' Christmas* || Two very old dolls have their own | Christmas celebration. || *A Tale for Easter* | Lovely pictures of all the magic | things that happen on Easter. || *First Prayers* || Old and new prayers in an exqui- | site miniature volume. Protestant | and Catholic editions.

CONTENTS: Title page [3], Dedication page [5]: To | Bethany | and the | Lovely Fowl, penned in brown within the brown outline of a small card, overlaid with leaf and flower of the split leaf geranium.

ILLUSTRATIONS: Pp. [6-29] alternate between text on even numbered pages and twelve full color full page illustrations on odd numbered pages. Front endpapers carry the same image (reversed) of Edgar sitting on a branch. Rear endpapers are similar, but Edgar is a younger bird hunched on the branch. Title page shows a hungry Edgar with his mouth open ready to be fed. A single geranium leaf on page [33]. Pp. [2, 30-32, 34-35] are blank.

OTHER: *Edgar* was not only this book, but also a pet crow of the McCready family. A stuffed toy made in Edgar's likeness was also re-created and sold by the Jenny Wren Press, ca. 1993.

COPYRIGHT REGISTRATION: A 110823 granted to Oxford University Press, Inc., 114 Fifth Ave., N.Y. 11, N.Y. W. S. Gherton, agent for claimant, swears on Oct. 19, 1953:

EDGAR ALLAN CROW, by Tasha Tudor, a U.S. citizen born approx. 1910, was published Oct. 15, 1953. The book was printed by Kellogg and Bulkeley, Hartford, Ct, from type set and plates made by The Composing Room, Inc., N.Y., N.Y. and binding by H. Wolff Manufacturing Co., Inc., N.Y., N.Y. Application and affidavit and two deposit copies received at L.C. Oct. 23, 1953.

COPYRIGHT REGISTRATION: TXu-668-983

COPYRIGHT REGISTRATION: Vau-368-966

E3 _____. Overmann lists dark blue tweed cloth binding, which I have not examined.

E4 _____.

PAGINATION: [40] pages in 2 signatures, plus extra wood grain endpapers in a rebound ex-library copy with a rebinding dated July 1962. 6 1/2" x 6".

COVER: Federal blue buckram printed in black on front with the illustration of the original jacket. <u>BY had been omitted</u> before the illustrator's name.

CONTENTS: Title page is the third leaf; it was the second in the trade edition. Likewise, the last printed page with a green leaf is the third leaf from the end; it was the second from the end in the trade edition.

E5 _____.

PAGINATION: A rebound copy in which the binder saved only the textual pages [1] through [27], where [1] is the title page. Page [28] is blank. 2 signatures. 6 5/8″ x 6 1/4″.

COVER: Teal buckram

E6 **ENGLISH COTTAGE** | **GARDENING** | FOR AMERICAN GARDENERS | [6 13/16″ rule] | TEXT AND PHOTOGRAPHS BY MARGARET HENSEL | FOREWORD BY TASHA TUDOR || Including a Cultural Chart compiled with the help of Gary Koller, | Assistant Director of Horticulture at The Arnold Arboretum || With Garden Plans by Gordon Morrison || W.W. NORTON & COMPANY | NEW YORK • LONDON   [***Dedication*** | *This book is dedicated to all of the gardeners whose gardens* | *and love of gardening made it possible.* [photograph of rose bush at the window and door of a stone house] || Text and Photographs Copyright © 1992 by Margaret Hensel | All rights reserved. || The text of this book is composed in Galliard, | with the display set in Galliard. | Composition by the Maple-Vail Book Manufacturing Group. | Manufactured by Dai Nippon Printing Co., Ltd., Tokyo, Japan. | Book design by Marilyn Fowles Appleby. || Library of Congress Cataloging-in-Publication Data || Hensel, Margaret. | English cottage gardening for American gardeners / by Margaret Hensel. | p. cm. | Includes index. | 1. Cottage gardens, English. 2. Cottage gardens, English—United | States. 3. Cottage gardens, English—Pictorial works. I. Title. | SB405.H498 1992 | 712′.6—dc20   90-28433 | ISBN 0-393-03012-1 || W.W. Norton & Company, Inc., 500 Fifth Avenue, New York, N.Y. 10110 || W.W. Norton & Company, Ltd., 10 Coptic Street, London WC1A 1PU || 1 2 3 4 5 6 7 8 9 0]

PAGINATION: 239 + [1], plus free endpapers in 22 [?] signatures on white paper. Text pages are numbered, but the full-page illustrations are not. 10 9/32″ x 10 ¼″.

COVER: Gray rayon over board covers. Spine stamped in green: HENSEL ◊ ENGLISH COTTAGE GARDENING   NORTON

DUST JACKET: White dust jacket, one large photograph on front, seven of various flowers on the back. ENGLISH COTTAGE | GARDENING | FOR AMERICAN GARDENERS | [9 5/8″ violet rule | photograph of Westington House garden | 9 5/8″ violet rule] | TEXT AND PHOTOGRAPHS BY MARGARET HENSEL | FOREWORD BY TASHA TUDOR. Spine: HENSEL ◊ ENGLISH COTTAGE GARDENING   [logo] NORTON. Back: [7 5/8″ violet rule | layout of seven photographs | 7 5/8″ violet rule] | "Hensel's book is as ardent and generous as the gardens it presents, spilling | over with passionate pleasures and practical tips….With [this] inspira- | tional pattern book in hand, American gardeners at all levels of expertise | can convincingly re-create the enchanting English cottage gardens in their | own backyards." —*Horticulture* | [in the lower left corner] W·W· NORTON | [logo] | NEW YORK · LONDON |

174

Printed in Japan. [in the lower right corner] ISBN 0-393-03012-1   90000> | EAN [TWO BARCODES] | 9 780393 030129. Front flap: ISBN 0-393-03012 [corner clipped] || ENGLISH COTTAGE | GARDENING | FOR AMERICAN GARDENERS || TEXT AND PHOTOGRAPHS | BY MARGARET HENSEL | FOREWORD BY TASHA TUDOR || Thanks to the extraordinary photo- | graphs and gardening wisdom in this | book, the elegant intimacy of the En- | glish cottage garden look is now, at | last, a practical possibility for amateur | gardeners in diverse regions of the | United States. The author, whose pho- | tographs and articles on garden design | appear in *Horticulture* and many other | magazines, has analyzed the aesthetic | and horticultural elements in ten rep- | resentative cottage gardens—eight in | England and two in the United States | (including Tasha Tudor's at Corgi Cot- | tage in Vermont). Her spectacular | photographs render the look and atmo- | sphere of these gardens, while her text | focuses on easily grown, readily avail- | able plants that are adaptable to a wide | variety of climatic and soil conditions. | In the back of the book may be found | specific horticultural information on a | wide variety of cottage garden plants | commonly available in the United | States, glossaries of Latin and common | names, and a list of sources for old rose | varieties. ¶The gardens in this beautiful book | are not those of the great estates of | England, manicured by staffs of pro- | fessional gardeners. They are, instead, | labors of love on the part of individual | homeowners, many of whom started | with bleak, rubble-strewn lots and | went on to create the enchanted set- | tings pictured here. || 10-92. Back flap: [black and white photograph of Hensel] *Credit: Gingles Morse.* | MARGARET HENSEL is an accomplished | garden designer, photographer, and | writer. Born in Philadelphia, she re- | ceived her formal training in landscape | design at the Radcliffe Landscape De- | sign Program. A longtime contributor | to *Horticulture* magazine, her articles | on gardens and design have also ap- | peared in the *New York Times*, the | *Christian Science Monitor*, and *House | and Garden*. She lives in the Berk- | shires in western Massachusetts. || Jacket design by Marilyn Fowles Appleby | Jacket photographs by Margaret Hensel.

ILLUSTRATIONS: There are many un-numbered full-page color photographs.

CONTENTS: Title page [3]. Page 7 text by Tudor: FOREWORD | [5″ black rule and photograph of pinks] | IT WAS AT the Berkshire Botani- | cal Garden in Stockbridge, Massachu- | setts, that I first met Margaret Hensel. | She stood out in the usual garden | group like some exotic flower. She | had the looks of a fourteenth-century | painting and a delightful exuberance | for things horticultural. Needless to | say, I was impressed. ¶Over a number of years, she has | frequently photographed my garden, | so I have come to know her. It was | both an honor and a surprise to be | asked to write a foreword to *English | Cottage Gardening for American Gar- | deners.* ¶I thoroughly enjoy Margaret's | delight in exuberant gardens, gardens | overflowing with the old favorites— [column two] hollyhocks, foxgloves, poppies, for- | get-me-nots, sweet-scented shrub | roses, and even vegetables. She lets | the reader see, through her words, the | pleasing disorder of masses of lady's | mantle, pinks, violas, and fragrant | sweet alyssum—all spilling over warm | brick paths in happy profusion. ¶This book encourages that most rewarding of complaints, Garden | Fever. As I read the book this fall, it | made me wish to rush out and plant | dozens of blue and white campanulas | among my shrub roses, along with | more dozens of my favorite mignon- | ettes. In my eagerness to put some of | the book's ideas into practice in my | own garden, I for once regretted the | coming of winter's peace. Now, it is a [column three] special book that makes a lover of | winter long for spring in the autumn! ¶And, kind reader, do you not agree | with Margaret Hensel that it is time | for Americans to turn more often to | lovely flowers in their yards and along | their walks, turning away from the | dull shrub plantings that one all too | often sees? How boring those shrub | plantings are! How unimaginative! | "Yes," you may say, "but shrubs | require no care." Well, nothing truly | worthwhile is ever easy. But you will | be surprised by joy if you choose to | follow the spirit of this book and cre- | ate a small Eden of your own. || Tasha Tudor | Corgi Cottage 1990.

OTHER: Corgi Cottage is discussed and photographed in Chapter 9, AMERICAN COTTAGE GARDENS: CITY AND COUNTRY, pp. [144]-167. Photographs of Tudor's gardens appear with captions on pages [10]-11, [34], [144] - 145, [154]-167. Although the CIP data mentions an index, there is none. Have not examined a copy with price intact.

COPYRIGHT REGISTRATION: TX 3 443-893 granted to Margaret Hensel c/o Paul R. Reynolds Inc., 71 West 23rd St., N.Y., N.Y. 10010. Amanda Medina Murray, agent for Margaret Hensel, swears on Nov. 16, 1992:

ENGLISH COTTAGE GARDENING FOR AMERICAN GARDENERS, Text and photographs by Margaret Hensel, a U.S. citizen, was published Nov. 16, 1992. Fees charged to account DAO15350, W.W. Norton & Company, 500 Fifth Ave., N.Y., N.Y. 10110. Application and two deposit copies received Nov. 23, 1992.

E7   _____. [*Dedication* | *This book . . .* W.W. Norton & Company, Ltd., 10 Coptic Street, London WC1A 1PU ‖ 2 3 4 5 6 7 8 9 0]

E8   _____. [*Dedication* | *This book ...* Manufactured by Dai Nippon Printing Co., Ltd., <u>Hong Kong</u> ... London WC1A 1PU ‖ 3 4 5 6 7 8 9 0.

COVER: Gray rayon over board covers. Spine stamped in <u>gray</u>: HENSEL ◊ ENGLISH COTTAGE GARDENING   NORTON. Third printing, ca. 1996. The statement of geographic origin at bottom left of back cover now reads: *Printed in Hong Kong*. Other details as in second printing.

F1 FAIRY TALES ‖ from ‖ HANS CHRISTIAN ANDERSEN ‖ Illustrated by | TASHA TUDOR ‖ [snow flake] ‖ OXFORD UNIVERSITY PRESS | LONDON NEW YORK TORONTO. [Copyright 1945 | Oxford University Press | New York, Inc. ‖ PRINTED IN THE UNITED STATES OF AMERICA]

PAGINATION: 9 signatures, war-time paper: [i-iv] v-vii [viii] 9-273 [274-280] plus plain ivory end papers. Half-title on page [i]; CONTENTS, page v-vi; ILLUSTRATIONS, page vii. Blank pages: [ii, viii, 274-280] 9″h x 6 3/8″ w.

COVER: Blue cloth cover, silver snow flake stamped on front. Spine in silver: FAIRY | TALES | from | Hans Christian | ANDERSEN | [snowflake] | Illustrated by | TASHA | TUDOR ‖ [snowflake] ‖ OXFORD. Top edge is painted blue.

DUST JACKET: Blue cloudy dust jacket with white flaps. Front has snow flake border on sides and top, calligraphic text with large serifs. FAIRY | TALES ‖ [swan] ‖ FROM | Hans Christian | ANDERSEN | [in a white scroll] Illustrated by | TASHA TUDOR. Spine: FAIRY | TALES | from | Hans Christian | ANDERSEN ‖ [snow flake] ‖ Illustrated by | TASHA | TUDOR ‖ [snow flake] ‖ OXFORD. A white snow flake is centered on the back. Front flap most text printed in black, 4 lines in blue (Illustrated by | Tasha Tudor | OXFORD BOOKS | FOR BOYS AND GIRLS, and the initial O): Fairy Tales | from | HANS CHRISTIAN ANDERSEN ‖ Illustrated by | TASHA TUDOR ‖ OF ALL the fairy tales that have been | written for children, those of Hans | Christian Andersen are among the | most famous and the best loved. Boys and girls | all over the world know these tales from Den- | mark, and they have taken their place among | the classics of all times. ¶ Many artists have illustrated Andersen's | stories, but there is always place for another | edition. Tasha Tudor's pictures for this collec- | tion will stand beside other famous illustrations | in their beauty and their sympathetic interpre- | tation of the stories. Every child who reads of | the Little Mermaid, the Ugly Duckling, the | Real Princess and the countless other well- | loved people of these stories will find them | brought to life in Tasha Tudor's pictures with | just the humor and charm and pathos that the | author has given to his fairy tales. ¶There are twenty-eight stories in this vol- | ume. The E.V. Lucas translation has been | used for the large majority of them; for the | balance, that of the Oxford Standard Authors | has been used. This selection was made by the | illustrator and represents her favorite stories | among the many written by this great writer | of fairy tales. ‖ OXFORD BOOKS | for BOYS and GIRLS ‖ $3.50. Back flap (Other books by Tasha Tudor, and, The Calico Books, in blue): Other books by | Tasha Tudor ‖ MOTHER GOOSE | $2.00 ‖ THE WHITE GOOSE | $1.00 ‖ A TALE FOR EASTER | $1.00 ‖ SNOW BEFORE CHRISTMAS | $1.00 ‖ The Calico Books | Each $.75 ‖ ALEXANDER THE GANDER | PUMPKIN MOONSHINE | THE COUNTY FAIR | DORCAS PORKUS.

ILLUSTRATIONS: Thirty-one black and white illustrations (one on the first page of each story): pages 9, 15, 25, 32, 34, 48, 67, 76, 82, 86, 103, 114, 119, 123, 128, 137, 149, 153, 161, 169, 174, 179, 186, 193, 197, 221, 248, 251, 261, 264, 266. Ten full page color illustrations (blank on back) facing pages: 12, 32, 74, 88, 122, 142, 164, 182, 200, 248. "Illustrations," page [vii] lists colored illustrations facing pages 90 and 166. Both were actually bound one sheet forward.

OTHER: This book is difficult to find with a very good dust jacket. The jacket was printed on a poorer grade war-time paper, and the books were obviously heavily read. Therefore, the jackets show heavy wear, or are missing.

COPYRIGHT REGISTRATION: A 191370 granted to Oxford University Press, Inc., 114 Fifth Ave., N.Y., N.Y.

FAIRY TALES FROM HANS CHRISTIAN ANDERSEN, illustrated by Tasha Tudor, of U.S., was published Nov. 21, 1945. The book was printed by Kellogg and Bulkeley, Hartford, Ct. Deposit copies were received at L.C. Nov. 25, 1945; affidavit received Nov. 27, 1945.

COPYRIGHT RENEWAL REGISTRATION: R 545570 granted to the author, Tasha Tudor, Marlboro, Vt. Kuna Dolch, agent for claimant, swears, undated:

FAIRY TALES FROM HANS CHRISTIAN ANDERSEN, by Tasha Tudor, was originally published Nov. 21, 1945*; claimant was Oxford University Press. An asterisked footnote indicates an amendment by the Copyright Office, although there is no noticeable change; the Copyright Office probably supplied this date where Dolch left a blank space. Fees charged to account 6694 Walck, Inc., Henry Z., 19 Union Square West, N.Y., N.Y. 10003. Application received and effective January 30, 1973.

F2 _____.

   COVER: Blue cloth, without the gray hue as above, and with a sheen. As above.

   DUST JACKET: Have not examined one.

F3 _____. [Copyright 1945 | Oxford University Press | New York, Inc. || Second Printing, 1946 || PRINTED IN THE UNITED STATES OF AMERICA]

   PAGINATION: Still 9 signatures on a better grade ivory paper. Pagination and illustrations as before. 9″h x 6 3/8″w.

   COVER: Mauve cloth cover, same cover wording and decoration but stamped in black ink. Top edge is painted mauve. [A copy at the New Hampshire State Library has a $4 price penciled on flyleaf, accession number 141000, and a first date stamp: 11/21/1963.]

   DUST JACKET: Have not examined one with price intact.

   ILLUSTRATIONS: Thirty-one black and white illustrations as before. Ten full page color illustrations (verso blank) inserted and facing pages: 12, 32, 74, 90, 122, 142, 166, 182, 200, 248. Two earlier plates were bound a page forward.

F4 _____. . . . TUDOR || HENRY Z. WALCK, INCORPORATED NEW YORK [COPYRIGHT 1945 HENRY Z. WALCK, INC. LIBRARY OF CONGRESS CATALOG | CARD NUMBER : AC66-10721. | PRINTED IN THE UNITED STATES OF AMERICA.]

   PAGINATION: Half-title on page [i]; CONTENTS, page v-vi; ILLUSTRATIONS, page vii. Blank pages: [ii, viii, 274-280] 9″h x 6 3/8″ w.

   COVER: Mustard cloth cover. Top painted mustard. Spine stamped in gold: FAIRY | TALES | from | Hans Christian | ANDERSEN || Illustrated by | TASHA | TUDOR || WALCK . There are no snow flakes on this cover.

   DUST JACKET: Blue dust jacket with white flaps, text printed in black. On front, a twig border resembling heraldic panel reproduces the illustration (now in color) from page 128. The illustration has been separated with castle at top and swan boat at bottom, leaving a white space where title, author and illustrator are printed in black. The lettering is the same as the first Oxford edition, although the title and author statements are smaller and the 'Illustrated by TASHA TUDOR' is larger. Spine text same as spine of book. A gold crown is centered on back. Flaps have new text, all black. Front, upper corner clipped: FAIRY TALES | from | Hans Christian Andersen | Illustrated by | TASHA TUDOR || " ★★ Tasha Tudor has selected thirty- | one of her favorite Andersen tales to | illustrate. Ten exquisite illustrations in | color and thirty-one in black and white | make this a gift book to be cherished by | young and old. The E. V. Lucas transla- | tion has been used for the majority of the | tales, that of the Oxford Standard Authors for the balance . . . One of the | truly distinguished books." | -Library Journal || For this volume of her personal favorites, | Tasha Tudor has created a lovely new | jacket in full color, which further en- | hances an edition that is already consid- |ered a classic among fairy tale collections. || HENRY Z, WALCK, INC. || $4.00. Back flap: *Books illustrated| by Tasha Tudor* | FIRST GRACES | FIRST PRAYERS | MOTHER GOOSE | A CHILD'S GARDEN OF VERSES | *by Robert Louis Stevenson* | *Books written and illustrated | by Tasha Tudor |* A IS FOR ANNABELLE | ALEXANDER THE GANDER | AROUND THE YEAR | THE COUNTY FAIR | THE DOLLS' CHRISTMAS | DORCAS PORKUS | 1 IS ONE | PUMPKIN MOONSHINE | A TALE FOR EASTER | THISTLY B.

F5 _____ .

COVER: Spine is stamped in <u>black</u>.

DUST JACKET: Front flap clipped at top. Text identical to above, except, <u>$5.75</u> on lower corner. New text on back flap: *Books illustrated* | *by Tasha Tudor* | FIRST GRACES | FIRST PRAYERS |*Catholic and Protestant* | MORE PRAYERS | MOTHER GOOSE | A CHILD'S GARDEN OF VERSES | *by Robert Louis Stevenson* | *Books written and illustrated* | *by Tasha Tudor* | A IS FOR ANNABELLE | ALEXANDER THE GANDER | AROUND THE YEAR | THE COUNTY FAIR | THE DOLLS' CHRISTMAS | DORCAS PORKUS | 1 IS ONE | PUMPKIN MOONSHINE | A TALE FOR EASTER | THISTLY B.

F6 **The Family of Man** | *The photographic exhibition created by | Edward Steichen for the Museum of Modern Art* || Published for the MUSEUM of MODERN ART by SIMON AND SCHUSTER || in collaboration with the MACO MAGAZINE CORPORATION.   [And from the facing page: *Editor*: Jerry Mason | *Art Director*: Leon Lionni | *Art Assistant*: Frances Gruse | *Captions*: Dorothy Norman | *Production*: Allied Graphic Arts, Inc. | *Printing*: R.R. Donnelley & Sons Company || *Assistant to Edward Steichen*: Wayne Miller || *Theme photograph of Piper*: Eugene Harris, "Popular Photography" | *End papers*: Pat English, photographed in England for "Life" | Copyright 1955 by the Museum of Modern Art | Library of Congress Catalog Card Number: 55-8929].

PAGINATION: 207 pp.

COVER: Blue paper over boards, black linen spine wrap, in a glassine wrapper.

CONTENTS: Nell Dorr's <u>photograph of Tasha Tudor</u> and Bethany on page 24.

COPYRIGHT REGISTRATION: A 186063 granted to Museum of Modern Art, 11 West 53rd St., NY 19, N.Y. George H. Levy, agent for claimant and National Comics Publications, Inc., 480 Lexington Ave., NY 17, N.Y., swears on May 12, 1955:

THE FAMILY OF MAN, by Edward Steichen, Ridgefield, Ct., a U.S. citizen born in 1879, was published May 10, 1955. The book was printed and bound by R.R. Donnelly and Sons, Corp, Chicago, Il., from plates prepared by Allied Graphic Arts, N.Y., N.Y. Two deposit copies received at L.C. May 11, 1955; application received May 27, 1955.

Handwritten notes in the public record refer to registrations TX 1-210-249, ORKIW RE 240-940, RE 205-652, RE 176-861.

COPYRIGHT RENEWAL REGISTRATION: RE 205-652 granted to the Museum of Modern Art, 11 West 53 Street, N.Y., N.Y., 10019, Proprietor of a copyright in a work made for hire. Frances Keech, agent for claimant, swears, December 28, 1982:

THE FAMILY OF MAN, by The Museum of Modern Art as employer for hire of: Edward Steichen and Carl Sandburg, was originally published May 10, 1955. Fees charged to account DA 011320, The Museum of Modern Art, N.Y. Application received and effective January 10, 1983.

COPYRIGHT RENEWAL REGISTRATION: RE 176-861granted to The Museum of Modern Art, 11 West 53 St. New York, NY 10019, Proprietor of a copyright in a work for hire. Frances Keech, agent for The Museum, swears on August 31, 1983:

THE FAMILY OF MAN, by Edward Steichen and Carl Sandburg, was published May 10, 1955, registration A 186063. Renewal Application received at LC September 6, 1983, the effective date of registration. Fees charged to The Museum of Modern Art, NY, Account DA 011320.

COPYRIGHT RENEWAL REGISTRATION: RE 240-940 granted to Ruth Orkin, 65 Central Park West, N.Y., N.Y. 10023, swears, December 19, 1983:

"Cardplayers" and "Brothers, London" as published in the book FAMILY OF MAN, originally published May 10, 1955, by the Museum of Modern Art. These photographs from page 40 and 191, as well as "Nanette's Charmed," Apr 17, 1955, pp. 22-23, and "Appraisal at a Preview," Life mag. pp. 81, 82, 83, were typed into the second page of the application. They have been lined out and asterisked to this note: See Renewal File ccn 4-0440518(0). Application, remittance and effective date is December 27, 1983.

F7 _____. [And from the facing page: *Editor*: Jerry Mason . . . Norman | *Jacket design*: Harry Zelenko || *Assistant to Edward Steichen*: Wayne Miller || *Production*: Allied Graphic Arts, Inc. | *Printing*: Achrovure Div. Of Union Camp Corp. | *Binding*: H. Wolff Book Manufacturing Co. | *Jacket printing*: J. Miller Printing & Litho Corp. || Maco Publishing Co., Inc.: George H. Levy, president; Mel Bookstein, vice-president || *Theme photograph* . . . Number: 55-8929].

COVER: Navy buckram over boards, embossed in gold. Front: The Family of Man. Spine: The | Family | of | Man || created by | Edward | Steichen | for the | Museum | of | Modern | Art || prologue | by Carl | Sandburg || Simon and | Schuster. Back is plain.

DUST JACKET: White dust jacket with a design of four bars in the primary colors, rcd, ycllow, bluc and green. Each bar begins as one side of a frame around the photograph of 'The Piper' and extends to the extremity of the page. The yellow bar extends to the right onto the front flap, dividing the flap 8 ¾″ from the top between text and Steichen's signature. The blue bar extends to the top of the page. The green bar extends to the left, around the page and into the same design on the back of the dust jacket. The red bar extends to the bottom. The blue and green bars create an upper left panel bearing the title. The green and red bars create a lower left panel with this text: The greatest photographic | exhibition of all time- | 503 pictures from 68 countries- | created by Edward Steichen for the Museum of Modern Art | Prologue by Carl Sandburg. Spine is bisected by the green bar, with title printed laterally above, and SIMON AND SCHUSTER printed laterally below the bar. The design is repeated on the back of the jacket, but offset to the left. Dust jacket front flap: *I believe The Family of Man* | *exhibition*, produced and shown | first at the Museum of Modern Art | in New York and now being | circulated throughout the world, | is the most ambitious | and challenging project photography | has ever attempted. | The exhibition, now permanently | presented on the pages of this book, | demonstrates that the art | of photography is a dynamic | process of giving form to ideas | and of explaining man to man. | It was conceived as a mirror | of the universal elements | and emotions in the everydayness | of life—as a mirror of the | essential oneness of mankind | throughout the world. || Edward Steichen [reproduction of signature] || Deluxe Edition: $15.00. Back flap cites seven reviews, utilizing the primary colors in the source titles. "…the whole story | of mankind…" –*Philadelphia Inquirer* [blue] | "…as a vast | and lovely epic poem…" –*Baltimore News-Post* [green] | "…portraying the | emotions which | all members of the | human family share…" –*Life* [red] | "…a fantastically large, | rich and extensive | exhibition of human | anecdotes…" –*San Francisco Chronicle* [blue] | "…global in scope | and universal in | its theme…" –*New York Herald Tribune* [green] | "…which symbolize | the universality of | human emotions…" –*The New York Times* [red] | "…and…the beauty | and resources | of the earth…" – *Christian Science Monitor* [blue] || [yellow bar] || *Editor*: Jerry Mason | *Art Director*: Leo Leonni | *Art Assistant*: Frances Gruse | *Captions*: Dorothy Norman | *Production*: Allied Graphic Arts, Inc. | *Printing*: Achrovure, New Jersey | *Binding*: H. Wolff, New York | *Assistant to Edward Steichen*: Wayne Miller | *Jacket Design*: Harry Zelenko | *Theme photograph of Piper*: Eugene Harris, "*Popular Photography*" | *Published for the Museum of Modern*

Art, New York, | by Maco Publishing Co., Inc. | Distributed by Simon and Schuster | 630 Fifth Avenue | New York, New York.

F8 _____.

    PAGINATION: 192pp.

    COVER: <u>White paper over boards imprinted in gilt with block design</u>, black cloth spine wrap.

    DUST JACKET: White dust jacket with multi-colored blocks.

F9 _____.

    PAGINATION: 192pp. Thin paperback on grayish paper.

    COVER: MACO | $100 on front cover of paper wrapper.

F10 _____.

    PAGINATION: 256pp. Paperback in small size.

    COVER: A CARDINAL GIANT GC-51 ... THE COMPLETE BOOK.

F11 _____. . . . Copyright 1955 . . . renewed 1983.

    PAGINATION: 192pp.

    COVER: Navy blue cloth imprinted on front The Family of Man. In dj.

F12 _____. . . . Copyright 1955 . . . renewed 1983. <u>1986, 3rd printing 1990.</u>

    PAGINATION: 192pp. thick paperback.

    COVER: <u>$16.95   51695, on back.</u>

F13 _____. . . . Copyright 1955 . . . renewed 1983. <u>1986, 5th printing 1994.</u>

    COVER: <u>$18.50   51850, on back.</u>

F14 **FIRST CAROLS**. This book is incorrectly credited to Tudor on the back flap of *Take Joy!* Lutterworth edition, 1967. It may have been confused with *First Graces*. Lutterworth's 1964 *First Graces*, does cite *First Carols* and *First Hymns*, "both books illustrated by Brenda Meredith Seymour." There is no United States copyright for this title. See Related Books for full details.

F15 *First* | *Delights* | A Book About the Five Senses | BY | TASHA TUDOR || Platt & Munk, *Publishers* | NEW YORK [Copyright © 1966 by The Platt & Munk Co., Inc. | All rights reserved. Printed in the United States of America. | Library of Congress Catalog Card Number: 66-17113]

    PAGINATION: Two signatures of heavy paper, plus endpapers. [40] pp. cover to cover. 7 1/4″ x 9 7/16″.

    COVER: Reinforced cloth hinge. Fabric weave imprinted paper over boards, illustrated with a semi-circular border inside a larger rectangle border, both green garlands on a rose ground. Front cover in the semi-circle, girl holding a corgi puppy; back cover, baby bunny, corgi and duck. Black text on front: ⌐*First* ⌐*Delights* | TASHA TUDOR | A Book About the Five Senses; on spine: No. 550 [in blue] *First Delights   Tasha Tudor* | PLATT & MUNK; on back upper left cover: 550:0250. Four end paper illustrations are yellow panels bordered in a green ribbon with apples. Apple motif appears on pp. [1-6, 34-36].

DUST JACKET: Repeats the colors, illustrations and text of the cover, except, the number codes of spine and back cover are not printed on the jacket. Lower corner has been clipped from the front flap, whose text reads: $2.50 | TASHA TUDOR | ⌐*First* | ⌐*Delights* | Sally smells spring in daffodils and | damp earth, tastes summer in wild | strawberries warm in the sun, hears | autumn in the call of wild geese, | sees winter in new-fallen snow. With | every changing season, she discovers | new wonders of the world through | her five senses. ¶ Tasha Tudor, who is one of | America's best-loved illustrators, | presents Sally's joyous discoveries in | eloquent words and delicate, full- | color drawings that convey the en- | during richness of a little girl's life | in the country. In *First Delights* she | has created a memorable and endear- | ing book, one that the youngest | reader will take pleasure in over and | over again. || PLATT & MUNK, *Publishers* | New York, N.Y. 10010 || No. 550. Back flap: TASHA | TUDOR || Tasha Tudor lives in a large, old- | fashioned farmhouse in New Hamp- | shire with her husband and four | children. Present also are a seem- | ingly infinite assortment of animals | —horses, cows, pigs, chickens, ducks, | cats, dogs and, not too long ago, a | guinea pig. ¶ One of the world's foremost illus- | trators of children's books, Miss | Tudor has always had a special feel- | ing for rural scenes and for the | grace of children and animals, as is | apparent in her delicate and loving | text and illustrations for *First | Delights*. ¶ The daughter of Rosamond | Tudor, who was a portrait painter, | and W. Starling Burgess, who de- | signed yachts, Miss Tudor studied | at the Museum of Fine Arts in | Boston. Though she was born in that | city, she grew up on a farm in Con- | necticut, and she has never lost her | enthusiasm for country life. || © MCMLXVI. The Platt & Munk Co., Inc. | Made in the United States of America.

CONTENTS: Half-title, [5]; title page includes five vignettes of Sally shading her eyes to see, listening to a shell, smelling roses, tasting a candy cane and holding a corgi puppy [7]; preface, beneath a painting of an owl: "Alone and warming his five wits, | The white owl in the belfry sits." | *Alfred, Lord Tennyson*, [9].   Page [36]: *About Tasha Tudor* || Tasha Tudor lives in a large, old-fashioned | farmhouse in New Hampshire with her husband and | her four children (when they are not away at school). | Present also are a seemingly infinite assortment of | animals—horses, cows, pigs, chickens, ducks, cats, dogs | and, not too long ago, a guinea pig. All of these | creatures are subject to her charm and often serve as | models for her illustrations. ¶ One of the world's foremost illustrators of | children's books, Miss Tudor has always had a special | feeling for rural scenes and for the grace of children | and animals, as is apparent in her delicate and loving | text and illustrations for *First Delights*. ¶ The daughter of Rosamond Tudor, who was a | portrait painter, and W. Starling Burgess, who de- | signed yachts, Miss Tudor studied at the Museum of | Fine Arts in Boston. Though she was born in that city, | she grew up on a farm in Connecticut, and she has | never lost her enthusiasm for country life.

ILLUSTRATIONS: Every page is a watercolor scene of "Sally" sensing the four seasons of the year.

OTHER: The references to "her husband" which appear in this book are to Allan J. Woods, to whom Tudor was then married. Removing the spine of this book reveals two folded signatures sandwiched between two pieces of white buckram, attached by two staples and sewn from top to bottom. The spine of the first signature is imprinted **SERIES #550 TASHA TUDOR'S FIRST DELIGHTS SIG #2 PG.#5-20**; and the second, **SERIES #550 TASHA TUDOR'S FIRST DELIGHTS SIG #3 PG.#21-36.** From the binder's viewpoint, the first 2 sheets and the last 2 sheets, with accompanying buckram reinforcement are each considered a signature comprising pages 1-5 and 37-40, respectively. Thus, pages 1 and 40 are actually pasted to the binder's boards and are concealed in the binding. This is why the pagination for this book begins includes the covers. The first and last sheets are separate sheets of paper neither stapled nor sewn into the binding, rather they are simply pasted inside the front and back covers.

SEE ALSO: *Tasha Tudor's Five Senses* derived from this title.

COPYRIGHT REGISTRATION: A 845021 granted to The Platt & Munk Co., Inc., 200 Fifth Ave., N.Y. 10, N.Y. Bertha Shapiro, agent for claimant, swears on June 16, 1966:

FIRST DELIGHTS (#550) Retail price $2.50, by Tasha Tudor, R.D. #1, Contoocook, N.H., a U.S. citizen, was published April 1, 1966. Tasha Tudor is also cited as author of the illustrations & cover art. The book was printed and bound by American Book-Stratford Press, 75 Varick St., N.Y., N.Y. Application and affidavit, fees and two deposit copies received at L.C. June 23, 1966.

Reference is made to registration RE 734-231.

COPYRIGHT REGISTRATION: KK 195245 granted to The Platt & Munk Co., Inc., 200 Fifth Ave., N.Y. 10, N.Y. Bertha Shapiro, agent for claimant, swears, undated:

FIRST DELIGHTS (#550) a book by Tasha Tudor, R.D. #1, Contoocook, N.H., a U.S. citizen, was published April 1, 1966. Application and affidavit, fees and two deposit copies received at L.C. June 23, 1966.

COPYRIGHT RENEWAL REGISTRATION: RE 731-173 granted to Tasha Tudor, c/o Corgi Cottage Industries, P.O. Box 7281, Richmond, Va. 23221-0281. Kathyrn [*sic*] L. Barrett, Esq., 235 East 22ⁿᵈ St., Apt. 11C, N.Y., N.Y. 10010, agent for Tasha Tudor, swears on June 21, 1996:

FIRST DELIGHTS; A BOOK ABOUT THE FIVE SENSES, by Tasha Tudor was published April 1, 1966, and registered to Platt & Munk Co., Inc., KK195245. Renewal application received Aug. 9, 1996, the effective date of this registration.

COPYRIGHT RENEWAL REGISTRATION: RE 734-231 granted to Tasha Tudor, c/o Corgi Cottage Industries, P.O. Box 7281, Richmond, Va. 23221-0281, claiming as author. Kathryn L. Barrett, Esq., 235 East 22ⁿᵈ St., Apt. 11C, N.Y., N.Y. 10010, 212-684-6689, agent for Tasha Tudor, swears on June 21, 1996:

FIRST DELIGHTS; A BOOK ABOUT THE FIVE SENSES, by Tasha Tudor was published April 1, 1966, and registered to Platt & Munk Co., Inc., A845021. Renewal application received Aug. 9, 1996, the effective date of this registration. Mail certificate to Kathyrn L. Barrett [*sic*]; and correspondence to Kathryn L. Barrett, Esq. [Ms Barrett signed her name Kathryn - Ed.]

F16 _____.

COVER: The spine code is shortened from No.550 to <u>550</u>, and printed in <u>black</u>, not blue.

ILLUSTRATIONS: The colors of the plates are generally brighter; the cover is less so, perhaps fading from the missing dust jacket.

F17 _____. . . BY | TASHA TUDOR || 1969 FIRST CADMUS EDITION | THIS SPECIAL EDITION IS PUBLISHED BY | ARRANGEMENT | WITH THE PUBLISHERS OF THE REGULAR EDITION | PLATT & MUNK PUBLISHERS | BY | **E. M. HALE AND COMPANY** | EAU CLAIRE, WISCONSIN <u>[There is a 3/4″ 'seal' printed to the left and lower than the author's name: a circle of hash lines enclosing the large initials CEB with a device above and its inverse below. Printed around the inside of the circle is</u> CADMUS EDITORIAL BOARD • APPROVED •] [Copyright © 1966 by The Platt & Munk Co., Inc. | All rights reserved. Printed in the United States of America. | <u>Standard Book Number: 8382-1013-9</u> | Library of Congress Catalog Card Number: 66-17113 || <u>This edition lithographed in U.S.A. by Wetzel Brothers, Inc., Milwaukee, Wisconsin</u>]

PAGINATION: Two signatures of heavy paper. [36]pp. including flyleaves. 7 1/4″ x 9 <u>1/5</u>″.

COVER: Library binding with reinforced cloth hinge. Cloth cover with the same illustrations as first edition, but with variant text. Front, as before; spine: <u>TUDOR First Delights HALE-CADMUS</u>; back: <u>a 1 1/4″ CEB seal which appeared on the title page</u>. End papers as before.

CONTENTS: [2] [2 apples on a twig] **FIRST DELIGHTS | *A Book About the Five Senses* ||** *Written and illustrated by Tasha Tudor* || Sally finds there are wonderful things in the world | around her, just waiting to be found. You, like | Sally, have five senses, and all can bring delight to | you. When you hear a bird's song, taste a piece of | candy, see the bright fall leaves, pick a daffodil, | hug a puppy, all are exciting first experiences. | Seasons change and your senses keep enjoying the | new delights each season brings. || Classification and Dewey Decimal: Easy (E) || ***About the Author and Illustrator:*** | TASHA TUDOR, who grew up on a farm in Con- | necticut, now lives in a large, old-fashioned farm- | house in New Hampshire with her husband and | four children. On the farm are all kinds of animals. | Tasha Tudor studied at the Museum of Fine Arts | in Boston, Massachusetts, the city of her birth. Half-title, [3]; title page [5] and preface [7] illustrated as before. Page [34] is same apple motif as appeared on page [35] in the first edition. Here page [35] is blank.

OTHER: This reprint is on a lighter weight paper than the first edition.

F18 **FIRST | DELIGHTS** [red] | A Book About the Five Senses || [vignette in a 2 ¾" circle] || *By Tasha Tudor* || PLATT & MUNK, PUBLISHERS • *New York* | A DIVISION OF GROSSET & DUNLAP [black]. [Inside front cover: Copyright © 1988, 1978, 1966 by Platt & Munk, Publishers, | a division of Grosset & Dunlap, Inc. | All rights reserved. | Grosset & Dunlap is a member of | The Putnam Publishing Group, New York. | Published simultaneously in Canada. Printed in Hong Kong. | ISBN 0-448-09327-8. | Library of Congress Catalog Card Number 87-82515.]

PAGINATION: Two signatures, white paper. [28]pp. including flyleaves. 8 1/4" x 7 1/4".

COVER: Yellow paper over boards. Lighter yellow box outlined with a blue rule and apple motif, front and back. Front cover text: **FIRST DELIGHTS** [red] | A Book About the Five Senses | [vignette in 3 ½" circle] || *Tasha Tudor* [black]. Detail, in circle, of Sally and corgi from page [19]. Spine has a blue false band top and bottom, and between them the black text printed laterally: FIRST DELIGHTS   Tudor   Platt & Munk. Back cover, same colored panel with detail in circle from page [6]. UPC bar code at lower left, and beneath it, 0 70918 09327 2; at lower right, ISBN 0-448-09327-8. White end papers are joined in one .75" inch yellow band border.

DUST JACKET: Exactly like covers, plus two flaps printed in black. Front flap: $8.95 | [rule] | (12.50 CAN) | [apple bough and blue bird] | This is a year in Sally's life, | filled with the special delights | her five senses bring. | These delights can be yours, too, | when you smell a flower, | or hear a bird's song, | or see the stars on a quiet night. | Then, like Sally, you'll know | that the truly wonderful things | in the world are all around you, | waiting for you to find them. | —*Tasha Tudor* || ISBN 0-448-09327-8. Back flap reprints the biography from page [28]: Born in Boston, Tasha Tudor | grew up on a farm in | Connecticut, and her | impressions of rural New | England life are the inspiration | for her artwork. She has won | many awards and honors since | her first book was published in | 1938. More than sixty books | later, her gift is still unique. She | now lives in Vermont where she | is surrounded by her corgis, her | family, and her friends—and the | country pleasures so lovingly | depicted in her books. || *Platt & Munk Books by Tasha Tudor* || First Delights | A Book About the Five Senses | First Poems of Childhood | Tasha Tudor's Bedtime Book | Tasha Tudor's Fairy Tales || PLATT & MUNK | A division of Grosset & Dunlap | A member of | The Putnam Publishing Group | New York | Printed in Hong Kong.

CONTENTS: Page [28], biography as on back flap of dust jacket.

ILLUSTRATIONS: Text and the illustrations pp. [2-27] are identical to the original pp. [8-33] in first edition above. Vignette on title page is taken from page [22], and that inside the back cover from page [14].

184

F19 _____. [Copyright © 1988, 1978, 1966 ... <u>1989 Printing</u>]

COVER: Back cover lower left has <u>two</u> UPC bar codes. Above the smaller right one: 50895. Below the larger left, 9 780448 093277. Printed in larger type above both bar codes: ISBN 0-448-09327-8.

DUST JACKET: A duplicate of cover. Front flap of jacket: $8.95 | [rule] | (11.75 CAN) . . . —*Tasha Tudor* || <u>Jacket copyright © 1988 by Platt & Munk, Publishers.</u> || ISBN 0-448-09327-8.

F20 _____. [Copyright © 1988, 1978, 1966 ... <u>1991 Printing</u>]

COVER: Back cover lower left has <u>one large</u> UPC bar code beneath the same ISBN as before. Below the bar code, 0 70918 09327 2.

F21 **FIRST GRACES** || *Illustrated by* | TASHA TUDOR | | New York • Oxford University Press • 1955 [Copyright 1955 by Oxford University Press, Inc. | © Oxford University Press, Inc. 1955 | Printed in the United States of America | Library of Congress Catalog Card Number 55-11589]

PAGINATION: Pages [1-3] 4-47 [48] in 3 signatures on buff paper plus end papers. 5 3/8" x 4"

COVER: Blue cloth. Pink label pasted on front cover: [a robin hovering, above] FIRST GRACES | *Illustrated by* | TASHA TUDOR above [3 baby robins with mouths open sitting on a branch], all in an oval of flowers. stamped on spine in black: TASHA TUDOR   FIRST GRACES   Oxford. Each endpaper has an oval frame of lavender flowers on a lavender field. Within the frame of the verso is an illustration of 3 chicks, and within the recto, 3 bunnies feeding. Rear endpapers repeat the same designs.

DUST JACKET: Pink jacket reproduces cover label illustration and text. Front flap: FIRST | GRACES || *illustrated by* | TASHA TUDOR || A COMPANION vol- | ume to Tasha Tu- | dor's popular *First* | *Prayers,* this collec- | tion has been care- | fully selected from | both old and con- | temporary sources. | Over twenty pray- | ers of thanksgiving | are included in this | tiny volume. Chosen | with the advice of | educators in the re- | ligious field, these | prayers will develop | in the child a true | sense of gratitude | toward God. || Oxford Books | for Boys and Girls | 60-120 $1.75. [Upper corner was clipped from examination copy.] Back flap: FIRST | PRAYERS || *illustrated by* | TASHA TUDOR || THIS collection of | prayers for little | children has been | selected with care | and with advice | from educators in the | religious field. Here | are familiar, beau- | tiful words that be- | long in the hearts | and memories of all | of us. Some less fa- | miliar but no less | lovely prayers have | been included which | express simply for | little children the | ever-loving presence | of God. ¶ Available in both Protestant and Ca- | tholic editions. | $1.75.

CONTENTS: Title Page [1] has a lavender oval similar to endpapers, page [3] black and white dedication To | POLLY THAYER STARR | WITH LOVE AND | GRATITUDE in an ivy oval. Pages 36-37: a blue background with 18 stars. Page [36], the first American flag above, and a spread eagle below: ON THE FOURTH OF JULY | Our fathers' God, to thee, | Author of liberty, | To thee we sing: | Long may our land be bright | With freedom's holy light; Page [37], two girls and a boy in colonial dress singing, above: Protect us by thy might, | Great God, our King. | *Samuel F. Smith.* Pages 38-39 picture children from four cultures holding hands around a flag pole with the United Nations Flag and this verse: UNITED NATIONS DAY | North, South, East, and West, | May thy holy name be blessed: | Everywhere around the sun, | May thy holy will be done. Page 40: FOR THANKSGIVING | May God give us grateful hearts | And keep us mindful | Of the need of others. Page 42, ...Give Him my heart...Pages 46-47: WE OFFER sincere thanks to the various | publishers and copyright holders for per- | mission to reprint: "Dear...*Our First Music,* C.C. Birchard & Co.

185

ILLUSTRATIONS: Pages 4-47 are two-page illustrations beginning in color on page 4 and alternating with black and white every second page. Pages without text: 5, 7, 9, 11, 13, 17, 19, 21, 23, 25, 27, 31, 33, 35, 39, 41, 43, 45, [48].

COPYRIGHT REGISTRATION: A 219303 granted to Oxford University Press, Inc., 114 Fifth Ave., N.Y. 11, N.Y. John A. Begg, agent for claimant, swears on Dec. 19, 1955:

FIRST GRACES, by Tasha Tudor, Rt. 1, Contoocook, N.H., a US citizen, was published 10 November 1955. The book was printed by Kellogg and Bulkeley, Hartford, Ct. from plates and type prepared by Composing Room, N.Y., N.Y. and bound by H. Wolff Book Manufacturing Co., Inc., N.Y., N.Y. Application and affidavit, fees and two deposit copies received at L.C. Jan. 9, 1956.

F22 **FIRST GRACES** | | *Illustrated by* | TASHA TUDOR || New York • Henry Z. Walck, Incorporated • 1955 [Copyright 1955 by Henry Z. Walck, Inc. | Printed in the United States of America | Library of Congress Catalog Card <u>Number: 59-12017</u>]

PAGINATION: [1-3] 4-47 [48] pages in <u>3 signatures</u>, plus endpapers, on <u>buff</u> paper. 5 11/32″ x 3 7/8″.

COVER: Gray-blue <u>with label</u>, as above. Publisher on spine changes to: <u>Walck</u>.

DUST JACKET: Similar to first Oxford with these changes. Last two lines of the front flap read: <u>Henry Z. Walck, Inc. | 40-90</u>. Both corners, including prices, were clipped from the examination copy. There is <u>no price printed on the back flap</u> for *First Prayers*.

OTHER: Examination copy inscribed <u>Christmas 1960</u>.

F23 _____.

PAGINATION: [1-3] 4-47 [48] pages in <u>3 signatures</u>, plus endpapers, on <u>ivory</u> paper.

COVER: Gray-blue cloth <u>without label</u>.

DUST JACKET: Have not examined one.

OTHER: Examination copy inscribed <u>March 1967</u>.

F24 _____. *Illustrated by* | TASHA TUDOR || Henry Z. Walck, Inc. New York [<u>This impression, 1980</u>] || ISBN 0-8098-1953-8 || Copyright © 1955 by Henry Z. Walck, Inc. || Library of Congress Catalog Card <u>Number: 59-12017</u> | Manufactured in the United States of America.

PAGINATION: [1-3] 4-47 [48] pages in <u>2 signatures</u> on ivory paper. Contents and illustrations as above. 5 3/8″ x 4 1/8″.

COVER: <u>Yellow plastic-filled paper over board covers</u>, deer skin imprint, stamped in black on spine: FIRST GRACES | Tasha Tudor | Walck.

DUST JACKET: Have not examined one.

F25 _____. [<u>This impression, 1981</u>] || ISBN 0-8098-1953-8 || Copyright © 1955 by Henry Z. Walck, Inc. || Library of Congress Catalog Card <u>Number: 59-12017</u> | Manufactured in the United States of America.

PAGINATION: [1-3] 4-47 [48] pages in <u>2 signatures</u> on ivory paper. 5 3/8″ x 4 1/8″.

COVER: <u>Red plastic-filled paper over board covers</u>, deer skin imprint, stamped in gold on spine: FIRST GRACES | Tasha Tudor | Walck.

DUST JACKET: <u>White jacket</u> with an image of the paste-on label, text and illustrations from the first edition on front. Text in black, on spine: TUDOR | FIRST GRACES | Walck. Front flap: <u>$3.50</u> ||

FIRST | GRACES | *Illustrated by* | TASHA TUDOR || This collection, which is a | companion volume to *First* | *Prayers*, has been carefully se- | lected from both old and con- | temporary sources. | The delightfully illustrated | volume includes over twenty | prayers of thanksgiving that | will develop in the child a | true sense of gratitude toward | God. || 0-8098-1953-8. **Back flap:** FIRST | PRAYERS | *illustrated by* | TASHA TUDOR || "Lovely prayers, beauti- | fully illustrated for little | children."—*Christian* | *Herald.* | FIRST | GRACES | *illustrated by* | TASHA TUDOR || "This tiny exquisite book | ...contains twenty-one | prayers of thanksgiving." | —*Chicago Tribune* || Henry Z. Walck, Inc. | A Division of | David McKay Company, Inc. | New York

OTHER: This printing was sold as a boxed set with *First Prayers* (turquoise binding) and *More Prayers* (moss green binding) as *Tasha Tudor's TREASURE, q.v.* for a description of the slipcase.

F26 _____. [This impression, 1984...United States of America]

COVER: <u>Red plastic-filled paper over board covers</u>, deer skin imprint, imprinted in gold on the spine: FIRST GRACES   Tasha Tudor   Walck. 5 3/8″ x 3 15/16″

DUST JACKET: Have not examined a copy with the price intact.

F27 **FIRST GRACES** || *Illustrated by* | TASHA TUDOR || Random House [house logo] New York [Copyright © 1955 by Henry Z. Walck, Inc. All rights | reserved under International and Pan-American Copyright | Conventions. Originally published by Henry Z. Walck, Inc., | in 1955. Published in the United States by Random House, | Inc., New York, and simultaneously in Canada by Random | House of Canada Limited, Toronto. || *Library of Congress Cataloging-in-Publication Data:* | Tudor, Tasha. First graces. SUMMARY: Twenty-one short | graces include several for meals and ones for the New Year, | Easter, springtime, school, the Fourth of July, United | Nations Day, Thanksgiving, and Christmas. | 1. Children—Prayer books and devotions—English. [1. Prayer | books and devotions. 2.Grace at meals] I. Tudor, Tasha, | ill. BV265.F54 1989 242'.82 88-306731 | ISBN: 0-394-84409-2 || Manufactured in the United States of America | 1 2 3 4 5 6 7 8 9 0]

PAGINATION: <u>2 signatures, glued.</u> Pagination, text and illustrations are identical to the first edition. 5 1/2″ x 4″.

COVER: <u>Pink gloss laminate over paper over boards</u> with oval flower illustration and text. Spine printed in black: TASHA TUDOR   FIRST GRACES | Random House. Back cover, lower left has 1 ¼″ x 2″ <u>white box with two UPC bar codes</u>, 84409 over right smaller bar code and 0 79808 84409 3 under left larger bar code; ISBN 0-394-84409-2, beneath all. This edition has <u>white endpapers without illustrations</u>.

DUST JACKET: <u>Pink</u> gloss laminate dust jacket is identical to cover, has large white flaps, 3 1/2″ wide. <u>Text of 1984 Walck printing</u> is reset. Front flap reads: <u>$5.95 U.S.</u> || This collection ... carefully | selected ...and | contemporary sources. ¶ The delightfully...true | sense of gratitude toward | God. Back flap in new type: ...beautifully | illustrated for little chil- | dren." —*Christian Herald* | ...*Tribune* | Random House [house logo] New York | Jacket art copyright © 1955 Henry Z. Walck, Inc. || Manufactured in the U.S.A.

OTHER: A Review Copy, 1989 reissue, should have laid in a 4 x 5.5″ Review Copy Slip indicating a publication date of June 22, 1989, and a code number 118-75. Colophon wrongly attributes first publication to Henry Z. Walck, Inc., instead of Oxford University Press.

F28 _____. Have not examined a copy of the 2nd printing.

F29 _____. [Copyright...United States of America | 3 4 5 6 7 8 9 0.

DUST JACKET: Binding and jacket as above, but <u>the front flap has new text</u>: <u>$9.00 U.S. | $11.50 CAN.</u> || Here are familiar, beautiful | words that belong in the hearts | and memories of all of us, as

187

| well as some less well known | but no less lovely prayers. | They all express simply for | little children the ever-loving | presence of God.   Back of jacket has white box bar code as before, although I've seen a copy with a bookseller's gummed label placed over the printed one. The affixed label has a different bar code and the date 7/12/93 over the printed one.

F30 _____. [Copyright...United States of America | 4 5 6 7 8 9 0.]

PAGINATION: Size increased to 5 5/8″ x 4″.

DUST JACKET: Binding and jacket as in first Random House, but new text on front flap: $10.00 U.S. | $12.50 CAN. ‖ Here are . . . presence of God. Bar codes as before, but I've seen a copy with a bookseller's gummed label placed over the printed one. The affixed label has a different bar code and the date 07/94 over the printed one.

F31 _____. Random House announced a reprint for 1997, ISBN 0679887873 and LC card number 97-65831. However, the Library of Congress had not yet received a copy as of March 3, 1998.

F32 **FIRST GRACES** ‖ *Illustrated by* | TASHA TUDOR ‖ Lutterworth Press [First published in Great Britain, 1964 ‖ ISBN 0 7188 0307 8 ‖ Copyright Henry Z. Walck Inc., 1955 ‖ *Printed in the Netherlands by Henkes Senefelder bv*]

PAGINATION: Pages [1-3] 4-47 [48] plus endpapers in 3 signatures on ivory paper. 5 1/4″ x 3 3/4″

COVER: Gray paper (buckram grain) over boards, imprinted in black: FIRST | GRACES [on cover] and [on the spine], FIRST GRACES   TASHA TUDOR   LUTTERWORTH.

DUST JACKET: Pink jacket has same illustration as first Oxford edition. Spine printed in black: TUDOR   FIRST GRACES   LUTTERWORTH. Front flap set with the same text as the 1984 Walck, except for ISBN . . . gratitude toward | God. ‖ 7188 0307 8. Lower corner clipped from examination copy. Back white flap: FIRST PRAYERS | 7188 0306 x | MORE PRAYERS | 7188 1364 2 | *Both books illustrated by* | TASHA TUDOR | "These books will give a lot of | pleasure to very young rea- | ders. Children will probably | know some of the lovely pray- | ers and graces, and will cer- | tainly be encouraged by the | enchanting little illustrations | to learn others, less familiar." | *Sunday School Chronicle* ‖ FIRST CAROLS | 7188 0309 4 | FIRST HYMNS | 7188 0308 6 | *Both books illustrated by* | BRENDA MEREDITH | SEYMOUR | Two exquisitely illustrated | books which little children | will treasure at all times of | the year. [Compare this text with the Lutterworth FIRST PRAYERS dj.]

ILLUSTRATIONS: Illustrations and text varies from first Oxford in that page 36 has been retouched to remove the American stars, flag and eagle.

CONTENTS: The hymn on page 36 has changed to: For the beauty of the earth, | For the beauty of the skies, | for the love which from out birth | Over and around us lies, | For the beauty of each hour, | Of the day and of the night, | Hill and vale, and tree and flower, | Sun and moon, and stars of light, | Gracious god, to Thee we raise | This our sacrifice of praise. | F.S.Pierpoint. Page 37 has no verse. Pages 38-39 have been redesigned from the American edition to have the book's only twig frame with this verse on 38: Thank You for the world so sweet, | Thank You for the food we eat, | Thank You for the birds that sing, | Thank You, God, for everything. | *E. Rutter Leatham.* Page 39 has a new picture of a girl and two corgis picnicking. Page 42: ...Give my heart... Pages 46-47 have been re-set with this text added to the end: ; | "Thank you for the world so sweet" by | E. Rutter Leatham, copyright holder | Mrs. Lorna Hill.

F33 _____.

COVER: The cover paper is darker gray, with a green cast. Type on spine has been recast to the extent that the "T" of Tudor and the "L" of Lutterworth are larger than other letters.

DUST JACKET: Dust jacket is a stronger pink than above. Front flap text includes ISBN 0 7188 0307 8. At the lower right of the complete flap: 50p. net has been canceled with a black bar, and printed below it is 60p. net.

OTHER: The violet color of the title page illustration is faint.

F34 _____. [This impression 1979 || ISBN 0-8098-1953-8 || Copyright Henry Z. Walck Inc., 1955 || *Printed in Hong Kong*]

PAGINATION: White paper.

COVER: Gray paper (linen imprint) over boards printed in black on spine: FIRST GRACES Tasha Tudor   WALCK.

DUST JACKET: As first Oxford edition. Text varies: last two lines of front flap, Henry Z. Walck, Inc. | 40-90. Both corners were clipped from examination copy. Price was stricken from the back flap in this printing.

ILLUSTRATIONS: Text and illustrations identical to the Lutterworth editions.

OTHER: Inscribed inside front fly leaf June 1, 1980. This curious piece is the Lutterworth imprint, even though the spine and dust jacket carry the name   Walck. The ISBN on the verso of title page is slightly larger than previously.

F35 _____.

DUST JACKET: The background of the front illustration is white with no clouds. Changed text on the front flap matches the 1984 Walck with the addition of ISBN in front of the same code number. Lower corner has been clipped. There is no text on the 3″ wide back flap.

F36 _____. [*First published in great Britain, 1964* | This impression 1979 || ISBN 0 7188 0307 8 || Copyright Henry Z. Walck Inc., 1955 || *Printed in Hong Kong*]

DUST JACKET: Varies, cloudless illustration. The front flap is three inches wide with small changes from F31. . . . toward | God || ISBN 0 7188 0307 8 || 75 p. net. Back flap has one change from Lutterworth F30: *Sunday School Chronicle* || FIRST A B C | 7188 1597 1 | FIRST HYMNS . . .

F37 _____. [*First published in Great Britain, 1964* | This impression 1985 ||L [in circle logo] || Lutterworth Press | 7 All Saints' Passage | Cambridge CB2 3LS | England || ISBN 0 7188 0307 8 | Copyright © Henry Z. Walck Inc., 1952 || *Printed in Singapore*]

PAGINATION: White paper.

COVER: Blue paper (fine buckram imprint) cover printed in gold on spine: TUDOR   FIRST GRACES   Lutterworth.

DUST JACKET: Gloss film laminate rose dust jacket as 1st Lutterworth, and on the back, lower left:, ISBN 0-7188-0307-8 | [UPC bar code] | 9 780718 803070. At lower right, back: Lutterworth Press | 7 All Saints' Passage | Cambridge CB2 3LS | England. Jacket is complete, front white flap reproduces the text from first Lutterworth, minus the ISBN, and this price in lower right corner: £L2.25 net. Back flap: More delightful books in this beautiful series | for little children: FIRST PRAYERS |

0 7188 0306 x | MORE PRAYERS | 0 7188 1364 2 | *Illustrated by* | TASHA TUDOR || FIRST HYMNS | 0 7188 0308 6 | Illustrated by | BRENDA MEREDITH | SEYMOUR.

F38 _____. [*First published in Great Britain, 1964* | This impression <u>1989</u> || [L in circle logo] || Lutterworth Press | P.O. Box <u>60</u> | Cambridge <u>CB1 2NT</u> | England || ISBN 0 7188 <u>2561 6</u> | Copyright © Henry Z. Walck Inc., 1952 || *Printed in Singapore*]

   PAGINATION: White paper.

   COVER: White paper impressed with a fine buckram weave, over boards. The only printing is the title, FIRST | GRACES, impressed in gilt, and centered in a gilt stamping of the floral oval from the title page.

   DUST JACKET: In a white box. The lid has a background of alternating pink and blue vertical stripes. A colorful floral oval (not a Tudor design) is laid over the striped background. FIRST | GRACES is centered on a white field within this oval. At the lower right of the box bottom: FIRST GRACES | ISBN 0-7188-2561-6 | [bar code] | 9 780718 825614. A PUBLISHERS PRICE (red) label at the left of the bar code bears the price five pounds forty-five.

F39 _____. . . . <u>The</u> Lutterworth Press [*First published in Great Britain, 1964* | This impression <u>1991</u> ||[L in circle logo] || <u>The</u> Lutterworth Press | <u>P.O. Box 60</u> | Cambridge <u>CB1 2NT</u> | England || ISBN 0 7188 0307 8 || Copyright © Henry Z. Walck Inc., 1952 || *Printed in <u>Hong Kong by Colorcraft Ltd</u>*]

   COVER: Light blue paper (fine weave pattern) over boards printed <u>in gold on spine</u>: TUDOR FIRST GRACES   [L in circle logo].

   DUST JACKET: Gloss film laminate <u>hot pink</u> dust jacket as before with two changes. Insignia at base of spine is Lutterworth's 'L in a circle' logo. Publisher's statement on back changes to: <u>The</u> Lutterworth Press | <u>P.O. Box 60</u> | Cambridge <u>CB1 2NT</u> | England. The lower corner was clipped from the examination copy.

   OTHER: First incorrect attribution to 1952 copyright year. Sold as part of the set *A TREASURY OF FIRST BOOKS*, in either the girl's pink box, or the boy's blue box.

F40 EERSTE DANKEBEDE

Elsa Naude', Editor, Children's Books, Human & Rousseau (PTY) LTD, Cape Town, South Africa, in her letter to the editor, 16 March 1992: "The only other Human & Rousseau editions of books illustrated by Tasha Tudor that I can trace, are EERSTE GEBEDE (FIRST PRAYERS) and EERSTE DANKGEBEDE (FIRST GRACES), originally published by David McKay Co. Inc., New York. We published these in 1978 and reprinted in 1979 but the books are now out of print. In both cases the Afrikaans text was done by a local author, I.L. de Villiers." Tudor and Holmes are fairly well known in South Africa, mainly due to their books being available in local libraries.

F41 FIRST POEMS | OF CHILDHOOD | Illustrated by TASHA TUDOR || [boy and girl under umbrella] || PLATT & MUNK, *Publishers* NEW YORK [Copyright © 1967 by The Platt & Munk Co., Inc. | All rights reserved. Printed in the United States of America. | Library of Congress Card Number: AC 67-10586]

PAGINATION: Three signatures of heavy ivory paper: [1-7] 8-45 [46-48] pp. plus green endpapers. 7 1/8″w x 8 1/8″h.

COVER: In 1/2 light gray paper over boards in linen weave stamp. Gilt embossing on front cover, a bear in a 1 1/2″x1 1/8″ rectangle. Spine, wraps 3″ dark gray paper (also linen weave) onto covers, and stamped in gold: *First Poems of Childhood* | TUDOR | PLATT & MUNK. Green end papers; reinforced white cloth hinge.

DUST JACKET: Green dust jacket printed in green on front, First Poems | OF CHILDHOOD | *Illustrated by TASHA TUDOR*. Illustration of young girl and boy sitting back-to-back reading, above the text; below text, a rag doll, basket of flowers, and a teddy bear in blue pants and yellow sweater. There are sprays of flowers in the upper corners. Back cover, rag doll and teddy bear sitting together looking at a book. Spine text in black: [yellow nasturtium] *First Poems of Childhood*   TUDOR   PLATT & MUNK [yellow nasturtium]. Front white flap with black text: $1.95 || First Poems | OF CHILDHOOD || *Illustrated by* | TASHA TUDOR || Tasha Tudor has illustrated with | grace and delicacy this collection | of favorite poems for the very | young. Animals, holidays, the sea- | sons, farm and forest, the magic | world of fantasy—all the world of | childhood is beautifully illumined | by Miss Tudor's genius. ¶ Here are the verses of such fa- | vorite poets of childhood as Robert | Louis Stevenson, Edward Lear, | Henry Wadsworth Longfellow, | Eugene Field, and many others. ¶ For its wonderful words, and for | Tasha Tudor's warm and colorful | expression of the beauty that is | poetry, this should be every child's | first book. || PLATT & MUNK, *Publishers* | New York, N.Y. 10010 | No. 505 [Lower corner clipped from examination copy] Back white flap with black text: TASHA | TUDOR || Tasha Tudor lives in a large, old- | fashioned farmhouse in New | Hampshire. One of the world's | foremost illustrators of children's | books, Miss Tudor has always had | a special feeling for rural scenes | and for the grace of children and | animals. ¶ The daughter of Rosamond | Tudor, who was a portrait painter, | and W. Starling Burgess, who de- | signed yachts, Miss Tudor studied | at the Museum of Fine Arts in Bos- | ton. Though she was born in that | city, she grew up on a farm in Con- | necticut, and she has never lost her | enthusiasm for country life. || © MCMLXVII THE PLATT & MUNK CO., INC. | Made in the United States of America.

ILLUSTRATIONS: Pp. [1, 4 and 48] are blank, white pages. Pp. [2 and 47] are blank blue paper. Pp. [3 and 46] are blue with an identical watercolor chipmunk centered in a white torn edge panel. Page [5] Title page, in color, boy and girl standing under an umbrella. Text in black. Illustrations are mostly in color and were drawn to accompany the poems. Color on pages: [3], [7], 8-15, 18-23, 26-27, 30-37, 42-43, [46]. Pencil drawings on pages 16-17, 24-25, 28-29, 38-41, 44-45. Panel illustration printed across two pages: 20-21, 36-37. Title page illustration reappears on page 21. Boy reading from page [7] is reprinted on page 20. Same rose motif used on pp. 8 and 9. In all, 62 separate images.

CONTENTS: Page [7], an untitled table of contents, headed by a boy reclining on his right elbow reading: BABY *George MacDonald* 8 | THE SLUMBER BOAT *Alice C.D. Riley* 10 | THE ROCK-A-BY LADY *Eugene Field* 12 | THE STAR *by Jane Taylor* 15 | THE MOON 16 | WHAT WILL ROBIN DO? 17 | WHO HAS SEEN THE WIND? *Christina G. Rossetti* 18 | THE MONTHS *Richard B. Sheridan* 20 | DAIRY CHARM 22 | THE HAYLOFT *Robert Louis Stevenson* 23 | THE ARROW AND THE SONG *Henry Wadsworth Longfellow* 24 | PUSSY WILLOW *Kate Brown* 27 | A DOG AND A CAT WENT OUT TOGETHER 28 | PUSSY-CAT, PUSSY-CAT 29 | AT THE SEASIDE *Robert Louis Stevenson* 31 | WINGS 32 | MONDAY'S CHILD 33 | THE TABLE AND THE CHAIR *Edward Lear* 34 | THANKSGIVING DAY *Lydia Maria Child* 36 | THE OWL AND THE PUSSY-CAT *Edward Lear* 38 | A VISIT FROM ST. NICHOLAS *Clement C. Moore* 42

OTHER: Four puzzles were derived from the illustrations, copyright 1968 and sold in a red box as *POEM PUZZLES BY TASHA TUDOR*. Three are pictured here: At the seashore, The Star, and Pussy Willow. The Arrow and the Song is illustrated in the book in pencil drawing. The puzzle is a new version in watercolor.

This book is an expansion of the original twelve poems and illustrations included in Dana Bruce's *My Brimful Book*, Platt & Munk (1960).

COPYRIGHT REGISTRATION: A 929583 granted to The Platt & Munk Co., Inc., 200 Fifth Ave., N.Y. 10, N.Y. Sydell Drespel, agent for claimant, swears on Aug. 11, 1967:

FIRST POEMS OF CHILDHOOD #505 (Retail price $1.95), by Tasha Tudor, Route 1, Contoocook, N.H., a U.S. citizen, was published April 10, 1967. The book was printed by Duenewald-Konecky Litho., Inc., 45 West 19th St., N.Y., N.Y. and bound by American Book -Stratford Press, Inc, 75 Varick St., N.Y., N.Y. Application and affidavit received at L.C. Aug. 14, 1967; fees and two deposit copies received June 30, 1967.

COPYRIGHT RENEWAL REGISTRATION: RE 734-233 granted to Tasha Tudor, c/o Corgi Cottage Industries, P.O. Box 7281, Richmond, Va. 23221-0281, claiming as author (illustrator). Kathyrn [*sic*] L. Barrett, Esq., 235 East 22nd St., Apt. 11C, N.Y., N.Y. 10010, agent for Tasha Tudor, swears on June 21, 1996:

FIRST POEMS OF CHILDHOOD, the illustrations renewable matter by Tasha Tudor was published April 10, 1967, and registered to Platt & Munk Co., Inc., A929583. Renewal application received Aug. 9, 1996, the effective date of this registration. Mail certificate and correspondence to Kathyrn L. Barrett, Esq. [*sic*].

COPYRIGHT REGISTRATION: KK 201339 granted to The Platt & Munk Co., Inc., 200 Fifth Ave., N.Y. 10, N.Y. Sydell Drespel, agent for claimant, swears, undated:

FIRST POEMS OF CHILDHOOD, a book by Tasha Tudor, Route 1, Contoocook, N.H., a US citizen, was published April 10, 1967. Application and two deposit copies received at L.C. June 30, 1967.

COPYRIGHT RENEWAL REGISTRATION: RE 731-174 granted to Tasha Tudor, c/o Corgi Cottage Industries, P.O. Box 7281, Richmond, Va. 23221-0281, claiming as author. Kathyrn [*sic*] L. Barrett, Esq., 235 East 22nd St., Apt. 11C, N.Y., N.Y. 10010, 212-684-6689, agent for Tasha Tudor, swears on June 21, 1996:

FIRST POEMS OF CHILDHOOD, by Tasha Tudor was published April 10, 1967, and registered to Platt & Munk Co., Inc., KK201339. Renewal application received Aug. 9, 1996, the effective date of this registration. Certificate and correspondence to be mailed to Kathryn L. Barrett, and name signed likewise.

F42 _____.

COVER: Yellow-green cloth, stamped in gold, as above.

DUST JACKET: As above with an added ¾″ x 2 ¾″ silver foil label applied ¼″ from bottom. The label wraps from the spine onto the front of the dust jacket. It is imprinted with black (?) ink: three vertical bars adjacent to spine, a star ✳ , LIBRARY | BINDING.

OTHER: Examined a copy inscribed November 22, 1974.

F43 _____. [Copyright © 1967 by Platt & Munk All rights...AC 67-10586 | ISBN 0-8228-050-7 | **QUESTOR** ® | A QUESTOR COMPANY]

PAGINATION: As above. 7 1/4″ x 8 1/4″.

COVER: Printed matte paper in weave pattern over boards, <u>printed with illustration from first ed. dust jacket</u>. Upper right back in black: 505:0250. White end papers. White cloth reinforced hinge.

F44 _____.

COVER: Back cover text: **505:0295**.

DUST JACKET: Like first edition, but complete. The price $2.95 was printed on the front flap, but here it is covered with a <u>gold gummed label</u> screened in black to reveal: $3^{50}. Otherwise the cover and interior are the same as above.

F45 _____. . . . PLATT & MUNK, *Publishers* NEW YORK | A Division of Grosset & Dunlap [Copyright © 1967 by Platt & Munk | All rights reserved. Printed in the United States of America. | Library of Congress Card Number: AC 67-10586 | ISBN 0-448-40505-9 (Trade Edition) | ISBN 0-448-13021-1 (Library Edition)]

PAGINATION: Three signatures of ivory matte paper: [1-7] 8-45 [46-48] pp. <u>including covers</u>. 8 1/8″ x 7 1/8″.

COVER: Green jacket design, as above. Spine: *First* ... MUNK | 40505-9. Printed in black <u>on the back</u>, beneath illustration: Platt & Munk, Publishers/New York | A Division of Grosset & Dunlap; and in the lower left corner: ISBN 0-448-40505-9. Blue pages with chipmunks are the endpapers in this edition.

DUST JACKET: Sealed in gloss film laminate. Illustrations and text as before, with some changes. Upper corner of front flap has been clipped, and repriced with an <u>applied gold label overprinted in black</u>, $3^{50}. Have examined other copies with a <u>variant label</u> overprinted with a <u>black mask</u> to reveal $3^{50} in gold. There is no code at the bottom of front flap; the publisher statement is reset: Platt & Munk, Publishers/New York | <u>A Division of Grosset & Dunlap</u>. The back flap carries a new stylized <u>Platt&Munk</u> | <u>New York, N.Y.,</u> between the biography and copyright statement. Back, lower right: ISBN 0-448-40505-9, and at base of the spine: 40505-9. Examination copy includes handwritten <u>1980</u> on the front flyleaf.

F46 _____.

COVER: Glossier paper with a *fine weave imprint*.

DUST JACKET: Have not examined a copy

F47 FIRST | POEMS | OF | CHILDHOOD | Illustrated by | TASHA TUDOR ||

[locomotive logo] | Platt & Munk, Publishers/New York | A Division of Grosset & Dunlap [[ladybug, mouse and duck] Copyright © 1967 by Platt & Munk | All rights reserved. Printed in the United States of America. | Library of Congress Card Number: 78-68216 | **ISBN 0-448-49611-9**. (Originally published under the title, | *First Poems of Childhood*.) || Cover design by Julie Metz, A Good Thing, Inc.]

PAGINATION: Six sheets and cover stock folded and stapled into one paperback booklet. [24] pp. plus covers. <u>9 3/6″ x 8 1/32″</u>

COVER: Paper cover is largely the illustration of Dairy Charm. As on the title page, the title and author statement is in a calligraphic hand, large red F, rest of title is rust; illustration statement in blue: FIRST | POEMS | OF | CHILDHOOD | Illustrated by | TASHA TUDOR || Platt&Munk. A 7/8 x 3/5″ white lozenge in the upper left corner has the picture of a panda reading. Printed laterally to the left: Pandaback Book. Centered on a butterscotch back, a boy reading (from The Months) and at bottom in black: Platt & Munk, Publishers | A Division of Grosset & Dunlap   0-448-49611-9.   A label has been removed from upper left, back cover, of the examination copy.

CONTENTS: Page [3]: an untitled contents lists 13 of the previous 21 poems, most with authors. **Pussy Willow** Kate Brown | **Dairy Charm** | **The Hayloft** Robert Louis Stevenson | **Who Has Seen the Wind** Christina G. Rossetti | **The Slumber Boat** Alice C.D. Riley | **The Months** Richard B. Sheridan | **Baby** George MacDonald | **The Table and the Chair** Edward Lear | **Wings** A Psalm of David | **Monday's Child** | **The Star** Jane Taylor | **The Rock-a-by Lady** Eugene Field | **At the Seaside** Robert Louis Stevenson. Illustrations as with the poems in first edition, **except** the left hand page of At the Seaside is omitted in this edition.

F48 _____.

PAGINATION: Printed on heavier paper and cut slightly larger: 9 ¼″ x 8 1/16″.

COVER: The small Pandaback book lozenge in the upper left, front cover, here has 95ᶜ printed in upper left corner. Additional text at upper left, back corner: <u>49611:0095</u>.

F49 _____.

COVER: Lighter-weight paper. There is <u>no price</u> in the panda lozenge. Upper left back corner: <u>49611:0125</u>.

F50 _____.

COVER: Upper left back corner: <u>U.S.A.   0001.25</u> | <u>Canada 0001.50</u>.

F51 First Poems | OF CHILDHOOD | *Illustrated by Tasha Tudor* | [fine circle around boy with rooster] | PLATT & MUNK, PUBLISHERS • *New York* | A DIVISION OF GROSSET & DUNLAP

[Copyright © 1988, 1967 by Platt & Munk, Publishers, | a division of Grosset & Dunlap, Inc. | All rights reserved. | Grosset & Dunlap is a member of | The Putnam Publishing Group, New York. | Published simultaneously in Canada. Printed in Hong Kong. | ISBN 0-448-09326-X. | Library of Congress Card Number 87-82516]

PAGINATION: Two signatures of white paper: [1-6] 7-21 [22] 23-24 [25] 26-28 [29-32] including covers. 8 1/4″h x 7 1/4″w.

COVER: Printed paper over boards: a large yellow rectangle in a red line with apple motif (see FIRST DELIGHTS) on a green field front and back. Except for the spine First Poems is printed in blue ink in a shaded letter: title page, cover and dust jacket. Front cover: First Poems [blue] | OF CHILDHOOD | [detail of girl and boy reading <u>in a circle medallion outlined with one thin black line</u> from the first edition dust jacket] | *Tasha Tudor* [black]. Spine: red rule across the spine at top and bottom and between them in black: FIRST POEMS OF CHILDHOOD   Tudor   Platt & Munk. Back cover: detail <u>in circle</u> of doll and bear from first edition dust jacket and within the yellow field at bottom left, beneath the UPC bar code, 0 70918 09326 5. At lower back right: ISBN 0-448-19326-X. End papers, pp. [2-3] [30-31] and pp. [4-5] are edged in 3/4″ green border.

DUST JACKET: Duplicates cover. Green flaps with black text. Front flap: $8.95 | [rule] | (12.50 CAN) | [bluebird on apple bough] | In this timeless collection, | Tasha Tudor introduces young | children to the joys of poetry. | Favorite works by Robert | Louis Stevenson, Christina G. | Rossetti, Eugene Field, and | others are rendered with | affection and old-fashioned | charm. Together, poems and | paintings evoke the delights of | childhood to find the beauty in | the world around them. | ISBN 0-448-09326-X. Back flap text reprints the biography from page [30]: Born in Boston, Tasha Tudor | grew up on a farm in | Connecticut, and her | impressions of rural New | England life are the inspiration | for her artwork. She has won | many awards and honors since | her first book was published in | 1938. More than sixty books | later, her gift is still unique. She | now lives in Vermont where | she is surrounded by her corgis, | her family, and her friends— | and the country pleasures so | lovingly depicted in her books. || *Platt & Munk Books by Tasha Tudor* | First Delights | A Book About the Five Senses | First Poems of Childhood | Tasha Tudor's Bedtime Book | Tasha Tudor's Fairy Tales || PLATT & MUNK | A division of Grosset & Dunlap | A member of | The Putnam Publishing Group | New York | Printed in Hong Kong.

CONTENTS: Title page [3], page [5] in an untitled table of contents, listing only 13 poems, [6] and [29] are blank, poems on pages 7-28. Page [30]: Born in Boston, Tasha Tudor . . . These poems were deleted: The Moon, What will Robin do?, The Arrow and the Song, A Cat and A Dog Went Out Together, Pussy-cat, Pussy-cat, The Table and the Chair, The Owl and the Pussy-cat, A Visit from St. Nicholas. "Thanksgiving Day" is included but under the new title "Over the River and Through the Wood." <u>The new contents, page [5]:</u> Monday's Child . 7 | Baby *George MacDonald* . 8 | Pussy Willow *Kate L. Brown* . 13 | Who Has Seen the Wind? *Christina G. Rossetti* . 14 | At the Seaside *Robert Louis Stevenson* . 17 | Dairy Charm . 18 | The Hayloft *Robert Louis Stevenson* . 19 | Over the River and Through the Wood *Lydia Maria Child* . 20 | The Star *Jane Taylor* . 23 | The Rock-a-by Lady *Eugene Field*. 24 | The Slumber Boat *Alice C. D. Riley* . 26 | Wings. 28

ILLUSTRATIONS:. Title page: detail from page 7 in black line circle of banty rooster frightening boy with a dropped basket of eggs. Page [31] inside back cover is detail of page 10 in black line circle, boy with basket of apples. Contents picture is detail from page 10 of girl playing in leaf pile. Illustrations accompanying poems as in the first edition, but the colors are not as bright. This is especially noticeable where color washes to backgrounds are lost from the originals. All <u>pencil sketches were deleted</u> from this edition.

COPYRIGHT REGISTRATION: TX 2-325-732 granted to The Platt & Munk, Publishers, 51 Madison Ave., N.Y., N.Y. 10010. Louise Bates (212) 689-9200, agent for Platt & Munk, Publishers, swears on May 2, 1988:

FIRST POEMS OF CHILDHOOD, an abridgment of selections and illustrations by Platt & Munk, Publishers, employer for hire, a U.S. citizen, was completed in 1988 and published May 2, 1988. The book is derivative of FIRST POEMS OF CHILDHOOD originally published by Platt & Munk in 1967. LC is granted non-exclusive permission to make copies and phonorecords for the blind and physically handicapped. The book was manufactured by the South China Printing Co., Hong Kong. Fees charged to account DAO38288, Putnam Publishing Group (P&M), 51 Madison Ave., N.Y., N.Y. 10010. Application and two deposit copies received at L.C. May 3, 1988.

F52 _____. [. . . <u>1988 Printing</u>]

F53 _____. [. . . 1990 Printing]

> COVER: Back cover lower left: <u>ISBN 0-448-09326-X</u> | [two UPC bar codes.] Above the smaller right, <u>50895</u>. Beneath the larger left, <u>9 780448 093260</u>.

> DUST JACKET: Duplicate of cover including <u>the moved ISBN</u>. Front flap of jacket: $8.95 | [rule] | <u>(11.75 CAN)</u> | . . . the world around them. || <u>Jacket copyright © 1988 by Platt & Munk, Publishers.</u> ISBN 0-448-09326-X

F54 _____. [. . . 1992 Printing]

> COVER: Back cover lower left: <u>ISBN 0-448-09326-X</u> | [one UPC bar code] | <u>0 70918 09326 5</u>.

> DUST JACKET: Duplicates cover. Front flap of jacket: $9.95 | [rule] | <u>(11.75 CAN)</u> . . .

F55 [cherub with rose] | **FIRST | PRAYERS** | *Illustrated by* | TASHA TUDOR || [cross in flowers] || *OXFORD UNIVERSITY PRESS* [Copyright 1952 | OXFORD UNIVERSITY PRESS, INC. | PRINTED IN THE UNITED STATES OF AMERICA]

> PAGINATION: [1-2] 3-48 pp. in 3 signatures, plus end papers. 5 3/8″ x 3 7/8″

> COVER: Light gray-blue cloth cover in a course weave. Printed paper label (4 1/4″ x 2 3/4″) on front, [within a rose and ribbon border, 3 cherubs above the black title] | FIRST | PRAYERS | *Illustrated by* | TASHA TUDOR. Spine stamped in gold: Tudor   FIRST PRAYERS Oxford. Front and back end papers: an aqua field, both pages enclosed within a single white scalloped border. One of four different cherubs resting on a cloud on each end paper.

> DUST JACKET: Sky blue jacket imprinted same as front cover label. Same spine imprint in black.
> Front flap: FIRST | PRAYERS | *Illustrated by* | TASHA TUDOR || This collection of prayers | for little children has | been selected with care | and with advice from | educators in the religious | field. Here are familiar, | beautiful words that be- | long in the hearts and | memories of all of us. | Some less familiar but | no less lovely prayers | have been included | which express simply for | little children the ever- | loving presence of God. || *Oxford Books* | *for Boys and Girls* || <u>60-120</u>. Back flap is 2″ wide white paper without text.

> ILLUSTRATIONS: Color illustrations: Title page [1] (A pink ribbon upon a blue field, encloses an irregularly shaped white field bearing the text and two illustrations.), 4-5, 8-9, 12-13, 16-17, 20-21, 24-25, 28-29, 32-33, 36-37, 40-41, 44-45, 48. Pencil sketches: pp. 3, 6-7, 10-11, 14, 15, 18, 19, 22, 23, 26-27, 30-31, 34-35, 38-39, 42, 43, 46-47. Full page illustration with no printed text: pp. 3, 5, 8, 10, 13, 15, 17, 19 (hand lettered), 21, 23 (hand lettered), 25, 27, 29, 30, 35, 39, 43.

> CONTENTS: Dedication to Virginia Low Paine. Includes Tudor's first illustrations for The Twenty-Third Psalm on pp. 40-41.

OTHER: Examination copy has penciled price 1.50 at bottom of front dj flap.

RELATED EPHEMERA:

Have examined a folded order form (5 ¹/₈ x 3 ½″) which reproduces the cover label on a blue field. Center reproduces in color, pages 20 and 29, but without the page numbers. Text on back: FIRST PRAYERS [blue] | *Illustrated by* [black] | TASHA TUDOR [red] | THIS collection of prayers for little children has | been selected with care and with advice from edu- | cators in the religious field. Here are familiar, beau- | tiful words that belong in the hearts and memories | of all of us. Some less familiar but no less lovely | prayers have been included which express simply | for little children the ever-loving presence of God. | [red broken line] | **Tasha Tudor's | GINGER AND PICKLES STORE |** **R.F.D. No. 1 Contoocook, New Hampshire** | Please send me   copies of FIRST PRAYERS | at $1.50 each. | . Check enclosed   . Protestant edition | . Charge to my account   . Catholic edition | Name [rule] | Address [rule] | [rule] | PRINTED IN U.S.A. All type black, except, blue title on first line, red author on third line and red broken line.

COPYRIGHT REGISTRATION: A 70898 granted to Oxford University Press, Inc., 114 Fifth Ave., N.Y., N.Y. W. M. Gherton, agent for claimant, swears on Oct. 1, 1952:

FIRST PRAYERS, Protestant Edition, by Tasha Tudor, Contoocook, N.H., a U.S. citizen born approx. 1910, was published Sept. 11, 1952. The book's type set, plate making and printing were done by Kellogg and Bulkeley, Hartford, Ct.; it was bound by H. Wolff Book Mfg. Co. Inc., N.Y., N.Y. Application and affidavit and two deposit copies received at L.C. Oct. 6, 1952.

COPYRIGHT RENEWAL REGISTRATION: RE 67-990 granted to the author Tasha Tudor, Route 4, West Brattleboro, Vt. 05301. Lisa A. Checchi, David McKay Co., 2 Park Avenue, N.Y., N.Y. 10016, agent for Tasha Tudor, swears on Oct. 20, 1980:

FIRST PRAYERS (Protestant Edition) was published Sept. 11, 1952; A 70898, the original claimant, Tasha Tudor.* However, her name has been lined out and Oxford University Press, Inc. typed below it with an asterisked note, Amended by Copyright Office. Application received at L.C. Oct. 24, 1980, the effective date of this renewal.

F56 _____. [Copyright 1952 | OXFORD UNIVERSITY PRESS, INC. | PRINTED IN THE UNITED STATES OF AMERICA || *Nihil obstat* | John W. Sliney, D.C.L. | CENSOR LIBRORUM || *Imprimatur* | ✠ Matthew F. Brady, D.D. | BISHOP OF MANCHESTER]

COVER: Blue-gray course cloth with label. Top edge painted robin's egg blue. Gilt spine imprinted so that Tudor runs from ¾″ to 1 1/8″ from top of spine; title, 2″ to 3 ¼″ from top of spine; Oxford, 4 1/8 to 4 9/16″ from top of spine.

CONTENTS: This is the Catholic version with illustrations identical to Protestant. Text varies:

Page 32: O Lord Jesus Christ, I thank Thee, | That I am a baptised child. | Washed in the holy font, |Marked with the sacred sign. | May I always love Thy Church, | Wherein Thy Truth is stored, | And follow well Thy holy will, | O ever-loving Lord. Amen.

Page 33: Praise be to God, | The dear Father Who made me. || Praise to His son, | The Lord Jesus who saved me. || Praise to the Spirit for gifts | He doth send me. | Most Holy Trinity | Help and defend me. Amen.

Page 34: Lord, grant us faith, | the mother of love, | And love, | the mother of peace, | And peace, | the mother of blessedness, | Now and for ever.

Page 40: TWENTY-SECOND PSALM |The Lord ruleth me: and I shall want | nothing. He hath set me in a place of | pasture. | He hath brought me up, on the water of | refreshment: He hath converted my |soul. | He hath led me on the paths of justice, | for his own name's sake. | For

197

though I should walk in the midst of | the shadow of death, I will fear no | evils. For thou art with me.

Page 41: Thy rod and thy staff, they have | comforted me. | Thou hast prepared a table before me, | against them that afflict me. | Thou hast anointed my head with oil; | and my chalice which inebriateth me, | how goodly is it! | And thy mercy will follow me all the | days of my life. | And that I may dwell in the house of | the Lord unto length of days.

Page 44: O more than mighty cities known, | Dear Bethlehem, in thee alone | Salvation's Lord from heaven took birth | In human form upon the earth. || And from a star that far outshone | The radiant circle of the sun | In beauty, swift the tidings ran | Of God on earth in flesh of man.

Page 45: The wise men, seeing him, so fair, | Bow low before him, and with prayer | Their treasured orient gifts unfold | Of incense, myrrh, and royal gold. || The fragrant incense which they bring, | The gold, proclaim him God and King: | The bitter spicy dust of myrrh | Foreshadows his new sepulchre. || All glory, Lord, to thee we pay | For thine Epiphany today; | All glory, as is ever meet, | To Father and to Paraclete. Amen.

OTHER: Protestant versions include alternate text *Gentle Jesus, Meek and Mild*, pp. 32-33; Charles Wesley's *Let me above all fulfill*, p. 34; THE TWENTY-THIRD PSALM, pp. 40-41; and CRADLE HYMN by Martin Luther on pp. 44-45.

COPYRIGHT REGISTRATION: A 70899 granted to Oxford University Press, Inc., 114 Fifth Ave., N.Y., N.Y. W.S.Gherton, agent for claimant, swears on Oct. 1, 1952:

FIRST PRAYERS (Catholic Edition), by Tasha Tudor, Contoocook, N.H., a U.S. citizen born approx. 1910, was published Sept. 11, 1952. The book's type set, plate making and printing were done by Kellogg and Bulkeley, Hartford, Ct.; it was bound by H. Wolff Book Mfg. Co. Inc., N.Y., N.Y. Application and affidavit and two deposit copies received at L.C. Oct. 6, 1952.

COPYRIGHT RENEWAL REGISTRATION: RE 67-991 granted to the author Tasha Tudor, Route 4, West Brattleboro, Vt. 05301. Lisa A. Checchi, David McKay Co., 2 Park Avenue, N.Y., N.Y. 10016, agent for Tasha Tudor, swears on Oct. 20, 1980:

FIRST PRAYERS (Catholic Edition) was published Sept. 11, 1952; A 70899, the original claimant, Tasha Tudor.* However, her name has been lined out and Oxford University Press, Inc. typed above it with an asterisked note, Amended by Copyright Office. Application received at L.C. Oct. 24, 1980, the effective date of this renewal.

F57 _____. [The Catholic text.]

PAGINATION: As before. 5 5/16″ x 3 7/8″

COVER: The top edge is not painted. Cloth more gray-blue than before.

DUST JACKET: Have not examined one.

F58 _____. [The Catholic text.]

PAGINATION: As before. 5 5/16″ x 3 7/8″

COVER: Spine imprint is larger and placed so that Tudor is ¼″ from top of spine (others are ¾″); Oxford is 3/16″ from the bottom (others are 7/8″); and First Prayers is 1 5/8″ long (not 1 ¼″).

DUST JACKET: Front flap has a printed price $1.75 at the bottom right. A registration mark on back flap.

F59 _____. [The Catholic text.]

PIERPONT MORGAN LIBRARY copy, Julia P. Wightman collection JPW:3669, measures 3 15/16″ wide with a square spine. Paper label on cover is 4 7/32″ x 2 ½.″ Printer's registration mark at the left edge of rear dj flap. A personal gift note dated December 9, 1958 is laid in.

F60 _____. [. . . AMERICA | SECOND PRINTING, 1953]

PAGINATION: As before. 5 5/16″ x 3 7/8″

COVER: Robin's egg blue cloth.

DUST JACKET: As first printing, with the registration mark on back flap.

F61 _____.

COVER: Light blue cloth.

DUST JACKET: Back flap has white area only 1 ½″ wide. A penciled 1^{50} at top of front flap.

F62 _____. [. . . AMERICA | THIRD PRINTING, 1955]

DUST JACKET: Registration mark on back flap of dust jacket.

F63 **FIRST | PRAYERS** | *Illustrated by* | TASHA TUDOR | HENRY Z. WALCK, INC. [Copyright 1952 | HENRY Z. WALCK, INC. | PRINTED IN THE UNITED STATES OF AMERICA || Library of Congress Catalog Card Number: 59-9630]

PAGINATION: [1-2] 3-48 pp. in 3 signatures, plus end papers. 5 5/16″ x 3 7/8″.

COVER: Blue-gray cloth with paper label. Gold stamped spine.

F64 _____.

PAGINATION: 5 11/32″ x 3 7/8″.

COVER: Blue-gray cloth, without the paper label.

DUST JACKET: An updating of the Oxford 3rd printing, 1955, with these changes. The base of the spine substitutes Walck, as the new publisher. Front flap: top corner is clipped. Last three lines now read: … of God. || *Henry Z. Walck, Inc.* || *40-90 $1.95*. Rear flap: FIRST | GRACES || *Illustrated by* | TASHA TUDOR || A companion volume to | Tasha Tudor's popular | *First Prayers*, this collec- | tion has been carefully | selected from both old | and contemporary | sources. Over twenty | prayers of thanksgiving | are included in this tiny | volume. Chosen with the | advice of educators in | the religious field, these | prayers will develop in | the child a true sense of | gratitude toward God.

OTHER: Examined one with a gift inscription, "December 25, 1967."

F65 _____. [Copyright 1952 | HENRY Z. WALCK, INC. | PRINTED IN THE UNITED STATES OF AMERICA || Standard Book Number: 8098-1952-X || Library of Congress Catalog Card Number: 59-9630]

PAGINATION: [1-2] 3 [4] 5-48 pp. in 3 signatures, plus end papers. 5 5/16″ x 3 7/8″.

COVER: Light blue linen cover without paper label. Gold stamped spine.

DUST JACKET: Have not examined one.

OTHER: With a dated book plate: "October 12, 1969." Page 4, unnumbered.

F66 _____. . . . [floral spray <u>without cross</u>] | Lutterworth Press. [This impression **1979** || ISBN O-8098-1952-X || Copyright Henry Z. Walck Inc., 1952 || *Printed in Hong Kong*] [1-2] 3-48 pp. in 3 signatures. 5 5/16″ x 3 13/16″

COVER: <u>Gray</u> paper imprinted with linen weave over board covers. Front cover stamped in black: FIRST | PRAYERS. Spine stamped in BLACK: FIRST PRAYERS   Tasha Tudor WALCK.

DUST JACKET: Spine printed in black: TUDOR   FIRST PRAYERS   WALCK. Back cover, blue, as before. White front flap: FIRST . . . presence of God. || <u>ISBN</u> <u>0-8098-11952-X</u>. The lower corner was clipped from examination copy. Back flap is white, no text.

ILLUSTRATIONS: The pencil drawings are washed out to being nearly non-existent, especially pages 10-11 and 14-15.

OTHER: This curiosity appears to have been manufactured incorrectly in Hong Kong, confusing the English and American imprints. The title page Lutterworth and the nature of the paper over board covers both indicate the English edition. However, all other publisher citations are to Walck. The text is the Protestant version.

F67 _____. <u>Henry Z. Walck, Inc.   New York</u> [This impression, 1981 || ISBN 0-8098-1952-X || Copyright © 1952 by Henry Z. Walck, Inc. || Library of Congress Catalog Card Number: 59-9630 | Manufactured in the United States of America]

PAGINATION: As before. 5 3/8 x 4 1/8″.   The back cover measures 4 1/16″.

COVER: <u>Turquoise</u> paper over board cover, pigskin, spine stamped in gold: FIRST PRAYERS Tasha Tudor   Walck.

DUST JACKET: For the first time, the jacket is <u>white</u>, with the previous cover illustration printed in a ¼″ wide blue frame. Front flap: <u>$3.50</u> || FIRST . . . God. || <u>0-8098-1952-X</u>.   Back flap: FIRST | PRAYERS | *illustrated by* | TASHA TUDOR || "Lovely prayers, beauti- | fully illustrated for little | children." — Christian | Herald. | FIRST | GRACES *illustrated by* | TASHA TUDOR || "This tiny exquisite book | . . . contains twenty-one | prayers of thanksgiving." —Chicago Tribune || Henry Z. Walck, Inc. | A Division of | David McKay Company, Inc. | New York.

CONTENTS: This printing was sold as a boxed set with *First Graces* (red binding) and *More Prayers* (dark moss green binding) as *Tasha Tudor's TREASURE, q.v.* for a description of the slipcase.

F68 _____. [This impression, 1983...]

PAGINATION: 5 3/8″ x 4″

COVER: <u>Teal</u> paper blind stamped in <u>buckram weave</u>, over boards. Spine imprinted in gilt: FIRST PRAYERS Tasha Tudor Walck.

DUST JACKET: Upper right front flap: <u>$ 3.95</u>.

F69 _____. [This impression, 1984...]

COVER: Navy paper blind stamped in a leather grain. Spine imprinted in gilt: FIRST PRAYERS Tasha Tudor   Walck.

DUST JACKET: Upper right front flap: <u>$4.50</u>.

F70 _____. [This impression, <u>1986</u>...]

    COVER: <u>Blue-gray</u> plastic-filled paper, <u>pebble finish</u>.

    DUST JACKET: Price clipped from examination copy.

    OTHER: Dated inscription, July 12, 1987.

F71 _____. [This impression, <u>1986</u>...]

    COVER: <u>Teal</u> plastic-filled paper, <u>pebble finish</u>.

    DUST JACKET: Front flap, top: <u>$6.95</u>. <u>No ISBN</u>. Lower left back imprinted with <u>two bar codes</u>, 50695 above the small right one: 9 780809 819522 below the larger left code. Beneath all, ISBN 0-809-81952-X.

F72 **FIRST PRAYERS** | *Illustrated by* | TASHA TUDOR || HENRY Z. WALCK, INC.
[Copyright 1952 | HENRY Z.. WALCK, INC. | PRINTED IN THE UNITED STATES OF AMERICA || ISBN: 0-8098-1951-1 | Library of Congress Catalog Card Number: 59-9631 || *Nihil obstat* | John W. Sliney, D.C.L. | CENSOR LIBRORUM || *Imprimatur* | ✠ Matthew F. Brady, D.D. | BISHOP OF MANCHESTER]

    COVER: Light blue cloth imprinted in navy on spine: Tudor   FIRST PRAYERS   Walck.

    DUST JACKET: Similar to the 1st Oxford Spine: Tudor FIRST PRAYERS Walck. Top corner clipped from front flap. FIRST . . . *Henry Z. Walck, Inc.* || 40-90 <u>$2.50</u>. Back flap: FIRST | GRACES || *Illustrated by* | TASHA TUDOR || A companion volume to | Tasha Tudor's popular | *First Prayers*, this collec- | tion has been carefully | selected from both old | and contemporary | sources. Over twenty | prayers of thanksgiving | are included in this tiny | volume. Chosen with the | advise of educators in | the religious field, these | prayers will develop in | the child a true sense of | gratitude toward God.

    CONTENT: This is the Walck printing of the Catholic version with illustrations identical to Protestant, and the text of the Oxford Catholic printing.

F73 _____. [Copyright 1952...UNITED STATES OF AMERICA | <u>TENTH PRINTING, 1962</u> | | Library of Congress...]

    COVER: Light blue cloth imprinted on spine in gilt: Tudor FIRST PRAYERS   Walck

    DUST JACKET: Have not examined one.

F74 **FIRST | PRAYERS** || *Illustrated by* | TASHA TUDOR || Random House [emblem] New York
[Copyright © 1952 by Henry Z. Walck, Inc. Copyright | renewed 1980 by Tasha Tudor. All rights reserved under | International and Pan-American Copyright Conventions. | Originally published by Henry Z. Walck, Inc., in 1952. | Published in the United States by Random House, Inc., | New York, and simultaneously in Canada by Random House | of Canada Limited, Toronto. || *Library of Congress Cataloging-in-Publication Data:* | Tudor, Tasha. First Prayers. 1. Children–Prayer books and devotions– English. I. Tudor, Tasha, ill. | BV265.F56 1989 242'.82 88-30672 | ISBN: 0-394-84429-7 || Manufactured in the United States of America | 1 2 3 4 5 6 7 8 9 0]

    PAGINATION: [<u>1-3</u>] 4-48 pp. in 2 signatures, plus end papers. 5 3/8″ x 3 15/16″.

    COVER: Blue cover under gloss film laminate, over boards, imprinted with the original cover illustration and text in black. Spine printed in black: TASHA TUDOR   FIRST PRAYERS Random House. Lower left of back cover: White box with two UPC bar code, 84429 above the smaller right one; 0 79808 84429 1 under the smaller left. Beneath both bar codes, ISBN 0-394-84429-7. <u>This printing has white end papers without illustrations.</u>

DUST JACKET: Identical to printed cover. <u>Very wide, 3 1/2″, white flaps.</u> Front flap: $ 5.95 U.S. | Here are familiar...of God. [same text as before, but reset with new spacing.] Back flap: FIRST | PRAYERS | *Illustrated by* | TASHA TUDOR || "Lovely prayers, <u>beautifully</u> | illustrated for little | children." –Christian | Herald || FIRST | GRACES | *Illustrated by* | TASHA TUDOR || "This tiny exquisite book | contains twenty-one | prayers of <u>Thanksgiving</u>." | –*Chicago Tribune* || <u>Random House</u> <u>[emblem] New York | Copyright ©1952 by Henry Z. Walck, Inc. | Copyright renewed 1980 by Tasha Tudor. |</u> <u>Manufactured in the U.S.A.</u>

ILLUSTRATIONS: As Oxford, 2nd, above.

OTHER: Review copies were shipped with a 4″ x 5 ½″ red and white Review Copy slip announcing a publication date of June 15, 1989, and list price of $5.95. Coded 118-83.

F75 _____. Random House announced a reprint for 1997, ISBN 0679887873 and LC card number 97-65831. However, the Library of Congress had not yet received a copy as of March 3, 1998.

F76 [Cherub] | **FIRST | PRAYERS** || *Illustrated by* | TASHA TUDOR || [floral spray <u>without the cross</u>] | <u>Lutterworth Press</u> [First published in Great Britain, 1964 || Copyright HENRY Z. WALCK Inc., 1952]

PAGINATION: [1-2] 3-48 pages in 3 signatures. 5 5/16″ x 3 7/8″

COVER: Light <u>robin's egg blue</u> paper, homespun weave imprint, over boards. Stamped in navy, front cover: FIRST | PRAYERS; spine, FIRST PRAYERS TASHA TUDOR LUTTERWORTH

DUST JACKET: . Illustration same as Oxford, 2nd on blue field. Text: <u>FIRST PRAYERS</u> || *Illustrated by* | TASHA TUDOR (thinner type than US printings.) Spine in black: TUDOR FIRST PRAYERS Lutterworth. Front white flap: FIRST | PRAYERS || *Illustrated by* | TASHA TUDOR || Here are familiar, beau- | tiful words that be- | long in the hearts and | memories of all of us, | as well as some less | well known but no less | lovely prayers. | They all express simply | for little children the | ever-loving presence of | God. || 3s. 6d. | net. Rear flap: FIRST | GRACES || *Illustrated by* | TASHA TUDOR || This collection, which | is a companion volume | to First Prayers, has | been carefully selected | from both old and con- | temporary sources. | The delightfully illus-| trated volume includes | over twenty prayers of | thanksgiving that will | develop in the child a | true sense of gratitude | toward God. || 3s. 6d. | net.

OTHER: The type has been reset on an ivory matte paper and the text varies in places, sometimes running onto a second line which the Oxford imprint did not do: p. 4 ...and forgive us our trespasses as we forgive them that trespass against us, for ever and ever. Amen; p. 45 lacks the attribution to Martin Luther.

Inside back flyleaf, bottom: *Printed by Drukkerij Holland N.V., Amsterdam.*

F77 _____.

OTHER: Jeanette Knazek reports another binding with the same page [49] text, but whose cover is light <u>gray-green paper, asymmetrical weave imprint,</u> over boards, and stamped in black.

F78 _____. [First published in Great Britain, 1964 || ISBN 0 7188 0306 x || Copyright Henry Z. Walck Inc., 1952 | *Printed in the Netherlands by Henkes Senefelder bv*]

COVER: Pearl gray paper imprinted with buckram grain over boards. Front cover, stamped in black: FIRST | PRAYERS. Spine, in black: FIRST PRAYERS TASHA TUDOR LUTTERWORTH

DUST JACKET: Illustration same as Oxford, 2nd on blue field. Front flap text: <u>FIRST PRAYERS</u> ‖ *Illustrated by* | TASHA TUDOR (thinner type than US printings.) Spine in black: Tudor   FIRST PRAYERS   Lutterworth. Front white flap like the 1979 US copy: FIRST | PRAYERS . . God. ‖ ISBN <u>0 7188 0306 X</u> [Lower right corner has been clipped.] Back white flap: MORE PRAYERS | 7188 1364 2 | FIRST GRACES | 7188 0307 8 | *Both books illustrated by* | TASHA TUDOR ‖ "These books will give a lot of | pleasure to very young rea- | ders. Children will probably | know some of the lovely pray- | ers and graces, and will cer- | tainly be encouraged by the | enchanting little illustrations | to learn others, less familiar." | *Sunday School Chronicle* ‖ FIRST A B C | 7188 1597 1 | FIRST HYMNS | 7188 0308 6 | *Both books illustrated by* | BRENDA MEREDITH | SEYMOUR ‖ Two exquisitely illustrated | books which little children | will treasure at all times of | the year.

OTHER: The paper is white enamel finish.

F79 _____. [*First published in Great Britain, 1964* ‖ This impression <u>1985</u> ‖ L [in a circle logo] | Lutterworth Press | 7 All Saint's Passage | Cambridge CB2 3LS | England ‖ ISBN 0 7188 0306 X | Copyright © Henry Z. Walck Inc., 1952 ‖ *Printed in Singapore*]

PAGINATION: 5 ¼" x 3 11/16"

COVER: Blue paper imprinted with fine diamond weave over boards. Spine text as before, stamped in gold.

DUST JACKET: Gloss film laminate over same illustration and spine as before, robin's egg blue jacket. Back cover lower left: ISBN 0-7188-0306-X | [bar code] 9 780718 803063; and, lower right, Lutterworth Press | 7 All Saints' Passage | Cambridge CB2 3LS | England. White front flap, same text as above <u>without the ISBN</u>. In lower right, <u>L2.25 net.</u> White back flap text: More delightful books in this beautiful series | for little children: MORE PRAYERS | 0 7188 1364 2 | FIRST GRACES | 0 7188 0307 8 | *Illustrated by* | TASHA TUDOR ‖ FIRST HYMNS | 0 7188 0308 6 | Illustrated by | BRENDA MEREDITH | SEYMOUR .

F80 _____. . . . [flowers] | <u>The</u> Lutterworth Press. [*First published in Great Britain, 1964* ‖ This impression 19<u>91 | Reprinted 1994</u> ‖ [L in a circle logo] ‖ <u>The</u> Lutterworth Press | <u>P.O. Box 60</u> | Cambridge <u>CB1 2NT</u> | England ‖ ISBN 0 7188 0306 X ‖ Copyright © Henry Z. Walck Inc., 1952 ‖ *Printed in Hong Kong by Colorcraft Ltd*]

PAGINATION: [1-2] 3-48 pages in 3 signatures, plus endpapers. 5¼" x 3 13/16"

COVER: Blue paper imprinted with small weave over board covers. <u>This blue is lighter than above showing a slight gray-green.</u> Spine (<u>5/16</u>" wide) stamped in gold: Tudor FIRST PRAYERS [<u>L in circle logo</u>].

DUST JACKET: Glossy dust jacket is changed in three details. The jacket is <u>royal blue</u>. The spine carries the 'L in circle' <u>logo</u>, and the publisher's address on the back has changed: <u>The</u> Lutterworth Press | <u>P.O. Box 60</u> | Cambridge <u>CB1 2NT</u> | England.

OTHER: One of four volumes in the English boxed set *A TREASURY OF FIRST BOOKS, q.v.*

F81 _____. [*First published* . . . England ‖ ISBN 0 7188 2413 X . . . *Colorcraft Ltd*]

PAGINATION: 5 <u>5/16</u>" x 3 ¾"

COVER: White paper finished in leather texture, over boards. Spine: <u>7/16</u>" wide.   An oval of imprinted gilt flowers encloses the title and fills most of the front cover.   All edges gilt.

DUST JACKET: In a white box. The separate lid has a background of alternating pink and blue vertical stripes. A colorful floral oval (not a Tudor design) is laid over the striped background. FIRST | PRAYERS is centered on a white field within this oval. At the lower right of the box bottom: FIRST PRAYERS ‖ ISBN 0-7188-2413-X | [bar code] | 9 780718 824136. A PUBLISHERS PRICE (red) label at the left of the bar code bears the price five pounds forty-five.

F82 EERSTE GEBEDE. Cape Town, Human & Rousseau, 1978.

> OTHER: Have not examined a copy. Elsa Naude', Editor, Children's Books, Human & Rousseau (PTY) LTD, Cape Town, South Africa, in a letter, 16 March 1992: "The only other Human & Rousseau editions of books illustrated by Tasha Tudor that I can trace, are EERSTE GEBEDE (FIRST PRAYERS) and EERSTE DANKGEBEDE (FIRST GRACES), originally published by David McKay Co. Inc., New York. We published these in 1978 and reprinted in 1979 but the books are now out of print. In both cases the Afrikaans text was done by a local author, I.L. de Villiers. Tudor and Holmes are fairly well known in South Africa, mainly due to their books being available in local libraries."

F83 FLATFOOT. Thomas Leighton McCready, Jr.

This book was never published but is referred to in a certain STIPULATION dated April 5 and 17, 1961, in Equity Case No. 4796 before the Merrimack County, New Hampshire, superior court, to wit:

> [Tasha Tudor McCready] shall at times convenient to herself, during the calendar year 1961, complete and deliver to the publisher appropriate illustrations for an additional volume known as "Flatfoot" written by [Thomas Leighton McCready, Jr.] and to be published as a further work in the Farrar Straus and Cudahy series of books . . . , such illustrations to be comparable in number and nature to the art work done . . . for other works in the said series heretofore published.

> Flatfoot is referred to in *Yankee* magazine, (21:10 October 1957), page 38: "And there were other farm friends too, like Flatfoot and his family of Toulouse geese; . . ."

G1 **The Gentle Wit & Wisdom | of Tasha Tudor** [painting of mother holding a baby] | Reflections on life, art, gardening and | more from America's most beloved | author-illustrator. As well as, Tasha | reads "Corgiville Fair." [From the fourth panel: Created and produced by: | Donna M. Swajeski ‖ Recording directed by: | Michael V. Opelka ‖ Edited by: | R.J. Miles ‖ Artwork by: | Tasha Tudor ‖ Copyright 1996 | Donamar Productions, Inc.]

> PHYSICAL DESCRIPTION: 1 audiocassette in a plastic box, with a four panel paper liner. The box: 4 1/4″ x 2 1/4″. The liner: 4″ x 9 3/8″.

> LINER: A photo-reproduction on white paper, blank on the back. All type is black except for the title panel, which has inverse white lettering on a black background. Spine: the Gentle Wit and Wisdom of Tasha Tudor. First panel: Side One ‖ Tasha's reflections [then, column two] Side Two ‖ Tasha reads "Corgiville | Fair" with comments | [4″ vertical rule] | Copyright 1996 | Donamar Productions, Inc. / All Rights Reserved | mvo@inx.net. Third panel: **Meet Tasha Tudor** ‖ Going to Tasha's house is like stepping into a fairy | tale. The trees you pass in her Vermont woods | seem more like ancient, sleeping giants. And there | nestled in the forest is her snug wooden farm house | with a plume of smoke wafting from the chimney. | A black goat stands sentinel on a small hill. Dogs | begin to bark and Tasha's beloved Corgis race | through the field to herd you in. With Corgis at | your ankles, you pass a garden that is a fantastic | jungle of vines, berries, bursting flowers and | vegetables. Everywhere there is a riot of color… | hot pinks, sultry reds, the feathery peach of a | peony, startling whites. Tasha is always working at | something. Either feeding her hens, cooking a stew, | preserving peaches or sitting at the window, | drawing. She greets you wearing a long gingham | dress and a bandanna. *[sic]* ¶ Immediately, Tasha makes you feel at home. There | is tea waiting in a beautiful blue and white china | pot. We sit by her hearth in front of a blazing fire. | While she talks, her caged finches and parrots send | up beautiful arias in the background. ¶ These are the stories Tasha told me about her life. | I consider myself fortunate to be her confidante. | And even more so… | her friend. ¶ Donna M. Swajeski.

> CASSETTE: The clear plastic tape cassette is also imprinted in white: The Wit and Wisdom of Tasha Tudor ‖ Side A   [logo | rule] | CHROME ‖ Conversations with Tasha | Donamar Productions, Inc. [reverse side] The Wit and Wisdom of Tasha Tudor ‖ Side B   [logo | rule] | CHROME ‖ Tasha Reads Corgiville Fair | Donamar Productions, Inc.

> OTHER: Michael Opelka identifies this to be the true first edition which was created for distribution at the opening of "TAKE JOY!", the Tudor exhibition at the Abby Aldrich Rockefeller Folk Art Center November 1996-April 1997. For the opening weekend seminar, one hundred copies were taken to Williamsburg, Virginia. These were considered initial advertising and press release copies. Production problems delayed delivery until literally hours before the show. There was no copyright filed as of January 1998.

G2 _____.

> LINER: The general production liner is printed on a heavier enameled cover stock. The cover painting is clear and distinct where it was previously a blurred image. The type is reset to a larger Times New Roman with more space between lines, resulting in new line breaks. Spine: the Gentle Wit and Wisdom of Tasha Tudor. First panel: Side One ‖ Tasha's reflections [then, column two] Side Two ‖ Tasha reads "Corgiville Fair" ⌋with comments | [4″ vertical rule] | Tasha Tudor / Corgi CottageIndustries. All Rights Reserved | mvo@inx.net. Third panel: **Meet Tasha Tudor** ‖ Going to Tasha's house is like stepping into a fairy | tale. The trees you pass in her Vermont woods

seem⌊more like ancient, sleeping giants. And there nes-⌊tled in the forest is her snug wooden farm house with⌊ a plume of smoke wafting from the chimney. A⌊black goat stands sentinel on a small hill. Dogs | begin to bark and Tasha's beloved Corgis race | through the field to herd you in. With Corgis at your⌊ankles, you pass a garden that is a fantastic jungle of⌊vines, berries, bursting flowers and vegetables.⌊Everywhere there is a riot of color…hot pinks, sul-⌊try reds, the feathery peach of a peony, startling⌊whites. Tasha is always working at something.⌊Either feeding her hens, cooking a stew, preserving⌊peaches or sitting at the window, drawing. She⌊greets you wearing a long gingham dress <u>and ban-</u> | <u>dana.</u> ¶ Immediately_Tasha makes you feel at home. There | is tea waiting in <u>her</u> beautiful blue and white china | pot. We sit by her hearth in front of a blazing fire. | While she talks, her caged finches and parrots send | up beautiful arias in the background. ¶ These are the stories Tasha told me about her life. I⌊consider myself fortunate to be her confidante. And⌊even more so… | her friend. ¶ Donna M. Swajeski.

CASSETTE: As before.

OTHER: PAGINATION: A second dubbing of four hundred copies. Additional dubbings will be in quantities of two thousand.

G3 [printer's decorative leaf pattern] | **GINGER & PICKLES STORE** | **DOLL MUSEUM** | **Webster** | **New Hampshire** || **A country bookstore and doll museum** | **owned by Thomas L. McCready, Jr. &** | **Tasha Tudor McCready** | **P.O., R.F.D. No. 1, Contoocook** | **Telephone: Contoocook 11-13** || **Open Daily 1-5** | **Map, Directions & mileages given on back page** | [self-published, nd. ca. 1954/55]

PAGINATION: 6 ¼″ x 7″ cream laid paper, folded to form a 4-page booklet, 6 ¼″ x 3 ½″

ILLUSTRATIONS: The back panel is a hand-drawn (T.L. McCready?) and lettered map showing the location of the Ginger & Pickles Store.   The map displays the area between US Route 202 and Hopkinton village on the south to US Route 4 at Salisbury, N.H. on the north and includes such landmarks as the Hopkinton Post Office and Shell Gas Station, Davisville, Sandbank Farm, Stebbins Store and various cement and steel bridges over the Contoocook and Blackwater Rivers.

TEXT: Page [2]. **GINGER & PICKLES STORE** | ? | A small country bookstore founded in 1949 in | response to requests from all over the United | States for autographed Tasha Tudor books for | children and for Christmas Cards for adults de- | signed by the same artist. || ¶ Originally all sales were by mail until, before | long, new-found customers and friends began to | visit here when in New England. In 1954 a part | of this home was remodeled to serve as a store | and doll museum, and new items were added to | our shelves – English classic books for children, | such as the Beatrix Potter books and those time- | less favorites by Kate Greenaway, Randolph Calde- | cott, Leslie Brooke, Edward Lear, etc. We also added imported toys and stuffed animals. New | children's items of interest to people of discrim- | inating taste are being added from time to time. || ¶ For adults we expanded our Christmas Card | line in 1954 so as to include designs by other | artists as well as the large selection of Tasha | Tudor cards, and we plan as soon as possible to | carry greeting cards for other occasions, by Tasha | Tudor and other artists. Page [3]. **THE DOLL MUSEUM** | ? | Long before her marriage to Thomas L. Mc- | Cready, Jr., Tasha Tudor owned a few French | fashion dolls which she enjoyed as she does to | this day. In 1950 she wrote a children's book on | these dolls – "The Dolls' Christmas" – and, in | 1952, erected a two-story, nine-room doll house | which is twenty-five feet long and five feet high. | In 1954 this was moved to its new quarters next | to the Ginger & Pickles Store. This museum can be | seen by those coming to the store. No admission | is charged though the dolls do keep a "Contribu- | tion Box for Orphan Dolls" into which visitors | are permitted to donate as they wish. || *Location:* Webster (see map on back) is 14 miles | west of Concord, the State Capitol, and is within | easy driving range of any spot in central or south- | ern New Hampshire, southern Maine or Vermont, | as well as Boston and localities in northeastern | Massachusetts. || *Directions:* New Hampshire communities frown | on road signs, so we can not put out many. If | in doubt after studying our road map, stop at | Village Store-Post Office, Hopkinton; Shell Gas | Station, Contoocook; Stebbins Store, Webster, each | within six miles of our store.

See also the Ginger & Pickles Store catalog, described in Catalog section of the end of text.

G4 GIVE US | THIS DAY | THE LORD'S PRAYER || *Illustrated by* | *Tasha Tudor* || *PHILOMEL BOOKS* | *New York* [page [27]: *About Tasha Tudor* || Tasha Tudor is one of America's most distinguished and beloved artists; her | illustrations have brought her many honors and awards, and are cherished by | both children and adults. Her first book was published in 1938, and since | then she has illustrated more than sixty others, many of which she also | wrote. ¶ Ms. Tudor lives in southern Vermont in a charming house of her own | design, surrounded by her beautiful flower and vegetable gardens and or- | chards overlooking peaceful meadows and rich woodlands. She shares her | home with several corgi dogs, **an enormous Irish wolfhound,** over two dozen | birds, a trio of cats and a pet snake, as well as various temporary resi- | dents—farm or woodland creatures that often serve as her models. Several | of her children and grandchildren live near enough for frequent visits. ¶ Born in Boston, Ms. Tudor grew up in New England in the countryside | she so lovingly portrays in her illustrations. *Give Us This Day: The Lord's Prayer* | is a companion volume to her book *The Lord Is My Shepherd: The Twenty-Third* | *Psalm.* Both works express a deeply felt reverence that speaks to both old | and young. || Illustrations copyright © 1987 by Tasha Tudor. | Special contents copyright © 1987 by Philomel Books. | Published by Philomel Books, a member of The Putnam Publishing Group, | 51 Madison Avenue, New York, NY 10010. All rights reserved. | Published simultaneously in Canada by General Publishing Co., Limited, Toronto. | Design by Nanette Stevenson. Calligraphy by Jeanyee Wong | [rule] | Library of Congress Cataloging-in-Publication Data. Lord's prayer. English. | Give us this day. Summary: Presents the text of the most widely known version | of the Lord's prayer, with illustrations and brief commentary on the prayer's | origins and different versions. 1. Lord's prayer—Illustrations—Juvenile liter- | ature [1. Lord's prayer] I. Tudor, Tasha, ill. II. Title. BV232.L6713 1987 | 226'.96'00222 86-30557 ISBN 0-399-21442-9 First printing]

PAGINATION: Three signatures, white matte paper, [28] pp. endpaper to endpaper, plus paste downs inside both covers. 8 1/4″ x 6 7/8″

COVER: Continuous gloss laminate printed paper wrapped around boards. Deep green spine wrap is also printed on the cover. Front cover illustration: rectangular vine frame enclosing this tableau painted over a wash sky. A boy and girl are releasing twelve doves, and a penciled ghost of a 13th as the children sit back-to-back in a daisy bed. Their patch of earth is supported by a semi-circle of ribbon and evergreen suspended from a rainbow. Back cover illustration: a poppy garden with building and rainbow in a fine white frame on a taupe ground. Printed on the taupe at lower right: ISBN 0-399-21442-9 [computerized typeface]. Spine lettered in two colors on the green ground: *TASHA TUDOR* [mint green] *GIVE US THIS DAY The Lord's Prayer* [taupe] *PHILOMEL* [mint green].

DUST JACKET: Same design as cover without the green spine wrap; the front design continues around the spine until it meets the back. Lettered text overprinted on the front illustration, between the rainbow and the children: *GIVE US* | *THIS DAY* [purple] | *THE LORD'S PRAYER* [green] | *Illustrated by* | *Tasha Tudor* [purple]. Spine: *TASHA TUDOR* [black] *GIVE US THIS DAY The Lord's Prayer* [purple] *PHILOMEL* [black] Back text in black near the bottom edge, lower left: Printed in Hong Kong; and lower right: ISBN 0-399-21442-9 [computerized typeface].

Front ivory flap, all black text except the purple initial calligraphic *T*: $8.95 || *T*he best known of all Christian prayers | is illustrated here in sensitive watercolors | by one of America's foremost artists. Tasha | Tudor's interpretation captures the rever- | ent simplicity of the familiar and beloved | prayer. Although the images are drawn | from her own surroundings in rural New | England, they bespeak a universal faith. The | text is taken from the Book of Common | Prayer, which is based in turn upon the | words of Jesus as recorded in the New Tes- | tament in the Gospels of St. Matthew and | St. Luke. Ms. Tudor's illustrations elo- | quently express the faith and wisdom of the | words. Here is a book to share with all | members of the family, a book to be cher- | ished by young and old alike. Back flap: *Also illustrated by Tasha Tudor* || The

Lord | Is My Shepherd | The Twenty-Third Psalm ‖ The most celebrated of all psalms is inter- | preted here by one of America's best-loved | illustrators. The text of this superb expres- | sion of faith is in the familiar and beautiful | words of the King James Version. Tenderly | depicting gentle pastoral vistas and peaceful | village scenes, Tasha Tudor's watercolor | paintings complement the exquisite beauty | and simplicity of the verse and capture the | eternal comfort of its message. In a match- | ing format, this book is a perfect compan | -ion to *Give Us This Day: The Lord's Prayer.* ‖ *Jacket calligraphy by Jeanyee Wong* ‖ PHILOMEL BOOKS | *a member of the Putnam Publishing Group* | 51 Madison Avenue | New York, NY 10010 | 8709.

CONTENTS: Title Page [3]; dedication page [2], *for Beth*. The dedicatee is Tudor's Indiana business partner in the Jenny Wren Press, Beth Mathers.   Page [26], *About the Lord's Prayer* ; page [27], *About Tasha Tudor.*

ILLUSTRATIONS: 26 full-page color illustrations including two endpaper designs, which are repeated front and back. All 28 illustrations are in oval frames of vine and flowers, and most are signed *T. Tudor* at the lower right. Only pages [26-27] lack illustrations, and even these have green calligraphy titles. There are two pages of illustration for each phrase, although text is printed on only one of the pages, as follows:

Our Father,	who art in heaven,	[5]
Hallowed be thy Name,	[6]
Thy kingdom come,	[9]
Thy will be done,	On earth as it is in heaven.	[10]
Give us this day	our daily bread.	[13]
And forgive us	our trespasses,	[14]
As we forgive those	who trespass against us.	[16]
And lead us not	into temptation,	[19]
But deliver us from evil.	[21]
For thine is the kingdom,	[22]
and the power, and the glory,	for ever and ever.	Amen.	[24]

COPYRIGHT REGISTRATION: TX 2 222-610 granted to Philomel Books, 51 Madison Ave., N.Y., N.Y. 10010. Louise Bates (212) 689-9200, agent for Philomel Books, swears on Sept. 17, 1987:

GIVE US THIS DAY, THE LORD'S PRAYER, by Philomel Books, employer for hire and a U.S. citizen, completed in 1987, published Sept. 1, 1987, in the USA first. Philomel authored the text except for The Lord's Prayer, and added new text about the Prayer and about Tasha Tudor, the illustrator. L.C. is granted non-exclusive permission to make copies and phonorecords for the blind and physically handicapped. Printed by South China Printing Company, Hong Kong. Fees charged to deposit account DAO38288, Putnam Publishing Group (Phil), 51 Madison Ave., N.Y., N.Y. 10010. Application and two deposit copies received at LC Sept. 21, 1987, the effective date of registration.

COPYRIGHT REGISTRATION: VA 289 509 granted to Tasha Tudor, Route 4, Box 144, West Brattleboro, Vt. 05301. Louise Bates, agent for Tasha Tudor, swears on Sept. 17, 1987:

GIVE US THIS DAY, THE LORD'S PRAYER, illustrations (not a work for hire) by Tasha Tudor, a U.S. citizen. Work is derivative of The Lord's Prayer with new illustrations. Completion, publication, fees and receipt, as above.

G5 _____.

PAGINATION: [28] pp. from the trade edition including flyleaves are bound between <u>two ivory laid paper leaves added</u> at the front and back. The first and last of these are pasted to this binding's <u>green marbled endpapers</u>--creating extra heavy flyleaves with green linen hinges between them and the same marbled paper pasted inside the covers. 81/8″ x 65/8″.

COVER: The <u>publisher's presentation copy</u> to Tudor is bound in <u>green leather</u>. Leather cover is embossed with several gilt devices and wraps inside the covers forming a 3/8″ edge around the endpaper. This edge has a rule near the endpaper and beyond that a solid line ^{vvvvv} device. There is a blind stamped rule along the outsides of front and back covers. A frame of three rules sits a half-inch in from the edges; the first two more closely placed than the inner rule. A device of two heart-shaped leaves entwined is embossed inside each corner of the frame. Inside the lower front right corner are the two initials: *TT*. The back cover is the same as the front without the initials. The spine is more elaborate revealing two cord coverings at top and two at the bottom. Various gilt designs from top to bottom: two closely placed rules, a four-petaled flower, rule, ^^^, rule, rule, ^^^, rule, [text, laterally along spine] GIVE US THIS DAY   THE LORD'S PRAYER *Tasha Tudor*, rule, ^^^, rule, rule, ^^^, rule, a four-petaled flower, rule, two closely placed rules.

OTHER: Tudor inscribed at the top of the colored section of the first illustrated page (the trade flyleaf, above the girl and cat in a garden: To | Beth [Mathers, Mooresville, Indiana] | [a sketch of a dove holding a rose in its mouth]| A very special edition | of your book! | With a very special amount of | love! | from | Tasha.

G6 _____. Published simultaneously in Canada by General Publishing Co., Limited, Toronto. Have not examined a copy.

G7 _____. [page [27]: *About Tasha* . . . 51 Madison, New York, NY 10010. All rights reserved. | <u>Printed in Hong Kong by South China Printing Co.</u> | Design by Nanette . . . 86-30557 ISBN 0-399-21442-9. <u>Second printing</u>]

DUST JACKET: Lacks the phrase: Printed in Hong Kong. Examination copy had price clipped and a hand-written store label attached: 10.95.

G8 _____. [page [27]: *About Tasha* . . . Published by Philomel Books, a member of The Putnam Publishing Group, | <u>200</u> Madison Avenue, New York, NY 10016. All rights reserved. | Printed in Hong Kong by South China Printing Co. | <u>Published simultaneously in Canada.</u> | Design by Nanette . . . 0-399-21442-9 Third printing]

DUST JACKET: The dust jacket flaps have a deeper cream tone. Text of front flap is changed thus: <u>$8.95</u> | [7/8″ rule] | $12.50 (CAN) ‖ *T*he best known…   Back flap: *Also illustrated* . . . ‖ PHILOMEL BOOKS | <u>a division of the Putnam & Grosset Group</u> | <u>200</u> Madison Avenue | New York, NY 1001<u>6</u> | 8709.

G9 _____. Have not examined 4th printing.

G10 _____. Have not examined 5th printing.

G11 _____. Have not examined 6th printing.

G12 _____. [page [27]: *About Tasha* . . . Published by Philomel Books, a member of The Putnam <u>& Grosset | Book</u> Group, 200 Madison Avenue, New York, NY 10016. | <u>| All rights reserved. Published simultaneously in Canada.</u> | Printed in Hong Kong by South China Printing Co. <u>(1988) Ltd.</u> | Design by Nanette…ISBN 0-399-21442-9 | <u>7 9 10 8</u>]

COVER: A gray box (1 3/8″ x 2″) printed over the lower right corner of the back illustration and part of the mauve border. Within the box: ISBN 0-399-21442-9 | [a single bar code] | 0 48228 21442 7.

DUST JACKET: The same box and bar code as on cover. Flaps are white. Front flap: <u>$9.95</u> | [<u>11/16</u>″ rule] | $12.95 (CAN) ‖ *T*he best known . . . A double bar code at the bottom of front flap: <u>90000</u> [above the smaller right bar code] | [the two bar codes] | [and beneath the large left bar code] 9 780399 214424. Back flap: *Also illustrated. . .Give Us This Day: The Lord's Prayer.* ‖ *Jacket art*

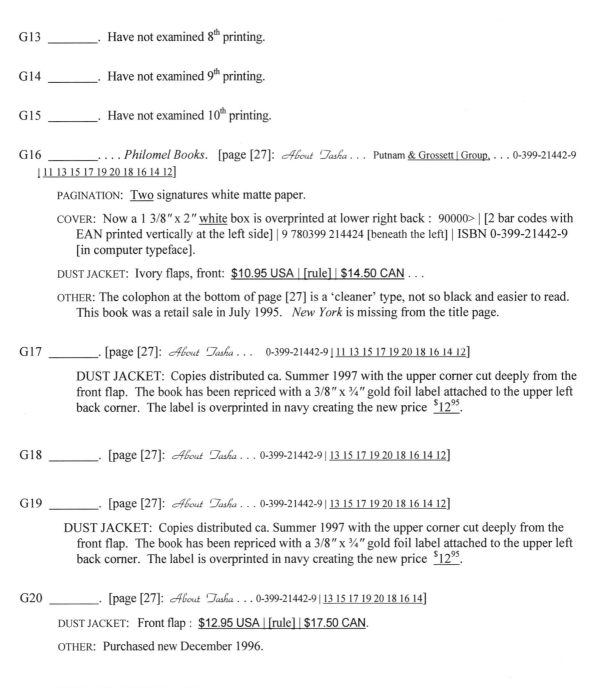

G13 _____. Have not examined 8th printing.

G14 _____. Have not examined 9th printing.

G15 _____. Have not examined 10th printing.

G16 _____. . . . *Philomel Books*. [page [27]: *About Tasha* . . . Putnam & Grossett | Group, . . . 0-399-21442-9 | 11 13 15 17 19 20 18 16 14 12]

    PAGINATION: Two signatures white matte paper.

    COVER: Now a 1 3/8″ x 2″ white box is overprinted at lower right back : 90000> | [2 bar codes with EAN printed vertically at the left side] | 9 780399 214424 [beneath the left] | ISBN 0-399-21442-9 [in computer typeface].

    DUST JACKET: Ivory flaps, front: $10.95 USA | [rule] | $14.50 CAN . . .

    OTHER: The colophon at the bottom of page [27] is a 'cleaner' type, not so black and easier to read. This book was a retail sale in July 1995. *New York* is missing from the title page.

G17 _____. [page [27]: *About Tasha* . . . 0-399-21442-9 | 11 13 15 17 19 20 18 16 14 12]

    DUST JACKET: Copies distributed ca. Summer 1997 with the upper corner cut deeply from the front flap. The book has been repriced with a 3/8″ x ¾″ gold foil label attached to the upper left back corner. The label is overprinted in navy creating the new price $12.95.

G18 _____. [page [27]: *About Tasha* . . . 0-399-21442-9 | 13 15 17 19 20 18 16 14 12]

G19 _____. [page [27]: *About Tasha* . . . 0-399-21442-9 | 13 15 17 19 20 18 16 14 12]

    DUST JACKET: Copies distributed ca. Summer 1997 with the upper corner cut deeply from the front flap. The book has been repriced with a 3/8″ x ¾″ gold foil label attached to the upper left back corner. The label is overprinted in navy creating the new price $12.95.

G20 _____. [page [27]: *About Tasha* . . . 0-399-21442-9 | 13 15 17 19 20 18 16 14]

    DUST JACKET: Front flap : $12.95 USA | [rule] | $17.50 CAN.

    OTHER: Purchased new December 1996.

G21 GIVE US | THIS DAY | THE LORD'S PRAYER ‖ *Illustrated by* | *Tasha Tudor* | [L in circle logo] | *LUTTERWORTH PRESS* | *Cambridge*. [page [27]: *About Tasha Tudor* | Tasha Tudor is one of America's most distinguished and beloved artists; her | illustrations have brought her many honours and awards, and are cherished | by both children and adults. Her first book was published in 1938, and since | then she has illustrated more than sixty others, many of which she also | wrote. Her work is known and loved in many parts of the world. ¶ **Tasha** Tudor **now** lives in southern Vermont, surrounded by her beautiful | flower and vegetable gardens and orchards. She shares her home with | several corgi dogs, an enormous Irish wolfhound, over two dozen birds, a | trio of cats and a pet snake, as well as various temporary residents— ⌐farm or woodland creatures that often serve as her models. Several of her⌐ children and grandchildren live near enough for frequent visits. ¶ Born in Boston, **Tasha** Tudor grew up in New England in the countryside | she so lovingly portrays in her illustrations. ¶ *Give Us This Day: The Lord's Prayer* is a companion volume to her book *The* | *Lord is My Shepherd: The Twenty-Third Psalm*. Both express a deep felt reverence⌐that speaks to young and old alike. || **Lutterworth Press | 7 All Saints' Passage | Cambridge CB2 3LS** || First published in Great Britain 1987 | Illustrations copyright © Tasha Tudor, 1987 | Special contents copyright © 1987 Philomel Books, | a member of The Putnam Publishing Group, | 51 Madison Avenue, New York, NY 10010. || British Library Cataloging in Publication Data | Give us this day: the Lord's Prayer. | 1. Lord's prayer—Juvenile literature | I. Tudor, Tasha | 226'.96'00222   BV232 | ISBN 0-7188-2685-X || All rights reserved. No part of this publication may be reproduced, | stored in a retrieval system or transmitted in any form or by any means.]

PAGINATION: Three signatures white matte paper, [28] pp. endpaper to endpaper, plus paste-downs to both covers. 8 5/16″ x 6 13/16″

COVER: Continuous gloss printed paper wrapped around boards, matching the US dust jacket illustrations, without the green spine wrap. Back cover, printed on the taupe at lower left: Lutterworth Press | 7 All Saints' Passage | Cambridge CB2 3LS | L4.95 net. Bottom, centered: Printed in Hong Kong. Lower right: above a single bar code, ISBN 0-7188-2685-X. and below the bar code, 9 780718 826857. Spine: *TASHA TUDOR* [black] *GIVE US THIS DAY* *The Lord's Prayer* [purple] [L in circle logo, black].

DUST JACKET: Have not examined one.

OTHER: Pagination and illustrations as in the US imprint.

MINIATURE EDITION

G22   GIVE US | THIS DAY | THE LORD'S PRAYER | *Illustrated by* | *Tasha Tudor* |

PHILOMEL BOOKS | *New York* [page 27: *About Tasha Tudor* || Tasha Tudor is one of America's most distinguished and beloved artists;⌐her illustrations have brought her many honors and awards, and are⌐cherished by both children and adults. Her first book was published in⌐1938, and since then she has illustrated more than sixty others, many of⌐which she also wrote. ¶ Ms. Tudor lives in southern Vermont in a charming house of her own | design, surrounded by her beautiful flower and vegetable gardens and⌐orchards overlooking peaceful meadows and rich woodlands. She shares⌐her home with several corgi dogs, over two dozen birds, a trio of cats and⌐a pet snake, as well as various temporary residents—farm or woodland⌐creatures that often serve as her models. Several of her children and⌐grandchildren live near enough for frequent visits. ¶ Born in Boston, Ms. Tudor grew up in New England in the countryside | she so lovingly portrays in her illustrations. *Give Us This Day: The Lord's* | *Prayer* is a companion volume to her book *The Lord is My Shepherd: The* | *Twenty-Third Psalm*. Both works express a deeply felt reverence that⌐speaks to both old and young. | [rule] | Illustrations copyright © 1987 by Tasha Tudor. | Special contents copyright © 1987 by Philomel Books, | a division of The Putnam & Grosset Group, | 200 Madison Avenue, New York, NY 10016. Miniature edition published by Philomel Books in 1989. | Published simultaneously in Canada. All rights reserved. | Printed in Singapore. Calligraphy by Jeanyee Wong | Library of Congress Number 86-30557. First miniature edition printing.]

PAGINATION: Two signatures white matte paper, [28] pp. including flyleaves. 5″ x 4 ¼″

COVER: Matte paper over boards. Front cover printed as dust jacket for first large edition, above. Back cover and spine are teal. Spine calligraphy and text as first, but white lettering.

DUST JACKET: Same design as cover. Text of front white flap has been reset from large edition. The initial T is now printed rather than calligraphy: The best known of all Christian prayers is⌐ illustrated here in sensitive watercolors by⌐one of America's foremost artists. Tasha | Tudor's interpretation captures the reverent⌐simplicity of the familiar and beloved prayer.⌐Although the images are drawn from her⌐own surroundings in rural New England,⌐they bespeak a universal faith. ¶ The text is taken from the Book of Common | Prayer, which is based in turn upon the | words of Jesus as recorded in the New Testa-⌐|ment in the Gospels of St. Matthew and St.⌐ Luke. Ms. Tudor's illustrations eloquently⌐express the faith and wisdom of the words.⌐Here is a book to share with all members of___⌐the family, a book to be cherished by young⌐and old alike. Back flap, with small changes: *Also illustrated . . .* perfect companion⌐to *Give Us This Day: The Lord's Prayer*. || Jacket art © 1987 by Tasha Tudor || PHILOMEL BOOKS | *a division of*

The Putnam & Grosset Group | 200 Madison Avenue | New York, NY 10016 || Printed in Singapore.

ILLUSTRATIONS: As in first large edition.

OTHER: Text on page [26] "About the Lord's Prayer" has also been reset; line breaks have changed. Sold with its companion book *The Lord Is My Shepherd* in a slip case, covered in the teal paper with the *Give Us This Day* front cover reproduced on both the front and back of the case. Both titles are superimposed:

GIVE US | *THIS DAY* [purple] | *The Lord's Prayer* [green] | [white rule] | THE LORD IS | MY SHEPHERD [purple] | *The Twenty-Third Psalm* [green] | Tasha Tudor [purple]. Spine lettering in white: TASHA | || *GIVE US* | *THIS DAY* | *The Lord's* | *Prayer* || [tilde] || *THE LORD* | *IS MY* | *SHEPHERD* | *The Twenty-Third* | *Psalm* || PHILOMEL. A white gummed label was affixed to the lower left of the case back, with this text: 51095 [above the smaller right of two bar codes] | [bar codes] 9 780399 218903 [beneath the left bar code] | ISBN 0-399-21890-4 [beneath both codes] | $10.95 | [rule] | $14.50 (CAN)

G23 _____.   Published simultaneously in Canada. Have not examined a copy.

G24 _____. Have not examined a 2^(nd) printing.

G25 _____. . . . *PHILOMEL BOOKS* . [page 27: *About Tasha* . . .   86-30557. | ISBN 0-399-21891-2 | 3 5 7 9 10 8 6 4]

   COVER: As above, but now, in a white rectangle, at lower right back: ISBN 0-399-21891-2 | [computerized typeface] | UPC [printed laterally left of bar code] | 0 48228 21891 3. Spine calligraphy and text as in large format 1st, but all white letters.

   DUST JACKET: Same design as cover. Front flap: $4.95 | [rule] | ($6.50 CAN) || The best known...

G26 _____. Have not examined a 4^(th) printing.

G27 _____. [page 26: *About Tasha Tudor*... | 5 7 9 10 8 6]

   DUST JACKET: UPC box has new text: ISBN 0-399-21891-2 | EAN [printed laterally to the left of two UPC bar codes] | 90000 [above the right code] | 9 780399 218910.

   OTHER: In a slip case, as in the first miniature.

G28 _____. [page 26: *About Tasha Tudor*... | 7 9 10 8 6]

G29 _____. [page 26: *About Tasha Tudor*... | 7 9 10 8 6]

   DUST JACKET: Another distribution. The price has been clipped from the dust jacket, and adjusted in the upper left back corner of the dust jacket by the application of a gold foil label overprinted in blue: $5^(95).

G30 _____. [page 26: *About Tasha Tudor* . . . 7 9 10 8 6]

   DUST JACKET: A new gold foil label on the back, imprinted $5^(95) | PUTNAM.   Distributed in 1996.

G31 _____. [page 26: *About Tasha Tudor* . . . <u>7</u> 9 10 8]

DUST JACKET: Front flap, new prices: <u>$5.95 USA | [rule] | $7.75 CAN</u> || The best known …

G32 _____. [page 26: *About Tasha Tudor* . . . 9 10 <u>8</u>]

DUST JACKET: Front flap, new prices: $5.95 USA | [rule] | <u>$7.95</u> CAN || The best known …

OTHER: Distributed new July 1997.

G33 GOOD MORNING AMERICA. [television program. American Broadcasting Corporation] December 17, 1997. 3 min.

OTHER: Broadcast as early as 7 a.m. Eastern Standard Time, Steve Aveson interviewed Tudor and included vignettes of goats, barn, weaving and tea by the fire. As short as it is, the segment contains errors in fact as when Aveson reports that Tudor wrote *Pumpkin Moonshine* <u>for her children</u>, or that her efforts were to assist her husband in raising <u>their three children</u>. Tudor says she has never taken a vacation in her life, because her whole life has been a vacation.

G34 GOOSEBERRY LANE || [sprig of flowers] || BY BETHANY TUDOR || J. B. LIPPINCOTT COMPANY | PHILADELPHIA   NEW YORK [*To* | *Mummy* | *and* | *Araminta* | *who really inspired* | *this book.* || Copyright © 1963 | by Bethany Tudor | Printed in the United States of America | Library of Congress Catalog Card No. 63-12405]

PAGINATION: Two signatures buff paper, [36] pp. including free endpapers.

COVER: Green wash paper over boards. Front, a large white oval in a ring of buttercup and purple blossoms. On a white field within the oval, GOOSEBERRY [curved above an illustration of the characters Samuel and Samantha, and below them] LANE. Centered at the bottom: by BETHANY TUDOR. Spine: Bethany Tudor   GOOSEBERRY LANE   Lippincott. Back: a bunch of flowers tied with a string. A different nosegay is drawn on green wash endpapers, verso and recto, and repeated at the back.

DUST JACKET: Reproduces cover, with white flaps. Front flap: **GOOSEBERRY LANE** || BY BETHANY TUDOR || Once upon a time there were two plush | ducklings, Samuel and Samantha. They | lived happily in a cardboard house until | one dreadful day when a heavy rainstorm | made it start to melt. ¶The poor ducklings were forced to hunt | for a new home. With the help of some | friendly birds and animals, they found and | moved into a delightful house. ¶Very small children will love these two | resourceful ducklings and will be enchant- | ed by their portraits that appear on every | page. || 0480 [corner clipped]. Back: This is Bethany Tudor's first book. Ever | since she was a very small child, she has | drawn pictures and loved small animals— | whether plush or real. She lives on a New | Hampshire farm with her mother, Tasha | Tudor, and two brothers and a sister, not | to mention many varieties of animals, who | have been her models as well as her friends. ¶Miss Tudor has studied art with her | mother and in Boston. She brings to her | writing and illustration not only youthful | freshness but real talent.

ILLUSTRATIONS: Most recto pages carry a full page illustration without text, pages [5-33]. Pages [5, 7] do have text. There are also illustrations and text on verso pages [6, 34].

CONTENTS: The text largely appears without illustration on verso pages [6-34]. As noted above, there is text on pages [5,7] and illustrations on pages [6,34].

OTHER: Have not examined a copy of the dust jacket with both corners and the price intact on the front flap. <u>AMERICAN BOOK PUBLISHING RECORD 1960-1964</u>, volume IV, page 5067: TUDOR, Bethany JUV | Gooseberry Lane. Philadelphia, Lippincott [c.1963] | unpaged, col.

213

illus. 18x22cm. 63-12405 bds., 2.75 | Two ducklings move into a new house with the help of | friendly birds and animals. Ages 4-8.

COPYRIGHT REGISTRATION: A 634401

COPYRIGHT RENEWAL REGISTRATION: RE 564 994 granted to Bethany Tudor, c/o HarperCollins Publishers, 10 East 53ʳᵈ St., N.Y., N.Y. 10011. Marilyn Small, agent for Bethany Tudor, swears on Dec. 20, 1991:

GOOSEBERRY LANE, by Bethany Tudor, was published June 10, 1963 under registration A 634401. Fees charged to account DA 064726, HarperCollins Publishers. Application received at LC Dec. 24, 1991.

G35 THE GREAT [green] **CORGIVILLE** [blue] KIDNAPPING [green] | by Tasha Tudor [red] | [newsdealer vending the latest special edition] | [*LB* and column logo] Little, Brown and Company | Boston   New York   Toronto   London [black] [*To Cyrus and Rebecca Harvey | and Piper* || [corgi between daffodils] || Copyright ©1997 by Tasha Tudor || All rights reserved. No part of this book may be reproduced in any form or by any electronic or mechanical | means, including information storage and retrieval systems, without permission in writing from the publisher, | except by a reviewer who may quote brief passages in a review. || First edition || Library of Congress Cataloging-in-Publication Data || Tudor, Tasha. | The great Corgiville kidnapping / by Tasha Tudor.—1ˢᵗ ed. | p. cm. | Summary: His instincts and his training as a part-time private investigator make Caleb Corgi suspi- | cious of a band of raccoons, especially when Corgiville's prize rooster disappears. | ISBN 0-316-85583-9 | [1.Dogs—Fiction. 2. Animals—Fiction. 3. Mystery and detective stories.] I. Title. | PZ7.T8228Gr 1997 | [Fic]—dc21   96-45412 | 10 9 8 7 6 5 4 3 2 1 || SC || Published simultaneously in Canada by Little, Brown & Company (Canada) Limited || Printed Hong Kong]

PAGINATION: [1-44] pp. including free endpapers. Three signatures white matte paper, four sheets in each signature. The first and last leaf of the first and last signatures are the pasted endpapers. 9 9/32″ x 12 1/8″

COVER: Illustrated paper under gloss lamination over boards. Federal blue with cream highlights, including the front lettering. A large panel illustration (balloon sailing across the sky) outlined in a thin red rule on the front, above it on a 1″ blue band: [3 1/16″ pink rule] **TASHA TUDOR** [3 1/16″ pink rule]. On a 1 1/16″ blue band at the bottom: THE GREAT **CORGIVILLE** KIDNAPPING. Cream spine, printed laterally: TUDOR [red] THE GREAT [green] **CORGIVILLE** [blue] KIDNAPPING [green] Little, Brown [black]. Back: A 4 ½″ x 6″ panel illustration, centered and outlined in a thin pink rule, showing Caleb sitting against the monument in town square reading a letter. A 1/16″ pink rule across the top of the back. In the lower left corner, 1 1/16″ x 2″ cream panel: ISBN 0-316-85583-9 | [two bar codes and over the smaller right one, 9000] | under the larger left, 9 780316 855839. Printed laterally at the left: EAN. Above the panel, also in cream: [two vertical rules] LITTLE, BROWN | REINFORCED BINDING.

The two-page endpapers show a Corgiville street scene, obviously influenced by Williamsburg, Virginia. Williamsburg has figured large in Tudor's life during the 1990s. Rustic Corgiville has been transformed from the Harrisville, N.H. countryside to the more sophisticated Southern town. The place has obviously prospered in the twenty-five year interval between books. A sign board features prominently in the lower right endpaper, just as the book is opened, and advertises the Tudor-Harry Davis partnership: TASHA'S TEA | HOUSE | [rule] | CORGIVILLE | WILLIAMSBURG | RICHMOND | [rule] | 804-674-9351. This is the working telephone number for Corgi Cottage Industries.

DUST JACKET: Front, back and spine reproduce the cover. Front cream-colored flap, with most text in black: **$15.95 FPT** | $21.95 in Canada | THE GREAT [green] | **CORGIVILLE** [blue] | KIDNAPPING [green] | by **TASHA TUDOR** [red] || C [blue] ALEB CORGI,

OUTSTANDING | student and part-time | private investigator, senses that | something is amiss in | Corgiville. He has noticed a | sudden increase in the number | of raccoons in town. They | claim they are tourists just | passing through, but Caleb | feels secrecy and conspiracy in | the air. ¶ Suddenly Caleb's suspicions | are confirmed. Babe, the prize | rooster who makes a yearly | sensation at the Corgiville Fair, | is reported kidnapped, and the | raccoons are overheard arguing | over the best way to stuff and | roast a large fowl. The town | is in a frenzy! Caleb knows he | must find and rescue Babe, but | how? || 09971545. [The initial 'C' is two lines high and blue.] Back cream flap: 2 1/8″ x 2 11/32″ color photograph of Tudor with a corgi. Laterally along the right side of the photograph: PATTI DENYS. [black] || TASHA TUDOR [red] is a | member of the pantheon of | the most prolific and revered | illustrators of all time. She | has written, illustrated, or | been the subject of more | than ninety books during a | career that has spanned | nearly three quarters of a | century. ¶ While many of Tasha | Tudor's books are intended | for children, they have | found a welcoming audience | among adults as well. Many | of these same adults have | also been inspired by Tasha | Tudor's unique vision of a | life lived in the style of the | 1830s. || Printed in the Hong Kong.

CONTENTS: Page [2] is blank.

ILLUSTRATIONS: Forty-eight color illustrations of varying sizes embellish the text and interpret the story through Tudor's imaginative eyes. Full-page illustrations, [3, 6, 25, 27, 33, 41]; double-page illustrations, endpapers, [20-21, 34-35].

OTHER: Tudor advertises her company on the endpapers, and on the wall of Megan's Market, page [11]: CORGI | COTTAGE | INDUSTRIES | CARDS FOR | ALL | OCCASIONS. The dedicatees are the Connecticut owners of the Crabtree & Evelyn company, and their corgi; all are alluded to in the book's first paragraph. Two errors appeared in the first edition. Page [16], grammatical: "Well, if I were you, I would go and make yourself a super-strong cup of Appletree and Emlyn's rosehip tea." Page [36], geographical: "I believe we're over Connecticut, northwestern part. . . Why, we're in Woodstock . . . " Woodstock is actually in the northeastern corner of the state.

A June 29, 1997, email communication from Corgi Cottage Industries announces "a leather bond [sic] edition of "The G.C.K." which will be available in our Christmas catalog. The book will have ¾″ morocan [sic] leather binding and corners with gold writing on spine. There will be 100 copies only which Tasha will sign and remarque. The price has not yet been determined but will be in the $300-500 range." The company's Christmas catalog didn't offer either this leather binding nor the trade binding of the book. They do appear in the Spring 1988 catalog. Another photograph by Patti Denys appears in *Animal Magnetism* (1998), *q.v.*

G36 _____. [*Also by Tasha Tudor: (TK)*] || (*Dedication TK*) || [corgi between daffodils] || Copyright ©1997 by . . . 96-45412 | 10 9 8 7 6 5 4 3 2 1 || IM || Published simultaneously in Canada by Little, Brown & Company (Canada) Limited || Printed in the United States of America]

PAGINATION: Three loose-page signatures, a "folded and gathered" (F&G) proof.

COVER: Only the dust jacket wrapped around signatures. Across top front: [3 1/16″ pink rule]
TASHA TUDOR [3 3/8″ pink rule]

DUST JACKET: Front cream-colored flap, with most text in black: **$00.00   FPT** | $00.00 in Canada | THE GREAT [green] . . . but | how? || 00000000. Back flap: . . . style of the | 1830s. || Printed in the U.S.A.

OTHER: A listing of Tudor titles is indicated on page [4], but none was printed here nor in the published book.

G37 _____.

COVER: Leather binding for a limited distribution of 100 copies. Have not examined a copy.

OTHER: Corgi Cottage Industries advertised this binding in its Spring 1998 catalog. Bound by the Harcourt Bindery, Boston, Ma., in three-quarter "green Morocco leather with cloth sides, raised bands to the spine, rich gold tooling, and vellum endpapers. This edi- | tion is limited to 100 numbered volumes, each signed by Tasha. Of the 100, the first 10 are for presentation, 90 are for | sale. This exquisite book will surely become one of the rarest and most treasured of Tasha's books. (#220 BOK) $350.00″ The cloth in the catalog illustration appears to be green-gray.

H1　TREASURY OF LITERATURE—READTEXT SERIES | HAPPINESS | HILL | Selected and Edited by | LELAND B. JACOBS | *Professor of Education* | *Teachers College, Columbia University* | *Specialist in Children's Literature* | *and* | JO JASPER TURNER | *Juvenile Editor* | *formerly elementary School* | *Teacher, principal, and Supervisor* | [two skunks] | CHARLES E. MERRILL BOOKS, INC. | Columbus, Ohio. [[a green and gray floral decoration with characters around the outside edges] TREASURY OF | Readtext Series [on a green ribbon] | LITERATURE | The books in this series are: | MERRY-GO-ROUND | • | HAPPINESS HILL | • • | TREAT SHOP | • • • | MAGIC CARPET | • • • • | ENCHANTED ISLES | • • • • • | ADVENTURE LANDS | • • • • • • | [floral decoration] | CHARLES E. MERRILL BOOKS, INC. | 1300 ALUM CREEK DRIVE • COLUMBUS 16, OHIO || © Copyright, 1960, by Charles E. Merrill Books, Inc. and Artists and Writers Press, Inc. | Printed in the U.S.A. by Western Printing and Lithographing Company. Published | simultaneously in Canada by Thomas Nelson & sons (Canada) Limited.]

PAGINATION: [1-6] 7-76 [77] 78-140 [141] 142-163 [164] 165-192 in twelve signatures plus free endpapers.　9 ¼″ x 6 7/8″ x 11/16″

COVER: Printed and sealed cloth. The image is a montage of many characters from the book converging up from the lower covers of both covers to a small hilltop two-thirds of the way up the spine. The green grass of the hill predominated under a yellow sky; a large purple tree forms most of the left edge of the back cover. Title in federal blue at top of front: **HAPPINESS | HILL**. Spine: HAPPINESS HILL　　MERRILL. Back cover near spine, 2 ½″ from top: **5320**. Turquoise endpapers with white line drawings of assorted characters and scenes in three horizontal panels. Cloth hinge.

CONTENTS: Pp. [3-5]. Fifty selections for second grade elementary school children in six groups: First things first, Going somewhere, Out in the open, Clever animals, Wits and wishes, and Just suppose. ACKNOWLEDGMENTS appear on page 192 and record some of the selections. Most credits appear at the foot of the first page of the story.

ILLUSTRATIONS: The new illustrations for each section are executed by six different artists. Catherine Scholz illustrated the last section of eight stories including Tudor's *The White Goose*, 1943. The drawings of Robin are a solid modern brown as opposed to Tudor's more antique and mysterious blue wash illustrations.

OTHER: *The White Goose* is retold in <u>nearly the same words</u> that Tudor chose.　This results in a loss of tone and rhythm as in these examples: *between night and dawning* becomes between the night and the dawn. *Over the hill he could hear the cowbells, and that other Robin, the echo of himself, calling from the mist* becomes Over the hill Robin could hear the cowbells. He could hear his own echo calling from the mist. . .

H2　_____. Teacher's Edition.

PAGINATION: The 192 pages cited above are separated from a TEACHER'S GUIDE | *for* | **HAPPINESS HILL** by an orange insert page. The latter is paginated: [I-ii] 1-62.　9 3/16″ x 6 13/16″ x 7/8″

COVER:　<u>Small additions</u> to the cover of previous entry. A line of black capitals at the top of cover: TEACHER'S EDITION, and the same 3 ¼″ up the spine: TEACHER'S | EDITION.　There is <u>no code on the back</u>.　The endpapers as above, but no cloth hinge.

CONTENTS: The *Teacher's Guide* has three parts: A Balanced Literature Program for Every Child, Teaching Suggestions for the Stories and Poems, and Supplementary Information including "About Some of the Authors,' and "About the Illustrators." The last page is Bibliography on Literature for Children. Suggestions for reading, understanding and interpreting *The White Goose* appear on pp. 49-50.

ILLUSTRATIONS: Four illustrations throughout this section.

OTHER: Tudor's erroneous biography (page 60) is one of twenty-one short sketches pp. 56-60. "Tasha Tudor was born in Boston, | but spent most of her youth in the | Connecticut countryside. There she | developed her fondness for country | auctions, gardening, and farming, and | for drawing pictures of everything | she saw. Miss Tudor began her seri- | ous career as an artist by illustrating | books written by her husband, Thomas L. McCready. They and their | three children have an old red farm- | house in New Hampshire, where she | continues to paint and write books | for children. Miss Tudor has illus- | trated the *Mother Goose Rhymes* and | *Andersen's Fairy Tales* in the deli- | cate soft colors for which she is fa- | mous. She has written and illustrated | close to a dozen children's books of | her own."

H3 HITTY'S ALMANAC ‖ [daffodils] ‖ BY | TASHA TUDOR | 1934.

PAGINATION: [78] unbound pages. 19 sheets (2 7/8″ x 5 ¾″) folded in half creating the book's dimensions, 2 7/8″ x 2 7/8″ x ¾″ thick. Three sheets are cut into two pieces and a single sheet forms the last page of the book.

COVER: Hand lettered and decorated, as is the entire book. The cover and pages [37, 45, 51] are reproduced in *Drawn from New England*, page 26.

CONTENTS: The book is probably Tudor's earliest manifestation of farm life and the calendar. Both themes recur throughout her *oeuvre* and are the subjects of numerous books as well as inspirations to her followers. Favored names Fillow, Bethany, Seth and Melinda all appear here. They demonstrate Tudor's inclination and ability to create an extended work of art at the age of nineteen.

ILLUSTRATIONS: Page [1] the cover/title page, is backed by a watercolor of a farmhouse on page [2], the verso. Pages [3-4] bear the opening text: Once upon a time there | was a little girl who | lived on a farm. Her | name was Hitty Fillow. ‖ In January it was very . . . From that point, versos of text alternate with rectos of watercolor paintings. Collation of the paintings:

[5]	parlor with a rag rug
[7]	red schoolhouse
[9]	kitchen and table
[11]	Brother Seth at the barn door
[13]	kitchen, mother, 3 girls, open cupboard with dishes
[15]	March . . . tapping maple trees
[17]	boiling sap
[19]	boiling sap at night in the moonlight
[21]	sleigh ride by moonlight
[23]	April plowing with oxen
[25]	Hitty and her hen in the woodshed
[27]	hen in a new coop
[29]	2 girls walking by a garden
[31]	Jane in the milkroom
[33]	planting corn
[35]	milking cows
[36]	text speaks of a calf named Bethany
[37]	Hitty and her father with geese
[39]	haying

OTHER: The book exists only as a unique manuscript which belongs to Bethany Tudor.

I1 **AN ILLUSTRATED STUDY** | of the **PEMBROKE WELSH CORGI STANDARD** ‖ This book is dedicated to the late Marjorie Butcher whose famed Cote de Neige | prefix is widely respected in the Corgi fancy. Mrs. Butcher, who conceived and | instigated this illustrated standard project, worked long and hard on it in the | months immediately preceding her death. ‖ Prepared by the Illustrated Standard Committee of the | Pembroke Welsh Corgi Club of America, Inc. ‖ the late Marjorie Butcher, Chairman | Mary Gay Sargent | Gladys Bundock | Lawrence Boersma ‖ Drawings by Pat deVore Wyatt | Poem illustration by Tasha Tudor ‖ *Corgi Fantasy* by Anne G. Biddlecombe reprinted with the permission of the | Welsh Corgi League. ‖ © Copyright 1975, the Pembroke Welsh Corgi Club of America, Inc.

> PAGINATION: White paper booklet, pp. [1] 2-32, plus a tan wrapper. 10″ x 6 13/16″

> COVER: Front cover has a Wyatt drawing (from page 14) showing the corgi in proper stance. Beneath the illustration: An Illustrated Study | of the | Pembroke Welsh Corgi Standard ‖ Prepared and Published by | The Pembroke Welsh Corgi Club of America, Inc. Back cover bears the insignia of the club, a corgi standing within a black circle on which is reverse-printed PEMBROKE WELSH CORGI CLUB • OF AMERICA INC •

> ILLUSTRATIONS: Tudor has three pen and ink drawings on page 2, each within its own black rule frame: a fairy riding a corgi, three children looking into a small woodland circle where two corgyn frolic, and 2 corgyn sitting in daffodils.

> COPYRIGHT REGISTRATION: A 664445 granted to The Pembroke Welsh Corgi Club of America, Inc. Lawrence Boersma, agent for claimant, swears on Aug. 25, 1975:

> > AN ILLUSTRATED STUDY OF THE PEMBROKE WELSH CORGI STANDARD, by Miss Mary Gay Sargent, 999 Lake Ave., Greenwich, Ct. 06830, Mrs. Gladys Bundock, 2405 Coffee Lane, Sebastopol, Ca. 95472 and Dr. Lawrence Boersma, 300 East 56th St., N.Y., N.Y. 10022, all US citizens, was published May 17, 1975. The book was manufactured by S & R Litho Co., 40 West 22nd St., N.Y., N.Y. Application and affidavit, fee and two deposit copies were received at LC Aug. 27, 1975.

I2 [page ii] THE ILLUSTRATED | TREASURY OF | **CHILDREN'S LITERATURE** [page iii] *Edited and with an introduction by Margaret E. Martignoni | formerly Superintendent of Work with Children | Brooklyn Public Library, New York* ‖ COMPILED WITH THE ORIGINAL ILLUSTRATIONS UNDER THE DIRECTION OF | P. EDWARD ERNEST | STAFF EDITORS: DORIS DUENEWALD • EVELYN ANDREAS • ALICE THORNE ‖ GROSSET AND DUNLAP • PUBLISHERS • NEW YORK. [The selections reprinted in this collection are used | by permission of and special arrangement with the | proprietors of their respective copyrights ‖ © Copyright, 1955, by Grosset & Dunlap, Inc. | All rights reserved under International and Pan-American Copyright Conventions. | Published simultaneously in Canada. Printed in the United States.]

> PAGINATION: vol. I. [i-iv], v-xii, 1-256 plus ivory endpapers with 18 full-color panels each illustrating a different story. vol. II. [i-iv], v-vi [vii-viii] 257-512, plus ivory endpapers as in volume one. The paper varies throughout the books, some light enamel, but mostly a lesser pulp paper. 10 ¼″ x 7 7/8″

> COVER: Matching covers: light blue half-linen overlapping navy blue cotton spine. A flower emblem twines between the four initials, I and T, C and L. Spines stamped in gold: [Harrison Cady's Peter Cottontail] | [a wide and a narrow gilt band] ‖ THE | ILLUSTRATED | TREASURY | OF | CHILDREN'S | LITERATURE ‖ VOL. I [II] ‖ Edited by |Margaret E. | Martignoni ‖ GROSSET

& | DUNLAP ‖ [narrow and wide gilt bands] ‖ [figure of Kate Greenaway's *Five Little Sisters*]. Blue and white headbands.

DUST JACKET: Have not examined one.

CONTENTS: This anthology represents a broad cross-section of reading for children and families at home. Contributions from 97 authors. Page v: *ACKNOWLEDGMENTS* ‖ Grateful acknowledgment is made to the following | publishers, authors, illustrators and other copyright | holders, for permission to reprint copyrighted ma- | terials: . . . OXFORD UNIVERSITY PRESS, INC. — Illustrations by Tasha | Tudor from *A Child's Garden of Verses*, by Robert Louis | Stevenson with pictures by Tasha Tudor, copyright 1947 by | Oxford University Press, Inc. . . . Page viii: *INTRODUCTION* . . . All in | all, eighty-five top ranking artists are | represented in the *Treasury* and a veritable | art education awaits boys and girls in its | pages. . .

ILLUSTRATIONS: The illustrations on pages 150-151 are "from a drawing by Tasha Tudor." Page 150 is a good pencil rendering [not from Tudor's hand] of the color plate which appeared on page [15] of *A Child's Garden* . . . ; and page 151 is after the ribboned illustration of page 13. A detail of the latter heads the *INTRODUCTION* on page ix.

COPYRIGHT REGISTRATION: A 212220   October 1, 1955

COPYRIGHT RENEWAL REGISTRATION: RE-164-297 granted to Grosset & Dunlap, Inc., 51 Madison Avenue, NY, NY 10010, Proprietor of copyright in a work made for hire. Louise Bates swears April 8, 1983:

THE ILLUSTRATED TREASURY OF CHILDREN'S LITERATURE by P. Edward Ernest and Staff, Editors and Margaret E. Martignoni, Author of introduction was renewed effective April 11, 1983. Fees charged to Deposit account DAO34886, Grosset & Dunlap, Inc.

I3 _____. [page iii] *Edited and with an introduction by Margaret E. Martignoni | formerly Superintendent of Work with Children | Brooklyn Public Library, New York* ‖ INCLUDING | POEMS FOR YOUNG CHILDREN | SELECTED BY NANCY LARRICK AND ILLUSTRATED BY KAY LOVELACE SMITH | COMPILED WITH THE ORIGINAL ILLUSTRATIONS UNDER THE DIRECTION OF | P. EDWARD ERNEST | STAFF EDITORS: DORIS DUENEWALD • EVELYN ANDREAS • ALICE THORNE | |
Volume One. [The selections reprinted in this collection are used | by permission of and special arrangement with the | proprietors of their respective copyrights ‖ © Copyright, 1955, by Grosset & Dunlap, Inc. | All rights reserved under International and Pan-American Copyright Conventions. | Published simultaneously in Canada. ‖ ©Copyright, 1965, by J. G. Ferguson Publishing Company | Special Edition | Selections by Nancy Larrick | Illustrations by Kay Lovelace Smith ‖ P-1168]

PAGINATION: vol. 1. [i-iv], v-xii, 1-256 plus ivory endpapers. vol. 2. [i-iv], v-vi [vii-viii] 257-512, plus ivory endpapers.

COVER: Turquoise plastic-filled paper, stamped in gilt and black ink. Front: **Beginner's Bookshelf** [three vertical olive fronds, underscored with a wide bar] [gilt] ‖ *The Illustrated Treasury of* | *Children's Literature* [black] | [gilt line drawings of Puss 'n Boots, Pinnochio, Raggedy Ann and a 'military' rabbit. Spine: [gilt bar] | **Beginner's Bookshelf** [gilt on a one-inch black band [three vertical olive fronds, underscored with a wide bar, in gilt] ‖ *The*

Illustrated Treasury of | *Children's Literature* [laterally, black] | 1 [gilt] | **𝓒**&**𝓢** [gilt] | [black bar]. Volume 2 carries '2' on the spine.

DUST JACKET: Have not examined one.

CONTENTS: *ACKNOWLEDGMENTS* is set in new type. *INTRODUCTION* contains new text, in part: "This special edition . . . includes Poems for Young Children selected by Nancy Larrick, who is greatly respected for her knowledge of literature for young readers, and illustrated by Kay Lovelace Smith, a talented newcomer to the group of distinguished illustrators of children's poems. . ."

ILLUSTRATIONS: The change noted above supplants illustrations by Kate Greenaway, C.B. Falls, Berta and Elmer Hader, *et alia* with Smith's colorful 'modern' images. The first thirty-three pages are a different selection of poems. We first encounter the original text with Palmer Cox's *Brownie Year Book* on page 34.

OTHER: The 'half-title' page [i]: [three vertical olive fronds] | **Beginner's Bookshelf** || *The Illustrated Treasury* | *of Children's Literature* || volume 1 || **C S** | *COMMUNICATION & STUDIES, INC.* | ATLANTA, GEORGIA 30303 | 1969. And volume 2 is so designated.

I4 **The | Illustrated Treasury | of | FAIRY | TALES** || Edited by T. A. Kennedy || *Art Direction and Book Design | by Natalie Provenzano* || Publishers • GROSSETT & DUNLAP • New York. [[floral device] *Grateful acknowledgement is made to Doug Cushman for permission to reprint | illustrations from* Giants © *1980 by Doug Cushman.* || Library of Congress Catalog Card Number: 82-81327. ISBN: 0-448-16578-3. | Copyright © 1982 by Grosset & Dunlap, Inc. All rights reserved. Published simultaneously in | Canada. Printed in the United States.]

PAGINATION: [i-x], 11-18, [19] 20-191, [192] plus white endpapers. 10 ¼″ x 7 ¾″

COVER: Pictorial boards show a montage of fairy tale scenes on white sealed paper with a imprinted tight weave. Title is printed on a white ribbon cascading across the middle. Spine and back are pink. Spine: **The Illustrated Treasury of FAIRY TALES** [printed laterally] || [GD logo] GROSSET | & | DUNLAP | 16578-3. Back cover has an inset box 3 7/8 x 3″ of a young page kneeling; at lower right, 0-448-16578-3.

DUST JACKET: Reproduces the design of the cover with this text on white flaps. Front: $9.95 || **The** | **Illustrated Treasury of** | **FAIRY TALES** || **Discover a world of magic…** || …a glistening, shimmering world | of handsome princes and beautiful | princesses, where fairies and elves | cavort in marvelous mischief and | pumpkins turn to gold with the | touch of a wand. || This collection brings that world to | life again with treasures like "Cin- | derella", "Rumplestiltskin" and | "The Snow Queen" . [*sic*] Generations of | classic illustrators bring the reader | a unique vision of a fairy tale | world, and each page sparkles with | nostalgia, humor and drama. || Each of these tales will be trea- | sured by young and old alike. For | the young child, it is a dazzling | entrance into the world of make | believe; for the old it is a chance to | recapture innocence and awe. But | for everyone, it is a chance to | believe in a world of enchantment. Back: **About the editor…** || *T.A. Kennedy* is currently the | Senior Editor of Children's Books | at Grosset & Dunlap, Inc. ¶ She lives in New York, and in | addition to her editorial work, has | authored articles, humor and fic- | tion on a variety of subjects. || **The** | **Illustrated Treasury** | **of Humor** | **for Children** || *Edited by Judith Hendra* ¶ Do you know about the old lady | who swallowed a fly? Or mean | Josephine? Or exploding gravy? ¶ A rollicking collection of giggles | and gasps, this glorious assortment | of stories and poems includes | works by Ogden Nash, Lewis Car- | roll, Edward Lear and a multitude | of others. ¶ Cheerfully illustrated by Doug | Cushman, Hilary Knight, Kate | Greenaway and more, this collec- | tion is guaranteed to brighten the | dullest of rainy days and bring a | smile to the sourest of faces. || Publishers • Grosset & Dunlap • New York.

ILLUSTRATIONS: Among other illustrations are these by Tudor:

Page 155   THE PRINCESS AND THE PEA, a detail from a head banner previously used on page [26] of *Tasha Tudor's BEDTIME BOOK*, 1977.

Page 167   THE SORCERER'S APPRENTICE, full-page, full-color illustration printed on page [17] in the same book.

COPYRIGHT REGISTRATION: TX-993-332 granted to Grosset & Dunlap, Inc. (Employer for hire). Louise Bates agent for Grosset & Dunlap, Inc., 51 Madison Ave., NY, NY 10010 (212) 689-9200, swears on August 25, 1982:

THE ILLUSTRATED TREASURY OF FAIRY TALES, entire work for hire, was published August 2, 1982. The book was manufactured by Danner Press Corporation, P.O. Box 8349, 1250 Camden Ave., Canton, Oh. 44709. Application and two copies received at the Library of Congress August 27, 1982, the effective date of this registration.

l5 The | Illustrated Treasury | of | Humor | for | Children ‖ Editor | **JUDITH HENDRA** ‖ **With introduction by** | **William Cole** ‖ Staff editor | NANCY CHRISTENSEN HALL ‖ Grosset and Dunlap Publishers   New York | A FILMWAYS COMPANY   [*To Tony, Kathy, and Jessica, with much love.* ‖ Library of Congress Catalog Number: 79-91869 | ISBN: 0-448-16429-9 (Trade Edition) | ISBN: 0-448-13616-3 (Library Edition) | Copyright © 1980 by Grosset & Dunlap, Inc. All rights reserved | Published simultaneously in Canada. Printed in the United States of America. | The selections reprinted in this collection are used by permission | of and special arrangement with the proprietors of their respective copyrights.]

PAGINATION: [i-ii] iii-x, [1]-244, [245-246] pp. plus white endpapers. 10 ¼ x 7 ¾″

COVER: Pictorial boards under gloss film laminate. Same illustration front and back is a montage of images from several of the 121 selections. The title is printed in blue on a yellow shield mounted in the middle of the illustration on the front cover. Spine: The Illustrated Treasury of | Humor for Children [blue] ‖ Edited by | JUDITH HENDRA [black] ‖ [GD logo [blue] | GROSSET | & | DUNLAP | 16429-9. Text of the back cover shield: A collection of children's stories and poems by masters | old and new, including selections by Hilaire Belloc, | Andrew Lang, Ogden Nash, Oliver Herford, Edward | Lear, Carolyn Wells, Lewis Carroll, E. Nesbit, Walter | de la Mare, Archy, and many others. With beautiful illus- | trations by Gyo Fujikawa, the Brothers Hildebrandt, | Tasha Tudor, Doug Cushman, Kate Greenaway, Tomi | Ungerer, Hilary Knight, and more. ‖ **With introduction by | William Cole** | Publishers • GROSSET & DUNLAP • New York | A FILMWAYS COMPANY ‖ 0-448-16429-9. A gold sticker at the upper left of back is overprinted with a navy mask with lettering in gold: $12^{95} | GROSSET.

ILLUSTRATIONS: Tudor's illustrations used in earlier books appear on:

Pages 6-7	THE THREE BILLY GOATS GRUFF
Pages [58-59]	THE OWL AND THE PUSSY-CAT
Pages [198]-199	THE TABLE AND THE CHAIR

COPYRIGHT REGISTRATION: TX-630-214 granted to Grosset & Dunlap, Inc. (Employer for hire). Louise Bates agent for Grosset & Dunlap, Inc., 51 Madison Ave., Ny, NY 10010 (212) 689-9200, swears on September 22, 1980:

THE ILLUSTRATED TREASURY OF HUMOR FOR CHILDREN, compilation, editing, introduction, was published September 5, 1980. The book was manufactured by Danner Press Corporation, P.O. Box 8349, 1250 Camden Ave., Canton, Oh. 44709. Application and two copies received at the Library of Congress January 21, 1981, the effective date of this registration.

16 INCREASE | RABBIT | *By T. L. McCready, Jr.* | ILLUSTRATIONS | *By Tasha Tudor* | ARIEL BOOKS • NEW YORK [to HAL VURSELL, | *an editor who lives in the city* | *but whose mind often strays to the country* || [painting of two little girls hugging a large brown rabbit within a grape vine frame] | © 1958 by Thomas L. McCready and Tasha Tudor. | Library of Congress catalog card no. 57-9634 | *Published simultaneously in Canada* | *by Ambassador Books, Ltd.* | MANUFACTURED IN THE U.S.A.]

PAGINATION: [52] pp. 4 signatures including fly leaves. 8 1/8" x 6 1/4".

COVER: Yellow cloth cover. Black-stamped rabbit above INCREASE RABBIT on front. Spine in black: McCready   INCREASE RABBIT   Ariel. 2-page color illustrated endpapers depict four (McCready/Tudor) children with Increase in a doll buggy, Biggity Bantam, Pekin White, Matilda, and Mr. Stubbs in a soup box wagon.

DUST JACKET: Yellow with two white flaps, all printing in black. Front: INCREASE | RABBIT | Increase in a circle of vegetables within a rope frame | By T. L. McCready, Jr. | Pictures by Tasha Tudor. Spine: McCready   INCREASE RABBIT   Ariel. Back is blank. Front flap has slight clips from both corners with no apparent loss of text. $2.75 || AN ARIEL EASY READING BOOK || 428 | $2.50 [which has been overprinted with a black bar] | INCREASE | RABBIT | *BY T. L. McCready, Jr.* | PICTURES BY *Tasha Tudor* || Increase Rabbit started life with | the unimpressive name of George. | He was one of two fine Belgian | hares which Mrs. Warner brought | home for the children to enjoy on | their New Hampshire farm. But | when, a few weeks later, "George" | was discovered to be the proud | mother of seven baby rabbits, the | children promptly renamed her In- | crease. || This was not the only time Increase | was to surprise the Warners, for | she turned out to be a very unusual | rabbit in many ways, and quite dif- | ferent from her rather stuffy hus- || (*continued on back flap*) || ARIEL BOOKS | FARRAR, STRAUS AND CUDAHY | 101 Fifth Avenue, New York 3, N. Y. Back flap: (continued from front flap) || band, Albert. The adventures In- | crease has when she decides to move | from the rabbit hutch into the | house, her friendship with the | Warners' tomcat Mr. Stubbs, and | the mischief she gets into because | of her uncontrollable love of | munching, make a delightful story | which is made even more enjoyable | by Tasha Tudor's pictures. || INCREASE RABBIT is a sequel to | BIGGITY BANTAM, PEKIN WHITE, | and MR. STUBBS by the same author | and illustrator. || ARIEL BOOKS | FARRAR, STRAUS AND CUDAHY | 101 Fifth Avenue, New York 3, N. Y.

ILLUSTRATIONS: Black and white illustrations: Pp. 2, 3 (title page), 6, 7, 10, 13-15, 19, 20-21, 23, 27, 30, 35, 38-41, 43, 46-47, 50-51. Colored illustrations: Pp. 4 (dedication in grape vine border, 8, 9, 17, 24-25, 29, 33, 37, 44-45, 48. Text only: Pp. 5, 11-12, 16, 18, 22, 26, 28, 31-32, 34, 36, 42, 48.

COPYRIGHT REGISTRATION: A 323791 granted to Thomas L. McCready, Jr., author, and Tasha Tudor, illustrator, Contoocook, N.H. H.D. Varsell, agent for claimants, swears on Feb. 13, 1958:

INCREASE RABBIT, by T. L. McCready, Jr. and Tasha Tudor, both U.S. citizens, was published Feb. 6, 1958. The book was manufactured by Monitor Press, New York City. Fees charged to Miss Anne Brooks Murray, Farrar, Straus & Cudahy, Inc. 101 Fifth Ave., N.Y. 3, N.Y. Application and affidavit and two deposit copies received at L.C. Feb. 17, 1958.

COPYRIGHT RENEWAL REGISTRATION: RE 313-229 granted to Tasha Tudor McCready, RD #4, Box 144, West Brattleboro, Vt. 05301, co-author and widow of the deceased author, Thomas L. McCready, and Efner Tudor Holmes, Rt. #1, Concord, N.H., child of the deceased author, Thomas L. McCready and Seth Tudor, Thomas Tudor and Bethany Tudor, RD#4, Box 144, West Brattleboro, Vt. 05301, children of the deceased author, Thomas L. McCready. Lucine Bellocchio, agent for Tasha Tudor McCready, Seth Tudor, Bethany Tudor and Efner Tudor Holmes [*sic*], swears on Dec. 10, 1986:

INCREASE RABBIT, ENTIRE TEXT BY T.L. McCready, Jr. and all illustrations by Tasha Tudor, was published Feb. 6, 1958, A 323791, and Thomas L. McCready, Jr. and Tasha Tudor were the original claimants. Fees charged to deposit account DAO13366, Farrar, Straus & Giroux, Inc. Application received at L.C., Dec. 12, 1986.

I7 _____.

PAGINATION: Increases to [56] pp.

COVER: A library pre-bound copy in a green painted cover. Front title painted in yellow, with the image of Increase and the right and lower portions of her vegetable border from the trade dust jacket. Cloth reinforced hinges and white endpapers, the previous pastedown endpapers now being loose.

CONTENTS: Title page [5], text runs through pages [7-53].

I8 _____. Published simultaneously in Canada | by Ambassador Books, Ltd.

Have not examined a copy.

J1 [a laurel leaf garland] | JACKANAPES | [two girls waving Union jacks] | By JULIANA HORATIA
EWING | Pictures by TASHA TUDOR | [Jackanapes galloping Lollo toward the reader, above a
laurel leaf garland] | OXFORD UNIVERSITY PRESS | *NEW YORK 1948* | COPYRIGHT 1948 OXFORD
UNIVERSITY PRESS, INC. | PRINTED IN THE UNITED STATES OF AMERICA   [Verso is blank.]

PAGINATION: 4 signatures ivory paper. [i-ii, 1-6] 7-16 [16a-16b] 17-22 [23] 24-40 [40a-40b] 41-42
[43] 44-50 [50a-50b, 51] 52-58 [58a-58b] 59-61 [62-64] 5 9/16″w x 7 7/8″h.

COVER: <u>Gray-green rayon-finish cloth cover</u>, <u>gold stamping</u> on spine: EWING JACKANAPES
OXFORD; on cover: JACKANAPES. A laurel garland encircles four different color
illustrations on the end papers.

DUST JACKET: A motif of the victor's green laurel wreath figures on the front and back of the dust
wrapper as well as the title page. The jacket is printed in red, blue, brown, yellow, black and
green. Front: JACKANAPES | By JULIANA HORATIA EWING, within a partial wreath open
at the bottom to a large wreath encircling the boy Jackanapes riding Lollo. Pictures by |
TASHA TUDOR, in a small enclosed wreath at the bottom and flanked by two union jacks, a
helmet, sword, drum and bugle. Text in black. Spine: EWING   JACKANAPES OXFORD.
Front flap: Jackanapes [blue] | by Juliana Horatia Ewing | Pictures by Tasha Tudor [red, main
text following in black] | Of all Juliana Ewing's stories of early nine- | teenth century England,
none is more be- | loved than *Jackanapes*. This story of a | bright-haired, high-spirited small boy,
who | rode Lollo across the village green and | who, as a young man, gave his life to save | his
best friend, has been loved and wept | over by generations of young readers. ¶For many years
there has been no new | edition of this perennial favorite. Tasha | Tudor, with her understanding
of the | period and her love of children, seems the | perfect artist to reinterpret this tale of |
courage and loyalty. The quiet humor of | the English village, the romance of the | Black
Captain, the smoke and blood of | battle are all in the pictures-both color | and black and white.
That she could give | us charming pictures of the English village | is not surprising, but even her
publisher | wondered how Tasha Tudor would handle | a battle scene. ¶readers who have loved
her earlier books | will find a vigor and action in these pictures | that earlier stories she illustrated
did not | call for. With each successive book, Tasha | Tudor has shown greater maturity and |
skill. *Jackanapes* will not prove to be an ex- | ception in this respect. [black] || Oxford Books |
for Boys and Girls [blue] |100-140 $2.00. Back flap: *Also Illustrated by Tasha Tudor* [red] ||
A Child's Garden | of Verses [blue] || By Robert Louis Stevenson [red] || "What Tasha Tudor can
do with color is | something to dream about, something to | feast the eyes upon again and again.
In | the many small black and white drawings | which grace the book, along with the full- | page
color plates, the artist captures the in- | nocence and tenderness of childhood in a | way that is
inimitably Tasha Tudor." | —*Philadelphia Inquirer* || "These lovely new pictures, meltingly soft |
in color, with Victorian children whose | faces are often rugged with character how- | ever pretty
their garments, are to the verses | what music might be-realization in an- | other form. . . . This
book marks, I think, | this artist's highest point in illustration." | —*New York Herald Tribune*
$2.50.

CONTENTS: Pp. [i] and [5] are half titles. Pages [ii] [2] [4] [6] [63-64] are blank.

ILLUSTRATIONS: Page [3] lists four full page color illustrations which are inserted following pages
16, 40, 50 and 58. Six pencil initials each in a laurel wreath introduce the chapters. Thirteen
pencil drawings interrupt the text on pages [3], 7, 11, 14, 19, 22, [23], 26, 29, 33, 48, 56, 60.
Two more color illustrations appear on the title page; a portion of one is the central figure of the
dust wrapper.

OTHER: The title page is tipped in.

COPYRIGHT REGISTRATION: A 27059 granted to Oxford University Press, Inc., 114 Fifth Ave., N.Y., N.Y.. Henry Z. Walck, agent for claimant, swears on Sept. 30, 1948:

> JACKANAPES, by Juliana Horatia Ewing, 1841-1885, a deceased British citizen and Tasha Tudor (illustrator), Contoocook, Webster, N.H., [*sic*] a U.S. citizen born approx. 1912, was published Sept. 30, 1948. Type was set and the book printed by Kellogg and Bulkeley, Hartford, Ct.; binding by American Book Stratford Press, Inc, New York, N.Y. Application and two deposit copies received at L.C. Oct. 7, 1948; affidavit received Nov. 5, 1948.

COPYRIGHT RENEWAL REGISTRATION: R 642886 granted to the illustrator Tasha Tudor c/o David McKay Company, Inc., 750 3rd Ave., N.Y., N.Y. 10017. Marguerite Gaignat, agent for claimant, swears, no date:

> JACKANAPES, by Juliana Horatia Ewing was published Sept. 30, 1948, original claimant Oxford University Press Inc.* (An asterisked footnote says amended by Copyright Office.) Tudor renews claim to 'new matter illustrations only,' and fees are charged to David McKay Company, Inc. Application received at L.C. Sept. 8, 1976.

J2 _____.

COVER: Identical except <u>bright</u> <u>green cloth cover</u> with <u>black stamping</u>.

DUST JACKET: Upper corner of front flap has been slightly clipped, others are whole.

J3 _____.

COVER: Rebound library copy. Sealed gray buckram cover with a painted image of the dominant theme from the original dust jacket: an hour-glass of laurel leaves displaying title, author and boy on pony. An example of later twentieth century rebinding, the examination copy bears a foil label inside the front cover: New Method Book Binder, Inc., Jacksonville, Illinois.

DUST JACKET: The examination copy seems to be a unique scanned and computer-generated jacket, ca. 1997. Two enlarged images are taken from the book, and not the original jacket. On the front, an image displays 90% of the title page, garland to garland. The image on the back is taken from the plate facing page 16, Jackanapes' parents at the wall.

The reader might also consult one of the Caldecott editions, e.g.

J4 **Ewing, Juliana Horatia. JACKANAPES.** WITH ILLUSTRATIONS BY RANDOLPH CALDECOTT. (*One Hundred and Thirty-Fourth Thousand.*) London | Society for Promoting Christian Knowledge, | Northumberland Avenue, Charing Cross, W.C. | 43, Queen Victoria Street, E.C. | Brighton: 135, North Street. | New York: E. & J. B. Young & Co.

OTHER: The Caldecott editions present instructive comparisons with Tudor's illustrations. See the frontispiece: Jackanapes on the battlefield leading his friend's horse by the reins. Tudor renders a soldier charging on his horse on page [Tudor] 48 and, a quite similar scene, the full color plate [50a] of Jackanapes rescuing Tony. The Caldecott title page poses Jackanapes and his parents against a backdrop of a blanket with zigzag border. Tudor uses the same device for her list of illustrations, page [T 3]. Tudor [T 23] draws a simpler baby Jackanapes following the young gosling to the pond (Caldecott 16). On the other hand, Caldecott's merry-go-round (C 22) shows only two horses, while Tudor's (T 29) is a full blown Fair attraction with children and parents and a man to push the wheel. From Caldecott's line drawing of Jackanapes racing on Lollo (C 30), Tudor develops her close copy into a full-page color plate (facing page 40). Tudor's charging soldier (T 48) is suggested in Caldecott's Boy Trumpeter sounding Retire (C 35) where soldiers with swords drawn are shadowed in the background. Both artists have rendered the death of Jackanapes. In Caldecott's (C 39), we see the Major with his hat fallen to the floor, but only Jackanapes hand. Tudor (T 56), makes Jackanapes the center of her drawing, and shows the Major with more composure. Again, Tudor begins with Caldecott's image of Miss Jessamine being drawn in her bath chair by Lollo (T 44). But her full-page color illustration is softer and more gallant. She places Tony and his fellow officer in their uniforms, which Caldecott did not, and depicts the second officer kissing Miss Jessamine's hand. A heavy black mustache is obvious. (Compare with pictures of Tudor's father Starling Burgess).

J5 The Jenny Wren | Book | of | Valentines | In which you will | find a delightful | Selection of cards | and sentiments. [Published by The Jenny Wren Press, Box 505, Mooresville, Indiana 46158 | Copyright © 1988 by Tasha Tudor | All Rights Reserved. | No part of this book may be reproduced in any form | without permission from the publisher. Printed in the USA || Library of Congress Catalog Card Number 88-51832 | ISBN 0-9621753-1-5]

PAGINATION: [16] pp. including the covers. 4 x 3 1/16″

COVER: Matte finish buff paper folded and stapled to the body. Title is centered between: top, two floral hearts and a wren in a green lace heart, all suspended on the same green ribbon' and bottom, a swag of blue flowers tied at each end with a green bow above a white dove, tiny letter in beak. This is all drawn on a lace edged pearl-colored panel which nearly fills the cover. The back has a small pink and brown heart centered, and printed at the lower right: ISBN 0-9621753-1-5. The title comes from the cover.

CONTENTS: The colophon is at the bottom of the last page [15]. This catalog of valentines reproduces one Tudor created for her children's dolls and bears.

ILLUSTRATIONS: The catalog contains 27 designs in full color, pp. [3-9]; and the 27 accompanying verses, pp. [10-15].

OTHER: One of the earliest offerings from The Jenny Wren Press (Indiana), the catalog was advertised in a February 18, 1989, mailing at $8.95, or $12.95 if autographed. Wholesale prices (12 or more) were $5.40 and $9.40. Copies were signed on the back.   An undated letter on buff paper to "Dear Customer" was folded and inserted with the books. Tasha Tudor and Beth Mathers thank you for purchasing the book.   The letter gives a brief history of how the small books came about; it announces plans to reprint the *Bouquet, The Mouse Mills Mail-Order Catalogue* and the *Christmas Annual.*

COPYRIGHT REGISTRATION: TX 2 562 528 granted to Tasha Tudor, R.R. 4, Box 205, West Brattleboro, Vt 05301. Beth Mathers (317-831-1415), 5 Daniel St., Mooresville, In. 46158, agent for Tasha Tudor, swears, no date:

THE JENNY WREN BOOK OF VALENTINES, by Tasha Tudor whose work is an anonymous contribution, an American citizen, was published Jan. 5, 1989. The work was completed in 1958 but had never been published. Library of Congress is granted non-exclusive permission to make copies and phonorecords for the blind and physically handicapped. Application and two deposit copies received at L.C. Dec. 23, 1988, the effective date of registration; application also received May 4, 1989. Certificate to be mailed to Beth Mathers/Jenny Wren Press, P.O. Box 505, Mooresville, In. 46158. [This application was hand written by Beth Mathers.]

J6 **Jenny Wren** | *Garden* | **Colouring Book** [in an oval of ribbon]. [Published by The Jenny Wren Press P.O. Box 505, Mooresville, Indiana 46158 | Copyright © 1991 The Jenny Wren Press All Rights Reserved. | No part of this book may be reproduced in any form without permission from the publisher | Printed in the U.S.A. Library of Congress Number in Publication Data [*sic*] ISBN 0-9621753-3-1]

PAGINATION: [12] pp. including the covers. 3 ¼ x 5 ¼″

COVER: Matte finish white cover stock folded and stapled to the body. Title is centered above three pots of flowers on front, within an oval of blue ribbon and roses. At the lower corners are garden tableau of tools and plants, the whole within. A wavy blue ribbon border surrounds the entire front. The back has one line centered at the bottom: © *Copyright 1991 The Jenny Wren Press* / ™ The title comes from the cover.

CONTENTS: The colophon is printed in its traditional proper place, at the bottom of the last page [10]. However, the statement confuses three different elements of contemporary book identification—the Library of Congress catalog card number, Cataloging-in-Publication data, and the International Standard Book Number. Neither LCCCN nor CIP data is given. The body of this book consists of the eight line drawings listed below, a child's coloring book.

ILLUSTRATIONS: The only color is the cover illustration: green lettering with a blue ribbon oval with pink roses, gray-brown garden tools at the bottom. A single brown line drawing of a garden tableau on each of the eight interior pages. The largest illustration, page [8], measures 4 3/8 x 1 7/8″

[3] Girl raking among flowering tulips, pots, watering cans and a crow

[4] Boy with trowel transplanting flowers, and a

[5] Boy looking at staked plants, wheelbarrow, hoe and crow

[6] Boy examining growing pumpkin, crow

[7] Girl picking flowers, crow with flower in mouth

[8] Procession of children bearing baskets of vegetables, crow with basket in mouth

[9] Girl between pots of flowers, tickling crow on head with a flower stem

[10] Crow sitting on pumpkin among other vegetables.

COPYRIGHT REGISTRATION: TX 3 216 412 granted to The Jenny Wren Press by written agreement between Tasha Tudor & Beth Mathers, co-owners of the Jenny Wren Press, P.O. Box 505, Mooresville, Indiana 46158.   Beth Mathers (317-831-1044) swears, November 5, 1991:

The Jenny Wren Coloring Book, by Tasha Tudor, an American citizen born 1915, was published Sept. 25, 1991. The work, a coloring book for small children, was completed in 1952 but had not been previously published.   Application and two deposit copies received at L.C. Dec. 18, 1991, the effective date of registration.   [This application was hand written by Beth Mathers.]

L1 **LADIES: 1962** | *And Other Talks At* | CONCORD ACADEMY || by ELIZABETH
B. HALL | *Headmistress of Concord Academy* | *And an Address by* ARCHIBALD MACLEISH |
Illustrations by TASHA TUDOR || PUBLISHED BY | THE BOARD OF TRUSTEES | OF CONCORD ACADEMY |
MCMLXII [COPYRIGHT © 1962 | BY THE BOARD OF TRUSTEES OF CONCORD ACADEMY || 𝕿𝖍𝖊 𝕽𝖎𝖛𝖊𝖗𝖘𝖎𝖉𝖊
𝕻𝖗𝖊𝖘𝖘 | CAMBRIDGE • MASSACHUSETTS | PRINTED IN THE U.S.A.]

PAGINATION: Six signatures. [i-x] 1-11 [12] 13-31 [32-33] 34-40 [41] 42-52 [53] 54-67 [68] 69-71
[72] 73-76 [77] 78-89 [90].

CONTENTS: [i] Half title; [ii] Frontispiece portrait of ELIZABETH B. HALL | CONCORD ACADEMY |
NOVEMBER 1962; [iii] Title page; [iv] reproduction of holograph note "Dear Mrs. Hall..."; [v-vi]
Foreword; [vii] Contents; [viii] Colophon; [ix] Half title; [x] blank; 1-[32], text; [33], blank;
34-40, text; [41], full page illustration; 42-71, text; [72] reproduction of holograph note "Dear
Mrs. Hall..."; 73-88, text; 89, *A Short Biographical Sketch* [of E. B. Hall]; [90], blank.

COVER: Mint green paper cover, outsize 6 1/4″ x 9 1/2″, binding pages 6 1/16″ x 9 1/4″. Text:
LADIES: 1962 | *And Other Talks At* | CONCORD ACADEMY | [child and dog at
schoolhouse door, from page 83] | ELIZABETH B. HALL | *And an Address by* | ARCHIBALD
MACLEISH.

ILLUSTRATIONS: Eleven line drawings to illustrate the talks at Concord [Massachusetts] Academy
where daughter Efner a student:

[vii]   Girl packing text books into crate labeled CONCORD ACADEMY

[12]   Girl sitting barefoot in the grass, clasping knees, hills.

22   Rose and hourglass

[41]   Boy (playing recorder) and girl sitting back-to-back in the moonlight

[53]   Girl and dog reading sign on closed door: No one under ten may enter here

61   Two mice wearing neck bows and dancing

[68]   "Justice" peeking

71   Corgi between a penny loafer and buckle galosh

[77]   A bird soaring above a valley, mountains in the background

83   A child with dog, holding open the left of double entrance doors looking inside the
building

88   A bird on its nest

COPYRIGHT REGISTRATION: A 610871 granted to Board of Trustees of Concord Academy, Concord,
Ma. Elizabeth B. Hall (Mrs. Livingston Hall, 80a Main Street, Concord, Ma.), agent for claimant,
swears on Feb. 12, 1963:

LADIES: 1962, by Elizabeth B. Hall, and Archibald MacLeish, Conway, Ma., both U.S. citizens,
was published Nov. 5, 1962 in Boston, Ma. The book was printed by the Riverside Press,
Cambridge, Ma. Two deposit copies received at L.C. Dec. 14, 1962; application and affidavit
and fee received Feb. 13, 1963.

L2 L̶I̶N̶S̶E̶Y̶ | W̶O̶O̶L̶S̶E̶Y̶ | *by Tasha Tudor* ‖ *New York* ‖ *Oxford University Press – 1946* [*Copyright 1946* | *Oxford University Press* | *New York, Inc.* | *Calligraphy by Hilda Scott* | *Printed in the United States of America*]

PAGINATION: 3 signatures ivory paper: [1-48] including front and back flyleaves. 4 3/4″ x 4″

COVER: White polka dots on yellow paper over boards, square spine. Red bordered white lozenge on front cover. On the white field: L̶I̶N̶S̶E̶Y̶ | W̶O̶O̶L̶S̶E̶Y̶ [red] | BY | TASHA TUDOR [black]. Front endpaper pictures a barefoot boy peering around the left side of red-framed bookplate, girl and lamb sitting at the right. Text of bookplate: *This Book* | *Belongs* | [rule] | *to.* Each of the other three endpapers has a different painting of three hollyhock stalks.

DUST JACKET: Ivory dust jacket, front: a lamb in dandelions between two curved ribbons on which are written the title in red letters, outlined in black; the superior, LINSEY, and the inferior, W̶O̶O̶L̶S̶E̶Y̶. Spine: *TUDOR - LINSEY WOOLSEY - OXFORD.* There is a small single rose centered on the back. Front flap: *A Calico Book* | *LINSEY WOOLSEY* | *by Tasha Tudor* ‖ *Other books in this series:* | *Pumpkin Moonshine* | *Alexander the Gander* | *County Fair* | *Dorcas Porkus* | *Each 75 cents* ‖ *OXFORD BOOKS* | *for* | *Boys and Girls* ‖ *40-60* Have not examined a copy with the lower corner of front flap present. Back flap: *You will want these books* | *by Tasha Tudor* ‖ *Snow Before Christmas* | *$1.00* ‖ *A Tale for Easter* | *$1.00* | *The White Goose* | *$1.00* ‖ *Mother Goose* | *$2.00* ‖ *Fairy Tales* | *from* | *Hans Christian Andersen* | *$3.50.*

CONTENTS: Title page [3], colophon [4], dedication, FOR BETHANY AND SETH [5], twenty full-page illustrations on the even-numbered pages [6-44], text on odd-numbered pages [7-45], blank pages [46-47].

ILLUSTRATIONS: In addition to the full-page textual illustrations and the endpapers and dust jacket, there are these. Title page has a straw bee hive, hollyhocks and other flowers. Dedication is written on a gift tag attached to a pink-ribboned white package sitting between a spray of cut flowers and a smaller wrapped present. The outline of a pink-brown ribbon and bow surround the dedication. Each initial on text pages is painted red, much larger than the rest of the text and embellished within a red box with vignettes from the story.

OTHER: Dedicatees are the two oldest McCready children.

COPYRIGHT REGISTRATION: A 6875 granted to Oxford University Press New York Inc., 114 Fifth Ave., N.Y. 11, N.Y. Henry Z. Walck, agent for claimant, swears on Oct. 25, 1946:

LINSEY WOOLSEY, by Tasha Tudor, Route #1, Contoocook, Webster, N.H., [*sic*] a U.S. citizen born in 1916, was published Oct. 24, 1946. The book was typeset and printed by Kellogg and Bulkeley Co., Hartford, Ct. and bound by Spiral Binding Co., Inc., N.Y., N.Y. Application and affidavit received at L.C. Oct. 27, 1946; two deposit copies received Nov. 1, 1946.

COPYRIGHT RENEWAL REGISTRATION: R 566630 granted to the author Tasha Tudor, Marlboro, Vt. 05344. Kuna Dolch, agent for Tudor and Walck, Henry Z., Inc., swears, undated:

LINSEY WOOLSEY, by Tasha Tudor, a U.S. citizen born approx. 1916, was originally published Oct. 24, 1946, A 6875 to Oxford University Press. Fee charged to deposit account #6694, Henry Z. Walck, Inc. Application received at L.C. Dec. 13, 1973.

L3 _____.   Overmann lists a Walck cloth cover in dust jacket. Have not examined one.

L4 _____. Warner Books planned to reprint *Linsey Woolsey* in a 4 ¼ x 3 ⅞″ paper over boards edition in April 1998. Part of the *Warner Treasures* series, the book, ISBN 0-446-91216-6, was to retail for $ 6.95. http://www.warnerbooks.com did not indicate the book as of March 3. 1998. A company spokesperson confirmed a few days later that Warner would not be reprinting the series; another employee speculated they might be published by Little, Brown. <u>A ghost.</u>

L5   A | LITTLE | PRINCESS | *By FRANCES HODGSON BURNETT* || [Sara at dormer window] || *Pictures by* | *TASHA TUDOR* || J. B. LIPPINCOTT COMPANY | *Philadelphia   New York* [Illustrations Copyright © 1963 by Tasha Tudor | Library of Congress Catalog Card No. 63-15435 | Foreword Copyright © 1963 by Phyllis McGinley | Printed in the United States of America]

PAGINATION: 13 signatures of ivory paper: [1-4] 5-6 [7-8] 9-17 [18] 19-52 [53] 54-86 [87] 88-109 [110] 111-126 [127] 128-136 [137] 138-156 [157] 158-185 [186] 187-202 [203] 204-221 [222] 223-238 [239] 240, plus fly leaves. 8 11/16″ x 6 11/16″. 13/16″ thick.

COVER: Green-gray cloth. Stamped in gilt: on the front, an illustration of Sara sitting reading within a wreath of ivy; spine, *Burnett* | [a rose] | A LITTLE PRINCESS [laterally] | [a rose] | *Lippincott*. Front and back endpapers the same two-page ink drawing of a Victorian street scene.

DUST JACKET: Dust jacket on ivory paper is a wrap-around color illustration of the schoolgirls walking in line down a London sidewalk against a brick rowhouse, a two-horse phaeton in the street. Over-printed in black on front: A LITTLE PRINCESS || *By FRANCES HODGSON BURNETT* | *Pictures by* | *TASHA TUDOR*. On spine: BURNETT | A | LITTLE | PRINCESS || LIPPINCOTT. Front flap: *The* | *Tasha Tudor Edition* || A | LITTLE | PRINCESS || By | FRANCES HODGSON BURNETT | *Illustrations by* TASHA TUDOR |*with a foreword by* | PHYLLIS McGINLEY || Sara Crewe did indeed seem like a | little princess when she arrived at | Miss Minchin's boarding school in | London. Her father who had brought | her from India had bought | her all | sorts of handsome clothes, she had a | French maid, a pony and a beautiful | doll, Emily, who was to become her | great friend. ¶ When Sara had been in school some | time a dramatic change took place in | her fortunes and her whole life. She | remained, however, a little princess | throughout. ¶ This story of Sara Crewe has been | a favorite with generations of chil- | dren. They have delighted in her | happiness and wept over her sorrows | and have been enchanted by the | mysterious events that bring about a | second great change in Sara's life. ¶ Tasha Tudor, whose pictures for || *The Secret Garden* have been so | much loved, has recreated for a whole | new generation of readers the Lon- | don of the last century and Sara, a | little princess. || 01014   <u>$5.00</u>. Back flap: *The Author* | FRANCES HODGSON BURNETT was a | born storyteller, and even when she | was a young child, living in Man- | chester, England, her greatest plea- | sure was in making up stories and | acting them out, using her dolls as | characters. When she was in her teens | her family, in search of better for- | tune, moved to Tennessee and there | young Frances had her first taste of | success, for two of her stories were | bought and published by an Amer- | ican magazine. From that point on | her career was assured, and until her | death in <u>1921</u> she wrote constantly | and produced more than forty books | and countless short stories. ¶ *The Artist* | Tasha Tudor's delicate color work, | her charming pencil drawings in | many books have made friends all | over this country. Children and | grown-ups alike have been drawn | to her nostalgic representation of a | world of another age. She has lived | in London and knows the square | where Miss Minchin's school was and | the streets where Sara walked. Best | of all she knows and loves this story | of another century. ¶ Tasha Tudor lives in an old farm- | house in New Hampshire which is | big enough to hold her four children | and many visiting friends and cousins. | There are animals, too, who are part | of the family, a garden, a grove of | sugar maples and blue New Hamp- | shire mountains in the distance. Examination copy bore a half-inch <u>vertical registration mark</u> centered at base of spine, back side of dust jacket.

CONTENTS: Page [1] Half title; [2] *By Frances Hodgson Burnett* || *Illustrated by* | *Tasha Tudor* || THE SECRET GARDEN | A LITTLE PRINCESS; [3] title page; [4] colophon; 5-6, foreword; [7] contents; [8] blank; 9-240, text.

ILLUSTRATIONS: Twelve full-page color illustrations: title page and pages [18, 53, 87, 110, 127, 137, 157, 186, 203, 222, 239], each with text printed on its back. Contents and 19 chapter heads are black ink drawings. A ribbon drape above each chapter head illustration contains the chapter number in Roman numerals; chapter title in capital letters below.

OTHER: This is one of the more problematic Tudor books to identify. There seem to be three points to verify the true first printing: 1) price, 2) Burnett's death date, 3) cloth color.

The true price is $5.00; and because this was a very popular gift book, purchasers often clipped the price. There is no pattern to the way the price was cut from the jacket.

Burnett's death date from the back flap of the jacket is sometimes stated to be 1921. This is in error; she died in 1924, which most jackets indicate. I can found no substantiating statement, but logic and book dealers generally agree that the error would have first been printed and when discovered, corrected. Thus, a true first would carry the 1921 date.

The editor has been forced to decide between three binding colors, all a jade green. I have decided the true first has a flat finish, and a relatively smooth weave. I adjudge that when that cloth was exhausted, the binder used a second similar fabric, but one with a more gray cast to the jade. The third state is a lighter sea-green cloth with a more distinct weave, like cheesecloth.

COPYRIGHT REGISTRATION: A 647284 granted to Phyllis McGinley, 12 Hazel Lane, Larchmont, N.Y. Charles C. Granade, Jr., agent for claimant, swears on Sept. 5, 1963:

A LITTLE PRINCESS, by Frances Hodgson Burnett, with foreword by Phyllis McGinley and illustrations by Tasha Tudor, Route 1, Contoocook, N.H., U.S. citizens, was published Aug. 29, 1963. New matter in this version: Foreword. The book was printed by Cornwall Press, Inc., Cornwall, N.Y. Fees charged to J.B. Lippincott Co., 227 South 6th St., Philadelphia, Pa. Two deposit copies, application and affidavit received at L.C. Sept. 16, 1963.

COPYRIGHT REGISTRATION: A 647285 granted to Tasha Tudor, Route #1, Contoocook, N.H. Charles C. Granade, Jr., agent for claimant, swears on Sept. 5, 1963:

A LITTLE PRINCESS, by Frances Hodgson Burnett, with illustrations by Tasha Tudor and foreword by Phyllis McGinley, U.S. citizens, was published Aug. 29, 1963. New matter in this version: illustrations. The book was printed Cornwall Press, Inc., Cornwall, N.Y. Fee charged to J.B. Lippincott Co., 227 South 6th St., Philadelphia, Pa. Two deposit copies, application and affidavit received at L.C. Sept. 16, 1963.

COPYRIGHT RENEWAL REGISTRATION: RE 521 838 granted to Tasha Tudor, RFD 4, West Brattleboro, Vt. 05301. Marilyn Small, agent for Tasha Tudor the author [sic], swears on Nov. 22, 1991:

A LITTLE PRINCESS, by Frances Hodgson Burnett with renewable illustrations by Tasha Tudor, was originally published Aug. 29, 1963, A 647285. Fees to be charged against account DA 064726, HarperCollins Publishers, 10 East 53rd St., N.Y., N.Y. 10022. Application received Dec. 13, 1991, the effective date of this registration.

L6 _____.

COVER: A gray cast to the jade green cloth.

DUST JACKET: $5.00, at bottom of front flap. Back flap: *The Author* . . . death in 1924 she wrote constantly . . .

L7 _____.

COVER: A slightly lighter and brighter sea-green in a coarser weave resembling cheesecloth.

DUST JACKET: Have not examined one with a price intact. Back flap: . . . death in <u>1924</u> . . .

L8 _____.

   PAGINATION: 7/8″ thick.

   COVER: <u>Bright emerald cloth.</u> Ivory kid paper.

   DUST JACKET: Ivory paper, top corner has been clipped. Bottom line of front flap: 01014 <u>$5.95</u>.
      [This jacket may have been from another book.]

   CONTENTS: Major parts of the dust jacket blurbs are repeated for the first time on the <u>Half title, page</u>
      <u>[1]</u>: A LITTLE PRINCESS ‖ **About the book** . . . ‖ . . . Sara Crewe did indeed seem like a little
      princess when she arrived at Miss ⌋ Minchin's boarding school in London. Her father who had
      brought her from ⌋ India had bought her all sorts of handsome clothes, she had a French maid, a ⌋
      pony and a beautiful doll, Emily, who was to become her great friend. ¶ When Sara had been in
      school some time a dramatic change took place in | her fortunes and her whole life. She
      remained, however, a little princess | throughout. ¶ This story of Sara Crewe has been a favorite
      with generations of children. ⌋ They have delighted in her happiness and wept over her sorrows
      and have ⌋ been enchanted by the mysterious events that bring about a second great ⌋ change in
      Sara's life. ‖ **THE AUTHOR** ‖ Frances Hodgson Burnett was a born storyteller, and even when
      she was a ⌋ young child, living in Manchester, England, her greatest pleasure was in mak- ⌋ ing up
      stories and acting them out, using her dolls as characters. When she was | in her teens her family,
      in search of better fortune, moved to Tennessee and ⌋ there young Frances had her first taste of
      success, for two of her stories were bought and published by an American magazine. From that
      point on her ⌋ career was assured, and until her death in 1924 she wrote constantly and ⌋ produced
      more than forty books and countless short stories. ‖ THE ARTIST ‖ Tasha Tudor's delicate color
      work, her charming pencil drawings in many ⌋ books have made friends all over this country.
      Children and grown-ups alike ⌋ have been drawn to her nostalgic representation of a world of
      another age. ⌋ She has lived in London and knows the square where Miss Minchin's school ⌋ was
      and the streets where Sara walked. Best of all she knows and loves this ⌋ story of another
      century.

   OTHER: Examined a copy inscribed 12/25/72.

L9 _____. [Illustrations . . . America | ISBN-0-397-30693-8]

   PAGINATION: <u>13/16″</u> thick.

   COVER: Emerald cloth cover, stamped as above.

   DUST JACKET: Have not examined one.

   OTHER: Examined a copy with <u>1974 inscription</u>.

L10 _____.

   PAGINATION: Book is <u>7/8″ thick</u>.

   COVER: Sea-green cloth in a coarse cheesecloth weave.

   DUST JACKET: Front flap has upper corner, lower corner clipped. Back flap: . . . mountains in the
      distance. ‖ ISBN-0-397-30693-8.

L11 _____.

PAGINATION: Have not examined the book issued with this dust jacket.

DUST JACKET: Flaps are <u>not clipped</u>. Front flap: . . . little princess. || 01014 <u>$6.50</u>. Back flap: . . . mountains in the distance. || ISBN-0-397-30693-8.

L12 _____.

PAGINATION: As before, on 13 signatures of <u>white</u> paper, <u>1″ thick</u>.

COVER: <u>Emerald</u> cloth, <u>white</u> endpapers.

DUST JACKET: <u>Buff kid-finish paper</u>. Front flap, last line, 01014 $8.95. ISBN bottom of back flap.

L13 _____.

COVER: Emerald-green cloth.

DUST JACKET: <u>White</u> paper. Complete, <u>$10.00</u> in lower right corner, front flap.

L14 _____.

PAGINATION: <u>8 25/32″ x 6 ½″ x 1 1/16″</u>.

COVER: "Library Binding" in a <u>jade green plastic-filled paper</u> over boards, deerskin design. The cover is stamped in gilt as before.

DUST JACKET: Have not examined a copy without price clipped.   A ¾″ x 4″ <u>gold foil label</u> wrapped around the base of spine imprinted: [a row of laurel leaves] | [rule] | *Library Binding*.

L15 _____.

PAGINATION: White <u>kid-finish</u> paper. <u>8 ¾″ x 6 7/16″ x 15/16″</u>.

COVER: <u>Sea-green cloth</u> , stamped in gold front and spine.

DUST JACKET: <u>New design</u>. White paper, printed pink except for flaps, under gloss lamination. Rose borders front and back, and black text except for the title. The A of title is a black fanciful swirl, all other letters are green outlined in black. Front: A | Little Princess | [detail of color illustration from page [49]] |. By Frances Hodgson Burnett | author of *The Secret Garden* | <u>Illustrated</u> by Tasha Tudor. Spine: Burnett [rose] || A LITTLE PRINCESS [laterally] || [rose] | *Lippincott*. Back: Also by Frances Hodgson Burnett | Illustrated by Tasha Tudor || THE SECRET GARDEN || The secret garden—mysterious, walled, and | locked—is the center of Frances Hodgson Bur- | nett's beautiful and moving story of a lonely, | willful little girl and how she finds friends, | health, and happiness when she comes to live in a | great house on the Yorkshire moors. It is a story | that has been loved by boys and girls since its first | publication in 1912, never losing its charm, its | magic, its deep satisfaction. || <u>Trade ISBN 0-397-30693-8</u> [in a computer typeface]. Front flap: THE | TASHA TUDOR | EDITION || A LITTLE PRINCESS | By Frances Hodgson Burnett | Illustr<u>ated</u> by Tasha Tudor | *with a foreword by Phyllis McGinley* | [printer's decoration] | <u>When</u> Sara Crewe <u>arrives</u> at Miss Min- | chin's <u>London</u> boarding school<u>, she does</u> | <u>indeed seem like a little princess. Before</u> | <u>leaving for India</u>, her father <u>got her lovely</u> | clothes, a French maid, a pony and a | beautiful doll <u>whom Sara names</u> Emily. | <u>Sara quickly becomes the darling of the</u> | school and is adored by her teachers and

| classmates until a dramatic change in her | fortunes throws her whole life into a | tumble of trouble and surprising adven- | tures. She remains, however, a little prin- | cess throughout. ¶ This story of Sara Crewe has been a | favorite with generations of children. | They have delighted in her happiness and | wept over her sorrows, and have been | enchanted by the | mysterious events that | bring about the second great change in | Sara's life. ¶ Tasha Tudor, whose pictures for THE | SECRET GARDEN have been treasured by | millions, has re-created for a whole new | generation of readers the unforgettable | images of nineteenth-century London | and Sara, a | little princess. || *J.B. Lippincott   New York*. Back flap: THE AUTHOR || FRANCES HODGSON BURNETT was a born | storyteller, and even when she was a young | child, living in Manchester, England, her | greatest pleasure was in making up stories | and acting them out, using her dolls as char- | acters. When she was in her teens, her family | moved to Tennessee in search of better for- | tune, and there young Frances had her first | taste of success—two of her stories were | bought and published by an American maga- | zine. From that point on her career was as- | sured, and until her death in 1924 she wrote | constantly and produced more than forty | books and countless short stories. || THE ARTIST | TASHA TUDOR'S delicate color work and | charming pencil drawings are loved by mil- | lions of readers who have been drawn to her | nostalgic representation of another time. She | has lived in London and knows the square | where Miss Minchin's school was and the | streets where Sara walked. ¶Now, Tasha Tudor lives in a Vermont | farmhouse big enough to hold her many vis- | iting children, grandchildren, and friends. | Readers of all ages will recognize the work | of one of America's most beloved artists | in this timeless classic, A LITTLE PRINCESS. | Jacket art © 1963, 1985 by Tasha Tudor.

L16 Frances Hodgson Burnett | A Little Princess | Illustrated by Tasha Tudor | [Sara at her attic window] || *J. B. Lippincott* | *New York.*   [A LITTLE PRINCESS | Illustrations copyright © 1963 by Tasha Tudor | Foreword copyright © 1963 by Phyllis McGinley | Printed in the U.S.A. All rights reserved. | [2 ¼″ rule] | Library of Congress Cataloging-in-Publication Data | Burnett, Frances Hodgson, 1849-1924. | A little princess. || Summary: Sara Crewe, a pupil at Miss Minchin's | London school, is left in poverty when her father dies, | but is later rescued by a mysterious benefactor. | [1. Schools—Fiction. 2. Orphans—Fiction. | 3. London (England)—Fiction I. Tudor, Tasha, ill. | II. Title. | PZ7.B934Lg 1985   [Fic] 85-13043 | ISBN 0-397-30693-8 | ISBN 0-31339-X (lib. bdg.) [2¼″ rule]]

> PAGINATION: 8 signatures of white enameled paper: [i-iv] v-vii [viii-x, 1-2] 3-11 [12] 13-48 [49] 50-86 [87] 88-109 [110] 111-118 [119] 120-134 [135] 136-157 [158] 159-187 [188] 189-204 [205] 206-227 [228] 229-243 [244] 245 [246], plus free endpapers. 6 ¼″ x 9 ¼″ x 5/8″ thick.

> COVER: Garnet cloth, stamped in gilt only on spine: Burnett || A LITTLE PRINCESS || *Lippincott* [all printed laterally]. The endpaper illustration now appears in garnet.

> DUST JACKET: The dust jacket is as above, but enlarged by paper 9 ¼″ high and revealing more pink area above and below the rose borders.

> CONTENTS: Half-title without additional text, as in the first printings, page [i]; *By Frances Hodgson Burnett* | *Illustrated by Tasha Tudor* || THE SECRET GARDEN | A LITTLE PRINCESS, [ii]; title page, [iii]; colophon, [iv]; foreword, v-vii; blank, [viii]; contents, [ix-x]; half-title, [1]; blank, [2]; text, 3-245.

> ILLUSTRATIONS: The same 12 color illustrations appear on different un-numbered pages in this new type setting, and now have captions beneath them. Arabic numerals on the chapter head ribbons.

> OTHER: Text entirely reset, expanding the book to 245pp. The title page has remained fairly stable through the many printings. Now, however, the original blue wash background is a light gray wash. Examination copy was autographed 1989.

L17 _____.

> DUST JACKET: A white rectangle is overprinted beneath the text on the back, and the previous black bar code is gone. The 1 7/16 x 2 1/8″ box is nearly filled by: [2 bar codes], 90000 [above the smaller

right] | 9 780397 306930 [beneath the larger left] | ISBN 0-397-30693-8 [beneath all]. TRADE is printed laterally along the left of the left bar code.

OTHER: Publisher's 1792 tree in a circle logo has been added beneath *New York* at the bottom of the colored panel on the title page.

L18 _____. [flame and wave logo] HarperCollins*Publishers*

PAGINATION: Whiter paper than the previous printing.

COVER: Wine cloth in a tighter weave than previous, and with a slight sheen. Slightly rounded spine.

DUST JACKET: At base of front flap: [flame and water logo] HarperCollins*Publishers*.

OTHER: Printed ca. 1996.

PAPERBACK PRINTINGS

L19 _____ . . . . Tudor | [Sara at her window] | *A Harper Trophy Book* | *Harper & Row, Publishers* | [. . . 85-13043 | ISBN 0-397-30693-8 | ISBN 0-397-31339-X (lib. bdg.) | ISBN 0-06-440187-3 (pbk.) | [2 3/16″ rule] | First Harper Trophy edition, 1987 | Published in hardcover by J. B. Lippincott, | New York]

PAGINATION: Perfect bound pulp paper in a paper wrapper: [i-x], [1]-[246] plus the wrapper. 5 1/4″ x 7 9/16″ 5/8″ thick.

CONTENTS: Blank pages [i-ii]; *By Frances Hodgson Burnett | Illustrated by Tasha Tudor* | THE SECRET GARDEN | A LITTLE PRINCESS, [iii]; blank, [iv]; half-title, [v]; blank, [vi]; title, [vii]; colophon, [viii]; contents, [ix-x]. Colophon cites foreword copyright, but there is none; the foreword has been omitted from this printing.

COVER: New information, top front, above the rose border: HARPER TROPHY $2.50. Spine printed laterally in black ink: J187 Burnett A LITTLE PRINCESS Harper & Row. Back cover, new black text on a white panel within a green frame outlined in black on the pink ground of cover: Beloved by generations of young readers | [3 ½″ rule] | Ages 9 and up || Ten-year-old Sara Crewe wasn't really a princess. But | she seemed like one when she first arrived at Miss | Minchin's London boarding school. Her father had | given her all sorts of beautiful clothes before he had | returned to India, as well as a pony, a French maid, and | a wonderful doll named Emily. Sara wasn't spoiled, | though—almost everyone wanted to be her friend. ¶ Suddenly a terrible misfortune left Sara penniless— | and, she thought, forgotten. She had to wear old rags, | live in a dingy attic, and work for her living. It wasn't a | very happy life for a young girl. Then mysterious | changes began, showing Sara she had never really been | all alone. || **Frances Hodgson Burnett** is the author of the | classic THE SECRET GARDEN, also illustrated by Tasha | Tudor and available in a Harper Trophy edition. | 0287 | 0[bar code]1 | 46594 00250 | ISBN 0-06-440187-1 [in a 'computer' typeface]

L20 _____ . . . . Tudor | [Sara at her window] | [torch logo] HarperTrophy | *A Division of* HarperCollins *Publishers* [...ISBN 0-06-440187-1 (pbk.) | [2 3/16″ rule] | First ... New York]

COVER: Top front, HARPER TROPHY $3.50 US | $4.95 CDN. Spine: Burnett A LITTLE PRINCESS Harper Trophy. Back: . . . [2 bar codes], above the right, 40187; beneath the larger left, 0 46594 00350 8. . . Two different bar codes are printed sideways at the lower left corner, inside front cover: above the right 50350; beneath the left 9 780064 401876 || ISBN 0-06-440187-1.

L21 _____. [A LITTLE PRINCESS | Illustrations copyright ©1963 by Tasha Tudor | Foreword copyright ©1963 by Phyllis McGinley | All rights reserved. No part of this book may be used | or reproduced in any manner whatsoever without | written permission except in the case of brief | quotations embodied in critical articles and reviews. | Printed in the United States of America. | For information address HarperCollins | Children's Books, a division of HarperCollins | Publishers, 10 East 53rd Street, New York, NY 10022. | [2 3/16″ rule] | Library of Congress . . .   ISBN 0-06-440187-<u>1</u> (pbk.) | [2 3/16″ rule] | Published in hardcover by <u>HarperCollins Publisher.</u> | First Harper Trophy edition, 1987]

    COVER: Upper left above the rose border: HARPER TROPHY; and upper right, <u>$3.95 US | $5.25 CDN</u>. Printed in black on an <u>over-printed round green seal</u> at lower right: By the | author of | THE SECRET | GARDEN. Spine as before. Back cover continues the pattern of the paperbacks but has <u>omitted the headline</u> from this printing: Ten-year-old Sara…Harper Trophy edition. | [within a black line box] Now a WONDER WORKS sm television **presentation**. | [Two bar codes, above the right <u>50395></u>; beneath the larger left, <u>9 780064 401876</u>. At right of bar-codes: **HarperTrophy | $3.95 US / $5.25 CDN** | 9 up | ISBN 0-06-440187-1. Two different bar codes are printed sideways at the lower left corner, inside front cover. Above the right, <u>50305></u>; beneath the larger left <u>9 780064 401876 | ISBN 0-06-440187-1</u>. Inside front cover, upper left: **HarperTrophy | $3.95 US / $5.25 CDN.**

    <u>The inside back cover is an elaborate advertisement</u> within a double-ruled rectangle within a leafy border, all black. NOW ON VIDEO! [inverse in a black lozenge centered in the top of the border]. **1990 Parents' Choice Award Winner |** *A Little Princess* | ***From WonderWorks*** | "The best family drama series on television today." | –T.V. Guide || — • — || Frances Hodgson Burnett's classic is lovingly brought to life | in this critically acclaimed **WonderWorks** production, starring | Nigel Havers and Amelia Shankley. || "The story is good, the telling is great, | the children are unforgettable." | – The Washington Post || **Deluxe two-tape set only $29.95** | LIT120 || To order, Call | **TOLL FREE (800) 262-8600** | or ask your local video, book or record store. || — • — || **Public Media Video** | Box 800 | Concord, MA 01742 || [Public Media | Video logo] [**WONDERWORKS** | FAMILY MOVIE logo] || ©1992 Public Media Video. A Public Media Incorporated Release. All rights reserved.

L22 _____.

    PAGINATION: 7 5/8″ x 5 1/8″ x 5/8″

    COVER: HARPER TROPHY   <u>$4.50 US | $5.95 CDN</u>. The bar-codes are smaller, 5/8″ and 1/2″ high, and above the right, <u>50450</u>; else as before. The coding and text inside the front cover have <u>changed to reflect price increase,</u> and the bar-codes are smaller. The inside back cover has no text, without the WONDERWORKS ad.

L23 _____.

    HarperCollins plans to reissue a hard cover edition with updated typography, and color in Spring 1999.

L24 _____.

    HarperCollins plans to reissue a paperback edition with updated typography, and color in Spring 1999, without a locket.

L25 _____.

    HarperCollins plans to release the same paperback, but with a locket on a chain in Spring 1999. See Secret Garden for the corresponding key and chain.

L26 *Little Women* || BY LOUISA M. ALCOTT || *Illustrated by* | TASHA TUDOR || THE WORLD PUBLISHING COMPANY | NEW YORK AND CLEVELAND [Published by the World Publishing Company | 110 East 59th Street, New York, New York 10022 | Published simultaneously in Canada by | Nelson, Foster & Scott Ltd. | Library of Congress catalog card number: 75-82776 | Illustrations copyright © 1969 by Tasha Tudor | All rights reserved. No part of this book may be reproduced | in any form without written permission from the publisher, except for | brief passages included in a review appearing in a newspaper | or magazine. Printed in the United States of America.]

PAGINATION: [i-ii, 1-5] 6 [7-12] 13-121 [122] 123-267 [268-270] 271-544 pp. plus endpapers and full-page plates. 6 ½″ x 9 ½″.

COVER: Carmine cloth, illustration from page 534 <u>stamped in gilt</u> on front, as is the spine: ALCOTT | Little Women [printed laterally] | WORLD. <u>Top edge is painted yellow.</u> Mustard end papers with 2 pencil drawings in olive, repeated front and back: two adolescent girls and piano in parlor, and two young ladies sewing and reading. These drawings do not appear elsewhere in the book

DUST JACKET: Buff paper with black text, highlights in red. Watercolor (four adolescent girls sitting in a pine grove high above a village –Concord, Massachusetts ?) wraps around back, spine and front. Front: Little | Women [red] || Illustrated by | TASHA TUDOR || LOUISA M. ALCOTT [black]. Spine, Little Women [red, laterally] | ALCOTT || WORLD; and at lower back right, A3163 [black]. Front flap, $ 5.95 [black], The Tasha Tudor Edition of | Little Women | LOUISA MAY ALCOTT | *Illustrated by* | TASHA TUDOR [red] || "Christmas won't be Christmas without | any presents," grumbled Jo. With their | father away in the army, the March | family's finances were low—but nothing | could keep down their irrepressible high | spirits for long. ¶ Tomboy Jo, romantic Meg, artistic | Amy, and gentle Beth are the four teen- | aged March sisters who have been be- | loved by generations of readers since | this book was first written over one hun- | dred years ago. Humor, tragedy, ro- | mance, and realism make their story as | lively and appealing today as when it | was written. Louisa Alcott wrote frankly of things she had herself experienced, | and readers will respond to the ring of | truth in this warm story of a loving | family. ¶ Tasha Tudor has enriched the narrative | with over fifty of her finest pencil draw- | ings and eight exquisite watercolor | paintings. Based on careful research as | to place and period, the illustrations | spring from the artist's lifelong love of | this book, and express the characters | exactly as Louisa May Alcott herself | must have seen them. ¶ Now at last the most famous and popu- | lar of all American stories for girls has | been given its ideal interpretation in this | classic edition, with beautiful pictures by | America's favorite illustrator of books for | young people. [black] || The World Publishing Company | NEW YORK AND CLEVELAND [red]. Bottom corner clipped.

Back flap: [pencil sketch of a Victorian lady writing at a parlor table, a fireplace, a window] | LOUISA MAY ALCOTT [red] was born in | 1832 in Pennsylvania, but the family | soon moved to Concord, Massachusetts, | where she spent the happiest years of | her life. She had to work to help her | family's strained finances, and, like Jo | in the book, wrote many stories and | books, of which *Little Women*, pub- | lished in 1868, is best known. [black] || TASHA TUDOR [red] is America's most fa- | mous and beloved illustrator. She has | written and illustrated children's books | that tell of her own family's life in rural | New England, and has illustrated many | fairy tales and classics, among them | Kenneth Grahame's *The Wind in the | Willows. Take Joy: The Tasha Tudor | Christmas Book* is a perennial favorite | with young and old. Mrs. Tudor, who | has four children, lives in a lovely old | New Hampshire farmhouse where, in | addition to her painting, she cultivates | the traditional arts of good living as well | as a most beautiful flower garden. [black] || The World Publishing Company | NEW YORK AND CLEVELAND [red].

CONTENTS: Half-title, page [i]; blank pages, [ii, 1, 8, 10, 12, 268, 270]; title page, [3]; contents, [5] -6; list of illustrations, [7]; preface, [9]; Part First [11]; Part Second [269].

ILLUSTRATIONS: Eight full-page color illustrations: Frontispiece, *"Play something, Amy."* and, facing pages 16 *"I hate to think I've got to grow up..."*, 45 *They had a grand polka*, 147 *"Welcome to Camp Laurence!"*, 177 *"I wish I was a horse..."*, 406 *"Oh, Teddy, I'm so sorry, so desperately sorry..."*, 438 *"Mornin' now," announced Demi.*, 475 *...waiting for Laurie to come.* Black and white vignettes on pages [5], [7] and 47 chapter heads with Arabic chapter numbers.

OTHER: Printing stamp at bottom of page 544: 1 2 3 4 5 73 72 71 70 69.

COPYRIGHT REGISTRATION: A 111205 granted to Tasha Tudor, Route 1, Contoocook, NH 03229 for illustrations. Linda F. Hersh, agent for claimant, swears on Oct. 31, 1969:

LITTLE WOMEN, with new illustrations by Tasha Tudor, a U.S. citizen, was published Oct. 31, 1969. The book was printed by World Publishing Press, 2231 West 110 St., Cleveland, Oh. Fees to be charged to The World Publishing Co., 110 East 59th St., N.Y., N.Y. 10022. Application and affidavit and to deposit copies received Nov. 1969 [illegible].

L27 _____.

COVER: **World Library Binding**. The top edge is unpainted. The pictorial cloth cover is imprinted with the same illustration as the dust jacket from the trade edition. There are two changes to the type. The code at back bottom is A3163W. An additional black trademark appears above the horizon and to the right of the yellow leaves on the back cover illustration: WLB | WORLD LIBRARY BINDING. The L of the initial is elongated and stylized into a tree with a leafy top added. Its base sits on the bottom line separating the words "world" and "library."

DUST JACKET: Have not examined one.

CONTENTS: The body of the book is nearly identical to the first trade edition above.

ILLUSTRATIONS: This copy has one color plate misplaced; page [7] lists "Mornin' now..." opposite page 438. It is actually bound one sheet off opposite page 440.

L28 _____. Published simultaneously in Canada by Nelson, Foster & Scott Ltd. Have not examined a copy.

L29 _____. . . . TUDOR ‖ COLLINS [tree in circle logo] WORLD | Cleveland, Ohio 44111 [Published by Wm. Collins + World Publishing | 2080 W. 117th St., Cleveland, Ohio 44111 | Published simultaneously . . . United States of America.]

PAGINATION: [i-ii, 1-5] 6 [7-12] 13-121 [122] 123-267 [268-270] 271-544 pp. plus endpapers and full-page plates. 6 ½" x 9 ½". The first edition and much of this version was printed on ivory laid paid with a strong chain pattern. However, here certain signatures are printed on a buff paper with a kid finish, specifically pages i-16, 33-48, 177-192, 401-416, 465-480 and 529-544.

COVER: Carmine cloth, illustration from page 534 stamped in gilt on front, as is the spine: ALCOTT | Little Women [printed laterally] | WORLD. Top edge, plain. Ivory, plain end papers.

DUST JACKET: Illustrated as before. Publisher attributions change on spine and at the bottom of both flaps, all in black to: [tree in circle logo] | COLLINS | [very small rule] | WORLD. There is no price printed on the front flap.

ILLUSTRATIONS: As before, with one missing plate. *"Mornin' now,"* is listed on page [7], but is lacking from facing page 438.

OTHER: Printed from the same plates as the first edition, and therefore, bearing the string of numerals 1 through 5, and years 73 through 69 on page 544. However, the title page and dust jacket are imprinted with the correct publisher <u>Collins World</u>, belying this book's second state and publisher.

L30 _____. . . . TASHA TUDOR ‖ [tree in a circle logo] | **COLLINS** [Published by William Collins Publishers, Inc. | New York and Cleveland | ISBN 0-529-00529-8 | Library of Congress . . . United States of America.]

COVER: Spine, stamped in gilt: ALCOTT | Little Women [printed laterally] | <u>COLLINS</u>. Illustration from page 534 <u>blind stamped</u> on front cover. <u>Top edge unpainted</u>. <u>End papers are white</u>.

DUST JACKET: Designed as above with these changes: Code on back: A3163. Complete with <u>no printed price</u>, but an applied oval label has hand written 15.95. Red publisher's imprint at base of front flap: [tree in circle logo] | <u>COLLINS</u>. Back flap revised in larger type: TASHA TUDOR [red] is America's <u>most | famous</u> and beloved . . . lives in a lovely old | <u>Vermont</u> farmhouse where, in <u>addi- | tion</u> to her painting, she cultivates <u>the | traditional</u> arts of good living as well | as a most beautiful flower garden. ‖ [tree in circle logo] | <u>COLLINS</u> [both red] ‖ *Printed in U.S.A.* [black at lower left corner].

CONTENTS: The body of the book is nearly identical to the first trade edition above.

ILLUSTRATIONS: Color plate correctly bound facing page 438.

OTHER: Printer's mark on page 544 is **HB7J** running laterally at lower right gutter. This printing has a deep 3/16″ <u>square blind punch</u> at the lower right back, square. The dust jacket reference to an old Vermont farmhouse places this printing after 1972.

L31 _____.

DUST JACKET: Complete <u>without a printed price</u>.

OTHER: <u>No printer's mark on page 544.</u>

L 32 _____.

DUST JACKET: Lower left back, in black: <u>0-529-00529-8</u>. Front flap, upper corner: <u>$15.00</u>.

L33 *The Lord | Is My Shepherd* | THE TWENTY-THIRD PSALM | *Illustrated by* | *Tasha Tudor* | PHILOMEL BOOKS | NEW YORK [*Illustrations copyright © 1980 by Tasha Tudor.* | *Special contents copyright © 1980 by Philomel Books* | *Philomel Books are published by* | *The Putnam Publishing Group,* | *200 Madison Avenue, New York, NY 10016.* | *All rights reserved. Except for use in a review,* | *the reproduction or utilization of this work* | *in any form or by any electronic, mechanical, or other means,* | *now known or hereafter invented, is forbidden* | *without the written permission of the publisher.* ‖ Library of Congress Cataloging in Publication Data | Bible. O.T. Psalms XXIII. English. Authorized. | 1980. | The Lord is My Shepherd: | The Twenty-third Psalm. | SUMMARY: Presents an illustrated version | of the twenty-third Psalm. | [1. Bible. O.T. Psalms XXIII] I. Tudor, Tasha. | II. Title. | BS1450.23d.T8 1980 223'.205203 79-27134 | ISBN-0-399-20756-2]

PAGINATION: [28] pp. including free endpapers. 8 1/4″ x 6 7/8″.

COVER: Cream paper wrapped over boards. Illustration from page [7] is reproduced on the front cover to resemble a pasted label; likewise, page [2] on the back cover. All text in black, front, printed between church and the chipmunk: *The Lord | Is My Shepherd* | THE TWENTY-THIRD PSALM | *Illustrated by* | *Tasha Tudor*. Spine printed laterally: TASHA TUDOR The Lord is My Shepherd   PHILOMEL.

DUST JACKET: Identical to covers with the addition at lower right back, beneath the illustrated panel: *ISBN 0-399-20756-2*. Front flap: *ISBN 0-399-20756-2 $6.95* ‖ *The Lord Is My Shepherd* | THE TWENTY-THIRD PSALM | *Illustrated by Tasha Tudor* ‖ The most cherished of all psalms is inter- | preted here by one of America's most | beloved illustrators. The text of this su- | perb expression of faith is in the familiar | and beautiful prose of the King James | Version. Tenderly depicting gentle pas- | toral vistas and peaceful village scenes, | Tasha Tudor's watercolor paintings com- | plement the exquisite beauty and sim- | plicity of the verse and capture the eternal | comfort of its message. This is a book to | be treasured by all ages, one that will be | lovingly shared by all members of the | family. || [2 ¼″ color oval, a detail of a girl sitting and holding her knees from the page [25] illustration.] Back flap: [3 1/8″ x 2 5/8″ black and white photo of Tudor painting with corgi on her lap, along the right side]: *Photograph by Ulrike Welsch* | TASHA TUDOR'S illustrations have | been treasured by generations of people, | young and old. The author-artist of more | than fifty books, including *Take Joy!* and | *A Book of Christmas*, she is also the sub- | ject of the recently published biographi- | cal portrait *Drawn From New England:* | *Tasha Tudor*, by her daughter, Bethany | Tudor. Born in Boston, Tasha Tudor now | lives on a farm in Vermont. || PHILOMEL BOOKS || *are published by* | *The Putnam Publishing Group* | *200 Madison Avenue, New York, N.Y. 10016.*

CONTENTS: Title page, [3]; colophon, [4]; half-title, [5]; text as part of illustrations on pp. [7-8, 11-12, 14, 17-18, 20-22, 24]. *About the Twenty-Third Psalm* . . . , [26]. Only page [27] lacks an illustration and has this text: *About Tasha Tudor* | Tasha Tudor's illustrations are treasured by people of all ages, and she has | won many honors for her books. Born in Boston, she grew up in New | England, where she had ample opportunity to observe the beauty of the | rural scene and the animals and flowers of the countryside that she | depicts with such skill and love in her pencil drawings and delicate | watercolors. ¶ Her first book, "Pumpkin Moonshine," a tiny calico-covered vol- | ume which she both wrote and illustrated, appeared in 1938. She has | illustrated more than 50 books since then, including such classics as *The* | *Wind in the Willows* by Kenneth Grahame, and *Little Women* by Louisa | May Alcott, as well as books of her own authorship and anthologies such | as the perennially popular *Take Joy!* and the recent *A Book of Christmas.* | The Twenty-Third Psalm has always been her favorite of the psalms and | in 1965, she created the illustrations for a charming miniature edition. | For many years, however, she has longed to do a new, larger version that | would allow her the scope to render the scenes in full and sensitive detail. | The present volume is the happy fulfillment of her dream. ¶ Ms. Tudor now lives on a farm in Vermont. She is the subject of the | recently published biographical portrait, *Drawn from New England: Tasha* | *Tudor*, written by her daughter, Bethany.

ILLUSTRATIONS: Most pages including endpapers have a 6 3/4″ x 4 9/16″ color illustration featuring a large twig oval framing either text or a major subject. These pages are illustrations only: [6, 9-10, 13, 15-16, 19, 23, 25]. Page [26] reproduces an oval detail of cow, girl and corgi from page [11]. The illustrations have been changed in small part from the 1965 Achille St. Onge miniatures: sheep for a white horse, goats for horses.

COPYRIGHT REGISTRATION: VA 65-593 granted to Tasha Tudor, R.F.D. #4, West Brattleboro, Vt. Sarah W. Crane, agent for Tasha Tudor, swears on Nov. 12, 1980:

THE LORD IS MY SHEPHERD: THE TWENTY-THIRD PSALM, with illustrations by Tasha Tudor a U.S. citizen, was completed in 1980 and published Oct. 31, 1980. Fee charged against deposit account DAO 22438, G.P. Putnam's Sons for Philomel Books, 200 Madison Ave., N.Y., N.Y. 10016. Application and deposit received at L.C. Dec. 1, 1980.

L34 _____. [*Illustrations copyright... Philomel Books* | *a member of* | *The Putnam Publishing Group,* | *51 Madison Avenue, New York, NY 10010* | *All rights reserved . . .*]

COVER: Background color changed to butterscotch.

DUST JACKET: Front flap: *ISBN 0-399-20756-2 $8.95* . . . Back flap: . . . **PHILOMEL BOOKS** | a member of | The Putnam Publishing Group | 51 Madison Avenue, New York, N.Y. 10010

OTHER: This is the second impression, even though it is not so labeled.

L35 _____. [. . . ISBN-0-399-20756-2 | <u>Third impression</u>]

COVER: Texture resembles a lightly pebbled leather, probably from an applied finish.

OTHER: The paper of the book also has a pebbly appearance under light.

L36 _____. [...*written permission of the publisher.* | <u>*Published simultaneously in Canada.*</u> || *Library of Congress Cataloging in Publication Data* | *Bible. O.T. Psalms XXIII. English. Authorized.* | *1980.* | *The Lord is My Shepherd:* | *The Twenty-third Psalm.* | *SUMMARY: Presents an illustrated version* | *of the twenty-third Psalm.* | *[1. Bible.O.T. Psalms XXIII] I. Tudor, Tasha.* | *II. Title.* | *BS1450.23d.T8 1980 223'.205203 79-27134* | *ISBN-0-399-20756-2* | *Fourth impression*]

COVER: Gloss laminate finish over boards.

DUST JACKET: Front flap, upper corner: <u>*$8.95*</u> | [rule] | *$12.50 (Can)* . . .

OTHER: Verso has been reset entirely <u>in italic</u>. The paper has a <u>dull smooth finish</u>.

L37 _____. Have not examined a *fifth impression.*

L38 _____. [. . . *Special contents copyright © 1980 by Philomel Books* | *a division of* | <u>*The Putnam &*</u> <u>*Grosset*</u> *Group* | *200 Madison Avenue,* New York, NY <u>*10016*</u> . . . *without the written permission of the publisher.* | <u>*Published simultaneously in Canada*</u> . . . *Data* | *Bible. O.T. Psalms XXIII, English* . . . <u>*Sixth impression*</u>]

COVER: Gloss laminate finish over boards.

DUST JACKET: Have not examined one with price intact. Gloss laminate over paper. Back of jacket, lower right corner overlapping the illustration, a bar code device in a white field 2″ x 1 3/8″: ISBN 0-399-20756-2 | 50895 [over the smaller right bar code] | [two bar codes] | 9 780399 207563 [under the larger left bar code]. Back flap: . . . lives on a farm in Vermont. || *Jacket art c 1980 by Tasha Tudor* || **PHILOMEL BOOKS** || *A DIVISON OF* | *The Putnam & Grosset Group* | *200 Madison Avenue, New York, NY 1001<u>6</u>.* The ISBN is no longer printed <u>under</u> the illustrated panel.

L39 _____. [...*Special contents copyright © 1980 by Philomel Books,<u>_</u>* | *a <u>division of</u> The Putnam &* Grosset *Group* | *200 Madison Avenue, New York, NY 10016.* | <u>*Published simultaneously in Canada.*</u> | *All rights reserved. Except for use in a review,* | *the reproduction or utilization of<u>this work in any</u>* | *form or by any electronic, mechanical, or other means,* | *now known or hereafter invented, is forbidden* | *without the written permission of the publisher.* || *Library of Congress..ISBN 0-399-20756-2* | <u>*Seventh impression.*</u>]

COVER: The bar code box is printed on the back for the first time, as well as the dust jacket. ISBN 0-399-20756-2 | <u>90000</u> [above the smaller right code] | [two bar codes] | 9 780399 207563 [under the larger left bar code.

DUST JACKET: Front flap of dust jacket: <u>$9.95</u> | [3/4″ rule] | $12.95 (CAN) || *The Lord Is My Shepherd* . . . Back flap: . . . lives on a farm in Vermont. || *Jacket art © 1980 by Tasha Tudor* | [1 5/8″ rule] | <u>*Reinforced for Library Use*</u> || PHILOMEL BOOKS | *a division of* | *The Putnam & Grosset Group* | *200 Madison <u>Avenue</u>* | *<u>New</u> York, NY 10016.* Lower right back, the bar code box as on the cover.

OTHER: The data on the title page verso is in italic and reduced in size.

243

L40 _____. [*Illustrations copyright . . . ISBN 0-399-20756-2* | *9 10 8*]

> COVER: Re-designed bar code. Lower right back, a 1 3/8″ x 2″ white box with: ISBN 0-399-20756-2 | [bar code] | UPC [printed laterally at left of bar code] | 0 48228 20756 6.

> DUST JACKET: Bar code matches the book. Have not examined a copy with price intact. Examined one with a hand-written store price label: 10.95, suggesting the printed price was lower and had been clipped.

L41 _____. [*Illustrations copyright . . . ISBN-0-399-20756-2* | *9 10*]

> DUST JACKET: Front flap: $9.95 | [3/4″ rule] |$12.95 (CAN) || *The Lord Is* . . .

L42 _____. [*Illustrations copyright...ISBN-0-399-20756-2* | *10*]

> COVER: New bar code on back: 90000> [above smaller right code] | [2 bar codes] | EAN [laterally along left side of bar codes] | 9 780399 207563 [beneath the larger left bar code] | ISBN 0-399-20756-2.

> DUST JACKET: Same bar coding as cover. Price clipped from examination copy, which has a handwritten store label applied: 9/95   12^{95}.

L43 _____. [*Illustrations copyright...ISBN-0-399-20756-2* | *11 13 15 17 19 20 18 16 14 12*]

> DUST JACKET: Front flap, upper corner: $12.95 USA | [3/4″ rule] | $17.50 CAN.

L44 _____. [*Illustrations copyright...ISBN-0-399-20756-2* | *13 15 17 19 20 18 16 14 12*]

> DUST JACKET: Back flap ends with a new phrase: *New York, New York 10016* || *Printed in Hong Kong.*

L45 *The Lord* | *Is My Shepherd* | THE TWENTY-THIRD PSALM | *Illustrated by* |

Tasha Tudor || LUTTERWORTH PRESS | Guildford Surrey | England   [First published in Great Britain 1982 || Illustrations copyright © 1980 by Tasha Tudor | Special contents copyright © 1980 by | Philomel Books (Putnam Publishing Group, New York) || ISBN 0-7188-2541-1 || All rights reserved. No part of this publication | may be reproduced, stored in a retrieval system, | or transmitted, in any form or by any means, | electronic, mechanical, photocopying, recording or | otherwise, without the prior permission of | Lutterworth Press, Farnham Road, Guildford, Surrey || Printed in Hong Kong | by Colorcraft Ltd]

> PAGINATION: [28] pp. including free endpapers. 8 1/4″ x 6 7/8″.

> COVER: Buff paper under gloss laminate wrapped over boards. Illustrations like 1st US edition. Spine printed laterally: TASHA TUDOR The Lord is My Shepherd   [Double L | P logo. Two L's back-to-back above two P's back-to-back].

> DUST JACKET: Illustrations and text of front, spine and back as cover. Front flap: *The Lord Is My Shepherd* | THE TWENTY-THIRD PSALM | *Illustrated by* | *Tasha Tudor* || The best-loved of all the psalms is inter- | preted here by a favourite artist. Tasha | Tudor has chosen the familiar and beauti- | ful prose of the Authorised Version. The | tranquil fields and woods, the peaceful | village homes, in her watercolours, com- | plement the beauty and simplicity of the | verse and capture the eternal comfort of | its message. || A book to be shared by all the family and | treasured by all ages. || Illustrated in full colour throughout. || ISBN 0-7188-2541-1. [lower corner clipped]   Back flap: Other books by | TASHA TUDOR || 'First Books' contain prayers and graces | chosen for their direct simplicity and | illustrated with delicacy and charm, to | delight the youngest members of the | family: || FIRST PRAYERS || FIRST GRACES || MORE

PRAYERS || 'For the very young. Presented and illus- | trated in a delightful manner.' | - *Sunday School Chronicle* || 'The prayers express simply for little | children the ever-loving presence of | God.'   - *Baptist Times* || [double L | P logo, as on spine] || LUTTERWORTH PRESS | Luke House, Farnham Road | Guildford, Surrey

CONTENTS: Like the New York imprint, and page [27] has the illustration of girl and night sky detail from page [25], as well as this abbreviated text: *About Tasha Tudor* | Tasha Tudor's illustrations are treasured by people of all ages, and she has | won many honors for her books. Born in Boston, she grew up in New | England, where she had ample opportunity to observe the beauty of the | rural scene. ¶ Her first book, "Pumpkin Moonshine," a tiny calico-covered vol- | ume which she both wrote and illustrated, appeared in 1938. She has | illustrated more than 50 books since then, including such classics as *The | Wind in the Willows* by Kenneth Grahame, and *Little Women* by Louisa | May Alcott, as well as books of her own authorship and anthologies such | as the perennially popular *Take Joy!*

ILLUSTRATIONS: The only change from the New York imprint is including the gazing girl detail, previously on the front flap of dust jacket to page [27].

OTHER: Examined a copy inscribed 9th December 1984.

L46   _____. . . . *Illustrated by* | *Tasha Tudor* | LUTTERWORTH PRESS   [First published in Great Britain 1982] Reprinted 1985 || Lutterworth Press | 7 All Saints' Passage | Cambridge CB2 3LS || Illustrations copyright . . . Printed in Singapore]

COVER: Yellow paper wrapped over boards. Illustrations like 1st US edition. Spine printed laterally: TASHA TUDOR The Lord is My Shepherd   [L in circle logo]. Additional text on back, lower left: £3.95 net; bottom center, Lutterworth Press | 7 All Saints' Passage | Cambridge CB2 3LS; right, ISBN 0-7188-2541-1 | [7/8″ x 1 5/16″ white box overlaps pictorial panel slightly, contains bar code and number] | 9 780718 825416].

DUST JACKET: Have not examined one; probably never issued. Price label applied to cover.

OTHER: A paper label was placed over the printed net price on the back cover, with this text: PUBLISHERS PRICE [red] | £5.95.

MINIATURE EDITION

L47 THE LORD IS | MY SHEPHERD [teal] | The Twenty-Third Psalm [carmine] | ILLUSTRATED BY | Tasha Tudor [teal] | PHILOMEL BOOKS | New York [gray]   [Illustrations copyright © 1980 by Tasha Tudor. | Special contents copyright © 1980 by Philomel Books, | a division of The Putnam & Grosset Group, | 200 Madison Avenue, NY, NY 10016. Miniature | edition published in 1989 by Philomel Books. | Published simultaneously in Canada. | All rights reserved. Printed in Singapore. | Calligraphy by Jeanyee Wong | Library of Congress number: 79-21734 | First miniature edition printing.]

PAGINATION: [28] pp. including free endpapers. 5″ x 4 3/16″

COVER: Teal paper wrapped over board covers and spine. A new front cover illustration in a green wash employs the twig border now as a high arch gate leading into a meadow where an ox-drawn hay cart is being loaded; dogs, chicken and children nearby. Cover text is Wong's calligraphy like the title page, but the colors have been reversed. Main title and illustration statement are carmine, not teal; sub-title is teal not carmine. Spine printed in white in the same hand: TASHA TUDOR THE LORD IS MY SHEPHERD The Twenty-Third Psalm PHILOMEL. Plain back, no text.

DUST JACKET: Identical to cover. Front flap, only the blurb from the first edition, and it has been reset: The most cherished of all psalms | is interpreted here by one of America's | most beloved illustrators. The text of | this superb expression of faith is in the | familiar and beautiful prose of the King | James Version. Tenderly depicting gen– | tle pastoral vistas and peaceful village | scenes, Tasha Tudor's watercolor | paintings complement the exquisite | beauty and simplicity of the verse and | capture the eternal comfort of its mes– | sage. This is a book to be treasured by | all ages, one that will be lovingly | shared by all members of the family. Back flap: TASHA TUDOR'S illustrations have | been treasured by generations of peo-⌊ple, young and old. The author-artist⌊of more than fifty books, including *Take* | *Joy!* and *A Book of Christmas*, she is also⌊the subject of the biographical portrait⌊*Drawn From New England: Tasha Tudor,*⌊by her daughter, Bethany Tudor. Born⌊in Boston, Tasha Tudor now lives⌊in Vermont. ‖ Jacket art ©1989 by Tasha Tudor ‖ PHILOMEL BOOKS | *a division of The Putnam & Grosset Group* | 200 Madison Avenue | New York, NY 10016 ‖ Printed in Singapore.

ILLUSTRATIONS: As in the larger 1980 edition, plus the new cover/dust jacket illustration.

CONTENTS: Pages [26-27], teal calligraphy titles and the text has been re-set creating these new line breaks: Page [26]: About The Twenty-Third Psalm | . . . best- | loved . . . the | Book of . . . praise." | Almost . . . one | or another . . . thousand | years . . . the | conviction . . . have | made . . . King | David . . . James | Version . . . it | is this translation . . . Tudor | has chosen for this book. Page [27]: About Tasha Tudor | . . . ages,⌊and . . . Boston,⌊she . . . opportunity⌊to . . . and⌊flowers . . . and⌊ love. . . watercolors . . . calico-covered⌊volume . . . 1938.⌊She has illustrated more than 60 books since then, including such⌊classics . . . and *Lit-* | *tle Women* . . . own⌊authorship . . . *Take* | *Joy!*, *A Book of Christmas*, and the keepsake *Advent Calendar*. The⌊Twenty-Third . . . Psalms. | She created the larger version, from which this miniature ver- | sion was created, in 1980. ¶ Ms. Tudor now lives . . . subject⌊of the. . . *Tasha* | *Tudor* . . . Bethany.

OTHER: A companion volume to and issued in a slip case with *Give Us This Day, The Lord's Prayer*, *q.v.* for a description of slipcase.

COPYRIGHT REGISTRATION: VA 371 181 granted to Tasha Tudor, Rt. #4, Box 144, West Brattleboro, Vt. 05301. Louise Bates, Putnam Publishing group, 200 Madison Avenue, N.Y., N.Y. 10016, agent for Tasha Tudor, swears on Oct. 25, 1989:

THE LORD IS MY SHEPHERD, THE TWENTY-THIRD PSALM jacket art illustrated by Tasha Tudor, a U.S. citizen, was published Oct. 16, 1989. This new jacket art was completed in 1989 as derivative work for THE LORD IS MY SHEPHERD, THE TWENTY-THIRD PSALM (1980). Fees to deposit account DAO 38288, Putnam Publishing Group (Phil). Application and deposit copy received Oct. 30, 1989, the effective date of this registration.

L48 _____. Have not examined 2nd printing.

L49 _____. Have not examined 3rd printing.

L50 _____. Have not examined 4th printing.

L51 _____. . . . Tasha Tudor [teal] | PHILOMEL BOOKS [Illustrations copyright . . . 79-21734 | ISBN 0-399-21892-0 | 5 7 9 10 8 6]

COVER: UPC codes in a white box 2″ x 7/8″ at lower right back: ISBN 0-399-21892-0 | 90000 [over smaller right bar code] | [2 bar codes] EAN [laterally along the left code] | 9 780399 218927 [beneath the larger left bar code].

DUST JACKET: UPC white box as on cover. Front flap: $4.95 | [7/16″ rule] | ($6.50 CAN).

OTHER: New York does not appear at the foot of the title page. From the boxed set.

L52 _____. [Illustrations copyright © 1980... 79-21734 | ISBN 0-399-21892-0 | 7 9 10 8 6]

OTHER: Purchased new, without box or companion volume, June 1996.

L53 _____. [Illustrations copyright © 1980... 79-21734 | ISBN 0-399-21892-0 | _7_ 9 10 8]

DUST JACKET: Front flap: $5.95 USA | [3/4″ rule] | ($7.75 CAN).

OTHER: Purchased new, without box or companion volume, November 1996.

L54 _____.

DUST JACKET: Seventh printing, another distribution. The upper corner of the front flap has been clipped to remove an earlier price. A publisher's <u>gold foil label</u> applied to the upper left back: overprinted in blue to reveal the gold price, $ 5 ⁹⁵.

L55 _____. [Illustrations copyright © 1980...79-21734 | ISBN 0-399-21892-0 | 9 10 _8_]

DUST JACKET: Front flap: $5.95 USA| [3/4″ rule] | ($7.<u>95</u> CAN).

OTHER: Purchased new, without box or companion volume, February 1997.

L56 **THE LORD WILL | LOVE THEE** | Sara Klein Clarke || *Illustrated by Tasha Tudor* [a child in a caftan praying] | **THE WESTMINSTER PRESS • PHILADELPHIA.** [COPYRIGHT, MCMLIX, BY W. L. JENKINS || *All rights reserved*– no part of this book may be reproduced in any | form without permission in writing from the publisher, except | by a reviewer who wises to quote brief passages in connection | with a review in magazine or newspaper. || *A Prayer:* from *First Prayers for Children*, by John Oxenham | and Roderic Dunkerly. Used by permission. || Scripture quotations, unless otherwise indicated, are from | the Revised Standard Version of the Bible, copyright, 1946 and | 1952, by the Division of Christian Education of the National | Council of Churches, and are used by permission. || PRINTED IN THE UNITED STATES OF AMERICA]

PAGINATION: [1-2] 3-38 [39] 40-41 [42-46] 47-48 in four signatures of buff paper, plus free endpapers. First and last signatures are glued to the free endpapers. 8 1/8″ x 8 1/16″.

COVER: A course-weave ochre cloth wraps over the rounded spine and over the boards of this thin (5/16″) book. The front stamped in blue: THE LORD | WILL LOVE THEE | [a stylized cross and clover-leaf].

DUST JACKET: Blue, with ivory flaps, under gloss finish. Front: 5 1/4″ x 6 3/8″ color illustration in a yellow frame suggestive of Tudor's future twig frames, a Middle-eastern boy and girl and five sheep overlook a desert valley, hills and a rainbow. Above the frame in purple block letters: THE LORD WILL LOVE THEE. Remaining jacket text is black including, below the illustration: *Text by Sara Klein Clarke* • *Illustrated by Tasha Tudor.* Spine printed laterally: THE LORD WILL LOVE THEE   WESTMINSTER.

Back, right, 6″ x 4″ black and white photograph of Tudor sitting on a sofa holding a tiger cat. Beneath the photograph: *Photograph by Nell Dorr* . Centered across the bottom: THE WESTMINSTER PRESS • PHILADELPHIA. Block of text at left of photograph:

|| Born in Boston, Massachusetts, this noted illus- | trator, portrait painter, author, and lecturer | lives with her husband, Thomas L. McCready, | Jr., and their four children on a farm in Webster, | New Hampshire. Miss Tudor was educated | mostly by private tutor up to the time that she | attended the Boston Museum School of Fine | Arts. All available time, she reports, is spent | with the family enjoying the woods, fields, and | river (swimming and skating) on their property, | her love of the farm and outdoors clearly show- | ing in her art. When she is not illustrating either | her own or her husband's books, Miss Tudor is | very likely to be creating Christmas cards, | giving illustrated talks, caring for the farm | animals, or pursuing one of the many interests | —spinning, weaving, cooking, making doll's | clothes—that help form her enviable pattern of | the good life.

Front flap: *The Lord* | *Will Love Thee* | illustrated by | TASHA TUDOR | *Text by Sara Klein Clarke* || In this book Tasha Tudor departs from | the whimsical, delicate, inexpressibly | personal style of drawing that so typ- | ifies and endears her work to countless | admirers of all ages.

247

Now, revealing | her versatility, the present illustra- | tions are boldly defined and brilliant- | ly colored—dramatic accompaniments | to the Old Testament incidents retold | here briefly and simply, yet in the | biblical tone, to help pre-schoolers | understand that it is only through | God's love that all other love becomes | possible. ¶ The passages selected for retelling | enable the young child to identify | such family incidents as moving to a | new home, visiting grandfather, fam- | ily worship, bringing gifts to the | church, working together in the church; | they also show ways of being thought- | ful, kind, and concerned for those in | need. || 46-1227   **$2.50**

Back flap: *And It Was So* | illustrated by | TASHA TUDOR || Tasha Tudor's feeling for the warm, | eternal unity of man with man and of | mankind with the great natural world | —God's creation, all—could not mani- | fest itself more beautifully or more | clearly than in this book, a companion | volume to THE LORD WILL LOVE THEE. | Here she illuminates for the youngest | children the Bible's most basic mean- | ings, "translating" brief, carefully se- | lected Scriptural passages into the | language of her sensitive, unique, | timeless art. ¶ A child's first questions are also | those of the thoughtful adult his life | long: Who made us? Where do we | come from? Why? What can we do? | For each of these the Bible has ultimate | answers, in some of the most thrilling | words ever written. Now Tasha Tudor | illustrates the words in a way to remain | memorable for child and adult. They | speak of God, the Creator and Sus- | tainer of life, of our praise to him for | his goodness, of Jesus and his teaching | and why he came to us, of the church | in which we learn about God and worship him.

CONTENTS: The text, pages 3-48, largely synopsizes the story of Israel from Jacob through the building of King Solomon's temple. Most pages have a 5 x 7 1/2″ illustration at the top of the page illustrating the 3-6 lines of text at the bottom.

ILLUSTRATIONS: Full color illustrations on pages [1] 3, 6-7, 10, 12-13, 15, 18-19, 22, 24-25, 27, 30-31, 34, 36-37, [39, 42-43] 48; black and white on pages 4-5, 8-9, 11, 14, 16-17, 20-21, 23, 26, 28-29, 32-33, 35, 38, 40-41, [44-46] 47. These pages with views of King Solomon's temple have larger illustrations and no text: [39, 42]. In this book, atypical of her general style, Tudor transports the reader to the desert habitat of the Israelites of 4,000 years ago - camels, tents, and caftans. However, she digresses into mid-twentieth dress and houses of worship on pages [44-45] and 48. Page 48, in fact, is her familiar view of Mount Kearsarge and surrounding hills as seen from the rock in the McCready pasture in Webster, New Hampshire. The end papers, printed in blue, reproduce the illustrations from pages 32 and 9.

COPYRIGHT REGISTRATION: A 407771 granted to W.L. Jenkins, 915 Witherspoon Bldg., Philadelphia 7, Pa. John H. Chipman, agent for claimant, swears on Sept. 14, 1959:

THE LORD WILL LOVE THEE, by Sara Klein Clarke, , 51 Alexander St., Apt., 1211, Toronto, Ontario, and Tasha Tudor (Illustrator), Mrs. T.L. McCready, Route #1, Contoocook, N.H., U.S. citizens, was published Aug. 18, 1959. The book was printed by R.R. Donnelly & Sons Co., Crawfordsville, In. Fees on account, the Board of Christian Education of the United Presbyterian Church U.S.A. Application and affidavit received at L.C. Sept. 18, 1959; two deposit copies received Sept. 21, 1959.

COPYRIGHT RENEWAL REGISTRATION: RE 342-360 granted to The Westminster Press, 925 Chestnut St., 6th floor, Philadelphia, Pa. 19102, claiming as proprietor of copyright in a work made for hire. Dorothy C. Postowski, agent for The Westminster Press, swears on June 19, 1987:

THE LORD WILL LOVE THEE, by Sara Klein Clarke, author, and Tasha Tudor, illustrator, was originally published Aug. 18, 1959, copyright A 407771 registered to W. L. Jenkins. Fees charged to deposit account DAO 10693, Publications Unit/Program Agency, Presbyterian Church (U.S.A.) Renewal application received at L.C. June 26, 1987, the effective date of this renewal.

L57 _____.

PAGINATION: As above, in paper wrapper. 7 7/8″ x 7 7/8″

COVER: Two sheets of blue cover stock stapled at the top and bottom of the gathering of pages, with a tan paper spine wrap. The front reproduces trade dust jacket, but only imprinted with the title. Inside the front cover: A PRAYER ‖ Thank you, God, for all I have, | Keep and bless all those I love, | Help me always, God, to do | Just as you would wish me to. ‖ [A white pre-printed bookplate (1 1/4″ x 3 1/8″) at the lower right is imprinted in blue: *My Book and My Name* | [2 3/8″ rule].

Back cover printed in black text. ***To the homes in which this book will be used:*** [two paragraphs either side of a church/home illustration; on the left,] *The Lord Will Love Thee* is a | very simple telling, in words | and pictures, of incidents and | passages from the Old Testa- | ment that speak of God's con- | tinuing, sustaining love for his | people and their response to | him. The passages were selected | so that a young child can iden- | tify such family incidents as | moving to a new home, travel- | ing to see his grandfather, going | as a family to worship, bringing [second column] gifts to a church, working to- | gether in the church; and ways | of being thoughtful, kind, and | concerned for those in need in | any way. ¶ The young child will begin | to understand that love to God | and fellow man is possible be- | cause of God's love, which is | the promise in the words "The | Lord will love thee" -a love | which is given freely and for- | ever. [Between the two paragraphs is an image of a square tower, above this uncial title chRistiAn | fAith | And Life | A pRogRAm

for | chuRch And home, above a Cape Cod house with an outside chimney centered on the front. At bottom left corner: 45-1227.

Inside the back cover, a 3 1/4″ x 4 1/2″ white box printed in blue, two columns of references connecting each page of text to Scripture: The text is based on the following verses: | Page | 3 Genesis 12:1–2 | 4– 5 Genesis 33:12–14 | 6– 7 Genesis 48:8–11 | 8– 9 Genesis 49:28, 50:22; | Exodus 4:14 | 10–11 Exodus 12:50–51 | 12–13 Exodus 18:1–7 | 14–15 Exodus 35:4–9 | 16–17 Exodus 35:7–8; 36:7 | 18–19 Exodus 35:30–35 | 20–21 Exodus 35:25–26 | 22–23 Exodus 39:22–26 | Numbers 15:37–40 | 24 Numbers 10:2–3 | 25 Numbers 3:5–8; 4:47 [second column] Page | 26–27 Numbers 32:16, 24, 26 | 28–29 Deuteronomy 6:4–9 | 30 Deuteronomy 15:7–8 | 31 Deuteronomy 22:1–3 | 32 Deuteronomy 22:4 | 33 Leviticus 19:33-34 | 34–35 Leviticus 19:9–10 | 36 I Kings 5:1–5 | 37 I Kings 6:14–22 | 38-39 I Kings 7:15–16, 51 | 40–41 I Kings 8:22–23, 28-29 | 42–43 I Kings 8:38–40 | 44-45 I Kings 8:41–43 | 46–47 I Kings 8:65–66 | 48 Numbers 6:24–26.

OTHER: Paperback edition for use in Sunday Schools.

M1 *"Magical Moments In Time",* | *A Very Special Presentation By The Tudor Women, Tasha, Bethany and Efner* [pencil illustration of a mother holding a small boy and reading as they sit in a rocking chair] | —this original art by Tasha Tudor ‖ Arranged by Mori Books . 141 Route 101A . Amherst, NH 03031 . 603.882.2665.

> PAGINATION: A single 8 ½ x 11″ white paper folded to form an event program.

> COVER: "Title page" taken from front cover. The central illustration is encircled by a flowered ribbon tied at the top. Pencilled on the bow: MORI BOOKS, and at the bottom, MOTHER'S DAY | 1995.

> CONTENTS: Page [2] contains three panels placed above each other: a map to the Amherst shop, <u>DRIVING DIRECTIONS</u> and <u>Auction Rules</u>. Page [3] <u>The Program</u> announces for !:00 PM "The Tudor Women" Efner Tudor Holmes, Bethany Tudor, Tasha Tudor, A Live Auction of original Tudor art drawn on stage this afternoon, Questions and Answers , 3:30 pm Book Signing by the "Tudor Women" at Mori Books. "A special exhibit of original "Tudor" art and personal, family "Tudor Gifts" will be on display at Mori Books, courtesy of Bethany, Efner and Tasha. This one-day exhibit of family treasures has never before been publicly displayed. Page [4], a pencil drawing of an owl on a branch reading to a duckling, a rabbit and two birds on the ground. —this original art by Bethany Tudor . A bottom panel contains this quotation: "What would the world be, once bereft | Of wet and wilderness? Let them be left, | O let them be left, wilderness and wet, | Long live the weeds and the wilderness yet." ‖ — Gerard Manley Hopkins | *Inversnaid* | —this quotation—from "Springs of Joy"——selected by Efner Tudor Holmes.

> OTHER: The text fails to mention that the talk and auction were held in a school auditorium in Nashua, New Hampshire, three miles distant from the book shop.

M2 **Mr. Stubbs** | [5 pencil drawings of a cat encircling text] | *by* | T. L. McCREADY, Jr. | *Illustrated* | *by* | TASHA TUDOR ‖ FARRAR, STRAUS & CUDAHY   NEW YORK [ARIEL BOOKS, opposite FARRAR . . . on preceding page]   [TO MARY DAVIS | *who loves Stubbs and all cats* ‖ [4 children at gate with cat who has a tail] ‖ © 1956 BY THOMAS L. MCCREADY AND TASHA TUDOR. | LIBRARY OF CONGRESS CATALOG CARD NO. 56-9445. | PUBLISHED SIMULTANEOUSLY IN CANADA BY | AMBASSADOR BOOKS, LTD.]

> PAGINATION: Three signatures: [i-ii, 1-2] 3-16 [17] 18 [19] 20-26 [27] 28-30 [31] 32-34 [35] 36-40 [41] 42-44 [45] 46-48 [49-50] including free endpapers. 8 1/8″ x 6 1/8″.

> COVER: Carmine cloth over boards printed in black: front, **MR. STUBBS**, under full illustration of cat with short tail; spine, printed laterally, **McCready • MR. STUBBS • Ariel**. Two-page color illustration is repeated on front and back endpapers: a flower border in front of a rail and woven wire fence. Mr. Stubbs and Edgar Allan Crow walk the top rail, Biggity Bantam watches from the gate post and Pekin White and Matilda from the ground. Alexander the Gander and Araminta are craning their necks through the gate and Increase Rabbit sits watching on the ground.

> DUST JACKET: Red jacket with full white panel printed on front containing a blue-gray line frame around: **MR. STUBBS** | [gray cat's head encircled by two stalks of catnip] | **By T. L. McCready, Jr.** | **Pictures by Tasha Tudor**. Front flap: $2.50 | 40-80 ‖ *Mr. Stubbs* | *by* | T. L. McCREADY, Jr. | *Illustrated by* TASHA TUDOR ‖ Never was there such a cat as Mr. | Stubbs. What he lacked in tail he | more than made up for in spirit. | And the Warner

children, whose | pet he was, kept right up with him, | inventing games for him to play and | chariots for him to pull. He truly | was a cat of cats and his story right- | fully belongs with the other Warner | farm chronicles, BIGGITY BANTAM | and PEKIN WHITE, (see back flap) | also written by Mr. McCready and | illustrated by Mrs. McCready, who is the famous Tasha Tudor. || **ARIEL BOOKS** | FARRAR, STRAUS AND CUDAHY | 101 Fifth Avenue   New York 3, N.Y. Back flap: **BIGGITY BANTAM** | "There's nothing like Bantams as pets, | for those with space to own | them, and we hope this gay little story | will persuade some parents to give their | children bantams. The author has caught | the 'biggity' character of these creatures | very well, and the many pictures in both | line and full color are Tasha Tudor at | her best." — Louise Bechtel, *New York* | *Herald Tribune.* || **PEKIN WHITE** | "PEKIN WHITE by T. L. McCready, Jr., | concerns a fine pair of white ducks, who | really live on the McCreadys' farm in | New Hampshire, as does Biggity Bantam, | their rooster. Filled with rollicking good | humor and family fun, the adventures | (which are many) of the large and hand- | some white drake Pekin White and his | beautiful wife, Matilda Paddleford, are | enjoyable reading for children of early | school years. Generously and with a nice | freshness Tasha Tudor (Mrs. McCready) | has illustrated their book with a real | New Hampshire touch."—*The Christian* | *Science Monitor.* || **ARIEL BOOKS** | FARRAR, STRAUS AND CUDAHY | 101 Fifth Avenue   New York 3, N.Y.

ILLUSTRATIONS: Color illustrations: endpapers, [2] 6, 7, 10-11 (the Webster farmstead), 14, 15, 22-23, 26 [27], [31], [35], 38, 39, [42-43], 46, 47. Black and white pencil drawings: 6 studies of Mr. Stubbs on [ii and 1] 4-5, 8, 9, 12, 13, 16, [17], [19], 20, 21, 24, 25, 28, 29, 32, 33, 36-37, [41], [45].

OTHER: No text on pages [17], [19], [27], [31], [35], [41], [45], 48. Page [49] is blank.

COPYRIGHT REGISTRATION: A 251342 granted to Thomas L. McCready and Tasha Tudor, Route #1, Contoocook, N.H. H.D. Varnell, agent for claimants, swears on Sept. 11, 1956:

MR. STUBBS, by Thomas L. McCready, illustrated by Tasha Tudor, U.S. citizens, was published Aug. 17, 1956. The book was printed by Connecticut Printers, Hartford, Ct., and bound by American Book Stratford, N.Y., N.Y. Fees charged to the account of Farrar, Straus & Cudahy, Inc., c/o Miss Beverly Jane Loo, 101 Fifth Avenue, N.Y. 3, N.Y. Two deposit copies received at L.C. Sept. 12, 1956; application and affidavit received, Sept. 13, 1956.

COPYRIGHT RENEWAL REGISTRATION: RE 220-594 granted to Tasha Tudor McCready, R.D. #4, Box 144, West Brattleboro, Vt. 05301, the author and the widow of the deceased author, Thomas L. McCready; Seth Tudor, Thomas Tudor and Bethany Tudor of the same address, and Efner Tudor Holmes, Rt. #1, Concord, NH, children of the deceased author, Thomas L. McCready. Elizabeth Besobrasow**, agent for Tasha Tudor McCready, Seth Tudor* [and in the margin: * Thomas Tudor, Bethany Tudor and Efner Tudor Holmes], swears on Oct. 16, 1984: [* Amended by Copyright Office, ** See Renewal File. Besobrasow failed to sign the application.]

MR. STUBBS, by Thomas L. McCready - author and Tasha Tudor - illustrator, was originally published Aug. 17, 1956 and registered A 251342 to Thomas L. McCready [and Tasha Tudor *]. Fees charged to deposit account DAO 13366, Farrar, Straus & Giroux. Renewal application received at L.C. Oct. 18, 1984, the effective date of this renewal.

M3 _____. PUBLISHED SIMULTANEOUSLY IN CANADA BY AMBASSADOR BOOKS, LTD.

Have not examined a copy.

M4 _____. Overmann lists a cloth binding from Warne, United Kingdom. Have not examined a copy.

M5 MORE | PRAYERS || *Illustrated by* | TASHA TUDOR || [song sparrow on wild flower bouquet] || New York   Henry Z. Walck, Inc.   1967 [Grateful acknowledgment is made to | J.M. Dent & Sons Ltd. for permission to | reprint "Immanence" by Evelyn Underhill. || Copyright © 1967 by Henry Z. Walck, Inc. All rights reserved. | Library of Congress Catalog Card Number: 67-19929 | Printed in the United States of America]

PAGINATION: [1-3] 4-10 [11] 12-20 [21] 22-26 [27] 28-30 [31] 32-34 [35] 36 [37] 38 [39] 40 in two signatures and one gathering of buff paper, plus endpapers. 5 5/16″ x 3 7/8″

COVER: Light blue cloth. Gilt spine imprint: TUDOR   MORE PRAYERS   WALCK. Two endpaper illustrations are repeated front and back: a song sparrow singing on a rose, on left; another guarding a nest beneath the rose, on right. Free endpapers are blank on their reverse sides.

DUST JACKET: Lavender with buff flaps. Front: Black text on a white field within an oval of daisies and harebells: [sparrow on a twig] | MORE | PRAYERS || *Illustrated by* | TASHA TUDOR. Spine, printed laterally: TUDOR   MORE PRAYERS   WALCK. Front flap: MORE | PRAYERS | *illustrated by* | TASHA TUDOR || HERE are prayers for | young children, in a com- | panion volume to *First* | *Prayers* and *First Graces*. | The selection, made with | advice from educators in | the religious field, in- | cludes a few short pas- | sages from the Psalms as | well as familiar and less | well-known verses. The | direct simplicity of these | prayers and the delicate | illustrations by Tasha | Tudor will delight chil- | dren and will help them | to recognize God's pres- | ence in the world around | them. || *Henry* | *Z. Walck, Inc.* || *50-100.*   Both corners clipped on examination copy, but the editor has seen a copy with the lower right corner: **$1.95**. Back flap: FIRST | PRAYERS | *Illustrated by* | TASHA TUDOR || "Lovely prayers, beauti- | fully illustrated for little | children." — *Christian* | *Herald.* Available in | Protestant and Catholic | editions. || FIRST | GRACES | *Illustrated by* | TASHA TUDOR || "This tiny exquisite book | . . . contains twenty-one | prayers of thanksgiving." | —*Chicago Tribune.*

CONTENTS: Page [3] dedication features a tussie-mussie and beneath it in hand script, To | dear | Cousin Nan. Nan was a relative of Tudor's Hopkinton, NH, friend Marcia Cunningham. Page 40 is blank.

OTHER: *More Prayers* is the only Tudor book to have been first published by Henry Z. Walck, Inc. *American Book Publishing Record* (1967:88): *More Prayers.* Illus. by Tasha j,242.8 [*sic*]|| Tudor. New York, Walck, 1967. 38p. illus. | (pt. col.) 14cm. [BV265.M66] 67-19929 1.95 || *1. Children-- Prayer-books and devotions.* | I. Tudor, Tasha, illus.. | Originally published in paperback in 1965.

The statement from ABPR notwithstanding, we have not found a paperback.

COPYRIGHT REGISTRATION: A 974924 granted to Henry Z. Walck, Inc., 19 Union Square West, N.Y., N.Y. 10003. Henry Z. Walck, claiming for himself, swears on February 8, 1968:

MORE PRAYERS, by Tasha Tudor, Route 1, Contoocook, N.H., a U.S. citizen, was published Sept. 20, 1967. The book was printed by Kellogg and Bulkeley, 85 Trumbull St., Hartford, Ct., from type set by The Composing Room, Inc., 130 West 46th St., N.Y., N.Y., and bound by H. Wolff Book Mfg. Co. Inc., 508 West 26th St., N.Y., N.Y. Fees charged to Henry Z. Walck, Inc. #6694. Application and affidavit received Feb. 16, 1968. Two deposit copies received March 11, 1968.

COPYRIGHT RENEWAL REGISTRATION: RE-734-234 granted to Tasha Tudor, c/o Corgi Cottage Industries, P.O. Box 7281, Richmond, Va. 23221-0281 claiming as author (illustrator). Kathryn L. Barrett, Esq., 235 East 22nd St., Apt. 11C, N.Y., N.Y. 10010, 212-684-6689, agent for Tasha Tudor, swears on June 21, 1996: [*sic*]

MORE PRAYERS, illustrations as renewable matter by Tasha Tudor was published September 20, 1967, and registered to Henry Z. Walck, Inc., A974924. Renewal application received Aug. 9, 1996, the effective date of this registration. Certificate and correspondence to be mailed to Kathyrn L. Barrett [*sic*].

M6 _____.

COVER: In a courser deeper <u>robin's egg blue cloth</u>, spine ink is navy blue.

DUST JACKET: Examination copy had both corners clipped from front flap, as above. A penciled price was added: <u>2.50</u>.

M7 _____.

COVER: <u>Light moss green</u> leather-textured paper over boards, sprayed lacquer finish. Spine imprinting, as above in navy ink, although the letters are thinner than before.

DUST JACKET: Both corners clipped from front flap. For the first time, <u>$2.95</u> is printed at the <u>upper left</u> of flap.

M8 _____. Henry Z. Walck, Inc. New York [This impression, 1980 || Grateful acknowledgment is made to | J.M. Dent & Sons Ltd. for permission to | reprint "Immanence" by Evelyn Underhill. || <u>ISBN 0-8098-1954-6</u> || Copyright © 1967 by Henry Z. Walck, Inc. || Library of Congress Catalog Card Number: 67-19929 | <u>Manufactured in the United States of America</u>]

PAGINATION: [1-3] . . . [39-<u>40</u>] in two signatures white kid-finish paper, not as smooth as first printing, plus endpapers. 5 5/16″ x 3 7/8″

COVER: <u>Wine plastic-filled paper</u> in deerskin pattern over boards. Spine stamped in gilt: <u>MORE PRAYERS   Tasha Tudor   Walck</u>.

DUST JACKET: White paper, with illustrated <u>lavender panel on front</u>; the rest of the jacket is white. Front flap: $ 2.95 MORE PRAYERS…around | them. || *Henry Z. Walck, Inc.* | <u>ISBN 0-8098-1954-6</u>. A pre-printed round label $3⁵⁰ was applied over the price printed on the jacket. These labels dry with age and may fall off leaving a circular residue.

ILLUSTRATIONS: The colors of the endpapers and title page are washed out from previous.

M9 _____. [This impression, 1981 …]

PAGINATION: A smooth white matte paper. Two signatures 5 3/8″ x <u>4 1/16″</u>

COVER: <u>Dark moss green</u> paper cover in simulated deerskin, spine as before.

DUST JACKET: Front flap: <u>$3.50</u> [upper <u>right corner</u>] || MORE PRAYERS…around | <u>them.</u> || <u>ISBN</u> 0-8098-1954-6 back flap: . . . *Christian* | <u>*Herald.*</u> | FIRST | GRACES . . . —*Chicago Tribune* || <u>Henry Z. Walck, Inc. | A Division of | David McKay Company, Inc. | New York</u>.

OTHER: This is the first time the back flap has not indicated both Catholic and Protestant editions of *First Prayers*. This printing was sold in a boxed set with *First Graces* (red binding) and *First Prayers* (turquoise binding) as *Tasha Tudor's TREASURE, q.v.* for a description of the slipcase.

M10 _____. [This impression, 1984 …]

PAGINATION: 5 3/8″ x <u>3 15/16″</u>.

COVER: <u>Dark moss green</u> plastic-filled paper over boards, simulated deerskin.

DUST JACKET: Front flap: <u>$4.50</u> . . .

M11 _____. [This impression, 1984 …]

COVER: <u>Yellow plastic-filled paper, with linen imprint</u>, over boards; spine printed in black as above. The <u>endpapers are white</u> with no illustrations, for the first time. <u>5 5/16″ x 3 7/8″</u>.

DUST JACKET: The upper corner is clipped from dj front flap and a new price <u>$4.95</u> has been printed just to left of cut corner.

M12 _____. [This impression, 1986 …]

PAGINATION: <u>[i-ii]</u> [1-3] 4-10 [11] 12-26 [27] 28-30 [31] 32-34 [35] 36 [37] 38 [39-46] in two signatures, plus endpapers. <u>5 7/16″ x 3 7/8″</u>.

COVER: <u>Yellow coated paper</u> cover imprinted with a fine weave pattern; spine as before, black ink.

DUST JACKET: Front flap, not clipped: <u>$4.95</u> . . .

CONTENTS: Text as above, plus: <u>A half-title page [i] precedes the title page</u>. <u>Additional pages</u> include reviews: [41] OTHER STORIES | BY TASHA TUDOR | [wren, in color]; [42] THE DOLLS' CHRISTMAS | *"A cheerful little tale of the dolls' Christ- | mas celebration in an unusual doll house | large enough for foot high dolls. Little | girls thoroughly enjoy all the doll details."* | − Elementary English; [43] PUMPKIN MOONSHINE | *"A reissue of Miss Tudor's Hallowe'en | classic, first published in 1938, the tale of | a little girl who looked for the biggest | pumpkin on the farm to make a pumpkin | moonshine....Little children will love | Miss Tudor's delicately colored illustra- | tions."* −Publishers Weekly; [44] [angel and rose from title page of *First Prayers*, followed by an enlargement of the back flap blurb from earlier editions of *More Prayers*, including the reference to Catholic editions] FIRST PRAYERS | *illustrated by* | TASHA TUDOR | "Lovely prayers, beauti- | fully illustrated for little | children." — *Christian Herald*. Available in | Protestant and Catholic | editions. ; [45] [rabbits from the endpaper of *First Graces*] FIRST GRACES | *illustrated by* | TASHA TUDOR | "This tiny exquisite book | . . . contains twenty-one | prayers of thanksgiving." |—*Chicago Tribune*; [46] *A* | *Tale for Easter* | "Children . . . take delight in the lovely | childlike character of this small book | which carries the thought of springtime. | . . . Many delicate pictures of rabbits, lambs, chickens and daffodils, in close as- | sociation with little children, are sprin- | kled over the pages, while a wonderful | fawn brings a happy climax to the story. | Precise in detail and exquisite in color, Tasha Tudor's little books are truly Amer- | ican in tone, suggesting a loving obser- | vation akin to that of Beatrix Potter." | −*The Horn Book*.

M13 MORE | PRAYERS || *Illustrated by* | TASHA TUDOR || [song sparrow on wild flower bouquet] || <u>Lutterworth Press</u> [*First published in Great Britain, 1964* | This impression 1976 || ISBN 0 7188 1364 2 || Copyright © Henry Z. Walck Inc., 1957 || *Printed in Hong Kong*]

PAGINATION: [1-3] 4-10 [11] 12-26 [27] 28-30 [31] 32-34 [35] 36 [37] 38 [39-40] in two signatures, plus endpapers. 5 ¼″ x 3 ¾″

COVER: <u>Pearl gray paper over boards</u>, with a fine buckram weave.   Black imprint on spine: MORE PRAYERS   Tasha Tudor   LUTTERWORTH.   White paper endpapers illustrated as in the first edition.

DUST JACKET: Spine: TUDOR   MORE PRAYERS   Lutterworth. Text of front flap : MORE | PRAYERS | *Illustrated by* | TASHA TUDOR || HERE are prayers for young ⌊children, in a companion vol -⌋ ume to *First Prayers* and *First* ⌊ *Graces*. The selection includes⌋ a few short passages from the ⌊Psalms as well as familiar and⌊ less well-known verses. The | direct simplicity of these | prayers and the delicate <u>illus-</u> | <u>trations</u> by Tasha Tudor will⌊ delight children and will help | them to recognize God's pres- | ence in the world around | them. || ISBN 0 7188 1364 2 || 60 p net.   Back flap: FIRST PRAYERS | FIRST GRACES | *Both books illustrated by* | TASHA TUDOR || "These books will give a lot of | pleasure to very young rea- | ders. Children will probably know some of the lovely pray- | ers and graces, and will cer- | tainly be encouraged by the enchanting little illustrations to learn others, less familiar." *Sunday School Chronicle* || FIRST ABC | FIRST

HYMNS | *Both books illustrated by* | BRENDA MEREDITH | SEYMOUR || Two exquisitely illustrated | books which little children | will treasure at all times of | the year.

M14 _____. . . . The Lutterworth Press [*First published in Great Britain, 1964* | This impression 1991 || [L in circle logo] || The Lutterworth Press | P.O. Box 60 | Cambridge CB1 2NT | England || ISBN 0 7188 1364 2 || Copyright © Henry Z. Walck Inc., 1952 [*sic*] || *Printed in Hong Kong by Colorcraft Ltd*]

PAGINATION: Two signatures and one gathering, plus endpapers. 5 5/16″ x 3 13/16″

COVER: Robin's egg blue paper over boards, with a fine buckram weave. Gilt imprint on spine: TUDOR MORE PRAYERS [L in circle logo]. White paper endpapers illustrated as in the first edition.

DUST JACKET: Dust jacket is yellow with black text and white flaps; front illustration as on US editions. Spine: TUDOR MORE PRAYERS [L in circle logo]. Back has a bar code at lower left, and printed above it in a 1 3/4″ line: ISBN 0-7188-1364-2. Beneath the bar code: 9 780718 813642 Lower right corner: The Lutterworth Press | P.O. Box 60 | Cambridge CB1 2NT | England. Front flap, bottom corner clipped. Back flap: More delightful books in this beautiful series | for little children: | FIRST PRAYERS | 0 7188 0306 x | FIRST GRACES | 0 7188 0307 8 | *Illustrated by* | TASHA TUDOR || FIRST HYMNS | 0 7188 0308 6 | *Illustrated by* | BRENDA MEREDITH | SEYMOUR.

OTHER: See *A Treasury of First Books* for other copies in slipcase.

M15 _____. [First published … England || ISBN 0 7188 2627 2 || Copyright… Colorcraft Ltd]

COVER: White simulated leather binding. Gilt cover text: MORE | PRAYERS, in a floral oval. All edges gilt.

OTHER: In a white lightweight cardboard box. The detached lid is decorated with alternating pink, white and blue vertical stripes. The stripes are overlaid with a 5″ high full-color floral oval, not Tudor's design and different from the book cover. In the center: MORE | PRAYERS. In the lower right corner of the back of the box: MORE PRAYERS || ISBN 0-7188-2627-2 | [bar code] | 9 780718 826277. A price label with a rubber-stamped price has been applied beside the bar code: PUBLISHERS PRICE [red] | £5•45.

M16 **MOTHER | AND CHILD** | BY | NELL DORR [opposite title page: HARPER & BROTHERS • PUBLISHERS • NEW YORK] [COPYRIGHT 1954 BY NELL DORR || *Printed in the United States of America* || All rights in this book are reserved. No part of the book may | be used or reproduced in any manner whatsoever without | written permission except in the case of brief quotations | embodied in critical articles and reviews. For information | address Harper & Brothers, 49 East 33rd Street, New York 16. | [2 11/16″ tapered rule] | THE PHOTOGRAVURE AND COLOR CO. | THE SPIRAL PRESS • NEW YORK]

PAGINATION: Eleven signatures, ivory matte paper. [92] pages including free endpapers. See Contents below for collation and identification of photographs. 8 7/16″ x 7″

COVER: A different abstract black and white photograph on each printed cloth cover. The spine is black cloth wrapped 1/2″ onto covers, and edged with a silver rule where the spine wrap meets the printed cloth. Spine imprint in silver: NELL DORR MOTHER AND CHILD HARPER. Two double-page endpapers carry the same blurred image of stalks of Queen Ann's lace.

DUST JACKET: Ivory, black and white photograph of Tasha Tudor and daughter Bethany and Tasha's sister-in-law Polly Tudor with daughters Rosamond and Mary playing 'ring-around-the-rosy.' The photograph is divided by the red spine and fills all of the front and the right two-thirds of the back. Printing is mostly black, with rubrics; spine. reveal printing. Front cover (in red): MOTHER | AND | CHILD BY | NELL | DORR. Spine lettered as book. The back of the jacket has a gray panel on the left one-third and printed in the bottom third of the panel is: Mother and Child

[red] | BY NELL DORR [black] | HARPER AND BROTHERS [red] | *Publishers* NEW YORK [black]. Front flap: $4.50 | NELL DORR'S PICTURES [red] | are memorably powerful in their some- | times awesome stillness and in their con- | tained love of childhood, of nature and its | flowers and seasons. There is a humility | here which is as profound as it is uni- | versal. Her work is that of a mature artist | and is the flame of truth as she sees it. ¶ Her text is a prose poem in praise of | motherhood and of the home where God | is honored and the simple events of the | day are glorified by the gift of grace. ¶ In private life Nell Dorr is the wife of | the internationally known scientist and | inventor, Dr. John Van Nostrand Dorr. The Dorrs divide their time when in this | country between their homes in New | York, Connecticut and New Hampshire. | Mrs. Dorr is the mother of three daugh- | ters and has six young grandchildren. She | is the author of that Florida fantasy of | youth, *In A Blue Moon*, published by | G. P. Putnam's Sons in 1939 and of the | color film on the modern dance, *The* | *Singing Earth*, now in the film library | of the Museum of Modern Art. She also | directed the international documentary | color film, *The Dorr Way*. She is a Fellow | of the Royal Photographic Society of | London, England. Back flap: IN A BLUE MOON [red] | BY NELL DORR ‖ "I have heretofore avoided reviewing | books about photography or illustrated by | photography. But a photographic book | has recently been born that brings a new | note into photographic books and does it | with such exquisite grace and loveliness | that I cannot resist the temptation to talk | about it. . . . One would have to go deep | into the works of the poets to find an | equivalent expression of lyric loveliness. | Here is a document in photography that | is the opposite of what is generally la- | belled documentary photography today, | just as subjective is opposite to objective. | Here is the autobiography of a sensitive, | strong woman, a book containing essences | distilled from a mingling of cool waters | and warm earth." | EDWARD STEICHEN | From: *U. S. Camera*, 1939.

CONTENTS: This book is an album of full page black and white photographs, black predominating; page [54] is completely black with no image at all. Many of the images are abstract and impressionistic.

[1]	Front free endpaper - Queen Ann's lace
[2]	blank
[3]	2″ x 2 3/8″ Tasha Tudor sitting on settle and holding baby
[4]	Publisher's statement
[5]	Title page
[6]	Colophon, gray image
[7]	Dedication: TO MY BELOVED DAUGHTER	BETS	1915 – 1954 [Elizabeth Dorr Howe]
[8]	Gray image of window, plants, dolls
[9]	Text, beginning: [in red] THE STORY [remainder in black] is from everlasting to everlasting . . .
[10-11]	Abstract, probably of flowers
[12-13]	OUT OF THE CRADLE [red] endlessly rocking . . .[black]
[14-15]	Two images of Nell Dorr
[16-17]	EACH DOOR-STEP [red] has its own blossoms	And these are mine . . .[black]
[18]	A[red]nd I say to myself . . .[black]
[19]	Baby's face, *Katherine Howe*
[20-21]	A white image and swan
[22]	Tasha Tudor and her daughter Bethany
[23]	Elizabeth Dorr in her wedding dress, daughter 'Bets' of the dedication

[24]   The bed canopy crocheted by Tasha

[25]   Tasha and Bethany in bed

[26]   A flower

[27]   Tasha nursing Bethany

[28]   Bethany beside bed

[29]   Bethany standing at dresser

[30]   Mary Denny Burnett (Dady) peeking in at doorway

[31]   Tasha dressing Bethany *in Rosamond Tudor's Redding, Ct., summer house*

[32]   Seth Tudor in bed, *about 1942, Redding , Ct.*

[33]   Tasha Tudor, Mary Tudor and Bethany leaning over *Webster* banister, *ca. 1947*

[34]   Seth standing at foot of stairs with hammer, *Redding, Ct., ca. 1943*

[35]   Bethany sitting on bottom step, *Redding, Ct., ca. 1943*

[36]   A pantry scene

[37]   Bethany in a chair looking at bird cage suspended in window, *Dorr home, Westport, Ct.*

[38-39] Tasha at her clothesline, with geese *Alexander* and Araminta, *Redding, ca. 1943*

[40]   Tasha with her chickens, *Redding, ca. 1943*

[41]   Bethany holding a chicken, *Redding, ca. 1943*

[42]   The upstairs banister, *Dorr summer home, Hopkinton, NH*

[43]   Bethany beginning to climb the stairs, *ditto*

[44]   An image in light

[45]   Elizabeth 'Bets' Howe holding her daughter Katherine (Kitten)

[46]   Pantry window with jelly jars

[47]   Tasha in her pantry, *making jelly in the Redding kitchen*

[48]   At an evening table. *McCready family. Portrait shows T. L. McCready's grandmother in portrait. Tasha is before the lamp playing her zither to our children and a neighbor baby sitter (on extreme left). Tasha has had a zither all her life.*

[49]   Bethany sewing a button on a sweater

[50]   Katharine Howe examining a piano

[51]   Barbara Howe playing the piano. *Picture on page 155 of "The Family of Man"*

[52]   A night image of the moon

[53]   Nell Dorr holding Katharine Howe, nicknamed Kitten

[54]   A black page

[55]   Nell holding Katharine. *McCready said probably Christopher Ashe, Westport, Ct.*

[56]   A flower image

[57]   Nell holding grandson Chris Ashe

[58]   A flower image

[59]   Nell and Peter Ashe. *McCready says Christopher Ashe.*

[60]   A flower image

[61]   Katharine with hibiscus in her hair

[62]   A milkweed image ?

[63]   Winifred Ashe with her son Peter

[64]   Grandson Rob Tenery eating. *Robin Tenery son of Dr. R.M. Tenery and Barbara Tenery. Robbie was Tasha's model for R. L. Stevenson when she illustrated "A Child's Garden of Verses" – Oxford Press [sic]*

[65]   Bethany drinking from a dipper

[66]   A trout lily ?

[67]   Katharine lying in the grass

[68]   A butterfly on a rose

[69]   Katharine and Barbara standing in the grass in straw hats. *Hayfield at Nell's summer home, Hopkinton, N.H. 90 mile view off toward Franconia Notch, N.H.*

[70]   Barbara and Katharine in straw hats

[71]   Katharine walking beside a stone wall

[72]   An apple branch in bloom

[73]   Katharine playing a recorder. *Memo: check with Nell Dorr if ever wanting to use anything. She develops own prints.*

[74]   Six children playing on a hillside. *All of Nell's grandchildren on field to south of Nell's home, Hopkinton, N.H. Panoramic sweep of central N.H. mountains in background.*

[75]   Three girls walking on a hillside, Katharine in the lead

[76]   A pantry curtain

[77]   Bethany and Tasha before two large windows, *Redding kitchen, ca. 1943*

[78]   Two ducks beside a chicken wire fence, *Redding ca. 1943*

[79]   Bethany sitting on a straight-backed chair

[80]   A squirrel outside a window

[81]   Katharine sitting on an antique chair

[82]   A tree blowing on the hilltop

[83]   Tasha in cape walking behind a goose, *Rosamond Tudor's summer home, ca. 1943*

[84]   Mary Denny Burnett. *McCready's note: an old lady in Scotland*

[85]   Tasha brushing Bethany's hair, *ca. 1944*

[86]   Judy Moulton tying Bethany's neck ribbon, *Webster, ca. 1950*

[87]   Tasha, *Our best bedroom*

[88-89]   Rosamond Tudor's house, Redding, Ct., *where Tasha Tudor met and married T. L. McCready, Jr., in May 1938. Picture taken by Nell early 1940 or so.*

[90]   A flower image

[91]   B[red]lue smoke, smelling of promises, . . . [black]

[92]   Queen Ann's lace on endpaper

OTHER: There was laid in the examination copy a folded sheet of four pages reproduced from the book. Page [1] carries the large baby's face image of page [19]; page [4], the boy with hammer from page [34] of the book. Pages [2-3], this text with rubric: Mother and Child [red] is the adventure in motherhood of one | woman. She tells her story in picture and words–more in pictures than | words. ¶ To her, a mother is the instrument of far spheres. Something beyond | is seeking to work through her . . . the destiny of the human race is in her | hands. If only she could see this clearly, she would be perfectly quiet in her | mind. From out of the depths would come wisdom and strength and beauty | to her. She would know the consecration and high adventure of the scien- | tist and of the man of knowledge; of the musician and the artist; of religion | and pure revelation. Such knowledge is primitive and primeval and comes | directly to her. Mother and Child is a book that takes you gently by the | hand and leads you into this luminous world. ¶ Nell Dorr's pictures are memorably powerful in their sometimes awesome | stillness and in their contained love of childhood, of nature and its flowers | and seasons. There is a humility here which is as profound as it is universal. | Her work is that of a mature artist and is the flame of truth as she sees it. ¶ Her text is a prose poem in praise of motherhood and of the home | where God is honored and the simple events of the day are glorified by the | gift of grace. ¶ In private life Nell Dorr is the wife of the internationally known sci- | entist and inventor, Dr. John Van Nostrand Dorr. Mrs. Dorr is the mother | of three daughters *[Elizabeth Howe, Barbara Tenery and Winifred Ashe - ed.]* and has six grandchildren. She is the author of that | Florida fantasy of youth, *In A Blue Moon*, published by G. P. Putnam's   [page (3)] Sons in 1939 and of the color film on the modern dance, *The Singing | Earth*, now in the film library of the Museum of Modern Art. She is a Fel- | low of the Royal Photographic Society of London, England. ¶ ARTHUR RUSHMORE of The Golden Hind Press, Madison, New Jersey, | writes: "I have watched with interest the instinctive reactions of folk who have | been here and casually pick up 'Mother and Child' from the library table. | Some read the title and put it down — what could be new in that title! Some | leaf through it; cannot get beyond the grim fact that Queen Anne's Lace is | just wild carrot (and a damn nuisance!) — put it down. Then there are two | more kinds of people, those who know life, its ecstasy and its agony, and the | others are those who are emotionally geared for the good life, but missed it | through happenstances. Both these groups love this book, lingering through | it page by page. ¶ "The text and pictures evoke by suggestion what lies deep hidden in the | reader's mind — that quality of the masterpiece of art. It is just paint and | printer's ink — OR, it is the strong solvent that cuts through the coasting of com- | monplace life to the shy heart beneath." ¶ "Nell Dorr, who both dances and sings with her camera." | CARL SANDBURG ¶ "The lines are beautiful in their almost Biblical simplicity — their English | is pure and luminous — a feeling of inspiration in every line." | SIR HAROLD HARTLEY ‖ 6 7/8 x 8 1/4 INCHES 88 PAGES 82 PHOTOGRAPHS $4.50 PER COPY | [4 1/2″ red rule] | HARPER & BROTHERS · PUBLISHERS · NEW YORK.   Examination copy (believed to have been found in England) is inscribed and autographed on the half-title: To | Frederick F. Lovejoy | My lawyer, and also my friend - | Nell Dorr ‖ November - 2 - 1954.

We gratefully acknowledge the assistance of Bethany Tudor, Efner Holmes and Barbara Howe in identifying themselves and their families in the photographs. T.L. McCready, Jr. provided posthumous assistance with the *italicized* statements from his ca. 1955 notes generously loaned by Mr. and Mrs. Hugh Sanborn.

THE DORR FOUNDATION, 99 Park Avenue, New York 16, N.Y. distributed four mimeographed sheets with 21 brief reviews of the book headed: THE DORR FOUNDATION feels that you might enjoy sharing some of the comments about "Mother and Child" which have been brought to our attention.   Included are comments from Carl Sandburg, Lady Bullard, England, Prof. Henicker, Stuttgart, Germany (I can't believe this is photography), H.V. Kaltenborn, Erica Anderson, Lambaréné, Africa, etc.

COPYRIGHT REGISTRATION: A 153542 granted to Nell Dorr (Virginia Nell Dorr), 30 East 37th St., N.Y., N.Y. Frank S[ilver] MacGregor, President, Harper & Brothers, swears on Sept. 23, 1954:

MOTHER AND CHILD, by (Virginia) Nell Door, a U.S. citizen born in 1893, was published Sept. 22, 1954. The book's plates, typesetting, and printing were by the Photogravure and Color

Company, N.Y., N.Y.; binding by the Spiral Press, N.Y., N.Y. Certificate to be mailed to Harper & Brothers, 49 East 33rd St., N.Y. 16, N.Y. Application and affidavit received at L.C. Sept. 24, 1954. Two deposit copies received Sept. 23, 1954.

COPYRIGHT RENEWAL REGISTRATION: RE 134-204 granted to Nell Dorr, VillaSerena, Nettleton Hollow Road, Washington, Ct. 06793, claiming as author. Megan McNulty, agent for Nell Dorr, swears on July 27, 1982:

MOTHER AND CHILD, by (Virginia) Nell Dorr was published Sept. 22, 1954, A 153542. Renewal fee to be charged to account DAO17744 (?), Harper & Row, Publishers, Inc., 10 East 53rd St., N.Y., N.Y. 10022.

M17 _____.

DUST JACKET: Like the "black spine" state, and with front flap headed $4.50 || NELL DORR'S . . .

COVER: Another binding. The impressionistic images of the front and back covers are printed on a cream paper over boards. The result is a softer, antique look. The spine is red cloth, but retains the silver text.

CONTENTS: This version has two additional pieces tipped in. A light-weight bi-fold of Japan paper (6 3/4″ x 4 7/8″) is tipped in centered on page [2] with this text on the first and third surfaces. FROM | THE AUTHOR | TO | THE READER | [3¼″ red rule tapers from center] | Language is a matter of symbols. If one understands | the symbols, he understands the language. The sym- | bols may be written or spoken words; they may be mu- | sical sounds; or they may be pictures. Pictures that are | born in the mind of an artist are not easily translatable. | But pictures that are "camera born" (if they are taken | true) are as universal a language as there is. ¶ It is with this sobering thought in mind that I send | these small pictures out into the world. They speak | from the heart of one mother and are dedicated to the | memory of one who has joined that greater family | which needs no language. ¶ On the cover of my book I say this with symbols — | the living branch and the seed (the mother and child) | springing out of the unknown — the eternal mystery [page 3] — or God. Three times in the pages of the book I re- | peat these symbols. I speak of the spirit — of voices and | of listening to voices. This is not easy to do with a cam- | era — but I had to speak of these things. They may take | longer to understand . . . but I believe they are more | easily understood than they are explained; therefore I | shall not try. It is not important — I tell you only in | case you may wonder. ¶ The rest of the book needs no explaining. You may | even be surprised to see that life is not as different in | the Unites States of America as you had been led to | believe. It is not different at all. (These might almost | be your rooms — these might almost be your children.) ¶ I have had the same feeling in your homes and I | wished that I might share mine with you. This is a way. | A little book can travel far — just as easily as a letter. | Perhaps you will send me a letter in return and we will | know each other better. Write me about your home. | "Care of The Dorr Foundation" will always reach me. || Nell Dorr [simulated signature].   And tipped into the center of page [4] is a 4″ x 3 3/8″ paper with this message: The personal story of this American | mother speaks in a language that is un- | derstood by mothers the world over. Since | understanding is the greatest thing in the | world, The Dorr Foundation offers this | gift in the spirit of friendship between | the women of the United States and the | women of other lands. | [2 1/4″ rule tapers from the center] | THE DORR FOUNDATION | 99 PARK AVENUE · NEW YORK 16, N.Y.

M18 **MOTHER | AND CHILD || Nell Dorr** [© 1972 The Scrimshaw Press | 149 Ninth Street, San Francisco 94103 | L.C. number 72-76271 | ISBN 0-912020-2307 | Second edition. The first edition was | published under the same title by | Harper & Brothers (1954). || Designed by Nell Dorr | Typographic design by Jack W. Stauffacher. | Set in Hunt Roman display and Monotype | Bembo types by Peters Typesetting, Inc. || Five thousand copies printed | by Hallcraft Lithographers and bound by | Mountain States Bindery.]

PAGINATION: [108] pages. Six signatures on a paper with enamel finish. Endpapers are thick matte stock. 10″ x 8 1/4″.

COVER: The half-paper over boards are illustrated with a black and white photograph not included in the first edition but from the same shooting. Black text at the upper right: MOTHER | AND CHILD | Nell Dorr. The spine is wrapped 1 1/4″ onto both covers with red binders cloth, and stamped in silver: MOTHER AND CHILD   Nell Dorr   Scrimshaw.

DUST JACKET: Same image as the covers, but revealing more because a gray spine is narrower than was the cover's cloth wrap. Spine black type matches the book spine. A white adhesive store label has been attached to the upper corner of the front flap, printed in blue: DISTRIBUTED BY | TWO CONTINENTS | 30 East 42nd Street | New York, New York 10017. Front flap text in black: MOTHER AND CHILD | Nell Dorr || Several years ago, Grace Mayer asked her friend, | Nell Dorr, for her statement of beauty's meaning | to her. This is in part what she wrote: || "What does bread mean to me—or health, or | home, or country, or my fellow-man? What | does it all mean—Life? Without the one thing, | beauty, I think I could not endure to live. With it, | I can endure all. I find it equally in joy and in | sorrow. In the greatest of each, in birth and in | death I find an almost unbearable beauty . . . . | [There] is beauty in a calm so deep there is no | bottom. There is beauty in silence. There is beauty | just in the green world. What does it mean to me | —this beauty? It means everything that nourishes | my faith in life and in my brother-man. It means | all the priceless memories of my childhood. . . . | There must have been *un*-beautiful days—but | they are forgotten—only beauty remains. It | means the beauty of NOW . . . . Every day to | wake to it—to feel myself part of it—playing my | flute—dancing my part—in tune with the uni- | verse—in rhythm with the stars—a camera in my | hand. To work itself is holy. The camera cannot | see it. You have to see it and not depend too much | on exposures. See it. Feel it. Somehow it will | come through—a part of it will be there . . . . It | does not matter *what you see, but how*. One must | come closer. Look deeper. . . .To try to share this | beauty in pictures is only another way of giving | a loaf of bread. The world is being fed with so | much fear and horror (along with its wonders) | that someone must distribute a simple loaf of | bread—and that I feel is my task." || $8.95. Back flap: **Nell Dorr** | was born in Cleveland, Ohio, in 1895. Her father, | John Jacob Becker, was a photographic pioneer | and chemist. It was literally at his knee that she | learned the magic and the joy of the darkroom. ¶ Her books include *In a Blue Moon* (1939), | *Mother and Child* (first edition, 1954), *The Bare | Feet* (1962), *Of Night and Day* (1968) and now this | new edition of *Mother and Child*. Perhaps this | book shows in small measure what it is to be a | wholly unified person.

ILLUSTRATIONS: There are new images in this edition, some first edition photographs have been dropped, pages have been reorganized, images reversed. And the rubrics have been replaced with black ink. An interesting comparison to see how Dorr revised her work twenty years after the initial publication. First edition pages in brackets at end of line.

[1]   Front free endpaper - Queen Ann's lace

[2]   blank

[3]   3 1/2″ x3 ″ Tasha Tudor sitting on settee and holding baby with this quotation beneath: I have had my invitation to this world's festival, | and thus my life has been blessed. My eyes have | seen and my ears have heard. || It was my part at this feast to play upon my | instrument, and I have done all I could. | Tagore.

[4]   A new photograph of milkweed fluff ?

[45]   Bethany standing in a chair looking at bird cage suspended in window [37]

[46]   Tasha with her chickens [40]

[47]   Bethany holding a chicken [41]

[48-49]   Tasha at her clothesline, Alexander and Araminta [38-39]

[50]   A flower image [58]

[51]   Nell and Peter Ashe [59]

[52]   A flower image not used in the first edition

[53]   Elizabeth 'Bets' Howe with her daughter Katharine [45]

[54]   A flower image   not used in first edition

[55]   Katharine with hibiscus in her hair [61]

[56]   Bethany closing the curtains not in first edition

[57]   Tasha brushing Mary Tudor's hair not in first edition

[58]   Rob Tenery eating [64]

[59]   Bethany drinking from a dipper [65]

[60]   A trout lily ?? [66]

[61]   Katharine lying in the grass [67]

[62]   An apple branch in bloom [72]

[63]   Katharine playing a recorder   different image, similar to [73]

[64]   A butterfly on a rose [68]

[65]   Katharine and Barbara Howe standing in the grass in straw hats enlarged [69]

[66]   Barbara and Katharine in straw hats [70]

[67]   Katharine walking beside a stone wall [71]

[68-69]   Tasha with Bethany, Mary, Seth (dressed) and Rico Tudor among trees not   in 1st edition

[70]   Six children playing on a hillside [74]

[71]   Three girls walking on a hillside, Katharine in lead [75]

[72]   Barbara (Dorr) Tenery on a hill top not in first edition

[73]   Barby and Kitten Howe, Susie Tenery playing on a hilltop not in first edition

[74-75]   Tasha with Seth, Rico, Mary and Bethany at table not in first edition

[76]   A pantry curtain

[77]   Bethany and Tasha before two large windows

[78]   A squirrel outside a window [80]

[79]   Nell laying a loaf of bread in a pan not in first edition

[80]   A flower image not in first edition

[81]   Tasha bathing Bethany not in first edition

[82]   Two ducks (Pekin White and Matilda) beside a chicken wire fence [78]

[83]   Bethany sitting on a straight-backed chair changed image from [79]

[84]   Mary Denny Burnett

[85]   Tasha brushing Bethany's hair

[86]   A night image of the moon   [52]

[87]   Nell holding Katharine   [53]

[88]   A flower image   not in first edition

[89]   Tasha holding   not in first edition

[90]   Pantry window with jelly jars   [46]

[91]   Tasha in her pantry   [47]

[92]   Katharine examining a piano book   [50]   enlarged

[93]   Katharine and Barbara at the piano   changed image from [51]

[94]   Black page

[95]   Tasha and child on settle   [3]   frontispiece

[96]   At an evening table   [48]

[97]   Bethany sewing a button on a sweater[49]

[98]   A tree blowing on the hilltop   [82]

[99]   Tasha in cape walking with a goose   [83]

[100]   Judy Moulton tying Bethany's neck ribbon   [86]   reversed

[101]   Tasha   [87]

[102]   Tasha, Bethany and Seth in bed   not in first edition

[103]   Bethany and Seth in bed   not in first edition

[104-105]   Rosamond Tudor's house in Redding, Connecticut…[88-89]

[106]   Blue smoke, smelling of promises   [91]

[107]   A flower image…not in first edition

[108]   Queen Ann's lace on endpaper   [92]

These pages from the first edition were omitted in the second:

[44]   An image in light

[56]   A flower image

[60]   A flower image

[62]   A milkweed image?

[63]   Win Ashe and Peter

[81]   Katharine sitting on an antique chair

[90]   A flower image

OTHER: Examined a copy inscribed on page [2]: For | David Porter — | My trusted advisor and my friend. | These are my children and | my children's children, whose | future I would love | to help. | In friendship | Nell Dorr || January 5 — 1973.

In its Spring 1992 mailing the Jenny Wren Press announced a new reprinting of *Mother and Child.* Plans were to re-issue the book in late Fall 1992 or early Spring 1993 with a special introduction by Tudor. However, the re-issuing did not occur. Among Tudor fans it was understood that copyright permission was withheld because Jenny Wren Press wished to reprint without certain pictures of the nude children.

M19 [floral garland and goose] | MOTHER GOOSE | [circle of ribbon] | *Seventy-seven Verses with Pictures by* | *TASHA TUDOR* | [characters and pig] | OXFORD UNIVERSITY PRESS [Copyright 1944 | OXFORD UNIVERSITY PRESS | New York, Inc. || PRINTED IN THE UNITED STATES OF AMERICA]

PAGINATION: Five signatures of ivory "war time" paper: [1-9] 10-87 [88] pp. plus free endpapers. 7 1/2" x 6 3/4."

COVER: Moss-green cloth, like rayon, with gilt embossing: boy and girl with goose on front cover; spine, TUDOR   MOTHER GOOSE   OXFORD, laterally. The endpapers are buff without decoration.

DUST JACKET: Buff paper, black text, except for blue calligraphy on the front cover around and below a central illustrated medallion: MOTHER GOOSE | *Illustrated by* | TASHA TUDOR. Front medallion: Mother Goose with 7 goslings in a dandelion oval. A ribbon border around the entire page supported by characters from the verses. Spine: TUDOR   MOTHER GOOSE   OXFORD, laterally. Small clump of dandelions centered on back similar to those on page 66. Front flap: MOTHER | GOOSE || *Seventy-seven Verses* || *Selected and Illustrated by* | TASHA TUDOR || There is always room for a new | Mother Goose and this edition | will be particularly welcome for | Tasha Tudor's beautiful draw- | ings bring to the well-loved | verses a fresh and charming in- | terpretation. Boys and girls who | have this book as one of the first | in their libraries will treasure it, | and long after they have out- | grown the Mother Goose age | will go back to its lovely pic- | tures, both the color and black | and white. || OXFORD BOOKS FOR | BOYS AND GIRLS. [The price has been clipped from lower corner of examination copy.]   Back flap: *Do you know these picture books* | *by Tasha Tudor?* || THE WHITE GOOSE | A lovely fairy tale with exquisite moon- | lit pictures. | $1.00 || A TALE FOR EASTER | A picture book of all the enchanting | things that happen at Easter. | $1.00 || SNOW BEFORE CHRISTMAS | A New England Christmas of long ago. | $1.00 || *THE CALICO BOOKS* | *Each 75 cents* | Tiny calico-covered books about Sylvie | Ann and her adventures. || PUMPKIN MOONSHINE | ALEXANDER THE GANDER | COUNTY FAIR | DORCAS PORKUS.

CONTENTS: Pages [1] and [9] are half titles. Pages [2], [8] and [88] are blank as are the insides of both fly leaves. Dedication page [7]: *To Mary Denny Burnett* in a circle of 11 purple thistles. Burnett, known as Dady, was Tudor's Scottish nanny. She is pictured in *Mother and Child* and *Drawn From New England*.

ILLUSTRATIONS: Eighty-three illustrations. One 2-page spread of London Bridge, pp. 58-59. Beginning at page 10, the illustrations alternate 2 pages color, 2 pages black and white. Title page: a hatted goose sitting on a dandelion swag, above the title, above a ribbon and dandelion oval which encloses a woman, four children and a cat; above *Seventy-seven . . .* ,above a boy and a girl and a sheep on ground looking to center, above the publisher. Tudor's signature is reproduced with the illustrations on many pages.

OTHER: *Mother Goose* was a Randolph Caldecott Honor Medal winner in 1945, one of four runners-up when Elizabeth Orton Jones received the Caldecott Medal for illustrating Rachel Field's *Prayer For A Child.* This is not a rare book; it has been popular for fifty-four years and appears in many reprintings. However, indicative of the love and affection afforded by past owners, it is a difficult book to find in a good dust jacket. Jackets are generally missing or showing extreme wear. See also *ABC GO!*, v. 1 of the set *Collier's Junior Classics*, Crowell-Collier, 1962, for reproductions of certain of the illustrations accompanying Mother Goose rhymes. The individual rhymes used in *ABC GO!* vary from those printed here. "Old Mother Hubbard" is pictured in *Yankee* magazine, June 1954, page 31.

M20 _____.

PAGINATION: "Special" edition. <u>On heavy paper in slipcase.</u> 7 1/2″ x 6 3/4″ x ½″

COVER: Smooth <u>green linen, with square spine</u> gilt lettering as before. Spine has <u>6 extra flowers</u> stamped in lavender ink: TUDOR [3 lavender flowers] MOTHER GOOSE [3 lavender flowers] OXFORD. Each of four endpapers is framed in green ribbon and dandelion border with bows at the corners. A central dandelion ring medallion similar to the cover is topped with a green bow and pictures a nursery rhyme character in color: front left, Jack jumping over the candlestick, but a different picture than on page 40; front right, Mary, Mary watering her garden, but different from page 31; rear left, My maid Mary, different from page 19; rear right, Little Jack Horner, different from page 54. The book is in a 7 3/4″ x 6 7/8″ <u>slip case</u>, green paper over pasteboard. A white label (3 1/4″ x 3 1/4″) on the top side of the box as it lies flat, opening to the left, reproduces the ring of thistle from the dedication page encircling: *MOTHER | GOOSE | by | TASHA TUDOR*.

DUST JACKET: As above.

CONTENTS: A block of text above center on page [88]: *This edition of Mother Goose | consists of 500 copies specially | printed and bound for private | distribution, and autographed | by the illustrator, Tasha Tudor.* [Tudor's holograph signature from a fountain pen is just below this block.]

OTHER: Examined a copy inscribed on the Dedication page: Dearest Dady, ¶ This is the "special" Mother Goose, | and this copy is especially "special" as it | goes to you, the subject of the dedication. ¶ With no end of love and gratitude | for all you have ever done for me, | I feel you are in many ways responsible | for my being able to do this book. ¶ I love you! | Your Tash | December, 1944 | Tasha Tudor   [at twenty-nine years of age]

COPYRIGHT REGISTRATION: A 183852 granted to Oxford University Press, New York, Inc., 114 5th Ave., N.Y. 11, N.Y.

MOTHER GOOSE, Selected and Illustrated by Tasha Tudor, a U.S. citizen, was published Oct. 19, 1944. The book was printed by The Kellogg & Bulkeley Co., Hartford, Ct. Affidavit received at L.C. Oct. 31, 1944. Two deposit copies received Sept. 25, 1944.

COPYRIGHT RENEWAL REGISTRATION: R 515375 granted to Tasha Tudor, Contoocook, N.H., claiming as author. Kuna Dolch swears:

MOTHER GOOSE, by Tasha Tudor was originally published Oct. 19, 1944. Fees for renewal to be charged to account # 6694, Henry Z. Walck, Inc., 19 Union Square West, N.Y., N.Y. Copyright Office has added a note, "Selected and Illustrated by ---." Application and fee received [illegible].

M21 _____. [Copyright 1944 | OXFORD UNIVERSITY PRESS | New York, Inc. | SECOND PRINTING, JULY, 1944 || PRINTED IN THE UNITED STATES OF AMERICA]

PAGINATION: Paper has a <u>smoother finish.</u> 7 1/2″ x <u>6 11/16″</u>.

COVER: As before, <u>$2.00 at bottom corner of front flap</u>

M22 _____. [Copyright 1944 | OXFORD UNIVERSITY PRESS | New York, Inc. || SECOND PRINTING, JULY, 1944 | THIRD PRINTING, OCTOBER, 1944 || PRINTED IN THE UNITED STATES OF AMERICA]

COVER: Green cloth. 7 1/2″ x <u>6 5/8″</u>.

M23 _____. [Copyright . . . | THIRD PRINTING, OCTOBER, 1944 || PRINTED... AMERICA]

    COVER: Another binding in sky blue linen. 1944 | THIRD PRINTING, OCTOBER, 1944 || PRINTED IN THE UNITED STATES OF AMERICA]

    DUST JACKET: Have not examined a copy.

M24 _____. [Copyright 1944 | OXFORD UNIVERSITY PRESS | New York, Inc. || SECOND PRINTING, JULY, 1944 | THIRD PRINTING, OCTOBER, 1944 | FOURTH PRINTING, JANUARY, 1945 | PRINTED IN THE UNITED STATES OF AMERICA]

    PAGINATION: A better grade, less transparent, buff paper.

    COVER: Teal cloth.

    DUST JACKET: Have not examined one.

M25 _____. [Copyright 1944 . . . FOURTH PRINTING, JANUARY, 1945 . . . AMERICA]

    COVER: Another binding in the green fabric of the earlier printings. Endpapers are blank buff paper.

    DUST JACKET: As before, $2.00.

M26 _____. [Copyright 1944 | OXFORD UNIVERSITY PRESS | New York, Inc. || SECOND PRINTING, JULY, 1944 | THIRD PRINTING, OCTOBER, 1944 | FOURTH PRINTING, JANUARY, 1945 | FIFTH PRINTING, OCTOBER, 1945 | PRINTED IN THE UNITED STATES OF AMERICA]

    PAGINATION: Six signatures on buff paper. Page 55 is not numbered in this printing.

    COVER: Green fabric of the earlier printings, with pictorial endpapers.

M27 _____. Have not examined a SIXTH PRINTING, MAY, 1946.

M28 _____. [Copyright 1944 | OXFORD UNIVERSITY PRESS | New York, Inc. || SECOND PRINTING, JULY 1944 | THIRD PRINTING, OCTOBER, 1944 | FOURTH PRINTING, JANUARY, 1945 | FIFTH PRINTING, OCTOBER, 1945 | SIXTH PRINTING, MAY, 1946 | SEVENTH PRINTING, FEBRUARY, 1953 || PRINTED IN THE UNITED STATES OF AMERICA]

    PAGINATION: Six signatures on smooth ivory paper. Page 55 is numbered.

    COVER: Light blue cloth , imprinted as before.

    DUST JACKET: Price has been clipped from lower right front flap, and 2.20 penciled in. The same previous bookseller has lined out all prices on back flap and adjusted them: . . . THE WHITE GOOSE . . . 1.50 . . . A TALE FOR EASTER . . . 1.75 . . . SNOW BEFORE CHRISTMAS . . . 1.50 . . . THE CALICO BOOKS | Each 1.25 . . .

M29 _____. [Copyright 1944 . . . SEVENTH PRINTING, FEBRUARY, 1953 . . . UNITED STATES OF AMERICA]

    COVER: Light green "normal texture" cloth, not the dark silky rayon of previous bindings.

    DUST JACKET: An improved grade of ivory paper. The jacket is whole, but has no prices printed on either flap.

M30 _____. [Copyright 1944 | OXFORD UNIVERSITY PRESS | <u>New York, Inc.</u> || EIGHTH PRINTING, NOVEMBER, 1955 || PRINTED IN THE UNITED STATES OF AMERICA]

    COVER: Light green cloth as above.

    DUST JACKET: Have not examined one.

    OTHER: A dated inscription indicates this was a <u>1956</u> Christmas gift.

M31 _____. [Copyright . . . Inc. || EIGHTH PRINTING, NOVEMBER, 1955 . . . UNITED STATES OF AMERICA]

    PAGINATION: Six signatures on smooth ivory paper.

    COVER: <u>Lime green</u>, smooth, starched cloth, a yellow cast. Stamping as in previous printings. The spine is almost flat, a slight rounding, but unlike previous printings

    DUST JACKET: An even whiter paper than before, but still a definite ivory, not pure white. The text is exactly like the last examined 7th printing, although both front flap corners of the examination copy had been clipped.

M32 _____. . . . [characters and pig] | **HENRY Z. WALCK, INC.** [Copyright 1944 | **Henry Z. Walck, Inc.** || LIBRARY OF CONGRESS CATALOG CARD NUMBER: 58-59523 | *Printed in the United States of America*]

    PAGINATION: Six signatures on buff paper, as before. 7 1/2″ x 6 5/8″

    COVER: <u>Yellow-green cloth,</u> a shade between the previous 8th Oxford printings — more green than the lighter, more yellow than the darker. Gilt embossing: front as before. Spine: TUDOR MOTHER GOOSE   <u>WALCK</u>.

    DUST JACKET: Smooth ivory paper (kid). The upper corner of the front flap was clipped from the examination copy. Spine, in black: TUDOR   MOTHER GOOSE   <u>WALCK</u>. Front flap: MOTHER | GOOSE || *Seventy-seven*...black | and white. || <u>HENRY Z. WALCK, INC</u> || $3.50. Back flap: *Also by Tasha Tudor* || A IS FOR ANNABELLE || "The perfect gift for a little girl is this | enchanting new alphabet book...." | —*Chicago Tribune* || 1 IS ONE || "This exquisite counting book is a perfect | companion to the author-artist's alphabet | book, *A Is For Annabelle*." | —*Cleveland Press* || AROUND THE YEAR || "A companion piece to Miss Tudor's other | beautiful books, *A Is For Annabelle* | and *1 Is One*, this hand-lettered and | delightfully illustrated book gives a verse | for each month of the year." | —*San Francisco Chronicle*.

    CONTENTS: Text as in 1st Oxford. Page 55 is numbered.

    ILLUSTRATIONS: As in first Oxford.

    OTHER: Examined a copy inscribed on page [2]: ... <u>July 5th 1966</u>. I determined this to be the first Walck state by the slight changes of text, the nearness of the cloth color to the last Oxford printings, and the increased price indicative of a new publishing entity.

M33 _____.

    PAGINATION: As before, <u>perfect bound</u>. 7 3/8″ x 6 ½″

    COVER: <u>Paper over boards</u>. The former paper dust jacket is glued to raw-edged boards, each about 1/20″ thick. The flaps have been excised totally. In placing the spine perfectly, the front cover design is pushed to the extreme forward edge of the book, and was trimmed into the border leaving only about ½ of the girl in the blue dress. Endpapers as before, but trimmed closer to the design.

DUST JACKET: None

OTHER: One of the <u>rarer Tudor printings</u>. We purchased the only copy we've seen from a New Hampshire book dealer.

M34 _____.

PAGINATION: 7 ½″ X 6 5/8″

COVER: <u>Mint green cloth,</u> close in hue to M29. Ivory paper. The green of the endpaper illustrations are washed out from previous printings.

DUST JACKET: Have not examined one.

M35 _____.

COVER: Mint cloth with <u>navy</u> stamping.

DUST JACKET: Ivory kid-finish paper. Front flap: MOTHER | GOOSE . . . color and black | and white. || **HENRY Z. WALCK, INC.** || <u>$4.00.</u>   Back flap as in 1ˢᵗ Walck.

OTHER: Examined a copy with a **Christmas 1972** inscription. First NAVY stamping.

M36 _____. [A 2 15/16″ x 4 7/8″ <u>catalog card</u>: 398.8   Mother Goose | M
Seventy-seven verses with pictures | by Tasha Tudor.   Walck,
1944 | 87p. illus. || A charming book of some of the best- |
loved nursery rhymes. || 1. Nursery rhymes   I. Illus. II.
Title | [a circle simulating the hole in a library catalog card]] | This Main Entry catalog card may be reproduced without permission. || Copyright 1944 Henry Z. Walck, Inc. | <u>Copyright © renewed 1972 by Tasha Tudor</u> | ISBN: <u>0-8098-1901-5</u> | Library of Congress Catalog Card Number: 58-59523 | Printed in the United States of America]

PAGINATION: Six signatures on ivory paper. This printing changed the structure of the endpapers. The exterior sheet of the first signature comprises the front pasted endpaper and pp. 11-12. The exterior sheet of the last signature comprises pp. 77-78 and the rear pasted endpaper. Previously, endpapers were an added sheet beyond the book's body.

COVER: <u>Moss-green pebble-finish plastic-filled paper</u> over boards. <u>Navy stamping</u> as before.

DUST JACKET: White kid-finish paper with changed publisher citation. Rest of text as before. <u>Have not examined a copy with price intact.</u> Front flap: MOTHER . . . black | and white. || <u>Henry Z. Walck, Inc.,</u> | a Division of | DAVID McKAY COMPANY, INC., | <u>New York</u>. Back flap as before.

OTHER: Examination copy has a 5/8″ x 3/4″ white paper label at bottom of front flap: MARSHALL FIELD | & COMPANY | 86 | 5.50. A library copy records the acquisition date, 1/2/1979.

M37 _____.

COVER: <u>Khaki green matte paper over boards,</u> blind stamped in buckram weave. Illustration and spine in <u>light blue ink</u> stamping: front tableau and on spine, <u>TUDOR | MOTHER GOOSE</u>.

DUST JACKET: As before, price clipped.

OTHER: Examination copy has a dated inscription on half-title, <u>Spring 1979</u>.

M38 _____.

    COVER: <u>Dark forest green plastic-filled paper,</u> deer skin imprint. Light blue ink. Endpapers as above, poorly placed.

    DUST JACKET: Have not examined a copy with price intact.

M39 _____.

    PAGINATION: Six signatures bound and glued tightly in a rounded spine. Endpapers continue as the outer sheets of the first and last signatures. 7 ½″ x 6 ¾″

    COVER: <u>Bright grass green paper</u> over boards, fine <u>silk weave</u> imprint.

    DUST JACKET: Slightly darker hue of ivory paper. Whole dust jacket, with price in upper right corner, front flap: <u>$7.95</u>.

M40 _____.

    PAGINATION: 7 7/16″ x 6 5/8″

    COVER: <u>Robin's egg blue cloth.</u> <u>Black ink</u> on spine, TUDOR   MOTHER GOOSE <u>WALCK</u>. There is <u>no design</u> on the front cover.

    DUST JACKET: Have not examined one.

M41 _____.

    PAGINATION: 7 ½″ x 6 11/16″

    COVER: <u>Yellow-green grass cloth impressed paper</u> over boards. There is a heavy embossing of <u>white cross-threads</u> in the patterned paper. <u>Square spine.</u>

    DUST JACKET: Front flap complete: **<u>$8.95</u>** | MOTHER | GOOSE . . .

M42 _____. . . . [characters and pig] | <u>RANDOM HOUSE [house logo] NEW YORK</u> [Copyright 1944 by Henry Z. Walck, Inc. Copyright renewed 1971 by Tasha Tudor. All | rights reserved under International and Pan-American Copyright Conventions. <u>Originally | published by Henry Z. Walck, Inc., in 1944. Published in the United States by Random | House, Inc., New York, and simultaneously in Canada by Random House of Canada | Limited, Toronto.</u> || *Library of Congress Cataloging-in-Publication Data:* | Tudor, Tasha. Mother Goose. SUMMARY: The noted artist illustrates a selection of | seventy-seven traditional nursery rhymes. 1. Nursery rhymes. 2. Children's poetry. | {1. Nursery rhymes} I. Tudor, Tasha, ill. II. Title. PZ8.3.M85 1989b 398'.8 88-30674 | ISBN: 0-394-84407-6; 0-394-94407-0 (lib. bdg.) || Manufactured in the United States of America 1 2 3 4 5 6 7 8 9 0]

    PAGINATION: Six signatures on <u>ivory matte</u> paper. Pagination and signatures as before. The endpapers are the outermost sheets of first and last signatures. 71/2″ x 6 11/16″.

    COVER: <u>White paper, gloss film lamination,</u> over boards. For the first time, the original dust jacket <u>design is printed into the covers.</u> Spine printed laterally in black: TASHA TUDOR MOTHER GOOSE   [logo] Random House. Back cover, lower left corner: [2 UPC bar codes] and 84407 [above the small right code]; 0 7980884407 9 [under the larger left code]. Beneath all: ISBN 0-394-84407-6.

    DUST JACKET: White gloss laminated paper jacket reproduces the cover exactly. Front flap: $8.95 <u>U.S.</u> || MOTHER | GOOSE | *Seventy-seven Verses | Selected and Illustrated by |* TASHA TUDOR || Tasha Tudor's beautiful illustra- | tions bring to these well-loved | verses a fresh and charming in- | terpretation. Boys and girls who | have this book as one of the first | in their libraries will treasure it. | Long after they have outgrown | the Mother Goose age, children | will go back to its lovely pictures, | both color and black and white. Back flap: *Also by Tasha Tudor* ‖ A TALE FOR EASTER | "Many delicate pictures of rabbits, lambs, | chickens and daffodils, in close association | with little children, are sprinkled over the | pages, while a wonderful fawn brings a happy | climax to the story." —*Horn Book* ‖ FIRST PRAYERS | "Lovely prayers, beautifully illustrated for | little children." —*Christian Herald* ‖ FIRST GRACES | "This tiny exquisite book contains twenty- | one prayers of Thanksgiving." | —*Chicago Tribune* ‖ Also available in Gibraltar Library Binding ‖ Random House [logo] New York ‖ Cover illustration copyright © 1944 | by Henry Z. Walck, Inc. | Copyright renewed 1971 by Tasha Tudor. ‖ Printed in the U.S.A.

OTHER: The colophon perpetuates the error of Henry Z. Walck, Inc. having been the first publisher. Rights eventually passed through Walck to David McKay, but the first publisher was Oxford University Press. The colors of the illustrations take on less distinct green, yellow and black tones in these new photographic reproductions. The color illustrations have lost their vibrancy.

M43 _____.

PAGINATION: [i-iv, 1-9] 10-87 [88-92]. 7 ½" x 6 9/16" x 9/16"

COVER: Gibraltar Library Binding. White decorated paper impressed with a weave pattern and shellacked. Lower right back carries logo: an elephant standing on an opened book, in a double ring. The book lies above: GIBRALTAR | LIBRARY | BINDING. Beneath the logo: 394-94407-0. The signatures are all top sewn with two pieces of white buckram hinge at both ends. The hinges are glued under the white endpapers.

DUST JACKET: Have not examined a copy.

M44 _____. [Published simultaneously in Canada by Random House of Canada, Limited, Toronto] Have not examined a copy.

M45 _____. [Copyright 1944 . . . 2 3 4 5 6 7 8 9 0]

PAGINATION: 7 17/32" x 6 5/8"

M46 _____. [Copyright 1944 . . . 3 4 5 6 7 8 9 0]

PAGINATION: White matte paper.

DUST JACKET: A 2" silver Caldecott Honor Book round seal is affixed to the lower right front. New prices at top of front flap: $10.00 U.S. | $12.50 CAN.

M47 _____. [Copyright 1944 . . . 4 5 6 7 8 9 0]

DUST JACKET: Heavier gloss finish. Price on front flap, upper corner: $12.00 U.S. | $15.00 CAN.

M48 _____. [Copyright 1944 . . . 5 6 7 8 9 0] Have not examined a copy.

M49 _____. [Copyright 1944 . . . 6 7 8 9 0]

DUST JACKET: Price on front flap, upper corner: $14.00 U.S. | $17.50 CAN. Coding on back of dust jacket changes to 51400> over the right bar code, and 9 780394 844077, under the left bar code. Otherwise, as before.

M50 _____. [Copyright 1944 . . . 7 8 9 0]

M51 _____. [Copyright 1944 . . . <u>8 9 0</u>]

> DUST JACKET: Price on front flap, upper corner: $14.00 U.S. | <u>$18.00</u> CAN. || MOTHER . . . black and white. || <u>Random House | http://randomhouse.com/</u>.

> OTHER: Some plates have enhanced color, not always to the benefit of the image. This book was new in 1997.

M52 [within a frame of six oval portraits] A | MOUSE FAMILY | ALBUM || Written and illustrated by | Pamela Sampson || [publisher's globe and dividers logo] | Rand McNally & Company | Chicago · New York · San Francisco   [*To Captain and Mrs. Thaddeus Crane with love* || Library of Congress Cataloging in Publication Data | Sampson, Pamela. A mouse family album. | SUMMARY: A family album, put together from | memorabilia found in an attic trunk, portrays life of | Amelia Woodmouse's family at the turn of the century. | [1. Mice—Fiction] I. Title. | PZ7.S168Mo [E] 80-15585 | ISBN 0-528-82294-2 || Copyright © 1980 by Rand McNally & Company | All rights reserved | Printed in the United States of America by Rand McNally & Company | First printing, 1980]

> PAGINATION: [60] pp. ivory matte paper including free endpapers. The pasted endpapers are the first and last leaves of the first and last signatures. 12″ x 9 3/16″

> COVER: Cream paper over board covers imprinted with a fine linen weave. The front cover is framed in a brown stick border entwined with ivy. A female artist mouse stands at an easel as a family group of four poses for the painting. A fifth child-mouse plays with the artists tubes of color in the foreground. The title is printed in red in the same type as the title page above this tableau: A | MOUSE FAMILY | ALBUM. Beneath the illustration, in black: by Pamela Sampson. The spine is printed laterally: A MOUSE FAMILY ALBUM   Sampson   Rand McNally   [globe and dividers logo]. The back cover is framed in a similar stick and ivy border although it is less foliate than the front. The five member mouse family is pictured in a centered oval as the finished portrait from the front cover setting. The ISBN is printed in black at the upper left outside the border: 528-82294-2. The inner panels within the frames are slightly lighter in color than the spine and the covers outside the frames.

> CONTENTS: The story line and costumes are set a century ago. *A Mouse Family Album* is an extended fantasy including three generations of the Woodmouse family whose genealogy forms the front endpapers. A map of Middleshire, the family's home, forms the double-spread rear endpapers. The dedication [page 4] is to Tudor's two dolls Thaddeus and Melissa Crane, whose own "wedding" is recorded in *Life,* September 12, 1955, pp. 153-156, *q.v..* The dedication and other copyright information is printed on a large painted panel simulating a vellum sheet. Characters from the book examine it. Professor Phineas Plum supposedly discovered the material on which the book is based and with his artist niece Letitia Plum created the book. He writes somewhat erroneously in his "Dear Reader" letter on page [5]: "Miss Plum was responsible for the arrangement of the pictures and also added drawings and embellishments of her own where needed. The result is the completion, at last, of the Woodmouse family album begun so many years ago by Miss Amelia Woodmouse—to whom we most humbly dedicate this book . . . "

> Tudor's style is similar to that of her friend Pamela Sampson, born in Windsor, England. Sampson's elaborate full-color scenes of stores, the countryside, and home life are nearly all set in colored frames, but, as a rule, not so intricate as Tudor's. Small tableau appear throughout the book. Flower sprigs accent some pages, there are layouts of paper doll clothing for some of the mice. And the last page embellishment is even a very Tudoresque yellow primrose. Five illustrations and the front cover are initialed **P.S.**

> OTHER: Have examined an autographed copy dated by Sampson, 1980.

M53 MOUSE MILLS| CATALOGUE| FOR| SPRING || Put out by | The | Mouse Mills | Rocking Chair Court | Greenwillow | East of the Sun, West of the Moon [from inside the back cover: Published by The Jenny Wren Press, Box 505, Mooresville, Indiana 46158 | Copyright © 1989 by Tasha Tudor and The Jenny Wren Press | All rights reserved. No part of this book may be reproduced in any form | without permission from the publisher. Printed in the USA. || Library of Congress Catalog Card Number 89-050061 | ISBN 0-9621753-2-3]

PAGINATION: 40pp stapled into printed cover stock wrapper. 4 1/16″ x 3″

COVER: Simulated calico print of orange berries with green-bordered label superimposed, green script: Mouse Mills | Catalogue | for | Spring. Printed T. Tudor signature at bottom of label. Back cover, a green grosgrain (or possibly, taffeta) ribbon-bordered pocket with a simulated order blank tucked in and lettered: To | Mouse Mills. Another label in the center of the cover/pocket is embellished with a scalloped border and inscribed: Order Blanks

OTHER: This is a replica of a small book that Tudor created for her children and friends. The Jackie, a dress for a bear is described on page [9] and is politically interesting when one remembers that this small book was created in 1962. "Very chic saque | for the formal | tea when you | must look your | best." Various Tudor toys appear throughout.

10,080 copies were printed on 80# Mohawk Superfine Softwhite Text; the cover is 65# Mohawk Superfine Softwhite Cover. Printing was completed April 13, 1989.

COPYRIGHT REGISTRATION: TXu 378 101 granted to Tasha Tudor and The Jenny Wren Press, transfer by written agreement. Beth Mathers, P.O. Box 505, Mooresville, In. 46158 (317-831-1415), other copyright claimant and agent for Tasha Tudor, swears March 1989 [sic]:

MOUSE MILLS CATALOGUE FOR SPRING, an anonymous child's mail order catalogue for dolls ducks & bears by Tasha Tudor, born in 1916 [sic]was completed in 1962. No publication date is given. Applications were received at L.C. March 16 and July 28, 1989. Two deposit copies received March 16, 1989, the effective date of this registration.

M54 MY BRIMFUL BOOK || FAVORITE POEMS OF CHILDHOOD | MOTHER GOOSE RHYMES | ANIMAL STORIES | [rose] | Edited by DANA BRUCE | *Illustrated by* | TASHA TUDOR | MARGOT AUSTIN | WESLEY DENNIS || PLATT & MUNK, *Publishers* | [3 15/16″ rule] | NEW YORK [Copyright © 1960. || The Platt & Munk Co., Inc. New York 10, N.Y. || All rights in this book are reserved. No copyrighted material in this book | may be reproduced or used in any manner without written permission of | the publisher, except by a reviewer who, with proper credit, may quote brief | passages and reproduce not more than three illustrations in a review to be pub- | lished in a newspaper or magazine or to be broadcast by radio or television. || Printed in the United States of America. || Library of Congress Catalog Card Number: 60-9213]

PAGINATION: [76] pp. including free endpapers in five signatures side stitched. 12¼″ x 10 1/8″

COVER: Vertical red-striped paper over boards. Front cover: 3 brown stylized picture frames enclose title, sub-title and illustrators printed black on a yellow field: first, MY BRIMFUL BOOK; second, *An All-New Collection | of All-Time Favorites* | *POEMS OF CHILDHOOD |

*MOTHER GOOSE RHYMES | *ANIMAL STORIES; third, *Illustrated by* | TASHA TUDOR | MARGOT AUSTIN | WESLEY DENNIS. Overprinted in the lower right corner: A PLATT & MUNK CLASSIC. Color illustrations of a rooster, a shepherdess, a farm boy and a donkey. Red spine: MY BRIMFUL BOOK [white, centered, 6 ¼″ long], and [in black] 2008 [at top] | PLATT | & | MUNK [at bottom]. Back cover, upper left: 2008:0295, MY BRIMFUL BOOK [in frame]. End papers and fly leaves are two separate sheets, outlined in the same frame motif from front cover, are vertical stripes of green ink over butterscotch, decorated with Austin and Dennis illustrations and colored ribbons; signed MALTA. Reinforced buckram hinges.

CONTENTS: An anthology presenting three books in one with color illustrations on most pages. Title page [3]. Contents text, page [5] is overprinted in 5 horizontal color bars: red, blue, yellow, orange, lime. Section title pages: [7] yellow, Favorite Poems | of Childhood | *Illustrated by Tasha Tudor*; [27] orange, Mother Goose Rhymes | *Illustrated by Margot Austin*; [51] lime, Animal Stories | *Illustrated by Wesley Dennis*.

ILLUSTRATIONS: Tudor illustrations with "Poems of Childhood," pp. [2-3, 6-25]; Austin illustrations with "Mother Goose Rhymes," pp. [4, 26-49]; Dennis illustrations with "Animal Stories," pp. [50-74]. Tudor illustrations include girl and baby in a rose oval [2, 19], rose on the title page, a boy reading on page [6], seashore [8], a windy day [9], child with sled and star (full page) [10], small color wash of child and sled and cat [11], mother rocking child [12], 12 months [13], chipmunk [14], boy and dog on rock (full page) [15], 8 vignettes for "The Table and the Chair" [16-17], mother and children on stairs (full page) [18], bird on pussy willow branch [20], girl picking pussy willows (full page) [21], 2 page Christmas border on blue pages [22-23], toys and poppies and The Rock-a-by Lady border [24], 2 babies in slumber boats on a blue field [25].

OTHER: Austin and Dennis full-page illustrations are overprinted in small black type: © THE PLATT & MUNK CO. INC. <u>Tudor's are not</u>. These twelve poems and their illustrations have been given an interesting life by their publisher Platt & Munk. They were the basis for an expanded collection of twenty-one poems issued as Tudor's 1967 book *FIRST POEMS OF CHILDHOOD*. Two later versions, a 1967 paperback and a redesigned 1988 edition, use 13 of the poems, but not the exact same thirteen. Four of Tudor's full-age illustrations also were packaged as *Poem Puzzles*, die cut puzzles in frames, by Platt & Munk: "Pussy Willows" with the fine portrait of Bethany and the Webster farmstead, "The Arrow and The Song," The Star," "At the Seaside."

COPYRIGHT REGISTRATION: A 454576 granted to The Platt & Munk Co., Inc., 200 5th Ave., N.Y. 10, N.Y. Norman R. Harelick and Lillian Gluskin, agents for the claimant, swear on July 7, 1960:

No. 2008 - MY BRIMFUL BOOK (Retail price - $2.95), edited by Dana Bruce, 2 Sherman Ave., White Plains, NY, and illustrated by Tasha Tudor, Contoocook, N.H., Margot Austin, Danbury, Ct., and Wesley Dennis, Warrenton, Va., with cover and endpaper designs by Vincent Malta, 1960-60th St., Brooklyn, N.Y., U.S. citizens, was published June 1, 1960. Printing, engraving and plates were by Brett Lithographing Co., 47-07 Pearson Place, Long Island City, N.Y., from type set by Howard O. Bullard, Inc., 150 Varick St., and Philmac Typographers, 318 West 39th St., N.Y., N.Y. Van Reese Bookbinding Co., 304 Hudson St., N.Y. 13, N.Y., bound the books. Application and affidavit, fees and two deposit copies received at LC July 11, 1960.

COPYRIGHT RENEWAL REGISTRATION: RE 381 642 granted to Platt & Munk, Publishers, 51 Madison Ave., N.Y., N.Y. 10010, proprietors of copyright in a work made for hire. Louise Bates, agent for the claimant, swears on April 4, 1988:

MY BRIMFUL BOOK, Editor Dana Bruce; Illustrators, Tasha Tudor, Margot Austin, Wesley Dennis and Vincent Malta (cover and endpapers design) was originally published June 1, 1960. Fees charged to account DAO38288, Putnam Publishing Group, 51 Madison Ave., N.Y., N.Y. 10010. Renewal application received April 11, 1988, the effective date of this registration.

M55 _____.

    PAGINATION: <u>Enameled paper</u>. 12 1/4″ x <u>10 3/32″</u>

    COVER: <u>Gloss film laminate</u>. Back cover is <u>not coded</u>, but printed at bottom left: <u>Copyright ©</u> <u>MCMLX The PLATT & MUNK CO., INC., New York, N. Y.</u> Endpapers are printed on <u>double-page</u> sheets of paper.

    OTHER: Examined a copy inscribed March 1962.

M56 _____. [Copyright © <u>1969</u> . . . 60-9213]

    PAGINATION: <u>[68] pp.</u> in <u>4</u> signatures ivory matte paper, including free endpapers. 12 3/16″ x <u>9 5/8″</u> <u>x 7/16″</u>

    COVER: The stripes are a deeper red than before. Back cover: <u>2008:0295</u> [at top left], <u>Copyright ©</u> <u>MCMLX The PLATT & MUNK CO., INC., New York, N. Y.</u> [bottom left]. <u>Butterscotch</u> <u>endpapers, separated sheets</u>. Reinforced <u>buckram hinges</u>. Spine title is in smaller letters, the line is <u>4″ long</u>.

    CONTENTS: <u>Page [2] is blank</u>. These first edition stories of Dennis have been omitted: [58-59] "Big Sheep, Woolly Sheep, Where Are You Going?," [62-63] "The Chicken Family, the Happiest in the Barnyard," [64-65] "Donkeys at Work | and at Play."

    OTHER: Examined a copy dated Christmas 1969

M57 _____. [Copyright © <u>1969</u> …]

    PAGINATION: 12 ¼″ x <u>9 9/16″ x 13/32″</u>

    COVER: Have not examined a copy with back cover code intact. <u>Buff endpapers, plain</u>. Reinforced buckram hinges.

M58 _____. [Copyright © <u>1969</u>...]

    PAGINATION: 12 1/4″ x <u>9 9/16″ x 15/32″</u>

    COVER: The colors are not so intense, stripes salmon color. Back has only the <u>2008 code</u> in the upper left corner above title frame, <u>without the publisher's copyright statement</u>. <u>White endpapers</u>. Reinforced white buckram hinges.

M59 _____. [Copyright © <u>1969</u>...]

    PAGINATION: 12 1/4″ x <u>9 9/16″ x 15/32″</u>

    COVER: Back code as above. <u>Buff endpapers</u>.

M60 _____. . . . PLATT & MUNK, *Publishers* | [3 <u>7/8″</u> rule] | A Division of Grosset & Dunlap | NEW YORK [Copyright © 1960. || The Platt . . . Number: 60-9213 | ISBN 0-448-42008-2]

    PAGINATION: 4 signatures top stitched. <u>12 9/32″</u> x 9 9/16″ x 15/32″.

    COVER: <u>Gloss film laminate on illustrated paper</u> over boards. The stripes are a <u>dark rose</u>. Spine code has been moved from top to an inch above PLATT | & | MUNK: <u>42008-2</u>, printed laterally in black. Back cover: <u>42008:0395</u> [at top left] || MY BRIMFUL BOOK [in frame] || Platt & Munk Publishers | A Division of Grosset and Dunlap   ISBN 0-448-42008-2. The hinge was <u>top-sewn</u> through the book, before the exterior ivory matte sheets were glued down as pasted endpapers.

M61 _____.

PAGINATION: 12 ¼″ x 9 9/16″ x 3/8″

COVER: <u>Gloss film laminate.</u> <u>New cover design</u>: Five (1970s) children looking into a toy shop window, signed *Tier* ®. An inch-wide arched white ribbon forms the top of the page and the top of a toy shop window: **My Brimful Book** [red]. Overprinted in blue, in the top two window panes: Illustrated by Tasha Tudor, | Margot Austin and | Wesley Dennis ‖ Platt & Munk [bottom center]. Green-brown spine: **My Brimful** Book [red, top; and near the bottom, in blue] 42008-2 **Platt & Munk**. Back cover as front with this changed text in blue at bottom: Platt & Munk, Publishers | A Division of Grosset and Dunlap ISBN 0-448-42008-2. White endpapers top-sewn, but bound tighter. Only a few stitches show at the back when the book is opened.

M62 **MY SADIE** [2 7/8″ rule] | [drawing of horse and foal, from page 108] | By Efner Tudor Holmes | Illustrated by Ying-Hwa Hu ‖ [book logo] CHECKERBOARD PRESS | NEW YORK. [Text copyright © 1993 Efner Tudor Holmes. | Illustrations copyright © 1993 Checkerboard Press, Inc. | All rights reserved. | Published by Checkerboard Press, Inc., 30 Vesey Street, New York, NY 10007. | No part of this book may be reproduced or transmitted in any form or by any means, | electronic or mechanical, including photocopying, recording, or by any information | storage and retrieval system, without permission in writing from the publisher, except | by a reviewer, who may quote brief passages in review. | Printed in USA ISBN: 1-56288-350-X | Library of Congress Catalog Card Number: 92-56154 | E(5/5) 0 9 8 7 6 5 4 3 2 1]

PAGINATION: [1-4] 5-24 [25] 26-87 [88] 89-119 [120] 121-128. 8¼ X 5 ¼″

COVER: Full-color paper wrapper, light blue background. Front: $3.50 [black] ‖ MY SADIE [red shaded letters] ‖ Efner Tudor Holmes [black]. Spine: MY SADIE [red] Efner Tudor Holmes CHECKERBOARD PRESS [black] [book emblem]. Back: When Jill McCullough was ten years old, | her parents gave her Sadie, the first foal | ever born on their farm. ‖ Now, two years later, Sadie--a one-ton | black Percheron draft horse--is the most | important thing in Jill's life. When school | is complicated and overwhelming, Jill | knows she can always count on Sadie to life | her spirits. ‖ And while she cares for and trains Sadie, | Jill herself learns about responsibility, | dedication, and love. ‖ By Efner Tudor Holmes | Illustrated by Ying-Hwa Hu ‖ [11/8 x 1 ½″ white box with UPC code, lower left: bar code | 0 14121 00350 5 | ISBN 1-56288-350-X] [lower right: [book logo]] | CHECKERBOARD PRESS | NEW YORK.

ILLUSTRATIONS: Pencil drawings, pages [1,4] 5, 11 [25] 27, 34, 45, 56, 62, 65, 75, 81 [88] 91, 93, 101, 103, 108, 112, 113, 115 [120] 121-128.

OTHER: This is Holmes' story of a girl and her draft horse set in the New Hampshire towns where Holmes has always lived.

COPYRIGHT REGISTRATION: There was no copyright on file in January 1998.

M63 *MYTH, MAGIC, AND | MYSTERY* ‖ ONE HUNDRED YEARS OF | AMERICAN CHILDREN'S BOOK ILLUSTRATION ‖ Introductory Essay by Michael Patrick Hearn ‖ Essays by Trinkett Clark and H. Nichols B. Clark ‖ ROBERTS RINEHART PUBLISHER | *in cooperation with* | THE CHRYSLER MUSEUM OF ART [IN MEMORY | OF | JAMES MARSHALL | AND | MARGOT TOMES | MPH ‖ FOR CHARLOTTE ALLEGRA RICE CLARK | AND | HER GRANDPARENTS | DOROTHY BLAKE CLARK AND CHARLES ARTHUR CLARK, JR. | ROSEMAE SAIBEN CLARK AND CLINTON RICE CLARK | WHO OPENED SO MANY DOORS AND MINDS ‖ TC AND HNBC ‖ Copyright © 1996 by The Chrysler Museum of Art |

International Standard book Numbers 1-57098-079-9 (paper) | and 1-57098-080-2 (cloth) | Library of Congress Catalog Card Number 96-67396 || Published by Roberts Rinehart Publishers | 5455 Spine Road, Mezzanine West, Boulder, Colorado 80301 || Published in the UK and Ireland by Roberts Rinehart Publishers | Trinity House, Charleston Road, Dublin 6, Ireland || Distributed in the U.S. and Canada by Publishers Group West || Book design by Frederick R. Rinehart and E. Jack Van Zandt || Printed in Hong Kong || Exhibition schedule for *Myth, Magic, and Mystery: One Hundred Years | of American Children's Book Illustration:* || The Chrysler Museum of Art, Norfolk, Virginia: June 2, 1996-September 8, 1996 | The Memphis Brooks Museum of Art, Memphis, Tennessee: | November 3, 1996-January 6, 1997 | the Delaware Art Museum, Wilmington, Delaware: February 7, 1997-April 6, 1997.]

OTHER: Have not examined the hard cover binding. Examination from paperback edition.

M64 _____. Paperback edition.

PAGINATION: [i-iv] v [vi] vii-xii [1-2] 3-13 [14] 15-29 [30] 31-32 [33-34] 35-38 [39] 40-44 [45-46] 47-48 [a-j] 49-57 [58] 59-71 [72] 73-75 [76] 77-78 [79-80] 81-83 [84] 85-90 [91] 92-93 [94] 95-96 [97] 98-103 [104] 105-109 [110] 111-112 [113] 114-118 [119-120] 121 [122] 123-124 [125-126] 127-129 [130] 131-140 [141] 142-143 [144] 145-148 [149] 150-155 [156-158] 159-167 [168] 169 [170] 171-177 [178] 179-183 [184] 185-197 [198] 199-201 [202] 203-211 [212] 213-235 [236] 237-242 plus paper wrapper. 11 ½ x 9″

COVER: Full-color paper, gloss finish. A wide navy blue border is used at section titles throughout the book and is adapted to the front cover, the bottom rail missing. A double line rectangular frame is printed on the top rail in which is printed the title, all in yellow: MYTH, MAGIC, AND MYSTERY | *One Hundred Years of American Children's book Illustration.* The majority of the cover (9 5/8 x 7 5/16″) is N.C. Wyeth's *Rip Van Winkle* returning home (1921). Overprinted in gray letters, red shading, at the bottom: BY MICHAEL PATRICK HEARN | TRINKETT CLARK AND H. NICHOLS B. CLARK. Spine, a red panel printed in yellow: MYTH, MAGIC, AND MYSTERY   HEARN, CLARK, & CLARK   [a gray rhinoceros] Back: yellow panel within a frame, thin red, blue, red lines, text printed in blue ink with a black line illustration. Hilary Knight, "Eloise with Skibberdee," 1954 | unpublished drawing from *Eloise,* | collection of Mr. Hilary Knight || [drawing for the caption] || A STUNNING ACHIEVEMENT, *Myth, Magic, and Mystery* brings | together the work of nearly every prominent children's book illustrator of | the twentieth century. Developed for a nationwide, touring exhibit beginning | at the Chrysler Museum of Art in Norfolk, Virginia in June 1996, this book | stands alone as a portable encyclopedia of the "masters" of the genre. | Included here are the works of such popular illustrators as N. C. Wyeth, | Chris Van Allsburg, Maurice Sendak, Dr. Seuss, Edward Gorey, Tomi | Ungerer, and others; a special feature of the book is a complete "alphabet" | created from a selection of the classic ABC books by the likes of Richard | Scarry and *Curious George* creator H. A. Rey. ¶ *Myth, Magic, and Mystery* will be a volume to be treasured alongside | the classics themselves, a book to be sought after for moments of quiet | contemplation or recollections of sheer joy. || [printer's swirl] || TRINKETT CLARK was formerly the Curator of Twentieth-Century Art at | The Chrysler Museum of Art in Norfolk, Virginia. H. NICHOLS B. CLARK | currently serves as Curator of American Art at the Chrysler. Both have | written widely and coordinated exhibitions at a number of institutions. || [printer's swirl] || MICHAEL PATRICK HEARN is America's leading man of letters specializing in | children's literature and its illustration. Among his many books are the cult | classic *The Annotated Wizard of Oz* and, more recently, *The Porcelain Cat.* || FRONT COVER ART: N. C. Wyeth, "It was with some difficulty that he found his way to his own house," | 1921, from *Rip Van Winkle,* Millport Conservatory and Museum. || ROBERTS RINEHART PUBLISHERS | BOULDER, COLORADO | PUBLISHED IN COOPERATION WITH THE CHRYSLER MUSEUM OF ART.

A white panel (1 3/8 x 2 1/8″) printed over part of the central panel, the line borders and the wide blue bottom rail bears two bar codes: ISBN 1-57098-079-9 | [larger code and over the smaller, right hand code] 52995 | 9 781570 980794.

CONTENTS: An exhaustively illustrated review of twentieth century children's book illustration interpreted through this text: Foreword by Catherine H. Jordan, Acting Director of the Chrysler Museum of Art; Preface by the authors; Discover, Explore Enjoy by Michael Patrick Hearn; And the Dish Ran Away with the Spoon: A First Look at the World of Words, from Mother Goose to Dr. Seuss by Trinkett Clark; and three chapters written by H. Nichols B. Clark, Here and Now, Then and There: Stories for Young Readers; High Adventure and Fantasy: Art for All Ages; Happily Ever After . . . : Fairy Tales, Fables, and Myths. Notes, Checklist of Illustrations, Index.

ILLUSTRATIONS: Many illustrations, often two to a page, sometimes three or more. The majority are in color on a heavy coated stock with 2 ½″ outer margins. The captions for illustrations are often printed in these margins. Tudor illustrations appear on pp. 103, 118, 175 with accompanying text. A double page spread from *Corgiville Fair* is printed on page 103 with Tudor's hand-written text. This is the one sheet the editor did not see at the Morgan Library because it was touring with this exhibit at the time. Text: . . . Equally sympathetic [to animals, as are Garth Williams and Lillian Hoban - Ed.] is Tasha Tudor's *Corgiville Fair* (1970), which chronicles the | festivities of this annual event in a small town inhabited by corgis, cats, rabbits, and | goblins known as boggarts. The panoramic illustration of the fair [cat. No. 92] contains myriad details in carefully delineated watercolors that convey the spirit of celebration | as well as the artist's trademark aura of well-being. . .

Page 117: . . . Halloween is one of the most beloved of holidays and generates great | artistic appeal because of its potential for scary imagery. While Tasha Tudor includes | ghosts, witches, and goblins in the Halloween drawing for her charming book of holi- | days, *A Time to Keep* (1977), she tempers the potential for fright in order to reassure her younger readers [cat.no.118]. Nevertheless, children come away with a vivid sense of | the occasion that triggers the imagination. . . Page 118 carries the second two-page spread from "October" as painted by Tudor. This reproduction has more of a blue cast than does the published *A Time to Keep.*

Page 174: . . . NEW ENGLAND STOCK WITH OLD ENGLAND SOURCES || By contrast [with Gustaf Tenggren], Tasha Tudor has deep New England roots, and her preference for pen | and ink and soft, ethereal watercolors retains an allegiance to the tradition of Randolph | Caldecott, Walter Crane, Beatrix Potter, and Edmund Dulac. She elected to evoke the | ideals, beauty, and sentiment of a bygone era, and this devotion is borne out in the type | of books she has chosen to illustrate: Frances Hodson Burnett's *The Secret Garden* (1962) | and *Fairy Tales from Hans Christian Andersen* (1945), among others. From the last publi- | cation comes a tender realization of an episode in "The Real Princess," in which the | flaxen-haired guest is about to ascend the enormous mound of colorful mattresses and | feather beds that have been placed over a pea [cat. No. 194]. This ploy was intended to [page 175] test her royalty by assessing the sensitivity of her skin. Her finely chiseled features stand | in telling contrast to the ample countenance of the housekeeper. This affable matron is | accompanied by her young candle-bearing son, whose inclusion underscores the artist's | sentimental advocacy of domestic harmony. Tudor is deeply interested in theater and | costume, and she brings a fanciful sense of the stage set to her delicate execution. . .

OTHER: An advertising sheet indicates the book was to be published September 1996, $29.95 paper, and $50.00 cloth. The publisher's numbers are included: Tel:303-530-4400 FAX. 303-530-4488 rhinobooks@aol.com.

N1 THE | NEST || [a robin looking into its nest built in the crook of a branch] || by
Constantine Georgiou || **Illustrated by Bethany Tudor** || **Harvey House,**
Inc. | **Publishers** | **Irvington, New York   10533**. [*For Charles and Elizabeth* || *Copyright © 1972 by*
Harvey House, Inc. || *All rights reserved, including* | *the rights to reproduce this book* | *or portions thereof in any*
form. || *Library of Congress Catalog Card Number 72-76396* | *ISBN 0-8178-4891-6, Trade Edition. ISBN 0-*
8178-4892-4, Library Edition | *Manufactured in the United States of America* || *Harvey House, Inc., Publishers* |
Irvington, New York 10533]

PAGINATION: [1-7] 8-37 [38-40], buff textured paper, plus apple green endpapers. 9 ½ x 7 5/8″

COVER: Golden brown printed paper over boards, with a light gloss finish. Front cover is outlined
in a rectangular border of red apples and apple boughs. **Constantine Georgiou** [black] ||
[robin sitting on its nest] || **THE NEST** [brown letters edged in black] || **Illustrated by**
Bethany Tudor [black]. Spine printed in same black and brown scheme: **Georgiou**
[black]   **THE NEST** [brown letters edged in black] **Harvey House** [black]. The back is
blank. Back carries the same illustration but reversed. The only text just inside the lower right
border: ISBN 0-8178-4891-6.

DUST JACKET: Front, spine and back exactly like the book. Front flap: *ISBN 0-8178-4891-6 $3.95* ||
An EASY TO READ Picture Book || THE NEST | **by Constantine Georgiou** ||
Illustrated by Bethany Tudor || Young children will delight in this | warm and tender story
about a | mother robin and her efforts to build | her nest. Overshadowing the grim- | ness of city
classrooms, it is a simply- | told tale of innate care and provi- | sion for life outside the hard-
hitting | environments of today. || It is the kind of book that lifts the | youngest reader over the
rough | spots in his reading experience, help- | ing him to reach (without straining) | for word
recognition. Dr. Constan- | tine Georgiou, the author, is a rec- | ognized authority and teacher in
the | field of children's literature. || **Harvey House, Inc.** | **Publishers** | **Irvington, New York**
10533. Back flap: [1 3/16 x 1 ½″ photograph of Giorgiou] | An authority in the field of Chil- |
dren's Literature and Professor of | Education at New York University, | Dr. Constantine
Georgiou writes for | young readers with warmth and | clarity that stem from his knowledge | of
children and their books. A for- | mer elementary school teacher, Dr. | Georgiou is Chairman of
the Com- | mittee on the Children's Library at | NYU and Advisory Editor for *Chil-* | *dren and*
Their Literature. | [1 3/16 x 1 ½″ photograph of Tudor] | Bethany Tudor lives in an eight- | eenth
century New England farm- | house in Webster, New Hampshire, | where she pursues personal
intersts | in drawing, music, the study of nat- | ural history, and the domestic arts. | She has
attended Boston Univer- | sity, the Vesper George Art School | in Boston, and Kennington
School | of Art in London, England. Miss | Tudor credits her interst in illus- | trating children's
books to her | mother, Tasha Tudor, who is a well- | known artist in that field.

CONTENTS: Page [1]: About the Book || Young children will delight . . . field of children's literature.
Page [40] reproduces the text from the back flap: **About the Author** || An authority in the
field . . . Professor | of Education . . . Geor- | giou . . . that | stem . . . former | elementary . . . the |
Committee . . . Advisory | Editor . . . of | juvenile books . . . *Chil-* | *dren* . . . *Literature.* || **About**
the Artist || Bethany Tudor . . . England | farmhouse . . . pursues | personal . . . his- | tory, . . .
Univer- | sity, . . . Kennington | School . . . in- | terest in illustrating . . . Tasha | Tudor, who is a
well-known artist in that field.

ILLUSTRATIONS: Tudor has painted simple direct illustrations in green and brown watercolors of a
robin, an apple tree and a secure nest. One picture of a small rabbit appears on pages [2] and
[38]. An opposing illustration of the robin with a bit of twig in its mouth is on pages [3] and

[39]. The illustration on the title page [5] is 2 1/2″ x 3″. Each page of text [7] - 37 has a different illustration (ca. 4 1/2″ x 6″).

COPYRIGHT REGISTRATION: A 377480 granted to Harvey House, Inc., 5 South Buckhout St., Irvington, N.Y. 10533. Jeanne Gardner, agent for claimant, swears on Oct. 13, 1972:

THE NEST, text by Constantine Georgiou, 1 Washington Square Village, Apt. II-G, N.Y.C. 10012, and illustrations by Bethany Tudor, Route L [*sic*], Contoocook, N.H. 03229, both U.S. citizens, was published Sept. 14, 1972 . The book and jacket were printed by Film Exposures, 333 West 52nd St., N.Y.C., from type set by Howard Bullard, 150 Varick St., N.Y.C. and binding by Horowitz, Allwood Road, Clifton, N.J. Fees, application and affidavit and two deposit copies received at L.C. Oct. 24, 1972.

N1a _____.

OTHER: Examined another copy rebound in yellow buckram with the front cover full illustration painted to the buckram. 9 5/8″ x 7 9/16″ in rebound library copy.   **Tudor**. Spine printed in blue: THE NEST • GEORGIOU. The back is blank. An oval foil label has been attached at the bottom inside of the front cover: BOUND-TO-STAY-BOUND BOOKS | SINCE 1920 | JACKSONVILLE, ILLINOIS.

N2 *The New England* | BUTT'RY SHELF | ALMANAC | *being a Collation of Observations on* | *New England People, Birds, Flowers,* | *Herbs, Weather, Customs, and Cookery* | *of Yesterday and Today* | [13/16″ rule] | MARY MASON CAMPBELL | ILLUSTRATED BY | TASHA TUDOR | [tree-in-circle emblem] | THE WORLD PUBLISHING COMPANY | NEW YORK • CLEVELAND   [*Published by The World Publishing Company* | *Published simultaneously in Canada by* | *Nelson, Foster & Scott Ltd.* | *First Printing—1970* | *Copyright © 1970 by The World Publishing Company* | *All rights reserved* | *Library of Congress Catalog Card Number: 76-128491* | *Printed in the United States of America* || WORLD PUBLISHING | TIMES MIRROR || *The author and editor gratefully acknowledge* | *Imogene Wolcott, author of The Yankee Cook Book* | *published by Ives Washburn, Inc., for giving permission* | *to reprint the Christopher LaFarge verse,* | *"Rhode Island Clambake";* | *also Little, Brown and Company,* | *publishers of The Complete Poems* | *of Emily Dickinson, for cooperation.*]

PAGINATION: Ten signatures of ivory paper, pp. [1-7] 8-13 [14-15] 16-17 [18-26] 27 [28] 29-34 [34a-34b] 35 [36] 37-42 [43-46] 47 [48] 49-58 [59] 60-63 [64-68] 69 [70] 71-77 [78] 79-82 [83-85] 86 [87] 88-90 [91] 92-98 [98a-98b, 99] 100-104 [105-107] 108 [109] 110-111 [112] 113-123 [124] 125-129 [130, 130a-130b, 131-133] 134 [135] 136-137 [138] 139-147 [148] 149-154 [155-157] 158 [159] 160-161 [162 162a-162b] 163-171 [172] 173-177 [178-181] 182 [183] 184-186 [187] 188-194 [194a-194b] 195 [196] 197-201 [202-205] 206 [207] 208-210 [211] 212-221 [222] 223-225 [226-229] 230 [231] 232-233 [234] 235-243 [244] 245-249 [250-253] 254 [255] 256-257 [258] 259-267 [268] 269-271 [272-275] 276 [277] 278-280 [281] 282-291 [292] 293-296 [297] 298-302 [303-306] plus mustard endpapers. 7 1/2″ x 6 5/8″.

COVER: Aquamarine cloth stamped in gold on spine and front cover. Front: *The New England* | BUTT'RY SHELF | ALMANAC inside a rule box inside a larger box 3″ x 2 1/4″. Two acanthus leaf devices above and below the box. Spine: *Campbell*   The New England Butt'ry Shelf Almanac [tree in circle logo] WORLD.

DUST JACKET: Pictorial gloss film lamination, text in blue, red and black. Front, (six panels of farm scenes surrounding on oval of text, repeated on the back. Front text: *The New England* [blue] | *BUTT'RY SHELF* | *ALMANAC* [red] | *Being a Collation of Observations* | *on New England People, Birds,* | *Flowers, Herbs, Weather,* | *Customs, and Cookery* | *of Yesterday and Today* [blue] | *MARY MASON CAMPBELL* | *Illustrated by* | *Tasha Tudor* [red]. Spine, within a single large blue rule: *The New* | *England* [blue] | BUTT'RY SHELF ALMANAC [red] *Campbell* [GREEN, but some copies have faded to blue] [tree in circle logo] WORLD [blue]. Back: About | *The New England* | BUTT'RY SHELF COOKBOOK [red] | "This is a charming exercise | in nostalgia both in the text and the | recipes and in the warm illustrations by | Tasha Tudor . . . . This is the kind of food | I love because it never palls – N.Y. *Times* | " . . . a cookbook to treasure for its | esthetic as well as its | practical value." – *Concord Daily Monitor* | . . . required reading for all nostalgic | New Englanders by birth or proxy." | – *Library Journal* | "Good reading as well as good eating." | – Garden City N.Y. *Newsday* [blue]. Overprinted in black, lower right corner: A3408. Front flap text mostly black: $6.95 [black] | *The New England* [blue] | *BUTT'RY SHELF | ALMANAC* [red] | MARY MASON CAMPBELL | *Illustrated by Tasha Tudor* [blue] || "In a gentle mood of <u>nostaglia</u> [*sic*], *The New | England Butt'ry Shelf Almanac* has been | written in the hope that it will furnish | interesting and useful information to all | those who love New England, its cus- | toms, its people, its old houses and | ghosts, its hills and valleys and rivers and | coves, and its ways of keeping house and | garden."¶Mrs. Campbell has chronicled the sea- | sons, describing a bird for each month— | its habits, feeding, song—and a flower— | its cultivation and literary associations— | and then chatting in a personal way | about the landscape, historical events, | and anecdotes of rural life, quoting bits | of poetry, and giving recipes. She con- | cludes each month with a portrait of a | New England personage of note. ¶Mrs. Campbell writes from her own | experience and observation and her | seemingly endless knowledge of New | England lore. She tells us about feeding | chickadees in January, catching and cook- | ing shad in April, and cultivating roses in | June; about the wrens nesting in the | mailbox, the independent, long-lived | New England ladies and their legal | battles, Emily Dickinson, and New Eng- | land herb gardens. ¶Mrs. Campbell has set all this down in a lyric prose which is perfectly com- | plemented by Tasha Tudor's beautiful | illustrations. Back flap: MARY MASON CAMPBELL, [blue, remainder in black] a midwesterner | by birth, is a graduate of Yankton Col- | lege in South Dakota and did advanced | study at the University of Minnesota | and the Art Institute of Chicago. After | teaching for a year, she met Douglas | Campbell, a lawyer and native New | Englander, who introduced her to sum- | mers in New Hampshire. ¶Mr. and Mrs. Campbell now live most | of the year in their white eighteenth- | century New Hampshire farmhouse, sur- | rounded by old trees, flowers, and ex- | panses of green. ¶She is author of the delightful *New | England Butt'ry Shelf Cookbook*. [black] || TASHA TUDOR [blue] is a native New Englander, | born and raised in Connecticut. [*sic*] She re- | ceived no formal art training but was | taught by her mother, a portrait painter. | Mrs. Tudor has become well known as | an illustrator of books for young people, | among them the well-loved *The Wind in | the Willows*. ¶Mrs. Tudor has lived for many years in | a large farmhouse in Webster, New | Hampshire, a homestead in the true sense | of the word, where she raises cows, pigs, | chickens, and sheep, keeps a vegetable | garden, and tends bees. ¶Mrs. Tudor's background and interests | have made her the ideal illustrator for | *The Butt'ry Shelf Almanac*, and her work | is truly evocative of New England. [black] || [tree in circle logo] | WORLD PUBLISHING | [2 1/8" rule] | TIMES MIRROR | NEW YORK AND CLEVELAND.

CONTENTS: Half-title, page [1]. Dedication, POSIES | FOR MY | *Mother,* page [5]. Page [6]: ALSO BY | MARY MASON CAMPBELL | ILLUSTRATED BY | TASHA TUDOR || *The New England* | BUTT'RY SHELF COOKBOOK. *The Collation:* pp. [7]-13. *The Almanac:* pp. [15]-17. *Wedding Anniversaries:* p. [21]. *Index:* pp. [297]-302.

ILLUSTRATIONS: Full page pencil drawings: pp. [19, 20, 23, 43, 65, 83, 105, 131, 155, 179, 203, 227, 251, 273]. Small pencil drawings: Half-title [1], Dedication [5] pp. 13, 17 (with perhaps the tiniest corgi Tudor has drawn), 27, 35, 42, 54, 56, 58, 63, 86, 90, 98, 108, 121, 123, 134, 147, 158, 182, 186, 206, 221, 230, 243, 271, 276, 296. Full page water colors: pp. [Frontispiece 2, 34a, 98a, 130a, 160a, 194a] Each of four endpapers has a different pencil sketch of a jar and a dish holding flowers and fruit representative of one season. Blank pages: [14, 18, 22, 34b, 64, 98b, 130, 130b, 160b, 178, 194b, 202, 226, 250, 272, 303, 304, 305, 306]

OTHER: Some copies carry color plates on a courser paper. The illustration on page 86 is of Douglas and Mary Campbell at their picture window in Salisbury, N.H.; their home on page 17.

COPYRIGHT REGISTRATION: A 193825 granted to The World Publishing Company, 110 East 59th St., N.Y., N.Y. 10022. (Miss) Phoebe McKay swears on Nov. 23, 1970:

THE NEW ENGLAND BUTT'RY SHELF ALMANAC: being a Collation of Observations on new England People, Birds, Flowers, Herbs, Weather, Customs, and Cookery of yesterday and today by Mary Mason Campbell, 14 Fountain St., Wickford, R.I., a U.S. citizen, was published Oct. 30, 1970. The book was manufactured by Haddon Craftsmen, Inc., N.Y., N.Y. Fees charged to The World Publishing Company. Application and affidavit and two deposit copies received November 25, 1970.

N3 _____. Published simultaneously in Canada by | Nelson, Foster & Scott Ltd. Have not examined a copy.

N4 _____. . . . TASHA TUDOR || THOMAS Y. CROWELL COMPANY | NEW YORK • ESTABLISHED 1834. [*Copyright © 1970 by The World Publishing Company | All rights reserved | Library of Congress Catalog Card Number: 76-128491 | Printed in the United States of America | Published in Canada by | Fitzhenry & Whiteside Limited, Toronto | ISBN 0-690-00361-7 || 2 3 4 5 6 7 8 9 10 | The author and editor . . . for cooperation.*]

    COVER: Spine, change publisher to: CROWELL; back, lower right, 0-690-00361-7.

    DUST JACKET: Bottom of spine within rule: 0-690-00361-7 | CROWELL. Back lacks the overprinted code at lower right. New blue text, bottom of back flap: THOMAS Y. CROWELL COMPANY | Established 1834 | 666 Fifth Avenue | New York 10019. Have not examined a copy with price intact.

N5 _____. [*Copyright © 1970 by Thomas Y. Crowell Company, Inc, | All rights . . . ISBN 0-690-00361-7 || 3 4 5 6 7 8 9 10 | The author and editor ... for cooperation.*]

    COVER: Turquoise plastic-filled paper, prominent weave pattern, over boards. No ISBN on the back. White endpapers without decoration.

    DUST JACKET: Front flap: 0-690-00361-7, [price]. *The New England* . . . Have not examined a copy with the price intact.

N6 _____. . . . TASHA TUDOR || THE STEPHEN GREENE PRESS | Brattleboro, Vermont | Lexington, Massachusetts [Copyright © 1970 by The World Publishing Company, | © 1982 by Mary Mason Campbell || All rights reserved. No part of this book may be reproduced | without written permission from the publisher, except by | a reviewer who may quote brief passages or reproduce illustrations | in a review; nor may any part of this book be reproduced, | stored in a retrieval system, or transmitted in any form or by | any means electronic, mechanical, photocopying, recording, or | other, without written permission from the publisher. || This book is manufactured in the United States of America. It is | published by the Stephen Greene Press, Fessenden Road, Brattleboro, | Vermont 05301. **Library of Congress Cataloging in Publication Data** | Campbell, Mary Mason. | The New England butt'ry shelf almanac. || Includes index. | 1. Literary calendars. 2. New England—Social life | and customs. 3. Cookery, American—New England. | I. Title. | PN6245.C18 1983 974 83-11589 | ISBN 0-8289-0511-8]

    PAGINATION: Nine (?) signatures ivory paper, perfect bound. Color plates on enameled paper. 7 7/16″ x 6 3/8″

    COVER: Red paper impressed with cloth weave, over boards. Stamped in gold on spine only, within a wide gold rule within a narrow gold rule: CAMPBELL || THE NEW ENGLAND | Butt'ry Shelf Almanac || illustrated by | Tasha | Tudor || S | GP.

    DUST JACKET: Retains illustrations, with front and spine text reset. Front: THE NEW ENGLAND [black] || Butt'ry Shelf | Almanac [rust] || BEING A COLLATION OF OBSERVATIONS ON | [leaf] NEW ENGLAND PEOPLE [leaf] BIRDS [leaf] | FLOWERS [leaf] HERBS [leaf] WEATHER | [leaf] CUSTOMS AND COOKERY [leaf] | OF YESTERDAY AND TODAY || Mary Mason Campbell [black text, rust leaves] | *Illustrated by* | Tasha Tudor [rust]. Spine: a white panel with the same pattern as the book, but in color. The panel is outlined with a rust rule inside a black rule, half as wide. All text black except Butt'ry Shelf Almanac which is rust. Back text is black. Front flap: ISBN 0-8289-0511-8 T.N.E.B.S.A. $12.95 | The New England . . . Text exactly as before including misspelling, but all black with the exception of the one blue phrase, *Illustrated by Tasha Tudor*. Back flap: MARY MASON CAMPBELL . . . Mrs. Tudor has lived for some years in | a small farmhouse in Vermont — a charm- | ing homestead in the true sense of the | word— where she raises cows, pigs, chick- |ens, and sheep, keeps a vegetable and large | flower garden, and tends bees . . . evocative of New England. Publisher, black: THE STEPHEN GREENE PRESS | Brattleboro, Vermont 05301.

OTHER: A statement in the second printing, *q.v.*, dates this printing October 1983.

N7 _____. [. . . 83-11589 | ISBN 0-8289-0511-8 || PUBLISHED OCTOBER 1983 | *Second printing December 1983*]

PAGINATION: Cream paper. Perfect bound. Editor examined one which had dried and split.

DUST JACKET: Have not examined a copy with price intact, although the examination copy did have a gummed label just below the ISBN which read, $ 12.95.

N8 _____. [. . . PUBLISHED OCTOBER 1983 | *Second printing December 1983* | *Third printing August 1984*]

DUST JACKET: Have not examined a copy with upper corner, front flap, intact. This printing probably never carried the title initials. ISBN remains at upper left.

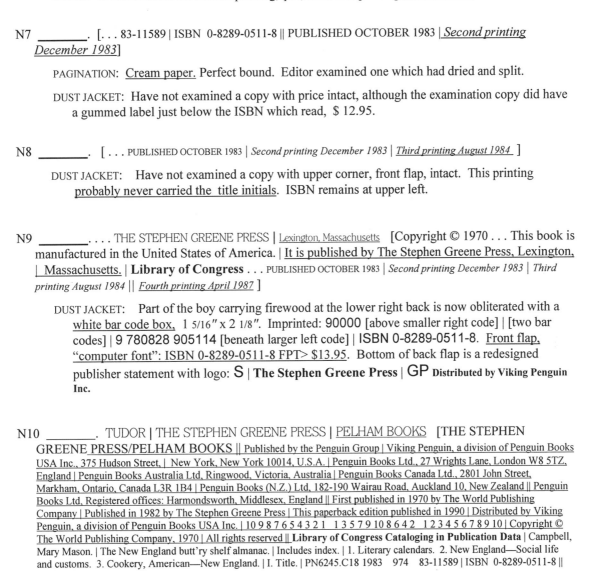

N9 _____. . . . THE STEPHEN GREENE PRESS | Lexington, Massachusetts [Copyright © 1970 . . . This book is manufactured in the United States of America. | It is published by The Stephen Greene Press, Lexington, | Massachusetts. | **Library of Congress** . . . PUBLISHED OCTOBER 1983 | *Second printing December 1983* | *Third printing August 1984* || *Fourth printing April 1987*]

DUST JACKET: Part of the boy carrying firewood at the lower right back is now obliterated with a white bar code box, 1 5/16″ x 2 1/8″. Imprinted: 90000 [above smaller right code] | [two bar codes] | 9 780828 905114 [beneath larger left code] | ISBN 0-8289-0511-8. Front flap, "computer font": ISBN 0-8289-0511-8 FPT> $13.95. Bottom of back flap is a redesigned publisher statement with logo: S | **The Stephen Greene Press** | GP **Distributed by Viking Penguin Inc.**

N10 _____. TUDOR | THE STEPHEN GREENE PRESS | PELHAM BOOKS [THE STEPHEN GREENE PRESS/PELHAM BOOKS || Published by the Penguin Group | Viking Penguin, a division of Penguin Books USA Inc., 375 Hudson Street, | New York, New York 10014, U.S.A. | Penguin Books Ltd., 27 Wrights Lane, London W8 5TZ, England | Penguin Books Australia Ltd, Ringwood, Victoria, Australia | Penguin Books Canada Ltd., 2801 John Street, Markham, Ontario, Canada L3R 1B4 | Penguin Books (N.Z.) Ltd, 182-190 Wairau Road, Auckland 10, New Zealand || Penguin Books Ltd, Registered offices: Harmondsworth, Middlesex, England || First published in 1970 by The World Publishing Company | Published in 1982 by The Stephen Greene Press | This paperback edition published in 1990 | Distributed by Viking Penguin, a division of Penguin Books USA Inc. | 10 9 8 7 6 5 4 3 2 1 1 3 5 7 9 10 8 6 4 2 1 2 3 4 5 6 7 8 9 10 | Copyright © The World Publishing Company, 1970 | All rights reserved || **Library of Congress Cataloging in Publication Data** | Campbell, Mary Mason. | The New England butt'ry shelf almanac. | Includes index. | 1. Literary calendars. 2. New England—Social life and customs. 3. Cookery, American—New England. | I. Title. | PN6245.C18 1983 974 83-11589 | ISBN 0-8289-0511-8 || PRINTED IN THE UNITED STATES OF AMERICA || Except in the United States of America, this book is sold subject to the condition that it shall not, by | way of trade or otherwise, be lent, re-sold, hired out, or otherwise circulated without the publisher's | prior consent in any form of binding or cover other than that in which it is published and without a | similar condition including this condition being imposed on the subsequent purchaser.]

PAGINATION: White paper, perfect bound paperback. 71/4″ x 6 1/4″ There are no endpapers.

COVER: For the first time, cover text (in rust, gray and black) appears in a vertical box obscuring part of the illustration. White box in a thin rust rule. This text: *The New England* [rust text and 2 1/4″ underscore] | BUTT'RY SHELF | ALMANAC [black] | [gray rule intertwined with hearts and vines] | OBSERVATIONS ON | [rust rule] | NEW ENGLAND PEOPLE, [leaf] BIRDS, [leaf] FLOWERS, | [leaf] HERBS, [leaf] WEATHER, [leaf] CUSTOMS, | AND COOKERY | OF YESTERDAY AND TODAY | [rule] | MARY MASON CAMPBELL [text is black, rules and leaf devices are rust] | [calligrapher's scroll device in gray] | [black rule] *Illustrated by* [rust] [black rule] | TASHA TUDOR [rust].   White spine, no box: MARY | MASON CAMPBELL [black] | THE NEW ENGLAND | BUTT'RY SHELF ALMANAC [rust] | 0-8289-0805-2 | STEPHEN GREEN PRESS | [rule] | PELHAM BOOKS [black].   Back top within a gray rule box, text in rust: "In a gentle mood of nostalgia, *The New England Butt'ry Shelf Almanac* has been | written in the hope that it will furnish interesting and useful information to all those | who love New England, its customs, its people, its old houses and ghosts, its hills and | valleys and rivers and coves, and its ways of keeping house and garden." | -From the introduction | [Below the box the gray rule with hearts and vine repeated from front cover. Then this text in black:] Enjoy a slice of New England life and lore in this fascinating collection of anecdotes, observa- | tions, history, <u>poety</u> [sic], and recipes from yesterday and today. A longtime New Englander, Mary | Mason Campbell captures the nuances of an old-fashioned lifestyle that still thrives in the | hearths of today's New England. Campbell chronicles the seasons, describing a bird and flower | for each month; tells us about feeding chickadees in January, catching and cooking shad in April, | and cultivating roses in June; and ruminates on wrens nesting in mailboxes, New England herb | gardens, and Emily Dickinson, Thoreau and other New Englanders of note. | [Gray calligrapher's scroll from front.] | Cover design by Todd Radom | Cover illustration by Tasha Tudor | S | GP | The Stephen Greene Press | Pelham Books | An imprint of Penguin USA | Americana || Aust. $19.99 | (recommended) | CAN. $14.95 | U.S.A. $10.95 | [lower right corner] ISBN 0-8289-0805-2 [above larger left bar code] | [2 barcodes] | 90000 [above smaller right code] | 9 780828 908054 [beneath left code].

ILLUSTRATIONS: Color plates on enameled paper.

OTHER: Purchased new, <u>February 1992</u>.

N11 _____. . . TUDOR | [stylized P in a circle] | A PLUME BOOK [PLUME | Published by the Penguin Group | Penguin Books USA Inc., 375 Hudson Street, | New York, New York 10014, U.S.A. | Penguin Books Ltd., 27 Wrights Lane, London W8 5TZ, England | Penguin Books Australia Ltd, Ringwood, Victoria, Australia | Penguin Books Canada Ltd, <u>10 Alcorn Ave., Suite 300</u>, Toronto, Canada M4V 3B2 | Penguin Books (N.Z.) Ltd, 182-190 Wairau Road, Auckland 10, New Zealand | Penguin Books Ltd, Registered offices: Harmondsworth, Middlesex, England | Published by Plume, an imprint of New American Library, a division of Penguin Books USA Inc. | Previously published in a Stephen Greene Press | Pelham Books edition, distributed by Viking Penguin | <u>First Plume Printing, May, 1991 | 10 9 8 7 6 5 4 3 2 1</u> | Copyright © The World Publishing Company, 1968 | All rights reserved. || [P in a circle] REGISTERED TRADEMARK-MARCA REGISTRADA || Printed in the United States of America | Without limiting the rights under copyright reserved above, no part of this publication may be | reproduced, stored in or introduced into a retrieval system, or transmitted, in any form, or by any | means (electronic, mechanical, photocopying, recording, or otherwise), without the prior written | permission of both the copyright owner and the above publisher of this book. | BOOKS ARE AVAILABLE AT QUANTITY DISCOUNTS WHEN USED T PROMOTE PRODUCTS OR SERVICES. FOR INFORMATION PLEASE WRITE TO PREMIUM MARKETING DIVISION, PENGUIN BOOKS USA INC., 375 HUDSON STREET, NEW YORK, NEW YORK 10014.]

PAGINATION: There are no endpapers.   71/4″ x 6 <u>1/16</u>″

COVER: Front: 'P circle' logo over PLUME in the lower right corner of the title panel.   Spine: **[P in circle]** | PLUME | MARY | MASON CAMPBELL [black] | THE NEW ENGLAND | BUTT'RY SHELF ALMANAC [rust] | <u>0-452-26735-8</u> | REFERENCE/REGIONAL [black]   Back: "In a gentle mood . . . From the <u>Introduction</u> . . .Tasha Tudor | **[P in circle]** | A PLUME BOOK | Reference/Regional | Z6735 || **$11.95.**   Lower right corner: <u>ISBN 0-452-26735-8</u> [over larger left code] 90000> [over smaller right code] | [2 barcodes] | 9 780452 267350 [under left code].

N12 *The New England* | BUTT'RY SHELF | COOKBOOK | *Receipts for* | *Very Special Occasions* || [rule] || MARY MASON CAMPBELL | ILLUSTRATED BY | TASHA TUDOR || THE WORLD PUBLISHING COMPANY | CLEVELAND • NEW YORK [*Published by the World Publishing Company* | *2231 West 110th Street, Cleveland, Ohio 44102* | *Published simultaneously in Canada by Nelson, Foster & Scott Ltd.* || FIRST PRINTING 1968 || *Library of Congress Catalog Card Number 67-22907* | *Copyright © 1968 by The World Publishing Company* | *All rights reserved. No part of this book may be reproduced in* | *any form without written permission from the publisher, except* | *for brief passages included in a review appearing in a newspaper* | *or magazine. Printed in the United States of America.*]

PAGINATION: 13 signatures [1-8] 9-12 [13] 14-15 [16] 17-25 [26] 27-31 [32] 33-43 [44] 45-51 [52] 53-63 [64, 64a-64h] 65-105 [106] 107-119 [120] 121-125 [126] 127-128 [128a-128h] 129-179 [180] 181-192. 7 ½″ x 6 ½″

COVER: Rust cloth stamped in gold on front cover in double rules, scroll above and below: *The New England* | BUTT'RY SHELF | COOKBOOK. Spine: *Campbell The New England Butt'ry Shelf Cookbook* [tree in circle and, W P] *World* . Mustard endpapers with six pencil drawings of buttery scenes, front and rear.

DUST JACKET: Color illustration of a stocked buttery repeated front and back. Front, top half: 2 ¼ x 3 3/8″ white panel superimposed, a wide and a narrow red rule surround around, *The New England* [blue] | *Butt'ry Shelf* | *Cookbook* (red) | *Receipts for* | *Very Special Occasions* [blue] | *MARY MASON CAMPBELL* [red]. Black calligraphy bottom center: *Illustrated by Tasha Tudor.* Spine: blue rule box enclosing: *The New* | *England* (blue) *Butt'ry Shelf Cookbook* (red) *Campbell* (green) *World* (blue). Back, lower right bottom: A1562. Flaps have the slightest angled cut from all four corners. Front flap: $5.95 [black] || *The New England* [blue] | *BUTT'RY SHELF* | *COOKBOOK* [red] | *Receipts for* | *Very Special Occasions* || MARY MASON CAMPBELL | *Illustrated by Tasha Tudor* [blue] | [remaining text black] In traditional New England houses the | buttery (pronounced "butt'ry") is a | small room located next to the kitchen, | its shelves laden with jars, crocks, plat- | ters, and plates filled with the richness | of country cooking. On a shelf nearest | the kitchen is kept the *Buttery Book,* | which is, in fact, a collection of books | containing rules and receipts that have | been handed down from generation to | generation. ¶For this unusual cookbook, Mary | Mason Campbell has chosen more than | two hundred treasured receipts from her | own *Buttery Book*—a collection that actu- | ally dates back to her great-grandmother's | time. These are the author's favorites, | and many of them have never before | been shared with anyone outside her | family. ¶The delectable treats described here | can easily be made today and provide a | faithful reminder of the days when holi- | (*continued on back flap*). Back flap: (*continued from front flap*) | days and family gatherings were always | a time for cooking and baking and filling | the buttery with good things to eat. ¶Mrs. Campbell invites you to enjoy | with her the fun and excitement of her | family traditions for celebrating festive | days—and to experience the rich and | wonderful tastes and smells of country | cooking that make each of these days a | "very special occasion." ¶The charming illustrations by Tasha | Tudor create an authentic picture of | New England farmhouse living at its | merriest and best. || MARY MASON CAMPBELL [blue] lives in New | Hampshire in a pre-Revolutionary farm- | house, which, of course, boasts a well- | filled buttery. Her interests are many, | but she especially enjoys working in her | garden, weaving on her eighteenth-cen- | tury looms, and preparing delightful | meals in her much-loved New England | kitchen for her family and good friends. | Mrs. Campbell and her husband spend | some time each year in Old Wickford, | on Narragansett Bay, Rhode Island, in | an 'acorn-sized fisherman's cottage," | built in 1802, which they have recently | restored. || TASHA TUDOR [blue] is one of America's best- | loved illustrators. She is a friend | and neighbor of Mrs. Campbell, and is very | much at home with the subject of this | book, for she too lives in New Hampshire | in an eighteenth-century red-clapboarded | farmhouse with a fine buttery and a busy | kitchen.

CONTENTS: Half-title, [1]. Title page, [3]. Dedication, [5]: A SUGAR COOKY | FOR | *Douglas* AND THE | *Mason Girls*. Contents, [7]. Color Illustrations, [8]. Glossary, 181-182. Index, 183-192.

285

ILLUSTRATIONS: Eight full page color illustrations on ivory matte paper between pages 64 and 65: New Year's Day Open House, Valentine's Day, Easter Breakfast, May Basket Day, Afternoon Tea Parties, Wedding Reception, Wedding Anniversary Dinner for Two, Picnic by the River; eight more are bound between pages 128 and 129: Breakfast Under the Apple Tree, Fourth of July, Mountain Cookout, Birthdays, Thimble Tea and the Quilting Bee, Hallowe'en, Thanksgiving, Christmas. The scheme is a scene in a twig bordered shield, often with flowers, ribbons and other ornaments. Other appropriate ornaments are beneath each shield. Pencil drawing on title page [3] depicts two tall hollyhocks framing the title and a row of four stoneware crocks at the bottom of the page. Other pencil drawings on pages [5] 9 [13] full-page, 17, 25, 27, 31, 33, 43, 45, 47, 51, 53, 54, 58, 63, 65, 66, 68, 70, 73, 78, 79, 85, 89, 98, 99, 107, 115, 119, 121, 127, 155, 159, 169, 171, 175, 176, 182. Pages [2, 6, 16, 26, 32, 44, 52, 64, 106, 120, 126, 180] are blank. Sketches on endpapers also appear on pages [13] 25, 70, 98, 139, 169. Same pansy drawing on pages 54 and 58. Illustration on page 66 is reversed and reduced on page 68. Illustration on page 171 is reduced on page 176.

COPYRIGHT REGISTRATION: A 20639 granted to The World Publishing Company, 2231 West 110th St., Cleveland, Oh. 44102. Jean M. Chapman, The World Publishing Company, 119 West 57th St., N.Y., N.Y. 10019, swears on Oct. 2, 1968:

THE NEW ENGLAND BUTT'RY SHELF COOKBOOK Today by Mary Mason Campbell, South Road, Salisbury, N.H., and Tasha Tudor (Illustrator), Route 1, Contoocook, N.H., both U.S. citizens, was published August 15, 1968. The book was manufactured by V & M Typographers, Brooklyn, N.Y., Halliday Lithographers, N.Y., N.Y., and World Publishing Co., Cleveland, Oh. Fees charged to The World Publishing Company. Application and affidavit received at L.C. Oct. 7, 1968; two deposit copies received Sept. 17, 1968.

COPYRIGHT RENEWAL REGISTRATION: RE 734-235 granted to Tasha Tudor, c/o Corgi Cottage Industries, P.O. Box 7281, Richmond, Va. 23221-0281 claiming as author (illustrator). Kathryn L. Barrett, Esq., 235 East 22nd St., Apt. 11C, N.Y., N.Y. 10010, 212-684-6689, agent for Tasha Tudor, swears on June 21, 1996:

THE NEW ENGLAND BUTT'RY SHELF COOKBOOK, RECIPES [sic] FOR VERY SPECIAL OCCASIONS, by Tasha Tudor and Mary Mason Campbell was published August 15, 1968, and registered World Publishing Co., A20639. Renewal application received Aug. 9, 1996, the effective date of this registration.

N13 _____. [Published by the World... SECOND PRINTING 1968 || Library of Congress Catalog Card Number 67-22907|Copyright ©1968 . . . Printed in the United States of America.]

N14 _____. [Published by the World... THIRD PRINTING 1969 . . . Printed in the United States of America]

PAGINATION: Six signatures buff paper.

N15 _____. . . . TUDOR [tree in a circle logo] | WORLD PUBLISHING | [rule] | TIMES MIRROR | NEW YORK. [Published by the World Publishing Company | Published simultaneously in Canada by Nelson, Foster & Scott Ltd. || Fourth printing-1972 | Copyright © 1968 by The World Publishing Company | All rights reserved | ISBN 0-529-00376-7 | Library of Congress catalog card number: 67-22907 | Printed in the United States of America | WORLD PUBLISHING | [rule] | TIMES MIRROR]

PAGINATION: Six signatures and two small gatherings. This printing on a whiter paper before.

COVER: Spine logo printed upright for the first time; beneath it, WORLD.

DUST JACKET: Front flap: $6.95 . . .

N16 _____. [*Published by the World Publishing Company | Published simultaneously in Canada by Nelson, Foster & Scott Ltd. || Fifth printing-1973 || Copyright . . .* TIMES MIRROR]

      PAGINATION: Six signatures and two small gatherings. Ivory paper.

N17 _____. . . . TUDOR || THOMAS Y. CROWELL COMPANY | Established 1834 | New York 10019 [*Copyright © 1968 by The World Publishing Company | All rights reserved | Library of Congress Catalog Card Number 67-22907 | Printed in the United States of America | Published in Canada by Fitzhenry | & Whiteside Limited, Toronto | ISBN 0-690-00362-5 | 5 6 7 8 9 10*]

      PAGINATION: 8 signatures. 7 1/2" x 6 1/2"

      COVER: Spine: *Campbell   The New England Butt'ry Shelf Cookbook*   CROWELL;   Back cover, lower right: 0-690-361-7.

      DUST JACKET: Spine: CROWELL [laterally, in blue].

      OTHER: The second appearance of a fifth printing. Examined a copy with a Mary Mason Campbell gift inscription, and dated in a different hand, Oct. 20, 1974. A spring of Rosemary was scotch-taped to the title page, accompanying Campbell's inscription. A printed and dated 1974 Christmas note with two Tudor illustrations is laid in and signed "Mary and Doug Campbell." The note is on buff light-weight artist's paper, printed in sepia, green and red. The dominant image is a ring of butt'ry implements encircling a plum pudding. The pudding, in turn, sits in a ring of holly printed in green and red. A green Christmas tree, ¼" high, decorates page [3] beneath the greeting.

N18 _____. . . . TUDOR || THE STEPHEN GREENE PRESS | Brattleboro, Vermont | Lexington, Massachusetts [Copyright ©1968 by The World Publishing Company, | ©1982 by Mary Mason Campbell || All rights reserved. No part of this book may be reproduced | without written permission from the publisher, except by | a reviewer who may quote brief passages or reproduce illustrations | in a review; nor may any part of this book be reproduced, | stored in a retrieval system, or transmitted in any form or by any means electronic, mechanical, photocopying, recording, or | other, without written permission from the publisher. || This book is manufactured in the United States of America. It is published by | The Stephen Greene Press, Fessenden Road, Brattleboro, Vermont 05301 || LIBRARY OF CONGRESS CATALOGING IN PUBLICATION DATA || Campbell, Mary Mason. | The New England Butt'ry shelf cookbook. || Includes index. | 1. Cookery, American—New England. I. Tudor, Tasha. | II. Title. | TX715.C1893 1982   641.5'68 82-9287 | ISBN 0-8289-0490-1   AACR2]

      PAGINATION: 7 1/2" x 6 1/2"

      COVER: Navy paper stamped with linen weave over boards. Gold stamping, front in double-rule frame: THE NEW ENGLAND | Butt'ry Shelf | Cookbook | Receipts for Very Special Occasions || Mary Mason Campbell. Spine in double rules: The | New England   Butt'ry Shelf Cookbook   Campbell | Tudor   S | GP. White endpapers without decoration.

      DUST JACKET: White title label has new color and type font. A brown rule inside a black rule frame surrounding: THE NEW ENGLAND [brown] | Butt'ry Shelf | Cookbook [red] | Receipts for Very Special Occasions || Mary Mason Campbell [brown]. Oval gummed gold foil seal attached bottom center: Illustrated by | Tasha Tudor.   Spine, a brown rule within a thin black rule, enclosing| THE | NEW ENGLAND [brown]   Butt'ry Shelf Cookbook [red]   Campbell | Tudor [brown]   S | GP [black]. Back, lower right printed laterally against the spine, from the bottom up, black: 0-8289-0490-1. Except for the illustrator statement, all text on front flap is black: T.N.E.B.S.C. $12.95 | 0 - 8289 - 0490 - 1 || [a thick black rule within a thin black rule] THE NEW ENGLAND | Butt'ry Shelf | Cookbook | Receipts for Very Special Occasions || Mary Mason Campbell [Below the box, in blue] *Illustrated by Tasha Tudor* || In traditional . . .   The text is largely as before, but the biographies on the back flap have been revised. MARY MASON CAMPBELL [blue] . . . Campbell and her husband spend | some time each year in Rhode Island. || TASHA TUDOR [blue] is one of America's best- | loved illustrators. She is an old friend | of Mrs. Campbell, and is very much at | home with the subject of this book, for she | too lives in a farmhouse with a fine buttery | and a busy kitchen.

ILLUSTRATIONS: Colored illustrations are now on enameled paper.

N19 _____. [Copyright ©1968 by The World . . . AACR2 || PUBLISHED OCTOBER 1982 *Second printing February 1983*]

   PAGINATION: Ivory paper. 71/2″ x 6 1/2″

   COVER: White end papers.

   DUST JACKET: A second smaller pre-printed white panel at center bottom, red inside a brown rule and a black rule frame: Illustrated by | Tasha Tudor.

N20 _____. Have not examined a third printing.

N21 _____. Have not examined a fourth printing.

N22 _____. . . . THE STEPHEN GREENE PRESS || Lexington, Massachusetts [Copyright ©1968 by The World . . . It is published by | The Stephen Greene Press, Lexington, Massachusetts. | Distributed by Viking Penguin | LIBRARY OF CONGRESS . . . Published October 1982 | 10 9 8 7 6 5]

   PAGINATION: 71/2″ x 6 1/2″

   DUST JACKET: Front flap: CAN $21.95 | U. S. A. $15.95. [two-rule box] . . . Back, lower right, 1 3/16″ x 2 1/16″ white panel: ISBN 0-8289-0490-1 [above the larger left code] 90000 [above the smaller right code] | [2 bar codes] | 9 780828 904902 [beneath the left code. Back flap text has been raised enough to allow this new text at bottom: S | GP | The Stephen Greene Press | Distributed by Viking Penguin.

N23 _____. . . . TUDOR || THE STEPHEN GREENE PRESS | PELHAM BOOKS [THE STEPHEN GREENE PRESS/PELHAM BOOKS || Published by the Penguin Group | Viking Penguin, a division of Penguin Books USA Inc., 375 Hudson Street, | New York, New York 10014, U.S.A. | Penguin Books Ltd., 27 Wrights Lane, London W8 5TZ, England | Penguin Books Australia Ltd, Ringwood, Victoria, Australia | Penguin Books Canada Ltd, 2801 John Street, Markham, Ontario, Canada L3R 1B4 | Penguin Books (N.Z.) Ltd, 182-190 Wairau Road, Auckland 10, New Zealand || Penguin Books Ltd, Registered Offices: Harmondsworth, Middlesex, England || First published in 1968 by The World Publishing Company | Published in 1982 by The Stephen Greene Press | This paperback edition published in 1990 | Distributed by Viking Penguin, a division of Penguin Books USA Inc. | 10 9 8 7 6 5 4 3 2 1 1 3 5 7 9 10 8 6 4 2 1 2 3 4 5 6 7 8 9 10 Copyright © The World Publishing Company, 1968 | All rights reserved | [CIP data is printed here verbatim from N22, but in a new font.] || PRINTED IN THE UNITED STATES OF AMERICA || Except in the United States of America, this book is sold subject to the condition that it shall not, by | way of trade or otherwise, be lent, re-sold, hired out, or otherwise circulated without the publisher's | prior consent in any form of binding or cover other than that in which it is published and without a | similar condition including this condition being imposed on the subsequent purchaser.]

   PAGINATION: 7 ¼″ x 6 ¼″

   COVER: No end papers. White paper cover, gloss film lamination. Easter Breakfast, page [64c] on the cover. [The gentleman at the table with the large mustache seems a close representation of Tasha Tudor's father Starling Burgess.-Ed.] Superimposed beige title boxes on front cover in brown rules. At top: *The New England* [brown] | [brown rule] BUTT'RY SHELF | COOKBOOK [brown rule with leaf] | RECEIPTS FOR | VERY SPECIAL OCCASIONS | [brown rule] | MARY MASON CAMPBELL [black]. At bottom: [3/4″ rule] *Illustrated by* [3/4″ rule], [brown] | TASHA TUDOR [black]. | Spine: MARY | MASON CAMPBELL [black] THE

NEW ENGLAND | BUTT'RY SHELF COOKBOOK [brown] 0-8289-0806-0 STEPHEN
GREENE PRESS | [rule] | PELHAM BOOKS. A 5/14″ yellow rule is printed across the spine
separating author and title. Back of cover: Experience the rich and wonderful tastes | and smells
of New England country cooking | and farmhouse living. I [rule and leaf] brown. Remaining
Text, black: In traditional New England houses, the buttery (pronounced butt'ry) is a small
pantry | located next to the kitchen. Its shelves are laden with jars, crocks, platters, and plates
filled | with the richness of country cooking. It is also where you'll find the Butt'ry Book, a |
collection of recipes handed down from generation to generation. For this unusual | cookbook,
Mary Mason Campbell has chosen more than 200 treasured recipes from her own | Butt'ry
Book—a collection that dates back to her great-grandmother's time. The | delectable treats
described here provide a faithful reminder of the days when holidays and | family gatherings
were always a time for cooking and baking and filling the buttery with good things to eat. || "A
charming exercise in nostalgia both in the text and the recipes." —*The New York Times* || "A
cookbook to treasure for its esthetic was well as its practical value." | —*Concord Daily Monitor* ||
"Good reading as well as good eating." —*New York Newsday* || MARY MASON CAMPBELL is
the author of *The New England Butt'ry Shelf Almanac* and of | *A Basket of Herbs,* both from the
Stephen Greene Press. She lives in Rhode Island. || TASHA TUDOR is one of America's best-
loved illustrators and lives in Vermont. || Cover design by Todd Radom | Cover illustration by Tasha Tudor || **S** | **G**
| **P** | **The Stephen Greene Press** | **Pelham Books** | **An Imprint of Penguin USA** | Food and Cooking ||
AUST. $19.99 | **(recommended)** | **CAN. $14.95** | **U.S.A. $10.95**. Lower right, back: black ruled box
(1 ¼″ x 2 1/16″) ISBN 0-8289-0806-0 [above larger left code] 90000 [above smaller right code] |
[two bar codes] | 9 780828 908061.

N24 _____. . . . TUDOR || [P in a circle logo] | A PLUME BOOK [PLUME | Published by the Penguin Group |
Penguin Books USA Inc., 375 Hudson Street . . . Penguin Books Canada Ltd, <u>10 Alcorn Ave., Suite 300, Toronto, Canada M4V</u>
<u>3B2</u> | Penguin Books (N.Z.) Ltd . . . Middlesex, England || Published by <u>Plume, an imprint of New American Library</u>, a division
of Penguin Books USA Inc. | Previously published in a Stephen Greene Press/Pelham Books edition, distributed by Viking |
Penguin. || <u>First Plume Printing, May, 1991</u> | <u>10 9 8 7 6 5 4 3 2 1</u> || Copyright © The World Publishing Company, 1970 | All
rights reserved. || [P in circle logo] REGISTERED TRADEMARK—MARCA REGISTRADA || Printed in the United States
of America || Without limiting the rights under copyright reserved above, no part of this publication may be | reproduced, stored
in or introduced into a retrieval system, or transmitted, in any form, or by any | means (electronic, mechanical, photocopying,
recording, or otherwise), without the prior written | permission of both the copyright owner and the above publisher of this book. |
BOOKS ARE AVAILABLE AT QUANTITY DISCOUNTS WHEN USED TO PROMOTE PRODUCTS OR SERVICES. FOR |
INFORMATION PLEASE WRITE TO PREMIUM MARKETING DIVISION, PENGUIN BOOKS USA INC., 375 HUDSON |
STREET, NEW YORK, NEW YORK 10014.]

PAGINATION: 7 1/4″ x 6 1/8″

COVER: Spine: [P in circle logo] | PLUME | MARY | MASON CAMPBELL [black] | [yellow rule] |
THE NEW ENGLAND | BUTT'RY SHELF COOKBOOK [brown] | <u>0-452-26736-6</u> | <u>FOOD AND</u>
<u>COOKING</u> [black]. Back: "Experience the rich . . . Cover illustration by Tasha Tudor. || **[P in circle logo]** |
<u>A PLUME BOOK</u> | Food and Cooking | <u>Z6736</u> || **$11.95**. Lower right, box with two bar codes: <u>ISBN 0-</u>
<u>452-26736-6</u> [above larger left code] 90000> [above smaller right code] | [bar codes] | 9
780452 267367.

N25 NEW | ENGLAND || WILD | FLOWERS. [tiny lettering at the
bottom right of front cover: 1937 T.T.]

PAGINATION: [154] pp. in 35 folded vellum sheets and 5 single sheets and two covers. 13″ x 10″ x
2″

COVER: Artist's vellum as binding over two separate boards, drilled and tied with a string.

ILLUSTRATIONS: 74 images of wildflowers painted on gray paper. Each painting is glued to the
recto of a page of the vellum. See reproductions in *Drawn From New England*, page 23.

CONTENTS: Inside front cover [2] and page [4] are blank. Page [3], a purple flower not identified. Page [5], lupine, not identified. Page [6] "Wild senna . . . " [text] Page [7], the painting of the senna. From there to the end, each verso bears an identification and each recto the corresponding painting. The last painting is glued to the inside back cover.

[8-9]	No identification
[10-11]	Yellow clover, white clover, red clover
[12-13]	European bellflower
[14-15]	Harebell
[16-17]	Rue anemone
[18-19]	Traveller's joy
[20-21]	Cardinal flower
[22-23]	Horned bladderwort
[24-25]	Steepel bush
[26-27]	Bladder campion
[28-29]	Butter and eggs
[30-31]	Musk mallow, white
[32-33]	Common speedwell
[34-35]	Purple gerardia
[36-37]	Smooth false foxglove
[38-39]	No identification
[40-41]	No identification
[42-43]	No identification
[44-45]	No identification
[46-47]	Turtle head
[48-49]	Monkey flower
[50-51]	Blue vervain
[52-53]	Yellow star grass
[54-55]	Quaker ladies, partridge vine
[56-57]	Dog violet, Canada violet
[58-59]	Wood sorrel and yellow wood sorrel
[60-61]	Wild geranium
[62-63]	Wild lupine
[64-65]	Wild senna
[66-67]	Wild bean
[68-69]	Wild columbine
[70-71]	Night shade
[72-73]	Blue eyed grass
[74-75]	Jack-in-the-pulpit
[76-77]	Shin leaf
[78-79]	Trailing arbutus
[80-81]	Pink azalea, American cranberry
[82-83]	Sheep laurel
[84-85]	Mountain laurel
[86-87]	Water lily
[88-89]	Dog's tooth violet
[90-91]	Wood lily

[92-93]	Turk's cap lily
[94-95]	Rattlesnake plantain
[96-97]	Ladies tresses
[98-99]	Large round leaf orchis
[100-101]	Green orchis
[102-103]	Pink lady's slipper
[104-105]	Yellow lady's slkipper
[106-107]	Jewel weed
[108-109]	Self heal
[110-111]	False dragon head
[112-113]	Bee balm
[114-115]	Motherwort
[116-117]	Basil
[118-119]	Wild morning glory
[120-121]	Common yarrow
[122-123]	White aster
[124-125]	New England aster
[126-127]	Robin's plantain
[128-129]	White aster #1
[130-131]	Daisy fleabane
[132-133]	White aster #2
[134-135]	Burr thistle
[136-137]	Blazing star
[138-139]	Devil's paint brush
[140-141]	Tansy
[141-142]	Black eyed Susan
[143-144]	Golden rod
[145-146]	Viper's bugloss
[147-148]	Queen Anne's lace
[149-150]	Closed gentian
[151-152]	Common St. John's wort
[153-154]	Wild ginger (glued to back cover)

OTHER: Tudor's second book exists in a single unique manuscript. Bethany Tudor writes of her mother March 10, 1997, ". . . When she was nineteen she decided to collect and paint all the Conn. Wildflowers in the area. It took two or three summers but the results: "New England Wildflowers" is a most amazing, well filled book. It was not published but remains a thing of beauty." And in *Drawn From New England*, page 23, ". . . Then, of course, she did a lot of drawing during the summer. She loved to paint wild flowers. In her late teens she set herself the task of painting all the Connecticut wild flowers she could find. This project took her quite a few summers to complete, but she enjoyed searching for plants through the lovely fields and woods. [And this caption to three illustrations and the cover of the book] .. *Drawing and painting were now primary and pleasurable pursuits. Shown here are pages from a portfolio of carefully researched paintings of New England wild flowers.*"

N26 New Hampshire Authors' Luncheon | *held in connection with* | THE BOOK FAIR | *sponsored by* | The Woman's College Club | *of* | CONCORD, NEW HAMPSHIRE ‖ [open book emblem] || NEW HAMPSHIRE HIGHWAY HOTEL | Concord, New Hampshire | September 13, 1955   1:00 P.M.

PAGINATION: [4] pp. folded card stock.   8 ½ x 5 ½″

COVER: Buff textured cover stock.

CONTENTS: Page [2] lists a menu and Courtesies. Among the latter *For Souvenir Books* | The Reader's Digest. This would explain why another bi-fold off-print *Reader's Digest (*June 1954) "Are You a Litterbug? Is inserted in the program. *Reader's Digest* was one of the largest accounts of a local printing plant. Page [3]: *Authors* | WHO HAVE INDICATED THEY WOULD BE PRESENT | Henry Darracott Allison | Clarence William Anderson | Kenneth Andler | Priscilla Ayers | Donald Babcock | Shirley Barker | Ella Shannon Bowles | Burnham Carter | George Calvin Carter | Mildred Criss | Bertha Damon | Fairfax Downey | William Plumer Fowler | Corey Ford | Margery Harkness | Carolyn Bailey Hill | Laurie Hillyer | Raymond P. Holden | Harry Elmore Hurd | Woodland Kahler | Eric P. Kelly | Donald MacNaughton | Loulie Albee Mathews | Nyleen Morrison | Paul Scott Mowrer | Guy Murchie | Thomas McCready | Harriet Chase Newell | Catherine Parmenter Newell | Walter Collins O'Kane | Louise Owen | Clement E. Philbrook | Mildred I. Reid | Marion Nichols Rawson | Elizabeth Ripley | Duane Bradley Sanborn | J. Duane Squires | Elva S. Smith | Tasha Tudor | Ann Tufts | Richard Upton | Herbert Franklin West | Polly Webster | Stephen Winship | Mason Wade.   Page [4] lists committee chairs and Hostesses.

N27 *THE | NIGHT BEFORE | CHRISTMAS* | *by* | CLEMENT C. MOORE |
illustrated by | TASHA TUDOR | ACHILLE J. ST. ONGE | WORCESTER [© 1962 BY ACHILLE J. ST. ONGE]

PAGINATION: [36] pp. including free end papers. 3 11/16″ x 2 5/8″

COVER: Full <u>red</u> calf, gilt frame and title on front: *THE* | *NIGHT* | *BEFORE* | *CHRIST'* | *MAS.* Four identical end papers: red string border centering a sprig of holly, on a yellow wash field. All edges gilt.

DUST JACKET: Buff jacket, brown printing, brown wash panel on front with Santa Claus [same as page 24] above the title: *THE | NIGHT BEFORE | CHRISTMAS* | BY CLEMENT C. MOORE | ILLUSTRATED BY TASHA TUDOR. Front flap: A book for a child | to treasure | *(and we're all | children at heart)* | and to invoke | memories of a | favorite person, | a favorite poem and | a favorite holiday | in years to come. || Illustrations by | the distinguished | American Artist... | Tasha Tudor || ACHILLE J. ST. ONGE | PUBLISHER | WORCESTER 6, MASS.

ILLUSTRATIONS: All illustrations in color: [6, 7, 10-31]. Full page illustrations on pp. [6, 10, 13-16, 18-20, 23-25, 27, 29, 31].

CONTENTS: No text on pp. [6, 13, 18, 20, 23, 27, 29, 31]. Blank pp. [2-4, 32, 34-35]. Half title: [5, 10]. Title page: [7]. Dedication page [9]: *To | E.B.H. | from | T.T.* Page [33]: *This edition of | The Night Before Christmas | was printed by | Joh. Enschede en Zonen, | Haarlem, Holland.*

OTHER: Dedicated to Edward B. Hills, Mill Hall, Pa., Tudor's first major patron, collector and dealer in original art. Robert E. Maasmann in *The Bibliomidgets of A. J. St. Onge.* Page 70: VIII. *The Night Before* [page 71] *Christmas*, by Clement C. | Moore. 1962. Full red calf, | gilt; a.e.g.; illustrated, col- | ored dust wrapper. 15,000 | copies issued. 3 11/16″ X 2 5/8″. ¶Printed by Joh. Enscede' | en Zonen, Haarlem, Holland. ¶Illustrated (endleaves, | dust wrapper, pages through- | out) in full color, by Tasha | Tudor. ¶1200 copies were bound in [page 72] red cloth, gilt; a.e.g., in the | same dust jacket as the lea- | ther edition.

COPYRIGHT REGISTRATION: A 8253 granted to Achille J. St. Onge, 7 Arden Road, Worcester 6, Ma., who claiming for himself, swears:

THE NIGHT BEFORE CHRISTMAS, by Clement Moore, with authorship claimed by Achille St. Onge, a U.S. citizen, was published Nov. 1, 1962. New matter in this version: The illustrations for this edition drawn by Tasha Tudor. The book was first published in Zurich, Switzerland. Fee and one deposit copy received at L.C. Jan. 21, 1963. Application received April 25, 1963.

N28 _____.

COVER: Have not examined one of the 1200 copies in <u>red cloth</u>.

N29 _____. [ALL RIGHTS RESERVED BY | ACHILLE J. ST. ONGE]

COVER: Wine calf.

OTHER: Page [33], additional text, bottom of the page: the St.Onge monogram.

N30 _____.

COVER: Another binding in scarlet calf.

N31 _____.

PAGINATION: [32] pp. including stiff free end papers created in binding when the first two leaves were pasted together evidenced by chain marks in paper. (One also sees this done in a reprinting of St. Onge *The Twenty Third Psalm*.) Minus the blank pages [2-4, 34-35] of previous printings. All text and illustrations as in the first St. Onge printing, but pagination is reduced by two, beginning with the half-title on page [3]. St. Onge monogram on page [31].

COVER: Wine calf.

N32 THE NIGHT | BEFORE CHRISTMAS | [Santa above a holly swag] | by CLEMENT CLARKE MOORE | [mistletoe] | Illustrated by | TASHA TUDOR | [two mice dancing] | Rand McNally & Company [Copyright © 1975 by Rand McNally & Company | All rights reserved | Printed in the United States of America | by Rand McNally & Company | Library of Congress Catalog Card Number: 75-8858 || First printing, 1975]

PAGINATION: Four signatures on white kid paper, [60] pages including free endpapers. The endpapers are the first and last leaves of the first and fourth signature, respectively, glued to the boards. Signatures are sewn and glued. 12" x 9 1/4"

COVER: White printed <u>paper over boards</u>, red, green and black flower border on front and back. Title on front in yellow out-lined letters: THE NIGHT | [Santa shaking paws with a corgi] | BEFORE | CHRISTMAS | Illustrated by TASHA TUDOR [black]. Spine: THE NIGHT BEFORE CHRISTMAS [red] MOORE [flower] TUDOR Rand McNally [black]. Back cover upper left above border: 528-82181-4; toys and gifts in a twig frame, centered.

DUST JACKET: No issued with a jacket.

CONTENTS: The Author | and the Illustrator [Author, and Illustrator, in red], pp. [56-58]. Page [58]: . . . Tasha Tudor, illustrator of this edition, is famed for the | delicacy of her watercolors and for the quaintness of her | period settings. Details in her illustrations reach straight to | the heart of childhood to appeal to children of any era. | Outdoors, owls and chipmunks and flying squirrels lead Santa | and his reindeer to a safe rooftop landing. Indoors, a cat and a | corgi make him welcome. A doll dances. A clown turns | cartwheels. The corgi dons Santa's cap and puffs on his pipe. | And under the floor—as every child knows there must be—is | an amusing and complete miniature house for a mouse. || Miss Tudor has given us a highly personalized version of "The | Night Before Christmas." The house, inside and out, is her | own Vermont farm home designed in exact detail after one of | 1740. Inside are to be found the rocking horse and the doll | carriage shown on the endpapers at the front of the book, the | doll that peeks from Santa's pack—"possessor of an extensive | wardrobe"—and the Noah's ark. The ornaments on the | Christmas tree date to the 1840s and once belonged to Miss | Tudor's grandmother. And naturally, in residence in the | house are a corgi and a cat. || A hundred and fifty years separate the author, Clement | Clarke Moore, and the illustrator, Tasha Tudor. Their talents | span the years and join to give today's children a delightfully | whimsical Christmas treat.

ILLUSTRATIONS: Two pages of black and white pencil drawings alternate with two pages of watercolor illustrations throughout the book. Endpaper illustrations: old gold field with an inset white line border, one of four different illustrations of children playing with toys, centered in a twig frame on each endsheet. Frontispiece is the opposing half of the title page featuring four children, a corgi and a cat on a bench watching a puppet tableau of Santa shaking hands with a corgi. The tableau is the reverse of the cover illustration. Pages [4-5, 24-25, 40-41, 52-53, 54-55] are double-page illustrations. Color, [4-5, 8-9, 12-13, 16-17, 20-21, 24-25, 28-29, 32-33, 36-37, 40-41, 44-45, 48-49, 52-53, 56-57]. B&W, [3, 10-11, 14-15, 18-19, 20-21, 26-27, 30-31, 34-35, 38-39, 42-43, 46-47, 50-51, 54-55, 57-59]. One pencil drawing is repeated on pp. [11] and [57].

CONTENTS: Blank page: [2]. Half-title, b&w [3, 7]. Frontispiece and title page, [4-5]. Copyright, [6]. Text, [8-23, 26-39, 42-51, 54-58].

COPYRIGHT REGISTRATION: A 692241 granted to Rand McNally & Co., P.O. Box 7600, Chicago, Il. 60680. Richard G. Sanders [illegible], agent for the claimant, swears on Nov. 17, 1975:

THE NIGHT BEFORE CHRISTMAS, Tasha Tudor (Illustrator), Rt. 4, West Brattleboro, Vt., a U.S. citizen, was published Aug. 1,1975 . New matter in this version: new illustrations. The book was manufactured by Rand McNally & Co., Versailles, Ky, and Black Dot Typesetters, Crystal Lake, Il. Fees charged to Rand McNally & Co. Application and affidavit and two deposit copies received at L.C. Nov. 20, 1975.

N33 _____. [Copyright © 1975 . . . First printing, 1975 | Second printing, 1976]

COVER: White printed linen-weave paper over board covers.

ILLUSTRATION: "Author" "Illustrator" on page [57], a less intense red.

OTHER: Examined a copy with Dec. 25, 1976 inscription.

N34 _____.

PAGINATION: Four signatures, white kid paper, [68] pages including free endpapers. ½" thick.

COVER: White printed cloth, illustrated as first printing. Library binding.

ILLUSTRATIONS: Extra leaves have been added, pushing the former endpapers deeper into the book; they now appear as pages [4-5, 64-65] in this binding. Pages [8-9, 28-29, 44-45, 56-57, 58-59] are double-page illustrations. Color, [4-5, 8-9, 12-13, 16-17, 20-21, 24-25, 28-29, 32-33, 36-37, 40-41, 44-45, 48-49, 52-53, 56-57]. B&W, [14-15, 18-19, 22-23, 24-27, 30-31, 34-35, 38-39, 42-43, 46-47, 50-51, 54-55, 58-59, 61-62]. The Author | and the Illustrator, pp. [60-62].

CONTENTS: Blank pages: [1-3, 6, 66-68]. Half-title, b&w [7, 11]. Frontispiece and title page, [8-9]. Copyright page, [10]. Text, [12-27, 30-43, 46-55, 58-62].

N35 _____. Have not examined a third printing.

N36 _____. [Copyright © 1975 . . . First printing, 1975 | Second printing, 1976 | Third printing, 1976 | <u>Fourth printing, 1978</u>]

    PAGINATION: Four signatures, white paper, <u>[60] pages</u> including endpapers, as in first edition.

    COVER: White printed <u>paper over boards</u>, fine linen weave.

    CONTENTS: The <u>type font is larger</u> on the title page verso.

N37 _____. Have not examined a fifth printing.

N38 _____. [Library of Congress Cataloging in Publication Data || Moore, Clement Clarke, 1779-1863. | The night before Christmas. || SUMMARY: The well-known poem about an important | Christmas Eve visitor. | [1.Christmas poetry] I. Tudor, Tasha. II. Ti- | tle. | PZ8.3.M782N65 811'.2 75-8858 | ISBN 0-528-82181-4 | ISBN 0-528-80144-9 lib. bdg. || Copyright © 1975 by Rand McNally & Company | All rights reserved | Printed in the United States of America | by Rand McNally & Company | First printing, 1975 | Second printing, 1976 | Third printing, 1976 | Fourth printing, 1978 | Fifth printing, 1979 | <u>Sixth printing, 1980</u>]

    PAGINATION: [60] pp.

    COVER: Upper right front: A publisher's <u>gold foil label</u>, overprinted in black <u>$6⁹⁵</u>.

N39 _____. Have not examined a seventh printing.

N40 _____. [Library of Congress...First printing, 1975 | Second printing, 1976 | Third printing, 1976 | Fourth printing, 1978 | Fifth printing, 1979 | Sixth printing, 1980 | Seventh printing, 1982 | <u>Eighth printing, 1983</u>]

    COVER: A thinner paper. Book is <u>3/8″</u> thick.

N41 _____. [Library of Congress . . . 75-8858 | <u>ISBN 0-528-82181-4</u> || <u>Copyright</u> © 1975 ... First printing, 1975 | Second printing, 1976 | Third printing, 1976 | Fourth printing, 1978 | Fifth printing, 1979 | Sixth printing, 1980 | Seventh printing, 1982 | Eighth printing, 1983 | <u>Ninth printing, 1984</u>]

    COVER: <u>Red gloss film lamination</u>, with previous illustration. The previous red border expands to become the entire background and spine for the white illustrated panels. A gold foil label overprinted in black, top right front: $ 9⁹⁵. Title printed in white on red spine. Back: The ISBN in a 'computer' font has been moved inside the illustration, lower right: ISBN 0-528-82181-4.

N42 _____. . . . [two mice dancing] | Rand McNally & Company || [CP logo] CHILDRENS PRESS CHOICE | A Rand McNally title selected for educational distribution || ISBN 0-516-09847-0. [1984 SCHOOL AND LIBRARY EDITION || Library of Congress ... 75-8858 || ISBN 0-516-09847-0 || Copyright © 1975 . . . Ninth printing, 1984]

    PAGINATION: <u>[68]</u> pp. including <u>extra white free endpapers</u>.   12 x 9 <u>3/16″</u>

    COVER: Without price label. Spine: [author and title as before, and] CHILDRENS PRESS CHOICE [CP logo on a book]. Centered beneath the back cover illustrations is the black CP book logo and beneath it: CHILDRENS PRESS CHOICE | REINFORCED BINDING. Bottom right, back within the green floral border printed in a 'computer' type: ISBN 0-516-09847-0. Whereas the cover has previously been a smooth paper, this binding has gloss laminate over paper impressed with a cloth weave pattern. <u>Cloth hinges</u>.

CONTENTS: Blank pages: [1-3, 6, 66-68]. Half-title, b&w [7]. Frontispiece and title page, [8-9]. Copyright page, [10].   Rear endpapers, pp. [64-65].

OTHER: Examined a copy with an unidentified store label on the back cover: $17.95.

N43 _____. [Library of Congress . . . 75-8858 | ISBN 0-528-82181-4 || Copyright © 1975 ... First printing, 1975 | Second printing, 1976 | Third printing, 1976 | Fourth printing, 1978 | Fifth printing, 1979 | Sixth printing, 1980 | Seventh printing, 1982 | Eighth printing, 1983 | Ninth printing, 1984 | Tenth printing, 1986]

PAGINATION: [60] pp.

COVER: Red gloss film lamination, no gold foil label evident.

N44 _____. . . . MOORE || Illustrated by | TASHA TUDOR | [mistletoe] | Checkerboard Press | New York | [two mice dancing].   [Library of Congress ... 75-8858 | ISBN 0-528-82181-4 || Copyright © 1975 Checkerboard Press, a division of Macmillan, Inc. | All rights reserved. ISBN: 002-689413-0 || CHECKERBOARD PRESS and colophon are trademarks of Macmillan, Inc. || Printed in the United States of America   0 9 8 7 6 5 4 3 2 1]

PAGINATION: 4 signatures. [60] pp.   12″ x 9 ¼″

COVER: Spine: . . . TUDOR   Checkerboard Press.   Back: The normal lower left corner decoration has been removed and replaced by a single barcode. Immediately beneath the bar code: 0 14121 89413 4 || ISBN 0-02-689413-0. The body is bound deeper into the spine than ever before. The endpapers have a deep obvious gutter; they have lain flat when open in previous bindings.

OTHER: The cover, all body text (except for changes noted here) and illustrations correspond to the Rand McNally tenth printing.

N45 _____. . . . TUDOR | [mistletoe] | Macmillan Publishing Company | New York | [two mice dancing].   [Copyright © 1975 Checkerboard Press, a division of Macmillan, Inc. | All rights reserved. No part of this book may be reproduced or | transmitted in any form or by any means, electronic or mechanical, | including photocopying, recording, or any information storage and | retrieval system, without permission in writing from the Publisher. | Macmillan Publishing Company | 866 Third Avenue | New York, NY 10022 | Printed in United States of America 10 9 8 7 6 5 4 3 2 | Library of Congress Cataloging in Publication Data | Moore, Clement Clarke, 1779-1863. | The night before Christmas. | SUMMARY: The well-known poem about an important | Christmas Eve visitor. | [1.christmas poetry] I. Tudor, Tasha. II. Title. | PZ8.3.M782N65   811'.2 75-8858| ISBN 0-02-767643-9.]

PAGINATION: Pagination, paper, illustrations and endpapers are above. For the first time there are no folded signatures; the book is perfect bound.   12″ x 9 ¼″

COVER: Red bordered covers as above. Macmillan at base of spine. Back, lower left: 90000> [above the smaller right code] | [two bar codes] | 9 780027 676433 [below the larger left code] || ISBN 0-02-767643-9.

N46 **The Night | Before Christmas** | CLEMENT CLARKE MOORE || [Santa and swag] | ILLUSTRATED BY | TASHA TUDOR || [mistletoe] || SIMON & SCHUSTER BOOKS FOR YOUNG READERS || [mice]   [[sower logo] | SIMON & SCHUSTER BOOKS FOR YOUNG READERS | An imprint of Simon & Schuster Children's Publishing Division | 1230 Avenue of the Americas, new York, New York 10020 || Copyright c 1975 by Simon & Schuster Children's Publishing Division | All rights reserved including the right of reproduction in whole or in part in any form. | SIMON & SCHUSTER BOOKS FOR YOUNG READERS is a trademark of Simon & Schuster. | Typography by Heather Wood | The text for this book is set in Weiss. | The illustrations are rendered in watercolor. | Printed and bound in the United States of America | First Simon & Schuster Books for Young Readers Edition, 1997 | 1 3 5 7 9 10 8 6 4 2 || Library of Congress Cataloging-in-Publication Data | Moore, Clement Clarke, 1779-1863 | The night before Christmas / written by Clement Clarke Moore, illustrated by Tasha Tudor | p.   cm. | Summary: The illustrator's Vermont farmhouse and her pets are featured in the illustrations | of this well-known poem about an important Christmas Eve visitor. | ISBN 0-689-81375-9 | 1. Santa Claus—Juvenile poetry. 2, Christmas—Juvenile poetry. 3. Children's poetry, America. [1. Santa Claus—Poetry. | 2. Christmas—Poetry. 3. American poetry. 4. Narrative poetry.] I. Tudor, Tasha, ill. II. Title. | PS2429.M5N5 1997b 811'.2—dc21   96-48760]

PAGINATION: [60] pp. including endpapers. 12 x 9 ¼"

COVER: Dark green cloth, blind stamped on lower right front in same typography as title page and dust jacket: [floral tip] The Night [triangle decoration] | Before Christmas. Spine, in gilt: MOORE [diamond device] TUDOR   The Night Before Christmas SIMON & SCHUSTER.   Red satin place ribbon bound in.

DUST JACKET: Redesigned jacket in a deep red, a decorative blue line frame made of four crossed members, with stylized floral tips, on front and back. Most of the front is the large panel from page [49], Santa and corgi filling sock, on a night sky blue field. Four toys not previously on the cover have been added to the four corners of the blue panel: ballerina from page [45], cow and sheep, jack-in-the-box, ball and drum from pp. [40-41]. Title in yellow across the top; The Night | Before Christmas | [illustration] | CLEMENT | CLARKE MOORE | [rule] | ILLUSTRATED BY TASHA TUDOR. Spine: MOORE [floral tip] TUDOR [white] The Night Before Christmas [yellow shaded letters]   [sower emblem] Simon & Schuster [blue].   Back: same illustration doll on horse as before, but now on the red field. A yellow box (1 3/8 x 2 1/8") in lower portion of panel: 90000> [above smaller right bar code] | [two bar codes] | 9 780689 813757 [beneath larger left code] | ISBN 0-689-81375-9. EAN running laterally up the left inside of box.   Front flap, tall yellow panel within a blue line frame: $18.00 US | $24.50 CAN || *All ages* || *'Twas the night before Christmas | and all through the house . . .* | [two floral head from front] || C[blue]lement Moore's beloved | poem has been a cherished | part of the holidays for over | a hundred and fifty years, and | Tasha Tudor's delicate water- | colors make this book a gift | to her readers. Recreating her | own Vermont farm home, her | illustrations enliven the poem | with all the charm of an old- | fashioned country Christmas: | handmade gifts under a candle- | lit tree, stockings hanging by | an open fire, and a magical | visit from Saint Nicholas. ¶Tasha Tudor's affectionate | watercolors evoke the warmth | and gentleness of a simpler | time. Her whimsical characters | and period detail are the perfect | match for the world's most | beloved Christmas poem, | making this elegant gift edition | one that will be treasured by | families for generations. || *Guaranteed Reinforced Binding.* Back flap, tall yellow panel within a blue line frame: CLEMENT CLARKE MOORE [blue] wrote | his poem "An Account of a Visit From | Saint Nicholas," later called "The Night | Before Christmas," in 1822. Moore was | a professor of religion and the author of | several scholarly works, but it was the | warm-hearted poem he wrote as a | Christmas present for his children for | which he is best remembered. || [two floral tips] || A Caldecott Honor artist with over forty | books to her credit [black], TASHA TUDOR [blue] | has spent all of her life in New England, | and she celebrates the landscapes, | animals, and people of her home in her | artwork. In *A Night Before Christmas* [*sic*], she | recreates her own Vermont farmhouse | in her illustrations: The ornaments on | the tree are ones she inherited from her | grandmother, and her beloved cat and | corgi welcome Saint Nick as he drops | down the chimney. ¶Tasha Tudor is also the illustrator of | *A Time To Keep, A Child's Garden of Verses,* and *1 Is One,* a Caldecott Honor book. She lives in Vermont. || *Jacket illustrations copyright © 1975, 1997 by Tasha Tudor | Jacket design by Heather Wood* [black] || SIMON & SCHUSTER | BOOKS FOR YOUNG READERS [blue] | *Simon & Schuster* [floral tip] *New York.* [black]

ILLUSTRATONS: As before, with changes to dust jacket as noted above. The blue backgrounds are slightly darker, more intense than originally. Pencil drawing of cat has been moved from page [58] to page [56].

CONTENTS: Endpaper illustrations same, but the surround fields are deep red. Half-title on pages [3,7] gray ink. Title page [5]. Page [56], gray title: The Author and Illustrator ǁ Born July 15, 1779, Clement Clarke Moore was a | graduate of Columbia College and a professor of religion. | Several of his scholarly works had already appeared in print | by 1822, when he wrote a poem about a magical visit from Saint | Nicholas as a Christmas gift for his children. Moore likely never | meant his poem to have a wider audience than his own family. It was | probably a family friend who sent the poem to a local newspaper, | the Troy *Sentinel*, where it appeared anonymously with the title "A | Visit From Saint Nicholas." It was widely admired and reprinted | many times, and finally appeared in 1837, with Clement Moore's | name attached, in an anthology that also included several of his | other poems. ǁ "The Night Before Christmas," as the poem came to be called, first | appeared in book form in 1848, illustrated with austere line drawings | by T.C. Boyd. Many other illustrators have interpreted Moore's | poem, including Thomas Nash [*sic*], the political cartoonist who is also | responsible for the Republican elephant and the Democratic donkey. | His illustrations, done in the 1960s [*sic*] for *Harpers Weekly*, first showed | Santa in the familiar outfit we know today: a red suit with white trim | and a black belt and boots. [Page 57]: More than a hundred fifty years after "The Night Before | Christmas" was written, Tasha Tudor chose to illustrate the poem | in her characteristic period watercolors, with their soft colors and | elaborate borders. Her illustrations recreate her own Vermont | farmhouse, designed in exact detail after one of 1740. The | ornaments on the tree date to the 1840s and were once owned by | the artist's grandmother, and readers of her work will already be | familiar with her beloved pets, a cat and a corgi, who are present to | welcome St. Nicholas as he drops down the chimney.   [Page 58]: Filled with charming, whimsical detail —a barn owl who guides St. | Nicholas's sleigh to a safe landing, a cat who plays the fiddle so that | Santa and a corgi can dance—Tasha Tudor's delightful illustrations | are a perfect match for Clement Moore's classic Christmas poem.

OTHER: This is the second reprint of a Rand McNally volume that Simon & Schuster has issued in a cloth binding. Printed with a simulated Tudor autograph on the front free endpaper. A similar signature was printed on copies of *The Bouquet* by the Jenny Wren Press. There are various inaccuracies in the biographical paragraphs: Nast and 1860, e.g. The colophon incorrectly refers to Simon & Schuster as being the 1975 copyright holder.

N47 *The Night Before Christmas*. Little, Brown & Co., September 1999.

OTHER: Tudor indicated during 1997 that she was nearing completion of new illustrations for *The Night Before Christmas*. Corgi Cottage Industries announced it on their website July 9, 1998. Little, Brown has scheduled the book with 32 full color pages for September 1, 1999, John Keller, Editor. May be entitled *'Twas the Night Before Christmas*.

O1 [ON THE HORIZON]

WORLD | [diamond rule] **OF** [rule diamond] | **READING** ‖ [two mountain goats and a pig looking across a chasm at two more goats, with a radiant city in the background] | [diamond] ON THE [diamond] | [rule] HORIZON | [rule] ‖ P. DAVID PEARSON   DALE D. JOHNSON | THEODORE CLYMER   ROSELMINA INDRISANO   RICHARD L. VENEZKY | JAMES F. BAUMANN   ELFRIEDA HIEBERT   MARIAN TOTH | *Consulting Authors* | CARL GRANT   JEANNE PARATORE ‖ **SILVER BURDETT & GINN** | **NEEDHAM, MA •** **MORRISTOWN, NJ** | ATLANTA, GA • CINCINNATI, OH • DALLAS, TX | MENLO PARK, CA • NORTHFIELD, IL

[from page [2]: Grateful acknowledgment is made to the following publishers, authors, and agents for their | permission to reprint copyrighted material. Any errors or omissions in copyright notice are inadvertent and will be corrected in future printings as they are discovered. ‖ "Ali Baba Bernstein" excerpt adapted from *The Adventures of Ali Baba Bernstein* by Johanna | Hurwitz. Text copyright © 1985 by Johanna Hurwitz. By permission of William Morrow & | Co. ‖ *Amy's Goose* by Efner Tudor Holmes, illustrated by Tasha Tudor. (Thomas Y. Crowell) Copy- | right © 1977 by Efner Tudor Holmes. Illustrations copyright © 1977 by Tasha Tudor. | Adapted and reprinted by permission of Harper & Row, Publishers, Inc. ‖ "April Rain Song" from *The Dream Keeper and Other Poems* by Langston Hughes. Reprinted by permis- | sion of Alfred A. Knopf, Inc., and of the author's agents, Harold Ober Associates Incorpo- | rated. ‖ "Beethoven's Biggest Fan" from "Peanuts" by Charles Schulz. Reprinted by permission of | United Feature Syndicate, Inc. ‖ *The Big Orange Splot* written and illustrated by Daniel Manus Pinkwater. Copyright © 1977 | by Daniel Manus Pinkwater. Reprinted by permission of Scholastic Inc. ‖ Acknowledgments continue on pages 382-383, which constitute an extension of this copy- | right page. ‖ **©1989 Silver, Burdett & Ginn Inc. All rights reserved.** | Printed in the United States of America. This publication, or parts thereof, may not be reproduced in any form | by photographic, electrostatic, mechanical, or any other method, for any use, including information storage | and retrieval, without written permission from the publisher.   ISBN 0-663-46121-9]

PAGINATION: 12 signatures of white paper [1-3] 4-383 [384] pp. 10 1/4″ x 8 1/8″

COVER: The paper over board covers with gloss lamination embellishes on the icons of the title page. The cover design is an overall royal wallpaper with a white diamond pattern. A 7 3/8″ high enlargement of the title page illustration is printed on the front cover highlighted with metallic rays from the city and a metallic blue-silver river flowing down the middle of the cover. This scene has an 1/8″ wide red rule at top and bottom. Superimposed on the top rule is an orange box with the title printed in red. Likewise, a silver metallic box is superimposed on the bottom rule and bears the publisher's name in blue. An orange box outlined in silver runs down the spine with the title printed sideways in red. The back cover is centered with a variation of the diamond lozenge: two goats in a colorful square superimposed over a red square. At the bottom the title page diamonds are reprinted, a silver diamond superimposed on a red one, and carrying the black imprint as on the title page. This lozenge surmounts an orange rectangle outlined in silver and bearing the publisher's name in red. To the right of this is a white box with black lettering: LEVEL 9 | ISBN 0-663-46121-9 | 3/2. Blue endpapers.

CONTENTS: These Tudor references appear: A flying goose (the same as on page 242) is printed below the Contents entry for WORKING IT OUT on page 9, … **Amy's Goose** [logo] 242 | REALISTIC FICTION | written by Efner Tudor Holmes   READERS' CHOICE [in a small blue box] | illustrated by Tasha Tudor … Page 242-243 background is a reversed detail of Tudor's painting on pages [12-13] of the original book. Over this is printed: a 1 3/8″ x 1″ tan panel at the upper left corner of page 242 with the text, READERS' | [rule] CHOICE | [rule] | AWARD | [rule] | [a book]. To the right of this: *Amy finds a wounded goose, and a challenge unlike | any she has ever faced.* [Below the left flying goose] AMY'S | GOOSE | *written by Efner Tudor Holmes | illustrated by Tasha Tudor.* Page 243 has a rectangle in the upper right hand corner, set opposing the one on page 242, bearing two readers logo above READING CORNER. The text begins beneath three geese: Amy stood in the garden … there for the night. Pages 244-245 carry the opening illustration from pages [10-11] of the first edition. Text on page 244: They always did . . . wild creatures were her friends. Text on page 245: But now the geese . . . get that sack of corn." Page 246 text: "Aren't they beautiful?" . . . get these potatoes in." Below the text is the illustration of Amy and her father from original page [14]. Text on page 247: Dinner seemed to Amy . . . as they gabbled in alarm. The original illustration of pages [18-19] is printed across the tops of pages 248-249, and below that the text of 248: "It's a fox," . . . forgotten on the shore. Text on page 249: When Amy went . . . "You're safe here." Page 250 is headed with the original illustration of page [23]. Text below it: Amy spent most . . . giving bits of it to the goose. Page 251 text at top: Suddenly they heard . . .calling to his mate. At the bottom the original page [24] illustration of Amy feeding the goose. Text on page 252: She slipped out … into the night. A detail from page [28] of Amy hugging her goose is printed In the lower right corner. Page [29] illustration, slightly reduced, is printed in a block at the top of page 253, and below the concluding text: they stood silently . . . fly over her and into the water.

The editors have added five lines at the bottom of page 253 following the text: *If you liked* Amy's Goose, *you may want to read* | Carrie's Gift, *a book written by Efner Tudor Holmes.* || What Do You Think? [blue, above a blue rule on an orange serrated line] | Do you think Amy made the right choice? Would | you have done the same thing? Explain your reasons.

Amy's Goose has been transcribed completely with one change in the text. Spring, the twenty-second word from the end of the story was capitalized in the original printing. Here it has been printed with a lower case "s."

Page 371 has two author biographies on a tan ground: MARGARET HILLERT . . . EFNER TUDOR HOLMES || Efner Tudor Holmes was born in Boston, | Massachusetts. She is married and has two chil- | dren. She says that she writes about animals and | country living because she likes both these things. | She is also interested in farming, music, and | travel. Her mother, Tasha Tudor, is a well-known | illustrator of children's books. *(Born 1949)* AUTHOR | INDEX, page, 380 lists HOLMES, EFNER TUDOR, "Amy's Goose," 242. Page 383: . . . **ILLUSTRATIONS** . . . Tasha Tudor, 242-253; . . . A B C D E F G H I J -VHP-96 95 94 93 92 91 90 89 88.   [Another copy carries string: E F G H I J -VHP-96 95 94 93 92 91 90 89.

OTHER: This is a colorful school textbook with a complicated design. The title page, transcribed above, is actually a 7 1/2″ x 5 1/8″ rectangle superimposed on a royal blue field, and surmounted by a design of two cascading diamonds each in a different shade of blue, and the front diamond outlined in a thin black line. WORLD OF READING is printed in inverse white letters on the front diamond. The large box is also outlined in black and further sub-divided horizontally into four more rectangles. The goat illustration is printed in the upper box. The next rectangle down has the title in green on an orange field. The third and fourth are tan, the third listing the team of authors and the fourth the publisher. The cities of publication are printed on the navy field below the large rectangle.

A variety of materials were issued under this teaching title and several copyrights granted to Silver, Burdett & Ginn, Inc., 160 Gould St., Needham Heights, Ma. 02194-2310, e.g.,

SR 190-067	Interactive teaching kit audios	Pub. 11/14/1992	Reg. 5/6/1994
TX 2-710-294	Teacher's edition Grade 3.2 9	Pub.	Reg. 12/22/1989
TX 2-716-726	Unit skills test, A Manual	Pub. 7/23/1988	Reg. 1/2/1990
TX 2-718-291	Workbook, Teacher edition	Pub.	Reg. 2/2/1990
TX 2-722-192	Curriculum Connections	Pub. 10/27/1988	Reg. 1/17/1990
TX 2-722-193	Writing	Pub. 10/19/1988	Reg. 1/17/1990
TX 2-723-112	Unit Process Tests Manual	Pub. 7/23/1988	Reg. 12/28/1989
TX 2-723-125	Castles of Sand: Challenge	Pub. 10/27/1988	Reg. 1/17/1990
TX 2-723-595	Skills Practice	Pub. 8/2/1988	Reg. 1/2/1990
TX 2-723-983	Idea Factory for Teachers	Pub. 1/24/1989	Reg. 1/17/1990

| TX 2-724-059 | Achieving English Proficiency | Pub. 12/1/1988 | Reg. 1/17/1990 |
| TX 2-724-146 | Reteaching | Pub. 12/4/1988 | Reg. 1/17/1990 |

O2 _____. . . . & Ginn | [rule] | WORLD OF READING | [rule] | [diamond] VIDEOS [diamond] | [rule] | Units 3 and 4.

PAGINATION: Video tape to accompany textbook, above. Color/Approx. running time 20 min.

COVER: Title, above, is taken from the front of the cover stock title piece inserted into the sleeve of the white plastic container, which reproduces the book cover in a smaller size. Spine: WORLD OF READING VIDEOS [between two rules] || Grade 3-2 | Unit 3 | Unit 4 || SILVER BURDETT & GINN. Back: [diamond] UNIT | THREE [diamond] || WORKING IT OUT || [diamond] Learn how illustrator Tasha Tudor and her daughter, author | Efner Tudor Holmes, work together to create beautiful | picture books for children. || [diamond] Listen to Beethoven's "Ode to Joy" from his Ninth Symphony | as you learn how the famous composer worked out a plan | for writing music. || [diamond] Set to the music of Beethoven's Fifth Symphony, this | dramatization shows a group of friends working together. || [diamond] UNIT | FOUR [diamond] || WEATHER OR NOT || [diamond] Meet Salish Indian John Arlee, who shares with us some of | his people's beliefs about the weather. || [diamond] A montage of weather conditions shows both the power and | beauty of weather. || [diamond] Do you know a lot about the weather? Here are some | interesting and unique facts that may surprise you. || Color/Approx. Running Time 20 min. || Produced by Video One, Boston, MA in cooperation with Silver Burdett & Ginn || For information on this and other titles call toll free: 1-800-848-9500 or write: Silver Burdett | & Ginn Customer Service Center; P.O. Box 2649; 4343 Equity Drive; Columbus, OH 43216 || © 1990 Silver, Burdett & Ginn Inc. All rights reserved. Copying this material in whole or in part is strictly forbidden and a violation of the Federal Copyright Law. || **ISBN 0-663-51106-2** VHS. Black plastic video cassette has this 3 x 1 ¾″ white label, printed in blue: SILVER BURDETT & GINN | WORLD OF READING | [rule] | [diamond] VIDEOS [diamond] | [rule] || *Grade 3-2* || Unit 3: Working It Out | Unit 4: Weather or Not || ©1990 Silver, Burdett & Ginn Inc. | All rights reserved || ISBN 0-663-51106-2.

COPYRIGHT REGISTRATION: PA-688-560 granted to silver Burdett Ginn Inc., 160 Gould Street, Needham Heights, Ma 02194-2310. Claire E. Keenan swears for the company 1/18/1994 that the video was published September 24, 1992.

O3 ***Once Upon | A Time...*** [red]| Celebrating the Magic of Children's books | in honor of the Twentieth Anniversary of | READING IS FUNDAMENTAL || *G•P•Putnam's Sons | New York* [black] [*Copyright Acknowledgments* | Atheneum Publishers…Viking Penguin. || Copyright © 1986 by G. P. Putnam's Sons | 51 Madison Avenue, New York, NY 10010. All rights reserved. | Published simultaneously in Canada by General Publishing Co., Limited, Toronto. | printed in the United States of America by Arcata Graphics/Kingsport. | Typeset by Fisher Composition, Inc. | Book design by Nanette Stevenson | First impression || [4″ rule] | Library of Congress Cataloging-in-Publication Data | Once upon a time. Summary: An illustrated collection of true and fictional anecdotes, | stories, and reminiscences by well-known children's authors and illustrators about books | and the experience of reading. 1. Children-Books and reading. 2. Authors, American- | 20th century-Books and reading. 3. Illustrators-United States-Books and reading. | 4. Children's literature-Appreciation-United States. 5. Books and reading-United States. | {1. Books and reading. 2. Reading. 3. Authors, American. 4. Illustrators} | I. Reading is fundamental, Inc. Z1037.A1053 1986 028.5'5 86-18715 | ISBN 0-399-21369-4 ISBN 0-399-21370-8 (pbk.)]

PAGINATION: [1-9] 10-11 [12-14] 15 [16-17] 18-19 [20-21 22-25 [26] 27-29 [30] 31 [32] 33-35 [36] 37-39 [40-41] 42-45 [46-47] 48-51 [52] 53-59 [60-63] 64. 101/4″ x 8 3/8″

COVER: Half-red cloth wraps spine, half natural paper over boards stamped on front cover in gold calligraphic uncials by Jeanyee Wong: ***Once Upon | A Time...*** Spine, also stamped in gold: RIF ***Once Upon A Time...*** Putnam

DUST JACKET: Fully illustrated jacket shows Trina Hyman's Little Red Riding Hood in a gallery of trees leading to a children's library. She is looking at pictures included in the book. A 3″ x 6″ tan panel is overprinted 3/4″ from the top edge of the jacket front. The panel is edged in a red line which is outlined in thin black on both sides. The title in large green uncials appears in this panel above the black sub-title: *Once Upon | A Time...* | Celebrating the Magic of Children's books | in honor of the Twentieth Anniversary of | READING IS FUNDAMENTAL. A round white sticker, 1 3/4″, is attached to upper right corner of jacket front with this red script: all profits from this book | will be | donated to | RIF | Reading Is | Fundamental | Inc. The back of the jacket continues the illustration and is also overprinted with a 6″ x 4″ vertical panel colored like the front and imprinted: Natalie Babbitt • Stan and Jan Berenstain | Barbara Helen Berger • Judy Blume | Ashley Bryan • Beverly Cleary | Tomie dePaola • Leo and Diane Dillon | Jean Fritz • M. B. Goffstein | Edward Gorey • Virginia Hamilton | Jamake Highwater • Trina Schart Hyman | Steven Kellogg • Myra Cohn Livingston | Arnold Lobel • James Marshall | Katherine Paterson • Jack Prelutsky | Maurice Sendak • Dr. Seuss | Shel Silverstein • Margot Tomes | Jim Trelease • Tasha Tudor | Ed Young. Another small area overprints the illustration at the lower left back and has this text in black: ISBN 0-399-21369-4. Spine is overprinted in white, with the same text as book spine, but in white: RIF *Once Upon A Time...* Putnam. Front flap: $14.95 || Natalie Babbitt • Stan and Jan Berenstain | Barbara Helen Berger • Judy Blume | Ashley Bryan • Beverly Cleary | Tomie dePaola • Leo and Diane Dillon | Jean Fritz • M. B. Goffstein | Edward Gorey • Virginia Hamilton | Jamake Highwater • Trina Schart Hyman | Steven Kellogg • Myra Cohn Livingston | Arnold Lobel • James Marshall | Katherine Paterson • Jack Prelutsky | Maurice Sendak • Dr. Seuss | Shel Silverstein • Margot Tomes | Tasha Tudor • Ed Young | *with an introduction by* | Jim Trelease. || [rule] | These beloved authors and artists have gener- | ously contributed their talents to create this | unique book in celebration of the twentieth | anniversary of Reading Is Fundamental (RIF). | Warm-hearted memories, poignant stories, | and hilarious anecdotes all come alive in the | words and illustrations of this rich and varied | collection by some of today's most outstanding | creators of books for children. Most of the | selections have been created especially for this | book; a few have been published previously. | Some are based on real experiences, others are | fictional, but all celebrate the joys of reading | and the magic of children's books. || Here is a book designed for the lasting | pleasure of both children and adults: one that | will entertain and inspire children who are just | beginning to explore the magical world of | reading, rekindle the memories of adults, and | be cherished by everyone who loves children's | books. || [rule] || *All profits from this book will be donated to | RIF—a non-profit organization dedicated | to the promotion of reading.* Back flap: Reading is Fundamental, Inc. (RIF) is a non- | profit organization that works for a literate | America by inspiring young people to read | and to aspire through reading. RIF works | through a network of local projects that spans | all fifty states, Washington D.C., Puerto | Rico, the Virgin Islands, and Guam. This | grassroots network makes it possible for | millions of children to choose and to own | books that interest them without cost to them | or their families. With the help of over 90,000 | volunteers, including parents, educators, and | individuals from all walks of life, RIF con- | ducts dynamic activities that bring books alive | and make reading a meaningful experience for | children. RIF also provides publications and | services to help parents encourage reading in | the home. || Founded in 1966 by Mrs. Robert S. | McNamara, RIF is now the largest reading | motivation program in America. Since its | founding, it has brought more than 65 million | books into the hands of children. || *Jacket illustration by Trina Schart Hyman | Calligraphy by Jeanyee Wong.* || Reading Is Fundamental, Inc. | Smithsonian Institution | 600 Maryland Avenue, SW | Suite 500 | Washington, D.C. 20560 || [rule] || G. P. Putnam's sons | 51 Madison Avenue | New York, NY 10010 | 8610.

CONTENTS: Page 54 is Tudor's depiction of herself reading in the evening to five children, Page 54 is with Dickinson's poem "There is no Frigate like a Book." On page 55 she describes the picture ". . .one of the many, many delights of being an artist: you can depict the world as you wish." Same illustration and poem accompany the January entry in *Rosemary For Remembrance*. The image was also made into a 18 1/2″ x 34 1/2″ poster by The Vanessa Ann Collection, PO Box 9113, Ogden, Utah 84409 ©1981 Tasha Tudor.

O4 _____ .

PAGINATION: Pages as before in a paper wrapper. 10 X 7 7/8″

COVER: The <u>paper wrapper</u> is similar to the hardcover dust jacket, with small changes. The spine text is reset in black Roman capitals; Wong's calligraphy is missing from the spine, although it is preserved on the cover and title page. The round RIF seal is applied to the front upper corner. The tan box on the bottom of the back cover is enlarged to accommodate a changed ISBN and price: ISBN 0-399-21370-8 | >>$6.95.

P1 **A Partial List of Original** | WATER COLORS, DRAWINGS, | OILS, AND PASTELS |
BY TASHA TUDOR | *Together with the names of the owners* | *of most of the pieces* | [feather device] |
Compiled by | THE TASHA TUDOR ROOM | Mill Hall, Pennsylvania [feather device] | COPYRIGHT
1975 | Edward B. Hills and Gretchen Brown McKeever.

PAGINATION: [1] 2-76 on yellow kid-finish paper, folded and stapled into a peach dimpled cover
stock wrapper.

COVER: Printed in black ink, high on the cover: A PARTIAL LIST OF ORIGINAL | WATER
COLORS, DRAWINGS, | OILS, AND PASTELS | By | TASHA TUDOR | *Together with the*
names of the | *owners of most of the pieces* in a thin-line box within a thicker-line border,
resembling raised plate. 8 7/16″ x 5 1/2″

CONTENTS: Page 2: FORWARD [*sic*] ‖ We have collected the information for this compilation |
with Tasha Tudor's gracious permission and the friendly | cooperation of the many people who
responded to our | "Note to Owners of Original Art Works by Tasha Tudor" | in several issues of
our TASHA TUDOR ROOM CATALOGUE. ‖ With posterity and supplements to this list in
mind, we | shall be very glad to enter into correspondence with | owners of Tasha Tudor art who
are unknown to us and | who are willing to supply us with pertinent information | for inclusion in
such supplements or to whom we as de- | voted collectors of Tasha Tudor art for more than thirty
| years can possibly be helpful in such matters as dates, | identification, and preliminary sketches.
‖ Also, we shall appreciate any corrections in any of the | details of this list so we can incorporate
them into sub- | sequent publications. We are particulary [*sic*] interested in | keeping our records
accurate and current and hope to be | apprised of changes of ownership as they occur. ‖ To assure
the privacy of owners who have so kindly | supplied us with the information contained in this list
and | spare them the necessity of undue correspondence, we are | not publishing the addresses of
individual owners and | will not furnish them on request. However, we are willing | to forward
notes, inquiries, etc. to individual owners who | can thus use their discretion as to whether they
want to | enter into further correspondence.

ILLUSTRATIONS: There are no illustrations.

OTHER: The University of Hawaii library owns this letter on stationery of The Tasha Tudor Room, The
Dutch Inn Gift Shop, 211 North Water Street, Mill Hall, Pennsylvania 17751: February 28, 1975 |
University of Hawaii Library | Honolulu, Hawaii ‖ Dear Sirs: ‖ Over the past five years, with
posterity in mind, we have | been preparing a list of over 1500 original paintings and | drawings by
Tasha Tudor along with the names of current | owners, the places where the art work was first
published, | etc., the list to be printed in a substantial pamphlet, | about 8″ x 6″, soft cover,
copyrighted, the pamphlets to | be permanently deposited in several hundred cooperating | college
and university libraries through the United | States and Canada. ‖ We shall be glad to supply your
library with a copy of this | pamphlet at no charge other than the assurance that the | pamphlet will
be accessioned as a permanent part of your | library. If you wish to have this pamphlet with the |
understanding indicated above, will you please send us a | letter to that effect. ‖ Very truly yours, |
Edward B. Hills [signature] | Edward B. Hills | Gretchen Brown McKeever [signature] Gretchen
Brown McKeever.   The University responded with this typed reply in the lower margin of the
letter: March 12, 1975 ‖ The U;niversity [*sic*] of Hawaii Library would | be happy to receive the
pamphlet you are | preparing. Please ship the work to my | attention, so that I may ensure that the |
pamphlet is made a permanent part of the | collection. | Sincerely, Carol Schaafsma [signature] |
Carol Schaafsma | Acquisitions Divisions.

COPYRIGHT REGISTRATION: A 642066 granted to Edward B. Hills, 211 North Water St., Mill Hall, Pa. 17751 and Gretchen Brown McKeever, 211 North Water St., Mill Hall, Pa. 17751, claiming for themselves, swear on June 4,1975:

A PARTIAL LIST OF ORIGINAL WATER COLORS, DRAWINGS, OILS, AND PASTELS BY TASHA TUDOR TOGETHER WITH THE NAMES OF THE OWNERS OF MOST OF THE PIECES, by Edward B. Hills and Gretchen Brown McKeever, both United States citizens, was published June 2, 1975. The book was printed by Focht Printing Company, Lewisburg, Pa. 17837. Application and affidavit, fee and two deposit copies received at L.C. June 9, 1975.

P2 PEKIN WHITE || *By T. L. McCready, Jr.* || ILLUSTRATIONS || *By Tasha Tudor* || ARIEL BOOKS •NEW YORK (FARRAR, STRAUS runs at bottom of verso opposite the Ariel Books New York legend). [*To INGE SCHADE,* | *Pekin's best friend outside our family,* | *and a true duck lover* || [drawing of two white ducks] || COPYRIGHT 1955 BY THOMAS L. MC CREADY AND | TASHA TUDOR. ALL RIGHTS RESERVED. LIBRARY | OF CONGRESS CATALOG CARD NUMBER 55-6684.

PAGINATION: Three signatures: [i-ii] [1-2] 3-16 [17] 18-26 [27-28] 29-30 [31] 32-34 [35] 36-40 [41] 42-49 [50] 8 1/8″ x 6 1/4″

COVER: Mint green cloth stamped in black, on front: PEKIN WHITE, 3 1/4″ line, 4 1/2″ down from the top edge, and printed under a 2 5/8″ high drawing of a drake. McCready • PEKIN WHITE • Ariel, on spine.

DUST JACKET: Mint green dust jacket, white free-form square centered on front has within it a border of blossoms framing a duck's head. Black lettering: PEKIN WHITE (above), and By T. L. McCready, Jr. | Pictures by Tasha Tudor (below), on front; McCready PEKIN WHITE Ariel, down spine. White flaps, front: $2.50 | 40-80 | PEKIN WHITE | by T. L. McCREADY, Jr. | *Illustrated by* TASHA TUDOR | This is the story of Pekin White and his | wife Matilda on a New Hampshire farm. | Pekin is a handsome white drake whose | brave exploits are greatly admired by the | ducks. In fact, they often follow him into | extraordinary adventures, such as a dar- | ing trip to the river or cheer him on in | the mischief of splashing all the water | out of the cow tub. Tom McCready, in his second little | book about the Warner farm in New | Hampshire, (see back flap for BIGGITY | BANTAM) has again captured the charm | of country life and its fascinating sea- | sonal rhythm. He writes from actual ex- | perience because he and his family really | are the Warners of the story. Pekin and | his friend, Biggity Bantam, are very | much alive, as are the Warner children. | And, of course, Mrs. Warner is Mrs. | McCready, who is also the famous | painter and illustrator, Tasha Tudor. | Small wonder that the lovely water colors | in this book and in BIGGITY BANTAM | have a beauty and freshness all their | own, for Tasha Tudor is painting of | what she knows and loves best. | **Ariel Books** | Children's Book Division | FARRAR, STRAUSS AND COMPANY | 100 Fifth Avenue New York 3, N.Y. Back flap: *If you like PEKIN WHITE,* | *you will like* BIGGITY BANTAM | *by* T. L. McCREADY, Jr. | *Illustrated by* TASHA TUDOR | "There's nothing like Bantams as pets, | for those with space to own them, and | we hope this gay little story will persuade | some parents to give their children Ban- | tams...The author has caught the 'biggity' character of these creatures | very well, and the many pictures in both | line and full color are Tasha Tudor at | her best." — Louise Bechtel, *New York* | *Herald Tribune.* "Biggity, the banty rooster, deserved his | name. In the city he drove the neighbors | crazy with his mischief, invaded their | yards and even stole a cherry pie. He | might have learned better manners when | he went to the country, but fierce, unruly | Biggity he remained -- a troublemaker | right to the end of the story....Never- | theless, this book has charm, for author | and artist have presented an attractive | picture of real life on their own New | Hampshire farm, generously illustrated | with Tasha Tudor's characteristic soft- | toned illustrations." — C.E. Van Nor- | man, *New York Times.* | **Ariel Books** | *Children's Book Division* | FARRAR, STRAUS AND COMPANY | 101 Fifth Avenue New York 3, N.Y.

CONTENTS: No text on pages [17], [27], [28], [31], [35], [41].

ILLUSTRATIONS: Watercolor illustrations: Front and rear end papers are same 2-page picture of 4 children playing at the river's edge with two white ducks swimming in the water; 2 ducks on grass [2]; 6, 7, 15, 22-23, [27], [31], [35], 42-43, 47. Black and white pencil drawing: pp. [ii-1], girl feeding ducks near a pump and catch basin; 4, 5, 8, 11, 12, 13, [17], 18-19, 21, 25, [28], 33, 36, 37, 38, 39, [41], 44, 48, 49.

OTHER: Examined a copy with labels of the Contoocook [N.H.] Library. The title page is autographed under the author's name. Penned into the gutter on page 3: 5-17-55 Gift. One suspects that McCready inscribed and gave this to the local public library.

A Ginger & Pickles Store advertising piece reproduces the front of the dust jacket. This text on the back: PEKIN WHITE and his wife, Matilda, are two "Pekin" ducks who | belong to the author's children. The book PEKIN WHITE is the second written | by T. L. McCready, Jr., and is illustrated by his artist wife, Tasha Tudor, who is very well known for her own work as an author-illustrator. ¶ As in T. L. McCready's first book, Biggity Bantam (Ariel Books), | the scenes and story contained in PEKIN WHITE depict the farm and life of the McCready family. ¶ The McCreadys have a store in the rear wing of their home which is | open to the public and, for those who can not get to it, a mail order business | is conducted. The Tasha Tudor books and those by her husband are all | available, each copy autographed. The name of the store is GINGER & | PICKLES STORE, named after Beatrix Potter's book of that title. This book | and others by Beatrix Potter are sold at the store. Adjoining this is the doll | house immortalized by Tasha Tudor in her book, *The Doll's Christmas*. || ❖ ❖ ❖ || PEKIN WHITE is 48 pages. For ages 4 to 8. | Price $2.50 (each copy autographed) || BIGGITY BANTAM is 48 pages. For ages 4 to 8. | It is also in color and black and white. | Price $2.50 (each copy autographed) || Orders shipped by mail || GINGER & PICKLES STORE | R.F.D. NO.1 | CONTOOCOOK | NEW HAMPSHIRE || *A price list of Tudor and McCready books as well as Tasha Tudor Christmas | cards and illustrated stationery sent on request. Announcement of Tasha Tudor | Christmas cards and her fall book for 1955 will be made in mid-summer.*

COPYRIGHT REGISTRATION: A 185760 granted to Thomas L. McCready and Tasha Tudor McCready, Contoocook, N.H. H.O. Varcell swears on April 6, 1955:

PEKIN WHITE, by Thomas L. McCready, born 1907, and Tasha Tudor McCready, both U.S. citizens, was published March 21, 1955. The book was lithographed and printed by Brett Litho, Long Island City, N.Y., and bound by American Book—Stratford, New York, N.Y. Application and affidavit received at LC April 12, 1955. Two deposit copies received April 14, 1955. Certificate to be mailed to Pat Van Doren, Farrar, Straus and Cudahy, Inc., 101 Fifth Ave., N.Y. 3, N.Y.

COPYRIGHT RENEWAL REGISTRATION: RE 158-656 granted to Tasha Tudor McCready, R.D #4, Box 144, West Brattleboro, Vt. 05301, widow of the deceased author Thomas L. McCready and as author, and Seth Tudor, Thomas Tudor and Bethany Tudor of the same address, children of the deceased author Thomas L. McCready, and Efner Tudor Holmes, Rt. 1, Concord, N.H., daughter of the deceased author Thomas L. McCready. Elizabeth Besobrasow, agent for the claimants swears on Jan. 27, 1983:

PEKIN WHITE, by Thomas L. McCready, and Tasha Tudor McCready, was originally published March 21, 1955. Renewal application received at LC Jan. 31, 1983, the effective date of this registration. Fees charged to account DAO 13366, Farrar, Straus and Giroux, Inc., 19 Union Square West, N.Y., N.Y. 10003

P3 _____.

COVER: Another binding, yellow cloth. All other features as above.

P4 _____.

PAGINATION: Changes to [i-iv, 1-2] 3-49 [50-52], plus two plain paste-downs. The two illustrations which were formerly the paste-down endpapers are missing. Pages [iii] and [50] are the former free endpapers each with one-half of the Blackwater River swimming scene. Current endpapers are ivory, interrupted with a heavy white cloth hinge.

COVER: Library binding. The cover is a brighter green cloth than before, and the illustration has been changed. The duck is the 3 1/4″ standing model pictured at the left on page [2]. The title text, like the duck, is still black, but has been enlarged to 4 1/2″ long and dropped to 5 1/8″ from the top edge. Spine imprinted in black capitals: PEKIN WHITE — MC CREADY.

P5 _____.

PAGINATION: Four extra pages at front and at rear adding pp. [i-vi] and [51-54]. Left half of front endpaper, and right half at rear endpaper illustrations have been lost in rebinding.

COVER: This copy at New Hampshire State Library, Accession no. 88499, has been rebound in orange buckram without dust jacket. Printed in cream with original jacket illustration. Text at top of front: PEKIN WHITE | T.L. McCREADY, Jr. Spine: PEKIN WHITE ~ McCREADY.

P6 *The Platt & Munk* | *Treasury of* | STORIES for CHILDREN. Edited by Nancy Christensen Hall | Cover illustration by Tasha Tudor | Title page illustration by George and Doris Hauman | Designed by Sallie Baldwin || Platt & Munk, Publishers/New York | A Division of Grosset & Dunlap [*For Amy and Kirsten—* | *the Country Mouse and the City Mouse* | ACKNOWLEDGMENTS . . . for permission to reprint copyrighted materials: . . . "The Owl and the Pussy-Cat" by Edward Lear from FIRST POEMS OF CHILDHOOD. Illustrated by Tasha Tudor. Copyright 1967 by Platt & Munk . . . "The Three Billy Goats Gruff" and "The Frog Prince" from TASHA TUDOR'S BEDTIME BOOK. Edited by Kate Klimo. Illustrated by Tasha Tudor. Copyright 1977 by Platt & Munk, Publishers . . . Library of Congress Catalog Number: 79-56868, ISBN: 0-448-47722-X (Trade Edition). Copyright ©1981 by Grosset & Dunlap, Inc. | All rights reserved. Published simultaneously in Canada. Printed in the United States of America. The selections reprinted in this collection are used by permission of and | special arrangement with the proprietors of their respective copyrights.]

PAGINATION: [i-viii] 1-40 [41] 42-43 [44] 45 [46] 47-48 [49-50] 51-52 [53] 54-55 [56-57] 58-102 [103] 104-114 [115-116]. 11 1/2″ x 9 1/4″.

COVER: Beige polished cotton in a gabardine weave imprinted on front cover: *The Platt & Munk* [black] | *Treasury of* | STORIES for | CHILDREN [red] | Edited by Nancy Christensen Hall [black]. Color illustrations: Two espaliered pear trees frame sides and top and at bottom, Snow White and Rose Red with bear, wolf, rabbit and birds. Spine: [apples] | Hall [red] | *The Platt & Munk Treasury of STORIES for CHILDREN* [black] Platt&Munk [red] 47722-X [black]. Back, centered: a circle of rose thorns enclosing Sleeping Beauty's castle, an old man, and the King's son horseback. || A collection of timeless children's stories including The Little | Engine That Could, The Country Mouse and the City Mouse, | Little Brown Bear, Uncle Wiggly, Snow-White and Rose-Red, | Puss-in-Boots, The Shoemaker and the Elves, and many more. | With beautiful illustrations by George and Doris Hauman, Lucille | and H.C. Holling, George Carlson, Tim and Greg Hildebrandt, | Eulalie Banks, Tasha Tudor, and others. || Platt & Munk, Publishers/New York | A Division of Grosset & Dunlap. | 0-448-47722-X [bottom right].

DUST JACKET: Have not examined one.

CONTENTS AND ILLUSTRATIONS: "The Owl and the Pussy-Cat" pp. 40-[41] with 4 pencil drawings. "The Three Billy Goats Gruff" pp. 66-67 with one pencil drawing across top of both pages. "The Frog Prince" pp. 102-[103]. Page [103] is a full page color illustration. End papers are brown watercolors by Tudor. Same front and back. Boy with dog and rooster raises his hand on the verso to greet a girl riding a donkey toward him, with a cat, on the recto of the facing page.

OTHER: Hall's dedication is to her daughter Kirsten.

COPYRIGHT REGISTRATION: TX 783-349 granted to Grosset & Dunlap, Inc., 51 Madison Ave., N.Y., N.Y. 10010. Louise Bates, agent for claimant, swears on Oct. 9, 1981:

THE PLATT & MUNK TREASURY OF STORIES FOR CHILDREN, by Grosset & Dunlap, Inc. (Employer for hire), a U.S. citizen and author of compilations, editing, illustrations was published Sept. 1, 1981. The work was completed in 1981, and was manufactured by Largene Press, 150 Lafayette St., N.Y., N.Y. 10013. Library of Congress is granted non-exclusive right to make copies and phonorecords for the blind and physically handicapped. Fees charged to account DAO34886, Grosset & Dunlap, Inc. Application and two deposit copies received Oct. 13, 1981, the effective date of registration.

P7 _____.

COVER: Printed gloss paper as before, but in a <u>linen weave</u>.

DUST JACKET: Exteriors repeat the cover designs and text. Front flap: *The Platt & Munk* [black] | *Treasury of* | *STORIES for* | *CHILDREN* [red] || Publishing houses, like people, take on | distinct personalities over the years. Dif- | ferent companies merge and/or acquire | one another, editors come and go, and | the line of books reflects the finest of | each "life" a publishing house has led. ¶This beautiful collection of illustrated | fairy tales for children represents over | one hundred years of Platt & Munk's | best stories and art. It begins with "The | Little Engine That Could," (Platt & | Munk's trademark), which was illus- | trated by George and Doris Hauman. | Many other artists, including Tim and | Greg Hildebrandt, the Hollings, and | Lois Lenski, have lent their distinctive | styles to the Platt & Munk line. A very | young Eulalie Banks did some of her | finest illustrations for Platt & Munk as | early as 1921, and she is still illustrating | popular children's books today. Tasha | Tudor, who did the cover of this volume, | is a relative newcomer to the line, hav- | ing illustrated her first Platt & Munk | storybook in 1961. ¶*The Platt & Munk Treasury* will enable | parents and grandparents to share with | their special children the same fairy | tales they cherished in their own youths. | Thus, the finest traditions of one gen- | eration survive and are passed on to | the next. Back flap: ABOUT THE EDITOR || Nancy Christensen Hall was appointed | Editor of Platt & Munk Books after it | was acquired by Grosset & Dunlap | Publishers. ¶One of her first official assignments | was to compile this collection from trea- | sured Platt & Munk classics and original | artwork, most of which had been stored | away for many years. ¶Ms. Hall has also written books for | children, including *Monsters, Creatures | of Mystery*, published by Platt & Munk | in 1980. She lives in New York City with | her husband and two children, Jonathan | and Kirsten. || Platt & Munk, Publishers/New York | A Division of Grosset & Dunlap.

Have not examined a dust jacket with price intact.

P8 _____. [*For Amy* . . . "Cinderella" . . . The Platt & Munk Co., Inc. . . . || 1982 PRINTING || Library of Congress . . . . their respective copyrights.]

COVER: The linen weave imprint.

DUST JACKET: Front flap: <u>$9.95</u> || *The Platt & Munk* [black] . . . PRINTED IN U.S.A.

P9 _____. [*For Amy* . . . "Cinderella" . . . The Platt & Munk Co., Inc. . . . || 1982 PRINTING || Library of Congress . . . . their respective copyrights.]

COVER: The gabardine weave imprint.

DUST JACKET: Front flap carries no price.

P10   Prime Time Live. ABC News. December 17, 1997. **"Four Seasons in Vermont, A Magical Garden through the Eyes of Tasha Tudor."**   Producer, Michael Bicks.   12 minutes.

> OTHER: Planned for a Thanksgiving broadcast but re-scheduled, this segment of the hour-long television program opens with Diane Sawyer: "We want to introduce you now to a very unusual woman who decided over 25 years ago to live a 19th-century life in a cabin in Vermont where she writes, draws and tends her magnificent garden. . . .Well, Jay Schadler was invited to visit that secret garden through all the seasons of this past year. . ." The transcript was found at http://www.abcnews.com/

P11   The Private World Of| *Tasha Tudor* || [printer's design] || by Tasha Tudor | and Richard Brown || [publisher's oval logo] | *Little, Brown and Company* | Boston Toronto London. [Copyright © 1992 by Richard Brown and Tasha Tudor || All rights reserved. No part of this book may be reproduced in | any form or by any electronic or mechanical means, including | information storage and retrieval systems, without permission in | writing from the publisher, except by a reviewer who may quote | brief passages in a review. || FIRST EDITION || Library of Congress Cataloging-in-Publication Data | Tudor, Tasha. | The private world of Tasha Tudor / by Tasha Tudor and | Richard Brown. — 1st ed. | p.   cm. | Includes bibliographical references. | 1. Tudor, Tasha. 2. Illustrators — United States — | Biography. | I. Brown, Richard, 1945—   . II. Title. | NC975.5.T82A2 1992 | 741.6'42'092 — dc20 | [B] 92-8735 {Second column} ACKNOWLEDGEMENTS || The authors are grateful for permission to reprint illustrations | from the following books: | Pages 30 and 54 from *A Time to Keep: The Tasha Tudor Book of* | *Holidays*, written and illustrated by Tasha Tudor. Copyright © | 1977 by Checkerboard Press. [*sic*] Reprinted with permission of | Macmillan Publishing Company. || Page 30 from *Corgiville Fair*, written and illustrated by Tasha | Tudor. Copyright © 1971 by Thomas V. Crowell Company. [*sic*] | Reprinted with permission of HarperCollins Publishers. || Page 76 from *Pumpkin Moonshine*, by Tasha Tudor. Copyright © | 1938 by Oxford University Press. Copyright renewed 1966 by | Tasha Tudor. Reprinted by permission of Henry Z. Walck, a | division of David Mckay Co., Inc. [*sic*] || Page 96 from *Drawn from New England*, copyright ©1979 by | Bethany Tudor. Illustration by Tasha Tudor. Reprinted by | permission of Philomel Books. || Pages 114 and 124 from *Tasha Tudor's Advent Calendar*, copyright | © 1988 by Tasha Tudor. Reprinted by permission of Philomel | Books. || 10 9 8 7 6 5 4 3 2 1 || IMAGO || Designed by Barbara Werden || Published simultaneously in Canada by | Little, Brown & Company (Canada) Limited || PRINTED IN HONG KONG]

> PAGINATION: [i-vi] vii-x [1-3] 4-5 [6-7] 8-13 [14-15] 16-17 [18-19] 20-21 [22-23] 24-27 [28-29] 30-31 [32-33] 34-35 [36-37] 38-41 [42-43] 44-45 [46-47] 48-51 [52-55] 56-59 [60-61] 62-63 [64-65] 66-67 [68-71] 72-73 [74-75] 76-77 [78-79] 80-81 [82-83] 84-89 [90-91] 92-93 [94-97] 98-99 [100-101] 102-105 [106-109] 110-113 [114-115] 116-125 [126-130] 131 [132] 133-134, not including end papers. Pages [130] and [132], blank. 10 3/4" x 8 7/8"

> COVER: Mauve half paper over boards, overlaps tan cotton spine wrap. Spine stamped in gilt: Tudor and Brown   The Private World of *Tasha Tudor*   Little, Brown. Red and white head and tail bands. Mauve calico end papers in small oak leaf wallpaper print.

> DUST JACKET: The front of the pink jacket bears a photograph of Tudor with fall leaves, and a superimposed pink panel at the upper right, within a white line: The | Private World | of | Tasha Tudor | [oak leaf] {in white} Tasha Tudor | and | Richard Brown {black}. Spine: The Private World of Tasha Tudor {white} Tudor and Brown {black} LITTLE, | BROWN {white} Back: three photographs, and at lower right, a white box with two bar codes: ISBN 0-316-11292-5 [over the larger left code] | 90000> [over the smaller right code]. EAN [printed laterally down the left edge of the box] | [two bar codes] | 9 780316 112925. Front flap: LIFESTYLE/GARDENING
>
> || TASHA Tudor has written and illus- | trated more than seventy-five | beloved children's books since her | first, *Pumpkin Moonshine*, in 1938. Now | seventy-seven years old, she lives on a | farm | in southern Vermont, where she has | recreated an early Victorian world. To | capture this intimate portrait of Tasha | Tudor, photographer Richard Brown fol- | lowed her throughout a year on her farm. | By interweaving Tudor's own words and | more than 100 color photographs, Brown | has evoked the essence of Tudor's uniquely | appealing personality and way of life. ¶ The inspiration for Tudor's art is evident | in her delightful surroundings. Foremost is | the magnificent garden she designed and | rightfully calls "paradise on earth." A | lively menagerie is

always underfoot, | indoors and out, including her trademark | corgies, the Nubian goats she milks twice a | day, the one-eyed cat Minou, the chickens, | fantail doves, and the cockatiels, canaries, | exotic finches, and parrots that inhabit a | virtual village of antique cages. ¶We watch Tudor at work in a corner of | her winter kitchen, her "chipmunk's nest," | on the delicate watercolors and drawings | that illustrate the books and calendars that | have charmed three generations. Exam- | ples of her work are scattered throughout | the book, including many drawings from | her sketchbook and vignettes never previ- | ously published. Her enchanting three- | story dollhouse is featured in detail as are | her handmade dolls and marionettes as | well as the candlelit tree that is the center- | piece of Tasha Tudor's old-fashioned New | England Christmas. | (*continued on back flap*) | 10923400   Back flap: Born in 1914 [*sic*] into Boston society (she sat | on Oliver Wendell Holmes's knee as a | child; Mark Twain and Albert Einstein | were also her parents' friends), Tudor felt | from an early age that she had lived before, | in the 1830s. She says, "Everything comes | so easily to me from that period, of that | time: threading a loom, growing flax, spin- | ning, milking a cow." ¶Dressed in antique clothing, spinning | and weaving her own linen, cooking on a | woodstove with nineteenth-century uten- | sils, Tudor inhabits a world that in these | evocative photographs speaks to all who | long for a simpler existence in harmony | with the seasonal rhythms of nature. || [Black and white 2 ¼ x 1 3/8″ photograph of Brown] || Richard Brown grew up near Boston | and graduated from Harvard College, | where he studied art and art history. He | moved to Vermont in 1968 and taught in a | small rural school before embarking on a | career as a photographer. His work has | appeared in *Harrowsmith Country Life, Audu-* | *bon, National Wildlife, The New York Times,* | *Country Journal,* and many other publica- | tions. His previous books are *The View from* | *the Kingdom, A Vermont Christmas, Moments in* | *Eden,* and *Pictures from the Country.* || *Jacket design by Steve Snider* | *Author photograph by Alden Pellett.*

ILLUSTRATIONS: Photographs on nearly every page; these carry Tudor illustrations: [i, vi] ix [1] 5 [7] 9, 20 [23] 24, 31, 34-35 [36-37] 38 [42] 51 [54-55] 56, 63 [69] 72-73, 76 [78] 81 [83] 87 [96] 104 [106] 110 [114-115] 118, 121-122, 124 [126] 134.

CONTENTS: "Selected Bibliography," page 131, lists 20 titles and ends with a paragraph urging one to buy Tudor creations from The Jenny Wren Press. From "Annotations," pp. 133-134: "The model for Corgiville was Harrisville, New Hampshire, but I took liberties with it."

COPYRIGHT REGISTRATION: TX 3 557 185 granted to Richard Brown, RFD #1, Barnet, Vt. 05821 and Tasha Tudor, RTE 4, Box 205, West Brattleboro, Vt. 05301. Karen L. Dane, agent for the claimants, swears on January 25, 1993:

THE PRIVATE WORLD OF TASHA TUDOR, a work completed in 1991 by Richard Brown, co-author of text and 100% of the photographs and Tasha Tudor, co-author of text, and drawings, both U.S. citizens, was published Oct. 14, 1992. L.C. is granted non-exclusive rights to make copies and phonorecords for the blind and physically handicapped. Fees charged to account DA 018775, The Little, Brown and Company (Inc.), 34 Beacon St., Boston, Ma. 02108 (617-227-0730). Application received Feb. 1 and May 4, 1993. Two deposit copies received Feb. 1, 1993.

P12 _____. [Copyright © 1992 ... Philomel | Books. |10 9 8 7 6 5 4 3 2 | IMAGO ...]

COVER: Spine cloth is maize.

DUST JACKET: Front flap: LIFESTYLE/GARDENING $35.00 FPT | $43.00 in Canada || TASHA...

P13 _____. Have not examined a third printing.

P14 _____. [Copyright © 1992 Philomel | Books. |10 9 8 7 6 5 4 | IMAGO ... Limited | **Printed in China**]

COVER: Spine cloth is tan.

P15 _____. [Copyright © 1992 ... Philomel | Books. | 10 9 8 7 6 5 | IMAGO ... Limited | **Printed in China**]

> OTHER: This printing probably from early 1994 evidenced from a contemporary shop label dated 08/94.

P16 _____. *Little, Brown and Company* | Boston <u>New York</u> Toronto London. [Copyright © 1992 ... Philomel | Books. | 10 9 8 7 6 | IMAGO ... Limited || <u>PRINTED IN HONG KONG</u>]

P17 _____. [Copyright © 1992 ... Philomel | Books. | 10 9 8 7 | IMAGO ... Limited || <u>PRINTED IN CHINA</u>]

P18 _____. [Copyright © 1992 ... Philomel | Books. | 10 9 8 | IMAGO ... Limited || <u>PRINTED IN CHINA</u>]

> OTHER: This printing was probably mid-1997. Caution to the reader: all copies of *The Private World* ... are labeled First Edition. This is technically correct, but pay attention to the print number because only the first represents the true first appearance of the book.

P19 PUMPKIN | MOONSHINE | BY | TASHA TUDOR | OXFORD UNIVERSITY PRESS | LONDON   NEW YORK   TORONTO [COPYRIGHT, 1938 | OXFORD UNIVERSITY PRESS | NEW YORK, INC. || PRINTED IN THE UNITED STATES OF AMERICA]

> PAGINATION: [44] pp. in 3 signatures on ivory paper, flyleaf to flyleaf. 4 3/4″ x 4″.

> COVER: Blue polka dot printed cloth cover, red title in a white oval within a red scalloped frame: PUMPKIN | MOONSHINE | BY | TASHA TUDOR. First endpaper is a red-orange scalloped book plate supported by Sylvie Ann and Wiggy: THIS BOOK | BELONGS | [rule] | TO. Front fly leaf has a watercolor illustration of a cornstalk, pumpkin and oak leaves. <u>Rounded spine.</u>

> DUST JACKET: Front, title scrolls (PUMPKIN above, and MOONSHINE below, in red/orange filled letters) enclose Sylvia Ann, a shock of corn and a pumpkin; hand lettering: BY | TASHA TUDOR, beneath the scroll at bottom. Back, vignette of a sparrow sitting on one of two wheat stems. Front flap in a calligraphic hand: PUMPKIN | MOONSHINE | BY TASHA TUDOR || SYLVIE ANN WANTED | A PUMPKIN MOONSHINE | FOR HALLOWE'EN. SO SHE | STARTED OUT TO FIND | THE BIGGEST PUMPKIN | THAT SHE COULD. HER | ADVENTURES WITH THE | PUMPKIN ARE TOLD IN | ENCHANTING PICTURES | AND EASY TEXT FOR | VERY SMALL PEOPLE. || OXFORD BOOKS | FOR BOYS AND GIRLS | $.75. An inked wheat stem motif appears on both sides of the title; a single stalk leans in toward the title on each side. Back flap is blank.

> CONTENTS: Page [3], title in orange lettering outlined in black in a scallop-edged oval. Page [5], title page with cornstalk, leaves and pumpkin. Page [6], imprint statement. Page [7] dedication: A WEE STORY | FOR A VERY SWEET WEE PERSON. Page [9], orange title, embellished initials, birds, and rye grass. Pages [2, 4] and [44] are blank.

> ILLUSTRATIONS: Each of the even numbered leaves [10] - [42] carries a single color illustration, odd numbered leaves [11] - [43] have hand lettered black text, each page beginning with an orange embellished initial. <u>The rear endpapers each carry</u> the same corn stalk design as the free front endpaper in the first edition.

> OTHER: *A PARTIAL LIST*... page 37 reports "All the art work, 69 pieces including paintings, hand- | lettered pages, illuminated capital letters, and several | alternate designs and pages. | E.B. Hills." Which is to say, that Edward B. Hills owned all the original art for *PUMPKIN MOONSHINE* in

1975. The dust jacket is reproduced in its original size in *the Private World of Tasha Tudor*, page 76.

COPYRIGHT REGISTRATION: A 121567 granted to Oxford University Press, 114 Fifth Avenue, New York City, whose agent H.Z. Walck swears on 19 September 1938:

PUMPKIN MOONSHINE, by Tasha Tudor a United States citizen, was published September 15, 1938. The book was printed by Jersey City Printing Company, Jersey City, N.J. from type set by the Jersey City Printing Company. The printing of the text was completed on April 1, 1938. Binding completed by Brownworth & Co., N.Y., N.Y., Sept. 15, 1938. Application and affidavit were received at the Library of Congress September 21, 1938, and two copies of the book were received September 22, 1938.

COPYRIGHT RENEWAL REGISTRATION: R 391355 granted to Tasha Tudor, Route 1, Contoocook, N.H., claiming as the author. Barbara L. Dammam swears:

PUMPKIN MOONSHINE, by Tasha Tudor was originally published Sept. 15, 1938. Renewal application received Aug. 11, 1966, and fee charged to account #6694, Henry Z. Walck, Inc., 19 Union Square West, N.Y., N.Y. 10003.

P20 _____. Have not examined a second printing.

P21 _____. [COPYRIGHT, 1938 | OXFORD UNIVERSITY PRESS | NEW YORK, INC. || THIRD PRINTING 1945 || PRINTED IN THE UNITED STATES OF AMERICA]

OTHER: THIRD PRINTING statement is cut type, while all else is hand lettered. The orange of this printing carries a much deeper red tinge than the earlier printings.

P22 _____. [COPYRIGHT, 1938 | OXFORD UNIVERSITY PRESS | NEW YORK, INC. || FOURTH PRINTING 1945 || PRINTED IN THE UNITED STATES OF AMERICA]

PAGINATION: Pages [2, 4, 8] and [44-47] are blank. Pages [3-18] and [35-48] are on thinner paper than [19-34]. 4 3/4″ x 4″

COVER: Cloth simulates first edition, but with squared spine. Blue cloth cover.

P23 _____. [COPYRIGHT, 1938 | OXFORD UNIVERSITY PRESS | NEW YORK, INC. || FIFTH PRINTING 1951 || PRINTED IN THE UNITED STATES OF AMERICA]

PAGINATION: [48] pp. in 3 signatures on ivory paper, flyleaf to flyleaf. Pages [2, 4, 8] and [44-47] are blank.

COVER: Paper over boards. Squared spine. 4 3/4″ x 4″

DUST JACKET: Dust jacket as above, but price has been clipped from front flap.

OTHER: Book is printed on thicker, but weaker stock than previous editions.

P24 _____. . . . TUDOR | HENRY Z. WALCK, INC. | NEW YORK [COPYRIGHT, 1938 | HENRY Z. WALCK, INC. | New York, Inc. || Library of Congress Catalog Card Number 58-13228 | PRINTED IN THE UNITED STATES OF AMERICA]

PAGINATION: [48] pp. matches fifth printing. 4 3/4″ x4″

COVER: Paper over boards.

DUST JACKET: Have not examined a copy.

OTHER: This is the first instance of Walck supplanting his own imprint in place of Oxford in the copyright statement. There is a shadow imprint immediately beneath Henry Z. Walck, like a palimpsest on both the title page and the verso. This is a whiter paper than the fifth printing.

P25 _____. HENRY Z. WALCK, INCORPORATED | New York [Copyright 1938 Henry Z Walck, Inc. <u>First published in this enlarged edition, 1962.</u> Library | of Congress Catalog Card Number: A62-8708. Printed in the United States of America.

PAGINATION: PAGINATION: [48] pages of buff paper in three signatures, including free endpapers. Ten stitches, top-sewn. <u>6 3/4″ x 6 3/16″</u>

COVER: <u>Yellow cloth</u>, stamped in brown on spine: Tudor   PUMPKIN MOONSHINE   Walck.

DUST JACKET: Have not examined one.

CONTENTS: Leaf 2, black line hollow lettering of title in an oval with scalloped edge; letters and border filled in orange. Page [5], title page <u>spells INCORPORATED in full</u>.

OTHER: *American Book Publishing Record 1960-1964*, IV:5067. TUDOR, Tasha   JUV | Pumpkin moonshine. [Enl. ed.] New York, Walck | [1962, c.1938] unpaged. col. illus. 18cm. A62-8708 | 2.75 | Back in print in an enlarged format. Ages 3-6.

Jack Smith, 11517 St. Mark, Cleveland, Ohio 44110, was granted copyright TXu 133-416 on August 4, 1983 for lyrics entitled "Pumpkin Moonshine." I have not seen the lyrics and have not determined if there might be a connection to Tudor's book.

P26 _____.

COVER: Overmann lists <u>orange cloth</u>, which I have not examined.

P27 _____. HENRY Z. WALCK, INCORPORATED | New York [{Top half, a full-size <u>catalog card Main Entry</u>} E   Tudor, Tasha | Pumpkin moonshine. Walck, 1938 | unp. illus. || A little girl looks for the | biggest pumpkin to make her jack- | o′-lantern. || 1. Halloween — Stories I. Title [hole] | This Main Entry catalog card may be reproduced without permission. || Copyright 1938 Henry Z Walck, Inc. <u>Copyright © renewed 1966 by Tasha Tudor.</u> First | published in this enlarged edition, 1962. All rights reserved. ISBN 0-8098-1085-9. Library | of Congress Catalog Card Number: A62-8708. Printed in the United States of America.

PAGINATION: [44] pages of white paper in <u>two signatures and four gatherings</u>, including free endpapers. Twenty-four stitches. 6 3/4″ x 6 7/8″

COVER: <u>Orange paper, weave imprint over boards.</u>

DUST JACKET: Dust jacket has sealed glossy finish. Front: blue wash in a vertical pattern within a blue line frame surrounding same vignette as early dust jackets. Title letters are red. Remaining jacket is white with same back illustration as before. Front flap: $6.95 | PUMPKIN MOONSHINE | *by Tasha Tudor* | Sylvia Ann wanted a Pumpkin Moon- | shine for Hallowe'en. So she started out | to find the biggest pumpkin that she could. | Her adventures with the pumpkin are told | in enchanting pictures and easy text for | very small people. ¶ A reissue, in an enlarged format, of the | 1938 edition. || HENRY Z. WALCK, INC. || 30-60. Spine: Tudor PUMPKIN MOONSHINE   Walck. Back flap: Other Books by Tasha Tudor | THE DOLLS' CHRISTMAS | FIRST GRACES | FIRST PRAYERS | MORE PRAYERS | MOTHER GOOSE | A TALE FOR EASTER.

CONTENTS: Images from pages 7 and 9 are combined for the first time onto page 7. The half-title appears above the dedication.

P28 _____.   HENRY Z. WALCK, <u>INC.</u> | New York   <u>[Copyright © 1938 by Tasha Tudor</u> || All rights reserved, including the right to reproduce | this book, or parts thereof, in any form, except for | the inclusion of brief quotations in a review. || Library of Congress Catalog Card Number: <u>A62</u>-8708 | ISBN: 0-8098-1085-9 || <u>10 9 8 7 6 5 4 3 2 1</u> | MANUFACTURED IN THE UNITED STATES OF AMERICA]

PAGINATION: [44] pp. including endpapers, ivory paper. 6 5/8″ x 6 7/8″

COVER: Orange paper with faintest weave imprint (<u>nearly smooth) over boards.</u>

DUST JACKET: Front flap: PUMPKIN MOONSHINE || *by Tasha Tudor* || *"The Kate Greenaway of today, with a | New England rather than an Old England | flavor, gives her small readers a small | book. Here's a natural for Halloween in | the story of how Sylvie Ann goes hunt- | ing the biggest pumpkin in her grand- | mother's field—and then has to roll it | back to the house— with catastrophic re-| sults. But the pumpkin survived to be-| come a Jack o'Lantern on a gate post. | Old fashioned charm."* –Kirkus Reviews || Henry Z. Walck, Inc. | <u>a division of</u> | DAVID <u>McKAY COMPANY, INC.</u> | New York. Back flap: OTHER STORIES WRITTEN | AND ILLUSTRATED | BY TASHA TUDOR || THE DOLLS' CHRISTMAS || *"Little girls of the doll-house age will | revel in the minute details....The author | has illustrated it in her customary style, | delicate, old-fashioned, but never over-| sweet."*—New York Times Book Review || A TALE FOR EASTER || *"Many delicate pictures of rabbits, lambs, | chickens and daffodils, in close associa- | tion with little children, are sprinkled | over the pages, while a wonderful fawn | brings a happy climax to the story."* | —Horn Book. Blank end papers. Have not examined a copy with price intact on front flap.

CONTENTS: Same oval title lozenge on page [3], but now the letters are black line hollow <u>without color.</u>

OTHER: For the first time the copyright statement has changed to '© 1938 by Tasha Tudor'.

P29 _____. [Copyright © 1938 by Tasha Tudor . . . Number: A62-8708 | ISBN: 0-8098-1085-9 <u>(cloth)</u> | ISBN: 0-8098-6375-8 (Paperback)</u> || <u>10 9 8 7 6 5 4</u> | MANUFACTURED IN THE UNITED STATES OF AMERICA]

PAGINATION: [40] pp. 6 1/2 x 6 1/2″

COVER: <u>Paper wrapper</u> has the blue wash reproduction of 1962 dust. Back imprinted black: <u>$2.95</u> [upper right], <u>0-8098-6375-8</u> [lower right].

CONTENTS: No endpapers nor are the old endpaper designs incorporated.

P30 _____.

COVER: Back: A <u>round green paper label</u> over printed price, stamped in black <u>$4.95</u>.

P31 _____.

COVER: Paper wrapper has imprinted, upper right back, <u>$4.95</u>.

OTHER: Purchased new in February 1989.

314

P32 _____. . . . Tudor || <u>Random House</u> [logo] New York [Copyright 1938 Henry Z. Walck, Inc. Copyright renewed 1966 by Tasha Tudor. All | rights reserved under International and Pan-American Copyright Conventions. Published | in the United States by Random House, Inc., New York, and simultaneously in Canada | by Random House of Canada, Limited, Toronto. || *Library of Congress Cataloging-in-Publication Data:* | Tudor, Tasha. Pumpkin moonshine / by Tasha Tudor. p. cm. SUMMARY: A little girl | visiting her grandparents sets out to find a fine pumpkin for Halloween, and it leads her | on a merry chase when it rolls down the hill. ISBN: 0-394-84588-9 [1. Halloween– | Fiction. 2. Pumpkin–Fiction] I. Title. PZ7.T8228Pu 1989 [E]–dc19 89-3543 || Manufactured in the United States of America 2 3 4 5 6 7 8 9 0]

> COVER: <u>Orange paper wrappers</u>, blank backs. The former title, author and cover illustration printed on a white field inside a green circular band on front; bird on wheat on a white field in a smaller green circular band centered on back. Lower left back, bar code in a white box: 84588 [over the smaller right code] | [two bar codes] | 0 79808 84588 5 [beneath the larger left code] | ISBN 0-394-84588-9. <u>Random House</u> $ 5.95 U.S.

P33 _____. Tudor || *The Jenny Wren Press* | *Mooresville, Indiana* [*1st Edition Copyright 1938 Henry Z. Walck, Inc.* | *Republished by Random House 1966. Copyright renewed 1966 by* | *Tasha Tudor* || *Special permission granted of this 55th Anniversary Edition by* | *Random House in 1993. Copyright © 1993 All rights reserved.* || *Library of Congress: Publication Data* [*sic*] | *I.S.B.N. 0-9621753-6-6*]

> PAGINATION: [48] pages including free endpapers in four signatures of white paper topsewn. 6 13/16 x 6 13/16″

> COVER: Butterscotch <u>leather binding</u> is stamped in gold. Front: The 55th Anniversary Edition || PUMPKIN [in scroll] [illustration] MOONSHINE [in scroll] BY | TASHA TUDOR. Spine: *Tudor Pumpkin Moonshine The Jenny Wren Press.* Back: Celebrating Tasha Tudor's 55th Year of Publishing | [rye grass] | [lower right] *I.S.B.N. 0-9621753-6-6.* Reinforced hinges.

> CONTENTS: Pp. [1-3, 46-48] are blank as are inside cover paste-downs. Page [4] illustration is the cornstalk from original ffep. Signed beneath cornstalk <u>T. Tudor</u> | 1993 and numbered at lower left 83 | 250. Page [5], half-title, orange lozenge; [6], the book plate as on original front paste-down. Text begins with title page, [7-43]. Pages [45-46] reproduce same cornstalk illustration which were the endpapers of the fourth and fifth printings.

> OTHER: A laid-in <u>blue-paper note</u> folded to 5 1/2 x 3 3/4″ reproduces the acknowledgment Sylvie Ann [Wallace] sent her Aunt Tasha McCready. ENDSTEAD | NOV. 21 | DEAR TASHA | THANK yOU | FOR My BOOK. | I LiKE iT | VERy MUCH. | I THiNK YOU ARE | VERy CLEVE- | R TO WRiTE | iT. THE [page 2-3] PUMPKiN FACES ARE VERY | FUNNY. MUMMY LOVES | iT TOO. WE READ iT TO | ALL OUR FRiENDS AND THEY | LiKE iT TOO. WiGGY HAS- | NT GOT A TAiL ONLY JUST | A TiNY BiT. | LOTS OF LOVE FROM SYLVi | +++SYLViE-AN | SYLViE-ANN | XXXXXXXOOO [page 4 blank].

The leather bound books were shipped wrapped in white tissue inside a cardboard folder such as those in which nylon stockings were once sold. <u>This</u> package was wrapped in a red calico gift wrap and closed with a gold foil Jenny Wren Press sticker with two green grosgrain ribbon drops.

The colophon errs in citing Walck as the 1938 copyright holder, and Random House as reprinting in 1966. Random House did not acquire rights until the late 1980s.

The Jenny Wren Press Spring-Summer 1993 catalog announces the 55th anniversary edition of 5000 copies. 250 copies were bound in leather, signed by Tudor and numbered. Numbers 1-50 with a remarque by Tudor sold for $200. Remaining leather bindings sold for $125. And the cloth bound, see below, listed for $14.95 or if signed, $29.95. The same catalog also advertised a 12″ hand-crafted Sylvie Ann doll, $75.00.

P34 _____.

    COVER: The trade binding in a <u>light blue cloth</u>. Identical in all other respects.

    DUST JACKET: White paper, cover text in black. Illustrations in color, and the title in orange letters outlined in black. Front flap: *Pumpkin Moonshine* | *by Tasha Tudor* || *Sylvie Ann wanted a Pumpkin* | *Moonshine for Halloween. So she* | *started out to find the biggest* | *pumpkin that she could. Her* | *adventures with the pumpkin are* | *told in enchanting pictures and an* | *easy text for all ages to share &* | *enjoy.* || *This special 55th Anniversary* | *edition is in celebration of Tasha Tudor's very 1st published book.* | <u>*Tasha Tudor is the oldest living*</u> | <u>*illustrator of*</u> <u>*childrens*</u> [sic] <u>*books in*</u> | <u>*America*</u>*...with over 80 books to* | *her credit.* Back flap: *History of the Book* || *The real Sylvie Ann was the 4 years* [sic] | *old niece of Tasha's husband to be at* | *the time the book was created. Tasha* | *enjoyed her greatly and as a surprise* | *made this little book to entertain* | *her! Eventually it was published by* | *Oxford Press* [sic] *in 1938 in a smaller* | *version, so that it could be enjoyed* | *by all!* || *With Gratitude:* | *The Jenny Wren Press would like to* | *thank Random House for the* | *privilege of issuing this 55th* | *Anniversary Edition.* || *This book & other treasures by* | *Tasha Tudor can be obtained by* | *writing to*: | The Jenny Wren Press P.M. | P.O. Box 505 | Mooresville, Indiana | 46158.

    OTHER: With the blue Thank You note laid in.

P35 _____. Warner Books announced plans to reprint *Pumpkin Moonshine* in a 4 ¼ x 3 7/8″ paper over boards edition in April 1998. Part of the *Warner Treasures* series, the book, ISBN 0-446-91246-8, was to retail for $ 6.95. http://www.warnerbooks.com did not list the book as of March 4, 1998. A company spokesperson confirmed a few days later that Warner would not be reprinting the calico books; another employee speculated the reprints might be published by Little, Brown.

R1 Henry A. Shute || **THE REAL DIARY OF A REAL BOY** | [1 ¾" rule] ||
Noone House | THE RICHARD R. SMITH CO., INC. | PETERBOROUGH, NEW HAMPSHIRE
[COPYRIGHT © 1967 BY | THE RICHARD R. SMITH CO. INC. | PETERBOROUGH, NEW
HAMPSHIRE || LIBRARY OF CONGRESS CATALOG CARD NO. 67-27745 || MANUFACTURED IN
THE UNITED STATES OF AMERICA].

PAGINATION: [i-iv] v [vi] vii-xiii [xiv] 1-10 [11] 12-37 [38] 39-57 [58] 59-72 [73] 74-105 [106]
107-109 [110] 111-122 [123] 124-131 [132] 133-152 [153] 154-158 [159] 160-162 [163] 164-
175 [176] 177-194 pages in seven signatures. 7 5/8" x 5 1/4".

COVER: Red cloth printed in black. Front: **Diry**. Spine: Shute | [vertical panel, printed sideways]
The Real Diary of a Real Boy | Tasha | Tudor   R•R | S. Pencil drawing of two-page street
scene used on both yellow endpapers. [Compare with endpapers of *The Great Corgiville
Kidnapping* - Ed.]

DUST JACKET: Cream dust jacket printed in black and red. Front is framed in wide red line outside a
narrow black rule, centered, large pencil medallion of boy at desk on front. Text: Henry A.
Shute [red] | THE REAL DIARY | OF A | REAL BOY [black] || [medallion] |
Illustrated by | TASHA TUDOR [red]. Spine like the book; only title and a new small
inkwell (between Tudor and R•R) are black. Remaining text and the rule around the title are red.
Front flap: $ 3.95 [black] || The Real Diary | of A Real Boy | by Henry A. Shute [red] || IN
THE winter of 1901-02, while rum- | maging in the shed-chamber of his | father's house, Judge
Henry A. Shute | unearthed a salt-box containing: a | popgun of pith elder and hoopskirt | wire, a
six-inch bean blower for school | use, a frog's hind leg (extra dry), and | a horde of other
treasures–among | them, a manuscript marked "Diry". ¶The diary was written–or so its | author
alleged–when he was an elev- | en-year-old boy growing up in the | 1860's in Exeter, New
Hampshire. ¶From the moment of its publication | in 1902, *The Real Diary of a Real Boy* | won
immediate popularity, and for | years to come was a favorite of read- | ers, young and old alike.
Now the | lively adventures of "Plupy", the real | boy, are re-issued in this new edition | with
delightful illustrations by Tasha | Tudor. ¶Plupy Shute's "Diry" makes up in | wit all that it loses
in spelling. It is | also an authentic chronicle of a boy's | world a century ago. That world may |
have vanished, but boys still grow up, | and they do it with much the same | gusto and spirit,
humor and imagina- | tion, as Plupy Shute. [black] || THE RICHARD R. SMITH, CO., INC. | NOONE
HOUSE | PETERBOROUGH, NEW HAMPSHIRE 03458 [and sketch of a colonial house with two
dormers and trees, all red].   Back flap, below 2 5/8 x 2 3/16" black and white photograph of
Shute: HENRY A. SHUTE   1856-1943 [red] || No one was more surprised than | Henry A.
Shute when his *Real Diary | of a Real Boy* became a best seller | after its publication in 1902. A
lawyer | and judge in Exeter, N.H., Shute's | career as a writer did not begin until | he was over
forty, and he regarded | his subsequent literary fame as some- | thing of a joke. The author of
nearly | twenty books, he was rated with Mark | Twain for his faithful portrayals of | boyhood life.
Revival of this volume | is a reminder that Judge Shute was | one of the great American
humorists. [black] || TASHA TUDOR'S [red] drawings for this | book capture vividly and
skillfully the | boyhood world of Plupy. One of the | world's foremost illustrators, she has |
drawn much of the material for her | work from her own New Hampshire | farmhouse and its
surroundings. No- | table among Miss Tudor's recent books | are *The Wind in the Willows* and
The | Tasha Tudor Book of Fairy Tales. <u>The back of the jacket is blank.</u>

ILLUSTRATION: Full page pencil drawings on pages [11, 38, 58, 73, 106, 110, 123, 132, 153, 159, 163, 176]. Sketch of boy at desk, page [ii]. Small drawing of a cornet on page 178.

COPYRIGHT REGISTRATION: A 946519 granted to The Richard R. Smith Co. Inc., Noone House, Peterborough, N.H. 03458. William L. Bauhan, President, swears on Oct. 20, 1967:

> THE REAL DIARY OF A REAL BOY, by Henry A. Shute 1856-1943, Exeter, N.H., a U.S. citizen deceased, and Tasha Tudor, Route 1, Contoocook, N.H., a U.S. citizen was published Oct. 15, 1967. New matter in this version: all illustrations (14) plus endleaves. Also: Foreword; revisions in text on about 15 pages; revisions pp. 179-194; new front matter. The book was printed by Murray Printing Co., Forge Village, Ma. from type set by the Scott Linotype Co., Boston, Ma. Binding by Colonial Press Inc., Clinton, Ma. Fees, application and affidavit and two deposit copies received Oct. 27. 1967.

COPYRIGHT REGISTRATION RENEWAL: RE 730-196 grants William L. Bauhan, Inc., P.O. Box 443, Dublin, N.H. 03444, 603-563-8020, Proprietor of copyright in a work made for hire renewal to the Illustrations, foreword, revision and new front matter, effective January 3, 1996. William L. Bauhan swears July 19, 1996:

> THE REAL DIARY OF A REAL BOY, was published October 15, 1967 and copyright to Richard R. Smith Co., Inc., A-946519. Authors of renewable matter are Tasha Tudor (Illustrations) (Forward [sic] and Revisions pp. 179-194 by Christopher D. Reed). Applications receied July 24, 1996 and January 3, 1996

COPYRIGHT RENEWAL REGISTRATION: RE 735-030 grants Tasha Tudor, c/o Corgi Cottage Industries, P.O. Box 7281, Richmond, Va, 23211-0281, claiming as author (illustrator). Kathyrn L. Barrett [sic], Esq., 235 East 22nd Street, Apt. 11C, New York, NY 10010, 212-684-6689, swears July 30, 1996:

> THE REAL DIARY OF A REAL BOY, was published October 15, 1967 and copyright to Richard P. Smith Co., Inc., [sic] A946519. Tasha Tudor is author of the renewable matter: Illustrations. Application received at LC August 9, 1996, the effective date of this registration. Certificate and correspondence to be mailed to Kathryn L. Barrett.

R2 _____.

DUST JACKET: 2nd state. Front flap: $3.95 . . .   Back imprinted in black: A Classic Tale for Young and Old . . . || "Us professional humorists have always known that Henry | Shute's *Real Diary of a Real Boy* was funnier than Mark Twain's | *Huck Finn* or *Tom Sawyer*, and it's about time we let the public | in on the secret."   – AL CAPP || "This was one of my favorite stories as a young boy." | – SAMUEL ELIOT MORISON || "In these troublesome times, what a relief to spend a few | minutes savoring those delightful days of an age gone by. Al- | though Plupy probably didn't intend it that way, he and his | friends remind us that there is a good case for 'boys being boys', | and that perhaps we should not be too discouraged if the pre- | sent young ones don't always perform in accordance with the | precepts of their elders." || – WALTER CRONKITE || "The 'diry' makes a vivid chronicle of a boy's world in the | 1860's and describes what passed for deviltry at that time . . . | It seemed the funniest book in the world when I was eleven." | – LOUIS M. LYONS || "Boys here have enjoyed *The Real Diary* for years. We look | forward to more readers with this attractive new edition." | – LOIS R. MARKEY, *Director* | *Public Library, Concord, N.H.* || "A picture of a vanished America. That America had fences, | alleyways, livery stables, and warts; in it boys 'fite' and 'dreen | marbles' and go 'bullfrogging' and yearn to be hack drivers . . . | Boys of Plupy's age still misspell, though not with his majestic | inconsistency. But whatever his orthography, Plupy had insight | into human psychology." – HOWARD MUMFORD JONES || Bottom left: Jacket printed by Sim's Press, Inc., | Peterborough, N.H.

R3 _____.

DUST JACKET: <u>3rd state</u>. Front flap: $3.95 . . .   Back imprinted in <u>red</u> and black, now has <u>seven</u> endorsements: A Classic Tale for Young and Old . . . [red] || "Us professional . . . MORISON || "The 'diry' makes a vivid . . . *Public Library, Concord, N.H.* || " A welcome revival. Times have changed since then, but | Judge Shute's *Diary* is as entertaining as ever . . ." | – ROBB SAGENDORPH, *Publisher | Yankee Magazine* || "A picture of a vanished . . . JONES || "Its merriment is so infectious that one cannot fancy a person | able to resist the spirit of this book." | – *The New York Journal* (c. 1902) ||. At bottom left: Jacket printed by Sim's Press, Inc., | Peterborough, N.H.

R4 _____.

COVER: <u>4th state,</u> a later distribution. <u>Ocher cloth,</u> and carries at the base of spine, <u>WLB</u>.

DUST JACKET: Front, spine and rear flap as before. <u>Price is clipped</u> from upper corner of front flap. Even though the new publisher's initials appear on the book spine, the jacket maintains the <u>R R S</u>. The house logo in red at bottom of front flap remains, but the three lines identifying the publisher are <u>overprinted with a thick black rule</u>. Back: <u>What the critics say about *The Real Diary of a Real Boy* . . .</u> "Us professional . . . Shute's ↓ . . . *Finn* ↓or . . . secret." ↓ – AL CAPP || "In these troublesome times, what a relief <u>to savor the</u> delightful ↓ days of an age gone <u>by.</u> Plupy and his friends remind us that there ↓ is a good case for 'boys being boys', and that perhaps we should ↓ not be too discouraged if the present young ones don't always per- ↓ form in accordance with the precepts of their elders." || – WALTER CRONKITE || <u>"One of the classics of New England boyhood, reissued in a new | format, and we've been enjoying again the same sort of laughs as | we did reading it some forty years ago.."</u> | - NEW HAVEN REGISTER || "Hoo raw. A NEW EDITION OF Plupy. With Pikchers . . . . *the | Real Diary* is way beyond funny. The funny stuff is all about 'fites' | and bean shooters and getting licked and other antics . . . The real | woolen goods is the straight story this kid comes over with about | 'How it really was' in a small New England town in the mid-19th | century." – RICHARD BISSELL IN THE NEW YORK TIMES || . . . . and its sequel *Brite and Fair:* || "*Brite and Fair* is a delightful book . . . recreating childhood life | in the 1860s. Plupy and his two friends have all the innocence, | imagination and ingenuity as they create havoc among the towns- | people and their own families." – PUBLISHER'S WEEKLY || *Brite and Fair* adds up to a fine and funny helping of nostalgia | for the simple, sunny summer days of old- time America. | – THE NEW YORK TIMES || "Tasha Tudor's illustrations capture perfectly the feeling of the | diary." – PROVIDENCE JOURNAL || *Both editions available from* | William L. Bauhan Publisher, Dublin, New Hampshire | (formerly Richard R., Smith Co., Noone House, Peterborough, NH.)

R5 _____.

COVER: <u>5th state</u>. Ocher cloth, <u>coarser weave</u> than above. Spine: the letters <u>W L B</u> are <u>spaced farther apart</u>.

DUST JACKET: Price is clipped from front flap.

R6 The Real Pretend [red]| [illustration of girl, cat and geranium on porch step] | By Joan Donaldson | Illustrated by Tasha Tudor [yellow] || Checkerboard Press | New York [black]. Colophon is printed on page [2]: [For Mary Rife || [photograph of girl on pony] | Thank you to Grandma Kathy, who told us | this true story and showed us the real photograph. | Looking back, she felt that her mother dealt with her | fairly and that no one had a brother who loved her more. —J.D. || Text © 1992 Joan Donaldson. Illustrations © 1992 Tasha Tudor. All rights reserved. | Published by Checkerboard Press, Inc., 30 Vesey Street, New York, NY 10007. | ISBN: 1-56288-158-2 Library of Congress Catalog Card Number: 91-73086 Printed in Singapore 0 9 8 7 6 5 4 3 2 1]

PAGINATION: [28] pages. Two signatures on white paper. 8 3/4 x 11 1/8 *"*.

COVER: Coral paper under gloss film laminate over boards. Most of the front cover is over-printed with a blue panel, centered upon which is a vignette of Kathy sitting in a wheelbarrow, with cats and pumpkins, within an oval frame of wild asters. Arched above the oval is the red title, The Real Pretend. Below it are arched two lines in yellow: By Joan Donaldson | Illustrated by Tasha Tudor. A gathering of wild flowers frames the whole on the left and right: maple leaves, asters, black-eyed Susans and Queen Ann's Lace. The spine is printed in blue: The Real Pretend   Donaldson/Tudor Checkerboard Press. Back, centered, a 4 3/4″ white medallion of Kathy reading her Larkin's catalog. The same illustration appears on the front free endpaper. At the lower left corner, a 1 1/4″ x 1 1/2″ white box enclosing a bar code and: 0 14121 00158 7 || ISBN 1-56288-158-2.

DUST JACKET: The dust jacket repeats the design and typography of the cover exactly. Additionally the two coral flaps carry this black text. Front flap: $12.95 || **E** [blue] veryone enjoys a game of | pretend. But when Kathy plays | salesperson for a mail-order | catalog, she and her brother, | Robert, face some unexpected | consequences. This heartwarming | tale, based on a true story, brings | home the true value of honesty | and love among family and | friends. || As always, Tasha Tudor's delicate | and charming illustrations make | this old-fashioned story come to | life. || [a small pantry scene]. Back flap: **Tasha Tudor** || Tasha Tudor is one of America's most beloved | illustrators. Born in 1915 in New England, she now | lives on her Vermont farm. Tasha's heartwarming | illustrations capture the serenity of her rural | nineteenth-century life-style, complete with period | clothing, numerous farm animals and household | pets, including her Welsh corgis, her renowned | garden, and her charming farmhouse. ¶Tasha has written and illustrated more than ninety | books that have delighted both children and adult | readers for many decades. Her works feature | children full of wonder, warm family scenes, and the | everyday charms of a country life. || **Joan Donaldson** || Joan Donaldson lives on her old-fashioned fruit | farm in southwestern Michigan. Teaching children, | quilting, gardening, and working on the family's | homestead fill most of her days. During her free | moments, Joan enjoys playing her Irish button | accordion, folk dancing, and nurturing friendships. | But most of all, Joan and her husband and two sons | seek to live a plain and pastoral life-style. ¶In 1987 Joan was chosen Homemaker of the year | by the Michigan State Fair. *The Real Pretend* is her | first book. || Checkerboard Press | New York.

CONTENTS: Page [1] is front free endpaper, [2] the dedication/colophon page, [3] the title page. Text begins on the title page verso running from page [4] to [27] where even numbered pages are text within a floral border, and odd numbered pages are full page illustrations within oval floral borders.

ILLUSTRATIONS: Full color illustrations on every sheet. Blue endpapers with a centered medallion: a leafy circle around a childhood vignette, each of the four a different illustration. Two are of Kathy and two her brother Robert.

OTHER: Joan Donaldson writes in *The LETTER* (11:1 Fall 1992, page 3) that this story was told by Kathy Klingheil at Michael Sull's 1989 Spencerian Script workshop attended by herself, Tudor and Carol Leuck. She says that after hearing the story, Tudor turned to her two friends and said, "One of you write that down as a story and we'll do it as a book together."

COPYRIGHT REGISTRATION: TX 3-741-719 granted to Tasha Tudor, Route 4, Box 205, West Brattleboro, Vt. 05301. Juwanda Ford, authorized agent for Checkerboard Press, Inc. 30 Vesey St., N.Y., N.Y. 10007 (212-571-6300), swears on June 16, 1993:

THE REAL PRETEND, illustrations not made for hire by Tasha Tudor, a U.S. citizen, was completed in 1992 and published Dec 1, 1992. Library of Congress is granted non-exclusive permission to make copies and phonorecords for the blind and physically handicapped. Application and two deposit copies received Jan 12, 1994.

COPYRIGHT REGISTRATION: TX 3-741-720 granted to Joan Donaldson, Pleasant Hill Farm, Fenneville, Mi. 49408. Juwanda Ford, authorized agent for Checkerboard Press, Inc. 30 Vesey St., NY, NY 10007 (212-571-6300), swears on June 16, 1993:

THE REAL PRETEND, not made for hire by Joan Donaldson, a U.S. citizen, was completed in 1992 and published Dec. 1, 1992. Library of Congress is granted non-exclusive permission to make copies and phonorecords for the blind and physically handicapped. Application and two deposit copies received Jan 12, 1994.

Selected Covers
and Dust Jackets

And It Was So
Top: A46, A48
Bottom: A47, A49, A50

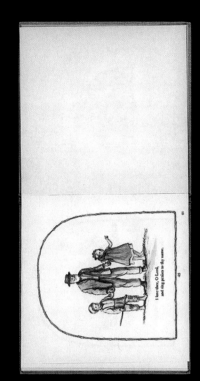

And It Was So
A46, note the code at lower right corner of page 48

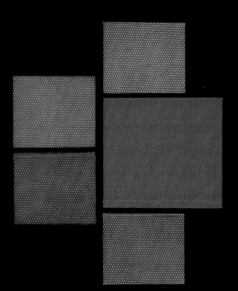

Alexander the Gander
Top: A23, A25
Bottom: A21, A27, A26

And It Was So
Top: A46 dust jacket
Bottom: A50 dust jacket

Plate 1

A Basket of Herbs
B1, B2 2 variant book plates

A Brighter Garden
Top: B52, dust jacket
Bottom: B56, B57, B56

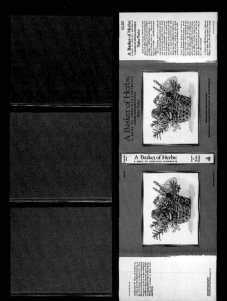

A Basket of Herbs
Top: B1, B2, B4
Bottom: B1 dust jacket

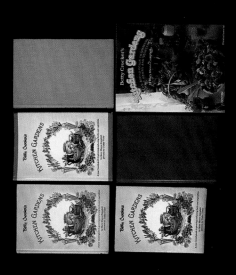

Betty Crocker's Kitchen Gardens
Top: B27, B30, B28
Bottom: B32, B30, B33

Plate 2

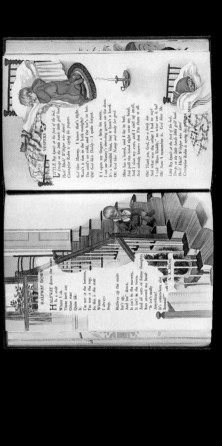

Childcraft: Poems of Early Childhood
C3: pp.144–145

The Christmas Cat
Top: C26, C32, C33
Bottom: C30, C34, C35

Brite and Fair
Top: B58, B59, B60
Bottom: B58, B59, B60 dust jackets

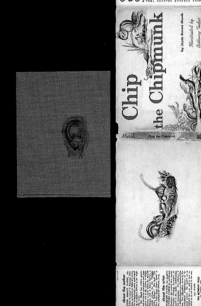

Chip the Chipmunk
C25, book and dust jacket

Plate 3

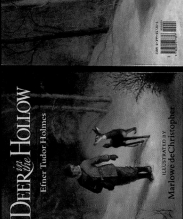

Deer in the Hollow
D1, front cover and back of dust jacket

English Cottage Gardening
E7, dust jacket; E6, cover

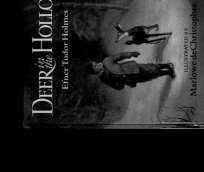

Collier's Junior Classics
A1, in two different bindings

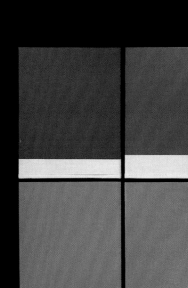

Drawn from New England
Top: D74, D76
Bottom: D75, D80

Plate 4

An Illustrated Study…
I1, front cover

Ladies: 1962
L1, front cover

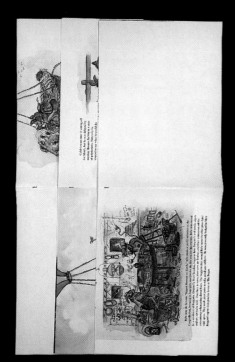

The Great Corgiville Kidnapping
G36, 3 signatures splayed to show check numbers at the folds

The Illustrated Treasury of Fairy Tales
The Illustrated Treasury of Humor for Children
I4, I5

Plate 5

The Lord Will Love Thee
Top: L56, L54 covers
Bottom: L53, dust jacket

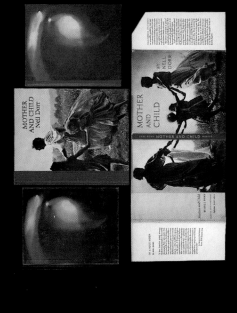

Mother and Child
Top: M16, M18, M17
Bottom: M17, dust jacket

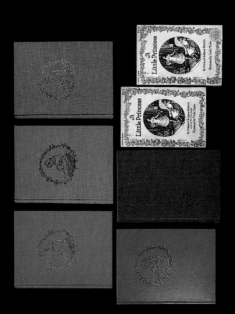

A Little Princess
Top: L5, L8, L10
Bottom: L14, L16, L20, L21

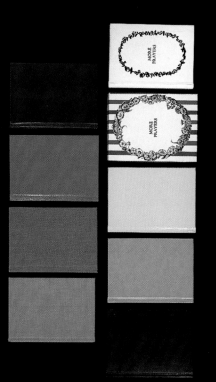

More Prayers
Top: M5, M6, M7, M8
Bottom: M9, M11, M12, M15 box, M15 cover

Plate 6

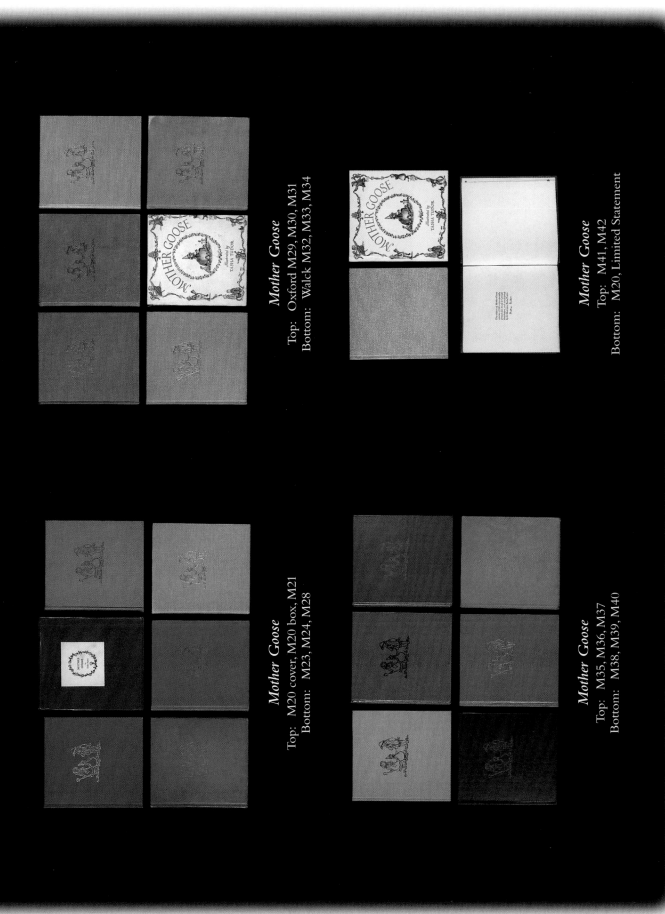

Mother Goose
Top: Oxford M29, M30, M31
Bottom: Walck M32, M33, M34

Mother Goose
Top: M41, M42
Bottom: M20, Limited Statement

Mother Goose
Top: M20 cover, M20 box, M21
Bottom: M23, M24, M28

Mother Goose
Top: M35, M36, M37
Bottom: M38, M39, M40

Plate 7

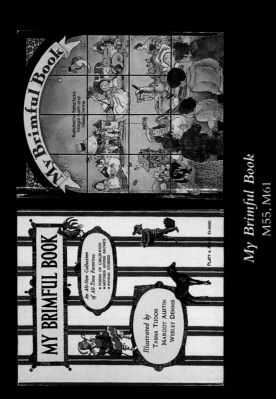

The Nest
N1

The New England Butt'ry Shelf Cookbook
Top: N12, N18, N23
Bottom: N17, N18, N22 dust jackets

My Brimful Book
M55, M61

The New England Butt'ry Shelf Almanac
Top: N2, N5, N6
Bottom: N9, N10, N11

Plate 8

On the Horizon
O1, O2

A Partial List...
P1

The Night Before Christmas
The Twenty Third Psalm
Top: N29, N30, N27
Bottom: St. Onge slipcase, T190, T192, St. Onge bibliography

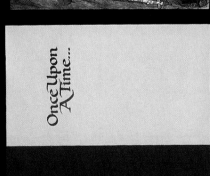

Once Upon a Time...
O3, O4

Plate 9

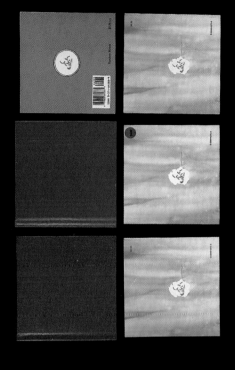

Pumpkin Moonshine
Top: P27, P28, P32
Bottom: P29, P30, P31

The Real Diary of a Real Boy
Top: R1, R3
Bottom: R4, R2

The Platt & Munk Treasury of Stories for Children
P6

The Real Diary of a Real Boy
Top: R1, R3
Bottom: R4, R2

Plate 10

Samuel's Tree House
Top: S4, S5
Bottom: S4, dust jacket

Samantha's Surprise
S1

Tasha Tudor's Seasons of Delight
Give Us This Day; The Lord's Prayer
Top: T155
Bottom: G5

Skiddycock Pond
S59

Plate 11

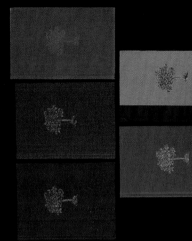

The Secret Garden
Top: S9, S15, S17
Bottom: S19, S20

The Secret Garden
Top: S34, S36, S41
Bottom: S49, S50, S51

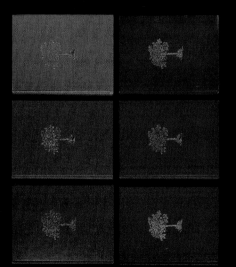

The Secret Garden
Top: S6, S7a, S7
Bottom: S8, S10, S12

The Secret Garden
Top: S6 dust jacket
Bottom: S22 dust jacket

Plate 12

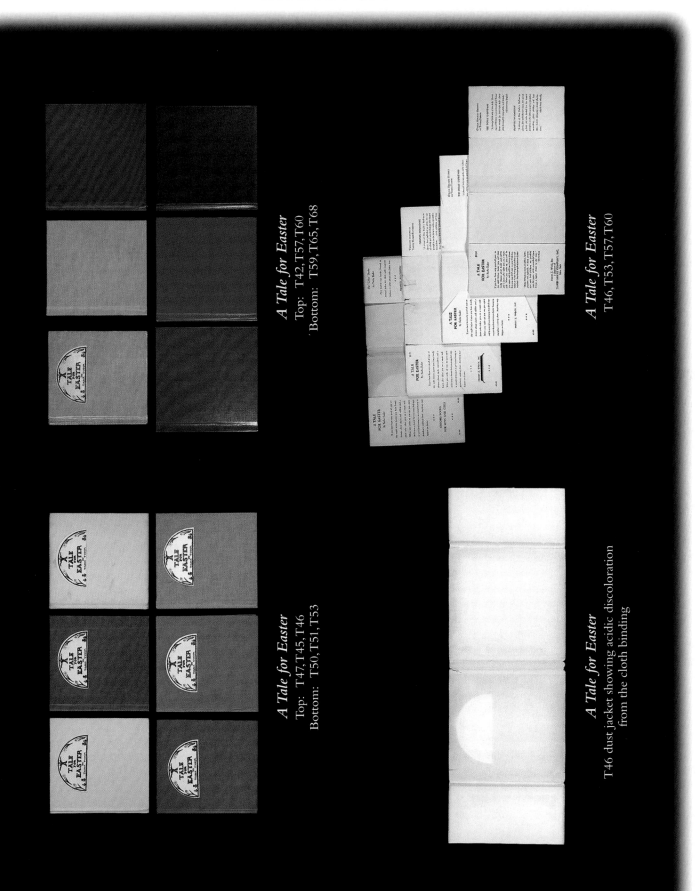

A Tale for Easter
Top: T42, T57, T60
Bottom: T59, T65, T68

A Tale for Easter
T46, T53, T57, T60

A Tale for Easter
Top: T47, T45, T46
Bottom: T50, T51, T53

A Tale for Easter
T46 dust jacket showing acidic discoloration
from the cloth binding

Plate 13

Tasha Tudor
T74

Tasha Tudor's Engagement Calendar
T109, T110

Take Joy! The Magical World of Tasha Tudor
T1, sleeve and videocassette

The Tasha Tudor Book of Fairy Tales
T78

Plate 14

Tasha Tudor's Garden
T135, T134

Thistly B
Showing Oxford and Walck title page versos
Top: T160
Bottom: T163

Tasha Tudor's Favorite Stories
Dust jackets for T119, T120, T123

Tasha Tudor's Sampler
Top: T146, T147
Bottom: T148, T152, T153

Plate 15

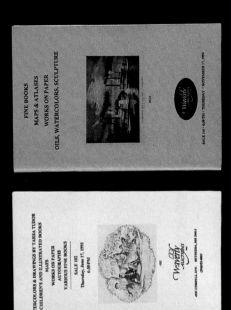

Waverly Auction Catalogs
Catalogs 102 and 116

Yankee
December 1951, June 1954
October 1957

The Twenty Third Psalm
Dedications: T190, T191, T194

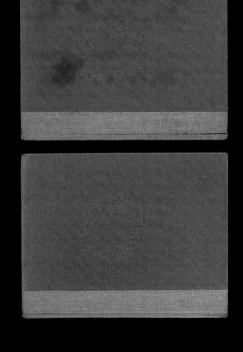

Wings from the Wind
W21, Two copies, the right displaying a red discoloration common to
this book

Plate 16

R7 ROSEMARY FOR | REMEMBRANCE [purple, remaining text black] || *A Keepsake Book* | TASHA TUDOR || PHILOMEL BOOKS | *New York* || [below the ribbon]

Copyright © 1981 by Tasha Tudor. All rights reserved. | Printed in the United States of America. [Page [2] To Linda, | the Renaissance woman [purple, remaining text is black] | [a wild rose] | *First edition, 1981* || *Published by Philomel Books | a division of The Putnam Publishing Group | 200 Madison Avenue, New York, N.Y. 10016* || *No part of this publication may be reproduced, | stored in a retrieval system, or transmitted, in any form or by any means, | without prior written permission of the publisher.* || *Information on last page of this book constitutes an extension of the copyright page.* | *ISBN 0-399-20812-7* | Designed by Sallie Baldwin / Antler & Baldwin Studio, Inc. || All the flowers and herbs that appear in the illustrations in this volume were painted from life, as they appeared | during the round of the year's seasons in Tasha Tudor's own garden. Among others, flower lovers may identify the following: | [rule] | **ON ENDPAPERS:** || *Artemisia* | *Campanula glomerata* | Feverfew (*Chrysanthemum parthenium)* | *Gypsophyla paniculata* | *Geranium Alpha* | Miniature rose | Maiden's blush rose (Cuisse de nymphe) | Bloomfield Dainty (a musk rose) | *Viola tricola* (Ladies' Delight) | Hidcote Beauty (a *Fuchsia*) | *Malva* (mallow) | Forget-me-not || **ON DEDICATION PAGE:** || Bloomfield Dainty rose || **ON TITLE PAGE:** || Rosemary | *Rosa nitidi* | *Campanula* [column 2] **JANUARY:** || Seed pods of *rosa multiflora* | Seed pods of *pinxter* bush (Azalea) | Seed pods of Sensitive fern | Seed pods of black-eyed Susan | Dried goldenrod || **FEBRUARY:** || Violet | Forget-me-not | *Convallaria majalis* (lily-of-the-valley) | Moss rose | Ivy | Bleeding heart | Hay fern | *Fuschia* || **MARCH:** || Pussywillows | Birch catkins | Fern fronds | Skunk cabbage [column 3] **APRIL:** || Pussywillow catkins | Birch catkins | *Narcissus poeticus* || **MAY:** || *Primula vulgaris* | Keys of Heaven (a *Primula*) | Daffodils | Bloodroot | Fiddleheads of Interrupted fern || **JUNE:** || *Rosa soulianna* | *Delphinium* | Regal lily | *Gypsophyla* | Interrupted fern | Shrub roses | Crested moss rose | (Chapeau de Napoleon) | Maidenhair fern [column 4] **JULY:** || Koenigen von Daenemarck | (Queen of Denmark) rose | *Geranium* "tree" | Old shrub rose || **AUGUST:** || *Artemisia* | Crane's-bill (*Geranium*) | *Valeriana* | Lilies, various | Lettuce poppies | Hollyhocks || **SEPTEMBER:** || Witch hazel blooms and pods | New England aster | Woodbine leaves and berries || **OCTOBER:** || Apples | Goldenrod | New England aster [column 5] **NOVEMBER:** || Interrupted fern | Bittersweet | British Soldier | Fairy cups || DECEMBER: || Oats | Wheat] Page [28]: Tasha Tudor and Philomel Books gratefully thank the following authors and publishers whose interest, cooperation and permission | to reprint have made possible the preparation of this volume. All possible care has been taken to trace the ownership of every | selection included and to make full acknowledgment for its use. If any errors have accidentally occurred, they will be corrected in | subsequent editions provided notification is sent to the publishers. | Holt, Rinehart and Winston, New York, for lines from (September) *Outermost House* by Henry Boston [*sic*], copyright © 1928 by Holt, Rinehart and Winston. | M.B. Yeats, Anne Yeats, and Macmillan Publishers Ltd., London; and Macmillan Publishing Company, Inc., New York, for lines | from the following poems by William Butler Yeats: (April) *The Song of the Wandering Aengus*; (June) *In Memory of Eva Gore-Booth and Con Markiewwicz*; | and (July) *To a Friend Whose Work Has Come to Nothing*, copyright © 1916, 1933 by Macmillan Publishing Company Inc., | renewed 1944, 1961 by Bertha Georgie Yeats.

PAGINATION: [28] pp. in two signatures including fly leaves. 8 1/2 x 11 1/4 ".

COVER: Printed paper under gloss film lamination over boards, in a pasteboard slipcase. Front cover headed by a title banner surmounted by five sparrows, edged with roses, small bouquets of rosemary *et alia* at both lower corners: ROSEMARY FOR | REMEMBRANCE [black]. Center illustration features a corgi, boy and girl holding hands behind a rosemary topiary, a cat, all in front of a flower garden. Beneath: *A Keepsake Book* [purple] | TASHA TUDOR [black]. Spine: [flower] Tudor [black] ROSEMARY FOR REMEMBRANCE [purple] Philomel [black] [flower]. Flesh background becomes more intense on the back cover which features an oval frame around a broach, fan, rose and bundle of letters. Back lower right corner: ISBN 0-399-20812-7. A light pasteboard slipcase shipped in cellophane shrink-wrap reproduces all features of the cover and adds text to the back. $ 10.95 [upper right] For those very special days in your life, | here is the perfect permanent record. | This beautiful album lists each day of the year, | providing spaces in which to make note of birthdays and anniversaries of family and friends, | as well as many other important events and recurring dates. | Distinguished American artist Tasha Tudor | has created exquisite watercolor paintings of scenes and activities for all the months, | and has chosen a favorite poem or apt quotation to accompany each. | In its own slipcase, | *ROSEMARY FOR REMEMBRANCE* | is designed to be a charming reminder of happy times past and to come, | a treasured and lasting keepsake. || [oval illustration] ||: **"There's rosemary, that's for remembrance..."** | —**William Shakespeare, *Hamlet*, IV, v, 174** || ISBN 0-399-20812-7.

CONTENTS: Title page [3], Copyright [2]. Odd numbered pages [5-27] are calendar pages, January through December, a line for each day. Even numbered pages [4-26], full page illustrations, representing an event of the month on the facing page, and a quotation from an author. Diary pages are enclosed in oval borders of flowers. Each facing illustration, except April, has a complimentary full or partial border. Acknowledgments, page [28].

ILLUSTRATIONS: All illustrations in color. A different tussy-mussy is centered on each of the four end papers. Title page oval white field surround by a pale green ribbon tied at top and embellished with roses, rosemary and campanula.

OTHER: Dedicated to Linda Allen who lived with Tudor for eleven years. Henry Besten is mistakenly attributed as "Henry Boston" on pages [22] and [28].

COPYRIGHT REGISTRATION: VA 94-068 granted to Tasha Tudor, RFD #4, West Brattleboro, Vt. Edith Menrad, agent for Tasha Tudor, swears:

ROSEMARY FOR REMEMBRANCE: A KEEPSAKE BOOK, watercolor paintings and compilation of text by Tasha Tudor, a U.S. citizen, completed in 1981 was published Nov. 20, 1981. Text was previously published, but illustrations and compilations of text are new to this version. Fees charged to account DAO38288, Putnam Publishing Group, 200 Madison Ave., N.Y., N.Y. 10016. Deposit copy received Feb. 3, 1982.

R8 _____. PHILOMEL BOOKS | *New York* [To Linda . . . Copyright © 1981 by Tasha Tudor. | All rights reserved. Published by Philomel Books, | a division of The Putnam & Grosset Book Group, 200 Madison Avenue, | New York, New York 10016. Published simultaneously in Canada. | Designed by Sallie Baldwin/Antler & Baldwin Studio, Inc. | Printed in Hong Kong by South China Printing Co. (1988) Ltd. | Information on the last page of this book consti- | tutes an extension of the copyright page. | ISBN 0-399-21816-5 | First Impression (revised edition) | [rule] | All the flowers . . . Oats | Wheat]

PAGINATION: [28] pp in two signatures including free endpapers. 8 1/2″ x 11 1/4″.

COVER: Printed paper front, no gloss. Green cloth hinge and back cover. Bird in circle and PHILOMEL BOOKS stamped in gilt, center bottom back. Price sticker on back lower right: 90000 [above smaller right code] | [2 bar codes] | 9 780399 218163 [beneath larger left code] | ISBN 0-399-21816-5 | $15.95 | [rule] | $20.95 (CAN). Maroon ribbon page marker.

OTHER: Title page border color is paler than the first edition and the copyright statement has been deleted from the title page.

R9 _____. [To Linda . . . ISBN 0-399-21816-5 | Second Impression (revised edition) | [rule] | All the flowers . . .]

COVER: A finer weave green cloth hinge and back cover. Price sticker on back lower right: U.S. $15.95   CAN $20.95 | [bar code] | 0 48228 21816 6 | ISBN 0-399-21816-5.

OTHER: Purchased new February 1993.

R10 *A Round Dozen* | STORIES BY | *Louisa May Alcott* | SELECTED AND WITH A FOREWORD BY | *Anne Thaxter Eaton* | ILLUSTRATED BY | *Tasha Tudor* | NEW YORK | *The Viking Press* [Copyright © 1963 by Anne Thaxter Eaton and Tasha Tudor | All rights reserved | First published in 1963 by The Viking Press, Inc. | Published simultaneously in Canada | by The Macmillan Company of Canada Limited || Library of Congress catalog card number: 63-18366 || PRINTED IN THE U.S.A.]

PAGINATION: 16 signatures of ivory paper: [1-5] 6 [7] 8-9 [10-13] 14-20 [21] 22-41 [42] 43-59 [60] 61 [62] 63-72 [73] 74-75 [76] 77-83 [84] 85-97 [98] 99-107 [108] 109-115 [116] 117-119 [120] 121-126 [127] 128-135 [136] 137 [138] 139-141 [142] 143-152 [153] 154-160 [161] 162-178\ [179] 180-184 [185] 186-195 [196] 197-204 [205] 206-236 [237] 238-256.   8 5/8″ x 6″

COVER: Mauve cloth stamped in blue: a nosegay on the upper right front, and on the spine: *Louisa* | *May* | *Alcott* || *A* | *Round* | *Dozen* || [flower] || *Viking*.

DUST JACKET: Pink front, blue spine and white back and flaps. Large front illustration is a stylized pocket watch with a circle of twelve vignettes in small flower borders; ribbon on stem at top. Inside the circle, black lettering on a white field: *A* | *Round Dozen* | STORIES BY | *LOUISA MAY ALCOTT* || SELECTED AND WITH A FOREWORD BY | *Anne Thaxter Eaton* | ILLUSTRATED BY | *Tasha Tudor*. Black spine lettering: *LOUISA* | *MAY* | *ALCOTT* || *A* | *Round* | *Dozen* || VIKING. Back, centered: a pencil drawing (from page [179]) of two girls climbing a dark staircase. Front flap: *A Round Dozen* [blue] | *Stories by Louisa May Alcott* | ILLUSTRATED BY | *Tasha Tudor* || For many, many years Louisa May Alcott's | short stories—collected in volumes with | delightful titles such as *Spinning Wheel* | *Stories, Aunt Jo's Scrap Bag* | and *Lulu's* | *Library*—were as much loved by readers | as the full-length books such as *Little* | *Women* and *Under the Lilacs* that are still | familiar favorites. ¶ But fashions change, and, one by one, | long ago, these collections went out of | print. ¶ Anne Thaxter Eaton, believing that | many good stories worth reading and re- | membering were lost along with the "peri- | od pieces" of only temporary interest, has | assembled an entrancing sampling of those | she herself likes best. Old-fashioned these | stories may be. But in the variety of their | plots and the liveliness of their style they | have the timeless appeal of all true story-telling. ¶Tasha Tudor's drawings, exquisite in | themselves, have a charming authenticity | of detail that will doubly endear to "mod- | ern" children the stories an earlier era | cherished. || 010015. Back flap: *Also chosen by* | *Anne Thaxter Eaton* | *Illustrated by Valenti Angelo* || WELCOME CHRISTMAS! | *A Garland of Poems* | "One of the loveliest holiday books. Not | all the poems were written expressly for | children, and therein lies the quality of the | book to grow on. It is plain that the poems | have been chosen 'because they suggest not | only a happy but a blessed Christmas.'" | —*New York Times* || THE ANIMALS' CHRISTMAS | "Everything about this book speaks the | simplicity and reverence, the peace and | beauty of the story of the Christ Child. | The stories are unusual ones, some known | and some printed for the first time....The | carols and poems are unusual, too....The book in both text and format is obviously | a 'labor of love.'...In the words and in | the drawings its message is joy and peace." | —*Saturday Review* || THE VIKING PRESS | *625 Madison Avenue* | *New York 22, N.Y.* ||PRINTED IN THE U.S.A.   Have not examined a copy with price intact.

ILLUSTRATIONS: Twenty-seven half-page pencil drawings: Title page [3], [13] [21] 36 [42] 58 [62] [73] [76] [84] [98] [108] [116] [120] [127] [136] [138] [142] [153] [161] [179] [185] [196] [205] 222 [237] 250.

CONTENTS: Page [1] is half-title.

COPYRIGHT REGISTRATION: A 663050 granted to Anne Thaxter Eaton, 118 East 31st St., N.Y., N.Y. and Tasha Tudor, Route 1, Contoocook, N.H. Phyllis Gelbman, agent for the claimants, swears on Nov. 15, 1963:

A ROUND DOZEN: STORIES BY LOUISA MAY ALCOTT with copyright claimed for the foreword, illustrations, and compilation by Eaton and Tudor, United States citizens, was published Nov. 7, 1963. The book was manufactured by Murray Printing Co., Forge Village, Ma. Fees charged to the Viking Press, Inc., 625 Madison Ave., N.Y. 22, N.Y. Application and affidavit received Nov. 18, 1963 and two deposit copies received Nov. 21, 1963.

COPYRIGHT RENEWAL REGISTRATION: RE 546 586 granted to Tasha Tudor, Route 4, Box 205, West Brattleboro, Vt. 05301, and Anne Eaton Brown, 814 Wellesley Ave., Los Angeles, Ca. 90049, next of kin of the deceased author, Ann Thaxter Eaton. Tsuyako Uehara, agent for the claimants, swears on Sept. 25, 1991:

A ROUND DOZEN: STORIES BY LOUISA MAY ALCOTT with copyright claimed for the foreword, illustrations, and compilation by Tudor and Brown, was published Nov. 7, 1963. Fees charged to Penguin Books USA, Inc., 375 Hudson St., N.Y., N.Y. 10014. Renewal application received Oct. 1, 1991, the effective date of this registration.

R11 _____. [Copyright © 1963…63-18366 || Second printing, November 1963 || PRINTED IN THE U.S.A.]

DUST JACKET: Have not examined a copy with price intact.

R12 _____. [Copyright © 1963…Limited || Third printing, July 1965 || SC 1. Short stories | Library of Congress catalog card number: 63-18366| PRINTED IN THE U.S.A.]

COVER: Pink cloth binding, rather than salmon.

DUST JACKET: More vivid colors than first edition. Front flap: $4.00 printed at top, the lower right corner clipped.

R13 _____. [Copyright © 1963…Limited || Fourth printing, July 1967 || SC 1 . . . PRINTED IN THE U.S.A.]

PAGINATION: Buff paper.

DUST JACKET: A more ivory hue than the white of 3rd printing.

R14 _____. [Copyright © 1963…Limited || Fourth printing, July 1967 || SC 1 . . . U.S.A.]

COVER: Library binding, pink cloth, imprinted on the front and spine with the illustrations from the dust jacket, sealed finish. Pink back and at lower right, VIKING | Library Binding logo – a ship sailing east. Cloth reinforced hinges.

DUST JACKET: Front flap, trade price clipped from the upper corner, retaining lower corner $3.77 net. Viking's gold foil seal (3/4″ x 2 3/4″) has been wrapped from the spine onto the front cover: **VIKING | Library | Binding** [printed sideways] at the left of the sailing ship logo; and to the right of the ship, **VIKING | Library Binding**.

S1 SAMANTHA'S SURPRISE | [ornaments on a branch of a Christmas tree] | by BETHANY TUDOR ‖ J.B. LIPPINCOTT COMPANY | Philadelphia and New York. [*To* | *Efner Tudor* | *the most* | *wonderful sister.* ‖ Copyright © 1964 by Bethany Tudor | Printed in the United States of America | Library of Congress Catalog Card No. 64-19060]

PAGINATION: [32] pp., 2 signatures buff paper plus red endpapers. 6 3/4″ x 8 11/16″.

COVER: Illustrated red paper over boards. The cover is dominated a 5 3/4″ x 7 1/2″ oval garland of greens and ornaments. On a white ground within this oval in black type: SAMANTHA'S | [ducks and owns dancing around a Christmas tree] | SURPRISE. Beneath the oval: by BETHANY TUDOR. Spine: Bethany Tudor   SAMANTHA'S SURPRISE   Lippincott.

DUST JACKET: The buff jacket reproduces the cover design, with added text on end flaps. Front flap: [Upper corner clipped from examination copy] SAMANTHA'S SURPRISE ‖ by ‖ Bethany Tudor ‖ It was early December when Samuel and | Samantha, two plush ducklings, began get- | ting ready for Christmas. ‖ The preparations were elaborate. There | was all the cleaning, the cooking, the dec- | orating and, last but not least, the PRES- | ENTS. ‖ Samuel was building a wonderful sur- | prise for Samantha. He worked so hard | planning and making the surprise, and | then a dreadful thing happened and Sa- | mantha almost had no surprise! ‖ Here is a Christmas tale with all the | right trimmings—the busy holidays filled | with suspense, the loveable [*sic*] ducklings and | their many happy friends and in the end, | of course, a party. ‖ 480 $2.75   Back flap: This is Bethany Tudor's second book. | Her first story about the little plush duck- | lings, *Gooseberry Lane*, was published in | 1963. ‖ Ever since she was a very small child, she | has drawn pictures and loved small animals | - whether plush or real. She lives on a New | Hampshire farm with her mother, Tasha | Tudor, and two brothers and a sister, not to | mention many varieties of animals who | have been her models as well as her friends. ‖ Miss Tudor has studied art with her | mother and in Boston. She brings to her | writing and illustration not only youthful | freshness but real talent. ‖ J. B. LIPPINCOTT COMPANY | *Good Books Since 1792* | Philadelphia and New York.

ILLUSTRATIONS: Fifteen full-color illustrations, fourteen of them occupy full pages on the on-numbered pages beginning with page [5]. Page [3] is a smaller illustration with the opening text at the foot of the page. Remaining text is printed on even-numbered pages [4] - [30]. Besides the cover and title page illustrations, one colored illustration of holly leaves and berries is reproduced on each of the

325

four endpapers. There are no black and white illustrations. Bethany Tudor presents in fresh illustrations scenes inspired, like her mother's, by the scenery of their every day life. There are the board floors of a colonial house, board walls of a work room, a country store, stone wall and the New Hampshire hills we came to know through Tasha Tudor's paintings.

OTHER: *American Book Publishing Record 1960-1964* volume IV, page 5067: TUDOR, Bethany *JUV | Samantha's surprise*. Philadelphia, Lippincott [c.1964, | 31p. col. illus. 17x22cm. 64-19060 2.75; lib. ed.,, 2.69 | About two ducklings and their Christmas preparations. Ages | 4-8. [The two commas after lib. ed. appear in the ABPR entry. Ed.]

COPYRIGHT REGISTRATION: A 712473 granted to Bethany Tudor, Route #1, Contoocook, New Hampshire. Charles C. Granade, Jr., swears August 13, 1964:

SAMANTHA'S SURPRISE by Bethany Tudor, a U.S. citizen, was published August 10, 1964. Manufactured by Gould Typographers Inc., 228 East 45th St., Ny 17, NY, Connecticut Printers Inc., 85 Trumbull St., Hartford, Conn. 06101, H. Wolff Book Manufacturing Co., Inc., 508 West 26th St., NY, NY 1000_. Application and affidavit and two copies received at Library of Congress, August 17, 1964.

COPYRIGHT RENEWAL REGISTRATION: RE 603 882 granted to Bethany Tudor (the author), Box 3, Jamaica, Vt. 05311. Marilyn Small swears on Nov. 23, 1992:

SAMANTHA'S SURPRISE by Bethany Tudor was originally published Aug. 10, 1964. Fees charged to account DAO 64726, HarperCollins Publishers, 10 East 53rd St., N.Y., N.Y. 10022. Renewal application received Nov. 30, 1992, the effective date of this registration.

S2 _____.

PAGINATION: Library cloth binding.

COVER: Red cloth with the same illustration as dust jacket and previous paper cover.

S3 _____.

PAGINATION: Rebound library copy, [40]pp. including free endpapers. 6 7/8 x 8 ¾"

COVER: Red sealed buckram imprinted with the original cover illustrations reduced to 5 3/8 x 6 7/8." The background of the medallion is white, the text blue. The original endpaper designs were removed and replaced by two blank sheets at each end of the book.

OTHER: A stamped date inside the back cover suggests this book was rebound in October 1982, although there is no indication of the binder's name.

S4 SAMUEL'S TREE HOUSE ‖ [sprig of wild flowers] ‖ Bethany Tudor ‖ COLLINS. [from page [2] preceding the title page: Tudor, Bethany. Samuel's tree house. | SUMMARY: A duckling made of plush builds a tree | house with the help of his friends. | [1. Toys—Fiction] I. Title. | PZ8.9.T78Sam [E] 78-12087 | ISBN 0-529-05435-3 ISBN 0-529-05522-8 lib. bdg. ‖ Published by William Collins Publishers, Inc., Cleveland and New York and simultaneously | by William Collins Sons & Company, Ltd., | London, Glasgow and Sydney. ‖ U.K. ISBN 0-00-183761-3 ‖ Copyright © 1979 by Bethany Tudor. | All rights reserved. | Printed in the United States of America.]

PAGINATION: [28] pp., including endpapers, in two signatures. 6 1/4″ x 6 1/8″

COVER: Royal blue paper over boards. Front, centered: a 4 3/16″ x 5 1/16″ white panel, a thin black rule surrounds a full color illustration of Samuel on a ladder and Samantha, Gweek and Mr. Owl. All printing black. At the top of the cover: SAMUEL'S TREE HOUSE; at the bottom, Bethany Tudor | COLLINS. Spine: Tudor   SAMUEL'S TREE HOUSE   Collins. Back centered, a 1 5/6″ x 2 3/8″ white panel, inset black rule and a painting of Samuel and Samantha. Centered at the bottom: ♥ MY LITTLE COLLINS BOOK ♥ [arched], above a line drawing of a bear reading to two rabbits.

DUST JACKET: Repeats the cover design and adds at the lower right back: U.S.A. ISBN 0-529-05435-3 | RB ISBN 0-529-05522-8 | U.K. ISBN 0-00-183761-3. Front flap with bottom corner clipped: U.S.A. ISBN 0-529-05435-3 $5.95 | U.K. ISBN 0-00-183761-3 £2.50. ‖ SAMUEL'S | TREE HOUSE ‖ Samuel was an independent sort of duck- | ling. When he decided to build a tree house | to live in, he was sure that he could do it | alone. He didn't what help from his sister | Samantha or his friend Gweek. And when | the birds and animals who lived in the tree | offered to lend a hand, he still said, "I can do | it myself, thank you." ‖ Carrying boards and tools up a tree is | hard work for a duckling, but at last the new | home was nearly finished…when suddenly | disaster struck. A heavy storm made a | wreck of Samuel's treehouse. What hap- | pened next is a heart warming surprise that | will have small readers cheering. ‖ Learning to do things alone is an essential | part of growing up. But knowing how to | accept help from family and friends is just as | important. Bethany Tudor's warm, appeal- | ing watercolor illustrations create a small, | special, and a totally believable world, and | her amusing, easy-to-read text simply and | lovingly reminds us all of this delicate but | rewarding balance. ‖ ISBN 0-529-05522-8. Back flap: BETHANY TUDOR has written and | illustrated four picture books for chil- | dren, and illustrated several books writ- | ten by other people. She grew up in a | family of artists and remembers spend- | ing many hours outdoors in summer | with a sketching pad on her knee. Her | mother is Tasha Tudor, one of America's | most beloved illustrators, and her sis- | ter, Efner Tudor Holmes, writes child- | dren's books. Bethany Tudor's own writ- | ing and drawing style has special appeal | for the very youngest of children, for it | reflects the warmth and feeling they | love. She lives in Vermont with her | small daughter. ‖ COLLINS | Cleveland ● New York ● London.

ILLUSTRATION: Dedication, page [4]: *For Laura | who loves the | ducklings as much as I do.* Below this is the illustration of Samuel and Samantha that is repeated on the back cover. Most pages have a 3/4 page illustration. Only the insides of the endpapers lack a color illustration. The endpapers repeat two wild flower designs.

OTHER: Dedicated to Bethany Tudor's daughter, Laura Dennis. The RB ISBN from the jacket back refers to a Reinforced Binding.

COPYRIGHT REGISTRATION: TX 329-478 granted to Bethany Tudor, RFD 4, West Brattleboro, Vt. 05301. Julia Smagorinsky, agent for Bethany Tudor, swears on Aug. 14, 1979:

SAMUEL'S TREE HOUSE text and illustrations completed in 1979 by Bethany Tudor, a U.S. citizen, was published March 15, 1979. The book was manufactured by Federated Lithographers, Providence, R.I., and Book Press, Brattleboro, Vt. L.C. is granted non-exclusive right to reproduce copies and phonorecords for the blind and physically handicapped. Fees charged to William Collins Publishers, Inc., 200 Madison Ave., Room 1405, N.Y., N.Y. 10016, DAO 34681. Application and affidavit and deposit received Sept. 14, 1979.

S5 _____ .

COVER: A reinforced library binding matches the trade binding in all but three aspects, the sewing, the cover and a jacket label. The book is top sewn before being glued to boards. The cover is yellow plastic-filled paper over boards, stamped in metallic blue ink on the spine. An image of Samuel with his ladder is blind stamped into the front cover. Stamped in the same blue ink at lower right back cover: (RB) 0-529-05522-8.

DUST JACKET: A gold foil label wraps from the back around the spine and onto the front of the dust jacket: 3/4″ x 2 7/8″. Printed in black ink from the left side of the label, sideways: CRB | CRB | CRB | CRB | CRB. Written larger on the right side, the front of the book: CRB [with a tree logo] | COLLINS REINFORCED BINDING. Have not examined a copy with corners of front flap intact.

S6 THE | SECRET GARDEN | *By* | *Frances Hodgson Burnett* | [a rose tree] | *Pictures by* | *Tasha Tudor* | J.B. LIPPINCOTT COMPANY | *Philadelphia New York* [Copyright 1911 by F.H. Burnett | Copyright Renewal 1938 by Verity Constance Burnett | Illustrations Copyright © 1962 by J.B. Lippincott Company | Library of Congress Catalog Card No. 62-17457 | Printed in the United States of America]

PAGINATION: Sixteen signatures, ivory paper: [1-6] 7-46 [47] 48-68 [69] 70-88 [89] 90-112 [113] 114-136 [137] 138-172 [173] 174-183 [184] 185-200 [201] 202-216 [217] 218-236 [237] 238-252 [253] 254-256. Half-title, [1]; [2] and [6] are blank; Title page, [3]; verso [4]; Contents, [5] 8 11/16″ x 6 5/8″ 7/8″ thick

COVER: Rose cloth cover. Rose tree stamped in gold on front cover. *Burnett* [rose] THE SECRET GARDEN [rose] *Lippincott* stamped in gold on the spine. Ivory end papers identical front and back: in green, rose tree on each paper with either fox and spade or crow and pitcher, all surrounded by rambling rose boughs.

DUST JACKET: Ivory paper printed green surrounding rose boughs, and in lighter panel on back, a rose tree. Inside a rose-bordered lighter panel on front: THE | SECRET GARDEN [an ivy ring around Mary with key at lock] BY *Frances Hodgson Burnett* | PICTURES BY *Tasha Tudor*. Spine same as book spine, but black ink. Front flap: THE | SECRET GARDEN | By | FRANCES HODGSON BURNETT | *Illustrated by* TASHA TUDOR || "It was the sweetest, most mysteri- | ous-looking place anyone could imag- | ine. The high walls which shut it in | were covered with the leafless stems | of roses which were so thick that they | matted together....*No wonder it's* | *still*, Mary whispered. *I am the first* | *person who has spoken in here for* | *ten years.*" || This is the secret garden, mysteri- | ous, walled and locked, that is the | center of Frances Hodgson Burnett's | beautiful and moving story of a lone- | ly, willful little girl and how she finds | friends, health and happiness when | she comes to live in a great house on | the Yorkshire moors. It is a story that | has been loved by boys and girls since | its first publication in 1912, never los- | ing its charm, its magic, its deep sat- | isfaction. || "It will rapt most children away, | for after fifty years its spell is just as | strong; a blend of power, beauty, | vivid interest and honest goodness. | Yes, if this is magic, it is good magic." | – RUMER GODDEN, *The New York* | *Times Book Review* | 01014 $5.00   Back flap: *The Author* | FRANCES HODGSON BURNETT was a | born storyteller, and even when she | was a young child, living in Man- | chester, England, her greatest pleas- | ure was in making up stories and | acting them out, using her dolls as | characters. When she was in her teens | her family, in search of better for- | tune, moved to Tennessee and there | young Frances had her first taste of | success, for two of her stories were | bought and published by an Amer- | ican magazine. From that point on her | career was assured and until her death | in 1921 she wrote constantly and pro- | duced more than forty books and | countless short stories. || *The Artist* | Tasha Tudor's delicate color work, | her charming pencil drawings in | many books have made friends all | over this country. Children and | grown-ups alike have been drawn | to her nostalgic representation of a | world of another age. In this book she | has brought to life children of the | early 1900's who live in a timeless | world of a secret garden. || Tasha Tudor lives in an old farm- | house in New Hampshire which is | big enough to hold her four children | and many visiting friends and cousins. | There are animals, too, who are part | of the family, a garden, a grove of | sugar maples and blue New Hamp- | shire mountains in the distance.

ILLUSTRATIONS: 27 black and white pencil drawings at the head of each chapter, draped with various ribbons carrying the chapter number in Roman numerals: 7, 13, 21, 26, 41, 49, 56, 62, 71, 80, 92, 100, 108, 121, 132, 144, 151, 158, 165, 177, 186, 196, 202, 213, 225, 232, 242. A similar bird with eggs in nest on page [5] under the ribbon "Contents." 11 full page color illustrations on pages [47, 69, 89, 113, 137, 173, 184, 201, 217, 237, 253]

COPYRIGHT REGISTRATION: A 582418 granted to J.B. Lippincott Co., 227 South Sixth St., Philadelphia 5, Pa. Charles C. Granade, Jr., agent for claimant, swears on Sept. 12, 1962:

THE SECRET GARDEN, illustrations by Tasha Tudor [reported as author], a U.S. citizen, was published Sept. 10, 1962. The book was manufactured by Connecticut Printers, Inc., 85 Trumbull St., Hartford 1, Ct., and Cornwall Press, Inc., Cornwall, N.Y. Fee charged to deposit account of J.B. Lippincott. Application and affidavit and two deposit copies received at LC, Sept. 17, 1962.

COPYRIGHT REGISTRATION: TX 1 879 368 corrects information on original registration A 582418. Mary D'Agnese, Copyright Department, Harper & Row, Publishers, Inc., 10 East 53rd St., N.Y., N.Y. 10022, agent for J.B. Lippincott Company, swears on June 24, 1986:

THE SECRET GARDEN, originally registered in 1962, was incorrectly attributed to Tasha Tudor. Author is now corrected to read, "J.B. Lippincott Company, employer for hire for the illustrations by Tasha Tudor." Fee charged to account DAO 56707, Harper & Row Publishers. Form CA received June 27, 1986, the effective date of supplementary registration.

S7 _____.

PAGINATION: Another state, thicker creamier paper. Book with dj is 1" thick.

DUST JACKET: Ivory dust jacket, price clipped.   Author's death from back flap: . . . her death in 1924 . . .

S7.5 _____.

COVER: Deep buff endpapers.

DUST JACKET: $5.00 price on front flap.

S8 _____.

    COVER: <u>Scarlet cloth. 7/8″ thick.</u> Ivory end papers.

S9 _____.

    COVER: <u>Carmine</u> cloth. Ivory paper.

    DUST JACKET: Upper right corner, front flap (ivory kid) dust jacket: <u>$ 6.25</u>. 29/32″ thick. <u>ISBN-0-397-30632-6 now appears on back of dj</u>, centered below rose border. Examined one inscribed: September 1977.

    CONTENTS: <u>ISBN-0-397-30632-6 now appears at top of page [4]</u>.

S10 _____.

    PAGINATION: 27/32″ thick.

    COVER: The cloth is smooth carmine fine weave. The <u>ink on endpapers is lime</u>.

    DUST JACKET: Kid finish buff paper. Have not examined a copy with price intact.

    CONTENTS: <u>This copy lacks a half-title between ffep and title page.</u>

S11 _____.

    PAGINATION: 27/32″ thick.

    COVER: The cloth is a <u>deeper red</u>. The ink on endpapers is <u>more khaki</u> than before.

    DUST JACKET: Have not seen one with price intact.

    OTHER: Examined a copy inscribed Christmas 1979.

S12 _____.

    PAGINATION: <u>1″</u> thick.

    COVER: <u>Carmine cloth</u>.

S13 _____.

    PAGINATIONS: 27/32″ thick.

    COVER: The endpapers are a deeper buff.

    DUST JACKET: Have not examined a copy.

S14 _____. [For the first time, the two cities are not printed on the title page. -Ed.]

    DUST JACKET: <u>Heavy buff kid has no printed price</u> front flap, upper right corner.

S15 _____.

    PAGINATION: <u>7/8″</u> thick.

    DUST JACKET: Buff kid paper imprinted <u>$10.00</u> in upper right corner of front flap.

S16 _____.

PAGINATION: <u>27/32″ thick</u>.

COVER: <u>Lighter red</u>.

DUST JACKET: Have not examined one.

CONTENTS: ISBN on p. [4], and <u>no cities on title page</u>.

S17 Frances Hodgson Burnett | The Secret Garden | <u>Illustrated</u> by | Tasha Tudor | *J.B.*
Lippincott   New York [THE SECRET GARDEN | <u>Text</u> copyright 1911 by F.H. Burnett | Copyright Renewal 1938 by
Verity Constance Burnett | Illustrations copyright © 1962 by J.B. Lippincott Company | <u>All right reserved.</u> <u>No part of this book</u>
<u>may be used or | reproduced in any manner whatsoever without written permission | except in the case of brief quotations</u>
<u>embodied in critical | articles and reviews.</u> Printed in the United States of America. | For information address J.B. Lippincott
Junior Books, 10 East 53rd | Street, New York, NY 10022. Published simultaneously in | Canada by Fitzhenry & Whiteside
Limited, Toronto. | Library of Congress Catalog Card No. 62-17457 | Trade ISBN 0-397-30632-6 | Library ISBN 0-06-32162-7]

PAGINATION: Twelve ? signatures, white paper: [i-viii, 1-2] 3-49 [50] 51-78 [79] 80-102 [103] 104-
134 [135] 136-166 [167] 168-210 [211] 212-221 [222] 223-241 [242] 243-265 [266] 267-286
[287] 288-306 [307] 308-311 [312].

COVER: <u>Lime green</u> cloth cover. Rose tree stamped in gold on front cover. *Burnett* [rose] THE
SECRET GARDEN [rose] *Lippincott* stamped in gold down spine. <u>White end papers,</u>
illustrations as before, but in a darker green ink. 9 1/4″ x 6 1/4″ <u>13/16″ thick</u>

DUST JACKET: A new design with a new rose bower border, still on a green ground similar to earlier
jacket. There is no rose tree on back cover. Inside panel <u>on front</u>: The | Secret Garden, above,
and By Frances Hodgson Burnett | Illustrated by Tasha Tudor, below this medallion, a detail
from illustration on page [79]: Mary is closing the gate as she leaves the garden carrying a jump
rope. Spine **same as** book spine. Front flap: <u>$8.95</u> | 1086185 | THE TASHA TUDOR |
EDITION | THE | SECRET GARDEN | By | Frances Hodgson Burnett | Illustrated by Tasha
Tudor[printer's ornament] | *It was the sweetest, most mysterious-looking | place <u>any one</u> could*
imagine. The high walls | which shut it in were covered with the leafless | stems of roses which
were so thick that they | matted together... "No wonder <u>it is</u> still," | Mary whispered. "I am the
first person who | has spoken in here for ten years." | This is the secret garden, mysterious, |
walled, and locked, the center of Frances | Hodgson Burnett's beautiful and moving | story of a
lonely, willful little girl and | how she finds friends, health and happi- | ness when she comes to
live in a great | house on | the Yorkshire moors. It is a | story that has been loved by boys and
girls | since its first publication in 1912, never | losing its charm, its magic, its deep | satisfaction.
J.B. Lippincott   New York   [The bottom corner has been clipped.] Back flap: THE AUTHOR
| FRANCES HODGSON BURNETT was a born | storyteller, and even when she was a young |
child, living in Manchester, England, her | greatest pleasure was in making up stories | and acting
them out, using her dolls as char- | acters. When she was in her teens, her family | moved to
Tennessee in search of better for- | tune, and there young Frances had her first | taste of success --
two of her stories were bought and published by an American maga- | zine. From that point on
her career was as- | sured, and until her death in 1924 she wrote constantly and produced more
than forty | books and | countless short stories. | THE ARTIST | TASHA TUDOR's delicate color
work <u>and</u> | charming pencil drawings <u>are loved by mil- | lions of readers who</u> have been drawn to
her | nostalgic representation of <u>another time.</u> In | this book she has brought to life children of |
the early 1900's who live in <u>the magical</u> | world of a secret garden. | Tasha Tudor lives in a
Vermont farmhouse | big enough to hold her <u>many visiting</u> chil- | dren, <u>grandchildren, and</u>
friends. <u>Readers of | all ages will recognize the work of one of |</u> America's most beloved artists
<u>in this time-</u> | less classic, THE SECRET GARDEN. | Jacket art ©1962 by J. B. Lippincott Company, |
©1985 by Tasha Tudor   Back of jacket: Also by Frances Hodgson Burnett | Illustrated by Tasha
Tudor | A LITTLE PRINCESS | *with a foreword by Phyllis McGinley* | Children and adults

alike have been drawn to the | story of Sara Crewe and her dramatic adventures | at Miss Minchin's boarding school in London. | They have delighted in her happiness and wept | over her sorrows and have been enchanted by the | mysterious events that bring about surprising | changes in Sara's fortune. | Tasha Tudor, whose pictures for THE SECRET | GARDEN have been treasured by millions, has | re-created for a whole new generation of readers | the unforgettable images of nineteenth-century | London and Sara, a little princess. [White paper label centered near bottom, covering a preprinted TRADE ISBN 0-397-30632-6]: TRADE ISBN 0-397-32165-1

CONTENTS: Half-title *The Secret Garden*, [i] and [1]; [ii], [viii] and [2] are blank; Title page, [iii]; verso [iv]; Contents, [v-vii]

ILLUSTRATIONS: Chapter illustrations (27) as before. Chapter numbers are now in Arabic numerals: 3, 10, 20, 26, 45, 54, 63, 71, 82, 94, 108, 118, 128, 144, 158, 173, 182, 191, 199, 213, 224, 236, 244, 258, 273 281, 293. A similar bird with eggs in nest on page [5] under the ribbon "Contents." Eleven full page color illustrations are brighter and clearer than in earlier editions: pages [50, 79, 103, 135, 167, 211, 222, 242, 266, 287, 307]

OTHER: Type for this edition has been completely reset. Title page reorganized.

COPYRIGHT REGISTRATION: TX 2 038 856 granted to Harper & Row, Publishers, Inc. Mary D'Agnese, agent for Harper & Row, Publishers, Inc., swears on March 5, 1987:

THE SECRET GARDEN, cover text by Harper & Row, Publishers, Inc. domiciled in the United States, was published February 20, 1987. The work was completed in 1986 and the book was manufactured by The Murray Printing Company, Westford, Ma. Fee charged to Account DAO 56707, Harper & Row, Publishers, Inc. There are correspondence, application and two deposit copies received at L.C. March 9, 1987. Funds received March 11, 1987, the effective date of this registration.

COPYRIGHT REGISTRATION: VA 224 547 granted to Tasha Tudor (this was not a work for hire). Megan McNulty, Copyright Department, Harper & Row, Publishers, Inc., 10 East 53rd St., N.Y., N.Y. 10022, agent for Tasha Tudor, swears on Oct. 30, 1985:

THE SECRET GARDEN, additions and revision to jacket art completed in 1985 by Tasha Tudor, a U.S., was published Oct. 16, 1985. The book had previously been registered although the year and registration number were unavailable. This derivative work is registered for additions and revisions to jacket art. Fee charged to account DAO 56707, Harper & Row, Publishers, Inc. Application received at L.C. Nov. 4, 1985 and April 14, 1986. Deposit copy received Nov. 4, 1985.

S18 _____.

COVER: Whiter kid paper, in a slightly brighter green cover.

DUST JACKET: The dust jacket carries no price at all. Two bar-codes in a 1 1/4″ x 2″ white box just above the rose border at the back bottom: 50895 [above the smaller right code] and 9 780694 002399 [below the larger left code. Running beneath both: ISBN 0-694-00239-9.

S19 _____. . . . Tudor | [torch logo] HarperCollins *Publishers* [THE SECRET GARDEN . . . For information address HarperCollins Children's Books, a division | of HarperCollins Publishers, 10 East 53rd Street, New York, N.Y. 10022. || Library of Congress Catalog Card No. 62-17457 | ISBN 0-397-32165-1.]

PAGINATION: White paper: [i-viii, 1-2] Remaining pagination as in S17 above. 9 1/4″ x 6 1/4″ x 3/4″ thick

COVER: Moss green cloth cover. Rose tree stamped in gold on front cover. Burnett [rose] THE SECRET GARDEN [rose] Lippincott stamped in gold down spine.

DUST JACKET: Jacket as in S17 except for these minor changes. Front flap has neither price nor code; text as above; last line: [flame logo] HarperCollins *Publishers* Back flap is identical to S17. The text on back of jacket is identical to S17, but ISBN coding is in a 2 3/16″ x 1 7/16″ white box. 90000 | Trade [printed down the left margin] [bar codes] 9 780397 321650 | ISBN 0-397-32165-1.

OTHER: The distinction of this printing is that eventhough the title page and dust jacket name the new publisher, the spine is still imprinted Lippincott.

S20 _____. [THE SECRET GARDEN | Text copyright 1911 by F.H. Burnett | Copyright Renewed 1938 . . . Card No. 62-17457 | ISBN 0-397-32165-1 | ISBN 0-397-32162-7(lib. bdg.)]

COVER: Smooth lime green half-paper over boards, maroon cloth wrapped around spine and overlaps the paper of covers. Rose tree stamped in gold on front cover. Spine: Burnett [rose] THE SECRET GARDEN [rose] HarperCollins, in gilt.

S21 _____.

PAGINATION: 7/8″ thick.

S22 _____.

COVER: Lime-green half-paper in a weave imprint. Printed *circa* 1996.

S23 _____. Have not examined a 1st paperback.

S24 _____. Have not examined a 2nd paperback.

S25 **The** | **Secret Garden** | Frances Hodgson Burnett | [rose tree] | *Decorations by Tasha Tudor* | A YEARLING BOOK [Published by | DELL PUBLISHING CO., INC. | 1 Dag Hammarskjold Plaza | New York, N.Y. 10017 | Copyright 1911 by F. H. Burnett | Copyright Renewal 1938 by Verity Constance Burnett | Illustrations Copyright © 1962 by J. B. Lippincott Company | All rights reserved | Reprinted by arrangement with J. B. Lippincott Company | Printed in the United States of America | Third Dell Printing - May 1973]

PAGINATION: [i-vi, 1] 2-7 [8] 9-17 [18] 19-23 [24] 25-42 [43] 44-50 [51] 52-58 [59] 60-65 [66] 67-75 [76] 77-87 [88] 89-100 [101] 102-110 [111] 112-120 [121] 122-135 [136] 137-149 [150] 151-163 [164] 165-172 [173] 174-181 [182] 183-189 [190] 191-202 [203] 204-212 [213] 214-224 [225] 226-231 [232] 233-245 [246] 247-259 [260] 261-268 [269] 270-280 [281] 282-298 pages on pulp paper. 7 9/16″ x 5 1/8″

COVER: Paperback in green wrapper with original illustration in a black line box 6 1/4″ x 4 3/4″ and the text: *The* | *Secret Garden* | *by Frances Hodgson Burnett* | *Decorations by Tasha Tudor.* Above the box: A DELL [colt and fence] YEARLING BOOK | $1.25 | *The enduring childhood classic.* Spine: DELL [black] | THE SECRET GARDEN [in green] FRANCES HODGSON BURNETT 440-07706-125 [in black] Back cover: [in green] THE SECRET GARDEN | [remaining text in black] Frances Hodgson Burnett | There are few books that have touched so deeply | the generations of readers as has Frances Hodgson | Burnett's immortal classic. Its special magic is best | explained by the book itself: "It was the sweetest, | most mysterious-looking place anyone could imag- | ine. The high walls which shut it in were covered | with the leafless stems of roses which were so thick | that they matted together....*No wonder it's still,* | Mary whispered, *I am the first person who has* | *spoken in here for ten years."* || Mary moves to a huge estate and meets the master | with a crooked back; his ailing son, Colin;

Martha, | the maid; and Dickon, the young gardener. Over a | million and a half copies of this classic have been | sold in hard-cover editions. This is the first paper- | back edition of THE SECRET GARDEN. || "A blend of power, beauty, vivid interest and honest goodness. | Yes, if this is magic, it is good magic." | —Rumer Godden, *The New York Times* || Frances Hodgson Burnett was reared in Manchester, England, | but moved to Tennessee in her teens. At that time two of her | stories were published by an American magazine. Thereafter | she wrote constantly, producing more than forty books and | countless short stories before her death in 1924. | A Yearling Book. Dell Publishing Co., Inc., New York | 010-014 | PRINTED IN USA [along lower right margin]

CONTENTS: Half-title, page [i]. Page [ii]: OTHER YEARLING BOOKS YOU WILL ENJOY: | *Charlotte's Web*, E.B. WHITE | *Stuart Little*, E.B. WHITE | *Island of the Blue Dolphins*, SCOTT O'DELL | *The Twenty-One Balloons*, WILLIAM PENE DU BOIS | *Roller Skates*, RUTH SAWYER | *Rabbit Hill*, ROBERT LAWSON | *Johnny Tremain*, ESTHER FORBES | *Strawberry Girl*, LOIS LENSKI | *The High King*, LLOYD ALEXANDER | *Harriet The Spy*, LOUISE FITZHUGH | *The Cricket in Times Square*, GEORGE SELDEN || YEARLING BOOKS are designed especially to entertain and | enlighten young people. The finest available books for chil- | dren have been selected under the direction of Dr. Charles F. Reasoner, Professor of Elementary Education, New York | University, and Dr. M. Jerry Weiss, Distinguished Professor | of Communications, Jersey City State College. || For a complete listing of all Yearling titles, | write to the Educational Sales Department, Dell Publishing Co., Inc., | 1 Dag Hammarskjold Plaza, New York, NY 10017. Pp. [v-vi], headed by the same illustration as before, but CONTENTS has been taken out of the ribbon and printed below it. Chapter heads: Roman numerals and illustrations.

S26 _____. Have not examined a 4th paperback.

S27 _____. Have not examined a 5th paperback.

S28 _____. Have not examined a 6th paperback.

S29 _____. Have not examined a 7th paperback.

S30 _____. Have not examined an 8th paperback.

S31 _____. [Published by . . . Ninth Dell Printing - September 1976]

COVER: Front: . . . A DELL [colt and fence] YEARLING BOOK | 1.50 | *The enduring childhood classic.* . . . Spine: DELL [black] | THE SECRET GARDEN [in green] FRANCES HODGSON BURNETT 440-07706-150 [in black] Back cover: as before.

CONTENTS: Half-title, page [i]. Page [ii]: OTHER YEARLING BOOKS YOU WILL ENJOY: | *A Little Princess*, FRANCES HODGSON BURNETT | *Island of the Blue Dolphins*, SCOTT O'DELL | *Strawberry Girl*, LOIS LENSKI | *Queenie Peavy*, ROBERT BURCH | *Confessions of an Only Child*, NORMA KLEIN | *Are You There, God? It's Me, Margaret*, JUDY BLUME | *A Room Made of Windows*, ELEANOR CAMERON | *Isabelle the Itch*, CONSTANCE C. GREENE | *Leo the Lioness*, CONSTANCE C. GREENE | *The Night Daddy*, MARIA GRIPE || YEARLING BOOKS are designed especially to entertain and enlighten | young people. The finest available books for children have been se- | lected under the direction of Charles F. Reasoner, Professor of | Elementary Education, New York University. || For a complete listing . . .

S32 _____. Have not examined a 10th paperback.

S33 _____. [Published by...| All rights reserved | ISBN: 0-440-47706-9 | Reprinted by arrangement with J. B. Lippincott Company | Printed in the United States of America | Eleventh Dell Printing - October 1977]

PAGINATION: As in the 9th printing

COVER: Spine: DELL [rule] 1.50 [black] | THE SECRET GARDEN [in green] FRANCES HODGSON BURNETT 0-440-47706-9 [in black] Back cover has this addition at bottom: ... Dell Publishing Co., Inc., New York | RL:5.4 | 010-014 | 0-440-47706-9 | PRINTED IN USA. 7 5/8″ x 5 1/8″

CONTENT: Pages [i-ii] and contents as above.

S34 _____. [Published by . . . United States of America | Twelfth Dell Printing—September 1978]

S35 _____. [Published by...| America | Thirteenth Dell Printing - March 1979 | MPC]

PAGINATION: 7 21/32″ x 5 1/8″

S36 _____. [Published by...| America | Fourteenth Dell Printing—October 1979 | MPC]

PAGINATION: As in the 9th printing. 7 21/32″ x 5 1/8″

COVER: 1.75   price at upper right front cover, and on spine.

S37 _____. Have not examined a 15th paperback.

S38 _____. Have not examined a 16th paperback.

S39 _____. [Published by...| America | Seventeenth Dell Printing—April 1981 | MPC]

PAGINATION: As in the 13th printing. 7 9/16″ x 5 1/8″ x 3/4″.

COVER: Upper right corner front cover, $1.75/$1.95 Canada; on spine: DELL | [rule] | 1.75 || THE SECRET. . . The ink of the back cover is somewhat blacker than the 13th printing.

S40 _____. Have not examined an 18th paperback.

S41 The | Secret Garden | Frances Hodgson Burnett || [printer's decoration, a line of ten 'flowers'.] || A YEARLING BOOK. [Published by...Constance Burnett | All rights reserved | Yearling ® TM 913705, Dell Publishing Co., Inc. || ISBN: 0-440-77706-2 || Book Club Edition || Reprinted by . . . America | Nineteenth Dell Printing June 1984]

PAGINATION: [i-vi] I, 2-261 [262-266] 6 3/4″ x 4 5/16″ x 1/2″

COVER: Paperback cover varies. Features are generally reduced in size since the book is smaller overall. Upper right front cover: U.S. $3.25 | CAN. $4.25. The black line panel on front measures 5 1/8″ x 4 1/4″ x 1/2″. There is no reference to Tudor on the cover or title page; and the chapter head illustrations are omitted from this printing. However, the cover design is as before, but reduced in size. Spine: DELL | [rule] | 3.25 | U.S. | [rule] | 4.25 | Can. ... THE ... 440-77706-2] The back cover carries most of the same text with changes in the heading and foot design ... THE SECRET GARDEN | by Frances Hodgson...in 1924. || [yearling in a circle logo, centered above text] | A Yearling Book • Dell Publishing Co., Inc. • New York | 010-014. Printed vertically along the spine at 1 1/8″ from the bottom: COVER PRINTED IN USA.

OTHER: The list of Other...has been revised on page [ii]. OTHER YEARLING BOOKS YOU WILL ENJOY: | A LITTLE PRINCESS, Frances Hodgson Burnett | BALLET SHOES, Noel Streatfield | DANCING SHOES, Noel Streatfield | THEATRE SHOES, Noel Streatfield | SKATING SHOES, Noel Streatfield MARY POPPINS IN CHERRY TREE LANE, P. L. Travers | HARRIET THE SPY, Louis Fitzhugh | THE LONG SECRET, Louise Fitzhugh | SPORT, Louise Fitzhugh FOURTH-GRADE CELEBRITY, Patricia Reilly Giff || YEARLING BOOKS are designed especially to entertain and | enlighten young people. Charles F. Reasoner, Professor | Emeritus of Children's Literature and Reading,

New | York University, is consultant to this series. || For a complete listing of all Yearling titles, write to | Promotion Department, Dell Publishing Co., Inc., P.O. Box 3000, | Pine Brook, NJ 07058.

S42 _____. [...Twentieth Dell printing—December 1982...]

PAGINATION: As in the 9th printing. 7 9/16" x 5 3/16"

COVER: Wrapper variations. Front: price changed to $2.95 U.S. / $3.75 Canada. Spine: DELL [rule] 2.95 etc. Back cover lacks the "Mary moves...SECRET GARDEN" paragraph. Information at bottom has been rearranged with a UPC bar code in a white box at lower left: 0 47706 | 71009 00295 | ISBN 0-440-47706-9. Lower right: the colt logo, A Yearling Book | Dell Publishing Co., Inc. | New York | RL:5.4 | 010-014 | 0-440-47706-9 | COVER PRINTED IN USA.

CONTENTS: Variations on page [ii]. The list of Other Yearlings reverts to the titles and centered typography of the 17th printing. OTHER YEARLING...YEARLING BOOKS are designed especially to entertain and | enlighten young people. Charles F. Reasoner, Professor | Emeritus of Children's Literature and Readings, New | York University, is consultant to this series. | For a complete listing of all Yearling titles, write to Ed- | ucation Sales Department, Dell Publishing Co., Inc., | 1 Dag Hammarskjold Plaza, New York, NY 10017.

S43 _____. Have not examined a 21st paperback.

S44 _____. Have not examined a 22nd paperback.

S45 _____. Have not examined a 23rd paperback.

S46 _____. Have not examined a 24th paperback.

S47 _____. Have not examined a 25th paperback.

S48 _____. Have not examined a 26th paperback.

S49 _____. [...America | September 1971 | 30 29 28 27 | MPC]

PAGINATION: Pagination and illustrations as in the 9th printing. 7 5/8" x 5 3/16"

COVER: Wrapper variations. Front: price changed to DELL•47706•U.S. $3.50 | CAN. $4.75 Spine: DELL | [rule] | FIC | [rule] | 3.50 | U.S. | 4.75 | Can. etc. Back cover as in the 20th printing.

CONTENT: Variations on page [ii]. The text is the same as the 19th printing with the OTHER YEARLING BOOKS...centered and slight changes in the line breaks of the last two paragraphs. || YEARLING BOOKS are designed especially to entertain and enlighten | young people. Charles F. Reasoner, Professor Emeritus of Child- | dren's Literature and Readings, New York University, is consultant | to this series. || For a complete listing of all Yearling titles, write to Dell Pub- | lishing Co., Inc., Promotion Department, P.O. Box 3000, Pine | Brook, NJ 07058 Otherwise like 9th printing.

S50 Frances Hodgson Burnett || THE SECRET GARDEN || Illustrated by Tasha Tudor || [rose tree] || A Harper Trophy Book | *Harper & Row, Publishers.* [THE SECRET GARDEN | Text copyright 1911 by F. H. Burnett | Copyright Renewal 1938 by Verity Constance Burnett | Illustrations copyright © 1962 by Harper & Row, Publishers, Inc. | All rights reserves. No part of this book may be used or | reproduced in any manner whatsoever without written permission | except in the case of brief quotations embodied in critical | articles and reviews. Printed in the United States of America. | For information address Harper & Row Junior Books, 10 East 53rd | Street, New York, NY 10022. | Library of Congress Catalog Card Number: 62-17457 | First Harper Trophy edition, 1987 | Published in hardcover by J. B. Lippincott, New York | ISBN 0-397-30632-6 | ISBN 0-06-32162-7 (lib. bldg.) | ISBN 0-06-440188-X (pbk.)

PAGINATION: [I-viii, 1-2] 3-311 [312] in a paper wrapper. 7 19/32″ x 5 1/16″ x 3/4″

CONTENTS: Pages [ii, viii and 2] are blank. Pages [I] and [1] are half-titles.

COVER: The cover is a reduced version of the dj from S17. Top centered above the rose border, HARPER TROPHY; and at the upper right, $3.50 US $4.95 CDN. Green spine with black lettering: Burnett   THE SECRET GARDEN   Harper & Row. Back cover is a large white field within a thin black line, within a pink border, within another thin black line, within a border of the same green as spine. On the white field this text: *Beloved by generations of young readers* | [3 1/2″ rule] | Ages 9 and up | *It was the sweetest, most mysterious-looking place any one could* | *imagine. The high walls which shut it in were covered with the* | *leafless stems of roses which were so thick, that they matted* | *together...."No wonder it is still," Mary whispered. "I am the* | *first person who has spoken in here for ten years."* || When orphaned Mary Lennox, sickly and lonely and | cross, comes to live at her uncle's great house on the | Yorkshire moors, she finds it full of secrets. Down a | corridor of empty rooms she hears someone crying in | the night. Outside, she meets Dickon, a magical boy | who can charm the wild animals and birds of the | countryside. And a robin Mary has befriended shows | her the way to a walled, locked garden that has been | completely forgotten for years and years. Is everything | within the garden dead, or can Mary make it grow | again? || **Frances Hodgson Burnett** is the author of the classic | A LITTLE PRINCESS, also illustrated by Tasha Tudor | and available in a Harper Trophy edition. | [2 bar codes] Above the smaller right one is 40188, and left or below the larger left one, 0 46594 00350 8 || ISBN 0-06-440188-X. Text printed at lower left corner on the green border: Cover art © 1962 by Harper & Row Publishers, Inc.; 1985 by Tasha Tudor | Cover © 1987 by Harper & Row Publishers, Inc. A two bar code array is printed inside the front cover at the lower left corner. Above the smaller right code: 50350. To the left or below the larger left code; 9 780064 401883. And in larger type beneath both: ISBN 0-06-440188-X.

OTHER: The colophon is centered on page [iv]. The body of this paperback reproduces the redesigned Lippincott/Harper & Row printing but in a smaller size on pulp paper. This is the first paperback to include the full-page illustrations, even though they are in black and white. Title page decorations are as in earlier paperbacks, but the type has been reset and includes the title in shaded letters as on the cover.

Purchased remaindered June 1996.

S51 _____. ... [rose tree] || [fire and water emblem] HarperTrophy | *A Division of* HarperCollins *Publishers*. [THE SECRET GARDEN ... Burnett | Illustrations copyright © 1962 by J. B. Lippincott Company | Illustrations copyright renewed 1990 by HarperCollins Publishers | All rights ... America. | For information address HarperCollins Children's Books, a division of | HarperCollins Publishers, 10 East 53rd Street, New York, NY 10022. | Library of Congress Catalog Card Number: 62-17457 | ISBN 0-397-32165-1 | ISBN 0-397-32162-7 (lib. bdg.) | ISBN 0-06-440188-X (pbk.) | Published in hardcover by HarperCollins Publishers. | First Harper Trophy edition, 1987.]

PAGINATION: 11/16″ thick.

COVER: There are three changes on the cover. 1) Price at upper right front: $3.50 US $4.75 CDN. Spine text: Burnett   THE SECRET GARDEN   HarperTrophy. The bar code on the back has been changed so that the number above the right one is 50350, and the number at left and below the left one is 9 780064 401883. However, this copy has what is probably the store's or distributor's label applied on top of the bar code and carrying this text: SECRET GARDEN-Tudor | 350 Burnett F | 288525 QP 92794 HARJ 1311 | 702 [bar code] | B3 4 2833 15>A85 85.

OTHER: Purchased new November 1996.

S52 _____.

COVER: Like S50, but front prices have been covered with a new label: [fire and water logo] USA $4.50 | [rule] | CANADA $5.95. Redesigned label at back bottom center: ISBN 0-06-440188-X [above larger left code] 50450> [above smaller right code] | [two bar codes] | 9 780064 401883 [beneath left code] | [fire and water logo] HarperCollins*Publishers.* An identical label has been applied over coding inside the front cover, bottom left.

OTHER: Purchased new July 1997.

S53 _____.

PAGINATION: ¾" thick.

COVER: Front no longer carries prices or the HarperTrophy citation. Back: the former second line "Ages 9 and up" has been eliminated from this printing. Following the text at lower right in bold print: **HarperTrophy | $3.50 US / $4.75 CDN**. A label has been placed over this pricing: **USA $4.50 | [rule] | CANADA $5.95**. Offset to the left of the HarperTrophy pricing the cover in imprinted with the same bar code and ISBN array as S50. A label has been placed over the entire barcode supplying this one instead: ISBN 0-06-440188-X, over the larger left code and, 50450> over the smaller right. At left and below the left code: 9 780064 401883. Another slightly smaller label (1 7/32" x 2 ¼") has been applied over this label masking all text and supplying this: BORDERS PRICE $4.50 | SECRET GARDEN-TUDOR | 851 [bar code] 085 | BURNETT F 1311 Ch Classics | 0288525 QP 0 101095 HARJ | 006440188X. A white label identical to that beginning "ISBN" from the back cover has been pasted inside the front cover obscuring the printed bar code reading 50350... Also the price label with $4.50 / $5.95 data.

OTHER: Purchased new November 1996.

S54 _____. . . . Manufactured in the United Kingdom . . .

COVER: Like S52, with new pricing and bar code on back: *Beloved by generations* | [rule] | Ages 9 and up | . . . in a Harper Trophy edition. || **US $5.95 / $7.95 CAN** | ISBN 0-694-01110-X | [above the smaller right barcode] 50595 | [two bar codes and a triangle sitting on its base ϰ] | [beneath the larger left bar code] 9 780694 011100.   Spine text: Burnett THE SECRET GARDEN HarperFestival.

OTHER: Purchased new November 1997. Books were shipped with a stiffening cardboard inside the back cover, 7 5/8" x 4 11/16". The cellophane shrinkwrap has one round label applied: a key in a white surround imposed on a larger green circle on which is written Includes you very own key! A gold colored metal key on 16" chain is taped to the front cover.

S55 _____. Audiocassette.

FORMAT: An audiocassette in a white pasteboard box that opens top and bottom. 7 1/16 x 4 5/16 x ¾"

COVER: Imprinted with the 'new' design of Mary coming out the garden, jump rope in hand. In a half-inch white band across the top: [red and blue flame and water logo] BOOK ON CASSETTE | [black line] | *The* | Secret Garden | [Mary in oval] | Frances Hodgson Burnett | *Performed by Claire Bloom.* The white 'band' and black line continue around the top of the box on all four panels. White spines are identical: [red and blue flame and water logo] | [rule] | Burnett/ | Bloom || The Secret Garden [laterally] | *Harper* | *Children's* | *Audio* || 1 cassette | CPN 1463. Back: BOOK ON CASSETTE [red and blue flame and water logo] | [rule] | A house full of mystery awaits orphaned | Mary Lennox when she comes to live | with her uncle on the Yorkshire moors. | At night she hears a distant crying that no | one will explain, and her uncle is strangely | unhappy. But when she meets Dickon, a | magical boy who charms both birds and animals, and | discovers a walled, locked garden, the secrets of | Missethwaite Manor begin to unfold. [Printed at the right of this block of text in a simulated gold seal: An ALA | Notable | Children's | Recording] ‖ **Frances Hodgson Burnett** is the author of over forty books, | including the classic *A Little Princess*. ‖ [black and white photograph of Bloom at the right of which are printed these four lines of text] **Claire Bloom** appeared in charles Chaplin's | movie masterpiece, *Limelight*. She has read | many classic stories on tape, including *Heidi* | and *Cinderella and other Fairy Tales*. ‖ [red and blue flame and water logo] HarperChildren's*Audio* | *A Division of* HarperCollins*Publishers* ‖ [two barcodes, 51195, over the smaller right bar code; 9781559 946506 and beneath the whole array, ISBN 1-55994-650-4] Printed at the right of the bar codes: $11.95 US/$15.95 CDN | Contents: 1 audiocassette in standard plastic case | total playing time: 1 hour (abridged) | P 1976 and © 1976, 1992 HarperCollins Publishers | All rights reserved. ‖ *The Secret Garden* is avilable in | hardcover and paperback editions | from HarperCollins Publishers.

Sold in shrinkwrap.

OTHER: Purchased new Feburary 1998.

S56 *The* | 𝒮ECRET | 𝒢ARDEN [rose tree] FRANCES HODGSON BURNETT ‖ *Illustrated by* | TASHA TUDOR ‖ [flame and water logo] HarperTrophy® | *A Division of* HarperCollins*Publishers*. [black and white illustration as before, but enlarged so as to reach nearly to the edges of the the page.] [HarperTrophy® is a registered trademark of | HarperCollins Publishers Inc. ‖ THE SECRET GARDEN . . . articles and reviews. Printed in the United States of America. | Typography by Alicia Mikles | For information address HarperCollins Children's Books, a division | of HarperCollins Publishers, 10 East 53ʳᵈ Street, New York, NY 10022. | http://www.harperchildrens.com | Library of Congress Catalog Card Number: 62-17457 | ISBN 0-397-32165-1 | ISBN 0-06-440188-X (pbk.) | Published in hardcover by Harper Collins Publishers | First Harper Trophy edition, 1987.]

PAGINATION: [i-vi] 1-59 [60] 61-90 [91] 92-114 [115] 116-149 [150] 151-189 [190] 191-253 [254] 255-276 [277] 278-302 [303] 304-326 [327] 328-354 [355] 356-358 [359-362] 7½ x 5 1/8″

COVER: All-over mint green paper wrapper, redesigned. The central motif of Mary exiting the garden gate is now encircled within an oval of rose briers and pink roses, similar to that which bordered the cover, but not from Tudor's hand. A key is contained at the bottom of the brier. The title is set in new type, placed above the oval motif, in green high-lighted letters, embossed; a pink rose at either side of the title. At bottom, *By* FRANCES HODGSON BURNETT | [rose bud] *Illustrated by* TASHA TUDOR [rose bud]. Spine: BURNETT [black] [rose bud] THE SECRET GARDEN [green] [rose bud] HarperTrophy [black]. Back: *Unlock the Magic of the Secret Garden* | [color vignette of Colin and Mary in garden, at the top of the rose oval from the front and enclosing this reworded text: *When* orphaned Mary Lennox, | lonely and sad, comes to live at her uncle's | great house on the Yorkshire moors, she finds | it full of secrets. At night, she hears the sound of | crying down one of the long corridors. Outside, | she meets Dickon, a magical boy who can charm | and talk to animals. Then, one day, with the help | of a friendly robin, Mary discovers the most | mysterious wonder of all—a secret garden, | walled and locked, which has been completely | forgotten for years and years. Is every- | thing in the garden dead, or can | Mary bring it back to life? ‖ [beneath the rose oval] HarperTrophy® | Ages 9 up | Cover art © 1962 by HarperCollins Publishers | Cover © 1998 by HarperCollins Publishers |Cover design by Alicia Mikles. A pink rectangle at the lower left corner is imprinted with the bar code data as in S54, above, except that the Canadian price has increased to $8.75. Inside the back cover: [wren on nest from chapter 25 head] | FRANCES HODGSON BURNETT was a born | storyteller. Even as a young child, her greatest | pleasure was in making up stories and activing them | out, using her dolls as characters. She wrote over | forty books, including the classic A LITTLE PRINCESS, | also illustrated by Tasha Tudor. ‖ TASHA TUDOR'S detailed, delicate artwork is well | loved by millions of readers. She lives in a Vermont | farmhouse big enough to hold her many visiting | children, grandchildren, and friends.

CONTENTS: Blank pages [359, 361-362]. The text and Tudor's chapter heads are as before. Chapter titles have been reset in the shaded script matching the title. Also, the title in the same script and a rose bud head each verso, from page 2 through 358. The rose bud and chapter title in Roman capitals head each recto, page 3 - 357.   Page [360]: *Other* | ᔕECRET ᏀARDEN | *titles you may enjoy:* || *The Secret Garden* | The Tasha Tudor edition | *By Frances Hodgson Burnett* | *Illustrated by* Tasha Tudor || *The Secret Garden* | A picture book adaptation of | *The Secret Garden by* Frances Hodgson Burnett | *Illustrated by* Mary Collier || *The Secret Garden Book and Charm* | *By* Frances Hodgson Burnett | *Illustrated by* Tasha Tudor || *The Secret Garden Paper Dolls* | Adapted from | *The Secret Garden by* Frances Hodgson Burnett | *Illustrated by* Judith Sutton || *Ask for these titles* | *at your favorite bookstore!*

ILLUSTRATIONS: Full-page black and white illustrations. Page [60] It was a curious sound . . .
   [91]   . . . she was inside the wonderful garden . . .
   [115]   A boy was sitting under a tree . . .
   [150]   "Who are you?" . . .
   [190]   They had come upon a whole clump . . .
   [254]   And the sun fell warm . . .
   [277]   Colin's flush grew deeper . . .
   [303]   "Your father will be very happy . . ."
   [327]   "I shall live for ever and ever and ever!"
   [355]   "It was the garden that did it . . ."

OTHER: Text is completely reset in this edition. Packed in shrinkwrap with the round applied label as S54 above, without cardboard insert. A gold colored metal key on 16″ chain is taped to the front cover. Purchased new April 1998. The official release date was April 30, 1998.

S57 _____.

COVER: Back, lower left. A pink rectangle imprinted with the bar code data. **US $4.95 / $6.95 CAN** | ISBN 0-06-440188-X || [2 bar codes, and above the small right code] 40188 | [beneath the larger left code] 0 46594 00495 6. [to the right of the bar codes, an isosceles triangle sitting on its base and containing an S.   A similar array is printed sideways at lower left inside the front cover. Now, however, the code above the right bar code is 50495, and that beneath the left is 9 780064 401883. White ground, not pink.

OTHER: Purchased new June 10, 1998, this copy does not have the locket. Corgi Cottage Industries, Spring 1988 catalog pictures this and offers for sale with a bookplate for $16.95. Also listed is a 10 x 15 ½″ print of the image of Mary leaving the garden gate. The advertising indicates this picture "has graced the image of almost 2 million volumes of The Secret Garden." We don't believe it was used earlier than 1995. All earlier Tudor editions carried the image of Mary trying the key in the gate lock. "For the first time, this delicate image is available as a fine art print. . . (#178 PRT)"   Prices are Unsigned $30, signed & numbered in an edition of 500 $65, and 25 artist's proofs (Each Artist's Proof is embellished with a small original sketch) at $175.   This catalog also pictures and offers for the first time a 13″ doll modeled from Tudor's illustrations of Mary Lennox. "Crafted of collector quality fine vinyl. (#001 DOL) $99.95 . . . Produced by Kids at Heart of Richmond . . ."

S58 **SIMPLE** | **ABUNDANCE** | [3/4″ square woodcut of a tree casting a shadow] | *A Daybook of* | *Comfort and Joy* | [3/4″ rule] Sarah Ban Breathnach || [W logo] | **WARNER BOOKS** | A Time Warner Company. [I would like to gratefully acknowledge all of the writers I have quoted in my meditations | for their wisdom, comfort and inspiration. An exhaustive search was done to determine whether | previously published material included in this book required permission to reprint. If there has | been an error, I apologize and a correction will be made in subsequent editions. || The following authors, their agents, and publishers have graciously granted permission to | include excerpts from the following: *Loving and Leaving the Good Life* ... *Copyright information continued on page 512.* || Copyright © 1995 by Sarah Ban Breathnach | All rights reserved. | SIMPLE ABNUDANCE ™ is a trademark of Sarah Ban Breathnach | Warner Books, Inc., 1271 Avenue of the Americas, new York, NY 10020 | [W logo] **A Time Warner Company** | Printed in the United States of America | First printing: November 1995 | 20 19 || **Library of Congress-in-Publication Data** [sic] | Ban Breathnach, Sarah. | Simple abundance: a daybook of comfort and joy / Sarah Ban | Breathnach. | p. cm. | ISBN 0-446-51913-8 (hardcover) | 1. Women—Religious life—Meditations. 2. Women—Conduct of life— | Meditations. 3. Simplicity. 4. Self-actualization (Psychology) | 5. Devotional calendars. I. Title. | BL625.7.B35 1995 | 158'.12—dc20   95-32330 | CIP || *Book design by Giorgetta Bell McRee.*

PAGINATION: Unpaged except for two page references. The colophon copyright acknowledgments [iv] indicate a continuation on page 512. This data is continued on the third unnumbered page from the end, and is headed: *Continued from p. iv.* 9 5/8" x 5 3/4"

COVER: Paper over boards is printed in an all-over mauve leaf design interrupted by a lined box on each cover and the spine. These gray-green boxes are outlined in a thin rule, all printing in charcoal. Front cover: SIMPLE | ABUNDANCE | [2" X 2" woodcut of the same tree motif from the title page] | [printer's rule with swirl] | A DAYBOOK | of | COMFORT | and JOY | [printer's rule with swirl] | Sarah Ban Breathnach. Spine: SIMPLE ABUNDANCE: A DAYBOOK of COMFORT and JOY | [printer's swirl] | Sarah Ban | Breathnach. And below the box: [W logo] | WARNER | BOOKS. Back cover: With the grace of Anne Morrow Lindbergh's | *Gift from the Sea* and the wisdom of M. | Scott Peck's *The Road Less Traveled,* SIMPLE | ABUNDANCE is a book of 366 evocative | essays—one for every day of your year—written | for women who wish to live by their own lights. ¶In the past a woman's spirituality has been sepa-| rated from her lifestyle. SIMPLE ABUNDANCE | shows you how your daily life can be an expression | of your authentic self . . . as you choose the tasti-lest vegetables from your garden, search for trea- | sures at flea markets, establish a sacred space in | your home for meditation, and follow the rhythm | of the seasons and the year. Here, for the first | time, the mystical alchemy of style and Spirit is | celebrated. Every day, your own true path leads | you to a happier, more fulfilling and contented | way of life—the state of grace known as . . . | SIMPLE | ABUNDANCE | *Embrace its gentle lessons, savor its sublime | common sense, dare to live its passionate truth, | and share its extraordinary and exhilarating gift | with every woman you encounter: the authentic | self is the Soul made visible.*

In the lower right back cover: [W logo] WARNER BOOKS | A Time Warner Company | Cover design by Diane Luger | COVER PRINTED IN U.S.A. | © 1995 WARNER BOOKS. A white gummed label (1 1/8" x 2 1/4") has been applied below the printed box: $18.95 US / $22.95 CAN. | ISBN 0-446-51913-8 [three rules, one above the next] | 51895> | [two bar-codes] | [beneath the larger left bar-code] 9 780446 519137. At the right side of the label, EAN is printed sideways atop the point of an equilateral triangle.

Red endpapers and a pink marker ribbon.

CONTENTS: A meditation for June 20 speaks of Frances Hodgson Burnett, her gardening within brick walls, and writing *The Secret Garden.* The June 23 meditation **Midsummer Night's Dreams** discusses Tasha Tudor and the Stillwaters, the "mock New England sect. . . the first commandment of the Stillwater religion, is to "Take joy" from each day." Breathnach makes two more references to Tudor. At the end of the June section in her **Joyful Simplicities for June,** she includes "Hold "The Great Party" on Midsummer's Night Eve (June 23) like | Tasha Tudor's Stillwater sect. If you are a fan of Tasha Tudor (and who | [next page] isn't?), have you seen a copy of the Tasha Tudor gift catalog from the Jenny | Wren Press? It features stationery products, artwork, reproductions of | Tasha's collection of eighteenth-century furniture, Corgi Cottage | Preserves, and much more. A one-year subscription can be ordered by call- | ing 1-800-552-WREN, or by writing the Jenny Wren Press, P.O. Box 505, | Mooresville, Indiana 46158. And in the **BIBLIOGRAPHY,** fourth page from the end is listed: Tudor, Tasha, and Richard Brown. *The Private World of Tasha Tudor.* Boston: Little, Brown, 1992.

OTHER: Dedication, page [v]: *Her eye, her ear, were tuning forks, burning glasses, | which caught the minutest refraction or echo of a | thought or feeling . . . . She heard a deeper vibration, | a kind of composite echo, of all that the writer | said, and did not say. || — WILLA CATHER || For | Chris Tomasino | with love and gratitude | and | Katie | who is the Deeper vibration | Always || One moved heaven for this book, | the other moved earth.*

There was no copyright on file at the Library of Congress, January 1998.

S59 **SKIDDYCOCK POND** ‖ by Bethany Tudor ‖ [a bunch of wildflowers] ‖ J. B. LIPPINCOTT COMPANY | Philadelphia and New York. [For Turkle ‖ Copyright © 1965 by Bethany Tudor | Printed in the United States of America | Library of Congress Catalog Card Number 65-21674]

PAGINATION: Two signatures of ivory paper: [1-32], plus free endpapers.

COVER: Blue paper over boards, overlapping a yellow cloth spine front and back. Front: SKIDDYCOCK POND, arched above an oval white vignette of Samuel, Samantha, Mr. Owl and Gweek in their sailboat. The oval is framed in yellow flowers in the manner of H. Willebeek Le Mair. Below the oval: by BETHANY TUDOR.   Spine imprinted in black: **Bethany Tudor   SKIDDYCOCK POND   Lippincott**.   Endpapers are a heavy blue wash or chalk over artist's paper, a water lily on the left paper, and a turtle on a rock with grass and water lily on the right. Pattern is repeated at rear.

DUST JACKET: Have not examined one. By comparison with Bethany Tudor's other Lippincott books, the jacket would probably be blue with a front identical to the book front.

ILLUSTRATIONS: Color illustrations begin on page [3], and except for page [3], each recto through page [31] is a full page illustration of the toy characters without text. The opening text is on page [3] and continues on versos {4} - [30]. Page [32] is blank.

OTHER: The dedicatee Turkle is Bethany Tudor's pet name for her sister Efner; the complement to Efner's Zelda. Tudor has occasionally sold signed color photocopies of the original art. *American Book Publishing Record Annual Cumulative 1965*, page 1283: TUDOR, Bethany JUV | Skiddycock Pond. Philadelphia, Lippincott [c.1965] | 1v. (unpaged) col. illus. 18x22cm. [PZ10.3.T8912Sk] | 65-21674 bds., 2.75; lib. ed., 2.69 | Two ducklings and their friends decide to go sailing. Ages | 4-8.

COPYRIGHT REGISTRATION: A 793453 granted to Bethany Tudor, Route #1, Contoocook, New Hampshire. Charles C. Granade, Jr., J. B. Lippincott Co., 227 South Sixth St., Philadelpha, Pa. swears on September 27, 1965:

SKIDDYCOCK POND by Bethany Tudor, a U.S. citizen, was published September 13, 1965. The book was produced by Connecticut Printers, Inc., 85 Trumbull St., Hartford, Conn., H. Wolff Book Manufacturing Co., 508 West 26th St., NY, NY, and Franklin Typographers, 255 W. 39th St., NY, NY.   Application and affidavit and two copies received at the Library of Congress Oct. 21, 1965.

S60 _____.

COVER: <u>Library binding in light blue sealed cloth</u> over boards; oversewn, twelve stitches. Back, lower center: **[LLB** logo]   This symbol identifies a | LIPPINCOTT | LONGLIFE BINDING | This binding is guaranteed to last as | long as the sheets, which are side-sewn | in picture books, and reinforced with | strong joint drill. Smythe-sewn books | are reinforced with muslin. The | cover is stain-resistant, washable | cloth, over top-grade binders board.

S61 SNOW | BEFORE | CHRISTMAS | BY | TASHA TUDOR || *OXFORD UNIVERSITY PRESS   London   New York   Toronto* [*Copyright 1941* | *Oxford University Press* | *New York, Inc.* || *Calligraphy by Hilda Scott* | *Printed in the United States of America*]

COVER: <u>Bright green cloth.</u> Colored title 2 1/8″ x 3 ¼″ label (in upper third of front cover) is framed in double black lines filled with red, as are all the letters. There is a hemlock sprig in each corner, and red 'swamp' berries in the lower corners.

DUST JACKET: Buff dust jacket. Front: SNOW | BEFORE | [three children and large ball of snow] | CHRISTMAS [red letters outlined in black]. Spine: TUDOR SNOW BEFORE CHRISTMAS OXFORD. Back: small sprig of winter berry with roots. Black text on front and rear flaps, front: SNOW BEFORE | CHRISTMAS || *By Tasha Tudor* || *Bethany and Muffin and Seth lived in an old* | *house with crooked window panes. In winter* | *they fed the birds and played Indians in the* | *woods.* | *They slid down hill and made snow* | *horses. And then of course there was school* | *which was taught by Uncle Adam. Most excit-* | *ing of all was Christmas when aunts and uncles* | *and cousins came from far and near to cele-* | *brate and exclaim over the beautiful Christ-* | *mas tree.* ¶*Tasha Tudor has made twenty of her love-* | *liest water-color illustrations for this story of* | *long ago. The clear cold of a New England* | *winter is here, and the warmth of an old house* | *where a family Christmas is about to be cele-* | *brated. Gay happy children play in the snow,* | *and kindly grown-ups help them enjoy them-* | *selves. This picture book of a winter long ago* | *will delight all ages.* || ☆ || OXFORD BOOKS | FOR BOYS AND GIRLS || ☆ || 40-80   <u>$1.00</u>.   Back flap: A TALE | FOR EASTER | *By Tasha Tudor* || *"In this new book Tasha Tudor has made some of* | *her loveliest drawings, pictures which have the* | *same fragile beauty of early Spring evenings.*¶*"It does not even pretend to be a story, it is* | *rather an evocation of those days before Easter* | *which the fortunate will always remember as hav-* | *ing a quivering anticipation, a newness of life* | *which makes Christmas seem almost garish by* | *comparison. Here is a little girl's first vague aware-* | *ness of the approaching day, taking shape with the* | *fitting of a new dress, with Hot Cross Buns, with* | *conferences with the chickens about the egg sup-* | *ply and as 'you never can tell what might happen* | *on Easter.' there are dreams of all the young* | *things of woods and pasture, waiting with sleek* | *coats and bright eyes for Easter morning. As slight* | *and simple a thing as the first*

narcissus, the book | *has the same unforgettable air of joy." ... . |* —*The New York Times* ‖ $1.00 ‖ ☆ ‖
The Calico Books | By Tasha Tudor | PUMPKIN MOONSHINE | ALEXANDER THE GANDER |
THE COUNTY FAIR | *Between the polka-dot covers of these tiny books* | *are lovely watercolor*
illustrations and simple tales | *of Sylvia Anne—charming picture books of coun-* | *try life a century ago.* ‖
☆ ‖ Each $.75.

CONTENTS: Title page [1] and dedication page [3] FOR |WEE |MARY are in color. The dedication
is printed in a circle of winterberry and one acorn. Efner Holmes reports that Mary is the
daughter of Tudor's brother.

ILLUSTRATIONS: All illustrations in color: four different field mice on each end paper, title page [1]
and dedication [3]. Full page illustrations on even-numbered pages [4]-[36]. Odd numbered
pages [5] - [37] contain the text in calligraphy. Blank: pp. [38-40] and inside both free
endpapers.

OTHER: The Pierpont Morgan Library, New York City, owns a copy like this, 6 1/4″ wide. The fact
that its Wightman Collection copy is green (and that green is a Christmas color) substantiates the
FIRST printing being in the bright green cloth. Definitely a square spine, accounting for the
extra measurement of this copy, which has not been subject to use and 'squashing.' The
Wightman cover label is slightly larger, 2 1/16″ high by 3 3/8″ wide, cut slightly low so that a part
of the bottom black line border has been cut while leaving a white paper beyond the top red
border; right side shows slightly more white than the left. The Wightman copy's dust jacket is
curiously discolored giving evidence that a chemical from the cloth has attacked the paper. The
entire back side of the jacket is a light vinegar brown, except for the portion adjacent to the
endpapers. The outside of the jacket does not exhibit the discoloration. (I have observed the
same effect to the dust jackets of *Jackanapes*.) The outside is near perfect, only a minor
bumping at the base of the spine. The spine also exhibits the slightest discoloration/sunning.
    JPW:3883

Examined a copy in this green cover, inscribed by Tudor to her nurse 'Dady' Burnett and dated
September 24, 1941 (a week before publication), making it one of the earliest Tudor signatures to
be positively dated. This also attests to the lighter green being the first binding, although this copy
has lost its front cover label.

The Chicago, Illinois, department store Marshall Field and Co. featured *Snow Before Christmas* in
the cover and dust jacket of its 1941 children's book catalog.

COPYRIGHT REGISTRATION: A 163315 granted to Oxford University Press, Inc., 114 Fifth Ave.,
N.Y., N.Y.

SNOW BEFORE CHRISTMAS by Tasha Tudor, a U.S. citizen, was published Oct. 2, 1941. The
book was printed or produced by The Haddon Craftsmen, Inc., Camden, N.J.   Affidavit
received Apr. 20, 1942; copies received Apr. 21, 1942.

COPYRIGHT RENEWAL REGISTRATION: R 454418 granted to the author Tasha Tudor, Route 1,
Contoocook, N.H. 03229. Patricia C. Lord, Henry Z. Walck, Inc., 19 Union Square West, N.Y.,
N.Y. 10003 swears:

SNOW BEFORE CHRISTMAS by Tasha Tudor was originally published Oct. 2, 1941, original
claimant Oxford University Press, Inc. Application received Jan. 27, 1969.

S62 _____.

PAGINATION: [40] pp. on ivory paper in two signatures, plus endpapers. 6 11/16″ x 6 3/16″

COVER: Blue-gray cloth over boards, course 'cheesecloth' weave, rounded spine. Same paper label as
before.

OTHER: Examination copy has poor registration in the illustrations of pages [28], [32] and [36]. Registration marks are preserved on the edge of page [38].

S63 _____.

   COVER: <u>Bound in dark green cloth</u>. Same paper label as before. Rounded spine.

   DUST JACKET: Have not examined one.

   OTHER: The binding glue tends to discolor the endpapers 5/8″ out from the gutter, front and back.

S64 _____. Have not examined a designated 2nd printing.

S65 _____. Have not examined a designated 3rd printing.

S66 _____. [*Copyright . . . New York, Inc.* || <u>*Fourth printing, 1946*</u> || *Calligraphy . . . United States of America*]

   PAGINATION: [40] pages plus decorated end leaves. 6 3/4″ x 6 1/8″

   COVER: <u>Gray-green silken cloth</u> with 2 1/8″ x 3 5/16″ label as before. Square spine

   DUST JACKET: Price at bottom of front flap: <u>$1.25</u>.

   ILLUSTRATIONS: Several plates out of registration: pp. [18, 20, 24, 36]

S67 ᴛᴴᴱ | SPRJNGS | OF JOY || by TASHA TUDOR || [a small girl, boy, cat and corgi surround a mother holding a baby] || Rand McNally & Company | Chicago · New York · San Francisco [**To F.B.S.** || Still the fair vision lives! Say nevermore | That dreams are fragile things. What | else endures | Of all this broken world save only dreams! | Unknown || [rose slip] || Library of Congress Cataloging in Publication Data | Tudor, Tasha | The springs of joy. || 1. Tudor, Tasha. 2. Joy in art. 3. Joy in | literature. I. Title. | NC975.5.T82A4 1979 741.9′73 79-66708 | ISBN 0-528-82047-8 | ISBN 0-528-82047-7 lib. bdg. || *Copyright © 1979 by Rand McNally & Company* | *All rights reserved* | *Printed in the United States of America by Rand McNally & Company* | *First printing, 1979* || In deference to the sensibilities of some readers, the publisher | has deleted several lines from the Walt Whitman poem contained herein.]

   PAGINATION: <u>[60] pp.</u> on white paper in four signatures <u>including fly leaves.</u> 12 x 9 1/4″

COVER: <u>Laid paper imprint</u> in fully printed paper over boards. Yellow ground with a large floral framed-illustration, front and back. Front cover: THE | SPRINGS | OF JOY [red calligraphic letters with curlicues], above, and by | Tasha Tudor [purple], below a color illustration of a woman, two boys, two girls and 2 corgis on a meadow picnic within a wildflower border. Spine: [yellow flower]   The Springs of Joy   Tudor   Rand McNally [purple] [yellow flower]. Back: bare-foot girl skipping rope within a circle of mushrooms in an arched border of violets. Upper left corner: <u>528-82047-8</u>. The front endpapers, a large yellow wild rose branch. The rear endpapers, a large fern leaf and pink wygelia (?) The free endpapers in this binding are the first and last leaves, respectively, of the first and last gatherings. Title page is bordered with roses and blue morning glories. Only the title is red, matching the cover; remaining text in black.

DUST JACKET: The book was not issued with a dust jacket.

CONTENTS: This is an anthology of quotations selected by Tudor and illustrated with some of her favorite themes: children, animals, flowers and contemplation in Nature. Each full color illustration illumines an accompanying credited quotation from literature, pp. [2, 4-57]. A few two-page illustrations. Several have appeared separately as prints, postal and Christmas cards. Tudor's Foreword, p. [5]: Joy and peace are a state of mind, easy for some to | come by, difficult for others. This book pictures a | few of the things that have brought, and still do | bring, intense joy to me. || This is not a storybook--it has no particular | beginning, no end, and definitely *no message*. | It is merely a statement of delight, drawn from | memory past and present. || May it bring you as much happiness in perusing its | pictures as it has given me in setting them down. || The pictures are my own, the quotations are "other | men's flowers." || Tasha Tudor | Corgi Cottage, 1979 || "Life is far too important a thing | to ever talk seriously about. || Oscar Wilde. Page [58]: Tasha Tudor || Clues to a unique way of life exist in abundance in Tasha Tudor's art. | Candle-lit rooms, food cooked at an open hearth, weaving, and | basketmaking find their way into her books, as do children and adults | dressed in charming styles of another day. The activities are usually | simple—picknicking [*sic*] in a meadow, canoeing in a secluded pond, | romping with the corgis, tending to goats and chickens. Friends look | through a new book as through a family album. The house in the | snow—that's the house in Redding, Connecticut, Tasha knew so | well as a child. There's granddaughter Laura on snowshoes, or | contemplating the cat. Grandson Winslow it is who hesitates before | jumping from the hayloft, or courteously offers a chair to a lady. Nate | dreams on a rock. Jenny is seated in the meadow. Jason gathers eggs. | Kim, framed by birch trees, studies his image in the water. And Laura, | July, Winslow, and Jenny enjoy tea with a beloved family friend, | Horatio Rabbit. Slyly, the artist even slips herself into a scene here and | there, included in a group, or herself as a young mother. And there she | is as a child admiring the fragile beauty of water lilies. || Asked how she arrived at a life-style rooted in values and customs of | the last century, Tasha Tudor is reticent. It cannot be explained, she | replies, other than to say that it is a "state of mind." Pressed further, | she speaks of her love of nature, of animals, of nearly lost handcrafts, | and particularly of books which have meant much to her. Quotations | from some of those books appear in this one. Speaking with "other | men's voices," Tasha Tudor reveals—perhaps unwittingly—much of | herself. || Many of the quotes have to do with dreams, with nature and animals. | These are to be expected. Others call upon solitude as "needful to the | imagination." The only true gift, we find, is "a portion of thyself." We | {p. [59]} also find that there cannot be in a creation—whether it be in a piece of | artwork, a gift for a friend, or a well-tended garden—"what in the | creator was not." || The wisdom in books exists only "according to the sensibility of the | reader." Peace? Nothing can bring it "but yourself." Happiness is "a | duty" to self and is found in "minute fractions." As for success—with | Thoreau, she greets each day with joy and finds that all nature is her | "congratulation." || Perhaps most revealing is a final quotation, from Elizabeth Barrett | Browning. Life the poet, Tasha Tudor learned to live with visions for | her company. With confidence and determination she has translated | those dreams into a life-style which, ultimately, has animated her art. | Living a life of loving detail, she speaks of herself as a happy woman. || Good, better, best; | Never rest | Till "good" be "better" | And "better" "best." || Mother Goose.

OTHER: Dedicated to a judicial <u>Pennsylvania</u> friend. See also *All for Love.*

COPYRIGHT REGISTRATION: TX 524-019 granted to Rand McNally & Company, Box 7600, Chicago, Il. 60680. Richard G. Sander, agent for the claimant swears on July 25, 1980:

THE SPRINGS OF JOY, illustrations and compilation of quotations by Tasha Tudor, a U.S. citizen, was published Oct. 12, 1979. The book, whose creation was completed in 1979, was manufactured by Rand McNally & Company, Hammon, In. and Versailles, Ky. Fees charged to account DA 019712, Rand McNally & Company. Application received July 28, 1980; and deposit received at L.C., January 2, 1980, the effective date of this registration.

S68 _____.

PAGINATION: <u>[68] pp. + endpapers</u>. Pp. [1-3] <u>and [66-68] blank,</u> reinforced with a stronger white end paper.

COVER: Library binding. Cover is heavily starched cloth. Back: top left code concealed with <u>a gold label imprinted with new code: 528-80047-7-6.97</u>

S69 _____. [**To F.B.S**.... ISBN 0-528-82047-8 || *Copyright © 1979 by Rand McNally & Company | All rights reserved | First printing, 1979 <u>Second printing, 1985 | Printed in Italy</u>* || In deference . . . contained herein.]

PAGINATION: [60] pp. white paper in four signatures <u>including free endpapers</u>. 12″ x 9 3/16″

COVER: Paper over boards sealed, <u>gloss film lamination</u>.

S70 _____. . . . TUDOR || [mother and children] || CHILDRENS PRESS CHOICE | [C P book logo] A Rand McNally title selected for educational distribution | ISBN 0-516-09832-2 [**To F.B.S.** . . . <u>ISBN 0-516-09832-2</u> || 1985 SCHOOL AND LIBRARY EDITION || *Copyright © 1979* . . . contained herein.]

PAGINATION: <u>[68] pp.</u> on white paper in four signatures <u>including fly leaves</u>. The four signatures are top sewn through a cloth hinge, heavy white end papers. 12″ x 9 1/4″

COVER: <u>Gloss film lamination over linen imprint</u> in printed paper over boards. <u>There are now two white boxes at the bottom of the cover.</u> Left: a 1 3/8″ x 1 1/2″ includes a large CP logo and beneath it: CHILDRENS PRESS CHOICE | REINFORCED BINDING. At lower right in a 1/2″ x 2″ box: <u>ISBN 0-516-09832-2.</u>

S71 _____. By TASHA TUDOR || [mother and children] || [checkered book logo] CHECKERBOARD PRESS | NEW YORK [**To F.B.S.** || . . .[rose] || Copyright © 1979 Checkerboard Press, a division of Macmillan, Inc. <u>09876543</u> | Checkerboard Press and colophon are trademarks of Macmillan, Inc. All rights reserved. | No part of this book may be reproduced or transmitted in any form or by any means, | electronic or mechanical, including photocopying, recording, or by any information storage | and retrieval system, without permission in writing from the Publisher. || **Printed in U.S.A.**]

PAGINATION: <u>[60] pp.</u> on white paper in four signatures <u>including free endpapers</u>. 12″ x 9 1/4″.

COVER: <u>Gloss film lamination on</u> paper over boards. <u>A round black price label</u> is attached to the upper right front. It is printed on a larger white circle, and 'overprinted' with $12^{95}. Back: a 1 15/16″ x 2 1/2″ <u>white box at the lower left bottom.</u> Beneath a bar code centered in the box: 0 14121 89092 1; and below that in a 'computer' font: <u>ISBN 0-02-689092-5.</u>

S72 _____. . . . [printer's swirl] **THE** [printer's swirl] | **SPRINGS** *of* **JOY** [red] | **T**ASHA **T**UDOR [blue] | [mother and children] | *Simon & Schuster Books for Young Readers* | [bird on nest] [To F.B.S. | [red printer's swirl] | Still the fair . . . <u>What else endures</u> | Of all . . . [rose] | [sower logo] | *Simon & Schuster Books for Young Readers* | An imprint of Simon & Scghuster Children's Publishing Division | 1230 Avenue of the Americas, New York, New York 10020 || Copyright ©1998 by Tasha Tudor | All rights reserved including the right of reproduction in whole or in part in any form. | SIMON & SCHUSTER BOOKS FOR YOUNG READERS is a trademark of Simon & Schuster. | Book design by Heather Wood. The text of this book is set in Horley Old Style. | The illustrations are renedered in wtercolor. | Printed and bound in the United States of America. | 10 9 8 7 6 5 4 3 2 1 | First Edition [*sic*] | Library of Congress Cataloging-in-Publication Data | the springs of joy / [compiled and illustrated] by Tasha Tudor. | p. cm. | Summary: A collection of quotations from a variety of authors whose inspirational | words find further expression in the joyful watercolors which accompany the text. | 1.Joy-Quotations, maxims, etc. [1.Joy-Quotations, maxims, etc. 2.Happiness- | Quotations, mexims, etc.] I. Tudor, Tasha, ill. | PN6084.J65T 1998   082-dc21   97-16198   CIP AC]

PAGINATION: [60] pp. on white paper in four signatures <u>including free endpapers</u>. 12″ x 9 3/16″.

COVER: <u>Purple cloth</u> over boards, mint green satin marker ribbon bound at the middle. Front blind stamped at lower right: [printer's swirl] **THE** [printer's swirl] | **SPRINGS** | *of* **JOY**. Spine stamped in gilt: **TUDOR   THE SPRINGS** *of* **JOY   Simon & Schuster**.

DUST JACKET: Violet front, mint green spine, back and flaps. The image is the girl jumping rope within a circle of mushrooms from the back cover of the Rand McNally edition. The Text and swirls are enlarged from the title page. THE | [lilac] | SPRINGS | of JOY | [girl jumping rope] | TASHA TUDOR, within the twig violets and forsythia border. Spine: **TUDOR** [violet] **THE SPRINGS** *of* **JOY** [coral] [sower logo] *Simon & Schuster*. Back: an amalgam of three images from the book, the blue circle ["To see a world in a grain of sand …"] around the girl and corgi ["Beloved Pan and all ye other gods . . ."] and embellished with the hollyhocks ["There is no duty we so much underrate . . ."] as well as their mirror image. A 1¼″ x 1 7/8″ white box beneath this image includes two black bar codes. Above the smaller right bar code: 90000>. At the right side EAN, and beneath the larger left bar code: 9 780689 818820. Beneath it all: ISBN 0-689-81882-3. Front flap: [hollyhocks leaning right] $18.00 US | $24.50 CAN || *All Ages* || "The gloom of the world | is but a shadow; behind it, | yet within our reach, is joy. | Take joy." —*Fra Giovanni* || [swirl and initial in coral] **I**n the words | of writers as diverse as William | Shakespeare, Henry Thoreau, and | Mother Goose, Tasha Tudor | admonishes her readers to "take | joy." The splendor of nature, the | warmth of the human heart, and | the power of dreams are all | proclaimed by some of the greatest | writers in the English language. | And Tasha Tudor brings their | words home with her delicate | watercolors, many featuring her | own beloved grandchildren and | even herself as a child. ¶ "There is no duty we so much | underrate as the duty of being | happy," Robert Louis Stevenson | says. In this wise, inspirational, | and touching collection of words | and pictures, embodying the | innocence of childhood and the | simple pleasures of times past, | Tasha Tudor reminds us of the | joy that is all around us. || *GUARANTEED REINFORCED BINDING / 0498*. Back flap: a Caldecott Honor artists with | over forty books to her credit, || **TASHA TUDOR** [violet] || has spent all of her life in new | England, and she recreates the | landscapes, animals, and people | of her home in her artwork. In | *the Springs of Joy,* she celebrates | her own family with tender and | touching portraits of he grand- | children. Her pets, the graceful | cats and ever-exuberant corgis, | also romp through the pages. ¶ Tasha Tudor is the illustrator | of *A Time to Keep, The Night* | *Before Christmas, A Child's* | *Garden of Verses,* and *1 is* | *One,* a Caldecott Honor | book. She lives in | Vermont. [hollyhock image inverted] || Jacket illustrations © 1979, 1998 by Tasha Tudor || Jacket design by Heather Wood || [a line rectangle around] VISIT US ON THE WORLD WIDE WEB | www.SimonSaysKids.com || *Simon & Schuster* | *Books for Young Readers* [coral] | *Simon & Schuster* [violet] [coral swirl] *New York* [violet, other text black except as noted].

CONTENTS: The illustrations have been enlarged slightly so that some full-page images bleed off the edges and loose some detail that appeared in the first edition. Text has been reset in a new font. Pages [58-59] carry new text: [fuschia] || **TASHA TUDOR** [blue] || A New England native, Tasha Tudor weaves the traditions and history of | her home into her life and art. Her delicate watercolors celebrate the | warmth, family attachments, and values of the past, and bring her readers | along with her to embrace her love for nature, for animals, and for children. || [coral swirl] || Parts of Tasha's own life often find their way into her illustrations. Many | readers are familiar with her beloved pets, the corgis, who romp and play | through the pages of Tasha's picture books. Her own childhood home | in Redding, Connecticut, makes an appearance in *the*

349

windows. And Tasha's grandchildren appear throughout the book" there's | Laura on snowshoes, and, a few pages later, petting an adored silver tabby | cat; Winslow in the hayloft or politely offering a chair to a lady; Jenny | sitting in a flowering meadow; Jason gathering eggs; Kim, standing | between two birch trees, studying his reflection in the water. Laura, Julie, | Winslow, and Jenny are gathered together for tea with a beloved family | friend, Horatio Rabbit. And Tasha herself appears, as a child, admiring the | fragile beauty of water lilies.   [page 59] With Tasha's own affectionate watercolors illustrating quotations from | authors she has loved and been inspired by, *The Springs of Joy* sums up | Tasha Tudor's life as an artist, and also as a woman dedicated to finding | joy in fragrant lilacs and bright pansies, in tea parties and good books, in | pets and grandchildren and in tasks well done, in memories of the past and | details of the present. Sharing that joy with her readers is another of her | great pleasures. || [coral swirl] || Good, better, best; | Never rest | Till "good" be "better" | And "better" "best." || Mother Goose.

OTHER: Even though the colophon calls this the First Edition, it is, of course, a reprint. The only reference to the 1979 original is Tudor's dated introduction. Simon & Schuster scheduled a reprinting for April 1, 1998.

T1 𝒯AKE 𝒥OY! | [photograph of Tudor painting on her porch] | THE MAGICAL WORLD | of |
TASHA TUDOR. [the credits run only in the videotape, against a magenta ground: Written &
Directed | By | Sarah Justine Kerruish | Editor | Bob Sarles | Director of Photography | David Collier |
Original Piano Music | by | David J. Reading | Original musical and arrangements | of Folk Tunes by | Paul
Peabody on Violin | John Polinsky on Guitar | Director of Archives | Joanna Allen | Production Executives |
Nellie Rodgers | Peyton Wilson | Production Manager | Emily Detmer |Post-Production Supervisor | Julie
Van Hook | Director of Narration | Simon Firth | Sound Recording | Joel Shapiro | Sound Editing | Andrea
Stelter | Account Executive | Erica Durbin | Legal Services | Richard Solomon | Assistant Art Director |
Alisa Price | Title Design | Anya Bruno | Asylum | Photographer | Richard W. Brown | Equipment Donated |
By | Guy Jaconelli | The HB Group, Inc. | North Haven, CT | On-Line Editor | Loren Sorensen | Varitel |
Color-Correction | Randy Musgrave | Varitel | Re-Recording Mixer | Will Harvey | Music Annex | Studio
Sound Recording | Mary Ellen Perry | Music Annex | | Archival Material Provided | by | Nell Dorr "The
Golden Key" | Copyright | Amon Carter Museum | Fort Worth, Texas | Nell Dorr Archives || Film/Audio
Services | Bartlett Gould | LIFE Magazine Photography | Verner Reed | J. R. Eyerman | Barry MacKeracher
| The MIT Museum | Mystic Seaport Museum, Film and Video Archives | National Air and Space Museum
| Verner Reed | Archival Assistance Provided | by | Christopher Ash [sic]| Glenn H. Curtiss Museum of
Local History | Harvard University Archive | Lleylleyn Howland III | Independence Park Maritime Museum
| Peter Jakab | Maine Maritime Museum | The Marblehead Historical Society | Mystic Seaport Museum,
Rosenfeld Collection | National Aviation Museum of Canada | Department of the Navy | National Museum
of Naval Aviation | Newburyport Public Library | New England Air Museum | Leonard Opdycke | Peabody
Essex Museum || Special Thanks to | Steve Jarrett | Eleanor Jarrett | Margaret Sudduth | Marco di Miroz |
Joan De Gusto | Marley Sarles || This film is dedicated to William & Jill Kerruish | for giving me such a
wonderful childhood. || SPELLBOUND | *productions* | ©1996] 45:48 minute VHS videotape.

> COVER: Lavender pasteboard sleeve open at the bottom for inserting the videocassette. As new, the
> entire case was sealed in plastic shrink-wrap applied by the manufacturer. Printing on the sleeve is
> largely black, with carmine highlights to Take Joy! and Tasha Tudor, on the front and three sides of
> the sleeve. The word **of** is always printed as a fanciful typographical design. The long sides print
> the title in one line. At the top of the case the composition is: 𝒯AKE 𝒥OY! | THE MAGICAL
> WORLD | of | **TASHA TUDOR**. Back: [one inch oval painting of a cat sleeping in a
> yellow-ware bowl] | [carmine leaf design] You have read the stories and marveled at the | wonderful
> illustrations. Now is your chance to enter | the magical world of Tasha Tudor. For the first | time
> ever Tasha Tudor has permitted a film crew | unprecedented access to document her daily life. | The
> result, Take Joy! [carmine], | is an intimate and charming | portrait of one of America's best-loved
> artists. | [paintings of boy with chickens, girl churning butter and a larger pencil sketch of a guinea
> pig dressed as a lady] | Produced by **Spellbound Productions** | in association with | **Corgi Cottage
> Industries** | ©Spellbound Productions, 539 Broadway, S.F. CA. 94133, tel. 415-352-1550.

> OTHER: Videocassette label (1 13/16″ x 3″) has a lightly printed rose branch, on which is overprinted,
> <u>carmine ink</u>, applied to the 4″ x 7 3/8″ black plastic videocassette: 𝒯AKE 𝒥OY! | THE
> MAGICAL WORLD | of | **TASHA TUDOR**.

On the recommendation of her friend Nicholas Carr, in November 1995 Emily Detmer inquired of
these authors (Nick's aunt and uncle) how Spellbound Productions might contact Tasha Tudor to
create a film study of Tudor. We advised that a representative should be in New York City within
four days where Tudor would be appearing at the Metropolitan Children's Book & Antique Toy
Fair and Seminar the weekend of December 1-3, 1995. Contact was made and raw footage was

shot in Marlboro, Vermont, in June 1996. The finished video premiered Friday evening November 1, 1996, in Williamsburg, Va. Director Sarah Kerruish and her mother, with Tudor and her daughter Bethany, were in the audience at the first public viewing. It marked the opening of TAKE JOY! THE WORLD OF TASHA TUDOR SEMINAR and EXHIBIT at the Colonial Williamsburg Foundation. The accompanying exhibit of Tudor paintings, dolls, and household effects exhibited at the Abby Aldrich Rockefeller Folk Art Museum through April 6, 1997.

This videotape met a good reception. All parties were sufficiently encouraged to undertake a second project, one that would capture Tudor's noted Christmas celebrations. Footage was shot at Christmas 1996, for *Take Peace* (1997).

T2 **Take Joy!** [red] | **THE TASHA TUDOR CHRISTMAS BOOK** | | *Selected, edited, and illustrated by* [blue]| TASHA TUDOR [red] || [chickadee on a branch] | THE WORLD PUBLISHING COMPANY / CLEVELAND AND NEW YORK [blue, all within a Fall woodland border of ground plants, nuts, berries and evergreens] [COPYRIGHT ACKNOWLEDGEMENTS || [This in left column] The editor and The World Publishing Company herewith render thanks to | the following authors, publishers, and agents whose interest, co-operation, | and permission to reprint have made possible the preparation of *Take Joy: | The Tasha Tudor Christmas Book*. All possible care has been taken to trace | the ownership of every selection included and to make full acknowledgment | for its use. If any errors have accidentally occurred, they will be corrected | in subsequent editions, provided notification is sent to the publishers. || Charles Scribner's Sons, for "To His Saviour, a Child, a Present by a | Child" by Robert Herrick. Reprinted by permission of Charles Scribner's | Sons. ¶ Columbia University Press, for "Noel Sing We" from *Early English | Christmas Carols* edited by Rossell H. Robbins. Reprinted by permission of| Columbia University Press. ¶ D. E. Collins, and Messrs. J. M. Dent and Sons, Ltd., and Dodd, Mead | and Co., for "A Christmas Carol" by G. K. Chesterton from *The Wild | Knight and Other Poems*. Reprinted by permission of D. E. Collins, Messrs. | J. M. Dent and Sons, Ltd., and Dodd, Mead and Co. ¶Doubleday & Company, Inc., for "The Gift of the Magi" from *The Four | Million* by O. Henry. Reprinted by permission of Doubleday & Company, Inc. ¶ Flensted Publishers, for R. P. Keigwin's translation of "The Fir Tree" by | Hans Christian Andersen. Reprinted by permission of Flensted Publishers, | Odense, Denmark. ¶ Harper & Row, Publishers, Inc., for "The Caravan" from *This Way to | Christmas* by Ruth Sawyer, copyright 1916 by Harper & Row, Publishers, [*sic*]| [right column] Inc. Renewal, 1944, by Ruth Sawyer Durand. Reprinted by permission of | Harper & Row, Publishers, Inc. ¶ Harry and Eleanor Farjeon, for their poem "Our Brother is Born." Re- | printed by permission of the authors. ¶ The Macmillan Company, for "Christmas in London" from *Little Dog | Toby* by Rachel Field, copyright 1928 by The Macmillan Company. Re- | printed by permission of The Macmillan Company. ¶ New Directions Publishing Corporation, J. M. Dent and Sons, Ltd., and | the Literary Executors of the Dylan Thomas Estate, for an excerpt from | *A Child's Christmas in Wales* by Dylan Thomas, copyright 1954 by New | Directions. Reprinted by permission of the publishers, New Directions Pub- | lishing Corporation, J. M. Dent and Sons, Ltd., and the Literary Executors | of the Dylan Thomas Estate. ¶ Nora Burglon, for "The Christmas Coin." Reprinted by permission of| the author. ¶ Schmitt, Hall & McCreary Company, publishers, for "Here We Come | A-Caroling" arranged by Torstein O. Kvamme from *The*

Christmas Caroler's | Book in Song and Story. Reprinted by permission of Schmitt, Hall & Mc- | Creary Company, Minneapolis, Minnesota. ¶ The World Publishing Company, for "The Twelve Days of Christmas" | from *Best Loved Songs and Hymns* edited by James Morehead and Albert | Morehead, copyright 1965 by James Morehead. Reprinted by permission of | The World Publishing Company. || ¶The author also wishes to thank Wendy Worth and Joan Knight for their | help in preparing this volume. || Published by The World Publishing Company | 2231 West 110th Street, Cleveland, Ohio 44102 | Published simultaneously in Canada by | Nelson, Foster & Scott Ltd. | Library of Congress catalog card number: AC 66-10645 | <u>NE66</u> | Text copyright © 1966 by The World Publishing Company | Illustrations copyright © 1966 by Tasha Tudor | All rights reserved. No part of this book may be reproduced in any form without written | permission from the publisher, except for brief passages included in a review appearing in a | newspaper or magazine. Printed in the United States of America. | Designed by Jack Jaget] <u>Page [160]: 1 2 3 4 5 70 69 68 67 66</u>

PAGINATION: Ten signatures buff paper, [1-8] 9-18 [19] 20-34 [35] 36-42 [43] 44-157 [158-160]. 8 1/2″ x 11 1/4″

COVER: Red cloth imprinted in black on front and back: twig frame, Christmas tree, rabbit, jay and birds. Spine stamped in gold: TAKE JOY!   Tasha Tudor   World. Old gold end papers with two pencil sketches: wren on left, and field mouse on right, each in a holly wreath within a larger single-line border, holly at corners. Repeated on back end papers.

DUST JACKET: Deep blue with full color illustrations, boy and girl, corgi, cat, rooster, two lambs and Christmas tree on front. TAKE JOY! [yellow decorated letters above illustration] and **The Tasha Tudor Christmas Book** [red letters below illustration] on front cover. Spine: [holly] | **Tasha | Tudor** [yellow] | TAKE JOY! [laterally, red] | **World** [yellow] [holly]. Back, branch with candle, centered, <u>A1199</u> [white] lower right. <u>Front flap lower corner clipped: $ 4.95</u> [black] | Take Joy! | The Tasha Tudor | Christmas Book | *Selected, edited, and illustrated by* | TASHA TUDOR [red, remaining text is black] || This beautiful book is Tasha Tudor's gift | to everyone who loves Christmas. From | a wide range of sources this famous and | beloved artist has chosen a richly varied | collection of poems, carols, stories, leg- | ends, and even Christmas recipes and | decorations. ¶ Among the many selections are tradi- | tional favorites like "Away in a Manger," | Hans Christian Andersen's story of "The | Little Fir Tree," and Clement Moore's | "The Night Before Christmas," as well as | the Biblical account of the Nativity. Less | familiar are poems by Shakespeare, | Blake, and Herrick, Christmas stories by | Selma Lagerlöf, Ruth Sawyer, and Dylan | Thomas (to name but a few), and some | little-known, very moving carols. There | is an exquisite poem by Rumer Godden, | <u>never before published</u>, written for Tasha | Tudor's children. And there are wonder- | ful recipes from the artist's own family | cookbook for delicious holiday treats. ¶ The many full-color and black-and- | white pictures in this book are aglow | with the tenderness, reverence, and | beauty for which Tasha Tudor's work is | known, and her selections celebrate all | the joys of the season, both religious and | secular. This is truly a book for all mem- | bers of the family, young and old, one | that will be read and reread and cherished | for many years. Back flap: TASHA TUDOR [red, remaining text except bottom three lines, black] is the well-known il- | lustrator of many books for young peo- | ple, including Kenneth Grahame's *The | Wind in the Willows*. A native of New Eng- | land, she lives in a large farmhouse in | Webster, New Hampshire. ¶ The Tudor family's Christmas celebra- | tion is justly famous. It begins with the | hanging of the Advent calendars made | each year by Tasha Tudor for her four | children. In the days preceding Christ- | mas, homemade gifts and decorations are | prepared with loving care, cookies and | cakes are baked, the crèche is set up, the | tree is brought in from their own stand | of fir trees. Finally, neighbors and friends | are invited to sing carols and to see a mar- | ionette performance of a Christmas play | with puppets the Tudor family have made | themselves. ¶ In this book one of America's best- | loved artists shares with readers her own | delight in the most joyous of all seasons. || [Publisher's tree logo] | The World Publishing Company | CLEVELAND AND NEW YORK [last three lines red].

CONTENTS: Half-title, p. [1]. *For* | Ann Beneduce, p. [7]. <u>Table of contents incorrectly lists INDEX on page 156, and ABOUT THE AUTHOR, page 158</u>. The index is printed on pages 155-157. Page [158] contains two paragraphs: ABOUT THE ARTIST || [left column] TASHA TUDOR is the very popular author and illustrator of many | beautiful books for children. Although born in

353

Boston, she was | brought up on a farm in Connecticut and has never lost her love | for country life. She paints animals and children with a warmth | and delicate charm that have become her trademarks. Tasha | Tudor follows in the artistic footsteps of her parents; her mother | was Rosamond Tudor, the portrait painter, and her father, W. | Starling Burgess, was a famous yacht designer. Tasha Tudor | studied art in London and at the Boston Museum School of Fine | Arts. ¶ Now, with her own family, she lives in a lovely old red frame | [right column] farmhouse in New Hampshire. When she is not busy being a | housewife and mother and entertaining visiting friends and rela- | tives, Tasha Tudor tends the greenhouse and gardens and looks | after the many farm animals—among them ducks, geese, cows, | horses, dogs and cats—all "members of the family." Part of each | day, she writes and paints at a large and pleasantly cluttered table, | permanently set up at one end of her kitchen, where she can | enjoy from her window a view of gardens, fields and woods. | Yet, somehow, she always finds time for the fun of preparing for | festive traditional family celebrations and for enjoying seasonal | delights.

ILLUSTRATIONS: Black and white: [1, 5] 9, 12-13, 16, 21-22, 24-25, 29, 32-33, 36-39, 41, 45, 48, 52, 56-57, 60-61, 64-81, 84-85, 88-89, 92-93, 96-97, 100-101, 104-105, 108-109, 112-129, 132-133, 136, 140-141, 144-145, 148-149, 152-153, 155, 157.   Color: [2, 7] 10-11, 14-15, 23, 27, 30, 42-43, 46-47, 54-55, 58-59, 62-63, 82-83, 86-87, 90-91, 94-95. 98-99, 102-103, 106-107, 110-111, 130-131, 134-135, 138-139, 142-143, 146, 150, [158-159].

Full page color: [3, 19, 34] 111, 147, 151, 154. Three motifs: a twig frame around textual page, two vertical bands of decoration, especially at sides of carols, and miscellaneous illustrations to text. Several of the illustrations are from earlier greeting cards.

OTHER: Sally Wimberley, Woodbridge, Va., reports alterations from the original art to the printed versions. For example, the pencil border of the Contents page [5] is the top dressing of the page 153 original pencil sketch, recorded in Hills and McKeever's *A Partial List . . .* as being the property of the Rev. William M. Peterson. Likewise, the kissing ball is an addition to the watercolor on page 134, and does not appear in the original. See also entry C45 *Christmas with Tasha Tudor: Take Joy!* for a revision of the the 1966 book to be published Fall 2000.

COPYRIGHT REGISTRATION: A 988696 granted to Tasha Tudor, ILLUSTRATIONS, Route 1, Contoocook, N.H. Ralph S. Taylor, The World Publishing Co., 2231 West 110th St., Cleveland, Oh. 44102 swears on May 13, 1968:

TAKE JOY: THE TASHA TUDOR CHRISTMAS BOOK- ILLUSTRATIONS by Tasha Tudor, Editor and Illustrator, a U.S. citizen, was published Oct. 27, 1966. New matter in this version: illustrations. The book was manufactured by Wescott & Thomson, 1027 Arch St., Philadelphia, 5, Pa.; Johnson & Harden Co., 3600 Redbank St., Cincinnati, Oh.; Nielson Lithographing Co., Eastern Hills Lane, Cincinnati, Oh. Fees charged to The World Publishing Company. Two deposit copies received at L.C. March 27, 1968. Application and affidavit received May 16, 1968.

COPYRIGHT REGISTRATION: A 988697 granted to The World Publishing Co. - (Text), 2231 West 110th St., Cleveland, Oh. 44102. Ralph S. Taylor, swears on May 13, 1968:

TAKE JOY: THE TASHA ... New matter in this version: The Story CHRISTMAS DAY, Page 153. [other facts as above].

T3 _____.

COVER: Printed blue cloth imprinted with the design of the dust jacket. At the back, lower right, printed in white: WLB | WORLD LIBRARY BINDING, with a stylized L forming a tree.

T4 _____.

>   COVER: Rebound copy (ca. 1980) in sealed blue buckram reproducing the front illustration and title from the dust jacket with some color changes. Sub-title and spine type are reset. Front and back endpapers lost in rebinding and two new ivory sheets added.

T5 _____. Published simultaneously in Canada by | Nelson, Foster & Scott Ltd. Have not examined a copy.

T6 _____.

>   COVER: Yellow endpapers, with illustrations as before.

>   DUST JACKET: Price $4.95 in upper front flap corner, lower corner clipped. A small portion of the registration guide remains on the side of front flap.

>   OTHER: Second printing statement on page 160: 2 3 4 5 70 69 68 67

T7 _____. 3rd printing in 1968 ? Have not examined a copy.

T8 _____.

>   COVER: A duller scarlet cloth cover, but same decorations and inks. Still the lighter yellow mustard endpapers.

>   DUST JACKET: Price, upper front flap: $6.95.

>   OTHER: Fourth printing statement on page [160]: 4 5 70 69.

T9 _____.

>   DUST JACKET: Positioned above the code in lower right, and printed in white is WLB | WORLD LIBRARY BINDING. The L extends into the lower line, and above the WB to form a tree top.

>   OTHER: Fourth printing statement on page [160]: 4 5 70 69. This could be a switched jacket, although I have never seen a variant 'library binding' of this book. - *Ed.*

T10 _____. 5th printing. Have not examined a copy.

T11 _____. 6th printing. Have not examined a copy.

T12 _____.

>   PAGINATION: Ivory paper.

>   COVER: Same frame design stamped in red plasticized cloth with grained leather pattern. This may be a 'library binding' which has lost its dust jacket.

>   DUST JACKET: As other trade copies, above. Lower corner of front flap intact with not text, upper corner clipped from examination copy.

OTHER: Seventh printing statement wihtout a year on page [160]: <u>7</u>. Exained a copy inscribed <u>Christmas 1971</u>.

T13 _____.

> PAGINATION: Ivory paper.
>
> COVER: Same frame design stamped in <u>red plasticized cloth with pigskin leather pattern</u>.
>
> DUST JACKET: Blue jacket, as before; $6.95 upper corner, front flap.
>
> OTHER: Eighth printing statement on page [160]: <u>8</u>

T14 _____.

> COVER: Same design as above, but in <u>red plastic-filled paper</u>.
>
> DUST JACKET: Re-designed jacket is <u>matte</u> <u>white</u> with new illustrations front and back. Front: The Tasha Tudor | Christmas Book | TAKE JOY! [in red] | [centered within a thin blue rule is a horizontal Christmas card of 7 children caroling (Irene Dash FT94-40K).]   A fanciful printer's decoration in blue ink on either side of the illustration, and below: SONGS, STORIES, POEMS | THINGS TO DO FOR A FAMILY CHRISTMAS. Spine: Tasha | Tudor [black] || TAKE JOY![red] || [publisher's emblem] | WORLD [black]. Jacket back: a Nativity card (American Artists design P739) 7 9/16″ x 5 13/16″ within a thin blue rule, blue printer's devices as on front. Below the right corner of illustration in black: <u>A1199N</u>. Front flap: [corner clipped] <u>The Tasha Tudor | Christmas Book [black]</u> | TAKE JOY! [red] | *Selected, edited, and illustrated by* | TASHA TUDOR [black] | This beautiful . . . for many years. | *(continued on back flap)* [Lower corner has been slightly clipped.] Back flap: *(continued from front flap)* || TASHA TUDOR [black] . . . most joyous of all seasons. || *jacket design by Archie Bennett* [black] || [redesigned circle and tree logo] WORLD PUBLISHING | [rule] | TIMES MIRROR | NEW YORK [red]. Have not examined a copy with price intact, but probably $6.95.
>
> OTHER: Eighth printing statement on page [160]: <u>8</u>.

T15 _____.

> COVER: Same design as above, but in <u>a finer woven non-gloss sealed red cloth</u>. Back lower right inside frame, stamped in black: WLB [where the larger L becomes a tree crown above the monogram and extends down into the next line as a tree trunk]   1199W | WORLD ['trunk' L] <u>LIBRARY BINDING</u>.
>
> DUST JACKET: $6.95 || The Tasha Tudor . . .
>
> OTHER: Eighth printing statement on page [160]: <u>8</u>.

T16 _____. . . . THE WORLD PUBLISHING COMPANY / CLEVELAND AND NEW YORK

> PAGINATION: 8 9/16″ X 11 1/8″
>
> COVER: Red plastic-filled paper over boards, same design, simulated pigskin. Spine: . . . World.
>
> DUST JACKET: <u>Matt</u> white jacket reflects merger of publishers. Spine: Tasha . . . [publisher's emblem] | **COLLINS** | [rule] | **WORLD** [black]. Back flap: . . . *Bennett* [black] || **COLLINS** [circle and tree logo] **WORLD** [red]. Have not examined a copy with price intact.

OTHER: Disparity in citing publisher on title page and on dust jacket. Eighth printing statement on page [160]: <u>8</u>. Examined copy inscribed <u>Christmas 1976</u>.

T17 **Take Joy!** [red]‖ THE TASHA TUDOR CHRISTMAS BOOK ‖ *Selected, edited, and illustrated by* [blue] | TASHA TUDOR [red] ‖ [chickadee on branch] | **COLLINS** [tree in circle logo] **WORLD** / CLEVELAND AND NEW YORK [blue] [COPYRIGHT ACKNOWLEDGEMENTS ‖ The editor and The World Publishing Company...help in preparing this volume. ‖ Published by <u>Wm. Collins + World Publishing Co., Inc.</u> | 2080 West 117th Street, Cleveland, Ohio 44111 | Published simultaneously in Canada by | Nelson, Foster & Scott Ltd. | Library of Congress catalog card number: AC 66-10645 | <u>ISBN # (Trade) 0-529-24962-7</u> | Library 0-529-00208-6 | NE66...Designed by Jack Jaget]

PAGINATION: On ivory paper. <u>8 3/8″ X 11 3/16″</u>.

COVER: The <u>red plastic-filled paper</u> over boards has a pigskin imprint and gilt spine lettering: TAKE JOY! **Tasha Tudor World**. <u>White end papers and covers, have no design for the first time</u>.

DUST JACKET: <u>Gloss laminate film</u> on design as above. Front flap: <u>$7.95, in upper right corner</u> | The Tasha Tudor . . .

OTHER: Error persists on Table of Contents referring to INDEX and ABOUT THE AUTHOR, Page [158]. <u>Page [160]: 8</u>.

T18 _____.

PAGINATION: 8 17/32″ X 11 3/16″

DUST JACKET: <u>Gloss laminate</u>. Front flap: <u>$8.95, in upper right corner</u> | The Tasha Tudor . . .

OTHER: <u>Page [160]: 8</u>.

T19 _____. . . . **COLLINS** [tree in circle logo] **PUBLISHERS** / CLEVELAND AND NEW YORK [COPYRIGHT ACKNOWLEDGEMENTS ‖ The editor and <u>Collins Publishers</u> herewith render thanks to the <u>follow-</u> | ing authors, publishers, and agents whose interest, co-operation, <u>and</u> | <u>permission</u> to reprint have made possible the preparation of <u>Take Joy:</u> | <u>The Tasha Tudor Christmas Book</u>. All possible care has been taken to | trace the ownership of every selection included and to make full <u>ac-</u> | <u>knowledgement</u> for its use. If any errors have accidentally occurred, | they will be corrected in subsequent editions, provided notification is | sent to the publishers....help in preparing this volume. ‖ Published by <u>Wm. Collins Publishers Inc.</u> | 2080 West 117th Street, Cleveland, Ohio 44111 | Library of Congress Cataloging in Publication Data | Tudor, Tasha, ed. | Take joy! | 1. Christmas-Juvenile literature. 2. Christmas | stories. 3. Carols. I. Title | [GT4985.T83 1979] 394.2′68282 79-12981 | ISBN 0-529-04962-7 | ISBN 0-529-00208-6 pbk. | 140679 | Text copyright © 1966 by The World Publishing Company | Illustrations copyright © 1966 by Tasha Tudor | All rights reserved. No part of this book may be reproduced in any form without written | permission from the publisher, except for brief passages included in a review appearing in a | newspaper or magazine. Printed in the United States of America. | Designed by Jack Jaget]

COVER: Gilt spine lettering: TAKE JOY! Tasha Tudor <u>Collins</u>.

DUST JACKET: Front flap: <u>$9.95</u>; <u>there is not a (continued) note</u> ; bottom of the flap is slightly clipped. Back flap for the first time has <u>a photograph of Tudor</u> holding a corgi in her left arm and drawing. Reset black text: [photograph] | Photography by Ulrike Welsch | **TASHA TUDOR** is the well-known | illustrator of many books for young | people, including Kenneth Grahame's | *The Wind in the Willows.* and Louisa | May Alcott's *Little Women.* A native | <u>New Englander</u>, she <u>now</u> lives in <u>Vermont</u>. ¶ The Tudor family's Christmas cele- | bration is justly famous. It begins with | the hanging of the Advent calendars | made each year by Tasha Tudor for | her children <u>and grandchildren</u>. In the | days preceding Christmas, homemade | gifts and decorations are prepared with | loving care, cookies and cakes are | baked, the crèche is set up, the tree is |

357

brought in from their own stand of fir | trees. Finally, neighbors and friends | are invited to sing carols and to see a | marionette performance of a Christmas | play with puppets the Tudor family | have made themselves. ¶ In this book one of America's best- | loved artists shares with readers her | own delight in the most joyous of all seasons. | [Publisher's emblem] | COLLINS [emblem and name red].

CONTENTS: Page [158]: TASHA TUDOR is the very popular author and illustrator of many | beautiful books for children. Although born in Boston, she was | brought up on a farm in Connecticut and has never lost her | love for country life. She paints animals and children with the | warmth and delicate charm that have become her trademarks. | Tasha Tudor follows in the artistic footsteps of her parents; her | mother was Rosamond Tudor, the portrait painter, and her | father, W. Starling Burgess, was a famous yacht designer. Tasha | Tudor studied art in London and at the Boston Museum School | of Fine Arts. | With her own family, she lived for many years in New | Hampshire. Now she lives in a lovely cottage of her own de- | [2nd column] sign in a pleasantly secluded area of Vermont. Her children | and grandchildren live nearby. When she is not busy entertain- | ing visiting friends and relatives, Tasha Tudor tends the green- | house and gardens and looks after the many resident animals | which at various times have included ducks, geese, cows, horses, | birds, goats, pigs, dogs and cats—all "members of the family." | Part of each day, she writes and paints at a large and pleasantly | cluttered table, permanently set up at one end of her sitting | room where she can enjoy from her window a view of gardens, | fields and woods. Yet, somehow, she always finds time for the | fun of preparing for festive traditional family celebrations and | for enjoying seasonal delights.

OTHER: Error persists on Table of Contents referring to INDEX and ABOUT THE ARTIST. Margaret Coval of Denver, Colorado (*The LETTER*, 6:1, Fall 1986, page 8) notes this is the last printing to refer to Keithen's, Sudbury, Pa. on page 140. This source of "clear toys," a sparkling candy made from pure barley sugar, changes in the next printing. Page [160]: 8.

T20 _____ . . . . PHILOMEL BOOKS [black] [COPYRIGHT ACKNOWLEDGEMENTS || The editor and Philomel Books herewith render thanks to the follow-...help in preparing this volume. || Published by Philomel Books, The Putnam Publishing Group | 200 Madison Ave., New York, N.Y. 10016 | Library of Congress Cataloging in Publication Data | Tudor...79-12981 | ISBN 0-399-20766-X (Previous ISBN 0-529-04962-7) | ISBN 0-399-61169-X lib. bdg. (Previous ISBN 0-529-00208-6 lib. bdg.) | 150780 | Text copyright © 1966 by The World Publishing Company | Illustrations copyright © 1966 by Tasha Tudor | All rights reserved. No part of this book may be reproduced in any form without written | permission from the publisher, except for brief passages included in a review appearing in | a newspaper or magazine. Printed in the United States of America. | Designed by Jack Jaget.]

COVER: Gilt spine lettering: TAKE JOY! **Tasha Tudor Philomel**.

DUST JACKET: Spine: **Tasha | Tudor** [black] | TAKE JOY! [red] | [tree in circle logo] | **Philomel** [black] Jacket lower right back, ISBN 0-399-20766-X | ISBN 0-399-61169-X (GB). Front flap has new heading: ISBN 0-399-20766-X $10.95 | The Tasha Tudor | . . . Clipped bottom corner removed part of last line: ISBN 0-399-61169. Back flap publisher statement: PHILOMEL BOOKS | are published by | The Putnam Publishing Group | 200 Madison Ave., New York, NY 10016.

CONTENTS: Page [2]: *Also Illustrated by Tasha Tudor | A Book of Christmas | Carrie's Gift* by Efner Tudor Holmes | *Little Women* by Louisa May Alcott | *The Wind in the Willows* by Kenneth Grahame || *About Tasha Tudor | Drawn from New England: Tasha Tudor, | A Portrait in Words and Pictures* by Bethany Tudor. Page [160] is blank

OTHER: Errors persist in Table of Contents references to INDEX and ABOUT THE AUTHOR. The source for the "clear toys" discussed on page 140 is now listed as Murray's Dairy Store, Watsontown, PA . (*The LETTER*, 6:1, Fall 1986, page 8).

T21 _____. [COPYRIGHT...help in preparing this volume. || Published by <u>Philomel Books, The Putnam Publishing Group</u> | <u>51 Madison Ave., New York, N.Y. 10010</u> | <u>Published simultaneously in Canada by</u> | <u>General Publishing Co., Ltd., Toronto</u> | Library of Congress Cataloging in Publication Data | Tudor...79-12981 | <u>ISBN 0-399-20766-X</u> | 161082 | Text copyright © 1966 by The World Publishing Company | Illustrations copyright © 1966 by Tasha Tudor | All rights reserved. No part of this book may be reproduced in any form without written | permission from the publisher, except for brief passages included in a review appearing in | a newspaper or magazine. Printed in the United States of America. | Designed by Jack Jaget]

    PAGINATION: Yellow-white paper.

    COVER: Ivory endpapers.

    DUST JACKET: Spine: **Tasha | Tudor** [black] | TAKE JOY! [red] | [<u>bird in circle logo</u>] Philomel [black]. '<u>Computer type</u>' ISBN 0-399-20766-X on lower right back beneath illustration. Front flap: The Tasha Tudor | Christmas Book [black]... [Last line in computer type]: ISBN 0-399-20766-X >$ 12.95. <u>Corners are complete</u>. Back flap publisher's statement: PHILOMEL BOOKS | <u>*a division of*</u> | The Putnam Publishing Group | <u>51 Madison Ave., New York, NY 10010</u>.

    CONTENTS: The colophon has been reset in a smaller type size so that "All rights reserved. . ." line measures 4 ¼″ against the previous 5 1/16″

T22 _____.

    DUST JACKET: Front flap last line . . . >$ 14.95. <u>Corners are not clipped</u>

    CONTENTS: Page [2] : *Also Illustrated by Tasha Tudor* | *A Book of Christmas* | <u>*A Christmas Village*</u> | *Carrie's Gift* by Efner Tudor Holmes | *Little Women* by Louisa May Alcott | <u>*Rosemary for Remembrance, A Keepsake Book*</u> | *The Wind in the Willows* by Kenneth Grahame || <u>*Edited and Illustrated by Tasha Tudor*</u> | *All For Love* || *About Tasha Tudor* | *Drawn from New England: Tasha Tudor, A* | *Portrait in Words and Pictures* by Bethany Tudor.

T23 _____.

    PAGINATION: Another state on <u>ivory</u> paper.

    DUST JACKET: Price may have been <u>$15.95?</u> Have not examined a copy with price intact in upper corner. Front flap bottom left: square 'computer' type face, ISBN 0-399-20766-X, [without price].

T24 _____.

    DUST JACKET: Upper front flap: <u>$16.95 [line] ($23.95CAN</u>).

T25 _____. [Have not examined a fourth printing.]

T26 _____. [Have not examined a fifth printing.]

T27 _____. [COPYRIGHT...Illustrations copyright © 1966 by Tasha Tudor. | Published by Philomel Books, a division of The Putnam | & Grosset Group, <u>200 Madison Avenue</u>, New York, NY | 10016. Published simultaneously in Canada. | All rights reserved. Book design by Jack Jaget. | <u>Printed in Hong Kong by Wing King Tong</u>. | <u>Sixth</u> impression]

PAGINATION: White paper.

COVER: <u>Gloss film laminate over white paper</u> printed with previous dust jacket illustration. Lower right back: ISBN 0-399-20766-X | [two bar codes] | <u>90000</u> above the smaller right bar code and <u>9 780399 207662</u> below the larger left bar code.

DUST JACKET: Front flap upper right: <u>$18.95</u> | [rule] | <u>$24.95(CAN)</u>. Black flap additional wording above company name: . . . seasons. || *Jacket art © 1966 by Tasha Tudor* | *[rule]* | *Reinforced for Library use* || PHILOMEL BOOKS | a division of The Putnam & Grosset Group | <u>200 Madison Avenue,</u> New York, NY <u>10016</u>.

OTHER: Page [160] is blank.

T28   _____. [COPYRIGHT...Printed in Hong Kong by Wing King Tong. | <u>SEVENTH IMPRESSION</u>]

COVER: A single bar code on back above: 0 48228 20766 5.

DUST JACKET: Have not examined one with price intact, but probably as above.

T29   _____. [COPYRIGHT...Printed in Hong Kong by Wing King Tong. | <u>9 10 8</u>.]

T30   _____. [COPYRIGHT...Printed in Hong Kong by Wing King Tong. | <u>9 10</u>.]

T31   _____. . . . <u>LUTTERWORTH PRESS / LONDON</u> [blue] [COPYRIGHT ACKNOWLEDGEMENTS || The editor and <u>Lutterworth Press</u> herewith render thanks to the following | authors, publishers, and agents whose interest, co-operation, and permission | to reprint have made possible the preparation of *Take Joy: The Tasha Tudor* | *Christmas Book*. All possible care has been taken to trace the ownership of | every selection included and to make full acknowledgment for its use. If | any errors have accidentally occurred, they will be corrected in subsequent | editions, provided notification is sent to the publishers. || Charles Scribner's Sons, for "To His Saviour, a Child, a Prcscnt by a | Child" by Robert Herrick. Reprinted by permission of Charles Scribner's | Sons. | Columbia University Press, for "Noel Sing We" from *Early English* | *Christmas Carols* edited by Rossell H. Robbins. Reprinted by permission of| Columbia University Press. | D. E. Collins, and Messrs. J. M. Dent and Sons, Ltd., and Dodd, Mead | and Co., for "A Christmas Carol" by G. K. Chesterton from *The Wild* | *Knight and Other Poems*. Reprinted by permission of D. E. Collins, Messrs. | J. M. Dent and Sons, Ltd., and Dodd, Mead and Co. | Doubleday & Company, Inc., for "The Gift of the Magi" from *The Four* | *Million* by O. Henry. Reprinted by permission of Doubleday & Company, Inc. | Flensted Publishers, for R. P. Keigwin's translation of "The Fir Tree" by | Hans Christian Andersen. Reprinted by permission of Flensted Publishers, | Odense, Denmark. | Harper & Row, Publishers, Inc., for "The Caravan" from *This Way to* | *Christmas* by Ruth Sawyer, copyright 1916 by Harper & Row, Publishers, [next column] Inc. Renewal, 1944, by Ruth Sawyer Durand. Reprinted by permission of| Harper & Row, Publishers, Inc. | Harry and Eleanor Farjeon, for their poem "Our Brother is Born." Re- | printed by permission of the authors. | The Macmillan Company, for "Christmas in London" from *Little Dog* | *Toby* by Rachel Field, copyright 1928 by The Macmillan Company. Re- | printed by permission of The Macmillan Company. | New Directions Publishing Corporation, J. M. Dent and Sons, Ltd., and | the Literary Executors of the Dylan Thomas Estate, for an excerpt from | *A Child's Christmas in Wales* by Dylan Thomas, copyright 1954 by New | Directions. Reprinted by permission of the publishers, New Directions Pub- | lishing Corporation, J. M. Dent and Sons, Ltd., and the Literary Executors | of the Dylan Thomas Estate. | Nora Burglon, for "The Christmas Coin." Reprinted by permission of | the author. | Schmitt, Hall & McCreary Company, publishers, for "Here We Come | A-Caroling" arranged by Torstein O. Kvamme from *The Christmas Caroler's* | *Book in Song and Story*. Reprinted by permission of Schmitt, Hall & Mc- | Creary Company, Minneapolis, Minnesota. | The World Publishing Company, for "The Twelve Days of Christmas" | from *Best Loved Songs and Hymns* edited by James Morehead and Albert | Morehead, copyright 1965 by James Morehead. Reprinted by permission of | The World Publishing Company. || The author also wishes to thank Wendy Worth and Joan Knight for their | help in preparing this volume. || <u>First published in Great Britain 1967</u> | Text copyright © 1966 by The World Publishing Company | Illustrations copyright © 1966 by Tasha Tudor | All rights reserved. No part of this book may be reproduced in any form without written | permission from the publisher, except for brief passages included in a review appearing in a | newspaper or magazine. Printed in the United States of America. | Designed by Jack Jaget] Page [160]: blank.

PAGINATION: Ten signatures of ivory paper: [1-8] 9-18 [19] 20-34 [35] 36-42 [43] 44-157 [158-160], plus endpapers. 8 1/2″ x 11 1/8″.

COVER: Blue paper over board imprinted with weave design. Navy stamping on front: TAKE JOY! | TASHA TUDOR Spine stamped in gold: TAKE JOY! *Tasha Tudor* LUTTERWORTH. Yellow-green end papers with two pencil sketches as before: wren on left, and field mouse on right, each in a holly wreath within a larger single-line border, holly at corners. Repeated on back end papers

DUST JACKET: Deeper blue than the American edition, nearing violet, same illustrations. A1199 in white at lower right back. Spine: [holly] | **Tasha** | **Tudor** [yellow] | TAKE JOY! [laterally, red] | **Lutter-** | **worth** [red on a white band] [holly]. Front flap lower corner clipped; have not examined a copy with price intact. | Take Joy! | The Tasha Tudor | Christmas Book | *Selected, edited, and illustrated by* | TASHA TUDOR [red, remaining text black and reset from American ed.] || This beautiful book is Tasha Tudor's gift | to everyone who loves Christmas. From | a wide range of sources this famous and | beloved artist has chosen a richly varied | collection of poems, carols, stories, leg- | ends, and even Christmas recipes and | decorations. ¶ Among the many selections are tra- | ditional favourites like "Away in a | Manger", Hans Christian Andersen's | story of "The Little Fir Tree", and "The | Cratchits' Christmas Dinner" from *The* | *Christmas Carol*, as well as the Biblical | account of the Nativity. Less familiar are | poems by Shakespeare, Blake, and Her- | rick, Christmas stories by Selma Lagerlöf, | Ruth Sawyer, and Dylan Thomas (to | name but a few), and some little-known, | very moving carols. There is an exquisite | poem by Rumer Godden, never before | published, written for Tasha Tudor's | children. And there are wonderful reci- | pes from the artist's own family cook- | book for delicious holiday treats. ¶ The many full-colour and black-and- | white pictures in this book are aglow | with the tenderness, reverence, and | beauty for which Tasha Tudor's work is | known, and her selections celebrate all | the joys of the season, both religious and | secular. This is truly a book for all mem- | bers of the family, young and old, one | that will be read and reread and cher- | ished for many years. Back flap: TASHA TUDOR [red, as is the publisher, remaining blurb is black] is the well-known | illustrator of many books for young peo- | ple, including the much loved little | books, *First Prayers* and *First Carols*. ¶ The Tudor family's Christmas celebra- | tion is justly famous. It begins with the | hanging of the Advent calendars made | each year by Tasha Tudor for her four | children. In the days preceding Christ- | mas, homemade gifts and decorations | are prepared with loving care, biscuits | and cakes are baked, the crèche is set | up, the tree is brought in from their own | stand of fir trees. Finally, neighbours and | friends are invited to sing carols and to | see a marionette performance of a Christ- | mas play with puppets the Tudor family | have made themselves. ¶ In this book Tasha Tudor shares with | readers her own delight in the most joy- | ous of all seasons. [black] || LUTTERWORTH PRESS [red]

ILLUSTRATIONS: As before.

CONTENTS: Title page: Take Joy! [and] TASHA TUDOR in red; rest of text in blue. Half-title, p. [1]. "For Ann Beneduce," p. [7]. Table of contents incorrectly lists INDEX on page 156, and ABOUT THE AUTHOR, page 158. The index is printed on pages 155-157. Page [158] contains two paragraphs: ABOUT THE ARTIST || TASHA TUDOR is the very popular author and illustrator of many | beautiful books for children. Although born in Boston, she was | brought up on a farm in Connecticut and has never lost her love | for country life. She paints animals and children with a warmth | and delicate charm that have become her trademarks. Tasha | Tudor follows in the artistic footsteps of her parents; her mother | was Rosamond Tudor, the portrait painter, and her father, W. | Starling Burgess, was a famous yacht designer. Tasha Tudor | studied art in London and at the Boston Museum School of Fine | Arts. ¶ Now, with her own family, she lives in a lovely old red frame [second column] farmhouse in New Hampshire. When she is not busy being a | housewife and mother and entertaining visiting friends and rela- |

tives, Tasha Tudor tends the greenhouse and gardens and looks | after the many farm animals—among them ducks, geese, cows, | horses, dogs and cats—all "members of the family." Part of each | day, she writes and paints at a large and pleasantly cluttered table, | permanently set up at one end of her kitchen, where she can | enjoy from her window a view of gardens, fields and woods. | Yet, somehow, she always finds time for the fun of preparing for | festive traditional family celebrations and for enjoying seasonal | delights.

T32 TAKE JOY! THE WORLD OF TASHA TUDOR [red] | AN EXHIBIT AND RELATED PROGRAMS AT | COLONIAL WILLIAMSBURG | ABBY ALDRICH ROCKEFELLER FOLK ART CENTER | NOVEMBER 2, 1996 TO APRIL 6, 1997 [gray].

PAGINATION: [4] pp. brown cover stock, folded in half as advertising mailer. 16 x 5 ½"

ILLUSTRATIONS: Six color, mixed. Richard Brown photographs of Tudor in fine lace, and sewing beside her fireplace, a goat toy. Two photographs of Williamsburg gates, one with Tudor. A 3 ½ x 4" reproduction in color of an unpublished Advent calendar. Image of a yellow frame "Tweedies General Store", with a gas pump, resembles that at Webster, N.H.

OTHER: Postmarked from Colonial Williamsburg, September 16, 1996

T33 " *Take Joy!* | *The World of* | *Tasha Tudor*" [red, within a red rule frame] [no date, 1996]

PAGINATION: [4] pp. plastic press folder. 6 5/8 x 4 3/8"

ILLUSTRATIONS: Six color transparencies, nos. 1, 4, 5, courtesy of Richard Brown, nos. 2, 3, 6, courtesy of Colonial Williamsburg. These titles and a brief paragraph explaining each: 1. Hands with miniature letters, 2. Copper tea kettle, 3. Valentine's Day card, 4. Marionettes, 5. Emma and Thaddeus in dollhouse, 6. Watercolor of Christmas scene. Item 3 pictures the famous heart shaped valentine with nine flower pots. The nine separate flowers are displayed beside the card. Item 6 is the painting from *A Time To Keep*, "December": We lighted the Advent Wreath and had St. Nicholas cake for tea. All the art for *A Time To Keep* [the Rand McNally book] was exhibited at Williamsburg.

T34 FOR 60 YEARS TASHA TUDOR'S WORK HAS FILLED | STORYBOOKS. NOW IT'S FILLING A MUSEUM. [TAKE JOY! THE WORLD OF TASHA TUDOR | AN EXHIBIT AND RELATED PROGRAMS AT | COLONIAL WILLIAMSBURG | ABBY ALDRICH ROCKEFELLER FOLK ART CENTER | NOVEMBER 2, 1996 TO APRIL 6, 1997].

PAGINATION: [10] pp. tan paper accordion-folded, an advertising piece. 4 ¼ x 6 ¼" folded from 21 x 6 ¼"

ILLUSTRATIONS: Five color, mixed. Richard Brown photograph of Tudor in fine lace, a toy goat, paintings of tree and geese, children at a tea party and a tray after tea.

OTHER: Undated, but obviously mailed in advance of the events.

T35 FINAL PROGRAM AND INFORMATION | **Take Joy!** | THE WORLD OF | *Tasha Tudor* || [drawing of a corgi driving a goat-drawn buckboard toward a signpost heading towards Williamsburg, and away from Vermont.] || TAKE JOY! THE WORLD OF TASHA TUDOR | SEMINAR | NOVEMBER 1-3, 1996 || Hennage Auditorium | DeWitt Wallace Decorative Arts Gallery | *Williamsburg* | INSTITUTE.

PAGINATION: [12] pp. cream paper stapled into cream cover stock. 8 ½ x 5 ½″

COVER: Cream cover stock is the title page, quoted above. Back, plain.

ILLUSTRATIONS: Only that line drawing described on the title page.

CONTENTS: THIS PROGRAM BELONGS TO ‖ [rule], page [1]. TAKE JOY! THE WORLD OF TASHA TUDOR | SEMINAR, pp. [2-5]. TAKE JOY! THE WORLD OF TASHA TUDOR | SEMINAR INFORMATION, p. [6]: Please wear your … badge at all times … Exhibition Buildings and Historic Trade Sites, Lost and Found, Patriot's Passes. TAKE JOY! THE WORLD OF TASHA TUDOR | SEMINAR REGISTRANTS, pp. [7-11].   Please direct questions and comments concerning this program | to: ‖ Tasha Tudor Seminar … NOTES, pp. [12] and inside back cover.

OTHER: The Colonial Williamsburg three-day seminar included these events: world premiere of the videotape *Take Joy: The Magical World of Tasha Tudor,* opening dinner featuring recipes from *The Tasha Tudor Cookbook*, "That the Future May Learn from the Past: Perspectives on Colonial Williamsburg and Tasha Tudor," "Tasha Comes to Williamsburg," "Pinafores to Party Gowns: Inspirations from Tasha Tudor's Period Costumes," "Tasha Tudor Sits for a Silhouette," children's rare book fair, silhouette-cutting studio, "The Pursuit of Happiness," "Preview from Corgi Cottage Industries," "1830s Sisters," and book signing by Tudor. Participants included Carolyn Weekley, William Barker, Liza Guzler and Jan Gilliam of Colonial Williamsburg, Joan DeGusto, Nel and Helen Laughon, Harry Davis, Donna M. Swajeski, and Amelia Stauffer.

T36 **Take Joy!** | THE WORLD OF | Tasha Tudor | [corgi driving to Williamsburg]

PAGINATION: [4] pp. white linen cover stock. 5 x 6 15/16″

COVER: Quoted above. Back, plain.

ILLUSTRATIONS: The single black line drawing described on dinner menu folder for Friday November 1, 1996, with Nanny T.'s fish chowder and Barbara von Trapp's chocolate torte.

T37 **Take Joy!** | THE WORLD OF | Tasha Tudor | [corgi driving to Williamsburg] | A FAMILY GUIDE TO THE EXHIBIT ‖ ABBY ALDRICH ROCKEFELLER | FOLK ART CENTER ‖ NOVEMBER 2, 1996-APRIL 6, 1997 ‖ COLONIAL WILLIAMSBURG [teal].

PAGINATION: [6] pp. buff granite paper tri-fold brochure. 8 ¼ x 16 ½″

COVER: Quoted above.

ILLUSTRATIONS: Reproductions of seven line drawings and three photographs, including "Tasha's great-aunt's playhouse. This brochure was distributed to visitors to the exhibit.

T38 *Take Peace* | A Corgi Cottage Christmas | With Tasha Tudor ‖ Directed & Written by | Sarah Kerruish ‖ Executive Producer | Harry Davis ‖ Directors of Photography | David Collier | Dusty Powers ‖ Editor | Kiki Tourme ‖ Additional Editing | John Douglas White ‖ Original Music Composed & Performed By | David J. Reading ‖ Animation | David Delp | Lighting | John Chater | Tom Scott ‖ Sound | Howard Shack ‖ Carols Performed By | Vicki Lyle ‖ Production Designer | Jim Orum ‖ On-Line Editor | David Scott Smith ‖ Re-Recording Mixer | Lisa Baro ‖ IMC Animation | Carols Cabrales ‖ Production Executives | Peyton Wilson | Steve White ‖ Production Assistant | Deidre Snow Woo ‖ Marketing Director | Erica Durbin ‖ Production Accounting | Pamela Ball ‖ Legal Services | Richard Solomon ‖

Title Design | Anya Bruno || Photographer | Richard R. Brown || Equipment Donated By | Guy Jaconelli | The HB Group Inc. || Special Thanks to: | Colonel Tom and Eun In Tudor [*sic*] | Bethany Tudor | Bill & Jill Kerruish | Eleanor Jarret | Margaret Sudduth | Steve Jarrett | Whetstone Inn | Jennifer Ward || © Spellbound Productions, Inc.   [1997] 45 minute VHS videotape

> COVER: Gray-green pasteboard sleeve open at the bottom for inserting the videocassette. Sealed in plastic shrink-wrap by the manufacturer. Printing on the sleeve is largely white with ice-blue highlights to 'Tasha Tudor' and 'Spellbound Productions' [on the back]. Front: *T*AKE *P*EACE || [oval photograph of tudor hanging a gingerbread ornament on a tree as two girls look on] || A CORGI COTTAGE CHRISTMAS | *with* | TASHA TUDOR.   Top of slipcase: *T*AKE *P*EACE | A CORGI COTTAGE CHRISTMAS | *with* TASHA TUDOR. Both side panels repeat this text in one line laterally down the case. Back: [Santa driving sleight] | ✳ | *Rekindle the true spirit of Christmas with | a visit to the magical world of Tasha Tudor. For | over fifty years author/illustrator Tasha Tudor has | delighted generations of children and their parents | with her books, advent [sic] calendars, and Christmas | cards. Now you can step into her storybook world | and experience all the joys of a Corgi Cottage | Christmas. Hear Tasha read from 'A Night Before | Christmas' and see her latest illustrations of this | Christmas classic. Learn how to make a wreath, | Christmas cookie ornaments, and a yuletide feast. | Enjoy the beauty of winter in Vermont...and | remember that time in your life when magic was | real and anything seemed possible.* || [Santa and corgi shaking hands/paws] [painting of back of a village church, etc.] || Produced by Spellbound Productions | in association with | Corgi Cottage Industries || © Spellbound Productions, 539 Broadway, S.F. CA. 94133, tel. 415-352-1550.

> CASSETTE: Videocassette label (1 7/8″ x 3″) has pencil sketch of raindeer in harness, on which is overprinted, black ink, applied to the 4″ x 7 3/8″ black plastic videocassette: *T*AKE *P*EACE | A CORGI COTTAGE CHRISTMAS | *with* | **TASHA TUDOR.** The same legend is printed on a side label ¾″ x 5 ¾″.

> OTHER: Kerruish premiered Spellbound's *Take Joy!* videotape in early November 1996 during the opening weekend of a six-month retrospective of Tudor's art and life-style at the Abby Aldrich Rockefeller Folk Art Center, Colonial Williamsburg, Virginia.   Live shoots for a subsequent Christmas videotape were filmed in Vermont in December 1996. Tudor appears here with Corgi Cottage Industries personnel Harry Davis and Jim Journigan, children Tom and Bethany Tudor and Tom's wife Eun Im, plus assorted children. The final product was distributed in late November 1997.
>
> Cellar Door Books loaned books and Christmas cards used for stills in the videotape. However, Corgi Cottage Industries would not allow the videotape to be released with credit given for this courtesy. (Letter, Kerruish to Hare, 12/03/97)

T39 A | TALE | FOR | EASTER [green] || BY | TASHA TUDOR || *OXFORD UNIVERSITY PRESS* | *London New York Toronto* [black] [*Copyright 1941 | Oxford University Press | New York, Inc.* || *Calligraphy by Hilda Scott | Printed in the United States of America*]

> PAGINATION: [36] pp. in two signatures plus endpapers. 6 11/16″ x 6 3/16″ with square spine. Seventeen stitches, saddle-sewn.[Morgan Library copy matches]

COVER: Mint green cloth with a 3 3/4″ x 2 3/32″ semicircular paste-down label on front: A | TALE | FOR | EASTER [in green letters outlined in black] || BY | TASHA TUDOR [black] and flower decorations.

DUST JACKET: Ivory paper slightly discolored on the back from chemicals in the cloth, evident by the whiter mask of the front cover label. Dj front illustrated with a large oval floral and green garland being tied at the top by two blue birds. The garland rises from a fawn, two rabbits, two ducks amid spring flowers and encircles A | TALE | FOR | EASTER, in green letters outlined in black. Centered on back is a one-inch clump of crocus. Front flap, text black: A TALE | FOR EASTER | *By Tasha Tudor* || *If you have been very good all year on* | *the night before Easter you have lovely* | *dreams about ducks and rabbits and a* | *fawn who takes you on a magic ride.* | *When you wake up you are you again* | *and it was a dream but you may find eggs* | *in your best bonnet or an Easter bunny in* | *grandma's rocking chair. Anything may* | *happen on Easter.* || *** || OXFORD BOOKS | FOR BOYS AND GIRLS || *** || 40-80 $1.00. Back flap: *The "Calico" Books* | *by Tasha Tudor* || *Tiny pocket size books, bound in* | *printed polka dot cloth with exquisite* | *pictures in color about little Sylvie Ann.* || *** || *PUMPKIN MOONSHINE* | *A Hallowe'en adventure.* || *** || *ALEXANDER THE GANDER* | *Sylvie Ann has trouble with* *Alexander* | *and the heliotrope pansies.* || *** || *THE COUNTY FAIR* | *Sylvie Ann and her brother spend a* | *successful day at the fair.* || *** || Each 75c

ILLUSTRATIONS: All in color, those on versos are larger and more detailed than those on recto pages. Page [1] is title page. Page [3] is dedication *TO* | *LITTLE* | *ANN* | *NEWELL* within a green ribbon garland, a yellow duckling and 6 daffodils. No illustration on the colophon page [2]; pp. [34-36] are blank. Ivory endpapers; a different flowering Spring bulb is centered on each; grape hyacinths in each corner of each endpaper.

OTHER: Examined a copy inscribed "A Joyous Easter 1941."

PIERPONT MORGAN LIBRARY owns an identical copy bearing the 1 11/16″ x 2 3/32″ bookplate of their trustee Julia Parker Wightman. Gold imprint of three medieval kings riding two horses through a wood to the left in a large outlined panel. Ms. Wightman's name appears below the illustration in a smaller panel. The whole is enclosed in a single line frame. The dust jacket doesn't exhibit the amount of discoloration evident in SNOW BEFORE CHRISTMAS. JPW:3881

COPYRIGHT REGISTRATION: A 151307 granted to Oxford University Press, Inc., 114 Fifth Ave., NY, NY.

A TALE FOR EASTER by Tasha Tudor, a United States citizen, was published March 13, 1941. The book was manufactured by Colorgraphic Offset Co., NY, NY. Deposit copies received at LC March 14, 1941; affidavit received March 15, 1941.

COPYRIGHT RENEWAL REGISTRATION: R 454415 granted to Tasha Tudor, Route 1, Contoocook, N.H. 03229, claiming as author. Patricia C. Lord swears:

A TALE FOR EASTER by Tasha Tudor, was originally published March 13, 1941. The original copyright claimant was Oxford University Press [assigned to Henry Z. Walck, Inc.] [*sic*]. Fees charged to account 6694. Walck (Henry Z.) Inc., 19 Union Square West, NY, NY 10003. Renewal application received Jan 27, 1969.

T40 _____.

PAGINATION: <u>Buff paper</u>. Seventeen stitches, saddle-sewn.

DUST JACKET: Have not examined a copy.

T41 _____.

> PAGINATION: Eight stitches saddle-sewn.
>
> COVER: <u>Light green buckram-weave paper</u> over boards, paper label on front.
>
> DUST JACKET: Have not examined a copy with price intact. Front label masked in the general acidic discoloration. Greens are olive, not bright as before.

T42 _____.

> PAGINATION: <u>Ivory</u> paper oversewn. Ten stitches, oversewn.
>
> COVER: <u>Courser weave light green cloth</u> over boards, paper label on front.
>
> DUST JACKET: Have not examined a copy.

T43 _____.

> PAGINATION: [36] pp. in two signatures, <u>thin buff war-time paper</u>, plus endpapers. 6 11/16″ x 6 1/8″. Twelve stitches, saddle sewn.
>
> COVER: <u>Dark green cloth</u> with paste-down label, rounded spine.

T44 _____. Have not examined a second printing.

T45 _____. [*Copyright 1941* I *Oxford University Press* I *New York, Inc.* II <u>Third printing, 1943</u> II *Calligraphy by Hilda Scott* I *Printed in the United States of America.*]

> PAGINATION: Two signatures, thin buff paper. 6 ¾″ x 6 3/8″.
>
> COVER: <u>Mauve linen</u> over boards, same paste-down. Crimped, rounded spine.
>
> DUST JACKET: In the lower right of front flap: <u>$1.00.</u>

T46 _____.

> PAGINATION: Buff paper. 6 11/16″ x 6 1/8″. Nineteen stitches, saddle sewn.
>
> COVER: <u>Mint green cloth, square spine.</u>

T47 _____.

> PAGINATION: Nineteen stitches, saddle sewn.
>
> COVER: <u>Mint paper over boards</u>, square spine.
>
> DUST JACKET: Have not examined one with price intact.

T48 _____. Have not examined a fourth printing.

T49 _____. Have not examined a fifth printing.

T50 _____. [*Copyright 1941* | *Oxford University Press* | *New York, Inc.* || <u>**SIXTH PRINTING   1947**</u> || *Calligraphy by Hilda Scott* | *Printed in the United States of America.*]

    PAGINATION: Two signatures 6 3/4″ x 6 1/16″.

    COVER: <u>Green cloth</u> over boards, paste-down label. Crimped rounded spine.

    DUST JACKET: Front flap, lower right: <u>$1.25 [in a new typeface]</u>.

T51 _____. [*Copyright 1941* | *Oxford University Press* | *New York, Inc.* || <u>**SEVENTH PRINTING   1949**</u> || *Calligraphy by Hilda Scott* | *Printed in the United States of America*]

    COVER: <u>Green paper, buckram weave imprint</u> over boards. Square spine. 6 13/16″ x 6 1/4″.   Square spine.

    DUST JACKET: Last line, front flap: 40-80   <u>$1.50</u>.   Examined a copy wherein the price of the calico books on the back flap has been adjusted in ball point pen from 75 cents to 1.00. This was probably done by personnel at The Ginger & Pickles Store since the the book bears that shop label.

    OTHER: Slightly out of registration on ffep, pp. [4-5, 8-9, 12-13, 25, 26-27]. Examined a copy with the Contoocook shop label at top left inside back cover and autographed cursive on ffep below the daffodil.

T52 _____. Henry Z. Walck, Inc.

    COVER: Have not examined one.

    DUST JACKET: Front as above. Spine: TUDOR ✳ A TALE FOR EASTER ✳ <u>WALCK</u>. Front flap: the former Oxford statement now reads, . . . ✳✳✳ || <u>HENRY Z. WALCK, INC.</u> | *Successor to* | OXFORD BOOKS FOR BOYS AND GIRLS | ✳✳✳ || 40-80   <u>$ 2.75</u>. The back flap prints the same list of Tudor books, lower on the flap, <u>without price</u>.

    OTHER: Examined this dust jacket without a book.

T53 Ａ | ＴＡＬＥ | ＦＯＲ | ＥＡＳＴＥＲ [green] || BY | TASHA TUDOR || *HENRY Z. WALCK, Inc.* *New York* [black] [*© Henry Z. Walck, Inc., 1941* || *Calligraphy by Hilda Scott* | *Printed in the United States of America*]

    PAGINATION: [40] pp. topsewn in one signature, including end papers. 6 3/4″ x 6 1/4″

    COVER: <u>A light green</u> cloth with front pastedown semi-circular label as before. Inner corner decorations of endpapers are partially obscured by the top sewing.

    DUST JACKET: Ivory jacket illustrated as before with changed text. Front flap: <u>$2.75</u> [at upper right] || A TALE . . . *happen on Easter*. || ✳✳✳ || HENRY Z. WALCK, INC. | [a <u>heavy printer's bar device cancels</u> *Successor to*.] || ✳✳✳ || 40-80   [Lower corner clipped.] Back flap: TWO NEW EDITIONS OF | TASHA TUDOR FAVORITES || PUMPKIN MOONSHINE | *"A reissue of Miss Tudor's Hallowe'en* | *classic, first published in 1938, the tale* | *of a little girl who looked for the biggest* | *pumpkin on the farm to make a pumpkin* | *moonshine. . . . Little children will love* | *Miss Tudor's delicately colored illustra-* | *tions, and parents won't mind reading her* | *story aloud more than once."* | —Publisher's Weekly || ALEXANDER THE GANDER | *"...now in somewhat larger format than* | *the original (1939). Typical Tudor illus-* | *trations lend nostalgic charm to this story* | *of a gander's fondness for heliotrope pan-* | *sies and its consequences."* —Chicago Tribune || ✳✳✳

    CONTENTS: Pages [2, 36-39] are blank.

OTHER: Examined a copy inscribed Easter <u>1966</u>.

T54 _____. [<u>COPYRIGHT 1941</u> | HENRY Z. WALCK, INC. | COPYRIGHT © RENEWED 1969 BY TASHA TUDOR ||
<u>STANDARD BOOK NUMBER: 8098-1008-5</u> | <u>LIBRARY OF CONGRESS CATALOG CARD NUMBER: A62-8626</u> || *Calligraphy by*
Hilda Scott | *Printed in the United States of America*]

COVER: Light green cloth, <u>gilt stamping</u> on spine only.

DUST JACKET: Clipped, no price; but 40-80 at bottom of front flap.

OTHER: An acquisition date penciled on page [5] of the New York Public Library, Donnell Branch
copy: DCH <u>2/25/71</u>, indicating this printing was distributed in early 1971.

T55 _____. [COPYRIGHT 1941 HENRY Z. WALCK, INC. | COPYRIGHT © RENEWED 1969 BY TASHA TUDOR | ISBN: 0-8098-
1008-5 (HARDCOVER) | ISBN: 0-8098-1807-8 (PAPERBACK) | LIBRARY OF CONGRESS CATALOG CARD NUMBER A62-8626 ||
Calligraphy by Hilda Scott | *Printed in the United States of America*]

PAGINATION: [40] pp. including endpapers topsewn in three signatures of rich creamy kid finish
paper. <u>Flowers have been eliminated from corners of endpapers.</u> <u>6 3/4″ x 6 1/8″</u>.

COVER: <u>Mint green</u> cloth. This is the first issue <u>without the pastedown label.</u> Spine printed in <u>dark</u>
<u>green ink:</u> TUDOR   A TALE FOR EASTER   WALCK. Cloth <u>reinforced hinge.</u>

DUST JACKET: Front flap corners clipped. Neither the previous *Sucessor to* and the printer's bar
appear on this front flap. Back flap: OTHER HOLIDAY STORIES | BY TASHA TUDOR ||
THE DOLLS' CHRISTMAS | *"A cheerful little tale of the dolls' Christ- | mas celebration in an unusual*
doll house | large enough for foot high dolls. Little | girls thoroughly enjoy all the doll details."
|—Elementary English || PUMPKIN MOONSHINE | *"A reissue of Miss Tudor's Hallowe'en | classic,*
first published in 1938, the <u>tale of</u> | <u>a little</u> girl who looked for the biggest | pumpkin on the farm to make a
pumpkin | moonshine....Little children will love | Miss Tudor's delicately colored illustra- | tions."
—Publishers' Weekly

T56 _____.   Have not examined a paperback copy.

T57 _____. [an outlined catalog card in typewriter font] E   Tudor, Tasha | A tale for
Easter. Walck, 1941 | unp. illus. || You can never tell what might happen |
on Easter - especially if you have been | good the whole year through. || 1.
Easter - Stories   I. Title | [hole] || This Main Entry catalog card may be reproduced without permission. ||
COPYRIGHT 1941 HENRY ... *America*]

PAGINATION: [40] pp. endpapers in three signatures <u>ivory</u> kid finish paper. <u>6 3/4″ x 6 1/8″</u>

COVER: Light green cloth, cloth hinge.

T58 _____.

PAGINATION: [36] pp. perfect bound, in a paper wrapper. Pages [34-36] are blank. There is <u>no</u>
<u>endpaper design</u> inside covers. 6 <u>1/2″ x 5 7/8″</u>.

COVER: Front of wrapper has former jacket illustration. In upper right corner: <u>$ 1.50;</u> in lower right
corner: <u>$1.75 Can.,</u> both in brown ink. Spine, <u>without stars:</u> TUDOR   A TALE FOR EASTER
WALCK <u>1807</u>. Back cover in brown ink: A TALE FOR EASTER | *by Tasha Tudor* ||
"Children...take delight in the lovely childlike char- | acter of this small book which carries the thought of |
springtime....Precise in detail and exquisite in color, | Tasha Tudor's little books are truly American in

tone, | suggesting a loving observation akin to that of Beatrix | Potter." —Horn Book || Tasha Tudor was born in Boston and grew up in the | Connecticut countryside. The mother of two sons and | two daughters, she now lives in Marlboro, Vermont, | where she gardens, housekeeps, sews and cooks, in | addition to writing and illustrating many children's | books.

OTHER: After 1971, by the reference to Vermont on the back cover. The *Horn Book Magazine* citation is from v.17:3, May-June 1941, page 206.

T59 _____. | Henry Z. Walck, Inc. . New York. [Copyright © 1941 by Tasha Tudor || All rights reserved, including the right to reproduce | this book, or parts thereof, in any form, except for | the inclusion of brief quotations in a review. || Library of Congress Catalog Card Number: <u>A62-8626</u> | ISBN: 0-8098-1008-5 || 10 9 8 7 <u>6 5 4 3 2 1</u>| MANUFACTURED IN THE UNITED STATES OF AMERICA]

PAGINATION: [40]pp in two signatures, including endpapers topsewn. Pages [1-2, 38-40] are blank. The first three leaves and the last (ffep, half-title, title page, rfep) and the pasted endpapers are the same ivory paper as the dust jacket. Remaining text on a <u>white</u> paper. <u>Plain endpapers</u> have no design. Ten top-sewn stitches. <u>6 13/16" x 6 13/16"</u>.

COVER: Shiny <u>olive</u> paper over boards, distinct linen weave imprint. Black spine lettering.

DUST JACKET: <u>Ivory paper</u>, illustrated as before but the colors are washed out. Front flap: <u>$5.95</u> || A TALE | FOR EASTER | By Tasha Tudor || If you have been very good all year on | the night before Easter you have <u>|</u> lovely dreams about ducks and rabbits <u>|</u> and a fawn who takes you on a magic <u>|</u> ride. When you wake up you <u>will be |</u> you again and it <u>will have been</u> a dream, <u>|</u> but you may find eggs in your best <u>bon- |</u> net or an Easter bunny in grandma's <u>rock- |</u> ing chair. Anything may happen on Easter. || "Many delicate pictures of rabbits, lambs, | chickens and daffodils, in close associa- | tion with little children, are sprinkled | over the pages, while a wonderful fawn | brings a happy climax to the story." | —Horn Book || Henry Z. Walck, Inc. | <u>a division of</u> | DAVID McKAY COMPANY, INC. | <u>New York</u>.

CONTENTS: The half-title is extracted from the title page and printed in black and white. It also heads the dedication page in color. There is a difference in the capital E of Easter; on the half-title the deer's nibbling has been filled in but it was not on the dedication page. The ribbon which formerly encircled the dedication has been removed.

OTHER: Dates from ca. 1972 by Walck/McKay merger. The *Horn Book Magazine* citation is from v.17:3 May-June 1941, page 206.

T60 _____. [. . . <u>10 9 8 7 6 5 4 3 2 1</u> . . .]

PAGINATION: [40]pp in <u>three gatherings</u>, including endpapers topsewn. The endpapers have a creamy appearance; body of book on a more oyster shell paper. Ten stitches. 6 13/16" x <u>6 15/16"</u>.

COVER: <u>Olive</u> paper over boards, <u>matte finish</u>. Black spine lettering.

T61 _____. [. . . <u>10 9 8 7 6 5 4 3 2</u> . . .]

PAGINATION: [40]pp. Nine stitches, top sewn. 6 13/16" x <u>6 7/8</u> .

COVER: <u>Olive</u> gloss paper over boards, <u>linen weave imprint</u>.

DUST JACKET: $5.95 price top of front flap.

T62 _____. [. . . <u>10 9 8 7 6 5 4 3 2</u> . . .]

PAGINATION: [40]pp. 6 15/32" x 6 7/16".

COVER: White paper wrapper with design of previous dust jackets on front cover. Spine as before. Back: $2.50, upper right, yellow crocus centered and at lower right, 0-8098-1807-8.

OTHER: Examined copy inscribed 1980.

T63 _____. Have not examined a third McKay printing.

T64 _____. [. . . A62-8626 | ISBN: 0-8098-1008-5 (Cloth) | ISBN: 0-8098-1807-8 (Paperback) | 10 9 8 7 6 5 4 | MANUFACTURED IN THE UNITED STATES OF AMERICA]

PAGINATION: [36] pp. 6 1/2″ x 6 7/16″.

COVER: Perfect bound, in a paper wrapper. Back, upper right, $ 2.95; bottom right, 0-8098-1807-8.; Pages [2, 36] are blank.

T65 _____. [. . . A62-8626 | ISBN: 0-679-20414-8 || 10 9 8 7 6 5 | MANUFACTURED IN THE UNITED STATES OF AMERICA]

PAGINATION: [40] pp. in one signature top sewn, including plain end papers. Pages [1-2, 4, 38-40] are blank. Twenty-four stitches, top sewn. 6 5/8″ x 6 3/4″.

COVER: Blue deer-skin pattern plastic-filled paper over boards stamped only on the spine, in gilt: TUDOR * A TALE FOR EASTER * WALCK.

DUST JACKET: Front flap: $6.95. Lower right back, in black: ISBN 0-8098-1008-5.

CONTENTS: The half-title is in color with the nibble out of the capital E.

T66 _____. [. . . ISBN: 0-679-20414-8 || 10 9 8 7 6 5 | MANUFACTURED IN THE UNITED STATES OF AMERICA]

PAGINATION: [36] pp. in three gatherings (?) ivory paper, perfect bound. 6 ½″ x 6 5/8″.

COVER: Ivory wrapper in dust jacket design. Back, upper right: $4.95; lower right, 0-8098-1807-8.

T67 _____. Have not examined a sixth McKay printing.

T68 _____. [. . . ISBN: 0-679-20414-8 || 10 9 8 7 | MANUFACTURED IN THE UNITED STATES OF AMERICA]

PAGINATION: [36] pp. in two signatures white paper, buff parchment endpapers. 6 3/4″ x 6 3/4″.

COVER: Purple plastic-filled paper imprinted with a light weave pattern, gilt spine stamping.

DUST JACKET: Gloss film laminate. Have not examined one with price intact.

T69 A | TALE | FOR | EASTER [pale green] || BY | TASHA TUDOR [black] [Copyright 1941 by Tasha Tudor. [sic] Copyright renewed 1969 by | Tasha Tudor. All rights reserved under International and | Pan-American Copyright Conventions. Originally | published by Henry Z. Walck, Inc. in 1941. [sic] Published in | the United States by Random House, Inc., New York, and | simultaneously in Canada by Random House of Canada | Limited, Toronto. || Library of Congress Cataloging-in-Publication Data: | Tudor, Tasha. A tale for Easter. SUMMARY: You can guess | Easter is coming when you get a new dress, have hot | cross buns, and wake up to colored eggs, baby ducklings, | and a bunny rabbit. {1. Easter-Fiction} I. Title. | PZ7.T8228Tal 1989 {E} 88-30675 | ISBN: 0-394-84404-1; 0-394-94404-6 (lib. bdg.) || Manufactured in the United States of America | 1 2 3 4 5 6 7 8 9 0]

PAGINATION: [32] pp. in two signatures, plus board covers. 6 13/16″ [front] x 6 11/16″.

COVER: White gloss film lamination over the original jacket design. Spine, in black: TASHA TUDOR A TALE FOR EASTER [house logo] Random House. Centered on back beneath a clump of crocus: *If you have been very good all year, on the night before* | *Easter you will have lovely dreams about* | *ducks and rabbits and a fawn who takes you on a* | *magic ride. When you wake up . . . you may find eggs* | *in your best bonnet or an Easter bunny in* | *your basket. Anything can happen on Easter.* | At lower left: two UPC bar codes, 84404 above the smaller right code; 0 79808 84404 8, beneath the larger left code. Beneath both: ISBN 0-394-84404-1. At lower right: $ 5.95 U.S.

CONTENTS: Page [1] is title page. Page [3] is dedication. Plain front pasted endpaper. The last page of text is printed on the rear end paper.

T70 _____. Have not examined a Canadian imprint.

T71 _____. [Copyright 1941 by Henry Z. Walck, Inc. | Copyright renewed 1969 by Tasha Tudor. | All rights reserved under International and | Pan-American Copyright Conventions. Originally | published . . . United States of America | 3 5 7 9 10 8 6 4 2]

PAGINATION: [32] pp. in two signatures bound as above. Ten stitches, saddle sewn. 6 13/16″ x 6 11/16″.

T72 _____. Overmann lists a Random House paperback which I have not examined.

T73 *Tasha Tudor* [COPYRIGHT, 1973, BY | IRENE DASH GREETING CARD CO., INC. | PRINTED IN U.S.A.]

PAGINATION: 14 (?) leaves numbered on recto. 11 5/8 x 11 ¾″ looseleaf notebook.

COVER: Moss green course taffeta cover. *Tasha Tudor* stamped in gilt script on front, spine and back. A gilt area approx. 7 ½ x 5 ½″ probably originally had a card mounted there, although none remained on the examination copy. Medium green endpapers; front, with a 5 7/8 x 5 ¾″ black and white photograph (not ascribed) of Tudor and two corgis and this text. *Tasha Tudor* Daughter of the famous American Cup Yacht designer, W. Starling Burgess, | Tasha Tudor is well known as the creator of children's books which she writes and illustrates | with impeccable artistry, Tasha Tudor left her social life in Back Bay Boston [*sic*] | for the special beauty of a working farm in the scenic hills of New Hampshire and now, Vermont. | Her life there with her four children is reflected in her illustrations, which are characterized | by a rural nostalgia and quaint charm quite singular in this mechanized world. | Mother, artist, farmwife, writer and craftswoman, Tasha Tudor is truly an American original. || *These designs are created exclusively for this personalized Christmas card album.* | *They come to you hand-folded, ready for insertion in the envelopes.* [lower left] COPYRIGHT, 1973, BY | IRENE DASH GREETING CARD CO., INC. | PRINTED IN U.S.A. [lower right] Back endpaper has two columns of closely spaced ordering information, including instructions for inscriptions, inks, a U.S. map showing imprinting service from either Gardena, Ca., or New York City [east or west of the Mississippi River]. "White self-sealing envelopes may be ordered for all cards ... All orders postmarked after Saturday, December 8th ..."

CONTENTS: Description is from a partial notebook from which pages had been removed. Although there is no indication of the total number of cards included, it seems certain that there were 14 heavy gray paper pages, probably each with a card attached and described with a short paragraph and price data. The pages remaining are 2, CC35-59V *SLEIGH'S AWAY;* 3, EE 43-33R *CHRISTMAS DIORAMA;* 9, EE 39-51E, *NATURAL BAROQUE;* 11, HH 31-63DF *RUSTIC BEAUTY;* 12, CC 37-78V *A TIME TO SHARE;* 13, FF 41-25F *A BOUNTIFUL BORDER; 14,* CC 39-8V *THE COUNTRY STORE.*

OTHER: All versos are blank except for page 14, which caries a SCHEDULE OF PRICES FOR QUANTITIES OVER 100 CARDS. Pricing begins at 125 cards and is listed for five price ranges in two categories: Without Imprint and With Name Imprinted. The ranges and prices are C series, $30/$37.25; E series, 37.50/44.75; F series, 45/52.25; G series, 60/67.25; H series, 70/77.25.

See also item TASHA TUDOR CHRISTMAS CARDS for one copyright notice.

T74 **TASHA TUDOR** [Photographs by Ann K. Beneduce, Thomas Y. Crowell Company]

PAGINATION: [16] gloss paper stapled twice in cover stock. 8 15/16 x 6″

COVER: Front: black and white photograph of Tudor sitting in a grassy orchard with three corgi dogs. The only text is the title. Back: white with text at the bottom center, THOMAS Y. CROWELL COMPANY | 201 PARK AVENUE SOUTH | NEW YORK, NEW YORK 10003 || *Printed in U.S.A.*

CONTENTS: Pages [1-2] comprise an unsigned biographical essay by Tudor's editor Ann Beneduce. " . . . Now she has given [her corgis] a book of their own, CORGIVILLE FAIR, which she affectionately regards as her masterpiece . . . In 1971 she was awarded the Regina Medal of the Catholic Library Association for her outstanding contribution to the field of children's literature . . ."

ILLUSTRATIONS: Twenty-one black and white photographs including the cover, and a corgi birthday party beside the Blackwater River and with granddaughter Laura Dennis.

OTHER: Undated ca. 1971 booklet issued coincident with *Corgiville Fair*, and while still living in New Hampshire.

T75 *Tasha Tudor Bibliography*

PAGINATION: [8] White paper, 2 sheets folded and numbered. 8 15/16 x 7″

COVER: Front: Title and a paragraph describing how to interpret the list and its symbols. A photograph of Tudor drawing with corgi on lap. Also a drawing of a small girl drawing a posing corgi. Beneath the line drawing this caption: Illustrated in 1989 by Tasha Tudor for Elaine's Upper Story. Back: Title index to the list.

CONTENTS: Eighty-four numbered chronologic entries for books written or illustrated by Tudor, 1938 - 1989. The briefest annotations, some only 6 or 7 words long.   A separate slip of paper is laid in containing items 85 - 89, 1990 - 1994.

OTHER: This list was included in her mailings to customers by Elaine Hollabaugh, Rogers City, Michigan. Since Summer 1981, she has published *The Letter* devoted to Tasha Tudor interests. See *Serial Literature* for a complete abstract of *The Letter*. The Library of Congress has no copyright records for either the bibliography or the newsletter.

T76 The Tasha Tudor [page [6], remainder of title page on page [7]] Book of [gray] Fairy | Tales [red] || Selected, Edited and Illustrated | by TASHA TUDOR || PLATT & MUNK, *Publishers* | NEW YORK [black] [*Foreword* || FAIRY TALES are perennially the favorite literature of childhood. | They can be traced back, in the form we know, at least to 1697, | when Charles Perrault's book, *Contes de Ma Mère l'Oie* (Tales of | Mother Goose) was first published. Perrault's tales are still read and | told today, and two of them are included in this book. ¶ Children deserve, indeed require, the special charm and imagery | of the fanciful. It is for their particular delight that this edition is | published. No other collection of fairy tales published this century has | quite caught so fully the classical simplicity, warmth and magic of | fairy stories as has *The Tasha Tudor Book of Fairy Tales*. ¶ For this book is far more than a collection of favorite stories | illustrated by a favorite artist, although it is that as well. These are the | stories that Tasha Tudor loved as a child and has told to her children. | She has selected them, edited and shaped them, and with her own | unerring taste has illustrated them with affectionate care and delicate | grace. ¶ Here are represented the master storytellers, Perrault, Hans | Christian Andersen and the Brothers Grimm, as well as folk tales | from old Russia and the English. These stories, newly retold, blend | wit and sparkle and soaring imagination with the delightful artistry | of Tasha Tudor, who sees beauty and magic in everyday things of | the house, the woods and the fields, and weaves them all skillfully | into her interpretations. ¶ Throughout *The Tasha Tudor Book of Fairy Tales* is distin- | guished for its expansiveness of spirit and feeling and its elegance of | design and color.

PAGINATION: Six signatures of thick ivory paper: pages [1-10] 11-14 [15] 16-18 [19-20] 21-22 [23] 24-30 [31] 32-35 [36-37] 38-40 [41] 42-44 [45-46] 47-49 [50] 51-52 [53] 54-59 [60] 61-63 [64] 65-68 [69] 70 [71] 72 [73-74] 75-76 [77] 78-80 [81] 82 [83] 84-88 [89] 90-92 [93-96] including covers, topsewn in seventeen stitches. 12 1/4″ x 10 1/8″.

COVER: Yellow paper (fine cloth weave imprint) over boards. Title in red: The Tasha Tudor | Book of | Fairy | Tales. Twining rose brier from Sleeping Beauty's castle and motifs from five of the stories: Little Red Riding Hood, Rapunzel, Puss in Boots, Cinderella, and The Valiant Tailor. Variant drawings of the first two appear on pages [81] and [41]. Puss in Boots illustration is a detail from page [50]. The latter two appear only on covers. "T. Tudor" is visible in the lower right of front cover. Spine printed in black: 4200 [roses] The Tasha Tudor Book of [roses] Fairy Tales [roses] Platt & Munk. Back cover: an image (which does not appear elsewhere in the book) of Cinderella dancing with her blue waist-coated prince. Yellow end papers, each with the same painting of a rose tree, surrounded by and supporting twelve characters from the stories, as well as several birds.

ILLUSTRATIONS: Most pages have at least one colored illustration. Each of the twelve stories begins with an illuminated initial. Full page illustrations on pages [15, 19, 23, 31, 36, 41, 45, 50, 53, 60, 69, 73, 77, 81, 89]. Blank pages: [4, 10, 93]. Illustrations for "The Tinder Box" contain some of the earliest of Tudor's representations of Corgi dogs, although not true to the Corgi face.

CONTENTS: Pages [6-7] form a two-page title pages spread. A knight on the recto rides toward a castle on the opposing verso. Half-title, page [5]: The | Tasha Tudor | Book of Fairy Tales ‖ [a rose tree]. Contents, page [9]: Sleeping Beauty, Rumpelstiltskin, Mr. Samson Cat, The Valiant Taylor, The Emperor's New Clothes, Rapunzel, The Flying Trunk, Puss in Boots, Thumbelina, The Tinder Box, Jack and the Beanstalk, Mr. Bun, The Lame Duck, Red Riding Hood, Cinderella. Page 92 ABOUT TASHA TUDOR: Tasha Tudor is one of the world's foremost illus- | trators of children's books. Her adult years have been devoted almost entirely | to creating and capturing in word and color the special delights of childhood's | fancy. She comes gracefully and perhaps naturally to this achievement, for she is | the daughter of the portrait painter, Rosamond Tudor, and of W. Starling | Burgess, a designer of yachts. ¶ Miss Tudor studied at the School of the Museum of Fine Arts in Boston, where | she was born. Much of her material is drawn from her New England farmhouse | and the surrounding woods and fields. Her illustrations are unique for their | magic blend of the quaint and the real, for their soft colors, and their delicate | beauty of line. In *The Tasha Tudor Book of Fairy Tales* Miss Tudor has fulfilled | a lifelong dream of creating and illustrating her own book of fairy tales. ‖ ✳ ‖ THE TASHA TUDOR BOOK OF FAIRY TALES is set in 16 point Deep- | dene, one of 128 type faces created by Frederic W. Goudy. Its vertical elegance | and pleasing openness perfectly complement the fairy tale in story and illus- | tration. The titles are set in Eve Bold. ¶ This book was produced under the editorial supervision of Phyllis Braun, and | lithographed for Platt & Munk by the Niagara Lithograph Company, Buffalo, | NY; composition by Baxter & Spencer Inc., New York, NY; typography | and design by Joan Stoliar.

OTHER: *Publishers' Weekly* (December 18, 1961, page 18) quotes David B. Dreiman, president of the firm saying that this is the most successful single book ever published by Platt & Munk. *PW* also says the book was published October 12 (as opposed to the copyright statement) and that less than six weeks after publication, a second printing makes a total of 110,000 copies in print. A third printing is under way.

See Also *Tasha Tudor's Fairy Tales* for 1988 and 1990 derivative printings in blue boards. Two die cut sets of puzzles were also derived from the full-page illustrations of this book: a blue box and a pink box.

COPYRIGHT REGISTRATION: A 537301 granted to The Platt & Munk Co., Inc., 200 Fifth Ave., NY 10, NY. Lillian Gluskin, agent for the claimant, swears on Dec. 14, 1961:

THE TASHA TUDOR BOOK OF FAIRY TALES (#4200), selected, edited and illustrated by Tasha Tudor, Route 1, Contoocook, NH, a U S citizen, was published Aug. 25, 1961. Composition of the text by Baxter & Spencer, 110 Greenwich St., N.Y.,N.Y.; printing, plates, and engravings, text and cover by Niagara Lithograph Co., Buffalo, N.Y.; binding by Economy Bindery, 511 Joyce St., Orange, N.J.; and coating (covers) by Bove Finishing Co., 601 West 26th St., N.Y., N.Y. Application and affidavit and two deposit copies received at LC Dec. 19, 1961.

COPYRIGHT RENEWAL REGISTRATION: RE 432-199 granted to Tasha Tudor claiming as editor and illustrator, RFD 4, Box 205, West Brattleboro, Vt. 05301. Louise Bates, agent for Tasha Tudor, swears on April 14, 1989:

THE TASHA TUDOR BOOK OF FAIRY TALES by Tasha Tudor was originally registered Aug. 25, 1961. Fees charged to Putnam Publishing Group, 200 Madison Ave., NY, NY 10016. Renewal application received Apr. 20, 1989.

T77 _____.

COVER: Library edition with cloth reinforced hinge.

T78 _____.

PAGINATION: 11 5/8″ x 9 5/8″

COVER: A rebound volume in aqua library buckram is painted with castle illustration from page facing title page, without the approaching knight. Ivory end papers added, one of the original pictorial endpapers has been preserved and bound in as page [4]. Typography of title has been reproduced in white paint on front cover, but repositioned: The Tasha Tudor | Book of Fairy | Tales | by TASHA TUDOR. Spine: TUDOR | The Tasha Tudor Book of FAIRY TALES.

OTHER: Rebound ex-library copy demonstrating covers manufactured in the rebinding process.

T79 The Tasha Tudor | Book of [black] | Fairy Tales [red] | Selected, Edited and Illustrated by TASHA TUDOR | PLATT & MUNK, *Publishers* | NEW YORK [black] [*Foreword* | FAIRY TALES are perennially . . . design and color. | Copyright © 1961, 1965 The Platt & Munk Co., Inc., New York, N.Y. 10010 | All rights ... Card Number: 61-13221]

PAGINATION: Three signatures of ivory paper topsewn and with cloth hinge: pages [1-8] 9-18 [19] 20-23 [24] 25-27 [28] 29-32 [33] 34 [35] 36-38 [39-40] 41-42 [43] 44-48 [49] 50-51 [52] 53-56 [57] 58-60 [61-62] 63-65 [66] 67-68 [69-70] 71-72 [73] 74-76 [77-80] including covers. Twelve stitches top sewn. 12 1/4″ x 10 3/16″.

COVER: Library edition with reinforced cloth hinge. Ocher paper (fine cloth weave imprint) over boards. Back cover, upper left: 4200:0295

CONTENTS: <u>Thirteen stories, rearranged</u>; The Valiant Tailor and The Lame Duck have been omitted. Title Page [4]. Contents, page [6]: Thumbelina, Cinderella, The Tinder Box, Jack and the Beanstalk, Rumpelstiltskin, Mr. Samson Cat, Sleeping Beauty, The Emperor's New Clothes, Rapunzel, The Flying Trunk, Puss in Boots, Mr. Bun, Red Riding Hood, ABOUT TASHA TUDOR. Text begins on page 9. There is <u>no half-title</u>.

ILLUSTRATIONS: Title page in only page [5] here and reproduces the castle previously on the facing page while omitting the knight and the rose path.

OTHER: ABOUT TASHA TUDOR ends the book on page 76.

T80 _____. [Foreword . . . Copyright © <u>1961, 1965, 1969</u> The Platt & Munk Co., Inc., <u>Bronx, N.Y. 10472</u> | All rights . . . Card Number: 61-13221]

PAGINATION: <u>Four</u> signatures of ivory paper oversewn in library binding: pages [1-4] 5-14 [15] 16-17 [18] 19-23 [24] 25-27 [28-29] 30 [31] 32-36 [37] 38-40 [41] 42-45 [46] 47-48 [49] 50 [51] 52-54 [55] 56-57 [58] 59-61 [62] 63-64. Twelve stitches top sewn. <u>12 1/4″ x 9 3/4″</u>.

COVER: Back cover, upper left: 4200:0295. <u>Olive endpapers</u>. Reinforced cloth hinge.

ILLUSTRATIONS: Full page illustrations on pages [4], [15], [18], [28], [31], [37], [41], [46], [49], [55], [58], [62].

CONTENTS: "The Tinder Box" has been omitted. Title Page [1]. Contents, page [3] <u>Tudor biography and typography statements have been omitted. Book ends on page 64</u> with Little Red Riding Hood, The woodman and Grandma holding hands.

T81 _____.

OTHER: As above, and added at lower left back: <u>Copyright ©MCMLXI The Platt & Munk Co., Inc., New York, N.Y.</u>

T82 _____.

COVER: <u>Ivory endpapers</u>, cloth hinge. Back cover imprinted <u>4200</u> at upper left, and without the publisher's statement.

OTHER: Examined a copy inscribed 18 June 1973.

T83 _____. [Foreword...Number: 61-13221| <u>ISBN 0-8228-4200-9</u>]

PAGINATION: <u>Four signatures</u> top sewn and glued. Eighteen stitches. 12 1/4″ x 9 1/2″.

COVER: Illustrated boards under <u>gloss film laminate</u>. <u>The end papers are white. Back cover: upper left, 4200:0395.</u>

T84 _____.

COVER: As above, but with <u>white cloth hinges</u>, front and rear.

T85 _____. PLATT & MUNK, *Publishers* | <u>A Division of Grosset & Dunlap</u> | NEW YORK [Foreword...Number: 61-13221| <u>ISBN 0-448-44200-0 (Trade edition)</u> | ISBN 0-448-13036-X (Library edition)]

PAGINATION: <u>Page [64] is not numbered.</u>

COVER: <u>Back cover: upper left, 44200:0395;</u> bottom center, Platt & Munk Publishers | A Division of Grosset and Dunlap. <u>Lower right:</u> ISBN 0-448-44200-0, with the last digit in the gutter. Spine: [rose] ᏟhᏋ ᏟᗩᏕhᗩ Ꮯᑌᗪoᖇ ᗷook oℱ [rose] ℱᗩiᖇᎽ ᏟᗩⅼᏋᏕ [rose] <u>44200-0</u> ႥⅼᗩᏓᏓ & ᗰᑌnk. Spine and edges of front cover have faded from butterscotch to pink on examination copy.

T86 _____.

    COVER: A gold foil <u>price label</u> overprinted in navy ($4⁹⁵⁾ at upper right of front. Back cover: bottom center, **Platt & Munk** Publishers/<u>New York</u> | A Division of Grosset and Dunlap. Lower right: ISBN 0-448-44200-0, not in gutter. <u>There is no code at upper left.</u>

T87 _____. [Foreword...Copyright © 1961, 1965, 1969 The Platt & Munk Co., <u>Inc. | All</u> rights...(Library Edition)]

    PAGINATION: Pages are<u>perfect bound,</u> and not sewn to cover. Page <u>[64] is numbered.</u>

    COVER: Back cover: as above, plus <u>$ 5.95 at upper left.</u>

T88 _____. [Foreword...design and color. || <u>1980 Printing</u> | Copyright...]

    PAGINATION: <u>Signatures are sewn</u> to cover. Twenty-one stitches, top sewn.

T89 _____. [Foreword...design and color. || <u>1980 Printing</u> | Copyright...]

    PAGINATION: <u>Signatures and white endpapers are glued</u> to spine binding tape so tightly as to appear perfect bound.

    COVER: There is <u>no price printed</u> on the cover.

T90 _____. [Foreword...design and color. | <u>1984 Printing</u> | Copyright...]

    PAGINATION: Perfect bound.

    COVER: Back cover, upper left: <u>$5.95</u>

T91 _____. [Foreword...design and color. | <u>1986 Printing</u> | Copyright...]

    COVER: Back cover, upper left, <u>$8.95.</u> Lower left in a 1 1/16 x 1 3/8″ <u>white box: bar code</u> and under it, 0 70918 44200 1. Lower right in ½ x 2 1/16″ <u>white box in computer type</u> face, ISBN 0-448-44200-0.

T92 ᏟhᏋ ᏟᗩᏕhᗩ Ꮯᑌᗪoᖇ [page [6], remaining text on page [7]] ᗷook oℱ [gray] ℱᗩiᖇᎽ | ᏟᗩⅼᏋᏕ [red] || Selected, Edited and Illustrated | by <u>Tasha Tudor</u> || COLLINS | <u>LONDON AND GLASGOW.</u> [black] [*Foreword* || FAIRY TALES are perennially the <u>favourite</u> literature of childhood. | They can be traced back, in the form we know, at least to 1697, | when Charles Perrault's book, *Contes de Ma Mère l'Oie* (Tales of | Mother Goose) was first published. Perrault's tales are still read and | told today, and two of them are included in this book. ¶ Children deserve, indeed require, the special charm and imagery | of the fanciful. It is for their particular delight that this edition is | published. No other collection of fairy tales published this century has | quite caught so fully the classical simplicity, warmth and magic of | fairy stories as has *The Tasha Tudor Book of Fairy Tales*.

¶ For this book is far more than a collection of <u>favourite</u> stories | illustrated by a <u>favourite</u> artist, although it is that as well. These are the | stories that Tasha Tudor loved as a child and has told to her children. | She has selected them, edited and shaped them, and with her own | unerring taste has illustrated them with affectionate care and delicate | grace. ¶ Here are represented the master storytellers, Perrault, Hans | Christian Andersen and the Brothers Grimm, as well as folk tales | from old Russia and the English. These stories, newly retold, blend | wit and sparkle and soaring imagination with the delightful artistry | of Tasha Tudor, who sees beauty and magic in everyday things of | the house, the woods and the fields, and weaves them all <u>skilfully</u> | into her interpretations. ¶ Throughout *The Tasha Tudor Book of Fairy Tales* is distin- | guished for its expansiveness of spirit and feeling and its elegance of | design and <u>colour</u>. || <u>Copyright © 1961 The Platt & Munk Co., Inc.</u> | <u>Copyright © 1963 in Great Britain and the British</u> <u>Commonwealth | (except Canada) | William Collins Sons and Co. Ltd. | Published by agreement with The Platt and Munk Co. Inc. || PRINTED</u> <u>AND MADE IN GREAT BRITAIN BY | WILLIAM COLLINS SONS AND CO. LTD. | LONDON AND GLASGOW</u>]

PAGINATION: Six signatures of thick <u>buff</u> paper: pages [1-10] 11-14 [15] 16-18 [19-20] 21-22 [23] 24-30 [31] 32-35 [36-37] 38-40 [41] 42-44 [45-46] 47-49 [50] 51-52 [53] 54-59 [60] 61-63 [64] 65-68 [69] 70 [71] 72 [73-74] 75-76 [77] 78-80 [81] 82 [83] 84-88 [89] 90-92 [93-96] including covers, ten stitches saddle sewn. <u>12 1/8″ x 9 7/8″</u>.

COVER: Yellow paper (weave imprint) over boards. Design and title as Platt & Munk first edition. Spine printed in black: [roses] The Tasha Tudor Book of [roses] Fairy Tales [roses] Collins. The weave pattern is not so fine as the Platt & Munk. The hinge indentions on front and back covers are not as pronounced as the first edition.

CONTENTS: Page 92 ABOUT TASHA TUDOR: Tasha Tudor is one of the world's . . . capturing in word and <u>colour</u> the special delights. . . magic blend of the quaint and the real, for their soft <u>colours</u>, and their delicate. . . fairy tales. || ✳

OTHER: The New York statement concerning type and production was deleted from page 92.

T93 TASHA TUDOR CHRISTMAS CARDS. 1949.

OTHER: Bethany Tudor relates that her mother painted 13 cards each year from the 1940s into the 1970s. In *Take Peace*, Tudor says she painted 14 a year. See **Tasha Tudor** [Irene Dash Greeting Card Co.] for a partial description of the 1973 album. Here is the only copyright notice on file at the Library of Congress; it apparently is not the first in the series given the wording of the notice.

COPYRIGHT REGISTRATION: A 124624 granted to Irene Dash Greeting Card Co., Inc., 106 7th Ave., N.Y. 11, N.Y. Martin Dash swears on Aug. 8, 1949:

TASHA TUDOR CHRISTMAS CARDS, a new edition of a previously published book by Tasha Tudor, Contoocook, N.H., a U.S. citizen born ? [*sic*], was published June 1, 1949. The previous title was *1949 edition of annual Christmas Card catalogue*. Type setting and printing by Artcraft Lithograph & Printing Co., Inc., N.Y., N.Y.; binding by Michelman, N.Y., N.Y. Application and affidavit and two deposit copies received Aug. 9, 1949.

Tasha Tudor. Christmas Village, A Three Dimensional Advent Calendar. *See Christmas Village.*

T94 [butter print] THE TASHA TUDOR [red] | [6 ¼″ black rule] | COOKBOOK [red] | [4 3/8″ black rule] | *Recipes and Reminiscences | from Corgi Cottage* | [4 1/8″ black rule] | Written and illustrated by [black] | TASHA TUDOR [red]| with Carol Johnston Lueck | [LB logo] LITTLE, BROWN AND COMPANY | Boston   New York   Toronto   London [black] [Copyright © 1993 by Tasha Tudor || All rights reserved.

PAGINATION: Eight signatures of ivory paper. Pages [i-viii] ix-x [1-2] 3-8 [9] 10 [11-12] 13-21 [22-24] 25-36 [37]38-41 [42-44] 45-46 [47] 48-49 [50] 51- 58 [59-60] 61-62 [63] 64 [65] 66 [67-68] 69-71 [72] 73-74 [75] 76-77 [78-79] 80-87 [88] 89-96 [97] 98 [99-100] 101-102 [103] 104-110 [111] 112-116 [117] 118-122, [123-126].   9 1/4″ x 8 1/4″.

COVER: Yellow printed paper over boards. Front, a twig border wound with a red ribbon and decorated with various utensils, food and animals. The title is yellow letters outlined in orange; the remaining text is green. Tasha Tudor | THE TASHA TUDOR | COOKBOOK | [2 3/8″ orange rule] | *Recipes and Reminiscences from Corgi Cottage* | [2 3/8″ orange rule] | [a country cottage within a twig oval, red tablecloth and canton china] | Featuring More Than 80 of Tasha Tudor's | Favorite Family Recipes. Spine lettering font and color as on front: Tudor THE TASHA TUDOR COOKBOOK   Little, | Brown. Back cover: frontispiece illustration, 7 3/8″ x 6 3/8″, a mother in a summer kitchen with two children, two corgyn and two cats. Tan endpapers printed in a small wallpaper design of white oak leaves.

DUST JACKET: Duplicates the cover with the addition of a white box (1 1/4″ x 2 1/8″) with UPC bar codes centered at the bottom back: ISBN 0-316-85531-6 [above large code], 90000> [above small code] | 9 780316 855310 [below large code]. Front flap: COOKBOOK **$24.95 FPT** | $29.95 in Canada || Tasha Tudor, beloved children's book | author and illustrator, has at last written | her long-awaited cookbook. In words and | the enchanting watercolors for which she | is renowned, she shares the recipes she has | gathered over a lifetime — some that have | been passed down for generations and | some that she created specially for her | children and grandchildren. These tradi- | tional recipes recall an old-fashioned New | England lifestyle and summon up Tasha | Tudor's own warm family memories, which | she shares here with her readers. ¶ Tasha Tudor's recipe collection includes | summery picnic salads, hearty winter | soups, and breakfast treats like Great- | Grandmother Tudor's Cornbread, | Blueberry Coffee Cake, and Butterscotch | Rolls. Her main dishes — Roast Chicken with tarragon and sage, vegetable-laden | Beef Stew, and Salmon served with home- | grown peas — are the prelude to her irre- | sistibly rich desserts, including a luscious | dark chocolate torte and English Toffee | Bars. ¶ At Tasha Tudor's Corgi Cottage, Christmas celebrations are the high point | of the year, filled with the kind of food and | wholesome fun that harks back to an earl- | ier time. Her recipes bring family and | friends together to make her well-known | gingerbread Christmas tree ornaments | (which have been displayed on the White | House tree), and such seasonal favorites as | thumb cookies and pulled taffy for wrap- | ping as gifts or for putting in paper cornu- | copias to hang on the tree. || *(continued on back flap)*| 11932445. Back flap: All of these authentic, tried-and-true | recipes are presented for the first time with | some fifty original watercolor and pen- | and-ink drawings in this beguiling keep- | sake kitchen companion. || [2 3/4″ x 1 7/8″ black and white photograph of Tudor sitting holding a goat.] | Tasha Tudor has written and illustrated | more than seventy-five children's books | since her first, *Pumpkin Moonshine*, in 1938. | She is famous for her charming art- and | craftwork, including watercolor paintings | and handmade dolls. She is also famous for | the 1830s-style new England world she | has preserved on her farm in southern | Vermont. In a house built by her son, she | lives very much in the manner of the nine- | teenth century and engages in such tasks | as spinning and weaving flax, cooking on a | wood stove with antique utensils, and | tending her many animals, including her | trademark Corgis, chickens, Nubian goats, | and her collection of exotic birds. Her | lifestyle is memorably depicted in *The | Private World of Tasha Tudor*. || *Jacket design by Steve Snider* | *Author photograph by Richard Brown* || PRINTED IN SINGAPORE.

ILLUSTRATIONS: All pages [I]-[[124] are printed with a lavender corner reminiscent of the triangular gummed photo mount corners common in the twentieth century. The pattern is the same as the tan endpapers; there is a gold band along the inside edge of each corner. Full page color illustrations, without text: pp. [ii, viii, 9, 37, 47, 50, 63, 65, 72, 75, 78-79, 88, 97, 103, 111, 117]. Full page, full color, section titles: [1, 11, 23, 43, 59, 67, 99]. Smaller color illustrations on pages with text: [i, v] 5, 6-7, 8, 14-15, 16, 21, 26, 32, 34, 39, 40, 54, 56, 58, 66, 70, 73, 76, 80, 83, 86, 90, 91, 93, 94, 95, 98, 101, 102, 104-105, 112, 118. Sepia and white chalk illustrations: 19, 28, 31, 34, 53, 63, 84, 106, 108, 114, [123]. Recurring butter mold design: [iii, vii, ix] 3, 13, 25, 45, [61], 69, 119, [123] Blank pages: [vi, 2, 12, 22, 24, 42, 44, 60, 68, 100] Most of the illustrations are new for this book. However, a number have appeared previously on greeting cards and postal cards:

[v]	blue saltglaze teapot
[6-7]	"kitchen wreath" of wheat and hand utensils
16	1990, 6 jars, 2 plates on a shelf.
21	Canton blue and small baskets on wall shelves
32	bath scene with corgi in front of fire
[37]	farm buildings in a wheat ring with butt'ry stuff
[50]	farm buildings within a ring of food, topped by 'kitchen wreath'
56	little boy pulling wagon of vegetables, girl with large bouquet
[65]	girl and corgi at open cupboard filled with canning and crocks
76	plate and bowl, green and red goblets
[78-79]	four children in a butt'ry
[88]	girl churning, two corgyn, black cat
[97]	girls in brown dress, green dress, dancing with boy in brown and infant
104-105	two boys and girl packing Christmas tins of cookies, green ribbon and twig
[111]	pewter plates, jug, crock, candle stick, copper pitcher
112	three women, four children in country kitchen, turkey in open oven
[117]	small boy on stool watching girl string cranberries

CONTENTS: Page [123]. *Sources* | A wide assortment of Tasha Tudor's creations - calendars, | Christmas cards, valentines, reprints of early miniature | books made for her children, replicas of her sketch books, | lithographs, paper dolls, and illustrated books - | are available from: The Jenny Wren Press | P.O. Box 505 | Mooresville, Indiana | 46158.

OTHER: The recipe on page 69 is in error—line 7 of ingredients should be eliminated, it repeats line 3.

COPYRIGHT REGISTRATION: TX 3-700-704 granted to Tasha Tudor, Route 4, Box 208, West Brattleboro, Vt. 05301. Robyn I. Renahan, agent for Tasha Tudor, swears on December 27, 1993:

THE TASHA TUDOR COOKBOOK, not a work for hire and neither anonymous nor pseudonymous with recipes and illustrations by Tasha Tudor, a U.S. citizen, was completed in 1993 and published Nov. 9, 1993, by Little, Brown and Company, Inc. 34 Beacon St., Boston, MA 02108. Library of Congress is granted non-exclusive right to make copies and phonorecords for the blind and physically handicapped. Fees charged to account DA O18775, Little, Brown and Company (617-227-0730 x276). Application and two deposit copies received Jan. 4, 1994.

T95 [pencil sketch of boy's head] ‖ THE TASHA TUDOR SKETCHBOOK SERIES | FAMILY AND FRIENDS ‖ Text by TASHA TUDOR | Selected Drawings from the Personal Sketchbooks of TASHA TUDOR ‖ Corgi Cottage Industries | Richmond, Virginia. [[6″ x 8″ pencil sketch of three girls on fireside settle] | Library of Congress Number *[sic]* 95-072152 | Published by CORGI COTTAGE INDUSTRIES | P.O. Box 7281, Richmond, VA 23221-0281 | FIRST EDITION ‖ [right column] I.S.B.N. Number *[sic]* 1-888267-00-3 | Copyright © CORGI COTTAGE INDUSTRIES | Original artwork Copyright © TASHA TUDOR | All Rights Reserved ‖ [running beneath both columns] No part of this book may be reproduced in any form without written permission from the Publisher.]

PAGINATION: [1-2] 3-40 pp. 8″x 10″

COVER: Pasteboard, both faces a brown buckram weave print simulating an artist's sketchbook, wire-bound. Brown ink title on the front cover arches above and below an oval photograph of Tudor sketching: THE TASHA TUDOR SKETCHBOOK SERIES || [photograph] || FAMILY AND FRIENDS.

ILLUSTRATIONS: As many as thirteen of Tudor's pencil sketches are reproduced per page. The first is the head of a small boy on the title page. Tudor reminiscences about her sketching on nearly every page. She comments on drawing the various children. Pages 11, 13-14, 16, 19, 21, 27-28, 30, 33, 35 and 39 lack text and are sketches only.

CONTENTS: Page 40 at the left of the page: 4 1/2″ x 2 1/2″ black and white photograph of Tudor sitting on a fallen tree sketching. On the right two-thirds of the page: ABOUT THE ARTIST. . . | [4 1/2″ rule] || TASHA TUDOR is one of the most prolific author/illustrators of all | time. She has written, illustrated, or been the subject of almost eighty | books over a career spanning nearly three-quarters of a century. ¶ Her unique life-style has directly inspired her art to such an extent | that, today, they are almost interchangeable. Her skill in cooking and | gardening has exerted a strong influence on her work as has her | life-long affinity for clothing and antiques from the 1830s. ¶ Although many of TASHA TUDOR'S books might be described as | children's books, an interesting phenomenon occurs when those | children grow up — they remain enchanted by her work and pass on | their enthusiasm, in turn, to their children. ¶ TASHA TUDOR is truly one of America's National Treasures.

OTHER: This is a lovely family album of sketches, largely of children. Here one sees the seminal work which later became known through the published books; the girl and corgi on a plank bridge, for instance, which is printed in fully painted form on page [10] of THE SPRINGS OF JOY. The exulting last line of page 40 is a particularly interesting 'pat-on-the-back' when one considers that this is published by Tudor's own company.

T96 *Tasha Tudor: The Direction of Her Dreams.*   Wm John Hare | Priscilla T. Hare | Preface by Efner Tudor Holmes | Illustrations by Bethany Tudor | Photographs by Nell Dorr || Oak Knoll Press || New Castle, Delaware [Copyright 1998 by Wm John Hare and Priscilla T. Hare] 11″h x 8 ½″ w.

OTHER: The definitive Tudor bibliography and the book now laid before you. A work of some 15 years' compilation, the volume catalogs 1060 entries and more than fifty pages of periodical citations. Includes chapters by Tudor editors Dorothy Haas (Rand McNally) and Patricia Gauch (Philomel). A short article Tudor wrote for *Horn Book* magazine recounts her 1958 visit to the home of Beatrix Potter and is reprinted here for the first time. Cover art by Mary Torosian Graves, Peterborough, NH. Typesetting of the essays by Michael Höhne. Printing by Braun-Brumfield, Inc. in Ann Arbor, Michigan.

T97 _____.

COVER: A limited distribution of 25 numbered copies were signed by the contributors and bound in leather.

T98 *Tasha Tudor's* | **ADVENT CALENDAR** [green] | *A Wreath of Days* [red] || Philomel Books | New York [green] [Published in 1988 by Philomel Books, a division of | The Putnam & Grosset Group, 200 Madison Avenue, New York, NY 10016. | Text and illustrations copyright © 1988 by Tasha Tudor. All rights reserved. | Published simultaneously in Canada. Printed and bound in Singapore | by Tien Wah Press (Pte) Ltd. First impression]

PAGINATION: Twelve unnumbered and fully illustrated pages, including covers, on five sheets sewn into one gathering; the end sheet is glued to the cover boards. The two middle sheets are glued together enabling doors in the inner sheet to open revealing Advent calendar scenes printed on the sheet which backs it. 11 1/4″ h x 9 11/16″ w.

CONTENTS: [1]   Front cover: Christmas tree on village green in oak and pine oval wreath. *Tasha Tudor's* | ADVENT CALENDAR, in green ink, above the wreath. *A Wreath of Days*, in red ink within a small holly wreath at bottom. Five animals tableau surround the perimeter

[2]   Inside front cover. Corgis hanging Advent wreath, etc., wreath motif.

[3]   Title page with wreath, ribbons, birds and a miniature of this calendar at the bottom. All text within the predominant pine and oak

[4]   "For our family…" Advent wreath and vertical text panel above bird cage.

[5]   "It is impossible..." Pantry shelf and vertical text panel above a bird cage.

[6-7]   *Corgiville at Christmas* Advent calendar

[8]   "We cut..." Candles and colophon, a garland of greens, and bird cages.
[9]   Family holding hands around candle-lit Christmas tree in a parlor, bird cages.

[10]   Rabbit family gathered in their kitchen, within an oak and pine wreath.

[11]   Corgis, rabbits and Edgar Allen Crow at winter fair booth, in oak leaf wreath.
[12]   Back cover: Corgis, rabbits, and cats dancing under Advent wreath, border tableau. At bottom: ISBN 0-399-21471-2   US >>$9.95   CAN >>$13.95

COPYRIGHT REGISTRATION: TX 2 421 663 granted to Tasha Tudor, Route 4, Box 144, West Brattleboro, Vt. 05301. Louise Bates, agent for Tasha Tudor, swears on Oct. 11, 1988:

TASHA TUDOR'S ADVENT CALENDAR, not a work for hire with text and illustrations by Tasha Tudor, a U.S. citizen, was completed in 1988 and published Oct. 10, 1988. Library of Congress is granted non-exclusive right to make copies and phonorecords for the blind and physically handicapped. The book was manufactured by Tien Wah Press (Pte) Ltd., Singapore. Fees charged to account DAO 38288, Putnam Publishing Group, NY, NY 10016 (212-951-8719). Application and two deposit copies received Oct. 12, 1988.

T99 _____. [Published in 1988 . . . Tien Wah Press (Pte) Ltd. <u>Second impression</u>.]

PAGINATION: 11 1/4″ h x 9 5/8″ w.

COVER: Back cover in a pale blue rectangle centered at bottom: US$9.95   CAN$12.95 | 50995 [above the smaller right bar code] | 9 780399 214714 [beneath larger left bar code] | ISBN 0-399-21471-2.

T100 **Tasha Tudor's** [rust] | [printer's lime-green calligraphic swirl] | **Bedtime** | **Book** [rust] | Edited by Kate Klimo [lime-green] | [boy and girl as bookends, reading] | [publisher's locomotive emblem] | Platt & Munk, Publishers/New York [lime-green]. [from page [4] which precedes the title page: For Murray Rhein, | with respectful admiration || Copyright © 1977 by Platt & Munk, Publishers. | All rights reserved under International and Pan-American Copyright Conventions. | Printed in the United States of America | ISBN 0-8228-7217-X | Library of Congress Catalog Card Number: 77-85353]

PAGINATION: [46] pp, endpaper to endpaper in three signatures glued to the boards. Twelve stitches saddle sewn. 12 1/4″ x 10 1/8″.

COVER: Front and back covers are identical, gloss laminate paper over boards. A border of fourteen story vignettes around the center text panel. Spencerian pen flourishes printed in green, text in rust: [swirl] | **Tasha Tudor's** | [swirl] | **Bedtime** | **Book** | [swirl] Overprinted in black at bottom of front cover: **Platt & Munk**. Spine: **Tasha Tudor's   Bedtime Book** [rust] **Platt & Munk** [black] Back cover, upper left, <u>7217:0395</u>. Center panel has a different green swirl in each corner, titles in black ink: Goldilocks and the Three Bears | [swirl] Snow White [swirl] | The Shoemaker and the Elves | City Mouse and Country Mouse | Mother Hulda | The Billy Goats Gruff | The Frog Prince | The Traveling Musicians of Bremen | Babes in the Woods | Shingebiss | The Real Princess | Hansel and Gretel | The Sorcerer's Apprentice | [swirl] Star Dipper [swirl].

CONTENTS: The half-title [3] is reproduces author, title and swirl from title page. Pages [2, 42-43] are blank. There are illustrations on all pages [6-41], including boxed initials on many text pages. Full-page illustrations with no text: [9, 13, 17, 21, 25, 29, 33, 37, 41]. The stories are: Goldilocks and the Three Bears [6-7], The Frog Prince [8-9], The Three Wishes [10-11], Snow White and the Seven Dwarfs [12-13], Shingebiss [14-15], The Sorcerer's Apprentice [16-17], The Billy Goats Gruff [18-19], Mother Hulda [20-21], The Star Dipper [22-23], The Babes in the Wood [24-25], The Real Princess [26-27], Hansel and Gretel [28-29], The Country Mouse and the City Mouse [30-31], The Traveling Musicians of Bremen [32-33], The Shoemaker and the Elves [34-35], The Sugar-Plum Tree [36-37], The Owl and the Pussycat [38-39], Escape at Bedtime [40-41].

ILLUSTRATIONS: Front and back endpapers are identical brown watercolors: a boy with dog and rooster on the left, and on the right, a girl on a burro with a cat. Both are within a straight watercolor border, a device used throughout the book.

OTHER: See *Battered*, B5, for a motion picture adaptation of "Shingebiss." Murray Rhein was an editor.

COPYRIGHT REGISTRATION: A 914645 granted to Platt & Munk, Publishers, 1055 Bronx River Ave., Bronx, N.Y. 10472. Beverly Reingold swears on Nov. 14, 1977:

TASHA TUDOR'S BEDTIME BOOK by Tasha Tudor and Kate Klimo, both U.S. citizens, c/o Platt & Munk, Publishers was published Oct. 1, 1977. The book was manufactured by City Printing Company, 297 State Street N., New Haven, Ct. Application and affidavit and fee received Nov. 17, 1977; two deposit copies received Nov. 25, 1977.

T101 _____.

PAGINATION: Fourteen stitches, saddle sewn. 12 1/4" x <u>10 3/16"</u>.

COVER: Coded on back cover upper left: <u>7217:0495</u>.

CONTENTS: New text, page [43]: One of the world's foremost illustrators of children's | books, Tasha Tudor has always had a special feeling for | the world of folk and fairy tales. This has never been | more apparent than it is in her *Bedtime Book*. ¶ The daughter of Rosamond Tudor, who was a por- | trait painter, and W. Starling Burgess, who designed | yachts, Miss Tudor studied at the Museum of Fine Arts in | Boston. Though she was born in that city, she grew up | on a farm in Connecticut, and she has never lost her | enthusiasm for country life, especially for New England. | She now lives in Vermont in a house built by her son, | where she is surrounded by her corgis, her family, and | friends.

T102 _____. . . . [publisher's locomotive emblem] | **Platt & Munk, Publishers/New York** [green] | <u>A Division of Grosset & Dunlap</u> [black ink] [from page [4] which precedes the title page: For Murray . . . | All rights reserved.<u>|</u> Printed in the United States of America. | <u>Published simultaneously in Canada.</u> | <u>ISBN: 0-448-47217-1 (Trade Edition)</u> | ISBN: 0-448-13038-6 (<u>Library Edition</u>) | Library of Congress Catalog Card Number: 77-85353]

PAGINATION: 12 1/4" x <u>10 1/4"</u>.

COVER: A gummed label has been removed from front cover of examination copy. Spine: **Tasha Tudor's   Bedtime Book** [rust] <u>47217-1</u> **Platt & Munk** [black] Back cover: ... Star Dipper || <u>Platt & Munk, Publishers/New York | A Division of Grosset & Dunlap</u>. In the blue border at extreme lower right: 0-448-47217-1. The light panels which on other copies are a butter yellow color have a pink hue in this printing. The<u> back lacks price</u> coding.

T103 _____. [from page [4] which precedes the title page: For Murray . . . || *1980 Printing* | . . .   Catalog Card Number: 77-85353]

PAGINATION: 12 1/4″ x 10 3/16″.

COVER: <u>The front cover bears a blue on gold foil label, with price $5⁹⁵ in gold, applied to the center of the upper right vignette.</u>

T104 _____... [from page [4]: . . . admiration || *1982 Printing* | Copyright . . .]

PAGINATION: In <u>single signature, crimped and glued</u>.

T105 _____... [from page [4]: . . . admiration || *1984 Printing* | Copyright . . .]

COVER: A blue print on gold foil price label on back: $6⁹⁵ | GROSSET.

T106 𝒯𝒶𝓈𝒽𝒶 𝒯𝓊𝒹𝑜𝓇'𝓈 [black] | 𝔅𝔢𝔡𝔱𝔦𝔪𝔢 𝔅𝔬𝔬𝔨 [light blue] || [4 ½″ roundel detail from page 43] || Edited by Kate Klimo || Platt & Munk, Publishers/New York | A Division of Grosset & Dunlap [black]. [*For Murray Rhein, | with respectful admiration || Platt & Munk Books by Tasha Tudor ||* First Delights | A Book About the Five Senses | First Poems of Childhood | Tasha Tudor's Bedtime Book | Tasha Tudor's Fairy Tales || Copyright © 1988, 1969, 1965, 1961 by Platt & Munk, Publishers, a division of Grossett & Dunlap, | a member of The Putnam Publishing Group, New York. | All rights reserved. Printed in Hong Kong. | Printed simultaneously in Canada | ISBN 0-448-09328-6. Library of Congress Catalog Card Number 87-82517.]

PAGINATION: Three signatures including the endpapers: pages [1-7] 8-34 [35] 36-43 [44-48], cover to cover. 11″ x 9 1/4″.

COVER: 𝒯𝒶𝓈𝒽𝒶 𝒯𝓊𝒹𝑜𝓇'𝓈 [black] | 𝔅𝔢𝔡𝔱𝔦𝔪𝔢 𝔅𝔬𝔬𝔨 [light blue] Pink paper over boards. The front cover is outlined in a thin black line which frames the author and title and, a yellow rectangular field with the illustration of The Babes in the Wood from page 27. Spine printed in black: [horizontal rule] *Tasha Tudor's* **BEDTIME BOOK** Platt & Munk [horizontal rule]. Back cover is also outlined in a thin black line, framing, at the upper left: $10.95 | [rule] | (15.50 CAN). A 3 1/3″ roundel of the country mouse leaving his city cousin, and below it: *Included in This Collection* || Goldilocks and the Three Bears | Snow White | The Shoemaker and the Elves | The Country Mouse and the City Mouse | The Babes in the Woods | Hansel and Gretel | The Sorcerer's Apprentice. At the lower left: [a bar code] | 0 70918 09328 9. Lower right: ISBN 0-448-09328-6.

ILLUSTRATIONS: Front and back endpapers are identical and are edged in a half inch pink border around a thin border of the cover pink around one large two-page yellow panel. Centered in the left half is an oval of the Country Mouse and the City Mouse eating in the country. In the right half, an oval of Goldilocks looking into the bears' dining room. Full-page illustrations with no text now appear on pages 11, 15, 19, 23, 27, 31, [35], 39, 43.

CONTENTS: Pages [4] and [44] are blank. The previous edition has been photographically <u>reduced and most pages have been numbered</u>. Colors are brighter in this production. Page [7]: Contents || Goldilocks and the Three Bears · 8 | The Frog Prince · 10 | The Three Wishes · 12 | Snow White and the Seven Dwarfs · 14 | Shingebiss · 16 | The Sorcerer's Apprentice · 18 | The Billy

Goats Gruff · 20 | Mother Hulda · 22 | The Star Dipper · 24 | The Babes in the Wood · 26 | The Real Princess · 28 | Hansel and Gretel · 30 | The Country Mouse and the City Mouse · 32 | The Traveling Musicians of Bremen · 34 | The Shoemaker and the Elves · 36 | The Sugar-Plum Tree · 38 | The Owl and the Pussycat · 40 | Escape at Bedtime · 42 | [boy and girl bookends from previous title page].

The re-written biography of Tudor is printed in black on a white field within a black line border upon a yellow field within the cover pink thin border within the half-inch pink border, matching the endpapers. TASHA TUDOR, one of America's foremost illustrators ⌊ of children's books, has always had a special feeling for | the world of folk and fairy tales. Her fanciful interpre- | tations capture the wit and sparkle of these classic | stories. She sees beauty and magic in the everyday | things of the house, the woods, and the fields and | weaves them all skillfully into her illustrations. ¶ Born in Boston, Tasha Tudor grew up on a farm in ⌊ Connecticut, and her impressions of rural New England | life are the inspiration for her artwork. She has won | many awards and honors since her first book was | published in 1938. More than sixty books later, her gift | is still unique. She lives in Vermont where she is | surrounded by her corgis, her family, and friends—and | the country pleasures so lovingly depicted in her books.

OTHER: The copyright line for this book is in error. *Tasha Tudor's Bedtime Book* was first published in 1977 (not cited) with several reprints in the early 1980's. The dates 1969, 1965, 1961 rightfully belong to *The Tasha Tudor Book of Fairy Tales*.

COPYRIGHT REGISTRATION: TX 2 301 452 granted to Platt & Munk, Publishers, 51 Madison Ave., NY, NY 10010. Louise Bates swears on May 2, 1988:

TASHA TUDOR'S BEDTIME BOOK, neither anonymous nor pseudonymous by Platt & Munk, Publishers, employer for hire, a U.S. citizen, was published May 2, 1988. Platt & Munk's authorship was an abridgment of selections and illustrations completed in 1988, a derivative of TASHA TUDOR'S BEDTIME BOOK originally published by Platt & Munk in 1961. The book was manufactured by South China Printing Co., Hong Kong. Fee charged to account DAO38288, Putnam Publishing Group (P&M). Application and two deposit copies received May 3, 1988.

T107 *Tasha Tudor's Dollhouse.* Little, Brown & Company will publish this book in September 1999.

The Little, Brown and Company Advance Fact Sheet lists Jennifer Josephy, Editor, and Harry Davis, Agent. A 144-page book of five to ten thousand words and eighty to ninety four-color photographs. Approximately twenty line drawings and twenty watercolors. An initial print run of 30,000 copies, trim size 8 ½ x 10 7/8", expected price of $35.00. Anticipated delivery date, September 1, 1998. "Having collected its 1,000-piece contents since childhood, Tasha Tudor considers her dollhouse a lifetime achievement. Over the years many have contributed to its creation - craftspeople from the Colonial Williamsburg Foundation, family members and friends, and countless artisans including musicians, clockmakers, silversmiths, glass blowers, potters, yacht designers, and book binders. This book offers a fully illustrated presentation of Tasha Tudor's remarkable dollhouse, showing how it parallels, in miniature, the life she has created at Corgi Cottage. Photos of the tiny, identical replicas of Tasha's own furniture, glass, pottery, kitchen utensils, art, clothing, etc., combined with her commentary on the history of the pieces, will provide a unique look at Tasha Tudor's rare ability to make her life and art interchangeable."

T108 *Tasha Tudor's Dolls* || [photograph of doll] || *A Doll Postal Card—showing "Violet"* | *mailing a letter by "Sparrow Post."* [...*Doll collection owned by* | TASHA TUDOR | WEBSTER (R.F.D. NO. 1 Contoocook) | NEW HAMPSHIRE || GINGER & PICKLES STORE | ... [ca. 1953.]]

PAGINATION: 5 ½ X 7 ″ ivory enameled paper, folded in half to enclose 10 black and white
  enameled postcards. [4] pp.

FOLDER: Title page transcribed above. One reproduction of card No. 1 on the front sheet.
  Page [2]: THESE postcards are of the Shakespeare fam- | ily home life. The live in a truly magic
doll | house with eight rooms and a front hall. The | house is known as The Seven Year Plan House as
| it is taking that number of years to be built and | completed. ¶The Shakespeares became tired of
living in The | Hotel Maple Bureau, a select but cramped place | to spend one's days, so The Seven
Year Plan | came into being and, though it will not be com- | pleted until 1956, the Shakespeares have
moved in | and are enjoying their home to the full. ¶This doll house is not just one to be looked at, |
but one that really is used and played with by | children and dolls alike. Dinner parties, teas and |
dances really take place. Mrs. Shakespeare and her | sister-in-law, Nicey Melinda Shakespeare,
belong to The Spool and Thimble Club which sponsors | Literary Contests, Bazaars and Art Exhibits.
The | gallant Captain Shakespeare owns a store known | as Shakespeare & Lovelace, well stocked in
calicos, | laces and buttons to delight the eyes of any femi- | nine doll. ¶Then there is The Sparrow
Post: you may see | Violet on the post card mailing a letter. This | is a non-profit organization
handling only doll | mail. Mr. Augustus Sparrow is Post Master Gen- | eral. He is a very eccentric
bird who quite fre- | quently forgets to pay his various employees their | wage of eight butterscotch
drops, and always takes | vacations at his own convenience.
  Page [3]: ¶The Shakespeare family consists of Captain and | Mrs. Shakespeare, their three
daughters, Emily, | Violet and Rosebud, and Nicey Melinda Shake- | speare, the Captain's sister. ¶The
dolls and the furniture come from different | decades of the 19th and 20th centuries, many as | gifts,
but they have all come together to make a | happy doll household, which may distress the eye | of the
"perfectionist" of period pieces, but thor- | oughly pleases the children, of all ages, who know | and
love the Shakespeares. ¶As time goes on there will be more postcards | showing Miss Nicey Melinda
Shakespeare's wed- | ding, The Doll's Fair, Christmas Party and many | others. || FIRST SERIES | No.
1. This is Violet Shakespeare mailing a letter | by Sparrow Post to her Aunt Nicey Melinda. The |
Post office is in her father's store, Shakespeare & | Lovelace. | No. 2. Here Nicey and Mrs.
Shakespeare do the | family washing and ironing. Babby, the maid, is | apparently on vacation. | No.
3. Mrs. Shakespeare and Nicey get ready for | a trip to Saratoga. They are wondering how they | are
going to fit in their ball dresses. | No. 4. The Shakespeares are enjoying tea. Violet | is about to get a
cup for herself while Rosebud | sits in Nicey's lap. The Captain has just come | back on leave. He is a
Captain in The New | Hampshire volunteers.
  Page [4] No. 5. Nicey is making pies for her brother, the | Captain's, return. His two
daughters and the pussy, | whose name is Puddings, look on. | No. 6. This is Shakespeare &
Lovelace Store. The | Captain is waiting on his wife who has come to | buy some apples. Violet is
talking with her friend, | Henrietta Asquith. | No. 7. Nicey is giving Rosebud and Violet their |
Saturday night bath. Violet is urging Rosebud not | to take so long as they wish Papa to read them a |
long story. | No. 8 Nicey gives Henrietta Asquith a music | lesson while Violet waits her turn. Violet
plays | the zither however. | No. 9. The Captain and his wife and sister have | a quiet dinner party all
to themselves. | No. 10. Mrs. Shakespeare cooks cranberry sauce | while Nicey chops apples for the
mince pies. It | must be Thanksgiving. || *Doll collection owned by* | TASHA TUDOR | WEBSTER
(R.F.D. NO. 1 Contoocook) | NEW HAMPSHIRE || GINGER & PICKLES STORE | *Books, Christmas Cards, Doll*
Postals, | *Correspondence Cards, Old Dolls, Doll* | *Furniture and Accessories, Imported* | *Toys.* [ca. 1955.]]

  The folder encloses ten black and white postal cards. Legend from the backs of individual
cards: TASHA TUDOR'S OLD-FASHIONED DOLLS [the top line of card]. With this second line
on the respective postals: 1. Posting a Letter by Sparrow Post; 2. Wash Day; 3. Packing for a Trip to
Saratoga; 4. Afternoon Tea; 5. Rolling Pies; 6. Shopping; 7. Saturday Night Bath; 8. The Music
Lesson; 9. The Dinner Party; 10. Cooking.

T109 TASHA TUDOR'S [white] | Engagement Calendar [rose] | 1996 |
PHOTOGRAPHS BY RICHARD W. BROWN | TEXT BY TOVAH MARTIN |

ILLUSTRATIONS BY TASHA TUDOR ‖ Houghton Mifflin Company | Boston   New York ‖ [boy and dolphin emblem] [white]. [[from page [1]] Text copyright © 1995 by Tovah Martin | Photographs copyright © 1995 by Richard W. Brown | Illustrations copyright © 1995 by Tasha Tudor | All rights reserved]

PAGINATION: 112 unnumbered 170 gsm matte coated white paper pages. Specified trim size 8″ x 8″, although examination copies measure 7 15/16″ wide.

COVER: Four color process on 270 grams-per-square-meter art boards with gloss film lamination. White WIRE-O binding. The front cover shows Tudor arranging a lily in a bouquet before her mother's portrait. Cover (and title page) text white, except for rose *Engagement Calendar*. At the upper right: TASHA TUDOR'S | Engagement Calendar | 1996. Across the bottom: PHOTOGRAPHS BY RICHARD W. BROWN. The back cover is a detail of the rambler rose, title and inks as before, centered. At lower left corner in white: 6-97240 | FPT $14.95 | Printed in Italy. A white box 1 5/16″ x 2 1/4″ at the lower right includes two UPC bar codes, in black ink. Above the left one; ISBN 0-395-73327-8, and below it 9 780395 733271. Above the smaller right bar code: 90000.

CONTENTS: This is a derivative book from the earlier *Tasha Tudor's Garden* and *The Private World Of Tasha Tudor*. The full color process book is a week-by-week engagement calendar with a Richard Brown photograph on the verso and the week's blank schedule on the recto of each two-page spread. Each recto also includes a short narrative by Martin, and occasionally a Tudor water color.

OTHER: Printed in Italy with a first printing of 16,000 copies ordered for an August 7, 1995, release date. Copics were being delivered shrink-wrapped July 20, 1995. The brief title page inscription is overprinted in white on a photograph of Tudor with her goats in the lupine meadow on pp. [2-3]. Martin's introduction, pages [4-5].

ILLUSTRATIONS: Tudor illustrations on pages: [1, 9, 19, 29, 35, 41, 53, 63, 67, 71, 75, 79, 81, 85, 89, 91, 97, 101, 107, 111]. The page/illustration correlation of photographs in *...Engagement Calendar* to the earlier *... Garden* and *The Private World...* is:

ENGAGEMENT CALENDAR		*TT'S GARDEN*	*PRIVATE WORLD...*
Front cover	Tudor w/bouquet	[127]	
[1]	raspberries	120	
Title pages [2-3]	goats in meadow	74-75	
[5-6]	two brown bunnies		110
[7]	bird house w/winter sky	[28]	
[8]	Tudor sketching at fireplace	159	
[9]	painting of white hyacinth	32	
[10]	birds in cage		85
[12]	crab apple in snow		
[14]	Tudor pitching hay in barn		120
[16]	5 marionettes on wall		[52-53]
[18]	flowers in skirt		
[19]	painting of pink rose		
[20]	heirloom jewelry		13
[22]	Tudor with lantern and pail		
[24]	girl at dollhouse		
[26]	shelf of 19th century books		10
[28]	w/plate and parrot on shoulder	[39]	
[29]	painting of blue flower	158	
[30]	digging w/white crocus in garden		
[32]	fork on wheelbarrow, reversed	41	
[34]	white doves in cote	21	
[35]	drawing of dove	55	
[36]	Tudor with new bushes		

Back cover   rambler rose   [92]

OTHER: Print data determined on July 18, 1995.

COPYRIGHT REGISTRATION: TX 4-131-443 granted to Tovah Martin c/o Christina Ward Literary Agency, PO Box 515, North Scituate, Ma. 02060. Victoria Garbe, Houghton Mifflin Co., 222 Berkeley St., Boston, Ma. 02116 (617-351-5126), agent for Tovah Martin, swears on Oct. 4, 1995:

TASHA TUDOR'S ENGAGEMENT CALENDAR (6-97240) by Tovah Martin, domiciled in the U.S., a work completed in 1995 was published Aug. 8, 1995. The book was neither a derivative nor was it a work for hire. Fees charged to account DA 015539, Houghton Mifflin Company. Application and two deposit copies received Oct. 6, 1995.

COPYRIGHT REGISTRATION: VA 724-519 granted to Richard W. Brown c/o Doe Coover Agency ... swears on Oct. 4, 1995:

TASHA TUDOR'S ENGAGEMENT CALENDAR (6-97240) with photographs by Richard W. Brown, domiciled in the U.S., a work completed in 1995 was published Aug. 8, 1995. The book is derivative in that with the exception of some photos previously published, others are all new photos. Fees charged to account DA 015539, Houghton Mifflin Company. Application and two deposit copies received Oct. 6, 1995.

COPYRIGHT REGISTRATION: VA 724-520 granted to Tasha Tudor c/o Doe Coover Agency . . . swears on Oct. 4, 1995:

TASHA TUDOR'S ENGAGEMENT CALENDAR (6-97240) with 2-dimensional artwork by Tasha Tudor, domiciled in the U.S., a work completed in 1995 was published Aug. 8, 1995. Illustrations have been added to this work. Fees charged to account DA 015539, Houghton Mifflin Company. Application and two deposit copies received Oct. 6, 1995.

T110 TASHA TUDOR'S [white] | **Engagement Calendar** [rose] | 1997 ‖ PHOTOGRAPHS BY RICHARD W. BROWN | TEXT BY TOVAH MARTIN | ILLUSTRATIONS BY TASHA TUDOR ‖ Houghton Mifflin Company | Boston   New York [white]. [[from page [1]] Text copyright © 1996 by Tovah Martin | Photographs copyright © 1996 by Richard W. Brown | Illustrations copyright © 1996 by Tasha Tudor | Designed by Susan McClellan | All rights reserved | Printed in Italy]

PAGINATION: 112 unnumbered 170 gsm matte coated white paper pages.   8″ x 7 15/16″.

COVER: Four color process on 270 gsm art boards with gloss film lamination. White WIRE-O binding. Cover (and title page) text white, except for rose *Engagement Calendar*. At the upper left: TASHA TUDOR'S | Engagement Calendar | 1997. Across the bottom: PHOTOGRAPHS BY RICHARD W. BROWN. The front cover shows Tudor on a ladder, picking pears. She feeds a piece to a corgi, also on the ladder. The back cover is a detail of the Tudor's pond lilies, title inks as before centered in the lower half of the cover. At lower left corner in white: 6-97241 | FPT $15.95 | Printed in Italy. A white box 1 5/16″ x 2 1/4″ at the lower right includes two UPC bar codes, in black ink. Above the left one: ISBN 0-395-79126-X, and below it 9 780395 791264. Above the right: 90000>.

CONTENTS: This is a derivative book from the earlier *Tasha Tudor's Garden, The Private World Of Tasha Tudor* and *Tasha Tudor's Heirloom Crafts*. The full color process book is a week-by-week engagement calendar with a Richard Brown photograph or an occasional Tudor water color on the verso and the week's blank schedule on the recto of each two-page spread. Each recto also includes a short description by Martin. The brief title page inscription is overprinted on a photograph of a Spring bouquet with bird cage, pp. [2-3]. Martin's introduction is on pages [4-5]. A Tudor painting of a pear, in the margin of page [4].

ILLUSTRATIONS: Tudor illustrations on pages: [4, 22, 52] The page/illustration correlation of
...*Engagement Calendar* to ...*Garden, The Private World...* and ... *Heirloom Crafts* is:

ENGAGEMENT CALENDAR		TTG	PWTT	TTHC
Front cover	Tudor on			
[1]	painting of wildflower bouquet	G[5]		
Title pages [2-3]	parlor tulips, birdcage	G55		
[4]	painting of pear	G16		
[6]	stone wall in snow		P23	
[8]	tea with a young girl		P[106-107]	
[10]	sewing tools on linen			
[12]	2 marionettes on wall			C13
[14]	snowy clearing			
[16]	close-up of woman in dress			
[18]	camellias in a bowl	G35		
[20]	Tudor w/parrot on shoulder			
[22]	sketchbook of mice		P87	
[24]	Tudor and girl at window		P[18-19]	
[26]	kitchen pump and tulips			
[28]	close-up of kitchen wall stencil			Cdj
[30]	Tudor cleaning garden	G45		
[32]	chionodoxas with frost			
[34]	crocks and eggs			C36-37
[36]	girl spinning			C54,dj
[38]	daffodils and house		P[2-3]	
[40]	2 white doves at dove cote		P5	
[42]	tulips in bloom			
[44]	tulips in a bucket	G[46]		
[46]	Tudor and girl with goat		P[22-23]	
[48]	violet violas		P21	
[50]	Tudor gathering rhubarb			
[52]	painting of yellow roses			
[54]	Tudor and girl with pie			
[56]	clay planter in garden	G[12-13]		
[58]	Minou in a chair		P86	
[60]	Bourbon Variegata			
[62]	Tudor making daisy chain	G[98]		
[64]	combing hair		P62	
[66]	Summer bouquet	G[116]		
[68]	Tudor with scythe			
[70]	toy goat			C[148]
[72]	Tudor w/bowl of blueberries	G133		
[74]	Imperial Silver lilies on cloth	G126		
[76]	painting of apple tree and geese		P72	
[78]	tomatoes on outdoor table			C84
[80]	Tudor dipping candles			C[74]
[82]	Fall bouquet			
[84]	Tudor canoeing		P[94-95]	
[86]	gate under Fall maple		P92	
[88]	Tudor with red maple leaves			
[90]	ferns with first frost	G155		
[92]	pumpkin on a chair		P99	
[94]	Tudor w/kindling and Minou	G[156]-157		
[96]	girl lighting candles			C77
[98]	dried flower bouquet			C[43]

[100]	Kate Smith at fireplace		
[102]	salt glaze tea set		C46-47
[104]	frosting gingerbread		C92-93
[106]	red sled against tree	P111	
[108]	two girls at playhouse	P117	
[110]	Tudor in red cape in snow	P[108-109]	
[112]	1998 calendar and vole	P[1]	
Back cover	lily pond	G112	

COPYRIGHT REGISTRATION: TX 4-373-240 granted to Tovah Martin c/o Christina Ward Literary Agency, PO Box 515, North Scituate, Ma. 02060. Victoria Garbe, Houghton Mifflin Co., 222 Berkeley St., Boston, Ma. 02116 (617-351-5126), agent for Tovah Martin, swears on Oct. 21, 1996:

TASHA TUDOR'S ENGAGEMENT CALENDAR 1997 (6-97241) by Tovah Martin, domiciled in the U.S., a work completed in 1996 was published July 29, 1996. The book was neither anonymous, pseudonomous nor was it a work for hire. Fees charged to account DA 015539, Houghton Mifflin Company. Application and two deposit copies received Oct. 24, 1996, the effective date of registration.

COPYRIGHT REGISTRATION: VA 808-365 granted to Richard W. Brown c/o Rhoda Wyr Agency, 151 Bergen St., Brooklyn, NY 11217 . . . swears on Oct. 21, 1996:

TASHA TUDOR'S ENGAGEMENT CALENDAR 1997 (6-97241) With exception of some photos previously published, all new photographs by Richard W. Brown, domiciled in the U.S., a work completed in 1996 was published July 29, 1996. Other information as above.

COPYRIGHT REGISTRATION: VA 808-366 granted to Tasha Tudor c/o Doe Coover Agency, 58 Sagamore Ave., Medford, Ma 02155 . . . swears on Oct. 21, 1996:

TASHA TUDOR'S ENGAGEMENT CALENDAR 1997 (6-97240) with 2-dimensional artwork illustrations by Tasha Tudor, domiciled in the U.S., a work not made for hire completed in 1996 was published July 29, 1996. Other information as above.

T111 TASHA TUDOR'S [black] | Engagement Calendar [orange] | 1998 [black] ||

PHOTOGRAPHS BY RICHARD W. BROWN | TEXT BY TOVAH MARTIN | ILLUSTRATIONS BY TASHA TUDOR || Houghton Mifflin Company | Boston   New York [white on photographs]. [[from page [1]] [jar of wildflowers] Text copyright © 1997 by Tovah Martin | Photographs copyright © 1997 by Richard W. Brown | Illustrations copyright © 1997 by Tasha Tudor | Designed by Susan McClellan | All rights reserved | Printed in Italy]

PAGINATION: One hundred twelve unnumbered 170 gsm matte coated white paper pages and. Trim size to 8″ x 8″.   Examination copy measures 7 7/8 x 8 1/4″

COVER: Two 260 gsm gloss card stock covers, under film lamination in white WIRE-O binding. The front cover shows Tudor sitting in a rocker amidst the flowers in her dooryard sewing daisies. Two corgis and a potted fairy rose nearby. Cover text at top, white, except for (rose) *Engagement Calendar 1998*. Three rows: TASHA TUDOR'S | Engagement Calendar 1998 | *Photographs by* RICHARD W. BROWN. The back cover is a detail of raspberries and mint leaves in a blue bowl. Upper left corner: TASHA TUDOR'S [white]| Engagement Calendar [green] | 1998 [white].   At lower left corner in white: 6-81144 | $15.95 | Printed in Italy. A yellow box 1 5/16″ x 2 1/4″ at the lower right includes two UPC bar codes, in black ink. Above the larger left bar code: ISBN 0-395-86530-1, and below it 9 780395 865309. Above the right: 90000>.

CONTENTS: This is a derivative book from the earlier *Tasha Tudor's Garden*, *The Private World Of Tasha Tudor* and *Tasha Tudor's Heirloom Crafts*. The full color process book is a week-by-week engagement calendar with a Richard Brown photograph or an occasional Tudor water color on the verso and the week's blank schedule on the recto of each two-page spread. Each recto also includes a short narrative by Martin. The title page photograph pictures Tudor walking with two corgyn (Owen and Rebecca?) in her meadow with fall leaves, pp. [2-3]. Martin's introduction is on pages [4-5] with a Tudor painting of a tulip on each of these pages.

ILLUSTRATIONS: Tudor illustrations on pages: [1, 4, 5, 33, 61, 73, 83, 95, 112] The page/illustration correlation of ...*Engagement Calendar* to ... *Garden, The Private World* ... and ... *Heirloom Crafts* is:

ENGAGEMENT CALENDAR 1998		*TTG*	*PWTT*	*TTHC*
Front cover	Tudor in front 'yard'	G104-105		
[1]	painting of wildflower bouquet	G100		
Title pages [2-3]	Tudor in meadow			
[4]	painting of tulip	G58		
[5]	painting of tulip	G58		
[6]	house and gardens in snow			
[8]	Tudor in settle holding baby corgi	G33		
[10]	frost on window pane			
[12]	pantry scene with cookbook			C[82]
[13]	three tin cookie cutters			C10
[14]	Tudor in red cape with rooster	G29		
[16]	toy Horatio and Edgar on trunk			C146
[18]	snowshoes parked in snow	G27		
[20]	Tudor sewing at fireplace			Cdj,[114]
[22]	yarn in basket			C[94]
[24]	Tudor tending indoor hothouse			
[26]	Tudor walking down barn approach			
[28]	girl in white dress			C130
[30]	daffodils sprouting through oak leaves	G30		
[32]	Tudor with gray parrot on shoulder		P[82-83]	
[33]	brown sketch of parrot			
[34]	Tudor in boots holding pussy willows	G38		
[36]	purple crocus	G40		
[38]	Tudor in her bedroom		P8	
[40]	daffodils in blue jug		P16	
[42]	pink magnolias in bloom			
[44]	Tudor potting violets and primrose	G[43]		
46]	orange Icelandic poppy in garden			
[48]	bouquet of tulips	G10		
[50]	Tudor inspecting blooms			
[52]	Magic violas	G62		
[54]	bed of lupine, pinks and Elizabeth poppies		P[26]	
[56]	Tudor and girl with pink peonies			
[58]	strawberries		P44	
[60]	Tudor and Minou in garden		P39	
[61]	pencil sketch of Minou			
[62]	two girls in garden		P[64-65]	
[64]	Tudor holding Nubian kid		P25	
[66]	water lilies in bowl	G114		
[68]	Tudor and children picking raspberries	G118-119		
[70]	Tudor at lunch on the porch	G[18-19]		
[72]	pink hollyhocks	G123		
[73]	corgi sniffing at hollyhocks			

[74]	Tudor gathering sweet peas			
[76]	Tudor cleaning clay pots			
[78]	colchicum	G140		
[80]	girl in blue dress with dried flowers			
[82]	three Fall maples			
83]	painting of two maples leaves	G145		
[84]	Tudor with yoke and 2 water buckets			
[86]	Fall bouquet in crock	G150-151		
[88]	Kate Smith hatchelling flax, Minou in barn door way			C53
[90]	ferns with first frost			
[92]	house in late Fall		P98	
[94]	white rooster on the wood pile			C21
[95]	pencil sketch of two chickens			
[96]	close-up of kitchen wall		P103	
[98]	blue Canton platter			C39
[100]	Tudor at stove, parrot on shoulder		P[126-127]	
[101]	butter mold			C10
[102]	bottles in winter window			C49
[104]	Tudor knitting			
[106]	Tudor, girl and dog marionette			C134-135
[108]	detail of Christmas tree			
[109]	gingerbread squirrel			C92
[110]	Tudor in red cape and corgyn in snow		P[128-129]	
[112]	gooseberries			
Back cover	raspberries in blue bowl on red cloth	G17		

OTHER: Sfera, Milan, Italy, printed 17,500 copies; delivered in early July 1997.

T112 *Tasha Tudor's* | FAIRY TALES | [Rumpelstiltskin 4 13/16″ roundel] | Selected, Edited, and Illustrated by Tasha Tudor || Platt & Munk, Publishers/New York | A Division of Grosset & Dunlap. [*Platt & Munk Books by Tasha Tudor* || First Delights | A Book About the Five Senses | First Poems of Childhood | Tasha Tudor's Bedtime Book | Tasha Tudor's Fairy Tales || Copyright © 1988, 1969, 1965, 1961 by Platt & Munk, Publishers, a division of Grosset & Dunlap, | a member of The Putnam Publishing Group, New York. | All rights reserved. Printed in Hong Kong. | Published simultaneously in Canada. | ISBN 0-448-09329-4. Library of Congress Catalog Card Number 87-82518.]

PAGINATION: Three signatures white kid paper: [1-8] 9-15 [16] 17-21 [22-23] 24-26 [27] 28-30 [31] 32-37 [38] 39-43 [44] 45 [46-48] including covers. Eight stitches saddle sewn. 11″ x 9 1/4″.

COVER: Light blue with thin black rule around the design. Little Red Riding Hood illustration from page [16] on front, full size with title as on title page. Spine: [rule] *Tasha Tudor's* **FAIRY TALES** Platt & Munk [rule]. Back cover, upper left corner: $10.95 | rule | (15.50 CAN) || [roundel (upper center of Puss in Boots from page [44]] || *Included in This Collection* || Thumbelina | Red Riding Hood | Rumpelstiltskin | Sleeping Beauty | The Emperor's New Clothes | Cinderella | Puss in Boots || UPC code | 0 70918 09329 6 [lower left]   ISBN 0-448-09329-4 [lower right]. Back cover is also boxed with a thin black rule.

CONTENTS: End papers: pp. [2-3] [46-47]; page [46] has two paragraphs about Tasha Tudor, the other three have cameos cut from the Emperor's New Clothes illustration, page [31]. Pp. [2-3] are pale blue with darker blue box border. Pp. [46-47] are similar, but with white inside the border. Page [4] is blank white. Title page illustration is from page [22]. Instead of the previous *Foreword* on the title page verso, there is the list of Platt & Munk Books. Rumpelstiltskin illustration from page 19 is printed atop the contents box on page [7]. Five stories have been dropped which were in the 1969 edition. The following pages are reprinted with changed numbering. Correlation of pages between the . . .

	1988 edition	and the	1969 edition	is:
Thumbelina	[8]-13		[4]-9	
Red Riding Hood	14-18		60-64	
Rumpelstiltskin	19-[23]		25-[29]	
Sleeping Beauty	24-28		34-38	
The Emperor's New Clothes	29-32		39-42	
Cinderella	33-40		10-17	
Puss in Boots	41-45		52-56	

From page [46]: TASHA TUDOR, one of America's foremost illustrators of | children's books, has always had a special feeling for the world | of folk and fairy tales. Her fanciful interpretations capture | the wit and sparkle of these classic stories. She sees the beauty | and magic in the everyday things of the house, the woods, | and the fields and weaves them all skillfully into her | illustrations. || Born in Boston, Tasha Tudor grew up on a farm in | Connecticut, and her impressions of rural New England life | are the inspiration for her artwork. She has won many | awards and honors since her first book was published in | 1938. More than sixty books later, her gift is still unique. | She lives in Vermont where she is surround by her corgis, | her family and friends—and the country pleasures so | lovingly depicted in her books.

ILLUSTRATIONS: Full page color illustrations: [8], [16], [22], [27], [31], [38], [44]. Illustrations for Cinderella and Puss in Boots are slightly changed: Page 35 (the third page of the story) has the pumpkin design from the second page of the 1969 edition. It has been reversed on page 34. Flower borders of pp. 12-13 of the 1969 edition are not used. Wisteria cap hanging to the left on page 36 is used only once (it was on pages 14 and 16 in 1969), but it is reversed twice, on pages 37 and 39. (This right hanging version did not appear in 1969.) Wheat on page 43 is reversed from page 54 of the 1969 printing.

OTHER: A revision and re-issue of *The Tasha Tudor Book Of Fairy Tales* (1969) with the changes noted.

COPYRIGHT REGISTRATION: TX 2-301-453 granted to Platt & Munk Publishers, Inc., 51 Madison Ave., N.Y., N.Y. 10010, transfer by written agreement. Louise Bates, Putnam Publishing Group, 51 Madison Ave., N.Y., N.Y. 10010, agent for claimant, swears on May 2, 1988:

TASHA TUDOR'S FAIRY TALES, an abridged selection and illustrations by Tasha Tudor, a U.S. citizen, was completed in 1988 and published May 2, 1988. The book is derivative of TASHA TUDOR'S FAIRY TALES originally published by Platt & Munk in 1961. It was manufactured by South China Printing Co., Hong Kong. The Library of Congress is granted non-exclusive permission to make copies and phonorecords for the blind and physically handicapped. Fees charged to account DA038288, Putnam Publishing Group (The P&M). Application and two deposit copies received May 3, 1988.

T113 _____. [*Platt & Munk . . . Fairy Tales* || 1989 Printing | Copyright . . . 87-82518]

PAGINATION: Ten stitches saddle sewn.

COVER: Back, lower left: ISBN 0-448-09329-4 || [two bar codes, and above the smaller right one] 51095; beneath the larger left one: 9 780448 093291.

T114 _____. [*Platt & Munk . . . Fairy Tales* || 1990 Printing | Copyright . . . 87-82518]

COVER: Back, upper left: $10.95 | [rule] | (14.50 CAN).

T115 **Tasha Tudor's | Favorite | Christmas Carols** || [a Madonna] || *Illustrated by Tasha Tudor and Linda Allen* || DAVID McKAY COMPANY, INC. | New York [Illustrations by Tasha

Tudor, Courtesy of | American Artists Group, Inc. || *Design by Jane Preston* || **Library of Congress Cataloging in Publication Data** | Main entry under title: || Tasha Tudor's Favorite Christmas carols. || 1. Carols. 2. Christmas music. I. Tudor, | Tasha. II. Title: Favorite Christmas carols. | M2065.T23 [(M5400)] 783.6'55'2 77-29242 | ISBN 0-679-20975-1 || Copyright © 1978 by Tasha Tudor and Linda Allen || All rights reserved, including the right to | reproduce this book, or parts thereof, in any | form, except for the inclusion of brief quotations | in a review. || 10 9 8 7 6 5 4 3 2 1 | Manufactured in the United States of America]

PAGINATION: 4 signatures, cream paper. [i-viii] ix [x, 1] 2-3 [4] 5-6 [7] 8-9 [10] 11-12 [13] 14-15 [16] 17-19 [20] 21 [22] 23-24 [25] 26-27 [28] 29-31 [32] 33 [34] 35-36 [37] 38-40 [41] 42-43 [44] 45-46 [47] 48-49 [50] 51-52 [53-54] plus endpapers. 11 5/16″ x 8 1/2″.

COVER: Scarlet cloth with gilt title on front: TASHA TUDOR'S | FAVORITE | CHRISTMAS CAROLS. Spine stamped laterally in gilt: TASHA TUDOR'S FAVORITE CHRISTMAS CAROLS Tudor/Allen [McKay monogram] McKay. Textured, mustard end papers.

DUST JACKET: Wine with yellow lettering, front: TASHA TUDOR'S | FAVORITE | CHRISTMAS CAROLS | [an oval vignette, woman and three children singing at a parlor organ] | Illustrated by | Tasha Tudor and Linda Allen. Spine as on book, but in yellow. Back has a central wheat wreath; 0-679-20975-1 in lower right. Yellow flaps printed in wine, red and black. Front flap, top right, black: $7.95. TASHA TUDOR'S | FAVORITE | CHRISTMAS CAROLS || Illustrated by | Tasha Tudor and Linda Allen [wine] | [most of remaining text is black] Tasha Tudor, who is noted for evoking | the spirit of Christmas in many of her in- | comparable picture books, has chosen 17 | of her favorite Christmas carols for this | collection. Exquisite, detailed illustrations | by Miss Tudor and by her talented young | friend, Linda Allen, enhance the words | and simple piano arrangements. Included | are guitar chords, and a brief history of | each of the well-loved songs. || ¶TASHA TUDOR [red] was born and grew | up in New England, where she presently | lives. She attended the Boston Museum | School of Art and later studied at the | Kennington School of Art in London, but | she is largely a self-taught artist. Her first | book for children was *Pumpkin Moon-* | *shine,* published in 1938. Since that time, | she has illustrated several of the classics | for children and has written and illustrated | many of her own award-winning stories. | Miss Tudor has received numerous honors | for her work, including the Catholic | Library Association's Regina Medal for | her "continued distinguished contribution | to children's literature." ¶LINDA ALLEN [red] first met Tasha Tudor | in 1976. "I came to make slip covers for | Miss Tudor's furniture—supposedly a stay | of one week," she recalls. "I never left." ¶ Miss Allen, who has always lived in | New England, attended schools in New | Hampshire. In addition to painting and | drawing, she and Miss Tudor share many | interests, including spinning, weaving, and | other crafts and customs of the 19th | century. Back flap: *Other books written and* | *illustrated by Tasha Tudor* [red] || A IS FOR ANNABELLE | THE COUNTY FAIR | THE DOLLS' CHRISTMAS | 1 IS ONE | PUMPKIN MOONSHINE | A TALE FOR EASTER | TASHA TUDOR'S SAMPLER [black] || *Illustrated by Tasha Tudor* [red] || A CHILD'S GARDEN OF VERSES | FIRST PRAYERS | MORE PRAYERS | MOTHER GOOSE | FIRST GRACES || "No one makes lovelier picture books than | Tasha Tudor, whose delicate pictures sug- | gest Kate Greenaway and whose humor | suggests Beatrix Potter."—*Horn Book* || "What Tasha Tudor can do with color is | something to dream about, something to | feast the eyes upon again and again. . . . | The artist captures the innocence of child- | hood in a way that is inimitably Tasha | Tudor."—*Philadelphia Inquirer* [black] || *Jacket design by Linda Allen* [red] || DAVID McKAY COMPANY, INC. | 750 Third Avenue | New York, N.Y. 10017 [black].

CONTENTS: History of each song appears as on a gray broadside curling at the bottom, each on a separate page. Half-title, [i]; *Other Books Written and Illustrated by Tasha Tudor,* [v] lists same titles as back flap, except for spelling ONE IS ONE; and second list is reordered, A CHILD'S GARDEN OF VERSES | FIRST GRACES | FIRST PRAYERS | MORE PRAYERS | MOTHER GOOSE; Contents, [vii]; Preface, ix; Guitar chords, [54].

ILLUSTRATIONS: Color illustrations by Tasha Tudor from earlier Christmas cards: frontispiece [ii], title page [iii], [vi, 1, 13, 37, 41, 44, 53]. Illustrations by Linda Allen: in color [4, 16, 20, 25, 28, 32]; black and white [viii, 7, 10, 15, 23, 34, 47,50].

COPYRIGHT REGISTRATION: TX 124-214 granted to Tasha Tudor and Linda Allen, both of Route 4, West Brattleboro, Vt. 05031. H.J. Rabinovitz, David McKay Co., Inc., 750 Third Ave., N.Y., N.Y. 10017, agent for the authors, swears on Oct. 2, 1978:

TASHA TUDOR'S FAVORITE CHRISTMAS CAROLS, preface and illustrations by Tasha Tudor, illustrations by Linda Allen, both U.S. citizens, a work completed in 1978 was published Aug. 25, 1978. Pre-existing material is Christmas carols - words, music and author listed. Material added to this work: preface, illustrations, brief history of each carol. The book was manufactured by Automated Composition, 575 Lexington, Ave., N.Y., N.Y., Federated Litho. (Print.) 369 Prairie Ave., Providence, R.I. 02901, and Kennan Binders, Inc., 200 Pond Ave., Middlesex, N.J. 08846. Fees charged to account DA050830, David McKay Co., Inc. Application and deposit received at LC Oct. 10, 1978.

T116 _____.

DUST JACKET: The price on front jacket flap is $8.95. Otherwise, as above.

T117 _____. [Illustrations . . . review. || 10 9 8 7 6 5 4 3 2 . . . America]

PAGINATION: Ivory paper.

COVER: Wine cloth.

T118 _____. [Illustrations . . . *Preston* | First paperback edition: August, 1984 || **Library** . . . ISBN 0-679-20985-9 || Copyright © 1978. . . review. || 10 9 8 7 6 5 4 3 | Manufactured in the United States of America]

PAGINATION: 10 15/16″ x 8 1/4″.

COVER: Wine paper wrapper reproduces dj front of first edition. Yellow spine lettering as before, but slightly reduced in size. Back cover is yellow and reproduces an enlarged title, byline and first paragraph from the former dj front flap: $9.95 [black] || TASHA TUDOR'S ... Linda Allen [wine] || Tasha Tudor, who is noted for evoking the spirit of Christmas | in many of her incomparable picture books, has chosen 17 of | her favorite Christmas carols for this collection. Exquisite, de- | tailed illustrations by Miss Tudor and by her talented young | friend, Linda Allen, enhance the words and simple piano | arrangements. Included are guitar chords, and a brief history | of each of the well-loved songs. Tasha Tudor, who is noted for evoking...of each of the well-loved songs. || *Cover design by Linda Allen* || DAVID McKAY COMPANY, INC. | 2 Park Avenue | New York, NY 10016 || ISBN: 0-679-20975-1 ['computer' font in lower right rear].

T119 **TASHA TUDOR'S** | *FAVORITE* | *STORIES* | *Illustrated in Full Color* || **J. B. LIPPINCOTT COMPANY** | *Philadelphia and New York* [COPYRIGHT © 1965 BY TASHA TUDOR | PRINTED IN THE UNITED STATES OF AMERICA | LIBRARY OF CONGRESS CATALOG CARD NUMBER 65-21668 | FIRST EDITION || ACKNOWLEDGMENTS || Thanks go to the following publishers, agents, and individuals for their kind permission to | reprint material copyrighted or controlled by them: | Doubleday and Company, Inc., Mrs. George Bambridge, and the Macmillan Company of | Canada, Ltd. for "The Cat That Walked by Himself" from *Just So Stories* by Rudyard Kipling. | Houghton Mifflin Company for "Wicked John and the Devil" from *Grandfather Tales* by Richard | Chase, copyright 1948 by Houghton Mifflin Company. | Harold Ober Associates for "The Little Dressmaker" from *The Little Bookroom* by Eleanor | Farjeon, copyright © 1955 by Eleanor Farjeon, published by Henry Z. Walck, Inc.]

PAGINATION: [1-10] 11-18 [19] 20-23 [24] 25-29 [30] 31-46 [47] 48-55 [56] 57-62 [63] 64-72 [73] 74-83 [84] 85-88 [89] 90-91 [92] 93-98 [99] 100-115 [116] 117 [118] 119-128 [129] 130-131 [132] in 7 signatures, buff paper, plus the end papers. Blank pages: [2, 6, 10, 24, 56, 92, 118, 132]. 9 3/4″ x 7 3/4″.

COVER: Half-paper, light blue with a filament of black hair over boards, overlapping spine wrapped in green cloth. Stamping in carmine ink: an owl on a branch on the front; on spine, TASHA TUDOR'S *FAVORITE STORIES* LIPPINCOTT.

DUST JACKET: Dust jacket is green stone pattern printed with a wreath of oak leaves, acorns, pine needles and other around the front text. An acorn and cap centered on the front and back, and at the top and bottom of spine. Black printing: **TASHA TUDOR'S** | *FAVORITE* | *STORIES* ‖ [acorn] ‖ *Illustrated in* | *FULL COLOR*. Spine: **TASHA TUDOR'S** *FAVORITE STORIES* **LIPPINCOTT**. Jacket front flap clipped at bottom, no price evident. The initials LLB are not printed on this jacket. Front flap text in black (except as noted): **TASHA TUDOR'S** [red] | *FAVORITE* | *STORIES* | *Illustrated in Full Color* [red] ‖ "Tell me a story" is probably one | of the oldest requests in the world | and one which Tasha Tudor remem- | bers from her own childhood and | from her own children's voices. | Every person and every family have | their favorite stories, some old and | some new. To an artist of Tasha | Tudor's talents these favorites in- | spire a desire to paint the people, the | places, and the animals. ¶In this collection of stories, the | selections vary from fairy tales loved | by generations to folk legends rich | in the spirit of the past. Hans | Christian Andersen, Rudyard | Kipling, Eleanor Farjeon, and Mark | Twain are but a few of the many | authors represented. The ten stories | which Miss Tudor has chosen from | among her favorites are enhanced by | full-color illustrations and black-and- | white decorative drawings. ‖ All ages [bottom corner clipped]. Back flap headed by a 3 ½″ x 2 13/16″ black and white photo of Tudor with a cat under which appears: *Photo by Gerda Peterich* | Ever since her first book, *Pump-* | *kin Moonshine*, was published some | years ago, Tasha Tudor has had a | busy and distinguished career writ- | ing and illustrating books for young | readers. Her delicate color work and | charming pencil drawings have ap- | peared in many books, including new | editions of Frances Hodgson Bur- | nett's *The Secret Garden* and *A Little* | *Princess* and most recently, *Wings* | *From the Wind*, a poetry anthology | which is a companion volume to | *Tasha Tudor's Favorite Stories*. ¶Tasha Tudor lives in an old New | Hampshire farmhouse which is big | enough to hold her four children and | many visiting friends and cousins, not | to mention the animals, who are an | integral part of the family. There is a | garden, too, a grove of sugar maples, | and blue New Hampshire mountains | in the distance. ‖ J. B. LIPPINCOTT COMPANY | *Good Books Since 1792* | Philadelphia and New York.

ILLUSTRATIONS: Endpapers printed with a two-page border of twigs and berries in terracotta ink; a squirrel on a branch centered on the left page and an owl on a branch centered on the right. Repeated at back.

Full page color illustrations: Title page [3] a border of weeds, [19] She tied the thread to the little clap spindle-whorl | and drew it across the floor. [30] Harold could only stand and blubber hopelessly. [47] Rag flinched but plunged with a little 'ouch.' [63] Standin' in the door was the Old Boy himself, with his horns and | his tail and that old cow's foot of his'n. [73] Tom sat literally rolling in wealth. [84] Agamemnon fell to the ground. [89] The donkey, as the biggest, went to the window and looked in. [99] Making an elegant bow, he added, 'Duchess, | may I have the honour of this dance?' [116] It was a picnic tea, and we had it in Our Field. [129] From the thicket before him came three lovely white swans. Half page pencil drawings on pages [7] boy, girl and corgi at picnic, 11 - a stalking cat, 25 - a tea set, 33 - two rabbits, 57 - Wicked John and the beggar, 67 - Tom Sawyer with brush and bucket, 75- cannon, flag and fireworks, 86 - cat, dog, mule and rooster, 93 - an 18th century woman sewing, two boys, a girl and a corgi with rock and berries, a cat, hen and duckling beside a wooden basket,

CONTENTS: Half-title, pages [1, 9]. Dedication page [5] : To Virginia Lightner. CONTENTS [7-8]

OTHER: The dedicatee is a family friend, benefactor and resident of Marion, Ohio. A number of the citations to Ohio newspapers in the Periodicals section of this bibliography were gathered and organized by Mrs. Lightner, and were generously made available to us by Mary Rand Lightner. Virginia Lightner arranged for certain Tudor appearances in Ohio.

COPYRIGHT REGISTRATION: A 805370 granted to Tasha Tudor, Route 1, Contoocook, N.H. Charles Granade, Jr., J.B. Lippincott Co., 227 South Sixth St., Phila. Pa. 19106, agent for Tasha Tudor, swears on Nov. 10, 1965:

TASHA TUDOR'S FAVORITE STORIES, by Tasha Tudor, a U.S. citizen, was published Oct. 14, 1965. New matter in this version: illustrations, compilation. The book was manufactured by Reehl Litho, Inc., 305 East 45th St., N.Y., N.Y., Eastern Typesetting, 433 Church St., Hartford, Ct., and Economy Bookbinding Corp., 234 Schuyler Ave., Kearny, N.J. Fees charged to J. B. Lippincott Co. Application and affidavit and two deposit copies received at LC Dec. 3, 1965.

COPYRIGHT RENEWAL REGISTRATION: RE 646-745 granted to Tasha Tudor, c/o HarperCollins Publishers, Inc., 10 East 53rd St., N.Y., N.Y. 10022, claiming as the author. Joanne Fallert, HarperCollins, Publishers, Inc., 10 East 53rd St., 12th floor, N.Y., N.Y., agent for Tasha Tudor, swears on Dec. 9, 1993:

TASHA TUDOR'S FAVORITE STORIES, renewable illustrations and compilation by Tasha Tudor, was originally published Oct. 14, 1965. Fee charged to HarperCollins, Publishers, Inc. Renewal application received at LC Dec. 27, 1993.

AMERICAN BOOK PUBLISHING RECORD CUMULATIVE 1965, page 1283: TUDOR, Tasha, comp. *JUV | Favorite stories.* Philadelphia, Lippincott [c.1965] | 131p. illus. (pt. col.) 26cm. [PZ5.T8Fav] 65-21688 | 3.95; lib. ed., 3.79 | *1. Children's stories* | All ages.

HarperCollins Publishers archives contain:

Lippincott's COMPLETE CATALOG OF PUBLICATIONS…July 1, 1965 (page 55) lists Tudor as editor of this book "In Preparation" for (1965). Versions are indicated as j [junior] and LLB [Lippincott Longlife Binding] net. Another copy of the catalog in the HarperCollins archives has been hand annotated with the notations 11-29-65, 3.95 and LLB-3.79. The … July 1, 1966 - July 1, 1969 catalogs record the title with those prices and the further note, 119 pages. A pencil notation in 1969 catalog amends the W j price from 3.95 to 4.95. Catalogs June 1, 1970 - June 1, 1972 list at W j 4.95 | LLB 3.79. The June 1, 1972 CATALOG includes LC 65-21668, and ISBNs 0-397-30837-X and 0-397-30838-8 *for the first time.* The price for the trade edition increases to 5.95 in the June 1, 1973 CATALOG. The June 1, 1974-…1978 CATALOGS increase the trade price to 6.50. The LLB price always remains 3.79 net. LIPPINCOTT BOOKS FOR YOUNG READERS • 1977/78 also lists …FAVORITE STORIES with this new information: 7 1/2" x 9 1/2" and 132pp.

1.   A contract for THE TASHA TUDOR BOOK OF PROSE was signed by Tudor and Joseph W. Lippincott, Jr., December 3, 1964, and witnessed by Allan John Woods. Someone subsequently penciled a new title Tasha Tudor's Favorite Stories above the typed title.

2.   Tudor contracted "To deliver to the Publisher on or before March 1, 1965 two complete manuscript copies of said Work satisfactory to the Publisher in content and form, in length approximately 35,000 words, complete and ready for the printer, together with one set of illustrations therefor, and all necessary releases and permissions for the use of copyright materials."

3.   Tudor was to receive 6 free copies of the Work and could buy further copies at a 40%   discount for her own use, but not for resale.

4.   A Lippincott letter from Charles Granade to Tudor dated October 17, 1977 states that Lippincott stock is larger than needed to meet current demand, and copies may be remaindered. He offers

Tudor 10 complementary copies, and up to 20 more copies at $3.02 if she responds by October 26, 1977. In response, she checked her desire not to receive any copies of the book October 20, 1977.

T120 _____.

DUST JACKET: Top corner clipped from jacket front flap: LLB ‖ **TASHA TUDOR'S** … All ages $3.95. Otherwise, as above.

T121 _____.

COVER: The cloth covers are printed with the dust jacket design, glazed. This is a LIPPINCOTT LONGLIFE BINDING for sale to libraries. The body of the book as above; the same papers are used. The hinges are reinforced with white linen.

DUST JACKET: The price is clipped from the bottom of the front flap leaving the words All ages. Printed across the top of the flap is LLB $3.79 net, identifying this to be the binding for sale to libraries. Lippincott's gold foil label is wrapped around the spine near the bottom: LLB This symbol | identifies a | LIPPINCOTT | LONGLIFE BINDING. LIPPINCOTT | LONGLIFE | BINDING is printed twice more on the label, sideways on the spine, and sideways on the back.

T122 _____. Have not examined a 2nd printing.

T123 _____. [COPYRIGHT © 1965 BY TASHA TUDOR | PRINTED IN THE UNITED STATES OF AMERICA | LIBRARY OF CONGRESS CATALOG CARD NUMBER 65-21668 ‖ THIRD PRINTING ‖ ACKNOWLEDGMENTS…]

COVER: Half-paper is green, not blue.

DUST JACKET: No printing at top of front flap; the bottom text is: All ages $4.95.

T124 _____. [COPYRIGHT © 1965 BY TASHA TUDOR | PRINTED IN THE UNITED STATES OF AMERICA | LIBRARY OF CONGRESS CATALOG CARD NUMBER 65-21668 | Fourth Printing | ISBN-0-397-30837-X   Trade Ed. | ISBN-0-397-30838-8 LLB Ed. ‖ ACKNOWLEDGMENTS…]

COVER: Green paper over boards.

DUST JACKET: Dust jacket has no printing at the top; . . . white decorative drawings. ‖ Fourth Printing | All ages   [price clipped]. Back flap: . . . Philadelphia and New York | ISBN-0-397-30837-X   Trade Ed.

OTHER: Examined a copy inscribed: . . . 1973.

T125 _____. [COPYRIGHT © 1965 BY TASHA TUDOR | PRINTED IN THE UNITED STATES OF AMERICA | LIBRARY OF CONGRESS CATALOG CARD NUMBER 65-21668 | **Fifth Printing** | ISBN 0-397-30837-X   Trade ed. | ACKNOWLEDGMENTS | Thanks . . .]

PAGINATION: Seven signatures of ivory paper, plus the end papers. 9 3/4″ x 7 3/4″.

COVER: Half, mint green paper with a filament of black hair over boards, spine wrapped in green cloth. White endpapers printed in carmine as before.

DUST JACKET: Front flap: **TASHA TUDOR'S** . . . white decorative drawings. ‖ Fifth Printing | All ages $6.50.

T126 TASHA TUDOR'S | *Five* | *Senses*. Have not examined a hardcover copy of the first edition.

T127 TASHA TUDOR'S | *Five* | *Senses* | P&M [in locomotive outline] | PLATT & MUNK, PUBLISHERS/*New York*. From page [4]: [Copyright © 1978 by Platt & Munk, Publishers | All rights reserved. | Printed in the United States of America | Library of Congress Catalog Card Number 77-82326 | ISBN 0-8228-9601-X (paperback) | ISBN 0-8228-0550-2 (hardcover)]

PAGINATION: [28] pp. in one signature including wrapper, stapled. 9 9/32″ x 8 1/16″.

COVER: Full color wrapper, front is yellow. A girl holding a rabbit inside a floral and laurel half-round, inside and the lower half of a larger floral and laurel rectangle. Above the half-round: TASHA TUDOR'S [red] | *Five Senses* [black]. Below the half-round: **Platt** & **Munk** [black]. In the upper left corner: A Pandaback Book, printed laterally along the left side of a panda logo and 95c in a rectangle. Back cover, cream with illustration of bunny, corgi and duckling near bottom; upper left, 9601:0095.

ILLUSTRATIONS: Measure 7″ x 5 1/8″ and are on yellow or blue wash ground—most are blue sky over yellow 'ground.'

CONTENTS: Pages [2, 27] are blank. Page [3], half title with blue bird on an apple bough.

OTHER: Previously published as *First Delights, A Book About the Five Senses*. Text, revised from *First Delights,* pages [6-26]: [6] Sally lives on a farm. As the | seasons change from spring to | summer, from fall to winter, she | uses her five senses to enjoy the | things that happen there all year. [7] In spring, Sally sees the first | flowers, the new leaves. She | watches the fields and woods | turn soft and green. [8] She hears the robins singing, the | brooks running, and the frogs trilling in the pond. [9] She smells the daffodils and the | warm earth. [10] She touches her brand new | kittens. [11] She tastes syrup from the maple | trees, and she makes "sugar on | snow." [12] When spring has turned to | summer, Sally sees the hay cut | in the fields. [13] She hears the cowbells in the | green pastures. [14] She smells wild roses. [15] She touches fat puppies, with soft, | soft fur. [16] She tastes wild strawberries. [17] When summer has changed to | fall, Sally sees bright leaves | against blue sky. [18] She hears the call of wild geese. [19] She smells cornstalks and | pumpkins. [20] She touches smooth new acorns. [21] She tastes ripe red apples. [22] When fall becomes winter, | Sally sees the snow on field and | wood. [23] She hears sleigh bells. [24] She smells wood smoke. [25] She touches shining Christmas | balls. [26] She tastes a candy cane, enjoying | Christmas just as she does the | special moments of every season | on the farm.

COPYRIGHT REGISTRATION: TX 1-036-254 granted to Platt & Munk, Publishers, 51 Madison Ave., N.Y., N.Y. 10010. Louise Bates, Grosset & Dunlap, Inc., 51 Madison Ave., N.Y., N.Y. 10010 (212-689-9200), agent for claimant, swears on Nov. 15, 1982:

TASHA TUDOR'S FIVE SENSES, the entire work by Platt & Munk, Publishers (Employer for hire), a U.S. citizen, was completed in 1978 and published Dec. 15, 1978. L.C. is granted non-exclusive permission to make copies and phonorecords for the blind and physically handicapped. The book was manufactured by Danner Press Corp., PO Box 8349, 1250 Camden Ave., Canton, Oh. 44709. Fees charged to account DA034886, Grosset & Dunlap, Inc. Application and two deposit copies received Nov. 17, 1982.

T128 _____. From page [4]: [Copyright © 1978 by Platt & Munk, Publishers | All rights reserved. | Printed in the United States of America | Library of Congress Catalog Card Number 77-82326 | ISBN 0-448-13134-X | Special Library Edition | Distributed by Grosset & Dunlap.

PAGINATION: [28] pp. in one signature sewn into hardback with reinforced cloth hinge. 9 3/8″ x 8 1/8″.

COVER: Front cover has no publisher's name below the half-round and lacks price in the panda logo. Spine: GROSSET & DUNLAP 13134 [in black at base]. Back cover illustrated as above, upper left,

0-448-13134-X. A 3″ x 3 1/4″ white box outlined with a thin black rule is centered on the back cover. Within this box a black rule semicircle encloses an multi-colored array of GROSSET & DUNLAP'S SCHOOL & LIBRARY BINDING repeated 5.5 times above the GD logo and FOR CONSTANT EXTENDED USE. Beneath the semicircle: Distributed by | GROSSET & DUNLAP, INC. | Educational Division | 51 Madison Avenue, New York 10010 | A FILMWAYS COMPANY.

T129 _____. . . . PLATT & MUNK, PUBLISHERS/*New York* | **A Division of Grosset & Dunlap.** From page [4]: [Copyright © 1978 by Platt & Munk, Publishers | All rights reserved. | Printed in the United States of America | Library of Congress Catalog Card Number 77-82326 | ISBN 0-448-49601-1 (paperback) | ISBN 0-448-40550-4 (hardbound)]

PAGINATION: [28] pp. in three gatherings topsewn. 9 1/2″ x 8 1/8″.

COVER: Yellow paper over boards under gloss film lamination. Below the half-round: **Platt** & **Munk** | A Division of Grosset & Dunlap [black]. Spine: *Five Senses* [red]   TASHA TUDOR'S **Platt** & **Munk**   40550-4. Back cover, bottom right: ISBN 0-448-440550-4; upper left, 40550:0350. Cloth hinge.

CONTENTS: Pages [1-2, 27-28] are blank. Page [3], half title with blue bird on an apple bough.

OTHER: This printing was misbound. The middle two sheets were bound following the first four so that text pages are in this order: [6] Sally lives . . . [7] In spring, . . . [8] She hears . . . [9] She smells the daffodils . . . [10] She touches . . . [11] She smells cornstalks . . . [12] She touches smooth . . . [13] She tastes . . . [14] When fall . . . [15] She hears sleigh . . . [16] She smells wood . . . [17] She touches shining . . . [18] She tastes a candy cane . . . [19] She tastes syrup . . . [20] When spring . . . [21] She hears the cowbells . . . [22] She smells wild roses. [23] She touches fat puppies . . . [24] She tastes wild strawberries. [25] When summer . . . [26] She hears the call of wild geese.

T130 _____.

PAGINATION: [28] pp. in one signature stapled into a paper wrapper. 9 3/16″ x 8″.

COVER: Upper left front corner: A Pandaback Book, a panda logo and 95c in a rectangle. Back with illustration and at bottom right: 0-448-49601-1.

CONTENTS: Pages are gathered into one signature in the correct order.

T131 _____. . . . **A Division of Grosset & Dunlap** | Copyright © 1978 by Platt & Munk, Publishers. All rights reserved. Printed in the United States of America. | Published simultaneously in Canada. Library of Congress Catalog Card Number: 77-82326. | ISBN:0-448-40550-4 (Trade Edition); ISBN: 0-448-49601-1 (Paperback Edition); ISBN: 0-448-13134-X (Library Edition)."

PAGINATION: Topsewn without cloth hinge.   9 1/2″ x 8 3/16″.

COVER: Back, top left: 49550:0395; bottom right: ISBN 0-448-40550-4.

T132 _____.

PAGINATION: [28] pp. including paper wrapper. 9 1/4″ x 8 1/16″.

COVER: The Pandaback emblem is in the upper left cover, but without a price. Back, top left: 49601:0125; bottom right: 0-448-49601-1.

ILLUSTRATIONS: The skies are a strong blue color.

PAGINATION: [28] pp. on a thin paper including paper wrapper. 9 1/4″ x 8 1/16″.

COVER: The Pandaback emblem is in the upper left cover, but without a price. Back, only the illustration of bunny, puppy and duckling.

ILLUSTRATIONS: The skies are a light pallid blue color.

T134 Tasha Tudor's | GARDEN | [leaf design] | Text by Tovah Martin | Photographs by Richard W. Brown ‖ [boy and dolphin logo] | Houghton Mifflin Company | Boston New York | 1994. [Text copyright © 1994 by Tovah Martin | Photographs copyright © 1994 by Richard W. Brown | Illustrations copyright © 1994 by Tasha Tudor | All rights reserved ‖ Printed in Italy ‖ *Book design by Susan McClellan*]

PAGINATION: [1-6] 7-10 [11-13] 14-16, in a white cover stock wrapper, stapled. 10 1/2″ x 8 1/2″.

DUST JACKET: Mock-up jacket approximates that which was marketed on the first edition. It is smaller: 10 17/32″ versus the finished 10 7/8″. Type on the front is smaller. The title letters are 27/32″ high versus the published 7/8″, and the credits at the bottom of front are 7/32″ and not the published 5/16″. The front and back photographs are identical, gloss film lamination. There is no spine, and the back lacks the bar code box. The text of the flaps is nearly identical, before revision for the published

book. Price, coding and photographs are missing from the flaps. Front flap: TASHA TUDOR'S poignant art | has fascinated adults and children | for decades. Her 19th century New⌴England lifestyle is legendary. Gardeners are⌴especially intrigued by the profusion of⌴antique flowers - spectacular poppies, six-foot⌴foxgloves and intoxicating peonies - in the⌴cottage gardens surrounding her handhewn⌴house. ¶ Until now, we've only caught glimpses of | Tasha Tudor's landscape. In this gorgeous | book, two of her friends, the garden writer | Tovah Martin and the photographer Richard | Brown, take us in to the magical garden and | then behind the scenes. As we revel in the | bedlam of Johnny-jump-ups and cinnamon | pinks, the intricacy of the formal herb garden,⌴ and the voluptuousness of her heirloom roses,⌴we also learn Tasha's | gardening secrets. ¶ How does she coax forth her finicky | camellia blossoms in the dead of a Vermont | winter? How does she train those fantastic | standards to model for her artwork? How can⌴she keep her crown imperials from tumbling | in the winds? Tasha's garden reflects a wealth | of family lore, perfected through years and⌴years of working the soil. We may be dazzled | by the beauty of the garden but we come | away from this book with practical ideas | about improving our own plots of land. ¶ "Paradise on earth" is how Tasha describes | her garden and along with the flowers and⌴ vegetables that provide her food, her paradise⌴is filled with an enchanting menagerie —⌴corgis, Nubian goats, cats, chickens, fantail⌴doves and the forty or more exotic finches,⌴cockatiels, canaries, nightingales, and parrots⌴that inhabit her collection of antique cages. ¶Tasha's beautiful

watercolors and her⌴enchanting stories color this sublimely | beautiful book. Back flap: TOVAH MARTIN is the author of | *The Essence of Paradise: Plants for | Indoor Gardens, Victorian Moments in⌴the Garden,* and *Once Upon a Windowsill: | A History of Indoor Gardening.* A contributing editor⌴of *Victoria,* she writes regularly for this | country's leading gardening magazines. She is⌴staff horticulturalist [*sic*] for the 100-year-old | Logee's Greenhouses in

Danielson,⌴ Connecticut. ‖ RICHARD BROWN, like Tasha Tudor | before him, grew up in the Boston⌴area and left the city to make a life⌴in rural Vermont. A graduate of Harvard,⌴where he studied art and art history, he⌴taught school before embarking on a career⌴as a photographer. His books include | *The Private World of Tasha Tudor; Moments in⌴Eden; The View from the Kingdom; A Vermont⌴Christmas,* and *Pictures from the Country.*

OTHER: This mock-up was prepared for pre-publication advertising. There were editorial changes in the text of pages 7-16, *not described here*. Reminiscent of salemen's 'sample books' from a previous era.

T135 Tasha Tudor's | GARDEN | [leaf design] || Text by Tovah Martin | Photographs by Richard W. Brown || [boy and dolphin logo] | Houghton Mifflin Company | Boston New York | 1994. [Text copyright © 1994 by Tovah Martin | Photographs copyright © 1994 by Richard W. Brown | Illustrations copyright © 1994 by Tasha Tudor | All rights reserved || For information about permission | to reproduce selections from this book, write to | Permissions | Houghton Mifflin Company | 215 Park Avenue South | New York, New York 10003 || *Library of Congress Cataloging-in-Publication Data* | Martin, Tovah. | Tasha Tudor's garden / text by Tovah Martin ; photographs by Richard Brown. | p. cm. | ISBN 0-395-43609-5 | 1. Gardening – Vermont. 2. Tudor, Tasha – Homes and haunts – Vermont. | I. Brown, Richard, 1945- II. Title. | SB455.M369 1994 | 635.9'092 – dc20   94–7886 | CIP || SFE 10 9 8 7 6 5 4 3 2 1 | Printed in Italy || *Book design by Susan McClellan* || *Color separations by Sfera - Printing by Sfera / Garzanti* || Tasha Tudor's calendar's, cards, lithographs, and books are available from | Jenny Wren Press, P.O. Box 505, Mooresville, Indiana 46851]

PAGINATION: [1-6] 7-10 [11-13] 14-17 [18-19] 20-23 [24] 25-27 [28] 29-35 [36] 37-38 [39] 40-42 [43] 44-45 [46] 47-48 [49] 50-51 [52-53] 54-55 [56] 57-58 [59] 60-64 [65] 66-67 [68] 69-70 [71] 72-77 [78] 79 [80-81] 82-84 [85] 86-87 [88-89] 90-91 [92] 93-95 [96-98] 99-100 [101] 102-107 [108] 109-115 [116] 117-120 [121-122] 123-126 [127] 128-133 [134] 135 [136-138] 139-141 [142] 143-147 [148-149] 150-151 [152] 153-160, plus mint green endpapers. 10 13/16″ x 8 13/16″.

COVER: Cased in 3mm binders boards with 1 piece brillanta 4038 pale green cloth (an Italian cloth) stamped in gold on spine: Tasha Tudor's Garden [leaf] Martin & Brown [boy and dolphin] HOUGHTON | MIFFLIN.

DUST JACKET: In 5 colors (4 color process plus PMS 712 cream) on 150 gsm gloss plus gloss film lamination. Front is full-page illustration of Tudor gathering sweet peas, overprinted in cream: Tasha Tudor's | GARDEN || Text by Tovah Martin | Photographs by Richard W. Brown. Lavender background on spine and back. Spine printed in black (except white leaf) same wording as book spine. Three photographs on back and in a white box 2 3/8″ x 1 3/8″ lower left: ISBN 0-395-43609-5 [above the larger left code] | 90000 [above the smaller right code] | [2 bar codes] | 9 780395 436097 [below the left]. Just to the right of box, 6-90931. White flaps printed in black.

Front flap: FPT $ 35.00 || TASHA TUDOR'S poignant art | has fascinated adults and children | for decades. Her nineteenth- | century New England lifestyle is legendary. | Gardeners are especially intrigued by the | profusion of antique flowers – spectacular | poppies, six-foot foxgloves, and intoxicating | peonies – in the cottage gardens surrounding | her hand-hewn house. ¶ Until now we've only caught glimpses of | Tasha Tudor's landscape. In this gorgeous | book, two of her friends, the garden writer | Tovah Martin and the photographer Richard | Brown, take us into the magical garden and | then behind the scenes. As we revel in the | bedlam of Johnny-jump-ups and cinnamon | pinks, the intricacy of the formal peony | garden, and the voluptuousness of her | heirloom roses, we also learn Tasha's | gardening secrets. ¶ How does she coax forth her finicky | camellia blossoms in the dead of a Vermont | winter? How does she train that fantastic | topiary to model for her artwork? How can | she keep her crown imperials from tumbling | in the winds? Tasha's garden reflects a wealth | of family lore, perfected through years and | years of working the soil. We may be dazzled | by the beauty of the garden, but we come | away from this book with practical ideas | about improving our own plots of land. ¶ "Paradise on earth" is how Tasha describes | her garden, and along with the flowers and | the vegetables that provide her food, her | paradise is filled with an enchanting | menagerie - corgis, Nubian goats, cats, | chickens, fantail doves, and forty or more | exotic finches, cockatiels, canaries, night- | ingales, and parrots, which inhabit her | collection of antique cages. ¶ Tasha's beautiful watercolors and her | enchanting anecdotes color this sublimely | beautiful book. || 10340094.

Back flap carries two small photographs of author and photographer. [photo, and printed

laterally at its right side] *Providence Journal - Bulletin Photo* | TOVAH MARTIN is the author of | *The Essence of Paradise: Plants for* | *Indoor Gardens, Victorian Moments* | *in the Garden,* and *Once Upon a Windowsill:* | *A History of Indoor Gardening.* A contribu- | ting editor of *Victoria*, she writes regularly | for leading gardening magazines and is staff | horticulturalist *[sic]* for Logee's Greenhouses in | Danielson, Connecticut. || [photo, and printed laterally at its right side] *Susan*

McClellan | RICHARD W. BROWN grew up in the | Boston area and left the city to make | a life in rural Vermont. A graduate of | Harvard, where he studied art and art history, | he taught school before embarking on a ca- | reer as a photographer. His books include | *The Private World of Tasha Tudor, Moments* | *in Eden, The View from the Kingdom, A Vermont Christmas*, and *Pictures from the* | *Country.* || *Jacket design by Susan McClellan* | HOUGHTON MIFFLIN COMPANY | 222 Berkeley Street | Boston, Massachusetts 02116.

ILLUSTRATIONS: There are 114 full-color photographs throughout the book. Unnumbered pages are full-page reproductions. Thirty Tudor color illustrations of flowers appear on pages [1, 5] 8, 15-16, 32, 44, 48, 54-55, 58, 63, 70, 75, 90, 94, 100, 107, 120, 128, 130, 143, 145, 157, 158, 160.

OTHER: Rizzoli Bookstore, Boston, sold copies signed by Tudor on the half-title and with a green rectangular label (1¾ x 2¾″): printed in white, an R inside a circle, above Autographed | Copy, inside a diamond.

COPYRIGHT REGISTRATION: VA 597-225 granted to Tasha Tudor, c/o Doe Coover Agency, 58 Sagamore Ave., Medford, Ma. 02155. Monica Rich, Houghton Mifflin Co., 222 Berkeley St., Boston, Ma. 02116, agent for Tasha Tudor, swears on Nov. 22, 1994:

TASHA TUDOR'S GARDEN (6-90931), 2-dimensional artwork completed in 1994 by Tasha Tudor, domiciled in U.S.A., was published Sept. 6, 1994. The book has no pre-existing matter and consists of all new illustrations. Fees charged to account DA 015539, Houghton Mifflin Co. Application and one deposit copy received at L.C. Nov. 29, 1994, the effective date of this registration.

COPYRIGHT REGISTRATION: VA 597-226 granted to Richard W. Brown, c/o Rhoda Wehr Agency, 151 Bergen St., Brooklyn, N.Y. 11217. Monica Rich, Houghton Mifflin Co., 222 Berkeley St., Boston, Ma. 02116, agent for Richard W. Brown, swears on Nov. 22, 1994:

TASHA TUDOR'S GARDEN, photographs completed in 1994 by Richard W. Brown, domiciled in U.S.A., was published Sept. 6, 1994. The book has no pre-existing matter and consists of all new photographs. Fees charged to account DA 015539, Houghton Mifflin Co. Application received at L.C. Nov. 29, 1994.

T136 _____. Have not examined a second printing.

T137 _____. Have not examined a third printing.

T138 _____. [Text copyright © 1994 by Tovah Martin.... CIP || SFE 10 9 8 7 6 5 4 ... Indiana 46851]

T139 _____. Have not examined a fifth printing.

T140 _____. [There is no date on the title page.] [Text copyright © 1994 by Tovah Martin.... CIP ‖ SFE 10
9 8 7 6̲ ... Indiana 46851]

> DUST JACKET: Front flap: $35.00 price, <u>without the three letter code.</u> There is no code number at
> the bottom of the front flap of dust jacket. All other features as in the fourth printing.

T141 **Tasha Tudors ǀ trädgård** ‖ *Text av Tovah Martin ǀ Fotografier av Richard W. Brown* ‖
Översättning av Margareta Eklöf ǀ Fackgranskning av Karin Berglund ‖ [double RP logo] ǀ Rabén Prisma.
[[double RP logo] ǀ Bokförlaget Rabén Prisma ǀ Besöksadress: Kungstensgatan 49 ǀ Box 45022 ǀ 104 30
Stockholm ǀ e-postadress: raben.prisma@raben.se ‖ För information on tillstånd att ǀ reproducera material ǀ
ur denna bok, skriv till: ǀ Permissions ǀ Houghton Mifflin Company ǀ 215 Park Avenue South ǀ New York,
New York 10003 ‖ Text © Tovah Martin 1994 ǀ Foto © Richard W. Brown 1994 ǀ Illustrationer © Tasha
Tudor 1994 ǀ Första upplagan 1997 ǀ Andra upplagan 1997 ǀ Originalets titel: Tasha Tudor's Garden ǀ
Published by agreement with Houghton Mifflin Company ǀ through Sane Töregård Agency. ǀ
Originalförlag: Houghton Mifflin Company, ǀ Boston, New York 1994 ǀ Översättning: Margareta Eklöf ǀ
Fackgranskning: Karin Berglund ǀ Formgivning: Susan McClellan ǀ Tryckt i Italien 1997 ǀ ISBN 91-518-
3343-3]

> PAGINATION: Eight signatures, pages match the English language edition, except that page [160] is not
> numbered. Page numbers and their decorations in reset type. 10 13/16″ x 8 13/16″.

> COVER: Illustrated paper over boards, gloss laminate. Reproduces the illustrations and design of
> the original English dust jacket, text translated. Front: Tasha Tudors ǀ TRÄDGÅRD ‖
> Text av Tovah Martin ǀ Fotografier av Richard W. Brown ‖ RABÉN PRISMA. Spine: Tasha
> Tudors trädgård Martin & Brown [double RP logo]. Back preserves the upper photograph
> but replaces the bottom two with the following text: Tasha Tudor är en av Amerikas populärare
> illustratörer och författ- ǀ tare till barn- och kokböcker. Hon lever som man gjorde i New ǀ
> England förr i tiden. Trädgårdsodlare förundras speciellt över ǀ hennes gammaldags blommor –
> magnifika vallmor, två meter höga ǀ fingerborgsblommor och doftande pioner – i trädgården som
> breder ut ǀ sig runt huset byggt av handbilat timmer. ¶Tasha Tudors trädgård ligger i Vermonts
> kallaste trakt och klimatet ǀ liknar vårt nordiska, med långa, ibland snörika vintrar. Alla
> odlingsråd ǀ går därför att tillämpa hos oss. ¶I denna underbara bok förs vi in i den förtrollade
> trädgården och se- ǀ dan bakom kulisserna av två vänner, trädgårdsskribenten *Tovah Martin* ǀ och
> fotografen *Richard Brown*. Samtidigt som vi hänger oss åt överflödet ǀ av styvmorsvioler och
> nejlikor, den eleganta piongården och de gammal- ǀ dags rosorna lär vi oss också Tashas
> odlarhemligheter. ¶ Tashas fina akvareller ock personliga anekdoter ger karaktär åt denna ǀ
> vackra bok. ‖ Lower left, small white box 11/16″ x 1 1/8″ and this text: ISBN 91-518-3343-3 ǀ
> [barcode] ǀ 9 789151 833439. Bottom center: [double RP logo] ǀ RABÉN PRISMA. Moss green
> endpapers as in the U.S. original.

> CONTENTS: Page [160] carries only the two watercolors; the nursery information has been eliminated.

> OTHER: Brit Østerud reports this Swedish translation. http://www.bokia.se lists the trade price at
> 358, the Lågpris at 298, as of June 27, 1998. Marilyn Rogers went to Stockholm to get the
> examination copy which carried a florescent orange shop label on the front: 980609 248.- ǀ
> **179.00** ǀ EXTRA ǀ PRIS **Bokia**

T142 TASHA TUDOR'S ǀ HEIRLOOM ǀ CRAFTS ‖ [small diamond design] ‖ Text by Tovah Martin ǀ
Photographs by Richard W. Brown ‖ Houghton Mifflin Company ǀ Boston   New York ǀ 1995. [Text copyright
© 1995 by Tovah Martin ǀ Photographs copyright © 1995 by Richard W. Brown ǀ Illustrations copyright ©
1995 by Tasha Tudor ǀ All rights reserved ‖ Printed in Italy ‖ *Book design by Susan McClellan*]

> PAGINATION: [1-6] 7-8 [9] 10-11 [12] 13-16, in a white cover stock wrapper. 10 1/2″ x 8 5/8″.

DUST JACKET: Similar to the dust jacket without a spine. The front matches the published book, although these colors are paler. By contrast, the back is a stronger butterscotch than the final book, both are imprinted with the same three photographs. The published code at the lower left, does not appear on this pre-print. The bar codes are slightly wider. Above the left code: ISBN 0-395-73327-8, and below it: 9 780395 733271. Above the right code: 90000.

Front flap. Variant text in black less the price: IN THIS MAGICAL SEQUEL to *Tasha | Tudor's Garden,* author Tovah Martin | and photographer Richard Brown | revisit America's beloved children's book | illustrator, this time to take us inside Corgi | Cottage to watch Tasha create the crafts that | are an integral part of her legendary 19th | century lifestyle. ¶ Surrounded by authentic American | antiques and collectibles and using original | tools and techniques, we see Tasha spinning | flax, dying wool, and weaving on one of her | seven looms; dipping candles, making | baskets, and soap, and cheese from her | Nubian goats. ¶ We watch her make marionettes—her | rambling cottage has its own marionette | theater—and see her fashion wooden toys as | well as dolls and furniture for her built-in | dollhouse. ¶ Whether she's repairing one of her antique | dresses, crocheting a piece of lace to edge her | own petticoat, sewing a dress copied from an | 1830 pattern, or working on a quilt, Tasha's | hands are never idle. And, of course, we see | her create the new paintings that appear in | this book. || Publication November, 1995 | 160 pp. 8 ½ x 10 ½ | 100 color photographs | watercolors by Tasha Tudor | ISBN 0-395-73527-0 | FPT $35.00 cloth. Back flap has an extra paragraph at the top: **Tovah Martin** and **Richard Brown** are the | author and photographer of *Tasha Tudor's | Garden* which won the Award of the Year | from the Garden Writers' Association of | America as well as first prize in both the | book and photography

categories. || TOVAH MARTIN is the author of | *The Essence of Paradise, Victorian | Moments in the Garden, Once Upon | a Windowsill,* and other garden books. A | contributing editor of *Victoria,* she writes | regularly for the country's leading gardening | magazines. She is staff horticulturalist *[sic]* for | the hundred-year-old Logee's Greenhouses | in Danielson, Connecticut. ||

RICHARD W. BROWN, like Tasha | Tudor before him, grew up in | Boston and left the city for rural | Vermont. A graduate of Harvard, where he | studied art, he taught school before turning | to photography. His books include *The | Private World of Tasha Tudor, Moments in | Eden, The View from the Kingdom, A | Vermont Christmas,* and *Pictures from the Country.* He lives in Peacham, Vermont. || *Jacket design by Susan McClellan* || **HOUGHTON MIFFLIN COMPANY** | 222 Berkeley Street | Boston, Massachusetts 02116.

CONTENTS: There are textual changes to the sample pages; page 16 is radically different, with the painting which was eventually printed on page 95 of the published book. While similar, the table of contents reads thus: CONTENTS | [splint basket] | Made by Hand 7 | INTRODUCTION || Wood and Clay 19 | BASKETS [device] POTTERY [device] WOODWORKING || Field and Garden 43 | DRIED FLOWERS [device] HERBS [device] TEAS || All Creatures Great and Small 61 | DAIRYING [device] SOAP & CANDLEMAKING [device] WOOL || Culinary Arts 83 | OPEN HEARTH COOKING [device] CANNING [device] CIDERMAKING || Goldenrod and Indigo 103 | DYEING [device] WEAVING [device] KNITTING || A Stitch in Time 125 | QUILTING [device] LACE [device] ANTIQUE DRESSES || The World in Miniature 145 | MARIONETTES [device] TOYS [device] DOLLHOUSES.

OTHER: This advertising pre-print is an earlier stage of the first 16-page signature of the next entry. There were editorial changes in the text, *not described here.* Compare to any publishers' sample books, in general.

T143 TASHA TUDOR'S | HEIRLOOM | CRAFTS || [small diamond floral design] || Text by Tovah Martin | Photographs by Richard W. Brown || [boy and porpoise emblem] | Houghton Mifflin

Company | Boston New York | 1995. [Text copyright © 1995 by Tovah Martin | Photographs copyright
© 1995 by Richard W. Brown | Illustrations copyright © 1995 by Tasha Tudor | All rights reserved | For
information about permission to reproduce selections from this book, write to | Permissions, Houghton
Mifflin Company, 215 Park Avenue South, New York, New York 10003 || *Library of Congress
Cataloging-in-Publication Data* | Martin, Tovah. | Tasha Tudor's heirloom crafts / text by Tovah Martin
; photographs by Richard W. Brown | p. cm.| ISBN 0-395-73527-0 | 1. Tudor, Tasha — Themes,
motives. 2. Handicraft — United States. | I. Title. | NK839.T84M37 1995   95-18605 | 745.5'092 —
dc20   CIP || SFE 10 9 8 7 6 5 4 3 2 1 | Printed in Italy || *Book design by Susan McClellan | Color
separations by Sfera* || ACKNOWLEDGMENTS || Seth Tudor, the woodworker | Guy Wolff, the potter |
Rosemary Gladstar, the herbalist | Kate Smith, the weaver | Joan DeGusto, the seamstress | Andy Rice, the shepherd
| Amelia Stauffer, the candle-maker | Linda Allen, the marionette maker | Isabelle Hadley, the herbalist | Steve
Davie, the gardener | Our gratitude to all the models who patiently lent their time.]

PAGINATION: Eight signatures of 150 gsm wood free matte coated white paper, Smythe sewn. [1-6]
7-8 [9] 10-11 [12] 13-17 [18] 19-27 [28] 29 [30] 31-39 [40] 41 [42-43] 44-47 [48] 49-55 [56]
57-67 [68] 69-73 [74] 75-77 [78] 79-81 [82] 83-93 [94] 95-96 [97] 98-99 [100] 101-108 [109]
110-113 [114] 115-117 [118] 119-122 [123] 124-125 [126] 127-131 [132] 133-136 [137] 138-
139 [140] 141-147 [148] 149-152. 8 3/4″ x 10 3/4″.

COVER: The cover is Brillanta 4202 brown cloth over 3mm binders boards. Gold stamping on
spine: TASHA TUDOR'S HEIRLOOM CRAFTS   Martin & Brown   [boy and porpoise
emblem] HOUGHTON | MIFFLIN. Endpapers are 1 color PMS 4645 brown *[a light color]* on
white wood-free endpaper stock.

DUST JACKET: Five color; 4 color plus PMS 727 brown on 150 gsm white gloss, covered with gloss
film lamination. Front reproduces the photograph from page [114]: Tudor sewing a quilt before
her fireplace. The photograph is overprinted in white at the top, TASHA TUDOR'S |

HEIRLOOM CRAFTS, and at the lower left, PHOTOGRAPHS BY | Richard W. Brown
|| TEXT BY | Tovah Martin. Spine reproduces the book spine, but in brown ink. Back, three
photographs, a 4 3/4″ x 7″ variation of the sewing table from page 120-121, a 3 3/4″ x 2 1/2″
reproduction of the page 54 photo, and a 2 1/8″ x 3 1/4″ portion of Linda Allen's kitchen
stenciling which is not used in the book. Beneath the stenciling at lower right is a 1 5/8″ x 2 1/4″
white box containing two bar codes. Above the larger left UPC: ISBN 0-395-73527-0, and
beneath it 9 780395 735275. Above the small right hand UPC: 90000>. At the lower left
corner of the jacket in black: 6-90930.

Front flap text in black: FPT $ 35.00 || IN THIS MAGICAL SEQUEL TO *Tasha* | *Tudor's Garden,*
author Tovah Martin | and photographer Richard W. Brown | revisit Corgi Cottage, this time
taking us | inside to watch Tasha create the handmade | items that are an integral part of her
legendary | nineteenth-century lifestyle. ¶ Surrounded by authentic American | antiques and
collectibles and using original | tools and almost forgotten techniques, Tasha | spins flax, dyes
wool, and weaves on one of | her seven looms. With the help of friends, she | dips candles,
makes soap, and concocts herbal | creams and lotions. She harvests wood for | making baskets
and fruit for canning, presses | cider and dries herbs and flowers. ¶ Her Nubian goats supply her
with milk for | cheese and butter. Her bantam hens offer eggs | for cooking and decorating. As a
good Yankee, | Tasha lets nothing go to waste; stray feathers | from her guinea hens end up as
part of her toy | owls. Her rambling cottage has its own | marionette theater and a built-in
dollhouse, | and all of the actors and the dollhouse in- | habitants were made by Tasha. ¶
Whether Tasha is crocheting a piece of lace | to edge her petticoat, sewing a dress copied | from
an 1830s pattern, knitting intricately | patterned mittens and socks, or working on a | quilt, her
hands are never idle. For this book, | she has created a series of new paintings in the | style that
has made her one of America's best- | loved children's book illustrators. || 1195.

Back flap: [2 1/8″ x 1 5/8″ photograph of Martin] ‖ TOVAH MARTIN is the author of *The* |
Essence of Paradise, Victorian Moments | *in the Garden, Once Upon a Windowsill,* | and other
garden books. A contributing editor | of *Victoria*, she writes regularly for the country's | leading
gardening magazines. She is staff | horticulturist for the hundred-year-old Logee's |

Greenhouses, in Danielson, Connecticut. ‖ [2 1/8″ x 1 5/8″ Brown photograph] ‖ RICHARD W.
BROWN, like Tasha | Tudor before him, grew up in Boston | and left the city for rural Vermont.
A | graduate of Harvard, where he studied art, he | taught school before turning to photography. |
His books include *The Private World of Tasha* | *Tudor, Moments in Eden, The View from the* |
Kingdom, A Vermont Christmas, and *Pictures* | *from the Country.* He lives in Vermont's |
"Northeast Kingdom." ‖ *Jacket design by Susan McClellan* ‖ HOUGHTON MIFFLIN COMPANY |
222 Berkeley Street | Boston, Massachusetts 02116.

CONTENTS: Page [1] is half-title with watercolor of a cat asleep on a quilt and a pile of folded fabric.
Title page [3], Contents [5], Introduction 7-17.

ILLUSTRATIONS: Full page photographs: [2, 6, 9, 12, 18, 28, 40, 42-43, 48, 56, 68, 74, 78, 82, 94,
97, 100, 109, 114, 118, 123, 126, 132, 137, 140, 148] Tudor is featured on: [6, 28, 40, 56, 68,
74, 78, 97, 114, 118, 126, 140]. Tudor illustrations are reproduced as 2 1/2″ x 3″ vignettes on
pp. [1] 7, 19, 41, 57, 79, 95, 115, 133, the first page of some chapters. There are 135 Brown
photographs throughout the book on every page except these: [1, 3, 4] 7, 19, 26, 41, 57, 79, 83,
95, 115, 133.

OTHER: The first printing of 50,000 copies was to be delivered to the publisher September 25, 1995
for publication November 16, 1995. A piece of homespun pictured on page 104 derives from
Reginald Bacon. A photograph of the original *The Jenny Wren Book of Valentines* appears on page
142, a book reprinted by the Jenny Wren Press in 1988, *q.v.*

COPYRIGHT REGISTRATION: TX 4-191-880 granted to Tovah Martin c/o Christina Ward Literary
Agency, PO Box 515, Scituate, Ma. 02060. Victoria Garbe, Houghton Mifflin Company, 222
Berkeley St., Boston, Ma. 02116 (617-351-5126), agent for Tovah Martin, swears on Nov. 29,
1995 :

TASHA TUDOR'S HEIRLOOM CRAFTS (6-90930), text by Tovah Martin, domiciled in the
U.S., was completed in 1995 and published Sept. 7, 1995. Fee charged to account DA 015539
Houghton Mifflin Company. Application and two deposit copies received Dec. 1, 1995, the
effective date of registration.

COPYRIGHT REGISTRATION: VA 751-388 granted to Tasha Tudor c/o Doe Coover Agency, 58
Sagamore Ave., West Medford, Ma. 02155. Victoria Garbe, Houghton Mifflin Company, 222
Berkeley St., Boston, Ma. 02116 (617-351-5126), agent for Tasha Tudor, swears on Nov. 29,
1995 :

TASHA TUDOR'S HEIRLOOM CRAFTS (6-90930), 2-dimensional artwork by Tasha Tudor,
domiciled in the U.S., was completed in 1995 and published Sept. 7, 1995. Rest as above.

COPYRIGHT REGISTRATION: VA 751-389 granted to Richard W. Brown c/o Doe Coover Agency, 58
Sagamore Ave., West Medford, Ma. 02155. Victoria Garbe, Houghton Mifflin Company, 222
Berkeley St., Boston, Ma. 02116 (617-351-5126), agent for Richard W. Brown, swears on Nov.
29, 1995 :

TASHA TUDOR'S HEIRLOOM CRAFTS (6-90930), photographic artwork by Richard W.
Brown, domiciled in the U.S., was completed in 1995 and published Sept. 7, 1995. Rest as
above.

T144 Tasha Tudor's | OLD-FASHIONED GIFTS || Presents and Favors for All Occasions || *Tasha Tudor and Linda Allen* || DAVID McKAY COMPANY, INC. | New York. [Illustrations by Tasha Tudor on pages iii, vi, 69, 97, 101, 105, 113, | and 117, Courtesy of American Artists, Inc. || Copyright © 1979 by Tasha Tudor and Linda Allen || All rights reserved, including the right to | reproduce this book, or parts thereof, in any | form, except for the inclusion of brief quotations | in a review. || Library of Congress Cataloging in Publication Data || Tudor, Tasha. | Tasha Tudor's Old-fashioned gifts. || SUMMARY: Instructions for making a variety of gifts | for different holidays throughout the year. | 1. Handicraft. 2. Cookery. 3. Gifts. | [1. Handicraft. 2. Cookery. 3. Gifts.] I. Allen, Linda, | joint author. II. Title. III. Title: Old-fashioned gifts. | TT157.T83 745.5 79-2053 | ISBN 0-679-20981-6 || 1 2 3 4 5 6 7 8 9 10 || Manufactured in the United States of America || Book design by Jane Preston]

PAGINATION: [i-viii] ix-x, 1-8 [9-10] 11-12 [13] 14-16 [17] 18-23 [24] 25-28 [29] 30 [31] 32 [33] 34-36 [37] 38-40 [41] 42-46 [47-49] 50-52 [53] 54 [55] 56 [57] 58-64 [65] 66-68 [69] 70-71 [72] 73-80 [81-83] 84 [85] 86-87 [88-90] 91-92 [93] 94-96 [97] 98-100 [101-102] 103-104 [105] 106 [107] 108 [109] 110 [111] 112 [113] 114 [115] 116 [117] 118, ivory paper in 8 signatures. 10″ x 6 7/8″.

COVER: Red cloth stamped in gold on front: Tasha Tudor's | OLD-FASHIONED | GIFTS; and on the spine: Tudor/Allen   Tasha Tudor's OLD-FASHIONED GIFTS   [DM monogram in a box] McKay. Mustard end-papers.

DUST JACKET: White with red, wine and black printing. Front: Tasha Tudor's | OLD-FASHIONED | GIFTS [wine] | [Allen's color illustration of woman and two children 'crafting'] | Presents and Favors | for All Occasions || Tasha Tudor and Linda Allen [black]. Spine: Tudor/Allen [black] Tasha Tudor's OLD-FASHIONED GIFTS [wine] [monogram in a box] McKay [black]. Back, an Allen colored tree frame with gifts and sewing box encloses list of black text gifts, punctuated with light blue dots. CONTENTS [red] | Wool Rabbit • Doll's Band Box | Miniature Nesting Boxes • Cloth Book | Child's Pinafore • Stuffed Dog • Sunbonnet | Pocket • Patterned Mittens • Patchwork Potholders | Patterned Slipper-Socks • Paper hats and Crowns | Patchwork Pillow • Potpourri • Sachets | Holiday or birthday Snappers • Advent Calendar | Straw Star-and-Wreath Mobile | Paper-Lace Valentine and Envelope | Valentine Mobile • Cornucopia • Cashew Butter Toffee | Thanksgiving Garden Relish • Fondant | Wintergreen Patties • Satin Taffy | Ruth's Chocolate Fudge • Linda's Butter-Jam Cookies | Popcorn Balls • Almond Brittle • Hot Cross Buns • Halloween Candied Apples | Rye Bread • New England Cranberry Sauce | Toffee Bar Cookies • Raisin Gingerbread Cakes || 0-679-20981-6 [beneath frame, lower right].

Front flap: $10.95 [black] || Tasha Tudor's | OLD-FASHIONED | GIFTS [red] || Presents and Favors | for All Occasions [black] || Tasha Tudor and Linda Allen [red] || "The personal touches you give your | homemade gifts are what make them | such treasures," say Tasha Tudor and | Linda Allen. Their profusely illustrated | book contains clear, step-by-step instruc- | tions, pictures, and diagrams for making | a wide variety of presents, favors, and | decorations for many occasions—birth- | days, Christmas, Valentine's Day, and | Halloween among them. The more | than thirty projects include: personalized, | unique wearing apparel; appealing toys | and household gifts; imaginative mobiles | and party favors; and old-fashioned recipes | for cookies, candy, and other edibles. || ¶*Horn Book* has written that "no one | makes lovelier picture books than TASHA | TUDOR." The author and illustrator of | many award-winning books, she has re- | ceived numerous honors for her work, in- | cluding the Catholic Library Association's | Regina Medal for her "continued distin- | guished contribution to children's litera- | ture." || ¶LINDA ALLEN, Tasha Tudor's talented | collaborator, is also the co-illustrator of | *Tasha Tudor's Favorite Christmas Carols.*

Back flap: *Also written and illustrated by | Tasha Tudor and Linda Allen . . .* [black] || TASHA TUDOR'S FAVORITE | CHRISTMAS CAROLS [red] || "Seventeen carols so well chosen that it's | difficult to imagine that anyone's favorite | is missing."   —*Washington Post* || "A beautiful book with delicate illustra- | tions in pastel colors, which give deepened | meaning to the familiar words and printed | music. . . . Enchanting pictures painted in | the incomparable Tudor style." | —*Los Angeles Times* ‖ "Chances are, families where Tudor's col- | lection finds a home will discover that her | favorites are theirs too. She has embel- | lished her preface, the brief histories of | the carols and the songs themselves with | the cozy, old-fashioned illustrations in | color that have made her works so popu- | lar. The arrangements, for piano and | guitar, are easy for almost anybody to | master." —*Publishers Weekly* ‖ *Jacket illustrations by Linda Allen* | *Jacket design by Jane Preston* ‖ David McKay Company, Inc. | 2 Park Avenue | New York, N.Y. 10016

ILLUSTRATIONS: (Underlined pages have illustrations by Linda Allen. Most Tudor pictures are reproductions from earlier greeting cards; some are from Pumpkin Moonshine. Tudor illustrations in bold.) Color illustrations, pages [iii (Title), vi] **1**, 4-5, 7, **[10]** 14-<u>15</u>, 18-**19**, <u>[24]</u> 25, **28** [29] [33] 36 <u>[37]</u> <u>[41]</u> 44-45 <u>[49]</u> <u>52</u> <u>[53]</u> 56 **[57]** **60** <u>[65]</u> **68** **[69]** 74-**75**, 78 [82-83] 86 <u>[89]</u> **[93]** **[97]** **[101-102]** **[105]** **[107]** **[109]** **[113]** **[117]**. Black and white, pages **[v]** 2-4, 6, **8**-9, 12 **[13]** 16-18, 20-23, 25-27 [31] 34, 36, 38-39, 42-43 [47-48] 50-51 [55] **58-59**, 61-64, 66-67, 71 [72] 73, 76-80 **[81]** 84 [85] 87 [88] **[90]** <u>111</u> <u>[115]</u>.

CONTENTS: Page [I] is half-title.

COPYRIGHT REGISTRATION: TX 344-488 granted to Ms. Tasha Tudor and Ms. Linda Allen, both of Route 4, West Brattleboro, Vt. 05301. H.J. Rabinovitz, David McKay Co., Inc., 2 Park Ave., N.Y., N.Y. 10016, agent for Tasha Tudor and Linda Allen swears on Oct. 1, 1979:

TASHA TUDOR'S OLD-FASHIONED GIFTS, partial text and some illustrations by Tasha Tudor and Linda Allen, both U.S. citizens, was completed in 1979 and published Oct. 1, 1979. The book was manufactured by Fisher Composition Co., Inc., 461 Park Ave. South, N.Y., N.Y. 10016, Rae (Printing), 282 Grove Ave., Cedar Grove, N.J. 07009, and Keenan Binders, Inc., 200 Pond Ave., Middlesex, N.J. 08846. Fees charged to account DA050830, David McKay Co., Inc. Application and deposit copy received at L.C. Oct. 10, 1979.

T145 _____. [Copyright © 1979 by Tasha Tudor and Linda Allen ‖ All rights reserved, including the right to | reproduce this book, or parts thereof, in any | form, except for the inclusion of brief quotations | in a review. ‖ <u>First paperback edition:</u> <u>September 1981</u> ‖ Illustrations by Tasha Tudor on pages iii, vi, 69, 97, 101, 105, 113, | and 117, Courtesy of American Artists, Inc. ‖ Book design by Jane Preston ‖ Library of Congress Cataloging in Publication Data ‖ Tudor, Tasha. | Tasha Tudor's Old-fashioned gifts. ‖ SUMMARY: Instructions for making a variety of gifts | for different holidays throughout the year. | 1. Handicraft. 2. Cookery. 3. Gifts. | [1. Handicraft. 2. Cookery. 3. Gifts.] I. Allen, Linda, | joint author. II. Title. III. Title: Old-fashioned gifts. | TT157.T83 745.5 79-2053 ‖ <u>ISBN 0-679-20984-0</u> ‖ 1 2 3 4 5 6 7 8 9 10 ‖ Manufactured in the United States of America]

PAGINATION: 9 ¾" x 6 ¾".

COVER: Ivory paper wrapper under gloss film lamination, with illustrations from jacket of hard-cover edition. McKay monogram on spine is not boxed. Back cover has the same illustration as before, but now encloses most of the text [black] from the previous dust jacket font flap with altered line breaks: **$ 7.95** ...home- | ...treas- | ... Allen. | ...contains | ...and | ...pres- | ...oc- | ...Valentine's | ...more | ... personalized, | ...and | ...and | ...for | ...edibles. ‖ ...one | ...TASHA | ...many | ...nu- | ...the | ...Medal | ...contribu- | ...literature. ‖ *Cover illustrations by Linda Allen* | *Cover design by Jane Preston* [black] ‖ David McKay Company, Inc., | 2 Park Avenue | New York, N.Y. 10016 [green] ‖ 0-679-<u>20984-0</u>, below the frame at right [black].

TASHA TUDOR'S SAMPLER

T146 **TASHA** [red] | *A Tale for Easter* [black] | **TUDOR'S** [red] | *Pumpkin Moonshine* [black] | **SAMPLER** [red] | *The Dolls' Christmas* [black] ‖ written and illustrated by Tasha Tudor ‖ David McKay Company, Inc. | New York   [A TALE FOR EASTER © 1941 by Tasha Tudor | THE DOLLS' CHRISTMAS ©1950 by Tasha Tudor | PUMPKIN MOONSHINE © 1938 by Tasha Tudor ‖ All rights reserved, including the right to reproduce | this book, or parts thereof, in any form, except for | the inclusion of brief quotations in a review. ‖ Library of Congress Catalog Card Number 77-00018 | ISBN 0-679-20412-1 ‖ 10 9 8 7 6 5 4 3 2 1 | MANUFACTURED IN THE UNITED STATES OF AMERICA]

PAGINATION: [104] pp. in seven gatherings and three folded inserts, including endpapers. Ten stitches top sewn. 6 3/4″ x 6 7/8″.

COVER: Brown paper over boards. Gilt stamped spine: **xxx   TASHA TUDOR'S SAMPLER** [McKay monogram] **McKay**.

DUST JACKET: Ivory jacket, front and spine printed in cream background. Front cover alternates lines of the main title in large red capitals (as does the title page) with an illustration and the individual titles in a black calligraphic hand thus: **TASHA** | [a chick and two eggs in grass] | *A Tale for Easter* | **TUDOR'S** | [a jack o'lantern, a pumpkin and seeds on a green ground] | *Pumpkin Moonshine* | **SAMPLER** | [a small wrapped gift, a blue candlestick and pine boughs] | *The Dolls' Christmas*. Spine labeling duplicates book spine, but here the xxx and the McKay monogram are red, remainder black. Back of jacket: *Written and illustrated by Tasha Tudor* [red] || A IS FOR ANNABELLE | AROUND THE YEAR | THE COUNTY FAIR | THE DOLLS' CHRISTMAS | 1 IS ONE | PUMPKIN MOONSHINE | A TALE FOR EASTER [black] || *Illustrated by Tasha Tudor* [red] | A CHILD'S GARDEN OF VERSES | FIRST GRACES | FIRST PRAYERS | MOTHER GOOSE [black]. Front flap: $ 7.95 [black] || **Tasha Tudor's | Sampler** [red] || *A Tale for Easter | Pumpkin Moonshine | The Dolls' Christmas* || Tasha Tudor's incomparable pictures in | exquisite color, enriched with tiny de- | tails that children love, make this collec- | tion of three of her most popular stories | a book for all seasons. || "It is not only the children who take | delight in the lovely childlike character | of a *Tale for Easter*, which carries the | thought of springtime."—*Horn Book* || "For those 3-6's who like their Hallow- | eens as gentle and charming as late | fall sunshine, there is *Pumpkin Moon- | shine*."—*Christian Science Monitor* || "Little girls of the doll-house age will | revel in the minute details of *The Dolls' | Christmas*."—*New York Times Book Re- | view* [black]. Back flap: about Tasha Tudor . . . [red] || *Horn Book* has written that "no one | makes lovelier picture books than Tasha | Tudor, whose delicate pictures suggest | Kate Greenaway and whose humor sug- | gests Beatrix Potter." ¶Tasha Tudor was born and grew up in | New England, where she presently lives. | She attended the Boston Museum School | of Art and later studied at the Kenning- | ton School of Art in London, but she is | largely a self-taught artist. Her first book | for children was *Pumpkin Moonshine*, | published in 1938. Since that time, she | has illustrated several of the classics for | children and has written and illustrated | many of her own original stories. ¶Miss Tudor has received numerous | honors for her work, including the Cath- | olic Library Association's Regina Medal | for her "continued distinguished contri- | bution to children's literature." || *Jacket design by George Infante* [black] || David McKay Company, Inc. | New York [red]

CONTENTS: Half-title, p. [3]. Title page, [5]. Pages [7-37] reproduce *A Tale for Easter*. Title and dedication have been brought together on page [7] with a bunny, a mouse and two bluebirds. Text and illustrations reproduce the original, but the colors are much washed out. Only the illustration from the last page has been modified. Page [38] is blank. Pages [39-73] reproduce *Pumpkin Moonshine*. Page [39] combines the original pages [7] and [9], half-title (less one shock of corn) and dedication. Page [64] illustration is reversed, Sylvia Ann standing at Grandpawp's left. Page [74] is blank. Pages [75-101] reproduce *The Doll's Christmas*. Page [75] combines the title and the dedication page from original. Pages [102-104] are blank. Original end paper illustrations are reproduced on pages [100-101].

T147 _____.

PAGINATION: Ten stitches, top sewn 6 13/16″ x 6 15/16″.

COVER: <u>Red</u> plastic-filled paper over boards, with fine weave design. Spine stamped in black

DUST JACKET: Evidence of a round price label having been removed from front of jacket.

T148 _____. [A TALE . . .   ISBN 0-679-20412-1‖ 10 9 8 7 6 5 4 3 **2** | MANUFACTURED IN THE UNITED STATES OF AMERICA]

   PAGINATION: [104] pp. in <u>six signatures and two fold</u>ed inserts, including endpapers. Ivory paper. Nine stitches, top sewn. 6 13/16″ x 6 3/4″.

   COVER: Deep red <u>course</u> weave-imprint (like screeing) paper over boards.

   DUST JACKET: Have not examined a copy with price intact.

   CONTENTS: In this printing, the <u>half-title follows the title page</u> rather than preceding.

T149 _____.

   PAGINATION: [104] pp. in <u>six signatures and two fold</u>ed inserts, including endpapers. Buff paper. Thirteen stitches, top sewn. 6 13/16″ x 6 3/4″.

   COVER: <u>Red-orange</u> matte paper over boards. White cloth hinges.

   DUST JACKET: <u>$7.95</u> ‖ Tasha Tudor's . . .   Lower right back: . . . GOOSE ‖ 0-679-20412-1.

   CONTENTS: In this printing, the <u>half-title precedes the title page</u>.

T150 _____. Have not examined a third printing.

T151 _____. [A TALE . . . 10 9 8 7 6 5 **4** | MANUFACTURED IN THE UNITED STATES OF AMERICA]

   PAGINATION: [104] pp. in six gatherings and four folded inserts, including endpapers. Nine stitches top sewn. 6 11/16″ x 6 13/16″.

   COVER: <u>Red plastic-filled paper, pigskin imprint, over boards.</u>

   DUST JACKET: Front flap: <u>$8.95</u> . . . Lower right back: . . . GOOSE ‖ <u>ISBN 0-679-20412-1</u>.

   CONTENTS: The <u>half-title precedes the title page</u>.

T152 _____. [A TALE . . . 10 9 8 7 6 **5** | MANUFACTURED IN THE UNITED STATES OF AMERICA]

   PAGINATION: Twelve stitches, top sewn.   6 3/4″ x 6 13/16″.

   COVER: Pigskin imprint. <u>Gold</u> stamping on spine.

   DUST JACKET: Front flap: <u>$9.95</u> . . .

T153 _____.

   PAGINATION: Slightly more enameled finish to paper. Twelve stitches, top sewn. 6 13/16″ x 6 3/4″.

   COVER: Impressed fine weave pattern.

   DUST JACKET: <u>$ 9.95</u> . . .

T154 Tasha Tudor's | [2 rules] | Seasons | of Delight | [2 rules] | A Year on an Old-Fashioned Farm | A Three-Dimensional Pop-Up Picture Book. [Tasha Tudor's | Seasons of Delight | A Year on an Old-Fashioned Farm ‖ Philomel Books • New York | Text and illustrations copyright

PAGINATION: [1-14] cardboard pages and three sheets of cover stock folded and glued together at gutter, including covers. 8 13/16" x 8 3/4".

COVER: Front cover: four children and animals outside a rectangular twig and vine frame surrounding mostly black text. Title on front and spine is <u>butterscotch, remaining text is black</u>. Spine: Tasha Tudor's Seasons of Delight   PHILOMEL BOOKS [with bird in first O]. Back cover: [A twig circle encloses four children and pets with a snow horse above black text.] Colorful three-dimensional pictures by distinguished American artist Tasha Tudor | vividly depict the pleasures of life in the country throughout the year—the simpler | pleasures that can still be experienced today, as this book shows and tell us, for Mrs. | Tudor herself lives in this manner in her home in northern New England, with her | garden, her animals, and her many grandchildren. || Library of Congress Cataloging-in-Publication Data | Tudor, Tasha. | Tasha Tudor's Seasons of delight. | "A three-dimensional pop-up book"—Cover. | Summary: Three-dimensional pictures depict the pleasures of life in the country throughout the year. | 1. Farm life—Juvenile literarure.2.Seasons—Juvenile literature.3.Toy and movable | books—Specimens. [1.Seasons.2.Toy and movable books] I. Title. II. Title: Seasons of delight. | S519.T83 1986 574.5'43 85-28534 | ISBN 0-399-21308-2 || PHILOMEL BOOKS | a division of The Putnam Publishing Group | 51 Madison Avenue, New York, NY 10010 || <u>Produced in Mexico</u> for Intervisual Communications, Inc., Los Angeles, CA 90045. $13.95   ISBN 0-399-21308-2 [price and ISBN in square 'computer' type face.]

ILLUSTRATIONS: Pop-ups include moving panels, Tudor's farm buildings in Marlboro, Vermont and Tudor, herself, churning butter.

OTHER: The 'title page' description is actually taken from the front cover. The points to identify a first edition are: Cover title is butterscotch; Last line of back cover: Produced in Mexico…, $13.95 ISBN 0-399-21308-2; There is no bar code on the first edition.

COPYRIGHT REGISTRATION: TX 1 813 707 granted to Tasha Tudor, Route 4, Box 144, West Brattleboro, Vt. 05301. Louise Bates, agent for Tasha Tudor, swears on May 1, 1986:

SEASONS OF DELIGHT, a work not made for hire with text and illustrations by Tasha Tudor, a U.S. citizen, was completed in 1986 and published May 1, 1986. L.C. is granted non-exclusive right to make copies and phonorecords for the blind and physically handicapped. Fee charged to account DAO 38288, Putnam Publishing Group (Phil), 51 Madison Ave., N.Y., N.Y. 10010 (212-689-9200). Application and two deposit copies received May 7, 1986.

T155 _____.

PAGINATION: Publisher's presentation copy to Tudor in a specially crafted navy blue leather box, 10 5/16" x 9 7/8" wide, 1 7/16" deep.

COVER: Front and back cover are tooled identically: three concentric square gold rules set 1/2" in on the perimeter of the cover. A single gold leaf design is stamped inside each corner of these rules. A blind rule is drawn 1/8" in from the three outer edges of front and back covers, but not along the spine. The gold initials **T T** are stamped 1 3/4" in and up from the lower right corner of the front cover. The spine bears two gold horizontal rules at the top, one at the bottom and two more set 3/8" above the bottom. Title and author are printed in gold laterally down the spine: SEASONS OF DELIGHT   Tasha Tudor. The box is lined in a white artist's vellum.

OTHER: Inscribed to Beth [Mathers], 1992.

T156 _____.

COVER: All printing, including <u>title, in black.</u> Back cover, bottom line: <u>Printed and bound in Colombia, S.A.</u> for Intervisual Communications, Inc., Los Angeles, CA 90045. $13.95 [There is no ISBN]

T157 _____. [Tasha Tudor's ... Published in the United States by Philomel Books, a division of | The Putnam & Grosset Book Group, 200 Madison Avenue, New York, New York 10016. | Published simultaneously in Canada.]

    COVER: Black text. Back cover: Colorful three-dimensional pictures . . PHILOMEL BOOKS | a division of The Putnam & Grosset Book Group | 200 Madison Avenue, New York, New York 10016 || Printed and bound in Colombia, S.A. for Intervisual Communications, Inc., Los Angeles, CA 90045. Lower left: $14.95 | [rule] | ($19.50 CAN) Lower right: ISBN 0-399-21308-2 [in square 'computer' type face] above two UPC bar codes | 90000 [above the smaller right code] | [bar codes] | 9 780399 213083 [below larger left code.]

T158 **Tasha Tudor's** | [oval photograph of Tudor sitting and drawing beside a path with a small kid looking on, within a thin white border] | **Sketchbook** | [From inside the back cover: *Library of Congress Number 89-051276 | I.S.B.N. No. 0-9621753-0-7 | Published by the Jenny Wren Press | P. O. Box 505, Mooresville, Indiana 46158 | 1st Printing | Copyright © 1989 The Jenny Wren Press | All Rights Reserved | No part of this book may be reproduced | in any form without written permission from the Publisher. | Printed in the United States of America. || A special thank you to Marjorie Tudor for permission to use the photo appearing on the cover.*]

    PAGINATION: [20] leaves of 100# uncoated White Simpson offset wire-O bound at the left end between 4 ply 18 point C1S Cast Coated covers in the style of an artist's sketch book. 9" x 12"

    COVER: The covers are blue outside and white inside. Each copy was sold in a white envelope. Reproductions of pencil sketches from Tudor's sketchbooks appear on every page and both sides of the back cover. The front board verso is blank, although some copies were sold with an extra original sketch, signed and dated on this surface. Page [10] carries this caption with 16 sketches: *Sketches for one of my first books Linsay Woolsay* [sic]. In addition to family members, there are sketches of Linda [Allen] on page [26] and Eliza G., page [35]. The Redding, Ct., house dated January 12, 1945, page [11]. An annotated *Study of winter Kitchen at Christmas*, page [24]. *Thirsk Market Square*, Sept. 29, 1976, page [25].

The white envelopes for the copies with extra illustrations have an applied label of a Victorian design, not Tudor's. Hand-writing on this label indicates the subject of the extra illustration. Editors has seen 'Boy with Cat Carrying Wood,' and Little Girl with Doves." Each book was shipped in wrapping paper.

    OTHER: The Hilltop Press of Indianapolis completed printing 2,500 copies August 30, 1989. A single page Jenny Wren Press letter dated August 1st, 1989, and postmarked July 24, 1989, lists the *Sketchbook* as item 2 of 9: *Tasha Tudor Sketch Book*, 9" x 12", 40 pages. Wholesale $10.25 (12 or more items), Single Price $14.25, Retail Suggested Unsigned $16.95 and Retail Signed $20.95. These prices good until October 15th. The same item 2 and price options appears in an expanded formalized order form for 16 items headed Holiday Enchantments, and dated Oct. 14, 1989.

A further undated printed two-sheet advertisement was mailed October 18 and 24, 1989. It announces a public appearance on Dec. 1-3 in Durham, NC, requests orders for Christmas by November 25, 1989 and has this added description of the Sketchbook: "This outstanding collectible is the best of a 'lifetime collection of Tasha Tudor's most outstanding sketches. Take a look into this joyful private side of Tasha's artwork . . . you'll see sketches of Corgi's family, friends, her home & other enchantments . . . represented beautifully by the pencil of Tasha Tudor. In the format of an actual sketchbook . . . 9" x 12", 40 pages long. Price $16.95, with signature $20.95." And at the top of the reverse: " ♥ Original Artwork by Tasha ♥ | Tasha has hand sketched 35 pictures & signed them in sketchbooks! This unique offering gives you the chance | to own an original pencil sketch of her choice . . . This offering is very special . . . & only 35 sketchbooks at | this time are offered — a perfect gift for Someone Special at Christmas . . . | price for sketchbook — $ 1 5 0 . 0 0 | with original sketch.

The sketchbook without the extra illustration is listed in catalogs dated *Spring & Summertime [1990]. Spring & Summertime 1991* lists only the unsigned version.

Tasha Tudor's Christmas Valentines Holiday Collection 1990 - 1991 includes the Sketchbook as item 26, $16.95 or $20.95 with autograph. 26A <u>Tasha Tudor's Sketchbook</u> with an original pencil sketch done by Tasha! Only 40 will be | offered this holiday. A lovely gift for someone special, $150.00 each.

The Christmas 1991/Spring 1992 catalog lists the $16.95 Sketchbook as item B007. This boxed announcement also appears on page [5]: ♥ At Christmas we always offer 30 sketch books that have an original pencil sketch inside the cover done by Tasha - A <u>very</u> special gift & a wise investment . . . #BS07 – Sketchbook Original – $150.00 each ♥♥♥

Spring-Summer 1992 catalog lists only the $16.95 Sketchbook with the added note on the order form that the Sketchbook is not available wholesale.

A June 17, 1992, mailing to *Wholesale Customers* offers one copy of the Sketchbook with the extra illustration, a $150.00 value, to the gift/book shop with the winning display of Jenny Wren Press merchandise.

Fall-Winter 1992-1993 includes the $16.95 Sketchbook, and With original sketch by Tasha, $135.00 each BB057 offered Holiday Time only. The price continues in the *Spring-Summer 1993* catalog. The book is last pictured in the *Fall-Winter 1993-94* catalog without a price and overprinted: Temporarily | Out of Stock.

COPYRIGHT REGISTRATION: TX 2-786-873 granted to The Jenny Wren Press, PO Box 505, Mooresville, IN 46158 by written agreement between T. Tudor and Beth Mathers, co-owners of Jenny Wren Press. Beth Mathers, other copyright claimant and agent for Tasha Tudor swears on Jan. 15, 1990:

TASHA TUDOR'S SKETCHBOOK, text and compilations of illustrations by Tasha Tudor, an American citizen born 1916 *[sic]*, was completed in 1989 and published Sept. 15, 1989. Application received at LC Jan. 23, 1990 and April 19, 1990. Two deposit copies received Jan. 23, 1990.

T159 **Tasha Tudor's** | **TREASURE** | [small girl and boy praying, doll and teddy bear] | FIRST PRAYERS | FIRST GRACES | MORE PRAYERS || Henry Z. Walck, Inc. [1981]

PAGINATION: Three volumes in a slipcase, 5 5/8 x 4 3/16 x 1 5/16″

COVER: Each book in a simulated pigskin plastic-filled paper over board covers: *First Prayers,* turquoise; *First Graces,* red; *More Prayers,* moss green.

SLIPCASE: The four titles are within an oval of daisies on a lavender field with ivory paper revealed at all edges. The slipcase is covered to be held in the right hand, the books sliding out the left side. A label duplicating the front illustration is pasted to the "back" of the slipcase with the Walck name printed at the bottom edge of the lavender field. A four inch double column of flowers climbs the ivory spine, topped by a single cherub with its arms folded and its wings extended. The same floral motif is printed on the white top, reduced in size (3 5/8″), less the cherub. On the ivory bottom is ISBN: 0-679-20983-2/9.95.

DUST JACKET: Each of the three dust jackets is priced <u>$3.50</u> on the front flap, and with an individual ISBN at the bottom of flap. The back flaps are identical on all three dj's: ads for FIRST PRAYERS and FIRST GRACES, and in very small type: Henry Z. Walck, Inc. | A Division of | David McKay Company, Inc. | New York.

CONTENTS: On the title page verso of each book: <u>This impression, 1981</u>. See the specific title entries for descriptions of the books themselves.

OTHER: A three-volume boxed set of the 1981 reprints of these three Tudor books.

T160 *Thistly* | *B* | BY TASHA TUDOR | New York | OXFORD UNIVERSITY PRESS | 1949
[Copyright 1949 | OXFORD UNIVERSITY PRESS, INC. | PRINTED IN THE UNITED STATES OF AMERICA]

PAGINATION: Two signatures of ivory paper: [1-32] plus endpapers. Eight stitches, saddle sewn. 6 3/4 ″ x 6 1/8 ″.

COVERS: <u>Wine paper</u> over boards, linen imprint. White label on front, green ribbon and purple asters and yellow flowers encircling *Thistly* | *B* | BY TASHA TUDOR. Spine stamped in yellow: TUDOR   THISTLY B   OXFORD.

DUST JACKET: Buff dust jacket, front: *Thistly* | *B* | BY TASHA TUDOR, and a canary inside a circle of the green ribbon embellished with purple asters and yellow flowers. Spine: TUDOR THISTLY B   OXFORD. Back, centered, a small yellow flower and purple aster. Front flap: *Thistly B* || BY TASHA TUDOR || Thistly B was a canary but not | an ordinary one. He belonged to | Efner and Tom Tom who allowed | him to fly in and out of his cage as | he wished. One day Godmummy | arrived with a present for the chil- | dren. It was another canary — a wife | for Thistly B. ¶The story of how they raised a | family is told with delicate pictures | such as only Tasha Tudor can draw. || *Oxford Books* | *for Boys and Girls* || 40-70 $1.50. Back flap: *Also by Tasha Tudor* || *A Tale for Easter* | Lovely pictures of all the magic | things that happen on Easter. || *Snow before Christmas* | A family of long ago celebrate | a country Christmas. || *The White Goose* | A tale of moonlight and Robin | who saw a white goose. ||*Mother Goose* | Some of Tasha Tudor's most beau- | tiful pictures illustrate these | nursery rhymes.

ILLUSTRATIONS: All illustrations are in color. Each endpaper has the circle of green ribbon tied at the top enclosing: front left, Thistly B; front right, Yellow Bird on a nest; rear left, three baby birds facing right with their mouths open; rear right, baby bird facing left with its mouth open very wide. Half title [1], same flowers as jacket back. Title page [3], Thistly B and Yellow Bird tying the green ribbon rising from a bed of flowers. Dedication [5], smaller ribbon, 5 canaries, each holding a small card printed with one of the following names: To 'Molly' 'Susan' 'Peter' 'Jimmy' 'and' 'Tom Tom.'   Tom-Tom is Tom [McCready] Tudor, Peter [Smith] was son of Nancy and George Smith, St. Paul's School, Concord, NH, Susan could be Moulton whose parents rented space in the Webster house in the McCreadys' early years there.

CONTENTS: Text on even (left) pages [6] - [28]. Odd (right) pages [7] - [29] carry one illustration each. Pages [30 - 32] are blank.

COPYRIGHT REGISTRATION: A 36121 granted to Oxford University Press, Inc., 114 Fifth Ave., NY, NY. Henry Z. Walck swears on Sept. 12, 1949 :

THISTLY B by Tasha Tudor, a United States citizen BORN APPROX. 1915, was published Sept. 8, 1949. The book was typeset and printed by Kellogg and Bulkeley, Hartford, Ct. and bound by Spiral Binding Co., N.Y., N.Y. Application and affidavit and two deposit copies received at LC Sept. 20, 1949.

COPYRIGHT RENEWAL REGISTRATION: R 669304 granted to Tasha Tudor, Marlboro, Vt. 05344, claiming as the author. Marguerite Gaignat, David McKay Co., Inc., 750 Third Ave., NY, NY 10017, swears:

THISTLY B by Tasha Tudor was originally published Sept. 8, 1949. Fee paid by David McKay Co., Inc. Application received at LC Aug. 8, 1977.

T161 _____.

PAGINATION: Eight stitches, saddle sewn.

COVER: Mint green cloth binding with navy ink on spine. Same paper label on front cover.

DUST JACKET: Have not examined one.

T162 _____.

PAGINATION: [1-42] pp. including end papers. 6 5/8″ x 6 1/8″.

COVER: Library pre-bound copy. Wine buckram, black imprint on front cover: wreath, title, author and bird. Black printing on spine: THISTLY B —TUDOR.

DUST JACKET: Have not examined one.

ILLUSTRATIONS: Former fly leaf illustrations are now pages [2-3] and [38-39].

CONTENTS: Half title page is missing from examination copy. Title page is [7] in this pagination. Text: even-numbered pages [10-32]. Illustrations: odd-numbered pages [11-33]. Blank pages [1,4, (5-6 are missing), 34-37].

T163 _____. New York | Henry Z. Walck, Inc. | 1949 [Copyright 1949 | HENRY Z. WALCK, INC || Library of Congress Catalog Card Number: 61-7759 || PRINTED IN THE UNITED STATES OF AMERICA]

PAGINATION: Two signatures of ivory paper: [1-28]. White end papers pasted down; there are no fly leaves, and no endpaper illustrations. Title page is [1]. Page [28] is blank. Seven stitches, saddle sewn. 6 3/4″ x 6 1/8″.

COVER: Bright green cloth over boards, with label. Spine in black: TUDOR   THISTLY B WALCK.

DUST JACKET: Ivory dust jacket, spine: TUDOR   THISTLY B   WALCK. Front flap: *Thistly B* ... can draw. || *Henry Z. Walck, Inc.* || 40-70. Have not examined a copy with price intact. Back flap: Other books by Tasha Tudor | A Is For Annabelle | Alexander The Gander | Amanda And The Bear | Andersen's Fairy Tales | Around The Year | The County Fair | The Dolls' Christmas | Dorcas Porkus | Edgar Allan Crow | First Graces | First Prayers | CATHOLIC | PROTESTANT | Linsey Woolsey | Mother Goose | 1 Is One | Pumpkin Moonshine | A Tale for Easter.

T164 _____.

PAGINATION: [30] pp, including pasted endpapers. Title page on page [3].

COVER: Library binding, on a slightly courser and lighter green cloth. Without label, but with a 3″ x 3″ blind stamped square where the label would be. Cloth hinges, top sewn.

DUST JACKET: Examined a copy with front flap corners clipped and $3.75 penciled at bottom.

T165 _____.

PAGINATION: [32] pp, including endpapers. Title page on page [3]. Text runs to page [28], last illustration page [29].

COVER: Cloth hinge, top sewn. Navy ink on spine. Impressed cover, with a label.

DUST JACKET: Printed price at top of front flap, dj, $2.75. Lower front flap corner clipped.

T166 _____.

PAGINATION: [36] pp, including endpapers which were added in a rebinding. Paper has the repeated pattern, a child sitting on a foot stool reading and the words HUNTTING BOUND.

COVER: Gray painted buckram with the original jacket design in yellow and black. Cloth hinge, top sewn. Navy ink on spine.

CONTENTS: Title page on page [5]. Text runs to page [30], last illustration page [32].

DUST JACKET: Front flap, lower corner clipped from examination copy. Typed code on library book pocket 296., which I interpret to mean the cost, $2.96.

T167 _____.

PAGINATION: [32] pp, including endpapers.

COVER: Navy ink on spine. Impressed cover, no label.

DUST JACKET: Both corners clipped from front flap, but $3.75 penciled on front flap and typed on library book pocket.

T168 _____. New York | Henry Z. Walck, Inc. [Copyright 1949 | HENRY Z. WALCK, INC || ISBN: 0-8098-1022-0 || Library of Congress Catalog Card Number: 61-7759 | PRINTED IN THE UNITED STATES OF AMERICA]

PAGINATION: Two signatures, ivory paper: [1-32]. Pasted buff endpapers. Ten stitches, top sewn. 6 3/4″ x 6 3/16″

COVER: Mint green cloth, without label and impression . Navy ink on spine. White hinges.

DUST JACKET: Front flap, top corner clipped. Lower corner, $4.00. Back flap: Other books by Tasha Tudor | A IS FOR ANNABELLE | ALEXANDER THE GANDER | ANDERSEN'S FAIRY TALES | AROUND THE YEAR | THE COUNTY FAIR | THE DOLLS' CHRISTMAS | DORCAS PORKUS | FIRST GRACES | FIRST PRAYERS | (Catholic and Protestant) | MORE PRAYERS | MOTHER GOOSE | 1 IS ONE | PUMPKIN MOONSHINE | STEVENSON'S GARDEN OF VERSES | A TALE FOR EASTER.

T169 _____.

PAGINATION: Seven stitches, top sewn.

COVER: Grass green cloth. 3/8″ cloth hinge.

T170 **A** | **TIME** ᴛᴏ **KEEP** [red] | **Tʜᴇ Tᴀsʜᴀ Tᴜᴅᴏʀ** | **Bᴏᴏᴋ ᴏꜰ Hᴏʟɪᴅᴀʏs** [green] |
Written and Illustrated | by TASHA TUDOR ‖ [boy, book and corgyn] ‖ Rand McNally &
Company | *Chicago   New York   San Francisco* [black]   [Library of Congress Cataloging in Publication Data |
Tudor, Tasha. | A time to keep. ‖ SUMMARY: Describes traditional holiday celebrations | throughout the year in a New England household. | 1.
Holidays—New England—Juvenile literature. | (1.Holidays—New England) I. Title. | GT4805.T83   394.2'6974   77-9067 | ISBN 0-528-82019-2 |
ISBN 0-528-80213-5 lib. bdg. ‖ *Copyright © 1977 by Rand McNally & Company | All rights reserved | Printed in the
United States of America by Rand McNally & Company | First printing 1977*].

PAGINATION: [60] pp. heavy stock including free endpapers. Fourteen stitches, saddle sewn. 12″ x
9 3/16″. 7/16″ thick

COVER: Pressed linen weave printed paper over board covers, simulating two large white labels on a
pink ground. Front: leaf border of small items representing various holidays (and corgi and cat)
framing three children and text, in green, **A** | **TIME TO KEEP** | **Tʜᴇ Tᴀsʜᴀ Tᴜᴅᴏʀ Bᴏᴏᴋ ᴏꜰ
Hᴏʟɪᴅᴀʏs.** Spine text in red: [oak leaves and acorns] **Tᴜᴅᴏʀ** [mouse] **A TIME TO KEEP** [mouse]
Rᴀɴᴅ McNᴀʟʟʏ [oak leaves and acorns]. Back: holiday border surrounding small boy who is
tearing sheets from a calendar, with corgi and cat, and in upper left (black): 528-82019-2. Each of
four end papers features a seasonal flower border and a centered floral illustration for one season of
the year.

CONTENTS: Tudor's text answers the question — "Granny, what was it like when Mummy was like
me?" — by relating how she celebrated holidays with her family. Her text is interspersed with
literary quotations. Page [59]: **Tᴀsʜᴀ Tᴜᴅᴏʀ** | And that's how it still is. Holiday traditions rooted in
Tasha Tudor's own | childhood were recreated, with embellishments, for her own four children. Now | they are
renewed for her grandchildren. The Sparrow Post Office is still in use for | valentines. Advent calendars
appear each December 6. Marionettes are | refurbished and newly costumed for plays. Melissa, the special
love of the artist's | childhood, reappears at dolls' fairs. ¶ Tasha Tudor, one of America's most loved
illustrators, was born in Boston and | grew up in Connecticut, the daughter of a portrait painter and a designer
of | yachts. She has lived her entire life in New England, for many years in New | Hampshire and at present in
Vermont. Her first book, *Pumpkin Moonshine,* | appeared in 1938. There have been more than 40 books since
that time. ¶ *A Time To Keep* brings together all the qualities for which Tasha Tudor is famed. | The delicacy of
her watercolors. The nostalgic and imaginative settings. The | intricate borders with which she prefers to
surround her illustrations. Avid | gardeners will recognize flowers, grasses, and herbs of New England.
Friends and | acquaintances will recognize her home, her corgis, her family and friends. ¶ For all who would
know more of Tasha Tudor, she is a spinner, a weaver, a | seamstress, an admirer of the art of Eastman Johnson
and Winslow Homer, a | cook, an omnivorous reader, a "passionate" gardener. Above all, she is a painter |
who is able to translate her joy in a flower, her happiness in a task performed well, | her pleasure in the turning
of seasons, her appreciation of traditional values, into | a form that speaks eloquently to readers everywhere.

ILLUSTRATIONS: Borders of vines, flowers, twigs or other vegetation frame each page. Some pages are
divided into two or three framed panels. Other single frames enclose a double-page illustration. In
all, 99 illustrated tableau excluding the borders.

COPYRIGHT REGISTRATION: A 930920 granted to Rand McNally & Company, P.O. Box 7600,
Chicago, Il. 60680. Richard G. Sanders [?], agent for claimant, swears, Dec. 20, 1977:

A TIME TO KEEP by Tasha Tudor, Route 4, West Brattleboro, Vt. 05031, a U.S. citizen, was
published Sept. 16, 1977. The book was manufactured by Pearson Typographics & Schwauk
Graphics, both of Chicago, Il., Veritone Co., Des Plaines, Il., and Rand McNally & Co., Hammond,
In. Fees charged to Rand McNally & Co. Application and affidavit and two deposit copies
received at LC Dec. 28, 1977.

T171 _____.

PAGINATION: [70] pp. including pasted endpapers. Fourteen stitches, saddle sewn.

COVER: More pronounced buckram weave stamped in printed paper cover over heavier boards. An
extra heavy white sheet inserted as front and back end papers, so that former decorated

endpapers become pages [5-6]. ISBN is in same position, upper left white corner of back cover, but in a <u>gray</u> ink, rather than black. <u>1/2″ thick.</u> Gold foil price label (3/8″ x 3/4″) overprinted in black, showing a black price: $5⁹⁵, on front cover, upper right. On the back cover, upper left, another gold foil label (3/8″ x 1 1/8″) covers the printed ISBN and is printed in black: 528-80213-5-5.97.

OTHER: This is the <u>library binding</u>, but it doesn't have the corresponding ISBN <u>printed</u> on it. The correct ISBN is applied with the gold label.

T172 _____.

PAGINATION: [66] pp. including pasted endpapers. Fourteen stitches.

COVER: On the back cover, upper left: evidence of a label approx. ¾″ x 2″ having been removed.

OTHER: <u>Library binding</u>, but with a binding error. The rear illustrated endpaper is pasted to the board, as in the trade edition. This diminishes the page count by four. The front has the correct <u>four white pages</u> before reaching the decorated 'endpapers.'

T173 _____. [*Copyright © 1977 by Rand McNally & Company | All rights reserved | Printed in the United States of America*].

PAGINATION: [60] pp. including free endpapers. Pasted endpapers are the first and last leaves of the three signatures, without the white added endpapers. Fourteen stitches. 12″ x 9 3/16″ x <u>5/16″ thick.</u>

COVER: Smooth, semi-gloss finish. Back, lower right [black]: *Book Club | Edition | 3277*. Rear endpaper was creased in manufacture.

CONTENTS: This issue on thinner paper. Illustrations, text as before, although pp. [2-3] are slightly more pink than flesh.

T174 _____. [Library of Congress . . . *First printing, 1977 | Second printing, 1978*].

COVER: Fine linen imprint.

T175 _____. [Library of Congress . . . *First printing, 1977 | Second printing, 1978 | Third printing, 1978*].

T176 _____. [Library of Congress . . . *First printing, 1977 | Second printing, 1978 | Third printing, 1978 | Fourth printing, 1979*]

PAGINATION: [60] pp. including flyleaves in <u>four signatures</u>. 12″ x 9 1/4″ x <u>3/8″ thick.</u>

COVER: Remnant of price sticker on front cover.

T177 _____. [Library of Congress . . . *First printing, 1977 | Second printing, 1978 | Third printing, 1978 | Fourth printing, 1979 | Fifth printing, 1981*].

T178 _____. . . . by TASHA TUDOR ‖ [boy, book and corgyn] ‖ [book logo] CHECKERBOARD PRESS | NEW YORK [black]. [Copyright © 1977 Checkerboard Press, a division of Macmillan, Inc. | Checkerboard Press and colophon are trademarks of Macmillan, Inc. All rights reserved. | No part of this book may be reproduced or transmitted in any form or by any means, | electronic or mechanical, including photocopying, recording, or by any information storage | and retrieval system, without permission in writing from the Publisher. ‖ <u>Printed in U.S.A.</u>]

PAGINATION: [60] pp. including free endpapers. Fourteen stitches, but much more closely spaced than before, saddle stitched. 12″ x 9 3/16″.

COVER: Continuous gloss film over paper on boards. Front, upper right: a black and white round label: $ 12.95. Spine: . . . CHECKERBOARD PRESS [logo]. Back, lower left: [1 1/2″ x 1 1/4″ bar code] | 0 14121 89091 4 ‖ ISBN 0-02-689091-7.

T179 _____. [. . . from the Publisher. *Printed in Italy*]

COVER: A gold foil label, front upper right corner: $ 12.^{95}. Back, lower left corner, [1 1/4″ x 1″ bar code] | 0 14121 89091 4 | ISBN 0-02-689091-7.

T180 _____. . . . by TASHA TUDOR ‖ [boy, book and corgyn] ‖ **MACMILLAN PUBLISHING COMPANY** | **NEW YORK** [black] [Copyright © 1977 Checkerboard Press, a division of Macmillan, Inc. | All rights reserved. No part of this book may be reproduced or transmitted in any form or by | any means, electronic or mechanical, including photocopying, recording, or any information | storage and retrieval system, without permission in writing from the Publisher. | Macmillan Publishing Company | 866 Third Avenue | New York, NY 10022 | Printed in the United States of America | ISBN 0-02-789502-5 | 10 9 8 7 6 5 4 3 2]

COVER: Back, lower left: 90000> [above smaller right code] | [two bar codes] | 780027 895025 [beneath larger left code] | ISBN 0-02-789502-5. Spine: . . . MACMILLAN.

T181 _____.

COVER: A white label, 3/8″ x 1 1/4″ on back, upper right corner. Black type: MPC | > $13.95.

T182 *A* | *Time to Keep* | THE TASHA TUDOR | BOOK OF HOLIDAYS ‖ *Written and illustrated by* | *Tasha Tudor* ‖ [boy with book and corgis] ‖ SIMON & SCHUSTER | BOOKS FOR YOUNG READERS [[logo] | *SIMON & SCHUSTER BOOKS FOR YOUNG READERS* | An imprint of Simon & Schuster Children's Publishing Division | 1230 Avenue of the Americas, New York, New York 10020 ‖ Copyright © 1977 by Macmillan, Inc. | All rights reserved including the right of reproduction in whole or in part in any form. | SIMON & SCHUSTER BOOKS FOR YOUNG READERS is a trademark of Simon & Schuster. | Typography by Heather Wood | The text for this book is set in Stempel Schneidler. | The illustrations are rendered in watercolor. | Printed and bound in the United States of America | First Simon & Schuster Books for Young Readers Edition, 1996 | 1 3 5 7 9 10 8 6 4 2 ‖ Library of Congress Catalog Card Number 96-92212]

PAGINATION: A light blue satin marker ribbon is bound in. Sixteen stitches, saddle sewn. 12″ x 9 3/16″.

COVER: Navy blue cloth, blind stamped near the bottom of front cover: *A Time to Keep,* above a printer's decorative bar. Spine, gilt: *Tudor   A Time to Keep   Simon & Schuster.* Plain back.

DUST JACKET: First appearance of the book with a jacket which is adapted from the previous illustrated covers, with several alterations. The illustrated panels are printed against a pink background, previously on white. The ground within the border remains white. The front and back central figures are smaller than before; the borders have been expanded to eleven inches. The text is the same, but reset in new type: *A* | *Time to Keep* | [three children, two birds] | THE [green] | *Tasha Tudor* [carmine] | BOOK OF HOLIDAYS [green]. There are small evidences of retouching the illustrations at the top center. A large A has been removed, the pink link in the paper chain to the right shows the sparrow's tail still drawn over the link, and the break in the grass beneath the small girl's feet where the corgi's nose was previously. Spine: *Tudor* [carmine] *A Time to Keep* [green] [logo] *Simon & Schuster* [blue]. The back cover border is enlarged, the central motif smaller, and the Easter basket in the lower left corner of the frame has been excised and replaced with oak leaves and the stuffed blue bunny in a blue jacket. Beneath the central illustration is a two bar code array. EAN running vertically at the left of the larger of the two bar codes. Above the smaller right bar code: 90000>. Beneath the larger left: 9 780689 811623. Beneath all: ISBN 0-689-81162-4.

Text on flaps is mostly black, with high lights in green, blue and carmine on a pink field. Front flap upper right corner: $18.00 US | $24.50 CAN | *All Ages* [black] || [green printer's rule as on front cover] | *"Granny, what was it like | when Mummy was me?"* [sic] || *"Oh, there were lots of joyful times."* [blue] | [green printer's rule] || *T*[carmine initial, remaining text black] here were homemade | valentines and Easter eggs, Fourth | of July picnics and family birthdays. | Thanksgiving brought visits from | relatives—so many, the children | had to sleep in the barn! And | finally there was Christmas, the | best of all "times to keep," with | handmade presents, an Advent | calendar, and a "beautiful tree in | a shine of candles." ¶ Month by month, Tasha Tudor's | delicate illustrations bring to life | the holidays of an earlier time. A | warm-hearted celebration of family | and tradition, this treasury of | "times to keep" will be cherished | and enjoyed all year long. || [right white dove with heart from front] || *Guaranteed Reinforced Binding.* Back flap: Tasha Tudor [carmine] 's own family | history was the inspiration for many of | the holiday traditions in *A Time To Keep.* | A Caldecott Honor artist with over forty | books to her credit, Tasha Tudor has spent | all of her life in new England, and she | celebrates the plants, animals, landscapes, | and history of her home in her artwork. | Her appreciation for the beauties of nature | and the traditions of the past have made | her warm, delicate, and detailed watercolors | a favorite of readers everywhere. ¶Tasha Tudor is also the illustrator of *A | Child's Garden of Verses* by Robert Louis | Stevenson and her own *1 Is One*, a Caldecott | Honor book. She lives in Vermont. || [left while dove with heart from front cover] || *Jacket illustrations copyright © 1977, 1996 | by Tasha Tudor || Jacket design by Heather Wood* [black] || *Simon & Schuster | Books for Young Readers* [green] | *Simon & Schuster* [black] [green leaf device] *New York* [black].

CONTENTS: Page [59]: [printer's flower device] TASHA TUDOR [printer's flower device reversed] || And that's how it still is. Holiday traditions rooted in Tasha Tudor's own | childhood were recreated, with embellishments, for her own children. Now | they are renewed for her grandchildren. The Sparrow Post Office is still in ⌐use for valentines. Advent calendars appear each December 6. Marionettes⌐are refurbished and newly costumed for plays. Melissa, the special love of⌐the artist's childhood, reappears at dolls' fairs. ¶ Tasha Tudor, one of America's most loved illustrators, was born in⌐Boston and grew up in Connecticut, the daughter of a portrait painter and⌐a designer of yachts. She has lived her entire life in New England, for many⌐years in New Hampshire, and at present in Vermont. Her first book, *Pumpkin⌐Moonshine*, appeared in 1938. There have been more than forty books since⌐that time. ¶ *A Time To Keep* brings together all the qualities for which Tasha Tudor⌐is famed. The delicacy of her watercolors. The nostalgic and imaginative⌐settings. The intricate borders with which she prefers to surround her illus-⌐trations. Avid gardeners will recognize flowers, grasses, and herbs of New⌐ England. Friends and acquaintances will recognize her home, her corgis, and⌐her family. ¶ For all who would know more of Tasha Tudor, she is a spinner, a weaver,⌐a seamstress, an admirer of the art of Eastman Johnson and Winslow⌐Homer, a cook, an omnivorous reader, a "passionate" gardener. Above all,⌐she is a painter who is able to translate her joy in a flower, her happiness in⌐a task performed well, her pleasure in the turning of seasons, her apprecia-⌐tion of traditional values, into a form that speaks eloquently to readers⌐everywhere.

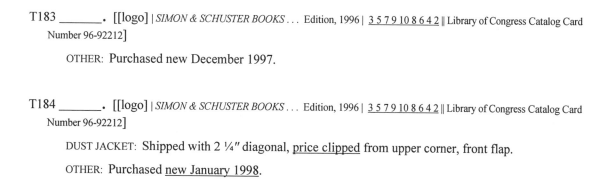

T183 _____. [[logo] | *SIMON & SCHUSTER BOOKS . . .* Edition, 1996 | 3 5 7 9 10 8 6 4 2 || Library of Congress Catalog Card Number 96-92212]

OTHER: Purchased new December 1997.

T184 _____. [[logo] | *SIMON & SCHUSTER BOOKS . . .* Edition, 1996 | 3 5 7 9 10 8 6 4 2 || Library of Congress Catalog Card Number 96-92212]

DUST JACKET: Shipped with 2 ¼″ diagonal, price clipped from upper corner, front flap.

OTHER: Purchased new January 1998.

T185 1980 | Tasha Tudor | Calendar | [4 1/8″ rule] | with fourteen reproductions | of full-color paintings | from *A Time To Keep* | [sprigs of rosemary and an hourglass] | *To e'very thing there is a season, | and a time to e'very purpose under the hea'ven: l...a time to keep.* —Ecclesiastes || [globe and dividers logo] Rand McNally & Company | Chicago • New York • San Francisco || Contents from A TIME TO KEEP | Copyright ©1977 by Rand McNally & Company | All rights reserved | Printed in the United States of America | by Rand McNally & Company.

PAGINATION: Fourteen artist's board sheets in a white spiral wire binding, [28] pp. A 3/32″ hole for hanging the calendar has been punched in the center at the edge opposite the binding. 10 5/8″ x 12 7/8″

COVER: Cover [page 1] is the white panel from the book cover with an additional pink panel (5 1/4″ wide) to the right on which is superimposed a smaller green title panel (5 1/4″ x 3 3/16″) with white text: 1980 | Tasha | Tudor | Calendar | [2 1/4″ rule] | with | fourteen | reproductions | of full-color | paintings. The back has only the small boy tearing sheets from a calendar, on a white field.

CONTENTS: Each sheet is printed in multi-color on even-numbered versos pp. [4-26], and black and white matte finish monthly calendars on the rectos pp. [5-27]. Most of the sheets (not in the same proportion as the book) reproduce one illustration from *A Time To Keep*, with additional color and text added at the right. Tudor's reminiscent text has been eliminated, but the two-line phrase still appears within the 'month box' at the top of each sheet. New verses appear here for the first time in the colored panels at the right.

ILLUSTRATIONS: Illustrations correspond to the following scheme: Title page [2], backed by JANUARY with a green panel and "The Year" by Coventry Patmore. FEBRUARY [6], yellow panel and "My Valentine" by Robert Louis Stevenson. MARCH [8], flesh panel and "*from* The First Spring Day" by Christina Rossetti. APRIL [10], yellow panel and "*from* The Poet's Calendar" by Henry Wadsworth Longfellow. MAY [12], green panel and "Song: On May Morning" by John Milton. JUNE [14], rose panel and "*from* The Poet's Calendar" by Longfellow. JULY [16], green panel and "*from* The Argument Of His Book" by Robert Herrick. AUGUST [18], green panel and "Under The Greenwood Tree" by William Shakespeare. SEPTEMBER [20], yellow panel and "Autumn" by Emily Dickinson. OCTOBER [22], pink panel and "*from* "When The Frost Is On The Punkin"" by James Whitcomb Riley. NOVEMBER [24], pink panel and "Up in the Morning Early" by Robert Burns. DECEMBER [26], green panel and "*from* Old Christmastide | *Marmion*" by Walter Scott. Page [28], small boy ripping pages from a calendar. The border around the boy was on the book but is not reproduced on the calendar.

T186 TO A MOUSE (On Turning Her Up In Her Nest With the Plough), November 1785. By Robert Burns. Unpublished Tudor manuscript, 1938

PAGINATION: Five leaves, plus covers. 6 ¾″ x 4 ¾″

COVER: Paper covered boards, marbled endpapers, lacking back free endpaper.

CONTENTS: Five leaves of stiff board. Stab-holes at left margins with portion of original cord which was used to fasten the leaves together.

ILLUSTRATIONS: Five watercolors, each with a protective tissue-guard.

OTHER: This description is taken from Doris Frohnsdorff's *Catalog 32* in which she offers this manuscript as item 202, listed at $1500. "The poem is lettered on recto of the first leaf. It is written in a minute hand and is illustrated with a small watercolor drawing of a mouse. Each of the remaining four watercolors are of mice, painted on watercolor paper, and mounted to the rectos of the other four leaves. Each is signed and dated '38." Believed to be owned by a Pennyslvania collector.

T187 A | TREASURY | OF | FIRST BOOKS.

COVER: Slip case title for Lutterworth's four-title set, 1994? 5 1/2″ x 3 7/8″ x 1 5/8″.   Two boxes were marketed with thumb cut-outs at the open edge, blue for boys and pink for girls. Books are identical in each. The boys' box is covered in blue paper top and bottom and has a 5 1/8″ gloss paper wrapped around the sides. This large label has a floral border and beneath the title on the front: a boy pumping water as a corgi laps from one of the buckets, the central motif of page 32, *More Prayers*. The title is repeated on the spine. Back centers the singing bird from the left endpaper of *More Prayers*. Printed above a single bar code in the lower right corner: ISBN 0-7188-2828-3; and below the bar code, 9 780718 828288. There is also a price label applied at the bottom: PUBLISHERS PRICE | L13•50.   The girls' box varies in that the floral border is more delicately colored, the front image is the girl sewing, page 13, *First Prayers*. Top and bottom gloss papers are pink and the bar code has changed slightly. Printed above: ISBN 0-7188-2829-1; and below the bar code, 9 780718 828295. Price label: PUBLISHERS PRICE | £13•50.

CONTENTS: The set includes *First Prayers*, 1994 printing, and 1991 printings of *More Prayers, First Graces* and *First Hymns*. See main title entries for the three Tudor titles. FIRST HYMNS follows here. This box unit was probably created about 1995/96.

T188 FIRST HYMNS ‖ *illustrated by* | BRENDA MEREDITH SEYMOUR ‖ The Lutterworth Press. [First published, 1967 | This impression 1991 ‖ The Publishers wish to make acknowledgement | to the following for the right to include hymns | of which they control the copyright: The | Methodist Youth Department ("To the Baby | Jesus" by Vivienne Sage); Miss M. Cropper | ("Jesus' Hands were kind Hands" by Margaret | Cropper; ‖ [L in a circle logo]‖| The Lutterworth Press | P.O. Box 60 | Cambridge CB1 2NT | England ‖ ISBN 0 7188 0308 6 | Copyright © 1967 The Lutterworth Press | *Printed in Hong Kong by Colorcraft Ltd*]

PAGINATION: [1-3] 4-40, plus free endpapers. 5 1/4″ x 3 13/16″.

COVER: Blue paper over board covers, a fine linen imprint. The spine is stamped in gilt: SEYMOUR FIRST HYMNS [L in circle logo].

DUST JACKET: Gloss lamination over green dust jacket. Front: FIRST HYMNS ‖ *Illustrated by* ‖ BRENDA MEREDITH | SEYMOUR, on a white oval field within a decorated oval of birds and flowers. Spine: SEYMOUR FIRST HYMNS [L in circle logo]. At the lower left back: a single bar code and above it, ISBN 0-7188-0308-6; below it, 9 780718 803087 >. In the lower right corner: The Lutterworth Press | P.O. Box 60 | Cambridge CB1 2NT | England. Front flap: FIRST HYMNS | *Illustrated by* | BRENDA MEREDITH | SEYMOUR ‖ Children adore hymns which | express their knowledge of | Jesus and His love for them | in simple terms. They 'love | to hear the story" of the birth | of Baby Jesus, to know that He | is 'a friend for little children | whose love will never die', | to recognize that 'all good | gifts around us are sent from | Heaven above', and to un- |derstand that when Christ | was crucified He 'died to | save us all'. ¶ This little book, which con- | tains a collection of these | favorite hymns exquisitely | illustrated by Brenda Meredith | Seymour, is a volume that | every child will treasure. [Have not examined a copy with lower corner price intact.] Back flap: More delightful books in this beautiful series | for little children: | FIRST PRAYERS | 0 7188 0306 x | MORE PRAYERS | 0 7188 1364 2 | FIRST GRACES | 0 7188 0307 8 | Illustrated by TASHA TUDOR.

ILLUSTRATIONS: The illustrations strongly suggest Tudor, with floral borders and sweet children. Seymour's children tend to have more cartoon-like mouths, round spots rather than intricately drawn mouths. The title page features a singing angel above the title playing a lute. The title page is decorated with a classic wreath of flowers, a bow at the bottom closed end. Two pages of black and white illustrations alternate with two pages of color illustrations, [2-3] through 40, except that 33 is black and white.

T189 *THE | TWENTY THIRD | PSALM | illustrated by | Tasha Tudor* | ACHILLE J. ST. ONGE | WORCESTER [© 1965 BY ACHILLE J. ST. ONGE]

PAGINATION: Four gatherings of buff linen weave paper: [36] pp., plus paste-down endpapers. [5] Half title [8] Copyright statement [9] *To my husband | Allan John Woods* [30] blank [31] *This edition of | The Twenty Third Psalm | was printed by | Joh. Enschedé en Zonen | Haarlem, Holland* [32-35] blank. Four stitches, saddle sewn. 3 5/8″ x 2 9/16″.

COVER: <u>Smooth dark green</u> leather stamped in gold on front, outlined twig encircling the title. All edges gilt. Yellow wash panel endpapers with large oval twig encircling a rabbit [on the left] and a gopher [on the right].

DUST JACKET: Light weight buff paper with a chain laid paper watermark. Front illustration on a blue wash field is the same on that printed on page [11]: Twig border, sides and top, surrounding a country church above the black text: *THE | TWENTY THIRD | PSALM | illustrated by Tasha Tudor* [rabbit, chipmunk and gopher at bottom]. Front flap text in black: *The Bible's finest | expression of faith, | in the familiar and | beautiful prose of the | King James version. | The prayer of our | childhood and the | universal favorite of | all English speaking | people, beautifully | illustrated in | full color by | Tasha Tudor. || Achille J. St. Onge | Publisher | Worcester 6, Mass.*

ILLUSTRATIONS: All illustrations share a single motif, a twig oval on a blue wash field framing a pastoral vignette, sometimes with text, as follows:

[i]   front endpaper, rabbit in ferns

[1]   front free endpaper, gopher in ferns

[6]   frontispiece, geese flying over pasture

[7]   Title page, chipmunk running under a blue sky

[10]   child and doll with corgi praying

[11]   country church "The Lord | is my shepherd"

[12]   beehive, bread and pitcher "I shall not want"

[13]   girl at table eating, corgi suckling young

[14]   girl and corgi lying in a pasture

[15]   girl with cow and corgi "He maketh me | to lie down in | green pastures

[16]   farm house by pond "He leadeth me | beside the | still waters"

[17]   girl and corgi watching white horse graze by a stream

[18]   girl and corgi walking past a fenced cape with floral dooryard "He restoreth my soul | He leadeth me in the | paths of righteousness | for his name's sake"

[19]   lane leading past a pond up to a country church and yard

[20]   girl and corgi walking up a dark cemetery lane to church

[21]   Hawk soaring "Yea, though I walk | through the valley | of the shadow of death, | I will fear | no evil"

[22]   girl and corgi gazing into a stream "For thou are with me; | thy rod and thy staff | they comfort me"

[23]   girl with sun streaming into dense woods

[24]   a bunny under briars, around the border an owl, a fox, hound and mink "Thou preparest a table | before me in the presence | of mine enemies"

[25]   girl kisses corgi's head "Thou anointest | my head with oil"

[26]   boy and girl sitting back-to-back with corgi and flute "My cup | runneth over"

[27]   girl with animals under an apple tree

[28]   night sky "Surely | goodness and mercy | shall follow me | all the days of my life: | and I will dwell | in the house | of the Lord | for ever"

[29]   girl and corgi sitting on a rock gazing at night sky

[36]   rear free endpaper, rabbit in ferns

[xxxvii] rear endpaper, gopher in ferns

OTHER: Robert E. Massmann cites this title in his *The Bibliomidgets of Achille J. St.Onge* (1979), page 75 , Entry XIII: *The Twenty Third Psalm*. 1965. Full green calf, gilt; a.e.g. Illustrated. 3 11/16″ x 2 5/8″ in colored dust wrapper. First issue, 14,000 copies. Printed by Joh. Enschede' en Zonen, Haarlem, Holland. Endleaves, dust wrapper, pages through-out in full color, by Tasha Tudor. Six copies bound in cloth, various textures and colors, gilt; plain edges. Also one copy in white leather. Examined a copy of the green in grained leather, thick boards, thin end leaves. 2 11/16″ wide. [Massmann doesn't mention a tan binding. Perhaps St. Onge left no records of such a binding. - Ed.]

COPYRIGHT REGISTRATION: AI 10108 granted to Achille J. St. Onge, 7 Arden Road, Worcester, Ma. 01606, a U.S. citizen. Achille J. St. Onge swears:

THE TWENTY THIRD PSALM by Tasha Tudor, Route 1, Contoocook, N.H., a U.S. citizen, was published Dec. 6, 1965 in Haarlem, Holland. New matter in this version: art work done especially for this edition by Tasha Tudor. Application received at L.C. May 16, 1966; one deposit copy received May 31, 1966.

COPYRIGHT REGISTRATION RENEWAL: RE-734-230 grants Tasha Tudor, c/o Corgi Cottage Industries, P.O. Box 7281, Richmond, Va. 23221-0281, claiming as author. Kathryn L. Barrett, Esq., 235 East 22nd St., Apt. 11C, New York, NY 10010, 212-684-6689 swears June 21, 1996:

TWENTY THIRD PSALM, was published December 6, 1965, [the Copyright Office has supplied the original claimant * Achille J. St, Onge] registration AI10108 [*sic*]. The renewable matter is: Illustrations and compilation.   Application received August 9, 1996, the effective date of this registration.

T190 _____.

PAGINATION: Endpapers have the linen appearance. Dedication present.

COVER: Tan kid leather over thin boards.

DUST JACKET: Thin paper, with fine linen appearance.

T191 _____.

PAGINATION: Coarser paper, nearly chain pattern. Dedication. 3 5/8 x 2 5/8″

COVER: Tan leather, with a more discernable grain, dull finish.

T192 _____.

    PAGINATION: [36]pp. including dedication on page [9]. 3 11/16 x 2 5/8″

    COVER: <u>Smooth green leather</u>, light grain. Pigskin, with dull finish.

    OTHER: Examined one copy with St. Onge signature in blue-black fountain pen ink beneath the colophon.

T193 _____.

    PAGINATION: [36]pp. Dedication. 3 11/16 x 2 11/16″

    COVER: <u>Pebbled grass green leather</u>,.

T194 _____.

    PAGINATION: [36]pp. <u>lacking dedication</u>. The paper has laid chain marks.

    COVER: <u>Smooth dark green leather</u>,.

T195 _____.

    PAGINATION: <u>[32] pages</u> plus paste-down endpapers. Blank sheets [2-4] and [32-35] <u>are not in</u> this printing. Consequent page numbers are two less than pagination of : half-title is [3], title [5], colophon [29]. Page [7] is blank without dedication.

    COVER: Smooth green leather with a very light texture. Thicker boards and <u>fewer pages</u>. The end leaves appear to be a heavier stock than the earlier printings; they are actually free endpapers and adjoining leaf pasted together.

    OTHER: There is no dedication.   Probably Massmann's entry XIIIa: The Twenty Third psalm. (<u>1975</u>). Full green calf, gilt; a.e.g Illustrated, colored dust wrapper. New issue, 4657 copies. 3 11/16″ x 2 5/8″. <u>This issue does not have the dedication inscription; the leather is lighter in color; and the boards are thicker than those in the first issue.</u>

see *The Lord Is My Shepherd* for the 1980 and 1989 adaptations, in large format.

V1 *The Victory Garden*. Public Broadcast System. November 25, 1995.

    OTHER: A thirteen minute segment of the television series with Holly Shimizu interviewing Tudor.

W1 The | Way of | the World ‖ **Bernard J. Weiss** | Reading and Linguistics ‖ **Eldonna L. Evertts** | Language Arts ‖ **Loreli Steuer** | Reading and Linguistics ‖ **Janet Sprout** | Educational Consultant ‖ **Lyman C. Hunt** | General Editor — Satellite Books | [device] | Level 10 ‖ HOLT, RINEHART AND WINSTON, PUBLISHERS | New York • Toronto • London • Sydney [Copyright © 1980, 1977, 1973 by Holt, Rinehart and Winston, Publishers | All Rights Reserved | Printed in the United States of America ‖ ISBN: 0-03-047826-X | 0123 071 98765432 ‖

Acknowledgments: *Grateful acknowledgment is given to the following authors and publishers:* | Addison-Wesley … Thomas Y. Crowell Company, for adaptation of the text of *Amy's Goose* by Efner Tudor Holmes | Copyright © 1977 by Efner Tudor Holmes. For "Company Clothes," from … *Town and Countryside Poems* by John Travers Moore. Copyright © 1968. Used by permission.]

PAGINATION: Approximately 298 pp. Have not examined a copy.

ILLUSTRATIONS: The story appears with new illustrations by Jane Clark, not the original Tudor paintings. Clark paints these images: Amy watching geese in formation, Amy and father watching fox capture goose, Amy holding wounded goose, Amy in barn, Amy watching goose fly off and watching flock of geese leaving, Amy waving farewell to goose.

OTHER: The adaptation of Holmes' story is printed on pages 246-255. This eighteen-word opening {Amy was standing in the garden when she heard the cry she had been waiting for all fall.} replaces the sixty-one word opening page of Holmes' book. {Amy stood in the garden watching the sun sink behind the hills. She had been helping her parents dig the last of the potatoes. The air smelled of cool damp earth mixed with the scent of the gold and orange leaves that fell silently and incessantly to the ground. Then Amy heard the cry she had been waiting for all fall.}

W2 THE | WHITE | GOOSE | *By* | *Tasha Tudor* ‖ *OXFORD UNIVERSITY* | *PRESS* ‖ *LONDON* • *NEW YORK* • *TORONTO* [*Copyright 1943* | *Oxford University Press* | *New York, Inc.* | [bunch of 4 cattails] | *Printed in the United States of America* | *Calligraphy by Hilda Scott*]

PAGINATION: [36] pp. in two signatures including free endpapers. 6 ¾ x 6 ¼″

COVER: Gray cloth. Title and two witch hazel branches printed in blue on front ivory paper label (2 5/8″ x 3 1/2″). Ivory end papers with four animal motifs (grouse, raccoon, rabbit, field mouse), each in a blue line frame.

DUST JACKET: Have not examined one.

CONTENTS: Pages [2-4] and [32-35] are blank. Title is page [5]. "To Nell" in oak leaves on page [7]. All text is black ink calligraphy, except the title which is blue block letters outlined in black. Text begins on page [8] and continues on versos through [30]. Text pages have blue borders, and there is a small blue drawing at the bottom of each text except for [26].

ILLUSTRATIONS: Twelve blue full-page illustrations (5 1/4″ x 4 3/4″), rectos, [9] - [31]. Versos carry hand-lettered text within the blue line frame and a botanical/zoological sketch at the bottom of each, excepting page [24] which has no painting.

OTHER: Dedicated to friend Nell Dorr, photographer-author of *Mother and Child.*

COPYRIGHT REGISTRATION: A 176093 granted to Oxford University Press, Inc., 114 Fifth Ave., N.Y. 11, N.Y.

THE WHITE GOOSE by Tasha Tudor of the United States, was published Sept. 30, 1943. The book was manufactured by The Kellogg and Bulkeley Co., Hartford, Ct. Copies received at L.C. Sept. 4, 1943. Affidavit received Oct. 15, 1943.

COPYRIGHT RENEWAL REGISTRATION: R 499023 granted to Tasha Tudor, Route 1, Contoocook, N.H., claiming as author. Kuna Dolch, Henry Z. Walck, Inc., 19 Union Square West, NY, NY 1003 swears:

THE WHITE GOOSE by Tasha Tudor was originally published Sept. 30, 1943. Fee charged to account 6694, Walck, Inc., Henry Z. Application received at L.C. Jan. 15, 1971.

W3 _____. . . . *By* | *Tasha Tudor* || FARRAR & RINEHART, INC. | *Distributed by* || *OXFORD UNIVERSITY* | *PRESS* || *LONDON •NEW YORK •TORONTO* [*Copyright 1943* | *Oxford University Press* | *New York, Inc.* | SECOND PRINTING 1943 | [bunch of 4 cattails] | *Printed in the United States of America* | *Calligraphy by Hilda Scott*]

PAGINATION: [36] pp. in two signatures including loose endpapers. 6 ¾ x 6 ¼″

COVER: Khaki green cloth over boards, with same front label.

DUST JACKET: THE | WHITE | GOOSE | *By* | *Tasha Tudor.* Title letters outlined in black, filled with blue; author in black. Surround by large botanical frame of witch hazel, mushrooms, maple seeds and ground plants. Spine in blue, *TUDOR THE WHITE GOOSE   OXFORD.* Back: two blue oak leaves and acorns. Front flap: *THE WHITE GOOSE* | *By Tasha Tudor* || *The little white goose had flown away.* | *Robin picked up several of her feathers* | *one moonlight night and followed the* | *cry of the wild geese. Down in the marsh* | *he saw a magic sight.* ¶*This story with its pictures of moon-* | *light is a rare and lovely addition to* | *fairytale picture books. We know that* | *readers who delight in this artist's* | *other books will agree that this is per-* | *haps her most beautiful.* || *OXFORD BOOKS* | *FOR BOYS AND GIRLS* || *$1.00. Back flap: Other Books by Tasha Tudor* || — || *SNOW BEFORE CHRISTMAS* | *$1.00* || *A TALE FOR EASTER* | *$1.00* | *The Calico Books* || *PUMPKIN MOONSHINE* || *ALEXANDER THE GANDER* || *THE COUNTY FAIR* || *DORCAS PORCUS* [sic] || *Each 75 cents.*

W4 *The Wind* | *in the* | *Willows* || *Kenneth Grahame* | *illustrated by* | *Tasha Tudor* || THE WORLD PUBLISHING COMPANY | CLEVELAND AND NEW YORK [Published by The World Publishing Company | 2231 West 110th Street, Cleveland, Ohio 44102 | Published simultaneously in Canada by | Nelson, Foster & Scott Ltd. | Library of Congress catalog card number: 66-14847 | CPHL | The special contents of this edition | copyright © 1966 by the World Publishing Company | Illustrations copyright © 1966 by Tasha Tudor | All rights reserved. No part of this book may be reproduced in any | form without written permission from the publisher, except for | brief passages included in a review appearing in a newspaper | or magazine. Printed in the United States of America. | Designed by Jack Jaget] Page [256] bottom: 1 2 3 4 5 70 69 68 67 66.

PAGINATION: Sixteen signatures on ivory paper, pages [1-7] 8-14 [15-16] 17-19 [20-22] 23-29 [30] 31-32 [33] 34-37 [38] 39-42 [43] 44-45 [46] 47 [48] 49-51 [52] 53-61 [62-63] 64-68 [69] 70 [71] 72-77 [78] 79-92 [93] 94-95 [96] 97-116 [117] 118-123 [124] 125-133 [134] 135-139 [140] 141 [142] 143-153 [154] 155-167 [168] 169-171 [172] 173-177 [178] 179-180 [181] 182-193 [194] 195 [196] 197-213 [214] 215-221 [222] 223-225 [226] 227-228 [229] 230-232 [233] 234-240 [241] 242-244 [245] 246-255 [256] plus endpapers. 9 3/8″ x 6 3/8″

COVER: Front and back endpapers are identical: green printed river bank scene on yellow paper. Moss green linen stamped in gold: illustration of Toad, Mole and Water Rat from page 255 on front cover. Spine: Graham THE WIND IN THE WILLOWS World.

DUST JACKET: Ivory vellum with two full size illustrations and text in red, green, blue and black.
Front: **THE WIND** | **IN THE WILLOWS** [red Victorian letters] || **Kenneth Graham** || **ILLUSTRATED BY** [green] || **Tasha Tudor** [blue] on a river scene within a branching willow, mole and rat picnicking. Spine: **THE WIND IN** | **THE WILLOWS** [red] || **Grahame** || [seedling in circle] [green] || **World** [blue]. Back: mole and rat boating on the river within a vine border. Lower right back corner: A 1029. Front flap, top corner, **$4.95**, in black as is all text, except the heading and footer which are blue: The Wind | in the Willows | BY KENNETH GRAHAME | *Illustrated by* | TASHA TUDOR [blue] || The delightful escapades of the four fa- | mous friends — Mole, Rat, Badger, and | Toad — have enchanted children, and | grownups too, for more than fifty years. | In this beloved book, Kenneth Grahame | created an imaginary world that is as real | and vivid as life itself. Bashful Mole, | emerging from his dark home to discover | the sunlit meadow and the exhilarating | joy of springtime; his worldly-wise friend | Rat; boastful, rash, yet endearing Toad; | practical Badger, and all the other crea- | tures of the Wild Wood remain in the | reader's mind as lifelong friends. The | story of their adventures is a rich heritage | of the imagination which should be part | of everyone's experience. ¶Kenneth Grahame said that he wrote | not only for children but for "adults who | remember what it is like to be children." | *The Wind in the Willows* has inspired | many outstanding artists to illustrate it, | but never before has it found so perfect | an interpreter as Tasha Tudor. Like the | author, Tasha Tudor is one who remem- | bers, who understands children from the | inside, who can see the world as children | see it. Her sensitive, delicate pencil draw- | ings and exquisite watercolor paintings | make this the classic edition of Mr. Gra- | hame's timelessly appealing story. || The World Publishing Company | CLEVELAND AND NEW YORK [blue]. Back flap text is black, except for the names of the author, the illustrator and the publisher's statement: Kenneth Grahame [blue] (1859-1932) was born | in Edinburgh, Scotland. Orphaned at an | early age, he was sent to Berkshire, Eng- | land, to be brought up by relatives there. | Though he hoped for an academic career, | he could not afford the necessary univer- | sity education, and instead had to go to | work as a clerk for the Bank of England. | In spite of his disappointment, he had a | long and successful career as a banker. | He came to think of banking as his pri- | mary occupation, but he sought out and | enjoyed the company of men of letters. ¶In 1899 Mr. Grahame married Elspeth | Thomson, a Scotswoman who shared his | love of fantasy and literature, and it was | for their son, Alastair, that *The Wind in* | *the Willows* was written in 1908. Although | he is most famous for this well-loved clas- | sic, Kenneth Grahame also wrote two | other books, *Dream Days* and *The Golden* | *Age*. [black] || Tasha Tudor, [blue] who is well known as the | artist-author of many beautiful children's | books, has always wanted to illustrate | *The Wind in the Willows*. She lives with | her large family in an old farmhouse in | Webster, New Hampshire. When she is | not writing or illustrating, she divides | her time between being housewife and | mother, entertaining visiting friends and | relatives, gardening and taking care of | her many farm animals, and looking after | a grove of sugar maples. [black] || The World Publishing Company | CLEVELAND AND NEW YORK.

CONTENTS: Half-title [1] [15], CONTENTS [5], LIST OF ILLUSTRATIONS [7]-8, FOREWORD 9-10, INTRODUCTION 11-14. Blank pages: [2, 6, 16] Twelve chapter titles carry both Arabic chapter and page numbers, a printer's swirl, the title and a pencil illustration. There are 89 other black and white drawings throughout and, when at the top of the page, there is no page number. A few occupy the lower third of the page. Page numbers are printed in opposing upper corners of two-page spreads, except that on chapter title pages the numbers are on the lower outside. Sixteen full page color illustrations are tipped in: frontispiece (faces title page [3]) and facing pages 25, 48, 64, 81, 96, 113, 121, 136, 145, 160, 176, 193, 208, 225, 240.

OTHER: From page 13: ...TASHA TUDOR, who is well known as the artist-author of | many beautiful children's books, has always wanted to illus- | trate *The Wind in the Willows*. She lives with her large | family in an old farmhouse in Webster, New Hampshire. | When she is not writing or illustrating, she devotes her time | to being housewife and mother, entertaining visiting friends | and relatives, gardening and taking care of her many farm | animals, and looking after a grove of sugar maples. The bottom corner of the dust jacket is clipped. One will probably never find a jacket with both corners present as a trade price and a library price were printed on opposing corners, the appropriate one to be clipped for sale.

COPYRIGHT REGISTRATION: A 864672 granted to The World Publishing Co., 2231 West 110th St., Cleveland, Oh. Donna A. Hoecker, agent for the claimant swears on Oct. 5, 1966:

THE WIND IN THE WILLOWS by Kenneth Grahame (deceased) was published June 20, 1966. The World Publishing Company, a U.S. citizen, files as author with this new matter: introduction and arrangement of illustrations within public domain text. The book was manufactured by Harry Sweetman, South Hackensack, N.J., Connecticut Printers, Hartford, Ct., Halliday, West Hanover, Ma, and American Book-Stratford Press, N.Y., N.Y. Fee charged to The World Publishing Co. Two deposit copies received at L.C. Sept. 12, 1966. Application and affidavit received Oct. 6, 1966.

COPYRIGHT REGISTRATION: A 864673 granted to Tasha Tudor (Illustrations), Route 1, Contoocook, N.H. Donna A. Hoecker, agent for the claimant swears on Oct. 5, 1966:

THE WIND IN THE WILLOWS by Kenneth Grahame (deceased) was published June 20, 1966. Tasha Tudor, a U.S. citizen, files as author. The book was manufactured by Harry Sweetman, South Hackensack, N.J., Connecticut Printers, Hartford, Ct., Halliday, West Hanover, Ma., and American Book-Stratford Press, N.Y., N.Y. Fee charged to The World Publishing Co. Two deposit copies received at L.C. Sept. 12, 1966. Application and affidavit received Oct. 6, 1966.

COPYRIGHT RENEWAL REGISTRATION: RE-734232 grants Tasha Tudor, c/o Corgi Cottage Industries, P.O. Box 7281, Richmond, Va., 23221-0281, claiming as author (illustrator). Kathryn [sic] L. Barrett swears June 21, 1996:

WIND IN THE WILLOWS [sic], was published June 20, 1966 and copyright to Tasha Tudor, A864673. Renewable matter are the illustrations. Certificate to be mailed to Kathryn L. Barrett [sic], correspondence to Kathryn L. Barrett, Esq. Application received at LC August 9, 1996, the effective date of this registration.

W5 _____.

DUST JACKET: Back, lower right corner, printed in black 2″ above edge: **WLB** | WORLD LIBRARY BINDING. The monogram **L** extends above the other two initials into a stylized tree. It also extends down between WORLD and LIBRARY.

OTHER: The editor examined this mis-matched book and jacket. The book is clearly the green cloth trade binding; the jacket indicates a library binding (see next entry). And the examination copy suggests the two have been together for many years. Since these jackets are not often switched, it is probable that some copies were distributed with the "wrong" jacket.

W6 _____.

PAGINATION: 9 7/8 x 6 1/2″

COVER: World Library Binding. Fine sealed cream cloth imprinted with the jacket design. Printed in black 2″ above back lower right corner: **WLB** | WORLD LIBRARY BINDING. The monogram L extends above the other two initials into a stylized tree. It also extends down into the next line between WORLD and LIBRARY.

DUST JACKET: As , except <u>upper corner of front flap is clipped.</u> The bottom corner, with black text: <u>$4.61 NET</u> .

OTHER: Examined a copy accompanied by contemporary REVIEW COPY card. The 5″ x 4 1/4″ gray laid paper sheet is printed in red, with information specific to this book (editor's bold) <u>typed</u> on the pre-printed form: [tree growing from ground in circle logo] REVIEW COPY ‖ TITLE `THE WIND IN THE WILLOWS` ‖ AUTHOR `Kenneth Graham` ‖ PUBLICATION DATE `June 20, 1966` ‖ PRICE `$4.95` | `World Library Binding $4.61 net` ‖ *Please do not release your review before publication | date. We would appreciate two copies of your review.* ‖ The World Publishing Company | 2231 WEST 110ᵀᴴ STREET • CLEVELAND 2 • OHIO. The Reviewer ? penciled in the gutter of page [5]: <u>6/11/1966 LMW from JHA   rev. 6/18/66.</u>

W7 _____. Have not examined one published simultaneously in Canada by | Nelson, Foster & Scott Ltd.

W8 _____. Have not examined a 2ⁿᵈ printing.

W9 _____. Page [256] carries only this publication data: <u>3 4 5 70 69 68 7 67.</u>

COVER: Green cloth as in first printing, top edge yellow.

DUST JACKET: Without the World Library Binding emblem. The A 1029 code is printed at lower right back corner of the dust jacket. <u>Both corners of front flap were clipped from examination copy.</u> A penciled notation was added at top of front flap: <u>5⁹⁵</u>.

OTHER: Printing ink splattered on page 192 and facing blank, and at base of back dj flap.

W10 _____. Page [256] carries only this publication data: <u>3 4 5 70 69 68 7 67.</u>

COVER: Green cloth as in first printing, top edge yellow.

DUST JACKET: Without the World Library Binding emblem. The A 1029 code is printed at lower right back corner of the dust jacket. <u>Both corners of front flap were clipped from examination copy.</u> A penciled notation was added at top of front flap: <u>5⁹⁵</u>.

OTHER: Printing ink splattered on page 192 and facing blank, and at base of back dj flap.

W11 _____.

PAGINATION: 9 7/16 x 6 9/16 x1 1/16″ thick.

COVER: <u>Brown</u> buckram, imprinted as before <u>in green ink.</u>

DUST JACKET: World Library Binding, <u>with the emblem,</u> and A 1029 code. Neither code appears on the book cover itself. Corners clipped from front flap of examined jacket.

CONTENTS: Page [256] is blank. There is no indication of printing, but the body and other text are like the first edition, <u>on a lighter ivory paper than before.</u>

W12 _____. [Published by The World...Foster & Scott Ltd. | The special contents...United States of America]

PAGINATION: Seven signatures porous 'book club' paper: pp. [1-9] <u>10-224.</u> <u>8 1/2″ x 5 3/4″</u>

COVER: <u>Green</u> cloth with <u>Badger</u> stamped in gilt on the <u>lower front.</u> Spine stamped in gold: Kenneth Grahame THE WIND IN THE WILLOWS World. <u>Top edge, green.</u>

DUST JACKET: Dust jacket carries same illustration as above, no code on back. Front flap text, black only with variations and lacking the publisher statement: ... world as children | see it. Her exquisite watercolor paintings | make this the classic edition of Mr. | Grahame's timelessly appealing story. || *Book Club | Edition.* Back flap text, black, varies slightly: ... *The Wind in the Willows.* She lives with | her large family in an old farmhouse in | Contoocook, New Hampshire. When she ... sugar maples. || PRINTED IN THE U.S.A.

ILLUSTRATIONS: Ivory end papers have river scene as in first edition, in olive. Sixteen full page colored illustrations are printed back-to-back following pages 32, 64, 96, 128, 160, 192. Untrimmed deckle fore-edge. None of the pencil drawings appear in this edition, including the tree formerly on the title page.

OTHER: Colophon lacks LCCN, CPHL and Designed by Jack Jaget.

W13 _____. JUNIOR DELUXE EDITIONS | GARDEN CITY, NEW YORK.

COVER: Plastic-filled paper in a pigskin imprint, half-tan with aqua spine wrap. Both covers stamped green title in orange frame and two illustrations: from first edition pages 53, and detail of Mr. Badger reversed from the illustration facing page 113, (p. 96 in this edition). Spine stamped in green and orange: [detail of three birds from first edition, page 164] || THE WIND | IN THE | WILLOWS || [rat with knapsack from first edition page [172]] || KENNETH GRAHAME || JUNIOR DELUXE | EDITIONS.　　Top edge, green.

W14 _____.

COVER: The tan and aqua plastic-filled paper, but without the decorative stamping front and back. The tan paper is 4 1/2″ wide across the cover instead of the 5″ in W11, Spine as above. Top edge, green.

W15 _____.

COVER: Mint green plastic-filled paper, pigskin imprint. Spine stamped in navy, within a rectangle formed of printers' curlicues: THE WIND IN THE WILLOWS • *GRAHAME.* Below the box, printed laterally across the base of spine; WORLD. Top edge, green.

OTHER: Examined a copy with a 1971 inscription.

W16 _____.

COVER: Tan plastic-filled paper, pigskin imprint. Spine stamped in navy, as before. Top edge, green.

DUST JACKET: Gloss spray finish. Bottom two lines of back flap: **PRINTED IN THE U.S.A.** | 4040.

W17 _____. **COLLINS** [tree in circle logo] **WORLD** [Published by William Collins & World Publishing Company, Inc. | 2080 West 117th Street, Cleveland, Ohio 44111 | Library of Congress catalog card number: 66-14847 | The special contents . . . Jack Jaget]

COVER: Green with illustration from page 255. Base of spine: WORLD.

OTHER: Ruby Miller of Portland, Oregon, provided this description. It was sold before we could examine it.

W18 _____. **COLLINS** [tree in circle logo] **WORLD** | CLEVELAND, OHIO [Published by The William Collins | & The World Publishing Company, Inc. | 2080 West 117th Street, Cleveland, Ohio 44111 | Published simultaneously . . . United States of America]

> PAGINATION: Fourteen signatures porous 'book club' paper: pp. [I-iv, 1-9] 10-222 [223-236]. 8 7/16 x 5 5/8″

> COVER: Flesh plastic-filled paper in a smooth deerskin pattern. Spine stamping in navy as in W13, but the box is 6 7/8″. Base of spine: COLLINS | [rule] | WORLD.

> DUST JACKET: Base of spine: [tree in circle logo] | COLLINS | [rule] | WORLD [blue]. Illustrations as before. Flap text reverts to the blue and black type of the previous trade editions. Front flap: The Wind . . . delicate pencil draw- | ings and exquisite watercolor paintings | make this the classic edition of Mr. Gra- | hame's timelessly appealing story. || *Book Club* | *Edition.* Back flap: Kenneth . . . has always wanted to illustrate | *The Wind in the Willows.* When she is | . . . sugar maples. || *Printed in the U.S.A.* | 2 3 5 9. There is no price printed on the jacket of this printing. Gloss spray finish.

> OTHER: Examined a copy inscribed Christmas '78.

W19 _____. . . . *Tudor* || [tree in circle logo] | **COLLINS**. [Published by William Collins Publishers, Inc. | New York and Cleveland | Library of Congress catalog card number: 66-14847 | ISBN No. 0-529-00119-5 | The special contents of this edition . . . United States of America. | Designed by Jack Jaget]

> PAGINATION: As in first edition, W3. 9 3/8″ x 6 3/8″

> COVER: Light green cloth stamped in green ink, illustration of mole, rat and toad as first. Spine: Grahame THE WIND IN THE WILLOWS COLLINS. Endpapers are a deep pastel green with the same illustration as always.

> DUST JACKET: Gloss film laminate. Spine: COLLINS | WORLD below the tree in a circle logo [in blue]. Back, lower right corner: A 1029 Back flap , same text as previous Collins World Book Club edition with these two bottom lines: a grove of sugar maples. || COLLINS [tree in circle logo] WORLD. [blue]

> CONTENTS: Frontispiece now faces page [5] and not the title page, as in previous trade editions.

> OTHER: This edition returns to the size, typography, and iconography of the first edition.

W20 _____.

> DUST JACKET: Varies from above in only two points. All publisher references to World are gone and the single word COLLINS appears at the base of the spine and as the last line of the back flap, both in blue. The tree in circle logo is only on the spine above COLLINS.

W21 **WINGS** | *from the* | **WIND** | *An Anthology of Poems* | *Selected and Illustrated by* | **TASHA TUDOR** | J. B. Lippincott Company | Philadelphia New York [*To Eunice Blake* || Copyright © 1964 by Tasha Tudor | Printed in the United States of America | Library of Congress Catalog Card Number 64-19059 | First edition || ACKNOWLEDGMENTS || Thanks go to the following publishers, agents and individuals for their kind | permission to reprint material copyrighted or controlled by them: Brandt & Brandt for "A Nonsense Song" from ...] [There are 16 acknowledgments printed on pages [4-5] -*Ed.*]

> PAGINATION: Six signatures of ivory paper: [1-10] 11-18 [19] 20-23 [24] 25-32 [33] 34 [35] 36-42 [43] 44-45 [46-47] 48-63 [64-65] 66-69 [70-71] 72-78 [79-81] 82 [83] 84-93 [94] 95 [96-97] 98-105 [106-107] 108-109 [110-111] 112-119 [120] plus ivory endpapers. 7 3/4″ x 9 3/4″

COVER: <u>Half olive paper</u>, wildflower wreath blind stamped on front. <u>Mustard linen</u> wrapped spine imprinted in red: *Tasha Tudor*   WINGS FROM THE WIND   *Lippincott*

DUST JACKET: Mustard color with red high bush cranberry embellishments front, spine and back. Front has large border of fall leaves and berries, two male golden-crowned kinglets at bottom corners and one in flight, top center. Black text, except [red] author, fills the enclosed space: **WINGS** | *from the* | **WIND** | [two red berries] | *An Anthology* | *of Poems* | *Selected and Illustrated by* | [one red berry] | TASHA TUDOR. Black spine text as on book, but with a single red cranberry top, and bottom. Cranberry sprig centered, back. Front flap printed in black on ivory, except TASHA TUDOR in red: WINGS | *from the* | WIND | *An Anthology of Poems* | *Selected and Illustrated by* | TASHA TUDOR ‖ Tasha Tudor has selected poems | for fun, for beauty, for pleasure. | Her own family spent many happy | hours enjoying poetry together and | for years this artist has longed to | illustrate some of her favorites. ¶Over fifty poets are represented | in this volume, and each poem has | been interpreted artistically by one | of the foremost illustrators of chil- | dren's books today. The poems are | ageless, including such classics as | "The Tiger" by William Blake | and "Calico Pie" by Edward Lear. ¶The Title *Wings from the Wind* is | quoted from "Matin Song" by | Thomas Heywood. It well ex- | presses the aim of this collection: ‖ "Wings from the wind to please | her mind, | Notes from the lark I'll borrow: | Bird, prune thy wing! Nightin- | gale, sing! | To give my Love good-morrow! | To give my Love good-morrow! | Notes from them all I'll borrow." ‖ All ages $ 3.95. [Top corner clipped.] Ivory back flap black text: [3 3/8 x 2 13/16″ photograph of Tudor with kitten] | *Photo by Gerda Peterich* ‖ Ever since her first book, *Pumpkin* | *Moonshine*, was published some | years ago, Tasha Tudor has had a | busy and distinguished career writ- | ing and illustrating books for young | readers. Recent books in which her | delicate color work and charming | pencil drawings have appeared are | new editions of Frances Hodgson | Burnett's *The Secret Garden* and *A* | *Little Princess*. ¶Tasha Tudor lives in an old New | Hampshire farmhouse which is big | enough to hold her four children | and many visiting friends and | cousins, not to mention animals, | who are an integral part of the | family. There is a garden, too, a | grove of sugar maples, and blue | New Hampshire mountains in the | distance. ‖ J.B. Lippincott Company | *Good Books Since 1792* | Philadelphia and New York.

ILLUSTRATIONS: Full-page color illustrations - [3, title page] and section titles on pages [9, 47, 81, 111]. Full-page black and white illustrations without text, pages [19, 33, 35] 41 [43] 53, 55, 63 [71, 79, 83] 99, 105. One of 114 other black drawings appear on most pages. Pages 26-27, 48-49, [64-65] [70-71] 92-93, [94]-95, [106-107] are two-page illustrations. Pages [2, 6, 10, 46, 80, 120] are blank.

Tudor has drawn a barn for page 22 with a sign over its door: ALLAN WOODS | HORSE SHOEING; and a picture of a blacksmith on page [24] Allan John Woods was Tudor's second husband. See also the dedication to *The Twenty Third Psalm*, St. Onge. An early boggart is pictured on a swing on page [111], seven years before the publication of *Corgiville Fair*. A drawing of the Purvis house appears on page 76.

OTHER: Eunice Blake was Tudor's editor at Oxford University Press beginning in 1938. Lippincott first lists this title at 3.95 (trade) and 3.79 (library binding) in its July 1, 1964 catalog. It is listed at those prices in each of the next ten years. In the June 1, 1975, and June 1, 1976 catalogs, prices are 4.95 (trade) and 3.79 (library binding). In the June 1, 1977, and June 1, 1978, catalogs, only the Longlife Binding is listed, still at 3.79. LIPPINCOTT BOOKS FOR YOUNG READERS 1977/78, again lists LLB $3.79; $4.95. ISBNs and Library of Congress catalog card numbers are reported for the first time in the June 1, 1972 catalog, with explanations of those and the Cataloging in Publication program on the catalog cover. "LC cataloging data is included on the copyright pages of virtually all books published since February 1972."

Because of a chemical reaction between the cover, its paper and the dust jacket, this book often has red splotches of varying intensity on its green cover.

COPYRIGHT REGISTRATION: A 724280 granted to Tasha Tudor, Route 1, Contoocook, N.H. Charles G. Granade, agent for Tasha Tudor, swears on Oct. 21, 1964:

WINGS FROM THE WIND by Tasha Tudor, a U.S. citizen, was published Oct. 2, 1964. New matter in this version: illustrations, compilation. The book was manufactured by Reehl Litho, Inc., 305 E 45 St., N.Y., N.Y. 10017, and The Cornwall Press, Inc., 75 Varick St., NY, NY 10013. Fee charged to J. B. Lippincott Company. Application and affidavit and two deposit copies received at LC Oct. 24, 1964.

COPYRIGHT RENEWAL REGISTRATION: RE 611 329 granted to Tasha Tudor, RFD 4, West Brattleboro, Vt. 05301, claiming as the author. Marilyn Small, HarperCollins Publishers, 10 East 53rd St., N.Y., N.Y. 10022, agent for Tasha Tudor, swears on Nov. 23, 1992:

WINGS FROM THE WIND with renewable illustrations and compilation by Tasha Tudor was originally published Oct. 2, 1964. Fee charged to account DA 064726, HarperCollins Publishers. Renewal application received at LC Nov. 30, 1992, the effective date of this registration.

W22 _____.

COVER: Lippincott Longlife Binding. White linen reinforcing hinges. The sealed linen cover is imprinted with the same design as dust jacket, plus this paragraph printed on the back cover.

LLB This symbol identifies a | LIPPINCOTT | LONGLIFE BINDING | This binding is guaranteed to last as | long as the sheets, which are side sewn | in picture books, and reinforced with | strong joint drill. Symthe sewn books | are reinforced with muslin. The | cover is stain-resistant, washable | cloth, over top-grade binders board.

DUST JACKET: The Longlife features of the dust jacket are these. The trade price was factory clipped from the lower corner of the front flap. And the upper corner, missing from the trade edition, is whole on this copy: LLB $3.79 net. There is a 1″ x 3″ gold foil label, placed just below Lippincott and covering the berry at the base of the spine. The label wraps the spine and is printed on the front: LLB This symbol | identifies a | LIPPINCOTT | LONGLIFE BINDING. Running laterally down the spine: LIPPINCOTT | LONGLIFE | BINDING; and laterally down the back: LIPPINCOTT | LONGLIFE | BINDING   LIPPINCOTT | LONGLIFE | BINDING.

W23 _____. [*To Eunice Blake* || Copyright © 1964 by Tasha Tudor | Printed in the United States of America | Library of Congress Catalog Card Number 64-19059 | Second Prinitng || ACKNOWLEDGMENTS . . .]

COVER: Trade binding, green paper, mustard spine.

DUST JACKET: Top corner front flap clipped, $3.95 at bottom.

W24 _____. [*To Eunice Blake* || Copyright © 1964 by Tasha Tudor | Printed in the United States of America | Library of Congress Catalog Card Number 64-19059 | THIRD PRINTING || ACKNOWLEDGMENTS . . .]

DUST JACKET: Top corner front flap clipped, $3.95 at bottom.

W25 _____.

COVER: LIPPINCOTT LONGLIFE BINDING as first edition above.

DUST JACKET: As first edition above.

W26 _____. [**To Eunice Blake** ‖ Copyright © 1964 by Tasha Tudor | Printed in the United States of America | Library of Congress Catalog Card Number 64-19059 | <u>FOURTH PRINTING</u> ‖ ACKNOWLEDGMENTS . . .]

DUST JACKET: Upper corner of dj front flap clipped. Lower corner: $3.95.

OTHER: Examined a copy inscribed Dec. 25, <u>1967</u>.

W27 _____. [**To Eunice Blake** ‖ Copyright © 1964 by Tasha Tudor | Printed in the United States of America | Library of Congress Catalog Card Number 64-19059 | <u>FIFTH PRINTING</u> ‖ ACKNOWLEDGMENTS . . .]

DUST JACKET: Trade jacket with front flap upper corner clipped. Pre-printed price at the bottom of front flap is still $3.95, although someone has penciled a line through it and written below it $2^{00}. Someone had already penciled <u>5-70</u> at the top of the front free endpaper of the examination copy.

OTHER: Examined the <u>publisher's file copy</u> sold through a Philadelphia book dealer. There are two red rubber stamp impressions on the front fly leaf: <u>FILE COPY | NOT TO BE REMOVED | FROM OFFICE</u>. Probably among books sold in Philadelphia when Lippincott was purchased by Harper & Row in New York City. Besides other seller's marks, there is a pen note: BIW | 353 on the ffep.

W28 _____.

COVER: Lippincott Longlife Binding. Cover, jacket, gold band and statement as in the first printing.

DUST JACKET: Price, $3.79, upper right front flap.

W29 *With My Love, Tasha*. Produced Exclusively by The Jenny Wren Press 1991 | All Rights Reserved. [Filmed at Conner Prairie Museum, Noblesville, Indiana, August 16-17, 1991. Special thanks to: | Polly Jontz | Kate Bend | Nancy Pugh | and the entire Conner Prairie Staff ‖ Production and Post production Facilities Provided by: | Video Post Graphics, Inc. | Dayton, Ohio.]

PAGINATION: 45 minute videotape, color.

COVER: Black plastic videocassette with two labels. 1 13/16″ x 3 1/16″ while label printed in yellow: *With My Love, Tasha | Copyright © The Jenny Wren Press 1991*. 1 ½″ round white label printed in red: ENCODED WITH AN | ANTI-COPYING PROCESS: ‖ MACROVISION^{TM} ‖ To ensure best play, your VCR | must be directly connected | to your TV or monitor. Use of | two or more VCR's linked | together could result in | distorted playback. | Patent #4,631,603

DUST JACKET: Mustard-colored cardboard slipcase for plastic videocassette. Front panel is a photograph of Tudor in a yellow calico dress with lace cap and collar working her old dog marionette, against a yellow backdrop. Back text: *With My Love, Tasha ‖ This enchanting video captures beloved illustrator of Children's Literature Tasha Tudor. | This video is of her last public speaking appearance at Conner Prairie Museum in | Noblesville, Indiana in August of 1991. ‖ Tasha's whimsical stories of "Having a career & raising children at the same time" — | will warm your heart! There are wonderful scenes of Tasha sketching as she "rambles" | of her own children, home, animals and Captain Deglar—her African Grey Parrot | who behaves himself "most of the time"! ‖There are also scenes of four of her enchanting Marrionettes [sic] created by Tasha...that | were used in family productions to entertain her dolls & special family friends...Tasha shares with the audience her wonderful skill of making them "come alive" to the viewers | delight.—There are other surprises too.... ‖ "With My Love, Tasha" is a true keepsake to be treasured by all that love and | admire her....copyright © 1991 by The Jenny Wren Press*

OTHER: This was marketed and the event staged as Tudor's last appearance. In fact, she continued to tour and perform actively throughout 1997.

No copyright notice was on file at the Library of Congress, January 1998.

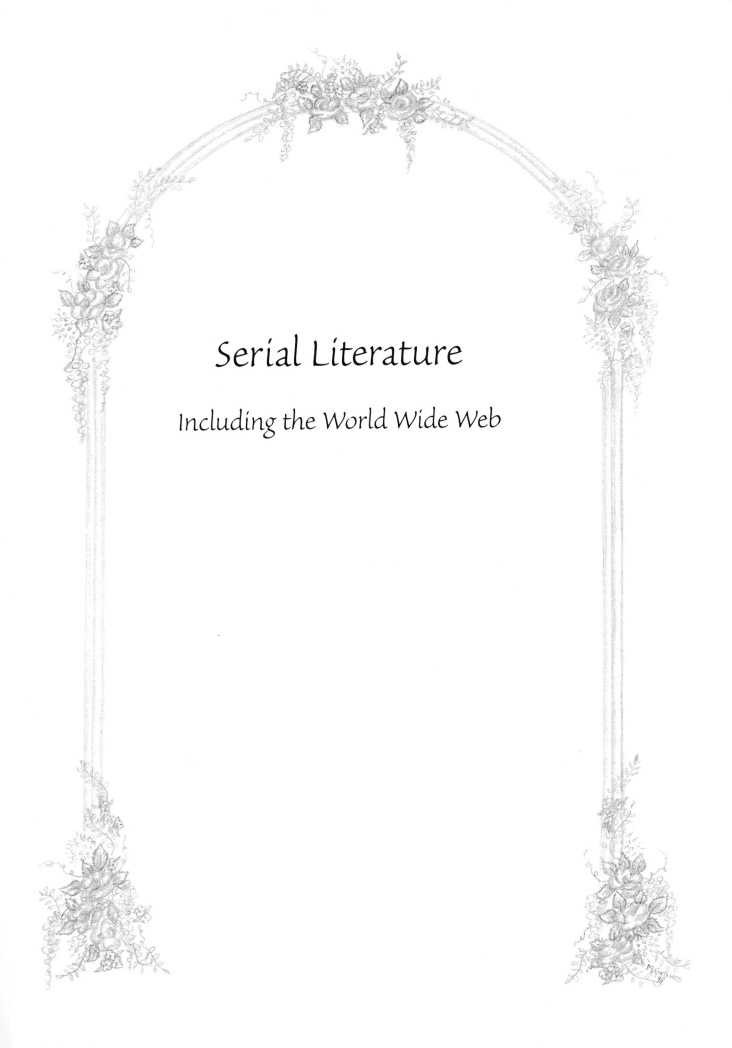

Serial Literature

Including the World Wide Web

AB Bookman's Weekly. 96:20. November 13, 1995. AB Bookman's Weekly, P.O. Box AB, Clifton, NJ 07015 201-772-0020.

> **"Tasha Tudor, Children's Author and Illustrator,"** by William [*sic*] John Hare. Pages 1864-1883. Presents the first comprehensive overview of Tudor's publishing history. Black and white photographs of Hare and Tudor.

Akron, Ohio. ca. 1955. Unidentified news photo shows Tudor and three children with this caption: The excitement of meeting an author and artist was experienced by Fairlawn School pupils at the annual PTA Book Fair. Among those who gathered around Tasha Tudor as she read from one of her books [*A is for Annabelle*] are (from left) Sally White, Margie Silver and Michael McCabe. Sally is the daughter of the Jay Whites, Margie's parents are the R.B. Silvers and Michael is the son of Mr. and Mrs. William McCabe."

ALA Booklist. cited on the wrapper of *Amy's Goose.* See *Booklist.*

American Bookseller. March 1982.

> **"Touring with Tasha Tudor,"** by Jim Roginski, Marketing Director of Children's Books, Putnam's Publishers. Condensed in *The LETTER* 2:1, Summer 1982.

American Country Collectibles. 5:2 Summer 1997. GCR Publishing Co., 1700 Broadway, New York, NY 10019

> **"The smart shopper's price guide to collectible children's books,"** by Ann Rooney Heuer. Pages 55-62. Discusses attributes of collectible children's books with brief descriptions, photographs and price guides to 37 books including *A Time to Keep*, Rand McNally, 1977, $15; and *A Tale for Easter*, Henry Walck, Inc., 1969, $8.

American Libraries. 2:3 March 1971

> Regina Medal to Tasha Tudor.

Antiques & Collecting Magazine. 101:9 November 1996.

> **"The Abby Aldrich rockefeller Folk Art Center presents Take Joy! The World of *Tasha Tudor*."** Page 6. Announces exhibit November 2, 1996 - April 6, 1997.

Atlanta Journal Constitution. November 27, 1997.

> **"Cozy treasures stoke family reading traditions,"** by Julie Bookman and Carolyn Nizzi Warmbold. Page L, 5:1. " . . .this year offers a bumper crop of special keepsakes to bring out year after year. . . "The Night Before Christmas" . . . Tasha Tudor (Simon & Schuster Books for Young Readers, all ages, &18). . . Tudor's snug farmhouse scenes bring a new charm to the story of the jolly old elf and his sleigh full of toys."

————. October 27, 1996.

> **"Tasha Tudor takes tradition to heart,"** by Paula Crouch Thrasher. Page K, 6:1. Williamsburg exhibit "focusing on the belief of the 81-year-old author-illustrator in individual freedom and personal integrity . . ."

The Baltimore Sun. Live October 31, 1996. The Baltimore Sun, 501 North Calvert Street, Baltimore, MD 21278

> **"Daytrip, Marionettes and more,"** by Lori Sears, page 6. One black and white photograph of three marionettes and this text: A world of things designed for smaller beings will be put on display this weekend at the Abby Aldrich Rockefeller Folk Art Center in Williamsburg, Va., as children's book illustrator Tasha Tudor shows off her best creations. The exhibit, "Take Joy! The

World of Tasha Tudor," will feature not only her doll family and 18-foot-long doll-house with furnishings and accessories, but also a marionette stage with painted backdrop, stage, orchestra pit and Corgi band. Original watercolors, early sketches, calendars and cards will be exhibited as well as teawares, toys and hand-made textiles from Tudor's collections. From Saturday through April 6, 1997. Daily hours are 10 a.m. to 6 p.m. The center is on South England Street in Williamsburg, Va. Admission is $10; $6.50 for ages 6 to 12. Call (757) 220-7698 or (757) 220-7255.

Baptist Times. Unkown date.
> Reviews *First Prayers.* Cited on dust jacket of *The Lord Is My Shepherd.*

Better Homes And Gardens® Holiday Crafts®. Fall/Winter 1997. 112pp in wrapper. Meredith
> Corporation, 1716 Locust Street, Des Moines, Ia.
> "Seasons of Joy: Tasha Tudor's Holiday Memories," produced by Linda T. Stueve, Photography by Ross Chapple. Some interview information was supplied by Beth Wheeler. Pp. 4, 16-25. The article grew from interviewing Tudor at the November 1997 opening of the Tudor retrospective at Colonial Williamsburg. Features 25 photographs, gingerbread recipe and pattern and instructions for a cross-stitch adaptation of a Tudor illustration *A Time to Share.*

Book Source Monthly. 9:5 August 1993. 34 pp. in wrapper. 2007 Syossett Drive, Cazenovia, NY 13035-
> 9753.
> **"Auction reports, Waverly Auctions...,"** page 9. "At Waverly Auctions' June sale . . . This sale included a group of Tasha Tudor original drawings and watercolors. Of the 15 offered, four sold for prices ranging from $335 to $1,540 and two others sold just after the sale to buyers unable to attend or bid by mail. Despite keen interest, evidenced by an advance sale of 50 catalogues to Tudor enthusiasts and by the presence of five Tasha Tudor bidders on the floor, the balance went unsold due to strong reserves. However, interest in the original art spilled over to several lots of Tudor illustrated books, most of which sold well above their high estimates. One lot of 7 brought an amazing $1,430, more than *eleven times* the high estimate." [Among those in attendance were Doris Frohnsdorf, Alicia Miller and Wm John Hare. -ed]

Booklist. ca. Octobre 1977 Review of *Amy's Goose,* excerpted on the wrapper of A41.

Booklist. 74:8 December 15, 1977. Pp. 645-716 in wrappers. American Library Association, 50 East
> Huron St., Chicago, Il. 60611. "A review in *Booklist* constitutes a recommendation for library purchase. ★ beside a title is a mark of quality, not necessarily of wide appeal or usefulness, and indicates an item selected by the staff as particularly good in its genre. YA at the end of an imprint denotes a books also recom- | mended in the books for Young Adults section..." From the **booklist editorial policy**, on the title page.
> "★ **Tudor, Tasha.** | **A time to keep: the Tasha Tudor book** | **of holidays.** Illus. by [the author]. 1977. | [57] p. col. Illus. 31cm. Rand McNally, | paper-covered boards, $5.95 | (0-528-82019-2; lib. Ed., $5.97 | (0-528-80213-5). | Nostalgic memories of days long ago | shimmer across the pages . . . soft delicate watercolors . . . fas- | cinating minutiae found in the artist's own | home. This glimpse into yesterday will be | a book to keep for years to come. Ages | 4-8. BE . . . " by Barbara Elleman, reviewer, children's books. Page 686

> _____. 76:10 January 15, 1980. Pp. 685-740 in wrappers.
> **"nonfiction | the arts | Tudor, Bethany. | Drawn from New England: Tasha Tudor. | A portrait in words and pictures.** Collins, | $10.95. | . . . Adult readers enthralled with Tasha Tu- | dor's old-fashioned illustrations will enjoy browsing through this biography . . . daughter Bethany's memories | and photographs and with Tudor's paint- | ings. The spirit in which Tudor has whole- | heartedly embraced an authentic rural | life-style . . . is reflected in her charming | portrayals of children and animals enjoy- | ing nature. See also p. 723." Page 692

"arts and crafts," reviewed by Barbara Jacobs . . . Tudor, Tasha and Allen, Linda. | Tasha Tudor's old-fashioned gifts. 1979. | 118p. illus. (part col.) McKay, 2 park | Ave., New York, NY 10016, $10.95 | (0-679-20981-6) . . . nowhere else can one find pat- | terns that convey more of the handcrafted | personal touch that is part of the spirit of giving. . . very suitable | "gifts for all seasons" book. Illustrations | are tasteful and directions are clear enough for almost any beginner who un- | derstands the rudiments of sewing and | knitting . . . " Page 694.

"Tudor, Bethany. | Drawn from New England: Tasha Tudor. | A portrait in words and pictures. 1979. | 95p. illus. (part col.) Collins, $10.95. | (0-529-05531-7). Galley. [i.e., reviewed from galley proofs] | Bethany Tudor, oldest daughter of well- | loved illustrator Tasha Tudor . . . smooth- | flowing narrative, old and contemporary | photographs, and samples of the artist's | work. . . admired | by child and adult alike. . . beautifully | composed depiction serves not only as a | biographical portrait of a woman follow- | ing her own dream and a commentary on | a contemporary artist, but also as a | glimpse into a world people lived in a hun- | dred years ago. Gr. 4-8. BE . . . " by Barbara Elleman. Page 723

_____. 76:11 February 1, 1980. Pp. 741-796 in wrappers.
"Tudor, Tasha | The springs of joy. 1979. [57] p. col. | illus. 31cm. Rand McNally, | paper-covered boards, $6.95 | (0-528-82047-8); lib. Ed., $6.97 | (0-528-80047-7). | Quotations from widely varied sources . . . Chosen for their reflection of | the philosophy, goals, and innermost con- | cerns of her life, the selections comple- | ment full-color paintings that are beauti- | fully reproduced in the pale, shimmering | shades, expressive details, and wistful not- | talgia long associated with the artist. The | sometimes excessive botanical borders | that Tudor uses are mostly gone, allowing | a clear focus and providing a sweep to the | pictures. . . portray a | life-style even more subtly and evocative- | ly than the biographical text of Bethany | Tudor's *Drawn from New England (Book-* | *list* 76:723 Ja 15 80). A book for sharing. | All ages. BE. . . " by Barbara Elleman.

Booklist Including Reference Books Bulletin. 81:11 February 1, 1985.
"Children's | books . . . All for love. Ed. And illus. By Tasha Tudor. | 1984. 93p. col. Illus. Putnam/Philomel, $15.95 (0-399-21012-1). YA | Gr. 6-9. Romantics take note . . . celebrating the state of love and festively gar- | nished with Tasha Tudor's special brand of sen- | timent. The selections will be most appreciated | by junior high students in the throes of first | love, though the pciture-book format may de- | ter some. . . the author also supplies some | folkloric wisdoms and sayings about love and | concludes with a description of her own fami- | ly's Valentine Day celebration . . . Nostalgic full-page | spreads, sweet cameo portraits, and ethereal | margin drawings—all in lush colors—are often | beautifully framed with garlands of ribbons or [page 785] flowers. Tudor has always steeped her work in | old-fashioned romantic ambience; here, she de- | livers her own special valentine to the world. | BE. . . " by Barbara Elleman. Pp. 784-785.

_____. 93:21 July 1997.
"Media: Versions of pastoral," by Sue-Ellen Beauregard. Page 1825. 2" review of *Take Joy: The Magical World of Tasha Tudor* and *A Visit with Tomie dePaola.* "Ages 10-adult. Two award-winning author/illustrators are visited in their rustic new England homes. Octogenarian Tasha Tudor lives in "Corgi Cottage" surrounded by sumptuous gardens and a menagerie of pets. In the engaging *Take Joy*, the "intensely private" artist (who wears her characteristic period clothing—shawl, long dress, apron, and a bonnet) is seen gardening, milking her goats, sewing doll clothes, working with marionettes, and creating her distinctive book illustrations. Voice-over narration provides details on the author's background and her successful and quaint lifestyle. Home movies, family photographs, and relaxing background music are soothing ingredients in this unusually good profile of the engaging, rather eccentric Vermonter. . ."

_____. 94:4 October 15, 1997.

"Tudor, Tasha. The Great Corgiville Kidnapping," by Helen Rosenberg. Page 406. 3 ½″ review. "Gr. 4-6. . . picture book for older readers . . . This is a clever story told by a master storyteller and illustrated with the sort of charming illustrations for which Tudor is known, but the audience for this book is unclear. The lengthy text contains language well beyond a younger reader's vocabulary, but the story, however charming, is not really developed enough for older readers. At the same time, much of the humor is adult, as when the raccoons argue over whether the *Joy of Cooking* or Julia Child's cookbook contains the best recipe for cooking a large bird. However, tried-and-true Tudor fans won't be disappointed. Younger readers light like the Mr. Pin books, featuring a penguin detective."

Boston Globe.   October 6, 1994
"House and garden circa 1830," by Carol Stocker. Page A, 1;1. Interview.

_____.   December 4, 1997
"Planting ideas rounding up this year's crop of garden gift books," by Carol Stocker. Page F, 1;2. Mentions Tudor in reviewing Richard Brown's *My Kind of Garden; Photographs and thoughts on cultivating the ideal garden.*

Boston Globe.   See also *Boston Sunday Globe*

Boston Herald. 155:86 Wednesday March 26, 1924.
"Girl Christens Yacht Argyll: East Wind Nips Legs of Pipers As Beauty Yacht Is Launched." Page 9. " . . . 1000 persons were in and about the place . . . The launching part included W.W. Lufkin, collector of the port of Boston, G.R. Agassiz, Horace Binney, Bryce Metcalf, F.C. McKenzie, W. Starling Burgess, Capt. Ben Pine, Marion Cooney, Horace Burnham, Mrs. W. Starling Burgess, Mrs. Aldred Warren. . . AS she disappeared roud a bend in the Clam Town district the pipes were doing homage to "Annie Laurie" and the wind was oh, so cold and scarching. Mr. Dominick plans to use the schooner on the New England coast this summer with headquarters at Newport and under colors of the New York Yacht Club." Photograph of 8-year-old Miss Natasha Burgess with roses. *Cf. Drawn From New England*, page 13, where this article is mistakenly cited as 1923.

_____. [After September 8, 1949]
Review of *Thistly B* excerpted on the back flap of *Amanda and the Bear.*

Boston Herald Traveler. 5:169 Friday, December 24, 1971.
"Tasha Tudor Leads Simple Life on Farm, Her Messages Bring Yule Joy," by Virginia Bohlin. Page 20. 16″ article speaks of farm life and corgis from Corgiville overtaking Santa's reindeer as Christmas icons. "Tasha Tudor is a very private person, who likes to keep her own life and location as protected as the . . . locale of Corgiville . . . Right now, while others are enjoying their 1971 Christmas cards, she's putting the finishing touches to the 12 designs she's doing for her 1972 collection." Two illustrations and four photographs including: Tasha takes time out to play with grandchild, Laura Dennis, 18 months, and the Corgis.

Boston Sunday Herald Traveler Magazine. December 17, 1967. Boston, Ma.
"Where Time Stands Still," by Betty Curtis. Pages 23-25, and recipes, **"Tasha Tudor's Christmas Goodies,"** page 13. Four photographs and text describe a winter's day at Tudor's Webster, NH, home.

Boston Post Magazine. 156:21 Sunday May 23, 1954.
"The House of Tudor: Tasha's "Mother Goose" bought it, an old New Hampshire farm for an exciting young family," by Frank G. Jason. Pages 4-5. 14″ article, six photographs and two drawings depict farm life. "More or less as a lark she did a book for a young niece of Tom's who was visiting from England. Through a relative the book found its way to a publisher and was

accepted . . . Her children . . . Bethany Wheelock, Seth Tudor, Thomas Strong and Efner Strong . . . Last year a former Radcliffe graduate tutored the children but this year Tom has taken over the task . . . Ginger and Pickles store . . . where the public may purchase autographed copies. This summer the entire house will be opened one day a week for public inspection and Tasha will demonstrate spinning and weaving, while her youngsters will be dress in old-fashioned costumes." Photos show Tudor drawing, chldren posing, family reading at the fire side, children in classroom, Bethany and Edgar, Bethany, Tom and Efner at loom.

Boston Sunday Globe. 163:60 Sunday, March 1, 1953. Boston, Ma.
"Their Dolls Have Birthdays, Weddings and Tea Parties," by Edgar Driscoll. Editorial and News Feature Service, page A-1. A 30″ interview by a bachelor with a different point of view. "Menage . . . includes a Radcliffe College graduate who teaches the children their three "r's" in an old-fashioned schoolroom located in the house . . . Edgar Allen Crow's relatives Rev. Crocus Bunion and Lady Cora Linsky." Recounts first illustrated letters and efforts with New York publishers. One ca. 1945 photograph of McCreadys and Bethany, Tom and Seth.

_____: New England section. 210:158 Sunday, December 5, 1976. Boston, Ma.
"Native cards," by Virginia Bohlin. Pages 46-47, 50. Discusses custom of Christmas cards from 1843 to the present and concentrates on New England artists Wallace Tripp, Tasha Tudor, Ellen Nelson, Charlotte Sternberg and Jim Anderson. Describes Tudor's lifestyle. Says Rtes 89 and 93 brought the 20th century too close, so she moved to Vermont. She has nearly finished her Christmas '77 collection of cards, a baker's dozen. "Thirteen is my lucky number," she says.

Boston Sunday Globe. Magazine. ca. February 1982. Boston, Ma.
"The renowned illustrator of "Little women" creates her first porcelain sculptures . . . Amy by Tasha Tudor." Page number missing. 8 x 5 ¾″ color illustration of Amy, a description of the set of four figures to be manufactured in Japan. To be made in a single limited edition, and sold at $75 each only to those who order by November 29, 1982, Alcott's 150th birthday. Order form from Franklin Porcelain, Franklin Center, Pa.

Another copy smaller in size from an undocumented national magazine, page 40, code NE6.

_____. undated.
"Q. Is it true that children's book illustrator Tasha Tudor lives in a house with no running water in the kitchen? G.W., Quincy." Page number missing. 3 ¾″ from Q&A. "A. True. The artist prefers a rural lifestyle and lives in a reproduction of a nineteenth-century farmhouse in Marlboro, Vermont. . . . She has illustrated more than forty children's books, including *A Time to Keep* and *Corgiville Fair*."

Bulletin Of The Center For Children's Books. July-August, 1962.

_____. May 1978.

Burlington Free Press. Ca. May 16, 1981. Reporting the conferring of an honorary doctorate by the University of Vermont. *Cf The Letter* 1:2.

C. Dickens, Fine, Rare & Collectible Books. JANUARY 23, 1997. Http://www.cdickens.com/tasha.html
"Accolade to Tasha Tudor," by Karen Book. Five paragraph description of Tudor and her art including references to 89 works, 2 Caldecott honor Awards, the Regina medal, an honorary doctorate and "a troublesome divorce was also reflected in her artwork at one point, giving her illustrations of that time a darkness and roughness not seen before or after."

Caged Bird Forum. Ca. 1990
"Ringed neck doves," by Bethany Tudor.

Caged Bird Hobbyist. 4:4 August 1996 Pet Business, Inc. 7-L dundas Circle, Greensboro, NC 27407. 66 pp. in wrapper.

> **"Pigeons and Doves, Ringneck Doves,"** by Bethany Tudor. Page 59. One-page article on raising and living with Streptopelia roseogrisea, the African ring dove.

Canadian Forum. December 1960.

Catholic Library World. 42:6 February 1971. Catholic Library Association, Haverford, Pa.

> **"Tasha Tudor,"** by Ilse L. Hontz. Pages 351-354. Reviews *Take Joy!, Becky's Birthday, First Delights, Wings from the Wind, Tasha Tudor's Favorite Stories, The Tasha Tudor book of Fairy Tales, A Child's Garden of Verses, The Twenty-Third Psalm.* Includes family details citing the 12/17/67 *Sunday Herald Traveler* article. "Tasha Tudor has given children a very special ray of sunshine . . . Walter de la Mare wrote: Only the rarest kind of best in anything can be good enough for the young, and Tasha Tudor has given this best to children throughout the world." Reproductions of three pieces of Tudor art.

_____. 42:11 July-August 1971.

> **"Regina Medal Presentation,"** by Sister Julanne Good. Pages 614-615. On the occasion of the April 13 award ceremony in Cincinnati. Two photographs of Sister Julanne, Tudor, Margaret Long, Marguerite de Angeli, Bishop Leibold.

Chicago Daily News. Ca. 1942. Review of *Dorkas Porkus.* Cited on *The County Fair,* Walck reprint, dust jacket.

Chicago Tribune. Unknown date, ca. 1942.

> Reviews DORCAS PORKUS . . . "an amusing story and delicate water-color illustrations. Lacks page.

_____. ca. 1954. Review of *A is For Annabelle.* Cited on jacket of Oxford *Around the Year.*

_____. ca. 1955. Review of *First Graces.* "This exquisite book . . . contains twenty-one prayers of thanksgiving." Excerpted on the dust jacket of *First Graces.*

_____ ca. Nov. 1956. Review of *1 is One.* Cited on jacket of Walck *Mother Goose.*

_____. ca. 1961.

> Reviews *Alexander the Gander.* "…somewhat larger format…" Lack date and page. [See dj to Walck *A Tale for Easter*]

_____. November 17, 1991.

> **"unretiring: Tasha Tudor draws on the past to illustrate her kind of world,"** by Melita Marie Garza. Section 6, page 13:1. "Tasha Tudor, 76, a renowned children's book illustrator, is profiled. Tudor clings to the customs of a more demure age."

Chicago Sunday Tribune. November 11, 1956.

> Cited in *Contemporary Authors* (81-84:573), and *Something About the Author* (20:187).

_____. 131ˢᵗ year, no. 331. Sunday, November 27, 1977.

> **"Tudor illustrations, A childhood joyland between book covers,"** by Mary Daniels. Section 11, page 2. 23″ account of Tudor Christmas celebrations drawing attention to *A Time to Keep* and *The Night Before Christmas.* "Her companion these days is her "semi-adopted daughter," Linda Allen . . . A collaborative book is scheduled for publication next fall. When there are no visitors to

the farm, Miss Tudor sits in a "special chair in what I call 'the window kitchen.' I won't let anyone else sit in it. I draw in my lap." Photo of Tudor and two book illustrations.

Children's Book Review Service. ca. October 1977. Review of Amy's Goose, excerpted on the wrapper of A41.

The Children's Historical Newsletter. 1:2, December 1994. 4 pages, green ink. The Jenny Wren Press, P.O. Box 505, Mooresville, Indiana
Dear Aunt Agatha, . . .Christmas shopping with Aunt Agatha, A pioneer Christmas, A Victorian table top Christmas tree, Be a Christmas Cook!, Always be a loving child especially at Christmas time, Aunt Lydia's "Did You Know?"

_____. 1:3, February 1995. 4 pages, red ink.
Dear Aunt Agatha, letters, Aunt Agatha's general store of treasures, Aunt Lydia's Did You Know? Little lesson in history, Have a special Queen of Hearts Valentine tea party! Make Victoria Valentines, Love tokens.

_____. 1:7, October, November 1995. 4 pages, black ink.
Dear Aunt Agatha, letters, This is Halloween! Halloween bread crust wishes, Aunt Lydia's Did You Know? Aunt Agatha's general store, Something old fashioned and yummy to make, Make a Thanksgiving day hamper, Dreaming of the future, Words of wisdom from Aunt Agatha, Indian symbols used in their art, Come to a Victorian Christmas celebration December

Christian Herald. Unknown date, ca. 1955.
Reviewing *First Graces.* "Lovely prayers, beautifully illustrated for young children." Excerpted on the dust jacket of *First Graces.*

The Christian Science Monitor. Unknown date, ca. 1938.
Reviewing Pumpkin Moonshine.

_____. 44:133 May 1, 1952. The Christian Science Publishing Society, 1 Norway Street, Boston, MA 02115
"Storybook Living Is Everyday Fare for New Hampshire Author and Family," by Harriet B. Blackburn, page 6. [page 10 in the Atlantic edition] 30″ of text, two Tudor drawings and three photographs. Reports of a drive to Contoocook for tea, two hours late. " . . . the children are starting in the public schools, each preparing to go to Milton Academy, Mass., later on . . . will become the Chipmunk Power and Light Company . . . it was his early story of a bantam rooster, "Biggity Bantam," illustrated by Tasha, and "almost accepted by a New York publisher" that encouraged the young couple to continue work on juveniles . . . involves shipping from Contoocook autographed Tasha Tudor books and other Ginger & Pickles Store items to all parts of the world."

_____. ca. 1955. Review of *Pekin White.* Cited on jacket of *Mr. Stubbs.*

_____. ca. 1962. Review of *Pumpkin Moonshine.* Cited on *The County Fair*, Walck reprint, dust jacket.

_____. 63:293 November 11, 1971.
"Going by way of the rainbow," by David Winder. Page B2. " . . . There is a Beatrix Pot- | terlike quality in those | delicately drawn rabbits | in Tasha Tudor's **Corgi- | ville Fair** (Crowell, $4.95), | which as you guessed is | less about rabbits than | corgis — those small dogs | the color of foxes wioth | short legs and cropped | tails. Mind you, the bog- | garts also get a good sho- | ing. Never heard of them? | They're trolls. Their hair | is moss, their ears are | leather, and their ears |

come off for convenience | when going down holes. . ." Cited in *Something About the Author* (20:188).

_____. Monday April 24, 1978
"Tasha's Tales From the Vermont Woods" by Sara Hoagland, page B2, B4. 15″ article with one black and white photograph of Tudor in profile holding *a Time to Keep.* "Gentle storybook painter . . . the supreme serenity of this woman . . . sharp and direct . . . as warm as her watercolors . . ." Of *Pumpkin Moonshine* she says, "I just had to earn a living, so I did it." "She is disdainful of reviewers and critics who search for profound inner meaning in her work. "I'm not trying to show anything - just please myself and earn a living," she states."

_____. 85:14. December 15, 1992
"The Home Forum, Christmas with Tasha Tudor" by Barbara Hall, pages 16-17. Text, plus two photographs by Richard W. Brown from *The Private World of Tasha Tudor*, published by Little, Brown and Company. One shows Tudor drawing in her kitchen, the other is one of her paintings on the familiar family-around-the-Christmas-tree theme.

The Cincinnati Post or *Inquirer.* Undated November 1977 clipping.
"Tasha Tudor, the beloved children's illustrator, is coming to Shillito's. Monday, November 7." Page number missing. A paid advertisement for two Tudor appearances at the Cincinnati department store, downtown at noon, and at the Kenwood Mall at 7:30. A picture of *A Time To Keep.*

Cleveland Press. Ca. 1956. Review of *1 is One.* Cited on jacket of Walck *Mother Goose.*

Colonial Homes. 24:5 September 1998.
"Calendar of Events, Exhibits: Styles of the Times." *Child in Fashion*, at the Abby Aldrich Rockefeller Folk Art Center at Colonial Williamsburg, examines children's clothing of the 19th century and explores the fashion trends and social mores that influenced garment styles. Items on display include 22 children's dresses and a boy's suit. Paintings and drawings detailing illustrator Tasha Tudor's use of these pieces for research also are on view, along with toys, dolls, and furniture of the 1800s. *Through August 31. Admission. (757) 220-7570.* One color photograph of a cream colored child's dress with embroidery.

Concord Monitor. New Hampshire. Unknown date, ca. 1968.
Review of *The New England Butt'ry Shelf Cookbook.* Cited on jacket of *The New England Butt'ry Shelf Almanac.*

_____. Friday, December 8, 1978. Concord, N.H.
"Efner Holmes Delivers Another Gift," by Katrina Richardson. Page 21. 12″ review of *Carrie's Gift.* ""The old man is someone I know," said Ms. Holmes. "The story could have happened easily enough. You write from your own experience and feelings and hope the public will like it. I lean on the sentimental side because that's the kind of person I am. You have to write from within you." Carrie is the name of Ms. Holmes' one-year-old niece for whom "Carrie's Gift" was written. And Heidi is the very image of Ms. Holmes' shepherd, Feisty."

_____. December 18, 1989.
"Family Tradition, Author Efner Holmes Puts her Own Stamp On The Tudor Style," by Lois Shea. Page D-1-2. 25″ discussion of Holmes Tudor instincts and her own accomplishments in the 20th century, not the 19th. Color photographs of Holmes and her Dutch oven nativity. "Tudor has illustrated each of Holmes' three books . . . A fourth collaboration, *Deer in The Hollow*, is to be published next year. Holmes' fifth book, *Night Shadows*, to be published in 1992, will not be illustrated by her mother. "That, to me, is a real accomplishment," she says. . . Holmes is trying to get a sixth story, *Roses By The Sea*, accepted by a publisher, but she's having

trouble, she says, because it deals with the topic of death and dying." [The latter two books have not been published. -*Ed.* 7/97]

_____. October 1991.   Undated,
"Fostering stigmas, rejected by state, the Janeways stand up for their gay kids," by Sarah Hodder. Page number missing. 6 ½ x 9 ½″ color photo and story. "The 200-year-old Webster farmhouse where Tasha Tudor once painted children's portraits is now empty of children, as are the neighboring fields and river banks."

_____. *Sunday Magazine.* November 7, 1993.
"Paul Reck: a life in theater," by Christine Hamm. Pages 1, 3-4. Discusses Reck and Grace and Kurt Graff's 1948 founding of Meadow Hearth, a summer theater in Hopkinton. "The three of them came to New Hampshire at the urging of the Graff's friend, Hopkinton resident Nell Dorr. Dorr, a photographer whose work was included in Edward Steichen's 1955 *Family of Man . . .* was part of an artistic community that emerged in the area during the late 1940s and '50s. Tasha Tudor, Dorr's subject in the book and herself a children's writer and illustrator, lived in nearby Webster . . . By 1956, as . . . television became more prevalent, audiences dropped off. When someone fell and sued the theater, the Graffs returned to Austria . . . " Two photographs of Reck, one of a Concord Community Player's 1965 production of *Brigadoon*, Reck dancing.

_____. July 5, 1996.
"Harrisville, history with a question mark," by Adolphe V. Bernotas. Pages B-1, B-8. 24″ article about the New Hampshire village which was the model for Corgiville. The article does not mention Corgiville, but does involve a mystery of its own in that the town's owner is attempting to locate the Harris family for whom the little village in a gorge was named.

_____. January 3, 1998.
"Wolfeboro, Life at Frost Corner recalls a quiet era. Reliving the 1830s is one woman's passion," by Gwen Filosa. Pages A-1, B1, B6. 16″ article about Virginia Taylor who grew up in Philadelphia, lived in the mid-West and worked for a time at the Conner Prairie Museum (Indiana) before moving to Wolfeboro, New Hampshire, to recreate a life of the past on a 200-year-old farm. Tudor is never mentioned, but her influence is obvious in the dress and style captured in the photographs, and from Taylor's Conner Prairie experience.   3 color photographs

Country Home. 11:5 September 1989. 150 pp. in wrapper. Meredith Corporation, 1716 Locust Street, Des Moines, Iowa 50336.
"Tasha Tudor, Celebrating 50 years of children's art," by Linda Joan Smith. Pages 6, 120-124, 128-129. Text, plus nine photographs, five colored illustrations, and six black and white drawings. Photographs by William Stites. *Sources,* page 127 refers readers to The Jenny Wren Press, Philomel Books and Elaine's Upper Story.

Country Living. December 1997
"TASHA TUDOR RETURNS," by Marie Proeller. Page 66, 271 word review of *The Great Corgiville Kidnapping.* One color photograph, Author and illustrator Tasha Tudor at play with one of her beloved corgis in Vermont.

Daily Press. 101st year, no. 308. Sunday November 3, 1996. The Daily Press, Inc., 7505 Warwick Blvd., Newport News, VA. 23607.
"Tudor's world, Exhibit showcases array of handmade items by children's book illustrator. The world of Tasha tudor, CW not content with exhibit limited to Christmas theme" by Mark St. John Erickson, pages A1, I1-I2. Text, plus seven photographs from the Colonial Williamsburg Foundation exhibit of November 1996-April 1997. There are two reproductions of Tudor paintings from A TIME TO KEEP four of parts of the exhibit, and one of Tudor and corgi taken at Williamsburg.

The Daily Review. 117th year. Friday, May 9, 1997. The Towanda Printing Co., 116 Main St., Towanda, Pa. 18848-0503.

"Area native writing book about children's author" by Nancy Coleman, page 3. 22″ text describes John Hare, his background and writings on Tasha Tudor. Photograph of Hare.

Dallas Morning News. Ca. 1961. Review of *Alexander the Gander*. Cited on *The County Fair*, Walck reprint, dust jacket.

The Day. Thursday, December 1, 1977. New London, Conn.

"She was too busy drawing to finish high school," by Barbara Reed. Page 30. 22.5″ with photograph of Tudor signing a copy of *The Night Before Christmas* and showing her most recent title *A Time To Keep*. Tudor signed books for Mali's Book Stores in Groton and Olde Mistick Village. Quotes Tudor on Pumpkin Moonshine, "I had to work at it. I went to every publisher—personally—because I believe in the personal touch." Quotes from several admirers of Tudor's art who attended the signing.

The Detroit Free Press. Ca. 1962. Review of *The Dolls House*. Cited on the wrapper of the Viking Seafarer paperback edition of that book.

Doll Life. Issue no. 7 December 1992. 82 pp. in wrapper. All American Crafts, Inc., 243 Newton-Sparta Road, Newton, N.J. 07860

"Tasha Tudor's Dolls," by Marian Schmuhl. Pages 72-[75], 65. Text, plus twelve photographs from previous publication: four from *Drawn From New England*, two from *The Dolls' Christmas*, two of the 1950s Shakespeare doll postal cards, two Jenny Wren Press products and one each from *A Is For Annabelle* and *A Time To Keep*. An ad for the JWP.

Doll Reader. Issue 3. March/April 1997.

Announces Williamsburg exhibit with background information on Tudor by Carolyn Cook. Pages 62-63.

Doll World. 20:5 October 1996. 64 pp. in wrapper. House of White Birches, 306 East Parr Road, Berne, IN 46711.

"Take joy! The World of Tasha Tudor," by Beth Wheeler. Pages 4, 6-7. This article summarized Tudor's life, pitches her Corgi Cottage Industries and describes the 1996 exhibit at the Abby Aldrich Rockefeller Folk Art Center, Williamsburg, VA. Three photographs of the doll house, marionettes and Tudor's toy goat. A short bibliography of Tudor books..

Dover Times. No date showing. Dover Township, Pa.

"New England Gardener/Artist Coming." 4″ text and one photograph announce Tudor's appearance at the Dover Intermediate School, May 9 [1987].

Early American Homes. 27:6 December 1996. [80] pp. in wrapper. Cowles History Group, 741 Miller Drive S.E. Suite D-2, Leesburg, VA. 22075

"Dollhouses at the Abby Aldrich Rockefeller Folk Art Center" by Carol McCabe, pages [52] - 57. One of eight photographs is a close-up of Tudor with a box of miniature letters and Valentines in her lap. A description of the 1996 Tudor exhibit at Williamsburg.

Early American Life. 10:6 December 1979. [112] pp. in wrapper. The Early American Society, Inc., Gettysburg, Pa. 17325

"A Visit with Tasha Tudor" by MH [Mimi Handler, Assistant editor], pages 24-25, 79. With reproductions of three Tudor drawings.

_____. 25:1 February 1994. [80] pp. in wrapper. Cowles Media Company, 6405 Flank Drive, Harrisburg, Pa. 17112

"Tasha Tudor's Sampler," Pages [1], 62. Four paragraphs and photograph of a reproduction of Tudor's 1931 sampler, which is now available as a kit from the Jenny Wren Press.

Early American Life Christmas 1982. [96] pp. in wrapper. Historical Times, Inc., 2245 Kohn Road, Harrisburg, Pa. 17105
"A Visit with Tasha Tudor" by Mimi Handler, pages 58-59. With reproductions of three Tudor drawings.

Elementary English. Unknown date, ca. 1950.
Reviews *The Dolls' Christmas.* "A cheerful little tale ... " [See dj Walck *A Tale for Easter*]

The Evening Bulletin. Tuesday, May 13, 1969. Philadelphia, Pa.
"Illustrator Tasha Tudor Gives Painting to Library Here," By Katrina Dyke. Page number missing. 12″, Tudor was in town to present an original painting from her book "Before Winter Comes" [*sic*] to the Free Library of Philadelphia. "Besides "Snow Before Winter" [*sic*] her books include ... " Mentions Tudor examining Beatrix Potter art at the library.

The Evening Chronicle. 135:286 Saturday, December 4, 1955. Allentown, Pa.
"An Artist prepares for Christmas," By Dorothy Roe, AP Women's Editor. Page 2. 6″, Tudor has six successful careers. ". . . member of the American Artists Group, . . . known throughout the country for her quaint, nostalgic greeting cards and her children's books, all of which are sold in the family's Ginger and Pickles Store and Doll Museum, whoch [*sic*] occupies one room of the big red farmhouse. . . Her husband acts as her business manager, runs the store and farm and supervises the education of the children. . ." Two photographs, Tudor painting and Tom, Bethany and Efner at loom; illustration of Christmas card showing Efner with birdcage, two cats, one beagle, one doll and a goldfish bowl.

Fairfield County Fair. Unknown date and pages, ca. 1954. Fairfield, Connecticut.
Reprint of **"A Mother-Artist And Her Camera,"** by Jo Matthews. 22″ article reprinted onto one sheet measuring 14 ½″ x 22″ with 3 photographs reproduced from *Mother and Child*, photograph of dust jacket, and a close-up of Nell Dorr. Discusses Dorr's photographic background, philosophy of motherhood, marriages and homes in New Hampshire, Connecticut and New York City. ".. the Dorr foundation, which ranges from providing scholarships for promising young engineering students to studying the problems of old age."

Firsts Magazine. 3:12 [no date available]
"*100 years / 100 books* Highspots of collectible children's books from 1863-1963," by Helen Younger. Younger includes Tudor's *Pumpkin Moonshine* as one of two 1938 entries in her list of 100 first appearances of children's books. The other entry for 1938 is Ludwig Bemelman's *Madeline.* Four pages found on the internet at http://www.clark.net/pub/alephbet/firsts.html October 5, 1997.

The Flint Journal. Wednesday, May 5, 1982. Flint, Michigan.
"Tudor knows the worth of her works," by James E. Harvey, Journal arts writer. 25″ of text and a 4x4″ photograph (Barry Edmonds) of Tudor reading *Drawn from New England* to 7-year-old Suzanne Carico. Appeared at 400-person luncheon at Hyatt Regency Hotel sponsored by Friends of the flint Public library and the flint Journal. Quoted as saying her interest is gain. "I'm not at all altruistic to my fellow human beings ... I much prefer Corgi dogs." She receives a large volume of fan mail at her isolated home, nine miles from Brattleboro. "The ones I don't want to answer seem to fall on the floor, where the dogs chew them up, or happen to fall into the fire ... I think they would be quite jolted if they knew what I really am ... He [Thomas McCready] doesn't count ... I guess he couldn't take my eccentricities ... I'm not making very good progress: I get stranger and stranger ... I like to draw people in fields because I don't do legs very well ... I have discovered, much to my amusement, that people are afraid of me — it's delightful."

Good News. Wednesday July 2, 1997. Coffeyville, Kansas.

> **"Chanute soon to be full of fame" Signature auction will be Aug. 2."** Unpaged. Tree of Life Southeast Kansas Support Group to hold benefit auction for a daycare center at the Rosebud Sioux Indian reservation. Among autographs gathered for the auction are John Travolta, Tasha Tudor and Chris Van Allsburg.

Greater Wilkes-Barre [Pa.] Chamber – December 1997 *Newsletter*. Http://www.wilkes-barre.org/news/dec97/small.htm. "Small Business Concerns: A message from the Tudor Book Shop & Café. Now that our Tasha Tudor event has taken place . . . both Tasha Tudor Teas were sold our four weeks prior to the event. Because of space constraints, we could only sell 450 tickets. Interestingly, almost half of the two groups of 225 attending the two teas were from out of town . . . over $1,000 was donated to both the Osterhout Free library and the Wyoming Historical and Geological Society . . . It was one of the most exciting programs that we have put together in the 20 year history of the book shop. — Lynn Gonchar." Reviewed from the web, March 4, 1998.

Greenbay News-Chronicle. Week of March 10, 1977. Green Bay, Wisconsin

> Reprint of **"A bit of 19th century living,"** by Angela Taylor from the N.Y. Times News Service. 15″ of text and a 6x7″ photograph of Tudor shaving ash splints. Page number missing. See *New York Times,* July 5, 1977.

Hagen For Alle. Nr. 1, Januar 1996. Bonniers, Abonnementsavdelinger, Postboks 2716 St. Hanshaugen, 0131 Oslo [Norway] 76 pp. including wrapper.

> **"Trend Gammeldags romantikk. I Tashas hage star tiden stille.** Tasha Tudor er en av Amerikas mest populaere illustratører og barnebokforfattere. Hennes livsstil fra 1800-tallets New England er legendarisk. Det er også hagen hennes med bare gammeldagse blomster. Så bli med til hennes fortryllende verden!" Pages 12-21. A translation of portions of Tovah Martin's text from *Tasha Tudor's Garden*, with Richard Brown photographs which appeared in . . . *Garden* on pages 21, 41, 90-91, [80-81], [20]-21, [65], 144, 151, 126, 114, 76, 61. A side panel on page 21 includes a map of New England and a discussion of **Klimaet I Tasha Tudors Vermont.**

The Hartford Times. Monday, August 15, 1955. Hartford, Connecticut.

> **"Children's book Illustrator's Dolls Find Counterpart in Plantation Story,"** by Edrie Van Dore. Page number missing. 18″ article and reproduction of dolls' baking postcard. "Neither ginger nor pickles did we find at the little store . . . Mr. McCready . . . was waiting on customers who bought books and cards. He said that he was sorry the artist could not be disturbed – she was working on a new book to be published this Fall. There was one child sick abed that day and the daily helper had not come. . . a national picture magazine had just spent several days at the McCready farm working on a color feature . . . a family of old dolls for whom she and her husband and father have built an enormous, completely furnished doll's house . . ." Reviews books *Plantation Doll, Surprise for Peter Pocket, On Their Own Two Feet, Arctic Hunter, Little Chief of the Gaspe* and *Search for Sammie*.

The Herb Companion. 7:2 December 1994/January 1995. 100 pp. in wrapper. Interweave Press, 201 East Fourth Street, Loveland, CO 80537

> **"Tasha Tudor, A simple life, a sprawling garden,"** by Kathleen Halloran. Photographs by Richard W. Brown, pages 1, 34-41 and front cover. Text, plus eight photographs of Tudor and her gardens, and one close-up of Christmas tree ornaments. Two recipes. Details from *Tasha's Herb Garden*, painted for the National Herb Society appear on the front cover and page 1. Further information on the painting, its genesis and off-spring prints are discussed on pages 36 and 38.

The Herb Society Of America Newsletter. 2:2 May/June 1997.

"Tasha Tudor Watercolor Sold." Page 1. Reports sale of Society's gift painting [see *The LETTER* 12:1, page 8] to a Californian through the efforts of Mr. and Mrs. John Hare, Cellar Door Books, Concord, N.H. Proceeds to the National Herb Garden Endowment Fund.

Home. 42:10. December 1996/January 1997.
    "News and notes." Page 22. Announces Tudor exhibit at Colonial Williamsburg.

The Horn Book Magazine. 14 Beacon Street, Boston, MA.
    "The Booklist" was a regular feature of the children's book review magazine *The Hornbook*, and especially under the byline of Alice M. Jordan during the 1940s was headed with this statement: The horn [*i.e., a hunting or Roaux horn - ed.*] against titles is a special honor indicating that the book so marked is outstanding in excellence in three counts - text, illustrations and bookmaking; or, on two counts, if there are no pictures." The symbol was later supplanted by the statement "All books listed are recommended . . . " and then, "Most books listed are recommended . . . " None of the Tudor reviews was ever designated with the horn symbol.

_____. 14:5 September-October 1938. 14 Beacon Street, Boston, MA.
    "New Books." Pages 289-310. In one of the earliest public notices of Tudor the artist/illustrator, *The Horn Book* (page 289) reproduces the illustration of Sylvie Ann telling her problem to Grandpawp at his tambour desk as Wiggie sniffs at a mouse hole in the baseboard.

_____. 15:5 September-October 1939.
    "The Booklist," by Alice M. Jordan. Pages 296-[305]. Thirty-five word notice of publication of *Alexander the Gander* by Oxford, $.75, p.297. Illustration of Sylvie Ann scolding Alexander, p. 301.

_____. 15:6 November-December 1939.
    Ad from Oxford University Press lists *Alexander the Gander* and eight other titles. Page 421.

_____. 17:1 January-February 1941.
    "A Bookseller Reviews ," by Lena Barksdale. Pages 56-63. "Tiny picture books have their own especial charm, and no one makes lovelier ones than Tasha Tudor, whose delicate pictures suggest Kate Greenaway, and whose humor suggests Beatrix Potter. *The County Fair . . .* ", p. 63.

_____. 17:3 May-June 1941.
    "The Spring Booklist," by Alice M. Jordan. Pages 206-216. *A Tale for Easter . . .* "the lovely childlike character of this small book which carries the thought of springtime rather than any religious note . . . precise in detail and exquisite in color, Tasha Tudor's little books are truly American in tone, suggesting a loving observation akin to that of Beatrix Potter," p. 206.

_____. date? A TALE FOR EASTER || "Many delicate pictures of rabbits, lambs, | chickens and daffodils, in close associa- | tion with little children, are sprinkled | over the pages, while a wonderful fawn | brings a happy climax to the story." | —Horn Book. [on flap of McKay Pumpkin Moonshine]

_____. 17:6 November-December 1941.
    "Illustrations Today in Children's Books," by Warren Chappell. Pages [444]-455. Chappell's note on *Snow Before Christmas* (Oxford $1.00): "A period piece, reminiscent of the English illustrators of the last century," p. 455
    "Christmas Booklist," by Alice M. Jordan. Pages 459-473. "*Snow Before Christmas . . .* many delicate pictures in the colors of the New England winter scene . . . ," p. 459.
    "Out of New England," by Tasha Tudor. Pages 483-484. Eight paragraph reminiscence of observing Nature and painting it. ". . . I drew pictures, and was taught and encouraged by my mother who is a painter . . . to my mother and my husband, and those blue and misty hills. I owe

any success I have ever gained." With a Dorr photograph of Tudor and goose, and an illustration from *Snow Before Christmas,* Tudor's newest book.

_____. 18:5 September-October 1942.
"New Books for Fall," by Alice M. Jordan. Pages 330-347. Announces *Dorcas Porcus* [*sic*] at $.75. "Another tiny book with delicate colored pictures tells of Sylvie Ann and one of her pets . . . " p. 332

_____. 19:6 November-December 1943.
"The Christmas 1943 Booklist," by Alice M. Jordan Pages [400a]-423. Announces *The White Goose,* Oxford $1.00. " . . . The delicate pictures are full of the magic Robin felt, but did not accept," p. 402.

_____. 20:6 November-December 1944.
"The Booklist," by Alice M. Jordan. Pages 472-493. Announces *Mother Goose*, Oxford $2.00. " . . . selected for fascinating illustration in soft and delicate colors. This is a book to be treasured in many homes," p. 475.

_____. 22:1 January-February 1946.
"The Booklist," by Alice M. Jordan. Pages 38-49. Announces as a New Edition, Hans Christian Andersen *Fairy Tales*, Lucas translation, Illustrated by Tasha Tudor. Knopf [*sic*] $3.50, p. 49.

_____. 22:2 March-April 1946.
"The Hunt Breakfast, The Greenaway-Caldecott *Horn Book.*" Page 74. Issue honoring the 100th birthdays of Kate Greenaway and Randolph Caldecott, both born in March 1846. "Of Kate Greenaway's influence in our own day, we could point to the drawings of Rachel Field and of Tasha Tudor . . . "

_____. 24:6 November-December 1948.
"New Books for Christmas," by Alice M. Jordan. Pages 451-468. Announces the New Edition of Juliana Horatia Ewing's *Jackanapes*, Oxford $2.00. Pictures by Tasha Tudor "A well-bound, well-printed and charmingly illustrated edition of this old favorite. J.D.L.," p. 467.

_____. 25:5 September-October 1949.
"Early Fall Booklist," Pages 401-426. Announces *Thistly B*, Oxford $1.50. " . . . delicate pictures accompany the gentle story of . . . a pet canary . . . This pretty book has an old-fashioned quality and appeal," p. 408.

_____. 26:6 November-December 1950.
"Christmas Booklist," by Jennie D. Lindquist and Siri M. Andrews. Pages 465-491. Announces *The Dolls' Christmas*, Oxford $1.50. " . . . more of a story than do some of Miss Tudor's books . . . Their home has something new in doll houses — a conservatory with tiny potted plants in it . . . " Illustration of girls at doll house from page [11], p. 478.

_____. 27:5 September-October 1951.
"I Do Feast Tonight," by Caroline M. Lord. Pages 309-314. Reminiscences of reading adventures and growing up. Page 313: "Not far from this famous knoll is a brook where a small boy and I sailed leaf boats one day. We watched them go under the bridge and come out on the other side, "with trees on either hand." At bedtime that evening of course I read Stevenson's "Where Go The Boats" and many another verse besides, in *A Child's Garden of Verses*, illustrated by Tasha Tudor. Does anyone know better than she what it feels like to be a song sparrow under a wet leaf?"

_____. 35:1 February 1959. *[See reprint in this book. -Ed.]*
"The Hunt Breakfast, A Letter with Drawings from Tasha Tudor." Pages 2, 4-5, 74. Tudor writes of visiting Beatrix Potter's home at Sawrey, England, and viewing her art and dolls at the home of Leslie Linder. Two Tudor illustrations, Pp. 4-5.

_____. 36:6 December 1960.
"Christmas Booklist," by Ruth Hill Viguers, Virginia Haviland, Margaret Warren Brown and Isaac Asimov. Pages 504-526. Announces *Becky's Birthday*, Viking $3.00. " . . . The pictures, half of them the author's typical soft water colors, and the spelled-out details in the text reveal a period picture of New England farm life in horse-and-buggy days . . ." p. 509.

_____. 37:6 December 1961.
"Another Christmas Book," [by Ruth Hill Viguers]. Page 616. Announces *Becky's Christmas*, Viking, $3.00, arrived too late to be included in the Christmas Booklist. " . . . Illustrations . . . have old-fashioned charm . . ." R.H.V. [*Becky's Christmas* was published October 23, 1961. - ed.]

_____. 39:1 February 1963.
"Late Winter Booklist: Recommended New Editions," by Ruth Hill Viguers, Virginia Haviland and Margaret Warren Brown. Pages 50-76. Rumer Godden, *The Dolls' House*, Viking $2.75, p. 75. Bottom of page 93 reproduces a small drawing of Tottie which headed chapter 1, page 11.

_____. 39:6 December 1963.
"Wild Rose, Briar Rose," by Mary Amos McMillan. Pages 622-628. "Tasha Tudor's little books and Lois Lenski's have been better received than giant picture books, which sometimes require a focal length of twenty feet between book and eye. These picture books have illustrations that belong on the wall of an exhibition hall rather than in the small scale of a child's possessions. Often the artistic intent seems to be gallery-oriented, not child-oriented . . . Books are included in the rush of every day at our house, in likely and unlikely places. Tasha Tudor's keepsake-like volumes go under pillows; . . . " pp. 622, 625.

_____. 40:2 April 1964.
"Early Spring Booklist: New Editions and Reissues," by Ruth Hill Viguers, Virginia Haviland, Ethel L. Heins and Priscilla L. Moulton. Pages 168-196. Alcott, L. M., A round Dozen, Viking, $4.00, " . . . charming, appropriate illustrations . . ."; F.H. Burnett, A Little Princess, Lippincott, $5.00. "The illustrator has obviously brought to this new edition her own childhood love for the story of Sara Crewe." With the illustration from Chapter 1, page 9, p. 196.

_____. 41:1 February 1965.
"Late Winter Booklist," by Ruth Hill Viguers, Virginia Haviland, Ethel L. Heins, and Priscilla L. Moulton. Pages 41-71. Reviews *Wings from the Wind: An Anthology of Poetry*, Lippincott $3.95, Library edition $3.79 net, pp. 63-64. " . . . Graceful and old-fashioned like her demure little girls and flower gardens . . . drawings that overflow with fragrant blossoms, affectionate companions, and responsive animals . . . " P.L.M. Illustration of "Twelfth Night" from page 17 is featured at the head of the review section, p. 41.

"Frances Hodgson Burnett: Episodes in her life," by Constance Buel Burnett. Pages 86-94. Reviews Burnett's literary life and contributions to copyright control to all authors. Two Tudor illustrations: from *A Little Princess*, page 150 and the dust jacket of *The Secret Garden*.

_____. 42:6 December 1966.
"Christmas Booklist," by Ruth Hill Viguers, Helen B. Crawshaw, Mary Silver Cosgrave, Virginia Haviland, Ethel L. Heins and Priscilla L. Moulton. Pages 699-730. Review of *Take Joy!* read from galley proofs. " . . . amply illustrated anthology of Christmas thoughts, stories, poems, carols, and

legends, with a description of Tasha Tudor's Christmas in rural New Hampshire . . . ," p. 702.
Announces Tudor edition of *The Wind in the Willows*, World $ 4.95, Library edition $ 4.61 net,
page 710.

_____. 45:6 December 1969.
"Christmas Booklist," by Paul Heins, Diane Farrell, Virginia Haviland, Ethel L. Heins, Sidney
D. Long and Ruth Hill Viguers. Pages 660-693. Recommended New Editions and Reissues.
Little Women, World $5.95, Library edition $5.61, p. 690.

_____. 54: 1 February 1978.
"Late Winter Booklist," by Ethel L. Hines, Mary M. Burns, Charlotte W. Draper,. Ann A.
Flowers, Virginia Haviland, and Paul Hines.   Pages 32-68. Announces *Tasha Tudor's Sampler:
A Tale for Easter / Pumpkin Moonshine / The Dolls' Christmas*. McKay, $7.95. New editions of
three stories originally published separately, in 1938, 1941, and 1950, p. 66.

_____. 58:6 December 1982.
"The Hunt Breakfast,"   Pages 594, 699-702 700. The theme of Children's Book Council's
newest year-round reading program is Nature. The materials for the program include a full-color
poster by Tasha Tudor, a full-color frieze by Carol Lerner, and a bookmark by Mary Azarian and
Patricia Lauber . . . ," p. 700.

_____. 62: 3 May-June 1986.
"New Editions and Reissues." Pages 343-348. *The Secret Garden*, Lippincott $8.95, library
edition $8.89. A reissue of the 1962 edition illustrated by Tasha Tudor.

_____. 63:4 July-August 1987.
"New Editions and Reissues." Pages 489-497. Burnett, *The Secret Garden* 287 pp.
Dell/Yearling 4.95.   CLASSICS Burnett, *The Secret Garden*, 311 pp. Harper Trophy 2.50
Illustrated by Tasha Tudor. *A Little Princess* 245pp. Harper Trophy 2.50 Illustrated by Tasha
Tudor.

_____. 64:3 May-June 1988.
"Shining Popocatapetl: Poetry for Children," by Rumer Godden.   Pages 305-314. A Tudor
drawing from page 63 of *The Dolls' House*, p. 314.

Horticulture. 67:6 June 1989. 72 pp. in wrapper. Horticulture Limited Partnership, 20 Park Plaza, Suite
1220, Boston, MA 02116.
"The Secret Garden of Tasha Tudor" by Wayne Winterrowd, pages 3, [32] -41 and front cover.
Text, plus eight color photographs, one of her famous bay standard, by Ivan Massar.

_____.   Another copy, this one with a re-set third line of text on the front cover, including reference
to a Canadian price of $2.95, and a bar code.
_____. 73:5 May 1995. 96 pp. in wrapper. Horticulture, Inc., 98 North Washington Street, Boston,
MA 02114-1913
"A spring visit with Tasha Tudor: May rings in the season in this storybook garden" by
Tovah Martin, pages 3, [40]-45. Text, plus seven photographs by Richard W. Brown excerpted
from *Tasha Tudor's Garden* © 1994 by Tovah Martin, published by Houghton Mifflin Company,
New York.

_____. 73:7 August/September 1995. Horticulture, Inc. as above.
"Letters" page 6 features a photograph of Tudor at her pansy hothouse and this paragraph: A
Word from Tasha Tudor. *Since the May 1995 publication of "A Spring Visit with Tasha Tudor,"
Tasha Tudor has received so many requests to visit her garden that she cannot possibly respond*

to them all. Although she was delighted to share her garden with kindred spirits through Horticulture, *she regrets that she cannot entertain the public at Corgi Cottage.—*Ed.

House Beautiful. 137:1 January 1995. House Beautiful, PO Box 7174, Red Oak, IA 51591
"In the garden, Beyond company, Author and illustrator Tasha Tudor took as her model an old-fashioned cottage garden, but this riot of runaway flowers is uniquely her own" by Hatsy Shields, pages [10] 34-36. Text, and six color photographs from *Tasha Tudor's Garden*, text by Tovah Martin, photographs by Richard W. Brown, published by Houghton Mifflin Company, Boston, Copyright © 1994 by Tovah Martin. Reprinted by permission.

Hudson, Ohio. An undocumented clipping. ca. 1965.
"And It Is: Hudson's Seymour House Belongs on a Christmas Card." 5″ article with photograph of house at 15 Prospect Street. Also a reproduction of a Tudor Christmas card of family on hall stairs first viewing the Christmas tree. Subjects are identified as Robin Burnham, Mary Duke, Betsy, Peter and Ann Guldan and Anna Lee.

Kalamazoo Gazette. 153:358 October 12, 1986. Kalamazoo, Michigan.
"Homespun: Tasha Tudor recreates warm world of the past," by Barbara Walters. Page G:1. 13″ article with drawings and photograph announces a Tudor visit for November 7, 1986, Grand Ball Room of the Student Center, Western Michigan University. Tickets are $7 for Michigan residents and $15 for out-of-state visitors. Notes on lifestyle and philosophy as indicated through *Rosemary for Remembrance.*

_____. 154:20. November 8, 1986.
"If I were ambitious, I would have you all for tea ," by Barbara Walters. Page A:3 12″ story and photograph of Tudor with marionettes. Crowd of 800 was much larger than expected to mark the 90th anniversary of the Public Library's children's room. Erroneously notes Tudor sold first book when she was 19 (she was actually 22), and that she is in her sixth decade (actually her eighth). Quotes various attendants.

_____. 160: 44. November 30, 1992.
"Author's childhood dream comes true: 'The Real Pretend' rings true for Fennville woman," by Rosemary Parker. Pages A:1, C:1. Two photographs of Joan Donaldson and a recounting of her friendship with Tudor and the publication of *The Real Pretend.* Donaldson met Tudor working on the Public Library's 1986 visit. They attended Spencerian handwriting workshop and learned the story. When the woman finished telling the two of her childhood experience, Tudor "turned to me and said 'you write it down and we'll do a book,'" Donaldson recalled."

Kirkus Reviews. October 15, 1971

_____. May 15, 1977

"The Kate Greenaway of today, with a | New England rather than an Old England | flavor, gives her small readers a small | book. Here's a natural for Halloween in | the story of how Sylvie Ann goes hunt- | ing the biggest pumpkin in her grand- | mother's field--and then has to roll it | back to the house--with catastrophic re- | sults. But the pumpkin survived to be- | come a Jack o'Lantern on a gate post. | Old fashioned charm." -Kirkus Reviews date ? [on flap of McKay Pumpkin Moonshine.]

Lady's Gallery, Fashion, Culture, Antiques. 4:2 February/March/April 1997. [82] pp. in wrappers. Lady's Gallery, Inc., P.O. Box 40443, Bay Village, Ohio 44140.

"Tasha Tudor Comes to Colonial Williamsburg," by Amelia Johanson. Pages 25-30, 66. Reviews the 1996/97 exhibition, reflects on Tudor's lifestyle and includes 10 color photographs and two black and white, two of Tudor paintings.

The LETTER. Loving Enthusiasts of Tasha Tudor Exchange Reflections. 1:1 Summer 1981. [8] pages, two folded sheets. Elaine's Upper Story, 1234 Larke Avenue, Rogers City, MI 49779. Elaine Hollabaugh, Editor-Publisher. *The LETTER* is a biannual publication (Summer and Winter) . . .
"Tasha Tudor is a Collector's Delight." Pages [1-3]. Photograph and recounting of Edward B. Hills' role in promoting Tudor. " . . . LONG AGO, Tasha Tudor remarked, "Ned Hills knows more about my work and me than I do myself!" Mrs. Tudor has confessed that she does not have a copy of each of her works and does not keep count of how many books she has illustrated . . . the earliest [Christmas] cards, the Ars Sacra designs published by Herbert Dubler, Inc., in the 1940s . . . . Tudor designed 13-14 cards each year through 1977.
"Tasha Tudor." Ann Beneduce photograph of Tudor; announces *Rosemary for Remembrance.* Page [4].
"Using Tasha Tudor Books With The Handicapped," by Inez Seaton. Page [4]
"Liberty Tea With Mary Mason Campbell," by Susan H. LePrevost. Page [5]
"The Dolls' Tea Party," by Melinda McClure. A party at Corgi Cottage. Page [6]
"Collecting Tasha Tudor Books Leads One Fan Into a New Hobby." Discusses Cecilia Owen of New Jersey and her doll house. Also Tudor's Bloomingdale visit in December 1977. Page [7]
"Cookie Crumbs," by Charlie Corgi. Discusses Kitto pubs in Oregon and cookie cutter in Emmaus, Pa. Page [8]
"From the Top of Elaine's Upper Story." Thank you and a photograph of Hollabaugh, her grandson and friend Becky Steere. Page [8]

_____. 1:2 Winter 1981. [4] pages, folded sheet.
"University of Vermont Honors Tasha Tudor." Page [1]. Front page and photograph of Tudor by Jym Wilson, *Burlington Free Press.* In large part a report of Mrs. Louise Swainbank's sponsoring Tudor for the UVM honorary Doctor of Humane Letters, *honoris causa,* May 15, 1981, in Burlington. Her declamation is reprinted and Tudor is quoted on age as saying, ". . . You can do anything you please. More people are scared of me. That's just delightful. And now that I'm a doctor, I can really intimidate them!"
"Antiques Mix Well With Tasha Tudor Art," by Patricia Bailey, North Carolina. Page [2]. Describes her first . . . *Annabelle* and drawing on the Tudor influence in a shop. Black and white photograph.
 "Anecdotes from Indiana," by Mildred Graves, librarian. Page [2]. Comments on *The Dolls' Christmas,* corresponded with Tudor in England, and visiting Tudor's booth at the 1978 convention of the American Library Association in Chicago. Photograph announcing Rand McNally's *A Child's Garden of Verses,* $ 7.95.
"A Tasha Tudor Christmas Exhibit," by Jean Beck. Page [3]. Beck reports on a December 1980 - January 1981 exhibit of items from the Tudor collections of Nellie Stein, Tasha Beck and herself. Exhibit staged at York College Special Collections Room. Art from *The White Goose, Take Joy!, Becky's Birthday.* Beck learned about Tudor through Ned Hills' English classes. Photograph of three women and display; advertising photograph of new book *Rosemary for Remembrance,* $10.95.
"A Book of Christmas Has A Worldwide Heritage." Page [4]. Reports that Waldo Hunt founded Intervisual Communications, Inc. in Los Angeles. ICI has published the pop-up *A Book of Christmas,* available in Danish, Dutch, English, Finnish, German, Italian, Japanese, Spanish and Swedish. Black and white photograph.
"Cookie Crumbs," by Charlie Corgi. Page [4]. Photograph of children with Corgi from the Indianapolis classroom of Rebecca McKenna. Mentions Patricia Sandy-Smith, Kalamazoo, Mi.
"Treasures." Page [4] includes announcement by Doris Frohnsdorff that sale of Ned Hills collection to being November 2, 1981.

_____. 2:1 Summer 1982. [4] pages, folded sheet.

"Thousands Enthralled by Tasha Tudor Exhibit." Pages [1-2]. Short article and 9 photographs reporting a six-week exhibit at the Indianapolis Children's Museum, which opened November 27, 1981. 8,000 people attended Tudor's appearances December 12, 13. Photo of Kate, a doll made by Tudor for her artist friend Pamela Sampson.

"A Tour With Tasha Tudor," by Jim Roginski, Marketing Director of Children's Books, The Putnam Publishing Group. Page [3] Reports of a book tour to Newport Beach, Santa Monica and Carmel, California, bookstores to promote *Rosemary for Remembrance*. "All of this is accepted graciously and calmly by Tasha. Her serenity amid the clamor is reassuring." One photograph.

"Treasures" and **"Old Books,"** advertisements. Page [4]

_____. 2:2 Winter 1982. [4] pages, folded sheet.

"Happiness Is Having An Autographed Tasha Tudor Book," by Suzanne Carrico, eight-year-old of Flint, Mi. Page [1]. Short article and photograph reporting a Friends of the Library luncheon and drawing at the Flint Hyatt Regency May 4, 1982. 500 people attended.

"Happy Birthday, Louisa May Alcott." Page [2]. On the 150th birth of Alcott, Hollabaugh discusses *Little Women*, Tudor's illustrations, the book's influence on Tudor and new porcelain figurines from the Franklin Mint. Tudor related closely to Amy and modeled the statue of Amy on one of herself at 12-years of age. One photograph of Alcott.

"Lavinia Loring: A Star Attraction Of Tasha Tudor Christmas Exhibit." Page [3]. Tudor exhibit at Packwood House Museum, Lewisburg, Pa., to include Tasha Hancock's doll Lavinia Loring. Exhibit runs Dec. 1, 1982 - Jan. 9, 1983 and features Tudor December 4 and 5. Tickets cost: dinner and reception, $10-$15; lecture and tour, $4 for adults, $2 for children, 6-16; tour of museum $2 for adults, $1 for children. Photograph of Loring by Charlotte Brown.

"The Cookbook's Back." Page [3]. Photograph and advertisement for the Stephen Greene Press reprint of *The New England Butt'ry Shelf Cookbook*, $12.95.

"Autographing Party At Metropolitan." Page [4]. Tudor to appear at New York City's Metropolitan Museum of Art, November 5, 1982, with seven other artists for autographing party; also at Wendy's Story 456 West Broadway on November 6.

"Cookie Crumbs." Page [4].   Mary Mason Campbell writes that her corgi Stedley Alexander Campbeil (Steddy) was a gift from Tudor. He is recorded as the ice cream man and a church member in *Corgiville Fair*; also the littlest angel at the top of the cover to *A Book of Christmas*.

"Aunt Jody's Christmas Bank." Page [4]. Describes unusual shops of Rossville, Ill., and Aunt Jody's Christmas Bank, located in an old bank building, with a Tasha Tudor room.

"Tasha Tudor Nature Poster." Pictures a poster *Nature* available from the Children's Book Council for its Year Round Reading Program.

_____. 3:1 Summer 1983. [4] pages, folded sheet.

"The Regina Medal Presentation Speech," by Sister M. Julanne Good, O.P. Page [1]. Reprints the June 1971 address. " . . . very pleased and highly honored to present *to someone very special* the Regina Medal Award for continued distinguished contribution in the field of children's literature."

"All About Lavinia Loring, A French Fashion Doll." Page [2]. Recognizing the 20th anniversary of a Tudor sending the doll Lavinia to Tasha Lee Brown Hancock at Mill Hall, Pa. Describes the fantasy world of the doll and various Sparrow Post letters concerning her moves.

"Rook Crow & Rook," by Horatio Rutabaga Rabbit. Page [3]. Text of adoption paper relating to Lavinia Loring, above.

"Summer Is Thyme To Collect A Basket Of Herbs." Reviews the book and reprints drawing for thyme from page [150]. Page [3]

"Cookie Crumbs," by Cricket Prydwen. Discusses life with the Bev and Joe Glennons "on the East Coast.". Page [4]

 "Treasures." Advertisements and wants. Page [4]

_____. 3:2 Winter 1983. [4] pages, folded sheet.

"Our Family's Love Affair With Tasha Tudor," by Bonnie Johnson, Maryland. Page [1]. Recounts family's admiration beginning at Dutch Inn and continuing through a Vermont visit. Mentions signings in Mill Hall, and the Packwood House Museum. Daughter Tasha Louise. " . . . My ancestors came from Salem, you know!" Two photographs.

"Katherine Elizabeth Knowlton: A Pictorial Essay," by an English Fashion Doll. Pages [2-3]. Eight photographs (three by Ann Beneduce) and description of doll made by Tudor for Pamela Sampson, table by Marjorie Tudor. Decorative border by Pamela Sampson.

"Cookie Crumbs," by Lamin Melody. Describes a tour through the herb garden of her mistress Susan LePrevost in Berkshire County, Massachusetts. Page [4].

"Tasha Tudor Sails in Nova Scotia." Page [4]. Short paragraph and Beneduce photograph of Tudor sailing (with grandsons Nathan and Jason Holmes) in 1982.

_____. 4:1 Fall 1984. [4] pages, folded sheet. *The LETTER is published each Fall . . .*

"Tasha Tudor Day In Duxbury," by Greg DiCenzo, eight-year-old Chandler School student. Page [1]. Reports Tudor's visit to the second-grade Massachusetts school room. "When the kids started to get a little noisy, Tasha Tudor said, "You have to give me great respect because I come from Vermont!" And suddenly, the room was quiet." 150 people attended a luncheon and book signing: 500 books were sold. Beneduce photograph.

"B Is For Bethany." Page [2]. Report of Louise and Bill Jolley of Pennsylvania, their collection of Tudor original paintings, and naming their second daughter Bethany. Photograph.

"A Homespun Tale," by Susan Showalter. Page [2]. Describes the Rhode Island woman's adoration of Becky's Christmas and how she finally traded a lap robe for a copy. Also photograph of Gail Blair reading to her kindergarten class in Highland Heights, Kentucky.

"New Tasha Tudor Collectibles." Page [3]. Describes the release of eleven enameled boxes by the English Crummles & Company. " . . . She actually came to our workrooms spending lots of time here and saw the way we painted the enamels . . . " Photographs of the eleven boxes and of Sarah Hollabaugh, Elaine's granddaughter, holding two of them.

"Cookie Crumbs," by Tudor Corgi. Page [4]. Report by the Rochester, NY, corgi of Virginia Bense.

"Treasures" and **"Old Books."** Page [4]. Advertisements and photograph of Jenny Klingshirn of Michigan making lemon drops.

_____. 5:1 Fall 1985. [4] pages, folded sheet .

"Tasha Tudor Vacations In The South Of France," by Miss Purrvis, the original model for "The Christmas Cat." Page [1]. Reports of six-month winter visit to Provence. " . . . she's working on a beautiful pop-up book of the four seasons at our Vermont farm . . . " Photographs by Tudor and Martin Kamen, and one of Tudor in Portland, Oregon, by Dr. Vera Peterson.

"Tasha Tudor Regards Randolph Caldecott A Genius Of Illustration," by Gwen Reichert. Page [2]. Report by the St. Augustine, Florida, school principal who discovered Caldecott's neglected grace in St. Augustine, and founded The Randolph Caldecott Society of America. Tudor letter about her regard for Caldecott. Photograph of Reichert with two students.

"Tasha Tudor Appearances." Page [2]. To be at the Metropolitan Museum of Art, NYC, November 16, 1985; and at the Kalamazoo, Michigan, Public Library in November 1986.

"Tasha Delights Dallas," by Steven VanVelzer and Ann Minton. Page [3]. Reports a Neiman-Marcus appearance of June 23, 1984. " . . . She is positively lovely, gracious, truly a person who is one in a million . . . elegant, ever-so-talented and exceptional lady . . . " Reprinted from *The Review*, August 1984, North Texas.

"For Microphiles." Page [3]. Photograph of Tudor kitchen scene as a miniature tableau by Dee Snyder of Florida, editor of *Nutshell News* magazine in which the scene will be featured.

"A New Jersey School Librarian Talks About Tasha Tudor." Page [3]. Gives talks in the area and thanks Cecilia Owen and Elaine Hollabaugh for loaning personal items. Two photographs.

"Cookie Crumbs," by Farley. Page [4]. Reporting from Col. and Marny Dilts, Delaware, Ohio, Chalet Lodge Herb Farm. Photograph of Marny and Farley.

"Treasures" and **"Old Books."** Page [4]. Advertisements.

"Something New By Tasha At Crabtree and Evelyn Stores." Page [4]. " . . . offers a Tasha Tudor-designed hexagonal tin . . . soap boxes: one holds a corgi-shaped soap, the other has a pink heart . . . "

_____. 6:1 Fall 1986. [8] pages, folded sheets .

"An Anniversary of Joy," by Anne Beneduce. Pages [1]-3. Reminiscing on the 25th anniversary of her association with Tudor. Three photographs and a drawing .

"Honeymoon In New Hampshire," by Barbara Smalstig. Page 3. Spent the night at the McCready house during November 1956 honeymoon. Photograph of house with Ginger & Pickles sign hanging from a maple tree.

"Magic of Garden Therapy." Page 4-5. Reviews the life of Frances Hodgson Burnett and her homes and the gardens she built in England, Bermuda and at Plandome on Long Island.

"Tasha Tudor Originals For Sale." Page 5. Reviews the Tudor-Brown relationship and upcoming sales of Ned Hills art and other items at the Packwood House Museum, Lewisburg, Pa. Two photographs ca. 1962.

"Have You Any Wool? From Linsey Woolsey" by Jenna Gove. Page 6-7. An 11-year-old girl from Cape Cod remembers her lamb who died, compares her to *Linsey Wollsey* and tells of learning to spin. Two photographs and three black and white illustrations from Linsey Woolsey.

"Old Books." Page 7. Directory of ten dealers.

"Cookie Crumbs," by Katy. Page 8. Having been moved from Corgi Cottage for Tudor's winter in France, Katy writes of her new home with Pamela Sampson in Carlisle, Ma. Born July 1, 1974, in Massachusetts since October 1984. One photograph of Sampson and Katy.

"Treasures." Page 8. Sale and want ads.

_____. 7:1 Fall 1987. [12] pages, folded sheets.

"Tasha Tudor Travels The Lecture Circuit." Page [1-3]. Reports appearances in Indianapolis, In., (9/86); Farmington, Ct., (10/86); Kalamazoo, Mi., (11/86); Whitewater, Wi., (3/87), New York, Tennessee, Pennsylvania and Vermont . Three photographs by Tudor by Gary Moore, Jerry Campbell and Carol Lueck.

"A Time To Keep," by Ann Reeves. Page [3]. Reports Kalamazoo, Michigan, talks.

"Heart of Country," by Alecia Marcum. Page [4-6]. Describes Nashville, Tennessee, appearances February 11-13, 1987. Reprints Resolution of the Tennessee House of Representatives. " . . . This is so nice. I've never met a politician before . . . and now lives in Brattleboro, Vermont [*sic*] . . . " Three photographs.

"A New England Butt'ry In Miniature," by Donna Turner, Klamath Falls, Oregon. Page [6]. Describes creating a miniature version of the dust jacket illustration of the *Butt'ry Shelf Cookbook.* Photograph.

"The Dolls' Bazaar, Recalled," by Gretchen Brown McKeever. Page [7-9]. " . . . It was the summer my father spent his vacation building [her first] lean-to greenhouse for Tasha . . . the library was the room where the bazaar was to be held that evening . . . My uncle had a Dutch Inn booth where there were miniatures he'd brought from his gift shop . . . " Four photographs of Brown and Efner McCready in 1961 with bears and souvenirs from the doll's bazaar.

"Linda Allen Leaves Vermont To Live In Rhode Island." Page [10]. Summary of Allen's life at Corgi Cottage studying with Tudor. Tudor dedicated *Rosemary for Remembrance* to Allen. Philomel Books to publish her own book *The Giant Who Had No Heart* in 1988 through editor Patricia Gauch. Born in New England, met husband Marlowe deChristopher at Rhode Island School of Design and married June 6, 1987 in Tasha's garden. Photograph of Connecticut book signing by Andrea Harris.

"The Becky Books." Page [10]. A plea for fans to write Ann Beneduce at Philomel Books to reprint the Becky books. Box notice.

461

"A Tasha Tudor Interest Group Is Formed In Farmington," by Barbara Gibson. Page [11]. Tudor visited in Connecticut October 17, 1986; an affinity group formed and met at the Farmington Library in April 1987.

"Treasures" and **"Old Books."** Page [11]. Advertisements.

"Cookie Crumbs." Page [12]. Class report from Mrs. Lewis' Montessori School about Chassis, the school pet in Rogers City, Michigan.

_____. 8:1 Summer 1989. [8] pages, folded sheets. The LETTER is an annual publication (one issue) . . . [There was no publication in 1988.]

"Congratulations, Tasha Tudor. Thank you for your 50 years of creating our favorite children's books We love you!" Page [1]. Large photograph of Tudor by Mary O'Hara.

"My Life In Two Centuries," by Emma. Pages 2-3. Tasha's doll writes of her life as a 19th century balletomane. " . . . In the Historical Dolls Museum in Provo, Utah, someone asked Tasha . . . many trips to Indiana to visit my cousin, Rose Finch. Beth Mathers made Rose . . . " Five photographs of Birdwhistle courtesy of Tasha Tudor.

"Love Letters." Page 3. Four congratulatory letters to the editor.

"A Golden Evening of Feasting & Merriment." Reports an Indiana party given by the Mathers to celebrate the 50th anniversary of *Pumpkin Moonshine*. Four photographs.

"How Jenny Wren Was hatched," by Beth Mathers. Page 5. "In the Fall of 1988 . . . Shirley Paxman said, "Beth, you've got to get Tasha to publish those wonderful books!" [small doll magazines] . . . I found a well-qualified [printer] Indianapolis Hill Top Press . . . We plan to print all 5 of Tasha's little books . . . " Tudor border by permission of Jenny Wren Press.

"A Wonderful Autumn Afternoon," by Doris Bullock. Page 6. Reports on an appearance of October 10, 1988, in Provo, Utah. Photograph of Bullock, Tudor and Beth Mathers.

"Post It." Page 6. Announcements of a boxed miniature gift set of books, a new book by Linda Allen, three magazine articles, and Tudor appearances at Durham, North Carolina, December 1-3, and Burlington, Vermont, December 9, 1989.

"Cookie Crumbs," by Nutmeg. Page 7. Writing from Becky Pugh's *Bone Jour Café-Boutique* in Washington, D.C. Photograph.

"Alexander's Fiftieth Anniversary." Page 7. Reprint of pages [24-25] and a paragraph description.

"Treasures" and **"Old Books."** Page 8. Advertisements.

_____. 9:1 Fall 1990. [12] pages, folded sheets.

"Tasha Tudor Creates A Masterpiece." Page [1]. Large photograph of Tudor. Notes 75th birthday.

"My Friendship with Tasha Tudor," by Rumer Godden. Pages 2-4. Recounts a friendship begun with exchange of letters from the Shakespeare family, visits between England, New Hampshire and Vermont. Photograph and two Tudor illustrations from *The Dolls' House*.

"Daisy Belle." Page 4. Photograph advertising a doll from the Jenny Wren Press.

"Williamsburg Christmas Show." Page 5 . Recounts Tudor appearance in Durham, N.C. December 1989 and plans for talks at the College of William and Mary, November 9-11, 1990, with a Tudor designed mail cachet. Tickets $10.50. Canceled envelopes, $3.00. Photograph of Wren Building, and one of Harry Davis reading President Bush's greeting to Tudor.

"Tasha Tudor in Toledo," by Barbara Zahrend, retired first grade teacher. Page 6. Recounts first buying *Mother Goose* in 1944, Ginger and Pickles Shop opening 1949, to the public in 1954. Visited McCready house in Webster, examined doll house, invited Tudor to Toledo Museum of Art presentation in 1960. Photograph of ad from *Yankee Magazine*, July 1959.

"One of Tasha Tudor's loveliest books . . ." Page7. Announcing *A Brighter Garden* with a large reproduction from the book.

"A Tasha Tudor Theme Luncheon." Page 8. Describes a bridesmaid luncheon patterned after Tudor, March 10, 1989, Bryan, Texas.

"Memorial Gift to Library." Page 8. Original pen and ink drawing for cover of *Mother Goose* given to Case Avenue Elementary School, Sharon, Pa. in memory of Louise Jolley.

"Post It." Page 8. Announcements of corrections to Elaine's bibliography; Tudor's schedules for Nashville, February 7-10, 1991, Sutton, Ma., April 26-27, 1991; Linda Allen's *Movable Mabeline; Rosemary for Remembrance* in a new edition; corgi information; and a new cookbook being written by Wayne Winterrowd.

 "The Golden Key Unlocks a Cache of Riches for Tasha Tudor Collectors," By Beth Mathers. Page 9. Announces a re-release of Nell Dorr's ca. 1955 film. 25 minutes long. Photograph of wedding procession leaving front door of house.

"Shops." Page 9. Fourteen item directory of businesses with Tudor interest.

"The County Fair Originated a Half-Century Ago." Page 10. Paragraph and reproductions of pictures from pages [16, 20] of the original book.

"Old Books." Page 10. Directory of twenty-four book dealers carrying Tudor stock, including Celler [*sic*] Door Books.

"Treasures." Page 11. Four columns of ads of books to buy/sell and, Jenny Wren Press catalog.

"Cookie Crumbs," by Owyn Tudor. Page 12. Dictated through Tudor's hand, Owyn, brought from England by Tudor in 1987, is unabashedly set on himself. Two photographs.

_____. 10:1 Fall 1991. [8] pages, folded sheets. First enameled paper, color photos, issue.

"Afternoon Tea with Tasha Tudor," by Heidi Helmke, niece of Elaine Hollabaugh. Pages [1], 8. A report on 4 p.m. tea, with three color photographs and Tudor and house. Speaks of 3 corgyn.

"Using Tasha Tudor Books in a Hospital," by Amy Dill, R.N. Page 2. Recounts the peaceful exchange of reading *The Dolls' Christmas* to a dying hospital patient*, and* with other patients. Tudor drawing of a corgi sitting for a drawing by a girl on a stool.

"Love Letter." Page 2. Gratitude from Elna Maness of Texas.

"Old Books." Page 2 . Directory of 14 dealers: Barn Loft, Aleph-Bet, Ten Eyck Books, etc.

"Cookie Crumbs," by Bonnie Toon, with George and Maggie Toon, Palm Harbor, Fl. Page 3. Therapeutic work with hospital patients, and visiting Corgi Cottage, August 1990. Photograph.

"Love Letter." Page 3. Gratitude from Margaret Klingler, Illinois. Tudor drawing.

 "Publisher's Party." Page 4. Describes a gathering in Marblehead, Ma. On the publication of *A Brighter Garden.* Color photos of Tudor, Monroe and Shirley Paxman, Charleen and Dan Perry and Michael Lueck.

"Admiring Miss Daisy." Page 5-6. Gwen Reichert, Doris Long, Serenity Fairchild and Sarah Linnet write about the Jenny Wren Press dolls, of 1990. Two color, three black and white photos, including Elaine Hollabaugh's granddaughters Emily and Sarah.

"Love Letter." Page 6. Gratitude from Eunice Russell, Rhode Island.

"Treasures." Page 7. Four columns of swap ads.

"Post It." Page 7. Announcements of clothing exhibit at Conner Prairie, In., June 8 - November 10, 1991; Tudor's last public appearance, at Conner Prairie, will be videotaped, August 16-18, 1991; *Tasha Tudor's Corgi Cottage Cookbook* [*sic*] and *The Private World of Tasha Tudor* to be published Fall 1992; back issues of *The Letter* for sale.

"Tasha's Chocolate Cookies Receipt." Page 8. From *Tasha Tudor's Corgi Cottage Cookbook* to be published by Atlantic Monthly Press, Fall 1992 [*sic*].

_____. 11:1 Fall 1992. [8] pages, folded sheets. Biennial publication (one issue every two years).

"Tasha Tudor: Our National Treasure," by Harry Davis. Pages [1]-2. Fascinating piece from two aspects. Reports on what was announced as Tudor's final public presentation — August 16, 17, 18 at Conner Prairie, Indiana. (Ticket demand increased the scheduled talk to three sessions.) "A last change to hear this remarkable artist speak candidly about her life and art and the inseparable nature of the two." In fact, Tudor has continued to perform until the present day. Secondly, the piece is written by Davis who was to become Tudor's next business partner three years later. He writes with the highest adulation of "a public farewell of epic proportions, reverential applause, a career totally without precedent, one of America's true national treasures, grand dame of American artists, standing ovation deafening in its tribute, one of the century's most fascinating personalities." He is equally laudatory of her forthcoming book *Corgi Cottage Cookbook* [*sic*] when he writes of its paintings . . . "Tasha's greatest accomplishment, breathtaking would be an understatement, has transcended the limitations of her medium, astounding, in the ranks of the greatest masters, an event of major proportions." One color, two black and white photographs.

"Love Letter." Page 2. Gratitude from Becky Steve, Mi., and Marion R. Smith, Ct.

"The Story Behind the Book," by Joan Donaldson, Fennville, Mi. Page 3. Tells how *The Real Pretend* grew from a story told by Kathy Klingheil at a 1989 Ohio workshop in Spencerian Script. Carol Lueck was writing the *Corgi Cottage Cookbook.* Two pictures of Michael Sull, Tudor, Donaldson and Lueck.

"Tasha Tudor's Genteel World of Antique Fashions," by Elaine Potter Hollabaugh. Page 4-5. Report of Conner Prairie exhibition of 50 of Tudor's 'frocks,' 21 of which are pictured and identified here in three color photographs. Quotes Tudor telling of getting good buys at auction when she was as young as nine, because people wouldn't bid against a little girl. Her wooden lady models her dresses for drawing.

"*Dorcas Porkus* is Fifty Years Old." Page 5. Illustration from page [26].

"Messages from Tasha Tudor," by Mary Ellen Monroe, musician from New York. Page 6. Recounts visits to Corgi Cottage in June 1987 and July 14, 1988, letters exchanged and working in a 'state-of-mind.' Make the most of the privileges we have, of living in so beautiful a world. Black and white photograph of Tudor in her September garden.

"Treasures." Page 7. Four columns of sale and want ads.

"Love Letter." Page 2. Gratitude from Ann Beneduce, New Jersey.

"Old Books." Page 2 . Directory of 14 dealers:

"Cookie Crumbs," by . Photograph.

"Post It." Page 7. Announcements of Tasha's cookbook, Winter 1993; *Vermont Magazine, Victoria, Country Home* articles; biennial *The Letter*; send SASE for books, cards, notes for sale.

"The Private World of Tasha Tudor." Page 8. "Autobiographical . . . intimate look at everything her fans have longed to know about . . . " Reviews new book to be published October 28, 1992. Color photograph of Tudor in her bedroom.

"Cookie Crumbs," by Crushed Velvet.

_____. 12:1 Fall 1994. [8] pages, folded sheets, plus a single page insert.

"Getting to Know Tasha," by Joan Donaldson. Pages [1]-2. Relates first meeting in Kalamazoo, 1986, and annual visits between the Donaldson and Tudor homes, including the 1992 summer solstice party with Tom Tudor. One black and white, two color photographs.

"[Letters]." Page 2. Gratitudes from Marilyn Atchison, British Columbia, Joy Wheeler, Oregon, Anne Medlock, Tennessee.

"A Word About Writing to Tasha." Page 2. A plea for 'instant pen-pals' not to write to Tudor, or ask questions of her. In summer she cannot eat supper before 10 p.m. " Wouldn't it be considerate to correspond less often . . . "

"Post It!." Page 3. Describes 1989-92, 1994 *Letters*; *English Cottage Gardening for American Gardeners*; *Vermont Magazine* and *Victoria.*

"*Dressing Miss Daisy,*" by Jan Lewandowski. Page 3. Describes her Solon, Ohio, business *La Petite Modiste* where she makes and sells costume doll clothes. Black and white photograph.

"How Excited I was the Day I met Tasha Tudor," by Elizabeth "Betsy Birdwhistle" Gerrard. Page 4. Recounts meeting Tudor at Conner Prairie, In., October 1, 1985, making her friendship and subsequent visits to Corgi Cottage. Gerrard plays interpretative roles at Conner Prairie. Two color photographs.

"Merry Christmas from Tasha Tudor." Page 5. Two 1945 Christmas cards in color.

"A Reminiscence," by Paul Peabody Sr. [*sic*], Nyack, NY. Tells of being invited to perform marionette show at Corgi Cottage in 1981 and ensuing visits. Tudor prodded Peabody to have his book *Blackberry Hollow* published by Philomel. Color and black and white photographs.

"Ben and Fido visit Elaine's Upper Story." Corgis belonging to Susie and Jack Smeyers, and Miller and Carl Riggs photographed with Hollabaugh's granddaughters, Sarah and Emily.

"Treasures." Page 7. Four columns of sale and want ads.

"Tasha's Herb Garden." Page 8. Discusses the friendship of Yvonne Snyder, Dover, Pa., and Tudor dating from 1980. Tudor created a painting of her herb garden for the Herb Society of America's 60th anniversary. 1000 prints of the painting are available for sale, as it the original art. Reproduction of the piece and an Ann Beneduce photograph of Tudor's garden. Notice of *Tasha Tudor's Garden*, and an herb Society appearance in Reading, Pa., June 25, 1995.

"Heart." Throughout . For the first time, there are outlined hearts crossed by ribands, each heart carrying a short Tudor fact, e.g. Tasha Tudor was born in Boston, August 28, 1915.

The insert sheet is headed with a large black and white close-up of Tudor and announces an appearance at the Nashville, Tn., antique show January 4-7, 1995. She will sell from her booth, autograph, will offer original toys she made for her children and herself, give an illustrated lecture, and auction her lecture sketches.

_____. 13:1 Fall 1996. [12] pages, folded sheets, <u>and stapled</u>.

"Visiting Tasha Tudor is lots of Fun," by Sarah Johnson, New York. Pages [1], 10. The fourteen-year-old model for Kathy in *The Real Pretend* tells of her skills at spinning, of her mother's correspondence with Tudor, and traveling to Corgi Cottage to model. She likes her 'Tudoresque' farm, seeing Corgi Cottage through the eyes of Benjamin Tudor, and putting on a marionette show. She was shocked by a real person standing in Tudor's attic room; it turned out to be Tudor's modeling mannequin. Three color photographs.

"Post It!." Page 2. Get back issues, 1989-96; *Victoria*'s artist-in-residence for 1996; *The Corgiville Kidnapping* [*sic*] ready for publisher.

"[Letters]." Page 2. Gratitudes from Barbie Dunning, Maryland, Maggie Page, Arkansas, Barbara Brown, New York, Adeline Herman, New Hampshire, Paul Peabody, New York and Jane Seegar, Maryland. Black and white photographs of Sarah Johnson, and Tudor's guinea-fowl-feather owls.

"Tasha Tudor's much-loved book, *A Time to Keep*, is back!" Pages [2a-2b]. Two identical box ads are printed on this 1 ¾″ strip, the front part of the sheet also containing pages 7-8.

"Collecting Tasha Tudor books in England," by Sheila James. Page 3. Tells of her children's book collection and Tudor's place in it. Mention several favorite titles.

"Sara Cardile recently portrayed Tasha Tudor in a fourth grade project in New Jersey." Page 3. Black and white photograph.

"Around the Year with Tasha Tudor," by Harry Davis, Tasha's partner in Corgi Cottage Industries. Pages 4-5. Reviews Tudor's 1996 appearances: January, Nashville, TN (her drawings set record prices, one selling for $1900); February, Columbus, Ohio; April, Bloomingdale's, NYC (3000 people, six back-to-back 15-minute presentations; planning and circumstances were less than perfect); June, Reading, Pa. (1000 fans plus Tudor's grandson Jan in the audience); November, Williamsburg, Va. (traveled with Bethany and Marjorie Tudor, neighbor Isabel Hadley and traveling companion Joan DeGusto; an original Tudor doll modeled after her grandmother Effie Fenno Tudor was purchased by Doris Long, South Carolina); December, New York City (four generations of one family came from Texas to the Metropolitan Book Fair). Four color photographs, including Effie Fenno Tudor, Texans Ruby Painter, Gloria Wade, Lesa, Jane and Megan, and Metropolitan organizer Rebecca Myers.

"Tasha Tudor is Coming to Williamsburg," by Jan Gilliam. Announces variety of events to be staged at Colonial Williamsburg, November 2, 1996 - April 6, 1997, with several appearances by Tudor. Black and white photograph of her doll Emma Birdwhistle.

"Corgi Cookie Crumbs," by Miss Basil. Page 6. Owned by Timothy Newcomer and Paul Mertel, Carlisle, Pa. Black and white photograph, nursing five pups. Visit our herb shop.

"Tasha Tudor and Spring came to Columbus, " by Dr. Regina Rosier, Professor of Education, Urbana University. Page 7. Reports of several hundred people coming to see Tudor at the February 1995 Home and Garden Show. One black and white photograph , Tudor and her roses.

[Hollabaugh tries to make Tudor's brownies.] Page 8. Short paragraph and plug for *The Tasha Tudor Cookbook*.

"**Treasures.**" Page 9. Four columns of sale and want ads, only that of Corgi Cottage Industries is printed in bold typeface.

[**Christmas card reproductions**] Pages 8, 10. Early '40s in color, two later black and white.

[**Heart**] Throughout . Eight re-designed ribbon hearts, each carrying a short Tudor fact, e.g. Vermont land was purchased with money earned from *Corgiville Fair*, her first royalty check for *Pumpkin Moonshine* was $75.

[No mention of Tudor's appearance at the Cincinnati Flower Show in April 1996. -*Ed.*]

Lexington Herald-Leader. April 20, 1996. Lexington, KY

"'**My whole life has been a vacation', Tudor's art, simple lifestyle capture national attention,**" by Beverly Fortune. Two and one-half pages found on the paper's Website - http://www.kentuckyconnect.com/heraldleader/news/sat/t10center.html. Announces Tudor's appearances scheduled for the next week at the 7th annual Cincinnati Flower Show. Tudor was scheduled to give two performances, but a third was added to meet the response. Quotes Tudor on aging, energy, personal questions (As long as they are not too personal. Any questions about religion or the kind of underwear I wear, I refuse to answer them.), high-tech society, environment, regrets and Martha Stewart. One posted photograph is cited as being from *The Private World of Tasha Tudor.* It is not; it pictures an avenue of hemlocks ending at a three-tiered iron fountain before a pergola.

Library Journal. Ca. 1945

Reviews *Fairy Tales from Hans Christian Andersen.*

_____. Unknown date, ca. 1968.

Review of *The New England Butt'ry Shelf Cookbook.* Cited on jacket of *The New England Butt'ry Shelf Almanac.*

_____. 122:11. June 15, 1997.

Reviews *Take Joy! The Magical World of Tasha Tudor.* By Chris Moesch and Bette-Lee Fox.

Life. 39:11 September 12, 1955. Time, Inc., 540 North Michigan Avenue, Chicago 11, Ill.

"**A Wedding in the land of dolls: New Hampshire youngsters turn make-believe into enchanting reality,**" photographed by Verner Reed, pages 153-[156]. Nine black and white photographs and nine paragraph captions. Pictures of Tudor and her children Bethany, Tom and Efner and friends Holly Hoofnagle, Katherine and Barbara Howe, Lucy, Richard and Inge Schade, Judy Moulton, Barbara Barker, Richard Webb.

See also Hilda Miloche and Wilma Kane's *The Paper Doll Wedding.* New York: Simon & Schuster, 1954. A Little Golden Activity Book A22. The story is very like the celebration Tudor created. This one takes place on the pages of the book; there are four pages of paper dolls to cut out and dress for the wedding ceremony and reception. Begins with invitations, baking and floral preparations.

Los Angeles Times. Unknown date, ca. September 1978.

"A beautiful book with delicate illustrations in pastel colors, which give deepened | meaning to the familiar words and printed music. . . . Enchanting pictures painted in the incomparable Tudor style." Quoted on the dust jacket of *Tasha Tudor's Old-Fashioned Gifts.*

The Magazine Antiques. 153:4. April 1998 pp. [473]-616 in wrappers.

"**Nineteenth-century children's costumes in Tasha Tudor's collection,**" by Linda Baumgarten and Jan K. Gilliam. Pages [564]-[571] Eighteen illustrations of paintings, Tudor's costumes and other old lore with text by these two Colonial Williamsburg curators.

Maine Antique Digest. 25:10 October 1997. P.O. Box 1429, Waldoboro, Me. 04572

"You're Invited. The Fabulous Fall Heart of Country Antiques Show, October 17 18 19 . . . A Visit with Tasha Tudor," page 37G. Full page ad announces Tudor's fourth (?) appearance at an antique show organized by Richard and Libby Kramer of St. Louis, Mo. Tudor slated to sign autographs on Thursday and Friday and will give her illustrated lecture at Saturday's $25 ticketed event. Mentions Tudor "grew up in a prominent Boston family surround by a circle of friends including Emerson, the Alcotts, Thoreau, Mark Twain and Oliver Wendell Holmes, Jr., all of whom influenced her early years."

Manchester Area Branch, American Association Of University Women, March 1998 Bulletin. One page tri-fold mailer.

"John Hare discussing Tasha Tudor. Tuesday, March 17, at 7:30 p.m. at the home of Hilda Berlinguette, 1588 Hall Street, Manchester telephone 627-1817. Hostesses: Elizabeth Hand, Phylliis [*sic*] Benoit, Brenda Watts ‖ John Hare is librarian at the New Hampshire Technical Institute. He has written a biography [*sic*] of Tasha Tudor and will begin his talk by discussing the influence of Beatrix Potter on Tasha Tudor. According to Phyllis Benoit, John is a fount of knowledge, absorbing everything in his path, and enjoys sharing as well---so he loves questions. Please come."

The Marion Star. Tuesday, November 18, 1952. Marion, Ohio

"Will Speak at Junior High Thursday, Tasha Tudor, Writer and Illustrator, to Talk Here." Page number missing. 14″ discussion of McCready farm, the doll house and Sparrow Post with a branch office in Marion operated by Mary Rand Lighter. McCreadys visiting Mr. and Mrs. John Lightner of 327 Bellefontaine Ave. "The Lightner family became acquainted with Miss Tudor and her family about two years ago . . . Mr. and Mrs. Lightner visited overnight in the New Hampshire farmhouse Oct. 31, 1951 . . . Miss Tudor's appearance here will be free of charge."

_____. Undated news clipping, ca. 1954.

"Tasha Tudor Discovers No Conflict in Doing Six Jobs at Once," by Dorothy Roe, Associated Press Women's Editor. Page number missing. 7 ½″ article re wife, mother, antique collector, storekeeper, artist and author. Children Efner, 5, Tom, 9, Sth [*sic*], 11, and Bethany, 13. With two photographs of Tudor painting, and Tom, Bethany and Efner at loom, under the headline, New Englander Has Home, Career Too. "As a member of the American Artists Group . . . "

_____. Another copy from a different unidentified newspaper also includes an illustration of a Christmas card with this caption: "NOSTALGIC CHIRSTMAS . . . The little girl pictured giving presents to the pets in the card above is little Efner McCready, daughter of the artist, Tasha Tudor."

_____. Friday, November 21, 1952. Marion, Ohio

"Chats on Homelife, Author and Illustrator Speaks on Personal Life," by Patricia Oshorn. Page number missing. Reviews previous evening's appearance at State Street Junior High School before an audience of 225, mostly female. Spoke of her life, made about 5 sketches of her children and animals, displayed Capt. And Mrs. Shakespeare and his sister Nicey Melinda. Told of illustrated letters to her future husband.

Martha's Kidlit Newsletter. 9:12, December 1997

"Tasha Tudor's Art; Baum & Gruelle Titles Popular at Waverly December Auction," p. 3. Tasha Tudor's original art sold well at the December 4 auction at Waverly's Auctions, of Bethesday, MD. . . Reports prices on several items.

Miniature Collector. 17:4 September/October 1994. Scott Publications, 30595 Eight mile Road, Livonia, MI 48152-1798

"Miniature Collector, So You Want Me To Make An Elephant Ladder," Story and photography by Harry Smith. Pages [40-43], and table of contents. Smith, renowned miniaturist, tells of receiving a tiny letter from Captain and Mrs. T. Crane, No. 1 Upstairs, Greenwillow requesting that he make a proper sized spinning wheel to make a new sweater for the Captain. Smith also fashioned the instruments played by the corgi band in *The Rose and The Ring*. Nine photographs including two of Melissa Crane and one of the corgi instruments.

Mori Books [Newsletter]. Undated January 1995 mailing. 1 sheet   109 Route 101A, Amherst, NH 03031
"Yes! Yes! Tasha Tudor's visit was a grand success."   Page [1].   Book signing "November 5 was greeted with one of those remarkable fall days, that her 400 enthusiastic fans and admirers will cherish for years." Mori dressed as Natty Bumpo in one of Tudor's woodsman costumes.

_____. Undated April 1995 mailing. Pp. [1-4] 141 Route 101A, Amherst, NH 03031
"Announcement of a VERY SPECIAL Event to take place on Mother's Day (May 14)."
Page [3]. A joint appearance of Tasha Tudor and her daughters Bethany and Efner Holmes. "This is the very first public presentation that the Tudor Women . . . will have done together . . . Bethany wrote the first bibliography of Tasha's work, Drawn from new England . . . Reserved seats at $20, General and Balcony seating $15. . ." Appearance at Elm Street Junior High School Auditorium, Nashua, N.H. followed by book signing at the Amherst shop.

NFSS Bulletin. March-April 1994.
"In Praise of Society Finches," by Bethany Tudor.   Tudor writes of the nature, care and experiences of raising these small birds.

_____. July-August 1994.
"A Special Starling, Tweedy: A Love Story," by Bethany Tudor.   Tudor relates her wonderful pet starling which she raised from a small hatchling in her chicken coop. The bird was Tudor's companion for eight years and lived the most extraordinary experience of traveling to England with the McCready family for 13 months in 1957-58.

New Bedford Standard-Times. Ca. 1967. Review of *The Real Diary of A Real Boy* cited on the dust jacket of *Brite and Fair*.

New Hampshire Profiles. 1:12 December 1952.
"At home with Tasha Tudor," by Pearle G. Covey. A visit to the McCready farm in Webster, NH. Four illustrations and a photograph of Tudor.

_____. 16:9 September 1967.   56 pp. in wrapper. New Hampshire Profiles Corp., One Pleasant Street, Portsmouth, NH 03801
"Autumn treasure hunt" by Mary M. Campbell. Sketches by Tasha Tudor, pages 22-23. With four reproductions of two Tudor drawings.

_____. 17:7 July 1968.   64 pp. in wrapper.
"The day of Independence" by Mary M. Campbell. Illustrated by Tasha Tudor, pages 19, 57-58. With a Tudor drawing of a small parade in a country street.

_____. 17:10 October 1968.   60 pp. in wrapper.
"Candles in the Jack O'Lantern" by Mary M. Campbell. Sketch by Tasha Tudor, pages 23, 52-53. With a Tudor drawing of a girl carving pumpkins beside a well (5 ½ x 6″), as well as a 2″ x 2 ¼″ miniature of the same drawing.

_____. 18:11 November 1969.   pp. in wrapper.
"Thanksgiving at Northwood" by Mary M. Campbell. Sketch by Tasha Tudor, pages [28] 29, 50-52. Comments on the origins of Thanksgiving and especially on Sarah Josepha Hale's novel *Northwood*. Also thoughts on the roasting process of the Thanksgiving turkey.

_____. 27:11 December 1978.   pp. in wrapper.

"**Of Boggarts, Beeswax & Christmas,**" by Efner Tudor Holmes. Pages 28-31. Recollections of Christmas and growing up in Webster, N.H. 3 illustrations from *Corgiville Fair.*

New Hampshire Sunday News. October 16, 1983.
"**Exeter's Plupy Shute and his 'Real Diary': Hometown History**" by George Woodbury. Page 4C. 28″ describing Shute and how he came to resurrect his diary of 1868-69. Mentions Noone House reprint.

New Haven Register. Ca. 1967. Review of *The Real Diary of a Real Boy* cited on dust jacket of *Brite and* Fair and The *Real Diary of a Real Boy..*

New York Herald Tribune Books. 101:34,510 May 11, 1941.
"**Books for Young People, Other books Chosen for Honor,**" edited by May Lamberton Becker. Section 9. Page 10. 2 ¾″ review of *A Tale for Easter*, 36 pp., Oxford, $1. "A jewel of prettiness, this little book is light in the hand, tidy in size, gentle in spirit. Its water-color pictures are not imitations of Kate Greenaway, but bring her to mind by making one happy in the same way. "You can never tell . . . begins the tale, in Hilda Scott's clear calligraphy . . . it is a tiny book to kept at hand for any Easter."

New York Herald Tribune Weekly Book Review. 104:35,791 November 12, 1944.
"**Books for Young People . . . Here Are Children's Classics,**" edited by May Lamberton Becker., Section VI, p. 12. 3 ½″ review of *Mother Goose*, 88 pp., Oxford, $2. "Tasha Tudor's place in contemporary illustration is established, and in the hearts of children quite as firmly. Her work has Victorian fragrance but is not Victorian in spirit: her pictures have charms like those of Kate Greenaway but greater reality. The page of this book is larger than the "pocket" or "stocking" size by which she is best known: there is a rhyme on each, with a picture either in warm, tender coloring or in soft grays. Each of these fulfills the first great requirement of Mother Goose pictures: you can tell at a glance, without glancing at the text, which rhyme it illustrates. For the characterization is perfect, and sometimes one feels she has seen deeper into the character than many of her predecessors."

_____. ca. 1947.
Review of *A Child's Garden of Verses* (1947) on the dust jacket of *Jackanapes.*

New York Herald Tribune Book Review. 110:37,982 November 12, 1950.
"**Books for Young People, for the Age That Looks and Listens,**" edited with reviews by Louise S. Bechtel. Section 7. Page 16. 3 ¾″ review of *The Dolls' Christmas,* 30 pp., Oxford, $1.50. ". . . all four had the great luck to own Pumpkin House, a marvelous dollhouse big enough for large dolls. It is probably the best dollhouse ever put into a book (of course, next to Queen Mary's and to the once-loved "Rackety Packety House"). . . Every detail is told and drawn in a way to enchant small girls . . . My only complaint about this charming book is that it is not twice as long. But there is enough to set off many a small doll owner on plans for the same sort of Christmas party. All the pictures are in full color, in the familiar Tudor style, and will enchant the many homes that collect her little books."

_____. Unknown date ca. 1954. Review of *Biggity Bantam.* "The author has caught the 'biggity' character of these creatures very well, and the many pictures in both line and full color are Tasha Tudor at her best. — Louise Bechtel." Cited on jacket of *Mr. Stubbs* and *Pekin White.*

_____. 114:39,445 November 14, 1954
"**Picture Books for Ages 4 to 8,**" by Louise S. Bechtel. Section VI, part II. Page 4. 4 ¾″ review of *A is For Annabelle*, 55pp. Oxford, $2.50 ". . . even the roses are chosen from grandmother's time. Other little girls, from about four (on and up, especially up to grandmothers and doll collectors) will gather, on inevitable second looking, affection for the little girls who show their joy

in these treasures. . . thanks to Tasha Tudor for the prettiest book of all she has made, for letting us share her own wonderful Annabelle and her own characterful small daughter."

116:48,180   November 18, 1956.
   "Books Offer Untold Delight, Fun, Beauty and Wisdom; fun and Beauty for the Youngest,"
   by Margaret Sherwood Libby. Section 6, Part II. Children's Book Week Number, page 5. 2 ¾"
   review of *1 is One*, 40 pp., Oxford, $2.75. "A picture book . . . reminiscent of "gift books" of the
   turn of the century. . . dainty . . . soft blurry sweetness about the flower-wreathed pages . . Children
   and birds and beasts illustrate a jingle that sing-songs the numbers from one to twenty. We find
   some charming, like the little mouse accompanist o the toadstool, but most are a bit too
   charming."

_____. 120:41,556   September 11, 1960.
   "For Boys and Girls," by Margaret Sherwood Libby. Section 6, page 9. 4" review of *Becky's
   Birthday*, 47 pp., Viking, $3.00. "As long as birthdays roll around, especially those very precious
   ones between five and twelve, children will forward to their own with a very special anticipation,
   and parents and friends will given them books about these happy events. Tasha Tudor in offering
   one provides a very different sort of pleasure from the slap-happy, jolly nonsense of Dr. Seuss in
   his book of last year, "Happy Birthday to You." . . . gentle, serene account . . . with a turn-of-the-
   century flavor that many a little girl of the sixties will long to share. . . in a setting worthy of the
   storied "wood near Athens" . . . this kind of book is a specialty of Tasha Tudor who pictures
   sweetly in soft water colors an idyllic country life, drawing on her experiences with her children."

New York Times. ca. Oct, 1954.
   Review of *A is for Annabelle*, excerpted on the dust jacket of *Around the Year*.

_____. 104:35,638   Sunday August 21, 1955.
   **"Lilliput mansion, The Shakespeares' Miniature Home Is a New Hampshire Tourist
   Novelty,"** by Morris Gilbert, PAGE X21. Introduces the Shakespeare and Crane family of dolls
   whose home with the McCreadys of Webster, N.H., is an advertised doll museum "open all year
   round from 1 to 5 P.M." Describes the doll house and furnishings and the addition built to hold it.
   No fee to inspect the dolls' house, but there is a contribution box, for those who wish to contribute
   to the upkeep of the Shakespeare family.

_____. ca. 1967.
   Richard Bissell reviews *The Real Diary of a real Boy*, excerpted on the dust jacket of *Brite and
   Fair*.

_____. 126:43,627   Tuesday, July 5, 1977.
   "An Illustrator Who Works at the Art of 19th-Century Living," by Angela Taylor. Page34.
   22" story datelined Marlboro, Vt. Discusses Tudor's lifestyle, her four-year-old house. "Seth is
   building another house for his sister Bethany down the road . . . Linda Allen spins wool, making
   some yarn from the corgis' fur . . . She and about 30 friends have formed a group called the
   Stillwaters, to try to relive that life. . ." Three photographs of Tudor shaving ash splints, weaving a
   basket and sketching as granddaughter Laura looks on. This article was syndicated and appears
   elsewhere under different headlines. There is also an unidentified (Ohio ?) copy, "The Past Is
   Future Enough."

New York Times Book Review. 90:30,234   November 3, 1940.
   "The New Books for Younger Readers . . . At the Fair," by Anne T. Eaton. Section 6, page 10.
   10" review of *THE COUNTY FAIR*, unpaged, Oxford, 75 cents. "As in the two preceding
   miniature volumes by Tasha Tudor . . . the very simple story is told as much by the pictures as by
   the text. The engaging Sylvie Ann (one notes that she has grown slightly older) . . . "Pumpkin
   Moonshine" tells a better story than either of the later books, but all three of these little volumes

have the same charm of clear and lovely color, the same pleasant out-of-door atmosphere and the same delightful drawings of children and farm animals. Children who have been to county fairs and those who have not will enjoy the pictures . . . for little children."

_____. 90: 30,381 March 30, 1941.
"The New Books for Younger Readers . . . A Picture Book," page 10. Reviews *A Tale for Easter.* " . . . she made some of her loveliest drawings, pictures which have the same fragile beauty of early Spring evenings. It does not pretend to be a story' it is rather an evocation of those days before Easter . . . As slight and simple a thing as the first narcissus, the book has the same unforgettable air of joy."

_____. 91:30,640 December 14, 1941.
"The New Books for Younger Readers . . .Country Christmas," by Anne T. Eaton. Page 10. 3 ½" review of *Snow Before Christmas*, unpaged, Oxford, $1. " . . . a brief text and many delightful pictures . . . make the New England scene very real. . . The pictures are charming in color and spirit, and Tasha Tudor has succeeded in capturing that feeling of anticipation in which, for the child, lies the joy of the Christmas season. For children 4 to 8." Cited in *Contemporary Authors* (81-84:573).

_____. 92: 30,955 October 25, 1942.
"The new Books for Younger Readers . . . Sylvie Ann's Pig," pages 10, 39. " . . . we find all the seasons represented in these small, appealing volumes with their exquisitely colored illustrations. . . the story is simplicity itself, yet it has lively action and eventfulness in line with a little child's interests. The drawings on every page add distinction and atmosphere and make the setting very convincing. The sunflower and Black-eyed Susans seem really to blossom . . . gracious golden green of a Summer landscape. These little stories are never dull nor perfunctory, for the artist-author has touched them with the magic of the changing seasons, of Spring meadows and falling snow, of firelight and candlelight, cozy kitchens and shady orchards. . ." Cited in *Contemporary Authors* (81-84:573).

_____. 93: 31,305 October 10, 1943.
"Children's Bookshelf | Tales of a Very Friendly Dragon, | A Goose and Other Creatures," by Anne T. Eaton, page 6. "Marsh Magic" review *The White Goose*, Oxford $1. "The many boys and girls and older readers who have taken pleasure in Tasha Tudor's charming little books, "Pumpkin Moonshine," "Snow Before Christmas," "Dorcas Porcus" and the rest, in which the artist-author has captured the joy of childhood in each of the year's seasons, will welcome this delicate moonlit addition to the list. . . Tasha Tudor has put real beauty into the drawings and she handles her story with a light and delicate touch. The tale is so slight it seems like a footnote done in moonlight to the author's other books. Children from 6 to 8 will enjoy it all the more if they make the acquaintance of one of the daytime stories as a companion piece."

_____. 97: 33,104 September 12, 1948.
"New Books for Younger Readers . . . THE DOLLS' HOUSE By Rumer Godden. Illustrated by Dana Saintsbury, 125 pp, Viking, $2.50." 5 ½" review by Ellen Lewis Buell, page 35. "To her first book for children, Miss Godden brings the same sensitive play of imagination and delicacy of characterization which mark her adult novels. . . There are genuine suspense and tensity of emotion in this miniature domestic drama because the dolls, each sharply individualized, are as alive as the little girls who gave them life by loving them. The real and the unreal are deftly mingled with a perfect logic and the whole is illumined by tenderness and humor."

_____. Unknown date for review of *The Dolls' Christmas* which was published October 5, 1950. "Little girls of the doll-house age will | revel in the minute details....The author | has illustrated it in her customary style, | delicate, old-fashioned, but never over- | sweet."—New York Times Book Review [on flap on McKay *Pumpkin Moonshine*]

_____. Unknown date for review of *Biggity Bantam* which was published February 23, 1954. "Nevertheless, the book has charm, for author and artist have presented an attractice picture of real life on their own New Hampshire farm, generously illustrated with Tasha tudor's characteristic soft-toned illustrations. — C.E. Norman." Cited on the dust jacket of *Pekin White*.

_____. 115: 39,383 November 21, 1965.
"For this Christmas...the illustrator young people love TASHA TUDOR ...," page 22. Lippincott advertisement for Tudor's new book *Tasha Tudor's Favorite Stories*, and pictures *Wings from the Wind, The Secret Garden* and *A Little Princess*.

_____. Unknown date, ca. 1967. Review of *The Real Diary of A Real Boy* cited on dust jacket of *Brite and Fair* and *The Real Diary of a Real Boy*.

_____. Unknown date, ca. 1968.
Review of *The New England Butt'ry Shelf Cookbook*. Cited on jacket of *The New England Butt'ry Shelf Almanac*.

_____. 121:41,560 November 7, 1971.
"We love these new books. Your children will too!" A Thomas Y. Crowell advertisement including *Corgiville Fair*, Ages 4-8 at $4.95. Section 7, Part II, *Children's Books*, page 23. "The finest children's literature in paperback. Yearling boks from Dell. . . There are now 137 delightful Yearling titles . . . " Just published | THE SECRET GARDEN | Frances Hodgson Burnett: illustrated by Tasha Tudor . . . All ages 95c, page 39. A Crowell ad for Corgiville Fair with photograph of the book superimposed on one of Tudor and her corgis, page 44. Cited in *Something About the Author* (20:188).

_____. 121:41,581 November 28, 1971.
"Corgiville Fair," by Ingeborg Boudreau, faculty of the Graduate School of Library and Information Science, Pratt Institute. Page 8. ". . . all is not so quiet as the dliecate, pastel pictures or your remembrance of the author's "The County Fiar" of 1940 might have you think. . . All told, it's a generous harvest of Mrs. Tudor's living, feeling and observing—a bounty of imaginative, delicate watercolors for as exuberant an aggregation of Americana as you'll find on land or paper." Two illustrations from the book.

_____. 122:42,085 April 15, 1973.
"Rabbit Roundup," by Judy Noyes, co-owner and children's book-buyer of the Chinook Bookshop, Colorado Springs, Co. Section 7, Page 8. "Tasha Tudor's *A Tale for Easter* is an old friend to keepers of children's book lists. Originally published in 1941, it has now been issued in paperback (Walck, $1.50) . . . "

_____. 125:43,051 December 7, 1975.
"Dasher, Dancer & Co.," by George A Woods. Page 8. "Parents, this is Old Nick. St. Nick, talking to you and have I got a sleigh-full of slightfulls—books with Christmas themes—for all of your little ones. Of course, giving such books on Christmas morn is like applying pre-emergent crabgrass control after the weeds have blossomed. These books are in anticipation of the holiday. What you should give as Christmas gifts are on page 66. Sad to relate, my publishing elves haven't done too well this year. By their work I'd judge they are growing old and tired, indulging in Christmas clichés, warming up the same old chestnuts. Take two, **THE NIGHT BEFORE CHRISTMAS** (Rand McNally, $4.95) illustrated by Tasha Tudor and the same title in a paperback (Random House/Pictureback, 95 cents0) illustrated by Douglas Gorsline. The former presents me elfin, with pointed ears. I'm more flattered by Gorsline, shown against handsome antique panoramas. I'll opt for this last reluctantly. So what else is new? . . . " Cited in *Something About the Author* (20:188).

_____. 126:43,393 November 14, 1976.
  "**You & Children & Crowell & Christmas.**" Page 45. A full-page ad of 40 children's books for Christmas gifts arrayed as a Christmas tree. *The Christmas Cat* forms the pinnacle.

_____. 127:43,842 February 5, 1978.
  "**A TIME TO KEEP,** *the Tasha Tudor Book of Holidays,* 64 pp. Rand McNally $5.95. (Ages 5 to 8). 10″ review by Anne Crompton. "Nostalgia is Tasha Tudor's middle name . . . Despite the subtitle . . . this is really a book of seasons, punctuated by holidays. Delicate watercolors intricately framed . . . The family is dressed for the rural 19th century. Someone must be busting blood vessels offstage cooking and cleaning, washing and weeding; but we see only happy, relaxed faces. The children are delighted to help with sugaring and harvesting; and the parents seem under no stress. They labor quietly, slowly, like nature itself. . . At first glance I decided "It's a fraud!" . . . According to the book, however, it's all true! Not only did the artist do these neat things in her childhood, and with her own children. She does them today with her grandchildren! In the light of this information, "A Time to Keep" takes on a downright sinister hue. It becomes dangerous, threatening, like the Walton television series. Exposed to it, a modern child is bound to ask "Why don't we live like this?" . . . what will arouse wonder and envy is . . . quiet joy and gentle activity. . . . [parents] may well be enticed to try once more, with feeling, to make of their children's childhood a time to keep."

_____. 140:4846. December 30, 1990.
  "**Brighter Garden,**" by Karla Kuskin. Page 19. 6 ½″ review. " . . . poetry unlike any other verse written before. . . forces her into a conventional mold: nature poet. . . 14 of the poems are excerpted . . . eliminates the possibility that a child might be touched by some meaning or music in a line even if it is not crystal clear. The look of the book compounds the myth of the maiden lady nature poet with Tasha Tudor's soft pastel watercolors. These delicate renderings of Victorian women and conneted children in softly pretty landscapes have nothing in common with Dickinson's passionate and eccentric poetry. . . "dramatic rather than lyrical, direct, vigorous, and so original that she suffered for it thoroughout her lifetime." It is unfortunate that 104 years after the end of that lifetime she, and her readers, are still suffering for it."

Newsday. Unknown date, ca. 1968.
  Review of *The New England Butt'ry Shelf Cookbook.* Cited on jacket of *The New England Butt'ry Shelf Almanac.*

_____. November 24, 1996.
  "**Cover story, Colonial Williamsburg, a Long Island child goes back in time**" by Paul Vitello, pages D8-[D9]. The text describes Colonial Williamsburg and historic recreations generally, but also includes one 7 x 10 ¾″ photograph where ... Children admire a collection of antique toys and dollhouses at the exhibit "Take Joy: The World of Tasha Tudor."

Nutshell News. December 1985
  "**For Microphiles.**" Report and photograph of Tudor kitchen scene as a miniature tableau by Dee Snyder of Florida, associate editor of *Nutshell News* magazine, is cited in *The Letter* 5:1, Fall 1985, page [3].

Parents Magazine. 22:12, December 1947.
  "**Old-Fashioned Christmas in New England,**" by Tasha Tudor. Pages 47, 52, 54. This is one of Tudor's earliest accountings of a year of preparations for Christmas baking, parties, guests and plays. "To us Christmas means not only the tree and presents, but the coming of cousins, the Dolls' Party, the Puppet Show; these events take time to prepare . . . " Card illustrations.

"The Pembroke in the Spotlight." **http://www.getnet.com/~kamir/eliz.htm**. Reviewed page last updated January 27, 1998. Nine paragraphs discussing Pembroke Welsh corgis, largely those belonging to Queen Elizabeth II. But also suggests other celebrated Corgi owners: ... Tasha Tudor, artist-author. Her enchanting illustrations appear in many joyful books, including the tiny, leather-bound *The Twenty-third Psalm.* Prince Philip purchased a copy while visiting America, and the Queen ordered more through a British bookseller. The Corgi model for each of the illustrations is Mrs. Tudor's Megan. . . ."

Philadelphia Inquirer. ca. 1947.
Review of *a Child's Garden of Verses* (1947) from the dust jacket of *Jackanapes.*

_____. Before 1978.
Quoted on the dust jacket of *Tasha Tudor's Favorite Christmas Carols:* "What Tasha Tudor can do with color is | something to dream about, something to | feast the eyes upon again and again. . . . | The artist captures the innocence of child- | hood in a way that is inimitably Tasha | Tudor."

Piecework, All This By Hand. 5:2, March/April 1997. Interweave Press, Inc., 201 East Fourth Street, Loveland, Co. 80537-5655.
"Take Joy! Tasha Tudor's costume collection," by Beth Wheeler. Pages 11-13. Discusses the 1996-97Colonial Williamsburg exhibit of Tudor's 50 costumes, and Tudor's life. Three color photographs, two of dresses, and one of Tudor with corgyn, a detail of which appears inside the front cover.

Pittsburgh, Pa. Unidentified news clipping. ca. November 1, 1963.
"Joseph Horne Co. Come Meet Tasha Tudor and Bethany Tudor." Page number missing. A mother-daughter Autograph Party, Tuesday, November 5, from 3:00 to 5:00 in our book department. Advertises *The* [sic] *Little Princess,* $5.00 and *Gooseberry Lane,* $2.75.

Plain Dealer. Wednesday, July 13, 1977. Cleveland, Ohio.
"Artist Tasha Tudor draws a life-style from another age," by Angela Taylor, New York Times. Page 1-C, 3-C. See *New York Times* July 5, 1977.

_____. Undated news clipping, ca. October, 1963.
"Like Mother, Like Daughter!" Page number missing. Black and white photographs of Tudor and close-up of Bethany. "Illustrations by Tasha Tudor (left) and her daughter, Bethany, are featured in two new books by Lippincott. Mrs. Tudor did the illustrations for a new edition of Frances Hodgson Burnett's classic, "A Little Princess." Bethany's first book, "Gooseberry Lane," tells of two resourceful ducks in text and pictures."

_____. Undated advertisement, ca. October, 1963.
"Higbee's You're invited to meet Tasha Tudor and her Daughter Bethany!" Page number missing. "Little Princess Gooseberry Lane . . . be our guests at a luncheon Friday Nov. 1 - 3-5 p.m. Tickets, 1.25 for children, 1.60 for adults.

_____. Undated advertisement, ca. October, 1963.
"Higbee's More distinguished guests at Higbee's!" Page number missing. "Meet Tasha Tudor and her daughter Bethany at a luncheon and autograph party on Saturday at 12 noon. Book signings at 1, 2:30 and 4:30 p.m. for *A Little Princess* and *Gooseberry Lane.* Tickets for the luncheon, 1.25 for children, 1.60 for adults."

_____. After December 2, 1963.
A photograph of the Tudors and 11 others with this caption: "Tasha Tudor and her daughter, Bethany, were guests recently at Higbee's, Cleveland, where a luncheon was given for them and

they autographed books for a large audience of parents and children." The photograph was previously published in *Publishers Weekly*, December 2, 1963.

_____. Undated news clipping, ca. November 5, 1966.
"For Children's Author: Farm's Like a Storybook," by Olive Gresmer. Page number missing. Describes Tudor as a woman born a generation too late. Discusses farm life, that youngest daughter comes closest to her mother's wish to share the fondness for the rural and primitive. Oldest daughter appears with Tudor on speaking engagements, one son teaches in Vermont, the other goes to Denison University. Tudor will appear this week at Higbee's Department Store.

Playthings. 95:12. December 1997
Reviews *The Great Corgiville Kidnapping.* Page 34.

Practical Homeschooling. Issue no. 5, 1994. Home Life Inc.
"Tasha Tudor's World," by Joan Donaldson [author of *The Real Pretend*]. Four pages found on Website - http://www.home-school.com/Articles/Tasha TudorsWorld/html. (A 9K file dated 9 October 1995.) Discusses Tudor's methods of raising her family, and concludes with two pages describing the Donaldson's own efforts at creating a meaningful life for their children without "television, radio and other forms of mass consumer media."

Providence Journal. Ca. 1967. Review of *The Real Diary of a Real Boy* cited on dust jacket of same.

_____. Ca. 1968. Review of *Brite and Fair* cited on dust jacket of same.

Publishers' Weekly. 180:25 December 18, 1961. 90pp. in wrappers.
"Huge Crowds Greet Tasha Tudor | in Tour of Stores, Schools." Pages 18-19. Describes *The Tasha Tudor Book of Fairy Tales* as the most successful single book ever published by Platt & Munk. Includes sales and audience figures from Tudor's appearances in Cleveland, Washington, D. C., Chicago, Rock Island and Chevy Chase. Three photographs.

_____. ca. 1962.
Reviews *Pumpkin Moonshine.* "A reissue of Miss Tudor's . . ." [See dj to Walck *A Tale for Easter*]

_____. 184: 23 December 2, 1963. 108pp. in wrappers.
"The Tudors at Higbee's." Pages 22-23. Reports Oct. 31-Nov. 2 book tour of Tasha and Bethany Tudor which began at four Cleveland schools, continued at Higbee's Department Store, then to Horne's in Pittsburgh, Hudson's in Detroit, Marshall Field in Chicago and an opening luncheon at Chicago's "Miracle of Books Fair." More than 500 copies of *A Little Princess* and *Gooseberry Lane* sold at the Higbee's luncheon and signing. Place mats at Higbee's luncheon were reproductions of one of the drawings from *Gooseberry Lane.* Radio and television appearances and articles in the Cleveland *Plain Dealer* and *Press.* Photographs of signing and a window display.

_____. ca. 1967. Review of *The Real Diary of a Real Boy* cited on dust jacket of same.

_____. ca. 1968. Review of *Brite and Fair* cited on dust jacket of same.

_____. 211:9 February 28, 1977. 130pp. in wrappers.
"Dorothy Haas of Rand McNally is enthu- | siastic at the prospect of publishing an- | other work by author-illustrator Tasha | Tudor: "A Time to Keep: the Tasha | Tudor Book of holidays." Based on | festivities observed in her household. . ." Cited in *Something About the Author* (20:188)

_____. Unknown date, ca. September 1978.

"Chances are, families where Tudor's collection finds a home will discover that her favorites are theirs too. She has embellished her preface, the brief histories of the carols and the songs themselves with the cozy, old-fashioned illustrations in color that have made her works so popular. The arrangements, for piano and guitar, are easy for almost anybody to master." Quoted on the dust jacket of *Tasha Tudor's Old-Fashioned Gifts.*

_____. 226:17 October 26, 1984. 1911 Rowland St., Riverton, N.J. 08077, 114 pp. in wrappers.
"CHRISTMAS VILLAGE | *Tasha Tudor, with her illustrations.* | Philomel; $8.95 ISBN 0-399-21088-1 | Every one of Tudor's creations has | been a bestseller during the course of | her long career, and it is a safe bet that | her quaint Advent calendar won't lin- | ger on any bookstore shelves. . . Be- | sides giving children the zest of discov- | ery and keeping track of the days be- | fore the holiday, the pop-up may serve | as an addition to home dcorations, | year after year. (All ages)" Page 105.

_____. 237:39. September 28, 1990.
"A Brighter Garden," reviewed by Diane Roback and Richard Donahue. Page 104.

_____. 239:53. December 7, 1992.
"THE REAL PRETEND." Page 62. 4″ review mistakenly attributes the story to Donaldson's grandmother. ". . . Although the tale is a bit long for the picture-book format, first-time author Donaldson's low-key style and Tudor's dainty, old-fashioned country scenes suggest an enjoyable summer afternoon spent poring over an album of faded family photographs. Both text and art are surrounded by gossamer oval borders depicting country flora and artifacts—a further harkening to halcyon days of yore. Ages 4-8. (*Dec.*)"

_____. 241:30. July 25, 1994.
"TASHA TUDOR'S GARDEN." Page 50. 4″ review. "The noted children's-book author and illustrator Tasha Tudor, "half naturalist, half gardener," lives with her dogs, Nubian goats and countless trees, plants and flowers on a 259-acre hilltop farm in Vermont. Her Martin (The Essence of Paradise) and Brown (the private World of Tasha Tudor) politely dog her trail during the growing months to learn the hows and whys of her gardening prowess. . . Tudor's "manure tea," an invention consisting of cow flops and water steeped all summer in a caldron for use as fertilizer. Tea or no, the book's roundly picturesque and dappled with full-color photos of Herself minding the peonies and strolling barefoot (by preference) past the daffodils. The text by Martin in friendly and informative. A list of Tudor's favorite nurseries is included. (*Oct.*)"

_____. 244:35. August 25, 1997.
"THE GREAT CORGIVILLE KIDNAPPING." Page 70. 4 ¼″ review. "Tudor returns to the scene of *Corgiville Fair* for this rather wordy tale starring dog detective Caleb Corgi. . . Displaying the wry humor her fans have come to expect, Tudor splashes her narrative with intentional melodrama, zippy puns and clever asides (a pointed reference to Gertrude Stein is just for parents). Yet a plot that wanders in many directions and overly long chunks of text will likely be off-putting to young readers (e.g., the opening paragraph extols Caleb's virtues in a long-winded résumé). Tudor's sprawling pictures are abundantly detailed—especially the book's endpapers and Megan's market, the town grocery store—depicting a buzzing Corgiville filled with nattily attired, anthropomorphic animals. Still, this is not the venerable artist's most memorable work. All ages. *(Sept.)*

_____. 245:4. January 26, 1998.
"THE SPRINGS OF JOY." Page 90. 5" review. ". . . The text is a collection of literary quotations about inspiration and happiness, while the watercolors, rendered in the artist's characteristically tender and nostalgic style, illustrate "a few of the things that [bring] joy" to the artist. . . An afterword explains that the models are Tudor's grandchildren and pets, the setting her New England home. The pastoral beauty and innocent view of childhood will certainly please the

artist's many fans, young and old, but the quotes will vary in their appeal. While Ralphs Waldo Emerson's maxim "The only gift is a portion of thyself" can easily find favor with children as well as adults, some selections, such as Coventry Patmore's "Winter" ("[I] Love Winter, and to trace/ The sense of the Trophonian pallor on her face"), seem rather sophisticated for the audience implied by the pictures. The overall sense here is of a very personal volume, the artist's illustrated commonplace book or diary, and readers will enjoy this offering to the extent that they already share Tudor's rosy vision. All ages. *(Apr.)*"

Reading Eagle/Reading Times. MONDAY, June 26, 1995. Reading, Pa.
   "There's nothing more delightful than getting old. You're all going to get that way. Tasha serves up her homespun wisdom" by Lisa Scheid, pages B1, B3. The 18″ text describes Tudor's speaking/sketching engagement at Northeast Middle School, Reading, Pa., the previous afternoon. Tickets were $15 reserved seating and $10 general admission. Photograph of Tudor.

Reflections On The Passing Show From A Bystander. Christmas 1995. Ken Sadler.
   Http://www.europa.com/~kbsadler/PSDec95.html. Comments onhis Christmases as a child. Cover reproduces Tudor's image of St. Nick coming in to a house roof for a landing, flying squirrels directly the landing process from chimney top.

The Republican-Courier. March 30, 1971. Findlay, Ohio.
   "Children's Book Illustrator Will Speak Here April 15." 9″ announcement of Tudor's appearance at the R.L. Heminger Auditorium, Findlay High School, April 15. Page number missing.

_____. Friday April 16, 1971
   "Tasha Tudor Lectures, Author-Illustrator Charms Youngsters," by Alice Moore. 18″ review of Tudor's appearance at the R.L. Heminger Auditorium, Findlay High School, the day before. She had been in Cincinnati just prior to receive the Regina Medal Award. Page number missing.

_____. April ?, 1971.
   "Tasha Tudor Will Sketch During Lecture." Announces Tudor's appearance at the R.L. Heminger Auditorium, Findlay (Ohio) High School, April 15. Sponsored by Mother Goose Book Shop and Mrs. Scott Elsea. Page number missing. Photograph of Tudor and corgi Megan.

_____. Friday April 16, 1971
   "Tea Party With Tasha," photograph by Howard Moyer. Pictures Tudor at tea with these girls: Laurie and Beth Cleary, Angela Conine, and Tracy and Shelley Miller. Page number missing.

_____. ca. November 12, 1976.
   "Tudors Autograph Children's Books." Page number missing. 4″ report: "Sutton and Lightner's Department Store was filled with excited mothers and wide-eyed children on Thursday November 11. The mother and daughter team of Efner Tudor Holmes and Tasha Tudor were autographing . . . *The Christmas Cat* . . . Efner Holmes and Tasha Tudor are on a tour to promote their collaboration throughout the East and Midwest, and will wind up the tour in Boston, Massachusetts.

The Review. August 1984, North Texas. ***Maybe, American Literary Review***
   Report of Tudor's visit to Neiman-Marcus, Dallas June 23, 1984, by Steven VanVelzer and Ann Minton. " . . . positively lovely, gracious, truly a person who is one in a million . . . elegant, ever-so-talented and exceptional lady . . . " Cited in *The Letter*, 5:1, Fall 1985. Page [3].

Rockwell Museum of Corning, N.Y. http://www.stny.lrun.com/RockwellMuseum/special.html "November 19, 1998 - March 14, 1999. Once Upon a Page: The Art of Children's Books. This exhibition features seventy works by some of the most distinguished American and international illustrators of children's books, all from the Dr. and Mrs. August C. Mazza collection at the University of Findlay, Findlay, OH. The collection, diverse in both style and medium, includes . . . Tasha Tudor"

Rutland Herald. December 14, 1992. Rutland, Vermont.
    "Life as Art, Tasha Tudor Charms Admirers With her 19th Century Sensibility." Pages 1, 14. Reports of a book signing in Manchester, Vt., featuring Tudor and Richard Brown who spent a year and a half photographing Tudor through the seasons . . . Mark Twain was a great friend of Papa's. But don't embarrass me, it's not good taste to boast . . . the house her son Seth built - an exact copy in reverse of a 1740 home she admired in Webster, N.H. [*sic*].

San Francisco Chronicle. Ca. 1957. Review of *Around the Year.* Cited on jacket of Walck *Mother Goose.*

Saturday Review. 44:45 November 11, 1961. 80 pp. in wrappers. Saturday Review Inc., 25 West 45th St., New York 36, NY.
    "BOOKS FOR YOUNG AMERICA | Stars in the Picture Books Sky," by Alice Dalgliesh. Pp. 37-44. One page essay and reviews of new children's books for the holiday season. "You can never tell about the artists who make our children's picture books. Some illustrators have been with us for years with scarcely a change in style or | technique, yet their names are household words, or at least library words. Others have | stayed because they have the ability to write their own books, or because their work | grows: they can change style and technique to suit the feeling of the book. . . They are children's books. This cannot be repeated too often. . . But again—all these are books for young children, and we must never let ourselves for- | get it. To live for any length of time, a child's book needs to communicate both in | text and pictures; lately some of them seem to talk to themselves, or to have paper-thin, almost invisible ideas. Give children a chance to have books with interesting pictures | of all kinds—and real stories, not all attempts at *mood.* Then we shall keep the child with | his book, the book for the child, and he may joyously share it with adults. . . [p. 37] *Folk Tales* | The Brothers Grimm hoped | their carefully collected "House-| hold Tales" would be a heritage in the | house, and that is what they became. ¶We do happen to have as our child- | dren's heritage a sturdy body of litera- | ture of which folk tales form substantial | pillars. These through the years have | had considerable kicking around and | bear some deep scars. At present they | are being commercialized and rewritten | to an uncomfortable degree. ¶The worst blow that has been dealt | them is the use of the name of a tele- | vision personality, or of an artist, as part | of the title of the book. Librarians have | usually stood firmly against this type of | thing: parents and teachers should. We | do have a group of delightful picture | books in which a single story is presented | with respect, as well as carefully made | collections by those who have the back- | ground for making them. But this year | we have two books to which any critic | with any standards would object. So that | we can contrast them with better books, | they are considered first. -A.D. || **SHIRLEY TEMPLE'S NURSERY TALES . . . THE TASHA TUDOR BOOK OF FAIRY TALES.** | *Platt & Munk. 96 pp. $3.95.* The foreword | states: "These stories, newly retold, blend | wit and sparkle and soaring imagination | with the delightful artistry of Tasha Tu- | dor." This wit, sparkle, etc. I do not see. | The stories are shortened and softened. | Rapunzel suffers by the complete expunga- | tion of her twins—who were the natural re- | sult of the Prince's nightly climb to her | tower. Why? Hans Christian Andersen's | stories are brashly retold, or shortened. | Why? To make more room for oversweet | pictures? We have known Tasha Tudor as | an illustrator and writer for some time. This | year she has a reissue in larger form of a | favorite story. "Alexander the Gander," | and a Christmas book with another pub- | lisher. Why do this inferior book? The | proper credits are, fortunately, given. || **THE THREE WISHES: A Folk Tale** . . . dates all the way back to | Greek mythology and has appeared in many versions and in many languages. This | telling is from 'More English Fairy Tales' | edited by Joseph Jacobs and reprinted by | permission of G. P. Putnam's Sons." Now that's the way to do it! . . . **TOLD IN NORWAY . . . TOLD IN RUSSIA . . . TOLD IN IRELAND . . . McCALL'S READ ME A STORY BOOK** . . ." Page 41.

School Library Journal. 17:7 March 1971. 184 pp. in wrappers. R.R. Bowker, 205 East 42th St., NY, NY 10017.

"**AWARDS** The 1971 Regina Medal Award, given by the Catholic Library Association, is going to Tasha Tudor, author and illustrator of children's books. The medal, presented annually since 1959, is given for continued distinguished contribution to the field of children's literature. Miss Tudor's books include *A is for Annabelle* (Walck, 1954), *One is One* (Hale, 1956), *First Graces* (Walck, 1955), *First Prayers* (Walck, 1952), *Pumpkin Moonshine* (Walck, 1962), and the *Tasha Tudor Book of Fairy Tales* (Platt, 1961). She has also illustrated *Wind in the Willows, Little Women,* and Hans Christian Andersen's *Fairy Tales.* The award will be presented April 13 during the CLA's annual convention in Cincinnati.

_____. 26:7 March 1980. 152 pp. in wrappers.

"**TUDOR, Tasha & Linda Allen.** *Tasha Tudor's Old-Fashioned Gifts: Pres ents and Favors for All Occasions.* Illus, some color, by authors. 118p. CIP. McKay. Oct. 1979. CSm $10.95 LC 79-2053. *Gr 6-7*—As quaintly and sweetly as ever, Tasha Tudor now offers directions for 36 "presents and favors . . . The co-author and co-illustrator, whose name is not in the title, is Linda Allen, who has done about half of the watercolors and pencil sketches which abound in this book. Her art is imitative of, but inferior to, Tudor's. The purpose of this fluffy, nostalgic book, stated in the introduction, is to inspire readers to make their own gifts and to be creative. There are other books which accomplish this more effectively; one of them is *Family Book of Crafts* by Hellegers and Kallem (Sterling, 1973).—*Carolyn K. Jenks,* | *University of New Hampshire, Durham*" Page 144. CSm = cloth bound, Smyth sewn

_____. 31:7 March 1985. 192 pp. in wrappers.

"**TUDOR, Tasha, sel.** *All for Love.* Illus. by sel. 93p. diags. Score. Index. CIP. Philomel. Oct. 1984. PSm (cl.sp.) $15.95. ISBN 0-399-21012-1. LC 83-21959. *Gr 10 Up*—Tudor's *All for Love,* in a pretty picture book format, may well become a classic gift for lovers and the favorite centerpiece of Valentine book displays. . . its pages are lavishly illustrated in watercolors with the artist's familiar garlands of posies surrounding lovers in antique costume. . . Essentially a gift item, *All for Love* may appeal to sentimental YAs.— *Janet French, Centennial School Dis-|trict libraries, Warminster, Pa.*" Page 183. PSm = paper over boards, Smyth sewn

_____. 43:12 December 1997.

"**TUDOR, Tasha.** *The Great Corgiville Kidnapping,*" reviewed by *Judith Gloyer, Milwaukee Public Library.* 4 ½" review. "Gr 1-4—In a quaint New England village populated by an array of animals done up in jackets à la Beatrix Potter, Caleb . . . The plot is predictable; it is the details that offer pleasure. Tudor uses colorfully descriptive language that brings richness to the story. . . The pictures are also a delight . . . Tudor's sketchy watercolors, both small scale and panoramic spreads, draw viewers in for a closer look at all of the homey details. With its slightly longer length and a more challenging vocabulary than most picture books, this title may appeal more to older children and the lucky adults who can share it with them."

School Library Media Activities Monthly. 11:8. APRIL 1995. LMS Associates, 17 East Henrietta St., Baltimore, Md., 21230.

"**Science/Art: Tasha Tudor, How Does Your Garden Grow?**" Pages 22-24. A school activity guide to lead students in discovering the art of Tasha Tudor and the rudiments of botany. Includes a 36-title list of Tudor books as well as related magazine articles and general gardening books. ". . . the class will illustrate a science report cover with watercolor pictures in a style similar to Tasha Tudor's paintings. . . 1830s-style New England world she has preserved on her farm in Southern Vermont. . . "I've always done borders of sticks or ribbons or flowers around my illustrations and I don't even know why I decided to. I don't even remeber when I didn't. . ." The class may create a greeting card with watercolors used to depict a sampling of flowers . . . Students who want to write to Tasha Tudor may send their letters to: Tasha Tudor; c/o The Jenny Wren Press; P.O. Box 505; Mooresville, IN 46158."

Single Mother. Issue 24. May/June 1995.
> **"Single Mothers of Invention: Meet women who have made important contributions to the world,"** by Karen Cimino and Andrea Engber. The authors discuss those who raised families and achievements emphasizing Maya Angelou, Isadora Duncan, Mary Wollstonecraft, Margaret Sanger and George Sand. A suggestion to read the biographies and diaries of women is followed by a list of 24 people to consider from Cleopatra to Catherine Deneuve and includes Tasha Tudor, children's book author and illustrator. They suggest Virginia Kelley, mother of Jacqueline Kennedy Onassis, editor, former First Lady . . . and George Sands [*sic*].
> The article can be found at http://www.parentsplace.com/readroom/nosm/may95sin.html.

Smithsonian. 23:8 November 1992.
> Review of *The Secret Garden*, by Kathleen M. Burke. Pictures by Tasha Tudor. Page 196.

Spring. November-December 1982. Rodale Press.
> Have not examined a copy, but it is reported the issue carries an ad for the Franklin Mint ceramic statuary *Amy*.

Story-A-Day. 1:2 October 1, 1953. Story-A-Day, Inc., 270 Park Avenue, New York, N.Y. Editorial Dept., 161 Newbury St., Boston 10, Mass. 32pp. in mustard pictorial wrapper.
> **"Peggy and the Postman,"** by Evelyn Ray Sickels. Pictures by Tasha Tudor. Pages [2]-5 with three pencil drawings with blue coloring.
> **"The Truly Magic Doll,"** by Gracye Dodge White. Pictures by Tasha Tudor. Pages 22-25 with five pencil drawings, three with yellow coloring and two with red.

Sturnus. 1:2 Spring-Summer 1993. The North American Starling Fanciers Association.
> **"Tweedy,"** by Bethany Tudor. The same article which is cited above in the NFSS BULLETIN.

Sunday School Chronicle. unknown date, ca. 1967
> Review excerpted on the dust jacket of *First Graces*, Lutterworth. "These books *[First Prayers, More Prayers]* will give a lot of pleasure to very young readers. Children will probably know some of the lovely prayers and graces, and will certainly be encouraged by the enchanting little illustrations to learn others, less familiar."

————.
> Reviews *First Prayers, First Graces, More Prayers*. Cited on the dust jacket of *The Lord is My Shepherd*.

T.V. Guide. Ca. 1990. Reviews WonderWorks *The Secret Garden*

Take Joy! 1:1 January/February 1997. 18 pp. in wrapper, pages 1 and 18, being the insides of the front and back covers. Take Joy!, Box 123, 50 Lexington Avenue, NY, NY 10010
> Premiere Issue of a Tudor-centered magazine engineered by Corgi Cottage Industries, but edited and published by Donna M. Swajeski and her husband Michael Opelka. Staff listing: Editress-in-Chief - Tasha Tudor, Publisher/Exec. Editor - Donna M. Swajeski; Managing Editor - Harry Davis; Senior Design Editor - Jim Journigan; Layout/Design - Michael Opelka & Brian Metz; Art Work - Tasha Tudor. The names of Mr. Journigan and Mr. Metz do not appear in subsequent issues. The initial issue has articles by Swajeski, Isabelle Hadley, Jan Gilliam, Gary Overmann, Amelia Stauffer, Janet Stampfl, Harry Davis and a page of classified advertisements. Photographs and art reproductions.

————. 1:2 March/April 1997. 22 pp. in wrapper, pages 1 and 22, being the insides of the front and back covers.

Articles by/about Amelia Stauffer, Isabelle Hadley, Pat Warthen, Donna M. Swajeski, Chris Vermeersch, Gary Overmann, Bethany Tudor, Marilu Diller, Winslow Tudor, Harry Davis and Sherry Pees. Classified advertisements. Photographs and art reproductions. Excerpt from *Cranford* by Elizabeth Gaskell.

_____. 1:3 May/June 1997. 22 pp. in wrapper, as above.
Articles by/about Jan Gilliam, Joan DeGusto, Gary Overmann, Isabelle Hadley, Sherry Pees, Suzy Mclennan-Anderson, Amelia Stauffer, Winslow Tudor, Crystal M. Trulove, Jan Robinson, Linda Harwood, Alice Morse Earle and Donna M. Swajeski. Classified advertisements, photographs and art reproductions. Excerpt from *Precious Bane* by Mary Webb.

_____. 1:4 July/August 1997. 22 pp. in wrapper, as above.
Articles by/about Tea time, Peachblow Two flowers, Charlestown, NH, Clara and Harry Fuchslocher, Harry Davis reviews *The Great Corgiville Kidnapping: Worth the Wait!*, Instant water garden, Thomas Tudor on August birthdays in Webster, Donna M. Swajeski on Paul Peabody and his puppets - and summer reflections, Isabelle Hadley writes of healing herbs, Joan Donaldson on Spencerian script, five recipes, Eun Im Kim Tudor on cornbread and growing up on a Korean island, Harry Davis on collecting and using antiques, Amelia Stauffer on visiting flower suppliers near Brattleboro, Margaret L. Been remembers knitting during World War II, Winslow Tudor gives instructions for building a coldframe. Classified advertisements, photographs and art reproductions. Excerpt from *The Mill on the Floss* by George Elliot. Tudor announces that *Prime Time Live* has taped Corgi Cottage for a November television broadcast. And she is signing bookplates for…*Kidnapping*.

_____. 1:5 September/October 1997. 22 pp. in wrapper, as above.
Articles by/about The perfect cup, Making apple cider by Joan Donaldson, Moonlit apples by John Drinkwater, Excerpts from a gardener's journal by Amelia Stauffer, A cottage garden, Susan's vegetable lasagna, Tea with Tasha! [in Wilkes-Barre, Pa], Simple soap making by Marilu Diller, Nature watch: Autumn husking bee by Winslow Tudor, Yellow ware mixing bowls by Harry Davis, The recipe file Cooking with pumpkins, The artist Dulac by Gary Overmann, The art of the cameo, From The Secret Garden Meet Rosemary Gladstar by Isabelle Hadley, The "Art of Living" as experienced by our readers by Marie Albert, Making a rustic flower pot, Notes from the back porch by Donna M. Swajeski. Classified advertisements, photographs and art reproductions. Excerpt from *Pamela* by Samuel Richardson.

_____. 1:6 November/December 1997. 22 pp. in wrapper, as above.
The issue is incorrectly numbered 5 on the front cover. Articles by/about Rings of Fancy: figural napkin rings, Home comfort [stoves] by Joan Donaldson, Timeless toys: Steiff animals, Excerpts from a gardener's journal by Amelia Stauffer, Tasha's Christmas cookies, November roses, Plan a perennial swappers club, Child in fashion by Jan Gilliam, A tribute to a very special Tasha Tudor fan (Virginia Elsea, Findley, Ohio, book shop owner [incorrectly implies Tudor was living in Vermont when she gave an Ohio presentation]), Coming next issue, A Valentine to dogs, Holiday cooking ideas, From The Secret Garden Very special cats by Isabelle Hadley, The "Art of Living" as experienced by our readers by Jan Robinson "Tussie Mussie's Christmas gift," the land of Oz by Gary Overmann, Holiday decorating by Judith Katz-Schwartz, Marking rustic bread by Dave Cerchio, Velvet Shoes by Elinor Wylie, Notes from the back porch by Donna M. Swajeski. Heartline advertisements, photograph of Tasha's Thanksgiving dinner table and art reproductions. Excerpt from *The Vicar of Wakefield* by Oliver Goldsmith.

_____. 2:1 January/February 1998. 22 pp. in wrapper, as above.
Articles by/about Knitting folk socks, Delectable mountains [quilt] by Joan Donaldson, Vintage tea linens: the care of your tea finery, Excerpts from a gardener's journal by Amelia Stauffer: On how to maintain beautiful house plants during the winter, A Valentine to dogs, Puppy love, The care of your dog, Pembroke Welsh corgis, What would Valentine's be without flowers?, The recipe file

Valentine candy treats, The Cinderella myth by Gary Overmann mistakenly cites 'Pierre' Perrault for Charles Perrault, The "Art of Living" as experienced by our readers by Lenore Rodeheffer "Charlie McCarthy," A Valentine wreath, From The Secret Garden by Isabelle Hadley, Notes from the back porch by Donna M. Swajeski. Classified advertisements, photographs and art reproductions. Excerpt from *Vanity Fair* by William Makepeace Thackeray. The back cover reproduces 'February' from *A Time to Keep*, but incorrectly attributes it to *All for Love*.

————. 2:2 March/April 1998. 22 pp. in wrapper, as above.
Articles by/about: Maple sugaring by Joan Donaldson, Jewels of Spring, Margutis and Pysanka eggs, A cozy tea room, Excerpts from a gardener's journal by Amelia Stauffer; Dog of the Month: Molly, a Bernese Mountain therapy dog belonging to John and Joan Harkins of Holland, Pa., Easter memories by Colonel Thomas Tudor, Making beeswax candlesby K. L. Epperly, A country kitchen, How to make flower petal note paper, The genius of Arthur Rackham by Gary Overmann, The recipe file, chocolate lover's dream, The "Art of Living" as experienced by our readers: Joyce Maloney, A Garden for all Seasons, From the Secret Garden by Isabelle Hadley, Notes from the back porch by Donna M. Swajeski. Classified advertisements, photographs and art reproductions. Excerpt from *Vanity Fair* by Thackeray.

Tasha Tudor's Corgi Cottage Industries. http://www.richmond.net/tashatudor/ Last modified May 21, 1997. Web site.
"It is with enourmous pleasure that I welcome you to Corgi Cottage Industries's first Web Site! We have enjoyed great success thanks to all my nice fans and we're endlessly grateful to everyone for their kind encouragement and support. . . . With the coming of Spring . . . I am currently working on a new edition of The Night Before Christmas . . ." Several pages advertising items for sale.

————. http://www.tashatudor.com/ Last modified December 12, 1997 [and unchanged 7/3/98]. Web site.
"It is with enourmous pleasure that I welcome you to Corgi Cottage Industries's Webs [*sic*] Site! . . . With the onset of Winter . . . I am almost finished with a new edition of The Night Before Christmas and am quite plesed with the illustrations. They are very different from any of my previous work . . ." Several pages advertising items for sale. Images of cards and prints for sale are dated June 14, 1997 and September 2, 1997. Included in the sub-age "Tasha's Bibliography": "*…We welcome you to the timeless art and private world of Tasha Tudor…*"

Time. 83:4 January 24, 1964.
"**Modern Living, Morals: The Second Sexual Revolution.**" Pages 1, 54-59 and cover. *Time*'s six-page commentary on the changed place of sex in contemporary American society and especially changes since 1920. Cover painting and nine photographs including Marilyn Monroe as 'Symbol,' For Eros, a "meaningful relationship;" and Nell Dorr's famous photograph of Tudor nursing labeled 'Reality,' From commitment, reverence and joy.

The Times. Monday May 18, 1987. Gettysburg, Pa.
"**She shares her gifts with others,**" by Janet M. Williams. Page number missing. 4″ review of Tudor's engagement at the Dover (Pa.) Intermediate School the previous Saturday. One photograph of Tudor at easel.

The Times Record. Saturday, December 24, 1977. Brunswick, Me.
"**Take Joy! A traditional Christmas,**" by Jeanette K. Cakouros. Page 1+. 39″ article about the John and Peggy Chapman family of Day's Ferry, Woolrich, Maine. Most of the discussion is of Preparing Christmas foods in the beehive oven and on the hearth of the family's ca. 1777 home built by Jonathan Preble. Indicates a Tudor friendship begun when "Peggy Chapman's brother and Mrs. Tudor's son were fellow college students." The family emulates Tudor's life style in many

ways, and actually owns two corgis which were formerly Tudor's – Farley and Corey of *Corgiville Fair* dedication fame. Five photographs of house and family.

Tudor Book Shop & Café. Wilkes-Barre, Pa. http://www.wilkes-barre.org/news/dec97/small.htm [*extant as of March 4, 1998*]
Small Business Concerns: A message. . . "Now that our Tasha Tudor event has taken place, I want to thank the Chamber for their support. We thought you might like to know that both Tasha Tudor Teas were sold out four weeks prior to the event. Because of space constraints, we could only sell 450 tickets. Interestingly, almost half of the two groups of 225 attending the e two teas were from out of town. Therefore, we believe that this benefitted [*sic*] downtown businesses. In addition, as a result of the tea, over $1,000 was donated to both the Osterhout Free Library and the Wyoming historical and Geological Society. We, of course, were extremely pleased with the book sales, the accompanying publicity, and the wonderful support from everyone who worked on and attended the event. It was one of the most exciting programs that we have put together in the 20 year history of the book shop. – Lynn Gonchar"

The Union Leader. Monday, September 1992. Manchester, N.H.
"Old Books Are Items of Treasure at This Fair," by Dale Vincent. Page number missing. 16″ article about the New Hampshire Antiquarian Book Fair held in Concord the previous day. Discusses Cellar Door Books, John Hare and the shop's Tasha Tudor specialty. Photograph of Hare and Joyce Apgar of West Sand Lake, N.Y.

Vermont Life. 48:2 Winter 1993. 80 pp. in wrapper. The State of Vermont, 6 Baldwin Street, Montpelier, VT 05602
"Vermont foods, Cooking in Tasha Tudor's World" by Andrea Chesman. Photographed by Richard W. Brown, pages 58-61. A full-page photograph of Tudor braiding onions, and receipts for macaroni and cheese, chocolate cookies and Robie's blueberry muffins, from Robie Mock, Webster, N.H.

_____. Another printing. This cover has four red article titles printed on the front cover.

Vermont Magazine. 3:6 November/December 1991. 96 pp. in wrapper. North Country Publishing, L.P., 14 School Street, Bristol, VT. 05443
"Tasha Tudor's Secret Garden, a conversation with the sorceress of Corgiville," by Julie Kirgo, pp. [36]-40, 67-70. Photos by James Gipe. The article includes two photographs of Tudor, one of her house, and two advertisements for her books and cards. She recounts how the Jenny Wren Press came to be, its projects and its mailing list of 40,000 names.

Victoria. 3:3 June 1989. 128 pp. in wrapper. The Hearst Corporation, 959 Eighth Avenue, New York, NY.
"Children's Corner, Tasha Tudor—By "Sparrow Post,"" page 36. Advertises the *Mouse Mills Catalog for Spring, The Bouquet* and *The Jenny Wren Book of Valentines* all from the Jenny Wren Press. " . . . Jenny Wren, who, at the urging of Tasha's dear friend Beth Mathers, has agreed to go back to press . . . "   Illustrations of the Mouse Mills catalog and the print *Mother and Child in Tasha's Garden.*

_____. 3:8 December 1989. 128 pp. in wrapper. The Hearst Corporation, 224 W. 57th St., New York, NY. 10019
"With Tasha Tudor, The advent of Christmas," pp. [74-85]. Photographs Toshi Otsuki. Fifteen photographs of Tudor's house and grounds at Christmas, and one of 'Laura in the Snow.' With advertisements for various Jenny Wren Press items, and *the Tasha Tudor Fan Club Newsletter* from Elaine's Upper Story.

_____. 4:8 August 1990. 128 pp. in wrapper

"At Tasha Tudor's, A peaceable kingdom," by Mary Durant, pp. 70-[81], 126. Photography by Toshi Otsuki.   Twenty-five stunning photographs of Tudor's gardens and animals.   Page 126 refers order for Little Rose 'poster' from the Jenny Wren Press.   The print is not pictured and the article on page 79 incorrectly refers to Tudor's first book as *Pumpkin Sunshine*.

_____. 6:9 September 1992. 128 pp. in wrapper

"Tasha Tudor, "I think I've done a good job of life …"," photographs by Richard Brown, pp. 82-89, 126. Six photographs of Tudor, one of her bookshelf and two paintings. The ordering information on page 126 advertises *The Private World of Tasha Tudor*, $15 extra for an autographed copy.

_____. 7:5 May 1993. 116 pp. in wrapper.

"Tasha Tudor: You must see my Pinks this year," by Tovah Martin, pp. 84-87, 114. Photography by Toshi Otsuki.   Twelve photographs of Tudor's gardens.

_____. 8:9 September 1994.

" Tasha Tudor's September garden," by Tovah Martin. Pages 98-[101]. Reveries of putting the gardens to bed for the winter. "Tasha's house looks as if it always commanded the crest of her hill, and that is just the impression Tasha wants to convey . . . I am crazy about potatoes—it must be my Irish ancestry . . . "   Seven photographs, two drawings.

_____. 9:3 March 1995.

"A Special Invitation To Our Readers," by Claire Whitcomb. Page 16. An invitation for readers to send a SASE requesting tickets to an April 1, noon to 2 p.m., Tudor appearance at Bloomingdale's, 59th and 3rd Avenue, NYC. A ticket for one adult and two children will be sent by return mail. "Tasha is currently at work on "Corgiville Kidnapping" . . . Attendees will receive a *Victoria* gift, which will include a signed copy of one of Tasha Tudor's children's books." Maria Genvesi subsequently sent a letter to those who would not receive tickets with a copy of the single column and this message: "Due to an overwhelming response, we regret that we are unable to accommodate all of our readers. We have chosen attendees on a first come, first serve basis . . . We invite you to attend a special book signing by Tasha Tudor at 3:00 p.m. in the Children's Department."

_____. 9:7 July 1995. 116 pp. in wrapper. The Hearst Corporation, 959 Eighth Avenue, New York, NY.

"Along the garden path, From Tasha Tudor's Garden Garlands of a Summer Day," adapted from "Tasha Tudor's Garden." Text by Tovah Martin,. Photography by Richard Brown. Pp. 38-[39]. Three paragraphs, three Brown photographs, one small Tudor illustration, floral garlands and wreaths.

_____. 9:10 October 1995.

"Tasha Tudor Celebrates Heirloom Crafts," adapted from "Tasha Tudor's Heirloom Crafts." Text by Tovah Martin. Photography by Richard Brown. Pp. [98-99] 100 [101]. Ten paragraphs of text and nine Brown photographs complemented by one Tudor painting.

_____. 9:11 November 1995.

"Tasha in Toyland [rule] Join Tasha Tudor in New York – a special offer to Victoria readers,"   page 18. Two paragraphs announcing Tudor's appearance at the Metropolitan Art & Antiques Children's Book and Antique Toy Fair, December 1 -3, 1995.

_____. 10:1 January 1996.

"Reader to Reader, A Special Invitation to Our Readers. Victoria Launches "Reader to Reader" Newsletter," page 17.   This advertisement for a further Victoria venture features two small photographs of Tasha Tudor at Bloomingdale's, New York City.

_____. 10:4 April 1996. 120 pp. in wrapper.
"Dear Friends, Your visit to Tasha Tudor's Garden," by Nancy Lindemeyer, editor in chief, page 10. Five paragraphs and one photograph of Tudor painting in her garden. Lindemeyer announces Tudor to be Artist-In-Residence at Victoria magazine for 1996.

_____. 10:5 May 1996. 128 pp. in wrapper.
"Artist in Residence, a Victoria Exclusive, Spring Comes to Tasha Tudor's Garden," page 46-47, 114. Three paragraphs and two photographs of Tudor's 'Spring' painting, and one of Tudor painting by her garden. Two more photographs of the print and ordering information ($79 framed or $19.95 unframed) appear on page 114.

_____. 10:7 July 1996. 116 pp. in wrapper.
"Artist in Residence, Gathering Wild Strawberries, A Tasha Tudor print just for you," pages 26-27, 99. Five paragraphs and two photographs of Tudor's 'Summer' print. The print is pictured again as well as 'Spring' with the order form on page 99.

_____. 10:8 August 1996. 120 pp. in wrapper
"Artist in Residence, Tasha Tudor: onward & Upward," by Katrina de Leon, Starr Ockenga, *et alia*. Pages 34-35. An 'advertorial' shows Tudor and 7 of her paintings. "Less than one year old, Corgi Cottage Industries is artist Tasha Tudor's latest venture, offering note cards and prints in her beguiling style. . ."

_____. 10:9 September 1996. 120 pp. in wrapper.
"Artist in Residence, Tasha Tudor's Vision of Fall," page 102-103, with order blank. Three paragraphs and three photographs of Tudor's 'Spring,' 'Summer' and 'Autumn' prints.

_____. 10:10 October 1996. 116 pp. in wrapper
"Our Private Collection, Victoria Books, Cassettes, and Tasha Tudor Prints," page 46. This advertisement includes only an order form for the three prints.

_____. 10:11 November 1996. 116 pp. in wrapper
"Artist in Residence, Christmas comes to Corgi Cottage," pages 98-99. Three paragraphs and five photographs, one of Tudor in her doorway and an order form for the four prints. 'Winter' is now included.

_____. 10:12 December 1996. 128 pp. in wrapper
"Our Private Collection, At Christmas, We've got you on our list," by Nicole Esposit and Luciana Pampalone. Pages 26-27, 121. Five paragraphs and three photographs of Tudor in her doorway (as above), her 'Winter' print and a cookie tin painted with the same image. Various Christmas gifts: tin, hollies and ginger cake. Order form on page 121.

_____. 11:1 January 1997. 116 pp. in wrapper
"Our Private Collection, Victoria gifts for you and your loved ones," page 110. This advertisement includes only an order form for the four prints and cookie tin.

_____. 11:2 February 1997. 120 pp. in wrapper
"Our Private Collection, Books and Guides, Prints and More," page 110. This advertisement includes only an order form for the four prints.

_____. 11:3 March 1997. 116 pp. in wrapper
"Our Private Collection, Victoria Books, Cassettes, and Scarf, Plus Tasha Tudor Prints," page 112. This advertisement includes only an order form for the four prints.

_____. 11:4 April 1997. 116 pp. in wrapper
"Our Private Collection, A Year With Tasha Tudor," page 106, 111. Pictures and describes the four prints painted in 1996 for Victoria. Includes a mailing address for Corgi Cottage Industries. Order form on page 111 lists the set of 4 at $65 or framed for $255.

_____. 11:5 May 1997. 120 pp. in wrapper
"Our Private Collection, Victoria Books, a Blue Rose, And Artist-in-Residence Prints," page 115. This advertisement includes only an order form for the four prints.

_____. 11:6 June 1997. 120 pp. in wrapper
"Our Private Collection, Victoria Books, Cassettes, And Artist-in-Residence Prints," page 112. This advertisement includes only an order form for the four prints.

_____. 11:7 July 1997. 116 pp. in wrapper, plus extra wrapper announcing *At Home With Roses.*
"Our Private Collection, Victoria Books, a Pique Rose, And Artist-in-Residence Prints," page 104. This advertisement includes only an order form for the four prints.

Washington Post. Unknown date.
"Seventeen carols so well chosen that it's | difficult to imagine that anyone's favorite | is missing." Quoted on dust jacket of *Tasha Tudor's Old-Fashioned Gifts.*

_____. ca. 1990. Reviews WonderWorks *the Secret Garden.*

_____. March 7, 1997.
"Stepping into an artist's life," by Mary Quattlebaum. Page WW, 52;1 Discusses Tudor's life style and the Colonial Williamsburg exhibit.

"Welcome to the Tasha Tudor Home Page!" http://opelka.com/~mvo/tasha1.html "The only officially licensed webpage dedicated to America's author-illustrator and master gardener, Tasha Tudor. Tasha would like to extend a special welcome to you! This website was created just for her Japanese fans. . . At 82, Tasha's also a well respected . . . Tasha Tudor welcomes your letters. (Written in English, please.) . . . "

The site includes photographs of Tudor and her house, porch, kitchen, best parlor, Meet the O'Hare family, and 13 pieces of recent art. Undated, documented February 20, 1997.

Wheaton Quarterly. Summer 1996. 32 pp. in wrapper. Wheaton College, Norton, MA 02766
"Course made good. She majored in classics. She dodged geometry and mathematics. So how did Marjorie Wolff '34 become America's only female naval architect?" by Brian Kologe, pages [12]-16. Discusses the design career of Starling Burgess' last wife. "In March of 1945, Marjorie and her mentor married. . . In the midst of this work Burgess died suddenly of a heart attack in 1947."

The Wichita Eagle-Beacon. Wednesday December 30, 1981.
"Illustrator Lives in 19th Century," by Brenda W. Rotzoll, United Press International. Page 12B. Interviewed for her Indianapolis Children's Museum appearance, Tudor reports still reading two hours a day after tea – just now it's Twain's *Roughing It.* Mentions Melissa Crane reading racy French novels.

Wilson Library Bulletin. 65:3. November 1990.
"A Brighter Garden," reviewed by Cathi MacRae. Page 128.

Wooden Boat. No. 37 November/December 1980. 144 pp. in wrapper. Wooden Boat Publications, Inc., P.O. Box 78, Brooklin, ME 04616

"The History of Small Yacht Design, Part I, SCHEMER and the skimming dishes," by Russell Clark, pages [42]-49. A paragraph of page 47 has Edward Burgess' recollections of yachting near Salem, MA, in the 1870s. Burgess was Tudor's father's father.

_____. No.46 May/June 1982. [168] pp. in wrapper

"A Farewell to Bror Tamm," by Llewellyn Howland III, pages 30-40. Tamm (1890-1981) a Dorchester, MA, yacht carpenter who reported to George Lawley and Son boat yard the morning the Titanic was reported sunk. Page 33 discusses Edward Burgess' designs of the 1880s. Page 35: William Starling Burgess [Tudor's father and namesake] , 1879-1947, whose younger brother Charles P. was named after Frank Paine's father, was the firm's [Burgess, Swasey and Paine] ranking member in reputation and experience. Discusses Herreschoff, photographs of Charles Franics Adams and Frank Paine.

_____. No. 56 January/February 1984. 160 pp. in wrapper.

"L. Frances Herreschoff, Part II," by Philip C. Bolger, pages 38-47. A paragraph of page 47: L. Frances Herreschoff was a proud man who considered that he had done some worthwhile things in his time; but he did not set himself above, or even as the equal, of such men as Starling Burgess and Charles E. Nicholson. I would place him much higher… .

_____. No. 65 July/August 1985. 160 pp. in wrapper.

"Varua, soul of the southern sea," by Timothy Mickleburgh, pages [44]-50. William Albert Robinson, for his 'dream ship',…began to look for a designer to tun his ideas into working drawings. Several were considered . . . but the commission went to W. Starling Burgess, who had designed the racing fisherman schooners MAYFLOWER, COLUMBIA and PURITAN, and had more recently been co-designer , with Olin Stephens, of the J-boat RANGER.

_____. No. 68 February 1986. 152 pp. in wrapper.

"A decade of legendary 12s," by Michael Adams, photographs by Morris Rosenfeld and Sons, pages 40-47. In 1928, however, the design firm of Burgess, Rigg, and Morgan created a 12-meter design (as well as an 8-meter). . .The first six Burgess-designed 12s . . .

_____. No. 71 August 1986. 160 pp. in wrapper.

"The Burgess legacy, Part I, The Early Years" by Llewellyn Howland III , pages 52-59. With an infant picture of Starling Burgess on page 52, and a chart of the 'Principal yachts and commercial vessels designed by Edward Burgess.'

_____. No. 72 September/October 1986. 152 pp. in wrapper.

"The Burgess legacy, Part II, The first ventures of W. Starling Burgess Co." by Llewellyn Howland III , pages 44-52. With a 1901 picture of Starling Burgess on page 44, diagrams and photographs of boats.

_____. No. 73 November /December 1986. 152 pp. in wrapper with a catalog bound in.

"The Burgess legacy, Part III, The second most wonderful sport in the world" by Llewellyn Howland, III , pages 32-40. With a 1914 picture of Starling Burgess on page 32.

_____. No. 74 February 1987. 152 pp. in wrapper.

"The Burgess legacy, Part IV, Conclusion" by Llewellyn Howland III , pages 42-52. The most biographical of the series, this discusses Burgess' various marriages and his work with other designers such as Glenn Curtis and Buckminster Fuller.

_____. No. 93   March/April 1990. 176 pp. in wrapper

"Whipping the Whippet into shape, those repairs old boats often need" by Maynard Bray, pages 77-84. Last year the 82-year-old knockabout sloop WHIPPET was completely restored . . . WHIPPET is one of nine Winter Harbor 21-class sloops, seven of which (including WHIPPET) were built by Burgess & Packard of Marblehead, Massachusetts, in 1907 for the Winter Harbor (Maine) Yacht Club. The design was by Alphaeus Packard, a gifted designer who has worked for the Herreschoff Manufacturing Co., and who in 1907 was teamed up with W. Starling Burgess.

Yankee. 15:12 December 1951. Yankee Magazine, Dublin, NH.

"Enchanted Farmhouse," by Richard D. Estes, pages 37-40. The article discusses the McCready family enterprise "on a backroad farm, between Contoocook and Webster, N.H. . . the doll family, which has temporary quarters and a general store in two upstairs rooms . . . they put out a quarterly *Dolls Magazine*, illustrated by Tasha . . . Sparrow Post, other offices of which are located in England, Texas, and Milton, Mass. . . They have put on many [marionette] shows in the last five years, appeared at the Museum of Natural History in New York last November for Children's Book Week, at the invitation of the New York *Times*, and on television in Richmond, Va., last April . . . Nell Dorr present[ed] them with the stage . . . Tasha has illustrated an assortment of over 30 Christmas Cards printed by the Irene Dash Greeting Card Co., a subsidiary of the American Artists' Group." Five Dorr black and white photographs and 3 illustrations of cards by Tudor.

_____. 18:6 June 1954.

"Yankee visits Mother Goose: The Legend of Mother Goose," by Laurie Hillyer, pages [23]-32. The article discusses Mother Goose rhymes, speculates on the Boston original of 'Mother Goose' and includes five Nell Dorr photographs of Tudor and family, and one Tudor drawing of Old Mother Hubbard.

_____. 21:10. October 1957.

"Storybook Farm." Pages 38-41. Concentrates on the farm life as recorded in McCready's books and "the Ginger and Pickles Store, which is located at one end of the large farmhouse. . . open May 30th to December 20th, daily from nine to five . . . write for the Ginger and Pickles Store catalog which contains a map." Three Tudor drawings and four black and white photographs by Anthony Anable, Jr.

_____. 23:7. July 1959

"Ginger and Pickles Store - Doll Museum." Pages 38-41. Paid ad for the enterprise with hours posted and a picture of Violet mailing a letter by Sparrow Post.

The York Daily Record. Friday, May 8, 1987. York, Pa.

"Noted illustrator Tudor to visit," by Anne McCracken. Page number B_ missing. 9″ of text announce engagement at Dover Intermediate School, Dover, Pa. B&W reproduction of Little Miss Muffet from *Mother Goose.*

The York Dispatch. Thursday, April 2, 1987. York, Pa.

"Articles connected with the books of author Tasha Tudor are displayed by members of the Shiloh Garden Club, Yvonne Snyder, left, Program chairman, and Beth O'Hara, publicity co-chairman. The club will sponsor a talk by Ms. Tudor at 1 p.m. May 9 at Dover Intermediate School." Page number missing.

York Sunday News. April 12, 1987. York, Pa.

"Of goslings and Tasha Tudor" by Kathryn Frydenborg. Page 1. 22″ text discussed Tudor's lifestyle, history, buying geese in York, Pa., and a May 9 speaking engagement in Dover. Tickets are $6 for adults and $3 for children. Three photographs of Tudor.

_____. May 10, 1987 (?). York, Pa.
"Tasha Tudor delights crowd." Page number missing. 1″ text and a 4x5″ close-up photograph of Tudor at her Shiloh Garden Club appearance. 600 people attended.

_____. undated 1987. York, Pa.
"Visit a Success" by Ruth Jones, Director of Public Relations, York County Library System. Page number missing. Thanks the Shiloh Garden Club for donation to the Dover Area Community Library resulting from Tudor's May 9 speaking engagement.

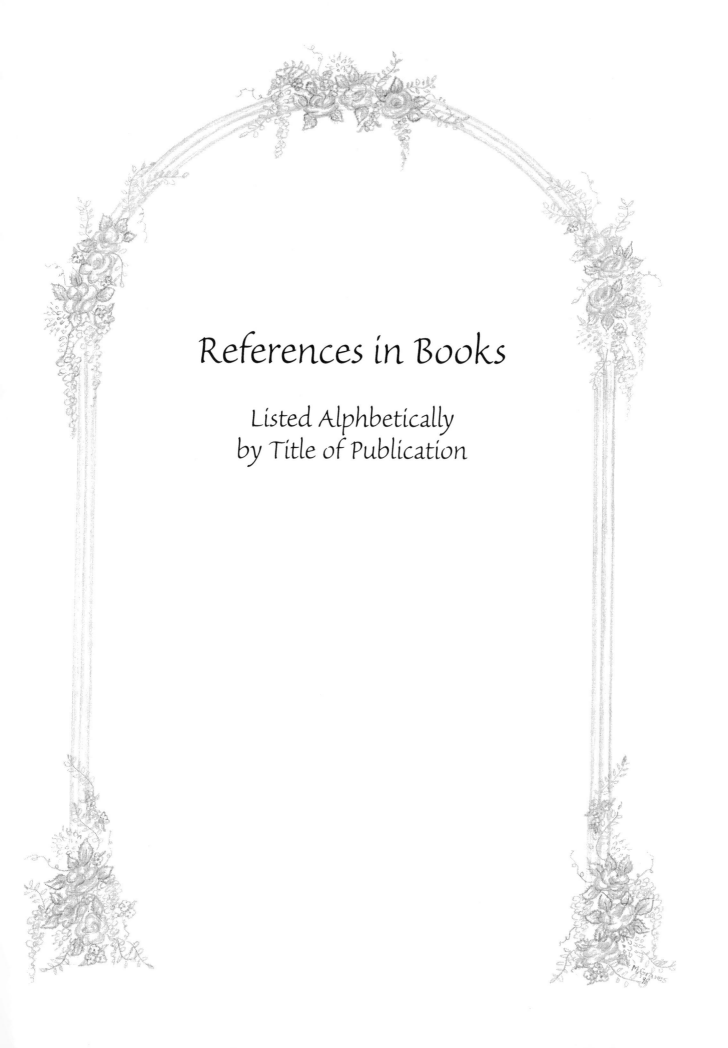

References in Books

Listed Alphbetically
by Title of Publication

A To Zoo Subject Access To Children's Picture Books, A Bibliographic Guide by Carolyn W. Lima and John A. Lima. 1993. 23 references to Tudor art and books, page 1143.

Best Books For Children Preschool Through Grade 6 by John Gillespie and Corinne Nadeseu. 1990. References (page 741) to *A is for Annabelle, The Dolls' Christmas, First Graces, First Prayers, 1 is One, Tasha Tudor's Sampler, A Time to Keep, Take Joy* and *Wings from the Wind.*

Children's Books And Their Creators. Anita Silvey, Editor. Boston and New York, Houghton Mifflin Company, 1995. 800 pp. Biographical information on hundreds of authors, each about a half-page long, 75 contributions from authors on their process and 175 illustrations. There are also genre entries, e.g. Sports stories, Picture books, Horror stories, etc. The entry on Tasha Tudor, pages 653-654, was written by Maryclare O'Donnell Himmel, a free-lance writer and reviewer.

Children's Literature From A To Z; A Guide For Parents And Teachers. Jon c. Stott. New York, McGraw-Hill Book Company, 1984. 318 +[1] pp. xx articles of varying length, a half page to three pages long. Mostly biographical, there are also discussions of genre and specific stories. Good scholarship by a Canadian children's literature professor. The entry on Tasha Tudor, pages 273-274, suggests relationships with Cooney/Hall's *Ox-Cart Man* and Blos' *A Gathering of Days.* Illustrations with some articles. Examined the paperback edition.

Children's Literature In The Elementary School by Charlotte S. Huck, Susan Hepler and Janet Hickman. 4th ed. New York, Holt, Rinehart and Winston, 1987.
College textbook in 13 chapters and 3 appendices. Twelve indexed references to Tudor, (42, 193, 387-8, 458, 460) are reading lists,
  - p. 114 "Tasha Tudor, Michael Hague, and Tomie de Paola have all created beautifully illustrated editions of this well-loved poem [*The Night Before Christmas*] for today's children."
  - p. 159 "The *Mother Goose* of Tasha Tudor is reminiscent of the work of Kate Greenaway. Her soft pastel pictures are quaint and charming; her characters, lovable. The costumes of the characters represent many periods: American colonial, pioneer, Kate Greenaway, and Elizabethan. Miniatures in flowered frames on the endpapers and title page add to the old-fashioned feeling of this book."
  - p. 165 "*A Is for Annabelle*, Delicate watercolors portray an old-fashioned doll with her different belongings representing difference letters."
  - p. 213 "Many [picture-book artists] do develop a recognizable personal style which may be identified by their preference for a particularly pictorial style of art, use of medium, even choice of content . . . The delicate old-fashioned style of Tasha Tudor's watercolors is as easily recognizable as the flowing, massive look of the watercolors of Warwick Hutton."
  - p. 407 "Both Tasha Tudor (192) nd Tomie de Paola (191) have created lovely old-fashioned picture-book editions of *The Night Before Christmas*."
  - p. 417 "Currently, some ten illustrated editions of *A Child's Garden of Verses* are in print. They range in interpretation from Tasha Tudor's (238) quaint pastel pictures that portray Stevenson as a young child to Brian Wildsmith's (239) edition that is a brilliant kaleidoscope of color."

_____. by Charlotte S. Huck, Susan Hepler, Janet Hickman and Barbara Z. Kiefer. 6th ed. Madison, Wi., Brown & Benchmark, 1997.
Revision of the college textbook in 14 chapters and 3 appendices. Six indexed references to Tudor, (42, 193, 387-8, 458, 460) are reading lists,
  - p. 98 As 114, above.
  - p. 153 "*Mother Goose* . . . Small, soft pastel pictures are quaint and charmingly reminiscent of the work of Kate Greenaway."
  - p. 159 As 165, above.
  - p. 217 As 213, above.

p. 400 "The most popular narrative poem in this country is Clement Moore's *The Night Before Christmas* (or *A Visit from St. Nicholas*). Every artist from Grandma Moses to Tasha Tudor to Tome de Paola and Wendy Watson has illustrated this Christmas story. Presently there are nearly forty editions of *The Night Before Christmas*.

p. 407 "Currently, some eighteen illustrated editions of *A Child's Garden of Verses* are in print. They range in interpretation from Tasha Tudor's quaint pastels, which portray Stevenson as a young child, to Brian Wildsmith's edition, a brilliant kaleidoscope of color."

Classics For Young Readers, Preschool Through Young Adult. Recommended and compiled by Stephanie Loer, Children's Book Editor, The Boston Globe. Illustrations by Linda Storm. Published by The Boston Globe, 1986. [32] pp. including ivory wrapper. A short essay introduces a title list of 209 'classic' books including on page [19] The Secret Garden by Frances Hodgson Burnett, illust. by Tasha Tudor (Lippincott).

Contemporary Authors. 81-84:572-573. Detroit, Gale Research Co., 1979
"**Tudor, Tasha 1915- .**" One page biography including Personal, Career, Writings, Sidelights, Biographical/Critical Sources.

A Goodly Heritage | *Children's Literature In* | *New England* | *1850-1950* || An exhibition from | the Alice M. Jordan Collection | of the Boston Public Library in observance | of the Year of the Young Readder | May 1989 | [printer's decorative flower] || BOSTON | BOSTON PUBLIC LIBRARY • 1989.
pp. 20-23: "Perhaps the most striking innovation of the period [1920-1950] was the emergence of the picture story book and the reissue of old favorites with new color illustrations by well-known artists. The establishment in 1938 of the Randolph Caldecott Medal for the most distinguished American picture book recognized the independent stature of the picture story book as a genre. Dr. Seuss, born Theodor Geisel in Springfield, Massachusetts, combined humor, fantasy, and learning in a long list of titles beginning in 1937 with *And to Think I Saw It on Mulberry Street*. Tasha Tudor brought a different style and tone to her picture books, as did C.W. Anderson in the *Billy and Blaze* series. It comes as something of a surprise that the enduring *Goodnight Moon* first appeared more than 40 years ago, authored by Margaret Wise Brown, a summer resident of Vinalhaven, Maine. Also in the 1940s two author-illustrators adorned the New England scene with books still in print and in demand. Virginia Lee Burton published *The Little House*, a testament to her early awareness of environmental concerns. And what exhibit of the goodly heritage of New England children's books from 1850 to 1950 could fail to include Robert McCloskey's *Make Way for Ducklings*.

Further, a chronology of children's publishing, pp. 23-35, includes as the 1938 entry: Tasha Tudor. Pumpkin Moonshine. Enlg. Ed. N.Y.: Henry Z. Walck, 1962.

Illustrators Of Children's Books, 1744-1945, compiled by Bertha E. Mahony and others. Boston, Horn Book, 1945.

_____, 1946-1956, compiled by B.M. Miller and others. Boston, Horn Book,. 1958.

_____, 1957-1966, compiled by Lee Kingman and others. Boston, Horn Book, 1968.

The Junior Book Of Authors. Second edition, revised. Edited by Stanley J. Kunitz and Howard Haycraft. New York, H. W. Wilson, 1951.
"**Tasha Tudor,**" autobiographical sketch, pages 288-289. "Uncle Adam . . . had previously taught our elder brothers . . . When I was twelve my family bought a place in Connecticut . . . my winters were spent at Spring Hill School in Litchfield, Connecticut, and in Boston . . . McCready . . . seriously started me on my career as an illustrator . . . " Tudor recalls showing illustrations to publishers in New York and Boston to no avail. But, having created *Pumpkin Moonshine*, had it

accepted for publication. "So Sylvie Ann did not receive her gift that Christmas, but only a late one, when the book came out . . . live with my husband and three children . . . pictures for the books are made . . . mostly due to the patience and help of a very understanding and delightful husband."

The New York Times Parent's Guide To The Best Books For Children. Revised and Updated. EDEN ROSS LIPSON. Times Books, Random House, 1991.
Among the 1033 entries are three by Tudor with one illustration. Item 322: *A Child's Garden of Verses* . . . Cloth: Checkerboard, 1981. ". . . illustrated in a sweet and rosy way. Artists who have taken difference approaches include Michael Foreman, Erik Blegvad, Jesse W. Smith, and Brian Wildsmith. Item 841: *A Little Princess*, Cloth: Lippincott/HarperCollins, Paper: Harper Trophy, 1963 ". . . For many years this was the only edition available in the United States. But, as with all the other Burnett novels, the copyright has expired and numerous editions in hard- and softcover have appeared. Avoid clumsy and unnecessary abridgments. . ." Item 909:
The Secret Garden, " . . . For many years this pretty [Tudor] edition was the only one available; however, the copyright on Burnett's work expired in 1987 and nearly a dozen illustrated editions appeared in both hard and soft cover. They all show essentially the same scenes in the same fashion, emphasizing the Victorian setting. Choose whichever version appeals, but do not choose one with an abridged text. . ." The illustration is the newer cover image of Mary exiting the garden gate.

Something About The Author. 20: 184-188. Detroit, Gale Research Co., **DATE ?**
"Tudor, Tasha." Much the same information as in *Contemporary Authors*, plus Hobbies and Other Interests, and a longer bibliography. Lists Religion as "Stillwater," and Residence, Marlboro, Vt. One photograph of Tudor, five illustrations from books.

Something About The Author: Facts & Pictures About Authors & Illustrations Of Books For Young People. 69: 195-199. Edited by Donna Olendorf. Detroit, Gale Research Co., 1992.
"Tudor, Tasha." A revised and longer bibliography. Bill Finney's photograph of Tudor, illustrations from *Mother Goose* and *The Night Before Christmas*. And extensive bibliography ends with *Deer in the Hollow* and contains a number of errors including the indication that Tudor illustrated *Deer in the Hollow*.

Related Books

None of these titles mention Tudor directly, although photographs of her kitchen do appear in the first. The others are related by subject and are contemporaneous from Tudor's publishers. Books that *refer* to Tudor's lifestyle, no matter how fleetingly, are included in the main body of the book, e.g. *Dolls of Three Centuries, The Family of Man.*

American Country Folk Crafts: 50 Country Craft Projects for Decorating Your Home. <u>Carol Endler</u>
<u>Sterbenz</u>, photography by Beth Galton. New York, Harry N. Abrams, Inc. [1987] 174pp.

A discussion of The Kitchen (29) describes an "accessible kitchen in a Massachusetts barn." The
kitchen pictured on page [28] and described on 29-30, 35 is actually Tudor's Marlboro, Vermont,
home. Compare with *The Private World of Tasha Tudor*, page 105. Page 42 also shows a
cupboard demonstrating Swedish wall painting, Linda Allen's initials and date [19]80. Compare
with *Private World . . .* pp. [126-127]. Directory of Craftsmen, pp. 157-165, lists Boxes by Linda
Allen, Rt#4, Box 205, West Brattleboro, Vt. on page 158; Needlework, and Painted Decoration,
Linda Allen, page 160. The author acknowledges, page 167, behind the scenes assistance of
several people including Cynthia Beneduce, of Cynthia Beneduce Antiques, New York, N.Y.
Beneduce is the daughter of Tudor's editor Ann Beneduce.

The Doll | *In The Window* | BY | PAMELA BIANCO | [small red wooden doll] | Oxford

University Press | NEW YORK . 1953 [Copyright 1953 | OXFORD UNIVERSITY PRESS | PRINTED
IN THE UNITED STATES OF AMERICA] For | **Eunice Blake**, page [5].

An association item is dedicated to Eunice Blake, Tudor's editor at Oxford University Press. The book
is bound in blue cloth and measures 7 1/8 x 7 1/8". The cover design, and cover type are similar to *The
Dolls' Christmas*. Have not examined a dust jacket. It would seem that Eunice Blake inspired doll
stories in writers/illustrators. Bianco is the daugther of Captain Francesco and Margery Williams
Bianco, author of *The Velveteen Rabbit*.

Copyright registration A 106599 granted to Oxford University Press, Inc., 114 Fifth Ave., N.Y. 11,
N.Y. W. S. Gherton [illegible], agent for the claimant, swears on Sept. 11, 1953:

THE DOLL IN THE WINDOW, by Pamela Bianco, 143 Waverly Place, N.Y., N.Y., a U.S.
citizen, born in 1905, was published Sept. 10, 1953. The book was printed by Kellogg and
Bulkeley Company, Hartford, Ct. from type set by The Composing Room, N.Y., N.Y., and
bound by H. Wolff Book Manufacturing Co., N.Y., N.Y. Application and two deposit copies
were received at LC Sept. 15, 1953.

The Dolls' House || By Rumer Godden | WITH PICTURES BY DANA SAINTSBURY || NEW YORK |

The Viking Press | 1948. [COPYRIGHT 1947 BY RUMER GODDEN | PUBLISHED BY THE VIKING PRESS IN
AUGUST 1948 | SECOND PRINTING NOVEMBER 1948 || PRINTED IN THE UNITED STATES OF AMERICA | BY VAIL-
BALLOU PRESS, INC., BINGHAMTON, N.Y.] 125 [126-128] pp.

COVER: Yellow cloth cover, red stamping.

DUST JACKET: Dj price $2.50.

ILLUSTRATIONS: There are five full page color illustrations: (Tottie standing in the doorway of a
doll house) on the front cover; "She liked to think of the tree of whose wood she was made,"
frontispiece and also reproduced on the jacket back (Tottie in front of a tree with three lavender
birds);""I don't think we shall ever have a house, " said Mr. Plantaganet" (four dolls and dog on
round rug in front of three houses marked FOR SALE) facing page 16; "On the center of one of
the long tables with the sampler behind her," (three dolls and sampler on display) facing page 64;
"She sat by the lamp and saw the shadow of the roses," (doll on sofa with table, lamp, roses and
picture on wall).

CONTENTS: Page [1] half-title; frontispiece tipped in; page [5] FOR | *Janaki Paula Mary Foster* |
WITH LOVE; page [7] Illustrations, page [9] half-title.

OTHER: This is the edition with Saintsbury illustrations which preceded the Tudor version. Instructive for comparison of the two illustrators' treatment of the same subject.

[A victor's wreath of flowers tied with a purple ribbon frames the title page, headed by an angel playing a lute] || FIRST CAROLS || *illustrated by* | BRENDA MEREDITH SEYMOUR || New York | Henry Z. Walck, Inc. | 1968. [Copyright © 1967 Lutterworth Press || Acknowledgments || The Publishers wish to make acknowledgement | to the following for permission to include | carols of which they control the copyright: | Oxford University Press ("Little Jesus, sweetly | sleep" and "Unto us a Boy is born" from the | *Oxford Book of Carols*); and Miss D. E. Collins ("How Far is it to Bethlehem?"). ||Library of Congress Catalog Card Number: || 68-13488 || All rights reserved. || PRINTED IN THE NETHERLANDS]

PAGINATION: [1-3] 4-11 [12] 13-27 [28] 29-40, plus endpapers.

COVER: Yellow paper over boards, homespun weave imprint. Gilt stamping, on front: FIRST | CAROLS. Spine: FIRST CAROLS   SEYMOUR   WALCK. Full-Color endpapers feature a different cherubic angel on the verso and recto, repeated at rear.

DUST JACKET: Butterscotch jacket with white endpapers. Front features an oval of flowers, lute and birds encircling FIRST CAROLS || *Illustrated by* | BRENDA MEREDITH | SEYMOUR. Spine: SEYMOUR FIRST CAROLS   Walck. Front flap: FIRST CAROLS || *Illustrated by* | BRENDA MEREDITH | SEYMOUR || This collection of best-loved | carols, which tell of the birth | of Jesus, of the star that shone | over Bethlehem, and of the | coming of the shepherds and | the Wise Men, will bring | pleasure to all young children. | Simple, familiar words and | appealing pictures convey the | meaning and the spirit of | Christmas. | This is a companion volume | to *First Hymns*, also illustrated | by Brenda Meredith Seymour. || Henry Z. Walck, Inc. 50-100. [Have not examined a copy with corners intact.]   Back flap: FIRST HYMNS || *Illustrated by* | BRENDA MEREDITH | SEYMOUR || Favorite hymns of faith, hope, | love and thankfulness have | been collected together in this | little book. Their simple lan- | guage will appeal to all small | children and will enable them | to join in singing God's | praises. || Printed in the Netherlands

ILLUSTRATIONS: Seymour's style is much like Tudor's and would explain the publisher's reason for teaming her two books - *First Hymns* and *First Carols* - with Tudor's *First Prayers, First Graces* and *More Prayers*. Both artists include birds, flowers and innocent children in their motifs. And the publishers employ the same techniques in all five books, i.e. full-color illustrations backed by black and white.

OTHER: This book is erroneously attributed to Tudor on the back flap of Lutterworth's *Take Joy!* Seymour's *First Hymns* is described with the three Tudor books which Lutterworth boxed as a unit and sold under the title *A Treasury of First Books*, q.v.

The | SECRET | GARDEN [green ink] | [rose branch] | *Adapted from the original novel by* | FRANCES HODGSON BURNETT || *Illustrations by* | MARY COLLIER || [flame and water logo] HARPERCOLLINS*PUBLISHERS* || Text copyright © 1998 by HarperCollins Publishers • Text adapted by Alix Reid from *The Secret Garden* by Frances Hodgson Burnett • Illustrations copyright © 1998 by | Mary Collier • All rights reserved. Printed in the U.S.A. • Library of Congress Cataloging-in-Publication Data • The secret garden / adapted from the original novel by | Frances Hodgson Burnett ; illustrations by Mary Collier.   • p. cm. • Summary: In this abridged adaptation of the classic novel, a lonely orphan discovers the | wonders of a mysterious garden and befriends her invalid cousin. • ISBN 0-06-027853-6 • [I. Orphans—Fiction. 2. Gardens—Fiction. 3. Physically handicapped—Fiction.] | I. Collier, Mary, date, ill. II. Burnett, Frances hodgson, 1849–1924. Secret garden. • PZ7.S4475 1998 • 97-20757 • [E]-dc21 • CIP • AC • Typography by Alicia Mikles [black]

PAGINATION: [32] pages in two signatures plus rose free end papers. 11 ¼ x 8 5/8″

COVER: Speckled apple green half-paper over boards, overlaps dark green cloth spine. Spine stamped in green-gold foil: BURNETT/COLLIER   **THE SECRET GARDEN**   [flame and water logo] Title as on title page and dust jacket, blind stamped into front cover. Deep rose endpapers.

DUST JACKET: <u>All-over mint green</u>, redesigned . The central motif of Mary trying the lock of the garden gate is now encircled within the same oval of rose briers and pink roses, as in entry S56, and here attributed to Mary Collier. At bottom, *Adapted from the original novel by* FRANCES HODGSON BURNETT | [rose bud] *Illustrations by* MARY COLLIER [rose bud]. Spine: BURNETT/COLLIER [black]   THE SECRET GARDEN [green]   [flame and water logo, black]. Back: [color vignette of robin and key in garden, within the rose oval. A pink rectangle at the bottom center is imprinted: **US $12.95 / $18.50 CAN** || ISBN 0-06-027853-6 || 51295 [over smaller right of two bar codes] Δ | 9 780060 278533 [beneath larger left of two bar codes]. Front flap, a white panel within double black line border and this text (initial and bottom line in green, rest in black) similar to S56: Ages 4-8 || 𝒲hen orphaned | Mary Lennox, lonely and | sad, comes to live at her | uncle's great, empty house, | she has nothing to do and | no one to play with. Then a | friendly robin shows her the | way to a mysterious garden, | that has been locked up and | forgotten for years. Mary is | determined to bring the | secret garden back to life and, | along the way, finds good | friends and discovers the | magic of making things grow. ¶ Francis hodgson Burnett's THE SECRET GARDEN has | been loved by generations | of chidlren since its first | PUBLICATION IN 1912. Now, | for the first time, young | readers can unlock the | mystery of the secret garden | with this very special picture | book, adapted from Burnett's | classic work. Mary Collier's | rich, glorious paintings, | inspired by the original | novel, bring all the magic | and wonder of the secret | garden flowingly to life. || [flame and water logo] HarperCollins*Publishers*. Back flap, a white panel within a double black line: *Frances Hodgson Burnett* [green] | was a born storyteller. | Growing up in Manchester, | England, she found her | greatest pleasure in making | up stories and acting | them out, using her dolls as | characters. Until her death in | 1924 she wrote constantly, | producing more than forty | books, including the much | beloved A LITTLE PRINCESS. || *Mary Collier* [green] has loved to | draw since she was a child. | She received her bachelor's | degree in art history from | California State University | at Long Beach. She has | illustrated several books for | HarperCollins, including | MY LITTLE HOUSE SEWING | BOOK and MY LITTLE HOUSE | CRAFTS BOOK. She lives in | California with her daughters, | Elizabeth and Emily, and | her husband, Phillip. || Jacket art © 1998 by Mary Collier | Jacket design by Alicia Mikles.

CONTENTS: Page [3]: *For Captain and Mrs. Moore* | *—M.C.*

ILLUSTRATIONS: Every page is illustrated, some with full-page bleeds, remaining are set in double black line frames.

OTHER: Purchased new April 1998, this book is referred to on the last page of S56.

Catalogs

Aleph-Bet Books, Inc. Helen and Marc Younger, 218 Waters Edge, Valley Cottage, NY 10989.   Phone 914-268-7410   Fax 914-268-5942

A dealer in fine children's books of a wide variety, the Youngers issue catalogs in various formats, sometimes a first-rate printed catalog, sometimes a single sheet quoting a particular author. Catalogue 51 was issued about May 20, 1996. The Tudor titles offered are always of a high quality and a premium price.

Barnstable Originals, Studios of Harry W. Smith, Artist, Author, Silversmith, Master Miniaturist. Since 1959. 50 Harden Avenue, Camden, Maine 04843. Phone 207-236-8162 or 800-298-4721. Fax: 207-236-8169   email: hwsmith@midcoast.com.

> Undated tri-fold 8 ½ x 11″ flyer reproduces two pictures of 3″ = 1′ scale instruments for Tasha Tudor, [bass, harp, violin, cello, flute, clarinet, trumpet and trombone], and Melissa's spinnng wheel [with Melissa] for Tasha Tudor.

Books of the Ages, Batavia, Ohio. Issues several catalogs a year, specializes in children's titles, especially strong in Jenny Wren Press pieces. Catalogue No. 1 was postmarked Jan (?) 5, 1994. Catalogue No. 16 was postmarked September 9, 1997

Cellar Door Books, Concord, New Hampshire. Two catalogs annually, exclusively Tudor material, specializing in out of print Tudor material, including original art and ephemera. Approximately 300 items per catalog.   Tudor listings predominate since 1994.

> *A Tasha Tudor Offering* from Cellar Door Books, Concord, NH, October, 1994. An 18-page listing of approximately 200 items, ten sheets of cream paper.

> *Cellar Door Books*, 61 Borough Road, Concord, NH 03303 (603) 225-2012. TERMS OF SALE . . . A TASHA TUDOR OFFERING . . . October, 1994. Another distribution, ten pages on five cream sheets listing 95 items.

> *A Tasha Tudor Catalog* from CELLAR DOOR BOOKS   ANTIQUARIAN BOOKS   EST. 1971 . . . November 15, 1994. Single pink sheet, four-fold listing 75 items.

> *Tasha Tudor At The End Of The Year 1995* . . . Catalog #6   December 20, 1995. Three sheets in a peach cover stock, folded and stapled, listing 134 items. 16 pp. Front cover illustration is that from the front of *Ladies;* back cover reproduces the Chapter II head from *A Little Princess.*

> *1996 A Spring Of Joy! A Tasha Tudor Offering* . . . Catalog #7   May 15, 1996. Five sheets in peach cover stock, folded and stapled, listing 172 items and a selection of greeting and postal cards. 24 pp.   The front cover reproduces the original art of girl and corgi on bridge from "Solitude," *The Springs of Joy*, page 10. Inside the back cover, art from a greeting card "Chickadee on fir branch."   Back cover, the National Herb Society print of "Tasha's Herb Garden."

> *1996 A Spring Of Joy! Greeting Cards, Postal Cards, Note Cards, A Tasha Tudor Offering . . . Catalog # 7 Addendum   May 15, 1996.* Eighteen sheets of various cards illustrated by Tudor.

> *1996 Was A Year Of Take Joy!   A Tasha Tudor Offering* . . . Catalog # 8   January 15, 1997. Five sheets in cream cover stock, folded and stapled, listing 183 items. Pp. [1] 2-20, plus wrapper. Front cover reproduces the children and goat sled art for the Irene Dash greeting card CC 35-59V. Page 20 reproduces in black and white the madonna from *Take Joy!* page 63. Back cover, a black and white reproduction of the Diaparene box illustration.

> *Spring 1997 Tasha Tudor Offering* . . . Catalog #9   May, 1997. Seven sheets and speckled egg shell cover stock, folded and stapled, listing 253 items. Pp. [1] 2-27 [28] plus wrapper. Front cover illustration as in Catalog # 8; back cover illustration, the *Take Joy!* madonna as above.

Page [28] reproduces in black and white, "Tasha's Herb Garden" print, and the knight and castle from *Tasha Tudor's Book of Fairy Tales*, title pages.

Peace! Of the Season, Our Latest Tasha Tudor Catalog . . . Catalog # 10   December 1997. For the first time, a web address is included on the front cover: http://www.cellardoorbooks.com. Seven sheets in sage cover stock, folded and stapled, listing 300 items including significant orginal art of Tudor family provenance, prints and miscellaneous. An extra red paper strip is inserted between pages 6-7 and 22-23 and advertises the two Spellbound videotapes *Take Joy!* and *Take Peace*, the *Life* magazine and greetings cards. Pictured on the front cover is a new painting of chickadees by Bethany Tudor. Page 27 shows the goat sled art as above. Black and white illustrations on page [28] depict a most unusual Corgiville Advent calendar, and a set of paper dolls from the 1950s. *Tasha Tudor, The Direction of Her Dreams* is announced here.

Spring 1998 || Tasha Tudor | Catalog . . . Catalog # 11   May 1998. Eight sheets in blue stone cover stock, folded and stapled, listing 316 items. An extra yellow paper strip is inserted inside the cover advertising LATE ADDITIONS. Pictured on the front cover is a new painting of two canaries by Bethany Tudor. Eight other B. Tudor watercolors are reproduced in black and white. Some copies were distributed in a buff cover.

Children's Book Shop, Rochester, New York.

Books for you | 1942 [within a thin-ruled box, with broken corners. A two-storey house logo | CHILDREN'S | BOOK SHOP forms the lower right corner of the box] | 293 Alexander Street | Rochester, New York [below the box]. The letter to Boys and Girls, pp. [3-7] is signed Beatrice de Lima Meyers, Director of the Children's Book Shop. [220] pages glued into casing. 4 3/16 x 3 ¾"
        Pasteboard covers, ivory, cased in a blue cloth tape spine and stamped in red on the front: Large logo of house imprinted CHILDREN'S | BOOK SHOP. Beneath the logo: 1942. There is no jacket. The individually cut pages are of pulp paper, as a paperback, which has yellowed with fifty-five years aging. Also, the glue has dried so that most of the pages are loose. A few still cling to each other.

THE CONTENTS:
[1]   title page
[2]   blue illustration from *The Star Spangled Banner | Ingri and Edgar Parin d'Aulaire*
[3]   Dear Boys and Girls: In the years to come when boys and | girls like you study history, they will | learn that this period through which we | are living today is one of the most | important in the history of the world. || It is important because at this time | the United States of America, itself | founded upon Freedom, decided that it | was the obligation of every man, woman | and child in this great country to see to | it that Freedom should ring all over the | world.
[4]   Today history is being made faster | than ever before. Boundaries of count- | tries, forms of government, ways of | living, are changing right before our | eyes. These are days of speed, excite- | ment and surprises. It will be our duty | to make sure that they do not end in | confusion. In order to accomplish this | we must know many things -and in | order to know many things, we must | read. || We must read books of history to | know what ideas and what events have | caused this frightful world upheaval.
[5]   We must read books about great men | and women and their accomplishments. | In this way we may learn what has been | done in the past and what may be done | now and in the future to make the world | a better place to live in. || We must read books about people in | other lands, so that we may know their | habits, their needs and their problems. || We must read books about our neigh- | bors in the other Americas, who, | because of the wonderful discoveries in | science, are closer to us than ever before.
[6]   We must read books that will tell us | about these discoveries and how they | grew out of the dreams of great men. | Then, in spite of the grave, strange | years through which we are living-or | perhaps, because of them-we will | surely include on our reading list books | of

506

poetry; books about fairies, full of | the lovely make-believe; nature books | and animal books; and lots and lots of | funny books, to make us laugh and | laugh and so keep us strong and well | for the duration of the war and ready | for the Peace that is to come.

[7]   There is a world of all such books | right here on our shelves awaiting you. || From the many hundreds of books | published during this important year of | 1942 we have selected the ones | described in this little book as the ones | we think you will enjoy especially. || We hope you will come in to see them soon, and that you will like the books | we have carefully selected || expressly for you || Beatrice de Lima Meyers | Director | Children's Book Shop.

[8]   THE TALL BOOK OF | MOTHER GOOSE | Pictures by | Feodor Rojankovsky

[9]   blue illustration and description

[10]   TOMMY TIPPET'S TOYS | by Louise Woodcock | illus. By Elizabeth Logan

[11]   blue illustration and text

[12]   THE INDOOR NOISY BOOK Story by Margaret Wise Brown | Pictures by Leonard Weisgard

[13]   blue illustration and description

. . .

[36]   [red] FLIP AND THE COWS | Written and illustrated by | Wesley Dennis

[37]   red illustration and description

[38]   WHO WANTS AN APPLE | by Quail Hawkins | illus. by | Lolita and David Granahan

[39]   blue illustration and description

[40] [red] DORCAS PORKUS | Written and illustrated | by Tasha Tudor | Oxford University press | $.75

[41]   red illustration from page [32], and first page of text from page [9]

[42]   MARSHMALLOW | Written and Illustrated by Clare Turlay Newberry

[43]   blue illustration and description

. . .

[82]   A WAR-TIME HANDBOOK for | YOUNG AMERICANS | Words and Pictures by | Munro Leaf

[83]   blue illustration and description

. . .

[208] WE LIVE TO BE FREE | by Emma Gelders Sterne

[209] blue description: . . . This | is a book to keep on one's table to go | to again and again, lest we forget, even | for a moment—what we are fighting | for.

[210] blank

[211] red *In the long vista of the years to roll, | Let met not see my country's honour | fade; . . .Keats*

[212] CHILDREN'S | BOOK SHOP, in a circular logo: •IF•ALL•GOES•WELL•WE'RE• SURE•THERE'LL•BE•MORE•BOOKS•FOR•YOU•IN•43••

[213] Blank

[214] [red] Now that you have read over this list | of books that we have selected for you, | there are

     . . .

[215] [red] 1. Select the books you want. | 2. Pull order blank out of book. | 3. Fill in your name . . .

[216] blank

[217] blue order form

[218] blank

[219] red order form

[220]   blank

This 'catalog' of children's titles was published by Beatrice de Lima Meyers as a buying guide to new books for children in 1942. Meyers was the Director of the Children's Book Shop and a decided patriot for the War effort. The small book is printed in red and blue inks and cased in white boards. Most of the odd-numbered pages reproduce one illustration from the advertised title. Unless noted red, the page is printed in blue ink.

The Tudor entry on pages [40-41] advertises DORCAS PORKUS and includes the illustration of Sylvie Ann mending her linens.

Debra Jop of the Rochester, N.Y., Public Library, confirmed the name of the proprietor from the 1942 city directory on March 22, 1997, and reported that the business no longer exists. The Rochester Public Library owns books from the 1970s-1980s entitled BOOKS FOR YOU. The Library does not own any such titles for the 1940s, nor does its catalog list any author Beatrice de Lima Meyers.

Corgi Cottage Industries, Richmond, Virginia. An initial four-page mailing (September 1995) was a letter from Tudor under the letterhead of Tasha Tudor, Harry Davis and Thomas Kuhn. A letterhead emblem of Corgi Cottage in a wreath of wild flowers, with a corgi. It announces flower seeds, new art prints and posters, a sketchbook, replicas of chairs and future appearances. Order blank.

Second mailing, February 19, 1996, announces a wet paper watercolor *Tasha's Hollyhocks.* Color postal reproduction included and order blank for four versions of the print: Unsigned, Signed and numbered, Signed, numbered and remarqued, Artist's Proof, signed and remarqued.

Third mailing, April 4, 1996 included order form for 28 products (one of which is marked SOLD OUT) and a sheet of color reproductions, Announces completion of illustrations for *The Great Corgiville Kidnapping.*

Tasha Tudor's Corgi Cottage Industries | [rule] | Summer 1996. [20] page catalog, including pictorial wrapper. Offers prints and note cards of Richard Brown photographs of Tudor, and artist's proofs of *A Brighter Garden.* Announces major exhibit to be staged at Colonial Williamsburg, November 1996-April 1997.

Tasha Tudor's Corgi Cottage Industries | [rule] | Christmas 1996. Six-panel (12 pp.) fold-out catalog, 7 x 6," mailed by postal permit December 1996. "Madonna in Blue" on front cover. Reprints letter signed Tasha Tudor, no other names appear in the folder. Announces *Take Joy!* (videotape and magazine), *A Time to Keep* (Simon & Schuster reprint), and *The Great Corgiville Kidnapping.* Also pictures a fall wreath illustration with this note: "After November 1, 1966, | all books sold by | Corgi Cottage Industries | will feature a full-color | bookplate signed by Tasha, | at no additional charge. | *Pictured above is one of four | new bookplates to be used.*"

Tasha Tudor's Corgi Cottage Industries | [rule] | 1997. Thirty-page stapled catalog, last two pages being tear-off order blank. Letter from Tasha Tudor, page [2]. Announces new Spellbound Productions videotape for Christmas 1997 and ABC television production taping to be aired November 27, 1997. Front is a green painting, "Family Portrait," of six corgi dogs.

Tasha Tudor's Corgi Cottage Industries | [rule] | Christmas 1997. Twelve-page multi-fold catalog, last two pages being tear-off order blank. 7" x 35 ¼." Letter from Tasha Tudor, page [2]. Announces ABC television broadcast for November 26, 1997. Among the new merchandize is a re-issue of *The Night Before Christmas,* "Tasha's Welsh Breakfast Tea," a $200 pink luster tea cup and saucer, "chosen" by Tasha, and Caleb, the first in a new series of porcelain figurines. Cover is a Tudor painting "Home for the Holidays."

Save 50% | See reverse side. A green postal card with an illustration of Corgi Cottage was mailed in April 1998. A note from Tudor indicates a February sale is being extended to other merchandize. ". . . I believe strongly in listening to my fans for they are the ones who have given me this wonderful career as an artist. From April 13th - May 13th, all our other prints and cards will be offered at the same sale price as in February..." The card lists a number of specific items.

Tasha Tudor's Corgi Cottage Industries | [rule] | *Spring 1998.* Twelve-page multi-fold catalog, last two pages being tear-off order blank. 7″ x 35 ¼.″ Letter from Tasha Tudor, page [2]. Among the new merchandize are re-issues of *The Secret Garden* and *Corgiville Fair.* , "Tasha's own Spring Bouquet moisturizing cream," leatherbound ...*Kidnapping*, Edgar Tomcat figurine, Caleb keychain, Corgiville prints, a Take Joy! coffee mug, miniature basket, Tasha's yellow ware bowl, and Mary Lennox doll. Also Overmann *Bibliography*, *Animal Magnetism and The Springs of Joy.* Cover is "Mary emerging from the garden," art from current cover of *The Secret Garden.*

the enchanted doll house • DOLLS • TOYS • BOOKS • GAMES • Manchester Center, Vermont 05255 • 1973 -1974.

Have examined only page 41 which pictures two dolls similar to those in *A is for Annabelle* with this text. **TWO DOLL KITS** . Old fashioned doll kits of fine china with different hair styles. These will be collector's items some day. Kit furnishes china head, arms and legs, muslin cloth for body, tape for attaching doll head and pattern for body and clothes. You'll have FUN. **"EMMA"** (Blonde 15″ doll) 41-Tudor $9.00 **"MEG"** (Auburn 12″ doll) 41-Tudor 7.00

the enchanted doll house • DOLLS • DOLLHOUSES • TOYS • BOOKS • GAMES • Manchester Center, Vermont 05255 •1974 • 1975.

Page 9 depicts the two books *A is for Annabelle* and *Becky's Birthday*, and this text: "A IS FOR ANNABELLE" Illustrated by Tasha Tudor. An alphabet book about Grandmother's doll, Annabelle. Everything is about Annabelle and her belongings. Delightful. 9-Walch [sic] $5.20 ppd. EXCLUSIVELY OURS! Our lovely ANNABELLE 17″ has been fashioned after the doll in the story. Exquisitely dressed in pale pink gingham with a touch of blue, bonnet to match, this Lady Doll is perfection from head to toe. One of Judy's dolls. 9-JR $30.00 [Marian E. Miller reports that Annabelle is signed "J.R.-1975" on lower right side of back below the waist.] "BIRTHDAY FOR BECKY" [sic] Illustrated by Tasha Tudor. A child' feeling of delight in little pleasures comes from a family's feeling of affection. 9-Viking $4.50 ppd. And here's BECKY 15″ Inspired by the book. 9-LBH $12.00

the enchanted doll house • DOLLS • DOLLHOUSES • TOYS • BOOKS • GAMES • Manchester Center, Vermont 05255 •1975-1976.

Page 26 features two dolls Mary and Laura patterned after *The Little House on the Prarie* with this statement. "Judy Rankine from Ohio is fabulous. Here are beautiful replicas of MARY and LAURA WILDER, 15 ½″ "

the enchanted doll house • DOLLS • DOLLHOUSES • MINIATURES • TOYS • BOOKS • GAMES • CRAFTS • Manchester Center, Vermont 05255 •1977-1978.

Page G10 features four dolls and text: "FOUR DOLL KITS. Make your veryown Reproductions of old china dolls; each with its own personality and hair style. Kit has head, legs, arms, muslin cloth for body, patterns, instructions for body and clothes. Use your own skills. Left to right: NELL !2″ Black TU4 $7.00 EMMA 15″ Blonde TU2 $9.00 MEG 12″ Auburn TU3 $7.00 SALLY 13″ Blonde TU1 $7.00"

Doris Frohnsdorff, Gaithersburg, Maryland. Catalogue 32, Tasha Tudor. © 1981. [48] pp. in cream wrapper with an illustration of *Jackanapes* on the front. Gretchen Brown McKeever wrote a Foreword to this 208 item dispersal of the Ned Hills collection of Tasha Tudor books and original art. Twenty-eight illustrations include Rosamond Tudor oil paintings of her daughter Tasha in 1922 and 1933, and an oil of Efner McCready by Tasha Tudor in 1960. Among the unpublished and rarely seen pieces is Tudor's holograph for *Becky's Christmas* (in part) and a drawing imagining Elizabeth Barrett Browning writing at her desk.

Catalogue 42, Tasha Tudor. © 1986. [16] pp. in pink wrapper with an illustration of *Jackanapes* on the front. " . . . the second of our catalogues to be devoted entirely to the work of the contemporary American illustrator, Tasha tudor. This catalogue contains a nearly complete collection of her illustrated books in first edition . . . the largest collection of first editions ever to have been offered for sale in a catalogue . . ." 125 items including 21 pieces of original art and 7 Tudor letters to a fan.

Ginger & Pickles Store, Contoocook, N.H. Venture of Thomas and Tasha McCready, at their Webster, New Hampshire, home.

New | STATIONERY and COMPANION NOTES | four-colr reproductions of six water colors | BY | Tasha Tudor | ∗ ∗ ∗ | NOTES | Two each of six designs, with twelve envelopes | $1.00 | STATIONERY | Four eachof six designs, | plus 12 plain sheets with | 24 envelopes | $1.75 | ∗ ∗ ∗ |GINGER & PICKLES STORE | R.F.D. No. 1, Contoocook | New Hampshire || POSTAGE: 15c for the first box plus 5c each additonal box within | 1,000 miles' 25c plus 10c beyond 1,000 miles or west of Mississippi. *[One page flyer]*

Fall, 1955 | Ginger & Pickles Store | AND DOLL MUSEUM | R.F.D. No. 1 | CONTOOCOOK, NEW HAMPSHIRE | Telephone Contoocook 11-13 | OPEN DAILY 1-5 P.M. | Orders Shipped by Mail || Tasha Tudor Books, Christmas Cards, and Com- | panion Notes and Stationery. Postals showing Tasha | Tudor's collection of old fashioned dolls and furni- | ture. Imported toys. || *Store Items:* BOOKS BY TASHA TUDOR || EACH COPY AUTOGRAPHED . . . COMPANION STATIONERY & NOTES by Tasha Tudor-1955 spring | series | No. 11-Twelve notes, 2 each of 6 water colors with envelopes $1.00. | No. 24-Twenty-four sheets, 4 each of 6 water colors with 12 blank | sheets and 24 envelopes $ 1.75. | CHRISTMAS CARDS BY Tasha Tudor | 1955 "Preview" box assortment. Twelve cards $1.75. We stock over 40 | Tasha Tudor card designs sold (not assorted) 25 cards (all alike) to a | box $3.75. We handle orders for imprinting your name if desired. | POSTAL CARDS - Regular size postals published in 1952 showing series | of ten scenes (in black and white) of Tasha Tudor's collection of old- | fashioned dolls and their furniture. Set of ten postals $1.00. Also three | Christmas scenes showing the dolls' own tree and creche 10c each. | *Minimum mail order one dollar.* | POSTAGE: See other side forpostage and order blank. *[The one page mailer is illustrated at the upper left front with the Webster pasture scene similar to the endpapers of Biggity Bantam. This, however, is a Christmas scene with 8 children, one of whom is pulling a tree across the snow up the pasture toward the rock and house. Captioned" Chirstmas card scene of | Tasha Tudor's Home. -Ed.]*

Ginger & Pickles Store | FOR | MAIL ORDERS EXCLUSIVELY | BOX 231 | CONTOOCOOK, NEW HAMPSHIRE | (Successor to Ginger & Pickles Store- | Doll Museum — closed 1959) | BOOKS AND TOYS FOR CHILDREN | CHRISTMAS CARDS FOR ADULTS . . . An 8 ¾″ x 18″ tri-fold white sheet of paper dated "New book by Tasha Tudor for fall 1960" and printed in black. The catalog lists twenty-three Tudor books, many consistently and erroneously listed as published by Walk. *Jackanapes* is listed at $2.50 and as published 1948, Walk. [We have never seen a Walck printing of this title.] Page [3]: BOOKS WRITTEN BY | T. L. McCREADY, JR. | . . . who founded the Ginger & Pickles | Store as a mail order business in 1949. This | series of books is about his family, their pets | and farm. The McCreadys are called "The | Warners" in the five books below. . . Regular size postals showing series of ten scenes (in black | and white) of Tasha Tudor's collection of old-fashioned dolls and their | furniture. Set of ten postals $1.00. Also three Christmas scenes showing the | dolls' own tree and creche 10c each." Page [5]: We specialize in the B. potter books and other | English children's book classics. Also this store | is perhaps the only one in the world carrying all | of the various Tasha Tudor books and those by | T. l. McCready, Jr., immediately available for | shipment by mail." Merchandise includes jigsaw puzzles, painting books, Medici book name plates, fur and wool miniature animals, Thoren's music boxes (Swiss), miniature doll furnishings (Kiddicraft of England).

A Preview for You! | HERE IS OUR CHOICE OF THE BEST | PERSONALIZED CHRISTMAS CARDS | [Tom Naegele's design of hanging ornaments] | **TASHA TUDOR'S | GINGER & PICKLES STORE | Route 1, Contoocook, New Hampshire.** [The Christmas cards shown | in this booklet come from | the studios of America's fore- | most artists. The miniature | reproductions at best only sug- | gest the distinctive quality of | each design; all cards litho- | graphed on fine vellum stock | and issued in limited editions | . . . you'll find on each page the | exact size of the card, the senti- | ment that appears inside, and | price schedule. Please use order | form on last page. || *Painting on cover by* TOM NAEGELE | *from the* DESIGNERS & ILLUSTRATORS ALBUM | available on Card No. F471 – 45 | *Same price schedule as opposite page* | SENTIMENT INSIDE: Christmas Greetings | and Best wishes for a Happy New Year]

> PAGINATION: [1-20]. 3 ½″ x 2 ½″. Five pages of ivory paper folded, one staple.

> COVER: Same paper as rest of catalog. Front as described above. Inside and outside of back cover form a tear-off order blank headed TASHA TUDOR'S GINGER & PICKLES STORE, Route 1, Contoocook, N.H. . .

> ILLUSTRATIONS: Seventeen color illustrations of cards for sale on the front cover and pages [3-18], as follows: Madonna by Dorothy Simmons FD91-T7 [3], Christmas Cake by Cecilia Staples CS88-42 [4], The Magi by Grant Reynard E443-32L [5], Holiday Time by Clarence Carter E434-22L [6], Holiday Mail by Eyvind Earle EE61-102 [7], Candle Service by Tasha Tudor CT81-21H [8], Holiday Welcome by Flora Smith E444-101L [9], Holly and Bells by Carl Tait FV48-83L [10], Christmas Music by Cecilia Staples CS86-2V [11], Christmas Landscape by Adolf Dehn D355-61V [12], Candlelight by Witold Gordon E411-52 [13], Christmas Cheer by Robert Lee D369-102 [14], Snow-clad Fir by Eyvind Earle FE68-52H [15], Pantry Shelf by Tasha Tudor CT84-45H [16], Coming Home by Dorothy Simmons CD75-63V [17], Tree of Good Wishes by Carl Tait [18].

> OTHER: There is no indication that anyone other than the McCreadys produced this tiny catalog. However, several of the card designs are attributed either to the DESIGNERS & ILLUSTRATORS ALBUM or to the AMERICAN ARTISTS GROUP ALBUM. The booklet was undoubtedly supplied by the American Artists Group to local retailers such as the Ginger & Pickles Store imprinted with the store name for local distribution and generating orders.

Highsmith, The Complete School & School Library Catalog 96-97. Catalog L91. Fort Atkinson, Wisconsin. A catalog of general library supplies, picturing *The Secret Garden* (green paperback copy) in an ad for poly tape, page 40.

Houghton Mifflin Company, 222 Berkeley Street, Boston, Ma. 02116 6-99190 FALL 1995/WINTER 1996 Page 49 announces *Tasha Tudor's Heirloom Crafts* at $35.00 cloth. A side panel: *Tasha Tudor's Garden* received the Garden Writers Association of America Award for best book and photography in 1994.

The Jenny Wren Press, Mooresville, In. Venture of Tasha Tudor and Beth Mathers

1. An 8 ½ x 11″ white sheet of paper dated February 18, 1989 and printed in black advertised the *Jenny Wren Book of Valentines*, a set of 20 Valentine cards, the *Mouse Mills Catalogue for Spring* and a print of *Mother and Child in Tasha's Garden*. The letterhead is a Tudor drawing of two wrens within a rectangular block with a lace Valentine border. A third small wren looks up from the lower right corner. The letter is signed . . . Beth.

2. An 8 ½ x 11″ ivory sheet was distributed before April 1989. Printed in a rust ink and addressed to Dear Customer: It thanks one for the purchase of the *Jenny Wren Book of Valentines*. Also announces the *Mouse Mills Mail-Order Catalogue*, a *Christmas Annual*, the *Bouquet*, and an expensive doll with

wardrobe. The illustrations are as above, and the letter speaks of "Beth Mathers, my partner in the Jenny Wren Press, and I." There are printed signatures of Tasha Tudor and Beth Mathers.

3.   An 8 ½ x 14″ white sheet, black printing, was postmarked April 18, 1989. It advertises and depicts the *Mouse Mills Catalogue,* the "Mother and Child in Tasha's Garden" print, and *the Book of Valentines* plus five small Valentines and a girl reading to a corgi.

4.   A stiffer white matte card, 8½ x 11″ drawn in black and white. A border of pussy willows encloses text and creates a nesting area for Jenny Wren. One copy was received May 20, 1989. It announces Tudor articles in *Victoria* magazine and *Country Homes,* a color 3x5 of Tasha in her kitchen, and a doll for $3000. Eight products are pictured on the back including a new print, *Elizabeth in Tasha's Barn.*

5.   A white card 6 x 4½″ was mailed with the products. Drawn in black and white is Miss Wren standing on a low stump to sing. This message in Tudor's hand writing: With joyous song | from J. Wren. | Aren't they lovely!

6.   A business card for The Jenny Wren Press has a color illustration of a girl in blue and white bending over to smell a rose bush.

7.   An 8 ½ x 11″ white sheet printed landscape announced the 50th Anniversary lithograph. Printed one side only in black. Received July 3, 1989.

8.   A white card (8½ x 14″) printed in black features a 50th Anniversary lithograph, Tasha Tudor's Sketch Book and the products which had been pictured on item 4 above. received July 27, 1989.

9.   An 8½ x 11″ white sheet dated August 1st, 1989 indicates that to "qualify for our wholesale prices, you must order 12 or more items." The advertisement lists nine products, is printed in black and has reproduced signatures of Tasha Tudor and Beth Mathers. The design is as number 1 above, but lacking the wren at the bottom.

10. An October 14, 1989 order form is printed black on a white sheet of paper, 8½ x 11″. The sheet lists sixteen items, the last three of which will be available before February 1st, 1990. The sheet is addressed Dear Customer . . . Welcome to our first Color mailer!!!

11. An October 18, 1989, mailing consisted of two 8 x 11″ sheets, and for the first time, one in full color. The colored sheet is headed Holiday Enchantments from the Jenny Wren Press. It pictures the prototype of the doll to be limited to 500 copies. Six prints are pictured on the reverse. A second black and white sheet more fully describes the products and includes an order blank. A note on this sheet announces that Tudor will make public appearances December 1-3 in Durham, N.C. Requests for tickets may be sent to Harry Davis, P.O. Box 15424, Richard, Virginia.

12.   A 5 ½ x 3 ¾″ white card with small boy and rooster. Thank you for your order. Unknown date.

13.   A single pink sheet outlined with a border of magenta flowers was hand addressed and dated March 8, 1990 to customers. It lists specifications for the limited edition doll Daisy Belle. No more than 500 copies will be made by doll master Brenda Stewart. A down payment of $900 is due April 10, 1990 and the remaining $1000 upon shipment in fate Fall 1990. A 5 x 3 ½″ color photograph was enclosed. Postmarked March 8, 1990.

14. 1990. *Spring & Summer Delights from | The Jenny Wren Press.* A tri-fold enameled paper brochure has eleven color photographs of products, including Miss Daisy Belle.   This and an associated black and white order form (Spring 1990) give various deadlines of May 10 and September

25, 1990. Announces a small shop at 19 South Indiana in Mooresville will be open by chance or appointment!

15. 1990-1991. *Tasha Tudor's | Christmas Valentines | Holiday 1990-1991 Collection*. Enameled paper 23 ½ x 10 ¼″ mailed folded twice lists 31 numbered items and shows eight un-numbered lithographs. "Celebration" lithograph from a Christmas card featured on front. Miss Daisy Belle is advertised and will "come with a butter churn, crock, a Corgi recreated just for Jenny Wren from Tasha's drawings, a tiny shaker basket, an enchanting box of stationery & an autograph album. Tasha will be hand painting each face . . . There <u>may be</u> a 1-1 ½ year waiting period . . . Reservations will be accepted through December 1991 only." Thirteen color pictures of merchandise and a black and white drawing on the address side: 3 corgis in a goat-drawn sleigh racing by a sign post. A similar image later appears on the 1996 Colonial Williamsburg *Take Joy!* literature. Separate pieces in this mailing: a 5 ¼ x 4″ impressed Thank You for Your Order! Card with a black and white reproduction of Little Bo Peep searching, within a circle of flowers; an order form to wholesale customers, Winter 1990; and an order form with an appearance schedule printed on the back . . . Williamsburg, Va., November 9, 10, 11, 1990, Heart of Country Antique Show, Nashville, Tenn. Feb. 8 & 9, Vaillancourt Folk Art - April 27th , Sutton, Ma., Conner Prairie, Noblesville, In., Fall of 1991.

16. 1991. *Tasha Tudor's Enchanting | Spring & Summertime | Collection | 1991*. Enameled paper, 23 ½ x 10 ¼″, folded twice with four listings of products A-S, A-L, A-I and A-B. A separate un-lettered offering announces the 30th anniversary reprints of *Becky's Christmas*. 14 color photographs of merchandise and one black and white drawing for the address label: two rabbits constructing and painting a bill board, with the help of two jays, a mouse and two chickadees. "Feather Friends" lithograph featured on front. Magenta printed envelopes. Mailed near the end of March 1991.

17. A black and white single sheet advertisement announces a poster and videotape of Tasha Tudor's Last Public Speaking Appearance at the Conner Prairie Museum, Noblesville, Indiana, August 1991. This appearance is part of the "<u>Once in a Lifetime Exhibit of Tasha Tudor's</u> Most Outstanding <u>Antique Dresses</u>, <u>paintings</u>, her <u>Doll Collections</u> & other <u>Enchantments!</u>" at the museum June 8 - November 10, 1991. Postmarked June 7, 1991.

18. 1991-1992. *Tasha Tudor's Holiday Collection | Ready Now for | Christmas 1991 || New in Spring | of | 1992*. [8] page stapled enameled paper catalog, 10 13/16 x 8 3/8″. Red cover, eighteen color pictures of merchandise plus a black and white drawing of three wrens and a lace-edged valentine's card as the address portion. A letter from Tudor and Mathers with their picture. Announces moving the New Jenny Wren Press Shop to 11 East Main Street, Mooresville, In., and opening December 7, 1991. Lists merchandise A-N, A-Y, A-H, ten un-lettered lithographs and reprints of *Becky's Birthday* and *Becky's Christmas*. Some mailings included a 9/24/91 letter to Wholesale customers on black and white Jenny Wren stationery, and a separate green Wholesale price list decorated with rabbits, corgis and other JWP merchandise images.

19. A magenta letter addressed to Dear Special Customer, included a $5 and $10 coupon to be used by February 25, 1992.

20. 1992. *Tasha Tudor's Timeless Treasures | Spring-Summer 1992 | Prices Effective Thru October 5, 1992*. Sixteen page color catalog [i-ii, 1] 2-13 [14], stapled enameled paper. Picture of and letter signed by Tasha Tudor & Beth & David Mathers, The officers of The Jenny Wren Press & the entire Jenny Wren Staff! Various merchandise including announcement for Fall '92 or Spring '93 reprint of *Mother and Child*. Catalog advertises furniture reproductions.

21. A black and white mailing dated May 15th, 1992 announces and pictures *The Private World of Tasha Tudor* and *The Real Pretend*.

22. A heavily decorated letterhead (9 ½ x 7 ¼″) mailed from Indiana June 17, 1992 welcomes shops back to wholesale pricing, and announces a contest for the best Tudor display in a gift shop. The letter is framed in fanciful trees and has birds, flowers, a boy and corgi and other Tudor insignia.

23. 1992-1993. *The Magical World of Tasha Tudor | Fall-Winter | 1992-1993 | A free gift comes <u>with</u> <u>every order</u> from this catalogue! Prices effective thru March 1993.* Sixteen page color catalog [i] 1-14 [15], stapled enameled paper. Picture of The Jenny Wren Press shop and of Tudor signing a book. *Mother and Child* reprint to be available late May 1993. Some copies include wholesale price list, and a magenta order form for *The Tasha Tudor Cookbook* and the 55th anniversary reprint of *Pumpkin Moonshine.*

24. 1993. *Celebrating Tasha Tudor's 55th Year of Publishing | the Jenny Wren Press Spring-Summer | 1993.* Sixteen page color catalog [i] 1-14 [15], stapled enameled paper. Closeup of Tudor signing a book. Includes 55th anniversary reprint of *Pumpkin Moonshine* and Corgi Cottage Preserves. Some copies include wholesale price list. A pink order form dated Spring 1993 was send to Dear Special Friends.

25. 1993-1994. *The Jenny Wren Press Fall-Winter 1993-94 || Celebrating Tasha's | 55th Year of | Publishing || Prices for these products are on back page. Prices effective thru March 1993.* Sixteen page color catalog [1] 2-15 [16], stapled enameled paper. New announcement for the 55th anniversary reprint of *Pumpkin Moonshine,* a Sylvie Ann doll, and the Tasha Tudor sampler kit. A 6 ¼ x 4 ½″ card with an elaborate Tudor ink drawing of a garden arbor was mailed around this time with text: Thank You | For Helping | Make The | Magic Continue! | Love, | The Jenny Wren Press | Tasha Tudor, | Beth Mathers & | Miss Jenny Wren. The same card was later photocopied and mailed with orders.

26. 1994. *The Jenny Wren Press Spring-Summer 1994 ||* New item! *Prices valid through September 15, 1994 See inside cover for book information. Copyright 1994 J.W.P.* Sixteen page color catalog [1] 2-15 [16], stapled enameled paper. New announcement for *Around the Year* reprint. Picture of two corgis who invite correspondence, and note of a new store *The Enchanting World of Tasha Tudor,* 75 Van Buren St., Nashville, Indiana. Beth Mathers gives a schedule for twice-monthly teas with talk at the Mooresville store, $20 per person.

27. A green ink mailer on buff paper dated April 1994 offers a $10 gift certificate. 3 Tudor drawings.

28. 1994-95. *The Jenny Wren Press Fall-Winter 94-95 ||* New Product *Pricing information on back of Catalogue | Copyright J.W.P. 1994-95.* Sixteen page color catalog [1] 2-15 [16], stapled enameled paper. While still heavily Tudor, this catalogue introduces a number of books, china, silver and garden gifts not originating from Tudor.

29. A black and white advertisement dated Summer '94 pictures *Tasha Tudor's Garden* and offers a free autographed book plate to the first 1000 to order.

30. A green ink advertisement dated November 1994 offers a special Christmas gift and gift certificate on order placed until December 31st, 1994.

31. A magenta ink advertisement dated January 1st, 1995, announces sales and new merchandise.

32. A black and white photocopied advertisement, two cherubs holding an antique oval frame announcing an Historical Newsletter for Children. The 11 x 8 ½″ piece is in Mather's handwriting but is signed "Happy Valentines from Aunt Agatha." Spring 1995.

33. 1995. *The Jenny Wren Press & Mrs. Fizziwigs Spring-Summer 1995 || Prices on Back of Catalogue © J.W.P. 1995 $2.50.* Sixteen page color catalog [1] 2-15 [16], stapled enameled paper. A garden bench and scene with merchandise on front. Some later distributions carried a gold foil label on front

514

announcing sales through September 10, 1995 and a special "Tasha Tudor Treasures" sale on Saturday, July 15.

34. A green ink advertisement, one sheet, pictures *Tasha Tudor's Heirloom Crafts* and *Tasha Tudor's Engagement Calendar 1996*, with order blank.

35. Two small mailings, one red and one white announce special Christmas sales to Special Customers. Tasha Treasure Christmas Sale on December 1 in Mooresville. Fall 1995.

36. 1995-1996. *The Jenny Wren Press & Mrs. Fizziwigs Fall - Winter Collection 1995-1996* || © *The Jenny Wren Press   Prices for these wonderful items are listed on the back cover $2.50.*   Sixteen page color catalog [1] 2-15 [16], stapled enameled paper. The merchandise on front includes books and toy airships, but no Tudor items. Fully a third of the catalog are non-Tudor.

37. Carmine ink mailing dated January 1996 to Dear Special Customer advertises ½ price for all in stock Tasha Tudor items.

38. A carmine ink mailing dated March, 1996 is addressed to Dear Friends of The Jenny Wren Press, This will be the last mailing you will receive from us . . . close the business on May 31, 1996. The Jenny Wren Press Catalogue Company, and retail shop plus Mrs. Fizziwigs in Nashville will all close on May 31, 1996. . . the Historical Newsletter will continue into the future . . and Hannah will be for sale only through May 30, 1996. Reply envelopes have designs that were not drawn by Tudor.

Jo Ann Reisler, Ltd | *Catalogue 39* | *[Autumn 1997]*   This is only one of Reisler's catalogues to list books by Tudor. It is announced as the largest catalog to date, 658 items with numerous black and white illustrations and 28 in color. Among the 17 Tudor items are several McCready books, and the original art from one page of *Skiddycock Pond* (pictured in color).

_____. *Catalogue 41* | *[Winter 1998]*   701 items with numerous black and white and color illustrations. Thirteen Tudor books and three pieces of art from *Mother Goose, Becky's Birthday* and More Prayers. Also a copy of *Samuel's Tree House.* The art is pictured in color.

_____. *Catalogue 44* | *[Spring 1998]*   359 items with numerous black and white and color illustrations. NineTudor books and black and white reproductions of original art from *Around the Year* and *Becky's Christmas.*

Little, Brown and Company . . . September 1992-March 1993.   *The Private World of Tasha Tudor* announced for October on page 12, with a picture of the illustrated dust jacket.

Marshall Field & Company . . . Fall 1941. *"A Tale of Tales for Children" Books for Christmas.* Tagboard cover in a dustjacket with color Tudor illustrations from *Snow Before Christmas.* From the front flap: this is our juvenile catalog, made to look like a child's book. It is the tale of this year's outstanding books for hcildren, selected from many. Back flap: ad for Tudor's new book Snow Before Christmas. 32 pp. 6 x 6 ½". Description courtesy of Barbara Rardin.

Metropolitan Children's Book & Antique Toy Fair and Seminar, December 1-3, 1995. 38 pp. program brochure in cream wrapper. "Sharing the Joy of Reading with Children," by Rebecca Myers, pp. 5-7. Tudor illustrations on pp. 16-17 announcing a $150 lecture luncheon on December 2.

My Bookhouse, Tiffin, Ohio. Catalog 46, ca. Spring 1997   The catalog reproduces on its front cover a Tudor drawing of a Valentine with a bit of Shakespeare quoted. It is described as an original charcoal drawing on newsprint type drawing paper, and lists at $2000. The back cover reproduces a Sparrow Post job application (ca. 1958) handwritten by Tudor. Actual letter measures 3 ½ x 2″ with an envelope also pictured. The letter is an application signed by Mary Rand Lightner, daughter of Tudor's friend and patron Virginia Lightner: I hereby wish to become Postmistress for the Ohio Branch Office of The Sparrow Post, and promise to comply with all the rules and regulations set forth by this organization. Also to do my duty in protecting the mails from the depredations of all Crows, Jays and Magpies. My Sign and Seal, Mary Rand Lightner. [on the recto] Kindly fill out the opposite page, both sides, and return to Augustus A. Sparrow, Postmaster General. | Address | The Red House | 1 Upstairs Street S. W. | Webster | New Hampshire. Matted and edged in gold rick rack. $510.00. 15 other Tudor books, some Jenny Wren Press items.

Catalog 48, ca. 1997, front cover reproduces an illustration from *Snow Before Christmas*. Lists one other title.

Platt & Munk, New York City. Books for Schools and Library, 1966 catalog (34pp. plus wrapper) features *First Delights* on page [1] with an illustration. The entire wrapper is also illustrated by Tudor with a different panel, front and back, featuring Sally eating an apple, and counting on her fingers. Frohnsdorff, Catalog 32, above, item 93 reproduces the art for the front cover and describes it as unused. The back cover is item 92 in the same catalog, and although not pictured, matches the description; again referred to as unused. 8 ½ x 5 ½″

Random House, New York City. 1992 Backlist Catalog lists Tudor's ". . . timeless prayers and stories. Ages 5-7″ on page 50. *Pumpkin Moonshine, A Tale for Easter, First Graces, Mother Goose*.

Spellbound Productions, 539 Broadway, San Francisco, Ca. 94133 (415) 353-1550 fax (415) 352-1558/9. A press kit in a white folder includes this two-page 11 November 1996 press release <u>Spellbound Creates Documentary On Life of Children's Illustrator Tasha Tudor</u>. Fourteen other pieces.

Spoken Arts, New Rochelle, New York. 40 Years of Excellence, Videos . Readalongs. Undated catalog including on page 4, *Emily Dickinson's A Brighter Garden*, video, audio-cassette and book. " . . . this collection of twenty-three Dickensen [*sic*] poems was conceived by Karen Ackerman, the 1989 Caldecott Medal winner . . ."

Take Joy! 50 Lexington Ave Box 123, New York, NY 10010.

> Undated, circa November 1996, single page flyer on simulated vellum. TASHA TUDOR announces the premiere of her new magazine | TAKE JOY! | A VERY SPECIAL HOME-GROWN MAGAZINE | [printer's decorative bar centered by 5 balls] | In response to all my fans' requests for more information, stories and ideas from Corgi Cottage, I have decided to launch a bi-monthly | magazine devoted to the Art of Living….as I see it. Along with a team of friends and experts in the field of home and hearth, I believe we've | created a wonderfuly entertaining magazine that encourages enjoying every moment and aspect of life. . . . The first issue will appear in December for the new year . . . With gratitude to all my fans, | Tasha Tudor.

Tasha Tudor Room Catalogue.

> The Forward to A PARTIAL LIST OF ORIGINAL WATER COLORS, DRAWINGS, OILS AND PASTELS BY TASHA TUDOR mentions "the friendly cooperation of the many people who

516

responded to our "Notes to owners of original Arts Works by Tasha Tudor" in several issues of our TASHA TUDOR ROOM CATALOGUE.

Gretchen McKeever reports that most years this was one piece of paper folded over. It listed merchandise for sale at the Dutch Inn.

The 1978-1979 Catalogue of Tasha Tudor Items Currently Available. 4pp. 16" x 10 3/8", not quite foolscap. Printed in green on buff paper. Page [1] announces new acquisitions at the shop, with a driving map; Books, p. [2]; Christmas Cards, p. [3]; Other Tasha Tudor Items Available at the Dutch Inn Gift Shop, p. [4]. From page [4]: "Again this year, we are offering a limited number of Tasha Tudor's preliminary Sketches for books illustrations and Christmas cards. Because these vary greatly in subject matter, general effectiveness, price etc. we recommend that interested people make their selections here at the Tasha Tudor Room rather than by mail."

The Virginia P. Lightner Collection | of 48 Tasha Tudor Originals | is being offered for sale . . . Sale details on last page || [b&w picture of boy and girl jumping brook] || quotation from Efner Tudor Holmes. Cover title: Virginia P. Lightner's | Collection of Tasha Tudor Originals | [Thumbelina] | Saturday, April 29, 1995. 24pp. in a paper wrapper. 11 x 8 7/16"

Text from page 24 reflects on the Tudor - Lightner friendship and the original paintings Mrs. Lightner collected. John C. Lightner as executor of his mother's estate is offering the collection for sale. Color photographs of four pieces are printed on the cover. Forty-six black and white reproductions display all but two of the pieces for sale which are referred to as "Brother & Sister Pastels." This was a private sale with exhibition of the art at the LaRue, Ohio, firehouse on April 29, 1995. Interested parties were encouraged to contact Mr. John Lightner at 614-499-3494. Sets of color photographs of the art were also offered in advance of the sale at $20 per set.

Waverly Auctions, Bethesda, Maryland. Watercolors & Drawings by Tasha Tudor, Children's and Illustrated Books, Maps, Works on Paper, Autographs, Various Fine Books. Sale 102 Thursday June 17, 1993. Five lots of books (36 pieces); and fifteen separate original works of art, drawings and paintings, only five of which sold. The remaining ten failed to meet the reserve price. Fourteen pieces of the art are pictured on the wrapper. Item 193 from *The Night Before Christmas* is the remaining half of one piece previously listed as pictured as item122 in Frohnsdorff's Catalog 32, above. In the intervening 12 years, the painting was obviously cut apart. It did not reach the reserve price in the Waverly sale.

Fine Books, Maps & Atlases, Works On Paper, Oils, Watercolors, Sculpture. Sale 116, November 17, 1994. Lots 118-127 list ten works of art from various books, all of which are pictured on the wrapper. All sold.

Fine Books, Maps & Atlases, Autographs, Sale 136, March 6, 1997. Lots 381, 382, 383 include 7 common Tudor titles.

Fine Books Some of the Estate of Lynd Ward Children's & Illustrated, Art & Architecture, First Editions, Natural History, Original Art by Tasha Tudor. Sale 143, December 4, 1997. Lots 389, 390 include 7 common Tudor titles. Lots 228 - 242 are original art, all pictured in black and white. See the Reisler Catalog 41 for the re-appearance of items 232, 233 and 238 from this sale, but pictured in color in Reisler's catalog.

Autographs, Works on Paper & Canvas, Book Miscellany incl. Children's Books from the Library of Carolyn Michaels. Sale 148, June 11, 1998. Lot 515 comprised 8 Tudor titles and realized $200 plus a $30 premium. Titles: *Tasha Tudor's Book of Fairy Tales* (1969), *Tasha Tudor's Sampler* (5th), *First Poems of Childhood* (1st gray and 1st library binding), *Snow Before Christmas* (without a dust jacket), *The Wind in the Willows* (3rd with damage), *Take Joy!* (7th dated 1971), *and Thistly B* (without a dust jacket).

[Bethany with chicken]

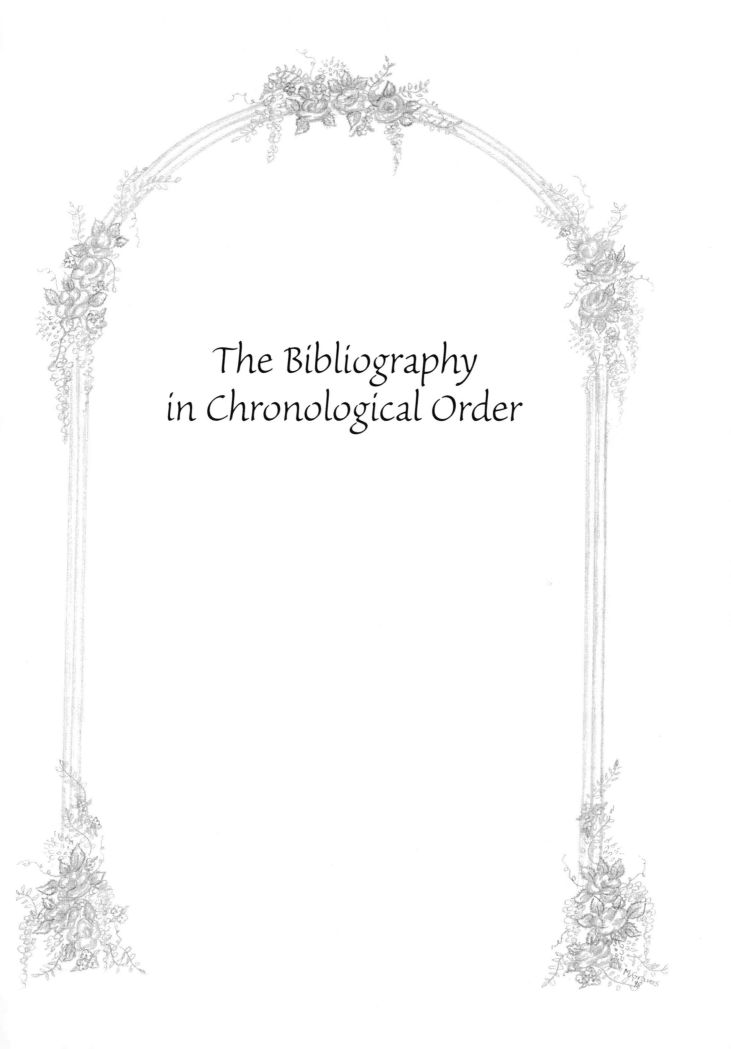

The Bibliography
in Chronological Order

The Titles Discussed in this Book
Listed by Publication Date (month and day in parenthesis)

1934 *Hitty's Almanac* [unpublished]
1937 *New England Wild Flowers* [unpublished]
1938 *Pumpkin Moonshine* (9-15)
    To a Mouse [unpublished]
1939 *Alexander the Gander* (10-16)
1940 *The County Fair* (9-26)
1941 *A Tale for Easter* (3-13)
    Snow Before Christmas (10-4)
1942 *Dorcas Porkus* (10-1)
1943 *The White Goose* (9-30)
1944 *Mother Goose* (10-19)
1945 *Fairy Tales from Hans Christian Andersen*
    (11-21)
1946 *Linsey Woolsey* (10-24)
1947 *Childcraft: Poems of Early Childhood* (3-10)
    A Child's Garden of Verses (Oxford, 9-25)
1948 *The Dolls of Yesterday* (3-15)
    Jackanapes (9-30)
1949 *Tasha Tudor Christmas Cards* (6-1)
    Thistly B (9-8)
1950 *The Dolls' Christmas* (10-5)
1951 *Amanda and the Bear* (8-16)
    Dolls of Three Centuries (10-15)
1952 *First Prayers* (9-11)
1953 *Tasha Tudor's Dolls* (ca. 3-15)
    Edgar Allan Crow (10-15)
    Diaparene toiletry box
1954 *Biggity Bantam* (2-23)
    Mother and Child (9-22)
    A is For Annabelle (10-21)
    Ginger & Pickles Doll Museum
1955 *Pekin White* (3-21)
    The Family of Man (5-10)
    New Hampshire Author's Luncheon (9-13)
    The Illustrated Treasury of Children's
        Literature (10-1)
    First Graces (11-10)
1956 *Mr. Stubbs* (8-17)
    1 is One (11-1)
1957 *Around the Year* (10-31)
1958 *Increase Rabbit* (2-6)
    And It Was So (4-29)
1959 *Adventures of a Beagle* (8-11)
    The Lord Will Love Thee (8-18)
1960 *My Brimful Book* (6-1)
    Becky's Birthday (8-15)
    Happiness Hill
1961 *The Tasha Tudor Book of Fairy Tales*
    (8-25)
    Becky's Christmas (10-23)
    A B C Go!

    Flatfoot [never published]
    Adventures of a Beagle (U.K.)
    Biggity Bantam (U.K.)
1962 *Chip the Chipmunk* (2-9)
    The Secret Garden (9-10)
    The Dolls' House (10-5)
    The Night Before Christmas (St. Onge, 11-1)
    Ladies: 1962… (11-5)
1963 *Gooseberry Lane* (6-10)
    A Little Princess (8-29)
    A Round Dozen (11-7)
1964 *Samantha's Surprise* (8-10)
    Wings from the Wind (10-2)
    First Graces (U.K.)
    First Prayers (U.K.)
1965 *Skiddycock Pond* (9-13)
    Tasha Tudor's Favorite Stories (10-14)
    The Twenty Third Psalm (St. Onge)
        (12-6)
1966 *First Delights* (4-1)
    The Wind in the Willows (6-20)
    Take Joy! (10-27)
1967 *First Poems of Childhood* (4-10)
    More Prayers (9-20)
    The Real Diary of a Real Boy (10-15)
    Take Joy! (U.K.)
1968 *Brite and Fair* (10-15)
    The New England Butt'ry Shelf Cookbook
        (8-15)
1969 *Little Women* (10-31)
1970 *The New England Butt'ry Shelf Almanac*
    (10-30)
1971 *Corgiville Fair* (8-30)
    Tasha Tudor (Crowell)
    Betty Crocker's Kitchen Gardens (10-18)
1972 *The Nest* (9-14)
1973 *Tasha Tudor* (Irene Dash Greeting Card
        Co.)
1974
1975 *A Partial List of Original Water Colors…*
    (6-4)
    The Night Before Christmas (Rand
        McNally, 8-1)
    An Illustrated Study of the Pembroke Welsh
        Corgi Standard (8-25)
1976 *The Christmas Cat* (9-28)
    The Secret Garden [audiotape]
1977 *A Time to Keep* (9-16)
    Tasha Tudor's Bedtime Book (10-1)
    Amy's Goose (10-14)
    Tasha Tudor's Sampler

1978 *Tasha Tudor's Favorite Christmas Carols*
        (8-25)
     Battered (9-11)
     Carrie's Gift (10-12)
     Tasha Tudor's Five Senses (12-15)
     Bettys Gas (Denmark)
     Elma Se Gans (South Africa)
     Eerste Dankebede (South Africa)
     Eerste Gebede (South Africa)
     Vildgasen (Sweden)
1979 *Samuel's Tree House* (3-15)
     A Book of Christmas (9-5)
     Tasha Tudor's Old Fashioned Gifts (10-1)
     The Springs of Joy (10-12)
     Drawn from New England (11-19)
     El Libro de Navidad (Columbia)
1980 *1980 Tasha Tudor Calendar*
     The Illustrated Treasury of Humor for
        Children (9-5)
     A Mouse Family Album (10-1)
     The Lord is My Shepherd (Philomel,
        10-31)
     The Way of the World
     Een boek voor de Kersttijd (Netherlands)
     Buon Natale (Italy)
     kurisumasu ni tsuite (Japan)
     Le livre de Noel (France)
     Wenn Weihnachten Ist (Germany)
1981 *A Child's Garden of Verses* (Rand
        McNally, 8-1)
     The Platt & Munk Treasury of Stories for
        Children (9-1)
     Rosemary for Remembrance (11-20)
     Tasha Tudor's Treasure
1982 *The Illustrated Treasury of Fairy Tales*
        (8-2)
     The Art of Making Furniture in Miniature
        (11-19)
     The Lord is My Shepherd (U.K.)
1983 *A Basket of Herbs* (2-17)
1984 *Christmas Village* (9-25)
     All for Love (10-22)
1985
1986 *Once Upon a Time*
     Tasha Tudor's Seasons of Delight (5-1)
1987 *Give Us This Day: The Lord's Prayer*
        (USA, U.K., 9-1)
1988 *Easter at the White House*
     Tasha Tudor's Fairy Tales (5-2)
     Tasha Tudor's Advent Calendar: A Wreath
        of Days (10-10)
     The Jenny Wren Book of Valentines
        (12-23)

1989 *And It Was So* (U.K.)
     Give Us This Day [miniature edition]
     Mouse Mills Catalogue for Spring (3-16)
     Tasha Tudor's Sketchbook (9-15)
     The Bouquet (ca. 10-31)
     Tasha Tudor Bibliography
     On the Horizon
1990 *A Brighter Garden* (9-5)
1991 *Jenny Wren Garden Colouring Book*
        (12-18)
     A Brighter Garden [audiotape]
     A Brighter Garden [videotape]
     With My Love, Tasha [videotape]
1992 *On the Horizon* [videotape] (9-24)
     The Private World of Tasha Tudor
        (10-14)
     English Cottage Gardening for American
        Gardeners (11-16)
     The Real Pretend (12-1)
1993 *The Deer in the Hollow* (10-27)
     The Tasha Tudor Cookbook (11-9)
     My Sadie
1994 *Tasha Tudor's Garden* (9-6)
     A Treasury of First Books
1995 *The 1995 Bibliography and Price Guide...*
     Magical Moments in Time (5-14)
     Tasha Tudor's Engagement Calendar, 1996
        (8-8)
     Tasha Tudor's Heirloom Crafts (9-7)
     The Victory Garden (11-25)
     Simple Abundance
     The Tasha Tudor Sketchbook Series: Family
        and Friends
1996 *Tasha Tudor's Engagement Calendar, 1997*
        (7-29)
     Myth, Magic, and Mystery
     Take Joy! The Magical World of Tasha Tudor
     The Gentle Wit & Wisdom of Tasha Tudor
     The 1996 Bibliography and Price Guide...
1997 *The Great Corgiville Kidnapping*
     Take Peace! A Corgi Cottage Christmas
     Tasha Tudor's Tragard
     Tasha Tudor's Engagement Calendar, 1998
     Good Morning America (12-17)
     Prime Time Live (12-17)
1998 *The 1998 Bibliography and Price Guide...*
     Animal Magnetism
     Tasha Tudor: The Direction of Her Dreams
        (10-1)
1999 *The Night Before Christmas* (Little,
        Brown, 9-1)
     Tasha Tudor's Dollhouse (9-1)
2000 *Christmas with Tasha Tudor: Take Joy!*
        (9-1)

Credits

Grateful acknowledgment goes to the following individuals and publishers for permission to reproduce the covers and dust jackets and to quote from the title pages and versos and the dust jackets and other noted sections of the books listed.

Linda Allen for Tudor, Tasha and Linda Allen. *Tasha Tudor's Favorite Christmas Carols.* David McKay, 1978. Tudor, Tasha and Linda Allen. *Tasha Tudor's Old-Fashioned Gifts.* David McKay, 1979.

Amon Carter Museum Archives for Dorr, Nell. *Mother and Child.* Harper & Brothers, 1954, and The Scrimshaw Press, 1972.

Anne Eaton Brown for Alcott, Louisa May. *A Round Dozen.* Viking Press, 1963.

Board Of Trustees, Concord Academy for Hall, Elizabeth B. *Ladies: 1962.* Concord Academy, 1962.

Marlowe deChristopher for Holmes, Efner Tudor. *Deer in the Hollow* with illustrations by Marlowe deChristopher. Philomel, 1993.

Joan Donaldson for Donaldson, Joan. *The Real Pretend.* Checkerboard Press, 1992.

From *Betty Crocker's Kitchen Gardens* 1979, 1971 Golden Books Publishing Company, Inc. Used by permission.

Grosset & Dunlap, Inc. for Hall, Nancy Christensen, *The Platt & Munk Treasury Of Stories For Children.* Platt & Munk, Publishers, 1981.

HarperCollins Publishers for examination of contract pertaining to *Tasha Tudor's Favorite Stories;* for permission to reproduce the cover, cover copy and dust jacket text of *The Christmas Cat;* cover and dust jacket text for *The Secret Garden;* cover and illustration from *A Little Princess.*

Efner Tudor Holmes
    Amy's Goose. Thomas Y. Crowell, 1977.
    Carrie's Gift. Collins + World, 1978.
    The Christmas Cat. Thomas Y. Crowell, 1976.
    Deer In The Hollow. Philomel Books, 1993.
    My Sadie. Checkerboard Press, 1993.

"A Letter With Drawings" by Tasha Tudor, The Horn Book Magazine, Feb. 1959 reprinted by permission of The Horn Book, Inc., 11 Beacon St., Suite 1000, Boston, MA 02108.

Houghton Mifflin for permission to reprint the covers, title page, and text from title page versos from *Tasha Tudor's Engagement Calendar, 1996, 1997, 1998.*

Jacket cover and title page from *Tasha Tudor's Garden.* Text copyright © 1994 by Tovah Martin. Photographs copyright © 1994 by Richard W. Brown. Illustrations copyright © 1994 by Tasha Tudor. Reprinted by permission of Houghton Mifflin Company. All rights reserved.

Jacket cover and title page from *Tasha Tudor's Heirloom Crafts.* Text copyright © 1995 by Tovah Martin. Photographs copyright © 1995 by Richard W. Brown. Illustrations copyright © 1995 by Tasha Tudor. Reprinted by permission of Houghton Mifflin Company. All rights reserved.

From *The Great Corgiville Kidnapping* by Tasha Tudor. Copyright © by Tasha Tudor. From The Private World of Tasha Tudor by Tasha Tudor and Richard Brown. Copyright © 1992 by Richard Brown and Tasha Tudor. By permission of Little, Brown and Company.

Gretchen Brown McKeever *The Tasha Tudor Room.* A Partial List Of Original Water Colors, Drawings, Oils, and Pastels by Tasha Tudor together with the names of the owners of most of the pieces by Edward B. Hills and Gretchen Brown McKeever, 1975.

New England Unit, Inc. of Herb Society of America, Inc. for permission to reproduce the cover and dust jackets and bookplate and to quote from title pages and versos, and dust jackets. Campbell, Mary Mason et alia, *A Basket Of Herbs, A Book Of American Sentiments.* Stephen Greene Press, 1983.

The Pembroke Welsh Corgi Club of America, Inc. for *An Illustrated Study Of The Pembroke Welsh Corgi Standard.* The Club, 1975.

From *THE NEW ENGLAND BUTT'RY SHELF ALMANAC* by Mary Mason Campbell, illustrated by Tasha Tudor. Copyright (1970 by the World Publishing Company. Copyright © 1982 by Mary Mason Campbell. Used by permission of The Stephen Greene Press, an imprint of Penguin Books USA Inc.

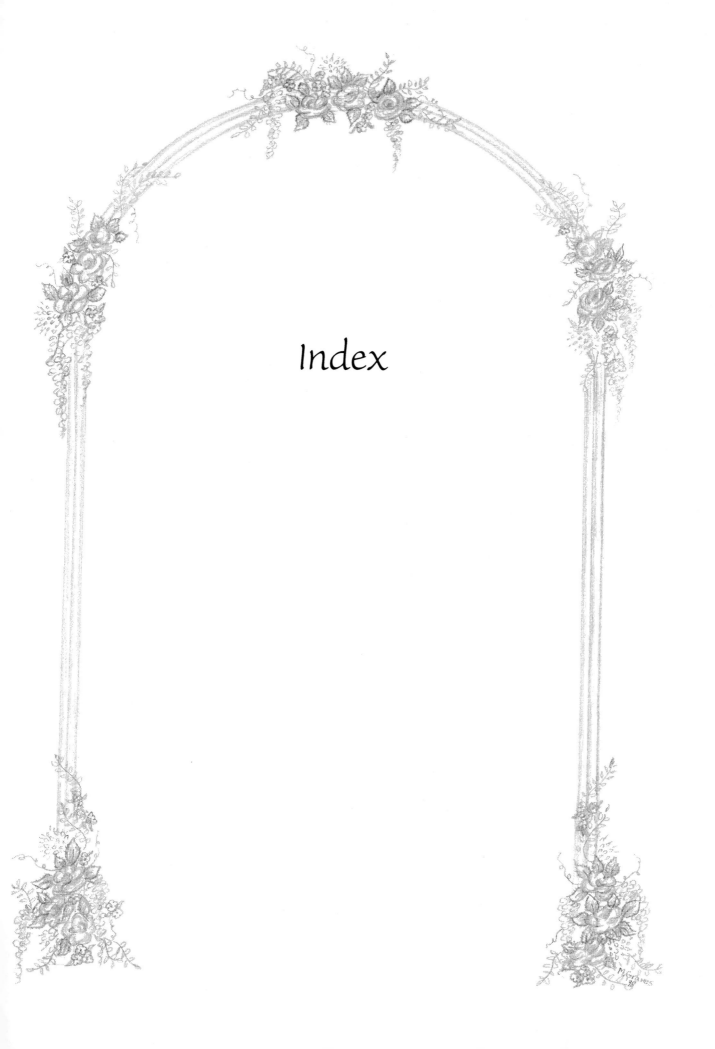

Index

Lippincott, Joseph W., Jr., 397
Lippincott Longlife Binding, 343, 398, 436
The Little Bookroom, 395
Little, Brown and Company, Boston, 73, 214,
  232, 280, 515
  Christmas with Tasha Tudor, Take Joy!, 136
  Corgiville Fair, 141
  The Night Before Christmas, 298
  The Private World of Tasha Tudor, 309
  *The Tasha Tudor Cookbook, Recipes and
    Reminiscences from Corgi Cottage*, 377
  Tasha Tudor's Dollhouse, 384
Little, Brown and Company (Canada) Limited,
  141, 214, 309, 378
Little, Brown Reinforced Binding, 141
Little Dog Toby, 352
"The Little Dressmaker", 395
Little Plum
  mentioned on cover, 160
A Little Princess, 12, 53, 63, 232
  dj blurb, 332
  mentioned on cover, 135, 140
  mentioned on dj, 396, 435
"Little Red Riding Hood" , 29, 301
Little Women, 4, 239, 242, 323
  mentioned on dj, 116, 121, 357
Livingston, Myra Cohn, 302
Livsey, Rosemary E., 64
Lobel, Arnold, 302
Lock Haven State Teachers College, Pa., 9
Logee's Greenhouses, Danielson, Ct., 401
Long, Doris, 465
The Long Secret, 336
Longfellow, Henry Wadsworth, 191
  "The arrow and the song", 192
Loo, Beverly Jane, agent, 251
*The Lord Is My Shepherd, The Twenty-Third
  Psalm*, 38, 169, 207, 241, 426
  mentioned on dj, 116
The Lord Will Love Thee, 247
  dj blurb, 82
Lord, Patricia C., agent, 345, 365
Lord, Priscilla Sawyer, 91
Los Angeles, Ca., 324
Los Angeles Times, 466
"A Love That Lasts", 73
Lovejoy, Frederick F., 259
Lovely Fowl [Edgar Allan Crow], dedicatee,
  173
Lubec, Me., 148
Lucas, E. V., translator, 177
Ludbrook, Mrs.
  at Mr. Linder's, 43
Ludlow, Vt., doll, 162
Lueck, Carol Johnston, 377
Lulu's Library, 323
Lunde, Oslo, Norway
  Min julebok, 113

Luther, Martin
  "Cradle hymn", 198
Lutterworth Press, Cambridge, 254
  And It Was So, 84
  First Carols, 500
  First Graces, 188
  First Hymns, 423
  First Prayers, 200, 202
  Give Us This Day, The Lord's Prayer, 210
  *The Lord Is My Shepherd, The Twenty-third
    Psalm*, 245
  A Treasury of First Books, 423
Lutterworth Press, Guildford, Surrey
  *The Lord Is My Shepherd, The Twenty-third
    Psalm*, 244
Lutterworth Press, London
  Take Joy! The Tasha Tudor Christmas Book,
    360
Lyle, Vicki, vocalist, 363
Lynd, Robert, 73
Lyos, Louis M., 318
Maasmann, Robert E., 292
MacDonald, George
  "Baby", 192
MacGregor, Frank Silver, agent, 259
MacKeracher, Barry, 351
MacLeish, Archibald, 230
The Macmillan Company of Canada Limited,
  94, 98, 159, 323
Macmillan Publishers Ltd., London, 321
Macmillan Publishing Company, New York,
  129, 296, 321, 419
  1 is One, 60
  A Child's Garden of Verses, 129
  The Night Before Christmas, 296
  *A Time to Keep, The Tasha Tudor Book of
    Holidays*, 420
MacNaughton, Donald, author, 292
MACO Magazine Corporation, 179
MACROVISIONTM, 437
Madison, James and Dolley, President, 172
magazine, 9
The Magazine Antiques, 466
Magic Carpet, 217
Magic In The Air. v. 3, 64
Magical Moments in Time, 250
The Magical World of Tasha Tudor, 514
Mague, Charles and Frances, vi
Mahony, Bertha E., 494
Mail Box Seeds, 105
Main, Pete, 167
Maine Antique Digest, 466
Maine Maritime Museum, 351
Malfait, Joan, vi
Malta, Vincent, designer, 274
"man dolls", 23
*Manchester Area Branch, American Association Of
  University Women, March 1998 Bulletin*, 467

Rife, Mary, dedicatee, 319
Riley, Alice C. D.
    "The Slumber Boat", 192
Rinehart, Frederick R., designer, 277
Rip Van Winkle, 277
Ripley, Elizabeth, author, 292
The Riverside Press, Cambridge, Ma., 230
Rizzoli Bookstore, Boston, 403
The Road Less Traveled, 342
Roads To Greatness, v.8, 64
Robbins, Rossell H., 352
Roberts Brothers, Boston, 116
Roberts Rinehart Publishers, Boulder, Co.,
    277
Roberts Rinehart Publishers, Dublin, Ireland,
    277
Robin
    character in *The White Goose*, 217
Rochester (N.Y.) Public Library, vi
"The Rock-A-By Lady", 192
Rockwell Museum, Corning, N.Y., 477
Rodgers, Nellie, production, 351
Rogers, Marilyn, 404
Rogers, Roy and Charlie, 86
Roller Skates, 335
"Rolling Pies, 5", 385
A Room Made of Windows, 335
Rooney, Mickey, 85
Rorick, Paige Biggers, 88
The Rose and the Ring, production, 90
Rosemary for Remembrance, A Keepsake Book, 53,
    169, 302, 321, 359
    mentioned on dj, 75
Rosetti, Christina G.
    "The Moon", 192
    "What will Robin do?", 192
    "Who has seen the wind?", 192
A Round Dozen, 12, 323
Royal Photographic Society, 256
Rubinstein, Helena, 163
"Rumpelstiltskin", 393
Rushmore, Arthur
    reviews *Mother and Child*, 259
Russell, Elizabeth G., Dr., vi
Russo, Dorothy Ritter, 49
"Rustic Beauty   HH 31-63DF", 371
Rutland Herald, 478
Ruttle, Shaw & Wetherill, Philadelphia, Pa.,
    162
S & R Litho Co., New York, 220
Sage, Vivienne, 423
Sagendorph, Robb, 319
Saintsbury, Dana, illustrator, 12, 158, 499
Salisbury, N.H., 206
    Campbell home, 281
Salish Indian, 301
Sally
    character in *First Delights*, 182

Samantha
    character in *Gooseberry Lane*, 213
Samantha's Surprise, 9, 325
sample books, 402, 405
sampler kit, 514
Sampson, Pamela, 13, 167, 272, 459, 460
Samuel
    character in *Gooseberry Lane*, 213
Samuel's Tree House, 24, 327
San Francisco Chro nicle, 478
    review on dj, 180
Sanborn, Duane Bradley, author, 292
Sanborn, Hugh, v, 259
Sandbank Farm, 206
Sandburg, Carl, 179
    reviews *Mother and Child*, 259
Sander, Richard G., agent, 273, 294, 348, 418
Sane Tregrd Agency, 404
Sardi, Francesco Saba, translator, 111
Sargent, Mary Gay, 220
Sarles, Bob, editor, 351
Sarles, Marley, 351
Satellite Books, 428
"Saturday Night Bath, 7", 385
Saturday Review, 478
Sawrey, 43
Sawyer, Diane, television journalist, 309
Sawyer, Ruth, 335, 352
Scarry, Richard, 277
Schaafsma, Carol, librarian, 304
Schade, Inge, 466
    dedicatee, 305
Schade, Lucy, 466
Schade, Richard, 466
Schadler, Jay, television journalist, 309
Schilo, Kristen, Gato & Maui Productions, 85
Schmocker, Ruth C., vi
Schoenhut dolls, 163
Scholastic Inc., 299
Scholz, Catherine, artist, 217
School and Library Edition, 295
School Library Journal, 58, 479
School Library Media Activities Monthly, 479
Schreiber, Joanne, 104
Schulz, Charles, 299
Schuster, Thomas E., 49
Schwauk Graphics, Chicago, Il., 418
Schweitzer, Albert
    quotation, 148
Scott, Hilda, calligrapher, 165, 166, 231, 344,
    364, 428
Scott Linotype Co., Boston, Ma., 318
Scott, Tom, lighting, 363
Scribner Press, New York, 162, 164
Searchlights and Nightingales, 73
Sears, Cynthia Lovelace, 93
*Seasons of Delight. See Tasha Tudor's Seasons of
    Delight, A Year on an Old-Fashioned Farm*

South China Printing Co., Hong Kong, 115, 147, 195, 208, 322, 384, 393

Sparrow Post Office, 418, 488, 516

Sparrow, Augustus, postmaster, 115, 385, 517

Spellbound Productions, San Francisco, Ca., 516

    Take Joy! The Magical World of Tasha Tudor, 351

    Take Peace, A Corgi Cottage Christmas with Tasha Tudor, 363

Spencerian Script workshop, 320

Spinning Wheel Stories, 323

spinning wheel, miniature, 90

Spiral Binding Co., Inc., New York, 231, 416

The Spiral Press, New York, 255, 260

Spoken Arts, Inc., St. Petersburg, Fl.

    A Brighter Garden, 117

Spoken Arts, New Rochelle, N.Y., 516

The Spool and Thimble Club, 385

Sport, 336

Spring, 480

Springer, Jo, 104

Springfield, Vt., 163

The Springs of Joy, 20, 33, 128, 169, 250, 346

Sprout, Janet, 428

Squires, J. Duane, author, 292

St. George, Eleanor, 161, 163

St. Jerome and the Lion, 156

St. Onge, Achille J., Worcester, Ma., 242

    The Night Before Christmas, 292

    The Twenty Third Psalm, 424

St. Paul's School, Concord, N.H., 77, 415

"The Star", 192, 274

"Star Dipper", 382

Starr, Polly Thayer, dedicatee, 185

Stauffacher, Jack W., typographer, 261

Stauffer, Amelia, candle-maker, 363, 406

Stebbins Store, 206

Steichen, Edward, photographer, 179, 256

Stelter, Andrea, sound editor, 351

Stephen Greene Press, Brattleboro, Vt.

    A Basket of Herbs, 91

    The New England Butt'ry Shelf Almanac, 282

    The New England Butt'ry Shelf Cookbook, 287

Stephen Greene Press, Lexington, Ma.

    The New England Butt'ry Shelf Almanac, 283

    The New England Butt'ry Shelf Cookbook, 288

Stephen Greene Press/Pelham Books

    The New England Butt'rty Shelf Almanac, 283

    The New England Butt'ry Shelf Cookbook, 288

Sterling Drug, Inc., New York, 149

Sternhagen, Frances, 117

Stettheimer Doll House, 163

Steuer, Loreli, 428

Stevenson, Nanette, designer, 74, 115, 207, 301

Stevenson, Robert Louis, 33, 123, 191, 349

    "At the seaside", 192

    "Dairy charm", 192

    "A dog and a cat went out together", 192

    "The hayloft", 192

    "Pussy-cat, pussy-cat", 192

Stewart, Brenda, dollmaker, 512

Stillwaters, 8, 342, 470

Stockton CAL Doll Club, 66

Stoliar, Joan, typographer-designer, 373

Story-A-Day, 480

The Story of Holly and Ivy

    mentioned on dj, 156

A Storycraft Book, 122

Strawberry Girl, 335

Streatfield, Noel, 336

Stuart Little, 335

"Study of winter Kitchen at Christmas," sketch, 413

Sturnus, 480

Sudduth, Margaret, 351, 364

"The Sugar-Plum Tree", 382

Sull, Michael, 320

Sullivan, Anne, agent, 164

Sullivan, Thelma L., 49

Sunday School Chronicle, 254, 480

    review on dj, 188

Sunny Brook Farms Nursery, 105

Suzette, a musical Jumeau doll, 161

Swajeski, Donna M., 205, 363, 480

Sweden

    origin of boggarts, 137

Sybilholme, Quechee, Vt., 164

Sylvie Ann, 125, 311. *See* Wallace, Sylvie Ann

    character in the calico books, 143, 165, 508

Sylvie Ann (doll), 514

T is for Tasha Tudor, 66

T.E. Schuster, 49

T.V. Guide, 480

"The table and the chair", 192, 223

Take Joy! [periodical] , 9 , 516, 480

    Take Joy! The Magical World of Tasha Tudor, 9, 351, 364

    premiere, 363

Take Joy! The Tasha Tudor Christmas Book, 12, 61, 136, 181, 242, 352

    mentioned on dj, 75, 121, 239, 242

Take Joy! The World of Tasha Tudor, xi, 205

    A Family Guide to the Exhibit, Nov. 2, 1996 - April 6, 1997, 363

    dinner menu, 363

    exhibit and seminar program, 352, 362

    press materials, 362

Take Peace, A Corgi Cottage Christmas with Tasha Tudor, 9, 352, 363, 377

Colophon

This book was typeset:

—the essays and index—
in Adobe Bembo
with Adobe San Vito heads
and John Ware's Regency Script titles
using QuarkXPress on a Macintosh computer

—the bibliography—
in a multitude of typefaces
using Microsoft Word on a Windows PC